Twipntact .com/ed

DATABASES AND TRANSACTION PROCESSING

An Application-Oriented Approach

DATABASES AND TRANSACTION PROCESSING

An Application–Oriented Approach

Philip M. Lewis

Arthur Bernstein

Michael Kifer

State University of New York at Stony Brook

Boston San Francisco New York
London Toronto Sydney Tokyo Singapore Madrid
Mexico City Munich Paris Cape Town Hong Kong Montreal

Senior Acquisitions Editor: Maite Suarez-Rivas
Project Editor: Katherine Harutunian
Executive Marketing Manager: Michael Hirsch
Production Supervisor: Diane Freed
Composition: Windfall Software
Copyeditor: Dianne Wood
Technical Art: George Nichols
Proofreader: Holly McLean-Aldis
Text Design: Gina Hagen
Cover Design: Susan Carsten Raymond
Cover Photo: Super Stock, Inc.
Design Manager: Gina Hagen
Prepress and Manufacturing: Caroline Fell

Access the latest information about Addison-Wesley titles from our World Wide Web site:
http://www.aw.com/cs

The programs and applications presented in this book have been included for their instructional value. They have been tested with care but are not guaranteed for any particular purpose. The publisher does not offer any warranties or representations, nor does it accept any liabilities with respect to the programs or applications.

Library of Congress Cataloging-in-Publication Data

Lewis, Philip M., 1931–
    Databases and transaction processing : an application-oriented approach / Philip M.
  Lewis, Arthur Bernstein, Michael Kifer.
       p.   cm.
    Includes bibliographical references and index.
    ISBN 0-201-70872-8 (pbk.)
    1. Database management. 2. Transaction systems (Computer systems). I. Bernstein,
  Arthur J. II. Kifer, M. (Michael), 1954– III. Title.
    QA76.9.D3 L485 2001
    005.74—dc21   2001033572

Printed in the United States of America.

1 2 3 4 5 6 7 8 9 10—HP—04030201

Contents

PART Two   53

Database Management

11 Physical Data Organization and Indexing   325

cs 12 Case Study: Completing the Student Registration System 377

PART Four   667

Transaction Processing

Preface

Database and transaction processing systems occupy a central position in our information-based society. Virtually every large system with which we interact in our daily lives has a database at its core. The systems range from those that control the most trivial aspects of our lives (e.g., supermarket checkout systems) to those on which our lives depend (e.g., air traffic control systems). Over the next decades, we will become increasingly dependent on the correctness and efficiency of these systems.

We believe that every computer scientist and information systems professional should be familiar with the theoretical and engineering concepts that underlie these systems. These are the people who will be designing, building, maintaining, and administering these highly complex systems.

This book is intended to be a text for any of the following courses in a computer science or technically oriented information systems curriculum:

- An introductory undergraduate or graduate course in databases

- An undergraduate or graduate course in transaction processing for students who have had an introductory course in databases

- An advanced undergraduate or a first graduate course in databases for students who have had an introductory course in databases

If only one course is to be taught covering both databases and transaction processing, the instructor can select material related to both topics.

Rather than focusing on how to build the database management system itself, our approach focuses on how to build applications. We believe that many more students will be implementing applications than will be building DBMSs. We believe that placing databases in the context of transaction processing accentuates this emphasis, since transactions provide the mechanism that applications use to access databases. Furthermore, we include substantial material describing the languages and APIs used by transactions to access a database, such as embedded SQL, ODBC, and JDBC.

While the book thoroughly covers conventional topics—relational databases, SQL, and the ACID properties of transactions—it also provides a very substantial treatment of less conventional and newer issues, such as object and object relational databases, XML and document processing over the Internet, and the transactional issues related to Internet commerce.

Although we cover many practical aspects of database and transaction processing applications, we are primarily concerned with the concepts that underlie these topics rather than on the details of particular commercial systems or applications. Thus, in the database portion of the book, we concentrate on the concepts underlying the relational and object data models rather than on any particular commercial DBMS. These concepts will remain the foundation of database processing long after SQL is obsolete. (Recall the generation of programmers who were trained in COBOL and found it extremely difficult to learn any other language.) In a similar way, in the transaction processing portion of the book, we concentrate on the concepts underlying the ACID properties and the technical issues involved in their implementation, rather than on any particular commercial DBMS or TP monitor.

To enhance students' understanding of the technical material, we have included a case study of a transaction processing application, the Student Registration System, which is carried through the book. While a student registration system can hardly be considered glamorous, it has the unique advantage that all students have interacted with such a system as users. More importantly, it turns out to be a surprisingly rich application, so we can use it to illustrate many of the issues in database design, query processing, and transaction processing.

A unique aspect of the book is a presentation of the software engineering concepts required to implement transaction processing applications, using the Student Registration System as an example. Since the implementations of many information systems fail because of poor project management and inadequate software engineering, we feel that these topics should be an important part of the student's education. Our treatment of software engineering issues is brief, as many students will take a separate course in this subject. However, we believe that they will be better able to understand and apply that material when they see it presented in the context of an information system implementation. Since the courses that use this text at Stony Brook are not software engineering courses, we do not cover this material in class. Instead, we ask the students to read it and require that they use good software engineering practice in their class projects. We do cover in class those aspects of the Student Registration System that illustrate important issues in databases and transaction processing.

OVERVIEW

There is sufficient material in the book for three one-semester courses. The first half of the book is a text for a first course on databases. For students who have completed such a course, the second half of the book concentrates on transaction processing and advanced topics in databases. At Stony Brook, we offer both an undergraduate (introductory) and a more advanced (graduate) database course as well as an undergraduate and graduate version of the transaction processing course.

The book is divided into parts so that the instructor can more easily organize the material. We have included a Chapter Dependency Chart to make it easier to design customized courses.

Part I: Introduction

Chapters 1 through 3 contain introductory material for a first course in databases. Chapter 1 serves as general introduction. Chapter 2 briefly covers SQL and the ACID properties of transactions. By introducing this basic material early, we are able to remove some constraints on the order of presentation of topics discussed later.

Chapter 3 begins our discussion of the Student Registration System and the software engineering concepts appropriate for its implementation. In particular, we discuss requirements and specification documents and the use of application generators to design graphical user interfaces. In the introductory database course at Stony Brook, we ask the students to read this material but do not cover it in class lectures. However, at this point in the course, we start the class project by asking students to write a Specification Document.

Part II: Database Management

Chapters 4 through 15 constitute the core of a first course in databases. Some of the topics covered are:

- The concept of a relation and the DDL features of SQL, including automatic constraint checking

- The Entity-Relationship Model and schema design, including methods (and their limitations) for converting E-R diagrams to relational schemas

- Relational algebra, calculus, and the DML features of SQL with particular attention to the semantics of complex SQL queries through relational algebra and calculus

- Functional dependencies and normalization, including algorithms for decomposing a schema into 3NF, BCNF, and 4NF

- Triggers and active databases, including triggers in SQL:1999

- The inclusion of SQL statements in a program written in a conventional programming language, including embedded SQL, dynamic SQL, ODBC, JDBC, and SQLJ. The recently standardized language for stored procedures, SQL/PSM, is also discussed

- Physical organization of the data and indexing, including B^+ trees, ISAM, and hash indices

- Query processing and optimization, including algorithms for computing selections and joins, and methods for estimating the cost of query plans

Software engineering issues, as applied to the Student Registration System, are integrated throughout these chapters. In Section 5.7, we present the database design for the system, including the E-R Diagram and relation schema. Chapter 12 presents material on Design Documents, Test Plan Documents, and project planning that is needed to complete the system. In Section 12.6, we present the detailed design and part of the Java/JDBC program for one of the transactions in the system.

Chapter 15 summarizes some of the material on transaction processing from later chapters. It can be used to enrich a database course if time permits.

Part III: Advanced Topics in Databases

Chapters 16 through 19 contain materials that can become part of an advanced database course. Such a course includes all the chapters in this part plus Chapter 27. In our experience, lack of time prevents one or more sections of Chapters 7, 8, 9, 10, 11, and 14 from being covered in a first database course, so this material can also be included. The topics covered in Part III include

- Object and object-relational databases, including the conceptual model, ODMG databases, object-relational extensions of SQL:1999, and CORBA

- Database aspects of document processing on the Web, including a detailed discussion of XML Schema, XPath, XSLT, and XQuery

- Distributed databases, including heterogeneous and homogeneous systems, multidatabases, fragmentation, semijoins, global query optimization, query design, and distributed database design

- Online analytic processing and data mining, including star schemas, the CUBE and ROLLUP operators, associations, and classification

Part IV: Transaction Processing

Chapters 20 through 27, together with portions of Chapters 9 and 10, contain material for a one-semester course in transaction processing. Many of the examples in these chapters refer to the Student Registration System design developed in Chapters 3 and 12 and in Section 5.7. We ask the students to read this material as appropriate.

Chapter 20 contains a detailed description of the ACID properties of transactions. Chapters 21 and 22 describe a variety of transaction models and the architecture of transaction processing systems in a distributed and heterogeneous client/server environment. Some of the topics covered are

- Models of transactions, including savepoints, chained transactions, transactional queues, nested and multilevel transactions, distributed transactions, multidatabase systems, and workflow systems

- Architectures for transaction processing systems, including, client-server organizations for both centralized and distributed databases, two-tiered and three-tiered architectures, TP monitors, and transaction managers. Transactional remote procedure call and peer-to-peer communication together with their use in organizing a transaction processing system are discussed

■ Implementation of transaction architectures and models in transaction processing applications on the Internet

Chapters 23 through 26 describe how the ACID properties of atomicity, isolation, and durability are implemented in both centralized and distributed systems. Some of the topics covered are

■ Concurrency controls for abstract databases, including strict two-phase locking, optimistic concurrency controls, timestamp-ordered concurrency controls, concurrency controls for object databases, and locking protocols to implement the different models of transactions

■ Concurrency controls for relational databases, including locking protocols for the different isolation levels, examples of correct and incorrect schedules at each isolation level, granular locking, index locking, and multiversion concurrency controls, including SNAPSHOT isolation

■ Logging and recovery, including write-ahead logs, dumps, and checkpoints

■ Distributed transactions, including the two-phase commit protocol, global serialization, global deadlocks, and synchronous and asynchronous algorithms for managing replicated data

Chapter 27 covers security and Internet commerce. Some of the topics covered are

■ Symmetric and asymmetric encryption, digital signatures, blind signatures, and certificates

■ The Kerberos protocol for authentication and key distribution

■ Internet protocols, including the SSL Protocol for authentication and session encryption, the SET Protocol for secure transactions, electronic cash protocols, and protocols that guarantee goods atomicity, certified delivery, and money atomicity

Our goals in Chapters 20 through 27 are

■ To make students aware of the architecture of the transaction processing systems with which their transactions must interact, so that they can better evaluate the features offered by competing system vendors

■ To describe the costs, measured in system resources and performance, involved in implementing the ACID properties of transactions

■ To describe techniques to decrease these costs—for example, granular locks, indices, denormalization, and table fragmentation.

■ To describe situations in which an application will execute correctly even though isolation is not total—for example, transactions that might execute correctly at an isolation level less stringent than SERIALIZABLE

We have also included an Appendix, which covers certain system issues that are important for understanding parts of the text. These include the ideas behind modular systems and encapsulation, the basics of the client/server architecture, multiprogramming and threads, and the basics of interprocess communication. Instructors might choose to present some of this material if the students have not covered it in previous courses.

DEPENDENCIES AMONG CHAPTERS

To help instructors tailor the material to the needs of their courses, we have identified certain sections that can be skipped without disrupting the flow of material in the corresponding chapters. Such sections are marked with an asterisk. Even though material covered in these sections is sometimes referenced in other chapters, these references can be ignored. In addition, exercises that are more difficult than the rest are marked with one or two asterisks, depending on the difficulty.

The text can be used in a number of different ways depending on the goals of the course. To provide some guidance to the instructor, the table on the next page shows the chapters that might be included in five different courses that address different student populations and attempt to emphasize different aspects of the subject. In this table, "yes" means that all parts of the chapter should be covered by the lectures. "Parts" means that the instructor can select only parts of the material presented in the chapter. "Read" means that the chapter can be given as a reading assignment to the students.

Column 1 marks chapters that would be covered in a slow-paced introductory database course. In such a course, for instance, only parts of Chapter 8 on normalization theory might be included—perhaps only the introductory sections. Similarly, only some parts of Chapter 10, on various ways in which SQL can be combined with a host language, might be covered—perhaps only one approach, the one required for the course project.

Columns 2 and 3 outline two more intensive introductory database courses. Column 2 expands the material covered in the introductory course in the direction of database applications, while Column 3 describes a more theory-oriented version of the course. It provides a more in-depth coverage of the normalization theory, foundations of query languages, and query optimization at the expense of the application-oriented material in Chapter 10. Although we have characterized this material as theory-oriented, we might also have characterized it as system-oriented, because it covers issues involved in the design of a DBMS. The courses in these two columns are the ones we teach in our undergraduate program at Stony Brook (depending on the interests of the instructor).

Column 4 describes an advanced database course. The course might start by reviewing or filling in material that the instructor judges the students might not have covered in a prerequisite, introductory database course. Such material would probably be found in Chapters 7, 8, 9, 10, and 14. The body of the course then continues with advanced database topics and some material on transactions in

Chapter	Courses				
	DB/Intro	DB/Applications	DB/Theory	DB/Advanced	Transactions
1	yes	yes	yes		yes
2	yes	yes	yes		
3	read	read			
4	yes	yes	yes		
5	yes	yes	yes		
6	yes	yes	yes		
7		parts	yes	parts	
8	parts	parts	yes	parts	
9		yes	yes	yes	yes
10	parts	yes		parts	yes
11	yes	yes	yes		
12	read	read			
13	parts	yes	yes		
14		parts	yes	parts	
15	yes	yes	yes		
16				yes	
17				yes	
18				yes	
19				yes	
20					yes
21					yes
22					yes
23					yes
24					yes
25					yes
26					yes
27				yes	yes

electronic commerce. At Stony Brook this course is taught to graduate students who had a database course in their undergraduate years.

Column 5 describes a course on transaction processing that also assumes that students have had an introductory database course as a prerequisite. At Stony Brook, we teach both an undergraduate and a graduate version of this course. The material on transaction processing is supplemented with related material that might not have been covered in the student's prerequisite database course, for example, some material from Chapters 9 and 10.

For further fine-tuning of courses, the chapter dependency diagram that follows can be of help. The figure identifies two kinds of dependencies. Solid arrows indicate that one chapter depends on much of the material presented in another chapter, except for the sections marked as optional. Dotted arrows indicate weak dependency, which means that only a few concepts developed in the prerequisite chapter are used in the dependent chapter, and those concepts can be covered quickly. The dependencies involving Chapter 27 are a special case. It can be taught either at the end of a transaction processing course, in which case it depends on Chapters 21, 22, and 25, or at the end of a database course, in which case it depends on Chapter 15.

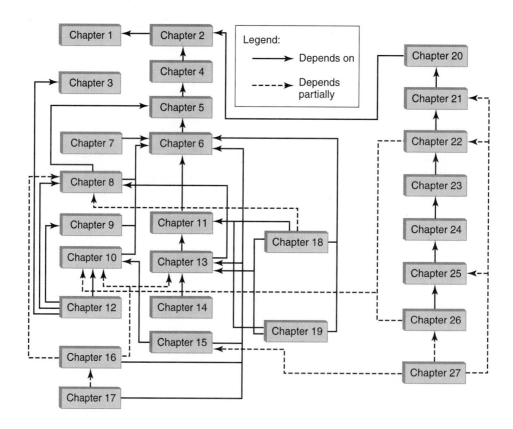

SUPPLEMENTS

In addition to the text, the following supplementary materials are available to assist instructors:

- Online PowerPoint presentations for all chapters

- Online PowerPoint slides of all figures

- An online solution manual containing solutions for the exercises

- Any additional references, notes, errata, homeworks, exams, and so forth, that we think might be of interest to our readers

For more information on obtaining these supplements, please check online information for this book at *www.aw.com/cssupport*. The solutions manual and Power-Point presentations are available only to instructors through your Addison-Wesley sales representative.

ACKNOWLEDGMENTS

We would like to thank the reviewers, whose comments and suggestions significantly improved the book:

Suad Alagic, Wichita University

Catriel Beeri, The Hebrew University

Rick Cattel, Sun Microsystems

Jan Chomicki, SUNY Buffalo

Henry A. Etlinger, Rochester Institute of Technology

Leonidas Fegaras, University of Texas at Arlington

Alan Fekete, University of Sidney

Johannes Gehrke, Cornell University

Jiawei Han, Simon Fraser Universtiy

Peter Honeyman, University of Michigan

Vijay Kumar, University of Missouri–Kansas City

Jonathan Lazar, Towson University

Dennis McLeod, University of Southern California

Rokia Missaoui, University of Quebec in Montreal

Clifford Neuman, University of Southern California

Fabian Pascal, Consultant

Sudha Ram, University of Arizona

Krithi Ramamritham, University of Massachusetts–Amherst and IIT Bombay

Andreas Reuter, International University in Germany, Bruchsal

Arijit Sengupta, Georgia State University

Munindar P. Singh, North Carolina State University

Greg Speegle, Baylor University

Junping Sun, Nova Southeastern University

Joe Trubicz, Consultant

Vassilis J. Tsotras, University of California, Riverside

Emilia E. Villarreal, California Polytechnic State University

We would also like to thank the following people who were kind enough to provide us with additional information and answers to our questions: Don Chamberlin, Daniela Florescu, Jim Gray, Pankaj Gupta, Rob Kelly, and C. Mohan.

Several people taught out of beta versions of the book and made useful comments and suggestions: David S. Warren and Radu Grosu. Joe Trubicz served not only as a reviewer when the manuscript was complete, but provided critical comments on early versions of many of the chapters.

A number of students were very helpful in reading and checking the correctness of various parts of the book: Ziyang Duan, Shiyong Lu, Guizhen Yang, and Yan Zhang.

Many thanks to the staff of the Computer Science Department at Stony Brook, and in particular Kathy Germana, who helped make things happen at work.

We would particularly like to thank Maite Suarez-Rivas, our editor at Addison-Wesley, who played an important role in shaping the contents and approach of the book in its early stages and throughout the time we were writing it. We would also like to thank the various staff members of Addison-Wesley, who did an excellent job of editing and producing the book: Katherine Harutunian, Pat Mahtani, Diane Freed, Regina Hagen, Paul Anagnostopoulos, and Jacqui Scarlott.

Last, but not least, we would like to thank our wives, Rhoda, Edie, and Lora, who provided much needed support and encouragement while we were writing the book.

DATABASES AND TRANSACTION PROCESSING

An Application-Oriented Approach

Part One

The introductory part of the book consists of three chapters.

In Chapter 1, we will try to get you excited about the fields of databases and transaction processing by giving you some idea of what the book is all about.

In Chapter 2, we will introduce many of the technical concepts underlying the fields of databases and transaction processing, including the SQL language and the ACID properties of transactions. We will expand on these concepts in the rest of the book.

In Chapter 3, we will begin our discussion of the case study application that we carry throughout the book, the Student Registration System. We will discuss many of the software engineering concepts involved in such an implementation project and will give the Requirements Document for the system.

Chapter 1

Overview of Databases and Transactions

1.1 WHAT ARE DATABASES AND TRANSACTIONS?

During your vacation, you stand at the checkout counter of a department store in Tokyo, hand the clerk your credit card, and wait anxiously for your purchases to be approved. In the few seconds you have to wait, messages are sent around the world to one or more banks and clearinghouses, accessing and updating a number of databases until finally the system approves your purchase. Over 20 million such credit card transactions are processed each day from over 10 million merchants through more than twenty thousand banks. Billions of dollars are involved, and the only record of what happens is stored in the databases on the network. The accuracy, security, and availability of these databases and the correctness and performance characteristics of the transactions that access them are critical to the entire credit card business.

What is a database?   To be precise, a **database** is a collection of data items related to some enterprise—for example, the depositor account information in a bank. A database might be stored on cards in a Rolodex or on paper in a file cabinet, but we are particularly interested in databases stored as bits and bytes in a computer. Such a database can be **centralized** on one computer or **distributed** over several, perhaps widely separated geographically.

An increasing number of enterprises depend on such databases for their very existence. No paper records exist within the enterprise; the only up-to-date record of its current status—for example, the balance of each bank customer's checking account—is stored in its databases. Many enterprises view their databases as their most important asset.

For example, the database of the company that manufactured the airplane on which you flew to Tokyo contains the only record of information about the engineering design, manufacturing processes, and subassembly suppliers involved in producing that plane ten years ago, together with every test made on it over its lifetime. If, at some time in the future, a test shows that a turbine blade on one of the plane's jet engines has failed, the company can determine from its database which subcontractor supplied that particular engine, and the subcontractor can determine from its database the date on which that turbine blade was manufactured, the machines and people involved, the source of the materials from which the blade was fabricated, and the results of quality assurance tests made while the blade was being manufactured. In this way it can determine the cause of the failure and increase the quality of future planes. The existence of that detailed historical database, as well as the ability to search it for information about the fabrication of a specific turbine blade in a specific jet engine on a specific airplane manufactured ten years ago, gives the airplane manufacturer a significant strategic advantage over any other manufacturer that does not maintain such a database.

In some cases, a database is the major asset of an enterprise—for example, the database of the credit history company that your credit card company consulted when you applied for your card. In other cases, the accuracy of the information in the database is critical for human life—for example, the database in the air traffic control system at the Tokyo airport.

To make access to them convenient, databases are generally encapsulated within a **database management system** (**DBMS**). The DBMS supports a high-level language in which the application programmer describes the database access it wishes to perform. The most commonly used language, and the one we study in this text, is the Structured Query Language (**SQL**). Its beauty lies in its declarative nature: The application programmer need only state what is to be done; the DBMS figures out how to do it efficiently. The DBMS interprets each SQL statement and performs the action it describes. The application programmer need not know the details of how the database is stored, need not formulate the algorithm for performing the access, and need not be concerned about many other aspects of managing the database.

What is a transaction?   Databases frequently store information that describes the current state of an enterprise. For example, a bank's database stores the current balance in each depositor's account. When an event happens in the real world that changes the state of the enterprise, a corresponding change must be made to the information stored in the database. With online DBMSs, these changes are made in real time by programs called **transactions**, which execute when the real-world event occurs. For example, when a customer deposits money in a bank (an event in the real world), a deposit transaction is executed. Each transaction must be designed so that it maintains the correctness of the relationship between the database state and the real-world enterprise it is modeling. In addition to changing the state of the database, the transaction itself might initiate some events in the real world. For example, a withdraw transaction at an automated teller machine (ATM) initiates the event of dispensing cash, and a transaction that establishes a connection for a telephone call requires the allocation of resources (bandwidth on a long-distance link) in the telephone company's infrastructure.

Credit card approval is only one example of a transaction that you executed on your vacation in Tokyo. Your flight arrangements involved a transaction with the airline's reservation database, your passage through passport control at the airport involved a transaction with the immigration services database, and your check-in at the hotel involved a transaction with the hotel reservation database.

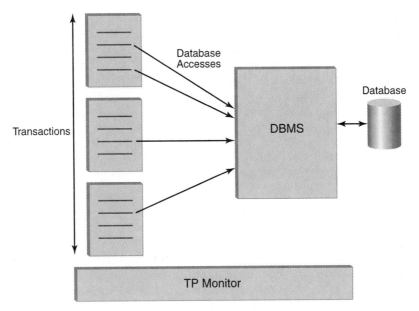

Figure 1.1 The structure of a transaction processing system.

Even the phone call you made from your hotel room to tell your family you had arrived safely involved transactions with the hotel billing database and with a long-distance carrier to arrange billing and to establish the call.

Other examples of transactions you probably execute regularly involve ATM systems, supermarket scanning systems, and university registration and billing systems. Increasingly, these transactions entail access to distributed databases: multiple databases managed by different DBMSs stored at different geographical locations. Your phone call transaction at the Tokyo hotel is an example.

What is a transaction processing system?   A system that manages transactions and controls their access to a DBMS is called a **TP monitor**. A **transaction processing system** (**TPS**) generally consists of a TP monitor, one or more DBMSs, and a set of application programs containing transactions (see Figure 1.1). The database is at the heart of a transaction processing system because it persists beyond the lifetime of any particular transaction. An increasing number of enterprises depend on such systems for their business. For example, one might say that the credit card transaction processing system *is* the credit card business.

1.2   FEATURES OF MODERN DATABASE AND TRANSACTION PROCESSING SYSTEMS

Modern computer and communication technology has led to significant advances in the architecture, design, and use of database and transaction processing systems. A comparison with older systems follows.

■ The databases in most new systems are based on the **relational model**, in which the data is stored in tables and can be accessed with a (relatively) simple query language such as SQL. In SQL the programmer need not be aware of the data's detailed physical layout. By contrast, older systems used a more complex database model, called the **network model**, in which the data records were linked by use of a complicated pointer structure through which the query language had to navigate, making queries much more difficult to design, program, and test.

■ The databases in many new systems can contain large multimedia objects, such as pictures and video clips, thus enabling a new generation of applications such as Internet-based catalogs and digital encyclopedias. Older databases could contain only alphanumeric data and thus were limited to a smaller class of applications.

■ Most new systems are **online**, whereas the older systems were often **batch** with paper backup of the computer database. For example, when you execute a withdraw transaction (online) at an ATM, your account balance is debited (in real time) before you receive the money. By contrast, in older systems withdrawals were done at the teller's window using paper withdrawal slips, and the bank closed at 2 P.M. so the bank's database could be updated overnight (offline).

■ Most new systems allow **concurrent access** by the transactions to the database. As a result, the operations of the transactions are interleaved in time. Older systems, on the other hand, permitted only **sequential access** to the database: One transaction was executed after the previous one completed. When transactions were processed sequentially, the average delay between the time the transaction was submitted and its completion time grew rapidly with the number of transactions trying to access the database. Similarly, the number of transactions that could be processed per second fell. This delay quickly became intolerable for an online system. Concurrent transaction execution provides more rapid response to the user.

■ Many new systems involve **distributed computation**. With the decreasing cost of computer hardware, it has become economical to place computing devices at a number of sites in an enterprise, and with the decreasing cost of communication, it has become economical to interconnect these sites. In particular, the terminals with which users interact now have significant intelligence and actively participate in the overall computation. In older systems, on the other hand, very little computation (except, perhaps, simple data formatting) was done at the terminals—hence, they were referred to as dumb terminals—and all the intelligence resided at the central computer. For example, the computer in the ATM terminal has the intelligence to gather the required information for a withdraw transaction before interacting with the bank's computer and then to respond to a request from the bank's computer to dispense the cash.

■ Many new systems involve **distributed data**. With the decreasing cost of storage devices, it has become possible for different components of an enterprise to maintain their own databases. The distribution of the data might reflect the organization chart of the enterprise, or the enterprise might be geographically distributed and the data might be distributed to sites where it is used most heavily. By contrast, in older systems all the data was stored at a central location. For example, during a credit card approval transaction, your credit card account might have been accessed at one site while the store's account was accessed at a different site—all while you were waiting for approval.

■ Older systems were **homogeneous**, involving modules of a single manufacturer. Hence, compatibility was not a problem, and modules could be interconnected in a straightforward way. Many new systems are **heterogeneous**, involving hardware and software modules produced by a variety of manufacturers. Systems have been "opened up," and the resulting competition has produced better products. As a consequence, however, the development of industry-wide interfacing standards is now a major issue.

■ Transactions in older systems were mainly executed by businesspeople in their place of business. The Internet is bringing transaction processing into the home, causing explosive growth in the number of transaction processing systems and in the number of transactions that have to be processed by each. The implications of this new capability on business and, indeed, on our every day lives will be profound.

These characteristics allow for substantially enhanced functionality of databases and transaction processing systems, which in many cases is reflected in important new business opportunities for the enterprises that deploy them. In turn, this new functionality implies a number of additional requirements on the operation of these systems.

■ **High availability**   Because the system is online, it must be operational at all times when the enterprise is open for business. In some enterprises, this means that the system must always be available. For example, an airline reservation system might be required to accept requests for flight reservations from ticket offices spread over a large number of time zones, so the system is never shut down. By contrast, in the offline banking system transactions are executed only during business hours. With online systems, failures can result in a disruption of business—if the computer in an airline reservation system is down, reservations cannot be made. The ability to tolerate failures depends on the nature of the enterprise. Clearly a flight control system has considerably less tolerance for failures than a flight reservation system has. Highly available systems generally involve replication of hardware and software.

■ **High reliability**   The system must accurately reflect the results of all transactions. This implies not only that transactions must be correctly programmed but also that errors must not be introduced because of concurrent execution of (correctly programmed) transactions or intercommunication of modules while the transaction is executing. Furthermore, large, distributed transaction processing systems include thousands of hardware and software modules, and it is unlikely that all are working correctly. The system must not forget the results of any transaction that has completed despite all but the most catastrophic forms of failure. For example, the database in a banking system must accurately reflect the effect of all the deposits and withdrawals that have completed and cannot lose the results of any such transactions should it subsequently crash.

■ **High throughput**   Because the enterprise has many customers who must use the transaction processing system, the system must be capable of performing many transactions per second. For example, a credit card approval system might perform thousands of transactions per second during its busiest periods. As we shall see, this requirement implies that individual transactions cannot be executed sequentially, but must be executed concurrently—thus significantly complicating the design of the system.

■ **Low response time**   Because customers might be waiting for a response from it, the system must respond quickly. Response requirements may differ depending on the application. Whereas you might be willing to wait fifteen seconds for an ATM to output cash, you expect a telephone connection to be made in no more than one or two seconds. Furthermore, in some applications, if the response does not occur within a fixed period of time, the transaction will not perform properly. For example, in a factory automation system the transaction might be required to actuate a device before some unit passes a particular position on the conveyor belt. Applications of this type are said to have **hard real-time** constraints.

■ **Long lifetime**   Transaction processing systems are complex and not easily replaced. They must be designed in such a way that individual hardware or software modules can be replaced with newer versions (that perform better or have additional functionality) without necessitating major changes to the surrounding system.

■ **Security**   Many transaction processing systems contain information about the private concerns of individuals (e.g., the items they purchase, their credit card number, the videos they view, and their health and financial records). Because these systems are accessible to a large number of people from a large number of places (perhaps over the Internet), security is important. Individual users must be authenticated (are they who they claim to be?), users must be allowed to execute only those transactions they are authorized to execute (only a bank teller can execute a transaction to generate a certified check), the information in the database must not be corrupted or read by an attacker, and the information transmitted between the user and the system must not be altered or overheard by an eavesdropper.

Our concern in this book is with the technical aspects of databases and the transaction processing systems that use them. Specifically, we are interested in the design and implementation of applications, including the organization of the application database, but we are not concerned with the algorithms and data structures used to implement the underlying DBMS and transaction processing system modules. Nevertheless, we must learn enough about these underlying systems so that we can use them intelligently in an application.

1.3   MAJOR PLAYERS IN THE IMPLEMENTATION AND SUPPORT OF DATABASE AND TRANSACTION PROCESSING SYSTEMS

A transaction processing system, together with its associated databases, can be an immensely complex assemblage of hardware and software, with which many different types of people interact in various roles. Examining these roles is a useful way of understanding what a transaction processing system is. First consider the people involved in the design and implementation of a transaction processing system.

System analyst.   The system analyst works with the customer of a proposed application system to develop formal requirements and specifications for it. He or she must understand both the business rules of the enterprise for which the application is being implemented and the database and transaction processing technology underlying the implementation, so that the application will meet the customer's needs and execute efficiently. The specifications developed by the system analyst are then refined into the design of the database formats and the individual transactions that will access the database.

Database designer.   The database designer specifies the structure of the database appropriate for an application. The database contains the information that describes the current state of the real-world application. The structure must support the accesses required by the transactions and allow those accesses to be performed in a timely manner.

Application programmer.   The application programmer implements the graphical user interface and the individual transactions in the system. He or she must ensure that the transactions maintain the correspondence between the state of the real-world application and the state of the database. Together with the database designer, the application programmer must ensure that the rules governing the workings of the enterprise are enforced. For example, in the Student Registration System, to be discussed later, the number of students enrolled in a course should not exceed the number of seats in the room assigned to the course.

Project manager.   The project manager is responsible for the successful completion of the implementation project. He or she prepares schedules and budgets, assigns people to tasks, and monitors day-to-day project operation. Project management is surprisingly difficult. According to a widely quoted report of the Standish Group, an Information Technology (IT) consulting group, of the more than eight thousand IT projects the group surveyed, only 16% completed successfully—on time and on budget. The primary reason for the failures was almost always poor project management.[1]

---

[1] For large companies, the success rate dropped to 9%. For projects that completed late or over budget, the average completion time was 222% of the scheduled time and the average cost was 189% of the budgeted cost. An astonishing 31% of the projects were canceled before they were completed. At the

The people interacting with (as opposed to building) an operational transaction processing system include the following.

User.   The user causes the execution of individual transactions, usually by interacting through some graphical user interface. The user interface must be appropriate to the capabilities of the intended class of users. As an example, the user interface presented by an ATM is simple enough that an average person can use the system to perform bank deposit and withdraw transactions without any training or instructions except those presented on the screen. By contrast, the interface to an airline reservation system, which is used by reservation clerks or travel agents, requires advanced training. In both cases, however, most of the complexities of the system are hidden from the user.

Database administrator.   The database administrator is responsible for supporting the database while the system is running. Among his or her concerns are allocating storage space for the database, monitoring and optimizing database performance, and monitoring and controlling database security. In addition, the database administrator might modify the structure of the database to accommodate changes in the enterprise or to handle performance bottlenecks.

System administrator.   The system administrator is responsible for supporting the system as a whole while it is running. Among the things he or she must keep track of are

■ **System architecture**   What hardware and software modules are connected to the system at any instant, and how are they interconnected?

■ **Configuration management**   What version of each software module exists on each machine?

■ **System status**   What is the health of the system? Which systems and communication links are operational or congested, and what is being done to repair the situation? How is the system currently performing?

Our main interest in this book lies at the application level. Thus, we are particularly concerned with the roles of the system analyst, the application programmer, and the database designer. However, in order for someone working at the application level to take full advantage of the capabilities of the underlying system, he or she must be knowledgeable about the other roles as well.

1.4   DECISION SUPPORT SYSTEMS—OLAP AND OLTP

Transaction processing is not the only application domain in which databases play a key role. Another such domain is **decision support**. While transaction processing

---

time this book was written, information about this study, called Chaos, could be found in [Standish 2000].

is concerned with using a database to maintain an accurate model of some real-world situation, decision support is concerned with using the information in a database to guide management decisions. To illustrate the differences between these two domains, we discuss the roles they might play in the operation of a national supermarket chain.

Transaction processing.   Each local supermarket in a chain maintains a database of the prices and current inventory of all the items it sells. It uses that database (together with a bar code scanner) as part of a transaction processing system at the checkout counters. One transaction in this system might be "3 cans of Campbell soup and 1 box of Ritz crackers were purchased; compute the price, print out a receipt, update the balance in the cash drawer, and subtract these items from the store's inventory." The customer expects this transaction to complete in a few seconds.

The main goal of such a transaction processing system is to maintain the correspondence between the database and the real-world situation it is modeling as events occur in the real world. In this case, the event is the customer's purchase and the real-world situation is the store's inventory and the amount of cash in the cash drawer.

Decision support.   The managers of the supermarket chain might want to analyze the data stored in the databases in each store to help them make decisions for the chain as a whole. Such decision support applications are becoming increasingly important as enterprises attempt to turn the *data* in their databases into *information* they can use to advance their long-term strategic goals.

Decision support applications involve queries to one or more databases, possibly followed by some mathematical analysis of the information returned by the queries. Decision support applications are sometimes called **online analytic processing** (**OLAP**), in contrast with the **online transaction processing** (**OLTP**) applications we have been discussing.

In some decision support applications, the queries are so simple they can be implemented as transactions in the same local database used for OLTP applications— for example, "Print out a report of the weekly produce sales in Store 27 for the past six months."

In many applications, however, the queries are quite complex and cannot be efficiently executed against the local databases. They take too long to execute (because the database has been optimized for OLTP transactions) and cause the local transactions—for example, the checkout transactions—to execute too slowly. The supermarket chain therefore maintains a separate database specifically for such complex OLAP queries. The database contains historical information about sales and inventory from all its branches for the past ten years. This information is extracted from the individual store databases at various times and updated once a day. Such a database is called a **data warehouse**.

A manager can enter a complex query about the data in the data warehouse—for example, "During the winter months of the last five years, what is the percentage of customers in northeast urban supermarkets who bought crackers at the same time they bought soup?" (Perhaps these items should be placed near each other on the shelves.)

Data warehouses can contain terabytes (10^{12} bytes) of data and require special hardware to maintain that data. An OLAP query might be quite difficult to formulate and might require query language concepts more powerful than those needed for OLTP queries. OLAP queries usually do not have severe constraints on execution time and might take several hours to execute. The warehouse database might have been structured to speed up the execution of such queries. The database need be updated only periodically because minute-by-minute correctness is not needed for the types of queries it supports—satisfactory responses might be obtained even if the database is less than 100% accurate.

Data mining.   A manager might also be interested in making a much less structured query about the data in the warehouse database—for example, "Are there *any* interesting combinations of items bought by customers?" Such queries are called **data mining**. In contrast with OLAP, in which requests are made to obtain specific information, data mining can be viewed as knowledge discovery—an attempt to extract new knowledge from the data stored in the database.

Data mining queries can be extremely difficult to formulate and might require sophisticated mathematics or techniques from the field of Artificial Intelligence. A query might require many hours to execute and might involve several interactions with the manager for obtaining additional information or reformulating parts of the query.

One widely repeated but perhaps apocryphal success story of data mining is that a convenience store chain used the above query ("Are there *any* interesting combinations . . . ") and found an unexpected correlation: In the early evenings, a high percentage of male customers who bought diapers also bought beer—presumably these customers were fathers who were going to stay home that night with their babies.

We discuss OLAP and data mining further in Chapter 19.

1.5   EXERCISES

1.1 Name three transaction processing systems with which you have interacted during the past month. For each of these systems state what transaction you executed, what real-world event caused you to initiate the transaction, and what change your transaction made in the database accessed by your transaction.

1.2 Name three types of business enterprise, not mentioned in the text, that critically depend on a transaction processing system for their business. For each, write a one-paragraph description of the transaction processing system and how the business depends on it.

1.3 Name three ways that supermarkets make additional profits by using an online scanner checkout system. For example, they might learn what items are bought together.

1.4 Some supermarkets give their customers ID cards that are scanned into the system at check out time and automatically give the customer any coupon discounts he or she is entitled to.

    a. Name three ways the supermarket benefits from this system (not including any savings involved in not having to deal with paper coupons). For example, it might learn what items you have bought and send you targeted ads.

    b. Describe three OLAP queries that might be made against this data.

1.5 Explain why clothing manufacturers often access the database of online checkout systems of major department stores.

1.6 The information systems used by multinational enterprises are usually available twenty-four hours a day, seven days a week. Why?

1.7 Give three examples each of applications requiring

    a. Highly reliable systems

    b. High-throughput systems

    c. Short response time systems

1.8 Explain the following:

    a. Why the checkbook you keep for your checking account is a database and

    b. how your checkbook database is related to the portion of the bank's database corresponding to your checking account.

1.9 Explain why an online material tracking system in a factory is more accurate than an offline system in which paper entries are kept during the day and entered into the computer at night. (That is, explain why the data in the system is more accurate each morning when the day starts, not more up to date during the day.) For example, any input errors can be detected as soon as they occur and can be immediately corrected.

1.10 Your school is planning a new automated student registration system. As a possible user, you are being interviewed by the system analyst doing a requirements analysis for the system.

    a. What transactions would you recommend be available to students? Include some query transactions, in which a student can request information from the system.

    b. Pick one of these transactions, and sketch the design of the forms the user interacts with when that transaction is run.

       c. What are some other classes of users in addition to students? What transactions do you think they would want?

1.11   a. Give three examples of OLAP queries that might be used by administrators in the student registration system described in the previous exercise.

       b. Give an example of a data mining query.

1.12 A number of Internet sites offer you free items if you fill out a detailed multipage registration form. Why?

Chapter 2

A Closer Look

2.1 CASE STUDY: A STUDENT REGISTRATION SYSTEM

Your university is interested in implementing a student registration system so that students can register for courses from their home PCs. You have been asked to build a prototype of that system as a project in this course. The registrar has prepared the following preliminary **Statement of Objectives** for the system.

The objectives of the Student Registration System are to allow students and faculty (as appropriate) to

1. Authenticate themselves as users of the system
2. Register for courses (offered for the next semester)
3. Obtain reports on a particular student's status
4. Maintain information about students and courses
5. Enter final grades for courses that a student has completed

This brief description is typical of what might be supplied as a starting point for a system implementation project, but it is not specific or detailed enough to serve as the basis for the project's design and coding phases. We will be developing the student registration scenario throughout this book and will be using it to illustrate the various concepts in databases and transaction processing.

Our next step is to meet with the registrar, faculty, and students to expand this brief description into a formal Requirements Document for the system. (We will discuss the Requirements Document in Chapter 3.) However, before we do that, we will take a closer look at some of the underlying concepts of databases and transaction processing.

2.2 INTRODUCTION TO RELATIONAL DATABASES

A database is at the heart of most transaction processing systems. At every instant of time, the database must contain an accurate description—often the only one—of the real-world enterprise the transaction processing system is modeling. For example, in the Student Registration System the database is the only source of information about which students have registered for each course.

Figure 2.1   The table STUDENT. Each row describes a single student.

StudId	Name	Address	Status
111111111	John Doe	123 Main St.	Freshman
666666666	Joseph Public	666 Hollow Rd.	Sophomore
111223344	Mary Smith	1 Lake St.	Freshman
987654321	Bart Simpson	Fox 5 TV	Senior
023456789	Homer Simpson	Fox 5 TV	Senior
123454321	Joe Blow	6 Yard Ct.	Junior

We are particularly interested in databases that use the **relational model** [Codd 1970, 1990], in which data is stored in **tables**. The Student Registration System, for example, might include the STUDENT table, shown in Figure 2.1. A table contains a set of **rows**. In the figure, each row contains information about one student. Each **column** of the table describes the student in a particular way. In the example, the columns are Id, Name, Address, and Status. Each column has an associated type, called its **domain**, from which the value in a particular row for that column is drawn. For example, the domain for Id is integer and the domain for Name is string.

This database model is called "relational" because it is based on the mathematical concept of a relation. A **mathematical relation** captures the notion that elements of different sets are related to one another. For example, John Doe, an element of the set of all humans, is related to 123 Main St., an element of the set of all addresses, and to 111111111, an element of the set of all Ids. A relation is a set of **tuples**. Following the example of the table STUDENT, we might define a relation called STUDENT containing the tuple (*111111111, John Doe, 123 Main St., Freshman*). The STUDENT relation presumably contains a tuple describing every student.

We can view a relation as a predicate. A **predicate** is a declarative statement that is either true or false depending on the values of its arguments—for example, the predicate "It rained in Detroit on date X" is either true or false depending on the value chosen for the argument X. When we view a relation as a predicate, the arguments of the predicate correspond to the elements of a tuple, and the predicate is defined to be true exactly when the tuple is in the relation. Thus, we might define the predicate STUDENT and say that STUDENT (*111111111, John Doe, 123 Main St., Freshman)* is true. Hopefully, the truth of this predicate implies that the individual with Id 111111111 does not have the name Bill Smith, and hence the tuple containing the values 111111111 and Bill Smith is not in the STUDENT relation.

The correspondence between tables and relations is now clear: The tuples of a relation correspond to the rows of a table, and the column names of a table are the names of the **attributes** of the relation. Thus, the rows of the STUDENT table can be viewed as enumerating the set of all 4-tuples (tuples with four attributes of the appropriate types) that satisfy the STUDENT relation (i.e., the Id, name, address, and status of a student).

In real applications, tables can become quite large—a STUDENT table for our university would contain over fifteen thousand rows, and each row would likely contain much more information about each student than is shown here. In addition to the STUDENT table, the complete database for the Student Registration System at our university would contain a number of other tables, each with a large number of rows, containing information about other aspects of student registration. Hence, the databases for most applications contain a large amount of information and are generally held in mass storage.

In most applications, the database is under the control of a database management system, which is supplied by a commercial vendor. When an application wants to perform an operation on the database, it does so by making a request to the DBMS. A typical operation might extract some information from the rows of one or more tables, modify some rows, or add or delete rows.

In addition to the fact that tables in the database can be modeled by mathematical relations, these operations on the tables can be modeled as mathematical operations on the corresponding relations. Thus, a particular unary operation might take a table, T, as an argument and produce a result table containing a subset of the rows of T. A particular binary operation might take two tables as arguments and produce a result table containing the union of the rows of the argument tables. A complex query against a database might be equivalent to an expression involving many such relational operations operating on many tables.

Because of this mathematical description, relational operations can be precisely defined and their mathematical properties, such as commutativity and associativity, can be proven. As we shall see in Chapter 14, this mathematical description has important practical implications. Commercial DBMSs contain a **query optimizer** module that converts queries into expressions involving relational operations and then uses these properties to simplify those expressions and thus optimize query execution.

An application describes the access that it wants the DBMS to perform on its behalf in a language supported by the DBMS. We are particularly interested in SQL, the most commonly used database language, which provides facilities for accessing a relational database and is supported by almost all commercial DBMSs.

The basic structure of the SQL statements for manipulating data is straightforward and easy to understand. Each statement takes one or more tables as arguments and produces a table as a result. For example, to find the name of the student whose Id is 987654321, we might use the statement

```
SELECT   Name
FROM     STUDENT
WHERE    Id = '987654321'
```
(2.1)

More precisely, this statement asks the DBMS to extract from the table named in the FROM clause—that is, the table STUDENT—all rows satisfying the condition in the WHERE clause—that is, all rows whose Id column has value 987654321—and then from each such row to delete all columns except those named in the SELECT

Figure 2.2 The database table returned by the SQL SELECT statement (2.2).

Id	Name
987654321	Bart Simpson
023456789	Homer Simpson

clause—that is, Name. The resulting rows are placed in a result table produced by the statement. In this case, because Ids are unique at most one row of STUDENT can satisfy the condition, and so the result of the statement is a table with one column and at most one row. Thus, the FROM clause identifies the table to be used as input, the WHERE clause identifies the rows of that table from which the answer is to be generated, and the SELECT clause identifies the columns of those rows that are to be output in the result table.

The result table generated by this example contains only one column and at most one row. As a somewhat more complex example, the statement

```
SELECT   Id, Name
FROM     STUDENT                    (2.2)
WHERE    Status = 'senior'
```

returns a result table (shown in Figure 2.2) containing two columns and multiple rows: the Ids and names of all seniors. If we want to produce a table containing all the columns of STUDENT but describing only seniors, we use the statement

```
SELECT   *
FROM     STUDENT
WHERE    Status = 'senior'
```

The asterisk is simply shorthand that allows us to avoid listing the names of all the columns of STUDENT.

In some situations the user is interested not in outputting a result table but interested in information *about* the result table. An example is the statement

```
SELECT   COUNT(*)
FROM     STUDENT
WHERE    Status = 'senior'
```

which returns the number of rows in the result table (i.e., the number of seniors). COUNT is referred to as an **aggregate** function because it produces a value that is a function of all the rows in the result table. Note that when an aggregate is used, the SELECT statement produces a single value instead of a table.

The WHERE clause is the most interesting component of the SELECT statement; it contains a general condition that is evaluated over each row of the table named in the FROM clause. Column values from the row are substituted into the condition, yielding an expression that has either a true or a false value. If the condition evaluates to true, the row is retained for processing by the SELECT clause and then stored in the result table. Hence, the WHERE clause acts as a filter.

Conditions can be much more complex than we have seen so far. A condition can be a Boolean combination of terms. If we want the result table to contain information describing seniors whose Ids are in a particular range, for example, we might use

```
WHERE   Status = 'senior' AND Id > '888888888'
```

OR and NOT can also be used. Furthermore, a number of predicates are provided in the language for expressing particular relationships. For example, the IN predicate tests set membership.

```
WHERE   Status IN ('freshman', 'sophomore')
```

Additional aggregates and predicates and the full complexity of the WHERE clause are discussed in Chapter 6.

The result table can contain information extracted from several base tables. Thus, if we have a table TRANSCRIPT with columns StudId, CrsCode, Semester, and Grade, the statement

```
SELECT   Name, CrsCode, Grade
FROM     STUDENT, TRANSCRIPT
WHERE    StudId = Id AND Status = 'senior'
```

can be used to form a result table in which each row contains the name of a senior, a particular course she took, and the grade she received. The first thing to note is that the attribute values in the result table come from different base tables: Name comes from STUDENT; CrsCode and Grade come from TRANSCRIPT. Second, the statement ensures that the rows of TRANSCRIPT for a particular student are associated with the appropriate row of STUDENT. This is guaranteed by the first conjunct of the WHERE clause which matches the Id values of the rows of the two tables. For example, if TRANSCRIPT has a row (987654321, CS305, F1995, C), it will match only Bart Simpson's row in STUDENT, producing the row (Bart Simpson, CS305, C) in the result table.

One very important feature of SQL is that the programmer does not have to specify in detail the algorithm the DBMS should use to satisfy a particular query. For example, tables are frequently defined to include auxiliary data structures, called indices, which make it possible to locate particular rows without using lengthy searches through the entire table. Thus, an index on the Id column of the STUDENT table might contain a list of pairs (*Id, pointer*) where the pointer points to the row of the table containing the corresponding Id. If such an index were present, the DBMS would automatically use it to find the row that satisfies the query (2.1). If the table also had an index on the column Status, the DBMS would use that index to find the rows that satisfy the query (2.2). If this second index did not exist, the DBMS would automatically use some other method to satisfy (2.2)—for example, it might look at every row in the table in order to locate all rows having the value senior in the Status column. The programmer does not specify what method to use—just the condition the desired result table must satisfy.

In addition to selecting appropriate indices to use, the query optimizer uses the properties of the relational operations to further improve the efficiency with which a query can be processed—again, without any intervention by the programmer. Nevertheless, programmers should have some understanding of the strategies the DBMS uses to satisfy queries so they can design the database tables, indices, and SQL statements in such a way that they will be executed in an efficient manner consistent with the requirements of the application.

The following three examples illustrate the SQL statements for modifying the contents of a table. The statement

```
UPDATE     STUDENT
SET        Status = 'sophomore'
WHERE      Id = '111111111'
```

updates the STUDENT table to make John Doe a sophomore. The statement

```
INSERT
INTO       STUDENT (Id, Name, Address, Status)
VALUES     ('999999999', 'Winston Churchill', '10 Downing St',
           'senior')
```

inserts a new row for Winston Churchill in the STUDENT table. The statement

```
DELETE
FROM       STUDENT
WHERE      Id = '111111111'
```

deletes the row for John Doe from the STUDENT table. Again, the details of how these operations are to be performed need not be specified by the programmer.

The STUDENT table itself could have been created with the SQL statement

```
CREATE TABLE   STUDENT(
Id             INTEGER,
Name           CHAR(20),
Address        CHAR(50),                                          (2.3)
Status         CHAR(10),
PRIMARY        KEY(Id) )
```

where we have declared the name of each column and the domain (type) of the data that can be stored in that column. We have also declared the Id column to be a **primary key** to the table, which means that each row of the table must have a unique value in that column and the DBMS will (most probably) automatically construct an index on that column. The DBMS will enforce this uniqueness constraint by not allowing any INSERT or UPDATE statement to produce a row with a value in the Id column that duplicates a value of Id in another row. This requirement is an example of an **integrity constraint** (sometimes called a **consistency constraint**)—an application-based restriction on the values that can appear as entries in the database. We discuss integrity constraints in more detail in the next section.

We have given simple examples of each statement type to highlight the conceptual simplicity of the basic ideas underlying SQL, but be aware that the complete language has many subtleties. Each statement type has a large number of options, that allow very complex queries and updates. For this reason, mastery of SQL requires significant effort. We continue our discussion of relational databases and SQL in Chapter 4.

2.3 WHAT MAKES A PROGRAM A TRANSACTION?

In many applications, a database is used to model the state of some real-world enterprise. In such applications, a transaction is a program that interacts with that database so as to maintain the correspondence between the state of the enterprise and the state of the database. In particular, a transaction might update the database to reflect the occurrence of a real-world event that affects the enterprise state. An example is a deposit transaction at a bank. The event is that the customer gives the teller the cash and a deposit slip. The transaction updates the customer's account information in the database to reflect the deposit.

Transactions, however, are not just ordinary programs. Requirements are placed on them, particularly on the way they are executed, that go beyond what is normally expected of nontransactional programs.

Consistency.   A transaction must access and update the database in such a way that it preserves all database integrity constraints. Every real-world enterprise is organized in accordance with certain rules that restrict the possible states of the enterprise. For example, the number of students registered for a course cannot exceed the number of seats in the room assigned to the course. When such a rule exists, the possible states of the database are similarly restricted.

The restrictions are stated as integrity constraints. The integrity constraint corresponding to the above rule asserts that the value of the database item that records the number of course registrants must not exceed the value of the item that records the room size. Thus, when the registration transaction completes, the database must satisfy this integrity constraint (assuming that the constraint was satisfied when the transaction started).

Although we have not yet designed the database for the Student Registration System, we can make some assumptions about the data that will be stored and postulate some additional integrity constraints.

IC0   The database contains the Id of each student. These Ids must be unique.

IC1   The database contains a list of prerequisites for each course and, for each student, a list of completed courses. A student cannot register for a course without having taken all prerequisite courses.

IC2   The database contains the maximum number of students allowed to take each course and the number of students who are currently registered for each course. The number of students registered for each course cannot be greater than the maximum number allowed for that course.

IC3   It might be possible to determine the number of students registered for (or enrolled in) a particular course from the database in two ways: The number is stored as a count in the information describing the course, and it can be calculated from the information describing each student by counting the number of student records that indicate that the student is registered for (or enrolled in) the course. These two determinations must yield the same result.

In addition to maintaining the integrity constraints, each transaction must update the database in such a way that the new database state reflects the state of the real-world enterprise that it models. If John Doe registers for CS305, but the registration transaction records Mary Smith as the new student in the class, the integrity constraints will be satisfied but the new state will be incorrect. Hence, consistency has two dimensions.

> *Consistency.* The transaction designer can assume that when execution of the transaction is initiated, the database is in a state in which all integrity constraints are satisfied. The designer has the responsibility of ensuring that when execution has completed the database is once again in a state in which all integrity constraints are satisfied and, in addition, that the new state reflects the transformation described in the transaction's specification.

SQL provides some support for the transaction designer in maintaining consistency. When the database is being designed, the database designer can specify certain types of integrity constraints and include them within the statements that declare the format of the various tables in the database. The primary key constraint of the SQL statement (2.3) is an example of this. Later, as each transaction is executed, the DBMS automatically checks that each specified constraint is not violated and prevents completion of any transaction that would cause a constraint violation.

Atomicity.   In addition to the transaction designer's responsibility for consistency, the TP monitor must provide certain guarantees concerning the manner in which transactions are executed. One such condition is atomicity.

> *Atomicity.* The system must ensure that the transaction either runs to completion or, if it does not complete, has no effect at all (as if it had never been started).

In the Student Registration System, either a student has registered for a course or he has not registered for a course. Partial registration makes no sense and might leave the database in an inconsistent state. For example, as indicated by constraint IC3, two items of information in the database must be updated when a student registers. If a registration transaction were to have a partial execution in which one update completed but the system crashed before the second update could be executed, the resulting database would be inconsistent.

When a transaction has successfully completed, we say that it has **committed**. If the transaction does not successfully complete, we say that it has **aborted** and the system has the responsibility of ensuring that whatever partial changes the transaction has made to the database are undone, or **rolled back**. Atomic execution implies that every transaction either commits or aborts.

Notice that ordinary programs do not necessarily have the property of atomicity. For example, if the system were to crash while a program that was updating a file was executing, the file could be left in a partially updated state when the system recovered.

Durability.   A second requirement of the transaction processing system is that it does not lose information.

> *Durability.* The system must ensure that once the transaction commits, its effects remain in the database even if the computer, or the medium on which the database is stored, subsequently crashes.

For example, if you successfully register for a course, you expect the system to remember that you are registered even if it later crashes. Notice that ordinary programs do not necessarily have the property of durability either. For example, if a media failure occurs after a program that has updated a file has completed, the file might be restored to a state that does not include the update.

Isolation.   In discussing consistency, we concentrated on the effect of a single transaction. We next examine the effect of executing a set of transactions. We say that a set of transactions is executed sequentially, or **serially**, if one transaction in the set is executed to completion before another is started. The good news about serial execution is that if all transactions are consistent and the database is initially in a consistent state, serial execution maintains consistency. When the first transaction in the set starts, the database is in a consistent state and, since the transaction is consistent, the database will be consistent when the transaction completes. Because the database is consistent when the second transaction starts, it too will perform correctly and the argument will repeat.

Serial execution is adequate for applications that have modest performance requirements. However, many applications have strict requirements on response time and throughput; often the only way to meet the requirements is to process transactions concurrently. Modern computing systems are capable of servicing more than one transaction simultaneously, and we refer to this mode of execution as concurrent. Concurrent execution is appropriate in a transaction processing system serving many users. In this case, there will be many active, partially completed transactions at any given time.

In concurrent execution, the database operations of different transactions are effectively interleaved in time, a situation shown in Figure 2.3. Transaction T_1 alternately computes using its local variables and sends requests to the database system to transfer data between the database and its local variables. The requests are made in the sequence $op_{1,1}$, $op_{1,2}$. We refer to that sequence as a **transaction schedule**. T_2 performs its computation in a similar way. Because the execution of the two transactions is not synchronized, the sequence of operations arriving at the database, called a **schedule**, is an arbitrary merge of the two transaction schedules. The schedule in the figure is $op_{1,1}$, $op_{2,1}$, $op_{2,2}$, $op_{1,2}$.

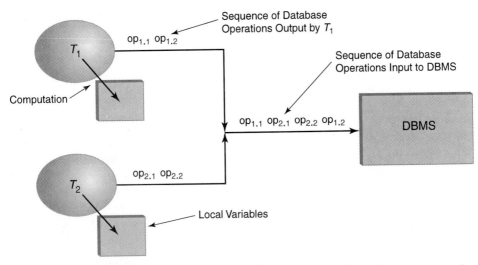

Figure 2.3 The database operations output by two transactions in a concurrent schedule might be interleaved in time. (Note that the figure should be interpreted as meaning that $op_{1,1}$ arrives first at the DBMS, followed by $op_{2,1}$, etc.)

Figure 2.4 A schedule in which two registration transactions are not isolated from each other.

T_1: $r(cur\_reg$: 29) $w(cur\_reg$: 30)

T_2: $r(cur\_reg$: 29) $w(cur\_reg$: 30)

When transactions are executed concurrently, the consistency of each one is not sufficient to guarantee that the database correctly reflects the state of the enterprise. For example, suppose that T_1 and T_2 are two instances of the registration transaction invoked by two students who want to register for the same course. A possible schedule of these transactions is shown in Figure 2.4, where time progresses from left to right and the notation $r(cur\_reg : n)$ means that a transaction has read the database object cur_reg, which records the number of current registrants, and the value n has been returned. (A similar notation is used for $w(cur\_reg : n)$). The figure shows only the accesses[1] to cur_reg.

Assume that the maximum number of students allowed to register is 30 and the current number is 29. In its first step, each of the two transactions will read this

---

[1] In a relational database, r and w represent **SELECT** and **UPDATE** statements.

value and store it in its local variable, and both will decide that there is room in the course. In its second step, each will increment its private copy of the number of current registrants; hence, both will calculate the value 30. In their write operations, both will write that same value, 30, into *cur_reg*.

Both transactions complete successfully, but the number of current registrants is incorrectly recorded as 30 when it is actually 31 (even though the maximum allowable number is 30). This is an example of what is often referred to as a **lost update**, because one of the increments has been lost. The resulting database does not reflect the real-world state, and integrity constraint IC2 has been violated. By contrast, if the transactions had executed sequentially, T_1 would have completed before T_2 was allowed to start. Hence, T_2 would find the course full and would not register the student.

As this example demonstrates, we must specify some restriction on concurrent execution that is guaranteed to maintain the consistency of the database and the correspondence between the enterprise state and the database state. One such restriction that is obviously sufficient follows.

> *Isolation.* Even though transactions are executed concurrently, the overall effect of the schedule must be the same as if the transactions had executed serially in some order.

The exact meaning of this requirement will be made clearer in Chapters 15, 23, and 24. However, it should be evident that if the transactions are consistent and if the overall effect of a concurrent schedule is the same as that of some serial schedule, the concurrent schedule will maintain consistency. Concurrent schedules that satisfy this condition are called **serializable**.

Isolation is usually achieved by requiring transactions to obtain locks on certain database items. If these locks have to be held for a long period of time, other transactions might have to wait until the transactions holding those locks complete, thus increasing response time and decreasing throughput. This is unacceptable for some applications. To accommodate such applications, most commercial DBMSs offer the option of executing at levels of isolation that are not serializable and are not equivalent to serial execution. We discuss these options in Chapters 10, 15, and 24.

As with atomicity and durability, ordinary programs do not necessarily have the property of isolation. For example, if programs that update a common set of files are executed concurrently, updates might be interleaved and produce an outcome that is quite different from that obtained if they had been executed in any serial order. That result might be totally unacceptable.

ACID properties. The features that distinguish transactions from ordinary programs are frequently referred to by the acronym **ACID** [Haerder and Reuter 1983].

Atomic   Each transaction is executed completely or not at all.

Consistent   Each transaction maintains database consistency.

Isolated   The concurrent execution of a set of transactions has the same effect as some serial execution of that set.

Durable   The effects of committed transactions are permanently recorded in the database.

When a transaction processing system supports the ACID properties, the database maintains a consistent and up-to-date model of the real world and the transactions supply responses to users that are always correct and up to date.

2.4   BIBLIOGRAPHIC NOTES

The relational model for databases was introduced in [Codd 1970, 1990]. The SQL language is described in the SQL-92 standard [SQL 1992]. The term *ACID* was coined by [Haerder and Reuter 1983], but the individual components of ACID were introduced in earlier papers—for example, [Gray et al. 1976] and [Eswaran et al. 1976].

2.5   EXERCISES

2.1 Given the relation MARRIED that consists of tuples of the form (a, b), where a is the husband and b is the wife, the relation BROTHER that has tuples of the form (c, d), where c is the brother of d, and the relation SIBLING, which has tuples of the form (e, f), where e and f are siblings, describe how you would define the relation BROTHERINLAW where tuples have the form (x, y) with x being the brother-in-law of y.

2.2 Design the following two tables (in addition to those in Figure 2.1) that might be used in the Student Registration System. Note that the same student Id might appear in many rows of each of these tables.

    a. A table implementing the relation COURSESREGISTEREDFOR relating a student's Id and the identifying numbers of the courses for which she is registered

    b. A table implementing the relation COURSESTAKEN relating a student's Id, the identifying numbers of the courses he has taken, and the grade received in each course

Specify the predicate corresponding to each of these tables.

2.3 Write an SQL statement that

    a. Returns the Ids of all seniors in the table STUDENT

    b. Deletes all seniors from STUDENT

    c. Promotes all juniors in the table STUDENT to seniors

2.4 Write an SQL statement that creates the TRANSCRIPT table.

2.5 Using the TRANSCRIPT table, write an SQL statement that

     a. Deregisters the student with `Id` = 123456789 from the course `CS305` for the fall of 2001

     b. Changes to an A the grade assigned to the student with `Id` = 123456789 for the course `CS305` taken in the fall of 2000

     c. Returns the Id of all students who took `CS305` in the fall of 2000

2.6 Write an SQL statement that returns the names (not the Ids) of all students who received an A in `CS305` in the fall of 2000.

2.7 State whether or not each of the following statements could be an integrity constraint of a checking account database for a banking application. Give reasons for your answers.

     a. The value stored in the `balance` column of an account is greater than or equal to $0.

     b. The value stored in the `balance` column of an account is greater than it was last week at this time.

     c. The value stored in the `balance` column of an account is `$128.32`.

     d. The value stored in the `balance` column of an account is a decimal number with two digits following the decimal point.

     e. The `social_security_number` column of an account is non-null and contains a nine-digit number.

     f. The value stored in the `check_credit_in_use` column of an account is less than or equal to the value stored in the `total_approved_check_credit` column. (These columns have their obvious meanings.)

2.8 State five integrity constraints, other than those given in the text, for the database in the Student Registration System.

2.9 Give an example in the Student Registration System where the database satisfies the integrity constraints IC0–IC3 but its state does not reflect the state of the real world.

2.10 State five (possible) integrity constraints for the database in an airline reservation system.

2.11 A reservation transaction in an airline reservation system makes a reservation on a flight, reserves a seat on the plane, issues a ticket, and debits the appropriate credit card account. Assume that one of the integrity constraints of the reservation database is that the number of reservations on each flight does not exceed the number of seats on the plane. (Of course, many airlines purposely overbook and so do not use this integrity constraint.) Explain how transactions running on this system might violate

     a. Atomicity

     b. Consistency

c. Isolation

d. Durability

2.12 Describe informally in what ways the following events differ from or are similar to transactions with respect to atomicity and durability.

a. A telephone call from a pay phone (Consider line busy, no answer, and wrong number situations. When does this transaction "commit?")

b. A wedding ceremony (Suppose that the preacher does not show up. Suppose that the groom refuses to say "I do." When does this transaction "commit?")

c. The purchase of a house (Suppose that, after a purchase agreement is signed, the buyer is unable to obtain a mortgage. Suppose that the buyer backs out during the closing. Suppose that two years later the buyer does not make the mortgage payments and the bank forecloses.)

d. A baseball game (Suppose that it rains.)

2.13 Assume that, in addition to storing the grade a student has received in every course he has completed, the system stores the student's cumulative GPA. Describe an integrity constraint that relates this information. Describe how the constraint would be violated if the transaction that records a new grade were not atomic.

2.14 Explain how a lost update could occur if, under the circumstances of the previous problem, two transactions that were recording grades for a particular student (in different courses) were run concurrently.

Chapter 3

Case Study: Starting the Student Registration System

3.1 **SOFTWARE ENGINEERING METHODOLOGY**

The implementation of the Student Registration System is proceeding on schedule. **CASE STUDY** A team consisting of faculty, students, and representatives of the registrar has met several times and has refined the informal Statement of Objectives given in Chapter 2 into a formal Requirements Document (which we reproduce in Section 3.2). Now it is time for us to begin our part of the project.

The implementation of a transaction processing system is a significant engineering endeavor. The project must complete on time and on budget, and, when operational, the system must meet its requirements and operate efficiently and reliably. The documentation and coding for the project must be such that the system can be maintained and enhanced over a long lifetime. Most important, it must meet the needs of its users.

On the basis of many years of experience with both successful and unsuccessful software projects, a number of procedures and methodologies have evolved that are generally agreed to be "good engineering practice" in carrying out such a project. Many books and entire courses are devoted to software engineering. Here we sketch one approach and apply it to the Student Registration System.

Projects usually begin with an informal Statement of Objectives as given at the beginning of Chapter 2. The next step is for the customers and users of the system, perhaps with the help of a system analyst, to expand these objectives into a formal **Requirements Document** for the system. The Requirements Document describes in some detail what the system is supposed to do, not how it will do it. In many contexts, the Requirements Document is a Request for Proposals (RFP) to the implementors, describing what the customer wants them to build.

Specification Document. The implementation group analyzes the Requirements Document in detail and produces a **Specification Document**, which is an expanded version of the Requirements Document that describes in still more detail what the system will do. In many contexts, the Specification Document is a contract proposal, describing exactly what the implementation group intends to build. The description is so precise that the User Manual and the Specification Document can be written and published at the same time. The following examples illustrate the different levels of detail in the Requirements and Specification Documents.

■ In the Requirements Document, the set of required interactions with users are listed, together with what each interaction is intended to do. In the Specification Document, the forms associated with each interaction are specified, together with exactly what happens when each button is pressed and each menu item is accessed.

■ The Requirements Document lists the information that must be contained in the system. The Specification Document includes the domains of all items of information.

Note that in the Requirements and Specification Documents we speak of interactions rather than transactions. An interaction is a deliberately vague term that refers to a function a user wants to perform—for example, register for a course or assign a grade. At this stage we do not yet know how many transactions will be required to implement an interaction—that is part of the design.

When the customer has signed off on the Specification Document, the design portion of the project can begin. In contrast with specifications, which describe *what* the system is supposed to do, the design describes how the system is to do what it does. We will discuss design in Chapter 12 and the specific issues involved in designing databases in Chapters 5 and 8. We will give a complete database design for the Student Registration System in Section 5.7 and the complete design and part of the code for the Registration Transaction in Section 12.6.

One reason so much time and effort is put into producing Requirements and Specification Documents is that experience has shown it to be surprisingly difficult to build a system that actually satisfies the customer's needs. Often the system's requirements are quite complex and the customer has difficulty articulating his needs in the precise manner needed for programming, or he leaves out important details (such as what is supposed to happen if a course is canceled after a number of students have registered for it) or specifies some feature and then is unhappy with that feature when it is implemented. It is cheaper and more efficient to work with the customer at the beginning of the project to sharpen and refine the specifications than it is to reimplement the system at the end of the project if it does not meet the customer's needs.

The next steps in the Student Registration System project.   In Section 3.2 we present the Requirements Document for the Student Registration System as given to us by our customer. Note that certain interactions can be performed only by faculty (e.g., assigning a grade) while others can be performed by both students and faculty (e.g., printing a report). This distinction is an example of the role of **authorization**—only certain people are authorized to perform certain activities. Authorization should be contrasted with **authentication**, which in this system uses passwords to ensure that a user is actually who she claims to be.

Note also that there are two categories of information stored in the database. Some information is required—for example, the Id number and password for each student. Other items of information are optional—they might not be available, or they might not have been decided on at the time data is entered. One example is the room number in which a course is to be taught, which might not be known at the time information about the course is entered into the system.

The next phase of the project is to analyze this Requirements Document and produce a formal Specification Document. Sections 3.4 through 3.7 deal with designing a graphical user interface—an essential part of the Specification Document. We will continue our discussion of the Specification Document in Section 3.8.

3.2   REQUIREMENTS DOCUMENT

I. Introduction

The objectives of the Student Registration System are to allow students and faculty (as appropriate) to

A. Authenticate themselves as users of the system

B. Register for courses (offered for the next semester)

C. Obtain reports on a particular student's status

D. Maintain information about students and courses

E. Enter final grades for courses that a student has completed

In this document, the term "enrolled" refers to courses a student is currently taking and the term "registered" refers to courses to be taken by the student in the following semester.

II. Related Documents

A. *Statement of Objectives* of the Student Registration System (including date and version number)

B. This university's *Undergraduate Bulletin* (including date)

III. Information to Be Contained in the System

A. The system shall[1] contain a name, an Id number, a password, and a status for each student and faculty member allowed to use the system. The status indicates whether the individual is a student or a faculty member. The password authenticates users and determines their status as students or faculty members. Id numbers are unique. It is assumed that at least one faculty member has been initialized as a valid user at startup time.

---

[1] Note that the requirements are numbered so that they can be referred to in later documents, such as the Test Plan, which must test that the system meets every one of its requirements. Also, requirements stated using words such as "shall" and "must" are mandatory. Words such as "should" and "can" do not connote a mandatory requirement and should be avoided unless the requirement is optional. For example, in one of the earliest recorded Requirements Documents (even then the requirements were numbered), the commandment is "Thou shall not kill," not "Thou should not kill."

B. The system shall contain the academic record of each student.

   1. Each course the student has completed, the semester the student took the course, and the grade the student received (all grades are in the set {A, B, C, D, F, I})

   2. Each course for which the student is enrolled this semester

   3. Each course for which the student has registered for next semester

C. The system shall contain information about the courses offered, and for each course the system shall contain

   1. The course name, the course number (must be unique), the department offering the course, the textbook, and the credit hours

   2. Whether the course is offered in spring, fall, or both

   3. The prerequisite courses (there can be an arbitrary number of prerequisites for each course)

   4. The maximum allowed enrollment, the number of students who are enrolled (unspecified if the course is not offered this semester), and the number of students who have registered (unspecified if the course is not offered next semester)

   5. If the course is offered this semester, the days and times at which it is offered; if the course is offered next semester, the days and times at which it will be offered. The possible values shall be selected from a fixed list of weekly slots (e.g., MWF10)

   6. The Id of the instructor teaching the course this semester and next semester (the Id is unspecified if the course is not offered in the specified semester; it must be specified before the start of the semester in which the course is offered)

   7. The classroom assignment of the course for this semester and next semester (the classroom assignment is unspecified if the course is not offered in the specified semester; it must be specified before the start of the semester in which the course is offered)

   All information shall be consistent with the *Undergraduate Bulletin*.

D. The system shall contain a record of all courses that have been taught, including the semester in which they were taught and the Id of the instructor.

E. The system shall contain a list of classroom identifiers and the corresponding number of seats. A classroom identifier is a unique three-digit integer.

F. The system shall contain the identity of the current semester (e.g., F1997, S1996).

IV. Integrity Constraints

The database described in Section III shall satisfy the following integrity constraints.

A. Id numbers are unique.

B. If in item III B2 (III B3) of Section 3.2 a student is listed as enrolled (registered) for a course, that course must be indicated in item III C2 as offered this semester (next semester).

C. In item III C4 of Section 3.2 the number of students registered or enrolled in a course cannot be larger than the maximum enrollment.

D. The count of students enrolled (registered) in a course in item III B2 (III B3) of Section 3.2 must equal the current enrollment (registration) indicated in item III C4.

E. An instructor cannot be assigned to two courses taught at the same time in the same semester.

F. Two courses cannot be taught in the same room at the same time in a given semester.

G. If a student is enrolled in a course, the corresponding record must indicate that the student has completed all prerequisite courses with a grade of at least C.

H. A student cannot be registered (enrolled) in two courses taught at the same hour.

I. A student cannot be registered for more than twenty credits in a given semester.

J. The room assigned to a course must have at least as many seats as the maximum allowed enrollment for the course.

K. Once a letter grade of A, B, C, D, or F has been assigned for a course, that grade cannot later be changed to an I.[2]

V. Interactions with the System

Interactions with the system are organized into sessions. A session starts when a user executes an Authentication interaction and ends when a user executes an End-of-Session interaction. During a session, a user can execute one or more interactions.

A. *Authentication.* Whenever a session starts, the user must be authenticated. The purpose of this interaction is to identify the user and to determine whether she is a student or faculty member. Subsequent interactions in the same session depend on this distinction. The input to the interaction is the Id number and password.

---

[2] This is an example of a *dynamic* integrity constraint, which limits the allowable changes to the state of a database, in contrast to a *static* integrity constraint, which limits the allowable states of the database. We discuss dynamic integrity constraints in Section 4.2.2.

B. *Registration.* This interaction can be performed only by students. Its purpose is to register the student in a course to be taught next semester. The input is a course number. The output shall include one of the following:

1. The course number if the student succeeded in registering for the course
2. The reason the student was unable to register

The registration shall not be successful for any of the following reasons, which shall be contained in the output.

1. There exists a prerequisite course that the student has not completed with a grade of at least C or is currently not enrolled in.
2. The number of students registered for the course would exceed the allowed maximum.
3. The initiator of the interaction is not a student.
4. The student has registered for another course scheduled at the same time.
5. The student is enrolled in the course or has taken the course and has received a grade of C or better.
6. The course is not offered next semester.
7. The student is already registered for the course.
8. The student would be taking more than 20 credits if the registration were to succeed.

C. *Deregistration.* The interaction can be performed only by students. Its purpose is to deregister the student from a course to be taught next semester for which that student previously registered. The input to this interaction is a course number. The deregistration will be unsuccessful if the student is not registered for the course.

D. *Get Grade History.* The purpose of this interaction is to produce a report describing the grade history of a student for each semester in which he has completed courses. It uses a student Id number. If a student is executing the interaction, the number need not be entered because the student can request only his or her own report and the Id of the invoker has been determined as part of authentication. If a faculty member is executing the interaction and an invalid student Id is input, the interaction shall not succeed. The report shall include

1. Current semester
2. Student name and Id number
3. List of courses completed with grade and instructor grouped by semester
4. Semester GPA and total number of credits for each semester in which the student has completed courses
5. Cumulative GPA and total number of credits of all courses completed so far

E. *Get Registered Courses.* The purpose of this interaction is to produce a report listing the courses for which a particular student has registered for the next semester. The interaction uses a student Id number. If a student is executing the interaction, the number need not be entered because the student can request only his or her own report and the Id of the invoker has been determined as part of authentication. If a faculty member is executing the interaction and an invalid student Id is input, the interaction shall not succeed. The report shall include

1. Student's name and Id number
2. Course number and credit hours
3. Time schedule for every course
4. Classroom assignment (if available)
5. Instructor (if available)

F. *Get Enrolled Courses.* The purpose of this interaction is to produce a report listing the courses in which a particular student is enrolled this semester. The interaction uses a student Id number. If a student is executing the interaction, the number need not be entered because the student can request only his or her own report and the Id of the invoker has been determined as part of authentication. If a faculty member is executing the interaction and an invalid student Id is input, the interaction shall not succeed. The report shall include

1. Student's name and Id number
2. Course number and credit hours
3. Time schedule for every course
4. Classroom assignment
5. Instructor

G. *Student Grade.* The purpose of this interaction is to assign or change a grade for a course a student has completed. The interaction can be performed only by the faculty member who taught the course. The inputs are a student Id number, a course number, a semester, and a grade.

1. The interaction shall not succeed if
   a. The invoker is not the faculty member who taught the course in the semester indicated.
   b. The student Id number is invalid.
   c. The student is not currently enrolled in the course or did not take the course in a previous semester.
   d. The interaction would change a grade (A, B, C, D, F) to an I.
2. If the interaction succeeds
   a. The student will no longer be shown as enrolled in that course, but will be shown as having completed that course.

b. If the course is a prerequisite for some course in the following semester for which the student is currently registered and if the grade is less than C, the student will be deregistered from that course.

H. *Student/Faculty Information.* The purpose of this interaction is to add, delete, or edit an entry specified in item III A. If an entry is to be added, the name, Id number, faculty/student status, and password must be supplied. If an entry is to be deleted or edited, the Id number must be provided as well as any fields to be changed. The interaction shall not succeed if the invoker is not a faculty member.[3]

I. *Course Information.* The purpose of this interaction is to display or edit the information describing an existing course (item III C) or to enter information describing a new course. The input to the interaction is a course number. This interaction can change any characteristic of a course, but cannot delete the course. Students shall be allowed only to display (not to enter or edit) information about a course. The interaction shall not succeed if the edited course information would violate any integrity constraint.

J. *End of Semester.* The purpose of this interaction is to end the semester. It can be invoked only by a faculty member. The interaction shall have the following effects:

1. The identity of the current semester as specified in item III F shall be advanced.

2. For each student, an I grade shall be assigned for all courses in which that student is currently enrolled and for which no grade has yet been assigned.

3. Each student shall be indicated as enrolled in those courses for which the database previously indicated that the student was registered.

4. For each course listed in item III C4, the number of students enrolled shall be set equal to the number registered and the number registered shall be set to 0.

The interaction shall fail if there will be a course taught next semester to which an instructor or classroom has not yet been assigned.

K. *Get Class Roster.* The purpose of this interaction is to produce a list of the names and Id numbers of students currently enrolled in or registered for a course. The interaction can be executed only by a faculty member. The input to the interaction is a course number and an indication of whether an enrollment or a registration list is requested. The interaction shall fail if an enrollment list for a course not currently being taught or a registration list for a course not to be taught next semester is requested.

---

[3] In a real system, this information would be controlled by a database administrator using a special set of transactions. In this project, we assume for simplicity that the database has been initialized with at least one faculty member's name, Id, and password.

L. *Room*. The purpose of this interaction is to display the size of an existing classroom (item III E) or to enter the identifier and size of a new classroom. The input to the interaction is a classroom identifier and the number of seats (if a new classroom is to be entered) or just the identifier (if the size of an existing classroom is requested). The interaction can be invoked only by a faculty member.

M. *OLAP Query*. The purpose of this interaction is to allow the user to input an arbitrary query from the screen. The interaction can be executed only by a faculty member (who, it is assumed, knows the database schema). The query is in the form of a single SELECT statement. The table produced by the query is output on the screen with attribute names (where possible) heading each column. The interaction fails if a statement other than a SELECT is input or if the statement is incorrect.

N. *End of Session*. The purpose of this interaction is to end the session. Any subsequent interactions with the system require a new authentication.

VI. System Issues

A. The system shall be implemented as a client/server system. The client computer shall be a PC on which the application programs will execute.

B. The application programs shall be implemented using an application generator.

C. The user interface shall be graphical and easy to use by students and faculty with little or no training.

D. The database can be any SQL database that executes on an available server computer and provides a transactional interface (in other words, it can perform the commit and abort operations).

VII. Deliverables

A. A Specification Document that describes in detail the sequence of events (input/output) that occurs for each interaction, including
   1. The forms and controls to be used
   2. The effect of using each control on each form, including any new forms that are displayed as a result of each possible action
   3. The errors for which the system checks and the error messages that are output
   4. Integrity constraints

B. A Design Document that describes in detail
   1. An Entity-Relationship (E-R) diagram that describes the system
   2. The declaration of all database elements (including tables, domains, and assertions)

   3. The decomposition of each interaction into transactions and procedures

   4. The behavior of each transaction and procedure

C. A Test Plan describing how the system will be tested, including how each of the numbered requirements and specifications will be tested

D. A demonstration of the completed system (including running the tests in the Test Plan)

E. Fully documented code for the system

F. A User Manual with separate sections for student and faculty

G. Version 2 of the Specification Document, the Design Document, and the Test Plan, describing the as-built system

3.3   REQUIREMENTS ANALYSIS—NEW ISSUES

Experience has shown that, no matter how carefully the Requirements Document is written, when the implementation team analyzes the requirements in order to prepare the Specification Document, a number of new issues will be identified. Parts of the Requirements Document will be found to be inconsistent or incomplete, and questions will be raised about the desired behavior of the system in certain previously unforeseen situations. The implementation team customarily presents these issues to the customer, who resolves them in a written document. The resolved issues then become part of a revised version of the Requirements Document and part of the initial version of the Specification Document. This entire scenario underscores the difficulties in precisely specifying the desired behavior of a proposed system.

When the Requirements Document given in the last section was analyzed by our local implementation team, a number of issues were identified. Below we present some of them together with their resolution. Your local implementation team is likely to discover other issues.

Issue 1.   What if, during the Course Information interaction, an attempt is made to add a new prerequisite for a course such that the prerequisites form a cycle? For example, course A is a prerequisite for course B, B is a prerequisite for course C, and C is a prerequisite for A. In other words, course A is a prerequisite for itself.

Resolution. A new database integrity constraint must be added to deal with this situation: There must not be a cycle of prerequisites. Any transaction that implements the Course Information interaction shall check for this condition, and, if it exists, the prerequisite shall not be added and an appropriate message shall be presented to the user. (The check for circularity in the general case is not simple. We might, however, require that the prerequisite for a course have a lower number than the course itself. Such a requirement eliminates the possibility of circularity.)

Issue 2. What if, during the Course Information interaction, an attempt is made to add a new prerequisite for a course and a student who does not have that prerequisite is already registered for that course?

Resolution. A new prerequisite for a course does not apply to the offering of the course (if any) in the following semester.

Issue 3. What if, during the Course Information interaction, the maximum number of students allowed in a course is reduced to a value that is less than the number of students who have already registered for the course?

Resolution. Room rescheduling is a fact of academic life, so this interaction must be allowed. However, the appropriate number of students must be deregistered from the course to bring the total number of registered students to the new maximum. The students shall be deregistered in the reverse order that they were registered. All deregistered students shall be notified in writing.

Issue 4. What if, during the Course Information interaction, an attempt is made to change the day and/or time a course is offered?

Resolution. A change in day and/or time does not apply to the offering of the course (if any) in the following semester.

Issue 5. What if, during the Course Information interaction, a course is canceled?

Resolution. Cancelation applies to the next semester. Students registered for the next semester shall be deregistered and notified in writing.

Issue 6. What if, during a Student/Faculty Information interaction, an attempt is made to change a student's Id number?

Resolution. An Id number (in contrast to a name or password) is permanently associated with an individual, so an attempt to change it makes no sense, except if it was originally entered in error. As a result, a change in Id number is allowed only if there is no other information relevant to the student in the system.

Issue 7. Several of the interactions, such as Get Grade History, Get Registered Courses, and Get Enrolled Courses, produce reports that describe the state of the database at a particular instant of time. Should those reports include the date and time they were produced?

Resolution. Yes, all such reports shall include the date and time.

Issue 8. Should the information in items III D and III F contain the year as well as the semester?

Resolution. Yes, and the End of Semester interaction shall appropriately update the year. This information shall be initialized at startup time.

Issue 9. How many digits should be used to indicate the year in the system?

Resolution. Four.

3.4 APPLICATION GENERATORS

The Student Registration System requires a sophisticated user interface, which must be specified in detail in the Specification Document. The user interface must contain forms, command buttons, menus, textboxes, and the like. Specifying and programming such an interface would appear to be a formidable task. Fortunately, there are a number of application generators that can considerably reduce the amount of programming knowledge and effort necessary to do the job. In this section, we discuss the basic concepts underlying these application generators.

An application generator usually contains the following components.

■ A Graphical User Interface (GUI) Designer that the application programmer can use to design the GUI to which users of the system will interface: forms, command buttons, menus, and so forth.

■ A programming language that can be used to write application programs, access databases, and execute transactions.

■ An Integrated Program Development Environment that includes a program editor and other tools to help the application programmer write programs and transactions and link them to the GUI.

■ A mechanism that allows the generated programs to connect to and access one or more DBMSs, either on the local computer or on some other computer across a network.

Some database application generators also contain facilities for automatically generating SQL statements from some graphical or tabular notation. However, we are interested only in how GUIs are generated and how they interact with application programs. We do not discuss any particular application generator, but use a notation similar to that used in many commercial systems. We distinguish between the designer of the application and the user of the application. (In this section, we use the term *designer* to refer to the application programmer who interacts with the application generator to design the user interface.)

3.5 GUIS AND OBJECTS

The GUI to a transaction processing system consists of a set of **forms**. For example, the form shown in Figure 3.1 can be used to authenticate users in the Student Registration System. Each form is represented within the system by an **object**. (We briefly discuss objects in the Appendix, Section A.1.1.) For example, the object corresponding to a particular form might have a method called Show that causes the form to be displayed on the screen. Each form contains a set of **controls**, such as

■ **Labels** that display text on the screen—for example, the heading in the figure.

■ **Textboxes** in which the user can enter information to be input to the application program and in which the application program can enter information to be

Welcome to the Student Registration System

Please enter your login Id and password

Id

Password

| OK | | Exit |

Figure 3.1   Introductory form for the Student Registration System.

output to the user. For example, in Figure 3.1, the user's Id and password are
input through textboxes.

■ **Command buttons** that the user can click with the mouse to cause the system to
take some action. In the figure, for example, when the command button labeled
OK is pushed, the system reads the information that has been entered in the
textboxes to authenticate the user.

■ **Menus**, **Checkboxes**, and **Optionboxes** that the user can click with the mouse
to express a choice.

The controls are also represented as objects within the system. For example, a
menu might have a method called `display_menu` that is executed when the menu
is clicked. The method causes the drop-down menu list to be displayed.

To design a user interface, the designer enters the GUI Designer and, with a
click of the mouse, asks it to create a blank form on the screen. Then the designer
can select an appropriate set of controls from a menu, place them on the form
with additional mouse clicks, and rearrange them with the usual drag-and-drop
operations. The GUI Designer might display a picture of a textbox, which the
designer can copy and then drag to its desired position on the form.

These controls and forms are represented by objects that have an associated visual representation on the screen. Thus, we refer to them as **visual objects**, which we can think of as encapsulating the following two data structures.

1. A data structure that represents the semantic (nonvisual) aspects of the object. For the textbox object, this data structure might contain two strings: Name, whose value is the name of the textbox (each visual object must have a unique name that can be used within the application program to refer to the object), and Text, whose value is the text stored in the textbox (and displayed on the screen).

2. A data structure that contains the information about the visual representation of the object. A command button object might have a label that is the text printed on the command button. Additional information might be stored in variables named Location, Color, Font, Typesize, and so forth.

Taken as a whole, the information in these two data structures is referred to as the **properties** or **attributes** of the object. During the design process, the application designer can ask the GUI Designer to display the properties of any object, perhaps in a table like that shown in Figure 3.2, which shows some properties of the textbox object.

When the object is initially created, some of its properties, such as the Name of the textbox, might be given default values—for example, Textbox1. To change the name, the designer just types the desired text into the Name entry in the property table. In a similar way, the designer can customize each object in each form by

Figure 3.2 Some properties of a textbox object.

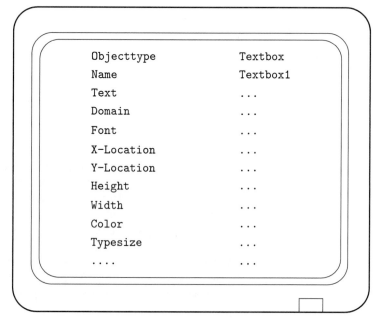

Objecttype	Textbox
Name	Textbox1
Text	. . .
Domain	. . .
Font	. . .
X-Location	. . .
Y-Location	. . .
Height	. . .
Width	. . .
Color	. . .
Typesize	. . .
. . . .	. . .

changing its properties. As we will see, properties can also be changed at run time by the application programs.

One of the properties of a textbox object might be the **domain** of the information—the allowable values that can be entered into the textbox at run time. For example, the domain of a textbox that is supposed to contain a Social Security number would be a nine-digit character string; the domain of a textbox that is supposed to contain the user's gender would be the character M or F. When the user enters the information, the system automatically checks whether the input is within the allowable domain and produces an appropriate error message if it is not.

In addition to the data structures containing its properties, a visual object also encapsulates a set of methods, which we might call a **drawing engine**, that uses the information in the data structures to draw the visual representation of the object on the screen. The method Show is an example. The drawing engine methods are called automatically when the object is displayed.

An important task of the drawing engine is to keep the visual representation and the data structure representation of the object consistent. Thus, for example, if the designer uses the table in Figure 3.2 to change from red to green the Color property of the data structure representation of a displayed textbox object, a drawing engine method is (automatically) called that changes from red to green the visual representation of the object on the screen. Similarly, if the designer uses the mouse to drag the visual representation of a textbox object from one location to another on the form, the drawing engine method that moves the object also changes the value of the Location property in the data structure representation of the object.

Thus, with very little effort the designer can create and customize a set of forms for a particular application. One reason this is so easy is that the methods for manipulating the objects, including their visual representation, have been supplied by the application generator and are encapsulated within the object modules. All the designer is doing is changing the object properties.

Most application generators supply a large library of visual object classes that can be used in various combinations on a form—all with a minimum amount of programming by the designer. In addition, most application generators allow the designer to enhance the properties of these classes by defining child classes or by editing the code within them—thus providing more flexibility at the expense of additional complication.

Creating GUIs without an application generator.   Many languages—Java is one example—include a library of visual objects (with appropriate drawing engines) that can be used to create GUIs without an application generator, using conventional programming techniques. For example, using the Java Abstract Window Toolkit (AWT) library, a program can create a new instance of a button object, explicitly set its properties, and place it on a window—all with method calls included in the library. Because the visual objects in the library include appropriate drawing engines, the designer need not be concerned with any details of how the objects are actually drawn. Using such a library, the designer can thus write a program that creates a GUI with surprisingly little effort beyond that required with an application generator.

To make the GUI respond to the user's inputs, the program uses the event handling mechanisms of the language. These mechanisms are also used when the GUI has been generated with an application generator and are the subject of the next section.

3.6 EVENTS AND PROCEDURES

Although a minimum amount of programming is needed to draw objects on the screen, the designer must implement procedures for performing the specific application-related functions that are executed at run time. These procedures, written in the language provided by the application generator, form the application program. An application procedure might

■ Cause a form to be displayed when the application starts

■ Gather and validate the information input through the forms

■ Change some property of an object on a form (e.g., its appearance on the screen)

■ Perform application-related computations and initiate the appropriate transactions to access the database (including executing SQL statements)

■ Display output information from transactions on the appropriate forms

■ Produce appropriate printed reports

■ Control devices that interact with the real-world application

The implementation of many of these functions involves invoking the methods of the forms and controls.

The application procedures are **event driven**. An **event** is an action usually (but not always) initiated by the user at run time. Each control has an associated set of events to which it responds. For example, a command button object responds when the mouse is clicked on it. A label object, for example, the heading in Figure 3.1, does not respond to a click. The designer can associate an application procedure with each event associated with an object. The application generator (or the implementation of the language used for the application procedures) provides a mechanism that, at run time, recognizes when an event occurs and what object the event is associated with, and then calls the associated procedure. We say that the event **triggers** the procedure call. In this way, the designer can associate a procedure with the event "The command button labeled OK in the form shown in Figure 3.1 is clicked." This procedure is then automatically called when the button is clicked at run time.

Events have names, such as Click for the click event. The association between the event and the application procedure to be executed when the event occurs might be made through the procedure's name. Thus, the application generator might require that the application procedure to be called when the command button labeled OK is clicked be named okbutton.Click, where okbutton is the unique (internal) name of the button (as distinguished from its external label, OK, printed on the screen)—that is, the value of its Name property.

CASE
STUDY

The designer must implement the application procedure so that it carries out the processing required by the event. The `okbutton.Click` procedure for the form shown in Figure 3.1 might

■ Execute an authentication transaction using the Id and password that have been entered in the textboxes in the form

■ Cause new forms to be displayed depending on whether the authentication transaction succeeds or fails

The designer can also associate application procedures with events that are not directly initiated by the user. An event might occur when the application is initiated, when a certain time period has elapsed, or when a system error occurs.

The next issue is how an application procedure accesses information on a form or changes the properties of an object. As we have seen, many properties of objects can be manipulated by methods that are supplied by the application generator and encapsulated within the object module. At design time, for example, the designer can change the `color` property of a command button object by modifying the color entry in the command button's property table. This modification results in the call of one of the methods of the object (supplied by the application generator), which modifies the color attribute within the object and then calls the appropriate drawing engine method to redraw the command button on the screen.

Methods can also be called from the application procedures and so can be executed at run time to change the appearance of forms or controls or to input or output information through textboxes. The organization of the routines is shown in Figure 3.3. As an example, an application procedure can cause a form named `form1` to be displayed at run time by invoking the procedure `form1.Show`.

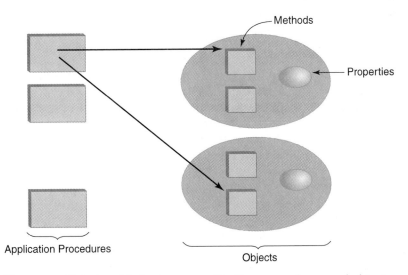

Figure 3.3 Relationship between application procedures and objects.

As another example, suppose that the (internal) name of the top textbox in Figure 3.1 is IDbox. One of the properties of a textbox is Text, which refers to the string of characters displayed in the textbox. An application procedure can access that string using the notation IDbox.Text. Thus, IDbox.Text appears to be a variable in the procedure. The procedure can read the value of that variable or assign a new value to it. If an application procedure wants to assign the text in IDbox to another variable, st, for example, it might use the statement

```
st = IDbox.Text
```

and if it wants to write text into a textbox used for output, named outbox, it might use the statement

```
outbox.Text = "This is the text."
```

In both cases, the execution of the assignment operator results in a call to an appropriate method of the object. In the first case, the effect of the method is to assign to the (program) variable st the value stored in the variable Text in the data structure of IDbox (the value of the Text property). (This is an example of an object method that does not affect the visual representation of the object.) In the second case, the assignment method assigns the specified string to the variable Text in the data structure of the textbox named outbox and then calls the appropriate drawing engine method to change the visual representation of outbox so that the specified string is displayed.

In general, a procedure can access any property of any object using the variable

```
object_name.property_name
```

and can execute a method of an object using the statement

```
object_name.method_name ( . . . arguments . . . )
```

Thus, as shown in Figure 3.3 an application program consists of a set of application procedures, which are called when certain specified events take place. Once called, a procedure can access and change the information on the screen using the properties and methods associated with the objects displayed. Note that the application procedures are not encapsulated within an object module (as are the methods described above). They access objects as they might access other globally declared data structures.

3.7 ACCESSING DATABASES AND EXECUTING TRANSACTIONS

Commercial application generators differ widely in the facilities they offer application programs for accessing databases and executing transactions. At a minimum, a generator should provide the ability for application programs to

■ Connect to a database on a local or remote server.

■ Execute SQL statements on the database.

■ Execute stored procedures within the server (if the server supports stored procedures).

■ Utilize the transactional facilities provided by the server.

More sophisticated application generators might allow a single transaction to access several databases on different servers. We will consider each of these capabilities in more detail in Chapter 10, when we discuss how SQL statements and other database calls can be included in application programs.

Automatically generating SQL statements.   Some application generators provide facilities for users to construct simple databases and generate simple queries using graphical notation. Queries constructed in this way are automatically translated into SQL or SQL-equivalent statements. We will discuss the conceptual framework underlying these visual query languages in Section 7.3.

Data forms.   Some application generators provide a high-level abstraction, which we might call a **data form** (also sometimes called a **data page**), in which it appears to the designer and the user that a particular form is directly connected to the database. When the form is initially displayed, textboxes on it are populated with appropriate database values. Whenever the user changes the value in one of these textboxes, the database is immediately updated to reflect that change.

Data forms can be easily implemented using the concepts of event programming. The display of the form is an event, and the application program that responds to that event contains a SELECT statement that reads information from the database and displays it in the form's textboxes. The application generator allows the user to specify the SELECT statement using graphical notation.

Similarly, when the user changes the value in some textbox and then moves the cursor out of that textbox, a **change-of-focus** event occurs, which causes the execution of a statement that updates the database appropriately. Again, the statement can be specified using graphical notation. The designer can thus create a data form without having to be concerned with the details of event programming or, if the graphical notation is simple enough, with the details of SQL programming.

Object-oriented application languages.   If the language provided by the application generator for writing application programs is object oriented, application-related entities can be represented as objects. In the Student Registration System, for example, the application programmer might implement an object class called `course` with a method called `register` for adding students to a course. Because the information about course registration is kept in the database, the `register` method must read and update the database.

Objects such as `course` or `student` are sometimes called **enterprise objects** because they correspond to the basic entities with which the enterprise is concerned. Access to the database can be encapsulated within these objects. The database itself might be relational or object oriented (see Chapter 16), but only the methods of the enterprise objects need be aware of the schema.

Application procedures that use enterprise objects respond to events that occur in the real world, and they enforce the rules of the enterprise in addition to invoking the methods of the visual objects in order to interact with the user through the GUI. For example, the application procedure for registering a student in a course might first call the methods of the `student` object (e.g., to determine whether the student has taken the prerequisite courses) and then call the `register` method for the `course` object.

Using enterprise objects, application procedures can be designed to implement the requirements of the enterprise without any knowledge of the database design. Thus, for example, the programmer who designs the procedure for registering students need not know the schema of the database.

3.8   SPECIFYING THE STUDENT REGISTRATION SYSTEM

Now that we have seen how easy it is to build a GUI, we can go back to preparing the Specification Document for the Student Registration System. One advantage of an application generator is that, during the requirements analysis phase of the project, while the forms and controls are being specified, the designer can quickly implement simple prototypes of the interface and show them to the customer. Although these prototypes do not contain the application procedures to implement interactions, they give the customer a feeling for how the system will appear. The customer can then make changes and improvements to make the interface more useful and intuitive to its users.

A Specification Document contains a complete description of what the system is supposed to do from the viewpoint of its end users—it is an expanded version of the Requirements Document. For a transaction processing system, the Specification Document should include

■ The integrity constraints of the enterprise

■ A picture of every form with every control specified

■ A description of what happens when each control is used, including
  ❏ What application procedure is executed
  ❏ What changes occur in the form or what new form is displayed
  ❏ What error situations can occur and what happens in each such situation

■ A description of each interaction, including
  ❏ The information input by the user and what events cause the interaction to be executed
  ❏ A textual description of what the interaction does (for example, the student is registered for the course)
  ❏ A list of conditions under which the interaction succeeds or fails, and what happens in each case

The Specification Document might also contain other information related to project planning (such as schedules, milestones, deliverables, cost information, etc.), information related to system issues (such as software and hardware on which the system must run), and any time or memory constraints. The Table of Contents for the Specification Document for the Student Registration System has the following sections.

CASE STUDY

I. Introduction
II. Related Documents
III. Forms and User Interactions
IV. Project Plans
A. Milestones

B. Deliverables

Note the relationship between the contents of the Requirements and Specification Documents.

In the following section, we present the initial part of Section III of the Specification Document. We give a database design for the Student Registration System in Section 5.7 and the design and part of the code for the Registration Transaction in Section 12.6.

3.9 SPECIFICATION DOCUMENT

Section III of the Specification Document—Forms and User Interactions—contains a detailed description of all interactions with users. Its initial part might look like the following.

III. Forms and User Interactions
A. When the Student Registration System is entered, Form 1, the Welcome Form (Figure 3.1) is displayed. In Form 1

    1. The Id and Password textboxes are filled in.

    2. The OK command button is clicked to run the *Authentication* interaction.

        a. If the *Authentication* interaction fails, Form 2, the Authentication Error Form, is displayed.[4] In Form 2, clicking the OK command button returns to Form 1.

        b. If the *Authentication* interaction succeeds, and the authenticated user is a student, Form 3, the Student Options Form, is displayed (see Specification B).

        c. If the *Authentication* interaction succeeds, and the authenticated user is a faculty member, Form 4, the Faculty Options Form, is displayed (see Specification C).

---

[4] We omit the figures for the other forms; they would be included in the actual specification.

3. The Exit command button is clicked to display Form 5, the Do You Really Want To Exit Form. In Form 5
    a. The Yes command button is clicked to exit the Student Registration System.
    b. The No command button is clicked to return to Form 1.

B. If the *Authentication* interaction succeeds, and the authenticated user is a student, Form 3, the Student Options Form, is displayed. In Form 3
    1. The Course description menu item is selected to run the *Get_Course_Names* interaction, which displays Form 6, the Course Name Form. In Form 6
        a. A course option box is selected.
        b. The OK command button is clicked to run the *Get_Course_Description* interaction, which displays Form 7, the Course Description Form.
        c. The Cancel command button is clicked to return to Form 3.

The remainder of Section III of the Specification Document is similar and is therefore omitted.

3.10   BIBLIOGRAPHIC NOTES

There are many excellent books on software engineering—for example, [Summerville 1996], [Pressman 1997], and [Schach 1990]. One of the very few books that address software engineering for database and transaction processing systems is [Blaha and Premerlani 1998].

3.11   EXERCISES

3.1 Prepare a Requirements Document for a simple calculator.

3.2 According to the Requirements Document for the Student Registration System, one session can include a number of interactions. Later, during the design, we will decompose each interaction into one or more transactions. The ACID properties apply to all transactions, but a session that involves more than one transaction might not be isolated or atomic. For example, the transactions of several sessions might be interleaved. Explain why the decision was made not to require sessions to be isolated and atomic. Why is a session not one long transaction?

3.3 Suppose that the database in the Student Registration System satisfies all the integrity constraints given in Section IV of the Requirements Document Outline (Section 3.2). Is the database necessarily correct? Explain.

3.4 The Requirements Document for the Student Registration System does not address security issues. Prepare a section on security issues, that might be included in a more realistic Requirements Document.

CASE
STUDY

3.5 In the resolution of issue 2 in Section 3.3, the statement was made that new prerequisites do not apply to courses offered in the next semester. How can a Registration Transaction know whether or not a prerequisite is "new"?

3.6 Suppose that the Student Registration System is to be expanded to include graduation clearance. Describe some additional items that must be stored in the database. Describe some additional integrity constraints.

3.7 Use your local application generator to implement the form shown in Figure 3.1.

3.8 List all of the properties of the command button object provided by your local application generator.

3.9 List all of the (user-visible) methods of the command button object provided by your local application generator.

3.10 List all of the control objects provided by your local application generator.

3.11 List all of the events that can be used to trigger procedure calls in your local application generator.

3.12 Describe the facilities provided by your local application generator to interact with databases.

3.13 Use your local application generator to implement a tic-tac-toe game in which the user plays against the system (and the user never wins).

3.14 Prepare a Specification Document for a simple calculator.

3.15 Use your local application generator to implement a simple calculator.

3.16 Prepare a Specification Document for the controls of a microwave oven. ■

Part Two

DATABASE MANAGEMENT

Now we are ready to begin our study of databases.

In Chapter 4, we will discuss how data items are specified in modern database management systems (DBMSs) and how they appear to the transactions that use them. In other words, we will learn a few things about data models and data definition languages.

In Chapters 6, 7, and 9, we will discuss how transactions access and modify data in a DBMS using data manipulation and query languages—in particular, SQL.

In Chapter 10, we will discuss how SQL statements can be performed from within a host language, such as C or Java.

In Chapters 5 and 8, we will talk about techniques for designing database structures and how database design affects the fundamental trade-off between read-only transactions (i.e., queries) and update transactions.

In Chapters 11, 13, and 14, we will discuss data organization and query processing techniques used in databases. These issues are important for tuning databases for performance. In Section 5.7 and Chapter 12, we will show how these ideas can be applied to the design of the Student Registration System.

In Chapter 15, we will give a brief overview of transaction processing, which is one of the most important application areas for databases.

Chapter 4

The Relational Data Model

This chapter is an introduction to the relational data model. First, we define its main abstract concepts, and then we show how these concepts are embodied in the concrete syntax of SQL. Specifically, this chapter covers the data definition subset of SQL, which is used to specify data structures, constraints, and authorization policies in databases.

4.1 WHAT IS A DATA MODEL?

Data independence. Ultimately, all data is recorded as bytes on a disk. However, as a programmer you know that working with data at that very low level of abstraction can be quite tedious. Few people are interested in how sectors, tracks, and cylinders are allocated for storing information. Most programmers much prefer to work with data stored in *files*, which is a more reasonable abstraction for many applications.

From a course on file structures, you might be familiar with a variety of methods for storing data in files. **Sequential** files are best for applications that access records in the order they are stored. **Direct access** (or **random access**) files are best when records are accessed in a more or less unpredictable order. Files might have **indices**, which are auxiliary data structures that enable applications to retrieve records based on the value of a **search key**. We will discuss various index types in Chapter 11. Files might also consist of fixed-length records or records that have variable lengths.

The details of how data is stored in files belong to the **physical level** of data modeling. This level is specified using a **physical schema**, which in the database field refers to the syntax that describes the structure of files and indices.

Early data-intensive applications worked directly with the physical schema instead of the higher levels of abstraction provided by a modern DBMS. This choice was made for a number of reasons. First, commercial database systems were rare and costly. Second, computers were slow and working directly with the file system offered a performance advantage. Third, most early applications were primitive by today's standards, and building a level of abstraction between those programs and the file system did not seem justified.

A serious drawback of this approach is that changes to the file format at the physical level could have costly repercussions for software maintenance. The "year 2000 problem" was a good example of such repercussions. In the 1960s and 1970s, it was common to write programs in which the data item representing the calendar year was hard-coded as a two-digit number. The rationale was that these programs would be replaced within fifteen to twenty years, so using four digits (or using a data abstraction for the DATE data type) was a waste of precious disk space. The result was that every routine that worked with dates expected to find the year in the two-digit format. Hence, any change to that format implied finding and changing code throughout the application. The consequence of these past decisions was the multibillion-dollar bill presented to the industry in the late 1990s for fixing outdated software.

If a data abstraction, DATE, had been used in those programs, the whole problem could have been avoided. Applications would have viewed years as four-digit numbers, even though they had been physically stored in the database as two-digit numbers. To adjust to the change of millennium, designers could have changed the underlying physical representation of years in the database to four-digit numbers by (1) building a simple program that converted the database by adding 1900 to every existing year field and (2) correspondingly changing the implementations of the appropriate functions within the DATE data type to access the new physical representation. None of the existing applications would have had to be modified because they could still use the same DATE data abstraction.

When the underlying data structures are subject to change (even infrequently), data-intensive applications design based on a bare file system becomes problematic. Even trivial changes, such as adding or deleting a field in a file, imply that every application that uses this file must be manually updated, recompiled, and retested. Less trivial changes, such as merging two fields or splitting a field into two, might impact the existing applications quite significantly. Accommodating such changes can be labor intensive and error prone. In addition, the data in the original file needs to be converted to the new representation, and without the appropriate tools such conversion can be costly.

Also, the file system offers too low a level of abstraction to support the development of an application that requires frequent and rapid implementation of new queries. For such applications, the **conceptual level** of data modeling becomes appropriate.

The conceptual model hides the details of the physical data representation and instead describes data in terms of higher-level concepts that are closer to the way humans view it. For instance, the **conceptual schema**—the syntax used to describe the data at the conceptual level—could represent some of the information about students as

Student (Id: INT, Name: STRING, Address: STRING, Status: STRING)

While this schema might look similar to the way file records are represented, the important point is that the different pieces of information it describes might be *physically* stored in a different way than that described in the schema. Indeed, these pieces of information might not even reside in the same file (perhaps not even on the same computer!).

The possibility of having separate schemas at the physical and conceptual levels leads to the simple, yet powerful, idea of **physical data independence**. Instead of working directly with the file system, applications see only the conceptual schema. The DBMS maps data between the conceptual and physical levels *automatically*. If the physical representation changes, all that needs to be done is to change the mapping between the levels, and *all* applications that deal exclusively with the conceptual schema will continue to work with the new physical data structures.

The conceptual schema is not the last word in the game of data abstraction. The third level of abstraction is called the **external schema** (also known as the **user** or **view** abstraction level). The external schema is used to customize the conceptual schema to the needs of various classes of users, and it also plays a role in database security (as we will discuss later).

The external schema looks and feels like a conceptual schema, and both are defined in essentially the same way in modern DBMSs. However, while there is a single conceptual schema per database, there might be several external schemas (i.e., views on the conceptual schema), usually one per user category. For example, to generate proper student billing information, the bursar's office might need to know each student's GPA and status and the total number of credits the student has taken, but not the names of the courses and the grades received. Even though the GPA and total number of credits might not be stored in the database explicitly, the bursar's office can be presented with a view in which these items appear as regular fields (whose values are calculated at run time when the field is accessed), and all fields and relations that are irrelevant to billing are omitted. Similarly, an academic advisor does not need to know anything about billing, so much of this information can be omitted from the advisor's view of the registration system.

These ideas lead to the principle of **conceptual data independence**: Applications tailored to the needs of specific user groups can be designed to use the external schemas appropriate for these groups. The mapping between the external and conceptual schemas is the responsibility of the DBMS, so applications are insulated from changes in the conceptual schema *as well as* from changes in the physical schema. The overall picture is shown in Figure 4.1.

Data models.   A **data model** consists of tools and languages for describing

1. **Conceptual and external schemas**. A schema specifies the structure of the data stored in the database. Schemas are described using a **data definition language (DDL)**.

2. **Constraints**. A constraint specifies a condition that the data items in the database must satisfy. A constraint specification sublanguage is usually part of the DDL.

3. **Operations on data**. Operations on database items are described using a **data manipulation language (DML)**. The DML is usually the most important and

Figure 4.1 Levels of data independence.

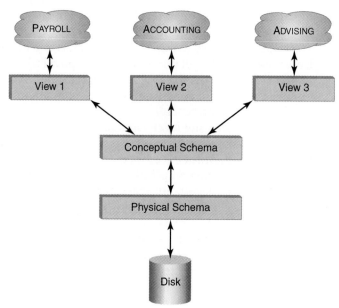

interesting part of any data model because it is the set of operations that ultimately gives us the high-level data abstraction.

In addition, all commercial systems provide some kind of **storage definition language** (**SDL**), which allows the database designer to *influence* the physical schema (although most systems reserve the final say). The SDL is usually tightly integrated with the DDL. Changes in the physical schema that might occur if the database administrator introduces new SDL statements into a database do not affect the semantics of the applications because physical data independence shields the application from physical changes. Hence, although the performance of an application might change, the results it produces do not.

In the following few sections, we describe the mother of all data models used by commercial DBMSs, the *relational model*, and the *lingua franca* these DBMS speak, *Structured Query Language* (**SQL**). Be aware, however, that despite its name SQL is not *just* a query language; it is a DML, a DDL, and an SDL—three for the price of one!

4.2   THE RELATIONAL MODEL

The *relational data model* was proposed in 1970 by E.F. Codd and was considered a major breakthrough at the time. In fact, database research and development in the 1970s and 1980s was largely shaped by the ideas presented in Codd's original work [Codd 1970, 1990]. Even today, most commercial DBMSs are based on the relational model, although they are beginning to acquire object-oriented features.

The main attraction of the relational model is that it is built around a simple and natural mathematical structure, the *relation* (or table). Relations have a set of powerful, high-level operators, and data manipulation languages are deeply rooted in mathematical logic. This solid mathematical background means that relational expressions (i.e., queries) can be analyzed. Hence, any expression can potentially be transformed (by the DBMS itself) into another, *equivalent,* expression that can be executed more efficiently, in a process called *query optimization.* Thus, application programmers need not study the nitty-gritty details of the internals of each database and need not be aware of how query evaluators work. The application programmer can formulate a query in a simple and natural way and leave it to the query optimizer to find an equivalent query that is more efficient to execute.

Nevertheless, query optimizers have limitations that can result in performance penalties for certain classes of complex queries. It is therefore important for both programmers and database designers to understand the heuristics they use. With this knowledge, programmers can formulate queries that the DBMS can optimize more easily and database designers can speed up the evaluation of important queries by adding appropriate indices and using other design techniques.

4.2.1 Basic Concepts

The central construct in the relational model is the **relation**. A relation is two things in one: a **schema** and an **instance** of that schema.

Relation instance. A **relation instance** is nothing more than a table with rows and named columns. When no confusion arises, we refer to relation instances as just "relations." The rows in a relation are called **tuples**; they are similar to *records* in a file, but unlike file records all tuples have the same number of columns (this number is called the **arity** of the relation), and no two tuples in a relation instance can be the same. In other words, a relational instance is a set of unique tuples. The **cardinality** of a relation instance is the number of tuples in it.

Figure 4.2 shows one possible instance for the STUDENT relation. The columns in this relation are named, which is the usual convention in the relational model. These named columns are also known as **attributes**. Moreover, because relations are *sets* of tuples, the order of their tuples is immaterial. Similarly, because columns

Figure 4.2 Instance of the STUDENT relation.

STUDENT	Id	Name	Address	Status
	111111111	John Doe	123 Main St.	Freshman
	666666666	Joseph Public	666 Hollow Rd.	Sophomore
	111223344	Mary Smith	1 Lake St.	Freshman
	987654321	Bart Simpson	Fox 5 TV	Senior
	023456789	Homer Simpson	Fox 5 TV	Senior
	123454321	Joe Blow	6 Yard Ct.	Junior

Figure 4.3 STUDENT Relation with different order of columns and tuples.

STUDENT	Id	Name	Status	Address
	111223344	Mary Smith	Freshman	1 Lake St.
	987654321	Bart Simpson	Senior	Fox 5 TV
	111111111	John Doe	Freshman	123 Main St.
	023456789	Homer Simpson	Senior	Fox 5 TV
	666666666	Joseph Public	Sophomore	666 Hollow Rd.
	123454321	Joe Blow	Junior	6 Yard Ct.

are named, their order in a table is of no importance. The relations in Figures 4.2 and 4.3 are thus considered to be the same relation.

We should note that the terms "tuple," "attribute," and "relation" are preferred in relational database theory, while "row," "column," and "table" are the terms used in SQL. However, it is common to use these terms interchangeably.

The value of a particular attribute in any row of a relation is drawn from a set called the attribute **domain**—for example, the Address attribute of the STUDENT relation has as its domain the set of all strings. One important requirement placed on the values in a domain is **data atomicity**.[1] Data atomicity does not mean that these values are not decomposable. After all, we have seen that the values can be strings of characters, which means that they *are* decomposable. Rather, data atomicity means that the relational model does not specify any means for looking into the internal structure of the values, so they appear indivisible to the relational operators.

This atomicity restriction is sometimes seen as a shortcoming of the relational model, and most commercial systems relax it in various ways. Some remove it altogether, which leads to a new breed of database models known as *object-relational*. We will return to the object-relational model in Chapter 16.

Relation schema.   A **relation schema** consists of

1. The **name** of the relation. Relation names must be unique across the database.

2. The names of the *attributes* in the relation along with their associated *domain names*. An **attribute** is simply the name given to a column in a relation instance. All columns in a relation must be named, and no two columns in the same relation can have the same name. A **domain name** is just a name given to some well-defined set of values. In programming languages, domain names are usually called *types*. Examples are INTEGER, REAL, and STRING.

3. The *integrity constraints (IC)*. **Integrity constraints** are restrictions on the relational instances of this schema (i.e., restrictions on which tuples can appear

---

[1] The notion of *data atomicity* has nothing to do (and should not be confused) with *transaction atomicity*.

in an instance of the relation). An instance of a schema is said to be **legal** if it satisfies all ICs associated with the schema.

To illustrate, let us revisit the schema that was mentioned before:

STUDENT(Id:INTEGER, Name:STRING, Address:STRING, Status:STRING)

This schema states that STUDENT relations must have exactly four attributes: Id, Name, Address, and Status with *associated domains* INTEGER and STRING.[2] As seen from this example, different attributes in the same schema must have distinct names but can share domains.

The domains specify that in STUDENT relations all values in the column Id must belong to the domain INTEGER, while the values in all other columns must belong to the domain STRING. Naturally, we assume that the domain INTEGER consists of all integers and that the domain STRING consists of all character strings. However, schemas can also have *user-defined* domains, such as SSN or STATUS, that can be constrained to contain precisely the values appropriate for the attributes at hand. For instance, the domain STATUS can be defined to consist just of the symbols "freshman," "sophomore," and so forth, and the domain SSN can be defined to contain all (and only) nine-digit positive numbers. The point of this discussion is that relation schemas impose so called *type constraints*.

A **type constraint** is a requirement that if **S** is a relation schema and **s** is a relation instance, then **s** must satisfy the following two conditions.

Column naming. Each column in **s** must correspond to an attribute in **S** (and vice versa), and the column names must be the same as the names of the corresponding attributes.

Domain constraints. For each attribute–domain pair, attr:DOM, in **S**, the values that appear in the column attr in **s** must belong to the domain DOM.

As we shall see, typing is just one of the several classes of constraints associated with relation schemas. To be legal, a schema instance must therefore satisfy typing as well as those additional constraints.

Relational database.   A **relational database** is a finite set of relations. Because a relation is two things in one, a database is also two things: a set of relation schemas (and other entities that we will describe shortly)—called a **database schema**—and a set of corresponding relation instances—called a **database instance**. When confusion does not arise, it is common to use the term "database" to refer to database instances only. Figure 4.4 depicts one possible fragment of a database schema for our Student Registration System. Figure 4.5 gives examples of instances corresponding to these relation schemas. Observe that each relation satisfies the type constraint specified by the corresponding schema.

---

[2] The Id attribute can also be stored as a string, and such a representation might be more appropriate for some universities. However, integer representation is more compact, and we choose to use it for illustrative purposes.

Figure 4.4 Fragment of the Student Registration database schema.

STUDENT (Id:INTEGER, Name:STRING, Address:STRING, Status:STRING)
PROFESSOR(Id:INTEGER, Name:STRING, DeptId:DEPTS)
COURSE (DeptId:DEPTS, CrsCode:COURSES, CrsName:STRING,
        Descr:STRING)
TRANSCRIPT (StudId:INTEGER, CrsCode:COURSES, Semester:SEMESTERS,
            Grade:GRADES)
TEACHING (ProfId:INTEGER, CrsCode:COURSES, Semester:SEMESTERS)

4.2.2 Integrity Constraints

We discussed the role that integrity constraints play in an application in Section 2.2. Now we have to fit these constraints into the database schema that supports that application. An **integrity constraint** (**IC**) is a statement about all *legal instances* of a database. That is, to be qualified as a legal instance a set of relations must satisfy all ICs associated with the database schema. We have already seen the type and domain constraints, and we will discuss several other kinds of constraints later.

Some integrity constraints are based on the business rules of the enterprise. The statement "Employees must not earn more than their bosses" is one example. Such constraints are often listed in the Requirements Document of the application. Other constraints, such as type and domain constraints, are based on the schema design and are specified by the database designer.

Since ICs are part of the database schema, they are usually specified in the original schema design. It is also possible to add or remove ICs later, after the database has been created and populated with data. Once constraints have been specified in the schema, it is the responsibility of the DBMS to make sure that they are not violated by the execution of any transactions.

An IC can be **intra-relational**, meaning that it involves only one relation, or it can be **inter-relational**, meaning that it involves more than one relation. The type constraint is an example of an intra-relational constraint; another example is a constraint that states that the value of the Id attribute in all rows of an instance of the STUDENT table must be unique. The latter is called a **key constraint** (discussed later). The constraint that asserts that the value of the attribute Id of each professor shown as teaching a course appear as the value of the Id attribute of some row of the table PROFESSOR is an inter-relational constraint called a **foreign key constraint** (discussed later). It expresses the requirement that each faculty member teaching a course be described by some row of the table that describes all faculty members. The rule that employees must not earn more than their bosses[3] can be intra-relational or inter-relational, depending on whether the salary information and the management structure information are stored in the same or different relations. This constraint

---

[3] For now, let us not worry about such subtleties as how this constraint applies to the company president, who has no boss.

Figure 4.5 A Fragment of a database instance.

PROFESSOR	Id	Name	DeptId
	101202303	John Smyth	CS
	783432188	Adrian Jones	MGT
	121232343	David Jones	EE
	864297531	Qi Chen	MAT
	555666777	Mary Doe	CS
	009406321	Jacob Taylor	MGT
	900120450	Ann White	MAT

COURSE	CrsCode	DeptId	CrsName	Descr
	CS305	CS	Database Systems	On the road to high-paying job
	CS315	CS	Transaction Processing	Recover from your worst crashes
	MGT123	MGT	Market Analysis	Get rich quick
	EE101	EE	Electronic Circuits	Build your own computer & save
	MAT123	MAT	Algebra	The world where $2 * 2 \neq 4$

TRANSCRIPT	StudId	CrsCode	Semester	Grade
	666666666	MGT123	F1994	A
	666666666	EE101	S1991	B
	666666666	MAT123	F1997	B
	987654321	CS305	F1995	C
	987654321	MGT123	F1994	B
	123454321	CS315	S1997	A
	123454321	CS305	S1996	A
	123454321	MAT123	S1996	C
	023456789	EE101	F1995	B
	023456789	CS305	S1996	A
	111111111	EE101	F1997	A
	111111111	MAT123	F1997	B
	111111111	MGT123	F1997	B

Figure 4.5 (continued)

Teaching	ProfId	CrsCode	Semester
	009406321	MGT123	F1994
	121232343	EE101	S1991
	555666777	CS305	F1995
	864297531	MGT123	F1994
	101202303	CS315	S1997
	900120450	MAT123	S1996
	121232343	EE101	F1995
	101202303	CS305	S1996
	900120450	MAT123	F1997
	783432188	MGT123	F1997
	009406321	MGT123	F1997

belongs to the class of *semantic constraints*, which we will also discuss later in this section.

The constraints up to this point were **static ICs**. **Dynamic ICs** are different: Instead of restricting the legal instances of a database, they restrict the evolution of legal instances. This type of constraint is particularly useful for representing the business rules of an enterprise. An example is a rule that salaries must not increase or decrease by more than 5% per transaction. Another example is a rule that the marital status of a person cannot change from single to divorced. A bank might have a rule that if an overdraft has been made, it must be covered by the end of the next business day through a transfer of funds from the line of credit account.

Unfortunately, the mainstream data manipulation languages (such as SQL) and commercial DBMSs provide little support for automatic enforcement of dynamic constraints. Therefore, application designers must provide code that enforces such constraints within the transactions that update the database. Because there is no easy way to verify that the transactions actually obey those rules, the integrity of such databases depends on the competence of the design, coding, and quality assurance groups that implement the transactions.

The situation with static ICs is much more satisfactory. Such constraints are both easier to specify and—in most cases—easier to enforce than dynamic ICs. In this section, we discuss the most common static integrity constraints. The following section shows how they are specified in SQL.

Key constraints.   We have already seen one example of a key constraint: Values of the Id attribute in an instance of the STUDENT table must be unique. For a more complex example, consider the TRANSCRIPT relation. Because it seems reasonable to assume that a student can get only one (final) grade for any course in any given semester, we can specify that {StudId, CrsCode, Semester} is a key. This specification ensures that for any given value for StudId, CrsCode, and Semester, there is *at most* one transcript record with these values. If such a tuple actually exists, it specifies the one and only grade that a given student got for a given course in a given semester.

With this intuition in mind, we can give a more precise definition of a key constraint. A **key constraint**, key($\overline{K}$), associated with a relation schema, **S**, consists of a subset, $\overline{K}$, of attributes of **S** with the following property: An instance, **s**, of **S satisfies** key($\overline{K}$) if it does not contain a pair of distinct tuples whose values agree on *all* of the attributes in $\overline{K}$.

Every key constraint, key($\overline{K}$), of schema **S** is assumed to have a certain *minimality property*: No subset of key($\overline{K}$) can be a key constraint for **S**. Therefore, it is an error to specify, for example, both {A} and {A,B}, where A and B are attributes, as keys in the same relation. Also, if {A,B} is a key, then at most one tuple can have a given pair of values, a and b, in attributes A and B. However, it is possible for two different tuples to have the same value in attribute A but not in B, and vice versa.

Thus, in the TRANSCRIPT relation it is quite possible to have two distinct tuples that record the same course taken by the same student, provided that this course was taken in *different semesters*. Likewise, there is no restriction on a particular student taking several *different courses* during the *same semester*.

Three points are important regarding the notion of a key.

1. If key($\overline{K}$) is a key constraint in schema **S** and $\overline{L}$ is a set of attributes in **S** that *contains* $\overline{K}$, then legal instance of **S** cannot contain *distinct* tuples that agree on every attribute in $\overline{L}$. Indeed, if t and s are tuples that have the same values for each attribute in $\overline{L}$, then they must have the same values for each attribute in $\overline{K}$. But because key($\overline{K}$) is a key constraint, t and s must be the same tuple.

   These ideas lead to the following notion: A set of attributes in **S** that contains a key is called a **superkey** of **S**. A superkey might happen to be a key, but there can be superkeys that are not keys. For instance, in our TRANSCRIPT example, {StudId, CrsCode, Semester} is a superkey that is also a key. {StudId, CrsCode, Semester, Grade} is a superkey but not a key. In other words, a superkey is like a key but without the minimality condition. Thus, we can say that a set of attributes, $\overline{K}$, forms a key if it is a superkey and no strict subset of $\overline{K}$ is a superkey.

2. Every relation has a key (and hence a superkey). Indeed, the set of all attributes in a schema, **S**, is always a superkey because if a legal instance of **S** has a pair of tuples that agree on all attributes in **S**, then these must be identical tuples. Because relations are sets, they cannot have identical elements. Now, if the set of all attributes in **S** is not a minimal superkey, there must be a superkey that is a strict subset of **S**. If that superkey is not a minimal superkey, there must be an even smaller superkey. As the number of attributes in a relation is finite, we will eventually hit the minimal superkey, which must then be a key by definition.

Figure 4.6 Fragment of the Student Registration database with key constraints.

```
STUDENT(Id:INTEGER, Name:STRING, Address:STRING, Status:STRING)
    Key: {Id}
PROFESSOR(Id:INTEGER, Name:STRING, DeptId:DEPTS)
    Key: {Id}
COURSE(CrsCode:COURSES, DeptId:DEPTS, CrsName:STRING,
        Descr:STRING)
    Keys: {CrsCode}, {DeptId,CrsName}
TRANSCRIPT(StudId:INTEGER, CrsCode:COURSES, Semester:SEMESTERS,
        Grade:GRADES)
    Key: {StudId,CrsCode,Semester}
TEACHING(ProfId:INTEGER, CrsCode:COURSES, Semester:SEMESTERS)
    Key: {CrsCode,Semester}
```

3. A schema can have several different keys. For instance, in the COURSE relation, CrsCode can be one key. But because it is unlikely that the same department will offer two different courses with the same name, we can specify that {DeptId, CrsName} is also a key in the same relation.

   If a relation has several keys, they are referred to as **candidate keys**. However, one key is often designated as the **primary key**. A primary key might or might not have any particular semantic significance in the application (often a primary key is just the first among equals). However, commercial DBMSs treat primary keys as requests to optimize the storage structures to enable efficient access to data whenever the value of a primary key is given, so the choice of primary key affects the physical schema.

Our fragment of the student registration database schema, with all of the key constraints included, is summarized in Figure 4.6. Note that the relation COURSE has two keys.

Referential integrity.   In relational databases, it is common for tuples in one relation to reference tuples in the same or other relations. For instance, the value 009406321 of ProfId in the first tuple in TEACHING (Figure 4.5) refers to Professor Jacob Taylor, whose tuple in the table PROFESSOR has the same value in the Id field. Likewise, the value MGT123 in the first tuple of TEACHING references the Market Analysis course described by a tuple in the COURSE table.

   In many situations, it is a violation of data integrity if the referenced tuple does not exist in the appropriate relation. For instance, it makes little sense to have a TEACHING tuple ⟨009406321, MGT123, F1994⟩ and not have the tuple describing MGT123 in the COURSE relation: Otherwise, which course is Jacob Taylor teaching? Likewise, if the PROFESSOR relation has no tuple with Id 009406321, who is the professor who is said to teach Market Analysis?

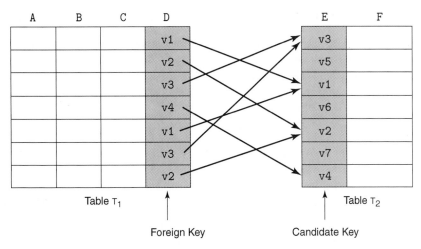

Figure 4.7 Attribute D in Table T_1 is a foreign key that refers to the candidate key, attribute E, in Table T_2.

The requirement that the referenced tuples must exist (when the semantics of the data so requires) is called **referential integrity**. One important type of referential integrity is the so-called *foreign key constraint*.[4]

Suppose that **S** and **T** are relation schemas, $\overline{F}$ is a list of attributes in **S**, and $\text{key}(\overline{K})$ is a key constraint in **T**. Suppose further that there is a known 1-1 correspondence between the attributes of $\overline{F}$ and $\overline{K}$ (but the names of the attributes in $\overline{F}$ and $\overline{K}$ need not be the same). We say that relation instances **s** and **t** (over schemas **S** and **T**, respectively) satisfy the **foreign key constraint** "**S**$(\overline{F})$ references **T**$(\overline{K})$" and that $\overline{F}$ is a **foreign key** if and only if, for every tuple $s \in$ **s**, there is a tuple $t \in$ **t** that has the same values over the attributes in $\overline{K}$ as does s over the corresponding attributes in $\overline{F}$.

The concept of a foreign key constraint is illustrated in Figure 4.7, where, in Table T_1, attribute D has been declared a foreign key that refers to attribute E in Table T_2. E must be a candidate (or primary) key of T_2, but note that the names of the referring and referenced attributes (D and E) in the two tables need not be the same. Note also that, although each row of T_1 must reference exactly one row of T_2, not all rows of T_2 need be referenced and two or more rows in T_1 can reference the same row in T_2.

In the next section, we will show how foreign key constraints are specified in SQL and discuss the precise semantics of such constraints (which is slightly more permissive than the definition we have just given).

---

[4] Keep in mind that the notion of referential integrity is more general than that of the foreign key constraint. Soon we will introduce *inclusion dependency*, which is an example of another type of referential integrity.

Figure 4.8 Some foreign key constraints for the Student Registration System.

TRANSCRIPT(StudId) <u>references</u> STUDENT(Id)
TRANSCRIPT(CrsCode) <u>references</u> COURSE(CrsCode)
TEACHING(ProfId) <u>references</u> PROFESSOR(Id)
TEACHING(CrsCode) <u>references</u> COURSE(CrsCode)
TRANSCRIPT(CrsCode,Semester) <u>references</u> TEACHING(CrsCode,Semester)

In a foreign key constraint, the referring and the referenced relations need not be distinct. For instance, in the schema

EMPLOYEE(Id:INTEGER, Name:STRING, MngrId:INTEGER)

with the key {Id} the supervisor is also an employee. Thus, we have the constraint "EMPLOYEE (MngrId) <u>references</u> EMPLOYEE(Id)." This constraint implies that in every tuple of the EMPLOYEE relation, for example, ⟨....., ..., 998877665⟩—the MngrId value 998877665 must occur in the Id field in this or some other tuple of the same relation.

For Figure 4.6, the foreign key constraints implied by the intended semantics of the data are shown in Figure 4.8. Three things are noteworthy here.

1. The attributes used to cross-reference relations need not have the same name. For instance, the attribute StudId of TRANSCRIPT references a STUDENT attribute named Id, not StudId. The foreign key constraint in the above EMPLOYEE relation is another example of the same phenomenon.

2. A foreign key might consist of more than one attribute, as illustrated by the last constraint in Figure 4.8. In plain English, this constraint states that if some student took a course in a particular semester, there must have been a professor who taught that course in that semester.

3. This point is more subtle. Contrary to a popular belief, professors do not teach empty classes—at least at some universities. In other words,

TEACHING(CrsCode,Semester)
      <u>references</u> TRANSCRIPT(CrsCode,Semester)   (4.1)

appears to be an appropriate constraint for our database: At least one student must have taken (or be taking) the course named in each tuple of TEACHING. Hence, (4.1) is a referential integrity constraint, but is it a foreign key constraint? The definition of foreign keys requires that the set of attributes *referred to* must be a candidate key in the *referenced* relation.

The set ⟨CrsCode, Semester⟩ is not a candidate key of TRANSCRIPT because there can be several different students taking the same course in any given semester. This example shows that there can be referential integrity constraints that are not foreign key constraints.

The above constraint is known as an **inclusion dependency** in database theory. A foreign key constraint is just a special kind of inclusion dependency, one where the referenced attribute set is a key. Unfortunately, because of the complexity of automatic enforcement of general inclusion dependencies, such dependencies are not part of SQL's DDL. However, they can be expressed using SQL's assertion mechanism. This is illustrated later in this chapter: The CREATE ASSERTION statement (4.4) is one possible representation of constraint (4.1).

Semantic constraints. Type, domain, key, and foreign key constraints are structural—they constrain the structure of the data. Other types of constraints might have little to do with structure, but rather might implement a business rule or convention in a particular enterprise. Such constraints are *semantic* because they are derived from the particular application domain being modeled by the database.[5]

A number of semantic constraints for the Student Registration System were discussed in Chapter 3. The number of students registered for a course must not exceed the capacity of the classroom where the course is scheduled to meet, a student registered for a course must meet all the prerequisites for the course, and so forth. As we will show later, SQL provides support for specifying a wide range of semantic constraints.

4.3   SQL—DATA DEFINITION SUBLANGUAGE

Having familiarized ourselves with the basic concepts of the relational model—tables and constraints—we are now ready to look at how these concepts are specified in the "real world"—the data definition sublanguage of SQL. We base our discussion on the SQL-92 standard, but be aware that most database vendors do not fully support this standard. Because most SQL manuals are hundreds of pages long (and the actual standard has several thousand pages), we discuss only the most salient points of the language. You will need a vendor-specific reference manual if you plan to undertake serious SQL projects.

Still, SQL-92 belongs to the past and you should be planning for the future. So to illustrate some concepts that are important for transaction processing, we also peek into the new standard, SQL:1999. We will discuss other parts of the SQL:1999 standard later in the book. The most significant of those are triggers in Section 9.2 and object-relational databases in Section 16.5. Some vendors are beginning to support parts of this standard in their latest releases.

Schemas are specified using the CREATE TABLE statement of SQL. This statement has a rich syntax, which we will introduce gradually. As a bare minimum, CREATE TABLE specifies the typing constraint: the name of a relation and the names of the attributes with their associated domains. However, the same statement can also specify primary and candidate keys, foreign key constraints, and even certain semantic constraints.

---

[5] The term "semantic constraint" might be somewhat misleading, because one can argue that keys and foreign keys are also semantic constraints that reflect certain business rules.

4.3.1 Specifying the Relation Type

The type for the STUDENT relation is defined as follows.[6]

```
CREATE TABLE  STUDENT (
Id            INTEGER,
Name          CHAR(20),
Address       CHAR(50),
Status        CHAR(10) )
```

You should have no difficulty relating this SQL schema to earlier examples. To make the reserved words more conspicuous, we highlight them in a different font.

4.3.2 The System Catalog

A DBMS must use information describing the structure of the database when it translates a statement of the DML into an executable program. It finds this information in the **system catalog**. Although its main purpose is to define a schema, the CREATE TABLE command also inserts rows describing the created table into the catalog. The catalog is a collection of special relations with their own schema. Figure 4.9 shows a table, COLUMNS, that could be part of a catalog. Each row of COLUMNS contains information about a column in some database table, and all columns in all database tables are described in this way. The four columns of the table COURSE, for example, are described by four rows in COLUMNS.

Because COLUMNS is also a table, its description must be recorded. Rather than creating a special set of tables for this purpose, it is convenient to describe COLUMNS (and the other tables of the catalog) as a set of tuples in the catalog itself! Thus, the first few rows of COLUMNS describe the schema of that relation. For example, the first row says that the first column of COLUMNS has the attribute name AttrName and the domain CHAR (255).

How then does all this referential complexity get bootstrapped? The catalog schema of a DBMS is designed by the vendor, and an instance of the catalog is created automatically whenever a new database is initialized (by the database administrator).

4.3.3 Key Constraints

Primary keys and candidate keys are specified in SQL using two separate statements: PRIMARY KEY and UNIQUE. For instance, the schema of the table COURSE might look like this:

```
CREATE TABLE  COURSE  (
CrsCode       CHAR(6),
DeptId        CHAR(4),
CrsName       CHAR(20),
Descr         CHAR(100),
PRIMARY KEY   (CrsCode),
UNIQUE        (DeptId,CrsName) )
```

---

[6] To avoid confusion, we use different fonts for relation names, attributes, and their types.

Figure 4.9 Catalog relation.

COLUMNS	AttrName	RelName	Position	Format
	AttrName	Columns	1	CHAR(255)
	RelName	Columns	2	CHAR(255)
	Position	Columns	3	CHAR(255)
	Format	Columns	4	CHAR(255)
	CrsCode	Course	1	CHAR(6)
	DeptId	Course	2	CHAR(4)
	CrsName	Course	3	CHAR(20)
	Descr	Course	4	CHAR(100)
	Id	Student	1	INTEGER
	Name	Student	2	CHAR(20)
	Address	Student	3	CHAR(50)
	Status	Student	4	CHAR(10)
	...	...	...	...

Notice that we changed the domain of DeptId from DEPTS to CHAR(4) and that of CrsCode from COURSES to CHAR(6). Do not worry—we will show later how to use the more informative domain names. The reason for this temporary move is that CHAR and INTEGER are built-in domains while DEPTS and COURSES must be defined by the user. Later we will discuss how this is done in SQL.

4.3.4 Dealing with Missing Information

Relations as we have defined them consist of tuples, which are in turn sequences of *known* values. For instance, in tuple ⟨111111111, Doe John, 123 Main St., freshman⟩, we have known values for Id, Name, Address, and so forth. In practice, the values of certain attributes might not be known. For example, when John Doe initially registers as a student we might not know his address. We might ask him to supply it as soon as possible, but we do not have to keep him out of our database until he complies. Instead, we use a placeholder, called NULL, and store it in place of the address until more information becomes available. Similarly, a tuple is entered in the TRANSCRIPT relation when a student registers for a course, but the Grade attribute for that tuple has no value specified until the semester completes.

The NULL placeholder is commonly referred to as a **null value**, but this is somewhat misleading because NULL is not a value, rather, it indicates the *absence* of a "normal" value. In database theory and practice, NULL is treated as a special value that is a member of every attribute domain but is different from any other value in any domain. In fact, as we will see in Chapter 6, NULL is not even equal to itself!

In our example, null values arise because of a lack of information. In other situations, they arise by design. For instance, the attribute MaidenName is applicable to females but not to males. A database designer might decide that the schema

EMPLOYEE(Id:INT, Name:STRING, MaidenName:STRING)

is an appropriate description of the enterprise at hand. If such a relation includes tuples that describe male employees, those tuples will not and cannot have any value for the MaidenName attribute. Again, we can use NULL here.

As we will show later, null values often introduce additional problems, especially in query processing. For these reasons and others, it is sometimes desirable not to allow null values in certain sensitive places, one such obvious place being the primary key. Indeed, how can we interpret a row of STUDENT of the form ⟨ NULL, Doe John, 123 Main St., freshman ⟩? What if John Doe is sharing a room with a friend, also John Doe, who attends the same university and is a freshman?

Most DBMSs reject an update that introduces a tuple with a null value in one of the attributes in the primary key. In addition to the primary key, there may be other places where NULL is inappropriate. For instance, while it might be barely acceptable not to specify an address, a missing student name would certainly be a problem.

In summary, database designers can deal with the null value problem by not allowing nulls in attributes that are deemed crucial to the semantic integrity of the database. We can, for instance, banish the nulls from the Name field as follows.

```
CREATE TABLE  STUDENT  (
     Id              INTEGER,
     Name            CHAR(20)  NOT NULL,
     Address         CHAR(50),
     Status          CHAR(10) DEFAULT 'freshman',
     PRIMARY KEY (Id) )
```

In this example, null values are not allowed in the primary key, Id (which we do *not* need to specify explicitly), or in Name (which we *do* need to specify). One additional feature to note: The user can specify a *default* value for an attribute. This value will be automatically assigned to the attribute of a tuple should the tuple be inserted without this attribute being given a specific value.

4.3.5 Semantic Constraints

Semantic constraints are specified using the CHECK clause, whose basic syntax is

CHECK (*conditional expression*)

The conditional expression can be any predicate or Boolean combination of predicates that can appear in the WHERE clause of an SQL statement. The integrity constraint is said to be violated if the conditional expression evaluates to false.

The CHECK clause is not used as a standalone statement. Either it is attached to a CREATE TABLE statement, in which case it usually serves as an intra-relational constraint on that particular relation, or it can be attached to a CREATE ASSERTION statement, in which case it is usually used as an inter-relational constraint.

The following example illustrates how the CHECK clause can limit the range of an attribute.

```
CREATE TABLE  TRANSCRIPT  (
    StudId   INTEGER,
    CrsCode  CHAR(6),
    Semester CHAR(6),                                    (4.2)
    Grade    CHAR(1),
    CHECK ( Grade IN ('A', 'B', 'C', 'D', 'F') ),
    CHECK ( StudId > 0 AND StudId < 1000000000 )  )
```

Restricting the applicable range of attributes is not the only use of the CHECK constraint in the above context. Using the somewhat contrived relation schema below, we can express the constraint that managers must earn more than their subordinates.

```
CREATE TABLE  EMPLOYEE  (
    Id           INTEGER,
    Name         CHAR(20),
    Salary       INTEGER,
    MngrSalary   INTEGER,
    CHECK ( MngrSalary > Salary )  )
```

The semantics of the CHECK clause inside the CREATE TABLE statement requires that *every tuple* in the corresponding relation satisfy all of the conditional expressions associated with all CHECK clauses in the corresponding CREATE TABLE statement.

One important consequence of this semantics is that the *empty relation*—a relation that contains no tuples—*always satisfies all* CHECK *constraints*, as there are no tuples to check. This can lead to certain unexpected results. Consider the following syntactically correct schema definition.

```
CREATE TABLE  EMPLOYEE  (
    Id           INTEGER,
    Name         CHAR(20),
    Salary       INTEGER,
    DepartmentId CHAR(4),                                (4.3)
    MngrId       INTEGER,
    CHECK ( 0 < (SELECT COUNT(*) FROM EMPLOYEE) ),
    CHECK ( (SELECT COUNT(*) FROM MANAGER)
             < (SELECT COUNT(*)FROM EMPLOYEE) ) )
```

Both CHECK clauses involve SELECT statements that count the number of rows in the named relation. Hence, the first CHECK clause presumably says that the EMPLOYEE relation cannot be empty. However natural this constraint may seem to be, it *does not* achieve the goal of checking that the relation is nonempty. Indeed, as we remarked, this condition is supposed to be satisfied by *every tuple* in the EMPLOYEE relation, *not* by the relation itself. Therefore, if the relation is empty, it satisfies every CHECK constraint, even the one that supposedly says that the relation must not be empty!

The second CHECK clause in (4.3) shows that in principle nothing stops us from trying to (mis)use this facility for inter-relational constraints. We have assumed that there is a relation, MANAGER, that has a tuple for each manager in the company. The constraint presumably says that there must be more employees than managers, which it in fact does, but only if the EMPLOYEE relation is not empty.

Apart from this subtle bug, the second constraint looks particularly unintuitive because it is symmetric by nature and yet is asymmetrically hard-wired into the table definition of just one of the two relations involved. To overcome this problem, SQL-92 provides one more way to use the CHECK clause—inside the CREATE ASSERTION statement. An assertion is a component of the database schema, like a table, so incorporating the CHECK clause within it puts the constraint in a symmetric relationship with the two tables. Thus, the two constraints can be restated as follows (and this time correctly!):

```
CREATE ASSERTION   THOUSHALTNOTFIREEVERYONE
      CHECK ( 0 < (SELECT COUNT(*) FROM EMPLOYEE) )
CREATE ASSERTION   WATCHADMINCOSTS
      CHECK ( (SELECT COUNT(*) FROM MANAGER)
                < (SELECT COUNT(*) FROM EMPLOYEE) ) )
```

Unlike the CHECK conditions that appear inside a table definition, those in the CREATE ASSERTION statement must be satisfied by the contents of the entire database rather than by individual tuples of the host table. Thus, a database satisfies the first assertion above if and only if the number of tuples in the EMPLOYEE relation is greater than zero. Likewise, the second assertion is satisfied whenever the MANAGER relation has fewer tuples than the EMPLOYEE relation has.

For another example of the use of assertions, suppose that the salary information about managers and employees is kept in different relations. We can then state our rule about who should earn more using the following assertion, which literally says that there must not exist an employee who has a boss who earns less. For the sake of this example, we assume that the MANAGER relation has the attributes Id and Salary.

```
CREATE ASSERTION   THOUSHALTNOTOUTEARNYOURBOSS
      CHECK ( NOT EXISTS
          (SELECT * FROM EMPLOYEE, MANAGER
          WHERE EMPLOYEE.Salary > MANAGER.Salary
             AND EMPLOYEE.MngrId = MANAGER.Id ))
```

An interesting question now is, what if, at the time of specifying the constraint THOUSHALTNOTFIREEVERYONE, the EMPLOYEE relation is empty? And what if, at the time of specifying THOUSHALTNOTOUTEARNYOURBOSS, there already is an employee who earns more than the boss? The SQL-92 standard states that if a new constraint is defined and the existing database does not satisfy it, the constraint is *rejected.* The database designer then has to find out the cause of constraint violation and either amend the constraint or rectify the database.[7]

Our last example is a little more complex.[8] It shows how assertions can be used to specify inclusion dependencies that are not foreign key constraints. More specifically, we express the inclusion constraint (4.1) using the assertion statement of SQL-92.

```
CREATE ASSERTION   CoursesShallNotBeEmpty
    CHECK  (NOT EXISTS (
        SELECT * FROM Teaching
        WHERE  NOT EXISTS (                                    (4.4)
            SELECT * FROM Transcript
            WHERE Teaching.CrsCode = Transcript.CrsCode
                AND Teaching.Semester = Transcript.Semester)))
```

The CHECK constraint here verifies that there is no tuple in the Teaching relation (the outer NOT EXISTS statement) for which no matching class exists in the Transcript relation (the inner NOT EXISTS statement). A tuple in the Teaching relation refers to the same class as does a tuple in the Transcript relation if in both tuples the CrsCode and Semester components are equal. This test is performed in the innermost WHERE clause.

Different assertions have different maintenance costs (the time required for the DBMS to check that the assertion is satisfied). Generally, intra-relational constraints come cheaper than do inter-relational constraints. Among the inter-relational constraints, those that are based on keys are easier to enforce than those that are not. Thus, for instance, foreign key constraints come cheaper than do general inclusion dependencies, such as (4.4).

The automatic checking of integrity constraints by a DBMS is one of the more powerful features of SQL. It not only protects the database from errors that might be introduced by untrustworthy users (or sloppy application programmers) but can simplify access to the database as well. For example, a primary key constraint ensures that at most one tuple containing a particular primary key value exists in a table. If a DBMS did not automatically check this constraint, an application program attempting to insert a new tuple or to update the key attributes of an existing tuple would have to scan the table first to ensure that the primary key constraint was maintained.

4.3.6 User–Defined Domains

We have already seen how the CHECK clause lets us limit the range of the attributes in a table. SQL-92 provides an alternative way to enforce such a constraint by allowing the user to define appropriate ranges of values, give them domain names,

---

[7] Unfortunately, many vendors do not comply with this requirement, so they might not warn the user when the existing data violates a newly specified constraint.

[8] It involves the use of a nested, correlated subquery. If you do not understand (4.4), plan to come back here after reading Chapter 6.

and then use these names in various table definitions. We could, for example, create the domain GRADES and use it in the TRANSCRIPT relation instead of using the CHECK constraint.

```
CREATE DOMAIN   Grades CHAR(1)
       CHECK ( VALUE IN ('A', 'B', 'C', 'D', 'F', 'I') )
```

The only difference between this and the previous constraint in (4.2) that was directly imposed on the Grade attribute of STUDENT is that here the special keyword VALUE is used instead of the attribute name (because there are no attributes here as the domain is not attached to any concrete table). Now we can add

```
Grade GRADES
```

to the definition of STUDENT. The overall effect is the same, but we can use this predefined domain name in many tables without repeating the definition (and, if necessary, at some later time we can change the domain definition and have that change automatically propagated to all the tables that use that domain). A domain is a component of the database schema, like a table or an assertion.

Note that, as with assertions, we can use complex queries to define fairly non-trivial domains.

```
CREATE DOMAIN   UpperDivisionStudent INTEGER
       CHECK ( VALUE  IN (SELECT Id FROM Student
                                 WHERE Status IN ('senior', 'junior')
                                 AND  VALUE IS NOT NULL )
```

The domain UPPERDIVISIONSTUDENT consists of student Ids that belong to students whose status is either senior or junior. In addition, the last clause excludes NULL from that domain. Observe that, in order to verify that the constraint imposed by this domain is satisfied, a query against the database is run. Since such queries might be quite expensive, not every vendor supports the creation of such "virtual" domains.

4.3.7 Foreign Key Constraints

SQL has a simple and natural way of specifying foreign keys. The following statement makes ProfId a foreign key referencing the PROFESSOR relation and makes CrsCode a foreign key referencing COURSE.

```
CREATE TABLE Teaching (
       ProfId    INTEGER,
       CrsCode   CHAR(6),
       Semester CHAR(6),
       PRIMARY KEY (CrsCode, Semester),
       FOREIGN KEY (CrsCode) REFERENCES Course,
       FOREIGN KEY (ProfId) REFERENCES Professor (Id)  )
```

If the names of the referring and the referenced attributes are the same, the referenced attribute can be omitted. The attribute CrsCode above is an example of this situation. If the referenced attribute has a different name than that of the referring attribute, both attributes must be specified. The term PROFESSOR (Id) in the second FOREIGN KEY clause shows how this is done.

It should be noted that, although the SQL standard does not require that the referenced attributes form a *primary* key (they can form *any candidate* key), some database vendors impose the primary key restriction.

In the above example, whenever a TEACHING tuple has a course code in it the actual course record with this course code must exist in the COURSE relation. Similarly, the professor's Id in a TEACHING tuple must reference an existing tuple in the PROFESSOR relation. The DBMS is expected to enforce these constraints automatically once they are specified. Thus, as part of the procedure for deleting a tuple in the PROFESSOR relation, a check is made to ensure that there is no corresponding tuple in the TEACHING relation.

In view of our discussion of null values, the following question is in order: What if, in a particular tuple, the value of an attribute in a foreign key is NULL? Should we insist that there be a corresponding tuple in the referenced relation with a null value in a key attribute? Not a good idea, especially if the referenced key is a primary key. Therefore, SQL *relaxes the foreign key constraint* by letting foreign keys have null values, in which case there need not be a corresponding tuple in the referenced relation.

Foreign key constraints raise a number of interesting issues. Consider the table EMPLOYEE defined in (4.3). Suppose that we also have a table that describes departments.

```
CREATE TABLE   DEPARTMENT   (
      DeptId    CHAR(4),
      Name      CHAR(40)
      Budget    INTEGER,
      MngrId    INTEGER,
      FOREIGN KEY (MngrId) REFERENCES EMPLOYEE (Id) )
```

Now, if we look back at the DepartmentId attribute of the EMPLOYEE table, it is clear that this attribute is intended to represent valid department Ids (i.e., Ids of the departments stored in the DEPARTMENT relation). In other words, the constraint

```
FOREIGN KEY (DepartmentId) REFERENCES DEPARTMENT (DeptId)
```

is in order as part of the CREATE TABLE EMPLOYEE statement.

The problem is that either EMPLOYEE or DEPARTMENT has to be defined first. If EMPLOYEE comes first, we cannot have the above foreign key constraint in the CREATE TABLE EMPLOYEE statement because it refers to the yet to be defined table DEPARTMENT. If DEPARTMENT is defined before EMPLOYEE, the DBMS will issue an error trying to process the foreign key constraint in the CREATE TABLE DEPARTMENT statement because this constraint references the table EMPLOYEE. We have produced the chicken and egg problem.

The solution is to *postpone* the introduction of the foreign key constraint in the first table. That is, if CREATE TABLE EMPLOYEE is executed first, we should not have the FOREIGN KEY clause in it. However, after CREATE TABLE DEPARTMENT has been processed, we can *add* the desired constraint to EMPLOYEE using the ALTER TABLE directive. This directive will be described in detail later in this section. Here we give only the final result.

```
ALTER TABLE  EMPLOYEE
    ADD CONSTRAINT EMPDEPTCONSTR
        FOREIGN KEY (DepartmentId) REFERENCES DEPARTMENT (DeptId)
```

If, after settling this circular reference problem, we now want to start populating the database, we are in for another surprise. Suppose that we want to put the first tuple, ⟨000000007, James Bond, 7000000, B007, 000000000⟩, into the EMPLOYEE relation. Since at this moment the DEPARTMENT table is empty, the foreign key constraint that prescribes that B007 refer to a valid tuple in the DEPARTMENT relation is violated.

One solution is to initially replace the DepartmentId component in all tuples in the EMPLOYEE relation with NULL. Then, when DEPARTMENT is populated with appropriate tuples, we can scan the EMPLOYEE relation and replace the null values with valid department Ids. However, this solution is awkward and error prone. A better way is to use a transaction and deferred checking of integrity constraints.

In Chapter 2, we pointed out that the intermediate states of the database produced by a transaction might be inconsistent—they might temporarily violate integrity constraints. The important thing is that constraints must be preserved when the transaction commits. To accommodate the possibility of temporary constraint violations, SQL allows the programmer to specify the mode of a particular integrity constraint to be either IMMEDIATE, in which case a check is made after each SQL statement that changes the database, or DEFERRED, in which case a check is made only when a transaction commits. Then, to deal with the cyclic reference problem, we can

1. Declare the foreign key constraints in the two tables, EMPLOYEE and DEPARTMENT, as INITIALLY DEFERRED to set the initial mode of constraint checking.

2. Make the updates that populate these tables part of the same transaction.

3. Make sure that when all updates are done the foreign key constraints are satisfied. Otherwise, the transaction will be aborted when it terminates.

The full details of how transactions are defined in SQL and how they interact with constraints will be discussed in Chapter 10.

4.3.8 Reactive Constraints

Typically when a constraint is violated, the corresponding transaction is aborted. However, in some cases other remedial actions are appropriate. Foreign key constraints are one example of such a case.

Suppose that a tuple ⟨007007007, MGT123, F1994⟩ is inserted into the TEACHING relation. Because the table PROFESSOR does not have a professor with the Id 007007007, this insertion violates the foreign key constraint that requires all non-

NULL values in the `ProfId` field of Teaching to reference existing professors. In such a case, the semantics of SQL is very simple: The insertion is rejected.

When constraint violation occurs because of deletion of a referenced tuple, SQL offers more choices. Consider the tuple $t = \langle 009406321, \text{MGT123}, \text{F1994}\rangle$ in table Teaching. According to Figure 4.5, t references Professor Taylor in the Professor relation, and the course Market Analysis in the Course relation. Assume that, because of a heavy teaching load, Professor Taylor did not publish enough so he "perishes" and must leave the university. What should happen to t? One solution is to temporarily set the value of `ProfId` in t to NULL until a replacement lecturer is found. Another solution is to have the attempt to delete Professor Taylor's tuple from the Professor relation fail, which might reflect the fact that a professor is not allowed to leave in the middle of a semester. Finally, if Professor Taylor is the only faculty member capable of teaching the course, we might remove MGT123 from the curriculum. By deleting the referencing tuple, t, the violation of referential integrity is resolved.

These possibilities can be rephrased in terms of a **reactive constraint**. This is a static constraint coupled with a specification of *what to do* if a certain event happens. For instance, the first alternative above is a constraint that requires that whenever a Professor tuple is deleted the field `ProfId` of all the referencing tuples in Teaching must be set to NULL. The second alternative is a constraint that asserts that if a referencing tuple exists it cannot be deleted. The third alternative asserts that all referencing tuples are deleted when the referenced tuple is deleted.

We can specify the appropriate response to an event using *triggers*, which are statements of the form

> WHENEVER *event* DO *action*

SQL-92 supports only very simple triggers, those associated with foreign key constraints. In fact, SQL-92 does not even mention triggers by name. Instead, it augments the FOREIGN KEY clause with options ON DELETE and ON UPDATE, which specify what to do if a referenced tuple is deleted or updated. To illustrate, let us revisit the table definition of Teaching.

```
CREATE TABLE   Teaching  (
     ProfId    INTEGER,
     CrsCode   CHAR(6),
     Semester  CHAR(6),
     PRIMARY KEY (CrsCode, Semester),
     FOREIGN KEY (ProfId) REFERENCES Professor
          ON DELETE NO ACTION
          ON UPDATE CASCADE ,
     FOREIGN KEY (CrsCode) REFERENCES Course (CrsCode)
          ON DELETE SET NULL
          ON UPDATE CASCADE  )
```

Here we have specified four triggers. One is **fired** (i.e., executed) whenever a Professor tuple is deleted, one whenever it is modified, one when a Course tuple is deleted, and one when it is modified. The clause ON DELETE NO ACTION means that any attempt to remove a PROFESSOR tuple must be rejected outright if the professor is referenced by a TEACHING tuple. NO ACTION is the default situation when an ON DELETE or ON UPDATE clause is not specified. The clause ON UPDATE CASCADE means that if the Id number of a PROFESSOR tuple is changed, the change must be propagated to all referencing TEACHING tuples (i.e., the new Id must be stored in the referencing tuples). Hence, the same professor is recorded as teaching the course. (Similarly, a specification ON DELETE CASCADE causes the referencing tuple to be deleted.) ON DELETE SET NULL tells the DBMS that, if a COURSE tuple is removed and there is a referencing TEACHING tuple, the referencing attribute, CrsCode, in that tuple must be set to NULL. Alternatively, the designer can specify SET DEFAULT (instead of SET NULL): If CrsCode was defined with a DEFAULT option (e.g., the Status attribute in the STUDENT relation), then it will be reset to its default value if the referenced tuple is deleted; otherwise, it will be set to NULL (which is the default value for the DEFAULT option).

Any combination of DELETE or UPDATE triggers with NO ACTION, CASCADE, or SET NULL/DEFAULT options is allowed in foreign key triggers. Even then, such triggers are not nearly powerful enough to capture the wide variety of situations that arise in database applications. For instance, we saw earlier a natural referential integrity constraint (4.1) that is *not* a foreign key constraint. More important, foreign-key triggers cannot even begin to address common needs such as preventing salaries from changing by more than 5% in a transaction.

To handle these needs, the major database vendors took destiny into their own hands and retrofitted their products with trigger mechanisms. Interestingly, the original design of SQL—before there was an SQL standard—did have relatively powerful triggers. Triggers were added back to the just completed SQL:1999 standard. We will briefly describe the general trigger mechanism here and leave the details to Chapter 9.

The basic idea behind triggers is simple: Whenever a specified *event* occurs, execute some specified *action*. Consider the following simple trigger defined in SQL:1999. The trigger fires whenever CrsCode or Semester is changed in a tuple in the TRANSCRIPT relation. When the trigger fires and the grade recorded for the course is not NULL, an exception is raised. Otherwise (if the grade *is* NULL), we interpret the change as a student dropping one course in favor of another, so the trigger does nothing and the change is allowed to take hold. This trigger is created with the statement

```
CREATE TRIGGER   CrsChangeTrigger
    AFTER UPDATE OF  CrsCode, Semester  ON Transcript
    WHEN   ( Grade IS NOT NULL )
        abortit('666', 'Grade must be NULL when registering')
```

This definition is self-explanatory except, perhaps, for the WHEN clause, which acts as a guard, i.e., a precondition that must be satisfied in order for the trigger to fire. If the precondition is true, the statements following WHEN are executed. In our case, the statement calls a user-defined procedure, abortit(), with error code 666 and a message text as arguments. Upon examining the error code, the `abortit()` procedure presumably aborts the transaction.

In general, many more details might need to be specified in order to define a trigger. For instance, should the action be executed just before the triggering update is applied to the database or after it? Should this action be executed immediately after the event or at some time later? Can a triggered action trigger another action? Moreover, to specify the guard in the WHEN clause, we might need to refer to both the *old* and the *new* values of the modified tuples (e.g., to check that salaries have not been changed by more than 5%). We postpone the discussion of these issues until Chapter 9, where many more examples of triggers will be given. In particular, we will discuss how general triggers can be used to maintain inclusion dependencies in the presence of updates (analogously to the use of the ON DELETE and ON UPDATE triggers to maintain foreign key constraints).

4.3.9 Database Views

In Section 4.1, we discussed the three levels of abstraction in databases: the physical level, the conceptual level, and the external level. We have already shown how the conceptual layer is defined in SQL. We now discuss the external (or view) layer of SQL. The physical layer will be discussed in detail in Chapter 11.

In SQL, the external schema is defined using the CREATE VIEW statement. In many respects, a view is like an ordinary table: You can query it, modify it, or control access to it. However, in several important ways a view is not a table. For one thing, the rows of a view are derived from tables (and other views) of the database. Thus, a view is in reality the repackaging of information stored elsewhere. Furthermore, the contents of a view do not physically exist in the database, instead, a definition of how to *construct* the view from database tables is stored in the system catalog. As we will see shortly, the view definition is a hybrid of the CREATE TABLE statement and the SELECT statement introduced in Chapter 2. Because of this, views are often called **virtual tables**.

To illustrate, consider the following view, which tells which professors have taught which students (a professor is said to have taught a student if the student took a course in the semester in which the professor offered it).

```
CREATE VIEW    PROFSTUD (Prof, Stud)  AS
SELECT Teaching.ProfId, Transcript.StudId
FROM TRANSCRIPT  Transcript, TEACHING                    (4.5)
WHERE Transcript.CrsCode = Teaching.CrsCode
        AND  Transcript.Semester = Teaching.Semester
```

The first line defines the name of the view and its attributes. The rest is just an SQL query that defines the contents of the view. The contents of this view with respect to the database instance of Figure 4.5 is shown in Figure 4.10. To help you understand where the tuples in the view come from, each tuple is annotated with a "justification." (A justification for $\langle P, S \rangle$ is a course code together with the semester in which student S took that course from professor P).

Figure 4.10 Contents of the view defined by SQL statement (4.5).

PROFSTUD	Prof	Stud		Justification
	009406321	666666666		MGT123,F1994
	121232343	666666666		EE101,S1991
	900120450	666666666		MAT123,F1997
	555666777	987654321		CS305,F1995
	009406321	987654321		MGT123,F1994
	101202303	123454321		CS315,S1997; CS305,S1996
	900120450	123454321		MAT123,S1996
	121232343	023456789		EE101,F1995
	101202303	023456789		CS305,S1996
	900120450	111111111		MAT123,F1997
	009406321	111111111		MGT123,F1997
	783432188	111111111		MGT123,F1997

PROFSTUD might be part of the external schema that helps the university keep in touch with its alumni. Establishing the relationship between students and professors through courses might be an important and frequent operation in such applications. So, instead of this relationship being defined in every single application, it can be defined once in the form of a view. Once it is defined, all applications can refer to the view as if it were an ordinary table. The rows of the view are constructed at the time it is accessed.

In Chapter 6, we will expand our discussion of the view mechanism and show how views can be used to modularize the construction of complex queries. The authorization mechanism is another important use of views. Later in this chapter, we will show that views can be treated as ordinary tables for the purpose of granting access rights to the information stored in them.

4.3.10 Modifying Existing Definitions

Although in theory the database schema for a particular application should not change over time, in practice schemas do evolve. Occasionally, new fields are added to relations or existing fields are dropped. New constraints or domains might need to be created, or some old ones might become invalid (perhaps because business rules change). Of course, we can always copy the old contents of a relation to a temporary relation, erase the old relation and its schema, and then create a new relation schema with the old name. However, this process is tedious and error prone. To simplify the task of schema maintenance, SQL provides the ALTER statement, which in its simplest form, looks like this.

```
ALTER TABLE  STUDENT
    ADD COLUMN  Gpa  INTEGER DEFAULT 0
```

This command adds a new field to the STUDENT relation and initializes the field's value in each tuple to 0. You can also use DROP COLUMN to remove a column from a relation and add or drop constraints. For instance,

```
ALTER TABLE   STUDENT
      ADD CONSTRAINT GPARANGE CHECK (Gpa >= 0 AND Gpa <= 4)
ALTER TABLE   TEACHING
      ADD CONSTRAINT TEACHKEY UNIQUE(ProfId, Semester, Time)
```

If the current instance of STUDENT violates the new constraint GPARANGE, or if TEACHING violates TEACHKEY, the newly added constraints must be rejected.

In order for constraints to be dropped from a table definition, the constraints must be named—an option we have not used until now.[9] We make up for this by naming every constraint in a revised definition of TRANSCRIPT.

```
CREATE TABLE   TRANSCRIPT   (
   StudId      INTEGER,
   CrsCode     CHAR(6),
   Semester    CHAR(6),
   Grade       GRADES,
   CONSTRAINT TRKEY PRIMARY KEY (StudId, CrsCode, Semester),
   CONSTRAINT STUDFK FOREIGN KEY (StudId) REFERENCES STUDENT,
   CONSTRAINT CRSFK FOREIGN KEY (CrsCode) REFERENCES COURSE,
   CONSTRAINT IDRANGE CHECK ( StudId > 0 AND
                              StudId < 1000000000 ))
```

Now we can alter the above definition by dropping any one of the specified integrity constraints. For example,

```
ALTER TABLE   TRANSCRIPT
      DROP CONSTRAINT TRKEY
```

When a table is no longer needed, its definition can be erased from the catalog. In this case, the schema of the table and its instance are *both* lost. Previously defined assertions and domains can also be dropped. For example,

```
DROP TABLE   EMPLOYEE   RESTRICT
DROP ASSERTION THOUSHALTNOTFIREEVERYONE
DROP DOMAIN GRADES
```

The DROP TABLE command has two options: RESTRICT and CASCADE. The RESTRICT option refuses to delete a table if that table is used in some other definition, such as an integrity constraint. The constraint THOUSHALTNOTFIREEVERYONE prevents us from deleting EMPLOYEE in this case. The CASCADE option, in contrast deletes a table definition along with any other definition that uses this table. So, for example,

---

[9] Explicit naming of constraints is optional. We will show later that there are other advantages to giving names to all constraints.

if we used CASCADE in the above DROP TABLE command, the assertion ThouShalt-NotFireEveryone would also be deleted (as well as the table Employee and the constraint WatchAdminCosts), and we would no longer need a separate DROP ASSERTION statement.

The DROP DOMAIN command has its own subtleties. For instance, deleting the domain Grades above will *not* leave the attribute Grade of Transcript in limbo. Instead, the effect is as if the definition of Grades is first copied over to all tables where this domain is used, after which the domain is erased from the system catalog.

4.3.11   SQL-Schemas

The structure of a database is described by a catalog. A catalog is SQL's version of a directory, whose elements are schema objects such as tables and domains. Thus, for example, Figure 4.9 on page 71 is a simplified version of part of the catalog for the Student Registration System. SQL-92 allows a catalog to be partitioned into SQL-schemas. An **SQL-schema**[10] is the description of a portion of a database that is under the control of a single user, who has the authorization to create and access the objects within it. For example,

CREATE SCHEMA SRS_StudInfo AUTHORIZATION JohnDoe

creates the SQL-schema SRS_StudInfo describing the part of the Student Registration System database that contains information about students. The AUTHORIZATION clause specifies the user (JohnDoe in our case) who controls the permissions for accessing tables and other objects defined in that SQL-schema. JohnDoe is said to be the **authorization Id** for that SQL-schema. An authorization Id is commonly understood (and implemented) in a way that allows several different user accounts to be assigned the same authorization Id.

The naming mechanism for SQL-schemas is similar to that used in the directory structure of an operating system. For example, if JohnDoe wants to create a Student table in the SRS_StudInfo SQL-schema, he refers[11] to it as SRS_StudInfo.Student.

SQL-92 does not specify the format in which the information in an SQL-schema must be stored, but it does require that each catalog contain one particular schema, named Information_Schema, whose contents are precisely specified. Information_Schema contains a set of SQL tables that repeat, in a precisely defined way, all of the definitions from all of the other SQL-schemas in the catalog. The information in Information_Schema can be accessed by any authorized user.

---

[10] Note that this use of the word "schema" is somewhat different than the sense in which we have been using it to describe a relation schema or database schema. We use the term "SQL-schema" to refer to SQL usage.

[11] SQL-92 has an elaborate default naming mechanism, so in many cases this two-level name qualification is not needed.

Finally, we note that SQL-92 defines a cluster as a set of catalogs. A cluster describes the set of databases that can be accessed by a single SQL program. Thus, our university might define a cluster describing all of the databases maintained by it that can be accessed by a single transaction.

4.3.12 Access Control

Databases often contain sensitive information. Therefore, the system must ensure that only those authenticated users who are authorized to access the database are allowed to and that they are only allowed to access information that has been specifically made available to them. Many transaction processing systems provide extensive authentication and authorization mechanisms. Authentication occurs prior to access. It might be the result of providing a password to the DBMS, or it can be a more elaborate scheme (such as the ones described in Chapter 27) involving a separate security server. In any case, once authentication has been completed, the user is assumed to be (correctly) associated with an authorization Id and access to the database can begin.

Authorization privileges are granted to specific authorization Ids. Of course, a set of users could have the same authorization Id, in which case they would all have the same privileges. The creator of a table or other object is assumed to own that object and has all privileges with respect to it. The owner can grant other users (i.e., other authorization Ids) certain specific privileges with respect to that object using the GRANT statement.

```
GRANT { privilege-list | All PRIVILEGES }
      ON object
      TO { authID-list | ALL } [ WITH GRANT OPTION ]
```

where WITH GRANT OPTION means that the recipient can subsequently grant to others the privileges she has been granted.

If the object is a table or a view, *privilege-list* can include

```
SELECT
DELETE
INSERT    [(column-comma-list)]
UPDATE    [(column-comma-list)]
REFERENCES   [(column-comma-list)]
```

The first four options grant the privilege of performing the specified statement. The options that include *(column-comma-list)* grant the privilege only for the specified columns. For example, if the INSERT privilege has been granted, only the values of the attributes named in *comma-list* can be specified in the inserted tuple. All *comma-lists* are optional, as indicated by the square brackets.

REFERENCES grants the privilege of referring to the table or column using a foreign key. It might seem strange to control this type of access, but security is not complete if foreign key constraints are not controlled. Two problems arise if foreign key constraints can be set up arbitrarily. Suppose that a student is permitted to create the table

```
CREATE TABLE  DontDismissMe  (
    Id    INTEGER,
    FOREIGN KEY (Id) REFERENCES Student)
```

If she inserts a single row in DontDismissMe containing her Id, the registrar will not be able to dismiss the student—that is, delete the student's row from Student—because a deletion would cause a violation of referential integrity and hence be rejected by the DBMS.

Unrestricted foreign key access can also create a security leak. Suppose that, in the interest of protecting student information, SELECT access to Student is not granted to anyone other than university employees in the registrar's office. If however, an intruder, were allowed to create the above table (perhaps with the name ProbeProtectedInfo), this restriction could be circumvented. If the intruder inserted the Id of a particular individual in the table and the insertion were permitted by the DBMS, the intruder could conclude that a row for that individual existed in Student (since referential integrity would otherwise be violated). Similarly, if the insertion were denied, the intruder could conclude that the individual was not a student. Hence, even though the intruder did not have permission to access the table through a SELECT statement, he was able to extract some information.

An example of a GRANT statement is

GRANT SELECT, UPDATE (ProfId) ON StudRegSystem.Teaching
        TO JohnSmyth, MaryDoe WITH GRANT OPTION

which grants to John Smyth and Mary Doe the permission to read a row and to update the ProfId column of a row (but not to delete or insert rows) of the Teaching relation. Furthermore, it gives them permission to pass on the same privileges to other users.

SQL allows control not only of direct access to databases but also of indirect access through views. For instance, the following statement gives all users who are classified as "alumnus" unrestricted query access to the ProfStud view defined in (4.5).

GRANT SELECT ON ProfStud TO Alumnus

However, alumni cannot pass their query rights to others, and they cannot update the view. What is more interesting is that these users might not even have the rights to access Transcript and Teaching—the two relations that supply the contents for the ProfStud view, although they have indirect access to parts of that information as represented by the view. Chapter 6 will have further discussion on this subject.

Privileges can also be granted for objects other than tables (for example domains). We omit the details.

Privileges, or the grant option for privileges, can be revoked using the REVOKE statement.

REVOKE [GRANT OPTION FOR] *privilege-list*
  ON *object*
  FROM *authID-list* {CASCADE | RESTRICT}

CASCADE means that if some user, U_1, who is assigned an authorization Id on *authID-list*, has granted those privileges to another user, U_2, the privileges granted to U_2 are also revoked, and so on (if U_2 has granted those privileges to still another user). RESTRICT means that if any such dependent privileges exist, the REVOKE statement is rejected.

In many applications, granting privileges at the level of database operations such as SELECT or UPDATE is not adequate. For example, only a depositor can deposit in a bank account and only a bank official can add interest to the account, but both the deposit and interest transactions might use the same UPDATE statement. For such applications, it is more appropriate to grant privileges at the level of subroutines or transactions. Many transaction processing systems control access at this level. We will return to this subject in Chapter 27.

4.4 BIBLIOGRAPHIC NOTES

The relational data model was introduced in [Codd 1970, 1990]. [Codd 1979] proposed various extensions to the original model, which allows capture of more semantic information.

These ideas were extended and implemented in the two early relational systems: System R [Astrahan et al. 1981] and INGRES [Stonebraker 1986]. Eventually, System R became DB2, a commercial product from IBM, and INGRES became a commercial product under the same name (currently sold by Computer Associates, Intl.).

A rich body of theory has been developed for relational databases, much of which found its way into research prototypes and commercial products. More indepth discussion as well as additional topics not covered in this book can be found in [Maier 1983, Atzeni and Antonellis 1993, Abiteboul et al. 1995].

4.5 EXERCISES

4.1 Define data atomicity as it relates to the definition of relational databases. Contrast data atomicity with transaction atomicity as used in a transaction processing system.

4.2 Prove that every relation has a key.

4.3 Define the following concepts:

  a. Key

  b. Candidate key

  c. Primary key

  d. Superkey

4.4 Define

    a. Integrity constraint

    b. Static, as compared with dynamic, integrity constraint

    c. Referential integrity

    d. Reactive constraint

    e. Inclusion dependency

    f. Foreign key constraint

4.5 Looking at the data that happens to be stored in the tables for a particular application at some particular time, explain whether or not you can tell

    a. What the key constraints for the tables are

    b. Whether or not a particular attribute is a key to a particular table

    c. What the integrity constraints for the application are

    d. Whether or not a particular set of integrity constraints is satisfied

4.6 Use SQL DDL to specify the schema of the Student Registration System fragment shown in Figure 4.4, including the constraints in Figure 4.8. Specify SQL domains for attributes with small numbers of values, such as `DeptId` and `Grade`.

4.7 Consider a database schema with four relations: SUPPLIER, PRODUCT, CUSTOMER, and CONTRACTS. Both the SUPPLIER and the CUSTOMER relations have the attributes `Id`, `Name`, and `Address`. An `Id` is a 9-digit number. PRODUCT has `PartNumber` (an integer between 1 and 999999) and `Name`. Each tuple in the CONTRACTS relation corresponds to a contract between a supplier and a customer for a specific product in a certain quantity for a given price.

    a. Use SQL DDL to specify the schema of these relations, including the appropriate integrity constraints (primary, candidate, and foreign key) and SQL domains.

    b. Specify the following constraint as an SQL assertion: *There must be more contracts than suppliers.*

4.8 Suppose that the system has two accounts: STUDENT and ADMINISTRATOR. Specify the permissions appropriate for these user categories using the SQL GRANT statement.

4.9 Explain why the REFERENCES privilege is necessary. Give an example of how it is possible to obtain partial information about the contents of a relation by creating foreign key constraints referencing that relation.

Chapter 5

Database Design I: The Entity-Relationship Model

Now that the Specification Document for the Student Registration System has been approved by the university registrar, we are ready to begin designing the database portion of the system. In Chapter 12, we will discuss the complete design process for an entire transaction processing application, including the final product of that process, the Design Document. Here we discuss the database portion of the design, of which the final product is the complete (compilable) set of CREATE statements that declare the database schema—tables, indices, domains, assertions, and so forth. We present the complete database design for the Student Registration System in Section 5.7.

The key issue in database design is to accurately model the appropriate aspects of a large enterprise as a relational database that can be efficiently accessed and updated by a large number of concurrently executing transactions in (perhaps) a number of distinct applications, some of which might also include decision support queries. As in other engineering disciplines, the design process can be facilitated if it is performed according to some specific methodology and can be evaluated according to some objective criteria.

In this chapter, we present a popular methodology for designing relational databases, the *entity-relationship (E-R) approach*, introduced by [Chen 1976]. Database design will be revisited in Chapter 8, where we present the *relational normalization theory*, which provides objective criteria for evaluating alternative designs.

It should be noted that many of the mechanisms underlying both the E-R approach and the relational normalization theory have been captured in computer programs, thereby relieving the designer of some routine aspects of carrying out a design. Still, this job requires a good deal of creativity, technical expertise, experience, and understanding of fundamental database design principles.

5.1 CONCEPTUAL MODELING WITH THE E-R APPROACH

To quash one very common misconception, we emphasize that the E-R approach is *not* a relative, a derivative, or a generalization of the relational data model. In fact, it is not a data model at all but a *design methodology*, which can be applied (but is not limited) to the relational model. The term "relationship" refers to one of the two main components of the methodology rather than to the relational data model.

The two main components of the E-R approach are the concepts of **entity** and **relationship**. Entities model the objects that are involved in an enterprise—for example, the students, professors, and courses in a university. Relationships model the connections among the entities—for example, professors *teach* courses. In addition, **integrity constraints** on the entities and relationships form an important part of an E-R specification, much as they do in the relational model. For example, a professor can teach only one course at a given time on a given day.

An **entity-relationship (E-R) diagram** (peek ahead at Figure 5.1, page 92, and Figure 5.3, page 96) is a graphical representation of the entities, relationships, and constraints that make up a given design. As in other visually oriented design methodologies, it provides a graphical summary of the design that is extremely useful to the designer, not only in validating the correctness of the design but also in discussing it with colleagues and in explaining it to the programmers who will be using it. Unfortunately, there is no standard drawing convention for E-R diagrams, and hence there is a good deal of variation among database texts in many aspects of this approach.

After the enterprise has been modeled with E-R diagrams (in any of their flavors), there are straightforward ways of converting these diagrams into sets of CREATE TABLE statements. Unfortunately, this conversion process does not yield a unique schema, especially in the presence of constraints, because some constraints that can be indicated in the E-R diagrams have no direct counterparts in SQL. These and related issues will be discussed in due time.

The creative part of the E-R methodology is deciding what entities, relationships, and constraints to use in modeling the enterprise. The simple examples we can include in a text might make these decisions look easy, but in practice designers must combine a detailed understanding of the workings of the enterprise with a considerable amount of technical knowledge, judgment, and experience.

An important advantage of the methodology is that the designer can focus on complete and accurate modeling of the enterprise, without (initially) worrying about efficiently executing the required queries and updates against the final database. Later, when the E-R diagrams are to be converted to CREATE TABLE statements, the designer can add efficiency considerations to the final table designs using normalization theory (Chapter 8) and other techniques to be discussed later in this chapter and in Chapter 13.

5.2   ENTITIES AND ENTITY TYPES

The first step in the E-R approach is to select the entities that will be used to model the enterprise. An entity is quite similar to an *object*, (see Appendix Section A.1.1) except that an entity does not have methods. It might be a concrete object in the real world, such as John Doe, the Cadillac parked at 123 Main Street, or the Empire State Building, or it might be an abstract object, such as the CitiBank account 123456789, the database course CS305, or the Computer Science Department at SUNY Stony Brook.

Similar entities are aggregated into **entity types**. For instance, John Doe, Mary Doe, Joe Blow, and Ann White might be aggregated into the entity type PERSON based on the fact that these entities represent humans. John Doe and Joe Blow might also belong to the entity type STUDENT because in our sample database of Chapter 4 these objects presumably represented students. Similarly, Mary Doe and Ann White might be classified as members of the entity type PROFESSOR.

Other examples of entity types include

■ CS305, MGT315, and EE101, entities of type COURSE

■ Alf and E.T., entities of type SPACEALIEN

■ CIA, FBI, and IRS, entities of type GOVERNMENTAGENCY

Attributes.   As with relations (and objects), entities are described using attributes. Every attribute of an entity specifies a particular property of that entity. For instance, the Name attribute of a PERSON entity normally specifies a string of characters that denotes the real-world name of the person represented by that database entity. Similarly, the Age attribute specifies the number of times the Earth had circled around the Sun since the moment that real-world person was born.

All of our examples of entity types have been semantic in nature; that is, the entity type consists of a semantically related set of entities. For example, it is usually pointless to classify people, cars, and paper clips in one entity type because they have little in common in a typical enterprise modeling. More useful is classifying semantically similar entities in one entity type, since such entities are likely to have useful common attributes that describe them. For example, in any enterprise people have many common attributes, such as Name, Age, and Address. Classification into entity types allows us to associate these attributes with the entity type instead of with the entities themselves.

Of course, different entity types have different sets of attributes. For instance, the PAPERCLIP entity type might have attributes Size and Price, while COURSE might have attributes CrsName, CrsCode, Credits, and Description.

Domains.   As in the relational model, the domain of an attribute specifies the set from which its value can be drawn. Unlike the relational model, however, E-R attributes can be *set-valued*. This means that the value of an attribute can be a set of values from the corresponding domain rather than a single value. For example, an entity type PERSON might have set-valued attributes ChildrenNames and Hobbies.

The inability to express set-valued attributes conveniently was one of the major criticisms of the relational data model that motivated the development of the object-oriented data model. However, the use of set-valued attributes in the E-R model is just a matter of convenience. Relations (as defined in Chapter 4) can be used to model entities with set-valued attributes with some extra effort.

Keys.   As with the relational model, it is useful to introduce the key constraints associated with entity types. A **key constraint** on an entity type, S, is a set of attributes, $\overline{A}$, of S such that

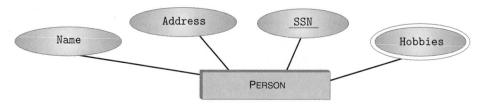

Figure 5.1 Fragment of the E-R diagram for the entity type PERSON.

1. No two entities in S have the same values for every attribute in $\overline{A}$ (for instance, two different COMPANY entities cannot agree on both the Name and the Address attributes).

2. No proper subset of the attributes in $\overline{A}$ has property 1 (i.e., the set $\overline{A}$ is *minimal* with respect to this property).

Clearly, this concept of entity keys is analogous to that of candidate keys in the relational model. One subtle point, though, is that attributes in the E-R approach can be set-valued and, in principle, such an attribute can be part of a key. However, in practice set-valued attributes that occur in keys are not very natural and often indicate poor design.

Schema.   As with the relational model, we define the **schema** of an entity type to consist of the name of that type, the collection of the attributes (with their associated domains and the indicator of whether each attribute is set-valued or single-valued), and the key constraints.

E-R diagram representation.   Entity types are represented in E-R diagrams as rectangles, and their attributes are represented as ovals. Set-valued attributes are represented as double ovals. Figure 5.1 depicts one possible representation of the PERSON entity type. Note that in this picture Hobbies is specified as a set-valued attribute and SSN is underlined to indicate that it is a key.

Representation in the relational model.   The correspondence between entities in the E-R model and relations in the relational model is straightforward. Each entity type is converted into a relation, and each of its attributes is converted into an attribute of the relation.

This simplicity might seem suspicious in view of the fact that entities can have set-valued attributes while relations cannot. How, then, can a set-valued attribute of an entity be turned into a single-valued attribute of the corresponding relation without violating the property of data atomicity (see Section 4.2) of the relational model?

The answer is that each entity that has a set-valued attribute is represented in the translation by a *set* of tuples, one for each element in the attribute value. To illustrate, suppose that the entity type PERSON of Figure 5.1 is populated by the following entities:

Figure 5.2 Translation of entity type PERSON into a relation.

Person	SSN	Name	Address	Hobby
	111111111	John Doe	123 Main St.	Stamps
	111111111	John Doe	123 Main St.	Coins
	555666777	Mary Doe	7 Lake Dr.	Hiking
	555666777	Mary Doe	7 Lake Dr.	Skating
	987654321	Bart Simpson	Fox 5 TV	Acting

⟨111111111, John Doe, 123 Main St., {Stamps, Coins}⟩
⟨555666777, Mary Doe, 7 Lake Dr., {Hiking, Skating}⟩
⟨987654321, Bart Simpson, Fox 5 TV, {Acting}⟩

In translation, we obtain the relation depicted in Figure 5.2.

The next question to ask is what keys of the relation are obtained by the above translation. If the entity type does not have set-valued attributes, the answer is simple: Each key (which is a set of attributes) of the entity type becomes a key of the corresponding relation schema. However, if one of the entity attributes is set-valued, determining the keys is a bit more involved. In the entity type PERSON, the attribute SSN is a key, because no two PERSON entities can have the same Social Security number and all hobbies are elements of a set that is the value of the Hobby attribute. However, in the PERSON relation (Figure 5.2) both John Doe and Mary Doe are represented by a pair of tuples and each Social Security number occurs twice. Therefore, SSN is not a key of that relation.

Clearly, the set-valued attribute Hobby is the trouble maker. To obtain a key of the relation in question, we must include the offending attribute. Thus, the key of the PERSON relation in Figure 5.2 is {SSN, Hobby}.

The following CREATE TABLE statement defines the schema for the PERSON relation.

```
CREATE TABLE  PERSON  (
      SSN        INTEGER,
      Name       CHAR(20),
      Address    CHAR(50),                        (5.1)
      Hobby      CHAR(10),
      PRIMARY KEY (SSN, Hobby) )
```

Even though we found a key in the end, a careful examination of the above table leaves us uneasy. Intuitively, it does not seem right that the Hobby attribute must be used to identify tuples in the PERSON relation. Furthermore, in the original entity type PERSON, any concrete value of SSN is known to uniquely identify the value of Name and Address. In the translation of Figure 5.2, we see that this property is still true, but it is not captured by the primary key constraint, which states that in

.ly determine a tuple, we must specify the value of both SSN and
.st, in the entity type PERSON the value of Hobby is not required to
value of Name and Address. This important constraint has been lost
on!

ing example is the first indication that the E-R approach alone is not
.ol for guaranteeing good relational design. Chapter 8 will provide a
tive criteria that can help the database designer evaluate the relational
ined by converting E-R diagrams into relations. In particular, the prob-
e relation in Figure 5.2 is that it is not in a certain "normal form" defined
in Chap. 8. That chapter proceeds to develop algorithms that can automatically
rectify the problem by splitting such offending relations into smaller relations that
are in a desired normal form.

5.3   RELATIONSHIPS AND RELATIONSHIP TYPES

The E-R approach makes a sharp distinction between the entities themselves and
the mechanism that relates them to each other. This mechanism is called **relationships**. Just as entities are classified into entity types, relationships that relate the
same types of entities and that have the same meaning are grouped into **relationship types**.[1]

For instance, STUDENT entities are related to PROGRAM entities via relationships
of type MAJORSIN. Likewise, PROFESSOR entities are related to the departments they
work for via relationships of type WORKSIN.

Once again, we emphasize that the concept of *relationship* in the E-R approach is
distinct from the concept of *relation* in the relational data model. Relationships are
just one of the modeling tools in the arsenal of the E-R approach. When it comes
to implementation, both entities and relationships are represented as relations (i.e.,
tables) in the DBMS.

Attributes and roles.   Like entities, relationships can have attributes. For instance,
the relationship MAJORSIN might have an attribute Since, which indicates the date
the student was admitted into the corresponding major. The WORKSIN relationship
might have the attribute Since to indicate the start date of employment.

Attributes do not provide a complete description of relationships. Consider the
entity type EMPLOYEE and the relationship REPORTSTO, which relates employees to
other employees. The first type of employee is the subordinate while the second is
the boss. Thus, if we just say that ⟨John, Bill⟩ is a relationship of type REPORTSTO,
we still do not know who reports to whom.

Splitting the EMPLOYEE entity type into SUBORDINATE and SUPERVISOR does
not help, because REPORTSTO might represent the entire chain of reporting in a
corporate hierarchy, making some employees subordinates and supervisors at the
same time.

---

[1] When there is a danger of confusion between relationships and entities on the one hand and relationship types and entity types on the other, we use the terms "relationship instance" and "entity instance"
instead of "relationship" and "entity," respectively.

The solution is to recognize that the various entity types participating in a relationship type play different roles in that relationship. For each such participating entity type, we define a **role** and give that role a name (for example, Subordinate). A role is similar to an attribute, but instead of specifying some property of the relationship it specifies in what way an entity type participates in the relationship. Both roles and attributes are part of the schema of the relationship type.

For example, the relationship type WORKSIN has two roles, Professor and Department. The Professor role identifies the PROFESSOR entity involved in a WORKSIN relationship, and the Department role identifies the corresponding DEPARTMENT entity in the relationship. Similarly, the relationship type MAJORSIN has two roles: Student and Program.

When all of the entities involved in a relationship belong to distinct entity types (as in WORKSIN and MAJORSIN), it is not necessary to explicitly indicate the roles, because we can always adopt some convention, such as naming the roles after the corresponding entity types (which is typical in practice).[2] However, such simplification is not possible when some of the entities involved are drawn from the same entity type, as is the case with the REPORTSTO relationship. Here, we have to explicitly indicate the roles, for example, Subordinate and Supervisor. Figure 5.3 shows several examples of relationships, including those where roles must be named explicitly.

To summarize, a **schema of a relationship type** includes

■ A list of attributes along with their corresponding domains. An attribute can be single-valued or set-valued.

■ A list of roles along with their corresponding entity types. Unlike attributes, roles are always single-valued.

■ A set of constraints, to be described later. (In Figure 5.3, constraints are represented as arrows, which will be explained later.)

The number of roles engaged in a relationship type is called the **degree** of the type.

We can now define the concept of a relationship more precisely. A relationship type **R** of degree n is defined by its attributes $A_1, \ldots, A_k$ and roles $R_1, \ldots, R_n$. The relationships populating **R** are defined to be tuples of the form

$$\langle \mathbf{e_1}, \mathbf{e_2}, \ldots, \mathbf{e_n}; a_1, a_2, \ldots, a_k \rangle$$

where $\mathbf{e_1}, \ldots, \mathbf{e_n}$ are entities that are values of the roles $R_1, \ldots, R_n$, respectively (these are the entities involved in the relationship) and $a_1, a_2, \ldots, a_k$ are values of the attributes $A_1, \ldots, A_k$, respectively. We assume that all of the values of the attributes in the relationship are in their respective domains as defined in the relationship type and all of the entities are of the correct entity types as defined in their respective roles.

---

[2] To avoid confusion, we use different fonts to distinguish entity types from the roles they play in various relationships.

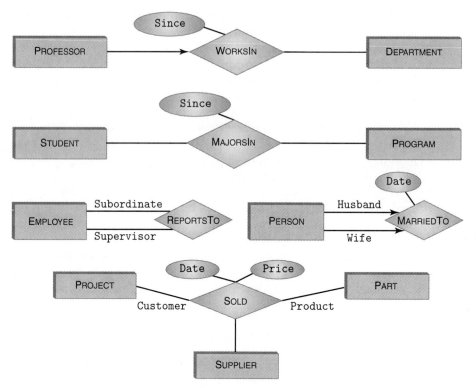

Figure 5.3 E-R diagrams for several relationship types.

For instance, the relationship type MAJORSIN can have the schema

⟨Student, Program; Since⟩

where Student and Program are roles and Since is an attribute. One instance in this relationship type might be

⟨Homer Simpson, EE; 1994⟩

This relationship states that the entity Homer Simpson is a student who is enrolled in the program represented by the entity EE and has been enrolled since 1994. The first two components in the tuple are entities, while the last one is a plain value drawn from the domain of years.

E-R diagram representation.   In E-R diagrams, relationship types are represented as diamonds and roles are represented as edges that connect relationship types with the appropriate entity types. If a role must be named explicitly (because some of the entities involved in the relationship are drawn from the same entity type), the name is included in the diagram. Figure 5.3 shows the E-R diagram for several of the relationships we have been discussing (we omitted all entity attributes to reduce clutter). The first three relationships in the figure are **binary** because they each relate two entity types. The last relationship is **ternary** because it relates three entity types. This last diagram also illustrates the point that sometimes the semantics of a diagram can be easier to convey if default role names (in this case `Project` and `Part`) are renamed (as `Customer` and `Product`, respectively).

Keys.   The key of a relationship enables the designer to naturally express many constraints easily and uniformly.[3] In the case of entity types, a key is just a set of attributes that uniquely identifies an entity. However, attributes alone do not fully characterize relationships. Roles must also be taken into account, so we define a **key of a relationship type**, **R**, to be a minimal set of roles and attributes of **R** whose values uniquely identify the relationship instances in that relationship type.

In other words, let $R_1, \ldots, R_k$ be a subset of the set of all roles of **R** and $A_1, \ldots, A_s$ be a subset of the attributes of **R**. Then the set $\{R_1, \ldots, R_k; A_1, \ldots, A_s\}$ is a key of **R** if the following holds.

1. *Uniqueness.* **R** does not have a pair of distinct relationship instances that have the same values for every role and attribute in $\{R_1, \ldots, R_k; A_1, \ldots, A_s\}$.

2. *Minimality.* No subset of $\{R_1, \ldots, R_k; A_1, \ldots, A_s\}$ has property 1.

In some cases, the key of a relationship takes a special form. Consider the relationship WORKSIN between entities of type PROFESSOR and type DEPARTMENT. It is reasonable to assume that each department has several professors but that each professor works for a single department. In other words, WORKSIN relates professors to departments in a **many-to-one** fashion. Because any given PROFESSOR entity can occur in at most one relationship of type WORKSIN, the role `Professor` is a key of WORKSIN. While there is no universally accepted representation for relationship keys in E-R diagrams, a relationship key that consists of just one role can be conveniently expressed by drawing this role as an arrow pointing in the direction of the relationship's diamond. Observe that there can be several roles that form a key, and so an E-R diagram can have several arrows pointing toward the same diamond. For instance, in Figure 5.3 both {`Husband`} and {`Wife`} are keys of the relationship type MARRIEDTO, so each of these roles is represented as an arrow.

Keys that consist of more than one role or attribute are usually represented textually, next to the diamonds that represent the corresponding relationship type. When representing such keys, we first list the roles and then the attributes. For example, in the last diagram of Figure 5.3 one key could be {`Customer`, `Product`; `Date`} (`Date` is included in the key because price may vary depending on the date).

In many situations, however, the relationship key turns out to be the set of all roles and is unique. In such a case, we do not specify the key in the diagram.

Representation in the relational model.   The following procedure can be used to map a relationship type **R** into a relation schema.

---

[3] Most texts define a limited form of relationship key under the guise of the *many-to-one* cardinality constraint.

■ *Attributes of the relation schema*. The attributes of the relation schema are

1. The attributes of **R** itself

2. For each role in **R**, the primary key of the associated entity type

Note that we use the primary key of the entity type, not the primary key of the relation schema constructed out of that entity type, because the goal is to identify the entity involved in the relationship. Thus, for example, in the case of a role associated with the entity type PERSON we use SSN and omit Hobby.

■ *Candidate keys of the relation schema*. In most cases, the keys of the relation schema are obtained by direct translation from the keys of **R** itself. That is, if a role, *R*, of **R** belongs to the key of **R** then the attributes of the primary key, *K*, of the entity associated with *R* must belong to the candidate key of the relation schema derived from **R**.

A slight problem arises when **R** has set-valued attributes. In that case, we resort to an earlier trick that was used for converting entity keys into relation keys: All set-valued attributes must be included in the candidate key of the relation (see the PERSON entity-to-relation translation) whether or not they are included in the key of **R**. Note that roles are always single-valued, so this special treatment of set-valued attributes does not apply to the roles.

■ *Foreign key constraints of the relation schema*. Because, in the E-R model, a role always refers to some entity (which is mapped to a relation), roles translate into foreign key constraints. The foreign keys of the relation schema corresponding to **R** are constructed as follows.

> For each role in **R**, the primary key of the associated entity type (which is among the attributes of the relation schema corresponding to **R**) becomes a foreign key that references the relation obtained from that entity type.

The only problem might be that the primary key of the entity type (e.g., SSN) need not be the primary key of the corresponding relation (e.g., {SSN, Hobby}), as we saw in the case of the PERSON entity type. Such problems are eliminated by the relational normalization theory of Chapter 8.

Figure 5.4 shows the CREATE TABLE commands that define the schemas corresponding to some of the relationships in Figure 5.3. Observe that, in the MARRIEDTo relation, we did not define the foreign key constraint because, although SSNhusband and SSNwife clearly reference the SSN attribute of the PERSON relation, SSN is not a candidate key for that relation, as explained earlier. The UNIQUE constraint in the schema guarantees that SSNwife is unique in any instance of the table and is hence a candidate key.

Note that when E-R diagrams are translated into tables, some of these tables describe entities and others describe relationships. Thus, the first E-R diagram of Figure 5.3 translates into three tables: one to describe the entity type of professors, one to describe the entity type of departments, and one to describe the relationship type that describes professors working for various departments.

Figure 5.4 Translations of some relationships.

```
CREATE TABLE   WORKSIN   (
    Since        DATE,
    ProfId       INTEGER,
    DeptId       CHAR(4),
    PRIMARY KEY (ProfId),
    FOREIGN KEY (ProfId) REFERENCES PROFESSOR (Id),
    FOREIGN KEY (DeptId) REFERENCES DEPARTMENT )


CREATE TABLE   MARRIEDTO   (
    Date         DATE,
    SSNhusband   INTEGER,
    SSNwife      INTEGER,
    PRIMARY KEY (SSNhusband),
    UNIQUE (SSNwife) )


CREATE TABLE   SOLD   (
    Price        INTEGER,
    Date         DATE,
    ProjId       INTEGER,
    SupplierId   INTEGER,
    PartNumber   INTEGER,
    PRIMARY KEY (ProjId, SupplierId, PartNumber, Date),
    FOREIGN KEY (ProjId) REFERENCES PROJECT,
    FOREIGN KEY (SupplierId) REFERENCES SUPPLIER (Id),
    FOREIGN KEY (PartNumber) REFERENCES PART (Number) )
```

5.4 ADVANCED FEATURES OF THE E-R APPROACH

5.4.1 Entity Type Hierarchies

Some entity sets might be closely related to others. For instance, every entity of the STUDENT entity set is also a member of the PERSON entity set. Therefore, all of the attributes of the PERSON set are applicable to such entities. Students can also have attributes that are not applicable to a typical PERSON entity (e.g., Major, StartDate, GPA). In this case, we say that the entity type STUDENT is a subtype of the entity type PERSON.

Formally, saying that an entity type R is a **subtype** of the entity type R' is the same as specifying an inter-entity constraint, which means that

1. Every entity instance in R is also an entity instance in R',
2. Every attribute in R' is also an attribute in R.

One important consequence of this definition is that any key of a supertype is also a key of all of its subtypes.

Note that subtyping is not only a constraint but also a relationship. It can be represented as a relationship with roles Sub(type) and Super(type) and is often called the IsA relationship. Thus, the names of the roles in the IsA relationship are fixed, but the ranges of these roles depend on the entity types that are related by each particular IsA relationship.

For instance, in the IsA relationship type that relates STUDENT and PERSON the range of Sub is STUDENT and the range of Super is PERSON. A particular instance of this relationship could be ⟨Homer Simpson, Homer Simpson⟩, which states that Homer Simpson is a student *and* a person. Note that the two entities involved in IsA are always identical.

So what is so useful about the IsA relationship? The answer lies in the fact that subtype constraints introduce a **classification hierarchy** in the E-R model. For instance, FRESHMAN is a subtype of STUDENT, which in turn is a subtype of PERSON. This property is *transitive*, which means that FRESHMAN is also a subtype of PERSON. The transitive property gives us a way to draw E-R diagrams in a more concise and readable manner. Because of property 2 of subtyping, every attribute of PERSON is also an attribute of STUDENT and, by transitivity, is also an attribute of FRESHMAN. This phenomenon is often expressed by saying that STUDENT **inherits** attributes from PERSON and that FRESHMAN inherits attributes from both PERSON and STUDENT.

Note that the inherited attributes (SSN, Name, etc.) are not specified explicitly for the entity types STUDENT and FRESHMAN, and yet they are considered valid attributes because of the IsA relationship. In addition to the inherited attributes, STUDENT and FRESHMAN might have attributes of their own, which their corresponding supertypes might not have. Figure 5.5 illustrates this idea. As STUDENT is a subtype of PERSON, this entity type inherits all of the attributes specified for PERSON, and so there is no need to repeat the attributes Name and D.O.B. (date of birth) for the STUDENT type. Similarly, FRESHMAN, SOPHOMORE, and so forth, are subtypes of STUDENT, and so we do not need to copy the attributes of STUDENT and PERSON over to these subtypes. Transitivity has the potential of greatly simplifying an E-R diagram. The EMPLOYEE branch of the IsA tree provides another example of attribute inheritance. The relationship EMPLOYEE IsA PERSON represents the fact that every EMPLOYEE entity has attributes Department and Salary. In addition, it states that every EMPLOYEE entity is also a PERSON entity and, as such, also has the attributes Name, SSN, and so forth.

Note that each IsA triangle in Figure 5.5 represents several relationship types. For instance, the upper triangle represents the relationship types STUDENT IsA PERSON and EMPLOYEE IsA PERSON. Although this notation makes the representation of the IsA relationship different from the representation of other kinds of relationships, it is used because there are a number of constraints associated with entity type hierarchies that can be naturally represented using such notation.

For instance, the union of the entities that belong to the entity types FRESHMAN, SOPHOMORE, JUNIOR, and SENIOR might be equal to the set of entities of type STUDENT (for example, in a four-year college). This constraint, called the **covering constraint**, can be handily attached to the lower right IsA triangle. In addition,

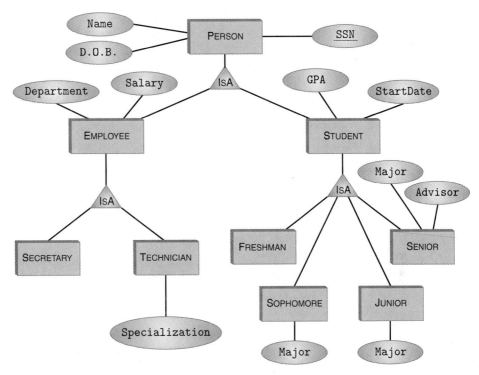

Figure 5.5 Example of an IsA hierarchy.

these entity sets might always be disjoint (they are in most American universities), and such a **disjointness constraint** can also be attached to the lower right triangle.[4]

Entity type hierarchies and data fragmentation.   Our discussion of the IsA relationship focused on conceptual organization and attribute inheritance. However, these hierarchies are also a good way to approach the issue of physical **data fragmentation** (or **data partitioning**). The need for data fragmentation often arises in distributed environments, where multiple geographically diverse entities must access a common database. Banks are a typical example because they often have many branches in different cities.

The problem that arises in such distributed enterprises is that of network delay: Accessing a database in New York City from a bank branch in Buffalo can be prohibitive for frequently running transactions. However, the bulk of the data needed by a local bank branch is likely to be of mostly local interest, and it might be a good idea to distribute fragments of such information among databases maintained at the individual branches. We will discuss data fragmentation for distributed

---

[4] There is no universally accepted way of representing covering and disjointness constraints in the E-R diagrams, so pick your own.

Figure 5.6 Using IsA for data fragmentation.

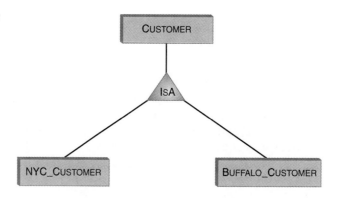

database in more detail in Chapter 18. Other uses of data fragmentation will be described in Section 24.3.1.

To see how data fragmentation can be addressed at the database design stage, consider an entity type, CUSTOMER, that represents the information about all customers of a bank. For each branch, we can create subtypes, such as NYC_CUSTOMER or BUFFALO_CUSTOMER, that are related to CUSTOMER as described in Figure 5.6.

Observe that the constraints associated with type hierarchies provide considerable expressive power in specifying how data might be fragmented. For instance, Figure 5.6 could be interpreted as a requirement that the New York City and Buffalo data must be stored locally. It does not say that the New York City database and the Buffalo customer database must be disjoint, but this restriction can be specified using the disjointness constraint introduced earlier. In addition, we can add the covering constraint to specify that the combined customer information at the branches includes all customers.

Representing IsA hierarchies in the relational model.   There are several ways to represent the IsA relationship using relational tables. One general way is to choose a candidate key for all entity types on a branch of the tree that represents the IsA hierarchy, add the key attributes to each entity type, and then convert the entities on that branch into relations, as discussed in Section 5.2. The choice of such a key is possible because, as mentioned earlier, a key of a supertype is also a key of a subtype.

For instance, in Figure 5.5 we can choose {SSN} as such a key and add the SSN attribute to each entity type. The subsequent conversion process will then yield the following relation schemas.

> PERSON(SSN, Name, D.O.B.)
>
> STUDENT(SSN, StartDate, GPA)
>
> FRESHMAN(SSN)
>
> SOPHOMORE(SSN, Major)
>
> JUNIOR(SSN, Major)
>
> SENIOR(SSN, Major, Advisor)

EMPLOYEE(SSN, Department, Salary)

SECRETARY(SSN)

TECHNICIAN(SSN, Specialization)

In the presence of various constraints, such as disjointness and covering, there are more efficient ways to represent the same information. For instance, if all subentities of STUDENT had the same set of attributes (i.e., if SENIOR did not have its private attribute Advisor), then instead of representing students using five relations we could have used just one with a special attribute Status whose range would be the set of constants {Freshman, Sophomore, Junior, Senior}.[5]

5.4.2 Participation Constraints

Consider a relationship type WORKSIN between entities of types PROFESSOR and DEPARTMENT. As discussed earlier, each department has several professors but each professor works for a single department, so the role Professor is a key of WORKSIN.

This key constraint ensures that no professor can occur in more than one relationship of type WORKSIN. However, it does not guarantee that each professor occurs in *some* relationship of this type. In other words, the key constraint does not rule out professors who do not work for any department (and possibly get away without teaching any courses!). To close this loophole, the designer can use *participation constraints*.

Given an entity type, **E**, a relationship type, **R**, and a role, ρ, a **participation constraint** of **E** in **R** in role ρ states that for every entity instance **e** in **E**, there is a relationship **r** in **R** such that **e** participates in **r** in role ρ.

Clearly, requiring that the entity type PROFESSOR participate in the relationship type WORKSIN in role Professor ensures that every professor works in some department.

For another example, we can try to ensure that every student takes at least one course. To this end, we can assume that there is a ternary relationship type, TRANSCRIPT, which relates STUDENT, COURSE, and SEMESTER. Our goal can be achieved by imposing a participation constraint on the STUDENT entity type.

In E-R diagrams, participation constraints are represented by a thick line connecting the participating entity with the corresponding relationship as shown in Figure 5.7. The thick arrow connecting PROFESSOR to WORKSIN indicates both that each professor participates in at least one relationship (denoted by the thick line) and that each professor can participate in at most one relationship (denoted by the arrow). Hence, a one-to-one correspondence between PROFESSOR entities and relationships is implied.

Representation in the relational model.   Conceptually, representing participation constraints using the relational model is easy. We have already seen, in Figure 5.4, page 99, the CREATE TABLE statement for the WORKSIN relationship. So,

---

[5] This transformation can be done even if SENIOR has its own attribute. However, in this case all students who have not reached the senior status will have their Advisor attribute set to NULL.

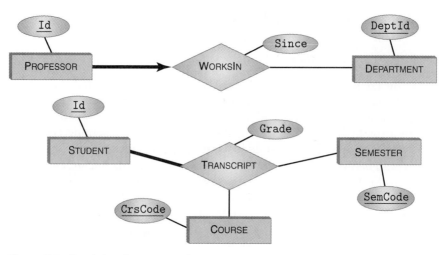

Figure 5.7 Participation constraints.

all it takes to enforce the participation constraint of PROFESSORS in WORKSIN is to specify the inclusion dependency[6] that states

> PROFESSOR(Id) <u>references</u> WORKSIN(ProfId)

Incidentally, this is also a foreign key constraint because ProfId is a key of WORKSIN. Thus, we can specify the above participation constraint in SQL-92 by simply declaring the Id attribute of PROFESSOR as a foreign key constraint.

```
CREATE TABLE   PROFESSOR   (
     Id         INTEGER,
     Name       CHAR(20),
     DeptId     CHAR(4),
     PRIMARY KEY (Id),
     FOREIGN KEY (Id) REFERENCES WORKSIN (ProfId) )
```

Note that this foreign key constraint does not rule out the possibility that Id can be a null, which means that in general a NOT NULL constraint for Id would be in order. However, in our case Id is declared as a primary key of PROFESSOR, so the NOT NULL constraint is redundant (at least, in SQL-92-compliant databases).

We could do an even better translation by noticing that Id is a key of PROFESSOR and also of WORKSIN (indirectly, through the foreign key constraint). Thus, we can merge the attributes of WORKSIN into the PROFESSOR relation (after deleting the attribute ProfId, as the same information is given by the attribute Id). This is possible because the common key of these tables guarantees that each PROFESSOR tuple has

---

[6] Inclusion dependencies were discussed in Section 4.2.2.

exactly one corresponding WorksIn tuple, so no redundancy is created by concatenating such related tuples. This yields the table PROFESSORMERGEDWITHWORKSIN:

```
CREATE TABLE   PROFESSORMERGEDWITHWORKSIN   (
    Id       INTEGER,
    Name     CHAR(20),
    DeptId   CHAR(4),
    Since    DATE,
    PRIMARY KEY (Id)
    FOREIGN KEY DeptId REFERENCES DEPARTMENT )
```

Although conceptually representation of participation constraints in the relational model amounts to nothing more than specifying an inclusion dependency, the actual representation in SQL-92 is not always as simple as in the previous example. The reason is that not all inclusion dependencies are foreign key constraints (see Section 4.2.2), and their expression in SQL-92 requires heavy machinery, such as assertions or triggers, which can have a negative effect on performance.

An example of this situation is the constraint on the participation of STUDENT in the TRANSCRIPT relationship, depicted in Figure 5.7. The translation of TRANSCRIPT to SQL-92 is

```
CREATE TABLE   TRANSCRIPT   (
    StudId    INTEGER,
    CrsCode   CHAR(6),
    Semester  CHAR(6),
    Grade     CHAR(1),
    PRIMARY KEY (StudId, CrsCode, Semester),
    FOREIGN KEY (StudId) REFERENCES STUDENT (Id),
    FOREIGN KEY (CrsCode) REFERENCES COURSE (CrsCode),
    FOREIGN KEY (Semester) REFERENCES SEMESTERS (SemCode))
```

As before, the foreign key constraints specified for the TRANSCRIPT table do not guarantee that every student takes a course. To ensure that every student participates in some TRANSCRIPT relationship, the STUDENT relation must have an inclusion dependency of the form

STUDENT(Id) <u>references</u> TRANSCRIPT(StudId)

However, since StudId is not a candidate key in TRANSCRIPT, this inclusion dependency cannot be represented by foreign key constraints. In Chapter 4, we illustrated how inclusion dependencies can be defined using the CREATE ASSERTION statement (see (4.4) on page 75).

Unfortunately, verifying general assertions is often significantly more costly than verifying foreign key constraints, so the use of constraints such as (4.4) should be carefully weighed against the potential overhead. For instance, if it is determined that including such an assertion slows down crucial database operations, the designer might opt for checking the inclusion dependency as part of a separate, periodically run transaction rather than one run in real time.

Figure 5.8 The IsA hierarchy of the PSSC enterprise.

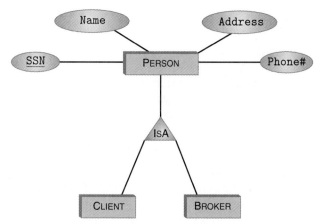

5.5   A BROKERAGE FIRM EXAMPLE

We have been using the Student Registration System to illustrate most of the concepts of the E-R model. In this section, we use a different enterprise as an additional illustration of these concepts.

The Pie in the Sky Securities Corporation (PSSC) is a brokerage firm that buys and sells stocks for its clients. Thus, the main actors are *brokers* and *clients*. PSSC has offices in different cities, and each broker works in one of these offices. A broker can also be an office manager (for the office she works in).

Clients own accounts, and any account can have more than one owner. Each account is also managed by some broker. A client can have several accounts and a broker can manage several accounts, but a client cannot have more than one account in a given office.

The requirement is to design a database for maintaining the above information as well as information about the trades performed in each account.

The basic information about brokers and clients is depicted in Figure 5.8. More information is shown in Figure 5.9. Here we make additional assumptions that a broker can manage at most one office and that each office has at most one manager. Notice that we did not specify a participation constraint for OFFICE in the relationship MANAGEDBY, so it is possible that an office might not have a manager (e.g., if the manager quits and the position remains vacant). Since each account can be maintained in exactly one office and by at most one broker, Figure 5.9 shows a participation constraint of entity ACCOUNT in the relationship IsHANDLEDBY by the arrow leading from ACCOUNT to IsHANDLEDBY. Thus, {Account} is a key of IsHANDLEDBY. Notice that the attributes that form a key of an entity are underlined and different keys are underlined differently. Thus, for instance, OFFICE has two keys: {Phone#} and {Address}.

However, after careful examination we can see that the diagram in Figure 5.9 has problems. For one, it requires every account to have a broker. This might or might

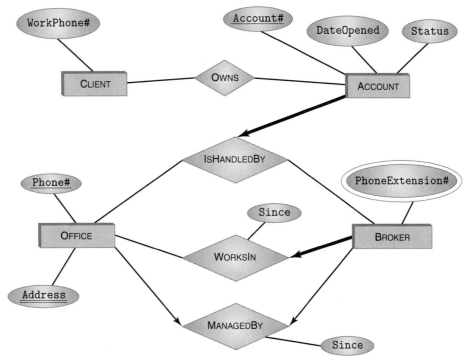

Figure 5.9 Client/broker Information: first attempt.

not be correct depending on company policy. For another, the requirement that a client cannot have two separate accounts in the same office is not represented in the diagram.

We might try to rectify these problems using the diagram depicted in Figure 5.10. Here we take a slightly different approach and introduce a ternary relation HASACCOUNT with {Client, Office} as a key. In addition, we maintain one more relationship, HANDLEDBY, which relates accounts and brokers but does not require that every account has a broker.

Unfortunately, even this diagram has problems. First, notice that the edge that connects ACCOUNT and HASACCOUNT does not have an arrow. Such an arrow would have made the role {Account} a key of the relationship HASACCOUNT, which contradicts the requirement that an account can have multiple owners. However, our new design introduces a different problem: the constraint that each account is assigned to exactly one office is no longer represented in the diagram. The participation constraint of ACCOUNT in HASACCOUNT says that each account must be assigned to at least one office (and at least one customer), but nothing here says that such an office must be unique. Furthermore, we cannot solve this problem by adding an arrow to this participation constraint because, as noted earlier, this would make it impossible to have multiple owners for the same account.

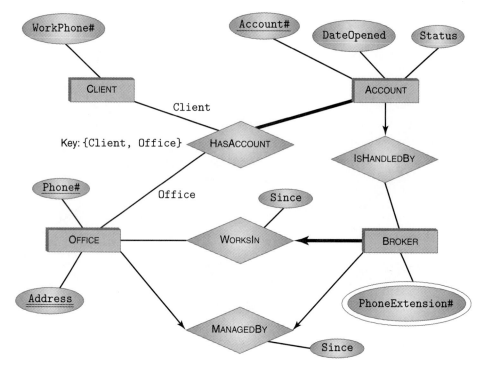

Figure 5.10 Client/broker Information: second try.

There is one more problem with our new design (which, in fact, was also present in our original design in Figure 5.9). Suppose that we have the following relationships:

⟨Client1, Acct1, Office1 ⟩ ∈ HasAccount

⟨Acct1, Broker1⟩ ∈ HandledBy

⟨Broker1, Office2⟩ ∈ WorksIn

What is there to ensure that Office1 and Office2 are the same (i.e., Account1's office is the same as that of the broker who manages Account1)? This last problem is known as a **navigation trap**: Starting with a given entity, Office1, and moving along the triangle formed by the three relationships HasAccount, HandledBy, and WorksIn, we might end up with a different entity, Office2, of the same type. Navigation traps of this kind are particularly difficult to avoid in the E-R model because doing so requires the use of participation constraints in combination with so-called *functional dependencies* (see Section 8.3), but these constraints are

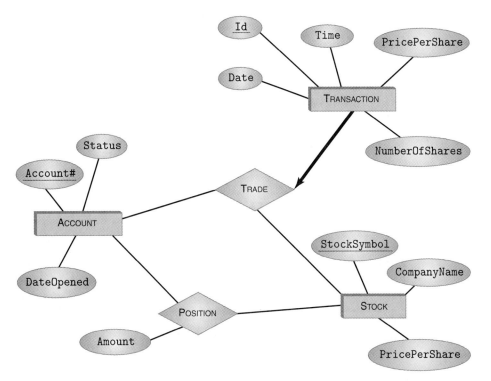

Figure 5.11 Trading information in the PSSC enterprise.

supported by the E-R model only in a very limited way: as keys and participation constraints.[7]

Note that we can avoid the navigation trap by removing the relationship HASAC-COUNT completely and reintroducing the OWNS relationship between clients and accounts. However, this brings back the problem that the constraint that a client cannot have more than one account in any given office is no longer represented.

Even though we have not yet obtained a completely satisfactory design for this part of the database, we now turn our attention to the part that deals with stock trading. On a bigger canvas, Figures 5.10 and 5.11 would be connected through the entity ACCOUNT.

---

[7] To neutralize the navigation trap in this example, we need an inclusion dependency of a fairly complex form. Loosely speaking, we want to ensure that in every tuple $t \in$ HASACCOUNT, the attribute Account refers to an account handled by some broker and the attribute Office refers to that broker's office. After learning the basics of relational algebra in Chapter 6, you will see that such an inclusion dependency can be formally specified as follows: $\pi_{\text{Office,Account}}(\text{HANDLEDBY} \bowtie \text{WORKSIN}) \supseteq \pi_{\text{Office,Account}}(\text{HASACCOUNT})$, where π is the *projection* operator (that chops off all attributes except Office and Account) and $\bowtie$ is the join operator (which "lines up" the tuples that correspond to the same broker in the relations HANDLEDBY and WORKSIN).

Trading information is specified using three entities, ACCOUNT, STOCK, and TRANSACTION. These entities are linked through the relationship POSITION, which relates stocks with the accounts they are held in, and the relationship TRADE, which represents the actual buying and selling of stocks. This information is depicted in Figure 5.11.

Notice that the role Transaction is a key of the relationship TRADE and that transactions do not exist outside of TRADE relationships. These constraints are expressed in Figure 5.11 using a thick arrow, which specifies the one-to-one correspondence between TRANSACTION entities and TRADE relationships.

5.6   LIMITATIONS OF THE E–R APPROACH

You have now seen two case studies of the use of the entity-relationship model for database design. If E-R design still does not seem completely clear to you, you are in good company. Although we have discussed several concepts that might provide general guidance in organizing enterprise data, applying these concepts in any concrete situation is still a mix of experience, art, and black magic. There is considerable freedom in deciding whether a particular datum should be an entity, a relationship, or an attribute. Furthermore, even after these issues are settled the various relationships that exist among entities can be expressed in different ways. This section discusses some of the dilemmas that often confront a database designer.

Entity or attribute?   In Figure 5.7, semesters are represented as entities. However, we could as well make TRANSCRIPT into a binary (rather than ternary) relation and turn SEMESTER into one of its attributes. The obvious question is which representation is best (and in which case).

To some extent, the decision of whether a particular datum should be represented as an entity or an attribute is a matter of taste. Beyond that, the representation might depend on whether the datum has an internal structure of its own. If the datum has no internal data structure, keeping it as a separate entity makes the E-R diagram more complex and, more important, adds an extra relation to your database schema when you convert the diagram into the relational model. On the other hand, if the datum has attributes of its own, it is possible that these attributes cannot be represented if the datum itself is demoted to the status of an attribute.

For instance, in Figure 5.7 the entity type SEMESTER does not have its own attributes, so representing the semester information as an entity appears to be overkill. However, it is entirely possible that the Requirements Document might state that the following additional information must be available for each semester: Start_date, End_date, Holidays, Enrollment. In such a case, the semester information cannot be an attribute of the TRANSCRIPT relationship, as there would then be no place to specify the information about the key dates and the enrollment associated with semesters (e.g., the total enrollment in the university during a semester is not an attribute of any particular transcript relationship).

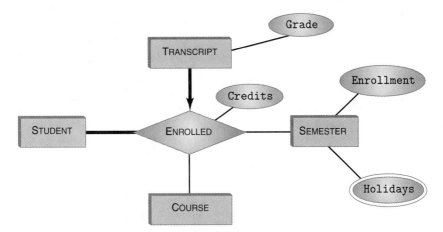

Figure 5.12 An alternative representation of the transcript information.

Entity or relationship?   Consider once again the diagram in Figure 5.7, where we treat transcript records as relationships between STUDENT, COURSE, and SEMESTER entities. An alternative to this design is to represent transcript records as entities and use a new relationship type, ENROLLED, to connect them. This alternative is represented in Figure 5.12. Here we incorporate some of the attributes for the entity SEMESTER, as discussed earlier. We also add an extra attribute, Credits, to the relationship ENROLLED.[8] Clearly, the two diagrams represent the same information (except for the extra attributes added to Figure 5.12), but which one is better?

As with the "entity versus attribute" dilemma, the choice largely depends on your taste. However, a number of points are worth considering. For instance, it is a good idea to keep the total number of entities and relations as small as possible because it is directly related to the number of relations that will result when the E-R diagram is converted to the relational model. Generally, it is not too serious a problem if two relations are lumped together at this stage because the relational design theory presented in Chapter 8 is geared to identifying relation schemas that must be split and to providing algorithms for doing that. On the other hand, it is much harder to spot the opposite problem: needlessly splitting one relation into two or more.

Coming back to Figure 5.12, we notice that there is a participation constraint for the entity TRANSCRIPT in the relationship type ENROLLED. Moreover, the arrow leading from TRANSCRIPT to ENROLLED indicates that the Transcript role forms a key of the ENROLLED relationship. Therefore, there is a one-to-one correspondence between the relationships of type ENROLLED and the entities of type TRANSCRIPT. This means that relationships of type ENROLLED can be viewed as superfluous,

---

[8] For instance, at Stony Brook some research courses can be taken for a variable number of credits.

because TRANSCRIPT entities can be used instead to relate the entities of types STU-
DENT, COURSE, and SEMESTER. All that is required (in order not to lose information)
is to transfer the proper attributes of ENROLLED to TRANSCRIPT after converting the
latter into a relationship.

As a result of this discussion, we have the following rule:

> Consider a relationship type, $\mathbf{R}$, that relates the entity types $\mathbf{E}_1, \ldots, \mathbf{E}_n$,
> and suppose that $\mathbf{E}_1$ is attached to $\mathbf{R}$ via a role that (by itself) forms a key
> of $\mathbf{R}$, and that a participation constraint exists between $\mathbf{E}_1$ and $\mathbf{R}$. Then
> it might be possible to collapse $\mathbf{E}_1$ and $\mathbf{R}$ into a new relationship type
> that involves only the entity types $\mathbf{E}_2, \ldots, \mathbf{E}_n$.

Note that this rule is only an indication that $\mathbf{E}_1$ can be collapsed into $\mathbf{R}$, not a
guarantee that this is possible. For instance, $\mathbf{E}_1$ might be involved in some other
relationship, $\mathbf{R}'$. In that case, collapsing $\mathbf{E}_1$ into $\mathbf{R}$ leaves an edge that connects two
relationship types, $\mathbf{R}$ and $\mathbf{R}'$, which is not allowed by the construction rules for
E-R diagrams. Such is the situation of the BROKER and ACCOUNT entities in Fig-
ure 5.10: The above rule suggests that BROKER can be collapsed into WORKSIN and
ACCOUNT can be collapsed into HANDLEDBY. However, both BROKER and ACCOUNT
are involved in two different relationships, and each such collapse leaves us with a
diagram where two relationships, WORKSIN and HANDLEDBY or HASACCOUNT and
HANDLEDBY, are directly connected by an edge. On the other hand, the TRANSAC-
TION entity type in Figure 5.11 can be collapsed into the TRADE relationship type.

Information loss.   We have seen examples where the arity of a relationship might
change by demoting an entity to an attribute or by collapsing an entity into a
relationship. In all of these cases, however, the transformations obviously preserve
the diagrams' information content. Now we are going to discuss some typical
situations where seemingly innocuous transformations cause **information loss**;
that is, they lead to diagrams with subtly different information content.

Consider the PARTS/SUPPLIER/PROJECT diagram of Figure 5.3. Some designers
do not like ternary relationships, preferring to deal with multiple binary relationships instead. Such a decision might lead to the diagram shown in Figure 5.13.

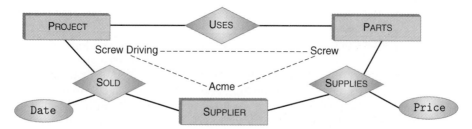

Figure 5.13   Replacing the ternary relationship SOLD of Figure 5.3 with three binary
relationships.

Although superficially the new diagram seems equivalent to the original, there are several subtle differences. First, the new design introduces a navigation trap of the kind we saw in the stock trading example: It is possible that a supplier, Acme, sells "Screw" and that Acme has sold something to project "Screw Driving." It is even possible that the screw driving project uses screws of the kind Acme sells. However, from the relationships represented in the diagram it is not possible to conclude that it was Acme who sold these screws to the project. All we can tell is that Acme *might* have done so.

The other problem with the new design is that the price attribute is now associated with the relationship SUPPLIES. This implies that a supplier has a fixed price for each item regardless of the project to which that item is sold. In contrast, the original design in Figure 5.3, page 96, supports different pricing for different projects (e.g., based on quantity). Similarly, the new design allows only one transaction between any supplier and project on any given day because each transaction is represented as a triple ⟨p, s; d⟩, so there is no way to distinguish among different transactions between the same parties on the same day. The original design, on the other hand, allows several such deals, provided that different parts are involved.

Having realized the danger of introducing navigation traps, we might be inclined to use higher-degree relationships whenever possible. For instance, in Figure 5.10 we might want to try eliminating the navigation trap caused by the relationships HASACCOUNT, WORKSIN, and HANDLEDBY by collapsing these three relationships into one. However, this transformation introduces more problems than it solves. For instance, if this transformation keeps the arrow that connects BROKER and WORKSIN, we unwittingly introduce the constraint that a broker can have at most one account and at most one client. If we do not keep this arrow, we lose the constraint that each broker is assigned to exactly one office. This transformation also makes it impossible to have brokers who have no accounts and accounts that have no brokers.

E-R and object databases.   Although we will not discuss object databases until Chapter 16, we briefly mention here that some of the difficult issues involved in translating E-R diagrams into schemas become easier for object databases.

- ■ In Section 5.2, we discussed the issues involved in representing entities with set-valued attributes in a relational database. The objects stored in an object database can have set-valued attributes, so the representation of such entities in the schema of the object database is considerably easier.

- ■ In Section 5.4, we discussed the issues involved in representing the IsA relationship in a relational database. Object databases allow a direct representation of the IsA relationship within the schema, so, again, representation of such relationships is considerably easier.

From these examples, it should be apparent that not only is it generally easier to translate E-R diagrams into schemas for object databases than into schemas for

Figure 5.14   An E-R diagram for the Student Registration System.

relational databases, but for many applications object databases allow a much more intuitive model of the enterprise than do relational databases.

5.7   CASE STUDY: A DESIGN FOR THE STUDENT REGISTRATION SYSTEM

In this section, we present a database design for the Student Registration System. This design might be included in the Design Document for the entire application, as will be discussed in Section 12.1.

The first step in the design process is to construct the E-R diagram shown in Figure 5.14, which is a model of the student registration enterprise as described in the Requirements Document (Section 3.2). Note from the figure that

■ STUDENT is related to CLASS through TRANSCRIPT, which signifies that a student is registered, is enrolled, or has completed a class in some semester.

CASE
STUDY

■ FACULTY is related to CLASS through TEACHES, meaning that a faculty member teaches a class in some semester and every class is taught by exactly one faculty member.

■ COURSE is related to COURSE through the relationship REQUIRES; that is, a course can be a prerequisite for another course in some semester. The attribute EnforcedSince specifies the date when the prerequisite became in force.

■ CLASS is related to CLASSROOM through TAUGHTIN; that is, a class is taught in a classroom in some semester.

■ A class (i.e., a particular offering of a course) uses at most one textbook, because the attribute Textbook is not part of the key of the entity CLASS. In Section 8.12, we will remove this restriction and discuss the impact of this decision on the system design.

On the basis of this E-R diagram and the list of integrity constraints given in the Requirements Document in Section 3.2.4, the next step is to produce the schema shown in Figures 5.15 and 5.16. The translation was done in a straightforward manner using the techniques described so far in this chapter. Note that tables were not created to correspond to the TEACHES and TAUGHTIN relationships because both have only roles, no attributes, and both are many-to-one. Therefore, the information about these relationships can be stored in the CLASS table—the tuple corresponding to each class in the CLASS table contains the ClasssroomId of the room where it is taught and the InstructorId of the faculty member who teaches it.

Note that some of the integrity constraints specified in the Requirements Document are checked within CREATE TABLE statements (specifically constraints 1, 3, 5, and 6 from Section 3.2.4). In the complete schema design, other integrity constraints are checked with separate CREATE ASSERTION statements and with one trigger. However, this part of the design requires SQL constructs that we have not yet discussed, and so we will complete the schema design in Section 12.6 after we cover these constructs.

We selected this particular design for inclusion in the book because it is straightforward and transparent. In practice, such a design might be a starting point for a number of enhancements whose goal is to capture more features and increase the efficiency of the final implementation.

Let us discuss a few possible enhancements and alternatives. Consider course dependencies. One obvious omission in our schema is the *corequisite* relationship and all of the constraints entailed by it. More subtly, university curricula change all the time: New courses are introduced, old courses are removed, and prerequisite dependencies between courses evolve in time. Thus, the REQUIRES relationship in Figure 5.14 might need two additional attributes, Start and End, to designate the period when the prerequisite relationship is effective. Even more interesting is the possibility that a particular prerequisite relationship might exist at different times. For instance, course A might be a prerequisite for course B between 1985 and 1990 and again between 1999 and the present. Modeling this situation is left to Exercise 5.10.

Figure 5.15 A schema for the Student Registration System—Part 1.

```
CREATE TABLE STUDENT   (
      Id             CHAR(9)  NOT NULL,
      Name           CHAR(20) NOT NULL,
      Password       CHAR(10) NOT NULL,
      Address        CHAR(50),
      PRIMARY KEY (Id) )

CREATE TABLE FACULTY   (
      Id             CHAR(9)  NOT NULL,
      Name           CHAR(20) NOT NULL,
      DeptId         CHAR(4)  NOT NULL,
      Password       CHAR(10) NOT NULL,
      Address        CHAR(50),
      PRIMARY KEY (Id) )

CREATE TABLE COURSE (
      CrsCode        CHAR(6)  NOT NULL,
      DeptId         CHAR(4)  NOT NULL,
      CrsName        CHAR(20) NOT NULL,
      CreditHours    INTEGER NOT NULL,
      PRIMARY KEY (CrsCode),
      UNIQUE (DeptId, CrsName) )

CREATE TABLE WHENOFFERED (
      CrsCode        CHAR(6)  NOT NULL,
      Semester       CHAR(6)  NOT NULL,
      PRIMARY KEY (CrsCode, Semester),
      CHECK (Semester IN ('Spring','Fall') ) )

CREATE TABLE CLASSROOM   (
      ClassroomId    CHAR(3)  NOT NULL,
      Seats          INTEGER NOT NULL,
      PRIMARY KEY (ClassroomId) )
```

Another interesting enhancement can be to account for the possibility that certain highly popular courses might be restricted to certain majors only. In this situation, the E-R diagram and the corresponding tables have to include information about the student majors (a set-valued attribute!), and this has to be consistent with the majors allowed in the courses. This enhancement is left to Exercise 5.11.

Enhancements to express more complex requirements are one source of modifications to the proposed design. Another source is the vast range of possible alternative designs, which might have implications for the overall performance of the system. We discuss one such alternative and its implications.

Figure 5.16 A schema for the Student Registration System—Part 2.

```
CREATE TABLE   REQUIRES    (
    CrsCode        CHAR(6)   NOT NULL,
    PrereqCrsCode CHAR(6)   NOT NULL,
    EnforcedSince DATE      NOT NULL,
    PRIMARY KEY (CrsCode, PrereqCrsCode),
    FOREIGN KEY (CrsCode) REFERENCES COURSE(CrsCode),
    FOREIGN KEY (PrereqCrsCode) REFERENCES COURSE(CrsCode)   )

CREATE TABLE   CLASS   (
    CrsCode        CHAR(6)   NOT NULL,
    SectionNo      INTEGER   NOT NULL,
    Semester       CHAR(6)   NOT NULL,
    Year           INTEGER    NOT NULL,
    Textbook       CHAR(50),
    ClassTime      CHAR(5),
    Enrollment     INTEGER,
    MaxEnrollment INTEGER,
    ClassroomId    CHAR(3),
    InstructorId   CHAR(9),
    PRIMARY KEY (CrsCode,SectionNo,Semester,Year),
    CONSTRAINT TIMECONFLICT
        UNIQUE (InstructorId,Semester,Year,ClassTime),
    CONSTRAINT CLASSROOMCONFLICT
        UNIQUE (ClassroomId,Semester,Year,ClassTime),
    CONSTRAINT ENROLLMENT
        CHECK (Enrollment <= MaxEnrollment AND Enrollment >= 0),
    FOREIGN KEY (CrsCode) REFERENCES COURSE(CrsCode),
    FOREIGN KEY (ClassroomId) REFERENCES CLASSROOM(ClassroomId),
    FOREIGN KEY (CrsCode, Semester)
        REFERENCES WHENOFFERED(CrsCode, Semester),
    FOREIGN KEY (InstructorId) REFERENCES FACULTY(Id)   )

CREATE TABLE   TRANSCRIPT    (
    StudId         CHAR(9)   NOT NULL,
    CrsCode        CHAR(6)   NOT NULL,
    SectionNo      INTEGER   NOT NULL,
    Semester       CHAR(6)   NOT NULL,
    Year           INTEGER   NOT NULL,
    Grade          CHAR(1),
    PRIMARY KEY (StudId,CrsCode,SectionNo,Semester,Year),
    FOREIGN KEY (StudId) REFERENCES STUDENT(Id),
    FOREIGN KEY (CrsCode,SectionNo,Semester,Year)
        REFERENCES CLASS(CrsCode,SectionNo,Semester,Year),
    CHECK (Grade IN ('A','B','C','D','F','I') ),
    CHECK (Semester IN ('Spring','Fall') )   )
```

Consider the attribute SemestersOffered of entity Course. Because it is a set-valued attribute, we translate it using a separate table, WhenOffered. We chose this particular design because we saw that it leads to a particularly easy way to express the constraint that the semester when any particular class is taught must be one of the semesters when that course is offered. For instance, it should not be possible for course CS305 to be offered only in spring semesters but for a certain class of this course to be taught in fall 2000. However, this should be allowed if CS305 is offered in both spring and fall semesters.

In our design, this requirement is expressed simply as a foreign key constraint in relation Class.

```
FOREIGN KEY (CrsCode, Semester)
        REFERENCES WhenOffered(CrsCode, Semester)
```

This constraint says that if a class of course with code crscode is offered during a semester, sem, then ⟨ csrcode, sem ⟩ should be a tuple in the relation WhenOffered; that is, sem must be one of the allowed semesters for the course.

Despite the simplicity of this design, one might feel that creating a separate relation for such a trivial piece of information is unacceptable overhead. Such a separate relation requires an extra operation for certain queries, additional storage requirements, and the like.[9] An alternative is to define a new SQL domain (introduced in Chapter 4), which contains just three values:

```
CREATE DOMAIN  Semesters CHAR(6)
      CHECK ( VALUE IN ('Spring', 'Fall', 'Both') )
```

The set-valued attribute SemestersOffered of the entity Course is now single-valued, but it ranges over the domain Semesters. The advantage is that the translation into the relational model is more straightforward and there is no need for the extra relation WhenOffered. However, it is now more difficult to specify the constraint that a class can be taught only in the semesters when the corresponding course is offered. Details are left to Exercise 5.12.

Finally, let us consider the possible alternatives for representing the current and the next semesters, as is required by some transactions specified in the Requirements Document in Section 3.2. In fact, our design has no obvious way to represent this information. One simple way to tell which semester is current or next is to create a separate relation to store this information. However, this would not be a good design because every reference to the current or to the next semester would require a relatively expensive database query. The right way to do this type of thing is to use the function CURRENT_DATE provided by SQL and the function EXTRACT to extract particular fields from that date. For instance,

```
EXTRACT(YEAR FROM CURRENT_DATE)
```

---

[9] In our particular case, none of these disadvantages seems to apply because, in all likelihood, the relation WhenOffered will be mostly used to verify the above foreign key constraint and having a separate relation for course-semester pairs is a very efficient way to check this constraint.

EXTRACT(MONTHS FROM CURRENT_DATE)

returns the numeric values of the current year and month. This should be sufficient to determine whether any given semester is current or next.   ■

5.8   BIBLIOGRAPHIC NOTES

The entity-relationship approach was introduced in [Chen 1976]. Since then it has
received considerable attention and various extensions have been proposed (see,
for example, research papers in [Spaccapietra 1987]). Conceptual design using the
E-R model has also been advanced significantly. The reader is referred to [Teorey
1992, Batini et al. 1992, Thalheim 1992] for comprehensive coverage.

More recently, a new design methodology called **Unified Modeling Language**
(UML) was developed and has been gaining popularity [Booch et al. 1999]. UML
borrows many ideas from the E-R model, but extends it in the direction of object-
oriented modeling. In particular, it provides means to model not only the structure
of the data but also the behavioral aspects of programs and how complex applications are to be deployed in complex computing environments. A succinct introduction to UML can be found in [Fowler and Scott 1999].

A number of tools exist to help the database designer with E-R and UML modeling. These tools guide the user through the process of specifying the diagrams,
attributes, constraints, and so forth. When all is done, they map the conceptual
model into relational tables. Such tools include *ERwin* from Computer Associates,
ER/Studio from Embarcadero Technologies, and *Rational Rose* from Rational Software. In addition, DBMS vendors provide their own design tools, such as *Oracle
Designer* from Oracle Corporation and *PowerDesigner* from Sybase.

5.9   EXERCISES

5.1 Suppose that you decide to convert IsA hierarchies into the relational model
by adding a new attribute (such as Status in the case of STUDENT entities,
as described in Section 5.4.1 on page 103). What kind of problems exist if
subentities are not disjoint (e.g., if a secretary can also be a technician)?
What problems exist if the covering constraint does not hold (e.g., if some
employees are not classified as either secretary or technician)?

5.2 Construct your own example of an E-R diagram whose direct translation into
the relational model has an anomaly similar to that of the PERSON entity (see
the discussion regarding Figures 5.1 and 5.2).

5.3 Represent the IsA hierarchy in Figure 5.5 in the relational model. For each IsA
relationship discuss your choice of the representation technique (i.e., either
the technique where each entity in the hierarchy is represented by a separate
relation or the one where the entity and its subentities are in the same relation
and are distinguished using a new attribute). Discuss the circumstances

when an alternative representation (to the one you have chosen) would be better.

5.4 Translate the brokerage example of Section 5.5 into an SQL-92 schema. Use the necessary SQL-92 machinery to express all of the constraints specified in the E-R model.

5.5 Identify the navigation traps present in the diagram of Figure 5.9.

5.6 Consider the following database schema:

SUPPLIER(SName, ItemName, Price)—supplier SName sells item ItemName at Price

CUSTOMER(CName, Address)—customer CName lives at Address.

ORDER(CName, SName, ItemName, Qty)—customer CName has ordered Qty of item ItemName from supplier SName.

ITEM(ItemName, Description)—information about items.

a. Draw the E-R diagram from which the above schema might have been derived. Specify the keys.

b. Suppose now that you want to add the following constraint to this diagram: *Every item is supplied by some supplier*. Modify the diagram to accommodate this constraint. Also show how this new diagram can be translated back to the relational model.

5.7 Use the E-R approach to model the operations of your local community library. The library has books, CDs, tapes, and so forth, which are lent to library patrons. The latter have accounts, addresses, and so forth. If a loaned item is overdue, it accumulates penalty. However, some patrons are minors, so they must have sponsoring patrons who are responsible for paying penalties (or replacing a book in case of a loss).

5.8 Design the E-R diagram for a real estate brokerage firm. The firm keeps track of the houses for sale, and it has customers looking to buy a house. A house for sale can be *listed* with this firm or with a different one. Being "listed" with a firm means that the house owner has a contract with an agent who works for that firm. Each house on the market has price, address, owner, and list of characteristics, such as the number of bedrooms, bathrooms, type of heating, appliances, size of garage, and the like. This list can be different for different houses, and some attributes can be present for some houses but missing for others. Likewise, each customer has preferences that are expressed in the same terms (the number of bedrooms, bathrooms, etc.). Apart from these preferences customers specify the price range of houses they are interested in.

5.9 A supermarket chain is interested in building a decision support system with which they can analyze the sales of different products in different supermarkets at different times. Each supermarket is in a city, which is in a state, which is in a region. Time can be measured in days, months, quarters, and years. Products have names and categories (produce, canned goods, etc.). Design an E-R diagram for this application.

5.10 Modify the E-R diagram for the Student Registration Schema in Figure 5.14 to include corequisite and prerequisite relationships that exist over multiple periods of time. Each period begins in a certain semester and year and ends in a certain semester and year, or it continues into the present. Modify the translation into the relational model appropriately.

5.11 Modify the E-R diagram for the Student Registration System in Figure 5.14 to include information about the student majors and the majors allowed in courses. A student can have several majors (which are codes of the various programs in the university, such as CSE, ISE, MUS, ECO). A course can also have several admissible majors, or the list of admissible majors can be empty. In the latter case, anyone is admitted into the course. Express the constraint that says that a course with restrictions on majors can have only those students who hold one of the allowed majors.

Alas, in full generality this constraint can be expressed only as an SQL assertion (introduced in Section 4.3) that uses features to be discussed in Section 6.2. However, it is possible to express this constraint under the following simplifying assumption: When a student registers for a course, she must state the major for which the course is going to be taken.

Modify the schema to reflect this simplifying assumption and then express the aforesaid integrity constraint.

5.12 Make the necessary modifications to the schema of the Student Registration System to reflect the design that uses the SQL domain SEMESTERS, as discussed at the end of Section 5.7. Express the constraint that a class can be taught only during the semesters in which the corresponding course is offered. For instance, if the value of the attribute SemestersOffered for the course CS305 is Both, then the corresponding classes can be taught in the spring and the fall semesters. However, if the value of that attribute is Spring then these classes can be taught only in the spring.

5.13 Design an E-R model for the following enterprise. Various organizations make business deals with various other organizations. (For simplicity, let us assume that there are only two parties to each deal.) When negotiating (and signing) a deal, each organization is represented by a lawyer. The same organization can have deals with many other organizations and it might use different lawyers in each case. Lawyers and organizations have various attributes, like address and name. They also have their own unique attributes, such as specialization and fee in case of a lawyer and budget in case of an organization.

Show how information loss can occur if a relationship of degree higher than two is split into binary relationship. Discuss assumption under which such a split does not lead to a loss of information.

Chapter 6
Query Languages I: Relational Algebra and SQL

Now that you know how to create a database, the next step is to learn how to query it to retrieve the information needed for some particular application. A *database query language* is a special-purpose programming language designed for retrieving information stored in a database.

Before relational databases, database querying was a dreadful task. To pose even a simple query (by today's standards), one would use a conventional programming language to write a program that could include multiple nested loops, error handling, and boundary condition checking. In addition, the programmer would deal with numerous details of the internal physical schema—in those days, data independence was only on the wish list.

The relational query language in which we are most interested is SQL (Structured Query Language). It is quite different from conventional programming languages. In SQL, you specify the properties of the information to be retrieved but not the detailed algorithm required for retrieval. For example, a query in the Student Registration System might specify retrieval of the names and Ids of all professors who have taught a particular course in a particular semester, but it would not provide a detailed procedure (involving while loops, if statements, pointer variables, etc.) to traverse the various database tables and retrieve the specified names. Thus, SQL is said to be *declarative*, as its queries "declare" what information the answer should contain, not how to compute it. Contrast this to conventional programming languages (e.g., C or Java), which are said to be *procedural* because programs written in them describe the exact actions to be performed to compute the answer.

As with other computer languages, a programmer can design simple queries after only a brief introduction to SQL, but the design of the complex queries needed in real applications requires a more detailed knowledge of the language and its semantics. Therefore, before we introduce SQL we study the *relational algebra*, which is another relational query language that is used by the DBMS as an intermediate language into which SQL statements are translated before they are optimized. In Chapter 7 we will introduce other relational languages—in particular, the relational calculus—and then relate these to SQL and the relational algebra.

6.1   RELATIONAL ALGEBRA: UNDER THE HOOD OF SQL

Relational Algebra is called an algebra because it is based on a small number of *operators*, which operate on relations (tables). Each operator operates on one or more relations and produces another relation as a result. A query is just an expression involving these operators. The result of the expression is a relation, which is the answer to the query. Thus, the result of the query for the Student Registration System posed in the previous section is a relation with two attributes giving the names and Ids of the professors who taught the specified course in the specified semester.

While SQL is a declarative language, meaning that it does not specify the algorithm used to process queries, relational algebra is procedural. A relational expression can be viewed as a specification of such an algorithm (although at a much higher level than the algorithms specified using traditional programming languages).

Thus, even when programmers use SQL to specify their queries, DBMSs use relational algebra as an intermediate language for specifying query evaluation algorithms. The DBMS parses the SQL query and translates it into an expression in relational algebra, which usually leads to a rather simplistic, inefficient algorithm. The **query optimizer** then converts this algebraic expression into one that is *equivalent* but that (hopefully) takes less time to execute.[1] On the basis of the optimized algebraic expression it produced, the query optimizer prepares a **query execution plan**, which is then transformed into executable code by the code generator within the DBMS. Because algebraic expressions have precise mathematical semantics, the system can verify that the resulting "optimized" expression is equivalent to the original. The semantics also makes it possible to compare different proposed query evaluation plans. A schematic view of query processing is shown in Figure 6.1.

The relational algebra is the key to understanding the inner workings of a relational DBMS, which in turn is essential in designing SQL queries that can be processed efficiently.

6.1.1 Basic Operators

Relational algebra is based on five basic operators:

■ **Select**

■ **Project**

■ **Union**

■ **Set difference**

■ **Cartesian product** (also known as **cross product**)

---

[1] Query optimizers do not really "optimize" (in the sense of producing the *most efficient* query evaluation algorithm) because this is generally an impossible task. Instead, they use heuristics known to produce equivalent expressions that are generally cheaper to evaluate.

Figure 6.1 Schematic
view of query processing

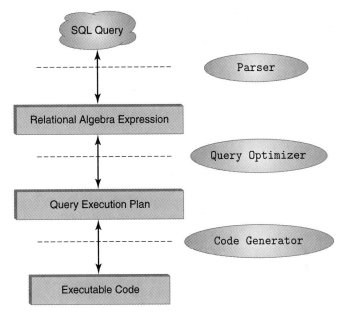

each of which we consider in turn. In addition, there are three *derived* operators (i.e., they can be represented as expressions involving the basic operators): **intersection**, **division**, and **join**. We also discuss the **renaming** operator, which is useful in conjunction with Cartesian products and joins.

Select operator. One of the most frequent operations performed on relations is selection of a subset of tuples (i.e., selection of some subset of the rows in a table). For instance, you might want to know who are the professors in the CS department. Surely, they are all listed in the PROFESSOR relation, but this relation might be large and a manual scan for the tuples of interest might be difficult. Using the select operator, this query can be expressed as

$$\sigma_{\text{DeptId} = \text{'CS'}} (\text{PROFESSOR})$$

The query reads as "Select all tuples from the PROFESSOR relation that satisfy the condition DeptId = 'CS'."

The syntax of the select operator is

$$\sigma_{\text{selection-condition}}(relation-name)$$

We will see later that the argument of the select operator can be more general than simply a name that identifies a relation. It can also be an expression that evaluates to a relation.

The selection condition can have one of the following forms:

■ *simple-selection-condition* (explained below)

■ *selection-condition* AND *selection-condition*

■ *selection-condition* OR *selection-condition*

■ NOT (*selection-condition*)

A simple selection condition can be any one of the following:

■ *relation-attribute* oper *constant*

■ *relation-attribute* oper *relation-attribute*

where oper can be any one of the following comparison operators: $=, \neq, >, \geq, <,$ and $\leq$. Each attribute participating in the comparison must be one of the attributes in the *relation name* argument of the selection operator.

It is important to realize that the above syntactic rules *must be followed*, in the same way that you follow the rules of syntax in any other programming language. A common syntax error is to write a query such as

$$\sigma_{\text{ProfId=PROFESSOR.Id AND PROFESSOR.DeptId='CS'}} (\text{TEACHING})$$

to list all courses taught by computer science professors. However natural this expression might seem, it is *syntactically incorrect*, because the selection condition uses attributes of the PROFESSOR relation where the syntax rules permit only the attributes of the TEACHING relation—the relation specified in the argument of the selection.

By itself, the expression $\sigma_{\text{selection-condition}}(\mathbf{R})$ is meaningless—it is just a string of characters. However, in a concrete database it can have a *value*, which is the *meaning* of the expression in the context of that database. Thus, we always assume that we are working in the context of some concrete database, which associates a concrete relation instance with each relation name.

Suppose that $\mathbf{r}$ is such a relation instance associated with $\mathbf{R}$. We define the *value* of the above expression with respect to $\mathbf{r}$, denoted $\sigma_{\text{selection-condition}}(\mathbf{r})$, to be the relation that consists of the set of all tuples in $\mathbf{r}$ that satisfy *selection-condition*. Thus, the value of the select operator operating on a relation is another relation.

For instance, the value of $\sigma_{\text{DeptId = 'CS'}}$ (PROFESSOR) with respect to the database of Figure 4.5 on page 63 is the relation CSPROF.

CSPROF	Id	Name	DeptId
	101202303	Smyth, John	CS
	555666777	Doe, Mary	CS

It should be clear what it means for a tuple in $\mathbf{r}$ to satisfy a selection condition. For instance, if the condition is $A > c$, where A is an attribute and c is a constant, a tuple, t, satisfies the condition if (and only if) the value of attribute A in t is greater than c.[2] When the selection condition is more complex (e.g., $cond_1$ AND $cond_2$), satisfaction is defined recursively: It is satisfied by t if and only if t satisfies both $cond_1$ and $cond_2$.

---

[2] We assume the existence of some ordering. In the case of numeric domains, the order is clear; in the case of domains of strings, we assume lexicographic order.

The condition $cond_1$ OR $cond_2$ is similar, except that t needs to satisfy only one of the subconditions. Analogously, t satisfies NOT $(cond)$ if t violates $cond$.

For instance, tuple 2 in the relation CSPROF satisfies the complex condition Id > 111222333 AND NOT (DeptId = 'EE') because it satisfies both of the following.

■ Id > 111222333, since 555666777 > 111222333.

■ NOT (DeptId = 'EE'), since 'CS' ≠ 'EE' (i.e., the tuple violates the condition DeptId = 'EE').

In contrast, tuple 1 in that relation violates the above complex condition because it violates the first term, Id > 111222333, of that condition (since 101202303 ≯ 111222333).

Here is a more complex selection:

$$\sigma_{\text{StudId} \neq 111111111 \text{ AND (Semester='S1991' OR Grade} = <'B')}(\text{TRANSCRIPT})$$

where the comparison among strings (Grade =< 'B') assumes lexicographic order. The value of this expression in the context of the database of Figure 4.5 is the relation

SUBTRANSCRIPT	StudId	CrsCode	Semester	Grade
	666666666	MGT123	F1994	A
	666666666	EE101	S1991	B
	123454321	CS315	S1997	A
	023456789	CS305	S1996	A

One obvious generalization of the selection condition is to allow conditions of the form $expression_1$ oper $expression_2$, where $expression$ can be either an arithmetic expression that involves attributes (which act as variables) and constants, or a string expression (e.g., pattern matching, string concatenation).

Examples of such expressions are EmplSalary > (MngrSalary * 2) and (DeptId + CrsNumber) LIKE CrsCode (here + denotes string concatenation and LIKE denotes pattern matching). The utility of such extended selections is obvious, and they are extensively used in database languages.

Project operator.   When discussing selection, we often refer to values of certain attributes in a tuple. In relational algebra, such references are very common, so we introduce special notation for them. Let A denote an attribute of a relation, $\mathbf{r}$, and let t be a tuple in $\mathbf{r}$. Then $t.A$ denotes the component of tuple t that corresponds to the attribute A. For instance, if t denotes tuple 1 in relation SUBTRANSCRIPT, then t.CrsCode is MGT123.

Also, we often need to extract a *subtuple* from a tuple. A subtuple, t, is a sequence of values extracted from t in accordance with some list of attributes. It is denoted as

$$t.\{A_1, \ldots, A_n\}$$

where $A_1, \ldots, A_n$ are attributes.

For instance, if t is tuple 1 in SUBTRANSCRIPT, then $t.\{$Semester, CrsCode$\}$ is the tuple $\langle$ F1994, MGT123 $\rangle$. Note that the order of attributes here does not (and need not) follow the order in which these attributes are listed in the relation SUBTRAN-SCRIPT. Moreover, sometimes it is convenient to allow duplicate attributes in the list. Thus, $t.\{$Semester, CrsCode, Semester$\}$ is $\langle$F1994, MGT123, F1994$\rangle$.

Now we are ready to define the projection operator, the general syntax of which is

$$\pi_{attribute\text{-}list} \ (relation\text{-}name)$$

For example, if $\mathbf{R}$ is a relation name and $A_1, \ldots, A_n$ are *some* (or all) of the attributes in $\mathbf{R}$, then $\pi_{A_1,\ldots,A_n}(\mathbf{R})$ is called the **projection** of $\mathbf{R}$ on attributes $A_1, \ldots, A_n$. (In other words, projection picks some subset of the columns in a table.)

As in the case of selection, the above expression can be assigned a value in the context of a concrete database. Suppose that $\mathbf{r}$ is a relation instance corresponding to $\mathbf{R}$ in such a database. Then the *value* of $\pi_{A_1,\ldots,A_n}(\mathbf{R})$, denoted $\pi_{A_1,\ldots,A_n}(\mathbf{r})$, is the set of *all* tuples of the form $t.\{A_1, \ldots, A_n\}$, where t ranges over all tuples in $\mathbf{r}$.

For instance, $\pi_{CrsCode,Semester}$ (TEACHING) is the relation

OFFERINGS	CrsCode	Semester
	MGT123	F1994
	EE101	S1991
	CS305	F1995
	CS315	S1997
	MAT123	S1996
	EE101	F1995
	CS305	S1996
	MAT123	F1997
	MGT123	F1997

Observe that the original TEACHING relation of Figure 4.5 (page 64) has 11 tuples, while OFFERINGS has only 9. What happened to the other tuples? The answer becomes apparent if we examine the original relation more closely. It is easy to see that tuples 1 and 4 are identical in their CrsCode and Semester attributes. The only difference between them is in the value of the ProfId attribute. The same is true of tuples 10 and 11. Applying the projection operator to tuples 1 and 4 (and to tuples 10 and 11) yields identical tuples, because the attribute ProfId is eliminated. Relations are sets and so do not allow duplicates; thus, only one copy in each group of identical tuples is kept.

The purpose of the projection operator is to help us concentrate on the relationships of interest and ignore the attributes that are irrelevant to a particular query. For instance, suppose that we wish to know which courses are offered in which semesters. The OFFERINGS relation shows this information clearly without diluting the answer with data that we did not ask for (i.e., `ProfId`). Projection also eliminates duplicates, which can save us time on analyzing the answer.

Now that we have seen two relational operators, we can combine them into a **relational expression**. This is not just an abstract mathematical exercise. Expressions are a general way of constructing queries in relational databases. For instance, we saw the query requesting all computer science professors; the result was the relation CSPROF. We could obtain just the names of those professors using the projection operator—π_{Name} (CSPROF)—but the advantage of the algebra is that operators can be combined just as in high-school algebra so we write

$$\pi_{\text{Name}}(\sigma_{\text{DeptId} = \text{'CS'}}(\text{PROFESSOR}))$$

without specifying the intermediate result and creating a temporary relation.

Set operations.   The next two operators are the familiar set operators **union** and **set difference**. Clearly, since relations are sets, these operators are applicable to them. The syntax is $\mathbf{R} \cup \mathbf{S}$ and $\mathbf{R} - \mathbf{S}$. If $\mathbf{r}$ and $\mathbf{s}$ are the relations corresponding to $\mathbf{R}$ and $\mathbf{S}$, then

■ The **value** of $\mathbf{R} \cup \mathbf{S}$ is $\mathbf{r} \cup \mathbf{s}$, the set of all tuples that belong to either $\mathbf{r}$ or $\mathbf{s}$.

■ The **value** of $\mathbf{R} - \mathbf{S}$ is $\mathbf{r} - \mathbf{s}$, the set of all tuples in $\mathbf{r}$ that *do not* belong to $\mathbf{s}$.

We can also use the **intersection** operator, $\mathbf{R} \cap \mathbf{S}$ (whose value on $\mathbf{r}$ and $\mathbf{s}$ is, naturally, $\mathbf{r} \cap \mathbf{s}$), but this operator is not independent of the rest. It can be represented as an expression built out of the basic five operators mentioned at the beginning of this section.

Unfortunately, we are not done yet. While the union of two sets is always a set, we cannot say the same about relations. Consider trying to compute the union of PROFESSOR with TRANSCRIPT. One problem is that relations are *tables* where all rows have the same number of items. However, the tuples in the PROFESSOR relation have three items each, while the tuples in the TRANSCRIPT relation have four. Since they have different arities, the collection of all of these tuples does not constitute a relation.

Even when the arities are the same, in order for the union to be meaningful all items in the corresponding columns must belong to the same domain. Consider the set-theoretic union of PROFESSOR and TEACHING. If we match the columns, `Id`, `Name`, and `DeptId` in PROFESSOR will correspond to `ProfId`, `CrsCode`, and `Semester`. In the union, the values in the first column are members of the same domain, so no problem there. However, the second and the third columns clearly do not belong to the same domain (e.g., people's names and course codes).

To overcome this problem, we limit the scope of the union operator and apply it only to *union-compatible* relations. Relations are **union-compatible** if their schemas satisfy the following rules.[3]

---

[3] Some texts relax this requirement by not insisting that the names of the attributes in both relations be the same (but still requiring that the domains correspond). Later in this section, we will introduce

Figure 6.2 Examples of set operators.

CrsCode	Semester
CS305	F1995

$$\pi_{\text{CrsCode,Semester}}(\sigma_{\text{Grade='C'}}(\text{TRANSCRIPT}))$$
$$-\pi_{\text{CrsCode,Semester}}(\sigma_{\text{CrsCode= 'MAT123'}}(\text{TEACHING}))$$

CrsCode	Semester
CS305	F1995
MAT123	S1996
MAT123	F1997

$$\pi_{\text{CrsCode,Semester}}(\sigma_{\text{Grade='C'}}(\text{TRANSCRIPT}))$$
$$\cup\ \pi_{\text{CrsCode,Semester}}(\sigma_{\text{CrsCode= 'MAT123'}}(\text{TEACHING}))$$

CrsCode	Semester
MAT123	S1996

$$\pi_{\text{CrsCode,Semester}}(\sigma_{\text{Grade='C'}}(\text{TRANSCRIPT}))$$
$$\cap\ \pi_{\text{CrsCode,Semester}}(\sigma_{\text{CrsCode= 'MAT123'}}(\text{TEACHING}))$$

■ Both relations have the same number of columns.

■ The names of the attributes are the same in both relations.

■ Attributes with the same name in both relations have the same domain.

We also require union compatibility for the difference and intersection operators.

Figure 6.2 illustrates some nontrivial uses of the set operators combined with select and project operators. The first query retrieves all course offerings *other than* MAT123, where some student received the grade C. The second query is a bit contrived, but is a good illustration; it yields all course offerings where either somebody got a C or the offered course was MAT123. The third query lists all offerings of MAT123 where somebody got a C.

One interesting aspect of these examples is that the original relations, TRAN-SCRIPT and TEACHING, are not union-compatible. However, they become compatible after the incompatible attributes are projected out. All expressions in this figure are evaluated in the context of our running example of Figure 4.5.

---

the *renaming operator*, which helps to smooth out the differences between these formulations of the requirement.

Figure 6.3   Two relations and their Cartesian product

Id	Name
111223344	Smith, Mary
023456789	Simpson, Homer
987654321	Simpson, Bart

A subset of $\pi_{\text{Id,Name}}$(STUDENT)

Id	DeptId
555666777	CS
101202303	CS

A subset of $\pi_{\text{Id,DeptId}}$(PROFESSOR)

STUDENT.Id	Name	PROFESSOR.Id	DeptId
111223344	Smith, Mary	555666777	CS
111223344	Smith, Mary	101202303	CS
023456789	Simpson, Homer	555666777	CS
023456789	Simpson, Homer	101202303	CS
987654321	Simpson, Bart	555666777	CS
987654321	Simpson, Bart	101202303	CS

Their Cartesian product

The Cartesian product and renaming.   The **Cartesian product** (also known as the **cross product**), **R** × **S**, is close to the cross product operation on sets: If **r** and **s** are relational instances corresponding to **R** and **S**, respectively, the *value* of this expression, denoted **r** × **s**, is the set of all tuples, t, that can be obtained by concatenation of some tuple, $r \in$ **r**, and a tuple, $s \in$ **s**.[4]

Figure 6.3 shows a Cartesian product of some subsets of $\pi_{\text{Id,Name}}$(STUDENT) and $\pi_{\text{Id,DeptId}}$(PROFESSOR). To make it clearer which parts of the tuples in the product come from which relations, we have marked the boundary with a double line.

We now must address the problem of attribute naming, which so far we have managed to ignore. The relations that are arguments to the algebraic expressions have their schema defined in the system catalog, so the names of their attributes

---

[4] The difference between the set-theoretic cross product operation on relations and the relational cross product operation is that in the former the result is a set of pairs of tuples of the form ($<a, b>, <c, d>$) while in the latter it is a set of concatenated tuples, i.e., $<a, b, c, d>$.

are known. In contrast, the relations produced by evaluating the expressions are created on the fly, and their schema is not explicitly defined. For some operations, such as σ and π, this does not present a problem, as we can simply reuse the schema of the argument relation. For $\cup$, $\cap$, and $-$, we do not have a naming problem either because the relations involved in these operations are union-compatible, and so have the same schema, which, again, can be reused for the query answer.

The Cartesian product is the first time we must deal with the naming problem. In Figure 6.3, observe that some attributes of the product relation suddenly change names. This is because the relations involved in the operation, $\pi_{\texttt{Id,Name}}$ (STUDENT) and $\pi_{\texttt{Id,DeptId}}$ (PROFESSOR) have an identically named attribute, Id, which would otherwise appear twice in the product. The relational model does not allow different columns to have the same name within the same relation, so we rename the attributes by specifying the relation of their origin.

In the above Cartesian product example, we managed to find a simple and natural renaming convention, and we will continue to disambiguate attribute names by prefixing relation names whenever appropriate. However, this convention does not always work—for instance, it breaks down in the case of a cross product of two instances of the PROFESSOR relation. Rather than invent increasingly complex naming conventions, we place the burden on the programmer, who now becomes responsible for the renaming. To this end, we introduce the **renaming operator**, which does not belong to the core of the algebra and has no standard notation. We choose the following simple notation:

$$\textit{expression}[A_1, \ldots, A_n]$$

where *expression* is an expression in relational algebra and $A_1, \ldots, A_n$ is a list of names to be used for the attributes in the result of that expression.

We assume that n represents the number of columns in the result of the expression. Moreover, we assume that there is some standard order of columns in the relation produced by evaluating the expression. For example, in the results of π, σ, $\cup$, $\cap$, and $-$ the order is the same as that in which the attributes are listed in the schema of the argument relations. For $\mathbf{R} \times \mathbf{S}$, the attributes should be listed as in Figure 6.3: the attributes of $\mathbf{R}$ followed by the attributes of $\mathbf{S}$. For instance,

$$(\pi_{\texttt{Id,Name}} (\textsc{Student}) \times \pi_{\texttt{Id,DeptId}} (\textsc{Professor}))$$
$$[\texttt{StudId,StudName,ProfId,ProfDept}]$$

renames the attributes of the product relation in Figure 6.3 to StudId, StudName, ProfId, ProfDept from left to right. In particular, the two occurrences of Id are renamed StudId and ProfId, respectively.

The renaming operator can also be applied to subexpressions. The following example is similar to the previous example, except that we rename the attributes of the PROFESSOR relation before applying other operators.

$$\pi_{\texttt{Id,Name}} (\textsc{Student}) \times \pi_{\texttt{ProfId,ProfDept}} (\textsc{Professor} \ [\texttt{ProfId,ProfName,ProfDept}])$$

The result is the same as before, but the names of the attributes (from left to right) are now Id, Name, ProfId, ProfDept. Also note that we have to change the attributes in the second π operator, because the attributes in the argument relation were changed as a result of the renaming.

The Cartesian product holds the distinction of being the most computationally expensive operator in relational algebra. Consider $\mathbf{R} \times \mathbf{S}$, and suppose that $\mathbf{R}$ has n tuples and $\mathbf{S}$ has m tuples. The Cartesian product has $n \times m$ tuples. In addition, each tuple in the product is larger in size. For concreteness, let both $\mathbf{R}$ and $\mathbf{S}$ have 1,000 tuples with 100 bytes per tuple. Then $\mathbf{R} \times \mathbf{S}$ has 1,000,000 tuples with 200 bytes per tuple. Thus, while the total size of the original relation is under half a megabyte, the product has 200 megabytes. The cost of just writing out such a relation on disk can be prohibitive. This is just a small example. We will soon see that it is not uncommon for a query to involve three or more relations. Even in the case of four tiny relations of 100 tuples with 100 bytes per tuple, the Cartesian product has 100,000,000 tuples with 400 bytes per tuple—40 gigabytes of data!

In a course on analysis of algorithms, you might have been taught that algorithms with polynomial time complexity are acceptable as long as the degree of the polynomial is not too high. As you can see from the above example, in query processing even quadratic algorithms are unacceptable if they operate on large volumes of data. Because of the potentially huge costs, query optimizers attempt to avoid cross products if at all possible.

6.1.2 Derived Operators

Joins. A **join** of two relations, $\mathbf{R}$ and $\mathbf{S}$, is an expression of the form

$$\mathbf{R} \bowtie_{join\text{-}condition} \mathbf{S}$$

The *join condition* is just a special form of the already familiar selection condition of the σ operator:

$$\mathbf{R}.A_1 \text{ oper}_1 \mathbf{S}.B_1 \text{ AND } \mathbf{R}.A_2 \text{ oper}_2 \mathbf{S}.B_2 \text{ AND } \ldots \text{ AND } \mathbf{R}.A_n \text{ oper}_n \mathbf{S}.B_n$$

Here $A_1, \ldots, A_n$ are a subset of the attributes of $\mathbf{R}$, and $B_1, \ldots, B_n$ are a subset of the attributes of $\mathbf{S}$. Finally, $\text{oper}_1, \ldots, \text{oper}_n$ are the comparison operators $=, \neq, >$, and so forth.

These restrictions imply that join conditions can have only the AND connective (no ORs or NOTs) and that no comparisons between attributes and constants are allowed.

Even though we use a new symbol to represent it, join is not a radically new operator. *By definition*, the above join is equivalent to

$$\sigma_{join\text{-}condition}(\mathbf{R} \times \mathbf{S})$$

However, as joins occur frequently in database queries, they have earned the privilege of having their own symbol.

Figure 6.4 is an example of a join of two relations. Note the join condition Id < Id which means that, in order to qualify for a join, the value of the Id attribute in the STUDENT tuple must be less than the value of the Id attribute in the PROFESSOR tuple.

Figure 6.4 Join of relations in Figure 6.3.

STUDENT.Id	Name	PROFESSOR.Id	DeptId
111223344	Smith, Mary	555666777	CS
023456789	Simpson, Homer	555666777	CS
023456789	Simpson, Homer	101202303	CS

$$\pi_{Id,Name}(\text{STUDENT}) \bowtie_{Id<Id} \pi_{Id,DeptId}(\text{PROFESSOR})$$

Note that the definition of a join involves a Cartesian product as an intermediate step. Therefore, a join is a potentially expensive operation. However, the silver lining is that the Cartesian product is hidden inside the join. In fact, Cartesian products rarely occur on their own in typical database queries. Thus, even though the intermediate result (the product) can potentially be very large, the final result is manageable, as only a small number of tuples in the product might satisfy the join condition.

For example, the result of the join in Figure 6.4 is half the size of the Cartesian product in Figure 6.3. It is not uncommon for the size of a join to be just a tiny fraction of the size of the corresponding cross product. The tricky part is to compute a join without having to compute the intermediate Cartesian product! This may sound like magic, but there are several ways to accomplish this feat, and query optimizers do so routinely.

The general joins described above are sometimes called **theta-joins** because in antiquity the Greek letter θ was used to denote join conditions. While theta-joins are certainly common in query processing (the query *List all employees who earn more than their managers* involves a theta-join), the more common kind is one where all comparisons are equalities:

$$\mathbf{R}.A_1 = \mathbf{S}.B_1 \text{ AND } \ldots \text{ AND } \mathbf{R}.A_n = \mathbf{S}.B_n$$

Joins that utilize such conditions are called **equijoins**.

Equijoins are essentially what gives relational databases their "intelligence" because they tie together pieces of disparate information scattered throughout the database. Using equijoins, programmers can uncover complex relationships hidden in the data with just a few lines of SQL code.

Here is how you can find the names of professors who taught a course in the fall of 1994:

$$\pi_{Name}(\text{PROFESSOR} \bowtie_{Id=ProfId} \sigma_{Semester='F1994'}(\text{TEACHING}))$$

The inner join lines up the tuples in PROFESSOR against the tuples in TEACHING that describe courses taught by the respective professors in fall 1994. The final projection cuts off the uninteresting attributes. Finding the names of courses and the professors who taught them in the fall of 1995 is almost as easy:

$$\pi_{\text{CrsName,Name}} \big($$
$$\big(\text{PROFESSOR} \bowtie_{\text{Id=ProfId}} \sigma_{\text{Semester='F1995'}} (\text{TEACHING}) \big)$$
$$\bowtie_{\text{CrsCode=CrsCode}} \text{COURSE}$$
$$\big)$$

The above query involves two joins. We placed parentheses around the first join to indicate the order in which the joins are to be computed. However, this was not necessary because join happens to be an *associative* operation, as can be proved using its definition.

$$\mathbf{R} \bowtie_{\text{cond}_1} (\mathbf{S} \bowtie_{\text{cond}_2} \mathbf{T})$$

$$= \sigma_{\text{cond}_1}(\mathbf{R} \times \sigma_{\text{cond}_2}(\mathbf{S} \times \mathbf{T})) \qquad \text{by definition of } \bowtie$$

$$= \sigma_{\text{cond}_1}(\sigma_{\text{cond}_2}(\mathbf{R} \times (\mathbf{S} \times \mathbf{T}))) \qquad \text{because } \sigma \text{ and } \times \text{ commute (check!)}$$

$$= \sigma_{\text{cond}_2}(\sigma_{\text{cond}_1}(\mathbf{R} \times (\mathbf{S} \times \mathbf{T}))) \qquad \text{because two } \sigma\text{'s commute (check!)}$$

$$= \sigma_{\text{cond}_2}(\sigma_{\text{cond}_1}((\mathbf{R} \times \mathbf{S}) \times \mathbf{T})) \qquad \text{by associativity of } \times \text{ (check!)}$$

$$= (\mathbf{R} \bowtie_{\text{cond}_1} \mathbf{S}) \bowtie_{\text{cond}_2} \mathbf{T} \qquad \text{by definition of } \bowtie$$

The above double-join query illustrates one additional point. Join conditions such as TEACHING.CrsCode = COURSE.CrsCode, which test for equality of attributes with the same name (but in different relations) are quite common. The main reason for this is that it is good design practice to assign the same name to attributes that denote the same thing but that belong to different relations. For instance, the semantics of CrsCode in COURSE, TEACHING, and TRANSCRIPT are the same (which is why we used the same name in all three cases!). Because finding hidden connections in the data often amounts to comparing similar attributes in different relations, the above design practice leads to equijoin conditions that equate identically named attributes.[5]

In fact, this design practice has the effect that most equijoins are of the variety in which the join condition equates *only* identically named attributes. In recognition of their importance, such joins received their very own name: the **natural join**. A natural join actually is a little more than that. First, the join condition equates *all* identically named attributes in the two relations being joined. Second, as the equated attributes really denote the same thing in both relations (as indicated by the identity of their names), there is no reason to keep both of the columns. Thus, one copy is always projected out. In sum, the **natural join** of **R** and **S**, denoted **R** ⋈ **S**, is defined by the following relational expression:

$$\pi_{\text{attr-list}}(\sigma_{\text{join-cond}}(\mathbf{R} \times \mathbf{S}))$$

---

[5] A natural question is why we used different names for the Id attributes in STUDENT (Id) and TRANSCRIPT (StudId)—in clear violation of the design rule previously mentioned. The answer is simple. We did it so that we could squeeze more examples out of a reasonably sized schema. In a well-designed database schema, StudId would be used in both places; likewise, ProfId would be used in both PROFESSOR and TEACHING; or, perhaps, Id would be used in all four places.

where

1. *attr-list* = *attributes*(**R**) ∪ *attributes*(**S**); that is, the attribute list used in the project operator contains all the attributes in the union of the argument relations *with duplicate attribute names removed*. Since duplicate attributes are deleted, there is no need to perform attribute renaming.

2. The join condition, *join-cond*, has the form

$$\mathbf{R}.A_1 = \mathbf{S}.A_1 \text{ AND } \ldots \text{ AND } \mathbf{R}.A_n = \mathbf{S}.A_n$$

where $\{A_1, \ldots, A_n\}$ = *attributes*(**R**) ∩ *attributes*(**S**). That is, it is the list of all attributes that **R** and **S** have in common.

Note that the notation for natural joins *omits the join condition*, because the condition is implicitly (and uniquely) determined by the names assigned to the attributes of the relations in the join.

A typical example of the use of natural joins is the following query:

$$\pi_{\text{StudId,ProfId}} \ (\textsc{Transcript} \bowtie \textsc{Teaching})$$

which lists all Ids of students who ever took a course along with the Ids of professors who taught them.

To further illustrate the difference between the natural join and the equijoin, it is instructive to compare the following two expressions:

$$\textsc{Transcript} \bowtie \textsc{Teaching}$$
$$\textsc{Transcript} \bowtie_{\text{Cond}} \textsc{Teaching}$$

where the equijoin condition Cond is Transcript.CrsCode=Teaching.CrsCode AND Transcript.Semester=Teaching.Semester. Both expressions are equijoins, and both use the same join conditions (the natural join uses it implicitly). However, the resulting relations have different sets of attributes.

Natural join

        StudId, CrsCode, Semester, Grade, ProfId

Equijoin

        StudId, Transcript.CrsCode, Teaching.CrsCode,

        Transcript.Semester, Teaching.Semester, Grade, ProfId

The two expressions represent essentially the same information. However, the schema of the equijoin has two extra attributes (which are duplicates of other attributes) and the natural join benefits from a simpler attribute naming convention.

Apart from finding hidden connections in the data, joins can be used for certain counting tasks. Here is how we can find all students who took at least two different courses:

$$\pi_{\text{StudId}} \ ($$
$$\quad \sigma_{\text{CrsCode} \neq \text{CrsCode2}} \ ($$
$$\qquad \text{TRANSCRIPT} \bowtie$$
$$\qquad \text{TRANSCRIPT}[\text{StudId}, \text{CrsCode2}, \text{Semester2}, \text{Grade2}]$$
$$\quad))$$

One obvious limitation of this technique is that if we want students who had taken fifteen courses, we have to join TRANSCRIPT with itself fifteen times. A better way is to extend the relational algebra with so-called *aggregate* functions, which include the counting operator. We do not pursue this possibility here, but we will return to aggregate functions in the context of SQL in Section 6.2.

The discussion of joins cannot be complete without mentioning that—rather unexpectedly—the intersection operator is a special case of a natural join. Suppose that **R** and **S** are union-compatible. It follows then directly from the definitions that $\mathbf{R} \cap \mathbf{S} = \mathbf{R} \bowtie \mathbf{S}$.

Division operator.   While the join operator brings intelligence to query answering, the division operator holds the distinction of being the most difficult to understand and use correctly.

The division operator becomes useful when you feel the urge to find out *which professors taught* **all** *courses offered by the Computer Science Department* or *which students took a class from* **every** *professor in the electrical engineering department*. The key here is that we are looking for tuples in one relation that match *all* tuples in another relation.

Here is a precise definition. Let **R** be a relation schema with attributes $A_1, \ldots,$ $A_n, B_1, \ldots, B_m$ and let **S** be a relation schema with attributes $B_1, \ldots, B_m$. In other words, the set of attributes of **S** is a subset of the attributes of **R**. The **division** of **R** by **S** is an expression of the form **R/S**. If **r** and **s** are relation instances corresponding to **R** and **S** in our database, the **value** of **R/S** in the database, denoted **r/s**, is a relation over the attributes $A_1, \ldots, A_n$ that consists of all tuples $<a>$ such that, *for every* tuple $<b>$ in **s**, the concatenated tuple $<a, b>$ is in **r**. A schematic view of this definition is depicted in Figure 6.5.

An equivalent way to define division is

$$<a> \in \mathbf{r/s} \text{ if and only if } \{<a>\} \times \mathbf{s} \subseteq \mathbf{r}$$

Thus, if we view $\times$ as multiplication, we can view division as multiplication's inverse.

As an example, consider the query *List all courses that have been taught by every computer science professor*. Here, by "every professor," we mean "every professor recorded in the database." That is, it is assumed that the database describes all we know about the situation. Not only does every tuple in the database assert a fact about the real-world enterprise being modeled, but there are no additional known facts that could be represented as tuples in the database relations. This is known as the **closed-world assumption** and is implicit in relational query processing.

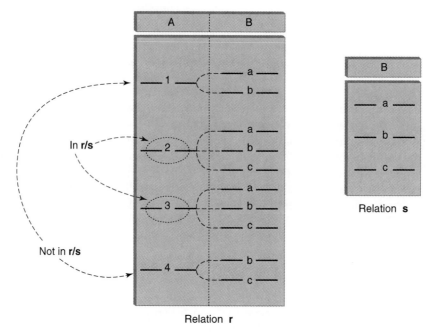

Figure 6.5 Division operator.

Figure 6.6 shows three relations. The relation

$$\text{ProfCS} = \pi_{\text{Id}}(\sigma_{\text{DeptId='CS'}}(\text{Professor}))$$

contains the Ids of all known computer science professors. The relation

$$\text{ProfCourses} = (\pi_{\text{ProfId,CrsCode}}(\text{Teaching}))[\text{Id,CrsCode}]$$

is a relationship between courses and professors who have taught them (at any time); it contains all known relationships of this kind. (Note that we have applied the renaming operator to make sure that the first attribute of PROFCOURSES has the same name as that of the attribute of PROFCS.) The third relation shows PROF-COURSES/PROFCS, the answer to the query.

Observe that before applying the division operator we carefully projected out some attributes (and renamed some others) to make the division operator applicable. This is one obvious situation in which projection must be performed.

To illustrate, let us consider the following query: *Retrieve all students who took a course from every professor who ever taught a course.* In the numerator we need a relation that associates the students with the professors who instructed them in some course. We can get this by taking the natural join of TRANSCRIPT and TEACHING:

$$\text{StudProf=Transcript} \bowtie \text{Teaching}$$

Figure 6.6 Anatomy of a Query: *Courses taught by every computer science professor*.

ProfCS	Id
	101202303
	555666777

All computer science professors: $\pi_{\text{Id}}(\sigma_{\text{DeptId='CS'}}(\text{PROFESSOR}))$

ProfCourses	Id	CrsCode
	783432188	MGT123
	009406321	MGT123
	121232343	EE101
	555666777	CS305
	101202303	CS315
	900120450	MAT123
	101202303	CS305

Who taught what: $(\pi_{\text{ProfId,CrsCode}}(\text{TEACHING}))[\text{Id,CrsCode}]$

CrsCode
CS305

The answer: ProfCourses/ProfCS

STUDPROF has attributes StudId, CrsCode, Semester, Grade, ProfId, which is more information than we want, so we eliminate unwanted columns using projection to get the numerator: $\pi_{\text{StudId,ProfId}}(\text{STUDPROF})$.

Because we are interested in students who took a course with "*every professor . . .* " we need a relation in the denominator that has a tuple for "*every professor . . . .*" Professors who have taught courses have their Ids inside the tuples of the TEACHING relation. (We do not want to use PROFESSOR here as this would include tuples for professors who have not done any teaching.) Hence, the denominator is $\pi_{\text{ProfId}}(\text{TEACHING})$ and the answer to our query is

$$\pi_{\text{StudId,ProfId}}(\text{STUDPROF}) \ / \ \pi_{\text{ProfId}}(\text{TEACHING}) \tag{6.1}$$

Here is one more example: *Find all students who took all courses that were taught by all computer science professors*. Here we need double division:

$$(\pi_{\text{Id,Name}}(\text{STUDENT}))[\text{StudId,Name}] \bowtie$$
$$(\pi_{\text{StudId,CrsCode}}(\text{TRANSCRIPT}) \ /$$
$$((\pi_{\text{ProfId,CrsCode}}(\text{TEACHING}))[\text{Id,CrsCode}] \ / \tag{6.2}$$
$$\pi_{\text{Id}}(\sigma_{\text{DeptId='CS'}}(\text{PROFESSOR}))) \ )$$

The second division here is our old friend from Figure 6.6, which yields all courses taught by every computer science professor. Therefore, the last three lines in the expression define the Ids of all students who took all such courses. The natural join in the first line is then used to obtain the names of these students. We had to rename the attributes of the STUDENT relation before taking the join.

We conclude by showing how the division operator can be expressed using other relational operators: projection, set difference, and cross product. Let **R** be a relation with attributes A, B, and let **S** be a relation over a single attribute B. (The construction, below, works even if A and B are disjoint lists of attributes.) The expression **R/S** can then be computed without the use of division as follows:

$T_1 = \pi_A(\mathbf{R}) \times \mathbf{S}$ All possible associations between A values in **R** and B values in **S**.

$T_2 = \pi_A(T_1 - \mathbf{R})$ All those A values in **R** that are **not** associated in **R** with every B-value in **S**. These are precisely those A values that should **not** be in the answer.   (6.3)

$T_3 = \pi_A(\mathbf{R}) - T_2$ *The answer*: all those A-values in **R**, that are associated in **R** with all B-values in **S**.

6.2 THE QUERY SUBLANGUAGE OF SQL

SQL is the most widely used relational database language. An initial version was proposed in 1974, and it has been evolving ever since. A widely used version, generally referred to as SQL-92, is a standard of the American National Standards Institute (ANSI). The language continues to evolve and SQL:1999 was recently completed. Like any rapidly changing language whose form is influenced by its many users, SQL has become surprisingly complex. The purpose of this section and the next is to introduce you to some of that complexity. However, you should understand that a full treatment of the language is well worth a book of its own. For example, [Melton and Simon 1992, Date and Darwen 1997] are more complete references to SQL-92; [Gulutzan and Pelzer 1999] describes SQL:1999. The unfortunate reality, however, is that commercial databases do not always adhere to the standards and a vendor-specific reference is almost always a must for serious application development.

SQL can be used interactively by submitting an SQL statement directly to the DBMS from a terminal. However, particularly in transaction processing systems, SQL statements are usually embedded in a larger program that submits the statements to the DBMS at run time and processes their results. The special considerations that relate to embedding will be discussed in Chapter 10.

6.2.1 Simple SQL Queries

Simple SQL queries are easy to design. Need a list of all professors in the electrical engineering (EE) department?—Happy to oblige:

```
SELECT   P.Name
FROM     PROFESSOR P
WHERE    P.DeptId = 'EE'
```

Note here the symbol P, which is referred to as a **tuple variable**. It ranges over the tuples of the relation PROFESSOR.[6] The tuple variable is actually unnecessary in this statement. We could equally well have not introduced it in the FROM clause and referred to the attributes as Name and DeptId instead of P.Name and P.DeptId, since there is no ambiguity. Or we could have used PROFESSOR.Name and PROFESSOR.DeptId, but this is rather cumbersome. Nevertheless, once the tuple variable has been introduced, you can no longer use the full table name anywhere in the statement.

We will see shortly that in some situations it is convenient to use tuple variables and in others it is essential. As a result, not using tuple variables in a SELECT statement is considered poor programming practice, often leading to subtle mistakes. Therefore, in this text we always declare all tuple variables.

Although this statement is rather simple, it is important to understand operationally how a SELECT statement might be evaluated. SELECT statements can become very complex, and following an operational flow through the statement is often the only way to figure out what is going on. Of course, different DBMSs might adopt different strategies for evaluating the same statement, but since they all produce the same result it is useful to describe a particularly simple strategy.

An evaluation strategy for simple queries.   The basic algorithm for evaluating SQL queries can be stated as follows:

Step 1.   The FROM clause is evaluated. It produces a table that is the Cartesian product of the tables listed as its arguments. If a table occurs more than once in the FROM clause, as in query (6.9) on p. 143, then this table occurs as many times in the product.

Step 2.   The WHERE clause is evaluated. It takes the table produced in step 1 and processes each row individually. Attribute values from the row are substituted for the attribute names in the condition, and the condition is evaluated. The table produced by the WHERE clause contains exactly those rows for which the condition evaluates to true.

Step 3.   The SELECT clause is evaluated. It takes the table produced in step 2 and retains only those columns that are listed as arguments. The resulting table is output by the SELECT statement.

As we discuss new features of the language, we will add additional steps to this strategy, but the basic idea remains the same. Each clause produces a table, which

---

[6] Mastering SQL often means stuffing one's head with redundant terminology. For instance, SQL variables are also known as "table aliases." We will see in Chapter 7 that these variables correspond to tuple variables of tuple relational calculus—the real theoretical basis of SQL.

is the input to the next clause to be evaluated. Certain steps need not be present in a particular evaluation. For example, step 2 might not have to be evaluated because a SELECT statement does not have to have a WHERE clause. Other steps might be trivial. For example, although every SELECT statement must have a FROM clause, if the clause names only a single relation, the Cartesian product is not required, and that relation is simply passed on to step 2.

The relational algebra equivalent of the above SQL query is.

$$\pi_{\text{Name}}(\sigma_{\text{DeptId='EE'}} (\text{Professor}))$$

Join queries.   Queries that express a join between two relations follow the same pattern as above. The following query, which returns the list of all professors who taught in fall 1994, involves a join.

```
SELECT   P.Name
FROM     Professor P, Teaching T                              (6.4)
WHERE    P.Id = T.ProfId  AND  T.Semester = 'F1994'
```

Note that the tuple variables in this example clarify the meaning of the statement because they identify the table from which each attribute is drawn. If the Id attribute of Professor were called ProfId instead of simply Id, we would have to use tuple variables to distinguish the two references.

Evaluation of the statement follows the steps outlined above. In contrast to the previous example, in this example processing the FROM clause involves taking a Cartesian product.

Take the time to convince yourself that this query is equivalent to the relational algebra expression.

$$\pi_{\text{Name}} (\text{Professor} \bowtie_{\text{Id=ProfId}} \sigma_{\text{Semester='F1994'}} (\text{Teaching})) \qquad (6.5)$$

which distinguishes a join condition from a selection condition. The join condition Id = ProfId ensures that related tuples in the two tables are combined. It makes no sense to combine a tuple from Professor that describes a particular professor with a tuple from Teaching that describes a course taught by a different professor. Hence, the join condition eliminates garbage. The selection condition Semester = 'F1994', on the other hand, eliminates tuples that are not relevant to the query.

The relationship between SQL and relational algebra.   The relational algebra expression

$$\pi_{\text{Name}}(\sigma_{\text{Id=ProfId AND Semester='F1994'}} (\text{Professor} \times \text{Teaching}))$$

is equivalent to (6.5), but it does not contain any join operator. Instead, it combines the join condition with the selection condition. Although the resulting expression leads to one of the least efficient ways of evaluating the corresponding SQL query, it is simple and uniform and, from a syntactic point of view, corresponds more closely to the equivalent SQL statement. More generally, the query template

```
SELECT   TargetList
FROM     REL₁ V₁, ..., RELₙ Vₙ                                (6.6)
WHERE    Condition
```

is roughly equivalent to the algebraic expression

$$\pi_{TargetList}\sigma_{Condition}(\text{Rel}_1 \times \ldots \times \text{Rel}_n) \tag{6.7}$$

"Roughly" means that we have to transform *Condition* into a relational algebra form. To be more concrete, consider the query *Find the names of the courses taught in fall 1995 together with the names of the professors who taught those courses.* Expressed in SQL we get

```
SELECT   C.CrsName, P.Name
FROM     PROFESSOR P, TEACHING T, COURSE C
WHERE    T.Semester = 'F1995' AND
         P.Id = T.ProfId AND T.CrsCode = C.CrsCode
```
(6.8)

The corresponding algebraic expression in the inefficient, but uniform, form described above is

$$\pi_{\text{CrsName,Name}}(\sigma_{Condition}(\text{PROFESSOR} \times \text{TEACHING} \times \text{COURSE}))$$

where *Condition* denotes the contents of the WHERE clause (modified to suit relational algebra).

```
Id = ProfId AND TEACHING.CrsCode = COURSE.CrsCode AND
    Semester = 'F1995'
```

Self-join queries.   Let us return to the query that we considered earlier, *Find all students who took at least two courses.* We expressed this in relational algebra as

$$
\pi_{\text{StudId}} \,(
$$
$$
\sigma_{\text{CrsCode} \neq \text{CrsCode2}} \,(
$$
$$
\text{TRANSCRIPT} \bowtie_{\text{StudId=StudId}}
$$
$$
\text{TRANSCRIPT}[\text{StudId,CrsCode2,Semester2,Grade2}]
$$
$$
) \,)
$$

Observe that we have joined the relation TRANSCRIPT with *itself*. To accomplish this in relational algebra, we have to apply the renaming operator to the second occurrence of TRANSCRIPT. In SQL, we must mention the TRANSCRIPT relation twice in the FROM clause and declare two different variables over this relation. Each variable is meant to represent a distinct occurrence of TRANSCRIPT in the join.

```
SELECT   T1.StudId
FROM     TRANSCRIPT T1, TRANSCRIPT T2
WHERE    T1.CrsCode <> T2.CrsCode AND T1.StudId = T2.StudId
```
(6.9)

The symbol <> in this query is SQL's way of saying "not equal." Note that we do need *two distinct tuple variables* to range over TRANSCRIPT; if we were to use just one variable, T, the condition T.CrsCode <> T.CrsCode would never be satisfied, making the answer to the query the empty relation. Therefore, there is no obvious way to do without tuple variables and still be able to express the query in an unambiguous way. This, then, is an example in which tuple variables are necessary.

Retrieving distinct answers. We already know from Chapter 4 that relations are sets, so no duplicate tuples are allowed. However, many relational operators can yield **multisets** (i.e., set-like objects that may contain multiple occurrences of identical elements) as an intermediate result of the computation. For instance, if we chop off the attribute Semester from the instance of the relation TEACHING depicted in Figure 4.5 (page 63), we get a list of tuples that contains duplicate occurrences of ⟨009406321, MGT123⟩ and of other tuples as well. As a consequence, in order for the SQL query

```
SELECT   T.ProfId, T.CrsCode
FROM     TEACHING  T                                          (6.10)
```

to return a relation (as required by the relational data model), the query processor must perform an additional scan of the result of the projection specified in the SELECT clause in which all duplicates are eliminated. In many cases, the application programmer is not willing to pay the price for duplicate elimination. Hence, the designers of SQL decided that, by default, duplicate tuples are not eliminated unless elimination is explicitly requested using the keyword DISTINCT.

```
SELECT   DISTINCT T.ProfId, T.CrsCode
FROM     TEACHING  T                                          (6.11)
```

Note that this query is missing the WHERE clause, which is *optional* in SQL. When it is missing, the WHERE condition is assumed to be true regardless of the values of tuple variables in the FROM clause.

While the WHERE clause is optional, the SELECT and the FROM clauses are not.

Comments. As with every programming language, the programmer may wish to annotate queries with comments. In SQL, comments are strings that begin with the double-minus sign, --, and end with a newline. For instance,

```
-- An example of  SELECT DISTINCT
SELECT   DISTINCT T.ProfId, T.CrsCode                         (6.12)
FROM     TEACHING T     --No WHERE clause!
```

Expressions in the WHERE clause. So far, the conditions in the WHERE clause have been comparisons of attributes against constants or other attributes. For numeric values, SQL provides the following comparison operators: = (equal), <> (not equal), > (greater than), >= (greater than or equal to), < (less than), and <= (less than or equal to).

All of these operators can be applied to numerals and character strings as well. (Strings can also be compared against patterns using the LIKE operator, which we will describe later.) Strings are compared character-wise, from left to right. For the purposes of this text, we limit our attention to ASCII symbols and assume that the ordering of characters in making comparisons between two strings is determined by the ASCII codes assigned to these characters.

The operands of these comparison operators can be **expressions**, not just single attributes or constants. For numeric values, expressions are composed of the usual operators, *, +, and the like. For strings, the concatenation operator, ||, can be used.

Assume, for instance, an appropriate EMPLOYEE relation with the attributes SSN, BossSSN, LastName, FirstName, and Salary. Then the query

```
SELECT    E.Id
FROM      EMPLOYEE  E, EMPLOYEE M
WHERE     E.BossSSN = M.SSN  AND  E.Salary > 2 * M.Salary
          AND E.LastName = 'Mc' || E.FirstName
```

returns all employees whose salary is more than twice that of their bosses's and whose last names are a concatenation of "Mc" and the first name (e.g., Donald McDonald).

Expressions and special features in the SELECT clause.   The SELECT clause has a number of special features, which we discuss next. In Section 2.2, we noted that the asterisk (*) represents the list of all attributes of all relations in the FROM clause. Note that when it is used and a relation appears twice (or more) in the FROM clause, its attributes appear twice (or more) as well. For instance, the query

```
SELECT    *
FROM      EMPLOYEE  E, EMPLOYEE M
```

is the same as

```
SELECT    E.SSN, E.BossSSN, E.FirstName, E.LastName, E.Salary,
          M.SSN, M.BossSSN, M.FirstName, M.LastName, M.Salary
FROM      EMPLOYEE E, M
```

Also, SQL permits expressions as part of the target list, not just in the WHERE clause (which we have seen). Suppose, for instance, that an audit office needs to produce the list of salary differences between employees and their immediate bosses. This can be accomplished with the following query, where the last element of the target list is an expression.

```
SELECT    E.SSN, M.SSN, M.Salary - E.Salary
FROM      EMPLOYEE E,  EMPLOYEE M
WHERE     E.BossSSN = M.SSN
```

If the above query is used interactively, most DBMSs display a table where the first two columns are labeled SSN and the last column has no label at all. Obviously, this is not very satisfactory since it requires the user to remember the meaning of the items in the SELECT clause. To alleviate this problem, SQL allows the programmer to change attribute names and assign names where they do not exist. This is accomplished with the help of the keyword AS. For example, we can modify the previous query as follows.

```
SELECT    E.SSN AS EmplId,
          M.SSN AS MngrId,
          M.Salary - E.Salary AS SalaryDifference
FROM      EMPLOYEE E, EMPLOYEE M
WHERE     E.BossSSN = M.SSN
```

This query is identical to the previous one in all but the form of the output. The attributes of the last query will be displayed as EmplId, MngrId, and SalaryDif-ference.

Negation.   Any condition in the WHERE clause can be negated with NOT. For instance, instead of T1.CrsCode <> T2.CrsCode in query (6.9), we could have written NOT (T1.CrsCode = T2.CrsCode). The negated condition need not be atomic—it can consist of an arbitrary number of subconditions connected with AND or OR, and it can even have nested applications of NOT, as in the following example.

```
NOT (E.BossSSN = M.SSN AND E.Salary > 2 * M.Salary
     AND NOT (E.LastName = 'Mc'|| E.FirstName))
```

6.2.2 Set Operations

SQL uses the set-theoretic operators from the relational algebra. Here is a simple query where set-theoretic operators can be used: *Find all professors who are working for the CS or EE departments.*

```
(SELECT   P.Name
 FROM     PROFESSOR P
 WHERE    P.DeptId = 'CS' )
 UNION
(SELECT   P.Name
 FROM     PROFESSOR P
 WHERE    P.DeptId = 'EE' )
```
(6.13)

The SQL formulation is self-explanatory. The query consists of two subqueries: one retrieving all CS professors and the other retrieving all EE professors. Their results are collected into a single relation using the UNION operator of the algebra.

   While this example illustrates the basic use of set-theoretic operators in SQL, the benefits of using UNION here are small. This query can be rewritten without UNION in a more efficient way.

```
SELECT   P.Name
FROM     PROFESSOR P
WHERE    P.DeptId = 'CS' OR P.DeptId = 'EE'
```
(6.14)

   Our next example, the query *Find all computer science professors and also professors who ever taught a computer science course*, is more involved, and the advantages of set-theoretic operators there are more substantial.

   Let us assume that all course codes in computer science begin with CS. In designing the query, we need to match patterns against strings (course codes). To verify whether a string matches a pattern, SQL provides the LIKE predicate. For instance, T.CrsCode LIKE 'CS%' verifies that the value of T.CrsCode matches the pattern that starts with CS and can have *zero or more* additional characters. SQL patterns are similar to wildcards in UNIX or DOS, although SQL's arsenal for building patterns is somewhat limited: Besides %, there is _, a symbol that matches an arbitrary *single* character.[7]

Without the UNION operator, CS professors or those who taught a CS course can be found as follows:

```
SELECT   P.Name
FROM     PROFESSOR P,  TEACHING T                              (6.15)
WHERE    (P.ProfId = T.ProfId  AND  T.CrsCode LIKE'CS%')
         OR (P.DeptId = 'CS')
```

We see that, as the WHERE condition gets longer and more complicated, it becomes harder to read and understand. With the UNION operator, we can rewrite this query in the following way:

```
(SELECT  P.Name
FROM     PROFESSOR P,  TEACHING T
WHERE    P.ProfId = T.ProfId AND  T.CrsCode LIKE'CS%')
UNION                                                          (6.16)
(SELECT  P.Name
FROM     PROFESSOR P
WHERE    P.DeptId = 'CS')
```

Although this query is no more succinct than (6.15), it is more modular and easier to understand.

If we want to change our query so that it retrieves all professors who taught a CS course without being a CS professor, we can easily modify (6.16) by replacing UNION with EXCEPT—the SQL name for the MINUS operator of relational algebra. Adapting (6.15) to the new query is more subtle: The WHERE clause of (6.15) has to be changed to

```
P.ProfId = T.ProfId AND T.CrsCode LIKE'CS%' AND P.DeptId <> 'CS'
```

Continuing with the discussion of the set operators, suppose that we need to find all students who have taken both the "transaction processing" course, CS315, and the "database systems" course, CS305. As a first try, we might construct the following query:

```
SELECT   S.Name
FROM     STUDENT S, TRANSCRIPT  T                              (6.17)
WHERE    S.StudId = T.StudId AND T.CrsCode = 'CS305'
         AND T.CrsCode = 'CS315'
```

---

[7] Suppose that you need to construct a pattern where the special characters % and _ stand for themselves. For instance, suppose you need to match all strings that start with _%. This is possible, albeit cumbersome: You have to declare an escape character and then prefix it to the special character to let SQL know that you want these characters to stand for themselves. For instance, C.Descr LIKE '_\%__$' ESCAPE '\' compares the value of C.Descr with a pattern that matches all strings that begin with _ %, followed by a pair of arbitrary characters and terminated with the symbol $. Here \ is declared as an escape character via the ESCAPE clause and then used to "escape" % and _.

On closer examination, however, we discover that this SQL query is not what we need because it requires that there be a tuple in TRANSCRIPT such that T.CrsCode is equal to both CS305 and CS315, which is never the case. This simple example illustrates one very common mistake—the failure to recognize the need for an additional tuple variable. The correct SQL query for our problem is

```
SELECT    S.Name
FROM      STUDENT S, TRANSCRIPT  T1, TRANSCRIPT T2
WHERE     S.StudId = T1.StudId AND T1.CrsCode = 'CS305'     (6.18)
          AND S.StudId = T2.StudId AND T2.CrsCode = 'CS315'
```

Observe that we used two distinct tuple variables over the relation TRANSCRIPT to express the fact that student S has taken two different courses.

What does this have to do with the original subject, set-theoretic operators of the relational algebra? It turns out that the INTERSECT operator lets us rewrite (6.18) in a more modular and less error-prone way.

```
(SELECT   S.Name
FROM      STUDENT S, TRANSCRIPT  T
WHERE     S.StudId = T.StudId  AND T.CrsCode = 'CS305')
INTERSECT                                                    (6.19)
(SELECT   S.Name
FROM      STUDENT S, TRANSCRIPT  T
WHERE     S.StudId = T.StudId AND T.CrsCode = 'CS315')
```

Notice that here we do not need multiple variables to range over the same relation, which somewhat reduces the risk of error. Instead, we write two simple, essentially similar queries and take the intersection of their answers.

Set constructor.   Finally, we mention one related feature, the constructor that enables the building of finite sets within SQL queries. The syntax of the set constructor is simple: *(set-elem$_1$, set-elem$_2$, . . . , set-elem$_n$)*. The operator IN lets us check if a particular element is within the set. For example, consider query (6.14), which, with the help of the set constructor, we can simplify as

```
SELECT    P.Name
FROM      PROFESSOR P                                        (6.20)
WHERE     P.DeptId  IN   ('CS','EE')
```

Note that if we take query (6.17) and replace its WHERE clause with

```
S.StudId = T.StudId  AND  T.CrsCode  IN ('CS305','CS315' )
```

we obtain a query with a meaning different from that of (6.17). This issue is further investigated in Exercise 6.13.

Negation and infix comparison operators.   Earlier we discussed the NOT operator. For some infix operators, such as LIKE and IN, SQL provides two forms of negation: NOT (X LIKE Y) and, equivalently, X NOT LIKE Y. Similarly, one can write X NOT IN Y instead of the more cumbersome NOT(X IN Y).

6.2.3 Nested Queries

SQL would be only half as much fun if there were only one way to do each task. Consider the query *Select all professors who taught in fall 1994*. One way to pose this in SQL was given in (6.4), but there is (at least) one other, radically different way: First compute the set of all professors who taught in fall 1994 using a **nested subquery**; then collect their names.

```
SELECT   P.Name
FROM     PROFESSOR P
WHERE    P.Id IN
         -- A nested subquery
         (SELECT T.ProfId
          FROM TEACHING T
          WHERE T.Semester = 'F1994')
```

Note that in this example the nested subquery is evaluated only once and then each row of PROFESSOR can be tested in the condition of the WHERE clause against the result of that evaluation.

The above example illustrates one way in which nested subqueries can be of help: *increased readability*. However, readability alone is not a sufficient reason for using this facility, as most query processors cannot optimize nested subqueries well enough. The major reason for nested subqueries is that they increase the expressive power of SQL—some queries simply cannot be formulated in a natural way without them.

Consider the query *List all students who did not take any courses*. In English this query sounds deceptively simple, but in SQL it cannot be done without the nested subquery facility.

```
SELECT   S.Name
FROM     STUDENT   S
WHERE    S.Id NOT IN                                        (6.21)
         -- Students who have taken a course
         (SELECT   T.StudId
          FROM     TRANSCRIPT T)
```

As a final example, a subquery can be used to extract a scalar value from a table. Suppose that you want to know which employees are paid a higher salary than you. Assuming that your Id is 111111111, you might use a subquery to return your salary from EMPLOYEE as follows:

```
SELECT   E.Id
FROM     EMPLOYEE   E
WHERE    E.Salary >                                         (6.22)
         (SELECT   E1.Salary
          FROM     EMPLOYEE E1
          WHERE    E1.Id = '111111111')
```

The overall query then finds all employees that earn more.

Correlated nested subqueries.   On the one hand, nested subqueries can often improve query readability. On the other hand, they are one of the most complex, expensive, and error-prone features of SQL. To a large extent, this complexity is due to **query correlation**—the ability to define variables in the outer query and use them in the inner subquery. Nesting and correlation are akin to the notion of begin/end blocks in programming languages and the associated idea of the scope of a variable.

To illustrate, suppose that we need to find student assistants for professors who are scheduled to teach in a forthcoming semester (for definiteness, let us say in fall 1999). For each professor, we compute the set of all courses she will be teaching during that semester and then find students who have taken one of these courses (and so are eligible to assist with them). The list of courses taught by professors can be computed in a nested subquery, and associating professors with students can be done in an outer query. Here is a realization of this plan in SQL:

```
SELECT   R.StudId,  P.Id,  R.CrsCode
FROM     Transcript R,  Professor P
WHERE    R.CrsCode  IN
         -- Courses taught by P.Id in F1999
         (SELECT  T1.CrsCode
          FROM    Teaching T1
          WHERE  T1.ProfId = P.Id AND T1.Semester = 'F1999' )
```

Here the scope of the variable T1 is limited to the subquery. In contrast, the variable P is visible in both the outer and inner queries. This variable parameterizes the inner query and correlates its result with the tuples of the outer query: For *each* value of P.Id, the inner query is computed independently *as if* P.Id *were a constant*. Each time an inner subquery is computed, the value of R.CrsCode is checked against the result returned. If this value belongs to the result, an output tuple is formed by the outer SELECT query.

Observe that, at a minimum, the inner query must be re-evaluated for each row of Professor. This contrasts with uncorrelated nested queries and explains the expense associated with query correlation.

Even though nested queries are a challenge for query optimizers, inexperienced database programmers sometimes tend to abuse them, substituting them for the much simpler ANDs, NOTs, and the like. Here is an example of how *not* to write the previous query (even though it is semantically correct):

```
SELECT   R.StudId,  T.ProfId,  R.CrsCode
FROM     Transcript R, Teaching T
WHERE    R.CrsCode  IN
         -- Courses taught by T.ProfId in F1999
         (SELECT  T1.CrsCode
          FROM    Teaching T1
          WHERE  T1.ProfId = T.ProfId AND
```

```
                     -- Bad style: unreadable and slow!
          T1.ProfId IN  (SELECT T2.ProfId
                         FROM   Teaching T2
                         WHERE  T2.Semester = 'F1999' ) )
```

The EXISTS operator. It is often necessary to check if a nested subquery returns no answers. For instance, we might wish to find *all students who never took a computer course*. A way to approach this problem is to compute the set of all computer courses taken by a student and then list only those students for whom this set is empty. This can be done with the help of correlated nested subqueries and the EXISTS operator, which returns true if a set is non-empty.

Here is one SQL formulation of this query:

```
SELECT   S.Id
FROM     Student S
WHERE    NOT EXISTS (
         -- All CS courses taken by S.Id                        (6.23)
         SELECT   T.CrsCode
         FROM     Transcript T
         WHERE    T.CrsCode LIKE'CS%'
                  AND   T.StudId = S.Id )
```

Once again, the variable **S** is global with respect to the inner subquery; this subquery is evaluated for each value of S.Id, which is treated as a constant during the evaluation. All values of S.Id for which the inner query has no answers constitute the answer to the outer query.

Expressing the division operator. We now show that query nesting can be of some help in expressing the relational division operator. For concreteness, consider the query *List all students who have taken all computer science courses*. We can solve the problem by first computing a single-attribute relation that has a row for each CS course (this is the denominator of the division operator). Then, for each student, we check if the student's transcript contains all of these courses.

To make the idea clear, we first realize our plan in mock SQL, a nonexistent language that differs from SQL in that it has one additional set operator, CONTAINS.

```
SELECT   S.Id
FROM     Student S
WHERE    -- All courses taken by S.Id
         (SELECT   R.CrsCode
           FROM     Transcript R
           WHERE    R.StudId = S.Id )
         CONTAINS
         -- All CS courses
         (SELECT   C.CrsCode
           FROM     Course C
           WHERE    C.CrsCode  LIKE'CS%' )
```

This looks simple enough, except that real SQL lacks CONTAINS. However, because *A* CONTAINS *B* is equivalent to NOT EXISTS (*B* EXCEPT *A*), this lack is not insurmountable. But, as a result, the real SQL formulation for the above query looks much more convoluted.

```
SELECT   S.Id
FROM     STUDENT S
WHERE    NOT EXISTS (
         (SELECT  C.CrsCode
          FROM COURSE C
          WHERE C.CrsCode LIKE'CS%' )
         EXCEPT
         (SELECT  R.CrsCode
          FROM    TRANSCRIPT R
          WHERE   R.StudId = S.Id ) )
```

Here is an even harder query:

Find all students who have taken a course from every *professor in the* CS *department.*

An SQL statement that produces an answer to this query is

```
SELECT   S.Id
FROM     STUDENT S
WHERE
    NOT EXISTS (
    -- CS professors who did not teach S.Id
    (SELECT  P.ProfId -- All CS professors
     FROM    PROFESSOR P
     WHERE   P.Dept = 'CS')                              (6.24)
    EXCEPT
    (SELECT  T.ProfId -- Professors who have taught S.Id
     FROM    TEACHING T, TRANSCRIPT R
     WHERE   T.CrsCode = R.CrsCode
             AND  T.Semester = R.Semester
             AND  S.Id = R.StudId) )
```

The variable S is global, and each time the subquery is evaluated the value of S is fixed. On the other hand, R ranges over all tuples in TRANSCRIPT. Therefore, the values of R.Semester and R.CrsCode correspond to all recorded enrollments of student S.Id, and T.ProfId is then successively bound to all professors who ever taught S.Id.

Set comparison operators.   Suppose that our STUDENT relation has one additional numeric attribute, GPA. We can ask the question *Is there a student in the university whose GPA is higher than that of* all *junior students?*
It turns out that nested queries are helpful here, too.

```
SELECT    S.Name, S.Id
FROM      STUDENT S
WHERE S.GPA >ALL  (SELECT  S.GPA                          (6.25)
                   FROM    STUDENT S
                   WHERE   S.Status ='junior')
```

Here > ALL is a comparison operator, which returns true whenever its left argument is greater than *every* element of the set to the right. If we replace it with >=ANY, we obtain a query about students whose GPA is greater than or equal to that of *some* junior student.

One other point is worth noting about this query: The variable S is declared in both the outer and the inner queries. So which one is referred to in the WHERE clause of the inner query? The answer, as with **begin/end** blocks, is that the inner declaration is valid within the inner query. (However, such declarations are poor programming practice.)

Nested subqueries in the FROM clause.   As if query (6.24) were not complex enough, SQL has more up its sleeve: you can have nested subqueries in the FROM clause! This works as follows: You write a nested subquery (it must not be correlated and hence cannot use global variables). This subquery can be used in the FROM clause as if it were a relation name. You can use the keyword AS to attach a tuple variable to it. (Actually, AS is optional here, but is highly recommended for readability.)

As an example, we can express a query similar to (6.24), but without NOT EXISTS (i.e., the answer consists of all students who were *not* taught by at least one CS professor), by moving the first nested subquery into the FROM clause (this move cannot be done for the second subquery, because it is correlated).

```
SELECT    S.Id
FROM      STUDENT S,
          (SELECT  P.ProfId -- All CS professors
           FROM PROFESSOR P
           WHERE P.Dept = 'CS') AS C
WHERE C.ProfId NOT IN                                    (6.26)
     (SELECT T.ProfId -- All S.Id's professors
      FROM TEACHING T, TRANSCRIPT R
      WHERE T.CrsCode = R.CrsCode
         AND T.Semester = R.Semester)
      AND S.Id = R.StudId )
```

The use of nested subqueries in the FROM clause should be avoided if at all possible, as it tends to produce queries that are hard to understand and verify, even for their author. A much better alternative is to use the view mechanism, which will be discussed in Section 6.2.6.

Apart from nested queries, SQL also permits explicit table joins in the FROM clause. However, we do not discuss this feature.

Figure 6.7 SQL aggregate functions.

COUNT([DISTINCT] Attr)	Count the number of values in column `Attr` of the query result. The optional keyword DISTINCT indicates that each value should be counted only once, even if it occurs multiple times in different answer tuples.
SUM([DISTINCT] Attr)	Sum up the values in column `Attr`. DISTINCT means that each value should contribute to the sum only once, regardless of how often it occurs in column `Attr`.
AVG([DISTINCT] Attr)	Compute the average of the values in column `Attr`. Again, DISTINCT means that each value should be used only once.
MAX(Attr)	Compute the maximum value in column `Attr`. DISTINCT is not used with this function, as it would have no effect.
MIN(Attr)	Compute the minimum value in column `Attr`. Again, DISTINCT is not used with this function.

6.2.4 Aggregation over Data

In many instances, it is necessary to compute average salary, maximum GPA, number of employees per department, total cost of a purchase, and so forth. These tasks are performed with the help of so-called **aggregate functions**, which operate on sets of tuples. SQL uses five aggregate functions which are described in Figure 6.7.

Aggregate functions cannot be expressed in pure relational algebra. However, the algebra can be extended to allow their use (these extensions are beyond the scope of this text).

To illustrate the use of aggregate functions, we assume that both STUDENT and PROFESSOR relations have the attribute Age and that the STUDENT relation also has the attribute GPA. We start with a few simple examples.

```
-- Average age of the student body
SELECT    AVG(S.Age)
FROM      STUDENT  S
```

```
-- Minimum age among professors in the management department
SELECT MIN(P.Age)
FROM PROFESSOR P
WHERE P.DeptId = 'MGT'
```

The above queries find only the average and the minimum ages, not the actual people who have them. If we need to find the youngest professor(s) within the management department, we can use a nested subquery.

```
-- Youngest professor(s) in the management department
SELECT    P.Name, P.Age
FROM      PROFESSOR P
```

```
WHERE    P.DeptId = 'MGT'   AND
         P.Age = (SELECT MIN(P1.Age)
                  FROM    PROFESSOR P1
                  WHERE   P1.DeptId = 'MGT'  )
```

The query (6.25) that returns the names and Ids of juniors with the highest GPA (previously written without aggregates) can be written alternatively with the use of MAX as follows:

```
SELECT   S.Name,S.StudId
FROM     STUDENT  S
WHERE    S.GPA >= (SELECT  MAX(S1.GPA)                       (6.27)
                   FROM STUDENT  S1
                   WHERE S1.Status = 'Junior')
```

The use of DISTINCT in aggregate functions can sometimes make a subtle difference in the query semantics. For instance,

```
SELECT   COUNT(P.Name)
FROM     PROFESSOR P                                         (6.28)
WHERE    P.DeptId = 'MGT'
```

returns the number of professors in the management department. On the other hand,

```
SELECT   COUNT(DISTINCT P.Name)
FROM     PROFESSOR P
WHERE    P.DeptId = 'MGT'
```

returns the number of distinct *names* of professors in that department, which can be different from the number of professors. Similarly,

```
SELECT   AVG(P.Age)
FROM     PROFESSOR P                                         (6.29)
WHERE    P.DeptId = 'MGT'
```

returns the average age of professors in the management department. However, if we write AVG (DISTINCT P.Age) in the above SELECT clause, the query result is the average age among *distinct* ages, which is statistically meaningless.

Now that you have seen the good things you can do with aggregates, you should also keep in mind the things you cannot do. It makes no sense to mix an aggregate and an attribute in the SELECT list, as in

```
SELECT   COUNT(*), S.Id
FROM     STUDENT S                                           (6.30)
WHERE    S.Name   = 'JohnDoe'
```

This is because the aggregate produces a single value that pertains to the entire set of rows corresponding to John Doe, while the attribute S.Id produces a distinct value for each row. (Note: There can be several people named John Doe.) In some cases, however, such associations can be made meaningful with the help of the GROUP BY construct, to be defined shortly.

While associating aggregates with attributes in the SELECT clause is not normally very useful, having multiple aggregates does make sense. For instance,

<pre>
SELECT   COUNT(*), AVG(P.Age)
FROM   STUDENT S   (6.31)
WHERE   S.Name = 'JohnDoe'
</pre>

counts the number of John Does in the student relation and also computes their average age. Finally, one might be tempted to rewrite statement (6.27) as

<pre>
SELECT   S.Name,S.StudId
FROM   STUDENT S
WHERE   S.GPA >= (MAX(SELECT S1.GPA
                       FROM   STUDENT S1
                       WHERE   S1.Status = 'junior'))
</pre>

but dare not—it is an invalid construct. Aggregates are not allowed in the WHERE clause.

Aggregation and grouping.   By now we know how to count professors in the management department. But what if we need this information for *each* department in the university? Of course, we could construct queries similar to (6.28) for each separate department. Each query would be the same, except that MGT in the WHERE condition would be replaced with other department codes. Clearly, this is not a practical solution, as even in a medium-size enterprise the number of departments can reach several dozen. Furthermore, each time a new department is created, we have to construct a new query, and when departments change their name we have to do tedious maintenance.

A better solution is provided in the form of the GROUP BY clause, which can be included as a component of a SELECT statement. This clause lets the programmer partition a set of rows into groups whose membership is characterized by the fact that all of the rows in a single group agree on the values in some specified subset of columns. The aggregate function then applies to the groups and produces a single row out of each group, as shown in Figure 6.8. For example, if we group the instance of the relation TRANSCRIPT shown in Figure 4.5 on page 63 based on the column StudId, five groups result. In any particular group, all rows have the same value in the StudId column but might differ in other columns.

For instance, the following query

<pre>
SELECT   T.StudId, COUNT(*) AS NumCrs,
         AVG(T.Grade) AS CrsAvg
FROM   TRANSCRIPT T
GROUP BY T.StudId
</pre>

produces the table

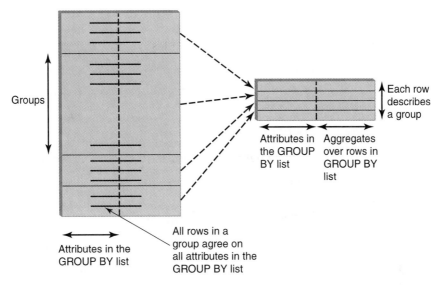

Figure 6.8 Effect of the GROUP BY clause.

TRANSCRIPT	StudId	NumCrs	CrsAvg
	666666666	3	3.33
	987654321	2	2.5
	123454321	3	3.33
	023456789	2	3.5
	111111111	3	3.33

Here is how to determine the number of professors in each department and (why not?) their average age:

```
SELECT    P.DeptId, COUNT(P.Name) AS  DeptSize,
          AVG(P.Age)  AS  AvgAge
FROM      PROFESSOR P
GROUP BY P.DeptId
```

The important point to note in these two queries is that each column in the SELECT clause either must be named in the GROUP BY clause or must be the result of an aggregate function.

The HAVING clause is used in conjunction with GROUP BY. It lets the programmer specify a condition that restricts which groups (specified in the GROUP BY clause) are to be considered for the final query result. Groups that do not satisfy the condition are removed before the aggregates are applied. Suppose that we wish to know the number of professors and the average ages of professors by department, as in the previous query, but this time only if the department has more than ten professors. This is accomplished as follows:

```
SELECT    P.DeptId, COUNT(P.Name) AS  DeptSize,
          AVG( P.Age)  AS  AvgAge
FROM      PROFESSOR P
GROUP BY P.DeptId
HAVING    COUNT(*) > 10
```

The HAVING condition (unlike the WHERE condition!) is applied to groups, *not* to individual tuples. So, for each group created by the GROUP BY clause, COUNT(*) counts the number of tuples. Only the groups where this count exceeds 10 are passed on for further processing. In the end, the aggregate functions are applied to each group to yield a single tuple per group.

Observe that the above queries use AS to give names to columns produced by aggregate functions. Furthermore, * is used with the COUNT function that appears in the HAVING clause. The * is often convenient in conjunction with aggregate functions, and it can be used in both the SELECT list and the HAVING clause. However, it should be noted that, in the above example, there are several alternatives: We can use P.Name and even P.DeptId instead of *, because SQL will not eliminate duplicates without an explicit request (DISTINCT).

If we want to consider candidates for the Dean's List on the basis of their grades for the 1997–1998 academic year, we might use

```
SELECT    T.StudId, AVG(T.Grade)  AS  CrsAvg
FROM      TRANSCRIPT T
WHERE     T.Semester IN ('F1997','S1998')
GROUP BY T.StudId
HAVING    AVG( T.Grade) > 3.5
```

In general, the HAVING clause is just a syntactic convenience—the same result can always be achieved with the help of nested queries in the FROM clause.

```
SELECT    Stats.DeptId, Stats.DeptSize, Stats.AvgAge
FROM      (SELECT  P.DeptId,
                  COUNT(P.Name) AS DeptSize, AVG(P.Age)
                      AS AvgAge
              FROM   PROFESSOR P
              GROUP BY P.DeptId) AS Stats
WHERE     Stats.ProfCount > 10
```

However, the use of nested queries in the FROM clause should be avoided.

Finally, the order of rows in the query result is generally not specified. If a particular ordering is desired, the ORDER BY clause can be used. For example, if we include the clause

```
ORDER BY CrsAvg
```

in the SELECT statement that produces the Dean's list, rows of the query result will be in ascending order of the student's average grade. In general, the clause takes as an argument a list of column names of the query result. Rows are output in sorted order on the basis of the first column named in the list. In the case in which multiple rows have the same value in that column, the second column named in the list is used to decide the ordering, and so forth. For example, if we want to output the candidates for Dean's List ordered primarily by average grade and secondarily by student Id, we might use the following SELECT statement:

```
SELECT    T.StudId, AVG(T.Grade)  AS  CrsAvg
FROM      TRANSCRIPT T
WHERE     T.Semester IN ('F1997','S1998')
GROUP BY T.StudId
HAVING    AVG(T.Grade) > 3.5
ORDER BY CrsAvg, StudId
```

The attributes named in the ORDER BY clause must be the names of columns in the query result. Thus, we refer to the second element as StudId (not T.StudId) in this example since, by default, that is the column name in the query result. Similarly, we cannot order rows primarily by average grade without introducing the column alias CrsAvg in the SELECT clause because without the alias the column has no name.[8]

Ascending order is used by default, but descending order can also be specified. If in the above example we had replaced the ORDER BY clause with

```
ORDER BY DESC CrsAvg, ASC StudId
```

the rows of the query result would have been presented in descending order of average grade and, for students with the same average grade, in ascending order of their Ids.

6.2.5 A Simple Query Evaluation Algorithm

The overall query evaluation process in the presence of aggregates and grouping is illustrated in Figure 6.9.

Step 1. The FROM clause is evaluated. It produces a table that is the Cartesian product of the tables listed as its arguments.

Step 2. The WHERE clause is evaluated. It takes the table produced in step 1 and processes each row individually. Attribute values from the row are substituted for the attribute names in the condition, and the condition is evaluated. The table produced by the WHERE clause contains exactly those rows for which the condition evaluates to true.

---

[8] Columns of the result table can be referred to by their ordinal position, but this convention is generally discouraged.

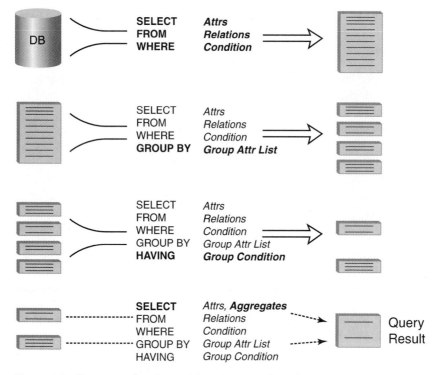

Figure 6.9 Query evaluation with aggregate functions.

Step 3.   The GROUP BY clause is evaluated. It takes the table produced in step 2 and splits it into groups of tuples, where each group consists precisely of those tuples that agree on all attributes of the group attribute list.

Step 4.   The HAVING clause is evaluated. It takes the groups produced in step 3 and eliminates those that fail the group condition.

Step 5.   The SELECT clause is evaluated. It takes the groups produced in step 4, evaluates the aggregate functions in the target list for each group, retains those columns that are listed as arguments of the SELECT clause, and produces a single row for each group.

Step 6.   The ORDER BY clause is evaluated. It orders the rows produced in step 5 using the specified column list. The resulting table is output by the SELECT statement.

Restrictions on GROUP BY **and** HAVING.   Like your apartment lease, grouping comes with several strings attached. The difference is, some of these restrictions actually make sense!

Consider a general form of SQL queries with aggregates:

SELECT   *attributeList, aggregates*
FROM   *relationList*
WHERE   *whereCondition*   (6.32)
GROUP BY *groupList*
HAVING   *groupCondition*

The purpose of the GROUP BY clause is to partition the result of the query into groups, with all tuples in the same group agreeing on each attribute in *groupList*. The aggregate functions in the SELECT clause, are then applied to each group to produce a *single* tuple. Since a single value is output for each attribute in *attributeList* in the SELECT clause (and that value is not an aggregate), all tuples in any given group must agree on each attribute in the list. This property is achieved in SQL by requiring that *attributeList* be a subset of *groupList*, which is a sufficient condition to ensure that each group yields a single tuple. (The condition is not necessary, but is general enough for most purposes.)

The second restriction concerns the HAVING condition. Intuitively, we need to ensure that *groupCondition* is either true or false for each group of tuples specified in GROUP BY. Generally, this condition consists of a number of atomic comparisons of the form $expr_1$ op $expr_2$, which are tied together by the logical connectives AND, OR, and NOT. For an atomic comparison $expr_1$ op $expr_2$, to make sense, both $expr_1$ and $expr_2$ must evaluate to a single value for each group. In practice, this means that for every column mentioned in *groupCondition* either of the following must hold:

1. It is in *groupList* (and thus it has a single value per group).
2. It appears in *groupCondition* as an argument to an aggregate function (thus, the expression sees a single value when the aggregation is computed).

Most DBMSs enforce the above syntactic restrictions.

We should also note that the order of the clauses in (6.32) is important—for instance, the HAVING clause cannot precede the GROUP BY clause. Also, the standard allows SQL statements that have the HAVING clause without the GROUP BY clause. In this case, the result of the SELECT-FROM-WHERE part of the query is treated as a single group and *groupCondition* in HAVING is applied to that group.

6.2.6 More on Views in SQL

The relations we have discussed up to this point are more technically referred to as **base relations**. They are the "normal" database relations. The contents of a base relation are physically stored on disk and are independent of the contents of other relations in the database.

As we already discussed in Chapter 4, a view is a relation whose contents are usually *not physically stored* in the database, instead, it is defined as the query result of a SELECT statement. Each time the view is used, its contents are computed using the associated query. Hence, the definition of the view (i.e., the query that determines the contents of the view) is stored (in the system catalog), not its contents.

Figure 6.10 Process of query modification by views.

```
SELECT    ... ... ...                                    Query that uses
FROM      VIEW1 V                                        a view, VIEW1
WHERE     ... AND V.Attr = 'abc' AND ...


          becomes


SELECT    ... ... ...                                    Query modified by
FROM      (definition of VIEW1) V                        the view definition
WHERE     ... AND V.Attr = 'abc' AND...
```

Because each view is the result of executing a query, its contents depend on the contents of the base relations in the database at the time the view is referenced.

The role of views in query languages is similar to that of *subroutines* in conventional programming languages. A view usually represents some meaningful query, which is used within several other, frequently asked queries, or it may have an independent interest. In either case, it makes sense to abstract the query and "pretend" that the database contains a relation whose contents precisely coincide with the query result.

Another important use of the view mechanism is to control user access to the data. This facility was briefly mentioned in Sections 4.1 and 4.3, and we will discuss it in more detail later in this section.

Using views in queries.   Once a view is defined, it can be used in SQL queries in the same way as any other table. Whenever it is used in a query, its definition is automatically substituted in the FROM clause, as illustrated in Figure 6.10.

Suppose that the university needs to find the department(s) where the average age of professors is the lowest. The application designer might determine that, in addition to the above query, a number of other queries compute the average age. In query processing, as in programming languages, this is a good enough reason to build a view for computing the average age.

```
CREATE VIEW AVGDEPTAGE(Dept,AvgAge) AS
    SELECT      P.DeptId, AVG(P.Age)
    FROM        PROFESSOR P
    GROUP BY    P.Dept
```

Like a subroutine, this view allows us to solve part of a larger problem separately. For example, we can now determine the minimum average age over all departments as follows:

```
SELECT    A.Dept
FROM      AVGDEPTAGE A                                              (6.33)
WHERE     A.AvgAge =    (SELECT MIN(A.AvgAge)
                        FROM AVGDEPTAGE A )
```

Views can make a complex SQL query easier to understand (and debug!). Consider query (6.24), page 152, which finds all students who have taken a course from each professor in the Department of Computer Science. The query uses two nested subqueries, one of which is correlated with the outer query. Because the issues of nesting and correlation are subtly intertwined, it might be hard to construct the right query the first time.

We can simplify the task with the help of views. The view

```
CREATE VIEW AllCSprofIDs(ProfId) AS
    SELECT    P.ProfId
    FROM      Professor P
    WHERE     P.Dept = 'CS'
```

constructs the set of Ids of all computer science professors. Next, we define a view to represent the second correlated subquery of (6.24). This subquery has a target list with only one attribute, ProfId, but it also uses a global variable, S, which parameterizes the sets of answers returned by the query. Each query execution returns the set of all professors who have taught a particular student. Since SQL does not allow the creation of views parameterized by a global variable, we improvise by including that variable's attributes in the target list. More precisely, we include only those attributes of the global variable that are actually used in the subquery. In our case, the global variable is S and the additional attribute is StudId. The result turns out to be our familiar view, ProfStud, defined in (4.5), page 81.

Unfortunately, we cannot subtract ProfStud from AllCSprofIDs yet, as they are not UNION-compatible. Furthermore, SQL allows the EXCEPT operator to be applied only to the results of subqueries—we cannot simply subtract one table from another. Therefore, we still must use nested subqueries. However, the subqueries are now much more manageable than in (6.24) since the views enable us to decompose a complex problem into smaller tasks.

```
SELECT    S.Id
FROM      Student S
WHERE

          NOT EXISTS (
              (SELECT P.ProfId FROM AllCSprofIDs P)
              EXCEPT
              (SELECT P.ProfId FROM ProfStud P
                WHERE P.StudId = S.Id))
```

Although the CREATE VIEW statement is quite different from the CREATE TABLE statement used for base relations, the deletion of views and tables from the system catalog uses similar statements: DROP VIEW for views and DROP TABLE for base tables.

What if we want to drop a view or a base table but the database has (other) views that were defined through this view or this table? The problem here is that dropping such a view or table means that all of the views defined through them will become "abandoned" and there will be no way to use them. In such a case, SQL leaves the decision to the designer of the DROP statement. The general format of the statement is

DROP {TABLE | VIEW } *table or view* {RESTRICT | CASCADE}

If the RESTRICT option is used, the drop operation fails if some view is dependent on the table or view being dropped. With the CASCADE option, all dependent views are also dropped.

Materialized views.   If a view becomes popular with many queries, its contents might be stored in a cache. Cached views are often referred to as **materialized views**. View caching can dramatically improve the response time of queries defined in terms of such views, but update transactions must pay the price. If a view depends on a base relation and a transaction updates the base relation, the view cache might need to be updated as well.

Consider view (4.5) on page 81, and suppose that a transaction adds tuple ⟨023456789, CS315, S1997, B⟩ to TRANSCRIPT. This tuple joins with tuple ⟨101202303, CS315, S1997⟩ in TEACHING to produce a view tuple, ⟨101202303, 023456789⟩. But this latter tuple is already in the view (see Figure 4.10, page 82), so this update does not change the view. Had we added ⟨023456789, MGT123, F1997, A⟩ to TRANSCRIPT, the view would have acquired new tuples, ⟨783432188, 023456789⟩ and ⟨009406321, 023456789⟩.

Consider now what might happen when tuples are deleted from the base relations underlying a materialized view. If a transaction deletes tuple ⟨123454321, CS305, S1996, A⟩ from TRANSCRIPT, one might think that tuple ⟨101202303, 123454321⟩ should also be deleted from the view cache. This is not the case, because ⟨101202303, 123454321⟩ can still be derived through a join between ⟨123454321, CS315, S1997, A⟩ and ⟨101202303, CS315, S1997⟩. Observe that Figure 4.10 indicates *two* reasons for tuple ⟨101202303, 123454321⟩ to be in the view, and the deletion of ⟨123454321, CS305,S1996, A⟩ removes only one of the reasons! However, if the transaction deleted ⟨123454321, MAT123, S1996, C⟩ from TRANSCRIPT, the tuple ⟨900120450, 123454321⟩ should be removed from the view cache.

Commercial DBMSs do not offer direct support for automatic maintenance of materialized views, but automatic deletion or insertion of tuples from or into the view cache can be accomplished with triggers (Chapter 9). Even so, triggers provide only the basic means for building support for view cache maintenance. As we have just shown, view cache maintenance is an algorithmically nontrivial task, especially if efficiency is the goal. We do not discuss these issues any further in this text. A number of algorithms have been proposed in the literature, for example, [Gupta et al. 1993, Mohania et al. 1997, Gupta et al. 1995, Blakeley and Martin 1990, Chaudhuri et al. 1995, Staudt and Jarke 1996, Gupta and Mumick 1995]. More research is still being conducted on the topic, because materialized views are becoming increasingly important for *data warehousing*.

Data warehouses are (infrequently updated) databases that typically consist of materialized views of the data stored in a separate production database. They are commonly used for online analytical processing (OLAP), which was briefly discussed in Chapter 1 and will be discussed in more detail in Chapter 19. In contrast to most production databases, data warehouses are optimized for querying, not transaction processing, and they are the primary beneficiaries of the advanced query capabilities of SQL discussed in this chapter. (In many transaction processing applications, rapid response time and high throughput requirements preclude the use of the complex queries.)

Access control and customization through views.   Database views are used not only as a subroutine mechanism but also as a flexible device for controlling access to the data. Thus, we might allow certain users to access a view but not some of the tables that underlie it. For instance, students might not be allowed to query the PROFESSOR relation because of the Social Security information stored there. However, there is nothing wrong with giving students access to the AVGDEPTAGE view defined earlier. Thus, while the access to PROFESSOR might be restricted to administrators, we might let students query the view AVGDEPTAGE:

```
GRANT SELECT ON AvgDeptAge TO ALL
```

Note that by using views we can repair a deficiency in the GRANT statement. In granting UPDATE (or INSERT) permission, we are allowed to (optionally) specify a list of columns that can be updated (or into which values can be inserted), but in granting SELECT permission SQL provides no way to specify such a list. We can get the same effect, however, by simply creating a view of accessible columns and granting access to that view instead of to the base table.

The creator (and thus the owner) of a view need not also be the owner of the underlying base relations. All that is required is that the view creator have SELECT privileges on all of the underlying relations. For instance, if the PROFESSOR relation is owned by *Administrator*, who in turn grants the SELECT privilege on PROFESSOR to *Personnel*, *Personnel* can create the view AVGDEPTAGE and later issue the above GRANT statement.

What happens if *Administrator* decides to revoke the SELECT privilege from *Personnel*? Notice that if *Administrator* revokes the privilege, the view becomes "abandoned" and nobody can query it. The actual result depends on how the REVOKE statement is issued. If the administrator uses the RESTRICT option in the REVOKE statement, revocation fails. If the CASCADE option is used, the revocation proceeds *and the view itself is dropped* from the system catalog.

Yet another use of views is customization, which goes hand in hand with access control. A real production database might contain hundreds of relations, each with dozens of attributes. However, most users (both "naive" users and application developers) need to deal with only a small portion of the database schema, the one that is relevant to the particular task performed by the user or the application. There is no benefit in subjecting all users to the tortuous process of learning large parts of the database schema. A better strategy is to create views customized to the various user categories so that, for instance, AVGDEPTAGE can be one of the views customized for the statisticians. The advantages of this approach are threefold.

1. *Ease of use and learning.* This speeds up application development and might prevent bugs that occur as a result of misunderstanding parts of the database schema.

2. *Security.* Various users and applications can be granted access to specific views, thereby reducing the possible damage from bugs, human errors, and malicious behavior.

3. *Logical data independence* (as discussed in Chapter 4). This benefit can result in huge savings in maintenance costs if later there is a need to change the database schema. Provided that schema reorganization does not lead to loss of information, none of the applications written against the views have to be changed—the only required change is in the view definitions.

6.2.7 The Null Value Quandary

In Chapter 4, we briefly discussed the concept of a **null value**. For instance, if we take the tuples in the TRANSCRIPT table to stand for courses taken in the past or those being taken in the current semester, some tuples may not have a valid value in the Grade attribute. NULL is a placeholder that SQL uses in such a case.

Null values are a (unfortunately unavoidable) headache in query processing. Indeed, what is the truth value of the condition T.Grade = 'A' if the value of T is a tuple that has a null in the Grade attribute?

To account for this phenomenon, SQL uses so-called *3-valued logic*, where the truth values are *true, false,* and *unknown* and where val_1 op val_2 (op being <, >, <>, =, etc.) is considered to be *unknown* whenever at least one of the values, val_1 or val_2, is NULL.

Nulls affect not only comparisons in the WHERE and CHECK clauses but also arithmetic expressions and aggregate functions. An arithmetic expression that encounters a NULL is itself evaluated to NULL. COUNT considers NULL to be a regular value (e.g., the statement (6.28) on page 155 counts NULL as well as normal values in producing the number of professors in the management department). All other aggregates just throw nulls away (e.g., statement (6.29) on page 155 ignores nulls in the Age column when computing the average). The following caveat holds, however: If such an aggregate function is applied to a column that has only NULLs, the result is a NULL.

Sadly, we have not reached the end of this confusing story. We also must decide what to do when a WHERE or a CHECK clause has the form $cond_1$ AND $cond_2$, $cond_1$ OR $cond_2$, or NOT *cond,* and one of the subconditions evaluates to *unknown* because of a pesky NULL hidden inside the subcondition. This issue is resolved by the truth tables in Figure 6.11, which shows the value of various Boolean functions depending on the values of subconditions.

If these tables seem bewildering, they should not be. The idea is very simple. Suppose that we need to compute the value of *true* AND *unknown.* Because *unknown* may turn out to be either *true* or *false,* the value of the entire expression can also be either *true* or *false* (that is, *unknown*). On the other hand, the expressions *false* AND

Figure 6.11   SQL's truth tables used to deal with the unknown.

$cond_1$	$cond_2$	$cond_1$ AND $cond_2$	$cond_1$ OR $cond_2$
true	true	true	true
true	false	false	true
true	unknown	unknown	true
false	true	false	true
false	false	false	false
false	unknown	false	unknown
unknown	true	unknown	true
unknown	false	false	unknown
unknown	unknown	unknown	unknown

cond	NOT cond
true	false
false	true
unknown	unknown

unknown and *true* OR *unknown* evaluate to *false* and *true*, respectively, regardless of whether *unknown* turns out to be *true* or *false*. The case of NOT is dealt with similarly.

SQL introduces one additional predicate, IS NULL, which is specifically designed to test if some value is NULL. For instance, T.Grade IS NULL is true whenever the tuple assigned to T has a null value in the Grade attribute; it evaluates to false otherwise. Interestingly, this is the only true 2-valued predicate in SQL!

So what happens when the entire condition evaluates to *unknown*? The answer depends on whether this is a WHERE or a CHECK clause. If a WHERE clause evaluates to *unknown*, it is treated as *false* and the corresponding tuple is not added to the query answer. If a CHECK clause evaluates to *unknown*, the integrity constraint is considered to be observed (i.e., the result is treated as *true*). The difference in the way the unknown values are treated in queries and constraints can be given a rational explanation. Indeed, it is assumed that the user expects the queries to return only the answers that are definitely *true*. On the other hand, a constraint of the form CHECK (condition) is viewed as a statement that the condition should *not* evaluate to *false*. Thus, the *unknown* truth value is considered acceptable.

We have presented only the general framework behind null values in SQL. Many details have been left out but can be found in most standard SQL references, such as [Date and Darwen 1997]. For instance, what is the impact of nulls on the LIKE condition, the IN condition, set comparisons (such as > ALL), the EXISTS feature, duplicate elimination (i.e., queries that use DISTINCT), and the like? Think of what might be reasonable in these cases and then compare your conclusions with those of [Date and Darwen 1997].

6.3   MODIFYING RELATION INSTANCES IN SQL

So far we have discussed the query sublanguage—by far the hardest part of SQL. However, databases exist not only for querying but also for entering and modifying the appropriate data. This section deals with the part of SQL that is used for data insertion, deletion, and modification.

Inserting data.   The INSERT statement has several forms, in the simplest of which the programmer specifies just the tuple to be inserted. The second version of this statement can insert multiple tuples and uses a query to tell which tuples to insert. To insert a single tuple, the programmer simply writes

```
INSERT INTO    PROFESSOR(DeptId,Id,Name)
VALUES ('MATH','100100100','Bob Parker')
```

The order of the attributes listed in the INTO clause need not correspond to the *default* order (i.e., the order in which they are listed in the CREATE TABLE statement). However, if you know the default attribute order, you can omit the attribute list in the INTO clause. Of course, the order of items in the VALUE clause must then correspond to the default attribute order. Despite the potential time saving, omitting the attribute list in the INTO clause is error prone (e.g., consider what happens if the schema is later changed) and is thus viewed as poor programming style.

The second form of the INSERT statement enables bulk insertion of tuples into relations. The tuples to be inserted are the result of a query in the INSERT statement. Note that, even though a query is used to define the tuples to be inserted into a relation, this mechanism is fundamentally different from defining views via queries (see Exercise 6.18).

As an example, let us insert some tuples into a relation called HARDCLASS. A hard class is one that is failed by more than 10% of the students. The attributes in HARDCLASS are course code, semester, and failure rate.

This query is actually quite complicated (because expressing the failure rate in SQL requires some thought), so we tackle it in steps by first defining two views.

```
--Number of failures per class
CREATE VIEW CLASSFAILURES(CrsCode, Semester, Failed) AS
      SELECT    T.CrsCode, T.Semester, COUNT(*)
      FROM      TRANSCRIPT T
      WHERE     T.Grade = 'F'
      GROUP BY T.CrsCode, T.Semester
```

Similarly, we can define the view CLASSENROLLED, which counts the number of students enrolled in each course.

```
--Number of enrolled students per class
CREATE VIEW CLASSENROLLED(CrsCode, Semester, Enrolled) AS
      SELECT    T.CrsCode, T.Semester, COUNT(*)
      FROM      TRANSCRIPT T
      GROUP BY T.CrsCode, T.Semester
```

Now, HARDCLASS can be populated as follows:

```
INSERT INTO HardClass(CrsCode, Semester, FailRate)
    SELECT   F.CrsCode, F.Semester, F.Failed/E.Enrolled
    FROM     ClassFailures F, ClassEnrolled E                    (6.34)
    WHERE    F.CrsCode = E.CrsCode AND F.Semester = E.Semester
                   AND (F.Failed/E.Enrolled) > 0.1
```

The final query looks simple, but imagine how complex it would be if not for the views!

There are a few more subtleties we must mention. First, if an INSERT statement inserts a tuple that violates some integrity constraint, the entire operation is aborted and no tuple is inserted (assuming that constraint checking has not been DEFERRED, as will be described in Section 10.3).

Second, it is possible to omit a value in the list of values in the VALUE clause (and the corresponding attribute in the attribute list) and an attribute in the SELECT clause if the CREATE TABLE statement does not specify NOT NULL. If the CREATE TABLE statement specifies a default for the missing attribute, that default value is used. Instead of omitting values, a better style is to use the more informative keywords DEFAULT or NULL (whichever is appropriate) in place of the missing values (e.g., (100100100, NULL, DEFAULT)).

Deleting data. Deletion of tuples is analogous to the second form of INSERT, except that now the keyword DELETE is used. For example, to delete the hard classes taught in the fall and spring of 1991 we use

```
DELETE FROM HardClass
WHERE Semester IN ('S1991','F1991')
```

Note that the DELETE statement does not allow the use of tuple variables in the FROM clause.

Suppose that, in order to improve teaching standards, the university decides to fire all professors with an excessively high failure rate in one of the courses. This turns out to be difficult (and not because of tenure!). Indeed, the DELETE statement has a very limited form of the FROM clause: The programmer can specify just one relation, the one whose tuples are to be deleted. (What would it mean to delete rows from the Cartesian product of two relations?) However, in order to find out who to fire we need to look inside the HARDCLASS relation, but there is no room for this relation in the FROM clause. So what are we to do? Use nested subqueries!

```
DELETE FROM Professor
WHERE Id IN
        (SELECT  T.ProfId
         FROM    Teaching T, HardClass H                     (6.35)
         WHERE   T.CrsCode = H.CrsCode
                 AND T.Semester = H.Semester
                 AND H.FailRate > 0.5)
```

Updating existing data.   Sometimes it is necessary to change the values of some attributes of existing tuples in a relation. For instance, the following statement changes the grade of student 666666666 for course EE101 from B to A:

```
UPDATE   TRANSCRIPT
SET      Grade ='A'
WHERE    StudId ='666666666' AND CrsCode = 'EE101'
```

Observe that, like DELETE, the UPDATE statement does not allow tuple variables and it uses only a limited form of the FROM clause (more precisely, UPDATE itself is a kind of FROM clause). As a result, some of the more complex updates require the use of nested subqueries. For instance, if, instead of firing them we decide to transfer all poorly performing professors to administration, we use a subquery similar to the one in (6.35).

```
UPDATE   PROFESSOR
SET      DeptId = 'Adm'
WHERE    Id IN
             (SELECT T.ProfId
              FROM TEACHING T, HARDCLASS H                    (6.36)
              WHERE T.CrsCode = H.CrsCode
                    AND T.Semester = H.Semester
                    AND  H.FailRate > 0.5)
```

And, yes, here is our favorite again: *Raise the salary of all administrators by 10%*:

```
UPDATE   EMPLOYEE
SET      Salary = Salary * 1.1
WHERE    Department = 'Adm'
```

Updates on views.   Because views are often used as a customization device that shields users and programmers from the complexity of the conceptual database schema, it is only natural to let programmers update their views. Unfortunately, this is easier said than done because of the following three problems:

1. Suppose that we have a simple view over TRANSCRIPT—a projection on the attributes CrsCode, StudId, and Semester. If the programmer wants to insert a new tuple in such a view, the value for the Grade attribute will be missing. This problem is not serious. We can pad the missing attributes with null values if the CREATE TABLE statement for the underlying base relation permits this; if it does not, the insertion command can be rejected.

2. Consider a view, CSPROF, over the PROFESSOR relation, which is obtained by a simple selection on DeptId = 'CS'. Suppose that the programmer inserts ⟨ 121232343, 'Paul Schmidt', 'EE'⟩. If we propagate this insertion to the underlying base relation (i.e., PROFESSOR), we can observe the anomaly that querying the view *after* the insertion does not show any traces of the tuple we just inserted! Indeed, Paul Schmidt is not a CS professor, so he does not appear in the view defined through the selection DeptId = 'CS'!

By default, SQL does not forbid such anomalies, but a careful database designer might include the clause WITH CHECK OPTION to ensure that the newly inserted or updated tuples in a view do, indeed, satisfy the view definition. In our example, we can write

```
CREATE VIEW CSProf(Id,Name,DeptId) AS
    SELECT   P.Id, P.Name, P.DeptId
    FROM     Professor  P
    WHERE    P.DeptId = 'CS'
    WITH CHECK OPTION
```

3. This problem is much more complex. It turns out that some view updates might have several possible translations into the updates of the underlying base relations. This is potentially a very serious problem, because the possibilities arising from a single view update might have drastically different consequences with respect to the underlying stored data.

To illustrate the third problem, consider the view PROFSTUD discussed earlier.

```
CREATE VIEW ProfStud(ProfId,StudId) AS
    SELECT   T.ProfId, R.StudId
    FROM     Teaching T, Transcript R
    WHERE    T.CrsCode = R.CrsCode
                AND T.Semester = R.Semester
```

The contents of this view were depicted in Figure 4.10 on page 82. Suppose that we now decide to delete the tuple ⟨101202303, 123454321⟩ from that view. How should this update be propagated back to the base relations? There are four possibilities.

1. Delete ⟨101202303, CS315, S1997⟩ and ⟨101202303, CS305, S1996⟩ from the relation TEACHING.
2. Delete ⟨123454321, CS315, S1997, A⟩ and ⟨123454321, CS305, S1996, A⟩ from the relation TRANSCRIPT.
3. Delete ⟨101202303, CS315, S1997⟩ from TEACHING and ⟨123454321, CS305, S1996, A⟩ from TRANSCRIPT.
4. Delete ⟨101202303, CS305, S1996⟩ from TEACHING and ⟨123454321, CS315, S1997, A⟩ from TRANSCRIPT.

For each of these possibilities, the join implied by the view does not contain the tuple ⟨101202303, 123454321⟩. The only problem is, which possibility should be used for the view update?

This example shows that, in the absence of additional information, it may not be possible to translate view updates into the updates of the underlying base relations. Much work has been done on defining heuristics aimed at disambiguating view updates, but none has emerged as an acceptable solution. SQL takes a simple-minded approach by allowing only a very restricted class of views to be updatable. The essence of these restrictions on the view definition is summarized here.

1. Exactly one table can be mentioned in the FROM clause (and only once). The FROM clause cannot have nested subqueries.

2. No aggregates, GROUP BY, or HAVING clauses are allowed.

3. Nested subqueries in the WHERE clause of the view cannot mention the table used in the FROM clause of the view definition (there is only one such table, because of case 1).

4. No expressions and no DISTINCT keyword in the SELECT clause are allowed.

Views satisfying these conditions (and some other rather obscure restrictions) are called **updatable** (in the SQL sense). Here is an example of an updatable view.

```
CREATE VIEW CANTEACH(Professor, Course)
    SELECT   T.ProfId, T.CrsCode
    FROM     TEACHING  T
```

Referring to the database of Figure 4.5, page 63, suppose that we delete ⟨09406321, MGT123⟩ from the view CANTEACH. There are two tuples in the underlying base relation (TEACHING) that give rise to the view tuple in question: ⟨09406321, MGT123, F1994⟩ and ⟨09406321, MGT123, F1997⟩. The translation of the view update into an update of TEACHING must therefore delete both of these tuples.

6.4 BIBLIOGRAPHIC NOTES

Relational algebra was introduced in Codd's seminal papers [Codd 1972, 1970]. SQL was developed by IBM's System R research group [Astrahan et al. 1981]. [Melton and Simon 1992, Date and Darwen 1997] are references to SQL-92, and [Gulutzan and Pelzer 1999] describe the extensions provided in SQL:1999.

The view update problem received considerable attention in the past. The following is a partial list of works that propose various solutions: [Bancilhon and Spyratos 1981, Masunaga 1984, Cosmadakis and Papadimitriou 1983, Gottlob et al. 1988, Keller 1985, Langerak 1990, Chen et al. 1995]. The maintenance problem for materialized views has also been an active research area [Gupta et al. 1993, Mohania et al. 1997, Gupta et al. 1995, Blakeley and Martin 1990, Chaudhuri et al. 1995, Staudt and Jarke 1996, Gupta and Mumick 1995]. More research is being conducted because of the importance of materialized views in data warehousing.

6.5 EXERCISES

6.1 Assume that **R** and **S** are relations containing n_R and n_S tuples, respectively. What is the maximum and minimum number of tuples that can possibly be in the result of each of the following expressions (assuming appropriate union compatibilities):

a. $R \cup S$

b. $R \cap S$

c. $R - S$

d. $R \times S$

e. $\mathbf{R} \bowtie \mathbf{S}$

f. $\mathbf{R} / \mathbf{S}$

g. $\sigma_{s=4}(\mathbf{R}) \times \pi_{s,t}(\mathbf{S})$

6.2 Assume that **R** and **S** are tables representing the relations of the previous exercise. Design SQL queries that will return the results of each of the expressions of that exercise.

6.3 Verify that the Cartesian product is an associative operator—i.e.,

$$\mathbf{r} \times (\mathbf{s} \times \mathbf{t}) = (\mathbf{r} \times \mathbf{s}) \times \mathbf{t}$$

for all relations **r**, **s**, and **t**.

6.4 Verify that selections commute—i.e., for any relation **r** and any pair of selection conditions $cond_1$ and $cond_2$, $\sigma_{cond_1}(\sigma_{cond_2}(\mathbf{r})) = \sigma_{cond_2}(\sigma_{cond_1}(\mathbf{r}))$.

6.5 Verify that, for any pair of relations **r** and **s**, $\sigma_{cond}(\mathbf{r} \times \mathbf{s}) = \mathbf{r} \times \sigma_{cond}(\mathbf{s})$, if the selection condition *cond* involves *only* the attributes mentioned in the schema of relation **s**.

6.6 Prove that, if **r** and **s** are union-compatible, then $\mathbf{r} \cap \mathbf{s} = \mathbf{r} \bowtie \mathbf{s}$.

6.7 Using division, write a relational algebra expression that produces all students who have taken all courses offered in every semester (this implies that they might have taken the same course twice).

6.8 Using division, write a relational algebra expression that produces all students who have taken all courses that have been offered. (If a course has been offered more than once, they have to have taken it at least once.)

6.9 An **outer join** of two relations **r** and **s** with join condition *cond*, denoted $\mathbf{r} \bowtie_{cond}^{outer} \mathbf{s}$, is defined as follows. As before, it is a relation over the schema that contains the union of the (possibly renamed) attributes in **R** (the schema of **r**) and **S** (the schema of **s**). However, the tuples in $\mathbf{r} \bowtie_{cond}^{outer} \mathbf{s}$ consist of three categories: (1) The tuples that appear in the regular join of **r** and **s**. (2) The tuples of **r** that do not join with any tuple in **s**. Since these tuples do not have values for the attributes that come from **S**, they are padded with NULL over these attributes. (3) The tuples of **s** that do not join with any tuple in **r**. Again, these tuples are padded with NULL over the attributes of **R**.

　　Construct a relational algebra query that produces the same result as $\mathbf{r} \bowtie_{cond}^{outer} \mathbf{s}$ using only these operators: union, difference, Cartesian product, general join (not outer join). You can also use constant relations, i.e., relations with fixed contents that does not depend on the rest of the database.

6.10 Express each of the following queries in (*i*) relational algebra and (*ii*) SQL using the Student Registration System schema of Figure 4.4.

a. List all courses that are taught by professors who belong to the EE or MGT Department.

   b. List the names of all students who took courses in spring 1997 and fall 1998.

   c. List the names of all students who took courses from at least two professors in different departments.

   d. List all courses taken by all students in department MGT.

 * e. Find every department that has a professor who taught all courses ever offered by that department.

6.11 Use the relational algebra to find the list of all "problematic" classes, where the failure rate is higher than 20%.

   Because the relational algebra does not have aggregate operators, we must add them to be able to solve the above problem. The additional operator you should use is $count_{A/B}(\mathbf{r})$.

   The meaning of this operator is as follows: A and B must be lists of attributes in $\mathbf{r}$. The *schema* of $count_{A/B}(\mathbf{r})$ consists of all attributes in B plus one additional attribute, which represents the counted value. The *contents* of $count_{A/B}(\mathbf{r})$ are defined as follows: for each tuple, $t \in \pi_B(\mathbf{r})$ (the projection on B), take $\pi_A(\sigma_{B=t}(\mathbf{r}))$ and count the number of tuples in the resulting relation ($\sigma_{B=t}(\mathbf{r})$ stands for the set of all tuples in $\mathbf{r}$ whose value on the attributes in B is t). Let us denote this number by $c(t)$.

   Then the relation $count_{A/B}(\mathbf{r})$ is defined as $\{< t, c(t) > | t \in \pi_B(\mathbf{r})\}$.

   You should be able to recognize the above construction as a straightforward adaptation of GROUP BY of SQL to the relational algebra.

6.12 State the English meaning of the following algebraic expressions (some of these queries are likely to yield empty results in a typical university, but this is beside the point):

   a. $\pi_{CrsCode,Semester}(\text{TRANSCRIPT}) / \pi_{CrsCode}(\text{TRANSCRIPT})$

   b. $\pi_{CrsCode,Semester}(\text{TRANSCRIPT}) / \pi_{Semester}(\text{TRANSCRIPT})$

   c. $\pi_{CrsCode,StudId}(\text{TRANSCRIPT}) / (\pi_{Id}(\text{STUDENT}))[\text{StudId}]$

   d. $\pi_{CrsCode,Semester,StudId}(\text{TRANSCRIPT}) / (\pi_{Id}(\text{STUDENT}))[\text{StudId}]$

6.13 Consider the following query:

```
SELECT   S.Name
FROM     STUDENT S, TRANSCRIPT T
WHERE    S.Id = T.StudId
         AND T.CrsCode IN ('CS305','CS315' )
```

What does this query mean (express the meaning in one short English sentence)? Write an equivalent SQL query without using the IN operator and the set construct.

6.14 Write query (6.33) on page 162 without the use of the views.

6.15 Express the following queries using SQL. Assume that the STUDENT table is augmented with an additional attribute, Age, and that the PROFESSOR table has additional attributes, Age and Salary.

a. Find the average age of students who received an A for *some* course.

b. Find the minimum age of A students *per course*.

c. Find the minimum age of A students per course among the students who have taken CS305 or MAT123. (Hint: a nested subquery in the HAVING clause might help.)

d. Raise by 10% the salary of every professor who is younger than 40 and had taught MAT123 in the spring 1997 or fall 1997 semester. (*Hint*: Try a nested subquery in the WHERE clause of the UPDATE statement.)

* e. Find the professors whose salary is at least 10% higher than the average salary of all professors. (*Hint*: Use views, as in the HARDCLASS example (6.34), page 169.)

** f. Find all professors whose salary is at least 10% higher than the average salary of all professors *in their departments*. (*Hint*: use views, as in (6.34).)

6.16 Express the following queries in relational algebra.

a. (6.14), page 146

b. (6.18), page 148

c. (6.21), page 149

6.17 Consider the following schema:

        TRANSCRIPT(StudId, CrsCode, Semester, Grade)
        TEACH(ProfId, CrsCode, Semester)
        PROFESSOR(ProfId, ProfName, Dept)

Write the following query in relational algebra and in SQL: *Find all student Ids who had taken a course from* each *professor in the MUS department.*

6.18 Define the above query as an SQL view and then use this view to answer the following query: *For each student who had taken a course from every professor in the MUS department, show the number of courses taken, provided that this number is more than* 10.

6.19 Consider the following schema:

        BROKER(Id, Name)   ACCOUNT(Acct#, BrokerId, Gain)

Write the following query in relational algebra and in SQL: *Find the names of all brokers who have made money in all accounts assigned to them (i.e., Gain > 0).*

6.20 Write an SQL statement (for the database schema given in Exercise 6.19) to fire all brokers who lost money in at least 40% of their accounts. Assume that every broker has at least one account. (*Hint*: Define intermediate views to facilitate formulation of the query.)

6.21 Explain why a view is like a subroutine.

6.22 Consider the following schema that represents houses for sale and customers who are looking to buy:

CUSTOMER(Id, Name, Address)
PREFERENCE(CustId, Feature)
AGENT(Id, AgentName)
HOUSE(Address, OwnerId, AgentId)
AMENITY(Address, Feature)

PREFERENCE is a relation that lists all features requested by the customers (one tuple per customer/feature; e.g., ⟨123, '5BR'⟩, ⟨123,'2BATH'⟩, ⟨432,'pool'⟩), and AMENITY is a relation that lists all features of each house (one tuple per house/feature).

A customer is *interested* in buying a house if the set of all features specified by the customer is a subset of the amenities the house has. A tuple in the HOUSE relation states who is the owner and who is the real estate agent listing the house. Write the following queries in SQL:

a. Find all customers who are interested in every house listed with the agent with Id 007.

b. Using the previous query as a view, retrieve a set of tuples of the form ⟨*feature, number_of_customers*⟩, where each tuple in the result shows a feature and the number of customers who want this feature such that:
   • Only the customers who are interested in every house listed with Agent 007 are considered
   • The number of customers interested in *feature* is greater than 3. (If this number is not greater than 3, the corresponding tuple ⟨*feature, number_of_customers*⟩ is not added to the result.)

6.23 Consider the schema PERSON(Id, Name, Age). Write an SQL query that finds the 100*th* oldest person in the relation. A 100*th* oldest person is one such that there are 99 people who are strictly older. (There can be several such people who might have the same age, or there can be none.)

6.24 The last section of this chapter presented four main rules that characterize updatable views in SQL. The third rule states that if the WHERE clause contains a nested subquery, none of the tables mentioned in that subquery can be the table used in the FROM clause of the view definition.

Construct a view that violates condition 3 but satisfies conditions 1, 2, and 4 for updatability, such that there is an update to this view that has two different translations into the updates on the underlying base relation.

6.25 Explain the conceptual difference between views and bulk insertion of tuples into base relations using the INSERT statement with an attached query.

Chapter 7

Query Languages II: Relational Calculus and Visual Query Languages

Relational algebra was used in Chapter 6 to explain how SQL queries are evaluated. In fact, DBMSs often use the relational algebra as a high-level intermediate code into which SQL queries are translated before being optimized. Conceptually and syntactically, however, SQL is based on a completely different formal query language, called **relational calculus** ("calculus" might seem a somewhat frightening name for such a relatively simple language). The relational calculus is a subset of classical predicate logic, a subject that had been well researched long before the relational model was born. One of the major contributions of E. F. Codd was his vision in realizing that this tool could be the basis for a powerful database query language.

There are two relational calculi. In the next section, we introduce the basics of **tuple relational calculus (TRC)**—the original, introduced in [Codd 1972]. TRC is important for a proper understanding of the query sublanguage of SQL. Indeed, as we shall see, SQL can be viewed as TRC with some of the mathematical symbols replaced with English words. For instance, [Date 1992] showed how TRC can be effectively used as an intermediate language for constructing complex SQL queries.

Then we sketch **domain relational calculus (DRC)** and discuss the visual query languages built around it. If you have studied the elements of the usual predicate logic, DRC should look familiar as it is essentially a subset of that logic. It was proposed as a language for database queries in [Lacroix and Pirotte 1977].

7.1 TUPLE RELATIONAL CALCULUS

Queries in TRC all have the form

   {T | Condition}

The part of the query to the left of the | is called the query **target**; the part to the right the query **condition** (or the *body* of the query).

The target consists of a **tuple variable**, T, which is just like the usual variables in high school algebra except that it ranges over *tuples of values* (such as relational tuples) rather than individual values (such as numbers and strings).

The query condition must be such that

■ It uses the variable T and possibly some other variables.

■ If a *concrete tuple* of values is substituted for each occurrence of T in *Condition*, the condition evaluates to a Boolean value of *true* or *false*.

Here is a simple example: *Find all teaching records for the courses offered in the fall of 1997.*

$$\{T \mid \text{TEACHING}(T) \text{ AND } T.\text{Semester} = \text{'F1997'}\}$$

The term TEACHING(T) is a test of whether tuple T belongs to the relation instance of TEACHING. T.Semester = 'F1997' is another test. It is easy to see that this TRC query corresponds to the SQL query

```
SELECT    *
FROM      TEACHING T
WHERE     T.Semester = 'F1997'
```

It should now be clear why we said earlier that SQL is essentially a syntactic variant of TRC. The target of a TRC query corresponds to the SELECT list of an SQL query. The query condition in TRC is split between two clauses in SQL: the FROM clause, which holds conditions of the form *Relation*(*Variable*) (which restricts particular variables to range over tuples of particular relations); and the WHERE clause, which holds all other conditions.

The easiest way to understand the meaning of TRC queries is to think of them *declaratively*, with no particular query evaluation algorithm in mind. You can consider this process as enumerating all possible choices for the target tuple variable T and then checking which choices turn the query condition into a true statement about the given database instance. This interpretation leads to the following definition:

> The *result* of a TRC query with respect to a given database is the set of all choices of values for the variable T that make the query condition a true statement about the database.

In fact, this definition is also a correct way to think about SQL queries (and sometimes the only sure way to verify that an SQL query does what the programmer intended).

Let us see how this definition works in more detail. Suppose that we choose ⟨009406321, MGT123, F1980⟩ as a possible answer for T in the above example. Substituting this for T yields

TEACHING(009406321, MGT123, F1980) AND 'F1980'= 'F1997'

Wrong guess. This tuple does not belong to the relation instance of TEACHING (check Figure 4.5, on page 63), and 'F1980' = 'F1997' is also not true. So this choice is discarded.

Another try: ⟨009406321, MGT123, F1994⟩. Substituting this for T yields

TEACHING(009406321, MGT123, F1994) AND 'F1994' = 'F1997'

A better choice but still a wrong guess. Although ⟨009406321, MGT123, F1994⟩ belongs to the instance of relation TEACHING (so that part of the query condition is true), the proposition 'F1994' = 'F1997' is still false.

Our third choice, ⟨009406321, MGT123, F1997⟩, yields

TEACHING(009406321, MGT123, F1997) AND 'F1997' = 'F1997'

which is a true statement about the current state of our database, so the last tuple belongs to the query result. In fact, only three tuples satisfy this query: ⟨009406321, MGT123, F1997⟩, ⟨783432188, MGT123, F1997⟩, and ⟨900120450, MAT123, S1997⟩, as can be verified by an exhaustive search of all possible elements of all domains.

Of course, DBMSs do not necessarily perform an exhaustive search. Instead, they use much more sophisticated algorithms (which are different for different DBMSs). However, we present the semantics of the language using exhaustive search as a teaching device because it is easy to understand and it can serve as a yardstick for more sophisticated query evaluation algorithms.

In addition, the exhaustive search semantics can be very helpful in verifying that a particular formulation of an SQL query does what we expect it to do—when writing complex SQL queries, we have seen how unreliable human intuition is.

We are now ready for the nuts and bolts of TRC. It may surprise you that we have already presented most of the underlying ideas. Only two things remain to be explained:

■ The syntax of query conditions

■ What it means for a condition to be true after substituting a guess-tuple for the tuple variable in the query target

Syntax of query conditions. The basic building blocks used in query conditions can be of one of these forms:

■ **P**(*T*), where **P** is a relation name and *T* is a tuple variable. Intuitively, **P**(*T*) is a test of whether tuple *T* belongs to the relation instance of **P** (of course, the test makes sense only after we choose a value for *T*). Example: STUDENT(T).

■ *T*.*A* oper *S*.*B*, where oper is a comparison operator (=, >, ≥, ≠, etc.), *T* and *S* are tuple variables, and *A* and *B* are attributes. The term *T*.*A* denotes the component of *T* corresponding to the attribute *A*. The intended meaning here is a comparison of one component of a tuple against another. Example: T.StudId ≥ S.ProfId.

■ *T*.*A* oper *const*. This is similar to the previous form, except that the comparison is with a constant rather than with a tuple component. Example: T.Semester = 'F1994'.

These basic building blocks are called **atomic conditions**. More complex query conditions are constructed recursively as follows:

■ C is a query condition if it is an atomic condition.

■ If C_1 and C_2 are query conditions, C_1 AND C_2, C_1 OR C_2, and NOT C_1 are also query conditions.

■ If C is a query condition, **R** is a relation name, and T is a tuple variable, then $\forall T \in \mathbf{R}$ (C) and $\exists T \in \mathbf{R}$ (C) are query conditions.

The symbol $\forall$ stands for "for all," and the symbol $\exists$ stands for "there exists." They are called the **universal quantifier** and the **existential quantifier**, respectively.

The intended meaning of the atomic conditions has been explained. The intended meaning of conditions in the second group should be obvious. For instance, C_1 AND C_2 is a condition that evaluates to true if and only if *both* C_1 and C_2 evaluate to true. The condition C_1 OR C_2 is true if and only if at least one of C_1 and C_2 evaluates to true. NOT C_1 is true if and only if C_1 is false.

The meaning of the quantified formulas can be read directly from the formulas. Let **r** be the relation instance of **R**. Then $\forall T \in \mathbf{R}$ (C) stands for: *For every tuple $t \in \mathbf{r}$, C becomes true if t is substituted for the variable T*. Similarly, $\exists T \in \mathbf{R}$ (C) stands for: *There exists tuple $t \in \mathbf{r}$, such that C becomes true after t is substituted for T.*

One more notion and we are done with the syntax. In the formulas $\forall T \in \mathbf{R}$ (C) and $\exists T \in \mathbf{R}$ (C), the variable T is said to be **bound** by the quantifier. Any variable that is not explicitly bound in this way is said to be **free**. For instance, in T.Name = S.Name both T and S are free, but in $\forall$S ∈ STUDENT (T.Name = S.Name) the variable S is bound and T is free.

What do all of these free and bound variables have to do with the semantics of queries? Consider the sentence *It rained on day* X. Here X is a free variable, and hence the phrase has no truth value until we make X concrete—that is, substitute a particular value for it. For comparison, consider the sentence *For all days* $X \in July$, *it rained on day* X. The English statement might sound awkward, but that is how you say it in logic (thereby eliminating possible ambiguity). Observe that we still have a variable in the second phrase, but now we intuitively feel that the phrase is either true or false (assuming that the context makes it clear which July and which location is meant). The main difference between the two sentences is that X is free in the first and bound in the second.

The implication of this discussion is that bound variables are used to make assertions about tuples in the database whereas free variables are used to specify the tuples to be returned by the query. These free variables can be used only in the query target, because the query answer is determined by substituting concrete values for the target variables and, after a substitution, the query condition is not supposed to have any free variables left (or else we are unable to tell whether a particular choice of values for the target variables makes the query condition true). Therefore, revisiting the definition of a TRC query {T | *Condition*}, we should add the following restriction:

T must be the *only* free variable in *Condition*.

Evaluation of query conditions.   So, how do we decide if a particular choice of a tuple satisfies a query condition? Let us look at a concrete example.

$$\{\ E\ |\ \text{Course}(E)\ \text{AND} \\ \forall S \in \text{Student}\ (\exists T \in \text{Transcript}(\\ \text{T.StudId = S.Id AND T.CrsCode = E.CrsCode}))\} \tag{7.1}$$

This query returns *all courses that have been taken by every student*.

Let us see if a particular choice for E satisfies the query condition. Because we know that a correct choice must be a tuple in Courses, we choose a concrete tuple in Figure 4.5, page 63, that belongs to this relation: ⟨MGT123, MGT, Market Analysis, Get rich quick⟩. After substituting this tuple for E, the query condition has no free variables but is still rather complex.

$$\text{Course(MGT123, MGT, Market Analysis, Get rich quick)}\ \text{AND} \\ \forall S \in \text{Student}\ (\exists T \in \text{Transcript}(\\ \text{T.StudId = S.Id AND T.CrsCode = 'MGT123'})) \tag{7.2}$$

To find out if this condition is true in our database, we evaluate it recursively by chipping off pieces of syntax in the order opposite to that in which the expression was built up from the atomic conditions. Since the first component of (7.2) is true in our database (the tuple ⟨MGT123, MGT, Market Analysis, Get rich quick⟩ does describe an existing course), we need only check if the second component is true.

The topmost piece in the second component is $\forall S \in$ Student. The purpose of this quantifier is to say that, for every concrete tuple $s \in$ Student, if we replace the variable S with tuple s, the subcondition

$$\exists T \in \text{Transcript}\ (\text{T.StudId} = s.\text{Id AND T.CrsCode = 'MGT123'}) \tag{7.3}$$

must be true. If this is the case, the expression (7.2) evaluates to true. If the subcondition (7.3) is false even for just one tuple in Student, the whole condition (7.2) evaluates to false.

Since we need to test (7.3) for all students, let us try the tuple from Figure 4.2 that describes John Doe (page 63). Because its Id component is 111111111, we have to evaluate (7.3) with s.Id replaced by 111111111. The topmost construct in (7.3) is $\exists T \in$ Transcript, so (7.3) evaluates to true if we can find a tuple $t \in$ Transcript such that, after substituting t for T, the condition

$$t.\text{StudId = 111111111 AND } t.\text{CrsCode = 'MGT123'}$$

becomes true. Incidentally, John Doe took MGT123 in fall 1997 and received a B, as evidenced by a tuple in Transcript. So, substituting this tuple for T, we get

$$\text{111111111 = 111111111 AND 'MGT123' = 'MGT123'}$$

which is true in our database, because each subcondition is true.

Are we done proving that our original choice, ⟨MGT123, MGT, Market Analysis, Get rich quick⟩, is an answer to the query? No! We have to verify that (7.3) is true for *every* tuple $s \in$ Student. So far, we have established only that this condition is true when s is the tuple describing John Doe.

Now let s be the tuple that describes Homer Simpson, Id 023456789. In order for s to satisfy (7.3), we need to verify that there is a tuple in TRANSCRIPT such that, if we substitute it for T, the following will be true in the database:

```
T.StudId = 023456789 AND T.CrsCode = 'MGT123'
```

We can try each tuple in TRANSCRIPT in turn, but we will save time by verifying that this relation has no tuple where the StudId attribute is 023456789 and the CrsCode attribute is MGT123. Therefore, substitution of Homer Simpson's tuple in (7.3) creates a condition that is false in our database, and thus (7.3) is *not* true for *every* student in our database. This means that (7.2) is false and so our original guess (of a tuple for COURSE) is *not* an answer to query (7.1).

If you have time, you can check that no choice satisfies the query condition in (7.1), so the answer is empty. But this need not necessarily be so. If we were to add appropriate transcript records for MGT123 so that all students in our database would have taken this course, the COURSE tuple that describes MGT123 would belong to the query result.

The above process, although tedious, is essentially what an expert might use to verify that a choice belongs to the query answer. With some experience, you will develop various shortcuts and time-saving devices ("optimizations"), but the above process will still serve as a "yardstick of correctness." A query designer might use some similar process to validate that a particular query design satisfies its intended requirements.

Examples.   The above procedure for verifying TRC queries is admittedly tedious, but you do not need to perform it each time you design a query (just as you do not execute a Java program manually for every record in a file to make sure that the program is correct). In most cases, queries can be verified by reading them in English, provided that you exercise rigor in their translation from TRC to English. This approach works well in many cases because humans have a certain inbred feeling for logical correctness. However, sometimes the English interpretation can get too complicated for complex queries, and this is where the above verification procedure may help.[1]

To get a better feel for TRC, we consider some queries that ordinarily require join, project, and select in relational algebra. In TRC, such queries require ∃ and AND. To simplify our queries, we slightly extend the syntax to allow more than one tuple variable in the target and to allow mixing of terms of the form *T.attribute* for different tuple variables. For example,

```
{S.Name, T.CrsCode | STUDENT(S) AND TRANSCRIPT(T) AND...}
```

---

[1] It is interesting to compare verifying TRC (or SQL) queries with verifying a Java program. In TRC, programs are short but individual statements are quite powerful. The difficulty is thus in verifying the combined meaning of a small number of powerful statements. In contrast, in Java, each individual command is easy to check but programs are large. It is thus hard to see all the consequences of executing a large number of simple statements.

This extension is just a notational convenience, as we could have written the same query in the old, more restrictive syntax by introducing a new tuple variable, R, with attributes Name and CrsCode.

```
{R | ∃S ∈ STUDENT (∃T ∈ TRANSCRIPT (
      R.Name = S.Name AND R.CrsCode = T.CrsCode AND...))}
```

The query *List the names of all professors who have taught* MGT123 is expressed as

```
{P.Name | PROFESSOR(P) AND
      ∃T ∈ TEACHING (P.Id = T.ProfId AND T.CrsCode = 'MGT123')}
```

Note that this query would involve the selection, projection, and join operators if we tried to express it in relational algebra. The corresponding SQL query is just a syntactic variant.

```
SELECT    P.Name
FROM      PROFESSOR P, TEACHING T
WHERE     P.Id = T.ProfId AND T.CrsCode = 'MGT123'
```

If we wanted the names of professors who had the distinction of teaching Homer Simpson, we would write

```
{P.Name | PROFESSOR(P) AND
      ∃T ∈ TRANSCRIPT (∃S ∈ STUDENT (∃E ∈ TEACHING(
      P.Id = E.ProfId AND T.StudId = S.Id AND
      E.CrsCode = T.CrsCode AND E.Semester = T.Semester
      AND S.Name = 'Homer Simpson')))}
```

The following query finds the Id numbers of all students who have taken the same course twice (but in different semesters):

```
{T.StudId | TRANSCRIPT(T) AND
      ∃T1 ∈ TRANSCRIPT(
           T.StudId = T1.StudId AND T.CrsCode = T1.CrsCode
           AND T.Semester ≠ T1.Semester)}
```

Notice that in this query we are using two tuple variables, one free and one bound, both ranging over TRANSCRIPT. In relational algebra, we would have joined TRANSCRIPT with itself (without using an equijoin).

Let us look at some queries that require the division operator in relational algebra. We have already discussed one such query in detail, query (7.1), which produces a *list of all those courses that have been taken by every student*. In discussing the division operator, we constructed query (6.1), page 139, which yielded *the list of all students who took a course from every professor who ever taught a course*. In TRC, this query is expressed as

```
{R.StudId | ∀T ∈ TEACHING (∃T1 ∈ TEACHING (TRANSCRIPT(R)
      AND T.ProfId = T1.ProfId AND T1.CrsCode = R.CrsCode          (7.4)
      AND T1.Semester = R.Semester))}
```

An explanation is in order here. A particular value of T.ProfId identifies a professor who has taught a course. A particular student, with Id R.StudId, has taken a course with that professor if there exists a tuple, T1, in TEACHING that states that the professor has taught a course (i.e., T.ProfId = T1.ProfId) and that the student has taken the course (i.e., T1.CrsCode = R.CrsCode AND T1.Semester = R.Semester). The student deserves to be in the query result if he or she has taken a course with all such professors (∀T ∈ TEACHING).

This query appears to be slightly more complex than the equivalent algebraic query (6.1). However, in TRC we do not need to introduce special operators to handle such queries (try to write query (6.1) without the division operator!), and the TRC query is more versatile. For instance, if we want to list student names rather than Id numbers, all we have to do is replace S.Id with S.Name. In contrast, in algebra, this would require one extra join with the COURSE relation.

Note that, if we omit the existentially quantified variable T1 and replace it with T in the rest of the query, we get all students who took all course offerings in the university (as opposed to a course from every professor). It is a useful exercise to go over this query and understand how it is different from query (7.4).

The SQL query corresponding to (7.4) is much harder to write because SQL designers considered universal quantifiers hard to use correctly so these quantifiers were eliminated from the language. (We should note, however, that SQL:1999 has introduced a limited form of universal and existential quantification, the FOR ALL and FOR SOME operators.) To compensate for this, SQL was given a number of features, such as nested subqueries and the EXISTS operator, that are even harder to use. Thus, the significant syntactic differences in expressing the above query in TRC and SQL have to do with the need to translate the universal quantifier into an equivalent statement that uses a nested subquery. Unlike SQL, TRC lacks the syntax to support nested subqueries. However, such subqueries can be represented using views, as described later in this section.

There are a few features of TRC queries that are important to note. First, adjacent existential quantifiers commute. Indeed, it does not matter whether we write

∃R ∈ TRANSCRIPT (∃T1 ∈ TEACHING (. . .))

or

∃T1 ∈ TRANSCRIPT (∃R ∈ TEACHING (. . .))

This can be verified using the method for evaluating query conditions given earlier.

Second, universal and existential quantifiers *do not* commute. A moment's reflection should convince us that saying "For every TEACHING tuple there is a TRANSCRIPT tuple such that statement *St* is true" is not the same as saying "There is a TRANSCRIPT tuple such that for all TEACHING tuples *St* is true."

Third, in relational calculus quantifiers are analogous to **begin/end** blocks in that they define the scope of variables. For instance,

$$\forall T \in \mathbf{R}_1 \, (U(T) \ \text{AND} \ \exists T \in \mathbf{R}_2 \, (V(T)))$$

is legal. The two occurrences of the variable *T* appear under the scope of different quantifiers. Therefore, as is the case with identically named variables that occur in nested **begin/end** blocks, these two occurrences are completely independent and the above expression is equivalent to

$$\forall T \in \mathbf{R}_1 \left(U(T) \quad \text{AND} \quad \exists S \in \mathbf{R}_2 \left(V(S) \right) \right)$$

where *S* is some other, new variable.

Views in TRC.   Now, suppose that we want to modify query (7.4) just slightly. Instead of listing students who took a course from *every* professor, we might want to see the students who took a course from *every computer science* professor. This seemingly minor change appears to cause serious difficulties for TRC (but not for the algebra!). The SQL formulation of this query was given in query (6.24), page 152.

Intuitively, the easiest way to modify (7.4) to handle such a query is to replace ∀T ∈ TEACHING with ∀T ∈ CSTEACHING, where CSTEACHING is a subset of TEACHING that corresponds to courses taught by computer science professors. This change is indeed correct *if* we have such a relation. However, such relation does not exist in our database, so we need to find a way around the problem.

We might want to change (7.4) by adding

$$\text{AND } \exists P \in \text{PROFESSOR (P.DeptId = 'CS' AND P.Id = T.ProfId)} \tag{7.5}$$

to the query condition (inside the innermost parentheses), but, unfortunately, this is wrong. Since T ranges over the entire TEACHING relation, the above addition to (7.4) must be true for all values of T.ProfId in TEACHING, which is possible only if every teaching professor in the database works in the Computer Science Department (which is not the case). The correct query is more complex, and it takes some patience to understand why.

```
{R.StudId | ∀T ∈ TEACHING (∃T1 ∈ TEACHING (TRANSCRIPT(R) AND
    NOT (∃P ∈ PROFESSOR (P.DeptId = 'CS' AND P.Id = T.ProfId))
      OR (T.ProfId = T1.ProfId AND T1.CrsCode = R.CrsCode          (7.6)
        AND T1.Semester = R.Semester)))}
```

The condition says that the value of R must be an element of TRANSCRIPT, and either T.ProfId is not a CS professor or R.StudId has taken a course with T.ProfId.

Fortunately, there is a simpler way to achieve the same result. Let us return to our first attempt: trying to use ∀T ∈ CSTEACHING. The problem here is that the seemingly natural relation CSTEACHING is not in our original database. However, we can *define* it using a query. We define a simpler relation instead.

```
CSPROF = {P.ProfId | PROFESSOR(P) AND P.DeptId = 'CS'}
```

which we can now use as a database view (or as a "subroutine") in a larger query.

```
{R.StudId | ∀P ∈ CSPROF (∃T1 ∈ TEACHING (TRANSCRIPT(R)
        AND P.ProfId = T1.ProfId AND T1.CrsCode = R.CrsCode     (7.7)
          AND T1.Semester = R.Semester))}
```

In fact, the complex query (7.6) is a TRC analog of taking query (7.7) and substituting in the definition of the view CSPROF. The complex result of such a substitution is not really surprising—think what would happen to a Java program if all subroutines were substituted in! A quick look at our examples of algebraic queries reveals extensive use of such subroutines, which is why some of those queries seem simpler than their TRC counterparts.

7.2 UNDERSTANDING SQL THROUGH TUPLE RELATIONAL CALCULUS

We have seen that SQL is essentially the language of tuple relational calculus, generously sprinkled with noise words whose intention is to hide the relationship to predicate logic.[2]

Beyond the pedigree, TRC is important for SQL because understanding it can help in writing complex SQL queries. Some SQL books rely on relational algebra to provide meaning to general SQL queries (as we did in Chapter 6). Unfortunately, the algebraic expressions are neither more intuitive than the equivalent TRC queries nor helpful with more advanced SQL. Indeed, translating the SQL queries of Section 6.2.3, which have nested subqueries, into algebra is not a straightforward task. More important, relational algebra is not a good vehicle to help translate SQL database queries into English to verify that they will function as intended.

Although an English description is not as formal as a mathematical specification, it has the advantage that both the customer and the programmer can easily understand it and hence confirm together that it corresponds to their intentions. The question then arises as to whether a given SQL query satisfies its English specification. We can reason as follows. An SQL query satisfies its English specification if and only if

1. For every tuple, t, that must be in the query result according to the English formulation, there is a way to assign tuples to the tuple variables mentioned in the FROM clause so that these tuples satisfy the WHERE condition and the query target list evaluates to t (after those tuples are substituted for the tuple variables).

2. Every tuple produced by the SQL query is in the result of the English formulation.

The main difficulty in applying these conditions is determining what it means for a particular assignment of tuples to variables to satisfy a WHERE condition. One can rely on intuition in simple cases, but this becomes increasingly error prone for more complex SQL queries, such as (6.24) on page 152.

---

[2] Back in the 1970s, when the first relational systems were being designed in research labs, there was hope that relational–calculus-based languages might be able to offer a sufficiently high level of programming that even nontechnical users, such as a company CEO, might be able to use them. Needless to say, even twenty years later this vision has not been fulfilled, while SQL keeps getting more and more complex with every new release.

Fortunately, this difficulty is resolvable because of the close correspondence between SQL and TRC. Given an SQL query, the idea is to first construct an equivalent TRC query that is then translated into English. As TRC is much closer to SQL than to English, there is a better chance to do the first step correctly. The next step, the translation of TRC to English, is actually a well-defined process (explained in many textbooks on predicate logic), which can be performed by a computer.

In this way, the problem of verifying SQL queries is reduced to the problem of translating SQL into TRC. For simple cases, this translation is easy, as illustrated earlier. We now illustrate the idea with a more complex example of an SQL query with a nested subquery. Consider the following query template, where, for definiteness, we assume that the attributes of REL1 are A, B and the attributes of REL2 are C, D, and that REL3 and REL4 have the attributes E, F and G, H, respectively.

```
SELECT   R1.A, R2.C
FROM     REL1 R1, REL2 R2
WHERE    Condition1(R1, R2) AND                              (7.8)
      R1.B IN (SELECT R3.E
                  FROM REL3 R3, REL4 R4
                  WHERE Condition2(R2,R3,R4))
```

In this template, the variables R3 and R4 are local to the subquery and the variables R1 and R2 are global. In addition, the WHERE condition in the subquery uses the variables R2,R3,R4 (which is what the notation Condition2(R2,R3,R4) is supposed to convey). Because R2 is a global variable used by Condition2, it parameterizes the inner subquery.

We assume that Condition1 is of the form palatable to TRC (i.e., it is a legal selection condition in relational algebra). However, the nested subquery is obviously not of the form TRC understands. Nevertheless, the translation into TRC is straightforward. To see this, recall the discussion of relational views on page 185.

Let us represent the inner subquery in (7.8) as a view—i.e., a named virtual relation (call it TEMP)—whose contents are not stored but rather computed by a query. One subtlety needs to be taken care of here: What is the right set of attributes to use with TEMP? We cannot take only the attributes from the target list of the inner subquery (i.e., E), because the inner subquery (and hence its result) is *parameterized* by the global variable R2. Recall that the free variables in the condition are those named in the target list (since the condition must evaluate to true or false once values of the target variables have been substituted). R2 must be free because it is assigned a value in the outer query. Therefore, the proper set of attributes for TEMP must include the attributes of REL2 (C and D) in addition to the attributes of the inner subquery's target list (i.e., E).[3] This reasoning leads to the following view definition for TEMP:

$$\text{TEMP} = \{\text{R3.E, R2.C, R2.D} \mid \text{REL2(R2) AND REL3(R3)}$$
$$\text{AND } \exists\text{R4}\in\text{REL4 } (\textit{Condition2}(\text{R2,R3,R4}))\} \tag{7.9}$$

The variables R2 and R3 are free here, but R4 must be quantified because it does not occur in the query target list.

Now the translation from (7.8) to TRC is

$$\{\text{R1.A, R2.C} \mid \text{REL1(R1) AND REL2(R2) AND } \textit{Condition1} \text{ AND}$$
$$\exists\text{R}\in\text{TEMP } (\text{R.E = R1.B AND R.C = R2.C} \tag{7.10}$$
$$\text{AND R.D = R2.D})$$

How does this TRC query express the condition R1.B IN (SELECT R3.E...)? Through the equality $\text{R.E} = \text{R1.B}$. Indeed, the assignment of tuple $\langle a,b\rangle$ to R1 and of tuple $\langle c,d\rangle$ to R2 satisfies the condition in (7.10) if and only if these tuples belong to the relations REL1 and REL2, respectively, and $\langle b,c,d\rangle$ is a tuple in TEMP—the relation representing the inner subquery in (7.8). But b is the value of R1.B, which means that b must be in the result of the inner subquery.

As another example, consider the more complex query (6.24) on page 152 that returns the Ids of all students who have taken a course from every professor in the Computer Science Department. Here we have to construct two views, one for each subquery of (6.24). The first view, CSPROF, is straightforward:

$$\text{CSPROF} = \{\text{P.ProfId} \mid \text{PROFESSOR(P) AND P.Dept ='CS'}\}$$

The result of this view is the set of Ids of all professors in the Computer Science Department. The second subquery of (6.24) returns the set of Ids of all professors who have taught a course taken by the student with Id R.StudId, where R is a variable that parameterizes the subquery. As explained earlier, the TRC view that corresponds to such a subquery must include R in the target list:

$$\text{PROFSTUD} = \{\text{T.ProfId, R.StudId} \mid \text{TEACHING(T) AND TRANSCRIPT(R) AND}$$
$$\exists\text{R1}\in\text{TRANSCRIPT } (\text{T.CrsCode = R1.CrsCode AND}$$
$$\text{T.Semester = R1.Semester AND}$$
$$\text{R.StudId = R1.StudId})\}$$

Finally, the whole of query (6.24) can be rephrased as follows: We are looking for those students, s, such that there does not exist professor c in CSPROF for whom the tuple $\langle c,s\rangle$ is not in PROFSTUD. Expressing this query in TRC is a bit cumbersome.

$$\{\text{S.StudId} \mid \text{STUDENT(S) AND NOT } (\exists\text{C}\in\text{CSPROF } (\text{NOT}(\exists\text{P}\in\text{PROFSTUD}$$
$$(\text{P.ProfId = C.ProfId AND P.StudId = S.StudId})))\}$$

---

[3] As a matter of fact, we need to include only those attributes of REL2 that are *actually used* in *Condition2*. That is, if *Condition2* uses R2.C but not R2.D, then R2.D need not be included in the attribute set of TEMP (but including it does no harm).

This expression can be simplified if we recall that in the standard logic NOT ∃X NOT is equivalent to ∀X:

{S.StudId | STUDENT(S) AND ∀C∈CSPROF ∃P∈PROFSTUD
(P.ProfId = C.ProfId AND P.StudId = S.StudId)}

In English this statement reads as follows: *A student Id,* s, *is in the result of this query if and only if, for every computer science professor,* c, *the tuple* ⟨c, s⟩ *is in the view* PROFSTUD; *that is,* c *has taught* s.

Now compare this with the original English formulation of (6.24): *Find all students who took a course from every professor in the* CS *department.* These two sentences have exactly the same meaning, which means that our complex SQL query has been validated.

7.3 DOMAIN RELATIONAL CALCULUS AND VISUAL QUERY LANGUAGES

Tuple relational calculus has become the basis of textual database query languages such as SQL. The other flavor of relational calculus, **domain relational calculus** (*DRC*), has become the basis of visual query languages such as IBM Query-By-Example and languages for PC databases such as Microsoft Access and Borland Paradox.[4]

DRC is quite similar to TRC. The main difference is that it uses **domain variables** rather than tuple variables in its queries. Recall that a tuple consists of a set of named attributes, each of which takes its values from some domain. A domain variable takes its values from the domain of some attribute. For example, a TEACHING relation might have an attribute named ProfId, with a domain consisting of valid Id numbers. Then Pid might be a domain variable, which takes its values from the domain of valid Id numbers.

As with TRC, the output of a DRC query is a relation and the general form of a DRC query is:

$$\{X_1, \ldots, X_n \mid Condition\}$$

where $X_1, \ldots, X_n$ is a list of (not necessarily distinct) domain variables, which form the **target** part of the query, and *Condition* is the query condition, which looks much the same as in TRC. Here is an example:

{Pid, Code | TEACHING(Pid,Code,F1997)}

This is essentially the same as the TRC query

{T | TEACHING(T) AND T.Semester = 'F1997'}

but it is simpler because we can put the constant F1997 directly into the condition TEACHING(Pid, Code, F1997), thereby eliminating the need for the conjunct

---

[4] There is nothing inherent in TRC or DRC that makes one formalism more suitable than the other for a particular query language. The choice of TRC as a foundation for SQL is merely a historical accident.

`T.Semester = 'F1997'`. Such substitution often makes DRC queries more compact and easier to understand than their TRC equivalents.

Because DRC and TRC are so close, many of the features and techniques they employ are either identical or very similar. Therefore, we do not discuss DRC at the same level of detail as we did TRC.

Syntax of DRC query conditions.   The general syntax of query conditions in DRC follows the outline of TRC. The basic building blocks have one of the following forms:

■ $\mathbf{P}(X_1, \ldots, X_n)$, where $\mathbf{P}$ is a relation name and $X_1, \ldots, X_n$ are domain variables. Intuitively, $\mathbf{P}(X_1, \ldots, X_n)$ represents a test of whether the tuple $\langle X_1, \ldots, X_n \rangle$ belongs to the relation instance of $\mathbf{P}$ (as in TRC, this expression is evaluated under a particular choice of values for $X_1, \ldots, X_n$). Example: STUDENT(Sid, N, A, S).

■ X oper Y, where oper is a comparison operator ($=, >, \geq, \neq$, etc.) and X and Y are domain variables. The intended meaning here is a comparison of the value of X against the value of Y. Example: `Sid ≥ Pid`. Note that since domain variables represent tuple components directly, we do not need to prefix X and Y with relation names as in TRC (for example, `A.Sid = B.Pid`).

■ X oper *const*, which is similar to the previous form, but here the comparison is with a constant rather than a variable. Example: $X = $ `'F1994'`.

These basic building blocks are called **atomic conditions**. More complex query conditions are constructed recursively as follows:

■ C is a query condition if it is an atomic condition.

■ If C_1 and C_2 are query conditions, C_1 AND C_2, C_1 OR C_2, and NOT C_1 are also query conditions.

■ If C is a query condition, $\mathbf{R}$ is a relation name, and X is a domain variable, then $\forall X \in \mathbf{R}.A(C)$ and $\exists X \in \mathbf{R}.A(C)$ are query conditions.

The quantifiers here are similar to those in TRC with one difference: The expression $\mathbf{R}.A$ denotes column A of relation $\mathbf{R}$, and the variable X ranges over the values that occur in that column. In other words, $\forall X \in \mathbf{R}.A$ (C) says that *for all* values that occur in column A of relation $\mathbf{R}$ (in the current database instance), the condition C must be true. The expression $\exists X \in \mathbf{R}.A$ (C) says that there is *at least one* value, x, in column $\mathbf{R}.A$ such that C becomes true if x is substituted for all occurrences of X.

The rules for free and bound variables are the same as those in TRC, and, as in TRC, the target variables are the only ones allowed to occur free in the query condition. To make the rules a bit more flexible, we allow constants to occur in the target as well. To summarize, in

$$\{X_1, \ldots, X_n \mid \textit{Condition}\} \tag{7.11}$$

each X_i, for $i = 1, \ldots, n$, is either a free variable that occurs in *Condition* or a constant. No other variable occurs free in *Condition*.

The *result* of query (7.11) on a given database is defined similarly to that of a TRC query: It is the set of *all* choices of tuples $\langle x_1, \ldots, x_n \rangle$ such that when x_1 is substituted for X_1, x_2 is substituted for X_2, and so on, *Condition* evaluates to true. If some X_i is a constant, no substitution occurs: The query result has this constant in the ith position in all tuples.

Examples. To illustrate the use of DRC and to highlight the differences between it and TRC, we use the same suite of queries as that used to illustrate relational algebra and TRC.

DRC queries often use more variables than do their TRC counterparts because DRC variables range over simple values, whereas TRC variables range over tuples. Thus, one TRC variable effectively stands for several DRC variables. As a result, DRC queries tend to use more quantifiers. However, the notation can be made more succinct in several ways. One is to introduce the **universal domain**, $\mathcal{U}$, which contains all values in all domains and instead of writing $\exists X \in \mathcal{U}$ (*Condition*) use a shorthand, $\exists X$ (*Condition*).

One reason why the universal domain is useful is that any expression of the form $\exists X \in \mathbf{R}.A_i(\mathbf{R}(\ldots, X, \ldots)\ldots)$, where A_i is the attribute of $\mathbf{R}$ that corresponds to the occurrence of X, is equivalent to $\exists X(\mathbf{R}(\ldots, X, \ldots)\ldots)$. In other words, we can replace the domain $\mathbf{R}.A_i$ with the universal domain $\mathcal{U}$. Certainly, $\mathcal{U}$ contains $\mathbf{R}.A_i$, but it can be much larger. However, any choice, x, for X that is outside of $\mathbf{R}.A_i$ cannot make $\exists X(\mathbf{R}(\ldots, X, \ldots)\ldots)$ into a true statement, since in order for $\mathbf{R}(\ldots, x, \ldots)$ to be true, x must be the value of A_i in some tuple in an instance of $\mathbf{R}$ and hence, x must belong to the domain of $\mathbf{R}.A_i$, for some i.

Let us now turn to the example queries of Section 7.1. The DRC equivalent of the query *List all names of professors who taught* MGT123 is

```
{N | ∃I∈Professor.Id ∃D∈Professor.DeptId (
            Professor(I,N,D) AND
            ∃S∈Teaching.Semester (Teaching(I, MGT123, S)))}
```

A cursory look at this query makes the utility of the universal domain apparent: Dropping the long domain names makes the query much shorter. We take advantage of this property in the following examples.

The next query returns the names of all professors who ever taught Homer Simpson.

```
{Pname | ∃Grd ∃Pid ∃Dept (Professor(Pid, Pname, Dept) AND
            ∃Grd ∃Crs ∃Sem ∃Sid ∃Addr ∃Stat (Teaching(Pid, Crs, Sem)
                AND Transcript(Sid, Crs, Sem, Grd)
                AND Student(Sid, Homer Simpson, Addr, Stat)))
```

It is instructive to compare the above two queries with their TRC counterparts. DRC queries typically require more quantified variables but fewer components of the form $\mathbf{R}_1.Attr_1 = \mathbf{R}_2.Attr_2$. However, commercial database languages built on top of DRC and TRC do not use quantifiers explicitly. Instead, all variables that *do not occur explicitly* in the target list of the query are assumed to be *implicitly quantified* with ∃ and range over the universal domain. Using this convention, all quantifiers in the above DRC queries can be dropped. So, for example, the second query becomes

```
{Pname | (PROFESSOR(Pid, Pname, Dept)
          AND TEACHING(Pid,Crs,Sem)
          AND TRANSCRIPT(Sid, Crs, Sem, Grd)
          AND STUDENT(Sid, Homer Simpson, Addr, Stat))}
```

In contrast, TRC quantifiers cannot be dropped without further adjustments to the query, because in some cases we might lose useful information about the corresponding quantified variables. To illustrate, let us revisit the TRC query about professors who taught MGT123.

```
{P.Name | PROFESSOR(P) AND
          ∃T∈TEACHING (P.Id = T.ProfId AND T.CrsCode = 'MGT123')}
```

Here, dropping ∃T ∈ TEACHING would leave T "undeclared," in the terminology of programming languages because we lose the information that the range of T is TEACHING. Range information is not lost in DRC, because undeclared variables are assumed to range over the universal domain. However, noticing that ∃T ∈ TEACHING (...) is equivalent to ∃T ∈ TEACHING (TEACHING(T) AND ...), we can rewrite the query as

```
{P.Name | PROFESSOR(P) AND
          TEACHING(T) AND P.Id = T.ProfId AND T.CrsCode = 'MGT123'}
```

This formulation is correct if we assume that the non-target variable T is implicitly quantified with ∃.

When existential quantifiers are dropped in either DRC or TRC there is potential ambiguity when ∃ and ∀ both occur in the same query. For example, consider ∀Y(LIKES(X,Y)), where LIKES(X,Y) means that X likes Y. The convention that X is implicitly quantified with ∃ still leaves us with a dilemma: Does this expression mean ∀Y∃X (LIKES)(X,Y) or ∃X∀YLIKES(X,Y)? A moment's reflection shows that these two expressions correspond to two very different English sentences: *Every* Y *is liked by some* X and *some* X *likes every* Y. Hence, in some cases quantification cannot be dropped. This ambiguity does not arise in SQL—it does not allow the use of ∀ because of the difficulties associated with optimizing such queries.[5] Instead, programmers are forced to jump through hoops if they need to ask queries that require ∀ or the division operator.

We studied techniques for overcoming this deficiency of SQL in Section 6.2, but before you are forced into the straightjacket of real-world languages, you can taste

---

[5] SQL: 1999 introduces a limited form of universal quantification.

freedom one last time and see how to use DRC to express our venerable query *Find all students who took a course from every professor*.

$$\{\texttt{Sid} \mid \forall \texttt{Pid}{\in}\textsc{Teaching}.\texttt{ProfId} \; (\exists \texttt{Crs} \; \exists \texttt{Sem} \; \exists \texttt{Grd} \; ($$
$$\textsc{Teaching}(\texttt{Pid, Crs, Sem}) \; \texttt{AND} \qquad\qquad (7.12)$$
$$\textsc{Transcript}(\texttt{Sid, Crs, Sem, Grd})))\}$$

This DRC query is substantially simpler than the corresponding SQL query (6.24), page 152, and the TRC query (7.4) on page 183. In particular, it is not necessary to have TEACHING mentioned twice. (Recall that in TRC TEACHING must occur twice for a nonobvious reason.) Note that in (7.12) we use $\exists$ explicitly, to avoid the ambiguity that arises when $\forall$ and $\exists$ occur in the same query.

One additional point is worth mentioning: We cannot replace the domain TEACHING.ProfId of the variable Pid with the universal domain $\mathcal{U}$. In general, $\forall X \in \mathbf{R}.A_i \; (\mathbf{R}(\dots, X, \dots))$ is *not* equivalent to $\forall X(\mathbf{R}(\dots, X, \dots))$. Using $\mathcal{U}$ instead of TEACHING.ProfId means that, in order for a particular value, sid, to be in the result of query (7.12), the condition TEACHING(pid, crs, sem) AND TRANSCRIPT(sid, crs, sem, grd) must be true for *all* values pid in $\mathcal{U}$ and for some values crs, sem, grd. This is clearly impossible when pid is a value in $\mathcal{U}$ that does not correspond to any professor Id ($\mathcal{U}$ must have such values, since it properly contains TEACHING.ProfId). However, as discussed earlier, in $\exists X \in \mathbf{R}.A_i$ domain $\mathbf{R}.A_i$ can be replaced with $\mathcal{U}$.

7.4 VISUAL QUERY LANGUAGES: QBE AND PC DATABASES

QBE (Query-by-Example) was the first widely acclaimed visual query language. Like SQL it was developed at IBM and at about the same time [Zloof 1975]. QBE is part of IBM's DB2 relational database product, and several other vendors have developed QBE clones. However, the greatest success of visual query languages came with the advent of PC databases, such as Borland Paradox and Microsoft Access.

In this section, we review QBE. Our goal here is to emphasize concepts, not to provide an exhaustive reference. At the end of the section, we briefly discuss Microsoft Access, whose interface is also based on domain calculus but more loosely than is QBE.

The basics of QBE.   QBE is one of the best illustrations of how a purely theoretical tool, the domain calculus, can be put to practical use. The main idea behind QBE is that the user (who is not necessarily a programmer) specifies a query by choosing relation templates from a menu and then filling these templates with "example tuples" that specify the desired answer. The example tuples in QBE consist of variables and constants, but even variables are made to look like "examples of constants"—QBE avoids programming notation as much as possible.[6]

---

[6] QBE goes out of its way to eliminate any semblance of programming terminology. It calls constants "example values" and variables "example elements."

Suppose that you want to find all professors in the MGT department. In QBE, you select a template corresponding to the PROFESSOR relation and then fill in the example tuple as follows:

PROFESSOR	Id	Name	DeptId
		P._John	MGT

It should be apparent that this QBE query is just a different, visual representation for the textual DRC query {Name | ∃I PROFESSOR(I, Name, MGT)}. The symbol _John is a domain variable in disguise, while MGT is a constant. Even though these two symbols might look similar to an unsuspecting user, the prefix _ betrays the special status of _John as a glorified variable. Furthermore, the operator **P.** meaning *print* indicates that _John is a target variable in the sense of relational calculus since it is output by the print command. QBE uses several operators, usually represented by a keyword followed with a period, but in this overview we use mainly **P.** —the mother of all QBE operators, which separates target variables from the rest.

Earlier we mentioned that commercial query languages do not quantify variables explicitly and, surely, we do not find quantifiers in QBE queries. Instead, all nontarget variables are assumed to be implicitly quantified with ∃. However, QBE goes one step further: Some nontarget variables, such as I in the DRC version of the above query, can be omitted. When this happens, the system invents a unique variable name and automatically substitutes it in.

In fact, even the variable _John is not necessary and we could drop it without affecting the final result. In that case the Name column contains just **P.** Thus, **P.** can occur in a query as a standalone operator. If the query result must be a relation with two or more attributes, we can put **P.** in several places in the query. If all attributes of a relation are to be output, we can put **P.** directly under the relation name instead of in each column.

PROFESSOR	Id	Name	DeptId
P.			MGT

Joins and advanced queries. The above query does not explicitly mention *any* variable. However, in general we cannot get away without using variables. If a variable needs to be mentioned twice or more in a query, it represents an equality between attributes in the same or different tuples and therefore cannot be omitted. This situation arises most often in specifying an equijoin. The following is a QBE version of the familiar query, *List all names of professors who taught* MGT123:

PROFESSOR	Id	Name	DeptId
	_123456789	P. _John	

TEACHING	ProfId	CrsCode	Semester
	_123456789	MGT123	

Here, _John is a target variable, as before, and _123456789 is a variable that is implicitly quantified with ∃. It is used in the query to specify an equijoin of two tables and therefore cannot be omitted. (In contrast, _John can be omitted, as before.)

We have seen that QBE lets the user specify simple selections simply by putting appropriate constants in the templates. QBE goes one step further by allowing the following syntax, which finds all professor names with Ids greater than the specified constant.

PROFESSOR	Id	Name	DeptId
	> 123456789	P.	

(Note the difference between the constant 123456789 and the variable _123456789.) However, more complex selections or join conditions cannot be specified in this way, so QBE provides a special template, called a **conditions box**, in which the user can write arbitrarily complex selection and join conditions using a syntax similar to that of relational algebra. For instance, to obtain the Ids of all students who have taken CS305 and received A or B, we can write

TRANSCRIPT	StudId	CrsCode	Semester	Grade		CONDITIONS
	P.	CS305		_G		_G = A OR _G = B

Since the result of a QBE query is a relation, there are certain restrictions on where the **P.** operator can occur. In particular, to avoid the possibility that **P.** is placed under two identically named attributes in different relational templates, QBE requires that all occurrences of **P.** must be in the same template.[7] How, then, can we specify the query *Find all professors together with the students they taught*? Since professors and students are stored in different relations, it does not appear possible to answer this query if all occurrences of **P.** are to appear in just one of the templates.

One solution is to allow users to construct *new* templates, so that they will not be restricted to just the templates of the relations that already exist in the database. To answer the above query, a user uses the menu system to define a new template, HASTAUGHT, as follows:

HASTAUGHT	Prof	Stud
I.	_123456789	_987654321

---

[7] This is a fairly serious restriction introduced to solve a relatively minor problem.

TRANSCRIPT	StudId	CrsCode	Semester	Grade
	_987654321	_CS305	_F1996	

TEACHING	ProfId	CrsCode	Semester
	_123456789	_CS305	_F1996

The operator **I.** (meaning *insert*) in the template HASTAUGHT specifies the tuples that should populate the corresponding table. The user can then query HASTAUGHT using the **P.** operator as follows:

HASTAUGHT	Prof	Stud
P.		

The price of a free lunch.   The earlier examples showed that the right choice of visual primitives and conventions can make the domain relational calculus accessible even to a nonspecialist. Unfortunately, as often happens in language design, features that make some things easy make other things hard. In the case of database query languages, the price is usually expressive power—that is, the inability to specify certain types of queries—or the awkwardness associated with doing so. In the case of QBE (and, in fact, SQL as well), the price is paid when one needs to ask queries that involve the division operator, such as *Find all courses taken by every student known to the database*. We will return to this query shortly.

Since QBE does not provide the universal quantifier ∀, it uses the *negation* operator to construct ¬∃¬ which is the same thing. To illustrate, let us consider the query *List all professors who did not teach any course in fall 1995*. In DRC this query can be stated either as

```
{Name|PROFESSOR (Id, Name, DeptId)
          AND ∀CrsCode (NOT(TEACHING (Id, CrsCode, F1995)))}
```

or as

```
{Name|PROFESSOR (Id, Name, DeptId)
          AND NOT (∃CrsCode (TEACHING (Id, CrsCode, F1995)))}
```

In both cases we have assumed that Id and DeptId are existentially quantified. QBE chooses the second formulation, which appears as

PROFESSOR	Id	Name	DeptId
	_123456789	**P.**	

TEACHING	ProfId	CrsCode	Semester
¬	_123456789		F1995

The symbol ¬ denotes the negation operator, and it occurs in the TEACHING template since we are requiring that there be no rows in TEACHING that match a particular Id in PROFESSOR. This negation roughly corresponds to set difference. The first template produces the names of all professors in the PROFESSOR relation and the second removes from that set those professors who taught a course in fall 1995. This query looks simple enough, but there are pitfalls. Previously, we said that all variables in QBE are implicitly quantified with ∃ and that the blank columns in the templates are really filled with system-generated variables (which are also implicitly quantified with ∃). Not so with negated example tuples! Indeed, if the system-generated variable, for example, _Crs123, that implicitly occurs in the column CrsCode were existentially quantified, we would have the following query:

$$\{\text{Name} \mid \exists\text{Id}\ \exists\text{DeptId}\ \exists\text{CrsCode}($$
$$\text{PROFESSOR(Id, Name, DeptId) AND}$$
$$\text{NOT TEACHING(Id, CrsCode, 'F1995'))}\}$$

This query returns an Id, say, 111111111, if there is a course, for example MGT123, such that the row ⟨111111111, MGT123, F1995⟩ is *not* in TEACHING. That is, it returns the Ids of all professors who did not teach *some* course in F1995—a different query than the one we posed! A correct formulation is

$$\{\text{Name} \mid \exists\text{Id}\ \exists\text{DeptId}\ \forall\text{CrsCode}($$
$$\text{PROFESSOR(Id, Name, DeptId) AND} \tag{7.13}$$
$$\text{NOT TEACHING(Id, CrsCode, 'F1995'))}\}$$

That is, the desired quantification of _Crs123 is universal.

The uncertainty of proper quantification of variables in negated tuples was an early source of semantic problems in QBE. Eventually, it was decided to assume all system-generated variables in negated tuples to be implicitly quantified with ∀. The reason behind this decision was the belief that, as in the previous example, universal quantification is what the user wants in most cases.

Unfortunately, this simple convention still does not completely resolve the issue because, as we already know, ∃ and ∀ do not commute. So there is a question of the order in which to arrange the quantification prefix. For instance, in (7.13) we could have ordered the quantifiers differently and obtained a different query:

$$\{\text{Name} \mid \forall\text{CrsCode}\ \exists\text{Id}\ \exists\text{DeptId}($$
$$\text{PROFESSOR(Id, Name, DeptId) AND} \tag{7.14}$$
$$\text{NOT TEACHING(Id, CrsCode, 'F1995'))}\}$$

It finds all professor names with the following property: For every course, there is a professor with that name who did not teach that particular course.

In the end, the semantics of QBE was resolved so that the quantification prefix is ordered in such a way that the existential quantifiers go first. Thus, the previous QBE query must be interpreted as (7.13).

Now that we understand negation in QBE, the query about the courses taken by every student can be expressed as follows. First, we need to find courses that have not been taken by at least one student. The relation containing all such courses, which we call NotAnswer, is constructed as follows:

NotAnswer	CrsCode
I.	_MGT111

Course	CrsCode	CrsName	Descr
	_MGT111		

Student	Id	Name	Status	Address
	_123456789			

Transcript	StudId	CrsCode	Semester	Grade
¬	_123456789	_MGT111		

Again, we used the insert operator to specify the tuples we wanted inserted into the relation NotAnswer. Thus, the contents of NotAnswer are described by the DRC query

$$
\begin{aligned}
&\{CrsCode \mid \exists CrsName\ \exists Descr\ \exists Id\ \exists Name\ \exists Status\ \exists Address \\
&\qquad \forall Semester\ \forall Grade (\\
&\qquad\qquad \text{Course}(CrsCode,\ CrsName,\ Descr)\ \text{AND} \\
&\qquad\qquad\qquad \text{Student}(Id,\ Name,\ Status,\ Address)\ \text{AND} \\
&\qquad\qquad\qquad \text{NOT\ Transcript}(Id,\ CrsCode,\ Semester,\ Grade))\}
\end{aligned}
$$
(7.15)

Finally, to obtain the answer to the original query we need to subtract NotAnswer from Course.

NotAnswer	CrsCode
¬	_MGT111

Course	CrsCode	CrsName	Descr
	_MGT111	P.	

Although we have covered most of its features, QBE has several aspects that we did not discuss (or mentioned only briefly). For instance, it has a very convenient data definition sublanguage, whose visual appearance is consistent with the query sublanguage. It also supports aggregate functions, such as counting, and averages, which are provided to the user in the form of operators (COUNT, AVG., etc.). Aggregate functions were discussed in detail in Section 6.2, although the focus there was on SQL, not QBE. Finally, we have seen the operator **I.**, which is a part of the data manipulation sublanguage of QBE. Similar operators are used to delete and modify tuples.

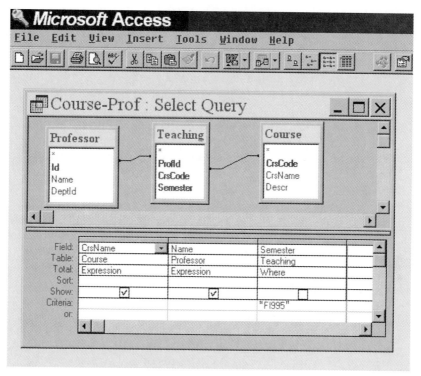

Figure 7.1 A visual query in Microsoft Access.

PC databases.   Conceptually, if you have seen one visual query language, you have seen them all. The main difference between QBE and Borland Paradox or Microsoft Access lies in the details of the graphical interface. Figure 7.1 depicts a query specified in the Access "design mode." The query returns all courses offered in fall 1995 along with the names of the professors who taught them.

Access tries hard to hide its relational calculus origins. To specify an equijoin, instead of using variables, the user drags one attribute into another, creating the graphical links seen in the figure, which represent join conditions (e.g., PROFESSOR.Id = TEACHING.ProfId). Access has an analog of QBE's conditions box (e.g., the criterion that TEACHING.Semester = 'F1995'). This box is used much more heavily than in QBE, particularly to specify things that QBE does with the help of operators, such as **P.** (See the line labeled "Show:" in Figure 7.1).

All in all, QBE is more flexible than Access and generally more intuitive to database specialists who are familiar with relational languages. However, for the drag-and-drop generation Access design mode is easier to use, at least for simple queries.

7.5   THE RELATIONSHIP BETWEEN RELATIONAL ALGEBRA AND THE CALCULI

We have presented a detailed overview of relational algebra and the two relational calculi. We have seen that some queries look simpler in one language than they do in another. A natural question is whether there are queries that can be written in only one of the languages.

Note that this is not an idle theoretic question. Recall that DBMSs use relational algebra as an intermediate code to which SQL queries are translated in order to be optimized. If TRC could express more queries than the algebra, some SQL queries possibly would not have algebraic counterparts and thus would be unimplementable. Similarly, if DRC could express more queries than TRC, it could be a better platform on which to base database languages.

The answer to the above question is that all three languages have exactly the same expressive power: Queries that can be asked in one language can also be asked in another—or almost so. In truth, the calculi are more expressive, but this added expressiveness is of little use in practical database queries.

To explain, consider the query $\{T \mid \text{NOT } Q(T)\}$, a request to return all tuples that are *not* in relation **Q**. Intuitively, this is not the kind of question normally asked about the data in a database. But, more important to our discussion, it has a very strange property. For example, suppose that **Q** is a relation that contains a set of student names and that the domain of names is CHAR(20). Then the result of $\{T \mid \text{NOT } Q(T)\}$ is the set of all strings up to 20 characters long, except those in **Q**. Now, suppose that the domain of names is later changed to become the set of all strings up to 30 characters long. Then the answer to the above query changes, even though the database instance does not!

Another situation where the answer to a query depends on the domain might arise when the query condition contains a disjunction. For instance, $\{T \mid \exists S(Q(T) \text{ OR } R(S))\}$ returns the set of all tuples in **Q** if **R** is an empty relation. However, if **R** contains even one tuple, the answer to this query is the set of all possible n-ary tuples, where n is the number of attributes in **Q**. In this case, then, the query answer depends on the domains of the attributes of **Q**.

Database queries whose result *does not* change when their domains change are called **domain-independent**. Exercise 7.4 shows that the queries expressed using relational algebra are always domain-independent. However, we have just seen that it is possible to use relational calculus to express a domain-dependent query. Even so, it turns out that

> Every domain-independent query in either one of the calculi has a translation into an equivalent query written in relational algebra, and vice versa.

The first part of this statement is not exactly obvious. A proof appears in [Ullman 1988]. However, the other direction, a translation from algebra into calculus, is easy and a worthwhile exercise, because it shows how the operators of relational algebra relate to the constructs in the relational calculi.

◼ *Selection*

> **Algebra:** $\sigma_{Condition}(\mathbf{R})$
>
> **TRC:** $\{T \mid \mathbf{R}(T) \text{ AND } Condition_1\}$
>
> **DRC:** $\{X_1, \ldots, X_n \mid \mathbf{R}(X_1, \ldots, X_n) \text{ AND } Condition_2\}$

In TRC, $Condition_1$ is obtained from $Condition$ by replacing attributes with the appropriate components of T. For instance, if $Condition$ is A = B AND C = d, where A, B, C are attributes and d is a constant, then $Condition_1$ is $T.A = T.B$ AND $T.C = d$.

In DRC, $Condition_2$ is obtained by replacing the attributes that occur in $Condition$ with appropriate variables. For instance, if A is the first attribute of $\mathbf{R}$, B is the second, and C is the third, then $Condition_2$ is $X_1 = X_2$ AND $X_3 = d$.

◼ *Projection*

> **Algebra:** $\pi_{A,B,C}(\mathbf{R})$
>
> **TRC:** $\{T.A, T.B, T.C \mid \mathbf{R}(T)\}$
>
> **DRC:** $\{X, Y, Z \mid \exists V \exists W(\mathbf{R}(X, Y, Z, V, W))\}.$

Here we assume that $\mathbf{R}$ has five attributes and that A, B, C are the first three.

◼ *Cartesian product*

> **Algebra:** $\mathbf{R} \times \mathbf{S}$
>
> **TRC:** $\{T.A, T.B, T.C, V.D, V.E \mid \mathbf{R}(T) \text{ AND } \mathbf{S}(V)\}.$

We assume, for definiteness, that $\mathbf{R}$ has attributes A,B,C and that $\mathbf{S}$ has attributes D, E.

> **DRC:** $\{X, Y, Z, V, W \mid \mathbf{R}(X, Y, Z) \text{ AND } \mathbf{S}(V, W)\}$

◼ *Union*

> **Algebra:** $\mathbf{R} \cup \mathbf{S}$
>
> **TRC:** $\{T \mid \mathbf{R}(T) \text{ OR } \mathbf{S}(T)\}$
>
> **DRC:** $\{X_1, \ldots, X_n \mid \mathbf{R}(X_1, \ldots, X_n) \text{ OR } \mathbf{S}(X_1, \ldots, X_n)\}$

Note that since $\mathbf{R}$ and $\mathbf{S}$ must be union-compatible for the $\cup$ operator to make sense, the two relation schemas must have the same arity.

◼ *Set difference*

> **Algebra:** $\mathbf{R} - \mathbf{S}$
>
> **TRC:** $\{T \mid \mathbf{R}(T) \text{ AND } (\text{NOT } \mathbf{S}(T))\}$
>
> **DRC:** Exercise 7.6

◼ No discussion of relational algebra is complete without saying something about the division operator.

> **Algebra:** $\mathbf{R}/\mathbf{S}$, where $\mathbf{R}$ has attributes A, B, and $\mathbf{S}$ has only B.
>
> **TRC:** $\{T.A \mid \mathbf{R}(T) \text{ AND } \forall X \in \mathbf{S} \ (\exists Y \in \mathbf{R} \ (Y.B = X.B \text{ AND } Y.A = T.A))\}$
>
> **DRC:** Exercise 7.6.

Figure 7.2   A list of Prerequisites.

PREREQ	Crs	PreCrs
	CS632	CS532
	CS505	CS213
	CS532	CS305
	CS305	CS213
	CS305	CS214
	CS214	CS114
	CS114	CS113
	CS305	CS220

7.6   RECURSIVE QUERIES IN SQL:1999

Limitations of relational query languages.   Numerous examples in this and preceding chapters illustrate the vast expressive power of relational query languages. Yet these languages are not expressive enough to allow the programmer to write complete applications in SQL. Surprisingly, SQL cannot even be used to express some very common queries, such as whether one course is a (possibly indirect) prerequisite of another.

To illustrate the problem, consider the relation PREREQ in Figure 7.2. Suppose that we want to find out if CS113 is a prerequisite course for CS632. With the relational algebra, we can try to approach the problem as follows. Let PREREQ_2 (Crs, PreCrs) denote the expression

$$\pi_{\text{Crs,PreCrs}}((\text{PREREQ} \bowtie_{\text{PreCrs=Crs}} \text{PREREQ})[\text{Crs},\text{P1},\text{C2},\text{PreCrs}])$$
$$\cup\ \text{PREREQ}$$

where, as before, [Crs,P1,C2,PreCrs] is attribute renaming. We can now compute the expression $\sigma_{\text{Crs='CS632' AND PreCrs='CS113'}}(\text{PREREQ}_2)$ and see if the result is nonempty. If it is, CS113 is a prerequisite of CS632 twice removed. However, it is easy to verify that in our concrete case the above expression evaluates to an empty relation, so we are not done yet.

We can try to see if CS113 is three prerequisites removed from CS632 by evaluating the following expression, which we denote PREREQ_3(Crs, PreCrs).

$$\pi_{\text{Crs,PreCrs}}((\text{PREREQ} \bowtie_{\text{PreCrs=Crs}} \text{PREREQ}_2)[\text{Crs},\text{P1},\text{C2},\text{PreCrs}])$$
$$\cup\ \text{PREREQ}_2$$

If $\sigma_{\text{Crs='CS632' AND PreCrs='CS113'}}(\text{PREREQ}_3)$ is nonempty, our hypothesis is confirmed. Again, however, this expression is empty so we have not yet established the indirect prerequisite relationship between the two courses. If we give the relation PREREQ the alias PREREQ_1, we start seeing the pattern that each iteration in the above process looks like, as follows:

$$\text{PREREQ}_{i+1} =$$
$$\pi_{\text{Crs,PreCrs}}((\text{PREREQ} \bowtie_{\text{PreCrs=Crs}} \text{PREREQ}_i)[\text{Crs,P1,C2,PreCrs}]) \quad (7.16)$$
$$\cup \text{ PREREQ}_i$$

Continuing in this vein, we create PREREQ_4, PREREQ_5, and so on. It is easy to verify by direct inspection that $\sigma_{\text{Crs='CS632' AND PreCrs='CS113'}}(\text{PREREQ}_5)$ is nonempty, and thus the two courses are five prerequisites removed.

Note that the above process can be used to provide negative answers as well. For instance, to verify that CS220 is *not* a direct or indirect prerequisite of CS505, we can compute PREREQ_2, PREREQ_3, and so on, and see that applying the selection $\sigma_{\text{Crs='CS505' AND PreCrs='CS220'}}$ yields an empty result in each case. How do we know that, for example, $\sigma_{\text{Crs='CS505' AND PreCrs='CS220'}}(\text{PREREQ}_{1000})$ is empty? That is simple: PREREQ_5, PREREQ_6, and so on, are all equal; that is, the join operation used in constructing these relations stops producing new tuples after several joins.

In view of the above discussion, it might seem that indirect prerequisites for courses can be found using the relational algebra alone. In our example, all we have to do is to check the contents of PREREQ_5. However, after more careful consideration things turn out to be more complex. What if, instead of the tuple $\langle \text{CS305,CS214} \rangle$, our PREREQ relation had the tuple $\langle \text{CS220,CS214} \rangle$? In this case, it would take one more iteration to establish the indirect prerequisite relation between CS632 and CS113; that is, $\sigma_{\text{Crs='CS632' AND PreCrs='CS113'}}(\text{PREREQ}_5)$ would still be empty, but $\sigma_{\text{Crs='CS632' AND PreCrs='CS113'}}(\text{PREREQ}_6)$ would not.

In other words, the number of iterations of the expression (7.16) needed to reach a stable state (where subsequent joins do not make a difference) is *data-dependent* and cannot be predicted in advance. Because of this, it is not easy to point to a single expression, such as $\sigma_{\text{Crs='CS632' AND PreCrs='CS113'}}(\text{PREREQ}_5)$, as one that will tell us whether or not CS113 is an indirect prerequisite of CS632 for all legal contents of the relation PREREQ. In fact, it is shown in [Aho and Ullman 1979] that *no relational expression can provide such an answer*! This result shows that relational languages, such as relational algebra, calculus, and SQL, have limited expressive power. In fact, as follows from exercise 7.14, checking prerequisites has polynomial time complexity, which implies that SQL cannot express certain polynomial time queries. The immediate practical consequence of this theoretical result is that it is not possible to write even simple database applications entirely in SQL. This is one reason why, in the real world, SQL is used from within a host language, such as C or Java, which provides the general application logic. (Chapter 10 will explain how this is done.)

Equation (7.16) is called **recurrent**, and queries expressed in its terms are called **recursive**. A recursive query is computed by applying the recurrence equation repeatedly, starting with some known initial value (PREREQ in our case), until a stable state is reached, that is, until PREREQ_{N+1} equals PREREQ_N for some N. In other words, the answer to our query about the prerequisites is the *stable state* of the recurrence equation (7.16). Thus, another interpretation of the aforesaid result in [Aho and Ullman 1979] is that the stable state of a recurrence equation cannot, in general, be represented as an expression in relational algebra.

Recursion in SQL.   The subfield of database research that studies the processing of recursive queries is known as **deductive databases**, and there is a vast literature on the subject (see [Ramakrishnan and Ullman 1995] for a survey). The need for processing recursive queries was eventually recognized by the SQL standards group and appropriate extensions were added to SQL:1999. We discuss these extensions next.

SQL:1999 does *not* use recurrent equations such as (7.16) to define recursive queries, because these equations correspond to the procedural view of *how* such queries are evaluated. Faithful to its original philosophy, SQL:1999 rather specifies what is to be retrieved *declaratively* rather than procedurally. Nevertheless, the connection between recurrence equations and the way SQL:1999 expresses recursive queries is clearly seen from the syntax, especially that of recursive views. For instance, the following view specifies all course-prerequisite pairs.

```
CREATE RECURSIVE VIEW INDIRECTPREREQVIEW(Crs, PreCrs) AS
SELECT * FROM PREREQ
UNION
SELECT P.Crs, I.PreCrs
FROM PREREQ P, INDIRECTPREREQVIEW I
WHERE P.PreCrs = I.Crs
```

The difference between a regular view and a recursive view is that the definition of a recursive view consists of two distinct parts.

■ *The nonrecursive subquery.* In our example, it is the first SELECT statement (above the UNION operator). It cannot contain references to the view relation being defined.

■ *The recursive part.* This part consists of the second subquery (below the UNION operator). Unlike the nonrecursive subquery, it references the relation INDIRECTPREREQVIEW, that is, the very view that is being defined by the CREATE RECURSIVE VIEW statement.

It should now be clear why such views are called recursive: Their definitions appear to be cyclic. However, their contents are well defined and best understood in terms of the recurrence equations mentioned earlier.

The purpose of the nonrecursive subquery in a recursive view definition is to specify the initial contents for the recursive relation used in the recurrence equation. In our case, this subquery states that the initial contents of INDIRECTPREREQVIEW are the contents of the relation PREREQ. Let us denote these contents as INDIRECTPREREQVIEW$_1$.

The recursive part specifies the actual recurrence equation. It says that, to obtain the next approximation of the contents of INDIRECTPREREQVIEW, one must evaluate this query assuming the current approximation. In other words, INDIRECTPREREQVIEW$_2$ is the relation computed by forming the union of INDIRECTPREREQVIEW$_1$ with the result of the query

```
SELECT P.Crs, I.PreCrs
FROM PREREQ P, INDIRECTPREREQVIEW₁ I
WHERE P.PreCrs = I.Crs
```

where we use the previous approximation, INDIRECTPREREQVIEW$_1$, to compute the value of INDIRECTPREREQVIEW$_2$. The stable state of this recurrence equation is considered to be the meaning of the recursive view. In our case, a stable state is reached when joining the current contents of INDIRECTPREREQVIEW with the original relation PREREQ no longer yields new course-prerequisite pairs, that is, when the result of the query

```
SELECT P.Crs, I.PreCrs
FROM PREREQ P, INDIRECTPREREQVIEW_N I
WHERE P.PreCrs = I.Crs
```

equals INDIRECTPREREQVIEW$_N$ for some $N > 0$.

Having defined a recursive view, we can now query it using a regular SELECT statement. For instance, to find out if CS113 is an indirect prerequisite of CS632, we can write

```
SELECT *
FROM INDIRECTPREREQVIEW I                                    (7.17)
WHERE I.PreCrs = 'CS113' AND I.Crs = 'CS632'
```

SQL:1999 also provides a syntax for recursive queries that does not rely on views. The overall idea is similar: A recursive query consists of two parts: the definition of a recursive relation and the query against this relation. The syntax of the first part is very close to the recursive view definition that we saw earlier, and the syntax of the second part is a regular SQL (nonrecursive) query. For instance, the query about the indirect prerequisite relationship between CS113 and CS632 can be expressed as follows:

```
WITH RECURSIVE INDIRECTPREREQQUERY(Crs, PreCrs) AS
        ((SELECT * FROM PREREQ)
         UNION
         (SELECT P.Crs, I.PreCrs
          FROM PREREQ P, INDIRECTPREREQQUERY I
          WHERE P.PreCrs = I.Crs))
SELECT *
FROM INDIRECTPREREQQUERY I
WHERE I.PreCrs = 'CS113' AND I.Crs = 'CS632'
```

Note that the top portion of this query is almost identical to the definition of the recursive view INDIRECTPREREQVIEW. The only essential difference is that a view definition is saved in the system catalog and can later be reused in other queries whereas the definition of the query INDIRECTPREREQQUERY is discarded by the system right after processing. The bottom portion of the above query corresponds to query (7.17) against the view INDIRECTPREREQVIEW.

Mutually recursive queries.   The transitive closure recursive queries considered so far do not illustrate the full power of the recursive query facility in SQL:1999. For a more complex example, consider that (out of sheer curiosity) we want to find prerequisite courses that are removed by an odd number of prerequisites. We can express this query by defining a relation, OddPrereq, that is **mutually recursive** with another relation, EvenPrereq (i.e., each relation is defined in terms of the other). Mutual recursion can be expressed with the help of the WITH statement as follows:

```
WITH
    RECURSIVE OddPrereq(Crs, PreCrs) AS
        ((SELECT * FROM Prereq)
        UNION
        (SELECT P.Crs, E.PreCrs
         FROM Prereq P, EvenPrereq E
         WHERE P.PreCrs = E.Crs)),
    RECURSIVE EvenPrereq(Crs, PreCrs) AS
        (SELECT  P.Crs, O.PreCrs
         FROM Prereq P, OddPrereq O
         WHERE P.PreCrs = O.Crs)
SELECT * FROM OddPrereq
```

In this query, the WITH statement defines two temporary relations, OddPrereq and EvenPrereq. The first relation has a nonrecursive subquery that says that every direct prerequisite is also an odd prerequisite. The recursive part of the definition of OddPrereq says that the rest of the odd prerequisites are obtained by joining the Prereq relation with the relation EvenPrereq that contains all of the even prerequisites. This latter relation is defined using the second recursive query. This query does not have a nonrecursive part, which means that the initial value of EvenPrereq is the empty relation. Subsequent approximations to EvenPrereq are obtained by joining Prereq with OddPrereq. Thus, OddPrereq and EvenPrereq depend on each other.

Restrictions on the use of recursion.   SQL:1999 has a number of restrictions on the use of recursion that seems to exist solely to give vendors a reprieve from the added cost of more esoteric features. However, some restrictions are motivated by technical considerations and the need to keep down the time complexity of query evaluation. The most important restriction in this category has to do with negation, which is expressed using the keywords EXCEPT and NOT. To illustrate, suppose that we want to find all *truly odd* prerequisites, that is, those, that are not even. (It is possible for a prerequisite to be both odd and even, because any pair of courses can be connected by more than one chain of prerequisites and the chains can have different lengths). We can *try* to express this query as follows:

```
WITH
    RECURSIVE OddPrereq(Crs, PreCrs) AS
        ((SELECT * FROM Prereq)
        UNION
```

```
      (SELECT P.Crs, E.PreCrs
       FROM PREREQ P, EVENPREREQ E
       WHERE P.PreCrs = E.Crs)
      EXCEPT                                              (7.18)
      (SELECT * FROM EVENPREREQ)),
    RECURSIVE EVENPREREQ(Crs, PreCrs) AS
      (SELECT P.Crs, O.PreCrs
       FROM PREREQ P, ODDPREREQ O
       WHERE P.PreCrs = O.Crs )
  SELECT * FROM ODDPREREQ
```

The problem in this query has to do with subtraction of the EVENPREREQ relation within the recursive part of the definition of ODDPREREQ. As we saw previously, the two relations are dependent on each other. So, in order to know what tuples are *in* ODDPREREQ, we need to know what tuples are *not in* EVENPREREQ, which requires knowing what is *in* EVENPREREQ. But the latter again requires knowing what is *in* ODDPREREQ—back to square one.

A commonly accepted solution to this problem (and the one used in SQL:1999) is to require the use of negation (such as EXCEPT and NOT) be **stratified**. That is, if the definition of a relation, **P**, depends on knowing the *complement* of a relation, **Q**, then the definition of **Q** must *not* depend on **P** (or on its complement). In particular, **P** cannot depend on its own complement. Note (exercise 7.15) that every use of negation in a nonrecursive query is stratified, so this restriction was not necessary in SQL-92.

The use of negation in query (7.18) is not stratified, so it is not legal in SQL:1999. To construct a legal query for retrieving all truly odd prerequisites, we must break mutual recursion in the definition of ODDPREREQ and EVENPREREQ.

```
  WITH
    RECURSIVE ODDPREREQ(Crs, PreCrs) AS
        ((SELECT * FROM PREREQ)
         UNION
         (SELECT P.Crs, E.PreCrs
          FROM PREREQ P, PREREQ P1, ODDPREREQ O
          WHERE P.PreCrs = P1.Crs AND P1.PreCrs = O.Crs)
         EXCEPT
         (SELECT * FROM EVENPREREQ)),
    RECURSIVE EVENPREREQ(Crs, PreCrs) AS
        ((SELECT P.Crs, P1.PreCrs
          FROM PREREQ P, PREREQ P1
          WHERE P.PreCrs = P1.Crs
          UNION
         (SELECT P.Crs, E.PreCrs
          FROM PREREQ P, PREREQ P1, EVENPREREQ E
          WHERE P.PreCrs=P1.Crs AND P1.PreCrs = E.Crs))
  SELECT * FROM ODDPREREQ
```

In this query, the two relations ODDPREREQ and EVENPREREQ are still recursive but not mutually so. ODDPREREQ depends on the complement of EVENPREREQ (because of the EXCEPT clause in its definition), but EVENPREREQ does not depend on ODDPREREQ. Therefore, the use of negation in this query is stratified and the query is allowed.

7.7   BIBLIOGRAPHIC NOTES

Tuple relational calculus was introduced in [Codd 1972] as a theoretical tool in the study of the expressiveness of relational algebra as a query language. [Date 1992] shows how TRC can be effectively used as an intermediate language for constructing complex SQL queries. Domain relation calculus was proposed as a language for database queries in [Lacroix and Pirotte 1977]. Query-by-example was introduced in [Zloof 1975]. A proof of the equivalence of domain-independent queries in either of the calculi with the relational algebra is due to Codd and can be found in [Ullman 1988]. Domain independence and related issues were studied in [Van Gelder and Topor 1991, Kifer 1988, Topor and Sonenberg 1988, Avron and Hirshfeld 1994] and others.

The proof that the transitive closure query cannot be expressed using relational algebra is due to [Aho and Ullman 1979]. Deductive databases are extensively discussed in [Ullman 1988, Abiteboul et al. 1995], and a number of research prototypes of deductive database systems are described in [Ramakrishnan et al. 1994, Sagonas et al. 1994, Vaghani et al. 1994]. Stratified negation was introduced in [Apt et al. 1988].

7.8   EXERCISES

7.1   a. Explain why tuple relational calculus is said to be declarative whereas relational algebra is said to be procedural.

b. Explain why, even though SQL is declarative, the query optimizer in a relational DBMS translates SQL statements into relational algebra, which is procedural.

7.2 Express in words the meaning of each of the following expressions (where TOOK has its obvious meaning). For example, the answer for one of them is "Every student has taken at least one course."

a. $\exists S \in$ STUDENT ($\forall C \in$ COURSE TOOK(S, C))

b. $\forall S \in$ STUDENT ($\exists C \in$ COURSE TOOK(S, C))

c. $\exists C \in$ COURSE ($\forall S \in$ STUDENT TOOK(S, C))

d. $\forall C \in$ COURSE ($\exists S \in$ STUDENT TOOK(S, C))

* 7.3 Prove that any query in tuple relational calculus has an equivalent query in domain relational calculus, and vice versa.

*7.4 Prove that relational algebra queries are domain-independent. *Hint:* Use induction on the structure of the relational algebra expression.

7.5 Consider the relation schema corresponding to the IsA hierarchy in Figure 5.5. Assume that this schema has one relation per entity, and each IsA relationship is also represented by a separate relation. (Consult Section 5.4 to refresh your memory about this type of translation of IsA hierarchies into the relational model.) Write the following queries both in tuple and domain relational calculus:

   a. Find all sophomores in the Computer Science Major.

   b. Find all students in the Computer Science Major.

   c. Find all departments where some technician has every specialization that any other technician (in the same or another department) has.

7.6 Write a domain relational calculus query that is equivalent to the following algebraic expressions:

   a. **R − S**

   b. **R/S**, where relation **R** has attributes *A, B* and **S** has only one attribute, *B*.

7.7 Express each of the following queries in relational algebra, tuple relational calculus, domain relational calculus, QBE, and SQL, using the schema of Figure 4.4, page 62.

   a. Find all courses that are taught by professors who belong to either of the departments EE and MGT.

   b. List the names of all students who took courses in spring 1997 and fall 1998.

   c. List the names of all students who took courses from at least two professors in different departments.

   d. Find all courses taken by all students in department MGT.

   *e. Find every department that has a professor who has taught all courses ever offered by that department.

   Compare the two calculi, QBE, and SQL with respect to the ease of their use for formulating the above queries.

7.8 If you have a copy of Paradox, Access, or a similar DBMS, design the above queries using the visual languages that come with them.

7.9 Write the query of Exercise 6.17 using TRC and DRC.

7.10 Write the query of Exercise 6.19 using TRC and DRC.

7.11 Write the query of Exercise 6.22 using TRC and DRC.

   a. Find all customers who are interested in every house listed with Agent '007'.

b. Using the previous query as a view, retrieve a set of tuples of the form ⟨feature, number_of_customers⟩ where each tuple in the result shows a feature and the number of customers who want this feature such that:

- Only the customers who are interested in every house listed with Agent '007' are considered; and
- The number of customers interested in "feature" is greater than 2. (If this number is 2 or less then the corresponding tuple ⟨feature, number_of_customers⟩ is not added to the result.)

This part of the query cannot be conveniently expressed by TRC or DRC because they lack the counting operator. However it is still possible (and is not hard).

7.12 Write SQL query (6.8), page 143, and query (6.9), page 143, using TRC and DRC.

7.13 Investigate the logical relationship between the SQL operator EXISTS and the TRC quantifier ∃. For concreteness, express query (6.23), page 151, using TRC.

*7.14 Show that the iterative process of computing the transitive closure of PREREQ terminates after a finite number of steps. Show that this process can compute the transitive closure in polynomial time, provided that the process is modified slightly so as to avoid redundant computation.

7.15 Show that in SQL-92 queries every use of negation is stratified.

7.16 Consider a relation DIRECTFLIGHT(StartCity, DestinationCity) that lists all direct flights among cities. Use the recursion facility of SQL:1999 to write a query that finds all pairs ⟨$city_1$, $city_2$⟩ such that there is an *indirect* flight from $city_1$ to $city_2$ with at least two stops in-between.

7.17 Use the recursion facility of SQL:1999 to express so-called "same generation" query: *Given a* PARENT *relation, find all pairs of people who have the same ancestor and are removed from her by equal number of generations.* (For example, a child is removed from her parent by one generation and from grandparent by two.)

7.18 Consider the following bill of materials problem: The database has a relation SUBPART(Part, Subpart, Quantity), which tells what subparts are needed for each part and in which quantity. For instance, SUBPART(mounting_assembly, screw, 4) means that the mounting assembly includes 4 screws. For simplicity, let us assume that parts that do not have subparts (the *atomic* parts) are represented as having NULL as the only subpart (for instance, SUBPART(screw, NULL,0)). Write a recursive query to produce a list of all parts and for each part the number of primitive subparts it has.

Chapter 8

Database Design II: Relational Normalization Theory

The E-R approach is a good way to start dealing with the complexity of modeling a real-world enterprise. However, it is only a set of guidelines that requires considerable expertise and intuition, and it can lead to several alternative designs for the same enterprise. Unfortunately, the E-R approach does not include the criteria or tools to help evaluate alternative designs and suggest improvements. In this chapter, we present the *relational normalization theory*, which includes a set of concepts and algorithms that can help with the evaluation and refinement of the designs obtained through the E-R approach.

The main tool used in normalization theory is the notion of *functional dependency* (and, to a lesser degree, *join dependency*). Functional dependency is a generalization of the key dependencies in the E-R approach whereas join dependencies do not have an E-R counterpart. Both types of dependency are used by designers to spot situations in which the E-R design unnaturally places attributes of two distinct entity types into the same relation schema. These situations are characterized in terms of *normal forms*, whence comes the term *normalization theory*. Normalization theory forces relations into an appropriate normal form using *decompositions*, which break up schemas involving unhappy unions of attributes of unrelated entity types. Because of the central role that decompositions play in relational design, the techniques that we are about to discuss are sometimes also called *relational decomposition theory*.

8.1 THE PROBLEM OF REDUNDANCY

Example is the best way to understand the potential problems with relational designs based on the E-R approach. Consider the CREATE TABLE PERSON statement (5.1) on page 93. Recall that this relation schema was obtained by direct translation from the E-R diagram in Figure 5.1. The first indication of something wrong with this translation was the realization that SSN is not a key of the resulting PERSON relation. Instead, the key is a combination (SSN, Hobby). In other words, the attribute SSN does not uniquely identify the tuples in the PERSON relation even though it does uniquely identify the entities in the Person entity set. Not only is this counterintuitive, but it also has a number of undesirable effects on the instances of the Person relation schema.

To see this, we take a closer look at the relation instance shown in Figure 5.2, page 93. Notice that John Doe and Mary Doe are both represented by multiple tuples and that their addresses, names, and Ids occur multiple times as well. Redundant storage of the same information is apparent here. However, wasted space is the least of the problems. The real issue is that when database updates occur, we must keep all the redundant copies of the same data consistent with each other, and we must do it efficiently. Specifically, we can identify the following problems:

Update anomaly. If John Doe moves to 1 Hill Top Dr., updating the relation in Figure 5.2 requires changing the address in both tuples that describe the John Doe entity.

Insertion anomaly. Suppose that we decide to add Homer Simpson to the Person relation, but Homer's information sheet does not specify any hobbies. One way around this problem might be to add the tuple ⟨023456789, Homer Simpson, Fox 5 TV, NULL⟩—that is, to fill in the missing field with NULL. However, Hobby is part of the primary key, and most DBMSs do not allow null values in primary keys. Why? For one thing, DBMSs generally maintain an index on the primary key, and it is not clear how the index should refer to the null value. Assuming that this problem can be solved, suppose that a request is made to insert ⟨023456789, Homer Simpson, Fox 5 TV, acting⟩. Should this new tuple just be added, or should it replace the existing tuple ⟨023456789, Homer Simpson, Fox 5 TV, NULL⟩? A human will most likely choose to replace it, because humans do not normally think of hobbies as a defining characteristic of a person. However, how does a computer know that the tuples with primary key ⟨111111111, NULL⟩ and ⟨111111111, acting⟩ refer to the same entity? (Recall that the information about which tuple came from which entity is lost in the translation!) Redundancy is at the root of this ambiguity: If Homer were described by at most one tuple, only one course of action would be possible.

Deletion anomaly. Suppose that Homer Simpson is no longer interested in acting. How are we to delete this hobby? We can, of course, delete the tuple that talks about Homer's acting hobby. However, since there is only one tuple that refers to Homer (see Figure 5.2), this throws out perfectly good information about Homer's Id and address. To avoid this loss of information, we can try to replace acting with NULL. Unfortunately, this again raises the issue of nulls in primary key attributes. Once again, redundancy is the culprit. If only one tuple could possibly describe Homer, the attribute Hobby would not be part of the key.

For convenience, we sometimes use the term "update anomalies" to refer to all of the above anomaly types.

Figure 8.1 Decomposition of the PERSON relation shown in Figure 5.2.

SSN	Name	Address
111111111	John Doe	123 Main St.
555666777	Mary Doe	7 Lake Dr.
987654321	Bart Simpson	Fox 5 TV

(a) PERSON1

SSN	Hobby
111111111	stamps
111111111	hiking
111111111	coins
555666777	hiking
555666777	skating
987654321	acting

(b) HOBBY

8.2 DECOMPOSITIONS

The problems caused by redundancy—wasted storage and anomalies—can be easily fixed using the following simple technique. Instead of having one relation describe all that is known about persons, we can use two separate relation schemas.

PERSON1(SSN, Name, Address)
HOBBY(SSN, Hobby)   (8.1)

Projecting the relation in Figure 5.2 on each of these schemas yields the result shown in Figure 8.1. The new design has the following important properties:

1. The original relation of Figure 5.2 is exactly the natural join of the two relations in Figure 8.1. In fact, one can prove that this property is not an artifact of our example—that is, that under certain natural assumptions[1] any relation, r, over the schema of Figure 5.2 equals the natural join of the projections of r on the two relational schemas in (8.1). This property, called *losslessness*, will be discussed in Section 8.6.1. This means that our decomposition preserves the original information represented by the PERSON relation.

2. The redundancy present in the original relation of Figure 5.2 is gone and so are the update anomalies. The only items that are stored more than once are SSNs, which are identifiers of entities of type PERSON. Thus, changes to addresses, names, or hobbies now affect only a single tuple. Likewise, the removal of Bart Simpson's hobbies from the database does not delete the information about his address and does not require us to rely on null values. The insertion anomaly is also gone because we can now add people and hobbies independently.

Observe that the new design still has a certain amount of redundancy and that we might still need to use null values in certain cases. First, since we use SSNs as tuple

---

[1] Namely, that SSN uniquely determines the name and address of a person.

Figure 8.2 The ultimate decomposition.

SSN
111111111
555666777
987654321

Name
John Doe
Mary Doe
Bart Simpson

Address
123 Main St.
7 Lake Dr.
Fox 5 TV

Hobby
stamps
hiking
coins
skating
acting

identifiers, each SSN can occur multiple times and all of these occurrences must be kept consistent across the database. So consistency maintenance has not been eliminated completely. However, if the identifiers are not dynamic (for instance, SSNs, which do not change frequently), consistency maintenance is considerably simplified. Second, imagine a situation in which we add a person to our Person1 relation and the address is not known. Clearly, even with the new design, we have to insert NULL in the Address field for the corresponding tuple. However, Address is not part of a primary key, so the use of NULL here is not that bad (we will still have difficulties joining Person1 on the Address attribute).

It is important to understand that not all decompositions are created equal. In fact, most of them do not make any sense even though they might be doing a good job at eliminating redundancy. The decomposition

> Ssn(SSN)
> Name(Name)
> Address(Address)   (8.2)
> Hobby(Hobby)

is the ultimate "redundancy eliminator." Projecting on the relation of Figure 5.2 yields a database where each value appears exactly once, as shown in Figure 8.2. Unfortunately, this new database is completely devoid of any useful information; for instance, it is no longer possible to tell where John Doe lives or who collects stamps as a hobby. This situation is in sharp contrast with the decomposition of Figure 8.1, where we were able to completely restore the information represented by the original relation using a natural join.

The need for schema refinement.   Translation of the Person entity type into the relational model indicates that one cannot rely solely on the E-R approach for designing database schemas. Furthermore, the problems exhibited by the Person example are by no means rare or unique. Consider the relationship HasAccount of Figure 5.10. A typical translation of HasAccount into the relational model might be

```
CREATE TABLE HasAccount (
AccountNumber INTEGER NOT NULL,
ClientId      CHAR(20),                    (8.3)
OfficeId      INTEGER,
```

```
PRIMARY KEY (ClientId, OfficeId),
FOREIGN KEY (OfficeId) REFERENCES OFFICE
... ... ... )
```

Recall that a client can have at most one account in an office and hence (ClientId, OfficeId) is a key. Also, an account must be assigned to exactly one office. Careful analysis shows that this requirement leads to some of the same problems that we saw in the PERSON example. For example, a tuple that records the fact that a particular account is managed by a particular office cannot be added without also recording client information (since ClientId is part of the primary key) which is an insertion anomaly. This (and the dual deletion anomaly) is perhaps not a serious problem, because of the specifics of this particular application, but the update anomaly could present maintenance issues. Moving an account from one office to another involves changing OfficeId in every tuple corresponding to that account. If the account has multiple clients, this might be a problem.

We return to this example later in this chapter because HASACCOUNT exhibits certain interesting properties not found in the PERSON example. For instance, even though a decomposition of HASACCOUNT might still be desirable, it incurs additional maintenance overhead that the decomposition of PERSON does not.

The above discussion brings out two key points: (1) Decomposition of relation schemas can serve as a useful tool that complements the E-R approach by eliminating redundancy problems; (2) The criteria for choosing the right decomposition are not immediately obvious, especially when we have to deal with schemas that contain many attributes. For these reasons, the purpose of Sections 8.3 through 8.6 is to develop techniques and criteria for identifying relation schemas that are in need of decomposition, as well as to understand what it means for a decomposition not to lose information.

The central tool in developing much of decomposition theory is **functional dependency**, which is a generalization of the idea of key constraints. Functional dependencies are used to define **normal forms**—a set of requirements on relational schemas that are desirable in update-intensive transaction systems. This is why the theory of decompositions is often also called **normalization theory**. Sections 8.5 through 8.9 develop algorithms for carrying out the normalization process.

8.3   FUNCTIONAL DEPENDENCIES

For the remainder of this chapter, we use a special notation for representing attributes, which is common in relational normalization theory, as follows: Capital letters from the beginning of the alphabet (A, B, C, D) represent individual attributes; capital letters from the middle to the end of the alphabet with bars over them $(\overline{P}, \overline{V}, \overline{W}, \overline{X}, \overline{Y}, \overline{Z})$ represent *sets* of attributes. Also, strings of letters, such as $ABCD$, denote sets of the respective attributes $(\{A, B, C, D\})$; strings of letters with bars over them, $(\overline{X}\,\overline{Y}\,\overline{Z})$, stand for unions of these sets $(\overline{X} \cup \overline{Y} \cup \overline{Z})$. Although this notation requires some getting used to, it is very convenient and provides a succinct language, which we use in examples and definitions.

A **functional dependency** (FD) on a relation schema, **R**, is a constraint of the form $\overline{X} \to \overline{Y}$, where $\overline{X}$ and $\overline{Y}$ are sets of attributes used in **R**. If **r** is a relation instance of **R**, it is said to **satisfy** this functional dependency if

> For every pair of tuples, t and s, in **r**, if t and s agree on all attributes in $\overline{X}$, then t and s agree on all attributes in $\overline{Y}$.

Put another way, there must not be a pair of tuples in **r** such that they have the same values for every attribute in $\overline{X}$ but different values for some attribute in $\overline{Y}$.

Note that the key constraints introduced in Chapter 4 are a special kind of FD. Suppose that $\text{key}(\overline{K})$ is a key constraint on the relational schema **R** and that **r** is a relational instance over **R**. By definition, **r** satisfies $\text{key}(\overline{K})$ if and only if there is no pair of distinct tuples, $t, s \in \mathbf{r}$, such that t and s agree on every attribute in $\text{key}(\overline{K})$. Therefore, this key constraint is equivalent to the FD $\overline{K} \to \overline{R}$, where $\overline{K}$ is the set of attributes in the key constraint and $\overline{R}$ denotes the set of all attributes in the schema **R**.

Keep in mind that functional dependencies are associated with relation schemas, but when we consider whether or not a functional dependency is satisfied we must consider relation instances over those schemas. This is because FDs are *integrity constraints* on the schema (much like key constraints), which restrict the set of allowable relation instances to those that satisfy the given FDs. Thus, given a schema, $\mathbf{R} = (\overline{R};\ Constraints)$, where $\overline{R}$ is a set of attributes and *Constraints* is a set of FDs, we are looking for a set of all relation instances over $\overline{R}$ that satisfies every FD in *Constraints*. Such relational instances are called **legal instances** of **R**.

Functional dependencies and update anomalies. Certain functional dependencies that exist in a relational schema can lead to redundancy in the corresponding relation instances. Consider the two examples discussed in Sections 8.1 and 8.3: the schemas PERSON and HASACCOUNT. Each has a primary key, as illustrated by the corresponding CREATE TABLE commands (5.1), page 93, and (8.3), page 214. Correspondingly, there are the following functional dependencies:

$$
\begin{array}{lll}
\text{PERSON:} & \texttt{SSN,Hobby} \to \texttt{SSN,Name,Address,Hobby} & \\
\text{HASACCOUNT:} & \texttt{ClientId,OfficeId} \to \texttt{AccountNumber,} & (8.4) \\
& \qquad\qquad\qquad\quad \texttt{ClientId,OfficeId} &
\end{array}
$$

These are not the only FDs implied by the original specifications, however. For instance, both `Name` and `Address` are defined as single-valued attributes in the E-R diagram of Figure 5.1. This clearly implies that one PERSON entity (identified by its attribute SSN) can have at most one name and one address. Similarly, the business rules of PSSC (the brokerage firm discussed in Section 5.5) require that every account be assigned to exactly one office, which means that the following FDs must also hold for the corresponding relation schemas:

$$
\begin{array}{lll}
\text{PERSON:} & \texttt{SSN} \to \texttt{Name, Address} & \\
\text{HASACCOUNT:} & \texttt{AccountNumber} \to \texttt{OfficeId} & (8.5)
\end{array}
$$

It is easy to see that the syntactic structure of the dependencies in (8.4) closely corresponds to the update anomalies that we identified for the corresponding relations. For instance, the problem with PERSON was that for any given SSN we could not change the values for the attributes Name and Address independently of whether the corresponding person had hobbies: If the person had multiple hobbies, the change had to occur in multiple rows. Likewise with HASACCOUNT we cannot change the value of OfficeId (i.e., transfer an account to a different office) without having to look for all clients associated with this account. Since a number of clients might share the same account, there can be multiple rows in HASACCOUNT that refer to the same account; hence, multiple rows in which OfficeId must be changed.

Note that in both cases, the attributes involved in the update anomalies appear on the left-hand sides of an FD. We can see that update anomalies are associated with certain kinds of functional dependencies. Which dependencies are bad? At the risk of giving away the secret, we draw your attention to one major difference between the dependencies in (8.4) and (8.5): The former specify key constraints for their corresponding relations whereas the latter do not.

However, simply knowing which dependencies cause the anomalies is not enough—we must do something about them. We cannot just abolish the offending FDs, because they are part of the semantics of the enterprise being modeled by the databases. They are implicitly or explicitly part of the Requirements Document and cannot be changed without an agreement with the customer. On the other hand, we saw that schema decomposition can be a useful tool. Even though a decomposition cannot abolish a functional dependency, it can make it behave. For instance, the decomposition shown in (8.1) yields schemas in which the offending FD, SSN → Name, Address, becomes a well-behaved key constraint.

8.4 PROPERTIES OF FUNCTIONAL DEPENDENCIES

Before going any further, we need to learn some mathematical properties of functional dependencies and develop algorithms to test them. Since these properties and algorithms rely heavily on the notational conventions introduced at the beginning of Section 8.3, it might be a good idea to revisit these conventions.

The properties of FDs that we are going to study are based on *entailment*. Consider a set of attributes $\overline{R}$, a set, $\mathcal{F}$, of FDs over $\overline{R}$, and another FD, f, on $\overline{R}$. We say that $\mathcal{F}$ **entails** f if every relation **r** over the set of attributes $\overline{R}$ has the following property:

If **r** satisfies every FD in $\mathcal{F}$, then **r** satisfies the FD f.

Given a set of FDs, $\mathcal{F}$, the **closure of** $\mathcal{F}$, denoted $\mathcal{F}^+$, is the set of all FDs entailed by $\mathcal{F}$. Clearly, $\mathcal{F}^+$ contains $\mathcal{F}$ as a subset.[2]

---

[2] If $f \in \mathcal{F}$, then every relation that satisfies every FD in $\mathcal{F}$ obviously satisfies f. Therefore, by the definition of entailment, f is entailed by $\mathcal{F}$.

If $\mathcal{F}$ and $\mathcal{G}$ are sets of FDs, we say that $\mathcal{F}$ **entails** $\mathcal{G}$ if $\mathcal{F}$ entails every individual FD in $\mathcal{G}$. $\mathcal{F}$ and $\mathcal{G}$ are said to be **equivalent** if $\mathcal{F}$ entails $\mathcal{G}$ and $\mathcal{G}$ entails $\mathcal{F}$.

We now present several simple but important properties of entailment.

Reflexivity.   Some FDs are satisfied by every relation no matter what. These dependencies all have the form $\overline{X} \rightarrow \overline{Y}$, where $\overline{Y} \subseteq \overline{X}$, and are called **trivial** FDs.

▪ The reflexivity property states that, if $\overline{Y} \subseteq \overline{X}$, then $\overline{X} \rightarrow \overline{Y}$.

To see why trivial FDs are always satisfied, consider a relation, **r**, whose set of attributes includes all of the attributes mentioned in $\overline{X}\,\overline{Y}$. Suppose that $t, s \in \mathbf{r}$ are tuples that agree on $\overline{X}$. But, since $\overline{Y} \subseteq \overline{X}$, this means that t and s agree on $\overline{Y}$ as well. Thus, **r** satisfies $\overline{X} \rightarrow \overline{Y}$.

We can now relate trivial FDs and entailment. Because a trivial FD is satisfied by every relation, it is entailed by every set of FDs! In particular, $\mathcal{F}^{+}$ contains every trivial FD.

Augmentation.   Consider an FD, $\overline{X} \rightarrow \overline{Y}$, and another set of attributes, $\overline{Z}$. Let $\overline{R}$ contain $\overline{X} \cup \overline{Y} \cup \overline{Z}$. Then $\overline{X} \rightarrow \overline{Y}$ entails $\overline{X}\,\overline{Z} \rightarrow \overline{Y}\,\overline{Z}$. In other words, every relation **r** over $\overline{R}$ that satisfies $\overline{X} \rightarrow \overline{Y}$ must also satisfy the FD $\overline{X}\,\overline{Z} \rightarrow \overline{Y}\,\overline{Z}$.

▪ The augmentation property states that, if $\overline{X} \rightarrow \overline{Y}$, then $\overline{X}\,\overline{Z} \rightarrow \overline{Y}\,\overline{Z}$.

To see why this is true, if tuples $t, s \in \mathbf{r}$ agree on every attribute of $\overline{X}\,\overline{Z}$ then in particular they agree on $\overline{X}$. Since **r** satisfies $\overline{X} \rightarrow \overline{Y}$, t and s must also agree on $\overline{Y}$. They also agree on $\overline{Z}$, since we have assumed that they agree on a bigger set of attributes, $\overline{X}\,\overline{Z}$. Thus, if s, t agree on every attribute in $\overline{X}\,\overline{Z}$, they must agree on $\overline{Y}\,\overline{Z}$. As this is an arbitrarily chosen pair of tuples in **r**, it follows that **r** satisfies $\overline{X}\,\overline{Z} \rightarrow \overline{Y}\,\overline{Z}$.

Transitivity.   The set of FDs $\{\overline{X} \rightarrow \overline{Y},\ \overline{Y} \rightarrow \overline{Z}\}$ entails the FD $\overline{X} \rightarrow \overline{Z}$.

▪ The transitivity property states that, if $\overline{X} \rightarrow \overline{Y}$ and $\overline{Y} \rightarrow \overline{Z}$, then $\overline{X} \rightarrow \overline{Z}$.

This property can be established similarly to the previous two (see the exercises).

These three properties of FDs are known as **Armstrong's Axioms,**[3] and their main use is in the proofs of correctness of various database design algorithms. However, they are also a powerful tool used by (real, breathing human) database designers because they can help them quickly spot problematic FDs in relational schemas. We now show how Armstrong's axioms are used to derive new FDs.

Union of FDs.   Any relation, **r**, that satisfies $\overline{X} \rightarrow \overline{Y}$ and $\overline{X} \rightarrow \overline{Z}$ must also satisfy $\overline{X} \rightarrow \overline{Y}\,\overline{Z}$. To show this, we can derive $\overline{X} \rightarrow \overline{Y}\,\overline{Z}$ from $\overline{X} \rightarrow \overline{Y}$ and $\overline{X} \rightarrow \overline{Z}$ using simple syntactic manipulations defined by Armstrong's axioms. Such manipulations can

---

[3] Strictly speaking, these are *inference rules*, because they derive new rules out of old ones. Only the reflexivity rule can be viewed as an axiom.

be easily programmed on a computer, unlike the tuple-based considerations we used to establish the axioms themselves. Here is how it is done:

(a) $\overline{X} \to \overline{Y}$ Given

(b) $\overline{X} \to \overline{Z}$ Given

(c) $\overline{X} \to \overline{Y}\,\overline{X}$ Adding $\overline{X}$ to both sides of (a): Armstrong's augmentation rule

(d) $\overline{Y}\,\overline{X} \to \overline{Y}\,\overline{Z}$ Adding $\overline{Y}$ to both sides of (b): Armstrong's augmentation rule

(e) $\overline{X} \to \overline{Y}\,\overline{Z}$ By Armstrong's transitivity rule applied to (c) and (d)

Decomposition of FDs. In a similar way, we can prove the following rule: Every relation that satisfies $\overline{X} \to \overline{Y}\,\overline{Z}$ must also satisfy the FDs $\overline{X} \to \overline{Y}$ and $\overline{X} \to \overline{Z}$. This is accomplished by the following simple steps:

(a) $\overline{X} \to \overline{Y}\,\overline{Z}$ Given

(b) $\overline{Y}\,\overline{Z} \to \overline{Y}$ By Armstrong's reflexivity rule, since $\overline{Y} \subseteq \overline{Y}\,\overline{Z}$

(c) $\overline{X} \to \overline{Y}$ By transitivity from (a) and (b)

Derivation of $\overline{X} \to \overline{Z}$ is similar.

Armstrong's axioms are obviously *sound*. By **sound** we mean that any expression of the form $\overline{X} \to \overline{Y}$ derived using the axioms is actually a functional dependency. Soundness follows from the fact that we have proved that these inference rules are valid for every relation. It is much less obvious, however, that they are also **complete**—that is, if a set of FDs, $\mathcal{F}$, entails another FD, f, then f can be derived from $\mathcal{F}$ by a sequence of steps similar to the ones above that rely solely on Armstrong's axioms! We do not prove this fact here, but a proof can be found in [Ullman 1988]. Soundness and completeness of Armstrong's axioms is not just a theoretical curiosity—this result has considerable practical value because it guarantees that entailment of FDs (i.e., the question of whether $f \in \mathcal{F}^+$) can be verified by a computer program. We are now going to develop one such algorithm.

An obvious way to verify entailment of an FD, f, by a set of FDs, $\mathcal{F}$, is to instruct the computer to apply Armstrong's axioms to $\mathcal{F}$ in all possible ways. Since the number of attributes mentioned in $\mathcal{F}$ and f is finite, this derivation process cannot go on forever. When we are satisfied that all possible derivations have been made, we can simply check whether f is among the FDs derived by this process. Completeness of Armstrong's axioms guarantees that $f \in \mathcal{F}^+$ if and only if f is one of the FDs thus derived.

To see how this process works, consider the following sets of FDs: $\mathcal{F} = \{AC \to B, A \to C, D \to A\}$ and $\mathcal{G} = \{A \to B, A \to C, D \to A, D \to B\}$. We can use Armstrong's axioms to prove that these two sets are equivalent, i.e., every FD in $\mathcal{G}$ is entailed by $\mathcal{F}$, and vice versa. For instance, to prove that $A \to B$ is implied by $\mathcal{F}$, we can apply Armstrong's axioms in all possible ways. Most of these attempts will not lead anywhere, but a few will. For instance, the following derivation establishes the desired entailment:

(a) $A \rightarrow C$ An FD in $\mathcal{F}$
(b) $A \rightarrow AC$ From (a) and Armstrong's augmentation axiom
(c) $A \rightarrow B$ From (b), $AC \rightarrow B \in \mathcal{F}$, and Armstrong's transitivity axiom

The FDs $A \rightarrow C$ and $D \rightarrow A$ belong to both $\mathcal{F}$ and $\mathcal{G}$, so the derivation is trivial. For $D \rightarrow B$ in $\mathcal{G}$, the computer can try to apply Armstrong's axioms until this FD is derived. After a while, it will stumble upon this valid derivation:

(a) $D \rightarrow A$ an FD in $\mathcal{F}$
(b) $A \rightarrow B$ derived previously
(c) $D \rightarrow B$ from (a), (b), and Armstrong's transitivity axiom

This shows that every FD in $\mathcal{F}$ entailed by $\mathcal{G}$ is done similarly.

Although the simplicity of checking entailment by blindly applying Armstrong's axioms is attractive, it is not very efficient. In fact, the size of $\mathcal{F}^+$ can be exponential in the size of $\mathcal{F}$, so for large database schemas it can take a very long time before the designer ever sees the result. We are therefore going to develop a more efficient algorithm, which is also based on Armstrong's axioms but which applies them much more judiciously.

Checking entailment of FDs.   The idea of the new algorithm for verifying entailment is based on *attribute closure*.

Given a set of FDs, $\mathcal{F}$, and a set of attributes, $\overline{X}$, we define the **attribute closure** of $\overline{X}$ with respect to $\mathcal{F}$, denoted $\overline{X}_{\mathcal{F}}^+$, as follows:

$$\overline{X}_{\mathcal{F}}^+ = \{A \mid \overline{X} \rightarrow A \in \mathcal{F}^+\}$$

In other words, $\overline{X}_{\mathcal{F}}^+$ is a set of all those attributes, A, such that $\overline{X} \rightarrow A$ is entailed by $\mathcal{F}$. Note that $\overline{X} \subseteq \overline{X}_{\mathcal{F}}^+$ because, if $A \in \overline{X}$, then, by Armstrong's reflexivity axiom, $\overline{X} \rightarrow A$ is a trivial FD that is entailed by every set of FDs, including $\mathcal{F}$.

It is important to understand that the closure of $\mathcal{F}$ (i.e., $\mathcal{F}^+$) and the closure of $\overline{X}$ (i.e., $\overline{X}_{\mathcal{F}}^+$) are related but different notions: $\mathcal{F}^+$ is a set of functional dependencies, whereas $\overline{X}_{\mathcal{F}}^+$ is a set of attributes.

The more efficient algorithm for checking entailment of FDs now works as follows: Given a set of FDs, $\mathcal{F}$, and an FD, $\overline{X} \rightarrow \overline{Y}$, check whether $\overline{Y} \subseteq \overline{X}_{\mathcal{F}}^+$. If this is so, then $\mathcal{F}$ entails $\overline{X} \rightarrow \overline{Y}$. Otherwise, if $\overline{Y} \not\subseteq \overline{X}_{\mathcal{F}}^+$, then $\mathcal{F}$ does not entail $\overline{X} \rightarrow \overline{Y}$.

The correctness of this algorithm follows from Armstrong's axioms. If $\overline{Y} \subseteq \overline{X}_{\mathcal{F}}^+$, then $\overline{X} \rightarrow A \in \mathcal{F}^+$ for every $A \in \overline{Y}$ (by the definition of $\overline{X}_{\mathcal{F}}^+$). By the union rule for FDs, $\mathcal{F}$ thus entails $\overline{X} \rightarrow \overline{Y}$. Conversely, if $\overline{Y} \not\subseteq \overline{X}_{\mathcal{F}}^+$, then there is $B \in \overline{Y}$ such that $B \notin \overline{X}_{\mathcal{F}}^+$. Hence, $\overline{X} \rightarrow B$ is not entailed by $\mathcal{F}$. But then $\mathcal{F}$ cannot entail $\overline{X} \rightarrow \overline{Y}$; if it did, it would have to entail $\overline{X} \rightarrow B$ as well, by the decomposition rule for FDs.

The heart of the above algorithm is a check of whether a set of attributes belongs to $\overline{X}_{\mathcal{F}}^+$. Therefore, we are not done yet: We need an algorithm for computing the

Figure 8.3 Computation of attribute closure $\overline{X}_{\mathcal{F}}^{+}$.

$closure := \overline{X}$
repeat
        $old := closure$
        if there is an FD $\overline{Z} \to \overline{V} \in \mathcal{F}$ such that $\overline{Z} \subseteq closure$ **then**
                $closure := closure \cup \overline{V}$
until $old = closure$
return $closure$

closure of $\overline{X}$, which we present in Figure 8.3. The idea behind the algorithm is enlarging the set of attributes known to belong to $\overline{X}_{\mathcal{F}}^{+}$ by applying the FDs in $\mathcal{F}$. The closure is initialized to $\overline{X}$, since we know that $\overline{X}$ is always a subset of $\overline{X}_{\mathcal{F}}^{+}$.

The soundness of the algorithm can be proved by induction. Initially, $closure$ is $\overline{X}$, so $\overline{X} \to closure$ is in $\mathcal{F}^{+}$. Then, assuming that $\overline{X} \to closure \in \mathcal{F}^{+}$ at some intermediate step in the **repeat** loop of Figure 8.3, and given an FD $\overline{Z} \to \overline{V} \in \mathcal{F}$ such that $\overline{Z} \subset closure$, we can use the *generalized transitivity rule* (see exercise 8.7) to infer that $\mathcal{F}$ entails $\overline{X} \to closure \cup \overline{V}$. Thus, if $A \in closure$ at the end of the computation, then $A \in \overline{X}_{\mathcal{F}}^{+}$. The converse is also true: If $A \in \overline{X}_{\mathcal{F}}^{+}$, then at the end of the computation $A \in closure$ (see exercise 8.8).

Unlike the simple-minded algorithm that uses Armstrong's axioms indiscriminately, the run-time complexity of the algorithm in Figure 8.3 is quadratic in the size of $\mathcal{F}$. In fact, an algorithm for computing $\overline{X}_{\mathcal{F}}^{+}$ that is *linear* in the size of $\mathcal{F}$ is given in [Beeri and Bernstein 1979]. This algorithm is better suited for a computer program, but its inner workings are more complex.

Example 8.4.1 (Checking Entailment)   Consider a relational schema, $\mathbf{R} = (\overline{R}; \mathcal{F})$, where $\overline{R} = ABCDEFGHIJ$, and the set of FDs, $\mathcal{F}$, which contains the following FDs: $AB \to C, D \to E, AE \to G, GD \to H, ID \to J$. We wish to check whether $\mathcal{F}$ entails $ABD \to GH$ and $ABD \to HJ$.

First, let us compute $ABD_{\mathcal{F}}^{+}$. We begin with $closure = ABD$. Two FDs can be used in the first iteration of the loop in Figure 8.3. For definiteness, let us use $AB \to C$, which makes $closure = ABDC$. In the second iteration, we can use $D \to E$, which makes $closure = ABDCE$. Now it becomes possible to use the FD $AE \to G$ in the third iteration, yielding $closure = ABDCEG$. This in turn allows $GD \to H$ to be applied in the fourth iteration, which results in $closure = ABDCEGH$. In the fifth iteration, we cannot apply any new FDs, so $closure$ does not change and the loop terminates. Thus, $ABD_{\mathcal{F}}^{+} = ABDCEGH$.

Since $GH \subseteq ABDCEGH$, we conclude that $\mathcal{F}$ entails $ABD \to GH$. On the other hand, $HJ \not\subseteq ABDCEGH$, so we conclude that $ABD \to HJ$ is not entailed by $\mathcal{F}$. Note, however, that $\mathcal{F}$ does entail $ABD \to H$. □

Figure 8.4 Testing equivalence of sets of FDs.

Input: $\mathcal{F}$, $\mathcal{G}$ – FD sets
Output: *true*, if $\mathcal{F}$ is equivalent to $\mathcal{G}$; *false* otherwise
for each $f \in \mathcal{F}$ **do**
      if $\mathcal{G}$ does not entail f **then return** *false*
for each $g \in \mathcal{G}$ **do**
      if $\mathcal{F}$ does not entail g **then return** *false*
return *true*

The above algorithm for testing entailment leads to a simple test for equivalence between a pair of sets of FDs. Let $\mathcal{F}$ and $\mathcal{G}$ be such sets. To check that they are equivalent, we must check that every FD in $\mathcal{G}$ is entailed by $\mathcal{F}$, and vice versa. The algorithm is depicted in Figure 8.4.

8.5 NORMAL FORMS

To eliminate redundancy and potential update anomalies, database theory identifies several **normal forms** for schemas such that, if a schema is in one of the normal forms, it has certain predictable properties. Originally, [Codd 1970] proposed three normal forms, each eliminating more anomalies than the previous one.

The **first normal form (1NF)**, as introduced by Codd, is equivalent to the definition of the relational data model. The **second normal form (2NF)** was an attempt to eliminate some potential anomalies, but it has turned out to be of no practical use, so we do not discuss it.

The **third normal form (3NF)** was initially thought to be the "ultimate" normal form. However, Boyce and Codd soon realized that 3NF can still harbor undesirable combinations of functional dependencies, so they introduced the so-called **Boyce-Codd normal form (BCNF)**. Unfortunately, the sobering reality of computational sciences is that there is no free lunch. Even though BCNF is more desirable, it is not always achievable without paying a price elsewhere. In this section, we define both BCNF and 3NF. Subsequent sections develop algorithms for automatically converting relational schemas that possess various bad properties into sets of schemas in 3NF and BCNF. We also study the trade-offs associated with such conversions.

Toward the end of this chapter, we show that certain types of redundancy are caused not by FDs but by other dependencies. To deal with this problem, we introduce the **fourth normal form (4NF)**, which further extends BCNF.

The Boyce-Codd Normal Form.   A relational schema, $\mathbf{R} = (\overline{R};\ \mathcal{F})$, where $\overline{R}$ is the set of attributes of $\mathbf{R}$ and $\mathcal{F}$ is the set of functional dependencies associated with $\mathbf{R}$, is in Boyce-Codd normal form if, for every FD $\overline{X} \rightarrow \overline{Y} \in \mathcal{F}$, either of the following is true:

■ $\overline{Y} \subseteq \overline{X}$ (i.e., this is a trivial FD).

■ $\overline{X}$ is a superkey of $\mathbf{R}$.

In other words, the only nontrivial FDs are those in which a key functionally determines one or more attributes.

It is easy to see that PERSON1 and HOBBY, the relational schemas given in (8.1), are in BCNF, because the only nontrivial FD is SSN → Name, Address. It applies to PERSON1 which has SSN as a key.

On the other hand, consider the schema PERSON defined by the CREATE TABLE statement (5.1), page 93, and the schema HASACCOUNT defined by the SQL statement (8.3), page 214. As discussed earlier, these statements fail to capture some important relationships, which are represented by the FDs in (8.5), page 216. Each of these FDs is in violation of the requirement to be in BCNF: They are not trivial, and their left-hand sides—SSN and AccountNumber—are not keys of their respective schemas.

Note that a BCNF schema can have more than one key. For instance, $\mathbf{R} = (ABCD; \mathcal{F})$, where $\mathcal{F} = \{AB \rightarrow CD, \ AC \rightarrow BD\}$ has two keys, AB and AC. And yet it is in BCNF because the left-hand side of each of the two FDs in $\mathcal{F}$ is a key.

An important property of BCNF schemas is that their instances do not contain redundant information. Since we have been illustrating redundancy problems only through concrete examples, the above statement might seem vague. Exactly what is redundant information? For instance, does the abstract relation

A	B	C	D
1	1	3	4
2	1	3	4

over the above mentioned BCNF schema $\mathbf{R}$ store redundant information?

Superficially it might seem so, because the two tuples agree on all but one attribute. However, having identical values in some attributes of different tuples does not necessarily imply that the tuples are storing redundant information. Redundancy arises when the values of some set of attributes, $\overline{X}$, necessarily implies the value that must exist in another attribute, A—a functional dependency. If two tuples have the same values in $\overline{X}$, they must have the same value of A. Redundancy is eliminated if we store the association between $\overline{X}$ and A only once (in a separate relation) instead of repeating it in all tuples of an instance of the schema $\mathbf{R}$ that agree on $\overline{X}$. Since $\mathbf{R}$ does not have FDs over the attributes BCD, no redundant information is stored. The fact that the tuples in the relation coincide over BCD is coincidental. For instance, the value of attribute D in the first tuple can be changed from 4 to 5 without regard for the second tuple.

A DBMS automatically eliminates one type of redundancy: Two tuples with the same values in the key fields are prohibited in any instance of a schema. This is a special case: The key identifies an entity and so determines the values of all attributes describing that entity. As the definition of BCNF precludes associations that do not contain keys, the relations over BCNF schemas do not store redundant information. As a result, deletion and update anomalies do not arise in BCNF relations.

Relations with more than one key still can have insertion anomalies. To see this, suppose that associations over ABD and over ACD are added to our relation as shown:

A	B	C	D
1	1	3	4
2	1	3	4
3	4	NULL	5
3	NULL	2	5

Because the value over the attribute C in the first association and over B in the second is unknown, we fill in the missing information with NULL. However, now we cannot tell if the two newly added tuples are the same—it all depends on the real values for the nulls. A practical solution to this problem, as adopted by the SQL standard, is to designate one key as primary and to prohibit null values in its attributes.

The Third Normal Form.   A relational schema, $\mathbf{R} = (\overline{R};\ \mathcal{F})$, where $\overline{R}$ is the set of attributes of $\mathbf{R}$ and $\mathcal{F}$ is the set of functional dependencies associated with $\mathbf{R}$, is in **third normal form** if, for every FD $\overline{X} \to A \in \mathcal{F}$, any one of the following is true:

■ $A \in \overline{X}$, (i.e., this is a trivial FD).

■ $\overline{X}$ is a superkey of $\mathbf{R}$.

■ $A \in \overline{K}$ for some key $\overline{K}$ of $\mathbf{R}$.

Observe that the first two conditions in the definition of 3NF are identical to the conditions that define BCNF. Thus, 3NF is a relaxation of BCNF's requirements. Every schema in BCNF must also be in 3NF, but the converse is not true in general. For instance, the relation HASACCOUNT (8.3) on page 214 is in 3NF because the only FD that is not based on a key constraint is AccountNumber $\to$ OfficeId, and OfficeId is part of the key. However, this relation is not in BCNF, as shown previously.[4]

If you are wondering about the intrinsic merit of the third condition in the definition of 3NF, the answer is that there is none. In a way, 3NF was discovered by mistake—in the search for what we now call BCNF! The reason for its remarkable survival is that it was found later to have some desirable algorithmic properties that BCNF does not have. We discuss these issues in subsequent sections.

Recall from Section 8.2 that relation instances over HASACCOUNT might store redundant information. Now we can see that this redundancy arises because of the functional dependency that relates AccountNumber and OfficeId and that is not implied by key constraints.

---

[4] In fact, HASACCOUNT is the smallest possible example of a 3NF relation that is not in BCNF (see Exercise 8.5).

For another example, consider the schema PERSON discussed earlier. This schema violates the 3NF requirements because, for example, the FD SSN → Name is not based on a key constraint (SSN is not a superkey) and Name does not belong to a key of PERSON. However, the decomposition of this schema into PERSON1 and HOBBY in (8.1), page 213, yields a pair of schemas that are in both 3NF and BCNF.

8.6   PROPERTIES OF DECOMPOSITIONS

Since there is no redundancy in BCNF schemas and redundancy in 3NF is limited, we are interested in decomposing a given schema into a collection of schemas, each of which is in one of these normal forms.

The main thrust of the discussion in the previous section was that 3NF does not completely solve the redundancy problem. Therefore, at first glance, there appears to be no justification to consider 3NF as a goal for database design. It turns out, however, that the maintenance problems associated with redundancy do not show the whole picture. As we will see, maintenance is also associated with integrity constraints,[5] and 3NF decompositions sometimes have better properties in this regard than do BCNF decompositions. Our first step is to define these properties.

Recall from Section 8.2 that not all decompositions are created equal. For instance, the decomposition of PERSON shown in (8.1) is considered good while the one in (8.2) makes no sense. Is there an objective way to tell which decompositions make sense and which do not, and can this objective way be explained to a computer? The answer to both questions is yes. The decompositions that make sense are called *lossless*. Before tackling this notion, we need to be more precise about what we mean by a "decomposition."

A **decomposition of a schema**, $\mathbf{R} = (\overline{R}; \mathcal{F})$, where $\overline{R}$ is a set of attributes of the schema and $\mathcal{F}$ is its set of functional dependencies, is a collection of schemas

$$\mathbf{R}_1 = (\overline{R}_1; \mathcal{F}_1), \quad \mathbf{R}_2 = (\overline{R}_2; \mathcal{F}_2), \quad \ldots, \quad \mathbf{R}_n = (\overline{R}_n; \mathcal{F}_n)$$

such that the following conditions hold

1. $\overline{R} = \cup_{i=1}^n \overline{R}_i$
2. $\mathcal{F}$ entails $\mathcal{F}_i$ for every $i = 1, \ldots, n$.

The first part of the definition is clear: A decomposition should not introduce new attributes, and it should not drop attributes found in the original schema. The second part of the definition says that a decomposition should not introduce new functional dependencies (but may drop some). We discuss the second requirement in more detail later.

The decomposition of a schema naturally leads to decomposition of relations over it. A **decomposition of a relation**, $\mathbf{r}$, over schema $\mathbf{R}$ is a set of relations

$$\mathbf{r}_1 = \pi_{\overline{R}_1}(\mathbf{r}), \quad \mathbf{r}_2 = \pi_{\overline{R}_2}(\mathbf{r}), \quad \ldots, \quad \mathbf{r}_n = \pi_{\overline{R}_n}(\mathbf{r})$$

---

[5] For example, a particular integrity constraint in the original table might be checkable in the decomposed tables only by taking the join of these tables—which results in significant overhead at run time.

where π is the projection operator. It can be shown (see exercise 8.9) that, if $\mathbf{r}$ is a valid instance of $\mathbf{R}$, then each $\mathbf{r}_i$ satisfies all FDs in $\mathcal{F}_i$ and thus each $\mathbf{r}_i$ is a valid relation instance over the schema $\mathbf{R}_i$. The purpose of a decomposition is to replace the original relation, $\mathbf{r}$, with a set of relations $\mathbf{r}_1, \ldots, \mathbf{r}_n$ over the schemas that constitute the decomposed schema.

In view of the above definitions, it is important to realize that *schema decomposition* and *relation instance decomposition* are two different but related notions.

Applying the above definitions to our running example, we see that splitting PERSON into PERSON1 and HOBBY (see (8.1) and Figure 8.1) yields a decomposition. Splitting PERSON as shown in (8.2) and Figure 8.2 is also a decomposition in the above sense. It clearly satisfies the first requirement for being a decomposition. It also satisfies the second, since only trivial FDs hold in (8.2), and these are entailed by every set of dependencies.

This last example shows that the above definition of a decomposition does not capture all of the desirable properties of a decomposition because, as you may recall from Section 8.2, the decomposition in (8.2) makes no sense. In the following, we introduce additional desirable properties of decompositions.

8.6.1 Lossless and Lossy Decompositions

Consider a relation, $\mathbf{r}$, and its decomposition, $\mathbf{r}_1, \ldots, \mathbf{r}_n$, as defined above. Since after the decomposition the database no longer stores the relation $\mathbf{r}$ and instead maintains its projections $\mathbf{r}_1, \ldots, \mathbf{r}_n$, the database must be able to reconstruct the original relation $\mathbf{r}$ from these projections. Not being able to reconstruct $\mathbf{r}$ means that the decomposition does not represent the same information as does the original database (imagine a bank losing the information about who owns which account or, worse, giving those accounts to the wrong owners!).

In principle, one can use any computational method that guarantees reconstruction of $\mathbf{r}$ from its projections. However, the natural and, in most cases, practical method is the natural join. We thus assume that $\mathbf{r}$ is reconstructible if and only if

$$\mathbf{r} = \mathbf{r}_1 \bowtie \mathbf{r}_2 \bowtie \cdots \bowtie \mathbf{r}_n$$

Reconstructibility must be a property of schema decomposition and not of a particular instance over this schema. At the database design stage, the designer manipulates schemas, not relations, and any transformation performed on a schema must guarantee that reconstructibility holds for all of its valid relation instances.

This discussion leads to the following notion. A decomposition of schema $\mathbf{R} = (\overline{R}; \mathcal{F})$ into a collection of schemas

$$\mathbf{R}_1 = (\overline{R}_1; \mathcal{F}_1), \ \mathbf{R}_2 = (\overline{R}_2; \mathcal{F}_2), \ldots, \ \mathbf{R}_n = (\overline{R}_n; \mathcal{F}_n)$$

is **lossless** if, for *every* valid instance $\mathbf{r}$ of schema $\mathbf{R}$,

$$\mathbf{r} = \mathbf{r}_1 \bowtie \mathbf{r}_2 \bowtie \cdots \bowtie \mathbf{r}_n$$

where

$$\mathbf{r}_1 = \pi_{\overline{R}_1}(\mathbf{r}), \ \mathbf{r}_2 = \pi_{\overline{R}_2}(\mathbf{r}), \ \ldots, \ \mathbf{r}_n = \pi_{\overline{R}_n}(\mathbf{r})$$

A decomposition is **lossy** otherwise.

In plain terms, a lossless schema decomposition is one that guarantees that any valid instance of the original schema can be reconstructed from its projections on the individual schemas of the decomposition. Note that

$$\mathbf{r} \subseteq \mathbf{r}_1 \bowtie \mathbf{r}_2 \bowtie \cdots \bowtie \mathbf{r}_n$$

holds for any decomposition (exercise 8.10), so losslessness really just states the opposite inclusion.

$$\mathbf{r} \supseteq \mathbf{r}_1 \bowtie \mathbf{r}_1 \bowtie \cdots \bowtie \mathbf{r}_n$$

The fact that

$$\mathbf{r} \subseteq \mathbf{r}_1 \bowtie \mathbf{r}_2 \bowtie \cdots \bowtie \mathbf{r}_n$$

holds, no matter what, may seem confusing at first. If we can get more tuples by joining the projections of **r**, why is such a decomposition called "lossy?" After all, we gained more tuples, not less! To clarify this issue, observe that what we might lose here are not tuples but rather information about *which tuples are the right ones*. Consider, for instance, the decomposition (8.2) of schema PERSON. Figure 8.2 presents the corresponding decomposition of a valid relation instance over PERSON shown in Figure 5.2. However, if we now compute a natural join of the relations in the decomposition (which becomes a Cartesian product since these relations do not share attributes), we will not be able to tell who lives where and who has what hobbies. The relationship among names and SSNs is also lost. In other words, when reconstructing the original relation getting more tuples is as bad as getting fewer—we must get exactly the set of tuples in the original relation.

Now that we are convinced of the importance of losslessness, we need an algorithm that a computer can use to verify this property, since the definition of lossless joins does not provide an effective test but only tells us to try every possible relation. This is not feasible or efficient.

A general test of whether a decomposition into n schemas is lossless exists, but is somewhat complex. It can be found in [Beeri et al. 1981]. However, there is a much simpler test that works for binary decompositions, that is, decompositions into a pair of schemas. This test can establish losslessness of a decomposition into more than two schemas, provided that this decomposition was obtained by a series of binary decompositions. Since most decompositions are obtained in this way, the simple binary test introduced below is sufficient for most practical purposes.

Testing the losslessness of a binary decomposition.   Let $\mathbf{R} = (\overline{R}; \mathcal{F})$ be a schema and $\mathbf{R}_1 = (\overline{R}_1; \mathcal{F}_1)$, $\mathbf{R}_2 = (\overline{R}_2; \mathcal{F}_2)$ be a binary decomposition of $\mathbf{R}$. This decomposition is lossless if and only if either of the following is true:

■ $(\overline{R}_1 \cap \overline{R}_2) \to \overline{R}_1 \in \mathcal{F}^+$.

■ $(\overline{R}_1 \cap \overline{R}_2) \to \overline{R}_2 \in \mathcal{F}^+$.

Figure 8.5 Tuple structure in a lossless binary decomposition: A row of r_1 combines with exactly one row of r_2.

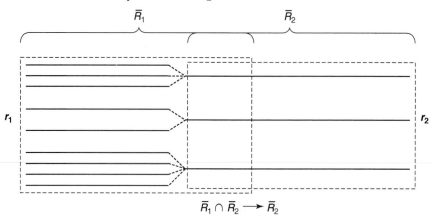

To see why this is so, suppose that $(\overline{R}_1 \cap \overline{R}_2) \to \overline{R}_2 \in \mathcal{F}^+$. Then $\overline{R}_1$ is a superkey of **R** since the values in a subset of attributes of $\overline{R}_1$ determine the values of all attributes of $\overline{R}_2$ (and, obviously, $\overline{R}_1$ functionally determines $\overline{R}_1$). Let **r** be a valid relation instance for **R**. Since $\overline{R}_1$ is a superkey of $\overline{R}$ every tuple in $\mathbf{r}_1 = \pi_{\overline{R}_1}(\mathbf{r})$ extends to exactly one tuple in **r**. Thus, as depicted in Figure 8.5, the cardinality (the number of tuples) in $\mathbf{r}_1$ equals the cardinality of **r**, and every tuple in $\mathbf{r}_1$ joins with exactly one tuple in $\mathbf{r}_2 = \pi_{\overline{R}_2}(\mathbf{r})$ (if more than one tuple in $\mathbf{r}_2$ joined with a tuple in $\mathbf{r}_1$, $(\overline{R}_1 \cap \overline{R}_2) \to \overline{R}_2$ would not be an FD). Therefore, the cardinality of $\mathbf{r}_1 \bowtie \mathbf{r}_2$ equals the cardinality of $\mathbf{r}_1$, which in turn equals the cardinality of **r**. Since **r** must be a subset of $\mathbf{r}_1 \bowtie \mathbf{r}_2$, it follows that $\mathbf{r} = \mathbf{r}_1 \bowtie \mathbf{r}_2$. Conversely, if neither of the above FDs holds, it is easy to construct a relation **r** such that $\mathbf{r} \subset \mathbf{r}_1 \bowtie \mathbf{r}_2$. Details of this construction are left to exercise 8.11.

The above test can now be used to substantiate our intuition that the decomposition (8.1) of PERSON into PERSON1 and HOBBY is a good one. The intersection of the attributes of HOBBY and PERSON1 is {SSN}, and SSN is a key of PERSON1. Thus, this decomposition is lossless.

8.6.2 Dependency-Preserving Decompositions

Consider the schema HASACCOUNT once again. Recall that it has attributes AccountNumber, ClientId, OfficeId, and its FDs are

$$\text{ClientId, OfficeId} \to \text{AccountNumber} \tag{8.6}$$
$$\text{AccountNumber} \to \text{OfficeId} \tag{8.7}$$

According to the losslessness test, the following decomposition is lossless:

$$\text{ACCTOFFICE} = (\text{AccountNumber, OfficeId};$$
$$\{\text{AccountNumber} \rightarrow \text{OfficeId}\}) \qquad (8.8)$$
$$\text{ACCTCLIENT} = (\text{AccountNumber, ClientId}; \{ \})$$

because AccountNumber (the intersection of the two attribute sets) is a key of the first schema, ACCTOFFICE.

Even though decomposition (8.8) is lossless, something seems to have fallen through the cracks. ACCTOFFICE hosts the FD (8.7), but ACCTCLIENT's associated set of FDs is empty. This leaves the FD (8.6), which exists in the original schema, homeless. Neither of the two schemas in the decomposition has all of the attributes needed to house this FD; furthermore, the FD cannot be derived from the FDs that belong to the schemas ACCTOFFICE and ACCTCLIENT.

In practical terms, this means that even though decomposing relations over the schema HASACCOUNT into relations over ACCTOFFICE and ACCTCLIENT does not lead to information loss, it might incur a cost for maintaining the integrity constraint that corresponds to the lost FD. Unlike the FD (8.7), which can be checked locally, in the relation ACCTOFFICE, verification of the FD (8.6) requires computing the join of ACCTOFFICE and ACCTCLIENT before checking of the FD can begin. In such cases, we say that the decomposition does not preserve the dependencies in the original schema. We now define what this means.

Consider a schema, $\mathbf{R} = (\overline{R}; \mathcal{F})$, and suppose that

$$\mathbf{R}_1 = (\overline{R}_1; \mathcal{F}_1), \ \mathbf{R}_2 = (\overline{R}_2; \mathcal{F}_2), \ \dots, \ \mathbf{R}_n = (\overline{R}_n; \mathcal{F}_n)$$

is a decomposition. $\mathcal{F}$ entails each $\mathcal{F}_i$ by definition, so $\mathcal{F}$ entails $\cup_{i=1}^{n}\mathcal{F}_i$. However, this definition does not require that the two sets of dependencies be equivalent—that is, that $\cup_{i=1}^{n}\mathcal{F}_i$ must also entail $\mathcal{F}$. This reverse entailment is what is missing in the above example. The FD set of HASACCOUNT, which consists of dependencies (8.6) and (8.7), is not entailed by the union of the dependencies in decomposition (8.8), which consists of only a single dependency AccountNumber $\rightarrow$ OfficeId. Because of this, (8.8) is not a dependency-preserving decomposition.

Formally,

$$\mathbf{R}_1 = (\overline{R}_1; \mathcal{F}_1), \ \mathbf{R}_2 = (\overline{R}_2; \mathcal{F}_2), \ \dots, \ \mathbf{R}_n = (\overline{R}_n; \mathcal{F}_n)$$

is said to be a **dependency-preserving decomposition** of $\mathbf{R} = (\overline{R}; \mathcal{F})$ if and only if it is a decomposition and the sets of FDs $\mathcal{F}$ and $\cup_{i=1}^{n}\mathcal{F}_i$ are equivalent.

The fact that an FD, f, in $\mathcal{F}$ is not in any $\mathcal{F}_i$ does not mean that the decomposition is not dependency preserving, since f might be entailed by $\cup_{i=1}^{n}\mathcal{F}_i$. In this case, maintaining f as a functional dependency requires no extra effort: If the FDs in $\cup_{i=1}^{n}\mathcal{F}_i$ are maintained, f will be also. It is only when f is not entailed by $\cup_{i=1}^{n}\mathcal{F}_i$ that the decomposition is not dependency preserving and so maintenance of f requires a join.

In view of this definition, the above decomposition of HASACCOUNT is not dependency preserving, and this is precisely what is wrong. The dependencies that exist in the original schema but are lost in the decomposition become inter-relational constraints that cannot be maintained locally. Each time a relation in

Figure 8.6 Decomposition of the HASACCOUNT relation.

AccountNumber	ClientId	OfficeId
B123	111111111	SB01
A908	123456789	MN08

HASACCOUNT

AccountNumber	OfficeId
B123	SB01
A908	MN08

ACCTOFFICE

AccountNumber	ClientId
B123	111111111
A908	123456789

ACCTCLIENT

Figure 8.7 HASACCOUNT and its decomposition after the insertion of several rows.

AccountNumber	ClientId	OfficeId
B123	111111111	SB01
B567	111111111	SB01
A908	123456789	MN08

HASACCOUNT

AccountNumber	OfficeId
B123	SB01
B567	SB01
A908	MN08

ACCTOFFICE

AccountNumber	ClientId
B123	111111111
B567	111111111
A908	123456789

ACCTCLIENT

the decomposition is changed, satisfaction of the inter-relational constraints can be checked only after the reconstruction of the original relation. To illustrate, consider the decomposition of HASACCOUNT in Figure 8.6.

If we now add the tuple ⟨B567, SB01⟩ to the relation ACCTOFFICE and the tuple ⟨B567, 111111111⟩ to ACCTCLIENT, the two relations will still satisfy their local FDs (in fact, we see from (8.8) that only ACCTOFFICE has a dependency to satisfy). In contrast, the inter-relational FD (8.6) is not satisfied after these updates, but this is not immediately apparent. To verify this, we must join the two relations, as depicted in Figure 8.7. We now see that constraint (8.6) is violated by the first two tuples in the updated HASACCOUNT relation.

The next question to ask is how hard it is to check whether a decomposition is dependency preserving. If we already have a decomposition complete with sets of functional dependencies attached to the local schemas, dependency preservation can be checked in polynomial time. We simply need to check that each FD in the original set is entailed by the union of FDs in the local schemas. For each such test, we can use the quadratic attribute closure algorithm discussed in Section 8.4.

In practice, the situation is more involved. Typically, we (and computer algorithms) must first decide how to split the attribute set in order to form the decomposition, and only then attach FDs to those attribute sets. We can attach the FD $\overline{X} \to \overline{Y}$ to an attribute set $\overline{S}$ if $\overline{X} \cup \overline{Y} \subseteq \overline{S}$. We state this more formally as follows.

Consider a schema, $\mathbf{R} = (\overline{R}; \mathcal{F})$, a relation, $\mathbf{r}$, over $\mathbf{R}$, and a set of attributes, $\overline{S}$, such that $\overline{S} \subseteq \overline{R}$. If $\overline{S}$ is one of the schemas in a decomposition of $\mathbf{R}$, the only FDs that are guaranteed to hold over $\pi_{\overline{S}}(\mathbf{r})$ are $\overline{X} \to \overline{Y} \in \mathcal{F}^{+}$ such that $\overline{X}\,\overline{Y} \subseteq \overline{S}$. This leads us to the following notion:

$$\pi_{\overline{S}}(\mathcal{F}) \;=\; \{\overline{X} \to \overline{Y} \mid \overline{X} \to \overline{Y} \in \mathcal{F}^{+} \text{ and } \overline{X} \cup \overline{Y} \subseteq \overline{S}\}$$

which is called the **projection** of the set $\mathcal{F}$ of FDs onto the set of attributes $\overline{S}$.

The notion of projection for FDs opens a way to construct decompositions knowing only how to split the attribute set of the original schema. If $\mathbf{R} = (\overline{R}; \mathcal{F})$ is a schema and $\overline{R}_1, \ldots, \overline{R}_n$ are subsets of attributes such that $\overline{R} = \cup_{i=1}^{n}\overline{R}_i$, then the collection of schemas $(\overline{R}_1; \pi_{\overline{R}_1}(\mathcal{F})), \ldots, (\overline{R}_n; \pi_{\overline{R}_n}(\mathcal{F}))$ is a decomposition. Since, given an attribute set in a decomposition, we can always determine the corresponding set of FDs by taking a projection, it is customary to omit the FDs when specifying schema decompositions.

Constructing decompositions thus involves computing projections of FDs. This computation involves calculating the closure of $\mathcal{F}$,[6] which can be exponential in the size of $\mathcal{F}$. If its cost is factored into the cost of checking for dependency preservation, this checking is exponential as well. In this regard, it is interesting that, in order to test a decomposition for losslessness, one does not need to compute the FDs that belong to the local schemas. The test presented earlier used the original set $\mathcal{F}$ of FDs and is polynomial in the size of $\mathcal{F}$.

To summarize, we considered two important properties of schema decomposition: losslessness and dependency preservation. We also saw an example of a relation (HASACCOUNT) that has a lossless but not dependency-preserving decomposition into BCNF (and which, as we shall see, does not have a BCNF decomposition that has both properties). Which of these two properties is more important? The answer is that losslessness is mandatory while dependency preservation, though very desirable, is optional. The reason is that lossy decompositions lose information

---

[6] There is a way to avoid computing the entire closure $\mathcal{F}^{+}$, but the worst-case complexity is the same.

contained in the original database, and this is not acceptable. In contrast, decompositions that do not preserve FDs only lead to computational overhead when the database is changed and inter-relational constraints need to be checked.

8.7 AN ALGORITHM FOR BCNF DECOMPOSITION

We are now ready to present our first decomposition algorithm. Let $\mathbf{R} = (\bar{R};\ \mathcal{F})$ be a relational schema that is not in BCNF. The algorithm in Figure 8.8 constructs a new decomposition by repeatedly splitting $\mathbf{R}$ into smaller subschemas, so that at each step the new database schema has strictly fewer FDs that violate BCNF than does the schema in the previous iteration (see exercise 8.13). Thus, the algorithm always terminates and all schemas in the result are in BCNF.

To see how the BCNF decomposition algorithm works, consider the HasAccount example once again. This schema is not in BCNF, because of the FD AccountNumber → OfficeId whose left-hand side is not a superkey. Therefore, we can use this FD to split HasAccount in the **while** loop of Figure 8.8. The result is, not surprisingly, the decomposition we saw in (8.8).

The next example is more complex and also much more abstract. Consider a relation schema, $\mathbf{R}=(\bar{R};\ \mathcal{F})$, where $\bar{R} = ABCDEFGH$ (recall that A, B, etc., denote attribute names), and let the set $\mathcal{F}$ of FDs be

$$ABH \rightarrow C$$
$$A \rightarrow DE$$
$$BGH \rightarrow F$$
$$F \rightarrow ADH$$
$$BH \rightarrow GE$$

To apply the BCNF decomposition algorithm, we first need to identify the FDs that violate BCNF—those whose left-hand side is not a superkey. We can see that the first FD is *not* one of these, because the attribute closure $(ABH)^+$ (computed with the algorithm in Figure 8.3) contains all schema attributes and so ABH is a superkey.

Figure 8.8 Lossless decomposition into BCNF.

Input: R $=\ (\bar{R};\ \mathcal{F})$
Decomposition := **R**
while there is a schema $\mathbf{S} = (\bar{S};\ \mathcal{F}')$ in *Decomposition* that is not in BCNF **do**
    /* Let $\bar{X} \rightarrow \bar{Y}$ be an FD in $\mathcal{F}$ such that $\bar{X}\bar{Y} \subseteq \bar{S}$
       and it violates BCNF. Decompose using this FD   */
    Replace **S** in *Decomposition* with schemas $\mathbf{S}_1 = (\bar{X}\bar{Y};\ \mathcal{F}_1)$
and $\mathbf{S}_2\ =\ (\bar{S} - \bar{Y}) \cup \bar{X};\ \mathcal{F}_2$, where $\mathcal{F}_1$ and $\mathcal{F}_2$ are all the FDs
from $\mathcal{F}'$ that involve only attributes in their respective schemas
end
return *Decomposition*

However, the second FD, $A \rightarrow DE$, does violate BCNF: The attribute closure of A is ADE, and so A is not a superkey. We can thus split **R** using this FD:

$$\mathbf{R}_1 = (ADE; \{A \rightarrow DE\})$$

$$\mathbf{R}_2 = (ABCFGH; \{ABH \rightarrow C, BGH \rightarrow F, F \rightarrow AH, BH \rightarrow G\})$$

Notice that we split $F \rightarrow ADH$ into $\{F \rightarrow AH, \ F \rightarrow D\}$ and $BH \rightarrow GE$ into $\{BH \rightarrow G, \ BH \rightarrow E\}$ and that some FDs fell by the wayside: $F \rightarrow D$ and $BH \rightarrow E$ no longer have a home, since none of the new schemas contains all the attributes used by these FDs. However, things are still looking bright, since the FD $F \rightarrow D$ can be derived from other FDs embedded in the new schemas $\mathbf{R}_1$ and $\mathbf{R}_2$: $F \rightarrow AH$ and $A \rightarrow DE$. Thus, if the validity of these two dependencies is maintained, the validity of $F \rightarrow D$ is necessarily maintained as well. Checking the two dependencies is easy because the attributes of each are confined to a single relation. Similarly, $BH \rightarrow E$ can still be derived because the attribute closure of BH, restricted to the FDs embedded in $\mathbf{R}_1$ and $\mathbf{R}_2$, contains E. (Verify using the algorithm in Figure 8.3!) The above decomposition is therefore dependency preserving.

It is easy to see that $\mathbf{R}_1$ is in BCNF, so the BCNF decomposition algorithm must concentrate on $\mathbf{R}_2$. The FDs $ABH \rightarrow C$ and $BGH \rightarrow F$ did not violate BCNF in **R** since both ABH and BGH are superkeys. As a result, they do not violate BCNF in $\mathbf{R}_2$ (which has only a subset of the attributes of **R**). The FD that clearly violates BCNF here is $F \rightarrow AH$, so the algorithm might pick it up and split $\mathbf{R}_2$ accordingly.

$$\mathbf{R}_{21} = (FAH; \{F \rightarrow AH\})$$

$$\mathbf{R}_{22} = (FBCG; \{\ \})$$

Now both schemas, $\mathbf{R}_{21}$ and $\mathbf{R}_{22}$, are in BCNF ($\mathbf{R}_{22}$ trivially so because it has no FDs). However, the price is that the FDs $ABH \rightarrow C$, $BGH \rightarrow F$, and $BH \rightarrow G$ that were present in $\mathbf{R}_2$ are now homeless. Furthermore, none of these FDs can be derived using the FDs that are still embedded in $\mathbf{R}_1$, $\mathbf{R}_{21}$, and $\mathbf{R}_{22}$. For instance, computing $(ABH)^+$ with respect to this set of FDs yields $ABHDE$, which does not contain C, so $ABH \rightarrow C$ is not derivable. Thus, we obtain a non-dependency–preserving decomposition of **R** into three BCNF schemas: $\mathbf{R}_1$, $\mathbf{R}_{21}$, and $\mathbf{R}_{22}$.

This decomposition is by no means unique. For instance, if our algorithm had picked up $F \rightarrow ADH$ at the very first iteration, the first decomposition would have been

$$\mathbf{R}_1' = (FADH; \{F \rightarrow ADH\})$$

$$\mathbf{R}_2' = (FBCEG; \{\ \})$$

This is not the end of the differences: While both of these schemas are in BCNF, some FDs that were present in the decomposition into $\mathbf{R}_1$, $\mathbf{R}_{21}$, $\mathbf{R}_{22}$ are now lost.

Properties of the BCNF decomposition algorithm. First and foremost, the BCNF decomposition algorithm in Figure 8.8 always yields a lossless decomposition. To see this, consider the two schemas involving attribute sets $\overline{X}\,\overline{Y}$ and $(\overline{S} - \overline{Y}) \cup \overline{X}$ that replace the schema $\mathbf{S} = (\overline{S}, \mathcal{F}')$ in the algorithm. Notice that $\overline{X}\,\overline{Y} \cap ((\overline{S} - \overline{Y}) \cup \overline{X}) = \overline{X}$ and thus $\overline{X}\,\overline{Y} \cap ((\overline{S} - \overline{Y}) \cup \overline{X}) \rightarrow \overline{X}\,\overline{Y}$ since $\overline{X} \rightarrow \overline{Y} \in \mathcal{F}$. Therefore, according to the losslessness test for binary decompositions on page 227, $\{\overline{X}\,\overline{Y},\ (\overline{S} - \overline{Y}) \cup \overline{X}\}$ is a lossless decomposition of $\mathbf{S}$. This means that at every step in our algorithm we replace one schema by its lossless decomposition. Thus, by Exercise 8.12, the final decomposition produced by this algorithm is also lossless.

Are the decompositions produced by the BCNF algorithm always dependency preserving? We have seen that this is not the case. Decomposition (8.8) of HASAC-COUNT is not dependency preserving. Moreover, it is easy to see that no BCNF decomposition of HASACCOUNT (not only those produced by this particular algorithm) is both lossless and dependency preserving. Indeed, there are just three decompositions to try, and we can simply check them all.

Finally, we have seen that the BCNF decomposition algorithm is nondeterministic. The final result depends on the order in which FDs are selected in the **while** loop. The decomposition chosen by the database designer might be a matter of taste, or it might be based on objective criteria. For instance, some decompositions might be dependency preserving, others not; some might lead to fewer FDs left out as inter-relational constraints (e.g., the decomposition $\mathbf{R}_1, \mathbf{R}_{21}, \mathbf{R}_{22}$ is better in this sense than the decomposition $\mathbf{R}'_1, \mathbf{R}'_2$). Some attribute sets might be more likely to be queried together so they better not be separated in the decomposition. The next section describes one common approach that can help in choosing one BCNF decomposition over another.

8.8 SYNTHESIS OF 3NF SCHEMAS

We have seen that some schemas (such as HASACCOUNT, in Figure 8.7) cannot be decomposed into BCNF so that the result is also dependency preserving. However, if we agree to settle for 3NF instead of BCNF, dependency-preserving decompositions are always possible (but recall that 3NF schemas might contain redundancies).

Before we present a 3NF decomposition algorithm, we introduce the concept of *minimal cover*, which is very simple. We know that sets of FDs might look completely different but nonetheless be logically equivalent. Figure 8.4 presented one fairly straightforward way of testing equivalence. Since there might be many sets of FDs equivalent to any given set, we question whether there is a set of FDs that can be viewed as "canonical." It turns out that defining a unique canonical set is not an easy task, but the notion of minimal cover comes close.

8.8.1 Minimal Cover

Let $\mathcal{F}$ be a set of FDs. A **minimal cover** of $\mathcal{F}$ is a set of FDs, $\mathcal{G}$, that has the following properties:

1. $\mathcal{G}$ is equivalent to $\mathcal{F}$ (but, possibly, different from $\mathcal{F}$).
2. All FDs in $\mathcal{G}$ have the form $\overline{X} \rightarrow A$, where A is a single attribute.

3. It is not possible to make $\mathcal{G}$ "smaller" (and still satisfy the first two properties) by either of the following:

a. Deleting an FD

b. Deleting an attribute from an FD

Clearly, because of the rule of decomposition for functional dependencies, it is easy to convert $\mathcal{F}$ into an equivalent set of FDs where the right-hand sides are singleton attributes. However, property 3 is more subtle. Before presenting an algorithm for computing minimal covers, we illustrate it with a concrete example.

Consider the attribute set $ABCDEFGH$ and the following set, $\mathcal{F}$, of FDs:

$$ABH \rightarrow C$$
$$A \rightarrow D$$
$$C \rightarrow E$$
$$BGH \rightarrow F$$
$$F \rightarrow AD$$
$$E \rightarrow F$$
$$BH \rightarrow E$$

Since not all right-hand sides are single attributes, we can use the decomposition rule to obtain an FD set that satisfies the first two properties of minimal covers.

$$ABH \rightarrow C$$
$$A \rightarrow D$$
$$C \rightarrow E$$
$$BGH \rightarrow F$$
$$F \rightarrow A \tag{8.9}$$
$$F \rightarrow D$$
$$E \rightarrow F$$
$$BH \rightarrow E$$

We can see that $BGH \rightarrow F$ is entailed by $BH \rightarrow E$ and $E \rightarrow F$, and that $F \rightarrow D$ is entailed by $F \rightarrow A$ and $A \rightarrow D$. Thus, we are left with

$$ABH \rightarrow C$$
$$A \rightarrow D$$
$$C \rightarrow E \tag{8.10}$$
$$F \rightarrow A$$
$$E \rightarrow F$$
$$BH \rightarrow E$$

It is easy to check by computing attribute closures that none of these FDs is redundant; that is, one cannot simply throw out an FD from this set without sacrificing equivalence to the original set $\mathcal{F}$. However, is the resulting set a minimal cover of $\mathcal{F}$? The answer turns out to be *no* because it is possible to delete the attribute A from

Figure 8.9 Computation of a minimal cover.

Input: a set of FDs $\mathcal{F}$
Output: $\mathcal{G}$, a minimal cover of $\mathcal{F}$

Step 1: $\mathcal{G} := \mathcal{F}$, where all FDs are converted to use singleton-attributes on
        the right-hand side
Step 2: Remove all redundant attributes from the left-hand sides
        of FDs in $\mathcal{G}$
Step 3: Remove all redundant FDs from $\mathcal{G}$

return $\mathcal{G}$

---

the first FD. $ABH \rightarrow C$ is entailed by the set

$$
\begin{aligned}
BH &\rightarrow C \\
A &\rightarrow D \\
C &\rightarrow E \\
F &\rightarrow A \\
E &\rightarrow F \\
BH &\rightarrow E
\end{aligned}
\tag{8.11}
$$

and $BH \rightarrow C$ is entailed by set (8.10). The first fact can be verified by computing the attribute closure of ABH with respect to (8.11) and the second by computing the attribute closure of BH with respect to (8.10). It then follows easily that the two sets are equivalent, and as a result (8.10) is not a minimal cover. Interestingly, after the removal of the redundant attribute A, the set (8.11) is still nonminimal because $BH \rightarrow E$ is redundant. Removing this FD yields a minimal cover at last.

    The algorithm for computing minimal covers is presented in Figure 8.9. Step 1 is performed by a simple splitting of the FDs according to their right-hand sides. For instance, $\overline{X} \rightarrow AB$ turns into $\overline{X} \rightarrow A$ and $\overline{X} \rightarrow B$.

    Step 2 is performed by checking every left-hand attribute in $\mathcal{G}$ for redundancy. That is, for every FD $\overline{X} \rightarrow A \in \mathcal{G}$ and every attribute $B \in \overline{X}$, we have to check if $(\overline{X} - B) \rightarrow A$ is entailed by $\mathcal{G}$—very tedious work if done manually. In the above example, we performed this step when we checked that $BH \rightarrow C$ is entailed by the FD set (8.10), which allowed us to get rid of the redundant attribute A in $ABH \rightarrow C$. Step 3 is accomplished by another tedious algorithm: For every $g \in \mathcal{G}$, check that the FD g is entailed by $\mathcal{G} - g$.

    An important observation about the algorithm in Figure 8.9 is that steps 2 and 3 cannot be done in a different order: Performing step 3 before 2 will not always return a minimal cover. In fact, we have already seen this phenomenon: We obtained set (8.10) by removing redundant FDs from (8.9); then we obtained set (8.11) by deleting redundant attributes. Nevertheless, the result still had a redundant FD ($BH \rightarrow E$). On the other hand, if we first remove the redundant attributes from (8.9), we get

$$BH \rightarrow C$$
$$A \rightarrow D$$
$$C \rightarrow E$$
$$BH \rightarrow F$$
$$F \rightarrow A$$
$$F \rightarrow D$$
$$E \rightarrow F$$
$$BH \rightarrow E$$

Then removing the redundant FDs $BH \rightarrow F, F \rightarrow D$, and $BH \rightarrow E$ yields the following minimal cover:

$$BH \rightarrow C$$
$$A \rightarrow D$$
$$C \rightarrow E \tag{8.12}$$
$$F \rightarrow A$$
$$E \rightarrow F$$

8.8.2 3NF Decomposition through Schema Synthesis

The algorithm for constructing dependency-preserving 3NF decompositions works very differently from its BCNF counterpart. Instead of starting with one big schema and successively splitting it, the 3NF algorithm starts with individual attributes and groups them into schemas. For this reason, it is called **3NF synthesis**. Given a schema, $\mathbf{R} = (\overline{R}; \mathcal{F})$, where $\overline{R}$ is a superset of attributes and $\mathcal{F}$ is a set of FDs, the algorithm carries out four steps.

1. Find a minimal cover, $\mathcal{G}$, for $\mathcal{F}$.

2. Partition $\mathcal{G}$ into FD sets $\mathcal{G}_1, \ldots, \mathcal{G}_n$, such that each $\mathcal{G}_i$ consists of FDs that share the same left-hand side. (It is not necessary to assume that different $\mathcal{G}_i$s have different left-hand sides, but it is usually a good idea to merge sets whose left-hand sides are the same.)

3. For each $\mathcal{G}_i$, form a relation schema, $\mathbf{R}_i = (\overline{R}_i; \mathcal{G}_i)$, where $\overline{R}_i$ is the set of all attributes mentioned in $\mathcal{G}_i$.

4. If one of the $\overline{R}_i$s, is a superkey of $\mathbf{R}$ (i.e., $(\overline{R}_i)_{\mathcal{F}}^{+} = \overline{R}$), we are done — $\mathbf{R}_1, \ldots, \mathbf{R}_n$ is the desired decomposition. If no $\overline{R}_i$ is a superkey of $\mathbf{R}$, let $\overline{R}_0$ be a set of attributes that constitutes a key of $\mathbf{R}$, and let $\mathbf{R}_0 = (\overline{R}_0; \{\})$ be a new schema. Then $\mathbf{R}_0, \mathbf{R}_1, \ldots, \mathbf{R}_n$ is the desired decomposition.

   Note that the collection of schemas obtained after step 3 might not even be a decomposition because some attributes of $\mathbf{R}$ might be missing (see example below). However, any such missing attributes will be recaptured in step 4, because these attributes must be part of the key of $\mathbf{R}$ (exercise 8.25).

It is easy to see that the result of the above algorithm is a dependency-preserving decomposition. By construction, every FD in $\mathcal{G}$ has a home, so $\mathcal{G} = \cup \mathcal{G}_i$. Since, by definition of minimal covers, $\mathcal{G}^{+} = \mathcal{F}^{+}$, $\mathcal{F}$ is preserved.

It also seems obvious that each $\mathbf{R}_i$ is a 3NF schema, because the only FDs associated with $\mathbf{R}_i$ are those in $\mathcal{G}_i$ and they all share the same left-hand side (which is thus a superkey of $\mathbf{R}_i$). It might seem that each $\mathbf{R}_i$ is also in BCNF but do not be fooled: The FDs in $\mathcal{G}_i$ might not be the only ones that hold in $\mathbf{R}_i$, because $\mathcal{G}^+$ might have other FDs whose attribute set is entirely contained within $\overline{R}_i$. To see this, consider a slight modification of our tried and true schema HASACCOUNT. Here $\overline{R}$ consists of the attributes AccountNumber, ClientId, OfficeId, DateOpened, and $\mathcal{F}$ consists of the FDs ClientId, OfficeId → AccountNumber and AccountNumber → OfficeId, DateOpened. The above algorithm then produces two schemas:

$$\mathbf{R}_1 = (\{\texttt{ClientId,OfficeId,AccountNumber}\},$$
$$\{\texttt{ClientId,OfficeId} \rightarrow \texttt{AccountNumber}\})$$
$$\mathbf{R}_2 = (\{\texttt{AccountNumber,OfficeId,DateOpened}\},$$
$$\{\texttt{AccountNumber} \rightarrow \texttt{OfficeId,DateOpened}\})$$

A careful examination shows that, even though AccountNumber → OfficeId is not explicitly specified for $\mathbf{R}_1$, it must nonetheless hold over the attributes of that schema because this FD is implicitly imposed by $\mathbf{R}_2$.

To understand why the FDs specified for $\mathbf{R}_2$ must be taken into account when considering $\mathbf{R}_1$, observe that the pair of attributes AccountNumber, OfficeId represents the same real-world relationship in both $\mathbf{R}_1$ and $\mathbf{R}_2$, so it is an inconsistency if the tuples in $\mathbf{R}_2$ obey a constraint over this pair of attributes while the tuples in $\mathbf{R}_1$ do not.

Coming back to the original issue, the above argument shows that schemas produced by our synthesis algorithm might have FDs with different left-hand sides and thus conformance to 3NF is not at all obvious. Nevertheless, it can be *proved* that the above algorithm always yields 3NF decompositions (see exercise 8.14).

The final question is whether the synthesis algorithm yields lossless decompositions of the input schema. The answer is yes, but proving this is more difficult than proving the 3NF property. Although it might not be obvious, achieving losslessness is in fact the only purpose of step 4 in that algorithm.

For a more complex example of 3NF synthesis, consider the schema with FDs depicted in (8.9) on page 235. A minimal cover for this set is shown in (8.12). Since no two FDs here share the same left-hand side, we end up with the following schemas: $(BHC; BH \rightarrow C)$ $(AD; A \rightarrow D)$, $(CE; C \rightarrow E)$, $(FA; F \rightarrow A)$, and $(EF; E \rightarrow F)$. Notice that none of these schemas forms the superkey for the entire set of attributes. For instance, the attribute closure of BHC does not contain G. In fact, the attribute G is not even included in any of the schemas! So, according to our remark about the purpose of step 4, this decomposition is not lossless (in fact, it is not even a decomposition!) To make it lossless, we perform step 4 and add the schema $(BCGH; \{\,\})$.

8.8.3 BCNF Decomposition through 3NF Synthesis

So, how can 3NF synthesis help design BCNF database schemas? The answer is simple: To decompose a schema into BCNF relations, do *not* use the BCNF algorithm first. Instead, use 3NF synthesis, which is lossless and guaranteed to preserve dependencies. If the resulting schemas are already in BCNF (as in our previous example), no further action is necessary. If, however, some schema in the result is not in BCNF, use the BCNF algorithm to split it until no violation of BCNF remains. Repeat this step for each non-BCNF schema produced by the 3NF synthesis.

The advantage of this approach is that, if a lossless and dependency-preserving decomposition exists, 3NF synthesis is likely to find it. If some schemas are not in BCNF after the first stage, loss of some FDs is inevitable (exercise 8.26). But at least we tried hard. Here is a complete example that illustrates the above approach.

Example 8.8.1 (Combining Schema Synthesis and Decomposition)
Let the attribute set be St (student), C (course), Sem (semester), P (professor), T (time), and R (room) with the following FDs:

```
St C Sem -> P
P Sem -> C
C Sem T -> P
P Sem T -> C R
P Sem C T -> R
P Sem T -> C
```

These functional dependencies apply at a university in which multiple sections of the same course might be taught in the same semester (so providing the name of a course and a semester does not uniquely identify a professor) and a professor teaches only one course a semester (so providing the name of a professor and a semester uniquely identifies a course) and all the sections of a course are taught at different times.

We begin by finding a minimal cover for the above set; the first step is to split the right-hand sides of the set of FDs into singleton attributes.

```
St C Sem -> P
P Sem -> C
C Sem T -> P
P Sem T -> C
P Sem T -> R
P Sem C T -> R
P Sem T -> C
```

Let $\mathcal{F}$ denote this set of FDs. The last FD is a duplicate, so we delete it from the set. Next we reduce the left-hand sides by eliminating redundant attributes. For instance, to check the left-hand side St C Sem, we must compute several attribute closures — $(St\ Sem)_{\mathcal{F}}^+ = \{St,\ Sem\}$; $(St\ C)_{\mathcal{F}}^+ = \{St,\ C\}$; $(C\ Sem)_{\mathcal{F}}^+ = \{C,\ Sem\}$ — which show that there are no redundant attributes in the first FD. Similarly, P Sem, C Sem T, and P Sem T cannot be reduced. However, checking P Sem C T brings some reward: $(P\ Sem\ T)_{\mathcal{F}}^+ = P\ Sem\ T\ C\ R$, so C can be deleted.

The outcome from this stage is the following set of FDs, which we number for convenient reference.

```
FD 1. St C Sem -> P
FD 2. P Sem -> C
FD 3. C Sem T -> P
FD 4. P Sem T -> C
FD 5. P Sem T -> R
```

The next step is to get rid of the redundant FDs, which are detected with the help of attribute closure, as usual. Since $(St\ C\ Sem)^+_{\{\mathcal{F}-FD\ 1\}} = St\ C\ Sem$, FD 1 cannot be eliminated. Nor can FDs 2, 3, and 5. However, FD 4 is redundant (because of FD 2), so it can be eliminated. Thus, the minimal cover is

```
St C Sem -> P
P Sem -> C
C Sem T -> P
P Sem T -> R
```

This leads to the following dependency-preserving 3NF decomposition:

```
(St C Sem P; St C Sem -> P)
(P Sem C; P Sem -> C)
(C Sem T P; C Sem T -> P)
(P Sem T R; P Sem T -> R)
```

It is easy to verify that none of the above schemas forms a superkey for the original schema; therefore, to make the above decomposition lossless we also need to add a schema whose attribute closure contains all the original attributes. The schema (St T Sem P; { }) is one possibility here.

If you trust that the 3NF synthesis algorithm is correct and that we did not make mistakes applying it, no checking for 3NF is necessary. However, a quick look reveals that the first and the third schemas are not in BCNF because of the FD P Sem → C embedded in the second schema.

Further decomposition of the first schema with respect to P Sem → C yields (P Sem C; P Sem → C) and (P Sem St; { })—a lossless decomposition but one in which the FD St C Sem → P is not preserved.

Decomposition of the third schema with respect to P Sem → C yields (P Sem C; P Sem → C) and (P Sem T; {})—another lossless decomposition, which, alas, loses C Sem T → P.

So, the final BCNF decomposition is

```
(P Sem C; P Sem → C)
(P Sem St)
(P Sem T)
(P Sem T R; P Sem T → R)
(St T Sem P)
```

This decomposition is lossless because we first obtained a lossless 3NF decomposition and then applied the BCNF algorithm, which preserves losslessness. It is not dependency preserving, however, since St C Sem → P and C Sem T → P are not represented in the above schemas. □

8.9 THE FOURTH NORMAL FORM

Not all of the world's problems are due to bad FDs. Consider the following schema:

$$\text{PERSON}(\text{SSN}, \text{PhoneN}, \text{ChildSSN}) \tag{8.13}$$

where we assume that a person can have several phone numbers and several children. Here is one possible relation instance.

SSN	PhoneN	ChildSSN
111-22-3333	516-123-4567	222-33-4444
111-22-3333	516-345-6789	222-33-4444
111-22-3333	516-123-4567	333-44-5555
111-22-3333	516-345-6789	333-44-5555
222-33-4444	212-987-6543	444-55-6666
222-33-4444	212-987-1111	555-66-7777
222-33-4444	212-987-6543	555-66-7777
222-33-4444	212-987-1111	444-55-6666

(8.14)

As there are no nontrivial functional dependencies, this schema is in 3NF and even BCNF. Nonetheless, it is clearly not a good design as it exhibits a great deal of redundancy. There is no particular association between phone numbers and children, except through the SSN, so every child item related to a given SSN must occur in one tuple with every PhoneN related to the same SSN. Thus, whenever a phone number is added or deleted, several tuples might need to be added or deleted as well. If a person gives up all phone numbers, the information about her children will be lost (or NULL values will have to be used).

It might seem that a compression technique can help here. For instance, we might decide to store only some tuples as long as there is a way to reconstruct the original information.

SSN	PhoneN	ChildSSN
111-22-3333	516-123-4567	222-33-4444
111-22-3333	516-345-6789	333-44-5555
222-33-4444	212-987-6543	444-55-6666
222-33-4444	212-987-1111	555-66-7777

Still, although this is more efficient, it solves none of the aforesaid anomalies. Also, it imposes an additional burden on the applications, which now must be aware of the compression schema.

In our discussion of BCNF, we concluded that redundancy arises when a particular semantic relationship among attribute values is stored more than once. In Figure 5.2 on page 93, the fact that the person with SSN 111111111 lives at 123 Main St. is an example of that—it is stored three times. In that case, the problem was traced back to the functional dependency that relates SSN and Address and the fact that SSN is not a key (and hence there can be several rows with the same SSN value). The redundant storage of a semantic relationship, however, is not limited to this situation. In the relation **r** shown in (8.14), the relationships SSN-PhoneN and SSN-ChildSSN are stored multiple times and there are no FDs involved. The problem arises here because there are several attributes—in this case PhoneN and ChildSSN—that have the property that their sets of values are associated with a single value of another attribute—in this case SSN. A relationship between a particular SSN value and a particular PhoneN value is stored as many times as there are children of the person with that SSN. Note that the relation satisfies the following property:

$$\mathbf{r} = \pi_{\text{SSN,PhoneN}}(\mathbf{r}) \bowtie \pi_{\text{SSN,ChildSSN}}(\mathbf{r}) \tag{8.15}$$

When (8.15) is required of all legal instances of a schema, this property is known as join dependency. A join dependency can arise when characteristics of an enterprise are described by sets of values. With the E-R approach to database design, we saw that such characteristics are represented as set-valued attributes and that translating them into attributes in the relational model is awkward. In particular, when an entity type or a relationship type has several set-valued attributes, a join dependency results.

Condition (8.15) should look familiar to you. It guarantees that a decomposition of **r** into the two tables $\pi_{\text{SSN,PhoneN}}(\mathbf{r})$ and $\pi_{\text{SSN,ChildSSN}}(\mathbf{r})$ will be lossless. That is certainly true in this case, but it is not our immediate concern. The condition also tells us something about **r**: A join dependency indicates that semantic relationships can be stored redundantly in an instance of **r**.

Formally, let $\overline{R}$ be a set of attributes. A **join dependency (JD)** is a constraint of the form

$$\overline{R} = \overline{R}_1 \bowtie \cdots \bowtie \overline{R}_n$$

where $\overline{R}_1, \ldots, \overline{R}_n$ is a decomposition of $\overline{R}$. Recall that earlier (page 216) we defined the notion of satisfaction of FDs by relational instances. We now define the same notion for JDs: A relation instance, **r**, over $\overline{R}$ **satisfies** the above join dependency if

$$\mathbf{r} = \pi_{\overline{R}_1}(\mathbf{r}) \bowtie \cdots \bowtie \pi_{\overline{R}_n}(\mathbf{r})$$

Let $\mathbf{R} = (\overline{R};\ Constraints)$ be a relational schema, where $\overline{R}$ is a set of attributes and *Constraints* is a set of FDs and JDs. As in the case of FDs alone, a relation over the set of attributes $\overline{R}$ is a **legal instance** of **R** if and only if it satisfies all constraints in *Constraints*.

Of particular interest are so-called **binary** join dependencies, also known as **multivalued dependencies** (*MVD*). These are JDs of the form $\overline{R} = \overline{R}_1 \bowtie \overline{R}_2$. The redundancy exhibited by the relation schema PERSON (8.13) was caused by this particular type of join dependency. The *fourth normal form*, introduced in [Fagin 1977], is designed to prevent redundancies of this type.

MVDs constrain instances of a relation in the same way that FDs do, so a description of a relation schema must include both. As a result, we describe a relation schema, **R**, as $(\overline{R}; \mathcal{D})$, where $\mathcal{D}$ is now a set of FDs and MVDs. **Entailment** of JDs is defined in the same way as entailment of FDs. Let $\mathcal{S}$ be a set of JDs (and possibly FDs) and d be a JD (or an FD). Then $\mathcal{S}$ **entails** d if every relation instance **r** that satisfies all dependencies in $\mathcal{S}$ also satisfies d. In the next section, we show how an MVD might be entailed by a set of MVDs. With this in mind, a relation schema, $\mathbf{R} = (\overline{R}; \mathcal{D})$, is said to be in **fourth normal form** (*4NF*) if, for every MVD $\overline{R} = \overline{X} \bowtie \overline{Y}$ that is entailed by $\mathcal{D}$, either of the following is true:

■ $\overline{X} \subseteq \overline{Y}$ or $\overline{Y} \subseteq \overline{X}$ (the MVD is trivial).

■ $\overline{X} \cap \overline{Y}$ is a superkey of $\overline{R}$ $((\overline{X} \cap \overline{Y}) \rightarrow \overline{R}$ is entailed by $\mathcal{D})$.

It is easy to see that PERSON is not a 4NF schema, because the MVD PERSON = {SSN PhoneN} $\bowtie$ {SSN ChildSSN} holds whereas SSN = {SSN PhoneN} $\cap$ {SSN ChildSSN} is not a superkey. What is the intuition here? If SSN were a superkey, then for each value of SSN there would be at most one value of PhoneN and one value of ChildSSN and hence no redundancy.

4NF and BCNF.   As it turns out, 4NF schemas are also BCNF schemas (i.e., 4NF closes the loopholes that BCNF leaves behind). To see this, suppose that $\mathbf{R} = (\overline{R}; \mathcal{D})$ is a 4NF schema and $\overline{X} \rightarrow \overline{Y}$ is a nontrivial functional dependency that holds in **R**. To show that 4NF schemas are also BCNF schemas we must demonstrate that $\overline{X}$ is a superkey of **R**. For simplicity, assume that $\overline{X}$ and $\overline{Y}$ are disjoint. Then $\overline{R}_1 = \overline{X}\,\overline{Y}$, $\overline{R}_2 = \overline{R} - \overline{Y}$ is a lossless decomposition of **R**, which follows directly from the test for losslessness of binary schema decompositions presented in Section 8.6.1. Thus, $\overline{R} = \overline{R}_1 \bowtie \overline{R}_2$ is a binary join dependency, i.e., an MVD that holds in **R**. But by the definition of 4NF it follows that either $\overline{X}\,\overline{Y} \subseteq \overline{R} - \overline{Y}$ (an impossibility) or $\overline{R} - \overline{Y} \subseteq \overline{X}\,\overline{Y}$ (which means that $\overline{R} = \overline{X}\,\overline{Y}$ and $\overline{X}$ is a superkey) or $\overline{R}_1 \cap \overline{R}_2 (= \overline{X})$ is a superkey. This means that every nontrivial FD in **R** satisfies the BCNF requirements.

It can also be shown (but it is harder to do so) that if $\mathbf{R} = (\overline{R}; \mathcal{D})$ is such that $\mathcal{D}$ consists only of FDs, then **R** is in 4NF if and only if it is in BCNF (see [Fagin 1977]). In other words, 4NF is an extension of the requirements for BCNF to design environments where MVDs, in addition to FDs, must be specified.

Designing 4NF schemas.   Because 4NF implies BCNF, we cannot hope to find a general algorithm for constructing a dependency-preserving and lossless decomposition of an arbitrary relation into relations in 4NF. However, as with BCNF, a lossless decomposition into 4NF can always be achieved. Such an algorithm is very similar to that for BCNF. It is an iterative process that starts with the original schema and at each stage yields decompositions that have fewer MVDs that violate 4NF: If $\mathbf{R}_i = (\overline{R}_i; \mathcal{D}_i)$ is such an intermediate schema and $\mathcal{D}_i$ entails an MVD, $\overline{R}_i = \overline{X} \bowtie \overline{Y}$, that violates 4NF, the algorithm replaces $\mathbf{R}_i$ with a pair of schemas $(\overline{X}; \mathcal{D}_{i,1})$ and $(\overline{Y}; \mathcal{D}_{i,2})$—neither of which have that MVD. Eventually, there will be no MVDs left that violate the requirements for 4NF.

Two important points regarding this algorithm need to be emphasized. First, if $\mathbf{R}_i = (\overline{R}_i; \mathcal{D}_i)$ is a schema and $\overline{S} \to \overline{T} \in \mathcal{D}$ (for simplicity, assume that $\overline{S}$ and $\overline{T}$ are disjoint), then this FD implies the MVD $R_i = \overline{S}\,\overline{T} \bowtie (\overline{R}_i - \overline{T})$. Thus, the 4NF decomposition algorithm can treat FDs as MVDs. The other non-obvious issue in the 4NF decomposition algorithm has to do with determining the set of dependencies that hold in the decomposition. That is, if $\mathbf{R}_i = (\overline{R}_i; \mathcal{D}_i)$ is decomposed with respect to the MVD $\overline{R}_i = \overline{X} \bowtie \overline{Y}$, what is the set of dependencies that is expected to hold over the attributes $\overline{X}$ and $\overline{Y}$ in the resulting decomposition? The answer is $\pi_{\overline{X}}(\mathcal{D}_i^+)$ and $\pi_{\overline{Y}}(\mathcal{D}_i^+)$—the projections of $\mathcal{D}_i^+$ on $\overline{X}$ and $\overline{Y}$. Here $\mathcal{D}_i^+$ is the **closure** of $\mathcal{D}_i$, i.e., the set of all FDs and MVDs entailed by $\mathcal{D}_i$ (the optional Section 8.10 provides a set of inference rules for MVD entailment). Projection of FDs on a set of attributes has been defined in Section 8.6.2. For an MVD, $\overline{R}_i = \overline{V} \bowtie \overline{W}$ in $\mathcal{D}_i^+$, its projection $\pi_{\overline{X}}(\overline{R}_i = \overline{V} \bowtie \overline{W})$ is defined as $\overline{X} = (\overline{X} \cap \overline{V}) \bowtie (\overline{X} \cap \overline{W})$, if $\overline{V} \cap \overline{W} \subseteq \overline{X}$, and it is undefined otherwise. It can easily be verified that the projection rule for MVDs is sound (see exercise 8.22).

To illustrate the algorithm, consider a schema with attributes $ABCD$ and the MVDs $ABCD = AB \bowtie BCD$, $ABCD = ACD \bowtie BD$, and $ABCD = ABC \bowtie BCD$. Applying the first MVD, we obtain the following decomposition: AB, BCD. Projection of the remaining MVDs on AB is undefined. Projection of the third MVD on BCD is $BCD = BC \bowtie BCD$, which is a trivial MVD, and projection of the second MVD on BCD is $BCD = CD \bowtie BD$. Thus, we can decompose BCD with respect to this last MVD, which yields the following final result: AB, BD, CD. Note that if we first decomposed $ABCD$ with respect to the third MVD, the final result would be different: AB, BC, BD, CD.

The design theory for 4NF is not as well developed as those for 3NF and BCNF, and very few algorithms are known. The basic recommendation is to start with a decomposition into 3NF and then proceed with the above algorithm and further decompose the offending (non-4NF) schemas. On a more sophisticated level, the work reported in [Beeri and Kifer 1986a, 1986b, 1987], among others, develop a design theory and the corresponding algorithms that can rectify design problems by synthesizing *new* (!) attributes. These advanced issues are briefly surveyed in the next section.

The fifth normal form. We are not going to cover the fifth normal form in this book. Suffice it to say that it exists, but that the database designer usually need not be concerned with it. 5NF is similar to 4NF in that it is based on join dependencies, but unlike 4NF it seeks to preclude all nontrivial JDs (not just the binary ones) that are not entailed by a superkey.

8.10 ADVANCED 4NF DESIGN*

The 4NF design algorithm outlined in Section 8.9 was intended to familiarize you with MVDs and 4NF, but it only scratches the surface of the 4NF design process. In this section, we provide more in-depth information, explain the main difficulties in designing database schemas in the presence of both FDs and MVDs, and outline the solutions. In particular, we explain why the 4NF decomposition algorithm does not truly solve the redundancy problem and why BCNF might be inadequate in the presence of MVDs. We refer you to the literature for more details.

8.10.1 MVDs and Their Properties

Multivalued dependencies are binary join dependencies. However, unlike general join dependencies they have a number of nice algebraic properties similar to those of FDs. In particular, a set of syntactic rules, analogous to Armstrong's axioms for FDs, can be used to derive new MVDs entailed by a given MVD set. These rules have a particularly simple form when we use a special notation for MVDs: It is customary to represent the multivalued dependency of the form $\overline{R} = \overline{V} \bowtie \overline{W}$ over a relation schema $\mathbf{R} = (\overline{R}, \mathcal{D})$ as $\overline{X} \twoheadrightarrow \overline{Y}$, where $\overline{X} = \overline{V} \cap \overline{W}$ and $\overline{X} \cup \overline{Y} = \overline{V}$ or $\overline{X} \cup \overline{Y} = \overline{W}$. Hence, $\overline{X} \twoheadrightarrow \overline{Y}$ is synonymous with $\overline{R} = \overline{X}\,\overline{Y} \bowtie \overline{X}(\overline{R} - \overline{Y})$.

Take a moment to understand the intuition behind this notation. An MVD arises when a single value of one attribute, for example, A, is related to a set of values of attribute, B, and a set of values of attribute C. Attribute A, contained in $\overline{X}$, can be thought of as an independent variable whose value determines (hence the symbol $\twoheadrightarrow$) the associated sets of values of both B and C, one of which is contained in $\overline{Y}$ and the other in the complement of $\overline{X}\,\overline{Y}$. For example, the MVD in the PERSON relation (8.13), SSN PhoneN $\bowtie$ SSN ChildSSN, can be expressed as SSN $\twoheadrightarrow$ PhoneN or SSN $\twoheadrightarrow$ ChildSSN.

In addition, it is often convenient to combine MVDs that share the same left-hand side. For example, $\overline{X} \twoheadrightarrow \overline{Y}$ and $\overline{X} \twoheadrightarrow \overline{Z}$ can be represented as $\overline{X} \twoheadrightarrow \overline{Y} \mid \overline{Z}$. It is simple to show that such a pair of MVDs is equivalent to a join dependency of the form $\overline{X}\,\overline{Y} \bowtie \overline{X}\,\overline{Z} \bowtie \overline{X}(\overline{R} - \overline{Y}\,\overline{Z})$. The representation $\overline{X} \twoheadrightarrow \overline{Y} \mid \overline{Z}$ is convenient not only for the inference system but also as a device that shows where the redundancy is: If the attributes of $\overline{X}$, $\overline{Y}$, and $\overline{Z}$ are contained within one relational schema, the associations between $\overline{Y}$ and $\overline{Z}$ are likely to be stored redundantly. We saw this problem in the context of the PERSON relation and will come back to it later.

With this notation, we now present an inference system that can be used to decide entailment for *both* FDs and MVDs. The extended system contains Armstrong's axioms plus the following rules.

FD–MVD glue.   These rules mix FDs and MVDs.

■ *Replication.* $\overline{X} \to \overline{Y}$ entails $\overline{X} \twoheadrightarrow \overline{Y}$.

■ *Coalescence.*   If $\overline{W} \subset \overline{Y}$ and $\overline{Y} \cap \overline{Z} = \emptyset$, then $\overline{X} \twoheadrightarrow \overline{Y}$ and $\overline{Z} \to \overline{W}$ entail $\overline{X} \to \overline{W}$.

MVD-only rules.   Some of these rules are similar to rules for FDs; some are new.

■ *Reflexivity.* $\overline{X} \twoheadrightarrow \overline{X}$ holds in every relation.

■ *Augmentation.* $\overline{X} \twoheadrightarrow \overline{Y}$ entails $\overline{X}\,\overline{Z} \twoheadrightarrow \overline{Y}$.

■ *Additivity.* $\overline{X} \twoheadrightarrow \overline{Y}$ and $\overline{X} \twoheadrightarrow \overline{Z}$ entail $\overline{X} \twoheadrightarrow \overline{Y}\,\overline{Z}$.

■ *Projectivity.* $\overline{X} \twoheadrightarrow \overline{Y}$ and $\overline{X} \twoheadrightarrow \overline{Z}$ entail $\overline{X} \twoheadrightarrow \overline{Y} \cap \overline{Z}$ and $\overline{X} \twoheadrightarrow \overline{Y} - \overline{Z}$.

■ *Transitivity.* $\overline{X} \twoheadrightarrow \overline{Y}$ and $\overline{Y} \twoheadrightarrow \overline{Z}$ entail $\overline{X} \twoheadrightarrow \overline{Z} - \overline{Y}$.

■ *Pseudotransitivity.* $\overline{X} \twoheadrightarrow \overline{Y}$ and $\overline{Y}\,\overline{W} \twoheadrightarrow \overline{Z}$ entail $\overline{X}\,\overline{W} \twoheadrightarrow \overline{Z} - (\overline{Y}\,\overline{W})$.

■ *Complementation.* $\overline{X} \twoheadrightarrow \overline{Y}$ entails $\overline{X} \twoheadrightarrow \overline{R} - \overline{X}\,\overline{Y}$, where $\overline{R}$ is the set of all attributes in the schema.

These rules first appeared in [Beeri et al. 1977], but [Maier 1983] provides a more systematic and accessible introduction to the subject. The rules are *sound* in the sense that in any relation where a rule premise holds, the consequent of the rule must also hold. For example, replication follows using the same reasoning we used for losslessness: If $\overline{X} \to \overline{Y}$ then the decomposition of $\overline{R}$ into $\overline{R_1} = \overline{X}\,\overline{Y}$ and $\overline{R_2} = \overline{X}(\overline{R} - \overline{Y})$ is lossless; hence, $\overline{R} = \overline{X}\,\overline{Y} \bowtie \overline{X}(\overline{R} - \overline{Y})$ and so $\overline{X} \twoheadrightarrow \overline{Y}$.

A remarkable fact, however, is that given a set, $\mathcal{S}$, that consists of MVDs and FDs and a dependency, d, which can be either an FD or an MVD, $\mathcal{S}$ entails d if and only if d can be derived by a purely syntactic application of the above rules (plus Armstrong's axioms) to the dependencies in $\mathcal{S}$. A similar property for FDs alone was earlier called *completeness*. Proving the soundness of the above inference rules is a good exercise (see exercise 8.21). Completeness is much harder to prove. The interested reader is referred to [Beeri et al. 1977, Maier 1983].

8.10.2 The Difficulty of Designing for 4NF

The inference rules for MVDs are useful because they can help eliminate redundant MVDs and FDs. Also, as in the case of FDs alone, using nonredundant dependency sets can improve the design produced by the 4NF decomposition algorithm described earlier. However, even in the absence of redundant dependencies things can go awry. We illustrate some of the problems on a number of examples. Three issues are considered: loss of dependencies, redundancy, and design using both FDs and MVDs.

A contracts example.   Consider the schema

CONTRACTS(Buyer, Vendor, Product, Currency)

where a tuple of the form ⟨John Doe, Acme, Paper Clips, USD⟩ means that buyer John Doe has a contract to buy paper clips from Acme, Inc., using U.S. currency. Suppose that our relation represents contracts of an international network of buyers and companies. Although the contract was consummated in dollars, if Acme sells some of its products in DM (perhaps it is a German company), it may be convenient to store the contract in two tuples: one with the financial information expressed in USD, the other information expressed in DM. In general, CONTRACTS satisfies the rule that, if a company accepts several currencies, each contract is described in each one. This can be expressed using the following combined MVD:

$$\text{Buyer Vendor} \twoheadrightarrow \text{Product} \mid \text{Currency} \tag{8.16}$$

To be explicit, this MVD means

CONTRACTS = (Buyer Vendor Product) ⋈ (Buyer Vendor Currency).

The second rule of our international network is that, if two vendors supply a certain product and accept a certain currency and a buyer of that product has a contract to buy certain product with one of the two vendors, then this buyer must have a contract for that product with the other vendor as well. For example, if, in addition to the above tuple, CONTRACTS contained ⟨Mary Smith, OfficeMin, Paper Clips, USD⟩, then it must also contain the tuples ⟨John Doe, OfficeMin, Paper Clips, USD⟩ and ⟨Mary Smith, Acme, Paper Clips, USD⟩. This type of constraint is expressed using the following MVD:

$$\text{Product Currency} \twoheadrightarrow \text{Buyer} \mid \text{Vendor} \tag{8.17}$$

Let us try to follow the 4NF decomposition algorithm. If we first decompose using the dependency (8.16), we get the following lossless decomposition:

(Buyer, Vendor, Product)
(Buyer, Vendor, Currency)   (8.18)

Observe that, once this decomposition is done, the second MVD can no longer be applied because no join dependency holds in either one of the above schemas.[7] The situation here is very similar to the problem we faced with the BCNF decomposition algorithm: Some dependencies might get lost in the process. In our case, it is the dependency (8.17). The same problem exists if we first decompose using the second dependency above, but in this case we lose (8.16).

Unlike losing FDs during BCNF decomposition, losing MVDs is potentially a more serious problem because the result might still harbor redundancy even if

---

[7] It is not quite obvious because we have not discussed the tools appropriate for verifying such facts. However, in this concrete example our claim can be checked using the definition of the natural join directly. We again recommend [Maier 1983] as a good reference for learning about such techniques.

every relation in the decomposition is in 4NF! To see this, consider the following relation for the CONTRACTS schema:

Buyer	Vendor	Product	Currency
B_1	V_1	P	C
B_2	V_2	P	C
B_1	V_2	P	C
B_2	V_1	P	C

It is easy to check that this relation satisfies MVDs (8.16) and (8.17). For instance, to verify (8.16) take the projections on decomposition schema (8.18).

Buyer	Vendor	Product
B_1	V_1	P
B_2	V_2	P
B_1	V_2	P
B_2	V_1	P

Buyer	Vendor	Currency
B_1	V_1	C
B_2	V_2	C
B_1	V_2	C
B_2	V_1	C

Joining these two relations (using the natural join) clearly yields the original relation for CONTRACTS. A closer look shows that the above relations still contain a great deal of redundancy. For instance, the first relation twice says that product P is supplied by vendors V_1 and V_2. Furthermore, it twice says that P is wanted by buyers B_1 and B_2. The first relation seems to beg for further decomposition into (Buyer, Vendor) and (Vendor, Product), and the second relation begs to be decomposed into (Buyer, Currency) and (Vendor, Currency). Alas, none of these wishes can be granted because none of these decompositions is lossless (for example, Vendor is not a key of the first relation). As a result, decomposition (8.18) suffers from the usual update anomalies even though each relation is in 4NF! Furthermore, since 4NF implies BCNF, even BCNF does not guarantee complete elimination of redundancy in the presence of MVDs!

A dictionary example.   For another example, consider a multilingual dictionary relation, DICTIONARY(English, French, German), which provides translations from one language to another. As expected, every term has a translation (possibly more than one) into every language, and the translations are independent of each other. These constraints are easily captured using MVDs.

$$\text{English} \twoheadrightarrow \text{French} \mid \text{German}$$
$$\text{French} \twoheadrightarrow \text{English} \mid \text{German} \qquad (8.19)$$
$$\text{German} \twoheadrightarrow \text{English} \mid \text{French}$$

The problem, as before, is that applying any one of these MVDs in the 4NF decomposition algorithm loses the other two dependencies, and the resulting decomposition exhibits the usual update anomalies.

A multilingual thesaurus example.   Let us enhance the previous example so that every term is now associated with a unique concept and each concept has an associated description (for the purpose of this example, ignore the language used for the description). The corresponding schema becomes DICTIONARY(Concept, Description, English, French, German), where the dependencies are

$$
\begin{aligned}
&\texttt{English} \rightarrow \texttt{Concept} \\
&\texttt{French} \rightarrow \texttt{Concept} \\
&\texttt{German} \rightarrow \texttt{Concept} \\
&\texttt{Concept} \rightarrow \texttt{Description} \\
&\texttt{Concept} \twoheadrightarrow \texttt{English} \mid \texttt{French} \mid \texttt{German}
\end{aligned}
\qquad (8.20)
$$

An example of a concept is A5329 with description "homo sapiens" and translations {human, man}, {homme}, and {Mensch, Mann}.

The 4NF decomposition algorithm suggests that we start by picking up an MVD that violates 4NF and then use it in the decomposition process. Since every FD is also an MVD, we might choose English → Concept first, which yields the schema (English, Concept) and (English, French, German, Description). Using the transitivity rule for MVDs, we can derive the MVD English ↠ French | German | Description and further decompose the second relation into (English, French), (English, German), and (English, Description).

The resulting schema has two drawbacks. First, it is lopsided toward English whereas the original schema was completely symmetric. Second, every one of the bilingual relations, such as (English, French), redundantly lists all possible translations from English to French and back. For example, if a and b are English synonyms, c and d are French synonyms, and a translates into c, then the English-French dictionary (English, French) has all four tuples: $\langle a, c \rangle$, $\langle a, d \rangle$, $\langle b, c \rangle$, and $\langle b, d \rangle$.

A better way to use the 4NF decomposition algorithm is to compute the attribute closure (defined on page 220) of the left-hand side of the MVD in (8.20) with respect to functional dependencies in (8.20) and derive the following MVD by the augmentation rule:

$$
\texttt{Concept Description} \twoheadrightarrow \texttt{English} \mid \texttt{French} \mid \texttt{German}
$$

We can then apply the 4NF decomposition algorithm using this MVD, which yields the decomposition (Concept, Description, English), (Concept, Description, French), and (Concept, Description, German). We can further decompose each of these relations into BCNF using the FDs alone, spinning off (Concept Description). Not only do we end up with a decomposition into 4NF, but also all dependencies are preserved.

8.10.3   A 4NF Decomposition How–To

The above examples make it clear that designing for 4NF is not a straightforward process. In fact, this problem was an active area of research until the early 1980s [Beeri et al. 1978, Zaniolo and Melkanoff 1981, Sciore 1983]. Eventually, all of this work was integrated into a uniform framework in [Beeri and Kifer 1986b]. While we cannot go into the details of this approach, its highlights can be explained with our three examples: contracts, dictionary, and thesaurus.

1. *The anomaly of split left-hand sides.* It is indicative of a design problem when one MVD splits the left-hand side of another, as in our contracts example. For instance, MVD (8.17) splits the left-hand side, (Buyer, Vendor), of (8.16), which indicates that Buyer and Vendor are unrelated attributes (every buyer is associated in some tuple with every vendor) and should not be in the same relation. This is precisely the reason for the redundancy that we observed in the decomposition of the CONTRACTS relation into (Buyer, Vendor, Product) and (Buyer, Vendor, Currency).

   One reason for the problem with this schema might be the incorrectly specified dependencies. Instead of the MVDs given in the CONTRACT schema, the join dependency

$$\text{Buyer Product} \bowtie \text{Vendor Product}$$
$$\bowtie \text{Vendor Currency} \bowtie \text{Buyer Currency}$$

   seems more appropriate. It simply says that each buyer needs certain products, each vendor sells certain products, a vendor can accept certain currencies, and a buyer can pay in certain currencies. As long as a buyer and a vendor can match on a product and a currency, a deal can be struck. This English-language description matches the requirements in the description of the contracts example, and the designer might have simply failed to recognize that the above JD is all that is needed.

2. *Intersection anomaly.* An intersection anomaly is one in which a schema has a pair of MVDs of the form $\overline{X} \twoheadrightarrow \overline{Z}$ and $\overline{Y} \twoheadrightarrow \overline{Z}$ but there is no MVD $\overline{X} \cap \overline{Y} \twoheadrightarrow \overline{Z}$. Notice that our dictionary example has precisely this sort of anomaly: There are MVDs English $\twoheadrightarrow$ French and German $\twoheadrightarrow$ French, but there is no dependency $\emptyset \twoheadrightarrow$ French. [Beeri and Kifer 1986b] argue that this is a design problem that can be rectified by inventing new(!) attributes. In this case, the attribute Concept is missing. In fact, our thesaurus example was constructed out of the dictionary example by adding this very attribute[8] plus the dependencies that relate it to the old attributes. Perhaps surprisingly, this type of anomaly can be corrected automatically—the new attribute and the associated dependencies can be invented by a well-defined algorithm [Beeri and Kifer 1986a, 1987].

3. *Design strategy.* Assuming that the anomaly of split left-hand sides does not arise,[9] a dependency-preserving decomposition of the schema $\mathbf{R} = (\overline{R}; \mathcal{D})$ into fourth normal form can be achieved in five steps.

   a. Compute attribute closure, X^+ the left-hand side of every MVD $X \twoheadrightarrow Y$ using the FDs entailed by $\mathcal{D}$. Replace every $X \twoheadrightarrow Y$ with $X^+ \twoheadrightarrow Y$.

---

[8] The other attribute, Description, was added to illustrate a different point. Ignore it for the moment.
[9] Any such anomaly means that the dependencies are incorrect or incomplete.

b. Find the minimal cover of the resulting set of MVDs. It turns out that such a cover is unique if $\mathcal{D}$ does not exhibit the anomaly of split left-hand sides.

c. Use the algorithm of [Beeri and Kifer 1986a, 1987] to eliminate intersection anomalies by adding new attributes.

d. Apply the 4NF decomposition algorithm using MVDs only.

e. Apply the BCNF design algorithm within each resulting schema using FDs only.

Every relation in the resulting decomposition is in 4NF and no MVD is lost on the way, which guarantees that no redundancy is present in the resulting schemas. Moreover, if the decompositions in the last stage are dependency preserving, so is the overall five-step process.

The transition from the dictionary example to the thesaurus example and then to the final decomposition of the thesaurus example is an illustration of the five-step process. To keep our examples simple, we applied step (c) first and then added an extra attribute, Description, to illustrate step (a) and to make step (e) more interesting. Since our examples do not have any redundant MVDs, step (b) is not necessary.

8.11   SUMMARY OF NORMAL FORM DECOMPOSITION

We summarize some of the properties of the normal form decomposition algorithms discussed.

■ *Third normal form* schemas might have some redundancy. The decomposition algorithm we discussed generates 3NF schemas that are lossless and dependency preserving. It does not take multivalued dependencies into account.

■ *Boyce-Codd* decompositions do not have redundancy if only FDs are considered. The decomposition algorithm we discussed generates BCNF schemas that are lossless but that might not be dependency preserving. (As we have shown, some schemas do not have Boyce-Codd decompositions that are both lossless and dependency preserving.) It does not take multivalued dependencies into account, so redundancy due to such dependencies is possible.

■ *Fourth normal form* decompositions do not have any nontrivial multivalued dependencies. The algorithm we sketched generates 4NF schemas that are lossless but that might not be dependency preserving. It attempts to eliminate redundancies associated with MVDs, but it does not guarantee that all such redundancies will go away.

Note that none of these decompositions produces schemas that have all of the properties we want.

8.12   CASE STUDY: SCHEMA REFINEMENT FOR THE STUDENT REGISTRATION SYSTEM

CASE STUDY

Having spent all that effort studying relational normalization theory, we can now use it to verify our design for the Student Registration System as outlined in Section 5.7. The good news is that we did a pretty good job of converting the E-R diagram in Figure 5.14, page 114, into the relations in Figures 5.15 and 5.16, so most of the relations turn out to be in Boyce-Codd normal form. However, you did not struggle through this chapter in vain—read on!

To determine whether a schema is in a normal form we need to collect all FDs relevant to it. One source is the PRIMARY KEY and the UNIQUE constraints. However, there might be additional dependencies that are not captured by these constraints or the E-R diagram. They can be uncovered only by careful examination of the schema and of the specifications of the application, a process that requires much care and concentration. If no new dependencies are found, all FDs in the schema are the primary and the candidate keys (or the FDs entailed by them), so the schema is in BCNF. If additional FDs are uncovered, we must check if the schema is in a desirable normal form and, if not, make appropriate changes.

In our case, we can verify that all relation schemas in Figure 5.16, except CLASS, are in BCNF, as they have no FDs that are not entailed by the keys. This verification is not particularly hard because these schemas have six or fewer attributes. It is harder in the case of CLASS, which has ten.

We illustrate the process using the CLASS schema. Along the way, we uncover a missing functional dependency and then normalize CLASS. First, let us list the key constraints specified in the CREATE TABLE statement for that relation.

1. CrsCode SectionNo Semester Year → ClassTime
2. CrsCode SectionNo Semester Year → Textbook
3. CrsCode SectionNo Semester Year → Enrollment
4. CrsCode SectionNo Semester Year → MaxEnrollment
5. CrsCode SectionNo Semester Year → ClassroomId
6. CrsCode SectionNo Semester Year → InstructorId
7. Semester Year ClassTime InstructorId → CrsCode
8. Semester Year ClassTime InstructorId → Textbook
9. Semester Year ClassTime InstructorId → SectionNo
10. Semester Year ClassTime InstructorId → Enrollment
11. Semester Year ClassTime InstructorId → MaxEnrollment
12. Semester Year ClassTime InstructorId → ClassroomId
13. Semester Year ClassTime ClassroomId → CrsCode
14. Semester Year ClassTime ClassroomId → Textbook
15. Semester Year ClassTime ClassroomId → SectionNo
16. Semester Year ClassTime ClassroomId → Enrollment

17. `Semester Year ClassTime ClassroomId → MaxEnrollment`
18. `Semester Year ClassTime ClassroomId → InstructorId`

Verifying that additional dependencies hold in a large schema can be difficult: One has to consider every subset of the attributes of CLASS that is not a superkey and check if it functionally determines some other attribute. This "check" is not based on any concrete algorithm. The decision that a certain FD does or does not hold in a relation is strictly a matter of how the designer understands the semantics of the corresponding entity in the real-world enterprise that is being modeled by the database, and it is inherently error prone. However, research is being conducted to help with the problem. For instance, FDEXPERT [Ram 1995] is an expert system that helps database designers discover FDs using knowledge about typical enterprises and their design patterns.

Unfortunately, we do not have an expert system handy, so we do the analysis the hard way. Consider the following candidate FD:

`ClassTime ClassroomId InstructorId → CrsCode`

It is easy to see why this FD does not apply: Different courses can be taught by the same instructor in the same room at the same time—if all this happens in different semesters and years. Many other FDs can be rejected through a similar argument. However, since in Section 5.7 we assumed that at most one textbook can be used in any particular course, the following FD is an appropriate addition to the set of constraints previously specified for CLASS:

$$\text{CsrCode Semester Year} \rightarrow \text{Textbook} \tag{8.21}$$

Although the textbook used in a course can vary from semester to semester, if a certain course is offered in a particular semester and is split in several sections because of large enrollment, all sections use the same textbook.[10]

It is now easy to see the problem with the design of CLASS: The left-hand side of the above dependency is not a key, and Textbook does not belong to any key either. For these reasons, CLASS is not in 3NF. The 3NF synthesis algorithm on page 237 suggests that the situation can be rectified by splitting the original schema into the following pair:

■ CLASS1, with all the attributes of CLASS, except Textbook, and FDs 1, 3–7, 9–13, 15–18 (these numbers refer to the numbered list of FDs provided earlier.)

■ TEXTBOOKS(CrsCode, Semester, Year, Textbook), with the single FD
`CrsCode Semester Year → Textbook`.

The resulting schemas are both in BCNF, since one can verify by direct inspection that all of their FDs are entailed by key constraints. The 3NF synthesis algorithm also guarantees that the above decomposition is both lossless and dependency preserving.

---

[10] Of course, this rule might not be true of all universities, but it is certainly true of many.

Let us now consider a more realistic situation in which classes can have more than one recommended textbook and all sections of the class in a particular semester use the same set of textbooks. In this case, FD (8.21) does not hold, of course. Observe that the textbooks used in any particular class are independent of meeting time, instructor, enrollment, and so forth. This situation is similar to the one in Section 8.9 relative to the PERSON relation shown in (8.14): Here, the independence of the attribute Textbook from the attributes ClassTime, InstructorId, and so forth, is formally represented through the following multivalued dependency,

```
(CrsCode Semester Year Textbook)
    ⋈ (CrsCode Semester Year ClassTime SectionNo
         InstructorId Enrollment MaxEnrollment ClassroomId)
```

or as

```
CrsCode Semester Year ↠ Textbook
```

using the notation of the optional Section 8.10. Like the schema of the PERSON relation, CLASS is in BCNF; even so, it contains redundancy because of the above multivalued dependency. The solution to the problem is to try for a higher normal form—4NF—and, fortunately, this is easy using the algorithm of Section 8.10. We simply need to decompose CLASS using the above dependency, which yields the following lossless decomposition (losslessness is guaranteed by the decomposition algorithm of Section) 8.10)

■ CLASS1(CrsCode, Semester, Year, ClassTime, SectionNo, InstructorId, Enrollment, MaxEnrollment, ClassroomId) with the FDs 1, 3–7, 9–13, 15–18

■ TEXTBOOKS(CrsCode, Semester, Year, Textbook) with no FDs

Note that the only difference between this schema and the one obtained earlier under the one-textbook-per-class assumption is the absence, in the second schema, of the FD

```
CrsCode Semester Year → Textbook
```

The result of applying relational normalization theory to the preliminary design for the Student Registration System developed in Section 5.7 is a lossless decomposition where every relation is in 4NF (and thus in BCNF as well). Luckily, this decomposition is dependency preserving, since every FD specified for the schema is embedded in one of the relations in the decomposition—something that is not always achievable with 4NF and BCNF design.   ■

8.13 TUNING ISSUES: TO DECOMPOSE OR NOT TO DECOMPOSE?

In this chapter, we have learned a great deal about schema decomposition theory. However, this theory was motivated by concerns that redundancy leads to consistency maintenance problems in the presence of frequent database updates. What if most of the transactions are read-only queries? Schema decomposition seems to make query answering harder, because associations that existed in one relation before the decomposition might be broken into separate relations afterward.

For instance, finding the average number of hobbies per address is more efficient using the monolithic relation of Figure 5.2 rather than the pair of relations of Figure 8.1, because the latter requires a join before the aggregates can be computed. This is an example of the classic time/space trade-off: Adding redundancy can improve query performance. Such a trade-off has to be evaluated in a particular application if the performance of a frequently executed query is found wanting. In this context, the term **denormalization** describes situations in which achieving certain normal forms incurs a punishing performance penalty and thus perhaps there should be no decomposition.

In general, no one recommendation works in all cases. Sometimes, simulation can help resolve the issue. Here is an incomplete list of conflicting guidelines that need to be evaluated against each particular mix of transactions.

1. Decomposition generally makes answering complex queries less efficient, because additional joins must be performed during query evaluation.

2. Decomposition can make answering simple queries more efficient, because such queries usually involve a small number of attributes that belong to the same relation. Since decomposed relations have fewer tuples, the tuples that need to be scanned during the evaluation of a simple query are likely to be fewer.

3. Decomposition generally makes simple update transactions more efficient. However, this may not be true for complex update transactions (such as *raise the salary of all professors who taught every course required for computer science majors*) since they might involve complex queries (and thus might require complex joins).

4. Decomposition can lower the demand for storage space, since it usually eliminates redundant data.

5. Decomposition can increase storage requirements if the degree of redundancy is low. For instance, in the PERSON relation of (8.14), suppose that, with few exceptions, most people have just one phone number and one child. In this situation, schema decomposition can actually increase storage requirements without bringing tangible benefits. The same applies to the decomposition of HASACCOUNT in Figure 8.6, which can increase the overhead for update transactions. The reason is that verification of the FD

```
ClientId OfficeId → AccountNumber
```

after an update requires a join because the attributes ClientId and OfficeId belong to different relations in the decomposition.

8.14   BIBLIOGRAPHIC NOTES

Relational normal forms and functional dependencies were introduced in [Codd 1970]. Armstrong's axioms and the proof of their soundness and completeness first appeared in [Armstrong 1974], although more accessible exposition can be found in [Ullman 1988, Maier 1983]. An efficient algorithm for entailment of FDs first appeared in [Beeri and Bernstein 1979]. A general test for lossless decompositions was first developed in [Beeri et al. 1981]. The algorithm for synthesizing the third normal form is due to [Bernstein 1976].

The fourth normal form was introduced in [Fagin 1977], which also presents a naive decomposition algorithm and explores the relationship between 4NF and BCNF. The fifth normal form is discussed in [Beeri et al. 1977], but we recommend [Maier 1983] as a more systematic introduction to the subject. The survey in [Kanellakis 1990] is also a good starting point. Other papers on 4NF are [Beeri et al. 1978, Zaniolo and Melkanoff 1981, Sciore 1983]. Eventually, all of this work on designing 4NF schemas in the presence of FDs and MVDs was extended and integrated into a uniform framework in [Beeri and Kifer 1986a and 1986b, 1987]. More recent works on 4NF are [Vincent and Srinivasan 1993, Vincent 1999].

In-depth coverage of the relational design theory is provided in texts such as [Mannila and Raäihä 1992, Atzeni and Antonellis 1993].

As illustrated in Section 8.12, one of the most difficult obstacles to applying the results discussed in this chapter to database design is finding the right set of dependencies to use in the schema normalization process. We mentioned the FDEXPERT system [Ram 1995], which helps discover functional dependencies using knowledge about various types of enterprises. Extensive work has also been done on the algorithms for discovering FDs, MVDs, and inclusion dependencies using the techniques from *machine learning* and *data mining* [Huhtala et al. 1999, Kantola et al. 1992, Mannila and Raäihä 1994, Flach and Savnik 1999, Savnik and Flach 1993]. We will introduce data mining in Chapter 19.

8.15   EXERCISES

8.1 The definition of functional dependencies does not preclude the case in which the left-hand side is empty—that is, it allows FDs of the form $\{\,\} \to A$. Explain the meaning of such dependencies.

8.2 Give an example of a schema that is not in 3NF and has just two attributes.

8.3 What is the smallest number of attributes a relation key can have?

8.4 A table, ABC, has attributes A, B, and C, and a functional dependency $A \to BC$. Write an SQL CREATE ASSERTION statement that prevents a violation of this functional dependency.

8.5 Prove that every 3NF relation schema with just two attributes is also in BCNF. Prove that every schema that has at most one nontrivial FD is in BCNF.

8.6 Prove that Armstrong's transitivity axiom is sound—that is, every relation that satisfies the FDs $\overline{X} \to \overline{Y}$ and $\overline{Y} \to \overline{Z}$ must also satisfy the FD $\overline{X} \to \overline{Z}$.

8.7 Prove the following *generalized transitivity rule*: If $\overline{Z} \subseteq \overline{Y}$, then $\overline{X} \to \overline{Y}$ and $\overline{Z} \to \overline{W}$ entail $\overline{X} \to \overline{W}$. Try to prove this rule in two ways:

❏ Using the argument that directly appeals to the definition of FDs, as in Section 8.4

❏ By deriving $\overline{X} \to \overline{W}$ from $\overline{X} \to \overline{Y}$ and $\overline{Z} \to \overline{W}$ via a series of steps using Armstrong's axioms

* 8.8 We have shown the *soundness* of the algorithm in Figure 8.3—that if $A \in$ *closure* then $A \in \overline{X}_{\mathcal{F}}^{+}$. Prove the *completeness* of this algorithm; that is, if $A \in \overline{X}_{\mathcal{F}}^{+}$, then $A \in$ *closure* at the end of the computation. *Hint:* Use induction on the length of derivation of $X \to A$ by Armstrong axioms.

8.9 Suppose that $\mathbf{R} = (\overline{R}, \mathcal{F})$ is a relation schema and $\mathbf{R}_1 = (\overline{R}_1; \mathcal{F}_1), \ldots, \mathbf{R}_n = (\overline{R}_n; \mathcal{F}_n)$ is its decomposition. Let $\mathbf{r}$ be a valid relation instance over $\mathbf{R}$ and $\mathbf{r}_i = \pi_{\overline{R}_i}(\mathbf{r})$. Show that $\mathbf{r}_i$ satisfies the set of FDs $\mathcal{F}_i$ and is therefore a valid relation instance over the schema $\mathbf{R}_i$.

8.10 Let $\overline{R}_1$ and $\overline{R}_2$ be sets of attributes and $\overline{R} = \overline{R}_1 \cup \overline{R}_2$. Let $\mathbf{r}$ be a relation on $\overline{R}$. Prove that $\mathbf{r} \subseteq \pi_{\overline{R}_1}(\mathbf{r}) \bowtie \pi_{\overline{R}_2}(\mathbf{r})$. Generalize this result to decompositions of $\overline{R}$ into $n > 2$ schemas.

8.11 Suppose that $\mathbf{R} = (\overline{R}; \mathcal{F})$ is a schema and that $\mathbf{R}_1 = (\overline{R}_1; \mathcal{F}_1), \mathbf{R}_2 = (\overline{R}_2; \mathcal{F}_2)$ is a binary decomposition such that neither $(\overline{R}_1 \cap \overline{R}_2) \to \overline{R}_1$ nor $(\overline{R}_1 \cap \overline{R}_2) \to \overline{R}_2$ is implied by $\mathcal{F}$. Construct a relation, $\mathbf{r}$, such that $\mathbf{r} \subset \pi_{\overline{R}_1}(\mathbf{r}) \bowtie \pi_{\overline{R}_2}(\mathbf{r})$, where $\subset$ denotes strict subset.

8.12 Suppose that $\mathbf{R}_1, \ldots, \mathbf{R}_n$ is a decomposition of schema $\mathbf{R}$ obtained by a sequence of binary lossless decompositions (beginning with a decomposition of $\mathbf{R}$). Prove that $\mathbf{R}_1, \ldots, \mathbf{R}_n$ is a lossless decomposition of $\mathbf{R}$.

8.13 Prove that the loop in the BCNF decomposition algorithm of Figure 8.8 has the property that the database schema at each subsequent iteration has strictly fewer FDs that violate BCNF than has the schema in the previous iteration.

* 8.14 Prove that the algorithm for synthesizing 3NF decompositions in Section 8.8 yields schemas that satisfy the conditions of 3NF. (*Hint:* Use the proof-by-contradiction technique. Assume that some FD violates 3NF and then show that this contradicts the fact that the algorithm synthesized schemas out of a minimal cover.)

8.15 Consider a database schema with attributes $A, B, C, D,$ and E and functional dependencies $B \rightarrow E, E \rightarrow A, A \rightarrow D,$ and $D \rightarrow E$. Prove that the decomposition of this schema into $AB, BCD,$ and ADE is lossless. Is it dependency preserving?

8.16 Consider a relation schema with attributes $ABCGWXYZ$ and the set of dependencies $\mathcal{F} = \{XZ \rightarrow ZYB, YA \rightarrow CG, C \rightarrow W, B \rightarrow G, XZ \rightarrow G\}$. Solve the following problems using the appropriate algorithms.

  a. Find a minimal cover for $\mathcal{F}$.

  b. Is the dependency $XZA \rightarrow YB$ implied by $\mathcal{F}$?

  c. Is the decomposition into $XZ\ YAB$ and $Y\ ABCGW$ lossless?

  d. Is the above decomposition dependency preserving?

8.17 Consider the following functional dependencies over the attribute set $ABCDEFGH$:

$$A \rightarrow E$$
$$AD \rightarrow BE$$
$$AC \rightarrow E$$
$$E \rightarrow B$$
$$BG \rightarrow F$$
$$BE \rightarrow D$$
$$BDH \rightarrow E$$
$$F \rightarrow A$$
$$D \rightarrow H$$
$$CD \rightarrow A$$

Find a minimal cover, then decompose into lossless 3NF. After that, check if all the resulting relations are in BCNF. If you find a schema that is not, decompose it into a lossless BCNF. Explain all steps.

8.18 Find a projection of the following set of dependencies on the attributes AFE:

$$A \rightarrow BC$$
$$C \rightarrow FG$$
$$E \rightarrow HG$$
$$G \rightarrow A$$

8.19 Consider the schema with the attribute set $ABCDEFH$ and the FDs depicted in (8.12), page 237. Prove that the decomposition $(AD; A \rightarrow D), (CE; C \rightarrow E),$ $(FA; F \rightarrow A), (EF; E \rightarrow F), (BHE; BH \rightarrow E)$ is not lossless by providing a concrete relation instance over $ABCDEFH$ that exhibits the loss of information when projected on this schema.

8.20 Consider the schema $BCDFGH$ with the following FDs: $BG \rightarrow CD$, $G \rightarrow F$, $CD \rightarrow GH$, $C \rightarrow FG$, $F \rightarrow D$. Use the 3NF synthesis algorithm to obtain a lossless, dependency-preserving decomposition into 3NF. If any of the resulting schemas is not in BCNF, proceed to decompose them into BCNF.

* 8.21 Prove that all rules for inferring FDs and MVDs given in Section 8.10 are sound. In other words, for every relation, $\mathbf{r}$, which satisfies the dependencies in the premise of any rule, R, the conclusion of R is also satisfied by $\mathbf{r}$ (e.g., for the augmentation rule, prove that if $\overline{X} \twoheadrightarrow \overline{Y}$ holds in $\mathbf{r}$ then $\overline{X}\,\overline{Z} \twoheadrightarrow \overline{Y}$ also holds in $\mathbf{r}$).

8.22 Let $\overline{X}, \overline{Y}, \overline{S}, \overline{R}$ be sets of attributes such that $\overline{S} \subseteq \overline{R}$ and $\overline{X} \cup \overline{Y} = R$. Let $\mathbf{r}$ be a relation over $\overline{R}$ that satisfies the nontrivial MVD $\overline{R} = \overline{X} \bowtie \overline{Y}$ (i.e., neither set $\overline{X}$ or $\overline{Y}$ is a subset of the other).

  a. Prove that if $\overline{X} \cap \overline{Y} \subseteq \overline{S}$ then the relation $\pi_{\overline{S}}(\mathbf{r})$ satisfies the MVD $\overline{S} = (\overline{S} \cap \overline{X}) \bowtie (\overline{S} \cap \overline{Y})$.

  b. Suppose $\overline{X}, \overline{Y}, \overline{S}$, and $\overline{R}$ satisfy all the above conditions, except that $\overline{X} \cap \overline{Y} \not\subseteq \overline{S}$. Give an example of $\mathbf{r}$ that satisfies $\overline{R} = \overline{X} \bowtie \overline{Y}$, but does not satisfy $\overline{S} = (\overline{S} \cap \overline{X}) \bowtie (\overline{S} \cap \overline{Y})$.

8.23 Consider a relation schema over the attributes $ABCDEFG$ and the following MVDs:

$$ABCD \bowtie DEFG$$
$$CD \bowtie ABCEFG$$
$$DFG \bowtie ABCDEG$$

Find a lossless decomposition into 4NF.

8.24 For the attribute set $ABCDEFG$, let the MVDs be:

$$ABCD \bowtie DEFG$$
$$ABCE \bowtie ABDFG$$
$$ABD \bowtie CDEFG$$

Find a lossless decomposition into 4NF. Is it unique?

8.25 Consider a decomposition $\mathbf{R}_1, \ldots, \mathbf{R}_n$ of $\mathbf{R}$ obtained via steps 1, 2 and 3 (but not step 4) of the 3NF synthesis algorithm on page 237. Suppose there is an attribute A is in $\mathbf{R}$ that does not belong to any of the $\mathbf{R}_i$, $i = 1, \ldots, n$. Prove that A must be part of every key of $\mathbf{R}$.

8.26 Consider a decomposition $\mathbf{R}_1, \ldots, \mathbf{R}_n$ of $\mathbf{R}$ obtained through 3NF synthesis. Suppose that $\mathbf{R}_i$ is *not* in BCNF and let $X \rightarrow A$ be a violating FD in $\mathbf{R}_i$. Prove that $\mathbf{R}_i$ must have another FD, $Y \rightarrow B$, which will be lost if $\mathbf{R}_i$ is further decomposed with respect to $X \rightarrow A$.

* 8.27 This exercise relies on a technique explained in the optional Section 8.10. Consider a relation schema over the attributes $ABCDEFGHI$ and the following MVDs and FDs:

$$D \rightarrow AH$$
$$G \rightarrow I$$
$$D \twoheadrightarrow BC$$
$$C \twoheadrightarrow B$$
$$G \twoheadrightarrow ABCE$$

Find a lossless and dependency preserving decomposition into 4NF.

Chapter 9

Triggers and Active Databases

In Chapter 4, we discussed triggers in the context of reactive constraints in databases. However, triggers have other uses as well. For example, they arise naturally in applications that require **active databases**, which are those that must react to various external events. In these applications, the general classes of possibly external events are known but their exact timings are not. This is what makes triggers a good paradigm for these applications.

Although triggers were not a part of the SQL-92 standard, a number of database vendors include some form of trigger in their product. Triggers are a part of the SQL:1999 standard, and we discuss that part of the standard in this chapter. More information on triggers in SQL:1999 can be found in [Gulutzan and Pelzer 1999].

9.1 SEMANTIC ISSUES IN TRIGGER HANDLING

A **trigger** is an element of the database schema, which has the following structure:

> ON *event* IF *precondition* THEN *action*

where *event* is a request for the execution of a particular database operation (e.g., insert a row in a table whose rows represent students registered for a course), *precondition* is an expression that evaluates to true or false (e.g., the class is full), and *action* is a statement of what needs to be done when the event occurs and the precondition is true (e.g., delete something from the database, send e-mail to the administrator). Because triggers are built out of the above three ingredients, they are sometimes called **event-condition-action**, or **ECA**, rules.

Surprisingly, a number of complex issues lurk behind this conceptual simplicity. First, several type of triggers are possible, each of which might be useful for different applications. Second, we will soon discover many nuances in how and when triggers are applied. Third, at any given point in time several triggers might be activated—how should a DBMS decide which to apply and in which order? Different choices can lead to different executions.

Finally, execution of a trigger might enable other triggers. Therefore, a single event can cause a chain reaction of trigger firing, and there is no guarantee that the process will ever stop. In practice, each DBMS has a limit on the depth of such chain reactions; for instance, if the depth exceeds 32, an exception is raised, the chain reaction stops, and all of the changes made by the original update statement and the triggers are rolled back. However, such a chain reaction is usually a symptom of poor design, and relying on the implementation limits imposed by the DBMS should be avoided. Some techniques for preventing chain reaction will be discussed later in the chapter.

Trigger consideration.   A trigger is **activated** when the triggering event is requested. The **consideration** of a trigger refers to when, after activation, the precondition specified in the trigger is checked. To see why consideration is an issue, assume that, when the triggering event is requested, the triggering precondition is true and so the trigger can fire. However, moments later the precondition might become false (because of updates made by this or other transactions). If the precondition is not checked immediately, the trigger will not fire.

Consider as an example the following trigger, whose purpose is to ensure that student registration does not exceed course capacity:

> ON *inserting a row in course registration table*
> IF *over course capacity*
> THEN *abort registration transaction*

When a student attempts to insert her name in the course registration table, the course might be full. Thus, if the precondition is checked when the registration attempt is made, the student's request will be rejected. However, at about the same time another student might execute a transaction to drop the course (or the registrar might have increased the course capacity), and this second transaction might commit before the first one. Therefore, if the trigger precondition is checked at the time the registration transaction commits, rather than at event time, our student will happily register for the course. In this example, deferring the consideration of trigger preconditions might be a suitable policy.

However, if our database is monitoring a nuclear power plant, the triggering event is a pressure increase, and the precondition is that the pressure not exceed a certain limit, then in all likelihood the immediate consideration of the trigger precondition is a better idea.

In summary, there are at least two useful strategies: A trigger can be considered **immediately** when the triggering event is requested, or consideration can be **deferred** until the transaction commits.

Trigger consideration is actually a little more subtle. Suppose that a trigger, T, is activated by an event, $\mathbf{e}$, that affects the relation R, and let C be the condition associated with T. Many systems (SQL:1999 included) make it possible for C to take into account the state of R immediately *before* $\mathbf{e}$ takes place and also immediately *after* $\mathbf{e}$ has been executed. Therefore, if C uses only these two states of R and does not refer to any other relation in the databases, the immediate and the deferred considerations of T yield the same result. Moreover, if C refers only to the before state of R, we can interpret this as that C is evaluated before $\mathbf{e}$ takes place! But if C does take into account database relations other than R, the two consideration modes might yield different results.

Trigger execution.   If trigger consideration is deferred, trigger execution is necessarily also deferred until the end of the triggering transaction. However, when triggers are considered immediately we have at least two options: We can execute the trigger immediately after its consideration, or we can defer execution until the end of the triggering transaction. Again, with a nuclear reactor immediate execution might be the way to go, but in less critical situations deferred execution might be a better option.

With immediate execution, there are the following further possibilities: The trigger can be executed *after* the triggering event, *before* it, or *instead* of it. At first glance, the last two possibilities seem quite strange: How can an action caused by a real-life event execute before or instead of that event? The answer lies in the fact that the event is a request to the DBMS issued by a transaction, so it is quite possible for the DBMS to ignore the request and execute the trigger instead. Or the system might execute the trigger first and then allow the requested action to occur.

Trigger granularity.   The issue here is what constitutes an event. **Row-level granularity** assumes that a change to a single row is an event, and changes to different rows are viewed as separate events that might cause the trigger to be executed multiple times. In contrast, **statement-level granularity** assumes that events are statements, such as INSERT, DELETE, and UPDATE, *not* the individual tuple-level changes they make. Thus, for instance, an UPDATE statement that makes no changes (because the condition in its WHERE clause affects no tuples currently in the database) is an event that can cause a trigger to execute!

At row-level granularity, a trigger might need to know the old and the new values of the affected tuple so it can test the precondition properly. In the case of a salary increase, for example, the old tuple contains the old salary and the new one contains the new salary. If both values are available, the trigger can verify that the increase does not exceed 10% and apply corrective actions as appropriate. Row-level triggers usually provide access to the old and the new values of the affected tuple through special variables.

At statement-level granularity, updates are collected in temporary structures, such as OLD TABLE and NEW TABLE. This allows the trigger to query both tables and act on the basis of the results.

Trigger conflicts.   It is possible for an event to activate several triggers at once. For instance, when a student registers for a course the following two triggers might be considered:

> ON *inserting a row in course registration table*
> IF *over course capacity*
> THEN *notify registrar about unmet demands*

> ON *inserting a row in course registration table*
> IF *over course capacity*
> THEN *put on waiting list*

In such situations, an important question is which trigger should be considered first. Two alternatives exist.

■ *Ordered conflict resolution.* Evaluate trigger preconditions in turn. When a condition is evaluated and found to be true, the corresponding trigger is executed; when that execution is complete, the next trigger is considered. In our case, the student might accept one of the alternative courses and abandon the request to add the course that is full. Therefore, by the time the second trigger is considered its precondition is no longer true, and the trigger will not fire.

■ *Group conflict resolution.* Evaluate all trigger preconditions at once and then schedule for execution all those whose preconditions are true. In this case, all scheduled triggers will be executed (one after another or concurrently), even if the preconditions attached to some triggers might become false shortly after their evaluation.

With the first option, the system can decide on trigger ordering or it can pick triggers at random. With the second option, trigger ordering is not necessary since all triggers can be scheduled to run concurrently, although most DBMSs do order triggers anyway.

Triggers and integrity constraints.   In Chapter 4, we discussed the possibility of updates to the database, which might violate referential integrity constraints. We saw that SQL has a way of specifying compensating actions (such as ON DELETE CASCADE) that the DBMS should take to restore integrity. These actions can be viewed as special triggers with very strict semantics: At the end of the execution, the integrity of the database must be restored. The situation is complicated by the fact that a compensating action might activate other triggers that can cause violations of referential integrity. In this case, the scheduling of all of these triggers must have the goal of ultimately restoring the integrity constraint. The problem of trigger scheduling does not have an obvious solution. We will discuss later how this issue is resolved in SQL:1999.

9.2   TRIGGERS IN SQL:1999

Creating the current SQL:1999 standard for trigger syntax and semantics was a rather long and painful process. First, the various database vendors already had triggers in their systems, so the standard had to offer sufficient benefits to convince the vendors to change their implementations. Second, as we have seen, the semantic issues associated with triggers are not trivial, and the standard would not have been accepted unless it offered reasonable solutions to the problems discussed earlier.

Armed with a new understanding of the issues associated with trigger handling, we can now approach the SQL:1999 standard systematically.

■ *Triggering events.* An event can be the execution of an SQL INSERT, DELETE, and UPDATE statement as a whole or a change to individual rows made by such a statement.

■ *Trigger precondition.* Any condition allowed in the WHERE clause of SQL.

■ *Trigger action.* An SQL query, a DELETE, INSERT, UPDATE, ROLLBACK, or SIGNAL statement, or a program written in the language of SQL's *persistent stored modules (SQL/PSM)*, which smoothly integrates procedural control statements with SQL query and update statements. We discuss SQL/PSM in the next chapter.

■ *Trigger conflict resolution.* Ordered: SQL:1999 assumes that all triggers are ordered and executed in some implementation-specific way. Since the order is likely to be different from one database product to another, applications must be designed so that they do not rely on trigger ordering.

■ *Trigger consideration.* Immediate: The preconditions of all triggers activated by an event are checked immediately when the event is requested.

■ *Trigger execution.* Immediate: Execution can be specified to be before or after the triggering event.

■ *Trigger granularity.* Row-level and statement-level granularities are both available.

Here is the general syntax of SQL:1999 triggers. Constructs in square brackets are optional; clauses in curly brackets specify a choice of one of the constructs separated by vertical lines.

```
CREATE TRIGGER  trigger-name
      {BEFORE | AFTER}
            {INSERT | DELETE | UPDATE [ OF column-name-list ]}
      ON  table-name
            [ REFERENCING[ OLD AS var-to-refer-to-old-tuple ]
                         [ NEW AS var-to-refer-to-new-tuple ] ]
                         [ OLD TABLE AS name-to-refer-to-old-table ] ]
                         [ NEW TABLE AS name-to-refer-to-new-table ] ]
      [ FOR EACH { ROW | STATEMENT } ]
      [ WHEN (precondition) ]
            statement-list
```

The syntax of SQL:1999 triggers closely follows the model discussed in the previous section. A trigger has a name; it is activated by certain events (specified by the INSERT-DELETE-UPDATE clause); it can be defined as a BEFORE or an AFTER trigger (indicating whether the precondition is to be checked in the state that exists before or after the event); and it can have a precondition (specified by the WHEN clause). The clauses FOR EACH ROW and FOR EACH STATEMENT specify the trigger granularity. If FOR EACH ROW is specified the trigger is activated by the changes to every individual tuple in the table watched by that trigger. If FOR EACH STATEMENT is specified (which is the default), the trigger is activated once per execution of an INSERT, DELETE, or UPDATE statement on the table being monitored, regardless of the number of tuples changed by that execution (it will be activated even if no changes occurred).

The *statement list* following the WHEN clause defines the actions to be executed when the trigger is fired. Usually, these actions are SQL statements (that insert, delete, or modify tuples), but in general they can be statements written in SQL/PSM, which can include SQL statements intermixed with if-then-else statements, loops, local variables, and so forth. We discuss SQL/PSM in the next chapter.

The REFERENCING *clause* is the means of referring to the pre-update and the post-update contents of the relation *table name*. This information can be used both in the WHEN condition and in the statement list that follows.

There are two types of references, depending on the granularity of the trigger. If the trigger has row-level granularity, we can use the clauses OLD AS and NEW AS, which define tuple variables to be used to refer to the old and the new value of the tuple that caused trigger activation. If the event is an INSERT, OLD is not applicable; if it is a DELETE, NEW is not applicable. If the trigger has statement-level granularity, SQL:1999 provides access to the old and the new value of the table affected by the triggering statement. Thus, the clause OLD TABLE names the table that contains the old state of the tuples affected by the update whereas the clause NEW TABLE defines the name under which the new state of these tuples can be accessed.

> **Note:**   NEW AS and OLD AS specify tuple variables that range *only over the tuples affected by the update*. That is, in tuple insertion, NEW AS refers to the inserted tuple; in tuple modification, it refers to the new state of the modified tuple. OLD AS refers to deleted tuples or to the old states of modified tuples.
>
> Likewise, OLD TABLE and NEW TABLE contain *only the tuples affected by the update*, not the entire old and new states of the table. If r was the state of a table before the update, the state after the update is $(r - old\ table) \cup new\ table$.

Finally, SQL:1999 imposes certain restrictions on what BEFORE and AFTER triggers can do.

BEFORE **triggers.**   All BEFORE triggers execute entirely before the triggering events. They are not allowed to modify the database, but can only test the precondition specified in the WHEN clause and either accept or abort the triggering transaction. Since BEFORE triggers cannot modify the database, they cannot activate other triggers.

A typical use of BEFORE triggers is to preserve application-specific data integrity. For example, in addition to the already familiar relation TRANSCRIPT, consider another relation, CRSLIMITS, which has the attributes CrsCode, Semester, and Limit with their usual meanings. The following is a trigger that works by monitoring tuple insertions into the TRANSCRIPT relation. An INSERT statement might insert several tuples involving different courses. The trigger specifies row granularity, so each insertion is treated as a separate event. The trigger checks that the course affected by the insertion is not filled to capacity. If it is, the insertion is rejected.

```
CREATE TRIGGER RoomCapacityCheck
   BEFORE INSERT ON Transcript
     REFERENCING NEW AS N
   FOR EACH ROW
```

```
WHEN
    ((SELECT COUNT(T.StudId) FROM TRANSCRIPT T
       WHERE T.CrsCode = N.CrsCode AND T.Semester = N.Semester)
    >=
    (SELECT L.Limit FROM CRSLIMITS L
       WHERE L.CrsCode = N.CrsCode AND L.Semester = N.Semester))
ROLLBACK
```

Note that the first SQL statement in the WHEN clause refers simultaneously to the new TRANSCRIPT tuples (through the tuple variable N) and to all tuples in the relation TRANSCRIPT (through the variable T). What state of the relation TRANSCRIPT is assumed while checking the validity of the WHEN condition? In the case of tuples referenced by N, the answer is clear: It must be the new state for each referenced tuple. However, it is less obvious what state is referenced by T. The answer is that BEFORE triggers assume that all referenced tables are in their old state while AFTER triggers assume the new state for each relation.

AFTER **triggers.**   AFTER triggers execute entirely after the triggering event has applied its changes to the database. They are allowed to make changes to the database and thus can activate other triggers (which can cause a chain reaction, as explained earlier). In this way, AFTER triggers serve as an extension of the application logic. They can take care of various events automatically, thereby relieving application programmers of the need to code all of these event handlers in each application.

The following examples illustrate the use of AFTER triggers. First we show how they enforce a constraint that caps at 5% any salary raises achieved by a single transaction. We assume that the database has a relation called EMPLOYEE with an attribute named Salary.

```
CREATE TRIGGER LIMITSALARYRAISE
    AFTER UPDATE OF Salary ON EMPLOYEE
    REFERENCING OLD AS O
                NEW AS N
    FOR EACH ROW
    WHEN (N.Salary − O.Salary > 0.05 * O.Salary)
        UPDATE EMPLOYEE
        SET Salary = 1.05 * O.Salary
        WHERE Id = O.Id
```

Whenever the Salary attribute in an EMPLOYEE tuple is updated, the trigger causes the DBMS to compare its old and new values and, if the raise exceeds the cap, to adjust the salary increase to just 5%. If the raise does not exceed the cap or if the update is a salary decrease, the trigger does not fire. Note that the tuple variables O and N in the above statement always *refer to the same tuple* that was affected by the database update that activated the trigger. The difference is that O refers to the old state of that tuple and N refers to the new state.

Notice that in this case when the trigger LIMITSALARYRAISE does fire and its action is executed, that action overrides the effect of the original event (which triggered LIMITSALARYRAISE). Furthermore, execution of the action is itself a triggering event for LIMITSALARYRAISE! The new event, however, does not lead to a chain reaction: When the trigger is checked the second time, the salary actually decreases (to become exactly 5% above the original). Thus, the WHEN condition is false and the trigger does not fire a second time.

We have seen several examples of triggers that have the granularity of a single row. However, some applications require that a trigger be fired only once per statement, after all updates specified in the statement have been processed. We illustrate the use of statement-level triggers with the following two examples.

Suppose that, after an across-the-board salary raise, we want to record the new average salary for all employees. We can achieve this with the help of the trigger

```
CREATE TRIGGER   RecordNewAverage
    AFTER UPDATE OF   Salary ON Employee
    FOR EACH STATEMENT
        INSERT INTO Log
        VALUES (CURRENT_DATE,
                (SELECT AVG(Salary) FROM Employee))
```

When this trigger is executed, it inserts a record into the table Log that gives the new average salary. The record also indicates the date on which the average was calculated (CURRENT_DATE is a built-in SQL function that returns the current date). Since it does not make sense to compute a new average after every individual salary change, statement-level granularity is better suited here than is row-level granularity.

The second example illustrates the use of statement-level triggers for maintaining inclusion dependencies. We discussed inclusion dependencies in Chapter 4 as a useful generalization of foreign key constraints, which occur frequently in practical settings. One such dependency, *No professor can be scheduled to teach a course that has no registered students,* was given in (4.1) on page 68. It is a referential integrity constraint that is *not* based on foreign keys, and its representation in SQL-92 requires the use of assertions (see (4.4) on page 75). We now show how AFTER triggers can help maintain this constraint in the presence of updates.[1]

The key idea is to construct an SQL view, IDLETEACHING, that includes precisely those tuples from the TEACHING relation that describe course offerings with no corresponding tuples in the TRANSCRIPT relation. In other words, the view contains precisely the tuples that violate the inclusion dependency. Designing such a view definition is left as an exercise.

The trigger works as follows: After one or more students drop a class (or several classes), the trigger deletes all tuples found in IDLETEACHING from TEACHING.

---

[1] The same technique can be used to emulate the ON DELETE and ON UPDATE clauses of foreign key constraints in systems that are not SQL-92 compliant.

```
CREATE TRIGGER  MAINTAINCOURSESNONEMPTY
        AFTER DELETE,UPDATE OF CrsCode,Semester ON TRANSCRIPT
        FOR EACH STATEMENT
            DELETE FROM  TEACHING
                WHERE                                              (9.1)
                    EXISTS (SELECT *
                        FROM IDLETEACHING T
                        WHERE Semester = T.Semester
                            AND CrsCode = T.CrsCode)
```

Similarly, we can construct a trigger to maintain the inclusion dependency when tuples are added to the TEACHING relation. This trigger should abort any transaction that tries to insert a tuple into TEACHING if there is no corresponding tuple in TRANSCRIPT.

Note that the above trigger might cause a chicken-and-egg problem. We cannot assign a course to a professor until somebody registers for it. However, in most schools the course schedule for the next semester is published before any student registers for any course, so some triggers might need to be created and then destroyed. The above trigger, for instance, might need to be in effect *only* between the registration deadline and the course add/drop deadline.

Summary of the trigger evaluation procedure.   Suppose that an event, **e**, occurs[2] during the execution of a statement, S, and this event activates a set of triggers, $\mathbf{T} = \{T_1, \ldots, T_k\}$. Then we can summarize the procedure for trigger processing as follows:

1. Put the newly activated triggers on the trigger queue, **Q**.
2. Suspend the execution of S.
3. Compute OLD and NEW if row-level granularity is used, or OLD TABLE and NEW TABLE if statement-level granularity is used.
4. Consider all BEFORE triggers in **T**. Execute those whose preconditions are true and place all AFTER triggers whose preconditions are true on **Q**.
5. Apply the updates specified in S to the database.
6. Consider each AFTER trigger on **Q** according to the (implementation-dependent) priority and execute it immediately if the triggering condition is true. If the execution of a trigger activates new triggers, execute this algorithm recursively, starting with step 1.
7. Resume the execution of statement S.

Triggers and foreign key constraints.   When the event that activates a trigger is invoked on a relation that has foreign key constraints with ON DELETE and ON UPDATE clauses, the compensating actions specified in these clauses are likely to cause updates of their own and as a result, the exact semantics of the system

---

[2] Remember that an event is a request to execute a database operation.

becomes quite complicated. In fact, it took several iterations for the designers of the SQL:1999 standard to find a satisfactory solution.

One might ask why foreign key constraints are not treated as regular triggers—in fact, in Chapter 4 we called them just that. The answer is that these constraints *are* triggers, but they have special semantics—they are intended to rectify states that violate foreign key constraints, and it is desirable to capture this semantics in the trigger evaluation procedure. To do so, we modify step 5:

5′.   Apply the updates specified in S to the database (as before). For each FOREIGN KEY constraint violated by the current (new) state

a. Denote the associated compensating action as **act** (i.e., CASCADE, SET DEFAULT, SET NULL, or NO ACTION). Note that **act** is an event that can in turn activate other triggers, $\mathbf{S} = \{S_1, \ldots, S_n\}$.

b. Consider all triggers in **S**. Execute the BEFORE triggers whose preconditions are true and place on **Q** all AFTER triggers whose preconditions are true.

c. Apply the updates specified in **act**.

Note that in (c) of step 5′, we did not say whether the unprocessed triggers from **S** should be placed in front of **Q** or appended to it. The reason for this is that SQL processes triggers according to their implementation dependent priority.

Observe that execution of AFTER triggers in step 6 can activate other triggers and also cause violation of foreign key constraints. In this case, steps 1 through 6 are invoked recursively.

Example.   The above algorithm is designed to handle very complex interactions of triggers and foreign key constraints—interactions that might involve dozens of triggers. Here we give a simple example that involves just two triggers and one foreign key constraint.

Let us assume that courses mentioned in the TRANSCRIPT relation must also be listed in the COURSE relation. Both of these relations are described in Figure 4.4 on page 62. The foreign key constraint between these relations, which we call CHECKCOURSEVALIDITY, can be expressed as follows:

```
CREATE TABLE TRANSCRIPT (
      StudId    INTEGER,
      CrsCode   CHAR(6),
      Semester  CHAR(6),
      Grade     grades,
      PRIMARY KEY (StudId, CrsCode, Semester),
      CONSTRAINT CHECKCOURSEVALIDITY
            FOREIGN KEY (CrsCode) REFERENCES COURSE (CrsCode)
                ON DELETE CASCADE
                ON UPDATE CASCADE )
```

CHECKCOURSEVALIDITY deletes or updates all TRANSCRIPT tuples if the corresponding COURSE tuple is deleted or updated.

Suppose, in addition, that there is an AFTER trigger, WATCHCOURSEHISTORY, that records all changes to the tuples in the COURSE relation. We leave it as an exercise to define this trigger in SQL. Finally, the trigger MAINTAINCOURSESNONEMPTY (9.1) is also part of the database scheme. Note that in this example we do not consider other foreign key constraints (in particular, those associated with the TEACHING relation—including such constraints would make a much more complex example).

Suppose now that some course code is changed in the relation COURSE, specifically CS305 becomes CS405 beginning with fall 2000. This change activates the trigger WATCHCOURSEHISTORY and the CHECKCOURSEVALIDITY foreign key constraint. Because WATCHCOURSEHISTORY is an AFTER trigger, it is placed on Q, and the trigger-processing algorithm handles the foreign key constraint first as required in step 5'(c). Therefore, all tuples in the TRANSCRIPT relation that have CS305 in them are changed to refer to CS405.

This change activates the second trigger, MAINTAINCOURSESNONEMPTY. Since CS305 has been changed to CS405, the professor who is listed as teaching CS305 in fall 2000 is left without a class. In other words, CS305 is listed in TEACHING for the fall 2000 semester, but TRANSCRIPT does not have any corresponding tuples. Therefore, the WHEN condition in MAINTAINCOURSESNONEMPTY is true and the trigger can be executed.

Because MAINTAINCOURSESNONEMPTY is an AFTER trigger, it is put on Q (step 5'(b)), which already contains WATCHCOURSEHISTORY. The order in which these two triggers in the queue are actually fired depends on the implementation of the particular DBMS being used and cannot be predicted.[3] When all triggers eventually fire, the record about the course change goes into the history log and the teaching assignment for CS305 is deleted.

Note that the interaction of the two triggers and the foreign key constraint described above might not yield the intended result in this example. For instance, it might be more reasonable to update the teaching assignment of CS305 to a teaching assignment of CS405.

9.3 AVOIDING A CHAIN REACTION

The possibility of a never-ending chain reaction in trigger execution is a serious concern. Trigger systems in which firing terminates in all cases are called **safe**.

Unfortunately, there is no algorithm that can tell whether any given set of triggers is safe. However, there are conditions that are sufficient to guarantee safety (i.e., if the conditions are satisfied, the triggers are safe), but they are not necessary (i.e., a set of triggers might be safe but not satisfy the conditions). The fact that there is no algorithm to test safety implies that there can be no necessary *and* sufficient condition for safety, which can be checked by an algorithm.

---

[3] Most vendors use scheduling strategies based on time stamps that reflect the time of trigger consideration. In our case, such time stamp ordering favors WATCHCOURSEHISTORY.

Figure 9.1 Trigger graph.

In view of this sorry state of affairs, we present one condition that is sufficient to guarantee safety but which rejects many perfectly safe trigger systems.

A **triggering graph** is a graph whose nodes are triggers (or foreign key constraints as a special case). An arc goes from trigger T to trigger T' if and only if execution of T is an event that can activate T'.

It is easy to see that one can use a simple syntactic analysis to determine whether one trigger might activate another trigger. Indeed, the events that enable a trigger are listed in the BEFORE/AFTER clause in the trigger definition (or in the ON DELETE/UPDATE clause in foreign key constraint definitions); the events *caused* by the triggers can be determined from the statements in the trigger body Figure 9.1 shows the triggering graph for some of the triggers discussed in this chapter.

Clearly, if the trigger graph is *acyclic*, it is not possible for the triggers to invoke each other in a nonterminating manner. By this criterion, the triggers WATCH-COURSEHISTORY, MAINTAINCOURSESNONEMPTY, and CHECKCOURSEVALIDITY cannot be involved in a chain reaction.

Even though this method can certify the safety of some systems, it fails in many cases. Indeed, the part of our triggering graph that involves LIMITSALARYRAISE is cyclic, because syntactic analysis shows that its execution activates this very trigger again. As shown earlier, however, this trigger will not fire the second time, because its WHEN condition is false. This analysis exposes the major weakness of the triggering graph method: It does not take into account the semantics of the triggering conditions associated with the triggers. For example, if one can verify that no cycle in the triggering graph can be traversed infinitely many times (as in our example), the trigger system is safe.

There are a number of enhancements to the triggering graph methods, but they are outside of the scope of this book.

9.4   BIBLIOGRAPHIC NOTES

The main concepts underlying triggers in databases are described in [Paton et al. 1993]. The algorithm for integration of triggers with foreign key constraints originates in [Cochrane et al. 1996]. The syntax of SQL:1999 triggers is described in recent guides to SQL, such as [Gulutzan and Pelzer 1999].

There is a vast body of literature on active databases; the information on SQL:1999 triggers provided here is only the tip of an iceberg. The interested reader is referred to [Widom and Ceri 1996] for a comprehensive study.

EXERCISES

9.1 Explain the semantics of the triggers that are available in your local DBMS. Describe the syntax for defining these triggers.

9.2 Give the exact syntactic rules for constructing the triggering graphs from the sets of SQL triggers and foreign key constraints.

9.3 Design a trigger that complements the trigger MAINTAINCOURSESNONEMPTY (see (9.1)) by precluding the insertion of tuples into the relation TEACHING when there are no corresponding tuples in the TRANSCRIPT relation.

9.4 Design a trigger that works like MAINTAINCOURSESNONEMPTY but is a row-level trigger.

9.5 Define the trigger WATCHCOURSEHISTORY that uses a table LOG to record all changes that transactions make to the various courses in the COURSE relation.

9.6 Define triggers that fire when a student drops a course, changes major, or when her grade average drops below certain threshold. (For simplicity, assume that there is a function, grade_avg(), which takes a student Id and returns the student average grade.)

9.7 Consider the IsA relationship between STUDENT(Id,Major) and PERSON(Id, Name). Write the triggers appropriate for maintaining this relationship: When a tuple is deleted from PERSON, the tuple with the same ID must be deleted from STUDENT; when a tuple is inserted into STUDENT, check whether a corresponding tuple exists in PERSON and abort if not. (Do not use the ON DELETE and ON INSERT clauses provided by the FOREIGN KEY statement.)

9.8 Consider a brokerage firm database with relations HOLDINGS(AccountId, StockSymbol, Price, Quantity) and BALANCE(AccountId, Balance). Write the triggers for maintaining the correctness of the account balance when stock is bought (a tuple is added to HOLDINGS or Quantity is incremented) or sold (a tuple is deleted from HOLDINGS or Quantity is decremented).

9.9 Consider an enterprise in which different projects use parts supplied by various suppliers. Define the appropriate tables along with the corresponding foreign key constraints. Define triggers that fire when a project changes a supplier; when a supplier discontinues a part; when a project stops using a part.

9.10 Consider triggers with immediate consideration and deferred execution. What do OLD AS and NEW AS refer to during consideration and during execution?

9.11 Give an example of an application where SQL:1999 triggers could be used for a purpose other than just maintaining integrity constraints.

Chapter 10

SQL in the Real World

In the previous chapters, we discussed SQL as an interactive language. You type in a query, anxiously listen to your hard drive, and then see the results appear on your screen (or more likely scroll by on the screen too quickly to be read). This mode of execution, called **direct execution**, was part of the original vision of SQL.

In most transaction processing applications, however, SQL statements are part of an application program written in some conventional language, such as C, Cobol, Java, or Visual Basic, and the program executes on a computer different from the one on which the database server resides. In this chapter, we discuss some advanced features of SQL that address the issues involved in this type of execution. Our goal is to present the basic concepts involved, not to cover all the syntactic options.

10.1 EXECUTING SQL STATEMENTS WITHIN AN APPLICATION PROGRAM

We are interested in creating programs that involve a mixture of SQL statements and statements from a conventional language. The SQL statements enable the program to access a database; the conventional language, called the **host language**, supplies features that are unavailable in SQL. These features include control mechanisms, such as the **if** and **while** statements, assignment statements, and error handling.

In our discussion of how SQL statements can be included in a host language, we must deal with two issues, discussed in the following paragraphs.

■ Prior to executing an SQL statement, a **preparation** step is performed. Preparation involves parsing the statement and then making a **query execution plan**, which determines the sequence of steps necessary for statement execution. In what order will tables be joined? Should the tables be sorted first? What indices will be used? What constraints will be checked? In Chapter 11, we will introduce the concept of an **access path**, which determines a technique for accessing the rows of a table. The query execution plan includes an access path for each table in the query. Because the execution of a single SQL statement can involve considerable computational and I/O resources, it is essential that it be carefully planned. The query execution plan is designed by the DBMS using the database schema and the structure of the statement: the statement type (e.g., SELECT, IN-SERT), the tables and columns accessed, and the column domains. Factors such as the number of rows in a table might also be taken into account in query optimization. The SQL statement is executed according to the sequence of steps outlined in the plan. These issues will be discussed in detail in Chapter 14.

■ SQL constructs can be included in an application program in two different ways.

Statement-Level Interface (SLI). The SQL constructs appear as new statement types in the program. The program is then a mixture of statements in two languages: the host language and the new statement types. Before the program can be compiled by the host language compiler, the SQL constructs must be processed by a **precompiler**, which translates the constructs into calls to host language procedures. The entire program can then be compiled by the host language compiler. At run time, these procedures communicate with the DBMS, which takes the actions necessary to cause the SQL statements to be executed.

The SQL constructs can take two forms. In the first, referred to as **embedded SQL**, they are ordinary SQL statements (e.g., SELECT, INSERT). In the second, they are directives for preparing and executing SQL statements, but the SQL statements *appear in the program as the values of string variables that are constructed by the host language portion of the program at run time*. Since in this case the actual SQL statements to be executed might not be known at compile time, this form is referred to as **dynamic SQL**. This is in contrast to embedded SQL, where the SQL statements are known at complile time and are written directly into the program. Hence embedded SQL is also referred to as **static SQL**. SQL-92 defines a standard for embedded SQL. We also discuss SQLJ—a version of SLI designed specifically for Java.

Call-Level Interface (CLI). Here, unlike static and dynamic SQL, the application program is written entirely in the host language. As with dynamic SQL, SQL statements are the values of string variables constructed at run time. These variables are passed as arguments to host language procedures provided by the CLI. Since no special syntax is used, no precompiler is needed.

We discuss two CLIs in this chapter: **JDBC** (Java DataBase Connectivity), which is specifically designed for the Java language, and **ODBC** (Open DataBase Connectivity), which can be used with many languages. The recently completed SQL:1999 standardizes the call-level interface. This standard is quite similar to ODBC, and it is expected that the two will converge.

10.2   EMBEDDED SQL

Embedded SQL is a statement-level interface that allows SQL statements to be embedded in a host language program. The schema of the database to be accessed by the program must be known at the time the program is written so that the SQL statements can be constructed. For example, the programmer must know the names of tables and the names and domains of columns.

Before the compilation of the program by the host language compiler, a precompiler (usually supplied by the vendor of the DBMS) scans the application program and locates the embedded SQL statements. These statements are not part of the host language, so they cannot be processed by the host language compiler. Instead they are set off by a special syntax so that the precompiler can recognize them. The precompiler translates each statement into a sequence of subroutine calls in the host language to a run-time library, which can be processed by the host language compiler at the next stage. Later, when the program is run and the SQL statement is to be executed, the subroutines are called and they send the SQL statement that was originally embedded in the application to the DBMS, which prepares and executes it.

It would be reasonable for the precompiler to check the form of each SQL statement and prepare a query execution plan, since that would eliminate a significant source of run-time overhead. However, most precompilers do not do this. Preparation requires the precompiler to communicate with the DBMS (to determine the schema of the database that the statement is accessing), and this communication might not be possible at compile time. Furthermore, since the query execution plan might depend on the size of tables, the closer in time the preparation is to the execution, the better.

In the best of all possible worlds, the embedded SQL constructs would be written in SQL-92 or SQL:1999, and the precompiler for each DBMS would perform any necessary translation to the dialect of SQL recognized by that DBMS. In the real world, however, most precompilers do not perform such translations, and the SQL constructs must be written in the exact dialect of the DBMS being accessed. In practice, then, the DBMS, as well as the database schema, must be known at the time the program is written.

Requiring the application program to use the exact dialect of the DBMS can be a disadvantage if, at some later time, it becomes necessary to change to a different DBMS with a different dialect. In some situations, however, using the dialect of the DBMS can be an advantage. Many DBMSs contain proprietary extensions to SQL. If the SQL embedded in the host language is exactly SQL-92, those extensions are not available to the programmer. Of course, if the proprietary extensions supported by a particular DBMS are used in an application, the difficulty of changing to a different DBMS at a later time increases.

The SQL-92 standard requires that all implementations of embedded SQL provide precompilers for at least seven host languages: Ada, C, COBOL, Fortran, M (formerly known as MUMPS),[1] Pascal, and PL/1. In practice, precompilers are available for other languages as well. Some application generators provide their own proprietary host language and their own dialect of embedded SQL, together with a compiler (or interpreter) that allows the SQL constructs to access any DBMS in a supported set of DBMSs.

---

[1] <u>M</u>assachusetts General Hospital <u>U</u>tility <u>M</u>ulti-<u>P</u>rogramming <u>S</u>ystem—if you really want to know.

Figure 10.1 Fragment of an embedded SQL program written in C.

```
EXEC SQL BEGIN DECLARE SECTION;
            unsigned long num_enrolled;
            char *crs_code, *semester;
            . . .
EXEC SQL END DECLARE SECTION;
```

  . . . *other host language declarations and statements* . . .
  . . . *get the values for* `semester` *and* `crs_code`. . .

```
EXEC SQL SELECT C.Enrollment
            INTO :num_enrolled
            FROM CLASS C
            WHERE C.CrsCode = :crs_code
                    AND C.Semester = :semester;
```

  . . . *the rest of the host language program* . . .

Figure 10.1 is a fragment of a C program with embedded SQL statements. Each embedded SQL statement is preceded by the words EXEC SQL, so it can be located by the precompiler. We use the syntax of SQL-92, but be aware that many database vendors use their own dialect of SQL (or a syntax from an older SQL standard).

All examples in this chapter come from the following two schemas:

CLASS(CrsCode:CHAR(6), Semester:CHAR(6),
          Enrollment:INTEGER, ProfId:CHAR(9), Room:CHAR(10))
The Key of CLASS: {CrsCode, Semester}
TRANSCRIPT(StudId:INTEGER, CrsCode:CHAR(6), Semester:CHAR(6),
          Grade:CHAR(1))
The Key of TRANSCRIPT: {StudId, CrsCode, Semester}

The domains of the attributes CrsCode, Semester, and Grade are the same as in Figure 4.5, page 63. That is, course codes are strings of the form MAT123 or CS305, semesters are strings of the form F1999 or S2000, and grades are letters of the form A or B.

For the application program as a whole to communicate with the database, host language statements and SQL statements must be able to access common variables. In that way, results computed by the host language portion of the program can be stored in the database and data extracted from the database can be processed by host language statements.

The first group of statements in the fragment of Figure 10.1 declares variables of the host program, or **host variables**, that are used for that purpose. The declarations are included between EXEC SQL BEGIN DECLARE SECTION and EXEC SQL END DECLARE SECTION so that they can be easily found and processed by the precompiler. However, the declarations themselves are *not* preceded by EXEC SQL. In this way, the declarations can be processed by both the precompiler and the host language compiler.

Host variables are used in the SELECT statement shown in the figure. Note the colon that precedes each use of a host variable in the SELECT statement to differentiate it from the table and column names of the database schema. The value of Enrollment is returned in the host variable num_enrolled and can be accessed by host language statements in the normal way after the SELECT statement has been executed.

Since CrsCode and Semester together form the primary key of CLASS, the SELECT statement returns a *single* row. This is an important point. If the SELECT statement returned more than one row, which one would be used to provide the value for the variable num_enrolled? For this reason, it is an error for a SELECT INTO statement to return more than one row. We address the case in which the result consists of multiple rows in Section 10.2.4.

We can think of the host language variables as parameterizing the SQL statement. They are used to communicate scalar values, not table or column names or structured data. Host language variables used in WHERE clauses correspond to **in parameters**, while those used in INTO clauses correspond to **out parameters**. When the statement is executed, the values of the *in* parameters are used to form a complete SQL statement that can be executed by the database manager. Note, however, that the SQL statement can be prepared before the values of the in parameters are determined because, for example, table and column names are known (they cannot be parameters). Therefore, the query execution plan used when the statement is first executed can be saved for subsequent executions of the same statement (since only the parameter values differ on each execution). This is an important advantage of embedded SQL. One function of the precompiler is to select routines that, at run time, move values into and out of host language variables and to handle formatting for communication with the DBMS.

10.2.1 Status Processing

In the real world, things do not always proceed smoothly. For example, when you attempt to connect to a database on a distant server, the server might be down or it might reject the connection. Or an INSERT statement that you attempt to execute might be rejected by the DBMS because it would cause a constraint violation. You might categorize these as error situations, since the requested action did not occur. In other situations, an SQL statement might execute correctly and return information describing the outcome of the execution. For example, the DELETE statement returns the number of rows deleted. SQL provides two mechanisms for returning information describing such situations to the host program: a five-character string SQLSTATE and a **diagnostics area**.

In Figure 10.2, we have added status processing to the fragment shown in Figure 10.1. SQLSTATE is declared within the declaration section, since it is used for

Figure 10.2 Adding some status processing.

```
#define OK "00000"
EXEC SQL BEGIN DECLARE SECTION;
     char SQLSTATE[6];
     unsigned long num_enrolled;
     char *crs_code, *semester;
EXEC SQL END DECLARE SECTION;
```

   ... *other statements*; *get the values for* `crs_code, semester` ...

```
EXEC SQL SELECT C.Enrollment
     INTO :num_enrolled
     FROM CLASS C
     WHERE C.CrsCode = :crs_code
         AND C.Semester = :semester;
if (strcmp(SQLSTATE,OK) != 0)
     printf("SELECT statement failed\n");
```

communication between the DBMS and the host language portion of the application.[2] This declaration is required in all embedded SQL programs.[3] The DBMS sends information to be stored in that string after each SQL statement is executed. The statement can then be followed by a (host language) conditional statement that checks the value of SQLSTATE. If that value is 00000, the last SQL statement executed successfully. If not, the particular exception situation can be determined and appropriate action can be taken. In the figure, a status message is printed.

Instead of checking status after each SQL statement, we can include a single WHENEVER statement anywhere before the first SQL statement is executed.

```
        EXEC SQL WHENEVER SQLERROR GOTO label;
```

Then any nonzero status in a subsequently executed statement causes a transfer of control to `label`. The WHENEVER statement remains in effect until another WHENEVER statement is executed.

More detailed information on the outcome of the last executed SQL statement can be retrieved from the diagnostics area using a GET DIAGNOSTICS statement. A single SQL statement can raise several exceptions. The diagnostics area records information about all exceptions raised.

Before this becomes a problem, we should mention one confusing issue: the difference in string notation in SQL (including all of its components, such as em-

---

[2] It is declared as a six-character string when SQL is embedded in C, to account for the additional null character that terminates strings in C. Note that SQLSTATE is not preceded by a colon when used in SQL statements, because it is recognized by the preprocessor as a special keyword.

[3] Earlier versions of SQL use a slightly different technique. Status is communicated through an integer variable, SQLCODE.

bedded SQL) and many of the host languages, such as C and Java. In SQL, strings are set in single quotes, while in C and Java they are set in double quotes. Thus, a C program with embedded SQL can have both kinds of notation. For instance, in

```
semester = "F2000";
EXEC SQL SELECT C.Enrollment
        INTO :num_enrolled
        FROM Class C
        WHERE C.CrsCode = 'CS305'
            AND C.Semester = :semester;
```

the string F2000 appears in a regular assignment statement and is processed by the C compiler, while CS305 occurs in an SQL statement and is handled by the SQL preprocessor.

10.2.2 Sessions, Connections, and Transactions

We introduce some terminology from the SQL standard. An **SQL agent** is simply the execution of an application program that includes SQL statements. It executes in an **SQL client**. Before the SQL-agent can perform any database operations, it must establish an **SQL connection** to an **SQL server**. That connection initiates an **SQL session** on the server. Once an SQL session has been established, the SQL agent can execute any number of **SQL transactions**, until it disconnects from the server, breaking the SQL connection and ending the SQL session.

SQL connections are established by executing a CONNECT statement (possibly implicitly), the general form of which is

CONNECT TO {DEFAULT | *db-name-string*}
        [AS *connection-name-string*] [USER *user-id-string*]

Phrases in square brackets are optional. Phrases in curly brackets refer to alternatives: One of the enclosed phrases separated by a vertical line must be chosen.

The option *db-name-string* is the name of the data source, *connection-name-string* is the name of the connection, and *user-id-string* is the name of the user (and can be used by the data source for authorization). The format used to specify a data source depends on the vendor. It can be a string that identifies the database by name on a local machine or something like

```
tcp:postgresql://db.xyz.edu:100/studregDB
```

on a remote machine.

A program can execute additional CONNECT statements to different servers, after which the new connection and the new session become current and the previous connection and session become dormant. The program can switch to a dormant connection and session by executing

SET CONNECTION TO {DEFAULT | connection-name-string}

SQL connections and SQL sessions are terminated by executing (possibly implicitly)

DISCONNECT {DEFAULT | *db-name-string*}

10.2.3 Executing Transactions

There is no explicit SQL-92 statement that initiates a transaction. A transaction is initiated automatically when the first SQL statement that accesses the database is executed within a session.[4] Transactions can be terminated with either COMMIT or ROLLBACK. The next SQL statement (after COMMIT or ROLLBACK) immediately starts a new transaction. This is referred to as **chaining**, which we will discuss in Chapter 21.[5]

The default mode of execution for transactions is READ/WRITE, meaning that the transaction can both read and make changes to the database. Alternatively, it can be restricted to READ ONLY access to protect the database from unauthorized changes.

In Chapter 2, we pointed out that, although only serializable schedules guarantee correct execution for all applications, less demanding levels of isolation can often be used for a particular application to improve performance. Hence, the default isolation level is SERIALIZABLE, but other levels are offered. We discuss these levels at some length in Chapters 15 and 24.

If a mode of execution other than the default mode is wanted, the SET TRANSACTION statement can be used. For example,

```
SET TRANSACTION READ ONLY
        ISOLATION LEVEL READ COMMITTED
        DIAGNOSTICS SIZE 6;
```

sets the mode to READ ONLY and the isolation level to READ COMMITTED. Any of the following isolation levels can be specified:

```
READ UNCOMMITTED
READ COMMITTED
REPEATABLE READ
SERIALIZABLE
```

The DIAGNOSTICS SIZE determines the number of exception conditions (caused by the last executed SQL statement) that can be described at one time in the diagnostics area.

Figure 10.3 illustrates the use of connection and transaction statements, as well as status processing. After the declarations, the next set of statements makes a connection to the server. The language does not provide an explicit statement for beginning a transaction; instead, a transaction is implicitly started once the connection is established.

The figure shows a fragment of the program that deregisters a student from a course. We assume that the host language variable semester contains the current semester, which can be determined through a call to the operating system, such as

---

[4] In SQL:1999, transactions can also be initiated by using a START TRANSACTION statement that initiates a transaction and specifies certain of its characteristics similarly to the SET TRANSACTION statement, described next.

[5] SQL:1999 also has COMMIT AND CHAIN and ROLLBACK AND CHAIN statements, which start a new transaction immediately after the commit or rollback completes, without waiting until the start of the next SQL statement.

Figure 10.3 The use of connection and transaction statements in a C program with embedded SQL statements whose purpose is to deregister a student from a course.

```
#define OK   "00000"
EXEC SQL BEGIN DECLARE SECTION;
     unsigned long stud_id;
     char *crs_code, *semester;
     char SQLSTATE[6];
     char *dbName;
     char *connectName;
     char *userId;
EXEC SQL END DECLARE SECTION;

// Get values for dbName, connectName, userId
dbName = "studregDB";
connectName = "conn1";
userId = "ji21";

     ... other statements ...

EXEC SQL CONNECT TO :dbName AS :connectName USER :userId;
if (strcmp(SQLSTATE,OK) != 0)
     exit(1);

... get the values for stud_id, crs_code, etc. ...

EXEC SQL DELETE FROM TRANSCRIPT
     WHERE StudId = :stud_id
          AND Semester = :semester
          AND CrsCode = :crs_code;

if (strcmp(SQLSTATE,OK) != 0)
     EXEC SQL ROLLBACK;
else {
     EXEC SQL UPDATE CLASS
          SET Enrollment = (Enrollment - 1)
          WHERE CrsCode = :crs_code
                    AND Semester = :semester;

     if (strcmp(SQLSTATE,OK) != 0)
          EXEC SQL ROLLBACK;
     else
          EXEC SQL COMMIT;
}
EXEC SQL DISCONNECT :connectName;
```

`time()`. The program makes two modifications to the database state: Deleting the row of Transcript that indicates that the student is registered in the course, and decrementing the `Enrollment` attribute of the course's tuple in Class. If either the DELETE statement or the UPDATE statement fails (and hence the value of SQLSTATE is not "00000" when the statement completes), the ROLLBACK command is executed.[6] Otherwise, the COMMIT command is executed. Then the transaction disconnects.

When an application executes either EXEC SQL COMMIT or EXEC SQL ROLLBACK, it is requesting that the database server, S, to which the application has a current connection, commit or roll back any changes it has made to the database at S. However, the application program might be executing a transaction that does more than just access a single database server. For example, by establishing several connections and switching among them, it might be accessing several database servers, or it might be putting the results of its computation into a local file system. The COMMIT and ROLLBACK statements are sent over the connection to S and therefore do not apply to these tasks.

If the program is connected to more than one database, the transactions at each can be separately committed or rolled back. However, the global transaction consisting of all of the separate transactions might not be atomic. We will discuss this issue further in Chapter 26.

10.2.4 Cursors

One of the advantages of SQL as a database language is that its statements can deal with entire tables. Thus, a SELECT statement might return table, which we refer to as the **query result** or **result set**. When the statement is executed in direct or interactive mode rather than embedded in an application program, the result set scrolls out on the screen. The following SELECT statement, for example, returns the Ids and grades of all students enrolled in a particular course in a given semester.

```
EXEC SQL SELECT T.StudId, T.Grade
     FROM Transcript T
     WHERE T.Semester = :semester
         AND T.CrsCode = :crs_code;
```

Suppose that we want to include such a statement in a host language program. The number of rows in the result set is not known until the statement is executed, so we face the problem of allocating storage within the program for an unknown number of rows. For example, if an array is to be used—how large should it be?

The SQL mechanism for solving this problem is the **cursor**, which allows the application program to deal with one row in a result set at a time. A cursor is similar to a pointer and can point to any row in a result set. A FETCH statement fetches the

---

[6] If the DELETE statement fails, no modification has been made to the database, which might lead us to think that the ROLLBACK command is not needed. However, the system must be notified that the transaction has completed so that, for example, an appropriate entry can be made in the system log and any locks acquired by the transaction can be released. The log is part of the mechanism the system uses to ensure transaction atomicity (Section 25.2), and locks are part of the mechanism the system uses to ensure isolation (Section 23.5).

Figure 10.4 Using cursors.

```
#define OK   "00000"
EXEC SQL BEGIN DECLARE SECTION;
    unsigned long stud_id;
    char grade[1];
    char *crs_code, *semester;
    char SQLSTATE[6];
EXEC SQL END DECLARE SECTION;

... input values for crs_code, semester, etc. ...

EXEC SQL DECLARE GETENROLLED INSENSITIVE CURSOR FOR
    SELECT T.StudId, T.Grade
        FROM TRANSCRIPT T
        WHERE T.CrsCode = :crs_code
            AND T.Semester = :semester;

EXEC SQL OPEN GETENROLLED;
if (strcmp(SQLSTATE,OK) != 0) {
    printf("Can't open cursor\n");
    exit(1);
}
EXEC SQL FETCH GETENROLLED INTO :stud_id, :grade;
if (strcmp(SQLSTATE,OK) != 0){
    printf("Can't fetch\n");
    exit(1);
}
EXEC SQL CLOSE GETENROLLED;
```

row pointed to by the cursor and assigns the attribute values in the row to host language variables in the program. In this way, variables need be allocated only for a single row. From the database schema, we know the types of the values in each row and so can declare variables of the appropriate type.

Figure 10.4 is a fragment of an embedded SQL program that uses cursors. The DECLARE CURSOR statement declares the name of the cursor as GETENROLLED, specifies it as INSENSITIVE (a qualification we discuss shortly), and associates it with a particular SELECT statement. It does not, however, cause that statement to be executed. The statement is executed when the OPEN statement is executed.

In the example, the associated SELECT statement is parameterized. Only tuples whose attributes CrsCode and Semester match the values stored in the host variables crs_code and semester are selected. When the OPEN statement is executed, parameter substitution takes place and then the SELECT statement is executed. Hence, changes to the parameters made after the cursor is opened have no effect

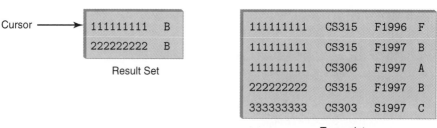

111111111	CS315	F1996	F
111111111	CS315	F1997	B
111111111	CS306	F1997	A
222222222	CS315	F1997	B
333333333	CS303	S1997	C

Transcript

Figure 10.5 With an insensitive cursor, the result set is effectively calculated when the cursor is opened and the underlying table is not accessed when rows are fetched.

on the tuples that are retrieved through it. OPEN positions the cursor prior to the first row in the result set.

When the FETCH statement is executed, the cursor is advanced. Thus, the FETCH statement in Figure 10.4 points the cursor to the first row in the result set, and the values in that row are fetched and stored in the host language variables stud_id and grade. The CLOSE statement closes the cursor. (In this example, only the first row of the result set is retrieved—clearly an artificial situation. The next example is more realistic.)

Each of the SQL statements in the program has a number of options. The general form of the DECLARE CURSOR statement is

DECLARE *cursor-name* [INSENSITIVE] [SCROLL] CURSOR FOR
       table-expression
       [ORDER BY *order-item-comma-list*]
       [FOR { READ ONLY | UPDATE [OF *column-commalist*] }]

where *table-expression* is generally a table, view, or SELECT statement.[7]

The option INSENSITIVE means that the execution of OPEN will effectively create a copy of the rows in the result set and all accesses through the cursor will be to that copy. The SQL standard uses the word "effectively" to mean that the standard does not specify how the INSENSITIVE option must be implemented, but whatever implementation is used must have the same effect as if a separate copy had been made. This type of returned data is sometimes called a **snapshot**.

INSENSITIVE cursors have a very intuitive semantics. The selection over the base tables implied by the SELECT statement is performed when OPEN is executed, and the result set is computed and stored. This copy can then be browsed at a later time using the cursor. The situation is shown for the cursor of Figure 10.4 for the fall 1997 semester and crs_code = 'CS315' in Figure 10.5.

Because an INSENSITIVE cursor accesses a copy of the result set, any modifications to the base tables by other statements in the same transaction (not through the

---

[7] Other alternatives are possible, but are beyond the scope of our discussion.

cursor) made after an INSENSITIVE cursor has been opened will not be seen through the cursor. For example, the transaction might execute

```
INSERT INTO Transcript
VALUES ('656565656', 'CS315', 'F1997', 'C');
```

after opening the cursor, thus inserting a new tuple directly (not through the cursor) into TRANSCRIPT. Although `crs_code` has the value CS315 and the current semester is F1997 at the time GETENROLLED is opened, the cursor cannot retrieve values from the new row. This is true even if the transaction executes an UPDATE statement that changes the attributes in one of the tuples in the result set after the cursor has been opened. Similarly, modifications of the base tables by concurrently executing transactions after the cursor has been opened will not be seen through the cursor.

The SQL standard does not specify what effects should be observed when changes are made to the base tables and the INSENSITIVE option has not been selected. Every database vendor is free to implement whatever it deems appropriate. Many vendors use the semantics called KEYSET_DRIVEN, which is part of the ODBC standard and is described in Section 10.6.

If INSENSITIVE is not specified, the cursor has not been declared READ ONLY, and the SQL query in the cursor declaration satisfies the conditions for an updatable view (see Section 6.3), the current row of the base table can be updated or deleted through the cursor, and the cursor is said to be "updatable." UPDATE or DELETE statements are used for this purpose, but the WHERE clause is replaced by WHERE CURRENT OF *cursor-name*. Thus, the general syntax is

```
UPDATE  table-name
SET  assignment-comma-list
WHERE CURRENT OF  cursor-name
```

and

```
DELETE
FROM  table-name
WHERE CURRENT OF  cursor-name
```

Because an INSENSITIVE cursor points to a copy of the result set, UPDATE and DELETE statements would have no effect on tables from which the result set was calculated. Hence, to avoid confusion, these operations cannot be performed through an INSENSITIVE cursor.

If a particular ordering of rows in the result set is desired, the ORDER BY clause can be used. If, for example, we include the clause

```
ORDER BY Grade
```

in the declaration of GETENROLLED, rows of the result set will be in ascending order of `Grade`.

The general form of the FETCH statement is

```
FETCH  [ [ row-selector ] FROM ]  cursor-name
INTO  target-commalist
```

where *target-commalist* is a list of host language variables that must match in number and type the list of attributes of the cursor's result set, and *row-selector* determines how the cursor is to be moved over the result set before the next row is fetched. The options are

> FIRST
> NEXT
> PRIOR
> LAST
> ABSOLUTE n
> RELATIVE n

If the row selector is NEXT, the cursor is moved to the next row of the result set and that row is fetched into the variables named in *target-commalist*. If the row selector is PRIOR, the cursor is moved to the preceding row and that row is fetched. Similarly, the FIRST row selector causes the cursor to be moved to the first row, and the LAST row selector causes the cursor to be moved to the last row. Finally, ABSOLUTE n refers to the nth row in the table, and RELATIVE n refers to the nth row after the row to which the cursor is pointing (n can be negative). If *row-selector* is omitted, NEXT is assumed. In that case, if the above ORDER BY clause is used in GETENROLLED, rows are fetched in ascending grade order.

The option SCROLL in the declaration of the cursor means that all forms of the FETCH statement are allowable. If SCROLL is not specified, only NEXT is allowable.

In Figure 10.6, we extend the example of Figure 10.4 so that all of the students enrolled in a particular course can be processed. The FETCH statement is now in a loop that terminates when the status returned indicates that execution was unsuccessful. The conditional statement following the loop checks for a "no data" condition (SQLSTATE has value "02000"), indicating that the result set has been completely scanned; it calls an error handling routine if this is not the case.

10.2.5 Stored Procedures on the Server

Many DBMS vendors allow **stored procedures** to be included as elements of the database schema. These procedures can then be invoked by an application at a client site and executed at the server site. Among the advantages of stored procedures are the following:

■ Since the procedure executes at the server, only its results need be transmitted from the server back to the application program. For example, a stored procedure might use a cursor to scan a large result set and analyze the rows to produce a single value that is returned to the application program. By contrast, if the cursor is used from within the application program, the entire result set must be returned to the application program for analysis, increasing communication costs and response time.

■ The SQL statements within a stored procedure can be prepared before the application is executed since the procedure is part of the schema stored at the server. By contrast, preparation of embedded SQL statements is generally done at run

Figure 10.6 Using a cursor to scan a table.

```
#define OK "00000"
#define EndOfScan "02000"
EXEC SQL BEGIN DECLARE SECTION;
     unsigned long stud_id;
     char grade[1];
     char *crs_code;
     char *semester;
     char SQLSTATE[6];
EXEC SQL END DECLARE SECTION;

EXEC SQL DECLARE GetEnrolled INSENSITIVE CURSOR FOR
     SELECT T.StudId, T.Grade
         FROM Transcript T
         WHERE T.CrsCode = :crs_code
             AND T.Semester = :semester
     FOR READ ONLY;

... get values for crs_code, semester ...

EXEC SQL OPEN GetEnrolled;
if (strcmp(SQLSTATE,OK) != 0) {
     printf("Can't open cursor\n");
     exit(1);
}

EXEC SQL FETCH GetEnrolled INTO :stud_id, :grade;
while (strcmp(SQLSTATE,OK) == 0) {
         ... process the values in stud_id and grade ...
     EXEC SQL FETCH GetEnrolled INTO :stud_id, :grade;
}

if (strcmp(SQLSTATE,EndOfScan) != 0) {
     printf("Something fishy: error before end-of-scan\n");
     exit(1);
}

EXEC SQL CLOSE GetEnrolled;
```

time. Hence, even if a stored procedure contains only a single SQL statement, that statement will execute more efficiently in the procedure than if it had been embedded directly in the application.

As explained in Section 14.6, this advantage can become a disadvantage because query plans tend to go stale. Thus, "old" stored procedures might avoid the overhead of query preparation but incur run-time overhead due to inefficient and out-of-date query plans. Some vendors (e.g., Sybase) provide an option, WITH RECOMPILE, that can be specified at the time of the procedure call. The application can thus periodically recompile stored procedures and keep query execution plans up to date.

■ Authorization can be checked by the DBMS at the level of the stored procedure using the GRANT EXECUTE statement, which extends the GRANT statement introduced in Section 4.3. Thus, even the users who are not authorized to access particular relations in the database might be authorized to execute certain procedures that contain statements that access those relations. For example, both the registration and grade changing transactions might invoke stored procedures that use a SELECT statement to access the same tuples in a particular table, but one stored procedure can be executed only by students and the other only by faculty.

In addition, a stored procedure can control what the user can do beyond the capabilities of the SQL GRANT statement. For example, the code within the stored procedure can enforce the requirement that only the student can execute a transaction to register himself.

■ The application programmer need not know the details of the database schema, since all database accesses can be encapsulated within the procedure body. For example, the registrar's office might supply the procedure body for the registration transaction. The application programmer need only know how to call it.

■ Maintenance of the system is simplified, since only one copy of the procedure, stored on the server, need be maintained and updated. By contrast, if the code contained in a procedure is part of a number of application programs, all of those copies have to be maintained and updated.

■ The physical security of the code for the procedure is enhanced because the code is stored on the server rather than with the application program.

We will discuss these advantages further in Section 22.2.1 along with the system architecture supporting stored procedures.

The original SQL-92 standard did not support stored procedures, but this support was added retroactively in 1996. We illustrate the language of stored procedures with the help of an example.

Figure 10.7 shows the DDL declaration of a stored procedure for the transaction that deregisters a student from a course. We assume that the application program

Figure 10.7 A stored procedure that deregisters a student from a course.

```
CREATE PROCEDURE Deregister (IN    crs_code CHAR(6),
                             IN    semester CHAR(6),
                             IN    student_id INTEGER,
                             OUT status INTEGER,
                             OUT statusMsg CHAR VARYING(100))
BEGIN ATOMIC
    DECLARE message CHAR VARYING(50)
        DEFAULT 'Houston, we have a problem: ';
    DECLARE Success INTEGER DEFAULT 0;
    DECLARE Failure INTEGER DEFAULT -1;

    IF 1 <> (SELECT COUNT(*) FROM CLASS C
            WHERE C.Semester = semester AND C.CrsCode = crs_code)
    THEN
        SET statusMsg = 'Course not offered';
        SET status = Failure;
    ELSE
        BEGIN    -- Block limits the scope of error handler
            DECLARE UNDO HANDLER FOR SQLEXCEPTION
                BEGIN
                    SET statusMsg = message || 'cannot delete';
                    SET status = Failure;
                END
            DELETE FROM TRANSCRIPT
                WHERE StudId = student_id
                    AND Semester = semester
                    AND CrsCode = crs_code;
        END
        BEGIN -- Block limits the scope of error handler
            DECLARE UNDO HANDLER FOR SQLEXCEPTION
                BEGIN
                    SET statusMsg = message || 'cannot update';
                    SET status = Failure;
                END
            UPDATE CLASS
                SET Enrollment = (Enrollment - 1)
                WHERE Semester = semester
                    AND CrsCode = crs_code;
        END
        -- Normal termination
        SET status = Success;
        SET statusMsg = 'OK';
    END IF;
END;
```

will connect to the DBMS before calling the procedure and will disconnect after the procedure returns.

The procedure body is written in the SQL **Persistent Stored Modules** language (**SQL/PSM**), as specified by the expanded SQL-92 standard.[8] The standard also provides for stored procedures written in other languages, such as C. Note that in this context SQL/PSM is simply another host language in which SQL statements are embedded. The procedure in the example has three *in* parameters, indicated by the keyword IN, and two *out* parameters, indicated by the keyword OUT. The standard also allows parameters that can be used both ways (INOUT).

The body of the procedure is enclosed in a BEGIN/END block. The option ATOMIC ensures that the entire block executes as a single atomic unit. Next follows a series of variable declarations, which are given initial value using the DEFAULT statement (which is optional). Note that neither the parameters nor the host variables (i.e., PSM variables declared within the stored procedure) have the : prefix. This is because SQL/PSM is a unified language whose compiler understands the host variable declarations, the control statements, and the SQL query and update statements. Our example illustrates the use of the variables both within and outside of the query and update statements. In particular, their value can be changed with the SET clause, and they can be part of arithmetic and string expressions.

PSM is a powerful, full-blown programming language that is well integrated with the rest of SQL. In our brief discussion, we omit many features, such as the looping constructs, the case statement, and cursors. A detailed treatment of PSM and stored procedures appears in [Melton 1997]; here we only touch upon error handling in PSM, which is somewhat different from that in embedded SQL.

Instead of checking the variable SQLSTATE after each update statement (or using the WHENEVER statement), in SQL/PSM one declares **condition handlers** for different values of SQLSTATE. A condition handler is a program that gets executed when an SQL statement terminates with the value for SQLSTATE that matches one of the values associated with that condition handler. In our case, we have two handlers associated with SQLEXCEPTION, which is a condition that matches any "error code" (an SQLSTATE value that does *not* begin with 00, 01, or 02). Each handler's scope is delimited by a BEGIN/END block, which allows us to associate different handlers with different SQL statements. Both handlers are UNDO handlers, which means that the DBMS will roll back the effects of the stored procedure and exit after the execution of the handler. UNDO handlers can occur only inside BEGIN ATOMIC blocks. If we specify CONTINUE handlers instead, the execution proceeds after the handler has been executed as if no error occurred. We can specify EXIT instead of UNDO, in which case the procedure will exit after the execution of the condition handler but the changes made by the procedure will *not* be rolled back.

---

[8] Other vendors provide similar languages, which precede SQL/PSM and differ from it in various ways. Oracle has PL/SQL, Microsoft and Sybase offer Transact-SQL, and Informix has the SPL language.

In direct (interactive) SQL (and inside another stored procedure), a stored procedure can be executed using the SQL statement

CALL *procedure_name* (*argument-commalist*) ;

In a host program with embedded SQL, a CALL statement is preceded by EXEC SQL. In that case, the procedure arguments are host language variables preceded by a :. For example, to execute the stored procedure Deregister(), we might use

EXEC SQL CALL Deregister(:crs_code,:semester,:stud_id);

where crs_code, semester, and stud_id are host variables.

10.3 MORE ON INTEGRITY CONSTRAINTS

A consistent transaction moves the database from an initial to a final state, both of which satisfy all integrity constraints. However, a constraint might be false in an intermediate state during transaction execution; for example, in the case of referential integrity, if the reference to a row is added before the row itself. Similarly, the state produced by the DELETE statement in the procedure Deregister (Figure 10.7) violates the integrity constraint that the number of students listed as enrolled in a course in TRANSCRIPT be equal to the NumEnrolled attribute value for the course in CLASS. If the DBMS checks constraints immediately after each statement is executed, the DELETE would be rejected.

To deal with this situation, SQL allows the application to control the mode of each constraint. If a constraint is in **immediate mode**, it is checked immediately after the execution of any SQL statement in the transaction that might make it false. If it is in **deferred mode**, it is not checked until the transaction requests to commit.

■ If constraint checking for a particular constraint is immediate and an SQL statement causes the constraint to become false, the offending SQL statement is rolled back and an appropriate error code is returned through SQLSTATE. The transaction can retrieve the name of the violated constraint from the diagnostics area.

■ If constraint checking for a particular constraint is deferred, the constraint is not checked until the transaction requests to commit. If the constraint is found to be false at that time, the transaction is aborted and an appropriate error code returned. Deferred constraint checking is obviously preferable to immediate checking if integrity constraints are violated in intermediate transaction states.

When a constraint is initially defined, it can be specified with options. For example, a table constraint conforms to the rule

[CONSTRAINT *constraint-name*] CHECK *conditional-expression*
    [{ INITIALLY DEFERRED | INITIALLY IMMEDIATE}]
    [{ DEFERRABLE | NOT DEFERRABLE }]

The first option gives the initial mode of the constraint. Thus, if INITIALLY DEFERRED is specified, the constraint is checked in the deferred mode until the mode is changed by an explicit SET CONSTRAINTS statement. The second option tells whether or not the constraint can be deferred by a subsequent SET CONSTRAINTS statement. The options NOT DEFERRABLE and INITIALLY DEFERRED are considered contradictory and cannot be specified together.

A DEFERRABLE constraint can be in IMMEDIATE or DEFERRED mode at different times. The mode switch is performed with the following statement:

SET CONSTRAINTS { *constraint-list* | ALL } { DEFERRED | IMMEDIATE }

where *constraint-list* is a list of constraint names, given in CONSTRAINT statements.

10.4   DYNAMIC SQL

With static SQL, an SQL statement to be executed is designed and embedded in the application program at the time the program is written. All of the details of the statement, for example, type (e.g., SELECT, INSERT), schema information (e.g., attribute and table names referred to in the statement), and host language variables used as *in* or *out* parameters are known at compile time.

In some applications, not all of this information is known when the program is written. To handle this situation, SQL-92 defines a syntax for including **directives** in a host language program to construct, prepare, and execute an SQL statement. The statement is constructed by the host language portion of the program at run time. The directives are collectively referred to as **dynamic SQL** to distinguish them from static SQL and to indicate that SQL statements can be (dynamically) constructed at run time. Since, as with static SQL, the directives use a syntax that sets them apart from the host language, dynamic SQL is also a statement-level interface. Static and dynamic SQL use the same syntax, so they can be processed by the same precompiler. An application program can include both static and dynamic SQL constructs.

The constructed SQL statement appears in the program as the value of a host language variable of type string and is passed to the DBMS at run time as the argument of a dynamic SQL directive for preparation. Once prepared, the statement can be executed. As with static SQL, the statement must be constructed in the dialect understood by the target DBMS.

Suppose that, for example, your university has a single student registration system that allows a student to register for any course at any of its campuses. Assume that each campus has its own course database with its own table and attribute naming conventions. When a student executes the registration interaction, the application program might construct, at run time, the appropriate SQL statements to perform the registration at the specified campus. For example, it might have string representations of the appropriate SELECT statements for each campus stored in a file. The correct string is retrieved from the file at run time, assigned to a host language variable, and then prepared and executed. Or the program might use a skeleton of an appropriate SQL statement, which was prepared in advance, and then fill in appropriate table and attribute names at run time.

In the above example, there might be some commonality among the schemas and the SQL statements that must be executed to register a student at all campuses. Hence, the application program might know something about the SQL statements that it is executing. As another example, consider an application that monitors a terminal and allows the user to input an arbitrary SQL statement for execution at some database manager. The application now has no advance information about the SQL statements that it is sending to the database, but must simply take the string that has been input to a variable and send it to the DBMS for processing. Similarly, consider an application in which a spreadsheet is connected to a database. At run time, the user might specify that the value of a particular entry in the spreadsheet is some expression involving database items that must be retrieved with queries. The queries might be expressed by the user in some graphical notation, but the application translates this notation into SELECT statements. Again, it has no advance information about the SQL statement to be executed and, possibly, about the schema of the database the statement is accessing.

This lack of information can create a problem, since the domains of the *in* and *out* parameters of the SQL statement must be known so that host language variables of the appropriate type can be used for parameter passing. For situations in which this information is not available to the application program at compile time, dynamic SQL provides directives that allow the program to query the DBMS at run time to obtain schema information.

10.4.1 Statement Preparation in Dynamic SQL

We illustrate the idea of dynamically constructed SQL statements with the following example:[9]

```
printf ("Which column of CLASS would you like to see? ") ;
scanf ("%s", column); // get user input Enrollment or Room)
// Incorporate user input into SQL statement
sprintf (my_sql_stmt,
    "SELECT C.%s FROM CLASS C \
        WHERE C.CrsCode = ? AND   C.Semester = ?",
    column);
EXEC SQL PREPARE st1 FROM :my_sql_stmt;
EXEC SQL EXECUTE st1
        INTO :some_string_var
        USING :crs_code, :semester;
```

Here, in addition to the fact that the values of CrsCode and Semester are not known at compile time, the exact form of the SELECT statement is also not known at that time since the column to be retrieved by the query depends on what the user inputs

---

[9] For readers who need some help with C, the function scanf() reads user input and puts the result in the variable column. The backslash in the SELECT clause indicates that the string continues on the following line. The function sprintf() substitutes the value of the variable column for the format symbol %s and puts the result in the variable my_sql_stmt.

at run time. The PREPARE statement sends the query string (in the variable my_sql_stmt) to the database manager for preparation and assigns the name st1 to the prepared statement. Note that st1 here is an SQL variable (used only in SQL statements), not a host language variable, so it is not preceded with :.

The EXECUTE statement causes the statement named st1 to be executed. The string has two *in* parameters marked with ?. The host language variables whose values are to be substituted for these parameters are named in the USING clause. In addition, the host variable to receive the result is named in the INTO clause. The ? marker is called a **dynamic parameter**, or **placeholder**, and can be used in SELECT, INSERT, UPDATE, and DELETE statements. Once prepared, st1 can be executed many times with different host language variables as arguments. The query execution plan created by the PREPARE statement is used for all subsequent executions during the current session.

Note that, just like SELECT INTO, EXECUTE INTO requires that the query result be a single row. If the result has more than one row, a cursor must be used instead of EXECUTE INTO. We describe cursors over dynamic SQL statements in Section 10.4.3.

Parameter passing in dynamic SQL is different from that in static SQL. Placeholders, instead of the names of host language variables, are used in the string to be prepared and the INTO clause is now attached to the EXECUTE statement instead of the SELECT statement. Why is parameter passing different in this case?

▓ With static SQL, the names of the host language variables serving as parameters are provided to the precompiler in the WHERE and INTO clauses of the SQL statements. The precompiler parses these clauses at compile time. The variables are described in the compiler's symbol table that is used to translate variable names to addresses (recall that declarations in the DECLARE SECTION are processed by both the precompiler and the host language compiler). The symbol table entries contain the mapping between variable names and addresses plus the type information needed by the precompiler to generate the code for converting data items from the database representation to these variables and back. This code is executed in the host language program at the time the SQL statement is executed.

▓ With dynamic SQL, as in the example, the SQL statement might not be available to the precompiler. Thus if host language variables to be used as parameters were embedded in the statement, they could not be processed using information contained in the symbol table. To make parameter information available at compile time, it is supplied in one of the two ways: through the *SQLDA* mechanism, explained later, and by supplying the input and output variables in the clauses USING and INTO, as in our example. In the latter case, the precompiler generates the code for fetching and storing the argument values from and to these variables for communication with the DBMS.

Applications should be designed using static SQL whenever possible, since dynamic SQL is generally less efficient. The separation of preparation and execution implies added communication and processing costs—although, if the statement is executed multiple times, the added cost can be prorated over the executions, because preparation need be done only once. Moreover, this cost can be eliminated in some cases. With certain SQL statement to be executed only once, we can combine preparation and execution using the EXECUTE IMMEDIATE directive:[10]

```
EXEC SQL EXECUTE IMMEDIATE
    'INSERT INTO Transcript '
    || 'VALUES ("656565656", "CS315", "F1999", "C") ';
```

More generally, as with EXECUTE, the SQL statement can be constructed in a host language string variable, in which case the EXECUTE IMMEDIATE statement takes the form

```
EXEC SQL EXECUTE IMMEDIATE :my_sql_stmt;
```

Note the : prepended to the variable my_sql_stmt. As before, it indicates that my_sql_stmt is a host language variable rather than an SQL variable.

EXECUTE IMMEDIATE is merely a shortcut that combines the PREPARE and EXECUTE statements into one and does not preserve the execution plan after the statement has been executed. This shortcut imposes additional syntactic restrictions—some logical and some not. For instance, it does not allow an associated INTO clause. Therefore, the statement to be executed cannot have any *out* parameters (i.e., it cannot retrieve any data) and so cannot be a SELECT statement.

EXECUTE IMMEDIATE also does not allow an associated USING clause, but this is not a serious limitation. The need for USING in the EXECUTE statement comes from the fact that the statement is prepared once, with dynamic *in* parameters marked as ?, and then is executed many times with different arguments. Since EXECUTE IMMEDIATE does preparation and execution in one step (and the prepared statement is not saved for posterity), the special dynamic parameters are not needed: We can simply *plug the appropriate* parameter *values* into the SQL statement (represented as a string in the host language) using the host language facilities and then pass the fully constructed statement to EXECUTE IMMEDIATE.

As in static SQL, SQLSTATE is used to return the status of PREPARE, EXECUTE, EXECUTE IMMEDIATE, and all other dynamic SQL statements.

10.4.2 Prepared Statements and the Descriptor Area

Even though the query in the example of Section 10.4.1 on page 295 is constructed at run time and the name of the output column is not known at compile time, the example is still fairly simple because the application knows that the query target list contains exactly one attribute name and that the WHERE clause has exactly two dynamic parameters. Knowing the number of outputs and inputs thus allows us

---

[10] Note the treatment of strings. INSERT INTO is part of the dynamic SQL statement, so we are using single quotes to denote strings. Since the statement is long, it is split into two strings, which are concatenated with the usual SQL concatenation operator, ||. To include a quote symbol in a string, it must be doubled, as in the case of ''656565656''. This enables the SQL parser to parse the string correctly. In the result, each occurrence of '' is replaced with a single quote, thus producing a valid SQL statement.

to use the EXECUTE statement and provide concrete variable names for the USING and INTO clauses. The precompiler can then supply such niceties as automatic format conversion. For example, if the user inputs Enrollment, which is an integer, conversion to the string format is automatic: The precompiler determines that the INTO variable is of type string. Since the DBMS provides, at run time, the type of the value returned by the SELECT statement, the nature of the conversion can be determined at that time.

Suppose now that, at run time, the application allows the user to specify the number of attributes in the target list and the condition in the WHERE clause. In this case we do not know the number of inputs and outputs at design time and will not be able to use the form of the EXECUTE statement described in Section 10.4.1, since we do not know how many variables to supply in the INTO and USING clauses at the time of writing the program.

To deal with this situation, dynamic SQL provides a run-time mechanism that the application program can use to request from the DBMS information describing the parameters of a statement. For example, suppose that an application allows the user to query any 1-tuple relation in the database:[11]

```
printf("Which table would you like to inspect? ");
scanf("%s", table); // get user input (e.g., Class or Transcript)
// Incorporate user input into SQL statement
sprintf(my_sql_stmt,
        "SELECT * FROM %s WHERE COUNT(*)=1",
        table);
```

This statement has no input parameters, but has an indeterminate number of output parameters, because the table to be used in the FROM clause is not known in advance. Thus, it is not known how many table attributes (i.e., *out* parameters) are represented by the * in the SELECT clause. Although the application knows nothing about these parameters, once the statement has been prepared, the DBMS knows all there is to know about them and can provide this information to the application. It does this through a descriptor area. The application first requests that the DBMS allocate a **descriptor area**, sometimes called an **SQLDA**, in which parameter information can be stored. After the statement has been prepared, the application can then request that the DBMS populate the descriptor with the parameter information. For the above example, we populate the descriptor area as follows:

```
EXEC SQL PREPARE st FROM :my_sql_stmt;
EXEC SQL ALLOCATE DESCRIPTOR 'st_output' WITH MAX 21;
EXEC SQL DESCRIBE OUTPUT st
        USING SQL DESCRIPTOR 'st_output';
```

---

[11] Our example uses the EXECUTE statement, which can handle only 1-tuple queries. For the general case, a cursor and the FETCH statement are needed. We discuss the use of cursors in dynamic SQL in the next section.

Here `st_output` is an SQL variable that names the descriptor area that has been allocated. The ALLOCATE DESCRIPTOR statement creates space in the database manager, which must be sufficient to describe at most 21 parameters of the statement (as specified by the WITH MAX clause). The descriptor can be thought of as a one-dimensional array with an entry for each parameter, together with a count of the *actual* number of parameters. Each entry has a fixed structure consisting of components that describe a particular parameter, such as its name, type, and value. All fields are initially undefined. The DESCRIBE statement causes the DBMS to populate the ith entry of the descriptor `st_output` with metainformation about the ith *out* parameter of the prepared statement st (which includes name, type, and length of the parameter). It also stores the number of these parameters in the descriptor.

Returning to our example, the application causes the prepared statement st to be executed using the directive

```
EXEC SQL EXECUTE st
        INTO SQL DESCRIPTOR 'st_output';
```

Execution causes the value of the ith attribute of the row returned to be stored in the *value field* of the ith entry in `st_output`. To retrieve the metainformation about the attributes as well as their values, the application can use the GET DESCRIPTOR statement, typically in a loop that inspects each column in the retrieved row, as illustrated in Figure 10.8. In the end, the program calls DEALLOCATE DESCRIPTOR to free the space occupied by the descriptor `st_output`.

Situations in which the SQL statement to be executed contains an unknown number of input parameters are rare. When they do occur, the application can use ALLOCATE and DESCRIBE INPUT to set up a descriptor area for the *in* parameters specified as ? placeholders. As before, this descriptor is essentially an array with an entry for each placeholder. The application then uses the DESCRIBE INPUT statement to request that the DBMS populate the descriptor area with the information about each *in* parameter: For example, its type, length, and name. In this case the value has to be supplied by the application using the SET DESCRIPTOR statement. We do not discuss the details of this procedure and refer the reader to SQL manuals such as [Date and Darwen 1997, Melton and Simon 1992].

10.4.3 Cursors

Like SELECT INTO, EXECUTE INTO has the problem that the result of the query must be a single tuple. A more likely situation is that the result of a query is a relation and the cursor mechanism is needed to scan it. Fortunately, cursors can be defined for prepared statements in dynamic SQL as they are in static SQL, although the syntax is slightly different. For instance, the following is equivalent to the program in Figure 10.4 in static SQL (for brevity we have not shown the status checks in this case):

```
my_sql_stmt = "SELECT T.StudId, T.Grade \
        FROM Transcript T \
        WHERE T.CrsCode = ? \
        AND T.Semester = ?";
```

Figure 10.8 Example of using GET DESCRIPTOR.

```
int collength, coltype, colcount;
char colname[255];
// arrange variables for different types of data
char stringdata[1024];
int intdata;
float floatdata;
... variable declarations for other types ...
// Store the number of columns in colcount
EXEC SQL GET DESCRIPTOR 'st_output' :colcount = COUNT;
for (i=0; i < colcount; i++) {
    // Get meta-information about the ith attribute
    // Note: type is represented by an integer constant, such as
    // SQL_CHAR, SQL_INTEGER, SQL_FLOAT, defined in a header file
    EXEC SQL GET DESCRIPTOR 'st_output' VALUE :i
      :coltype = TYPE,
      :collength = LENGTH,
      :colname = NAME;
    printf("Column %s has value: ", colname);
    switch (coltype) {
    case SQL_CHAR:
      EXEC SQL GET DESCRIPTOR 'st_output' VALUE :i :stringdata = DATA;
        printf("%s\n", stringdata); // print string value
        break;
    case SQL_INTEGER:
      EXEC SQL GET DESCRIPTOR 'st_output' VALUE :i :intdata = DATA;
        printf("%d\n", intdata); // print integer value
        break;
    case SQL_FLOAT:
      EXEC SQL GET DESCRIPTOR 'st_output' VALUE :i :floatdata = DATA;
    printf("%f\n", floatdata); // print floating point value
    break;
    ... other cases ...
  } // switch
} // for loop
```

```
EXEC SQL PREPARE st2 FROM :my_sql_stmt;
EXEC SQL DECLARE GETENROLL INSENSITIVE CURSOR FOR st2;
EXEC SQL OPEN GETENROLL USING :crs_code, :semester;
EXEC SQL FETCH GETENROLL INTO :stud_id, :grade;
EXEC SQL CLOSE GETENROLL;
```

As with static cursors, the DECLARE CURSOR statement has the options INSEN-SITIVE and SCROLL, and the FETCH statement has the option of allowing a row-selector to be specified for scrollable cursors. UPDATE and DELETE statements can also be performed through a dynamic cursor that is not insensitive.

10.4.4 Stored Procedures on the Server

Some DBMSs allow stored procedures to be called using dynamic SQL. To call the stored procedure of Figure 10.7, we might use

```
my_sql_stmt = "CALL Deregister(?,?,?)";
EXEC SQL PREPARE st3 FROM :my_sql_stmt;
EXEC SQL EXECUTE st3
     USING :crs_code, :semester, :stud_id;
```

The PREPARE statement prepares the call to the Deregister procedure. The EXEC SQL EXECUTE statement calls the procedure and supplies the values of host language variables as arguments.

10.5 JDBC AND SQLJ

JDBC[12] is an API to the database manager that provides a call-level interface for the execution of SQL statements from a Java language program. As in dynamic SQL, an SQL statement can be constructed at run time as the value of a string variable. JDBC was developed by Sun Microsystems and is an integral part of the Java language.

In contrast, SQLJ is a statement-level interface to Java analogous to static em-bedded SQL. Unlike JDBC, it was developed by a consortium of companies and has become a separate ANSI standard.

Both JDBC and SQLJ are designed to access databases over the Internet and are much more portable than the various implementations of embedded and dynamic SQL.

10.5.1 JDBC Basics

Recall that, in dynamic and static SQL, the target DBMS must be known at compile time since the SQL statements must use the target's dialect. With dynamic SQL, the schema need not be known at compile time. By contrast, in JDBC neither the DBMS nor the schema need be known at compile time. Applications use the JDBC dialect of SQL, independently of the DBMS being used, and, as with dynamic SQL,

---

[12] JDBC is a trademark of Sun Microsystems, which claims that it is not an acronym. Nevertheless, it is often assumed to stand for "Java Database Connectivity."

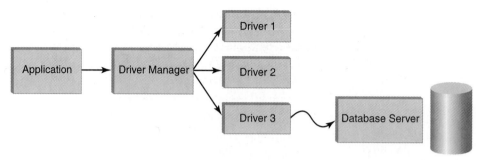

Figure 10.9 Connecting to a database through JDBC.

JDBC supplies features that allow the application to request information about the schema from the DBMS at run time.

The mechanism that allows JDBC programs to deal with different DBMSs at run time is shown in Figure 10.9. The application communicates with a DBMS through a JDBC module called a **driver manager**. When the application first connects to a particular DBMS, the driver manager chooses another JDBC module, called a **driver**, to perform whatever reformatting is needed to transform an SQL statement from the JDBC dialect of SQL to the dialect understood by that DBMS. JDBC maintains a separate driver for most commonly used DBMSs. The manager chooses the one corresponding to the particular DBMS being accessed. When an SQL statement is to be executed, the application program sends a string representation of the statement to the appropriate driver, which performs any necessary reformatting and then sends the statement to the DBMS, where it is prepared and executed.

The software architecture of JDBC consists of a set of predefined object classes, such as `DriverManager` and `Statement`. The methods of these object classes provide the call-level interface to the database. A JDBC program must first load these predefined object classes, then create appropriate instances of the object types, and then use the appropriate methods to access the database. The general structure of JDBC calls within a Java program is shown in Figure 10.10. We explain each statement as it appears:

- `import java.sql.*` imports all of the classes in the package `java.sql` and hence makes the JDBC API available within the Java program. The classes `Connection`, `Statement`, `DriverManager`, and `ResultSet` that occur in the figure are all in this package, as are `PreparedStatement`, `CallableStatement`, `ResultSetMetadata`, and `SQLException`. (`CallableStatement` is a subclass of `PreparedStatement`, which in turn is a subclass of `Statement`.)

- `Class.forName()` loads the specified database driver and registers it with the driver manager. Although the naming convention might not be intuitive, there is a class in the `java.lang` package, called `Class`, with methods that allow a class to be loaded into a program at run time. One of its static methods, `forName()`, can be used to load and register the specified driver. If the application wants

Figure 10.10 Skeleton of procedure calls needed for JDBC.

991-6804

```java
import java.sql.*;
... ... ...
  String  url,userId,password;
  Connection  con1;
  ... ... ...
  try {
    // use the right driver for your database
    Class.forName("sun.jdbc.odbc.JdbcOdbcDriver"); // load the driver
    con1 = DriverManager.getConnection(url, userId, password);
  } catch (ClassNotFoundException e) {
    System.err.println("Can't load driver\n");
    System.exit(1);
  } catch (SQLException e) {
    System.err.println("Can't connect\n");
    System.exit(1);
  }
  Statement stat1 = con1.createStatement(); // create a statement object
  String myQuery = ...some SELECT statement...
  ResultSet res1 = stat1.executeQuery(myQuery);
       ... process results ...
  stat1.close(); // free up the statement object
  con1.close();   // close connection
```

to connect to more than one database, Class.forName() is called separately for each.

This and the next statement are enveloped with the try/catch construct, which handles exceptions. We return to exception handling in Section 10.5.5.

■ DriverManager.getConnection() uses the static method getConnection() of the class DriverManager to connect to the DBMS at the given address. The method tests each of the database drivers that have been loaded to see if any are capable of establishing a connection to that DBMS. If so, it

1. Establishes the connection using the specified user Id and password
2. Creates a Connection object and assigns it to the variable con1, declared earlier

The parameter url contains the URL (uniform resource locator) of the target DBMS. This URL is obtained from the database administrator and looks something like

```
jdbc:odbc:http://server.xyz.edu/sturegDB:8000
```

The prefix jdbc specifies the main protocol for connecting to the database (JDBC, not surprisingly). The second component, odbc, specifies the subprotocol (which is vendor and driver specific). Next comes the address of the database server, followed by the communication port number on which the server is listening.

■ `con1.createStatement()` uses the `createStatement()` method of the Connection object `con1` to create a `Statement` object and assign it to the `Statement` variable `stat1`.

■ `stat1.executeQuery()` prepares and executes the SELECT statement provided as its argument, using the `Statement` object `stat1`. The SQL statement can have no *in* parameters, and the result set it returns is stored in the `ResultSet` object `res1`, which is created by the `executeQuery()` method. This method is analogous to the EXECUTE IMMEDIATE directive in dynamic SQL, since it combines both preparation and execution. A major difference is that the JDBC method creates an object for returning data, which EXECUTE IMMEDIATE cannot do. We discuss the `ResultSet` class in Section 10.5.3.

To execute an UPDATE, DELETE, or INSERT statement (or a DDL statement), the appropriate form is

```
stat1.executeUpdate(...some SQL statement...);
```

This function returns an integer denoting how many rows are affected (or 0 for a DDL statement, such as CREATE).

■ `stat1.close()` and `con1.close()` deallocate the `Statement` object and close the connection (deallocating the `Connection` object), respectively. After a statement has been executed, the `Statement` object that supported it need not be closed but can be reused to support another statement.

10.5.2 Prepared Statements

The calls to `executeQuery()` and `executeUpdate()` in Figure 10.10 both prepare and execute the specified statement. To prepare a statement and then execute it separately, the appropriate calls are

```
PreparedStatement ps1 =
     con1.prepareStatement(...SQL preparable statement...);
```

which returns a `PreparedStatement` object that is assigned to `ps1`, followed by either

```
ResultSet res1 = ps1.executeQuery();
```

or

```
int n = ps1.executeUpdate();
```

where `executeUpdate()` returns an integer denoting how many rows were updated.

`PreparedStatement` is a subclass of the class `Statement`. Note that both classes have methods with the names `executeQuery()` and `executeUpdate()`, but that the methods for `PreparedStatement` have no arguments.

As in dynamic SQL, the string argument of `prepareStatement()` can contain dynamic in parameters marked with the ? placeholders. Also as with dynamic SQL, the placeholders must be given concrete values before execution. This is done using the `setXXX()` methods. For instance,

```
ps1.setInt(1, someIntVar);
```

replaces the first ? placeholder with the value stored in the host language variable `someIntVar`. `PreparedStatement` has a number of `setXXX()` methods, where `XXX` specifies the type (e.g., `Int`, `Long`, `String`) to supply in arguments of different types.

10.5.3   Result Sets and Cursors

The execution of a query statement stores its result (the *out* arguments) in the specified `ResultSet` object. The rows in that result set are retrieved using a cursor. A JDBC cursor is implemented using the `next()` method of class `ResultSet`. When invoked on a `ResultSet` object, it scans the entire set tuple by tuple. In Figure 10.11, the result set object is stored in the variable `res2`, and `res2.next()` advances the cursor to the next row.

The program prepares the query, supplies arguments, and then executes the query. It then uses a while loop to retrieve all of the rows of the result set. The method `next()` moves the cursor and returns `false` when there are no more rows to return. In each iteration of the while loop, the result tuples are retrieved using calls to `getLong()` and `getString()`, which come in two forms: those that take attribute names as a parameter and those that takes positional arguments. Thus, we can use `getLong(1)` to obtain the student Id (since `StudId` is the first attribute in the result set `res2`) and `getString(2)` to obtain the grade (since `Grade` is the second attribute). The class `ResultSet` has `getXXX()` methods for all primitive types supported by Java.

JDBC defines three result set types. They differ in their support of scrolling and sensitivity.

■ A *forward-only* result set, as its name implies, is not scrollable (the cursor can move only in the forward direction). It uses the default cursor type (INSENSITIVE or nonINSENSITIVE) of the underlying DBMS.

■ A *scroll-insensitive* result set is scrollable and uses an INSENSITIVE cursor of the specified DBMS, so that changes made to the underlying tables after the result set is computed (either by the transaction that created the result set or by other transactions) are not seen in the result set.

■ A *scroll-sensitive* result set is scrollable and uses a not INSENSITIVE cursor. As we discussed in Section 10.2.4, the SQL standard does not define any required behavior when the INSENSITIVE option has not been selected. Database vendors are free to implement whatever semantics they deem appropriate, and JDBC generally provides the semantics supported in the DBMS it is accessing. Many vendors have implemented the semantics called KEYSET_DRIVEN, which is part of the ODBC specification and described in Section 10.6. In that semantics, row

Figure 10.11 Fragment of JDBC program using a cursor.

```java
import java.sql.*;
    ... ... ...
    Connection con2;
    try {
        // Use appropriate URL and JDBC driver
        String url = "jdbc:odbc:http://server.xyz.edu/sturegDB:800";
        Class.forName("sun.jdbc.odbc.JdbcOdbcDriver");
        con2 = DriverManager.getConnection(url, "pml", "36.ty");
    } catch ...  // catch exceptions

    // Use the "+" operator, for readability
    String query2 = "SELECT T.StudId, T.Grade " +
                    "FROM TRANSCRIPT T " +
                    "WHERE T.CrsCode = ? " +
                      "AND T.Semester = ?";

    PreparedStatement ps2 = con2.prepareStatement(query2);
    ps2.setString(1, "CS308");
    ps2.setString(2, "F2000");
    ResultSet res2 = ps2.executeQuery();

    long studId;
    String grade;
    while (res2.next()) {
      studId = res2.getLong("StudId");
      grade = res2.getString("Grade");
      ... process the values in studId and grade ...
    }

ps2.close();
con2.close();
```

updates and deletes made after the result set is created are visible but inserts are not. JDBC provides a variety of methods for querying the driver to determine what to expect.

If the target DBMS does not support the scrolling or sensitivity properties requested by an application, a warning is issued.

A result set can be read-only or updatable. With an updatable result set, the SQL query on which the result set is based must satisfy the conditions for updatable views (see Section 6.3). For example, the following variant of createStatement() creates a Statement object s3:

```
Statement s3 =
    con1.createStatement(ResultSet.TYPE_SCROLL_SENSITIVE,
                         ResultSet.CONCUR_UPDATABLE);
```

If the executeQuery() method of s3 is later invoked, the result set that will be created will be updatable and scroll-sensitive. Consult the description of classes ResultSet and Connection in your JDK documentation to see other options.

The current row of an updatable result set, res, produced by a SELECT statement that returns the value of a string attribute, Name, might be updated by assigning the value Smith to Name using

```
res.updateString("Name", "Smith");
```

As with the methods setXXX() and getXXX(), there is an updateXXX() method for every primitive type.

When the new value of the row has been completely constructed, the underlying table is updated by the execution of

```
res.updateRow();
```

Not only can rows in an updatable result set be updated and deleted but, in contrast to cursors in static and dynamic SQL, new rows can be inserted through the result set as well. The column values of the row to be inserted are first assembled in a buffer associated with the result set. The method res.insertRow() is then called to insert the buffered row in the result set res and in the database simultaneously.

10.5.4 Obtaining Information about a Result Set

As with dynamic SQL, information about a result set might not be known when the program is written. JDBC provides mechanisms for querying the DBMS to obtain such information. For example, JDBC provides a class ResultSetMetaData, whose methods can be used for this purpose. Thus

```
ResultSet rs3 = stmt3.executeQuery("SELECT * FROM TABLE3");
ResultSetMetaData rsm3 = rs3.getMetaData();
```

creates a ResultSetMetaData object, rsm3, and populates it with information about the result set rs3. This object can then be queried with such methods as

```
int numberOfColumns = rsm3.getColumnCount();
String columnName = rsm3.getColumnName(1);
String typeName = rsm3.getColumnTypeName(1);
```

The first method returns the number of columns in the result set, and the last two return the name and type of column 1. Using these methods, even without knowing the schema of a result set, one can iterate over the columns of each row in a loop, examine their types, and fetch the data. For instance, if rsm3.getColumnTypeName(2) returns "Integer", the program can call rs3.getInt(2) to obtain the value stored in the second column of the current row.

JDBC also has a class, DatabaseMetaData, which can be queried for information about the schema and other database information.

10.5.5 Status Processing

Status processing in JDBC uses the standard exception handling mechanism of Java. The basic format is

```
try {
        . . . code that might cause an exception goes here . . .
}
catch (SQLException e) {
        System.err.println("Bad things have happened:\n");
        System.err.println("Message: " + e.getMessage());
        System.err.println("SQLState: " + e.getSQLState());
        System.err.println("ErrorCode: " + e.getErrorCode());
};
```

In fact, in our examples all calls to executeQuery(), prepareStatement(), and the like, should have been enveloped with such a try statement.

The system *tries* to execute the statements within the try clause. Each such statement can contain method calls for Java or JDBC objects, and the declaration of each method can specify that, if certain errors occur during method execution, one or more named exceptions are **thrown**, where the name of the exception denotes the type of error that occurred. For example, the JDBC method executeQuery() throws the exception SQLException if the DBMS returns an access error during query execution. An access error occurs whenever there is an unsuccessful or incomplete execution of an SQL statement—more precisely, an execution for which the SQLSTATE returned has any value other than successful completion (of the form "00XXX"), warning (of the form "01XXX"), or no data ("02000").

If such an exception is thrown within the try clause, it is **caught** by the corresponding catch clause, which is then executed. In the example, an SQLException object, e, is created, whose methods can be used to print out an error message, return the value of SQLSTATE, or return any vendor-specific error code. When the catch clause completes, execution continues with the next statement following the clause.

10.5.6 Executing Transactions

By default, the database is in **autocommit mode** when a connection is created. Each SQL statement is treated as a separate transaction, which is committed when that statement is (successfully) completed. To allow two or more statements to be grouped into a transaction, autocommit mode is disabled using

```
con4.setAutoCommit(false);
```

where con4 is a Connection object.

Initially, each transaction uses the default isolation level of the database manager. The level can be changed with a call such as

```
con4.setTransactionIsolation(Connection.TRANSACTION_SERIALIZABLE);
```

Serialization levels TRANSACTION_SERIALIZABLE, TRANSACTION_REPEATABLE_READ, and the like, are constants (static integers) defined in class Connection.

Transactions can be committed or aborted using the `commit()` or `rollback()` methods of class `Connection`.

```
con4.commit();
con4.rollback();
```

After a transaction is committed or rolled back, a new one starts when the next SQL statement is executed (or, in the case of the first SQL statement in the program, when that statement is executed). This way of structuring transactions is called **chaining** and will be discussed further in Section 21.3.1.

If the program is connected to more than one DBMS, the transactions at each can be separately committed or rolled back. JDBC does not support a commit protocol that ensures that the set of transactions will be globally atomic. However, a proposed new Java package, JTS (Java Transaction Service), includes a TP monitor (and an appropriate API) that does guarantee an atomic commit of distributed transactions using JDBC. TP monitors are discussed in Chapter 22.

10.5.7 Stored Procedures on the Server

JDBC can be used to call a stored procedure if the DBMS supports this feature. For example, to call the stored procedure defined in Figure 10.7 on page 291 we might use the program fragment

```
CallableStatement cs5 =
      con5.prepareCall("{call Deregister (?,?,?,?,?)}");
cs5.setString(1, crs_code);
cs5.setString(2, semester);
cs5.setInt(3, stud_id);
cs5.getInt(4, status);
cs5.setString(5, message);
cs5.executeUpdate();
```

where con5 is a `Connection` object.

The first statement declares a `CallableStatement` object with the name cs5 and assigns to it the stored procedure `Deregister()`. The braces around the construct `{call Deregister(?,?,?,?,?)}` denote that the construct is part of the **SQL escape syntax** and signals the driver that the code within the braces should be handled in a special way. The values of the three *in* parameters of `Deregister()`, obtained from the Java variables `crs_code`, `semester`, and `stud_Id`, are specified with setXXX() method calls. (We omit the details of *out* parameters and return values, which are handled somewhat differently.) The final statement executes the call.

The DBMS might allow a stored procedure to return a result set, perhaps in addition to updating the database. A call to such a procedure is viewed as a query, in which case the last statement in the above program fragment is replaced by

```
ResultSet rs5 = cs5.executeQuery();
```

JDBC also has facilities for creating a stored procedure (as a string) and sending it to the DBMS.

Figure 10.12 A fragment of a Java program using JDBC.

```java
import java.sql.*;
    ... ... ...
    try {
        // Use the right JDBC driver here
        Class.forName("sun.jdbc.odbc.JdbcOdbcDriver");
    } catch (ClassNotFoundException e) {
        return(-1);   // Can't load driver
    }
    Connection con6 = null;
    try {
        String url = "jdbc:odbc:http://server.xyz.edu/sturegDB:8000";
        con6 = DriverManager.getConnection(url,"john","ji21");
    } catch (SQLException e) {
        return(-2);   // Can't connect
    }
    con6.setAutoCommit(false);
    Statement stat6 = con6.createStatement();
    try {
        stat6.executeUpdate("DELETE FROM TRANSCRIPT "
                         + "WHERE StudId = 123456789 "
                            + "AND Semester = 'F2000'   "
                            + "AND CrsCode = 'CS308'" );
    } catch (SQLException e) {
        con6.rollback();
        stat6.close();
        con6.close();
        return(-3);   // Can't execute
    }
    try {
        stat6.executeUpdate("UPDATE CLASS "
                         + "SET Enrollment = (Enrollment - 1) "
                            + "AND Semester = 'F2000' "
                            + "WHERE CrsCode = 'CS308'");
    } catch (SQLException e) {
        con6.rollback();
        stat6.close();
        con6.close();
        return(-4);   // Can't update
    }

    con6.commit();
    stat6.close();
    con6.close();
    return(0);   // Success!
```

10.5.8 An Example

Figure 10.12 is a fragment of a Java program containing calls to the JDBC API. The program performs roughly the same transaction as that of Figure 10.3, except that, for simplicity, it uses constants in the SQL statements instead of the ? placeholders.

10.5.9 SQLJ: Statement-Level Interface to Java

Although call-level interfaces, such as JDBC, can be used in static transaction processing applications (where the database schema and the format of the SQL statements are known at compile time), they are fundamentally less efficient at run time than statement-level interfaces, such as static SQL, because preparation and execution generally involve separate communication with the DBMS. For this reason, a consortium of companies developed a statement-level SQL interface to Java, called **SQLJ**, which is now an ANSI standard. An important goal of SQLJ is to obtain some of the run-time efficiency of embedded SQL for (static) Java applications while retaining the advantage of accessing DBMSs through JDBC.

SQLJ is a dialect of embedded SQL that can be included in Java programs. Such programs are translated by a precompiler into standard Java, and the embedded SQLJ constructs are replaced by calls to an SQLJ run-time package, which accesses a database using calls to a JDBC driver. An SQLJ program can connect to multiple DBMSs using different JDBC drivers in this way. As with embedded SQL, the precompiler can also check SQL syntax and the number and types of arguments and results.

We do not discuss the syntax of SQLJ in detail, but highlight some of the differences between SQLJ, embedded SQL, and JDBC.

1. In contrast to embedded SQL, in which each DBMS vendor supports its own proprietary version of SQL, SQLJ supports (essentially) SQL-92 and is much more portable across vendors.

2. SQL statements appear in a Java program as part of an **SQLJ clause**, which begins with #SQL (instead of EXEC SQL, as in embedded SQL) and can contain an SQL statement inside curly braces. For example, the SELECT statement of Figure 10.1 becomes in SQLJ:

```
#SQL {SELECT C.Enrollment
        INTO :numEnrolled
        FROM CLASS C
        WHERE C.CrsCode = :crsCode
          AND C.Semester = :semester};
```

3. Any Java variable can be included as a parameter in an SQL statement prefixed with :, as in static SQL. This method of passing parameters into an SQL construct (which, you will recall, is done at compile time) is considerably more efficient during run time than the method used in JDBC, in which the value of each argument must be bound to a ? parameter at run time.

4. In SQLJ, a query returns an **SQLJ iterator** object instead of a ResultSet object. SQLJ iterators are similar to result sets in that they provide a cursor

Figure 10.13 Use of an iterator in SQLJ.

```
import java.sql.*
    ... ... ...
    #SQL iterator GetEnrolledIter(int studentId, String studGrade);
    GetEnrolledIter iter1;

    #SQL iter1 = { SELECT T.StudId AS "studentId",
                          T.Grade AS "studGrade"
                   FROM TRANSCRIPT T
                   WHERE T.CrsCode = :crsCode
                         AND T.Semester = :semester };
    int id;
    String grade;
    while (iter1.next()) {
         id = iter1.studentId();
         grade = iter1.studGrade();
         ... process the values in id and grade ...
    }

    iter1.close();
```

mechanism.[13] In fact, both the SQLJ iterator object and the ResultSet object implement the same Java interface java.util.Iterator. An iterator object stores an entire result set and provides methods, such as next(), to scan through the rows in the set. Figure 10.13 shows an SQLJ version of the program fragment in Figure 10.6.

The first statement in the figure tells the SQLJ preprocessor to generate Java statements that define a class, GetEnrolledIter, which implements the interface sqlj.runtime.NamedIterator. This is an interface that extends the standard Java interface, java.util.Iterator, and provides the venerable next() method. The class GetEnrolledIter can be used to store result sets in which each row has two columns: an integer and a string. The declaration gives a Java name to these columns, studentId and studGrade, and (implicitly) defines the **column accessor** methods, studentId() and studGrade(), which can be used to return data stored in the corresponding columns.

The second statement declares an object, iter1, in the class GetEnrolled-Iter.

The third statement executes SELECT and places the result set in iter1. Note that the AS clause is used to associate the SQL attribute names in the result set with the column names in the iterator. These names do not have to be the same,

---

[13] SQLJ iterators can be converted into result sets, and vice versa.

but the sequence of columns in the result set and the iterator must correspond in number and type.

The `while` statement fetches the results one at a time into the host variables `id` and `grade` and processes them.

5. SQLJ has its own mechanism, which we do not discuss, for defining connection objects and for connecting to a database. A program can have several such connections active at the same time. Unlike in embedded SQL, each individual SQLJ statement can optionally designate a specific database connection to which that clause is to be applied. For example, the first SELECT statement in this section can be rewritten as

```
#SQL [db1] {SELECT C.Enrollment
            INTO :num_enrolled
            FROM CLASS C
            WHERE C.CrsCode = :crs_code
              AND C.Semester = :semester};
```

to specify that it is to be applied to the (previously defined) database connection named db1. If this option is not used, all SQL statements are applied to a default database connection, as in embedded SQL. Recall that, in JDBC, each SQL statement is always associated with a specific database connection *explicitly*, through its `Statement` object.

6. Just as static and dynamic embedded SQL statements can be included in the same host language program, SQLJ statements and JDBC calls can be included in the same Java program.

10.6 ODBC *

ODBC (Open DataBase Connectivity) is an API to the DBMS that provides a call-level interface for SQL statement execution. Our presentation is based on the ODBC specification developed by Microsoft, but be aware that some vendors do not support all of the features.

It should also be noted that the SQL standardization body has for quite a long time been working on a specification for a call-level interface, known as **SQL/CLI**, to replace the bulky dynamic SQL. ODBC is a branch of an earlier version of this specification, and it has much in common with the recently finalized release of SQL/CLI, which was included in SQL:1999. Microsoft has pledged to align ODBC with this newly adopted standard.

The software architecture of an ODBC application is similar to that of JDBC in that it uses a driver manager and a separate driver for each DBMS to be accessed. ODBC is not object oriented, however, and so it provides an interface to the DBMS that is much lower level. For example, in ODBC an application must specifically allocate and deallocate the storage it needs within the driver manager and the driver, whereas in JDBC that storage is automatically allocated when the appropriate objects are created. Thus, before an ODBC application calls the function

Figure 10.14 Skeleton of procedure calls needed for ODBC in a C program.

```
SQLAllocEnv(&henv);
SQLAllocConnect(henv, &hdbc);
SQLConnect(hdbc,database_name,userId, password);
SQLAllocStmt(hdbc, &hstmt);
SQLExecDirect(hstmt, ...SQL statement...);
... process results ...
SQLFreeStmt(hstmt, fOption);
SQLDisconnect(hdbc);
SQLFreeConnect(hdbc);
SQLFreeEnv(henv);
```

SQLConnect() to request a connection to a database manager, it must first call the function SQLAllocConnect() to request that the driver manager allocate storage for that connection. Later, after the application calls SQLDisconnect() to disconnect from the database manager, it must call SQLFreeConnect() to deallocate this storage. As a result, ODBC applications are prone to so-called **memory leaks**—an accumulation of garbage memory blocks that occurs when a program fails to free for ODBC structures that are no longer in use.

Figure 10.14 shows the structure of one version of the required function calls as they might appear in a C program.[14] Each function returns a value that denotes success or failure.

■ SQLAllocEnv() allocates and initializes storage within the driver manager for use as ODBC's interface to the application. It returns an identifying handle, henv. A **handle** is simply a mechanism the application can use to refer to this data structure. In C, a handle is implemented as a pointer, but other host languages might implement it differently. The environment area is used internally by the ODBC driver manager to store run time information.

■ SQLAllocConnect() allocates memory within the driver manager for the connection and returns a connection handle, hdbc.

■ SQLConnect() loads the appropriate database driver and then connects to the DBMS server using previously allocated connection, hdbc, the database name, user Id, and password.

   If the application wants to connect to more than one database manager, SQLAllocConnect() and SQLConnect() are called separately for each manager. The drivers (there might be more than one in this case) maintain separate transactions for each such connection.

---

[14] We have simplified the syntax in this and subsequent examples to emphasize the semantics of the ODBC interaction. For example, in reality, string parameters, such as database_name, are passed with an accompanying length field.

■ SQLAllocStmt() allocates storage within the driver for an SQL statement and returns a handle, hstmt, for that statement.

■ SQLExecDirect() takes a statement handle previously allocated using SQLAllocStmt() and a string variable containing an SQL statement, and asks the DBMS to prepare and execute the statement. The same handle can be used multiple times to execute different SQL statements.

  The SQL statement can be a data manipulation statement, such as SELECT or UPDATE, as well as a DDL statement, such as CREATE or GRANT. It cannot contain an embedded reference to a host variable, since variable names can be translated to memory addresses only at compile time. Note that SQLExecDirect() is related to but is more versatile than EXECUTE IMMEDIATE in dynamic SQL. Whereas the latter cannot return data to the application (see Section 10.4.1), the former can produce a result set using a SELECT statement, and this set can then be accessed through a cursor (see Section 10.6.2).

■ SQLDisconnect() disconnects from the server. This function takes the connection handle as an argument.

■ SQLFreeStmt(), SQLFreeConnect(), and SQLFreeEnv() release the handles and free up the corresponding storage space allocated by the corresponding Alloc functions.

10.6.1 Prepared Statements

Instead of calling SQLExecDirect(), the application program can call

```
SQLPrepare(hstmt, ...SQL statement...);
```

to prepare the statement and then

```
SQLExecute(hstmt);
```

to execute it.

  As in dynamic SQL, the statement argument of SQLPrepare() can contain the ? placeholders. Arguments can be supplied to those parameters using the SQLBindParameters() function. For example, the call[15]

```
SQLBindParameters(hstmt, 1, SQL_PARAMETER_INPUT,
                  SQL_C_SSHORT, SQL_SMALLINT, &int1);
```

binds the first parameter of the statement hstmt, which is an *in* parameter, to the host language variable int1, where int1 is of type short in the C language. The parameter's value replaces the first ? placeholder in hstmt when SQLBindParameters() is executed. SQLBindParameters() performs the conversion from type

---

[15] Again, we have simplified the syntax. The actual function SQLBindParameters() has no less than ten parameters!

short in C to type SMALLINT in SQL.[16] Since the procedure call is compiled by the host language compiler, references to host language variable int1 in the parameter list can be resolved at compile time. This contrasts with the use of SQLExecDirect(), where references to host variables are not allowed.

10.6.2 Cursors

The execution of a SELECT statement using SQLExecDirect() or SQLExecute() does not return any data to the application. Instead, data is returned through a cursor, which is maintained within the ODBC driver and referred to by the statement handle, hstmt, returned by SQLAllocStmt(). Additional ODBC functions must be called to bring the data into the application.

The program can optionally call SQLBindCol(), which binds a particular column of the result set to a specific host variable in the program. For example, we might use the following call[17] to bind the first column to the integer variable int2.

```
SQLBindCol(hstmt, 1, SQL_C_SSHORT, &int2);
```

When SQLFetch(hstmt) is called, the cursor is advanced and the values in the columns of the current row that had been bound to host variables are stored in those variables. If a column has not been bound to a designated host variable, the program can call SQLGetData() to retrieve and store its value. For example,[18] to store the value of the second column of the current row in the integer variable int3 we might use the call

```
SQLGetData(hstmt, 2, SQL_C_SSHORT, &int3);
```

Before executing the SELECT statement, the application can use SQLSetStmtOption() to specify one of the following three types for the cursor:

1. STATIC. As with the INSENSITIVE option for cursors in embedded SQL, when the SELECT statement is executed the driver effectively creates a copy of the rows in the result set. The cursor accesses that copy, as shown in Figure 10.5, page 286. This type of returned data is called a **snapshot**.

2. KEYSET_DRIVEN. When the SELECT statement is executed, the driver effectively constructs a set of pointers to the rows in the base table that satisfy the WHERE clause. If some other statement in this or a concurrent transaction *modifies* or *deletes* one of those rows, that change can be seen in a subsequent call to SQLFetch(). However, if some other statement in this or a concurrent transaction *inserts* a row that satisfies the WHERE clause, that change will not be seen by subsequent calls to SQLFetch() (since a pointer to that row is not in the set). Unfortunately, that is not the only anomaly that can occur. A change of an

---

[16] In a number of ODBC constructs, as in this one, the programmer must specify the desired conversion between the SQL data types used within the DBMS and the C language data types used within the application program.

[17] We have simplified the syntax.

[18] We have simplified the syntax.

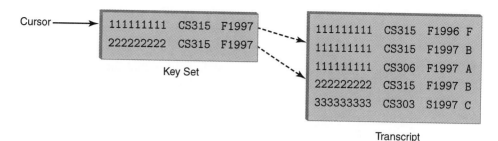

Figure 10.15 Effect of using a KEYSET_DRIVEN cursor to retrieve records from TRANSCRIPT.

attribute value in a row that previously satisfied the WHERE clause can cause the row to no longer satisfy the clause. However, the row will still be visible through the cursor. This type of returned data is sometimes called a **dynaset**. The situation is shown in Figure 10.15.

3. DYNAMIC. The data in the result set is completely dynamic. A statement in this or some other concurrently executing transaction cannot only change or delete a row in the result set after the SELECT statement is executed, but it can insert a row as well. Those changes will be seen in subsequent calls to SQLFetch().

The ODBC specification calls for the implementation of all of these cursor types. However the mechanisms made available to ODBC by a particular DBMS might make the implementation of a particular cursor type difficult, so a driver for that DBMS might support only a subset of cursor types. Clearly, DYNAMIC cursors are the most difficult to implement, and many drivers do not implement them.

The statement SQLSetStmtOption is used to request a cursor type as follows:

```
SQLSetStmtOption(hstmt,SQL_CURSOR_TYPE, Option);
```

where *Option* is one of the constants SQL_CURSOR_STATIC, SQL_CURSOR_DYNAMIC, or SQL_CURSOR_KEYSET_DRIVEN.

ODBC also supports positioned updates through a non-STATIC cursor. For such an update, the SELECT statement must be defined with a FOR UPDATE. For example,

```
SQLExecDirect(hstmt1,  "SELECT * \
                       FROM EMPLOYEE \
                       FOR UPDATE OF Salary");
```

uses a previously allocated statement handle, hstmt1, to prepare a query whose cursor will allow updates to the EMPLOYEE relation through the Salary attribute.

Now, suppose we have executed a number of SQLFetch(hstmt1) statements and the cursor is now positioned at the employee named Joe Public. To raise Joe's salary by $1,000, we might execute the following statement (where hstmt2 is a previously allocated statement handle):

```
SQLExecDirect(hstmt2, "UPDATE EMPLOYEE \
                       SET Salary = Salary + 1000\
                       WHERE CURRENT OF employee_cursor");
```

The only problem with the above statement is that the cursor name, employee_cursor, required by the WHERE CURRENT OF clause, comes out of the blue. In particular, it is not connected in any way to the cursor associated with the hstmt1 handle that we used to execute the SELECT statement. Thus, before executing the above UPDATE statement we must first give a name to that cursor. ODBC provides a special call to do just this:

```
SQLSetCursorName(hstmt1, employee_cursor);
```

As with dynamic SQL, information about the result set of a query might not be known when the program is written. ODBC thus provides a number of functions to obtain this information. For example, after a statement has been prepared, the program can call the function SQLNumResultCols(), to obtain the number of columns in a result set, and the functions SQLColAttributes() and SQLDescribeCol(), to provide information about a specific column in a result set.

ODBC also has a number of functions, called **catalog functions**, which return information about the database schema. For example, SQLTables() returns, in a result set, the names of all tables, and SQLColumns() returns column names.

10.6.3 Status Processing

The ODBC procedures we have been discussing are actually functions, which return a value, of type RETCODE, indicating whether or not the specified action was successful. Thus, we might have

```
RETCODE retcode1;
...
retcode1 = SQLConnect(...);
if (retcode1 != SQL_SUCCESS)    {
     ... do something ...
}
```

Additional information about the error can be found by calling SQLError().

10.6.4 Executing Transactions

By default, the database is in autocommit mode when a connection is created. To allow two or more statements to be grouped into a transaction, autocommit mode is disabled using

```
SQLSetConnectionOption(hdbc,
                       SQL_AUTOCOMMIT,
                       SQL_AUTOCOMMIT_OFF);
```

where hdbc is a connection handle. Initially, each transaction uses the default isolation level of the database manager. This level can be changed with a call such as

```
SQLSetConnectionOption(hdbc,
                       SQL_TXN_ISOLATION,
                       SQL_TXN_REPEATABLE_READ);
```

Transactions can be committed or rolled back using

```
SQLTransact(henv, hdbc, Action);
```

where `Action` is either `SQL_COMMIT` or `SQL_ABORT`.

After a transaction is committed or rolled back, a new transaction starts when the next SQL statement is executed (or, in the case of the first SQL statement in the program, when that statement is executed).

If the program is connected to more than one database, the transactions at each database can be separately committed or rolled back. ODBC does not support a commit protocol that ensures that the set of transactions will be globally atomic. However, Microsoft has introduced a new TP monitor, MTS (Microsoft Transaction Server), that includes a transaction manager (and an appropriate API) guaranteeing an atomic commit of distributed transactions using ODBC.

10.6.5 Stored Procedures on the Server

ODBC can be used to call a stored procedure if the DBMS supports this feature. For example, to call the stored procedure of Figure 10.7 on page 291 we might begin with the statement

```
SQLPrepare(hstmt, "{call Deregister(?,?,?,?,?)}");
```

which prepares the call statement. The braces around the call to `Deregister()` denote the SQL escape syntax discussed in Section 10.5.7. The parameters of `Deregister()` can be bound to host variables with `SQLBindParameter()` functions. Then the procedure call can be executed with

```
SQLExecute(hstmt);
```

As with embedded SQL, if the DBMS allows a stored procedure to return a result set, the application program can retrieve data from the result set using a cursor.

10.6.6 An Example

Figure 10.16 is a fragment of a C program containing ODBC procedure calls. It executes the same transaction as that in Figure 10.12. The constant `SQL_NTS`, when supplied as an argument to a procedure (`SQLConnect()` and `SQLExerDirect()` in the example) indicates that the preceding argument is a null-terminated string.

10.7 COMPARISON

We have discussed a variety of techniques for creating programs that can access a database—each has its own advantages and disadvantages. Here we summarize some of the issues involved.

Figure 10.16 A fragment of an ODBC program written in C.

```
HENV henv;
HDBC hdbc;
HSTMT hstmt;
RETCODE retcode;
SQLAllocEnv(&henv);
SQLAllocConnect(henv, &hdbc);
retcode = SQLConnect(hdbc, dbName, SQL_NTS, "john", SQL_NTS, "j121",
                          SQL_NTS);
if (retcode != SQL_SUCCESS){
    SQLFreeEnv(henv);
    return(-1);
}
SQLSetConnectionOption(hdbc, SQL_AUTOCOMMIT, SQL_AUTOCOMMIT_OFF);
SQLAllocStmt(hdbc, &hstmt);
retcode = SQLExecDirect(hstmt,
                     "DELETE FROM TRANSCRIPT \
                        WHERE StudId = 123456789 \
                                AND Semester = 'F2000' \
                                AND CrsCode = 'CS308'",
                     SQL_NTS);
if (retcode != SQL_SUCCESS) {
    SQLTransact(henv, hdbc, SQL_ABORT);
    SQLFreeStmt(hstmt, SQL_DROP);
    SQLDisconnect(hdbc);
    SQLFreeConnect(hdbc);
    SQLFreeEnv(henv);
    return(-2);
}
retcode = SQLExecDirect(hstmt,
                   "UPDATE CLASS \
                      SET Enrollment = (Enrollment - 1) \
                      WHERE CrsCode = 'CS308'",
                   SQL_NTS);
if (retcode != SQL_SUCCESS)    {
    SQLTransact(henv, hdbc, SQL_ABORT);
    SQLFreeStmt(hstmt, SQL_DROP);
    SQLDisconnect(hdbc);
    SQLFreeConnect(hdbc);
    SQLFreeEnv(henv);
    return(-3);
}
SQLTransact(henv, hdbc, SQL_COMMIT);
SQLFreeStmt(hstmt, SQL_DROP);
SQLDisconnect(hdbc);
SQLFreeConnect(hdbc);
SQLFreeEnv(henv);
```

■ In some cases (static SQL, SQLJ), the program contains SQL statements that use a special syntax; in others, the statements are values of variables (dynamic SQL, JDBC, ODBC). An advantage of the former is its simplicity, but a disadvantage is that the interaction with the database is fixed at compile time. In some applications, the statement to be executed cannot be determined until run time; in such cases, it is important that the application be able to construct SQL statements dynamically.

■ In some cases, the application must use the SQL dialect supported by the particular DBMS to which it is connected, making it difficult to port the application to a different vendor's product. In other cases (SQLJ, JDBC, ODBC), a single dialect is used in the application and modules are provided to translate it to each vendor's dialect. Portability is thus enhanced, but the application might not have access to the proprietary features supported by a particular vendor's product.

■ A number of factors are involved in assessing the run-time overhead incurred by each technique. These include the cost of communication, preparation, and parameter passing. In some cases, the cost depends on how a technique is implemented, but certain general observations can be made.

With a statement-level interface, the SQL statement has embedded parameter names that can be processed at compile time to generate parameter passing code. At run time, the statement can be passed to the server for both preparation and execution, so a single communication is sufficient. With a call-level interface and with dynamic SQL, parameter names are not included in the statement because the statement is not available at compile time when parameter names can be mapped to addresses using the symbol table. Instead, they are provided separately so that they can be dealt with at compile time. Except in special cases (e.g., EXECUTE IMMEDIATE), therefore, one communication is used to send the statement for preparation and one additional communication is needed for requesting execution. This issue is important, since communication is expensive and time consuming.

Preparation must take place at run time if the SQL statement is constructed dynamically (dynamic SQL, JDBC, and ODBC). However, even with static SQL, preparation is generally done at run time when the statement is submitted for execution. In all of these cases, if the statement is executed many times, the preparation cost can be prorated over each execution and might not be a major factor. The most effective way to avoid run-time preparation is to use stored procedures, in which case the DBMS can be instructed to create and store a query execution plan prior to execution of the application. Often, this is simply a separate plan for each SQL statement in the procedure. More sophisticated systems create an optimized plan for the procedure as a whole, since the sequence of SQL statements is known. Data structures created for one statement might be preserved for use by the next.

10.8 BIBLIOGRAPHIC NOTES

Embedded and dynamic SQL date back to prehistoric times, and every SQL manual covers them to some degree. The following references are good places to look: [Date and Darwen 1997, Melton and Simon 1992, Gulutzan and Pelzer 1999].

There is vast literature on ODBC. Microsoft publishes an authoritative guide [Microsoft 1997], but there are more accessible books, such as [Signore et al. 1995]. The history and principles behind SQL/CLI, the new SQL standard analogous to (and designed to replace) ODBC, are discussed in [Venkatrao and Pizzo 1995]. SQL stored procedures are discussed in [Eisenberg 1996, Melton 1997]. Information on JDBC and SQLJ is readily available on the Web at [Sun 2000] and [SQLJ 2000], but published references, such as [Reese 2000, Melton et al. 2000], are better places to learn these technologies.

10.9 EXERCISES

10.1 Explain the methods used by your local application generator to
   a. Include SQL statements in the host language
   b. Create database tables
   c. Connect and disconnect from a database
   d. Initiate, commit, and abort transactions
   e. Specify isolation levels
   f. Change the mode of constraint checking
   g. Grant a user the privilege of performing a SELECT statement on a particular table

10.2 a. Explain why a precompiler is needed for embedded SQL and SQLJ but not for ODBC and JDBC.
   b. Since the precompiler for embedded SQL translates SQL statements into procedure calls, explain the difference between embedded SQL and call-level interfaces, such as ODBC and JDBC, where SQL statements are specified as the arguments of procedure calls.

10.3 a. Explain why constraint checking is usually deferred in transaction processing applications.
   b. Give an example where immediate constraint checking is undesirable in a transaction processing application.

10.4 Explain the advantages and disadvantages of using stored procedures in transaction processing applications.

10.5 Write transaction programs in
   a. Embedded SQL
   b. JDBC

    c. ODBC

    d. SQLJ

that implement the registration transaction in the Student Registration System. Use the database schema from Figures 5.15 and 5.16.

10.6 Write transaction programs in

    a. Embedded SQL

    b. JDBC

    c. ODBC

    d. SQLJ

that use a cursor to print out a student's transcript in the Student Registration System. Use the database schema from Figures 5.15 and 5.16.

10.7 a. Explain why embedded SQL and SQLJ use host language variables as parameters, whereas dynamic SQL, JDBC, and ODBC use the ? placeholders.

    b. Explain the advantages of using host language variables as parameters in embedded SQL compared with ? placeholders.

10.8 Explain the advantages and disadvantages of using dynamic SQL compared with JDBC or ODBC.

10.9 Write a transaction program in

    a. Embedded SQL

    b. JDBC

    c. ODBC

    d. SQLJ

that transfers the rows of a table between two DBMSs. Is your transaction globally atomic?

10.10 Write a Java program that executes in your local browser, uses JDBC to connect to your local DBMS, and makes a simple query against a table you have created.

10.11 Suppose that, at compile time, the application programmer knows all of the details of the SQL statements to be executed, the DBMS to be used, and the database schema. Explain the advantages and disadvantages of using embedded SQL as compared with JDBC or ODBC as the basis for the implementation.

10.12 Section 10.6 discusses KEYSET_DRIVEN cursors.

    a. Explain the difference between STATIC and KEYSET_DRIVEN cursors.

    b. Give an example of a schedule in which these cursors give different results even when the transaction is executing in isolation.

c. Explain why updates and deletes can be made through KEYSET_DRIVEN cursors.

10.13 Give an example of a transaction program that contains a cursor, such that the value returned by one of its FETCH statements depends on whether or not the cursor was defined to be INSENSITIVE. Assume that this transaction is the only one executing. We are not concerned about any effect that a concurrently executing transaction might have.

10.14 Compare the advantages and disadvantages of the status processing (exception handling) mechanisms in embedded SQL, SQL/PSM, JDBC, SQLJ, and ODBC.

Chapter 11

Physical Data Organization and Indexing

One important advantage of SQL is that it is declarative. An SQL statement describes a query about information stored in a database, but it does not specify the technique the system should use in executing it. The DBMS itself decides that.

Such techniques are intimately associated with **storage structures**, **indices**, and **access paths**. A storage structure defines a particular organization of the rows of a table in a file. An index is an auxiliary data structure, perhaps stored in a separate file, that supports fast access to the rows of a table. An **access path** refers to a particular technique for accessing a set of rows. It uses an algorithm based on the storage structure of the table and a choice among the available indices for that table.

An important aspect of the relational model is that the result of executing a particular SQL statement (i.e., the statement's effect on the database and the information returned by it) is not influenced by the access path used in its execution. Thus, when designing the query the programmer does not have to be aware of the access paths available in the system.

Although the choice of an access path does not affect the result produced by a statement, it does have a major impact on performance. Depending on the access path used, execution time might vary from seconds to hours, particularly when the statement refers to large tables involving thousands, and perhaps hundreds of thousands, of rows. Furthermore, different access paths are appropriate for different SQL statements used to query the same table.

Because execution time is sensitive to access paths, most database systems allow the database designer and system administrator to determine which access paths should be provided for each table. Generally, the administrator takes into account the observed frequency with which different SQL statements are executed.

In this chapter, we describe a variety of access paths and compare their performance when used in the execution of different SQL statements.

11.1 DISK ORGANIZATION

For a number of reasons, databases are generally stored on mass storage devices rather than in main memory.

Size. Databases describing large enterprises frequently contain a huge amount of information. Databases in the gigabyte range are not uncommon, and those in the terabyte range already exist. Such databases cannot be accommodated in the main memory of current machines or of machines that are likely to be available in the near future.

Cost. Even in situations in which the database can be accommodated in main memory (e.g., when its size is in the megabyte range), the decision is generally to store it on mass storage.[1] The argument here is economic. The cost per byte of main memory is on the order of one hundred times that of disk.

Volatility. We introduced the notion of durability in Chapter 2 in connection with the ACID properties of transactions. The argument for durability goes beyond transactions, however. It is an important property of any database system. The information describing an enterprise must be preserved in spite of system failures. Unfortunately, most implementations of main memory are **volatile**: The information stored in main memory is lost on power failures and crashes. Hence, main memory does not naturally support database system requirements. Mass storage, on the other hand, is **nonvolatile**, since the stored information survives failures. Hence, mass storage forms the basis of most database systems. We will return to this issue in Chapter 25.

Since data on mass storage devices is not directly accessible to the system processors, accessing an item in the database involves first reading the item from the mass storage device into a buffer in main memory—at which point a copy exists on both devices—and then operating on the buffer. If the access involves changing the item, the copy on mass storage becomes obsolete and the buffer copy must be used to overwrite it.

The most commonly used form of mass storage is a disk. Since the strategy used to enhance the performance of a database system is based on the physical characteristics of a disk, it is important to review how a disk works in order to understand performance issues.

A disk unit contains one or more circular **platters** attached to a rotating spindle, as shown in Figure 11.1. One, and sometimes both, surfaces, of each platter are coated with magnetic material, and the direction of magnetism at a particular spot determines whether that spot records a one or a zero. Since information is stored magnetically, it is durable in spite of power failures.

Each platter (or surface) is accessed through an associated **read/write head** that is capable of either detecting or setting the direction of magnetism on the spot over which it is positioned. The head is attached to an arm, which is capable of moving radially, toward either the center or the circumference of the platter. Since platters rotate, this movement enables the head to be positioned over an arbitrary spot on the platter's surface.

---

[1] In applications requiring very rapid response times, the database is often stored in main memory. Such systems are referred to as **main memory database systems**.

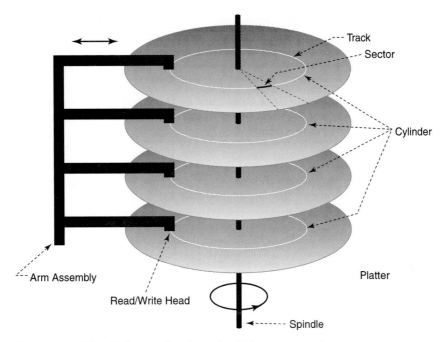

Figure 11.1 Physical organization of a disk storage unit.

As a practical matter, data is stored in **tracks**, which are concentric circles on the surface of the platter. Each platter has the same fixed number, N, of tracks, and the storage area consisting of the ith track on all platters is called an ith **cylinder**. Since there is a head for each platter, the disk unit as a whole has an array of heads and the arm assembly moves all heads in unison. Thus, at any given time all read/write heads are positioned over a particular cylinder. It would seem reasonable to be able to read or write all tracks on the current cylinder simultaneously, but engineering limitations generally allow only a single head to be active at a time. Finally, each track is divided into **sectors**, which are the smallest units of transfer allowed by the hardware.

Before a particular sector can be accessed, the head must be positioned over the beginning of the sector. Hence, the time to access a sector, S, can be divided into three components:

Seek time. The time to position the arm assembly over the cylinder containing S

Rotational latency. The additional time it takes, after the arm assembly is over the cylinder, for the platters to rotate to the angular position at which the start of S is under the read/write head of the platter containing S

Transfer time. The time it takes for the platter to rotate through the angle subtended by S

The seek time varies depending on the radial distance between the cylinder currently under the read/write heads and the cylinder containing the sector to be read. In the worst case, the heads must be moved from track 1 to track N; in the best case, no motion at all is required. If disk requests are uniformly distributed across the cylinders and are serviced in the order they arrive, it can be shown that the average number of tracks that must be traversed by a seek[2] is about $N/3$. Seek time is generally the largest of the three components, since it involves not only mechanical motion but overcoming the inertia involved in starting and stopping the arm assembly.

Rotational latency is the next largest component of access time and on average is about half the time of a complete rotation of the platters. Once again, mechanical motion is involved, although in this case inertia is not an issue. Transfer time is also limited by rotation time. The transfer rate supported by a disk is the rate at which data can be transferred once the head is in position; it depends on the speed of rotation and the density with which bits are recorded on the surface. We use the term **latency** to refer to the total time it takes to position the head and platter between disk accesses. Hence, latency is the sum of seek time and rotational latency.

A typical disk stores gigabytes of data. It might have a sector size of 512 bytes, an average seek time of 5 to 20 milliseconds, an average rotational latency of 2 to 10 milliseconds, and a transfer rate of several megabytes per second. Hence, a typical access time for a sector is on the order of 20 milliseconds.

The physical characteristics of a disk lead to the concept of the distance between two sectors, which is a measure of the latency between accesses to them. The distance is smallest if the sectors are adjacent on the same track, since latency is zero if they are read in succession. After that, in order of increasing distance, sectors are closest if they are on the same track, on the same cylinder, or on different cylinders. In the last case, sectors on tracks n_1 and n_2 are closer than sectors on tracks n_3 and n_4 if $|n_1 - n_2| < |n_3 - n_4|$.

Several conclusions can be drawn from the physical characteristics of a disk unit.

■ Most important, disks are extremely slow devices compared to CPUs. A CPU can execute hundreds of thousands of instructions in the time it takes to access a sector. Hence, in attempting to optimize the performance of a database system, it is necessary to optimize the flow of information between main memory and disk. While the database system should use efficient algorithms in processing data, the payoff in improved performance pales in comparison with that obtained from optimizing disk traffic. In recognition of this fact, in our discussion of access paths later in this chapter we estimate performance by counting I/O operations and ignoring processor time.

■ In applications in which an access to record A_1 will, with high probability, be followed next by an access to record A_2, latency can be reduced if the distance

---

[2] The problem can be stated mathematically: Suppose that we have an interval and we place two marks at random somewhere in the interval; how far apart are the marks on average?

between the sectors containing A_1 and A_2 is small. Thus the performance of the application is affected by the way the data is physically stored on the disk. For example, a sequential scan through a table can be performed efficiently if the table is stored on a single track or cylinder.

◼ To simplify buffer management, database systems transfer the same number of bytes with each I/O operation. How many bytes should that be? Using the typical numbers quoted earlier, it is apparent that the transfer time for a sector is small compared with the average latency. This is true even if more than one sector is transferred with each I/O operation. Thus, even though from a physical standpoint the natural unit of transfer is the data in a single sector, it might be more efficient if the system transfers data in larger units.

The term **page** generally denotes the unit of data transferred with each I/O operation. A page is stored on the disk in a **disk block**, or simply a block, which is a sequence of adjacent sectors on a track such that the page size is equal to the block size. A page can be transferred in a single I/O operation, with a single latency to position the head at the start of the containing block, since there is no need to reposition either the arm or the platter in moving from one sector of the block to the next.

A tradeoff is involved in choosing the number of sectors in a block (i.e., the page size). If, when a particular application accesses a record A in a table, there is a reasonable probability that it will soon access additional records close to A in the table (this would be the case if the table was frequently scanned), the page size should be large enough to accommodate these additional records to avoid a subsequent disk access. On the other hand, transfer time grows with page size, and larger pages require larger buffers in main memory. Hence, too large a page size cannot be justified since it is far from certain that information adjacent to A will actually be accessed. With considerations such as these in mind, a typical page size is 4,096 bytes (4 kilobytes). Note that our discussion here is motivated by the desire to reduce latency and seek time. In this case, the page size is adjusted so that related information is on the same page and hence on successive sectors (separated by a distance of 0).

The system keeps an array of page-size buffers, called a **cache**, in main memory. With page I/O, the following sequence of events occurs when an application requests access to a particular record, A_1, of a table. We assume that each table is stored in a **data file**. First, the database system determines which of the file's pages contains A_1. Then it initiates the transfer of the page from mass storage into one of the buffers in the cache (we modify this part of the description in a moment). At some later time (generally signaled by an interrupt from the mass storage device), the system recognizes that the transfer has completed and copies A_1 from the page in the buffer to the application.

The system attempts to keep the page in the buffer for some period of time for several reasons. First, the application might later decide to modify A_1. In that case, the copy of A_1 in the buffer must then be changed (other records in the buffer are left unchanged), and the buffer must then be used to overwrite the copy of the page on mass storage.

Second, this same application (or some other application) might request access to another record, A_2, in the same table. If A_2 resides on the same page as A_1, the system can return a copy without any additional I/O—an obvious win. The database system always tries to satisfy an application's request for database access by searching its cache before performing an I/O operation (this is the modification we referred to earlier).

When a requested page is found in the cache, the event is referred to as a **cache hit**. The potential for improving the performance of the system by maximizing the number of cache hits is enormous, and so considerable attention is paid to managing the (finite number of) cache buffers. When the cache is full (as it must be sooner or later) and a new page must be fetched, which buffer in the cache should be emptied? A number of algorithms have been developed to answer this question that attempt to maximize the number of hits. A common one is the **least recently used** (LRU) algorithm, which empties the buffer containing the page that has not been referenced for the longest time. The assumption is that pages referenced in the recent past are active, and the probability is high that they will be referenced again in the near future, so they should be retained in the cache.

11.2   HEAP FILES

We assume that each table is stored in a separate file, in accordance with some storage structure. The simplest storage structure is a **heap file**. With a heap file, rows are effectively appended to the end of the file as they are created. Thus the ordering of rows in the file is arbitrary. No rule dictates where a particular row should be placed. Figure 11.2 is a physical picture of the table TRANSCRIPT when stored as a heap file. Recall that the table has four columns: StudId, CrsCode, Semester, and Grade. We have modified the schema so that grades are stored as real numbers, and we have assumed that four rows fit in a single page.

The important characteristic of a heap file, as far as we are concerned, is the fact that its rows are unordered. We ignore a number of significant issues, since they are internal to the workings of the database system and the programmer generally has no control over them. Still, you should be aware of what these issues are. For example, we have assumed in Figure 11.2 that all rows are of the same length, and hence exactly the same number of rows fit in each page. This is not always the case. If, for example, the domain associated with a column is VARCHAR (3000), the number of bytes necessary to store a particular column value varies from 1 to 3000. Thus, the number of rows that will fit in a page is not fixed. This significantly complicates storage allocation. In general, whether rows are of fixed or variable length, each page must be formatted with a certain amount of header information that keeps track of the starting point of each row in the page and that locates unused regions of the page. We assume that the logical address of a row in a data file is given by a **row Id** (*rid*) that consists of a **page number** within the file and a **slot number** identifying the row within the page. The actual location of the row is obtained by

Figure 11.2 Transcript table stored as a heap file.

666666666	MGT123	F1994	4.0	
123454321	CS305	S1996	4.0	page 0
987654321	CS305	F1995	2.0	
111111111	MGT123	F1997	3.0	
123454321	CS315	S1997	4.0	
666666666	EE101	S1991	3.0	page 1
123454321	MAT123	S1996	2.0	
234567890	EE101	F1995	3.0	
234567890	CS305	S1996	4.0	
111111111	EE101	F1997	4.0	page 2
111111111	MAT123	F1997	3.0	
987654321	MGT123	F1994	3.0	
425360777	CS305	S1996	3.0	
666666666	MAT123	F1997	3.0	page 3

interpreting the slot number using the page's header information. The situation is further complicated if a row is too large to fit in a page.

The good thing about a heap file is its simplicity. Rows are inserted by appending them to the end of the file, and they are deleted by declaring the slot that they occupy as empty in the header information of the page in which they are stored. Figure 11.3 shows the file of Figure 11.2 after the records for the student with Id 111111111 were deleted and the student with Id 666666666 completed CS305 in the spring of 1998. Note that deletion leaves gaps in the file and eventually a significant amount of storage is wasted. These gaps cause searches through the file to take longer because more pages have to be examined. Eventually, the gaps become so extensive that the file must be compacted. Compaction can be a time-consuming process if the file is large, since every page must be read and the pages of the compacted version written out.

We can compare the efficiency of accessing a heap file with other storage structures, which we discuss later, by counting the number of I/O operations required to do various operations. Let F denote the number of pages in the file. First consider insertion. Before a row, A, can be inserted, we must ensure that A's key does not duplicate the key of a row already in the table. If a duplicate exists, it will be discovered in $F/2$ page reads on average, and at that point the insertion is abandoned. The entire file has to be read in order to conclude that no duplicate is present, and then the last page (with A inserted) has to be rewritten, yielding a total cost of $F + 1$ page transfers in this case.

Figure 11.3 TRANSCRIPT table of Figure 11.2 after insertion and deletion of some rows.

666666666	MGT123	F1994	4.0	
123454321	CS305	S1996	4.0	page 0
987654321	CS305	F1995	2.0	

123454321	CS315	S1997	4.0	
666666666	EE101	S1991	3.0	page 1
123454321	MAT123	S1996	2.0	
234567890	EE101	F1995	3.0	

234567890	CS305	S1996	4.0	
				page 2
987654321	MGT123	F1994	3.0	

425360777	CS305	S1996	3.0	
666666666	MAT123	F1997	3.0	page 3
666666666	CS305	S1998	3.0	

A similar situation exists for deletion. If a tuple, A, with a specified key is present, it will be discovered in $F/2$ page reads on average, and then the page (with A deleted) will be rewritten, yielding a cost of $F/2 + 1$. If no such tuple is present, the cost is F. If the condition specifying the tuples to be deleted does not involve a key, the entire file must be scanned since an arbitrary number of rows satisfying the condition can exist in the table.

A heap file is an efficient storage structure if queries on the table involve accessing all rows and if the order in which the rows are accessed is not important. For example, the query

```
SELECT   *
FROM     TRANSCRIPT
```

returns the entire table. With a heap storage structure, the cost is F, which is clearly optimal. Of course, if we want the rows printed out in some specific order, the cost is much greater since the rows have to be sorted before being output. An example of such a query is

```
SELECT   *
FROM     TRANSCRIPT T
ORDER BY T.StudId
```

As another example, consider the query

```
SELECT    AVG(T.Grade)
FROM      TRANSCRIPT T
```

which returns the average grade assigned in all courses. All rows of the table must be read to extract the grades no matter how the table is stored, and the averaging computation is not sensitive to the order in which reading occurs. Again, the cost, F, is optimal.

Suppose, however, a query requests the grade received by the student with Id 234567890 in CS305 in the spring of 1996.

```
SELECT    T.Grade
FROM      TRANSCRIPT T                                                (11.1)
WHERE     T.StudId = '234567890' AND
          T.CrsCode = 'CS305' AND T.Semester = 'S1996'
```

Since {StudId, CrsCode, Semester} is the key of TRANSCRIPT, at most one grade will be returned. If TRANSCRIPT has the value shown in Figure 11.2, exactly one grade (namely, 4.0) will be returned. The database system must scan the file pages looking for a row with the specified key and return the corresponding grade. In this case, it must read three pages. Generally, an average of $F/2$ pages must be read, but if a row with the specified key is not in the table, all F pages must be read. In either case, the cost is high considering the small amount of information actually requested.

Finally, consider the following queries. The first returns the course, semester, and grade for all courses taken by the student with Id 234567890, and the second returns the Ids of all students who received grades between 2.0 and 4.0 in some course. Since, in both cases, the WHERE clause does not specify a candidate key, an arbitrary number of rows might be returned. Therefore, the entire table must be searched at a cost of F.

```
SELECT    T.Course, T.Semester, T.Grade
FROM      TRANSCRIPT T                                                (11.2)
WHERE     T.StudId = '234567890'
```

```
SELECT    T.StudId
FROM      TRANSCRIPT                                                  (11.3)
WHERE     T.Grade BETWEEN 2.0 AND 4.0
```

The conditions in the WHERE clauses of statements (11.1) and (11.2) are equality conditions, since the tuples requested must have the specified attribute values. A search for a tuple satisfying an equality condition is referred to as an **equality search**. The condition in the WHERE clause of statement (11.3) is a **range condition**. It involves an attribute whose domain is ordered and requests that all rows with attribute values in the specified range be retrieved. The actual value of the attribute in a requested tuple is not specified in the range condition. A search for a tuple satisfying a range condition is referred to as a **range search**.

11.3   SORTED FILES

The last examples (11.2 and 11.3) illustrate the weakness of heap storage. Even though information is requested about only a subset of rows, the entire table must be searched since without scanning a page we cannot be sure that it does not contain a row in the subset. These examples motivate the need for more sophisticated storage structures, one of which we consider in this section.

Suppose that, instead of storing the rows of a table in arbitrary order, we sort them based on the value of some attribute(s) of the table. We refer to such a structure as a **sorted file**. For example, we might store TRANSCRIPT in a sorted file in which the rows of the table are ordered on StudId, as shown in Figure 11.4. A naive way to search for the data records satisfying (11.2) is to scan the data records in order until the first record having the value 234567890 in the StudId column is encountered. All records having this value would be stored consecutively, and access to them requires a minimum of additional I/O. In particular, if successive pages are stored contiguously on the disk, seek time can be minimized. In the figure, the rows describing courses taken by student 234567890 are stored on a single page. Once the first of these rows is made available in the cache, all others satisfying query (11.2) can be quickly retrieved. If the data file consists of F pages, an average of $F/2$ page I/O operations is needed to locate the records—a significant improvement over the case in which TRANSCRIPT is stored in a heap file. Note that the same approach works for query (11.1).

In some cases, it is more efficient to locate the record with a **binary search** technique. The middle page is retrieved first, and its Id values are compared to 234567890. If the target value is found in the page, the record has been located; if the target value is less than (or greater than) the page values, the process is repeated recursively on the first half (or last half) of the data file. With this approach, the worst-case number of page transfers needed to locate the record with a particular student Id is approximately log_2F.

The number of page transfers does not always reflect the true cost of searching sorted files. While doing a binary search, we might have to visit pages located on different disk cylinders, and this might involve considerable seek latency costs. In fact, under certain circumstances the seek-latency might dominate. Consider a sorted file that occupies N consecutive cylinders and in which successive pages are stored in adjacent blocks. A binary search might cause the disk head to move across $N/2$, then $N/4$, then $N/8$ cylinders, and so on. The total number of cylinders canvassed by the disk head will be about N, so the total cost of binary search will be

$$N \times seek\ time + log_2F \times transfer\ time$$

On the other hand, if we do a simple sequential search through the file, the average number of cylinders canvassed by the disk head will be $N/2$ and the total cost

$$N/2 \times seek\ time + F/2 \times transfer\ time$$

Figure 11.4 TRANSCRIPT table stored as a sorted file.

111111111	MGT123	F1997	3.0	
111111111	EE101	F1997	4.0	page 0
111111111	MAT123	F1997	3.0	

123454321	CS305	S1996	4.0	
123454321	CS315	S1997	4.0	page 1
123454321	MAT123	S1996	2.0	

234567890	EE101	F1995	3.0	
234567890	CS305	S1996	4.0	page 2
425360777	CS305	S1996	3.0	

666666666	MGT123	F1994	4.0	
666666666	MAT123	F1997	3.0	page 3
666666666	EE101	S1991	3.0	

987654321	MGT123	F1994	3.0	
987654321	CS305	F1995	2.0	page 4

Since seek time dominates transfer time, binary search is justified only if F is much larger[3] than N. In view of these results, neither sequential search nor binary search is considered a good option for equality searches in sorted files. A much more common approach is to augment sorted files with an index (see the next section) and use binary search within the index. Since the index is designed to fit in main memory, a binary search over the index is very efficient and does not suffer from the disk latency overhead described earlier.

Sorted files support range searches if the file is sorted on the same attribute as the requested range. Thus, the TRANSCRIPT file of Figure 11.4 supports a query requesting information about every student whose Id is between 100000000 and 199999999. An equality search for Id 100000000 locates the first tuple in the range (which might have Id 100000000 or, if such a tuple does not exist, will be the tuple with the smallest Id greater than this value). Subsequent tuples in the range occupy consecutive slots, and cache hits are likely to result as they are retrieved. If B is the

---

[3] We have ignored the rotational delay, which strongly favors sequential over binary search.

number of rows stored in a page and R is the number of rows in a particular range, the number of I/O operations needed to retrieve all pages of the data file containing rows in the range (once the first row has been located) is roughly R/B.

Contrast these numbers with a heap file in which each row in the range can be on a different page and it is necessary to scan the entire file to ensure that all of them have been located. If the data file has F pages, the number of I/O operations is F. Similarly, a sorted file supports the retrieval of tuples that satisfy query (11.3), although in this case the table must be sorted on Grade instead. It cannot be sorted on both search keys at the same time.

In practice, it is difficult to maintain rows in sorted order if the table is dynamic. A heavy I/O price must be paid if, whenever a new row is inserted, all of the following rows have to be moved down one slot in the data file (on average, half the pages have to be updated). One (partial) solution to this problem is to leave empty slots in each page when a data file is created to accommodate subsequent insertions between rows. The term **fillfactor** refers to the percentage of slots in a page that are initially filled. For example, the fillfactor for a heap file is 100%. In Figure 11.4 the fillfactor is 75% because three out of the four slots on a page are filled.

Empty slots do not provide a complete solution, however, since they can be exhausted as rows are inserted, and the problem then reappears for a subsequent insert. An **overflow page** might be used in this case, which Figure 11.5 illustrates using the TRANSCRIPT table. We have assumed that the initial state of the data file is as shown in Figure 11.4. Each page has a pointer field containing the page number of an overflow page (if it exists). In the figure, two new rows have been added to page 2 since the file was created. If an overflow page itself overflows, we can create an **overflow chain**: a linked list of overflow pages.

While the use of overflow chains helps keep files **logically sorted**, we lose the advantage of the sorted files being stored in contiguous space on disk because an overflow page can be distant from the page that links to it. This causes additional latency during a sequential scan that reads records in order, and hence the number of I/O operations necessary to transfer records in a range is no longer R/B. If performance of sequential scan is an important issue (and it usually is), the data file must be reorganized periodically to ensure that all of its records are stored in contiguous disk space. The lesson here is that maintaining a data file in sorted order can be expensive if the file is dynamic.

11.4   INDICES

Suppose that you have set up a database for an application and given it to a set of users. However, instead of receiving a check in the mail for your work, you start getting angry phone calls from the users complaining that the system is too slow. Some users claim that they have to wait a long time to get a response to their queries. Others claim that throughput is unacceptable. Queries are being submitted to the system at a rate greater than that at which the system is capable of processing them.

Figure 11.5 The TRANSCRIPT table stored as a sorted
file after the addition of several rows.

111111111	MGT123	F1997	3.0	
111111111	EE101	F1997	4.0	page 0
111111111	MAT123	F1997	3.0	

123454321	CS305	S1996	4.0	
123454321	CS315	S1997	4.0	page 1
123454321	MAT123	S1996	2.0	

Overflow: 5				
234567890	EE101	F1995	3.0	
234567890	CS305	S1996	4.0	page 2
234567890	LIT203	F1997	3.0	
425360777	CS305	S1996	3.0	

666666666	MGT123	F1994	4.0	
666666666	EE101	S1991	3.0	page 3
666666666	MAT123	F1997	3.0	

987654321	MGT123	F1994	3.0	
987654321	CS305	F1995	2.0	page 4

313131313	CS306	F1997	4.0	
				page 5

Indices can be used to improve this situation. An index over a table is analogous to a book index or a library card catalogue. In the case of a book, certain terms that are of interest to readers are selected and made index entries. In this case, each **index entry** contains a term (e.g., "gas turbines") and a pointer (e.g., "p. 348") to the location(s) in the book where the term appears. The entries are then sorted on the term to construct a table, called an **index**, for easy reference. Instead of having to scan the entire book for the locations at which a particular term is discussed, we can access the index efficiently and go directly to those locations.

The analogy is even closer in the case of a card catalogue. In this case, there might be several indices based on different properties of books: author, title, and subject. In each index, the entries are sorted on that property's value and each entry points to a book in the collection. Thus, an entry in an author index contains an author's name and a pointer (e.g., section, shelf) to a book written by her.

Similarly, an index on a database table provides a convenient mechanism for locating a row (data record) without scanning the entire table and thus greatly reduces the time it takes to process a query. The property to be located is a column (or columns) of the indexed table called a **search key**. Do not confuse a search key of an index on a table with a candidate key of the table. Remember that a candidate key is a set of one or more columns having the property that no two rows in any instance of the table can have the same values in these columns. A search key does not have this restriction, so, for example, TRANSCRIPT has more than one row for the student with Id 111111111, which means that the index on StudId will have several index entries with the search key value 111111111.

As with a candidate key, a search key can involve several columns. For example, the search key might include both the student Id and the semester. However, in contrast to a candidate key, the order of columns in a search key makes a difference, so you should think of a search key as a sequence (as contrasted with a set) of columns of the indexed table. You will see a context in which the ordering is important when we discuss partial key searches.

An index consists of a set of index entries together with a mechanism for locating a particular entry efficiently based on a search key value. With some indices, such as an ISAM index or a B^+ tree, the location mechanism relies on the fact that the index entries are sorted on the search key. A hash index takes a different approach. In either case, the data structure that supports the location mechanism, together with the index entries, can be integrated into the data file containing the table itself, as shown in Figure 11.6. This integrated data file is regarded as a new storage structure. Later we discuss ISAM, B^+ trees, and hash storage structures as alternatives to heap and sorted storage structures. With an integrated storage structure, each index entry actually *contains* a row of the table (no pointer is needed).

Alternatively, the index can be stored in a separate file, called an **index file**, in which each index entry contains a search key value and a rid.[4] This organization is

---

[4] With some indices, only the page Id field of the rid is stored. Since the major cost of accessing the data file is the cost of transferring a page, storing only the page Id in the index entry makes it possible to

Figure 11.6 A storage structure in which an index is integrated with the data records.

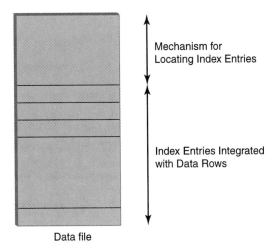

Mechanism for
Locating Index Entries

Index Entries Integrated
with Data Rows

Data file

shown in Figure 11.7. For example, the table TRANSCRIPT of Figure 11.2 on page 331 might have an index on StudId. Each index entry contains a value that appears in the StudId column in some row of the table and the rid of that row in the data file. Thus, the entry (425360777, (3,1)) is present in the index.

Integration saves space, since no pointer is needed and the search key does not have to be stored in both the index entry and the data record containing the corresponding row.

The SQL-92 standard does not provide for the creation or deletion of indices. However, indices are an essential part of the database systems provided by most vendors. In some, for example, an index with a search key equal to the primary key is automatically created when a table is created. Such indices are often integrated storage structures that make it possible to efficiently guarantee that the primary key is unique when a row is added or modified (and support the efficient execution of queries that involve the primary key).

In addition to indices that are automatically created, database systems generally provide a statement (in their own dialect) that creates an index explicitly. For example,

CREATE INDEX TRANSGRD ON TRANSCRIPT (Grade)

---

locate the correct page. Once the page has been retrieved, the record within it with the target search key value can be located using a linear search. The added computational time for this search is generally small compared to the time to transfer a page and might be justified by the saving of space in each index entry. With smaller index entries, the index can fit in fewer pages, and hence less page I/O is needed to access it. In some index organizations, a single index entry can contain several pointers. Since this feature only complicates the discussion without adding any new concepts, we do not consider it further.

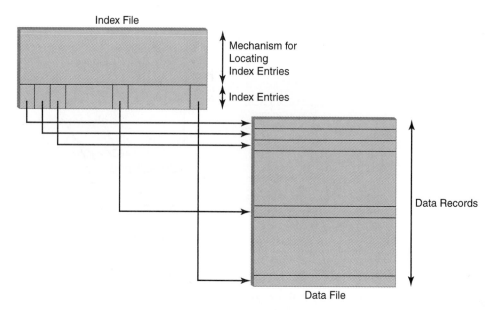

Figure 11.7   Index that references a separate data file.

creates an index called TRANSGRD on the table TRANSCRIPT with Grade as a search key. If CREATE INDEX does not provide an option to specify the type of index, a B+ tree is generally the result. In any case, the index created might be stored in an index file, as shown in Figure 11.7, and reference a table that has been integrated with another index in a storage structure. The data file might be organized in a storage structure that involves a location mechanism as shown in Figure 11.6, but for simplicity we do not consider this case.

The use of an appropriate index can drastically reduce the number of data file pages that must be accessed in a search, but accessing the index itself is a new form of overhead. If the index is small enough to fit in main memory, this additional overhead is small. However, if the index is large, index pages must be retrieved from mass storage, and these I/O operations must be considered as part of the net cost of the search.

Because they require maintenance, indices must be added judiciously. If the indexed relation is dynamic, the index itself will have to be modified to accommodate changes in the relation as they occur. For example, a new row inserted into the relation requires a new index entry in the index. Thus, in addition to the cost of accessing the index used in a search, the index itself might have to be changed as a part of operations that modify the database. Because of this cost, it might be desirable to eliminate an index that does not support a sufficient number of the database queries. For this reason, an index is named in CREATE INDEX so that it can be referred to by a DROP INDEX statement, which causes it to be eliminated.

Before discussing particular index structures, we introduce several general properties for categorizing indices.

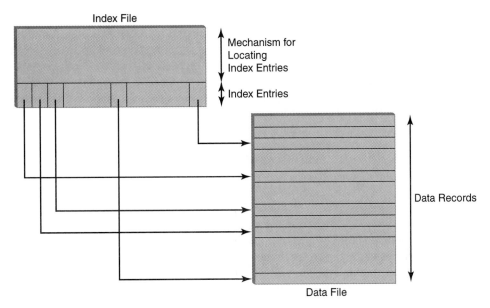

Figure 11.8 Unclustered index over a data file.

11.4.1 Clustered versus Unclustered Indices

In a *clustered* index, the physical proximity of index entries implies some degree of proximity among the corresponding data records. Such indices enable certain queries to be executed more efficiently than with unclustered indices. Query optimizer can use the fact that an index is clustered to improve the execution strategy. (Chapters 13 and 14 explain how clustering information is used by the query optimizer). Clustering takes different forms depending on whether index entries are sorted (as in ISAM and B+ trees) or not (as in hash indices). A sorted index is **clustered** if the index entries and the data records are sorted on the same search key; otherwise, it is said to be **unclustered**. Clustered hash indices will be defined in Section 11.6.1. These definitions imply that, if the index is structured so that its entries are integrated with data records, it *must* be clustered. The index shown in Figure 11.7 is an example of a clustered index in which the index and the table are stored in separate files (and therefore the data records are not contained in the index entries). The regular pattern of the pointers from the index entries to the records in the data file is meant to reflect the fact that both index entries and data records are sorted on the same columns. The index shown in Figure 11.8 is unclustered.

A clustered index is often called a **main index**; an unclustered index is also referred to as a **secondary index**.[5] There can be at most a single clustered index

---

[5] Clustered indices are also sometimes called **primary indices**. We avoid this terminology because of a potential confusion regarding the connection between primary indices and the primary keys of relations. A primary index is *not* necessarily an index on the primary key of a relation. For instance, the PROFESSOR relation could be sorted on the Department attribute (which is not even a key), and a

(since the data file can be sorted on at most one search key), but there can be several secondary indices. An index created by a CREATE TABLE statement is often clustered. With some database systems, a clustered index is always integrated into the data file as a storage structure. In this case, index entries contain data records, as shown in Figure 11.6. An index created by CREATE INDEX is generally a secondary, unclustered index stored in a separate index file (although some database systems allow the programmer to request the creation of a clustered index, which involves reorganizing the storage structure). The search key of the main index might be the primary key of the table, but this is not necessarily so.

A file is said to be **inverted** on a column if a secondary index exists with that column as a search key. It is **fully inverted** if a secondary index exists on all columns that are not contained in the primary key.

A clustered index with a search key, *sk*, is particularly effective for range searches involving *sk*. Its location mechanism efficiently locates the index entry whose search key value is at one end of the range and, since entries are ordered on *sk*, subsequent entries in the range are in the same index page (or in successive pages—we discuss this situation in Section 11.5). The data records can be retrieved using these entries.

The beauty of a clustered index is that the data records are themselves grouped together (instead of scattered throughout the data file). They are either contained in the index entries or ordered like them (see Figure 11.7). Hence, in retrieving a particular data record in the range, the probability of a cache hit is high since other records in the page containing that record are likely to have been accessed already. As described in Section 11.3, the number of I/O operations on the data file is roughly R/B, where R is the number of tuples in the range and B is the number of tuples in a page.

With a clustered index that is stored separately from the data, the data file does not have to be totally ordered to efficiently process range searches. For example, overflow pages might be used to accommodate dynamically inserted records. As each new row is inserted, a new index entry is constructed and placed in the index file in the proper place. The location mechanism of the index can then efficiently find all index entries in the range since they are ordered in one (or perhaps several) index pages. The cache hit ratio for retrieving data pages is still high, although it might suffer somewhat from the scattering of the rows that were appended after the data file was sorted.

Although the data file does not have to be completely sorted, index entries cannot simply be appended to the index file—they must be integrated into the index's location mechanism. Hence, we seem to have replaced one difficult problem (keeping the data file sorted) with another (keeping the index file properly organized). However, the latter problem is not as difficult as it appears. For one thing, index entries are generally much smaller than data records, so the index file is much smaller than the data file and therefore index reorganization requires less I/O. Further-

---

clustered index could be built, while the index on the Id attribute of that relation (which is also its primary key) will be unclustered, because rows will not be sorted on that attribute.

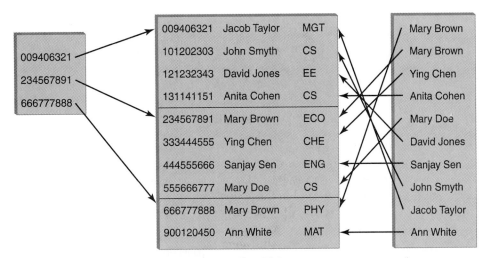

Figure 11.9 Sparse index (left) with search key Id; dense index (right) with search key Name. Both refer to the table PROFESSOR stored in a file sorted on Id.

more, as we will see, the algorithms associated with a B$^+$ tree index are designed to accommodate the efficient addition and deletion of index entries.

The index entries containing search key values in a range can be located even if an unclustered index on *sk* is used, since the entries are grouped together. The problem with an unclustered index is that the corresponding data records might be scattered throughout the data file. Thus, if there are R entries in the range, as many as R separate I/O operations might be necessary to retrieve the data records (we will discuss a technique for optimizing this number in a later section).

For example, a data file might contain 10,000 pages, but there might be only 100 records in the range of a particular query. If an unclustered index on the attributes of the WHERE clause of that query is available, at most 100 I/O operations will be needed to retrieve the pages of the data file (as compared with 10,000 I/O operations if the data is stored in a heap file with no index). If the index is clustered and each data file page contains an average of 20 data records, approximately 5 data pages will have to be retrieved. We have ignored the I/O operations on the index file in this comparison. We deal with index I/O in the individual discussions of different index structures.

11.4.2 Sparse versus Dense Indices

We have been assuming that indices are dense. A **dense index** is one whose entries are in a one to one correspondence with the records in the data file. A secondary, unclustered index must be dense; a clustered index need not be. A **sparse index** over a sorted file is one in which there is a unique index entry for each page of the data file, and vice versa. The entry contains a value that is less than or equal to all values in the page it refers to. The difference between a sparse and a dense index is illustrated using the table PROFESSOR in Figure 11.9. To simplify the figure we do

Figure 11.10 Sparse index with a problem: The search key is not a candidate key.

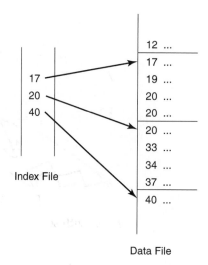

Index File

Data File

not show overflow pages in the data file and assume that all slots are filled. The data file is indexed by two separate index files. Only the index entries are shown in the index files, not the location mechanisms. Once again, we assume four slots per page. The Id attribute is the primary key of this table and is also the search key for the sparse index shown at the left of the figure. The Name attribute is the search key for the dense index at the right.

To retrieve the record for the faculty member with Id 333444555, we can use the sparse index to locate the index entry containing the largest value that is smaller than the target Id. In our case, the entry contains the value 234567891 and points to the second page of the data file. Once that page has been retrieved, the target record can be found by searching forward in the page. With a sparse index, it is essential that the data file be ordered on the same key as the index, since it is the ordering of the data file that allows us to locate records not referenced in the index. Hence, the sparse index must be clustered.

An important point concerning sparse indices is that the search key should be a candidate key of the table since, if several records exist in the data file with the same search key value and they are spread over several pages, the records in the first of those pages might be missed. The problem is illustrated in Figure 11.10. The search key of the sparse index is the first column of the table, which is not a candidate key. A search through the index for records having a search key value of 20 follows the pointer in the index having a search key value 20. Searching forward in the target page yields a single record with search key value 20 and misses the records with that value in the previous page of the data file.

Several techniques can be used to correct this problem. The simplest is to start the search through the data file at the prior page when the target value is equal to the value in the sparse index. Another approach is to create an index entry for each *distinct search key value* in the table (as opposed to one index entry per page). In that case, there might be several entries that point to the same page, but if there

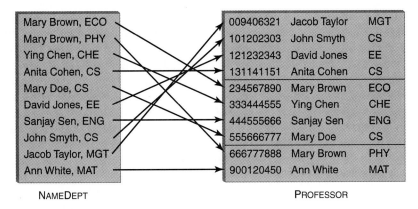

Figure 11.11 Dense index on PROFESSOR with search key Name, DeptId.

is considerable duplication of search key values in the rows of the table, this index will still be considerably smaller than a dense index.

Unclustered indices are dense. The index of Figure 11.9 is unclustered and, since an index entry exists for each record, the search key need not be a candidate key of the table. Therefore, several index entries can have the same search key value (as shown in the figure).

11.4.3 Search Keys Containing Multiple Attributes

Search keys can contain multiple attributes. For example, we might construct an index on PROFESSOR by executing the statement

        CREATE INDEX NAMEDEPT ON PROFESSOR (Name, DeptId)

Such an index is useful if clients of the supported application frequently request information about professors they identify by name and department Id. With such an index, the system can directly retrieve the required record. Not only is a scan of the entire table avoided, but records of professors with the same name in different departments are not retrieved (there might be two professors having the same name in a particular department, but this is unlikely).

A dense, unclustered index that results from this statement is shown in Figure 11.11. The index entries are lexicographically ordered on Name, DeptId (notice that the order of the two entries for Mary Brown is now reversed from their position in the dense index of Figure 11.9).

One advantage of using multiple attributes in a search key is that the resulting index supports a finer granularity search. NAMEDEPT allows us to quickly retrieve the information about the professor named Mary Brown in the economics department; the dense index of Figure 11.9 requires that we examine two data records.

A second advantage of multiple attributes arises if the index entries are sorted (as with an ISAM or B$^+$ tree index), since then a variety of range searches can be supported. For example, we can retrieve the records of all professors named Mary Brown in a particular department (an equality search), and in addition we can retrieve the records of all professors named Mary Brown in any department whose name is alphabetized between economics and sociology, or all professors named Mary Brown in all departments, or any professor whose name is alphabetized between Mary Brown and David Jones in all departments. All of these are examples of range searches. In each case, the search is supported because index entries are sorted first on `Name` and second on `DeptId`. Hence, the target index entries are (logically) consecutive in the index file and we are able to limit the range of entries to be scanned. The last two searches are examples of **partial key searches**—that is, the values for some of the attributes in the search key are not specified.

Note that a range search that is not supported by NAMEDEPT is one in which a value for `Name` is not supplied (e.g, retrieve the records of all professors in the economics department), since in that case the target index entries are not consecutive in the index file. This is precisely the reason that, in distinguishing a search key from a candidate key, we said that the ordering of attributes in a search key is important whereas it is not important for a candidate key. With partial key searches, values for a prefix of the search key can be used in the index search, while searching on a proper suffix of the key is not supported by the index.

For example, in the design of the Student Registration System given in Section 5.7, the primary key for the table TRANSCRIPT is `StudId, CrsCode, SectionNo, Semester, Year`. The Student Grade interaction can use an index whose search key consists of these attributes in the given order since, in assigning a grade to a student, all of this information must be supplied. However, the Class Roster interaction cannot use this index, since the search specifies the attributes `CrsCode, SectionNo, Semester, Year` but not `StudId`. The index is helpful for the Grade History interaction since `StudId` is supplied, but it is not optimal since the interaction uses a SELECT statement in which the WHERE clause specifies both `StudId` and `Semester/Year`. Unfortunately, the index does not support the use of `Semester/Year` without `CrsCode` and `SectionNo`. Reversing the order of the attributes in the primary key specification allows it to support both the Student Grade and the Grade History interactions. An additional index is needed for the Class Roster interaction.

In general, a tree index on table **R** with search key K supports a search of the form

$$\sigma_{attr_1 \mathrm{op}_1 val_1 \wedge ... \wedge attr_n \mathrm{op}_n val_n}(\mathbf{R}) \tag{11.4}$$

if some prefix of K is a subset of the attributes named in the search. For example, if the attributes of (11.4) are ordered so that $attr_1, \ldots, attr_s$, $s \leq n$, is a prefix of K, for some $s < n$, the search locates the smallest index entry satisfying $attr_1 = val_1 \wedge \ldots \wedge attr_s = val_s$ and scans forward from that point to locate all entries satisfying (11.4). Thus, a particular index can be used in different ways to support a variety of searches and can therefore be used in a variety of access paths to **R**.

Finally, search keys with multiple attributes show that an index can contain an arbitrary fraction of the information contained in the indexed table. A dense index has an index entry for each row and, with multiple attributes, can contain the values in an arbitrary number of the table's columns. The implication is that, for some queries, it is possible to find the requested information in the index *without accessing the table*. Thus, for example, the result of executing the query

```
SELECT   P.Name
FROM     PROFESSOR P
WHERE    P.DeptId = 'EE'
```

can be obtained from the index NAMEDEPT without accessing PROFESSOR by scanning the index entries. Such a scan is less costly than a scan of PROFESSOR, since the index is stored in fewer pages than is the table.

11.5   MULTILEVEL INDEXING

In previous sections, we discussed the index entries but not the location mechanism used to find them. In this section we discuss the location mechanism used in tree indices and then describe its use more specifically in the **index-sequential access method (ISAM)** and in **B$^+$ trees**.

To understand how the location mechanism for a tree index works, consider the dense index on the table PROFESSOR shown in Figure 11.9. Since the search key is Name, the index entries are ordered on that field, and since the data records are ordered differently in the data file, the index is unclustered. We assume that the list of index entries is stored in a sequence of pages of the index file. A naive location mechanism for the index is a binary search over the entries. Thus, to locate the data record describing Sanjay Sen, we enter the list of index entries at its midpoint and compare the value Sanjay Sen with the search key values found in that page. If the target value is found in the page, the index entry has been located; if it is less (or greater) than the values in the page, the process is repeated recursively on the first half (respectively, the last half) of the list. Once the index entry is located, the data page containing the record can be retrieved with one additional I/O operation.

It is important to note that a binary search on the list of index entries is a major improvement over one on a sorted data file, as described in Section 11.3, since data records are generally much larger than index entries. Thus, if Q is the number of pages containing index entries of a dense tree index and F is the number of pages in the data file, $Q \ll F$. The number of I/O operations needed to locate a particular index entry using binary search can be no larger than approximately $log_2 Q$.

We can further reduce the cost of locating the index entry by indexing the list of index entries itself. We construct a sparse index, using the same search key, on the index entries (a sparse index is possible because the index entries are sorted on that key) and do a binary search on that index. The entries in the second-level index serve as separators that guide the search toward the index entries of the first-level index. We thus use the term **leaf entry** to refer to index entries that reside in the lowest level of the tree and **separator entries** to refer to the entries that reside above.

The technique is illustrated in Figure 11.12, which shows a two-level index. To keep the figure concise, we assume a table with a candidate key having an integer domain, and we use that key as a search key for the index. We assume that a page of the index file can accommodate four index entries. Of course, in real systems

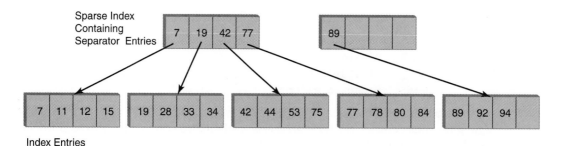

Figure 11.12 Two-level index.

one index page accommodates many more (e.g., 100), and the size of the index is relatively insignificant compared to the size of the data file.

In this and subsequent figures, we do not explicitly show the data records. The figures can be interpreted in two ways: (1) The index (leaf) entries contain pointers to the data records in a separate data file; (2) The index leaves contain the data records, and the figure represents a storage structure. In interpretation 1, the index file contains both index leaves and the second-level index, and one additional I/O operation is required to access the data record. In interpretation 2, locating an index leaf also retrieves the corresponding data entry, and no additional I/O is required. Our discussion of multilevel indices applies to both interpretations.

Finally, although in the figure the separators in the second-level index look identical to index leaves, this is not always the case. In interpretation 2, only index leaves, not separator entries, contain data records, and thus they are considerably larger than the separator entries. In interpretation 1, separators and leaf entries look identical, except that separators in the second level point to the nodes of the first level whereas leaf entries point to the records in the actual data file. The formats of these pointers will be different.

With a two-level index, we replace the binary search of the leaves by a two step process: first we do a binary search of the top-level sparse index to find the separator entry pointing to the page containing the target index leaf; second we retrieve that page to find the index entry (if it exists). Thus, if we are looking for a search key value of 33, we first do a binary search of the upper index to locate the rightmost separator with a value less than or equal to 33, which in this case is the separator containing 19. We then follow the pointer to the second page of index leaves and do a linear search in that page to find the desired index entry. If the target search key value were 32, we would perform the same steps and conclude that no row in the indexed table had value 32 in the candidate key field.

What have we achieved by introducing the second-level index? Since the upper-level index is sparse, it has fewer separator entries than there are leaf entries at the first level. If we assume separate data and index files, separator and leaf entries in the index are roughly the same size. Moreover, if we assume 100 entries in an index page, the second-level index occupies $Q/100$ pages (where Q is the number of leaf pages) and the maximum cost of accessing an index leaf entry using a binary search of the second-level index is roughly $log_2(Q/100)$ page I/Os plus 1 (for the

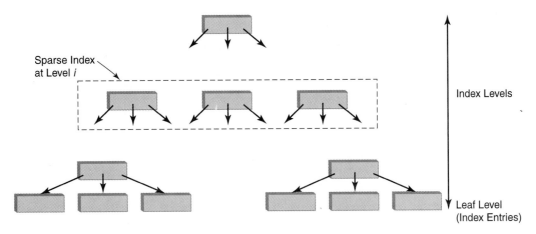

Figure 11.13 Schematic view of a multilevel index.

page containing the index leaf). This compares to log_2Q for a binary search over the index's leaf entries and represents a major savings if Q is large.

These considerations lead us to a multilevel index. If a two-level index is good, why not a multilevel index? Each index level is indexed by a higher-level sparse index of a smaller size, until we get to the point where the index is contained in a single page. The I/O cost of searching that index is 1, and so the total cost of locating the target index leaf entry equals the number of index levels.

A multilevel index is shown schematically in Figure 11.13. Each rectangular box represents a page. The lowest level of the tree contains the index leaves and is referred to as the **leaf level**. If we concatenate all of the pages at this level in the order shown, the index leaf entries form an ordered list. The upper levels contain separators and are referred to as **separator levels**. If we concatenate all of the pages at a particular separator level in the order shown, we get a sparse index on the level below. The root of the tree (the top separator level) is a sparse index contained in a single page of the index file. If index leaves contain data records, the figure shows the storage structure of a tree-indexed file.

We use the term **index level** to refer to any level of an index tree, leaf, or separator. We use the term **fan-out** to refer to the number of index separators in a page. The **fan-out** controls the number of levels in the tree: the smaller it is, the more levels the tree has. The number of levels equals the number of I/O operations needed to fetch an index leaf entry. If the fan-out is denoted by Φ, the number of I/O operations necessary to retrieve an index leaf is $log_\Phi Q + 1$.

If, for example, there are 10,000 pages at the leaf level and the fan-out is 100 (10^6 rows, in the data file assuming that leaf and separator entries are the same size), 3 page I/Os are necessary to retrieve a particular leaf. Thus, with a large fan-out, traversal of the index, even for a large data file, can be reduced to a few I/O operations. Since the root index occupies only a single page, it can often be kept in main memory, further reducing the cost. Even the second level index, which in this case occupies 100 pages, might be practical to keep in main memory.

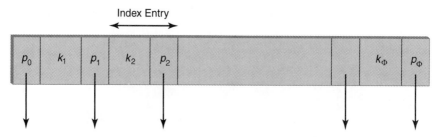

Figure 11.14 Page at a separator level in an ISAM index.

Multilevel indices form the basis for tree indices, which we discuss next, and these numbers indicate why tree indices are used so frequently. Not only do they provide efficient access to the data file, but, as we will see, they also support range queries.

11.5.1 Index–Sequential Access

The **index-sequential access method (ISAM)**[6] is based on the multilevel index. An ISAM index is a main index and hence it is a clustered index over records that are ordered on the search key of the index. Generally, the records are contained in the index leaves, so ISAM is a storage structure for the data file.

The format of a page at a separator level is shown in Figure 11.14. Each separator level is effectively a sparse index over the next level below. Each separator entry consists of a search key value, k_i, and a pointer, p_i, to another page in the index file. This page might be in the next, lower separator level, or it might be a page containing index leaves. The separators are sorted in the page, and we assume that a page contains a maximum of Φ separators.

Each search key value, k_i, separates the set of search key values in the two subtrees pointed to by the adjacent pointers, p_{i-1} and p_i. If a search key value, k, is found in the subtree referred to by p_{i-1}, it satisfies $k < k_i$; if it is found in the subtree referred to by p_i, it satisfies $k \geq k_i$. This is why search key values in an index page are called separators. It appears as if an ISAM index page contains an extra pointer, p_0, if we compare it with a page of a sparse index in a multilevel index.[7] Actually, a better way to compare a page of an ISAM index to an index page at the separator level is that the latter contains an extra search key value: The smallest search key value in the page, k_0, is actually unnecessary.

Figure 11.15 is an example of an ISAM index. In it, the tree has two separator levels and a leaf level. Search key values are the names of students, and the ordering is lexicographic. All search key values in the leftmost subtree (the subtree referred to by p_0 in the root page) are less than judy, and all search tree values in the

---

[6] The term *access method* is often used interchangeably with the term *access path*. We prefer *access path* since it conforms more closely to the concept.

[7] Note that the fan-out is now $\Phi + 1$. Since Φ is generally much greater than 1, we ignore the difference between Φ and $\Phi + 1$ in cost calculations.

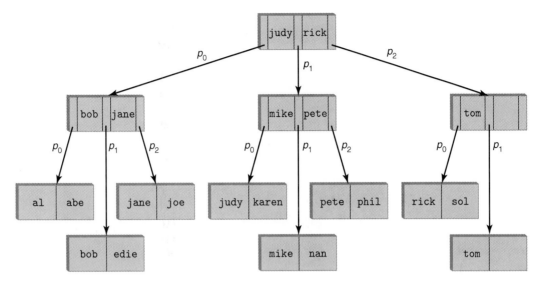

Figure 11.15 An example of an ISAM index.

middle subtree (the subtree referred to by p_1 in the root page) are greater than or equal to judy. An ISAM file is built by first allocating pages sequentially in the storage structure for the index leaf pages (containing the data rows) and then constructing the separator levels from the bottom up: The root is the topmost index built. Therefore, the ISAM index initially has the property that all search key values that appear at a separator level also appear at the leaf level.

A search for the data record containing the search key value karen starts at the root, determines that the target value is between judy and rick, and follows p_1 to the middle page at the next index level. From that page, it determines that karen is less than mike and follows p_0 to the leaf page in which the index leaf containing the record resides. If the goal were to retrieve all data records with search key values between karen and pete, we would locate the index leaf containing karen as before and then scan the leaf level until the entry containing pete was encountered. Because pages at the leaf level are stored sequentially in sorted order, the desired entries are consecutive in the file. If the goal were to retrieve all data records with search key values between kate and paul, we would scan the same leaf pages. In addition, the ISAM index supports keys with multiple attributes and partial key searches.

An ISAM index is characterized by the fact that the separator levels never change once they have been constructed. Although the contents of leaf level pages might change, the pages themselves are not allocated or deallocated and hence their position in the file is fixed. If a row of the table is deleted, the corresponding leaf entry is deleted from the leaf level but no changes are made to the separator levels. Such a deletion can create a situation in which a search key value in a separator entry has no corresponding value in a leaf entry. This would happen, for example, if the record for jane were deleted from Figure 11.15. Such an index might seem

Figure 11.16 Portion of the ISAM index of Figure 11.15 after an insertion and a deletion.

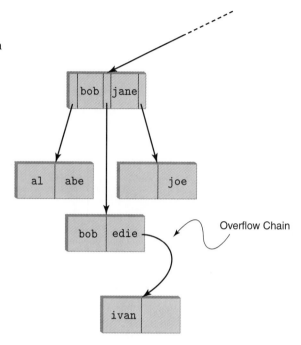

strange, but it still functions correctly and does not represent a serious problem (other than a potential waste of space where the deallocated leaf entry resided).

A more serious problem arises when a new row is added, since a new index leaf entry must be created and the appropriate leaf page might be full. This can be avoided by using a fill factor less than 1 (a fill factor of .75 is reasonable for an ISAM file), but overflow pages might ultimately be necessary. For example, if a row for ivan were inserted (and the row for jane deleted), the leftmost subtree of the resulting index would be as shown in Figure 11.16. Note that the new page is an overflow of a leaf-level page, *not* a new level or even a new leaf-level page. If a table is dynamic, with frequent insertions, overflow chains can become long and, as a result, the index structure becomes less and less efficient because the overflow chains must be searched to satisfy queries. The entries on the chains might not be ordered, and the overflow pages might not be physically close to one another on the mass storage device. The index can be reconstructed periodically to eliminate the chains, but this is expensive. For this reason, although an ISAM index can be effective for a relatively static table, it is generally not used when the table is dynamic.

11.5.2 B+ Trees

A B+ tree is the most commonly used index structure. Indeed, in some database systems it is the only one available. As with an ISAM index, the B+ structure is based on the multilevel index and supports equality, range, and partial key searches. Index leaves might contain data records, in which case the B+ tree acts not only

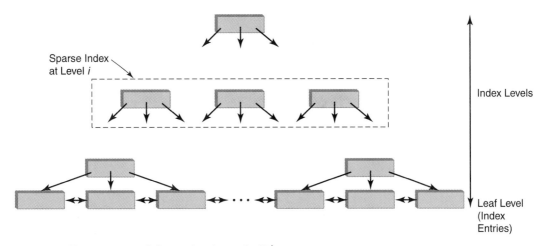

Sparse Index at Level *i*

Index Levels

Leaf Level
(Index
Entries)

Figure 11.17 Schematic view of a B$^+$ tree.

as an index but as a storage structure that organizes the placement of records in the data file. Or the tree might be stored in an index file, in which the index leaves contain pointers to the data file records. In the first case, the B$^+$ tree is a main index similar to an ISAM index since it is clustered. In the second case, it might be a main or a secondary index, and the data file need not be sorted on its search key.

Figure 11.17 shows a schematic diagram of a B$^+$ tree in which each page contains a sorted set of entries. The only difference between this figure and Figure 11.13 is the addition of **sibling pointers**, which link pages at the leaf level in such a way that the linked list contains the search key values of the records of the table in sorted order. In contrast to an ISAM index, the B$^+$ tree itself changes dynamically. As records are added and deleted, leaf and index pages have to be modified, added, and/or deleted, and hence leaf pages might not be consecutive in the file. However, the linked list enables the B$^+$ tree to support range searches. Once the index leaf at one end of a range has been located using an equality search, the other leaf entries that contain search key values in the range can be located by scanning the list. Note that this scheme works when the B$^+$ tree is used as either a main or a secondary index (in which case data records are not necessarily sorted in search key order). With the addition of sibling pointers, Figure 11.15 becomes a B$^+$ tree (keep in mind that leaf-level pages might or might not contain data records).[8]

Sibling pointers are not needed in an ISAM index because index leaf pages (which generally contain data records) are stored in the file in sorted order when the file is constructed and, since the index is static, that ordering is maintained. Hence, a range search can be carried out by physically scanning the file. Dynamically

[8] The difference between a B tree and a B$^+$ tree is that with a B tree we can have a pointer to a record in the actual data file at any level; that is, each index page can have a mixture of separator and leaf entries. This implies that a particular search key value appears exactly once in the tree. A B$^+$ tree does not possess this property.

Figure 11.18 Portion of the index of Figure 11.15 after insertion of an entry for vince.

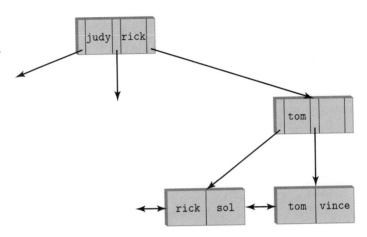

inserted index entries are not stored in sorted order, but can be located through overflow chains.

The second difference between a B^+ tree and an ISAM index is that a B^+ tree is a **balanced tree**. This means that, despite the insertion of new records and the deletion of old records, any path from the root to an index leaf has the same length as any other. Thus, the I/O cost of retrieving a particular leaf entry is the same for all index leaves. We have seen that, for multilevel indices with a reasonable fan-out, this cost can be surprisingly small. Φ is the maximum number of separator entries that can be fit in an index page. If we assume that the algorithms for inserting and deleting entries (to be described shortly) ensure that the minimum number of separators stored in a page is $\Phi/2$ (i.e., $\Phi/2$ is the minimum fan-out),[9] then the maximum cost of a search through a B^+ tree having Q leaf pages is $log_{\Phi/2}Q + 1$. (In general, the root node can have fewer than $\Phi/2$ separators, which affects this formula slightly.) Contrast this with an ISAM index with overflow chains. Because the length of a chain is unbounded, the cost of retrieving index leaves at the end of a chain is also unbounded.

Thus a major advantage of the B^+ tree over an ISAM index is its adaptation to dynamically changing tables. Instead of creating an overflow chain when a new record is added, we modify the index structure so that the tree remains balanced. As the structure changes, entries are added to and deleted from pages and the number of separators in a page varies between $\Phi/2$ and Φ.

Let us trace a sequence of insertions into the index of Figure 11.15, viewing that index as a B^+ tree. In this case, $\Phi = 2$. Figure 11.18 shows the rightmost subtree after a record for vince has been added. Since vince follows tom in search key order and

---

[9] In case Φ is odd, the minimum number of separators should really be $\lceil \Phi/2 \rceil$—the smallest integer greater than $\Phi/2$.

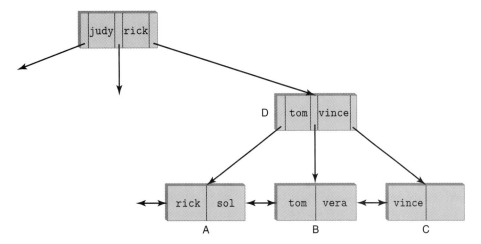

Figure 11.19 Index subtree of Figure 11.18 after the insertion of vera has caused the split of a leaf page.

there is room for an additional index leaf in the rightmost leaf page, no modification to the B$^+$ tree structure is required.

Suppose that the next insertion is vera, which follows tom. Since the rightmost leaf page is now full, a new page is needed, but instead of an overflow page (as in an ISAM index), we create a new leaf page. This requires modifying the structure of the index, which sets the B$^+$ tree solution apart from the ISAM solution. Because the ordering of search key values at the leaf level must be preserved, vera must be inserted between tom and vince. Hence, it is not sufficient simply to create a new rightmost leaf page containing vera. Instead, we must allocate a new leaf page and split the search key values in sorted order between the existing leaf page and the new page so that roughly half are stored in each. The result is shown in Figure 11.19. The smallest entry in the new leaf page, labeled C in the figure, is vince, so vince becomes a new separator in index page D (all entries in leaf page B are less than vince) which fortunately has enough room for that entry. In general, when a (full) leaf page containing Φ entries is split to accommodate an insertion, we create two leaf pages—one containing $\Phi/2 + 1$ entries and the other containing $\Phi/2$ entries—and we insert a separator at the next index level up. We refer to this as Rule 1. Note that we have both a separator and a leaf entry for vince.

If the next insertion is rob, the problem is more severe. The new index leaf must lie between rick and sol, requiring a split of page A, and four pointers are needed (to refer to the two pages that follow from the split as well as B and C) in page D. Unfortunately, a page can accommodate only three pointers, and therefore we must split D as well. Furthermore, following Rule 1, we must create a separator for sol. In the general case, an index page is split when it has to store $\Phi + 1$ separators (in this case sol, tom, and vince) and thus $\Phi + 2$ pointers to index pages at the next lower level. Each page that results from the split contains $\Phi/2 + 1$ pointers and $\Phi/2$

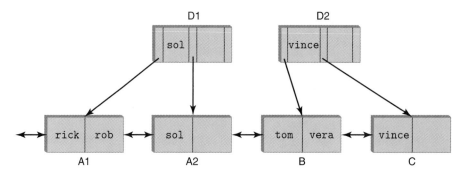

Figure 11.20 Index subtree of Figure 11.19 after the insertion of `rob` has caused the
split of a leaf page and of an index page.

separators. It might seem that we have misplaced a separator, but we are not done
yet.

The situation after the split of page A into A1 and A2 and page D into D1 and D2
is shown in Figure 11.20. Note that the total number of separator entries in pages D1
and D2—two—is the same as in page D, although the values are different: `sol` has
replaced `tom`. This number seems strange, since the number of separators required
to separate the pages at the leaf level is three (`sol`, `tom`, and `vince`). The explanation
is that `tom`, the separator that separates the values contained in the two subtrees
rooted at D1 and D2, becomes a separator at a higher level. In general, in splitting a
page at the separator level to accommodate $\Phi + 1$ separators, the middle separator
in the separator sequence is not stored in either of the two separator pages resulting
from the split, but instead is *pushed up* the tree. We refer to this pushing as Rule 2.

Hence, we are not finished. The separator has to be pushed and a reference has to
be made to the new index page (D2) at the next higher index level. In other words,
the process has to be repeated. In general, the process has to be repeated until an
index level is reached that can accommodate a new separator without requiring
a split. In our example, the next index level is the root page, and since it cannot
accommodate another separator, it will have to be split. In this case, the sequence
of separators that we are dealing with is `judy`, `rick`, and `tom`; using Rule 2, `rick`
must be pushed up to be stored in a new root page.

This completes the process and yields the B^+ tree shown in Figure 11.21. Note
that the number of levels has increased by 1 but that the tree remains balanced.
Four I/O operations are now required to access any index leaf and, if the table is
accessed frequently, the required number of I/O operations might be reduced by 1
by keeping the root page in main memory. Also note that, in splitting A, the sibling
pointer in B must be updated, which requires an additional I/O operation.

A node split incurs overhead and should be avoided, if possible. One way to do
this is to use a fillfactor that is less than 1 when the B^+ tree is created (a fillfactor of
.75 is reasonable). Of course, this might increase the number of levels in the tree.

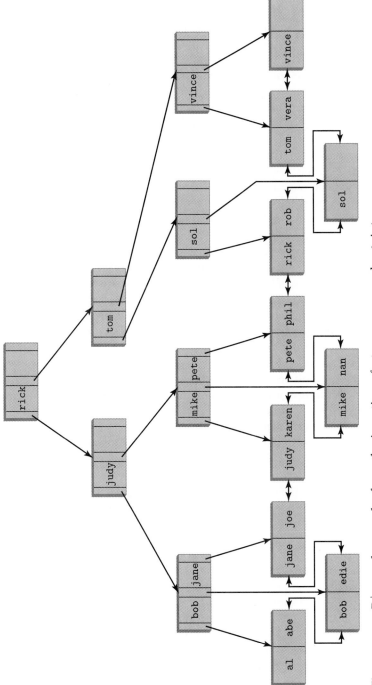

Figure 11.21 B+ tree that results from the insertion of vince, vera, and rob into the index of Figure 11.15.

One variation of the insertion algorithm that attempts to avoid a split involves redistributing index entries in the leaf-level pages. For example, if we insert a leaf entry for tony, in Figure 11.19 we might make room in page B by moving the entry for vera to page C (and replacing vince with vera as the separator in page D). Redistribution is generally done between neighboring pages at the leaf level that have the same immediate parent. Such pages are referred to as **siblings**.

The above discussion explains the main points of the process of *inserting* an entry into a B$^+$ tree. Exercise 11.12 asks you to formalize this process in an actual algorithm.

Deletion presents a different problem. When pages become sparsely occupied, the tree can become deeper than necessary, increasing the cost of each search down the tree and each scan across the leaf level. To avoid such situations, pages can be compacted. A minimum occupancy requirement of $\Phi/2$ entries per page is set for this purpose. When a deletion is made from a page with $\Phi/2$ entries, an attempt is first made to redistribute entries from the page's siblings. This is not possible if the siblings also have $\Phi/2$ entries, in which case the page is merged with a sibling to form a new page with $\Phi - 1$ entries and an index entry is deleted from the next higher level in the tree. Just as the effect of a split can propagate up the tree, so too can the effect of a merge. The deletion can cause the index page to fall below the threshold level, requiring separators to be redistributed or pages to be merged. If the effect propagates up to the root and the last separator in the root is deleted, the depth of the tree is reduced by 1. In exercise 11.13 you will formalize in an algorithm the process just described.

Since tables tend to grow over time, some database systems do not enforce the minimum occupancy requirement but simply delete pages when they become empty. If necessary, a tree can be completely reconstructed to eliminate pages that do not meet the minimum occupancy requirement.

Although we ignored this possibility in our previous discussion, when the search key is not a candidate key of the table, multiple rows might have the same search key value. Suppose, for example, that a record for another student named vince is added to the B$^+$ tree of Figure 11.18. Using Rule 1, the rightmost leaf node must then be split to accommodate a second index leaf with search key value vince, and a new separator must be created as shown in Figure 11.22. The first thing to note is that the search key values in page B are no longer strictly less than the value vince in the index entry in D. The second is that a search for vince terminates in leaf page C and therefore does not find the leaf entry for vince in B. Finally, if rows for additional students named vince are inserted, there will be several separators for vince at the lowest (and perhaps a higher) separator level. One way of handling duplicates is thus to modify the search algorithm to accommodate these differences. We leave the details of the modification to an exercise.

Another approach to handling the insertion of a duplicate is simply to create an overflow page if the leaf is full. In this way, the search algorithm does not have to be modified, although overflow chains can grow large and the cost estimates for using the tree described earlier will no longer apply.

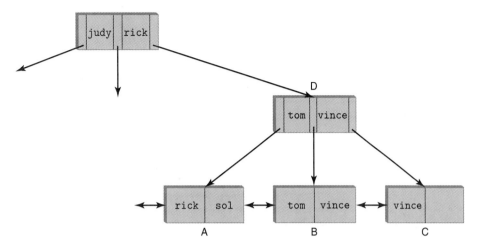

Figure 11.22 Index subtree of Figure 11.18 after the insertion of a duplicate entry for `vince` has caused the split of a leaf page.

11.6 HASH INDEXING

Hashing is an important search algorithm in many computer applications. In this section, we discuss its use for indexing database relations, looking at both **static hashing**, where the size of the hash table stays constant, and **dynamic hashing**, where the table may grow or shrink. The first technique is superior when the contents of a relation are more or less stable; the second, when indexing relations that are subject to frequent inserts and deletes.

11.6.1 Static Hashing

A hash index divides the index entries corresponding to the data records of a table into disjoint subsets, called **buckets**, in accordance with some **hash function**, h. The particular bucket into which a new index entry is inserted is determined by applying h to the search key value, v, in the entry. Thus, $h(v)$ is the address of the bucket. Since the number of distinct search key values is generally much larger than the number of buckets, a particular bucket will contain entries with different values. Each bucket is generally stored in a page (which might be extended with an overflow chain), identified by $h(v)$. The situation is shown in Figure 11.23.

An equality search for index entries with search key v is carried out by computing $h(v)$, retrieving the bucket stored in the referenced page, and then scanning its contents to locate the entries (if any) containing v. Since no other bucket can possibly contain entries with that key value, if the entry is not found in the bucket, it is not in the file. Thus, without having to maintain an index structure analogous to a tree, the target index entry of an equality search can be retrieved with a single I/O operation (assuming no overflow chain).

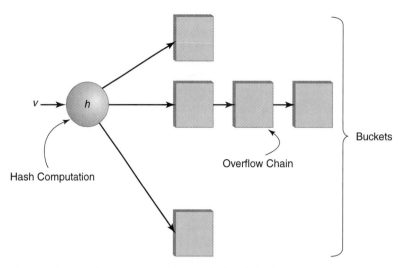

Figure 11.23 Schematic depiction of a hash index.

A properly designed hash index can perform an equality search more efficiently than a tree index can, since, with a tree index, several index-level pages must be retrieved before the leaf level is reached. If a succession of equality searches must be performed, however, a tree index might be preferable. Suppose for example, that it is necessary to retrieve the records with search key values $k_0, k_1, \ldots, k_l$, that the sequence is ordered on the search key (i.e., $k_i < k_{i+1}$), and that the sequence represents the order in which records are to be retrieved. Because the index leaves of a tree index are sorted on the key, the likelihood of cache hits when retrieving index entries is great. But with a hash index, each search key value might hash to a different bucket, so the retrieval of successive index entries in the sequence might not generate cache hits. The example shows that, in evaluating which index might improve an application's performance, the entire application should be considered.

Despite the apparent advantage that hash indices have for equality searches, tree indices are generally preferable because they are more versatile: Hash indices cannot support range or partial key searches. A partial key search is not supported because the hash function must be applied to the entire key. To understand why a range search cannot be supported efficiently, consider the student table discussed earlier. Suppose that we want to use a hash index to retrieve the records of all individuals in the file with names between paul and tom. Hashing can determine that there are no individuals with the name paul and retrieve the index entry for tom, but it is of no help in locating index entries for individuals with names inside the range because we have no recourse but to apply the hash function to every *possible* value in the range—only a few of which are likely to appear in the database. Successive entries in the range are spread randomly through the buckets, so the cost of evaluating such a range query is proportional to the number of entries in the range. In the worst case (when the number of such entries exceeds the number of pages in the file), the cost associated with the use of the index might exceed the cost of simply scanning the entire file!

In contrast, with a clustered ISAM or B$^+$ tree index the data records in the range can be located by first using the index to find the first record and then using a simple scan. A simple scan is possible because data records in the file are maintained in search key order. The cost of this search is proportional to the number of pages in the range plus the cost of searching the index. The important difference is that the I/O cost of a B$^+$ tree search depends on the number of *leaf pages* in the range, while the cost of a hash index search depends on the number of *records* in the range, which is much larger.

As in a tree index, an index entry in a hash index might contain the data record or might store a pointer to the data record in the data file. If it contains the data record, the buckets serve as a storage structure for the data file itself: The data file is a sequence of buckets. If it contains a pointer to the record, the index entries are stored as a sequence of buckets in an index file and the records in the data file can be stored in arbitrary order. In this case, the hash index is secondary and **unclustered**. If the data records referred to by the index entries in the same bucket are stored in the same or adjacent disk blocks, the hash index is **clustered**. This implies that data records with the same value of the search key are physically close to each other on mass storage.

Hash functions are chosen with the goal of randomizing the index entries over the buckets in such a way that, for an average instance of the indexed table, the number of index entries in each bucket is roughly the same. For example, h might be defined as

$$h(v) = (a * v + b) \bmod M$$

where a and b are constants chosen to optimize the way the function randomizes over the search key values, M is the number of buckets, and v is a string treated as a binary number in the calculation of the hash value. For simplicity, we assume M to be a power of 2 in all of the algorithms that follow (but in practice it is usually a large prime number).

The indexing scheme we have just described is referred to as a **static hash** because M is fixed when the index is created. The efficiency of static hashing depends on the assumption that all entries in each bucket fit in a single page. The number of entries in a bucket is inversely proportional to M: If fewer buckets are used, the average bucket occupancy is larger. The larger the average occupancy, the more unlikely it is that a bucket will fit in a page and so overflow pages will be needed. The choice of M is thus crucial to the index's efficient operation.

If Φ is the maximum number of index entries that can fit in a page and L is the total number of index entries, choosing M to be L/Φ leads to buckets that overflow a single page. For one thing, h does not generally divide entries exactly evenly over the buckets, so we can expect that more than Φ entries will be assigned to some buckets. For another, bucket overflow results if the table grows over time. One way to deal with this growth is to use a fillfactor less than 1 to enlarge the number of buckets. The average bucket occupancy is chosen to be $\Phi * fillfactor$ so that buckets with larger than average populations can be accommodated in a single page. M then becomes $L/(\Phi * fillfactor)$. Fillfactors as low as .5 are not unreasonable. The disadvantage of enlarging M is that space requirements increase because some buckets have few entries.

This technique reduces, but does not solve, the overflow problem, particularly since the growth of some tables cannot be predicted in advance. Therefore, bucket overflow must be dealt with, and this can be done with overflow chains as shown in Figure 11.23. Unfortunately, as with an ISAM index, overflow chains can be inefficient. Because an entire bucket must be scanned with each equality search, a search through a bucket stored in n pages costs n I/O operations. This multiplies the cost of a search by n over the ideal case. Fortunately, studies have shown that $n = 1.2$ for a good hash function.

11.6.2 Dynamic Hashing Algorithms

Just as B^+ trees are adapted from tree indices to deal with dynamic tables, dynamic hashing schemes are adapted from static hashing to deal with the same problem. The goal of dynamic hashing is to change the number of buckets dynamically in order to reduce or eliminate overflow chains as rows are added and deleted. Two dynamic hashing algorithms that have received the most attention are extendable hashing and linear hashing which we briefly discuss here.

Static hashing uses a fixed hash function, h, to partition the set of all possible search key values into subsets, S_i, $1 \le i \le M$, and maps each subset to a bucket, B_i. Each element, v, of S_i has the property that $h(v)$ identifies B_i. Dynamic hashing schemes allow S_i to be partitioned at run time into disjoint subsets, S_i' and S_i'', and B_i to be split into B_i' and B_i'', such that the elements of S_i' are mapped to B_i' and the elements of S_i'' are mapped to B_i''. By reducing the number of values that map to a bucket, a split has the potential of replacing one overflowing bucket with two that are not full. A change in the mapping implies a change in the hash function that takes into account the split of a single bucket (or the merge of two buckets). Extendable and linear hashing do this mapping in different ways.

Extendable hashing. Extendable hashing uses a sequence of hash functions, h_0, h_1, ..., h_b, based on a single hash function, h, which hashes a search key value into a b-bit integer. For each k, $0 \le k \le b$, $h_k(v)$ is the integer formed by the last k bits of $h(v)$. Stated mathematically,

$$h_k(v) = h(v) \bmod 2^k$$

Thus, the range of each function, h_k, is twice that of its predecessor, h_{k-1}. At any given time, a particular function in the sequence, h_k, directs all searches.

Unlike static hashing, dynamic hashing uses a second stage of mapping to determine the bucket associated with some search key value, v. This mapping uses a level of indirection implemented through a directory, as shown in Figure 11.24. The value produced by $h_k(v)$ serves as an index into the directory, and the pointer in the directory entry refers to the bucket associated with v. The key point is that distinct entries in the directory might refer to the same bucket, so $v1$ and $v2$ might be mapped to the same bucket even though $h_k(v1)$ and $h_k(v2)$ are distinct.

Figure 11.24 Extendable hashing maps the hash result to a bucket through a directory.

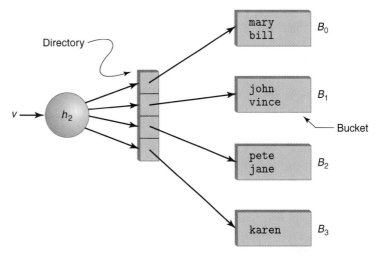

To see how this comes about, suppose that the range of h is the set of integers between 0 and $2^{10} - 1$. In Figure 11.24, we assume that a bucket page can hold two index entries. The figure depicts the algorithm at a point at which h_2 is used to hash search key values (and, thus, the directory contains $2^2 = 4$ entries). Since h_2 uses only the last two bits of the values in the range of h, the figure could be produced by the following function h:

v	$h(v)$
pete	1001111010
mary	0100000000
jane	1100011110
bill	0100000000
john	0001101001
vince	1101110101
karen	0000110111

Thus, h hashes pete to 1001111010, and since h_2 uses only the last two bits, it indicates the third directory entry, which refers to B_2.

Suppose that we now insert a record for sol into the table and that $h(\text{sol}) = 0001010001$. h_2 maps john, vince, and sol to B_1, causing an overflow. Rather than creating an overflow chain, extendable hashing splits B_1 so that a new bucket, B_5, is created, as shown in Figure 11.25. To accommodate five buckets, it is necessary to use a hash function whose range contains more than four values, so the index replaces h_2 with h_3. Since the high-order bit of $h_3(\text{john})$, 0, and $h_3(\text{vince})$, 1, differ (whereas the two low-order bits, 01, are the same), h_3 avoids overflow by mapping john and vince to different buckets (h_2 does not do this). In Figure 11.25, note that if both $v1$ and $v2$ are elements of B_1 (or B_5), $h(v1)$ and $h(v2)$ agree in their last three bits.

Figure 11.25 Bucket B_1 of Figure 11.24 has been split using extendable hashing.

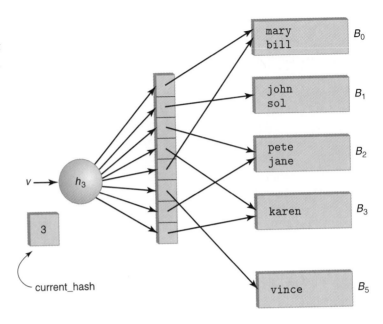

The directory is needed to compensate for the fact that only B_1 has been split. Indeed, h_3 not only distinguishes between john and vince, but also produces different values for pete (010) and jane (110). Hence, without a directory it would be necessary to split B_2 as well when h_2 is replaced by h_3. By interposing a directory between the hash computation and the buckets, we can map both pete and jane to B_2, which we do by storing a pointer to B_2 in both the third (010) and seventh (110) directory entries. As a result, in contrast to B_1 and B_5, if $v1$ and $v2$ are both elements of B_2, then $h(v1)$ and $h(v2)$ agree only in their last two bits.

The algorithm used in moving from Figure 11.24 to Figure 11.25 is quite simple.

1. A new bucket, B', is allocated and the contents of the overflowing bucket, B, is split between B and B' using the next hash function in the sequence.

2. A new directory is created by concatenating a copy of the old directory with itself.

3. The pointer to B in the copy is replaced by a pointer to B'.

Thus, the two halves of the directory in Figure 11.25 are identical except for the pointers in the second and sixth entry (which are the two halves of the bucket that has been split).

To give a complete description of the algorithm, we must deal with a few additional issues. First of all, how do we know which hash function in the sequence to use when a search has to be performed? That's easy. We simply store the index of the current hash function along with the directory. We assume a variable *current_hash* for this purpose, which is initialized to 0 (with only a single directory entry).

Figure 11.26 Bucket B_2 of Figure 11.25 is split, without enlargement of the directory.

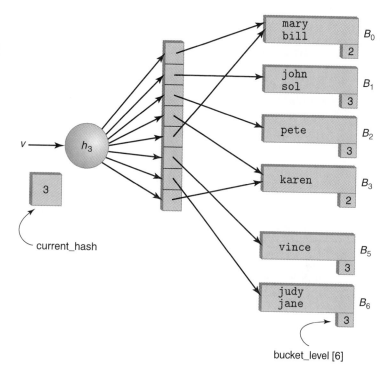

In general, the number of directory entries is $2^{current\_hash}$. The value of *current_hash* is 2 in Figure 11.24 (not shown) and 3 in Figure 11.25.

A more subtle problem arises if we consider what should happen if a row for judy is inserted next and $h(judy) = 1110000110$. judy is mapped to B_2 in Figure 11.25, causing the bucket to overflow and requiring it to be split. However, this situation is different from the one that caused us to replace h_2 with h_3, since h_3 itself is capable of distinguishing among index entries that are mapped to B_2 (recall that the hash values of the index entries in B_2 agree in only their last two bits). In the example, h_3 distinguishes judy and jane (110) from pete (010), so, instead of moving to a new hash function to deal with the overflow, we need only create a new bucket for judy and jane and update the appropriate pointer in the directory to refer to it. This is shown in Figure 11.26, in which the new bucket is labeled B_6.

There is a reason that the directory does not have to be enlarged this time. Each time it is enlarged, it becomes capable of storing pointers to accommodate the split of *every* bucket that exists at that time, whereas, in fact, only *one* bucket is actually split. Thus, when a directory is extended all but one of the pointers in its new portion simply point back to an existing bucket. The directory in Figure 11.25 was created to accommodate the split of B_1, so only entry 101 in the new portion of that directory refers to a new bucket. Since entries 010 and 110 both point to B_2, the directory can accommodate a split of B_2 without further enlargement.

We can detect this case by storing, along with each bucket, the number of times it has been split. We refer to this value as the *bucket level* and associate a variable, *bucket_level*[*i*] to store it. Initially *bucket_level*[0] is 0 and, when B_i is split, we use *bucket_level*[*i*] + 1 as the bucket level of both B_i and the newly created bucket. Because each time the directory is enlarged without splitting B_i, we double the number of pointers in the directory that refer to B_i, $2^{current\_hash-(bucket\_level[i])}$ is the number of pointers that point to B_i in the directory. Furthermore, when a bucket is split, the index entries are divided between the two resulting buckets so that, if *v*1 and *v*2 are both elements of B_i, then $h(v1)$ and $h(v2)$ agree in their last *bucket_level*[*i*] bits.

bucket_level[1] is 3 in both Figure 11.25 (not shown) and Figure 11.26, whereas *bucket_level*[2] is 2 in Figure 11.25 and is incremented to 3 in Figure 11.26.

The merge of two buckets can be handled using the inverse of the split algorithm. If the deletion of an index entry causes a bucket, B', to become empty, and B' and B'' were created when B was split, B' can be released by redirecting the pointer to B' in the directory so that it points to B'' and decrementing the bucket level of B''. In addition, when merging creates a state in which the upper and lower halves of the directory are identical, one half can be released and *current_hash* decremented. Merging is often not implemented since it is assumed that, although a table might temporarily shrink, it is likely to grow in the long term, and therefore a merge will ultimately be followed by a split.

Extendable hashing eliminates most of the overflow chains that develop with static hashing when the number of index entries grows. Unfortunately, though, it has several deficiencies. One is that additional space is required to store the directory. The other is that the indirection through the directory to locate the buffer requires additional time. If the directory is small, it can be kept in main memory, so neither of these deficiencies is major. In that case, directory access does not impose the cost of an additional I/O operation. Nevertheless, a directory can grow quite large and, if it cannot be kept in main memory, the I/O cost of extendable hashing is twice that of static hashing. Finally, splitting a bucket doesn't necessarily divide its contents and eliminate the overflow. For example, when the overflow is caused by multiple entries with the same search key value, splitting cannot remove the overflow.

Linear Hashing.   Because the deficiencies of extendable hashing are associated with the introduction of a directory, it is natural to search for a dynamic hashing scheme for which a directory is not required. A directory is needed with extendable hashing because, when a bucket is split, it might be necessary to switch to a hash function with a larger range: Search keys stored in different buckets must hash to different values. Thus, the range of h_{i+1} contains twice as many elements as the range of h_i, and therefore $h_i(v)$ and $h_{i+1}(v)$ might not be the same. However, if v is an element of a bucket that is not being split, the index must direct the search to that bucket before and after the split. The directory overcomes this problem.

Can this problem be overcome in a way that does not involve a directory? One possible way uses the same sequence of hash functions, $h_0, h_1, \ldots, h_b$, as

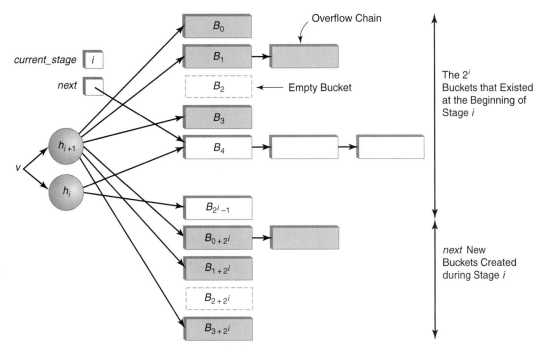

Figure 11.27 Linear hashing splits buckets consecutively. The shaded buckets are accessed through h_{i+1}.

extendable hashing does, but differently. h_i and h_{i+1} are used concurrently: h_i for values belonging in buckets that have not been split and h_{i+1} for values belonging in buckets that have. This approach has the advantage of providing the same mapping before and after the split for search keys that belong in buckets not involved in the split. The trick is to be able to tell, when initiating a search through the index, which hash function to use.

With linear hashing, bucket splitting is divided into stages. The buckets that exist at the start of a stage are split consecutively during the stage, so that there are twice as many buckets at the end of the stage as there were in the beginning. The situation is shown in Figure 11.27. Stages are numbered, and the number of the current stage is stored in the variable *current_stage*. In the figure, *current_stage* has value i, indicating that h_i and h_{i+1} are in use. Initially *current_stage* is 0 and there is a single bucket. The variable *next* indicates the next bucket in the sequence to be split.

When stage i is initiated, there are 2^i buckets and h_i, with range $\{0 \ldots 2^i - 1\}$, is used to hash search key values for an index search. A decision is made periodically to split a bucket (we return to this point shortly), and the value of *next* is used to determine which bucket among those that existed at the beginning of the stage is to be split. *next* is initialized to 0 at the start of the stage and incremented when the split occurs. Hence, buckets are split consecutively and *next* distinguishes those that have been split in the current stage from those that have not. Since *next* refers to the next bucket to be split, buckets with index less than *next* have been split in this stage. (Split buckets and their images are shaded in the figure.) Stage i is complete when the 2^i buckets that existed when the stage began have been split.

The new bucket created when B_{next} is split has index $next + 2^i$. Elements of B_{next} are divided using h_{i+1}: If v was an element of B_{next}, it remains in that bucket if $h_{i+1}(v) = h_i(v)$ and is moved to B_{next+2^i} otherwise. When the value of *next* reaches 2^i, a new stage is started by resetting *next* to 0 and incrementing *current_stage*.

When a search is to be performed on search key v, $h_i(v)$ is calculated. If $next \le h_i(v) < 2^i$, the bucket indicated by $h_i(v)$ is scanned for v. If $0 \le h_i(v) < next$, the bucket indicated by $h_i(v)$ has been split and $h_i(v)$ does not provide enough information to determine whether $B_{h_i(v)}$ or $B_{h_i(v)+2^i}$ should be scanned for v. However, since h_{i+1} was used to divide the elements when the split was made, we can decide which bucket to search using $h_{i+1}(v)$.

The important point to note about linear hashing is that the bucket that is split has not necessarily overflowed. We might decide to perform a split when a bucket, B_j, overflows, but the bucket that is split is B_{next}, and the value of *next* might be different from j. Note that in Figure 11.27 $next = 4$, which means that B_0, B_1, B_2, and B_3 have been split. In particular, B_2 was split when it was empty and certainly had not overflowed. Thus, linear hashing does not eliminate overflow chains (in this case, an overflow page must be created for B_j). Ultimately, however, B_j will be split because every bucket that exists at the start of the current stage is split before the stage completes. So, although an overflow chain might be created for a bucket, B, it tends to be short and is normally eliminated the next time B is split. The average lifetime of an overflow page can be decreased by splitting more frequently, although the price for doing that is lower space utilization since buckets that have not overflowed are split during each stage.

Given the assumption that a split occurs each time an overflow page is created, Figure 11.28 shows the sequence of states that a linear index goes through when it starts in the same state as shown for extendable hashing in Figure 11.24 and experiences the same subsequent insertions. In Figure 11.28(a) we have assumed that the index has just entered stage 2. Figure 11.28(b) shows the result of inserting sol into B_1. Although B_1 has overflowed, B_0 is split since *next* has value 0. Note that, since both mary and bill are hashed to B_0 by h_3, B_4 is empty. Figure 11.28(c) shows the result of inserting judy into B_2. B_1 is now split, eliminating its overflow chain, but a new overflow chain is created for B_2.

It might seem that linear hashing splits the wrong bucket, but this is the price that is paid for avoiding the directory. Splitting buckets in sequence makes it easy to distinguish the buckets that have been split from those that have not. Although overflow chains exist with linear hashing, there is no additional cost for fetching the directory.

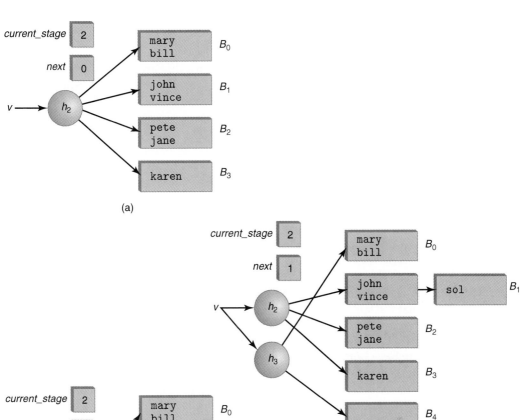

Figure 11.28 (a) State of a linear hash index at the beginning of a stage; (b) State after insertion of sol; (c) State after insertion of judy.

11.7   SPECIAL-PURPOSE INDICES

The index structures introduced so far can be used in a variety of situations. However, there are a number of index structures that are applicable only in very special cases, but can yield large savings in storage space and processing time. We consider two such techniques: bitmap and join indices.

11.7.1   Bitmap Indices

A **bitmap index** [O'Neil 1987] is implemented as one or more bit vectors. It is particularly appropriate for attributes that can take on only a small number of values—for example, the Sex attribute of the PERSON relation, which can take only two values: Male and Female. Suppose that PERSON has a total of 40,000 rows. A bitmap index on PERSON contains two bit vectors, one for each possible value of Sex, and each bit vector contains 40,000 bits, one for each row in PERSON. Thus, the ith bit in the Male bit vector is 1 if, in the ith row of PERSON, the Sex attribute has value Male. As a result, we can identify the row numbers of males by scanning the Male bit vector. Given the row number, we can calculate the offset from the beginning of the data file and find the desired row on disk by direct access.

Note that the space to store the example index is just 80,000 bits, or 10K bytes, which can fit handily in main memory. Because it is done entirely in main memory, searching such an index can be carried out quickly using sequential scan.

You may have noticed that bitmap indices seem to waste more space than they need to. Indeed, to encode the Sex attribute we use *two* bits, while only one bit suffices to encode all of its possible values. The reason for this is that bitmap indices are designed to trade space for efficiency, especially the efficiency of selecting on two or more attributes. To illustrate, suppose that our PERSON relation represents the result of a health survey and that there is an attribute Smoker and an attribute HasHeartDisease, both accepting just two values, Yes and No. One query might request the number of males in a certain age group who smoke but do not have heart disease. As part of this query, we have a selection with the following condition:

```
Sex = 'Male' AND Smoker = 'Yes' AND HasHeartDisease = 'No'
```

If all three attributes have bit indices, we can easily find rids of all tuples that satisfy this condition: Take the logical AND of the bit strings that correspond to the Male value of the Sex attribute, the Yes value of the Smoker attribute, and the No value of the HasHeartDisease attribute. The rids of the tuples that satisfy the condition correspond to the positions that have 1 in the resulting bit string.

More generally, bitmap indices can handle selection conditions that contain OR and NOT—all we have to do is compute an appropriate Boolean combination of the corresponding bit strings. For instance, suppose that the Age attribute has a bitmap index with 120 bit strings with a cost of 120 bits per PERSON record. This is quite acceptable, as a regular index will take at least 8 bytes (64 bits) per PERSON record anyway. Now we should be able to efficiently find all smoking males between the ages of 50 and 80 who never suffered from heart disease as follows: First compute the logical AND of the three bit strings as described above. Then compute the logical

OR of the bit strings corresponding to ages 50 to 80 in the bitmap index for the Age attribute. Finally, compute the logical AND of the two results. Again, the 1s in the final bit string give us the Ids of the records we need to answer the query.

Bitmap indices play an important role in data mining and OLAP (online analytical processing) applications, as discussed in Chapter 19. The reason for their popularity is that such applications typically deal with queries that select on low-cardinality attributes, such as sex, age, company locations, financial periods, and the like. It also has to do with the fact that these applications operate on data that is fairly static, and bitmap indices are expensive to maintain if the underlying data changes frequently (think of what it takes to update a bitmap index if records are inserted or deleted in the data file).

11.7.2 Join Indices

Suppose we want to speed up an equi-join of two relations, such as $\mathbf{p} \bowtie_{A=B} \mathbf{q}$. A **join index** [Valduriez 1987] is a collection that consists of all pairs of the form $\langle p, q \rangle$, where p is a rid of a tuple, t, in $\mathbf{p}$ and q is a rid of a tuple, s, in $\mathbf{q}$, such that $t.A = s.B$ (i.e., the two tuples join).

A join index is typically sorted lexicographically in ascending order of rids. Thus, the pair $\langle 3, 3 \rangle$ precedes the pair $\langle 4, 2 \rangle$. Such an index can also be organized as a B^+ tree or as a hash table. The values of the search key in the entries of a B^+ tree are the rids of the rows in $\mathbf{p}$. To find the rids of all rows of $\mathbf{q}$ that join with a row of $\mathbf{p}$ having rid p, one searches the tree using p. The leaf entries (if they exist) for p contain the requested rids. Similarly, a hash index hashes on p to find the bucket containing the entries for that rid. Those entries contain the rids of the rows in $\mathbf{q}$ that join with the row in $\mathbf{p}$ at rid p.

A join index can be thought of as a precomputed join that is stored in compact form. Although its computation might require that a regular join be performed first, its advantage (apart from its compact size) is that it can be maintained incrementally: When new tuples are added to $\mathbf{p}$ or $\mathbf{q}$, new index entries can be added to the join index without the entire join having to be recomputed from scratch (exercise 11.24).

Given a join index, $\mathcal{J}$, the system can compute $\mathbf{p} \bowtie_{A=B} \mathbf{q}$ simply by scanning $\mathcal{J}$ and finding the rids of $\mathbf{p}$ and $\mathbf{q}$ that match. Note that, if $\mathcal{J}$ is sorted on its $\mathbf{p}$ field, the rids corresponding to the tuples in $\mathbf{p}$ appear in ascending order. Therefore, the join is computed in one scan of the index and of $\mathbf{p}$. For each rid of a tuple in $\mathbf{q}$, one access to $\mathbf{q}$ is also needed.

Worth mentioning is one other variation on the join index, called a **bitmapped join index** [O'Neil and Graefe 1995]. Recall that a join index is typically organized as a sorted file, a hash table, or a B^+ tree in a way that makes it easy to find the rids of all rows of $\mathbf{q}$ that join with the row of $\mathbf{p}$ at rid p. We can combine these rids in $\mathbf{q}$ in the following (at first, unusual) way: For each rid p in $\mathbf{p}$, replace all tuples of the form $\langle p, q \rangle$ in $\mathcal{J}$ with a single tuple of the form

$$\langle p, \textit{bitmap for matching tuples in } \mathbf{q} \rangle$$

The bitmap here has 1 in the ith position if and only if the ith tuple in $\mathbf{q}$ joins with the tuple in $\mathbf{p}$ at the rid p. Attaching a bitmap might seem like a huge waste of space, because each bitmap has as many bits as there are tuples in $\mathbf{q}$. However, bitmaps are easily compressed, so this is not a major issue. On the other hand, bitmapped join indices can speed up multi-relational joins, as explained in Section 13.5, so the space–time trade-off might be justified.

11.8   TUNING ISSUES: CHOOSING INDICES FOR AN APPLICATION

Each type of index is capable of improving the performance of a particular category of queries. Hence, in choosing the indices to support a particular application it is important to know the queries that are likely to be executed and their approximate frequency. Adding an index to improve the performance of a rarely executed query is probably not wise, since each added index carries with it added overhead, particularly for operations that update the database.

For example, if query (11.2) on page 333, with the value of StudId specified as a parameter, is executed frequently, an index to ensure fast response might be called for. The search key for such an index is chosen from among the columns named in the WHERE clause (*not* the SELECT clause) because these are the columns that direct the search. In this case, an index on TRANSCRIPT with search key StudId is useful. Instead of scanning the entire table for rows in which the value of StudId is 111111111, the location mechanism finds the index entries containing the search key value. Each entry contains either the record or the rid of the record. Thus, while a scan requires that the system retrieve (on average) half the pages in the data file, access through the index requires only a single retrieval. On the other hand, an index on StudId is of no use in the execution of query (11.3) on page 333.

Suppose, however, that we need to support the query

```
SELECT    T.Grade
FROM      TRANSCRIPT T                                        (11.5)
WHERE     T.StudId = '111111111' AND T.Semester = 'F1997'
```

We might choose to create a multi-attribute index on StudId and Semester. If, however, we choose to limit ourselves to an index on a single attribute (perhaps to support other queries and avoid too many indices), which attribute should be its search key? Generally, the attribute that is most selective is chosen. If an index on StudId is created, the database system uses it to fetch all rows for the target student and then scans the result, retaining those rows for the target semester. This is more efficient than fetching all rows for the target semester, since there are likely to be many more rows for a given semester than for a given student. In general, columns that have only a few values in their domain (for example, Sex) are not likely to be very selective.

The following points provide some guidance in the choice of a search key:

1. A column used in a join condition might be indexed.
2. A clustered B^+ tree index on a column that is used in an ORDER BY clause makes it possible to retrieve rows in the specified order.

3. An index on a column that is a candidate key makes it possible to enforce the unique constraint efficiently.

4. A clustered B^+ tree index on a column used in a range search allows elements in a particular range to be quickly retrieved.

If the performance problem is one of throughput, we first have to identify the type of query causing the problem. One candidate is a query that is frequently invoked. Another is a long-running query that accesses many tables and does a significant amount of computation. In either case, once the problem query is identified, an appropriate index (or indices) can be added to speed its execution.

As we will see in Section 24.3.1, indices can also be used to improve performance by increasing the amount of allowable concurrency. Some concurrency controls use a locking protocol that involves locking index pages. The protocol can avoid locking an entire table if an appropriate index exists. Since locking an index is less restrictive than locking the entire table, such locks increase the number of database operations that can execute concurrently and thus improve performance. This type of performance improvement is sometimes the basis for index selection.

11.9 BIBLIOGRAPHIC NOTES

B-trees were introduced in [Bayer and McCreight 1972], and B^+ trees first appeared in [Knuth 1973]. The latest edition of that book, [Knuth 1998], contains much information on the material covered in this chapter. Hashing as a data structure was first discussed in [Peterson 1957]. Linear hashing was proposed in [Litwin 1980]; extendible hashing in [Fagin et al. 1979]. Index sequential files were analyzed in [Larson 1981].

Join indices were first proposed in [Valduriez 1987], and bitmap indices were first described in [O'Neil 1987]. Bitmapped join indices were introduced in [O'Neil and Graefe 1995].

11.10 EXERCISES

11.1 State the storage capacity, sector size, page size, seek time, rotational latency, and transfer time of the disk

a. On your local PC

b. On the server provided by your university

11.2 Explain the difference between an equality search and a range search.

11.3 a. Give an upper bound on the number of pages that must be looked at to perform a binary search for a particular name in the phone book for your city or town.

b. By how much is this number reduced if an index is prepared giving the name of the first entry on each page of the phone book? (Does that index fit on one page of the phone book?)

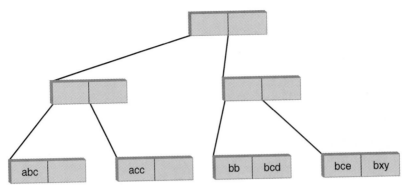

Figure 11.29 Partially specified B⁺ tree.

c. Conduct an experiment using your usual (informal) method to search for the name John Lewis in your local phone book, and compare the number of pages you look at with the number in exercise 3a.

11.4 Explain why a file can have only one clustered index.

11.5 Explain why a secondary, unclustered index must be dense.

11.6 Does the final structure of a B⁺ tree depend on the order in which the items are added to it? Explain your answer and give an example.

11.7 Starting with an empty B⁺ tree with up to two keys per node, show how the tree grows when the following keys are inserted one after another:

18, 10, 7, 14, 8, 9, 21

11.8 Consider the partially specified B⁺ tree in Figure 11.29.
   a. Fill in the internal nodes without adding new keys.
   b. Add the key bbb. Show how the tree changes.
   c. Delete the key abc from the result of (b). Show how the tree changes.

11.9 Consider the B⁺ tree in Figure 11.30. Suppose that it was obtained by inserting a key into a leaf node of some other tree, *causing a node split*. What was the original tree and the inserted key? Is the solution unique? Explain your answer.

11.10 Describe a search algorithm for a B⁺ tree in which the search key is not a candidate key. Assume that overflow pages are not used to handle duplicates.

11.11 Consider a hash function, h, that takes as an argument a value of a composite search key that is a sequence of r attributes, $a_1, a_2, \ldots, a_r$. If h has the form

$$h(a_1 \circ a_2 \circ \ldots \circ a_r) = h_1(a_1) \circ h_2(a_2) \circ \ldots \circ h_r(a_r)$$

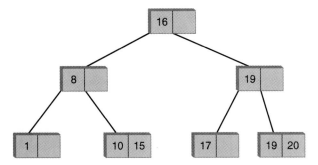

Figure 11.30 B$^+$ tree.

where h_i is a hash of attribute a_i and o is the concatenation operator, h is referred to as a **partitioned hash function**. Describe the advantages of such a function with respect to equality, partial key, and range searches.

11.12 Express the algorithm for insertion into a B$^+$ tree using pseudo-code.

11.13 Express the algorithm for deletion from a B$^+$ tree using pseudo-code.

11.14 Express the algorithm for insertion and deletion of index entries in the extendable hashing schema using pseudo-code.

11.15 Give examples of transactions that are

    a. Speeded up due to the addition of the B$^+$ tree index shown in Figure 11.21 on page 357.

    b. Slowed down due to the addition of the B$^+$ tree index shown in that figure.

11.16 Draw the B$^+$ tree that results from inserting `alice`, `betty`, `carol`, `debbie`, `edith`, and `zelda` into the index of Figure 11.21.

11.17 A particular table in a relational database contains 100,000 rows, each of which requires 200 bytes of memory. A SELECT statement returns all rows in the table that satisfy an equality search on a certain predicate. Estimate the time in milliseconds to complete the query when each of the following indices on that predicate is used. Make realistic estimates for page size, disk access time, and so forth.

    a. No index (heap file)

    b. A hash index (with no overflow pages)

    c. A B$^+$ tree index

11.18 Estimate the time in milliseconds to insert a new row into the table of the previous exercise when each of the following indices is used:

      a. No index (file sorted on the search key)

      b. A hash index (with no overflow pages)

      c. A B$^+$ tree index (with no node splitting required)

11.19 Estimate the time in milliseconds to update the search key value of a row in the table of exercise 11.17 when each of the following is used:

      a. No index (file sorted on the search key)

      b. A hash index (where the updated row goes in a different bucket than the original row's page, but no overflow pages are required)

      c. A B$^+$ tree index (where the updated row goes on a different page than the original row's pages, but no node splitting is required)

11.20 Estimate the amount of space required to store the B$^+$ tree of exercise 11.17 and compare that with the space required to store the table.

11.21 Explain what index types are supported by your local DBMS. Give the commands used to create each type.

11.22 Design the indices for the tables in the Student Registration System. Give the rationale for all design decisions (including those not to use indices in certain cases where they might be expected).

11.23 Explain the rationale for using fillfactors less than 1 in

      a. Sorted files

      b. ISAM indices

      c. B$^+$ tree indices

      d. Hash indices

11.24 Design an algorithm for maintaining join indices incrementally—that is, so that the addition of new tuples to the relations involved in the join do not require the entire join to be recomputed from scratch.

Chapter 12

Case Study: Completing the Student Registration System

Now that the Specification Document for the Student Registration System has been approved by the customer, we are ready to continue with the project. The next step is design.

12.1 THE DESIGN DOCUMENT

In contrast to specifications, which describe *what* the system is supposed to do, the design describes *how* the system is to do what it does. Thus, the design of a transaction processing system includes

- The declaration of every global data structure used in the system, including the database schema and any data structures kept by application programs between transaction invocations

- The decomposition of each interaction described in the Specification Document into transactions and procedures

- Detailed description of the behavior of every module, object, procedure, and transaction contained in the system

The results of the design phase are presented in a Design Document, which, in a sense, is an extension of the Specification Document. The Specification Document describes in detail the capabilities of the system, whereas the Design Document describes in detail how each of these capabilities is to be implemented.

The design process itself is often viewed as the most creative part of the implementation project. Good designs are simple and elegant. The designer formulates and evaluates various design alternatives to achieve the desired functionality (for example various table designs) and then, based on her judgment and experience, makes decisions that significantly influence the system implementation and its ultimate performance. Unfortunately, while making these decisions is the enjoyable part of the process, documenting the details in the Design Document is often one of the designer's more tedious (but nevertheless necessary) tasks.

Users of the Design Document include

- The coding group, who use it as their sole source of information in their coding

377

■ The quality control group, who use it, together with the Specification Document, to design tests and to determine what went wrong when an error is discovered

■ The maintenance group, who use it (at a later date) to implement enhancements to the system

An important part of the design process is to make all global decisions (i.e., those that affect multiple transactions and procedures) so that later, during the coding phase, each coder can implement each individual transaction or procedure with no knowledge of the overall system other than that provided in the Design Document. If the Design Document is incomplete to the extent that the coder of a particular transaction or procedure has to make a global decision, that decision is liable to be inconsistent with a decision made by the coder of another transaction or procedure about the same global issue—thus causing an error.

For example suppose an interaction, I, is decomposed into two transactions, T_1 and T_2, and that T_1 reads a database item, X, and saves its value in a variable, x, that is global to I. After T_1 commits, T_2 is initiated and uses the value of x, but unfortunately, the value of X might have been updated by the concurrent execution of another interaction. If T_2 assumes x has the current value of X, it might execute incorrectly.

During the design process, the global decision must be made as to whether this communication between T_1 and T_2 will be allowed or whether T_1 and T_2 should be combined into a single transaction. Perhaps, the designer will allow the communication, under the assumption that it is extremely unlikely that the communicated value will change between the execution of T_1 and T_2. For example, in the Student Registration System, X might be the semester Id. While it is possible that a concurrent interaction changes the semester Id, the designer might decide that the likelihood of this happening is so small that the value can be communicated in this way. The decision should be documented in the Design Document, so that it can be understood by the programmers and, if necessary, changed later if errors are reported and it is found that the assumption on which the decision was based is false.

12.1.1 The Document Structure

The sections of a design document for a transaction processing system might include

A. **Title, author(s), date, version number**

B. **Introduction**—a brief description of the goals of the system.

C. **Related documents**—references to the Requirements and Specification documents and to any other documents used in the design or implementation—for example, a Visual Basic user manual, an ODBC specification document, or a specification document for some object library used in the design.

D. **High-level design**—an informal description of the design so the reader can more easily follow the detailed descriptions in later sections. Among the items that might be included:

1. The decomposition of the system into modules or objects
2. The decomposition of the interactions defined in the Specification Document into transactions and procedures
3. A procedure calling tree
4. An E-R diagram for the database design, including the rationale for any choices made in designing the diagram

Also included in this section can be the rationale for any design decisions that need to be documented. Examples might include:

5. Why a session was decomposed into transactions in one way rather than in another, perhaps more intuitive, way
6. Why a table was normalized, denormalized, or fragmented[1] in a particular way, perhaps to meet some performance requirement
7. Why certain indices were defined
8. Why certain integrity constraints are to be checked by transactions rather than embedded in the database schema
9. Why certain transactions are allowed to execute at lower isolation levels
10. Any other decisions made to achieve performance requirements

E. **Declaration of the database schema and other global data structures**

1. *Database schema*
   a. The complete (compilable) set of statements that declare the database schema, including tables, indices, domain specifications, assertions, and access privileges—documented with the intended use of each table and column and the rationale for each index.
   b. A list of the integrity constraints, together with a description of where each constraint will be enforced: in the schema or by the individual transactions.

2. *Global Data structures*: The complete (compilable) declaration of any other global data structures; for example, those kept by an application program for use by the transactions it initiates. Each item must be documented with its intended use and any constraints on its values.

F. **Graphical user interface**—if an application generator had been used to design and implement the graphical user interface during the specification phase of the project and a description of that interface appears in the Specification Document, only a reference to the appropriate document section is needed.

---

[1] Fragmentation is discussed in Chapter 18.

Otherwise, any missing details of the user interface must be supplied here—including the specification of all events and objects (including their methods).

G. **Detailed description of transactions and procedures**—for each transaction and procedure,

1. *Transaction or procedure name*

2. *Description*—an informal, one-sentence description of what the transaction or procedure does. For example: "This transaction registers a student in a specified course, after checking that the prerequisites are satisfied." (The goal is to explain the general purpose of the transaction, not to give its detailed functional specification.)

3. *Arguments*—*in* and *out* arguments of the transaction or procedure. Each argument must be documented, with its type and intended use.

4. *Return Values*—the values that can be returned by the transaction or procedure, together with their type and intended use.

5. *Called from*—the procedures, or (GUI) events that call this transaction. (For example, a transaction might be called when a particular mouse-click event occurs on some form object.)

6. *Calls*—the procedures called by this transaction, including any events it causes and any exceptions it raises. (These last two items are useful when the design or code needs to be changed, and the designer or coder must propagate changes throughout the design.)

7. *Preconditions*—assumptions that the transaction or procedure can make (and does not have to check at run time) about the state of the database, the global data structure, and its arguments when it starts. For example, a transaction to register a student in a course might be able to assume that a previously executed transaction authenticated the student. As another example, a procedure invoked by a particular mouse-click event might be able to assume that an input value it needs was previously stored by the user in a particular field of a particular form object. (Most of the global errors in large system implementations occur because of miscommunication about preconditions.)

8. *Isolation Level*—the isolation level at which the transaction will execute.

9. *Actions*

   a. Textual description of the actions taken by the transaction or procedure. (Perhaps one or two paragraphs, compared to the one-sentence description given earlier—the goal here is to help the coder write the code.)

   b. Database tables and global data structures accessed, together with the changes the transaction or procedure is supposed to make. For example, after a successful registration transaction, the student must be listed in the appropriate table(s) as being registered for the course and the number of registrants for that course must be incremented.

c. Error situations

    i. Validity checks that the transaction or procedure must make about its arguments, the global data structure, or the database. For example, a transaction to register a student for a course might be required to check that the student has taken (or is taking) all the prerequisites for that course. Or a transaction accessing some field that is allowed to be null (for example, a registration transaction reading the course days and time) might be required to check that that field is not null at the time the transaction or procedure is executed. A description must be given of the actions to be taken when such a check fails.

    ii. Automatic constraint checks the system will make on the updates of this transaction and the actions to be taken if these updates fail.

    iii. Any other error or anomalous situations that might occur and the actions to be taken in each case. For example, what should happen if a database CONNECT statement fails? What exceptions should be raised and under what conditions?

d. Forms to be displayed in various circumstances—perhaps on successful completion or if some specified error situation occurs.

12.1.2 Design Review

Near the end of the design process, a formal **design review** is often held, in which all members of the design and quality assurance groups and perhaps some outside people participate. The participants are given the latest version of the Specification and Design documents before the review and are expected to have studied them before the meeting.

The designers make a formal presentation and the participants are expected to gain an understanding of the design and to identify issues such as:

■ Places where the Design Document is inconsistent with the Specification Document.

■ Places where the Design Document is incorrect, inconsistent, incomplete, or ambiguous.

■ Places where the efficiency of the design can be improved (perhaps by using a different table structure or a different indexing structure for a table).

■ Any areas of risk to the project in meeting its goals. For example, does a particular search algorithm meet the response time specifications? Does the design require a new version of a database driver that might not be available in time to meet the schedule? Does some suspect assumption underlie a global decision?

The goal of the design review is to identify issues, not resolve them. Each issue identified is assigned to a member of the design team for resolution by some specified date and for inclusion in a later version of the Design Document.

Any errors found during the design review are much easier and cheaper to correct than those found later, during the coding or testing phases. Errors found after the system has been delivered to the customer are still more expensive to correct.

The design review meeting might also include a review of the Test Plan, as described in the next section.

12.2   TEST PLAN

Testing is an important part of all software projects, not an informal ad hoc activity that the testers begin to think about only when the coding is complete. It is carried out in accordance with a formal Test Plan document, which is prepared during the design and coding phases of the project. The Test Plan document specifies the tests to be performed, the test data to be used, and the design of any test driver or scripting software needed to perform the tests.

The complete Test Plan might involve **module tests** performed by the coder of each individual module before the module is submitted for integration into the system, **integration tests** performed by the group that is integrating the modules into the system, and finally the **QA test set** performed by the quality assurance group on the completely integrated system.

We focus our attention on the final QA test set, but we first note an important aspect of module testing—testing the individual SQL statements within the module. These tests might include **code checks**, in which a colleague examines each SQL statement to verify that it satisfies its English-language specifications, as well as more conventional tests in which the SQL statements are executed against actual or test databases.

The design of an appropriate QA test set for a commercial transaction processing system is a significant endeavor. The test set might include tests designed using two different approaches.

Black box tests are designed from the Specification Document, without looking at the Design Document or the code. They assume that the system is just a "black box" and do not look inside. The goal is to verify that the system meets its specifications. Thus there must be at least one test for every specification in the Specification Document (including error situations). Some specifications might have several tests. For example, to test that the number of students registered for a course does not exceed the specified maximum, the designer might include tests in which a registration transaction is executed when the number of previously registered students is both one less than the maximum and exactly the maximum. The test should also include cases in which the number is far from the maximum. (What happens if the maximum is specified as 0 or 1?) Since it is impractical to include tests where the number of previously registered students and the maximum number of students both range over all possible integers (a completely exhaustive set of tests), the designer must use her experience to develop a test set that is representative of situations that might occur, meets the appropriate boundary conditions, and can be performed in the allotted testing time.

Because the user interface is specified in the Specification Document, the black box tests must test the user interface.

Glass box tests are designed using the Design Document and the code. They are called "glass box" because they look inside the system. The goal is to verify that the detailed coding is correct. Thus, glass box tests should visit every line of code, take every branch of the code, check the boundary conditions of every loop, invoke every event, execute every integrity check, and exercise all aspects of every algorithm. For example, the code to check whether a student has all the prerequisites for a course might contain a while loop, and the test designer might include tests to verify that the exit condition of that loop is correct. Note that the existence of this while loop and its exit condition is not evident from the Specification Document, which is why we need glass box tests in addition to black box tests. However, we also need black box tests since the designers might have misunderstood some portion of the Specification Document, and any test set based only on the Design Document would not find such errors. For example, a glass box text might show that the exit condition of a while loop corresponds to the Design Document, but the Design Document might be an incorrect interpretation of the specification.

The Test Plan might also include **stress tests** in which a (perhaps simulated) realistic load is placed on the system to verify that it meets its specifications for transaction throughput and response time. Such tests might uncover situations in which a large number of deadlocks occur or in which the database design needs tuning for other reasons to increase throughput or decrease response time.

If the application is built on a system that guarantees the ACID properties, we do not need additional tests to verify that the concurrent execution of transactions works correctly, assuming that we have already tested that each transaction works correctly when executed in isolation. However, if the application is being executed at some level of isolation less than SERIALIZABLE (see Section 10.2.3), additional tests might be necessary to ensure correctness under concurrent execution.

Often neglected in a Test Plan is testing the User Manual (and other deliverable documentation) to ensure that it corresponds to the specifications and to the delivered system.

The Test Plan document contains a script of all tests that are to be performed and the correct result of each. Since the Test Plan contains a large number of tests and must be executed many times during the testing and maintenance phases (after fixing some error or adding some new feature), it is highly desirable to employ a test driver or scripting mechanism to automate the Test Plan execution. If such a mechanism is used, the Test Plan document contains the appropriate inputs to the test driver. If a test driver is to be implemented as part of the project, its design must also be included.

The Test Plan document also contains a description of the testing protocol that will be used by the testers when performing the tests (or a reference to the company's standard testing protocol document). That protocol should include an **Error**

Report Form, which must be filled out when an error is found. The Error Report should include the tester's name, the date, the error description, and, most important, a detailed description of how to recreate the situation in which the error occurs. The Error Report is passed on to the person responsible for fixing the error, who fills in information about when and how the error was fixed and which version of the code contains the fix. The entire protocol must ensure that all errors that are found are eventually fixed and that some version of the code contains all of the fixes.

To design a Test Plan that is comprehensive (in the sense just described) and yet manageable takes a considerable amount of skill and experience. The actual size of the test set and the scope of the testing effort for any particular application are often marketing as well as technical decisions, dependent on a number of sometimes conflicting factors. For example,

■ How critical is the correctness of the system? Are people's lives at stake?

■ How important is time to market of the system? Is a competitive product about to be released or a trade show upcoming at which the system must be exhibited?

In some critical applications, half of the entire time allocated to the project is devoted to testing. Sometimes issues of professional ethics arise when management applies pressure to release an inadequately tested product.

In applications in which the system is being implemented by one group and delivered to another group, which will operate and maintain it, the test set, together with any drivers or scripting mechanisms, is often one of the deliverables, along with the code and the documentation.

Acceptance testing and beta testing.   In addition to the Test Plan, which is prepared and carried out by the system implementors, the customer often prepares and carries out an **acceptance test** before accepting the system (and perhaps making the final payment for it). An acceptance test is usually composed of realistic inputs and an actual customer database (in contrast with the implementor's Test Plan, which often involves boundary case inputs and test databases) and is intended to increase customer confidence that the system will fulfill its purpose. A savvy customer will spend considerable effort to design an acceptance test that comprehensively exercises the system in real-world situations.

If the system is a product with many customers, a small set of these customers is often selected to perform **beta testing**. In this context, the testing performed by the system implementors is called **alpha testing**. When the alpha testing has completed, the **beta test version** is supplied to customers, who use it on their actual applications and report any errors to the implementors. Because the beta test version might still contain serious errors, the customer might be at some risk in using it (implementation groups have been known to minimize the amount of alpha testing and rely on beta testing to find many of the errors in their system), but the customer gets the benefits of receiving an early version and might receive some other financial or technical incentives as well. The beta testing continues for some period of time, after which the initial release of the system is made to all customers.

Even after all of this testing, customers with critical applications often run a new system in parallel with their existing system for some period of time until they gain sufficient confidence that it can do its job reliably and correctly.

12.3 PROJECT PLANNING

Project planning is another important part of software engineering. While the Specification Document is being prepared, the project manager makes an initial version of the Project Plan. To make such a plan, the manager divides the project into a set of **tasks**, estimates the time required to complete each task, and then assigns each task to a specific person (or group) together with targeted start and completion dates.

A task might involve design, coding, testing, or documentation, but it must have the property that its completion can be precisely defined—for example, "The coding of module 3 is complete," not "Module 4 is 90% debugged." Estimating the time to complete a given task is quite difficult and requires understanding the complexity of the task and relating that complexity to the skill of the person assigned to carry it out.

An essential aspect of task scheduling is **task dependency**: Certain tasks cannot be started until certain others have completed. For example, the testing of a module cannot begin until its coding is finished.

Given the dependencies and estimated duration of tasks, a **Dependency Chart**, sometimes called a **PERT Chart** (Program Evaluation and Review Technique), can be constructed, as shown in Figure 12.1. Activities are represented by rectangles with the duration written above (sometimes maximal and minimal estimates of task duration are included), and dependencies represented by arcs. In this way, the chart shows which tasks can be done in parallel and which must be done sequentially. The longest path through this chart from start to end is called the **critical path** and is an estimate of the minimum time required to complete the project.

Other charts used to document the Project Plan include the following:

■ An **Activity Chart**, sometimes called a **Gantt chart** (named after its developer, Henry Gantt)—a bar chart showing when tasks are scheduled to start and complete (see Figure 12.2)

■ A **Staff Allocation Chart**—a bar chart showing the assignments of individual staff members to specific tasks, together with the scheduled start and completion dates (see Figure 12.3)

As the project proceeds, the project manager schedules periodic (perhaps weekly) project meetings at which implementation team members report on the status and expected completion date of each assigned task, compared with its scheduled completion date in the Project Plan. The project manager should encourage an environment in which team members feel comfortable in honestly reporting

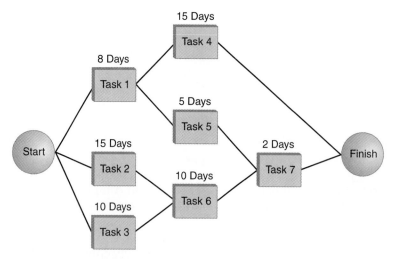

Figure 12.1 Dependency chart.

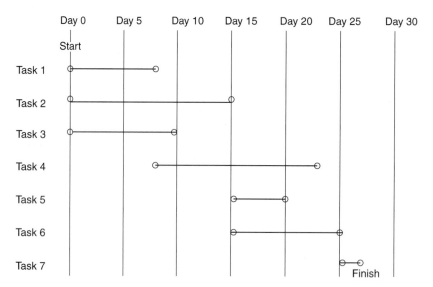

Figure 12.2 Activity chart.

when they are having trouble with their assigned task and might not be able to complete it on schedule. If necessary, the project manager then makes the appropriate decisions to ensure that the project completes on time. Tasks on the critical path must be monitored especially carefully. (Often the best people on the staff are assigned to them.) It is particularly important that minutes be kept of these meetings to document any decisions taken and any assignments made.

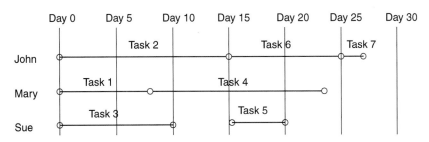

Figure 12.3 Staff allocation chart.

When the project is completed, many project managers hold a windup meeting with the entire team to discuss what went right and wrong with the planning and other aspects of the project. The goal is to learn from any mistakes and to increase the software engineering skills of the manager and the team members.

Although project management software is available to automate the production of project planning charts, the preparation and monitoring of a Project Plan require a considerable amount of skill and experience. Indeed, the main reason many software projects fail or are late is the lack of skill of the project manager in project planning and monitoring.

12.4 CODING

In most software projects, the time allocated for the coding phase is less than one-sixth of that allocated for the entire project. That fraction will become even smaller as application generators and reusable object libraries automate the production of code directly from the design.

A well-run IT department should have coding guidelines that every programmer follows. These guidelines vary from company to company, but there are many common rules. Some programming languages, such as Java, have their own coding styles, but this is usually only a small portion of what a typical set of coding standards mandates. One well-known example of such a set is known as the GNU Coding Guidelines [Stallman 2000]. Here we include some hints for producing professional quality code.

■ The two highest priorities in coding are *correctness* and *clarity*.[2] In addition to being correct, the code must be understandable to the large number of people (such as the quality assurance and maintenance groups) who will read it over its lifetime.

■ All of the coders should use the same style of variable definitions, indentation, and the like. Good text editors and integrated development systems provide tools for automatically indenting programs according to certain rules. The program for the entire system should look as if it had been written by a single coder.

---

[2] The third *c*, *cleverness*, has the lowest priority.

■ Variables and procedures should have application-oriented names that make their use self-evident—For example, not S, or Stu, or even Student, but Student_ Name or Student_ID_Number.

■ The use of comments

❏ The code for each module, procedure, and transaction should begin with a **preamble**, which is the same as its detailed description in the Design Document and can also include the author, date, and revision number. Some guidelines require that a **revision history** be included in the program file, which can include entries such as

```
1999-12-12: Mary Doe (md@company.com)
  foo.java (checkAll): added capability to check userids
1998-03-22: John Public (jp@company.com)
  foo.java (checkCredentials): fixed bug in while loop
```

However, keeping the revision history inside program files has become obsolete due to the development of sophisticated version control systems and as the complexity of software projects continues to increase. A better approach is to keep the revision history for all files in the same directory in a separate file, often called ChangeLog, which allows the developers to see the changes made to all files in one place and in chronological order. This style is superior when there are dependencies between the code in different files in the same directory. The history of individual files can typically be obtained from the version control system, which is a better place to keep it than inside the program file.

❏ Comments within a module, procedure, and transaction should be application oriented. For example, the following comment is useless

```
/* Increment number_registered */
number_registered = number_registered+1;
```

because it is self-evident from the code. If this line of code were part of the registration transaction and needed to be documented at all, a better comment might be

```
/* Another student has registered */
```

Not every statement needs to be commented. Some programming style books suggest that all loop and conditional statements be commented. For example, comments for a loop and conditional statement, respectively, might be

```
/* Give all employees making ≤ $10,000 a 5% raise. */
```

or

```
/* If the customer has exceeded the credit limit,
** then abort transaction. */
```

CASE
STUDY

❏ When the program needs to be changed because of bug fixes or enhancements, the appropriate comments should be updated along with the code.

■ System-specific data structures and code should be clearly documented as such. For example, some vendors supply their own version of the embedded SQL CONNECT statement

```
EXEC SQL CONNECT student_database IDENTIFIED BY pml
    DBMS_PASSWORD = 'z9t.56';
    /* ***System Specific: Ingres version of CONNECT */
```

Then, if the system must be ported to a different DBMS at some future time, the system-specific statements can be easily found with a text editor. If the CONNECT statement appears several times in the system, it can be encapsulated within a procedure, which can be called at the appropriate points. Then if the system must be ported, only the body of that procedure need be changed.

Prototype coding.   We have sharply differentiated the coding phase of the project from the requirements analysis and design phases. However, in practice prototypes of parts of the system are often coded during the earlier phases in order to aid in decision making. For example, in a transaction processing system implementation the following prototypes might be necessary:

During the Requirements Analysis Phase

■ Prototype of the user interface to evaluate its clarity and usability and to incorporate customer feedback.

■ Prototype of the DBMS access code to compare the relative speeds of various design choices—for example, stored procedures compared with those stored within the application program. These experiments can also be used to validate the specification of the expected transaction throughput of the final system, or they might be used to evaluate (and perhaps reduce) the time required to perform these tasks in the coding and testing phases.

During the Design Phase

■ Prototypes of possible designs for a specific table to evaluate the effect of various indexing schemes on the time required to execute particular SELECT or UPDATE statements.

■ Prototypes of other parts of the design to evaluate and reduce the risk involved in certain design decisions.

Sometimes this prototype code is later discarded. Sometimes it is used in the production version.

12.5   INCREMENTAL DEVELOPMENT

Most large implementation projects take several years to complete. During that time, the goals and needs of the enterprise sponsoring the project might change considerably. Therefore during the course of the project, the managers of the enterprise might request significant changes in the specifications of the system being built. An important issue is how the implementation team responds to such requests.

One approach is to continue building the system as originally specified. Unfortunately, even if the project is successfully completed, the resulting system might not completely satisfy the needs of the enterprise. Of course, implementation of the next version of the system, including some or all of the requested changes, can start as soon as the first version is completed and hopefully can be completed in a relatively short time.

Another approach is to try to keep up with the managers' requests, changing the specifications, design, and code many times during the project. Unfortunately, the project is often never successfully completed—the design is continuously being revised, the code is constantly being rewritten, and the project gets further and further behind schedule, with more and more money required to keep it going, until finally it is canceled. According to the Standish Group report, 31% of all information system projects are canceled before they are completed. Successful use of this approach requires discipline in limiting the number and scope of changes allowed and skill in negotiating with management on budget increases and schedule extensions.

Still another approach, called **incremental development**, involves building the system in stages. First a **core version** of the system is built based on a subset of the initial specifications, which can be implemented in a short period of time. Then successive versions are built, each including more of the specified functionality and some of the changes that the managers have requested, based on both the changed needs of the enterprise and the experience gained from running the previous versions. After several such incremental versions have been built, the system includes most of the requirements. Of course, it never includes all the requirements, since the managers tend to continually revise them.

The incremental approach is often better than the other two approaches. Risk is minimized because an operational system is available in a relatively short period of time, and any enhancements to it can be based on working experience. A potential disadvantage is that, unless the initial design is carefully done, design decisions made for early versions might be inappropriate for the increased functionality of later versions. Then the designers have the choice of changing the design (and rewriting large parts of the code) or using the old design, which might lead to an inefficient system.

Unfortunately, some designers use the incremental approach as an excuse to do no design at all and just hack together each version on top of the previous one. Needless to say, that approach can lead to disaster.

12.6 DESIGN AND CODE FOR THE STUDENT REGISTRATION SYSTEM

In Section 5.7, we discussed the design of the tables and some simple constraints suitable for the Student Registration System. In this section, we complete the design

by providing details of the more complex constraints and part of the code for the
registration transaction.

12.6.1 Completing the Database Design: Integrity Constraints

An important part of database design is listing the database integrity constraints
and deciding how each will be checked: automatically by the DBMS (in a CREATE
TABLE, CREATE ASSERTION, or CREATE TRIGGER statement) or in one or more of the
transactions. In the initial database design in Section 5.7, we did not fully discuss
this issue because we had not yet introduced some needed SQL constructs.

The following is a list of the database integrity constraints showing where each
is enforced: in the schema (shown in Figures 5.15, 5.16, and 12.4 on pages 116,
117, 393) or in the individual transactions. They are the same as those given in
the Requirements Document in Section 3.2, except that they have been expanded
to specify the attributes and tables involved in each constraint.

■ *Uniqueness of Ids.* Each Id in the STUDENT table, each Id in the FACULTY table,
and each CrsCode in the COURSE table must be unique. This is enforced by the
primary key constraints in the corresponding tables, as described in Section 5.7.

■ *If a student is listed as registered for a course in some semester/year, that course must
be offered at that time.* If a tuple exists in the TRANSCRIPT table with a particular
CrsCode, Semester, and Year, there must be a tuple in the CLASS table with that
CrsCode, Semester, and Year. This is enforced by the registration transaction,
Register(), in Section 12.6.3.

■ *Enforcement of the enrollment limit.* The value of the Enrollment attribute for a
tuple in the CLASS table cannot be larger than the value of the MaxEnrollment
attribute for that same tuple. This is enforced by a CHECK constraint in the CLASS
table, Section 5.7.

■ *Enrollment consistency.* The value of the Enrollment attribute for a class in the
CLASS table must be equal to the number of tuples in the TRANSCRIPT table
corresponding to students who have registered in that class for that semester and
year. This is enforced by the ENROLLMENTCONSISTENCY assertion in Figure 12.4.

■ *An instructor cannot be assigned to two courses taught at the same time in the
same semester.* Two tuples in the CLASS table cannot have the same ClassTime,
Semester, Year, and InstructorId. This is enforced by a UNIQUE constraint in
the CLASS table in Section 5.7.

■ *Two courses cannot be taught in the same room at the same time in the same semester.*
Two tuples in the CLASS table cannot have the same ClassroomId, Semester,
Year, and ClassTime. This is enforced by a UNIQUE constraint in the CLASS table
in Section 5.7.

■ *Students enrolled in a course must have completed all the prerequisites for it with a grade
of C or higher.* For each tuple, t_i, in the TRANSCRIPT table with attributes StudId,
CrsCode, Semester, and Year, if there are any tuples, t_r, in the REQUIRES table

with that same CrsCode value and the value of EnforcedSince preceding the semester designated in t_i then for each such t_r, there must be a tuple, t_n, in the TRANSCRIPT table with the same value of StudId, a CrsCode value equal to the value of the PrereqCrsCode attribute of t_r, an earlier value of Semester and Year, and a Grade of at least C. This is enforced by a call to the checkPrerequisites() method in the registration transaction in Section 12.6.3.

■ *A student cannot be registered for different courses taught at the same hour.* No pair of tuples in the TRANSCRIPT table with the same StudId can have values of CrsCode, SectionNo, Semester, and Year attributes, such that the tuples with the corresponding values of CrsCode, SectionNo, Semester, and Year attributes in the CLASS table have the same ClassTime. This constraint is not shown and is left as an exercise.

■ *A student cannot be registered for more than 20 credits in any given semester.* Let S be a set of all tuples in TRANSCRIPT having the same values in attributes StudId, Semester, and Year. Then the sum of the values of the CreditHours attribute in the COURSE table corresponding to the CrsCode values in tuples in S must be less than or equal to 20. This is enforced by a call to the method checkRegisteredCredits() in the registration transaction in Section 12.6.3.

■ *The room assigned to a course must have at least as many seats as the maximum allowed enrollment for the course.* If *cl* and *cr* are tuples in tables CLASS and CLASSROOM, respectively, with the same value of ClassroomId, then the value of MaxEnrollment in *cl* is less than or equal to the value of Seats in *cr*. This is enforced by the ROOMADEQUACY assertion, in Figure 12.4.

■ *A valid letter grade cannot be changed to an Incomplete.* Once a value of A, B, C, D, or F has been assigned to a Grade attribute in a tuple in the TRANSCRIPT table, it cannot be changed later to an I. This is enforced by the CANTCHANGEGRADEToI trigger in Figure 12.4.

Figure 12.4 completes the database design by defining the assertions and trigger portion of the schema.

12.6.2 Design of the Registration Transaction

We now present a design for the registration transaction in the format given in part G of Section 12.1.1. When a student wants to register for a particular course, she starts an application, which presents a GUI with a choice of courses offered in the next semester. When a particular course is selected, the GUI creates an instance object of the Java class ClassTable on page 396 using the constructor ClassTable(). Then, when the student presses the registration button on the GUI, the registration transaction (whose code is in the body of the Register() method of that class) is invoked on the new object.

1. **Transaction name**

```
public int Register(Connection con, String sid)
```

Figure 12.4 Some Constraints for the Student Registration System.

```
CREATE ASSERTION  ROOMADEQUACY
    CHECK ( NOT EXISTS (SELECT *
                        FROM CLASS C, CLASSROOM R
                        WHERE C.MaxEnrollment > R.Seats
                            AND C.ClassroomId = R.ClassroomId ) )


CREATE ASSERTION  ENROLLMENTCONSISTENCY
    CHECK (
        NOT EXISTS (SELECT *
                    FROM CLASS C
                    WHERE C.Year = EXTRACT(YEAR FROM CURRENT_DATE)
                        -- current_semester() is a user-defined function
                        AND C.Semester = current_semester()
                        AND C.Enrollment <>
                            (SELECT COUNT( * )
                            FROM TRANSCRIPT T
                            WHERE T.CrsCode = C.CrsCode
                                AND T.Year = C.Year
                                AND T.Semester = C.Semester)


CREATE TRIGGER  CANTCHANGEGRADETOI
    AFTER UPDATE OF Grade ON TRANSCRIPT
    REFERENCING  OLD AS O
                 NEW AS N
    FOR EACH ROW
    WHEN  (O.Grade IN ('A','B','C','D','F') AND N.Grade = 'I')
        ROLLBACK
```

This transaction is implemented as a method of class ClassTable. It is invoked on concrete instances of that class. The variables courseId and sectionNo are set by the class constructor, ClassTable(), to correspond to a particular class offering.

2. **Description**—This transaction registers a student in a course, after making a number of checks on the validity of the registration.

3. **Arguments**

   a. Connection con—the identifier of the database connection

   b. String sid—the Id of the student registering

4. **Return values**

   a. If registration is successful, returns the constant OK.

   b. If any of the checks described in **Actions**, below, fails, returns a string corresponding to the nature of the failure.

   c. If any database operation fails, returns the user-defined constant `FAIL`.

5. **Called from**—not relevant here because we do not give the complete design with the names of the other classes and methods.

6. **Calls**

   a. `checkCourseOffering()`

   b. `checkCourseTaken()`

   c. `checkTimeConflict()`

   d. `checkRegisteredCredits()`

   e. `checkPrerequisites()`

   f. `addRegisterInfo()`

   The first five of these procedures performs the checks described under **Actions**, below. If all the checks succeed, the last procedure updates the database to complete the registration.

7. **Preconditions**

   a. The student whose Id is contained in the argument `sid` has been authenticated.

   b. The database has been opened, and the connection `con` has been created.

   c. The JDBC method `setAutoCommit(false)` has been executed on the connection.

8. **Isolation level**—SERIALIZABLE: Set using the call to
`setTransactionIsolation(Connection.TRANSACTION_SERIALIZABLE)`

9. **Actions**

   a. **Textual description**

     i. The transaction checks that

       a. The course is offered the following semester.

       b. The student is not already registered for the course, is not currently enrolled in the course, and has not completed the course with a grade of C or better.

       c. The student is not already registered for another course scheduled at the same time.

       d. The total number of credits taken by the student the following semester will not exceed 20.

       e. The student has completed all of the prerequisites for the course with a grade of C or better (or is currently enrolled in some prerequisites).

     ii. If the student satisfies all of the checks, the transaction completes the registration by adding a new tuple for that student and class to the TRANSCRIPT table and incrementing the `Enrollment` attribute for that class in the CLASS table. It then commits and returns with status `OK`.

b. **Tables accessed**
  i. For the checks: STUDENT, COURSE, REQUIRES, CLASS, TRANSCRIPT
  ii. For the updates: TRANSCRIPT, CLASS

c. **Error situations**
  i. Validity checks
    If any of the checks described in **Actions** fails, the transaction aborts and returns with a status that identifies the failure. For example, if the student has already taken the course with a grade of C or better, the method checkCourseTaken() returns the user-defined constant Course-Taken as a status and the Register() transaction then returns with that status. Likewise, if a scheduling time conflict has been detected, the method checkTimeConflict() returns TimeConflict and the transaction then returns with that status. The calling method is responsible for producing an appropriate error message.
  ii. Automatic constraint checks performed by the system
    The number of students registered must not exceed the maximum allowable enrollment, MaxEnrollment, for the course. (This is enforced by an assertion.) If this check fails, the transaction is aborted by the DBMS and the calling procedure is responsible for producing an appropriate message.
  iii. Other anomalous situations
    If any database operation fails, the transaction aborts and returns FAIL. The calling procedure is responsible for producing an appropriate error message.

12.6.3 Partial Code for the Registration Transaction

The example that follows shows part of the Java program for the registration transaction. The program defines class ClassTable and, in particular, its key method Register(), which specifies the course registration transaction. In addition, the example provides the code for one consistency checking method, checkCourseTaken(), but omits the others, which are similar.

The method has been structured to make it easy to code and understand. First the required checks are performed to see if the requested registration is allowed. Each check is made by a separate procedure. If all of the tests succeed, the tables are updated by the procedure addRegisterInfo(). If the updates succeed, the transaction commits. The bulk of the database actions performed by the check and update procedures can be implemented as stored procedures on the database server.

As the design specifies, all error and success messages are produced not by the registration transaction but by the GUI program that calls the registration transaction, based on the value the transaction returns. This design has advantages because it allows the system to be implemented in a two- or three-tiered architecture consisting of a presentation server, which contains programs that manage the displays on the screen, and an application server, which contains the application programs that do the actual work. (We discuss the multitier architecture of transactions in

Chapter 22.) Using a three-tiered architecture for the Student Registration System, the GUI program executes on the presentation server, the register method executes on the application server, and the procedures listed in item G.6 (page 380) of the Design Document are stored procedures executed at the database server.

```java
public class ClassTable
{
    private String courseId;       // The course Id of the class
    private String sectionNo;      // The section number of the class
    ... ... ...
    // General return codes
    final public static int FAIL = -1;
    final public static int OK = 0;
    // Return codes for the various consistency checks
    final public static int CourseNotOffered = 1;
    final public static int CourseTaken = 2;
    final public static int TimeConflict = 3;
    final public static int TooManyCredits = 4;
    final public static int PrerequisiteFailure = 5;

    // The class constructor
    public ClassTable(String courseId, String sectionNo)
    {
        this.courseId = courseId;
        this.sectionNo = sectionNo;
    }

    // The registration transaction
    public int Register(Connection con, String sid)
    {
        int status = OK;          // return code of check*Status() methods
        int addResult = OK;       // return code of addRegisterInfo()

        try {
            // Make all the required consistency checks
            if ((status = checkCourseOffering(con,sid)) != OK) {
                con.rollback();        // Course not offered
                return status;
            } else if ((status = checkCourseTaken(con,sid)) != OK) {
                con.rollback();        // Course already taken
                return status;
            } else if ((status = checkTimeConflict(con,sid)) != OK) {
                con.rollback();        // Time conflict found
                return status;
            } else if ((status = checkRegisteredCredits(con,sid)) != OK) {
                con.rollback();        // Too many credits
```

```
    return status;
  } else if ((status = checkPrerequisites(con,sid)) != OK) {
    con.rollback();        // Lacks prerequisites
    return status;
  }
  // Consistency checks OK. Update tables now
  if ((addResult = addRegisterInfo(con,sid)) != OK) {
    // Failed to update tables—rollback
    con.rollback();
    return FAIL;
  }
  // Registration succeeded
  con.commit();
  return OK;
} catch (SQLException sqle) {
  // Catches exceptions raised during execution of commit or rollback
  return FAIL;
}    // try-catch

}    // Register()
```

The following program is an implementation of one of the checks performed in Register()—a check for whether the student has already taken the course and received a satisfactory grade.

```
// Another method of class ClassTable
private int checkCourseTaken (Connection con, String sid)
{
  // Construct the SQL command. Observe the use of single quotes
  // and spaces to produce a valid SQL statement
  // Also note: courseId is a variable defined in class ClassTable
  String SQLStatement = "select CrsCode from Transcript"
            + " where StudId ='" + sid
            + "' and CrsCode ='" + courseId
            + "' and Grade in ('A','B','C',NULL)";
  Statement stmt;
  try {
    stmt = con.createStatement();
    ResultSet rs = stmt.executeQuery(SQLStatement);
    // If the result set is non-empty, course has been taken
    if (rs.next()) {
      // course has been taken
      stmt.close();
      return CourseTaken;
    }
    // course has not been taken
    stmt.close();
```

```
      return OK;
  } catch(SQLException sqle) {
      // catches exceptions raised during execution of SELECT
      return FAIL;
  }    // try-catch
} // end of checkCourseTaken()
```

    // Other methods of class ClassTable are defined here

    ... ...
}   // end of class definition for ClassTable

12.7   BIBLIOGRAPHIC NOTES

Many of the issues in this chapter are discussed in greater detail in standard
software engineering texts such as [Summerville 1996, Pressman 1997, Schach
1990]. The particular issues involved in modeling and designing databases and
transaction processing applications are discussed in [Blaha and Premerlani 1998].

12.8   EXERCISES

12.1 Prepare a Design Document and Test Plan for a simple calculator.

12.2 a. Explain why black box testing cannot usually test all aspects of the
      specifications.

      b. Explain why glass box testing cannot usually test all execution paths
      through the code. (This does not mean that glass box testing cannot visit
      all lines and take all branches of the code.)

12.3 Explain why concurrent systems (such as operating systems) are difficult to
      test. Explain why transaction processing applications, even though they are
      concurrent, do not have these same difficulties.

12.4 Explain the advantages of incremental system development from the view-
      point of

      a. The managers of the enterprise sponsoring the project

      b. The project manager

      c. The implementation team

12.5 In the design of the registration transaction given in Section 12.6.2, some of
      the required checks are performed in the schema and some in the transaction
      program.

      a. Which of the checks performed in the program can be performed in the
      schema?

      b. For each such check, change the schema to perform that check.

12.6 Rewrite the program for the registration transaction in Section 12.6.3

    a. Using stored procedures for the procedures that perform the registration checks

    b. Using one stored procedure that performs all of the checks that are performed by individual procedures in the figure

    c. In C and embedded SQL

    d. In C and ODBC

12.7 Evaluate the coding style used in the program for the registration transaction in Section 12.6.3.

12.8 Prepare a test plan for the registration transaction given in Section 12.6.2.

12.9 For the deregistration transaction in the Student Registration System

    a. Prepare a design

    b. Write a program

    c. Prepare a test plan

Chapter 13

The Basics of Query Processing

An understanding of the principles and methods of query processing can help application designers produce better systems. In this chapter, we examine the methods used to evaluate the basic relational operators and discuss their impact on physical database design. Chapter 14 will deal with the more advanced part of query processing: query optimization.

13.1 EXTERNAL SORTING

Sorting is an important part of many algorithms used in computer programming and is at the very core of the algorithms that support relational operations. For instance, sorting is one of the most efficient ways to get rid of duplicate tuples, and is also the basis of some join algorithms. The sorting algorithms used to process queries in relational DBMSs are not the ones you might have studied in a basic algorithms course. The latter are designed to perform sorting when all data is stored in main memory, which usually cannot be assumed in the database context. When files are large and are kept in external storage, such as a disk, we use what is called **external sorting**.

The main idea behind external sorting is to bring portions of the file into main memory, sort them using one of the known in-memory algorithms (e.g., Quicksort), and then dump the result back to disk. This creates partially sorted file segments, which must be merged in order to create a single sorted file. Because the time to execute an I/O operation is several orders of magnitude greater than the time to execute an instruction, it is assumed that the cost of I/O dominates the cost of in-memory sorting. Hence, the computational complexity of external sorting is often measured only in the number of disk reads and writes. A typical external sorting algorithm consists of two stages: *partial sorting* and *merging*.

Partial sorting. The partial sorting stage is very simple. Suppose that we have a buffer in main memory that can accommodate M pages available for sorting and that the file has F pages. F is typically much larger than M. The first-stage algorithm is as follows:

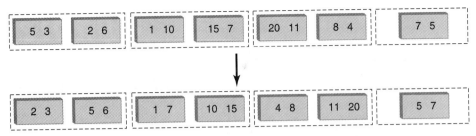

Figure 13.1 Partial Sorting of a file, $M = 2$, $F = 7$.

> **do** {
>   *read* M pages from disk into main memory
>   *sort* them in memory with one of the known methods (assume
>   that, apart from the M-page buffer, additional
>   memory is available for in-memory sorting)
>   *dump* the sorted file segment into a *new* file
> } **until** (end-of-file)

We use the term **run** to refer to a sorted file segment produced by one iteration of the above loop. The size of a run is the number of pages in the segment. Thus, the first stage produces $\lceil F/M \rceil$ sorted runs at the cost of $2F$ disk I/O operations (for simplicity, we assume that each I/O operation transfers exactly one page to or from main memory). (The symbol $\lceil\ \rceil$ here denotes the operation of rounding up to the nearest integer that is greater than or equal to F/M.) The partial sorting stage is illustrated in Figure 13.1, in which we assume that each block contains two records.

***k*-way merging.**   The next stage of the algorithm takes the sorted runs and merges them into larger sorted runs. This process can be repeated until we end up with just one sorted run, which is our final goal: the sorted version of the original file. A k-way merge algorithm takes k sorted runs of size R pages and produces one of size kR, as illustrated in Figure 13.2. The actual algorithm works as follows:

> **while** (there are nonempty input runs) {
>   *choose a smallest tuple* (with respect to the sort key) in each
>   run, and output the smallest among these
>   *delete* the chosen tuple from the respective input run
> }

Because each run is sorted, the choice step is simple since the smallest remaining element in a run is always its current head element. Figure 13.3 illustrates repeated application of the 2-way merge algorithm; Figure 13.4 does the same for the 3-way merge.

What is the cost of a k-way merge of k runs of size R? Clearly, each run must be scanned once and then the entire output must be written back on disk. The cost is thus $2kR$. Since we might start with more than k runs, we divide them into groups

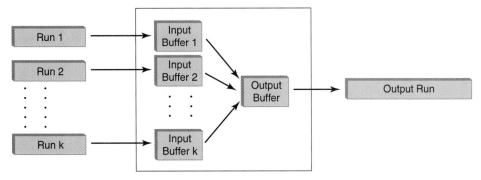

Figure 13.2 k-way merge.

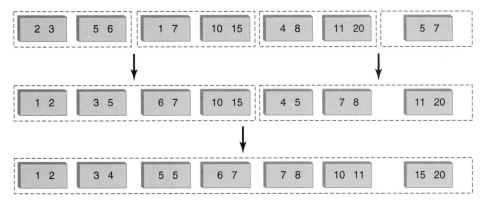

Figure 13.3 Merging sorted runs in a 2-way merge.

of k and apply the k-way merge separately to each group. If we refer to this process as a step and if we start with N runs, we have $\lceil N/k \rceil$ groups, and the upper bound on the total cost of the merge step is $2RN$. Note that this value does not depend on k. Moreover, since at the next merge step we start with $\lceil N/k \rceil$ runs, each with a maximum size kR, the cost of the merge again does not exceed $2RN$, and we are left with $\lceil N/k^2 \rceil$ runs. In fact, it is easy to show by induction that this upper bound on the I/O cost holds for every step of the merge algorithm.

The next question is what the value of k should be at the merging stage in an external sort algorithm. If we start with N runs and perform a k-way merge at each step, the number of steps is $\lceil log_k N \rceil$. Thus, the cost of the entire merging stage of the algorithm is bound by $2RN * log_k N$, where R is the initial size of a sorted run. Since, in our case, $R = M$ (i.e., we can use the entire buffer to produce the largest possible initial runs) and consequently $N = \lceil F/M \rceil$, we conclude that the cost is bounded by $2F * log_k \lceil F/M \rceil$.

Thus, it appears that the larger k is, the smaller is the cost of external sorting. Why, then, should we not take k to be the maximum possible—that is, the number

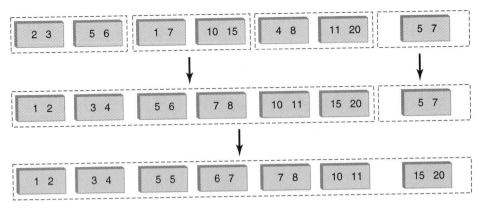

Figure 13.4 Merging sorted runs in a 3-way merge.

of initial sorted runs? The answer is that we are limited by the size M of the main memory buffer allocated for the external sort procedure. This reasoning suggests that we should utilize this memory in such a way as to make k as large as possible. Since we must allocate at least one page to collect the output (which is periodically flushed to disk) during the merge, the maximum value of k is $M - 1$. By substituting this value into the earlier cost estimate, we obtain the following estimate:

$$2F\,(log_{(M-1)}F - log_{(M-1)}M) \approx 2F(log_{(M-1)}F - 1)$$

Finally, by combining this cost with the cost of the partial sorting stage, we obtain an estimate for the entire procedure of external sorting:

$$2F * log_{(M-1)}F \qquad\qquad (13.1)$$

In commercial DBMSs, the external sorting algorithms are highly optimized. They take into account not only the cost of in-memory sorting of the initial runs but also the fact that transferring multiple pages in one I/O operation might be more cost-effective than performing several I/O operations that transfer one page at a time. For instance, if we have a buffer that holds 12 pages, we can either perform an 11-way merge reading one page at a time or a 3-way merge reading three pages at a time. Since reading (and writing) three pages takes almost the same time as reading one, it is reasonable to consider such a 3-way merge as an alternative. Another consideration has to do with delays when the output buffer is being flushed to disk during the merge operation. Techniques such as double or triple buffering might be used to reduce such delays. Despite all of these simplifications, however, the algorithm and the cost estimate developed in this section provide a good approximation for what is happening in real systems. Our discussion of the algorithms in the remainder of this chapter relies on the understanding of the cost estimates and on the details of the sorting algorithm developed here.

Sorting and B+ trees. The merge-based algorithm described above is the most commonly used sorting method in query processing because it works in all cases and does not require auxiliary data structures. However, when such structures are available sorting can be performed at a lower cost.

For instance, suppose that a secondary B$^+$ tree index on the sort key is available. Traversal of the leaf entries of the tree produces a sorted list of the record Ids (rids) for the actual data file. In principle, then, we can simply follow the pointers and retrieve the records in the data file in the order of the search key. Surprisingly, this might not always beat the merge-based algorithm!

The main consideration in deciding whether a B$^+$ tree index is worth considering for sorting a file is whether the index is clustered or unclustered. The short answer is, if the index is clustered, using a B$^+$ tree index is a good idea; otherwise, it might be a bad idea. If the index is clustered, the data file must already be almost sorted (by definition), so there is nothing we need to do. However, if the index is unclustered, traversing the leaves of a B$^+$ tree and following the data record pointers retrieves pages of the main file in random order. In the worst case, this might mean that we must transfer one page for each *record* in the index leaf (recall that our previous analysis was based on the number of pages in the file, not the number of records). Exercise 13.1 deals with estimating the cost of using unclustered B$^+$ trees for external sorting.

13.2 COMPUTING PROJECTION, UNION, AND SET DIFFERENCE

At first glance, computing the projection, union, and set difference operators is easy. With projection, for instance, we can just scan the relation and delete the unwanted columns. However, the situation is more complicated if the user query has the DISTINCT directive. The problem here is that duplicate tuples, which might arise as a result of the projection operation, must be eliminated. For instance, if we project out the attributes StudId and Grade of the relation TRANSCRIPT in Figure 4.5, the tuple ⟨MGT123, F1994⟩ will appear twice in the result. Thus, we must find efficient techniques to eliminate duplicate tuples.

The same problem with duplicates can arise in the computation of the union of two relations. In the case of the difference of two relations, r–s, duplicates cannot arise unless the original relation **r** had them all along. Nevertheless, the problem we are facing is similar: We must identify the tuples in **r** that are equal to tuples in **s**.

There are two techniques for finding identical tuples: sorting (which we discussed in the previous section) and hashing. We first apply these techniques to the projection operator and then discuss the modifications needed for union and set difference operators.

Sort-based projection. This technique first scans the original relation, removes the tuple components that are to be projected out, and writes the result back on disk. (We assume that there is not enough memory to store the result.) The cost of this operation is of the order $2F$, where F is the number of pages in the relation. Then the result is sorted at the cost of $2F * log_{(M-1)} F$, where M is the number of main memory pages available for sorting. Finally, we scan the result again (at the cost of

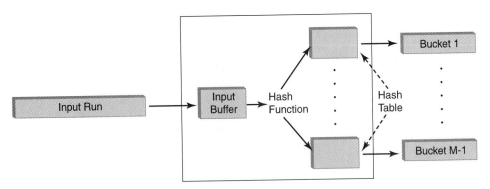

Figure 13.5 Hashing input relation into buckets.

$2F$), and, since identical tuples are right next to each other (because the relation is sorted), we can easily delete the duplicates.

In fact, we can do better than that if we combine sorting and scanning. First, we delete the unwanted components from the tuples during the partial sorting stage of the sorting algorithm. At that stage, we have to scan the original relation anyway, so removal of the tuple components comes at no additional cost in terms of disk I/O. Second, we eliminate the final scan needed to remove the duplicates by combining duplicate elimination with the steps in which sorted runs are output to the disk. Since each such step writes out blocks of sorted tuples, duplicate elimination can be done in main memory, at no additional I/O cost.

Thus, the cost of the sort-based projection is $2F * log_{(M-1)} F$. Furthermore, if we take into account that the first scan is likely to produce a smaller relation (of size αF, where $\alpha < 1$ is the reduction factor), the cost of projection is even lower (see exercise 13.2).

Hash-based projection.   Another way to quickly identify the duplicates is to use a hash function. Suppose that a hash function yields integers in the range of 1 to $M - 1$ and that there are M buffer pages in main memory, which includes an $(M - 1)$-page hash table and an input buffer. The algorithm works as follows. In the first phase, the original relation is scanned. During the scan, we chop off the tuple components that are to be projected out, and the rest of the tuple is hashed on the remaining attributes. Whenever a page of the hash table becomes full, it is flushed to the corresponding bucket on disk. This step is illustrated in Figure 13.5.

Clearly, duplicate tuples are always hashed into the same bucket, so we can eliminate duplicates in each bucket separately. This elimination is done in the second phase of the algorithm. Assuming that each bucket fits into the main memory, the second phase can be carried out by simply reading each bucket in its entirety, sorting it in main memory to eliminate the duplicates, and then flushing it to disk. The I/O complexity of the entire process is $4F$ (or $F + 3\alpha F$ if the size reduction factor due to projection, $\alpha (\alpha < 1)$, is taken into account). If the individual buckets do not fit in main memory, they must be sorted using external sorting, which incurs additional I/O overhead. Exercise 13.3 deals with the cost estimate in this case.

Comparison of sort-based and hash-based methods.   The assumption that every bucket can fit into main memory is realistic even for very large files. For instance, suppose that a 10,000-page buffer is available to the program to do the projection. Such a buffer requires only 40M of memory, which is well within the range of an inexpensive desktop computer. We can first use this buffer to store the hash table and then use it to read in the buckets. Assuming that each bucket will fit into the buffer, a $10,000 \times 10,000 = 10^9$-page file (400G) can be processed at the cost of just under 4×10^9 page transfers. Does the sort-based projection algorithm fare better? In this case, the cost is $2 \times 10^9 \, log_{10^4-1}10^9$, which is slightly higher.

   Thus, the possibility that we might have to externally sort the hash buckets is fairly remote. A much bigger risk is that the hash function we use will not distribute tuples to the buckets evenly. In this case, although the average bucket might fit in main memory, other buckets will not. In the worst case (which is unlikely), all tuples might fall into the same buffer, which will require external sorting. The cost will then be $2F$ to scan the original relation and copy it into the single bucket plus $2F \, log_{(M-1)}F$ to sort the bucket and eliminate the duplicates—a waste of $2F$ page transfers compared to sort-based projection.

Computing union and set difference.   Computing the union is similar to computing projection, except that we do not need to chop off unwanted attributes. To compute a set difference, **r–s**, we sort both **r** and **s** and then scan them in parallel, similarly to the merging process. However, instead of merging tuples, whenever we discover that a tuple, t, of **r** is also in **s**, we do not add it to the result.

   In hash-based set difference computation, we can hash **r** and **s** into buckets as described earlier. However, in each bucket we must keep the distinction between tuples that came from **r** and those that came from **s**. In the second stage, the set difference operation must be applied to each bucket separately.

13.3   COMPUTING SELECTION

Computing the selection operator can be much more complex than computing projection and the set operations, and a wider variety of techniques can be used. The choice of a technique for a particular selection operator can depend on the type of the selection condition and on the physical organization of the relation in question. Typically, the DBMS decides automatically on the technique it will use based on the heuristics that we describe next. However, understanding these heuristics gives the programmer an opportunity to request the physical organization that is most favorable to the selection types that occur most frequently in a particular application.

   We first consider simple selection conditions of the form *attr* op *value*, where op is one of the comparisons $=, >, <$, and the like, and then generalize our techniques to complex conditions that involve Boolean operators.

Database queries usually lead to two distinct kinds of selection: those based on equality (*attr=val*) and those based on inequality (such as *attr<val*). The latter are called **range queries** because they usually come in pairs that specify a range of values, for example, $\sigma_{c_1 < attr \leq c_2}(\mathbf{r})$.

13.3.1 Selections with Simple Conditions

One obvious way of evaluating a selection, $\sigma_{attr\ \text{op}\ value}(\mathbf{r})$, is to scan the relation **r** and check the selection condition for each tuple, outputting those that satisfy it. However, if only a small number of tuples satisfies the condition, the price of scanning an entire relation seems too high. In situations where more information is available about the structure of **r**, a complete scan is not needed. We consider three cases: (1) when no index is available on *attr*; (2) when there is a B$^+$ tree index on *attr*; and (3) when there is a hash index on *attr*. In case 3, only the equality selections (where op is =) can be handled efficiently. In case 2, both equality selections and range queries can be handled efficiently, although case 3 is generally better for equality selection. In case 1, complete scan of **r** is the only option unless the relation **r** is already sorted on *attr*. In this case, both equality and range conditions can be handled, although not as efficiently as when a B$^+$ tree index is available.

No index. In general, we might have no choice but to scan the entire relation **r** at the cost of F page transfers (the number of disk blocks in **r**). However, if **r** is sorted on *attr*, we can use binary search to find the pages of **r** that house the first tuple where *attr=value* holds. We can then scan the file in the appropriate direction to retrieve all of the tuples that satisfy *attr* op *value*.

The cost of such a binary search is proportional to $log_2 F$. To this, we must add the cost of scanning the blocks that contain the qualifying tuples. For instance, if **r** has 500 pages, the cost of the search is $\lceil log_2 500 \rceil$, that is, 9 page transfers (plus the number of disk blocks that contain the qualifying entries).

B$^+$ tree index. With a B$^+$ tree index on *attr*, the algorithm is similar to that for a sorted file. However, instead of the binary search, we use the index to find the first tuple of **r** where *attr=value*. More precisely, we find the leaf node of the B$^+$ tree that contains or points to the first row satisfying the condition. From there, we scan the leaves of the B$^+$ tree index to find all of the index entries that point to the pages that hold the tuples that satisfy *attr* op *value*.

The cost of finding the first qualifying leaf node of the index equals the depth of the B$^+$ tree. As before, we also have to add the cost of scanning the leaves of the index to identify all of the qualifying entries. Of course, this cost depends on the number of qualifying entries, which depends on the selection condition as well as on the actual data in the relation.

This is not the whole story, however. So far we have described only the process of getting the index entries. The cost of getting the actual tuples depends on whether or not the index is clustered. If the index is clustered, all of the tuples of interest are stored in one page or in several adjacent pages (this is true whether or not the index is integrated into the storage structure). For instance, if there are 1,000 qualifying tuples and each disk block stores 100 tuples, getting all these tuples (assuming that we already found the appropriate index nodes) requires 10 page transfers. On the other hand, if the index is unclustered, each qualifying tuple might be in a separate block, so retrieving all qualifying tuples might take 1,000 page transfers!

This raises the unhappy prospect of having to perform as many page transfers as the number of qualifying tuples in the selection, which can handily beat the number of pages in the entire relation **r**. Fortunately, with a little thought, we can do better than that. Let us first sort the record Ids of the qualifying tuples that we obtained from the index. Then we can retrieve the data pages from the relation in the ascending order of qualifying record Ids, which guarantees that every data page will be retrieved at most once. Thus, even with an unclustered index, the cost is proportional to the number of pages that contain qualifying tuples (plus the cost of searching the index and sorting the record Ids). In the worst case, this cost can be as high as the number of pages in the original relation (but no longer as large as the number of tuples there!). This is because the qualifying tuples are not packed into the retrieved pages as they would be with a clustered index: A retrieved page might only contain a single qualifying tuple. Hence, a clustered index is still greatly preferred.

Hash index. In this case, we can use the hash function to find the bucket that has the tuples where *attr=value* holds. Since two tuples which differ only slightly in *value* can hash to different buckets, this method cannot be efficiently used with range conditions, such as *attr<value*.

Generally, the cost of finding the right bucket is constant (close to 1.2 for a good hash function). However, the actual cost of tuple retrieval depends on the number of qualifying tuples. If this number is larger than 1, then, as in the case of B^+ tree indices, the actual cost depends on whether or not the index is clustered. In the clustered case, all qualifying tuples are packed into a few adjacent pages and the cost of retrieval is just the cost of scanning these pages. In the unclustered case, tuples are scattered through the data file and we face the same problem as with unclustered B^+ trees—sorting the record Ids results in a cost proportional to the number of pages that contain qualifying tuples.

13.3.2 Access Paths

The above algorithms for implementing the relational operators all assume that certain auxiliary data structures (indices) are available (or unavailable) for the relations being processed. These data structures, along with the algorithms that use them, are called **access paths**. So far, we have seen several examples of access paths that can be used to process a particular query: A *file scan* can always be used; a binary search can be used on files that are sorted on attributes specified in the query; a *hash index* or a B^+ tree can be used if the index has a search key that involves those attributes.

The access path for a given relational operation must be chosen with care. For instance, consider the TRANSCRIPT relation of Figure 4.5, page 63, and suppose that we have a hash index on the search key ⟨StudId, Semester⟩. The index is useful in computing $\pi_{\text{StudId,Semester}}$(TRANSCRIPT), since we can be certain that any duplicates created as a result of the projection originate from tuples that were stored in the same bucket. This greatly simplifies duplicate elimination, since the search for duplicates can be done one bucket at a time. If we compute $\pi_{\texttt{StudId,CrsCode}}(\textsc{Transcript})$, on the other hand, the index is of no help in eliminating duplicates. Although the projections of tuples t_1 and t_2 on $\langle\texttt{StudId, CrsCode}\rangle$ might be identical, t_1 and t_2 might be hashed to different buckets since the values of their $\texttt{Semester}$ attribute can differ. In order to use hashing for duplicate elimination, the entire search key of the hash index must be contained in the set of attributes that survive the projection (see exercise 13.4).

Nevertheless, the above hash index can be very useful for computing the expression $\sigma_{\texttt{StudId=666666666}\land\texttt{Grade='A'}\land\texttt{Semester='F1994'}}(\textsc{Transcript})$. We can use the hash index to retrieve the tuples that satisfy the partial condition $\texttt{StudId=666666666} \land \texttt{Semester='F1994'}$ and then scan the result (which presumably will be small) to find the tuples that additionally satisfy $\texttt{Grade='A'}$. However, the index is of no help in evaluating the expression $\sigma_{\texttt{StudId=666666666}}(\textsc{Transcript})$ since tuples satisfying that condition can be scattered over different buckets.

Finally, a hash index on $\langle\texttt{Grade, StudId}\rangle$ is not helpful for computing the relational expression $\sigma_{\texttt{Grade>'C'}}(\textsc{Transcript})$, but a B^+ tree index on the search key $\langle\texttt{Grade, StudId}\rangle$ can help (although a B^+ tree with search key $\langle\texttt{StudId, Grade}\rangle$ cannot). To use the hash function, we have to supply all possible values for $\texttt{StudId}$ and all values for $\texttt{Grade}$ above $\texttt{'C'}$, which is impractical. In contrast, since $\texttt{Grade}$ is a *prefix* of the B^+ tree search key, we can use this tree to efficiently find all of the index entries with the search key $\langle\texttt{g, id}\rangle$, where g is higher than $\texttt{'C'}$.

This discussion leads to the notion of when an access path *covers* the use of a particular relational operator. We define this notion precisely only for a selection operator whose selection condition is a conjunction of terms of the form *attr* op *value*. Projection and set difference operators are left as an exercise.

Covering relates access paths to relational expressions that can be evaluated using those paths. Consider a relational expression of the form

$$\sigma_{attr_1 \text{ op}_1 val1 \land...\land attr_n \text{ op}_n val_n}(\mathbf{R}) \tag{13.2}$$

where $\mathbf{R}$ is a relation schema. This expression is **covered** by an access path if and only if one of the following conditions holds:

▧ The access path is file scan. (A file scan can obviously be used to compute any expression.)

▧ The access path is a hash index whose search key is a subset of the attributes $attr_1, \ldots, attr_n$ *and* all op$_i$ operators in this subset are equality. (We can use the hash index to identify the tuples that satisfy some of the conjuncts in the selection condition and then scan the result to verify the conjuncts that remain.)

▧ The access path is a B^+ tree index with the search key $sk_1, \ldots, sk_m$ such that some prefix $sk_1, \ldots, sk_i$ of that search key is a *subset* of $attr_1, \ldots, attr_n$. (Section 11.4.3 explained how to use B^+ trees for partial key searches. This can help us find the tuples that satisfy some of the conjuncts in the selection. The rest of the conjuncts can be verified by a sequential scan of the result.)

■ The access path is binary search, and the relation instance at **R** is sorted on the attributes $sk_1, \ldots, sk_m$. The definition of covering in this case is the same as for B$^+$ tree indices.

Note that access paths based on hashing can be used only if all comparisons that correspond to the attributes in the search key are =. The other access paths can be used even if these comparisons involve inequalities, such as $\leq, <, >$, and $\geq$. If the comparison operator is $\neq$, the only applicable access path is a file scan since no index is effective in enumerating all the qualifying tuples in the relation.

As an example, consider the expression $\sigma_{a_1 \geq 5 \wedge a_2 = 3.0 \wedge a_3 = 'a'}(\mathbf{R})$ and assume that there is a B$^+$ tree with search key a_2, a_1, a_4 on **R**. We can use the index to find the leaf entry, e, in which a_2 has value 3.0 and a_1 has value 5 or, if such an entry is not present, the first entry in the index that would follow e. We can then scan the leaf entries from that point to find all of those in which, in addition, a_3 has value a.

One more notion before we proceed: The **selectivity** of an access path is the number of pages that will be retrieved if we use the evaluation method corresponding to that path. The smaller the selectivity, the better the access path. Selectivity is closely related to the cost of evaluating a query, although the query cost might involve other factors. For example, multiple access paths might be used (see Section 13.3.3) or it might be necessary to sort the result before output (if an ORDER BY clause is used). Clearly, for any given relational expression, access path selectivity depends on the size of the result of that expression and is always greater than or equal to the number of pages that hold the tuples in that result. However, some access paths have selectivity that is closer to the theoretical minimum, while others are closer to the cost of the entire file scan. The notion of when an access path covers an expression helps in identifying access paths whose selectivity seems "reasonable" for the given type of expression.

13.3.3 Selections with Complex Conditions

We are now ready to discuss the methods used to evaluate arbitrary selection.

Selections with conjunctive conditions. These are the expressions of the form (13.2) considered above. We have two choices:

■ *Use the most selective access path to retrieve the corresponding tuples.* Such an access path tries to form a prefix of the search key by using as many as possible of the attributes mentioned in the selection condition. In this way, it retrieves the smallest possible superset of the required tuples, and we can scan the result to find the tuples that satisfy the entire selection condition. For instance, suppose that we need to evaluate

$$\sigma_{\text{Grade}>'C' \wedge \text{Semester}='F1994'}(\text{TRANSCRIPT})$$

and there is a B$^+$ tree index with the search key $\langle \text{Grade}, \text{StudId} \rangle$. Since this access path covers the selection condition Grade$>$'C', we can use it to compute

$\sigma_{\text{Grade}> \, '\text{C}'}$ (Transcript). Then we can scan the result to identify the transcript records that correspond to the fall 1994 semester. If we had a B^+ tree index with the search key ⟨Semester, Grade⟩, we could use *it* as an access path, because this key covers both selection conditions.

■ *Use several access paths that cover the expression.* For instance, we might have two secondary indices whose selectivity is less than that of the plain file scan. We can then use both access paths to find the rids of the tuples that might belong to the query result and then compute the intersection of those sets of rids. Finally, we can retrieve the selected tuples and test them for the remaining selection conditions. For instance, consider the expression

$$\sigma_{\text{StudId}=666666666 \land \text{Grade}='\text{A}' \land \text{Semester}='\text{F1994}'} \, (\text{Transcript})$$

and suppose that there are two hash indices: on Semester and on Grade. Using the first access path, we can find the rids of the transcript records for the fall 1994 semester. Then we can use the second access path to find the rids for the records with grade 'A'. Finally we can find the rids that belong to both sets and retrieve the corresponding pages. As we scan the tuples, we can further select those that correspond to the student Id 666666666.

Selections with disjunctive conditions.   When selection conditions contain disjunctions, we must first convert them into *disjunctive normal form*. A condition is in **disjunctive normal form** if it has the form $C_1 \lor \ldots \lor C_n$, where each C_i is a conjunction of comparison terms (as in expression (13.2)).

It is known from elementary predicate calculus that every condition has an equivalent disjunctive normal form. For instance, for the condition

    (Grade='A' ∨ Grade='B') ∧ (Semester='F1994' ∨ Semester='F1995')

the corresponding disjunctive normal form is:

    (Grade='A' ∧ Semester='F1994') ∨ (Grade='A' ∧ Semester='F1995')
    ∨ (Grade='B' ∧ Semester='F1994') ∨ (Grade='B' ∧ Semester='F1995')

For conditions in disjunctive normal form, the query processor must examine the available access paths for the individual disjuncts and choose the appropriate strategy. Here are some possibilities.

■ *One of the disjuncts, C_i, must be evaluated using a file scan.* In this situation, we might as well evaluate the entire selection expression during that scan.

■ *Each C_i has an access path that is better than the plain file scan.* We have two subcases here:

  ❑ The sum of the selectivities of all of these paths is close to the selectivity of the file scan. In this case, we should prefer the file scan, because the overhead of the index search and other factors are likely to outweigh the small potential gain due to the use of more sophisticated access paths.

❏ The combined selectivity of the access paths for all disjuncts is much smaller than the selectivity of the file scan. In this case, we should compute $\sigma_{C_i}(\mathbf{R})$ separately, using the appropriate access paths, and then take the union of the results.

13.4   COMPUTING JOINS

The methods for computing projections, selections, and the like, are nothing but a prelude to a more difficult problem: evaluation of relational joins. With all of the attention given to the comparison of different access paths, the worst that can happen during the computation of a projection or selection is that we might have to scan or sort the entire relation. The result of such an expression is also well-behaved: It cannot be larger than the original relation.

Compare this to relational joins, where both the number of pages to be scanned and the size of the result can be *quadratic* in the size of the input. While "quadratic" might not seem too bad in applications in which some algorithms have exponential complexity, it is prohibitive in database query evaluation because of the large amounts of data and the relative slowness of disk I/O. For example, joining two files that span a mere 1,000 pages can require 10^6 I/O operations, which might be unacceptable even for batch jobs. For these reasons, joins are given special attention in databases query processing.

Consider a join expression $\mathbf{r} \bowtie_{A=B} \mathbf{s}$, where A is an attribute of $\mathbf{r}$ and B is an attribute of $\mathbf{s}$. There are three main methods for computing joins: nested loops, sort-merge, and hash based joins. We consider them in this order.

13.4.1   Computing Joins Using Nested Loops

One obvious way to evaluate the join $\mathbf{r} \bowtie_{A=B} \mathbf{s}$ is to use the following loop:

```
foreach t ∈ r do
    foreach t' ∈ s do
        if t[A] = t'[B] then output ⟨t,t'⟩
```

The cost of this procedure can be estimated as follows. Let $\beta_\mathbf{r}$ and $\beta_\mathbf{s}$ be the number of pages in $\mathbf{r}$ and $\mathbf{s}$, and let $\tau_\mathbf{r}$ and $\tau_\mathbf{s}$ be the number of tuples in $\mathbf{r}$ and $\mathbf{s}$, respectively. Then it is easy to see that the relation $\mathbf{s}$ must be scanned from start to end for each tuple in $\mathbf{r}$, resulting in $\tau_\mathbf{r}\beta_\mathbf{s}$ page transfers. In addition, $\mathbf{r}$ must be scanned once in the outer loop. All in all, there are $\beta_\mathbf{r} + \tau_\mathbf{r}\beta_\mathbf{s}$ page transfers. (In all cost estimates for the join operation, we ignore the cost of writing the final result to disk because this step is the same for all methods and also because the estimate at this stage depends on the actual size of the result. Trying to estimate this size takes us away from the main topic and is distractive at this stage.)

The above cost estimate teaches us two lessons:

■ *It involves a lot of page transfers!* Let $\beta_\mathbf{r} = 1{,}000$, $\beta_\mathbf{s} = 100$, and $\tau_\mathbf{r} = 10{,}000$. Our cost estimate says that the computation might require $1{,}000 + 10{,}000 \times 100 =$

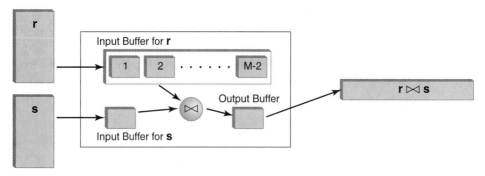

Figure 13.6 Block-nested loops join.

1,001,000 page transfers—too much to join such relatively small tables (about 166 minutes if one page I/O takes 10ms).

■ *The order of the loops matters.* Suppose that instead of scanning **r** in the outer loop, we scan **s** in the outer loop and **r** in the inner loop. Suppose that $\tau_s = 1,000$. Switching **r** and **s** in the cost estimate yield: $100 + 1,000 \times 1,000 = 1,000,100$. Although, in this example, the reduction in operations is minimal (a whopping 9 seconds!), it is easy to see that, if the number of tuples per page is the same in both relations, the smaller relation should be scanned in the outer loop and the bigger relation in the inner loop.

Block-nested loops join.   The complexity of the nested-loops join can be reduced considerably if, instead of scanning **s** once per tuple of **r**, we scan it once per each page of **r**. This will reduce the cost estimate to $\beta_r + \beta_r\beta_s$—a reduction of an order of magnitude from the above example. The way to achieve this feat is to output the result of the join for all tuples in the page of **r** that is currently in memory.

If we can reduce the number of scans of **s** to one per page of **r**, can we further reduce this number to one per group of pages? The answer is yes, provided we can use a little more memory. Suppose that the query processor has an M-page main memory buffer to do the join. We can allocate $M - 2$ of these pages for the outer loop relation **r** and one page for the inner loop relation **s**, leaving last page reserved for the output buffer. This process is depicted in Figure 13.6.

The cost of a block-nested loops join can be estimated similarly to our previous examples: The outer relation **r** is scanned once at the cost of β_r page transfers; the relation **s** is scanned once per group of $M - 2$ pages of **r**, that is, $\lceil \frac{\beta_r}{M-2} \rceil$. Thus, the cost (excluding the cost of writing the output to disk) is $\beta_r + \beta_s \lceil \frac{\beta_r}{M-2} \rceil$. In our example, if $M = 102$, the cost will go down to $1,000 + 100 \times 10 = 2,000$. And, if the smaller relation, **s**, is scanned in the outer loop, the cost will be even lower: $100 + 100 \times 10 = 1,100$ (or 11 seconds, assuming 10ms per page I/O)—quite a reduction from 10^6, the cost of the original, naive implementation.

Index-nested loops join.   The next idea is to use indices. This technique achieves particularly good results if the number of tuples in **r** and **s** that match on the attributes A and B is small compared to the size of the file.

Suppose that relation **s** has an index on attribute B. Then, instead of scanning **s** in the inner loop, we can use the index to find the matching tuples:

> **foreach** t ∈ **r do** {
>> *use the index on* B *to find all tuples* t' ∈ **s** *such that*
>> t[A] = t'[B]; *output* ⟨t,t'⟩
> }

To estimate the cost of this index-nested loops join, we have to take into account the type of index and whether it is clustered or not. The number of matching tuples in **s**, also matters.

If the index is a B^+ tree, the cost of finding the first leaf node for the matching tuple in **s** is 2 to 4, depending on the size of the relation. In a hash-based index, it is about 1.2, if the hash function is well chosen. The next question is how many I/O operations are required to fetch the matching tuples in **s**, and the answer depends on the number of matching tuples and whether the index is clustered or unclustered.

If the index is unclustered, the number of I/Os needed to retrieve all matching tuples can be as high as the number of matching tuples. So unclustered indices are not very useful for index-nested loops joins, *unless* the number of matching tuples is small (for instance, if B is a candidate key of **s**). For clustered indices, all matching tuples are likely to be in the same or adjacent disk blocks, so the number of I/Os needed to retrieve them is typically 1 or 2. Thus, in case of the clustered index the cost estimate is

$$\beta_{\mathbf{r}} + (\rho + 1) \times \tau_{\mathbf{r}}$$

where ρ is the number of I/Os needed to retrieve the leaf node of a B^+ tree index or to find the correct bucket of a hash index (we assume that the index is not integrated with the data file and that all matching tuples fit in one page, which is where the 1 comes from). In case of an unclustered index, the cost is

$$\beta_{\mathbf{r}} + (\rho + \mu) \times \tau_{\mathbf{r}}$$

where μ is the average number of matching tuples in **s** per tuple in **r**.

Let us return to our example and compare this cost with the cost of block-nested loops joins. Assuming that ρ is 2 (our relations are fairly small), we obtain $1,000 + 3 \times 10,000 = 31,000$ in the case of a clustered index—much higher than in the case of block-nested loops. However, if we switch **r** and **s** in the nested loop, the costs of index- and block-nested loops are much closer: $100 + 3 \times 1,000 = 3,100$ versus 1,100.

Still, in this example indices seem to be losing to block-nested loops by a large margin. Why consider indices at all? It turns out that indexed loops have one

Figure 13.7 Merge step of a sort-merge join.

Input: *relation* **r** *sorted on attribute* A;
           relation **s** *sorted on attribute* B
Output: $\mathbf{r} \bowtie_{A=B} \mathbf{s}$

```
Result := {}                        // initialize Result
t_r := getFirst(r)                  // get first tuple
t_s := getFirst(s)
while !eof(r) and !eof(s) do{
    while !eof(r) && t_r[A] < t_s[B] do
        t_r = getNext(r)            // get next tuple
    while !eof(r) and t_r[A] > t_s[B] do
        t_s = getNext(s)
    if t_r[A] = t_s[B] = c then     // for some const c
        Result := (σ_{A=c}(r) × σ_{B=c}(s)) ∪ Result;
}
return Result;
```

remarkable property: The cost is not significantly affected by the size of the inner relation, as can be seen from the above formulas. So, for example, if we use **s** in the inner loop and its size grows to 10,000 pages (100,000 tuples), the cost of block-nested loops joins grows to $1,000 + 10,000 \times 10 = 101,000$ page transfers. In contrast, the cost of index-nested loops join increases much more conservatively: $1,000 + 3 \times 10,000 = 31,000$. Thus, indexed joins tend to work better when relations in the join are fairly large and one is much larger than the other.

13.4.2 Sort-Merge Join

The idea behind sort-merge is to first sort each relation on the join attribute and then find matching tuples using a variation of the merge procedure, that is, scanning both relations simultaneously and comparing the join attributes. When a match is found, the joined tuple is added to the result. However, the actual process to do this is somewhat subtle. We show the algorithm in Figure 13.7.

According to the figure, the merging step of the algorithm works as follows: The relations **r** and **s** are scanned until the match on the attributes A and B is found. When this happens, all possible combinations (the Cartesian product) of the matching tuples are added to the result.

Let us now estimate the cost of a sort-merge join in terms of the number of page transfers. Obviously, we must pay the usual price to sort the relations **r** and **s**: $2\beta_r\lceil log_{M-1}\beta_r\rceil + 2\beta_s\lceil log_{M-1}\beta_s\rceil$ (assuming that M buffers are available). Computing the cost of the merging step is more subtle. At first sight, it seems that **r** and **s** are scanned only once. However, computing the Cartesian product might require several scans of the subrelation $\sigma_{B=c}(\mathbf{s})$ if we cannot fit both $\sigma_{A=c}(\mathbf{r})$ and $\sigma_{B=c}(\mathbf{s})$ in main memory. The best way to compute this product is then a block-nested loops join. The actual number of page transfers here depends on the sizes of these subrelations and on the amount of available memory. In typical cases, however, matching subrelations can be fit in main memory and multiple scans of the relation **s** can be avoided (for instance, if A and B are keys).

For our running example, we have the following relation sizes in blocks: $\beta_r = 1{,}000$, $\beta_s = 100$, and the buffer dedicated to our join operation has 102 pages. This means that sorting of **s** can be done in 200 page transfers and sorting of **r** can be done in $2 \times 1{,}000 \times \lceil log_{101}1000 \rceil$, or 4,000 page transfers. Merging takes one more scan (assuming that the matching tuples all fit in $(M-1)/2$ pages, so joining them does not involve additional scans). Thus, the whole join should take 5,300 page transfers. In fact, merging can be done during the final stage of the external sorting algorithm (as we did earlier for sort-based projection—details are left to exercise 13.9). In that case, the sort-merge join takes only 4,200 page transfers.

It may seem that the block-nested loops algorithm is better than sort-merge in this particular case. However, just as with the index-nested loops method, the asymptotic behavior of sort-merge is better than that of block-nested loops. When the sizes of **r** and **s** grow, the cost of block-nested loops grows quadratically—$O(\beta_r\beta_s)$—while the cost of sort-merge join increases much more slowly (assuming that $\sigma_{A=c}(\mathbf{r})$ and $\sigma_{B=c}(\mathbf{s})$ are small, as discussed above)—$O(\beta_r log\beta_r + \beta_s log\beta_s)$.

13.4.3 Hash Join

One way to compute a join, $\mathbf{r} \bowtie_{A=B} \mathbf{s}$, is to preprocess the relations **r** and **s** so that the tuples that possibly match will be placed on the same or adjacent pages. Such preprocessing eliminates the need for repeated scans of the inner loop relation and is the basic idea behind the sort-merge technique described above. However, sorting is just one of the possible preprocessing techniques. Alternatively, we can use hashing to make sure that matching tuples are placed close to each other. We used this technique earlier, when we needed to place duplicates tuples (that arise due to projection or set-theoretic operations) close to each other. Clearly, the problem of identifying the duplicates is a special case of the problem we now face: identifying the tuples that have the same value for one or more attributes (e.g., A and B above). The idea is illustrated in Figure 13.8.

The hash-join method first hashes each input relation onto the hash table, where **r** is hashed on attribute A and **s** is hashed on attribute B. This has the effect that the tuples of **r** and **s** that can *possibly* match are put in the same bucket.

In the second stage, the **r** half and the **s** half of each bucket are joined to produce the final result. If both halves fit in main memory, all of these joins can be done at the cost of a single scan of **r** and **s**. If the buckets are too large for main memory, other join techniques can be tried. Typically in this case, the **r** portion of each bucket is further partitioned by hashing on the attribute A using a different hash function. Then the **s** portion of the corresponding bucket is scanned. In the process, each tuple of **s** is hashed on attribute B using the new hash function and matching tuples in **r** are identified.

Assuming that each bucket fits in memory, we can join **r** and **s** at the cost of three scans for each of these relations. **r** and **s** must be input and the resulting buckets output (two scans for each relation), and then each bucket must be input to find the

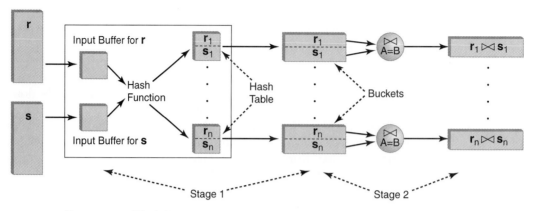

Figure 13.8 Hash join.

matching tuples (one scan for each relation—recall that we do not include the final output step in the cost). In our running example, the cost is 3,300 page transfers, which is higher than the cost of block-nested loops but the asymptotic behavior of hash join is better. In fact, if each hash bucket produced at the first stage of the algorithm fits in main memory, the cost is linear in the size of **r** and **s**. This makes hash join the best among all of the methods considered so far. However, it is important to realize that hash-join heavily depends on the choice of hash function and can be easily subverted by an unfortunate data skew (what if all tuples are hashed into the same bucket?). In addition, hash joins can be used only for equi-joins and are inappropriate for more general join conditions, such as inequalities.

13.5   MULTI-RELATIONAL JOINS

In Section 11.7, we discussed join indices and their use in computing joins. The algorithm for computing a join of the form $\mathbf{p} \bowtie_{A=B} \mathbf{q}$ works by scanning the join index and fetching the tuples whose rids are found in the index entries.

The actual computation is essentially similar to the indexed loop join, with **p** scanned in the outer loop, except that we use the join index to locate the tuples of **q** instead of a general-purpose index on attribute B of **q**. The advantage of the join index over other index types in this case is that it does not need to be searched: Since all matching tuples are already associated with each other, the index can simply be scanned, the pairs or rids of the matching tuples fetched, and the tuples joined.

The idea underlying join indices can be extended to multi-relational joins, where an index can be created to relate rids of more than two tuples. For instance, in a three-way join, $\mathbf{p} \bowtie \mathbf{q} \bowtie \mathbf{r}$, a join index consists of triples of the form $\langle p, q, r \rangle$, where p is a rid of a tuple in relation **p**, q is a rid of a matching tuple in **q**, and r is a rid of a matching tuple in **r**. The triples are sorted in ascending order of rids beginning with the first column of the index, then the second, and then the third (the index can also be a B^+ tree).

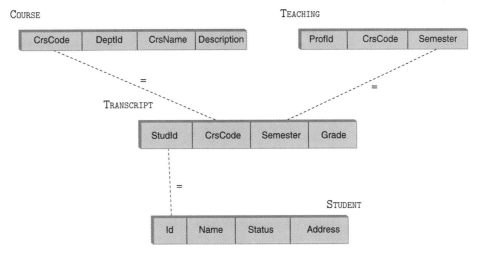

Figure 13.9 Star join.

With such an index, the join can be computed with a simple loop that scans the join index. For each triple $\langle p, q, r \rangle$ in the index, the tuples corresponding to the rids p, q, and r are fetched. Since the index is sorted on column 1 first, the join is performed in a single scan of the index and of the relation **p**. However, the relations **q** and **r** might have to be accessed many times. Indeed, if N is the average number of matching tuples in **q** per tuple in **p** and M is the average number of matching tuples in **r** per tuple in **p**, then, to compute the join, $| \mathbf{p} | \times N$ pages of **q** and $| \mathbf{p} | \times M$ pages of **r** might have to be retrieved.

Multiway join indices are especially popular for speeding up so-called *star joins*—a common type of join used in online analytical processing (OLAP, see Chapter 19).

A **star join** is a multiway join of the form $\mathbf{r} \bowtie_{cond_1} \mathbf{r}_1 \bowtie_{cond_2} \mathbf{r}_2 \bowtie_{cond_3} \cdots$, where each $cond_i$ is a join condition that involves the attributes of **r** and $\mathbf{r}_i$ only. In other words, there are no conditions that relate the tuples of $\mathbf{r}_i$ and $\mathbf{r}_j$ directly, and all matching is done through the tuples of **r**. An example of a star join is shown in Figure 13.9, where the "satellite" relations COURSE, TEACHING, and STUDENT are joined with the "star" relation TRANSCRIPT using equi-join conditions that do not match the attributes of the satellite relations to each other.

One reason that multiway join indices are good for computing star joins is that the join index of a star join is easier to maintain than the join index of a general multiway join (exercise 13.13). Furthermore, computing a general multiway join using a join index can be expensive. Consider a join, $\mathbf{r} \bowtie \mathbf{r}_1 \bowtie \mathbf{r}_2 \bowtie \ldots \bowtie \mathbf{r}_n$, and suppose that N is the average number of matching tuples in $\mathbf{r}_i$ per tuple in **r**. Then, using analysis similar to that for 3-way joins, a join index computation might need to access $| \mathbf{r} | \times N \times n$ pages.

Fortunately, star joins have more promising methods. One, described in [O'Neil and Graefe 1995], takes advantage of bitmapped join indices, introduced in Section 11.7.2. Instead of one join index that involves n relations, we can use one bitmapped join index, $\mathcal{J}_i$, for each partial join $\mathbf{r}_i \bowtie \mathbf{r}$. Each $\mathcal{J}_i$ is a collection of pairs $\langle v, bitmap \rangle$, where v is a rid of a tuple in $\mathbf{r}_i$ and $bitmap$ has 1 in the ith position if and only if the ith tuple in $\mathbf{r}$ joins with the $\mathbf{r}_i$'s tuple represented by v. We can then scan $\mathcal{J}_i$ and logically OR all of the bitmaps. This will give us the rids of all tuples in $\mathbf{r}$ that can join with *some* tuple in $\mathbf{r}_i$. After obtaining such an ORed bitmap for each satellite relation $\mathbf{r}_i$, where $i = 1, \ldots, n$, we can logically AND these bitmaps to obtain the rids of all tuples in $\mathbf{r}$ that join with some tuple in each $\mathbf{r}_i$. In other words, this procedure prunes away all tuples in $\mathbf{r}$ that *do not* participate in the star join. The rationale is that there will be only a small number of tuples left, so the join can be computed inexpensively by a brute-force technique like nested loops.

Join indices and star join optimization are supported by the recent versions of commercial DBMS from the major vendors, such as IBM's DB/2, Oracle's Oracle 8i, and Microsoft's SQL Server.

13.6   COMPUTING AGGREGATE FUNCTIONS

Generally, computing aggregate functions (such as AVG or COUNT) in a query involves a complete scan of the query output. The only issue here is the computation of aggregates in the presence of the GROUP BY *attrs* statement. Once again, the problem reduces to finding efficient techniques for partitioning the tuples according to the values of certain attributes. We have identified three such techniques so far.

- Sorting

- Hashing

- Indexing

All three techniques provide efficient ways to access the groups of tuples specified by the GROUP BY clause. All that remains is to apply the aggregate functions to the member tuples of these groups.

13.7   TUNING ISSUES: IMPACT ON PHYSICAL DATABASE DESIGN

How can the application designer translate the knowledge of computational techniques for relational operations into a better system design? One area where they can make a difference is in physical database design. Although the DBMS typically decides how to organize the data, it also takes hints from the database designer. In view of our discussion, the hints of particular interest are index declarations. Even though the SLQ standard does not address this area, most DBMS vendors allow the user to specify the attributes to be indexed, the type of index (hash, B^+ tree), and whether the index is clustered. These declarations can then be tailored to the particular mix of queries expected at each particular installation.

To illustrate this idea, consider the TRANSCRIPT relation (Figure 4.5, page 63) and suppose that most queries are expected to be selections and joins on the attribute Semester. The best strategy here is to request that the DBMS build a clustered index on that attribute. A B+ tree index ensures that the index leaf satisfying any particular selection (even for range queries) can be found quickly, and, because the index is clustered, the actual tuples of the relation can be retrieved with just a few page transfers. Moreover, when the DBMS needs to join on Semester, it can use a sort-merge join: Since the relation is already sorted on the right attribute (because the index is clustered), a significant part of the sorting step of the algorithm comes for free. Finally, since the table is dynamic, a B+ tree is preferable to an ISAM organization. Suppose that, in addition, selections and joins are expected on the StudId attribute. It is unlikely that range queries will be posed against the StudId attribute, so a secondary hash index is appropriate.

For a more interesting scenario (still involving the TRANSCRIPT relation), suppose that the most frequent access path is through the StudId, CrsCode combination (i.e., most queries use this path) and a less frequently used path is through Semester. Clearly, we must build one index on ⟨StudId,CrsCode⟩ and another on Semester. The question is, however, which index should be clustered? At first glance, it might seem that the index on ⟨StudId,CrsCode⟩ should be clustered because this is the main access path to the relation. However, a closer look at the semantics of this relation should convince us that, even though ⟨StudId, CrsCode⟩ is *not* a candidate key of this relation, the number of TRANSCRIPT records that agree on both of these attributes will be 1 in almost all cases—only when a student retakes a course can this number be larger than 1. Therefore clustering around ⟨StudId, CrsCode⟩ will not yield significant benefits. Also, it is not likely that range queries will be asked against this pair of attributes, so the overhead of a B+ tree index does not seem justified—a hash index is probably the best solution here. On the other hand, a clustered B+ tree index on Semester can greatly improve the efficiency of selections and joins on that attribute, and makes an excellent choice for a secondary access path.[1]

13.8 BIBLIOGRAPHIC NOTES

Sort-based evaluation techniques for relational operators are discussed in [Blasgen and Eswaran 1977]; hash-based techniques are covered in [DeWitt et al. 1984, Kitsuregawa et al. 1983]. Good surveys of techniques for evaluating relational operators and additional references can be found in [Graefe 1993, Chaudhuri 1998]. The use of join indices for computing multi-relational joins is studied in [Valduriez 1987], and techniques for computing various relational operators with the help of bitmap indices are discussed in [O'Neil and Graefe 1995, O'Neil and Quass 1997].

---

[1] Note that in this case the main index on the primary key ⟨StudId,CrsCode,Semester⟩ would not be clustered.

13.9   EXERCISES

13.1 Consider the use of unclustered B^+ trees for external sorting. Let R denote the number of data records per disk block, and let F be the number of blocks in the data file. Estimate the cost of such a sorting procedure as a function of R and F. Compare this cost to merge-based external sorting. Consider the cases of $R = 1, 10$, and 100.

13.2 Estimate the cost of the sort-based projection assuming that, during the initial scan (where tuple components are deleted), the size of the original relation shrinks by factor $\alpha < 1$.

13.3 Consider hash-based evaluation of the projection operator. Assume that all buckets are about the same size but do not fit in main memory. Let N be the size of the hash table in memory pages, F be the size of the original relation in pages, and $\alpha < 1$ be the reduction factor due to projection. Estimate the number of page transfers to and from the disk needed to compute the projection.

13.4 Give an example of an instance of the TRANSCRIPT relation (Figure 4.5) and a hash function on the attribute sequence $\langle \text{StudId}, \text{Grade} \rangle$ that sends two identical tuples in $\pi_{\text{StudId},\text{CrsCode}}(\text{TRANSCRIPT})$ into *different* hash buckets. (This shows that such a hash-based access path cannot be used to compute the projection.)

13.5 Clearly, the theoretical minimum for the selectivity of an access path is the number of pages that hold the output of the relational operator involved. What is the best theoretical upper bound on the selectivity of an access path when selection or projection operators are involved?

13.6 Based on the discussion in Section 13.3.2, give a precise definition of when an access path covers the use of projection, union, and set-difference operators.

13.7 Consider the expression

$$\sigma_{\text{StudId}=666666666,\text{Semester}='F1995', \text{Grade}='A'}(\text{TRANSCRIPT})$$

Suppose that there are the following access paths:

❑ An unclustered hash index on StudId

❑ An unclustered hash index on Semester

❑ An unclustered hash index on Grade

Which of these access paths has the best selectivity and which has the worst? Compare the selectivity of the worst access path (among the above three) to the selectivity of the file scan.

13.8 Compute the cost of $r \bowtie_{A=B} s$ using the following methods:

❑ Nested loops

❑ Block-nested loops

❏ Index-nested loops

where **r** occupies 2,000 pages, 20 tuples per page, **s** occupies 5,000 pages, 5 tuples per page, and the amount of main memory available for block-nested loops join is 402 pages.

* 13.9 In sort-merge join $\mathbf{s} \bowtie \mathbf{r}$, the extra scan in the merging phase seems unnecessary. We should be able to match the tuples of **s** and **r** during the last merging stage of the sorting algorithm. Work out the details of such an algorithm.

13.10 Estimate the number of page transfers needed to compute $\mathbf{r} \bowtie_{A=B} \mathbf{s}$ using a sort-merge join, assuming the following:

❏ The size of **r** is 1,000 pages, 10 tuples per page; the size of **s** is 500 pages, 20 tuples per page.

❏ The size of the main memory buffer for this join computation is 10 pages.

❏ The Cartesian product of matching tuples in **r** and **s** (see Figure 13.7) is computed using a block-nested loops join.

❏ $\mathbf{r}[A]$ has 100 distinct values and $\mathbf{s}[B]$ has 50 distinct values. These values are spread around the files more or less evenly, so the size of $\sigma_{A=c}(\mathbf{r})$, where $c \in \mathbf{r}[A]$, does not vary much with c.

13.11 The methods for computing joins discussed in this section all deal with equi-joins. Discuss their applicability to the problem of computing inequality joins, such as $\mathbf{r} \bowtie_{A<B} \mathbf{s}$.

13.12 Consider a relation schema, $\mathbf{R}(A, B)$, with the following characteristics:

❏ Total number of tuples: 1,000,000

❏ 10 tuples per page

❏ Attribute A is a candidate key, range 1 to 1,000,000

❏ Clustered B+ tree index of depth 4 on A

❏ Attribute B has 100,000 distinct values

❏ Hash index on B

Estimate the number of page transfers needed to evaluate each of the following queries for each of the proposed methods:

❏ $\sigma_{A<3000}$: sequential scan; index on A

❏ $\sigma_{A>3000 \wedge A<3200 \wedge B=5}$: index on A; index on B

❏ $\sigma_{A \neq 22 \wedge B \neq 66}$: sequential scan; index on A; index on B

13.13 Design an algorithm for incremental maintenance of a join index for a multiway star join.

13.14 Design a join algorithm that uses a join index. Define the notion of a *clustered join index* (there are three possibilities in the case of a binary join!) and consider the effect of clustering on the join algorithm.

Chapter 14

An Overview of Query Optimization

This chapter is an overview of relational query optimization techniques typically used in database management systems. Our goal here is not to prepare you for a career as a DBMS implementor but rather to make you a better application designer or data base administrator. Just as the knowledge of the evaluation techniques used in relational algebra can help do better physical design, an understanding of the principles of query optimization can help formulate SQL queries that stand a better chance of being improved by the query optimizer.

Relational query optimization is a fascinating example of tackling a problem of immense computational complexity with relatively simple heuristic search algorithms. A more extensive treatment of the subject can be found in [Garcia-Molina et al. 2000].

14.1 OVERVIEW OF QUERY PROCESSING

When the user submits a query, it is first parsed by the DBMS parser. The parser verifies the syntax of the query and, using the system catalog, determines if the attribute references are correct. For instance, TRANSCRIPT.Student is not a correct reference, because the relation TRANSCRIPT does not have Student as an attribute. Likewise, applying the AVG operator to the CrsCode attribute violates the type of that attribute.

Since an SQL query is declarative rather than procedural, it does not suggest any specific implementation. Thus, parsed queries must first be converted into relational algebra expressions, which can be evaluated directly using the algorithms presented in Chapter 13. As explained in Section 6.2.1, a typical SQL query such as

$$
\begin{array}{ll}
\text{SELECT} & \text{DISTINCT } \textit{TargetList} \\
\text{FROM} & \text{REL}_1 \ V_1, \ldots, \ \text{REL}_n \ V_n \\
\text{WHERE} & \textit{Condition}
\end{array}
\tag{14.1}
$$

is normally translated into the following relational algebraic expression:[1]

$$
\pi_{TargetList}(\sigma_{Condition'}(\text{REL}_1 \times \ldots \times \text{REL}_n))
\tag{14.2}
$$

---

[1] To simplify the notation, we ignore the possibility that some attributes might need renaming in the Cartesian product.

where Condition′ is Condition converted from SQL syntax to relational algebra form. For instance, the WHERE clause

```
T.Semester = 'F1995' AND P.Id = T.ProfId
         AND T.CrsCode = C.CrsCode
```

translates into the selection condition

```
Semester = 'F1995' AND Id = ProfId
         AND TEACHING.CrsCode = COURSE.CrsCode
```

Unfortunately, the algebraic expression (14.2), produced by the above straightforward translation from SQL, might take ages (literally!) to evaluate. For one thing, it contains a Cartesian product, so a join of four 100-block relations produces a 10^8-block intermediate relation, which, with a disk speed of 10ms/page, takes about 50 hours just to write out. Even if we manage to convert the Cartesian product into equi-joins (as explained later in this chapter), we might still have to grapple with the long turnaround time (dozens of minutes) for the above query. It is the job of the **query optimizer** to bring this time down to seconds (or, for very complex queries, a few minutes).

A typical query optimizer uses a combination of heuristics and cost estimates to choose among query execution plans. Thus, the two main components of a query optimizer are the **query execution plan generator** and the **plan cost estimator**. A **query execution plan** can be thought of as a relational expression with concrete evaluation methods (or *access paths*, as we called them in Chapter 13) attached to each occurrence of a relational operator in the expression. Thus, the main job of the query optimizer is to produce a single query execution plan that can evaluate the given relational expression. This plan can then be passed to the query execution plan interpreter, a software component directly responsible for query evaluation according to the given plan. The overall architecture of query processing is depicted in Figure 14.1.

14.2 HEURISTIC OPTIMIZATION BASED ON ALGEBRAIC EQUIVALENCES

The heuristics used in relational query evaluation are (for the most part) based on simple observations, such as that joining smaller relations is better than joining large ones, that performing an equi-join is better than computing a Cartesian product, and that computing several operations in just one relation scan is better than doing so in several scans. Most of these heuristics can be expressed in the form of relational algebra transformations, which take one expression and produce a different, equivalent, expression. Not all transformations are optimizations by themselves. Sometimes they yield "less efficient" expressions. However, relational transformations are designed to work with other transformations to produce expressions that are better overall.

We now present a number of heuristic transformations used by the query optimizers.

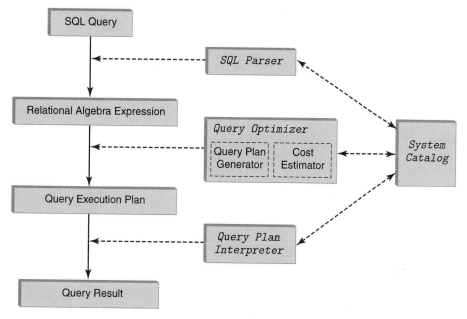

Figure 14.1 Typical architecture for DBMS query processing.

Selection and projection-based transformations.

■ $\sigma_{cond_1 \wedge cond_2}(\mathbf{R}) \equiv \sigma_{cond_1}(\sigma_{cond_2}(\mathbf{R}))$. This transformation is known as **cascading of selections**. It is not an optimization per se, but it is useful in conjunction with other transformations (see the discussion below of pushing selections and projections through joins).

■ $\sigma_{cond_1}(\sigma_{cond_2}(\mathbf{R})) \equiv \sigma_{cond_2}(\sigma_{cond_1}(\mathbf{R}))$. This transformation is called **commutativity of selection**. Like cascading, it is useful in conjunction with other transformations.

■ $\pi_{attr}(\mathbf{R}) \equiv \pi_{attr}(\pi_{attr'}(\mathbf{R}))$, if $attr \subseteq attr'$. This equivalence is known as **cascading of projections** and is used primarily with other transformations.

■ $\pi_{attr}(\sigma_{cond}(\mathbf{R})) \equiv \sigma_{cond}(\pi_{attr}(\mathbf{R}))$, if $attr$ includes all attributes used in $cond$. This equivalence is known as the **commutativity of selection and projection**. It is usually used as a preparation step for pushing a selection or a projection through the join operator (as explained below).

Cross-product and join transformations. The transformations used for cross-products and joins are the usual commutativity and associativity rules for these operators.

■ $\mathbf{R} \bowtie \mathbf{S} \equiv \mathbf{S} \bowtie \mathbf{R}$

■ $\mathbf{R} \bowtie (\mathbf{S} \bowtie \mathbf{T}) \equiv (\mathbf{R} \bowtie \mathbf{S}) \bowtie \mathbf{T}$

■ $\mathbf{R} \times \mathbf{S} \equiv \mathbf{S} \times \mathbf{R}$

■ $\mathbf{R} \times (\mathbf{S} \times \mathbf{T}) \equiv (\mathbf{R} \times \mathbf{S}) \times \mathbf{T}$

These rules can be useful in conjunction with the various nested loops evaluation strategies. As we saw in Chapter 13, it is generally better to scan the smaller relation in the outer loop, and the above rules can help maneuver the relations into the right positions. For instance, BIGGER ⋈ SMALLER can be rewritten as SMALLER ⋈ BIGGER, which intuitively corresponds to the query optimizer deciding to use SMALLER in the outer loop.

The commutativity and associativity rules (at least in the case of the join) can reduce the size of the intermediate relation in the computation of a multi-relational join. For instance, $\mathbf{S} \bowtie \mathbf{T}$ can be much smaller than $\mathbf{R} \bowtie \mathbf{S}$, in which case the computation of $(\mathbf{S} \bowtie \mathbf{T}) \bowtie \mathbf{R}$ might take fewer I/O operations than the computation of $(\mathbf{R} \bowtie \mathbf{S}) \bowtie \mathbf{T}$. The associativity and commutativity rules can be used to transform the latter expression into the former.

In fact, the commutativity and associativity rules are largely responsible for the many alternative evaluation plans that might exist for the same query. A query that involves the join of N relations can have $T(N) \times N!$ query plans just to handle the join, where $T(N)$ is the number of different binary trees with N leaf nodes. ($N!$ is the number of permutations of N relations, and $T(N)$ is the number of ways a particular permutation can be parenthesized.) This number grows very rapidly and is huge even for very small N.[2] A similar result holds for other commutative and associative relations (e.g., union) but our main focus is on join because it is the most expensive to compute.

The job of the query optimizer is to estimate the cost of these plans (which can vary widely) and to choose one "good" plan. Because the number of plans is large, it can take longer to find a good plan than to evaluate the query by brute force. (It is faster to perform 10^6 I/Os than 15! in-memory operations.) To make query optimization practical, an optimizer typically looks at only a small subset of all possible plans, and its cost estimates are approximate at best. Therefore, query optimizers are very likely to miss the optimal plan and are actually designed only to find one that is "reasonable." In other words, the "optimization" in "query optimizer" should always be taken with a grain of salt, since it does not adequately describe what is being done by that component of the DBMS architecture.

Pushing selections and projections through joins and Cartesian products.

■ $\sigma_{cond}(\mathbf{R} \times \mathbf{S}) \equiv \mathbf{R} \bowtie_{cond} \mathbf{S}$. This rule is used when *cond* relates the attributes of both $\mathbf{R}$ and $\mathbf{S}$. The basis for this heuristic is the belief that Cartesian products

---

[2] When $N = 4$, $T(4)$ is 5, and the number of all plans is 120. When $N = 5$, $T(5) = 14$, and the number of all plans is 1,680.

should never be materialized. Instead, selections must always be combined with Cartesian products and the techniques for computing joins should be used. By applying the selection condition as soon as a row of $\mathbf{R} \times \mathbf{S}$ is created, we can save one scan and avoid storing a large intermediate relation.

■ $\sigma_{cond}(\mathbf{R} \times \mathbf{S}) \equiv \sigma_{cond}(\mathbf{R}) \times \mathbf{S}$, if the attributes used in *cond* all belong to $\mathbf{R}$. This heuristic is based on the idea that if we absolutely must compute a Cartesian product, we should make the relations involved as small as possible. By pushing the selection down to $\mathbf{R}$, we hope to reduce the size of $\mathbf{R}$ *before* it is used in the cross product.

■ $\sigma_{cond}(\mathbf{R} \bowtie \mathbf{S}) \equiv \sigma_{cond}(\mathbf{R}) \bowtie \mathbf{S}$, if the attributes in *cond* all belong to $\mathbf{R}$. The rationale here is the same as for Cartesian products. Computing a join can be very expensive, and we must try to reduce the size of the relations involved. Note that if *cond* is a conjunction of comparison conditions, we can push each conjunct separately to either $\mathbf{R}$ or $\mathbf{S}$ as long as the attributes named in the conjunct belong to only one relation.

■ $\pi_{attr}(\mathbf{R} \times \mathbf{S}) \equiv \pi_{attr}(\pi_{attr'}(\mathbf{R}) \times \mathbf{S})$, if $attributes(\mathbf{R}) \supseteq attr' \supseteq (attr \cap attributes(\mathbf{R}))$, where $attributes(\mathbf{R})$ denotes the set of all the attributes of $\mathbf{R}$. The rationale for this rule is that, by pushing the projection inside the Cartesian product, we reduce the size of one of its operands. In Chapter 13, we saw that the I/O complexity of the join operation (of which $\times$ is a special case) is proportional to the number of pages in the relations involved. Thus, by applying the projection early we might reduce the number of page transfers needed to evaluate the cross product.

■ $\pi_{attr}(\mathbf{R} \bowtie_{cond} \mathbf{S}) \equiv \pi_{attr}(\pi_{attr'}(\mathbf{R}) \bowtie_{cond} \mathbf{S})$, if $attributes(\mathbf{R}) \supseteq attr' \supseteq (attr \cap attributes(\mathbf{R}))$ and $attr'$ contains all those attributes of $\mathbf{R}$ that are mentioned in *cond*. The potential benefit here is the same as for the cross product. The important additional requirement is that $attr'$ must include those attributes of $\mathbf{R}$ that are mentioned in *cond*. If some of these attributes are projected out, the expression $\pi_{attr'}(\mathbf{R}) \bowtie_{cond} \mathbf{S}$ will not be syntactically correct. This requirement is unnecessary in the case of the Cartesian product, since no join condition is involved.

The rules for pushing selections and projections through joins and cross products are especially useful when combined with the rules for cascading σ and π. For instance, consider the expression $\sigma_{c_1 \wedge c_2 \wedge c_3}(\mathbf{R} \times \mathbf{S})$, where c_1 involves the attributes of both $\mathbf{R}$ and $\mathbf{S}$, c_2 involves only the attributes of $\mathbf{R}$, and c_3 involves only the attributes of $\mathbf{S}$. We can transform this expression into one that can be evaluated more efficiently by first cascading the selections, then pushing them down and finally eliminating the Cartesian product:

$$\sigma_{c_1 \wedge c_2 \wedge c_3}(\mathbf{R} \times \mathbf{S}) \equiv \sigma_{c_1}(\sigma_{c_2}(\sigma_{c_3}(\mathbf{R} \times \mathbf{S}))) \equiv \sigma_{c_1}(\sigma_{c_2}(\mathbf{R}) \times \sigma_{c_3}(\mathbf{S})) \equiv \sigma_{c_2}(\mathbf{R}) \bowtie_{c_1} \sigma_{c_3}(\mathbf{S})$$

We can optimize the expressions that involve projections in a similar way. Consider, for instance, $\pi_{attr}(\mathbf{R} \bowtie_{cond} \mathbf{S})$. Suppose that $attr_1$ is a subset of the attributes in $\mathbf{R}$ such that $attr_1 \supseteq attr \cap attributes(\mathbf{R})$ and such that $attr_1$ contains all the attributes in *cond*. Let $attr_2$ be a similar set for $\mathbf{S}$. Then

$$\pi_{attr}(\mathbf{R} \bowtie_{cond} \mathbf{S}) \equiv \pi_{attr}(\pi_{attr_1}(\mathbf{R} \bowtie_{cond} \mathbf{S})) \equiv \pi_{attr}(\pi_{attr_1}(\mathbf{R}) \bowtie_{cond} \mathbf{S})$$

$$\equiv \pi_{attr}(\pi_{attr_2}(\pi_{attr_1}(\mathbf{R}) \bowtie_{cond} \mathbf{S})) \equiv \pi_{attr}(\pi_{attr_1}(\mathbf{R}) \bowtie_{cond} \pi_{attr_2}(\mathbf{S}))$$

The resulting expression can be more efficient, because it joins smaller relations.

Using the algebraic equivalence rules.   Typically, the above algebraic rules are used to transform queries expressed in relational algebra into expressions that are believed to be better than the original. The word "better" here should be taken with a grain of salt, because the criteria used to guide the transformation are heuristic. In fact, in the next section we will see that following through with all the suggested transformations might not yield the best result. Thus, the outcome of the algebraic transformation step should yield a set of candidate queries, which must then be further examined using cost estimation techniques discussed in the next section. Here is a typical heuristic algorithm for applying algebraic equivalences.

1. Use the cascading rule for selection to break up the conjunctions in selection conditions. The result is a single selection transformed into a sequence of selection operators, each of which can be applied separately.

2. The previous step leads to greater freedom in pushing selections through joins and Cartesian products. We can now use the rules for commutativity of selection and for pushing selections through joins to propagate the selections as far inside the query as possible.

3. Combine the Cartesian product operations with selections to form joins. As we saw in Chapter 13, there are efficient techniques for computing joins, but little can be done to improve the computation of a Cartesian product. Thus, converting these products into joins is a potential time and space saver.

4. Use the associativity rules for joins and Cartesian products to rearrange the order of join operations. The purpose here is to come up with the order that produces the smallest intermediate relations. (Note that the size of the intermediate relations directly contributes to overhead, so reducing these sizes speeds up query processing.) Techniques for the estimation of the size of intermediate relations are discussed in the next section.

5. Use the rules for cascading projections and for pushing them into queries to propagate projections as far into the query as possible. This can potentially speed up the computation of joins by reducing the size of the operands.

6. Identify the operations that can be processed in the same pass to save time writing the intermediate results to disk. This technique is called *pipelining* and is illustrated in the next section.

14.3   ESTIMATING THE COST OF A QUERY EXECUTION PLAN

As defined earlier, a query execution plan is more or less a relational expression with concrete evaluation methods (access paths) attached to each operation. In this section, we take a closer look at this concept and discuss ways to evaluate the cost of a plan to compute query results.

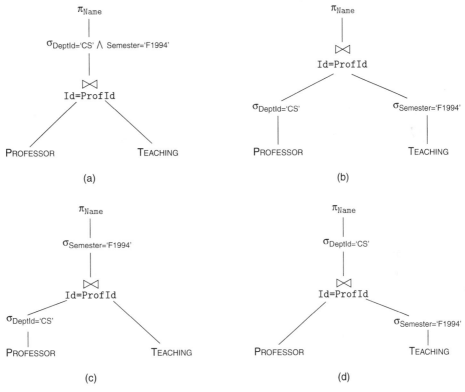

Figure 14.2 Query trees for relational expressions (14.3) through (14.6).

For discussion purposes, it is convenient to represent queries as trees. In a **query tree** each inner node is labeled with a relational operator and each leaf is labeled with a relation name. Unary relational operators have only one child, binary operators have two. Figure 14.2 presents four query trees corresponding to the following equivalent relational expressions, respectively:

$$\pi_{\text{Name}}(\sigma_{\text{DeptId}='\text{CS}' \wedge \text{Semester}='\text{F1994}'}(\text{PROFESSOR} \bowtie_{\text{Id=ProfId}} \text{TEACHING})) \qquad (14.3)$$

$$\pi_{\text{Name}}(\sigma_{\text{DeptId}='\text{CS}'}(\text{PROFESSOR}) \bowtie_{\text{Id=ProfId}} \sigma_{\text{Semester}='\text{F1994}'}(\text{TEACHING})) \qquad (14.4)$$

$$\pi_{\text{Name}}(\sigma_{\text{Semester}='\text{F1994}'}(\sigma_{\text{DeptId}='\text{CS}'}(\text{PROFESSOR}) \bowtie_{\text{Id=ProfId}} \text{TEACHING})) \qquad (14.5)$$

$$\pi_{\text{Name}}(\sigma_{\text{DeptId}='\text{CS}'}(\text{PROFESSOR} \bowtie_{\text{Id=ProfId}} \sigma_{\text{Semester}='\text{F1994}'}(\text{TEACHING}))) \qquad (14.6)$$

The relations PROFESSOR and TEACHING were described in Figure 4.5, page 63.

Expression (14.3), corresponding to Figure 14.2(a), is what a query processor might initially generate from the SQL query

```
SELECT   P.Name
FROM     PROFESSOR P, TEACHING T                              (14.7)
WHERE    P.Id = T.ProfId AND T.Semester = 'F1994'
         AND P.DeptId = 'CS'
```

The second expression, (14.4), corresponding to Figure 14.2(b), is obtained from the first by fully pushing the selections through the join, as suggested by the heuristic rules in the previous section. The third and fourth expressions, corresponding to Figure 14.2(c) and (d), are obtained from (14.3) by pushing only part of the selection condition down to the actual relations.

We are now going to augment these query trees with various query execution plans and estimate the cost of each.

Suppose that the following information is available on these relations in the system catalogue:

Professor

Size: 200 pages, 1,000 records on professors in 50 departments (5 tuples/page).

Indices: clustered 2-level B$^+$ tree on DeptId, hash index on Id.

Teaching

Size: 1,000 pages, 10,000 teaching records for the period of 4 semesters (10 tuples/page).

Indices: clustered 2-level B$^+$ tree index on Semester, hash index on ProfId

We need one additional piece of information before we can proceed: the weight of the attribute Id in the relation PROFESSOR and the weight of ProfId in the relation TEACHING. In general, the **weight** of an attribute, A, in a relation, $\mathbf{r}$, is the average number of tuples that match the different values of attribute A. In other words, weight is the average number of tuples in $\sigma_{A=value}(\mathbf{r})$, where the average is taken over all values of A in $\mathbf{r}$.

The weights for various attributes are typically derived from the statistical information stored in the system catalogue and maintained by the DBMS. Recent query optimizers go as far as maintaining *histograms* for the distribution of values in a particular attribute. Histograms give more precise information about how many tuples are likely to be selected for a given value of the attribute. Attribute weights are needed to estimate the cost of computing the join using index-based techniques, as well as to estimate the size of the result of all of the operations in our examples. Since intermediate results of the various operations might later be used as input to other operators, knowing the sizes is important for estimating the cost of each concrete plan.

Returning to our example, we first need to find realistic weights for the attributes Id and ProfId. For the Id attribute of PROFESSOR, the weight must be 1, since Id is a key. For the weight of ProfId in TEACHING, let us assume that each professor is likely to have been teaching the same number of courses. Since there are 1,000 professors and 10,000 teaching records, the weight of ProfId must be about 10. Let us now consider the four cases in Figure 14.2. In all of them, we assume that there is a 51-page buffer to evaluate the join plus a small amount of memory to hold some index blocks (the exact amount will be specified when necessary).

Case a: selection not pushed.   One possibility to evaluate the join is the indexed-nested loops method. For instance, we can use the smaller relation, PROFESSOR, in the outer loop. Since the indices on Id and ProfId are not clustered *and* because each tuple in PROFESSOR is likely to match some tuple in TEACHING (generally, every professor teaches something), the costs can be estimated as follows.

■ *To scan the* PROFESSOR *relation*: 200 page transfers.

■ *To find matching tuples in* TEACHING: We can use 50 pages of the buffer to hold the pages of the PROFESSOR relation. Since there are 5 PROFESSOR tuples in each such page, and since each tuple matches 10 TEACHING tuples, the 50-page chunk of the PROFESSOR relation can, on average, match $50 \times 5 \times 10 = 2,500$ tuples of TEACHING. The index on the ProfId attribute of TEACHING is not clustered, so record Ids retrieved from it will not be sorted. As a result, the cost of fetching the matching rows of the data file (leaving aside for the moment the cost of fetching the Ids from the index), can be as much as 2,500 page transfers. By sorting the record Ids of these matching tuples first, however (a technique described in Section 13.3.1), we can guarantee that the tuples will be fetched in no more than 1,000 page transfers (the size of the TEACHING relation). Since this trick must be performed 4 times (for each 50-page chunk of PROFESSOR), the total number of page transfers to fetch the matching tuples of TEACHING is 4,000.

■ *To search the index*: Since TEACHING has a hash index on ProfId, we can assume 1.2 I/Os per index search. For each ProfId, the search finds the bucket that contains the record Ids of all matching tuples (10 on average). These Ids can be retrieved in one I/O operation. Thus, the 10,000 matching record Ids of tuples in TEACHING can be retrieved 10 tuples per I/O—1,000 I/Os in total. The total cost of the index search for all tuples is therefore 1,200.

■ *Combined cost*: 5,200 page transfers.

Alternatively, we can use a block-nested loops join or a sort-merge join. For a block-nested loops join that utilizes a 51-page buffer of main memory, the inner relation, TEACHING, must be scanned 4 times. This leads to a smaller number of page transfers: $200 + 4 \times 1,000 = 4,200$. Note, however, that if the weight of ProfId is lower, the comparison between the index-nested and block-nested techniques is very different (exercise 14.4).

The result of the join is going to have 10,000 tuples (because Id is a key for PROFESSOR and every PROFESSOR tuple matches roughly 10 TEACHING tuples). Since every TEACHING tuple is twice the size of a PROFESSOR tuple, the resulting file will be 50% larger than TEACHING—in other words, it will have 1,500 pages.

Next we need to apply the selection and the projection operators. As the result of the join does not have any indices, we choose the file scan access path. Moreover, we can apply selection and projection during the same scan. Examining each tuple

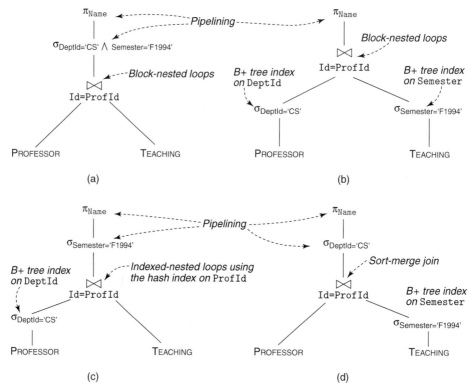

Figure 14.3 Query execution plans for the relational expressions (14.3) through (14.6).

in turn, we discard it if it does not satisfy the selection condition; if it does, we discard the attributes not named in the SELECT clause and output the result.

We could treat the join phase and the select/project phase separately, outputting the result of the join to an intermediate file and then inputting the file to do the select/project, but there is a better way. By interleaving the two phases, we can eliminate the I/O operations associated with creating and accessing the intermediate file. With this technique, called **pipelining**, join and select/project operate as coroutines. The join phase is executed until the available buffers in memory are filled, and then select/project takes over, emptying the buffers and outputting the result. The join phase is then resumed, filling the buffers, and the process continues until select/project outputs the last tuple. In pipelining the output of one relational operator is "piped" to the input of the next relational operator—without saving the intermediate result on disk.

The resulting query execution plan is depicted in Figure 14.3(a). All in all, using the block-nested loops strategy, evaluating this plan takes $4,200 + \alpha \times 1,500$ page I/Os, where 1,500 is the size of the join and α, a number between 0 and 1, is the reduction factor due to selection and projection. We study the techniques for estimating this reduction factor later in this chapter.

Case b: selection fully pushed. The query tree in Figure 14.2 (b) suggests a number of alternative query execution plans. First, if we push selections down to the leaf nodes of the tree (the relations Professor and Teaching), then we can compute the relations $\sigma_{\text{DeptId}='CS'}(\text{Professor})$ and $\sigma_{\text{Semester}='F1994'}(\text{Teaching})$ using the existing B$^+$ tree indices on DeptId and Semester. However, the resulting relations will not have any indices (unless the DBMS decides that it is worth building them). In particular, we cannot make use of the hash indices on Professor.Id and Teaching.ProfId. Thus, we must use block-nested loops or sort-merge to compute the join. The projection is then applied to the result of the join on the fly, while it is being written out to disk. In other words, we again use pipelining to minimize the overhead of applying the projection operator.

We estimate the cost of the plan, depicted in Figure 14.3(b), where the join is performed using block-nested loops. Since there are 1,000 professors in 50 departments, the weight of DeptId in the Professor relation is 20; hence, the size of $\sigma_{\text{DeptId}='CS'}(\text{Professor})$ is about 20 tuples, or 4 pages. The weight of Semester in Teaching is 10,000/4 = 2,500 tuples, or 250 pages. Because the indices on DeptId and Semester are clustered, computing the selection will take 4 I/Os (to access the two indices) + 4 + 250 I/Os (to access the qualifying tuples in both relations).

The join can be performed in one scan of each file (because the buffer is large enough to hold the entire Professor relation). Thus, the total cost is 4 + 4 + 250 + 4 + 250 = 512.

Case c: selection pushed to the Professor relation. For the query tree in Figure 14.2(c), a query execution plan can be constructed as follows. First, compute $\sigma_{\text{DeptId}='CS'}(\text{Professor})$ using the B$^+$ tree index on Professor.DeptId. As in case b, this prevents us from further using the hash index on Professor.Id in the subsequent join computation. Unlike case b, however, the relation Teaching remains untouched, so we can still use index-nested loops (utilizing the index on Teaching.ProfId) to compute the join. Other possibilities are block-nested loops and sort-merge join. Finally, we can pipe the output of the join to the selection operator $\sigma_{\text{DeptId}='F1994'}$ and apply the projection during the same scan.

The above query execution plan is depicted in Figure 14.3(c). We now estimate the cost of this plan.

■ $\sigma_{\text{DeptId}='CS'}(\text{Professor})$. There are 50 departments and 1,000 professors. Thus, the result of this selection will contain about 20 tuples, or 4 pages. Since the index on Professor.DeptId is clustered, retrieval of these tuples should take about 4 I/Os. Index search will take an additional 2 I/Os for a 2-level B$^+$ tree index. Because we intend to pipe the result of the selection into the join step that follows, there is no output cost.

■ *Indexed-nested loops join.* We use the result of the previous selection and pipe it directly as input to the join. An important consideration here is that, because we chose indexed-nested loops utilizing the hash index on Teaching.ProfId, the result of the selection does not need to be saved on disk even if this result is large. Once selection produces enough tuples to fill the buffers, we can immediately join the tuples with the matching PROFESSOR tuples, using the hash index, and output the joined rows. Then we can resume the selection and fill the buffers again.

As before, each PROFESSOR tuple matches about 10 TEACHING tuples, which are going to be stored in one bucket. So, to find the matches for 20 tuples, we have to search the index 20 times at the cost of 1.2 I/O per search. Another 200 I/Os are needed to actually fetch the matching tuples from disk since the index is unclustered. All in all, this should take $1.2 * 20 + 200 = 224$ I/Os.

■ *Combined cost.* Since the result of the join is piped into the subsequent selection and projection, these latter operations do not cost anything in terms of I/O. Thus, the total cost is: 4+2+224 = 230 I/Os.

Case d: selection pushed to the TEACHING relation. This case is similar to case c, except that selection is now applied to TEACHING rather than to PROFESSOR. Since the indices on TEACHING are lost after applying the selection, we cannot use this relation in the inner loop of the indexed nested loops join. However, we can use it in the outer loop of the index-nested loops join that utilizes the hash index on PROFESSOR.Id in the inner loop. This join can also be computed using block-nested loops and sort-merge. For this example, we select sort-merge. The subsequent application of selection and projection to the result can be done using pipelining, as in earlier examples. The resulting query plan is depicted in Figure 14.3(d).

■ *Join: the sorting stage.* The first step is to sort PROFESSOR on Id and $\sigma_{\text{Semester}='F1994'}$ (TEACHING) on ProfId.

❑ To sort PROFESSOR, we must first scan it and create sorted runs. Since PROFESSOR fits in 200 blocks, there will be $\lceil 200/50 \rceil = 4$ sorted runs. Thus, creation of the four sorted runs and storing them back on disk takes $2 \times 200 = 400$ I/Os. These runs can then be merged in just one more pass, but we postpone this merge and combine it with the merging stage of the sort-merge join. (See below.)

❑ To sort $\sigma_{\text{Semester}='F1994'}$ (TEACHING), we must first compute this relation. Since TEACHING holds information for about 4 semesters, the size of the selection is about $10,000/4 = 2,500$ tuples. The index is clustered, so the tuples are stored consecutively in the file in 250 blocks. The cost of the selection is therefore about 252 I/O operations, which includes 2 I/O operations for searching the index.

The result of the selection is not written to disk. Instead, each time the 50-page buffer in main memory is filled, it is immediately sorted to create a run and then written to disk. In this way we create $\lceil 250/50 \rceil = 5$ sorted runs. This takes 250 I/Os.

The 5 sorted runs of $\sigma_{\text{Semester}='F1994'}$ (TEACHING) can be merged in one pass. However, instead of doing this separately, we combine this step with the merging step of the join (and the merging step of sorting PROFESSOR, which was postponed earlier).

■ *Join: the merging stage.* Rather than merging the 4 sorted runs of PROFESSOR and the sorted runs of $\sigma_{Semester='F1994'}$ (TEACHING) into two sorted relations, the runs are piped directly into the merge stage of the sort-merge join without writing the intermediate sorted results on disk. In this way, we combine the final merge steps in sorting these relations with the merge step of the join.

The combined merge uses 4 input buffers for each of the sorted runs of PROFESSOR, 5 input buffers for each sorted run of $\sigma_{Semester='F1994'}$ (TEACHING), and one output buffer for the result of the join. The tuple p with the lowest value of p.Id among the heads of the 4 PROFESSOR's runs is selected and matched against the tuple t with the lowest value of t.ProfId among the tuples in the head of the 5 runs corresponding to $\sigma_{Semester='F1994'}$ (TEACHING). If p.Id=t.ProfId, p and t are removed from the runs and their join is placed in the output buffer. If p.Id<t.ProfId, p is discarded; else t is discarded. The process then repeats itself until all the input runs are exhausted.

The combined merge can be done at a cost of reading the sorted runs of the two relations: 200 I/Os for the runs of PROFESSOR and 250 I/Os, for $\sigma_{Semester='F1994'}$ (TEACHING) respectively.

■ *The rest.* The result of the join is then piped directly to the subsequent selection (on DeptId) and projection (on Name) operators. Since no intermediate results are written to disk, the I/O cost of these stages is zero.

■ *Combined cost.* Summing up the costs of the individual operations, we get: $400 + 252 + 250 + 200 + 250 = 1,352$.

And the winner is . . .   Tallying up the results, we can see that the best plan (among those considered—only a small portion of all possible plans) is plan c. The interesting observation here is that this plan is better than plan b, even though plan b joins smaller relations (because the selection is fully pushed). The reason for this is the loss of an index when selection is pushed down to the TEACHING relation. This illustrates once again that the heuristic rules of Section 14.2 are just that: heuristics. While they are likely to lead to better query execution plans, they must be evaluated within a more general cost model.

14.4   ESTIMATING THE SIZE OF THE OUTPUT

The examples in the previous section illustrate the importance of accurate estimates of the output size of various relational expressions. The result of one expression serves as input to the next, and the input size has a direct effect on the cost of the computation. To give a better idea of how such estimates can be done, we present a simple technique based on the assumption that all values have an equal chance of occurring in a relation.

The system catalog can contain the following set of statistics for each relation name **R**:

■ *Blocks*(**R**). The number of blocks occupied by the instance of table **R**

■ *Tuples*(**R**). The number of tuples in the instance of **R**

■ *Values*(**R**.*A*). The number of distinct values of attribute *A* in the instance of **R**

■ *MaxVal*(**R**.*A*). The maximum value of attribute *A* in the instance of **R**

■ *MinVal*(**R**.*A*). The minimum value of attribute *A* in the instance of **R**.

Earlier we introduced the notion of attribute weight and used it to estimate sizes of selection and equijoin. We now define a more general notion, reduction factor. Consider the following general query:

```
SELECT    TargetList
FROM      R₁ V₁, ..., Rₙ Vₙ
WHERE     Condition
```

The **reduction factor** of this query is the ratio

$$\frac{Tuples(\text{the result set})}{Tuples(\mathbf{R}_1) \times \cdots \times Tuples(\mathbf{R}_n)}$$

Although this definition seems cyclic (to find the reduction factor we need to know the size of the result set), the reduction factor is easy to estimate by induction on the query structure.

We assume that reduction factors due to different parts of the query are independent of each other. Thus,

$$reduction(Query) = reduction(TargetList) \times reduction(Condition)$$

where *reduction(TargetList)* is the size reduction due to projection of rows on the attributes in the SELECT clause and *reduction(Condition)* is the size reduction due to the elimination of rows that do not satisfy *Condition*.

Also, if *Condition* = *Condition₁* AND *Condition₂*, then

$$reduction(Condition) = reduction(Condition_1) \times reduction(Condition_2)$$

Thus, the size reduction due to a complex condition can be estimated in terms of the size reduction due to the components of that condition.

It remains to estimate the reduction factors due to projection in the SELECT clause and due to atomic conditions in the WHERE clause. We ignore nested subqueries and aggregates in this discussion.

■ $reduction(\mathbf{R}_i.A = value) = \frac{1}{Values(\mathbf{R}_i.A)}$, where $\mathbf{R}_i$ is a relation name and *A* is an attribute in $\mathbf{R}_i$. This estimate is based on the uniformity assumption—all values are equally probable.

■ $reduction(\mathbf{R}_i.A = \mathbf{R}_j.B) = \frac{1}{max(Values(\mathbf{R}_i.A), Values(\mathbf{R}_j.A))}$, where $\mathbf{R}_i$ and $\mathbf{R}_j$ are relations and *A* and *B* are attributes. Using the uniformity assumption, we can decompose $\mathbf{R}_i$ (respectively, $\mathbf{R}_j$) into subsets with the property that all elements of a subset have the same value of $\mathbf{R}_i.A$ (respectively, $\mathbf{R}_j.B$). If we assume that there are $N_{\mathbf{R}_i}$ tuples in $\mathbf{R}_i$ and $N_{\mathbf{R}_j}$ tuples in $\mathbf{R}_j$ and that every element of $\mathbf{R}_i$ matches an element of $\mathbf{R}_j$, then we can conclude that the number of tuples that satisfy the condition is $Values(\mathbf{R}_i.A) \times (N_{\mathbf{R}_i}/Values(\mathbf{R}_i.A)) \times (N_{\mathbf{R}_j}/Values(\mathbf{R}_j.B))$. In general, the reduction factor is calculated assuming (unrealistically) that each value in the smaller range always matches a value in the larger range. Assuming that $\mathbf{R}_i.A$ is the smaller range and dividing this expression by $N_{\mathbf{R}_i} \times N_{\mathbf{R}_j}$ yields the reduction factor.

■ $reduction(\mathbf{R}_i.A > value) = \frac{MaxVal(\mathbf{R}_i.A) - value}{Values(\mathbf{R}_i.A)}$. The reduction factor for $\mathbf{R}_i.A < value$ is defined similarly. These estimates are also based on the assumption that all values are distributed uniformly.

■ $reduction(TargetList) = \frac{\text{number-of-attributes}(TargetList)}{\text{number-of-attributes}(\mathbf{R}_i)}$. Here, for simplicity, we assume that all attributes contribute equally to the tuple size.

The weight of an attribute, $\mathbf{R}_i.A$, used in Section 14.3 can now be estimated using the notion of reduction factor:

$$weight(\mathbf{R}_i.A) = Tuples(\mathbf{R}_i) \times reduction(\mathbf{R}_i.A = value)$$

For instance, the reduction factor of the query PROFESSOR.DeptId = *value* is $1/50$, since there are 50 departments. As the number of tuples in PROFESSOR is 1,000, the weight of the attribute DeptId in PROFESSOR is 20.

14.5 CHOOSING A PLAN

In the previous section we looked at some query execution plans and showed how to compute their cost. However, we did not present a general technique for *producing* the candidate plans. Unfortunately, the number of possible plans can be quite large, so we need an efficient way of choosing a relatively small, promising subset. We can then compute the cost of each and choose the best. There are at least three major issues involved in this process.

■ Choosing a logical plan

■ Reducing the search space

■ Choosing a heuristic search algorithm

We discuss each of these issues in turn.

Choosing a logical plan. We defined a query execution plan as a query tree with the relational implementation methods attached to each inner node. Thus, constructing such a plan involves two tasks: choosing a tree and choosing the implementation methods. Choosing the right tree is the more difficult job because of the number of trees involved, which, in turn, is caused by the fact that the binary associative and commutative operators, such as join, cross product, union, and the like, can be processed in so many different ways. We mentioned in Section 14.2 that the subtree of a query tree in which N relations are combined by such an operator

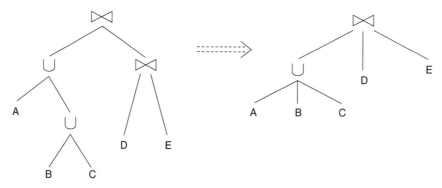

Figure 14.4 Transforming a query tree into a logical query execution plan.

can be formed in $T(N) \times N!$ ways. We want to deal with this kind of exponential complexity separately, so we first focus on **logical query execution plans**, which avoid the problem by grouping consecutive binary operators of the same kind into one node, as shown in Figure 14.4.

The different logical query execution plans are created from the "master plan" of the form (14.2) on page 425 by pushing selections and projections down and by combining selections and Cartesian products into joins. Only a few of all possible logical plans are retained for further consideration. Typically, the ones selected are fully pushed trees (because they are expected to produce the smallest intermediate results) plus all the "nearly" fully pushed trees. The reason for the latter should be clear from the discussion in the previous section: Pushing selection or projection down to a leaf node of a query tree might eliminate the option of using an index in the join computation.

According to this heuristic, the query tree in Figure 14.2(a) will not be selected, since nothing has been pushed. Section 14.3 then shows that the fully pushed query plan in Figure 14.3(b) is inferior to the nearly fully pushed plan in Figure 14.3(c), which has the least estimated cost. In this example, all joins are binary, so the transformation shown in Figure 14.4 does not pertain.

Reducing the search space.   Having selected candidate logical query execution plans, the query optimizer must decide how to evaluate the expressions that involve the commutative and associative operators. For instance, Figure 14.5 shows several alternative but equivalent ways of converting a commutative and associative node of a logical plan that combines multiple relations (a) into query trees (b), (c), and (d).

The space of all possible equivalent query (sub)trees that correspond to a node in a logical query plan is two-dimensional. First, we must choose the desired *shape* of the tree (i.e., we ignore the labels on the nodes). For instance, the trees in Figure 14.5 have different shapes, with (d) being the simplest. Trees of such a shape are called **left-deep query trees**. A tree shape corresponds to a particular parenthesizing of a relational subexpression that involves an associative and commutative operator. Thus, the logical query execution plan in Figure 14.5(a) corresponds to

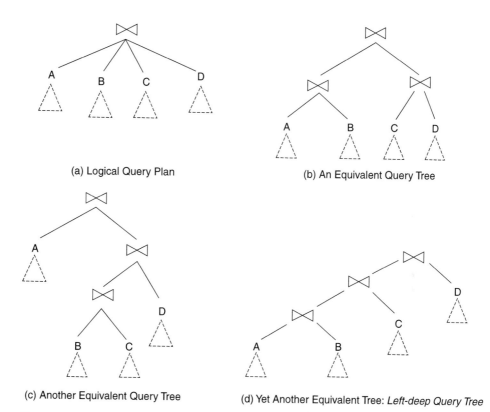

(a) Logical Query Plan

(b) An Equivalent Query Tree

(c) Another Equivalent Query Tree

(d) Yet Another Equivalent Tree: *Left-deep Query Tree*

Figure 14.5 Logical plan and three equivalent query trees.

the expression $A \bowtie B \bowtie C \bowtie D$, while the query trees (b), (c), and (d) correspond to the expressions $(A \bowtie B) \bowtie (C \bowtie D)$, $A \bowtie ((B \bowtie C) \bowtie D)$, and $((A \bowtie B) \bowtie C) \bowtie D$, respectively. A left-deep query tree always corresponds to an algebraic expression of the form $(\ldots ((E_{i_1} \bowtie E_{i_2}) \bowtie E_{i_3}) \bowtie \ldots) \bowtie E_{i_N}$.

Query optimizers usually settle on one particular shape for the query tree: left-deep. This is because, even with a fixed tree shape, query optimizers have plenty of work to do. Indeed, given the left-deep tree of Figure 14.5(d), there are still 4! possible ways to order the joins. For instance, $((B \bowtie D) \bowtie C) \bowtie A$ is another ordering of the join of Figure 14.5(d) that leads to a different left-deep query execution plan. So, if computing cost estimates for 4! query execution plans does not sound like a lot, think of what it would take to estimate the cost of 10! or 12! or 16! plans. Incidentally, all commercial query optimizers give up at around 16 joins.

Apart from the general need to reduce the search space, there is another good reason to choose left-deep trees over the trees of the form Figure 14.5(b): pipelining. For instance, in Figure 14.5(d) we can first compute $A \bowtie B$ and pipe the result to the next join with C. The result of this second join can also be piped up the tree without materializing the intermediate relation on disk. The ability to do this is very important for large relations because the intermediate output from a join can

Figure 14.6 Heuristic search of the query execution plan space.

Input: *A logical plan* $E_1 \bowtie \cdots \bowtie E_N$
Output: *A "good" left-deep plan* $(\ldots ((E_{i_1} \bowtie E_{i_2}) \bowtie E_{i_3}) \bowtie \ldots) \bowtie E_{i_N}$

```
1-Plans := all 1-relation plans
Best := all 1-relation plans with lowest cost
for (i := 1; i < N; i++) do
        // Below, ⋈ᵐᵉᵗʰ denotes join marked with an implementation method, meth*
        Plans := { best ⋈ᵐᵉᵗʰ 1-plan | best ∈ Best; 1-plan ∈ 1-Plans, where
                                        1-plan is a plan for some Eⱼ that has not
                                        been used so far in best }
        Best := { plan | plan ∈ Plans, where plan has the lowest cost }
end
return Best;
```

be very large. For instance, if the size of the relations **A**, **B**, and **C** is 1,000 pages, the intermediate relation can reach 10^9 pages just to shrink back to a few pages after joining with **D**. The overhead of storing such intermediate results on disk can be huge.

A heuristic search algorithm.   The choice of left-deep trees has reduced the size of the search space from immense to huge. Next we must assign relations to the leaf nodes of the left-deep tree. There are $N!$ such assignments, so estimating the cost of all is still a hopelessly intractable problem. Therefore, a heuristic search algorithm is needed to find a reasonable plan by looking only at a tiny portion of the overall search space. One such algorithm is based on *dynamic programming* and is used (with variations) in a number of commercial systems (e.g., DB2). We explain the main idea below; details are given in [Griffiths-Selinger et al. 1979]. A different heuristic search algorithm, described in [Wong and Youssefi 1976], is used in Ingres, another DBMS that was influential in the olden days.

A simplified version of the dynamic programming heuristic search algorithm is described in Figure 14.6. It builds a left-deep query tree by first evaluating the cost of all plans for computing each argument of an N-way join, $E_1 \bowtie \cdots \bowtie E_N$, where each E_j is a 1-relation expression. These are referred to as *1-relation plans*. Note that each E_j can have several such plans (due to different possible access paths; e.g., one might use a scan and another an index), so the number of 1-relation plans can be N or larger. The *best* among all these plans (i.e., those with lowest cost) are expanded into 2-relation plans, then 3-relation plans, etc., as follows. To expand a best 1-relation plan, p (for definiteness, assume that p is a plan for E_{i_1}) into a 2-relation plan, p is joined with every 1-relation plan, except the plans for E_{i_1} (because we already selected p as *the* plan for E_{i_1}). We then evaluate the cost of all such plans and retain the best 2-relation plans. Each best 2-relation plan, q (let us assume that it is a plan for $E_{i_1} \bowtie E_{i_2}$), is expanded into a set of 3-relation plans by joining q with every 1-relation plan, except the plans for E_{i_1} and E_{i_2} (since the latter are already accounted for in q). Again, only the lowest cost plans are retained for the next stage. The process continues until a left-deep expression corresponding to the logical plan $E_1 \bowtie \cdots \bowtie E_N$ is fully constructed.

We illustrate the overall process using our running example, query (14.7). First, the query processor generates a number of plausible logical plans—in our case, most likely the fully pushed tree of Figure 14.2(b) on page 431 plus the two partially pushed trees (c) and (d).

The shape of the trees depicted in Figure 14.2 are left-deep, but there are two query execution plans corresponding to each such tree: They differ in the order of relations in the join. Let us consider the query execution plans generated using the algorithm of Figure 14.6 starting with the logical plan of Figure 14.2(c).

The 1-relation plans for $\sigma_{\text{DeptId}=\,'CS'}(\text{PROFESSOR})$ can use the following access paths: a scan, the clustered index on PROFESSOR.DeptId, or a binary search (because PROFESSOR is sorted on DeptId). The best plan uses the index, so it is retained. For the expression TEACHING, scan is all that can be done. We now have two 1-relation plans. In the next iteration, the algorithm expands the chosen 1-relation plans to 2-relation plans. This amounts to generating the two expressions $\sigma_{\text{DeptId}=\,'CS'}(\text{PROFESSOR}) \bowtie_{\text{Id=ProfId}} \text{TEACHING}$ and $\text{TEACHING} \bowtie_{\text{ProfId=Id}} \sigma_{\text{DeptId}=\,'CS'}(\text{PROFESSOR})$ and deciding on the evaluation strategy to use for the join in each. We estimated the different plans for the former expression in Section 14.3 and concluded that the indexed-nested loops join is the best. The second expression cannot be evaluated in the same way because the order of the arguments indicates that the relation TEACHING is scanned first. This expression can be evaluated using sort-merge or block-nested loops. Both methods are more expensive, so they are discarded.

Once the best plan for evaluating the join is selected, we can consider the result of the join as a 1-relation expression, E, and we now have to find a plan for $\pi_{\text{Name}}(\sigma_{\text{Semester}=\,'F1994'}(E))$. Since the result of E is not sorted or indexed and since duplicate elimination is not requested, we choose a sequential scan access path to compute both selection and projection. Also, since E generates the result in main memory, we choose pipelining to avoid saving the intermediate result on disk.

The dynamic programming algorithm is likely to miss some good plans because it focuses on what is best at the current moment without trying to look ahead. One improvement here is to retain not only the best plans but also certain "interesting" plans. A plan might be considered interesting if its output relation is sorted or if it has an index, even if the cost of the plan is not minimal. This heuristic recognizes the fact that a sorted relation can significantly reduce the cost of subsequent operations, such as sort-merge join, duplicate elimination, and grouping. Likewise, an indexed relation can reduce the cost of subsequent joins.

14.6 TUNING ISSUES: IMPACT ON QUERY DESIGN

Database administration is a highly paid job for a reason. One of the important skills it requires is a good understanding of how query optimizers work and the ability to use this knowledge for tuning database designs and queries for performance.

Examining plans. In Section 13.7, we discussed how an understanding of the implementation of relational operators can affect design decisions at the physical level. That discussion focused on queries that involve a *single* operator, but a typical database workload consists of much more complex queries. Thus, to decide which operations can be speeded up with additional indices, one has to understand the query execution plans that a DBMS might choose for each particular query. In many cases, this requires a manual estimate of typical relation sizes and of value distributions in the join and selection attributes. Clearly, it is not possible to analyze any sizable number of query execution plans in this way, so the process requires a great deal of intuition and experience.

DBMS vendors usually supply various tools to help with tuning. The use of these tools normally requires creation of a mock-up database in which the different plans can be tried out. A typical tool in most DBMSs is the EXPLAIN PLAN statement, which lets the user see the query plans the DBMS generates. This statement is not part of the SQL standard, so the syntax varies among vendors. The basic idea is to first execute a statement of the form

```
EXPLAIN PLAN SET queryno=123 FOR
        SELECT    P.Name
        FROM      Professor P, Teaching T
        WHERE     P.Id = T.ProfId AND T.Semester = 'F1994'
                  AND T.Semester = 'CS'
```

which causes the DBMS to generate a query execution plan and store it as a set of tuples in a relation called PLAN_TABLE. queryno is one attribute of that table. Some DBMSs use a different attribute name, for example, id. The plan can then be retrieved by querying PLAN_TABLE as follows:

```
SELECT * FROM PLAN_TABLE WHERE queryno=123
```

Text-based facilities for examining query plans are extremely powerful, but these days they are used mostly by people who enjoy fixing their own cars. A busy database administrator uses text-based facilities only as a last resort, because many vendors provide flashy graphical interfaces to their tuning tools. For instance, IBM has Visual Explain for DB/2, Oracle supplies Oracle Diagnostics Pack, and SQL Server from Microsoft has Query Analyzer. These tools not only show query plans, but they can also suggest indices that can speed up various queries.

Index-only queries. Having identified the possible indices needed to support the various queries, the database designer must now decide what goes into the actual system. For instance, two different queries might require two different clustered indices for the same relation. Since only one index per relation can be clustered, something has to give. In this case, it is necessary to rank queries for their "importance," which can take into account the frequency with which the query occurs, the desired response time, and so forth.

Another way to work around the clustering conflicts is to force the optimizer to use **index-only strategies**. Suppose that Teaching already has a clustered B$^+$ tree index on Semester, but another important query requires a clustered index on

ProfId in order to quickly access the course codes associated with a given professor. Since the DBMS cannot create yet another clustered index on TEACHING, we can sidestep the problem by creating an *unclustered* B$^+$ tree index on TEACHING using the attribute sequence ProfId, CrsCode. Since our query needs only ProfId and CrsCode, the optimizer does not need to look into the TEACHING relation at all—all the information can be obtained from the index! Because the index is a B$^+$ tree, the values of CrsCode are clustered around the corresponding values for ProfId, which produces the same effect as that of a clustered index (in fact, it is more efficient because the index is smaller and there is no need to retrieve pages of the actual relation).

Index-only query processing might seem like an ultimate database tuning device. However, free computational lunches are rare: Keeping extra indices means storage overhead. More important, extra indices might significantly decrease the performance of update transactions, since every index must be updated whenever the corresponding relation is changed. Thus, adding indices might not be a good idea for highly dynamic relations.

Nested queries and query optimization. Nested queries are one of the most powerful features of SQL. They are also one of the hardest to optimize. Consider the following query:

```
SELECT   P.Name, C.CrsName
FROM     PROFESSOR P, COURSE C
WHERE    P.Department='CS' AND
         C.CrsCode IN
             SELECT T.CrsCode
             FROM TEACHING T
             WHERE T.Semester='F1995' AND T.ProfId = P.Id
```

that returns a set of rows in which the value of the first attribute is the name of a CS professor who has taught a course in the fall of 1995 and the value of the second is the name of one such course.

Typically, a query optimizer splits this query into two separate parts. The inner query is considered as an independently optimized unit; the outer query is also optimized independently (with the result set of the inner SELECT statement viewed as a database relation). Because of this separation, certain optimizations might not be considered by the query optimizer—for instance, the use of a clustered index on TEACHING with search key (ProfId, CrsCode) will not be considered, since the correlated nested query simply produces a set of course codes for each value of P.Id that is supplied. On the other hand, it is easy to see that the above query is equivalent to

```
SELECT   C.CrsName, P.Name
FROM     PROFESSOR P, TEACHING T, COURSE C
WHERE    T.Semester='F1995' AND P.Department='CS'
         AND P.Id = T.ProfId AND T.CrsCode=C.CrsCode
```

and the use of a clustered index *is* considered in optimizing this query.

It should be remarked that some query optimizers do, in fact, try to eliminate nested subqueries and take other steps to reduce the cost of processing them. However, it is still a good idea to avoid query nesting whenever possible.

Stored procedures. The advantages of stored procedures were discussed in Chapter 10. One of their important properties is that they are compiled by the DBMS and query execution plans for their embedded SQL statements are generated. This is good because the query optimizer need not be executed at run time. However, it is important to realize that the query execution plans generated at compile time represent the optimizer's best guess based on the statistics and physical organization then available. This means that, if indices are added or deleted at a later time or if the relevant statistics change drastically, the previously generated query plans might no longer be good or even applicable. Stored procedures should therefore not be used for queries that involve very dynamic relations, and it is highly recommended that these procedures be recompiled when indices change.

14.7 BIBLIOGRAPHIC NOTES

An extensive textbook treatment of query optimization can be found in [Garcia-Molina et al. 2000]. Heuristic search algorithms are described in [Griffiths-Selinger et al. 1979, Wong and Youssefi 1976].

For further reading on the latest query optimization techniques as well as additional references, see [Ioannidis 1996, Chaudhuri 1998].

14.8 EXERCISES

14.1 Can there be a *commutativity* transformation for the projection operator? Explain.

14.2 Write down the sequence of steps needed to transform $\pi_A((\mathbf{R} \bowtie_{B=C} \mathbf{S}) \bowtie_{D=E} \mathbf{T})$ into $\pi_A((\pi_E(\mathbf{T}) \bowtie_{E=D} \pi_{ACD}(\mathbf{S})) \bowtie_{C=B} \mathbf{R})$. List the attributes that each of the schemas $\mathbf{R}$, $\mathbf{S}$, and $\mathbf{T}$ *must* have and the attributes that each (or some) of these schemas must *not* have in order for the above transformation to be correct.

14.3 Under what conditions can the expression $\pi_A((\mathbf{R} \bowtie_{cond_1} \mathbf{S}) \bowtie_{cond_2} \mathbf{T})$ be transformed into $\pi_A(\pi_B(\mathbf{R} \bowtie_{cond_1} \pi_C(\mathbf{S})) \bowtie_{cond_2} \pi_D(\mathbf{T}))$ using the heuristic rules given in Section 14.2?

14.4 Consider the join PROFESSOR$\bowtie_{Id=ProfId}$ TEACHING used in the running example of Section 14.3. Let us change the statistics slightly and assume that the number of distinct values for TEACHING.ProfId is 10,000 (which translates into lower weight for this attribute).

a. What is the cardinality of the PROFESSOR relation?

b. Let there be an unclustered hash index on ProfId and assume that, as before, 5 PROFESSOR tuples fit in one page, 10 TEACHING-tuples fit in one page, and the cardinality of TEACHING is 10,000. Estimate the cost of computing the above join using indexed-nested loops and block-nested loops with a 51-page buffer.

14.5 Consider the following query:

```
SELECT DISTINCT E.Ename
FROM      EMPLOYEE E
WHERE     E.Title = 'Programmer' AND E.Dept = 'Production'
```

Assume that

❏ 10% of employees are programmers

❏ 5% of employees are programmers who work for the production department

❏ There are 10 departments

❏ The EMPLOYEE relation has 1,000 pages with 10 tuples per page

❏ There is a 51-page buffer that can be used to process the query

Find the best query execution plan for each of the following cases:

a. The only index is on Title, and it is a clustered 2-level B$^+$ tree.

b. The only index is on the attribute sequence Dept, Title, Ename; it is clustered and has two levels.

c. The only index is on Dept, Ename, Title; it is a clustered 3-level B$^+$ tree.

d. There is an unclustered hash index on Dept and a 2-level clustered tree index on Ename.

14.6 Consider the following schema, where the keys are underlined:

```
EMPLOYEE(SSN, Name,Dept)
PROJECT(SSN,PID,Name,Budget)
```

The SSN attribute in PROJECT is the Id of the employee working on the project. There can be several employees per project, but the functional dependency Pid → Name,Budget holds (so the relation is not normalized). Consider the query

```
SELECT    P.Budget, P.Name, E.Name
FROM      EMPLOYEE E, PROJECT P
WHERE     E.SSN = P.SSN AND
          P.Budget > 99 AND
          E.Name = 'John'
ORDER BY P.Budget
```

Assume the following statistical information:

❏ 10,000 tuples in EMPLOYEE relation

❏ 20,000 tuples in PROJECT relation

❏ 40 tuples/page in each relation

❏ 10-page buffer

❑ 1,000 different values for E.Name

❑ The domain of Budget consists of integers in the range of 1 to 100

❑ Indices:
- EMPLOYEE relation:
  On Name: Unclustered, hash
  On SSN: Clustered, 3-level B$^+$ tree
- PROJECT relation:
  On SSN: Unclustered, hash
  On Budget: Clustered, 2-level B$^+$ tree

a. Draw the *fully pushed* query tree.

b. Find the "best" execution plan and the second-best plan. What is the cost of each? Explain how you arrived at your costs.

14.7 Consider the following schema, where the keys are underlined (different keys are underlined differently):

PROFESSOR(<u>Id</u>, Name, Department)
COURSE(<u>CrsCode</u>, <u>Department, CrsName</u>)
TEACHING(ProfId, <u>CrsCode, Semester</u>)

Consider the following query:

```
SELECT   C.CrsName, P.Name
FROM     PROFESSOR P, TEACHING T, COURSE C
WHERE    T.Semester='F1995' AND P.Department='CS'
         AND P.Id = T.ProfId AND T.CrsCode=C.CrsCode
```

Assume the following statistical information:

❑ 1,000 tuples with 10 tuples/page in PROFESSOR relation

❑ 20,000 tuples with 10 tuples/page in TEACHING relation

❑ 2,000 tuples, 5 tuples/page, in COURSE

❑ 5-page buffer

❑ 50 different values for Department

❑ 200 different values for Semester

❑ Indices:
- PROFESSOR relation:
  On Department: Clustered, 2-level B$^+$ tree
  On Id: Unclustered, hash
- COURSE relation:
  On CrsCode: Sorted (no index)
  On CrsName: Hash, unclustered

- TEACHING relation:
  - On ProfId: Clustered, 2-level B$^+$-tree
  - On Semester, CrsCode: Unclustered, 2-level B$^+$ tree

  a. First, show the *unoptimized* relational algebra expression that corresponds to the above SQL query. Then *draw* the corresponding *fully pushed* query tree.
  b. Find the best execution plan and its cost. Explain how you arrived at your costs.

14.8 Consider the following relations that represent part of a real estate database:

    AGENT(Id, AgentName)
    HOUSE(Address, OwnerId, AgentId)
    AMENITY(Address, Feature)

The AGENT relation keeps information on real estate agents, the HOUSE relation has information on who is selling the house and the agent involved, and the AMENITY relation provides information on the features of each house. Each relation has its keys underlined.

Consider the following query:

    SELECT   H.OwnerId, A.AgentName
    FROM   HOUSE H, AGENT A, AMENITY Y
    WHERE   H.Address=Y.Address AND A.Id = H.AgentId
             AND Y.Feature = '5BR' AND H.AgentId = '007'

Assume that the buffer space available for this query has 5 pages and that the following statistics and indices are available:

❏ AMENITY:
- 10,000 records on 1,000 houses, 5 records/page
- Clustered 2-level B$^+$ tree index on Address
- Unclustered hash index on Feature, 50 features

❏ AGENT:
- 200 agents with 10 tuples/page
- Unclustered hash index on Id

❏ HOUSE:
- 1,000 houses with 4 records/page
- Unclustered hash index on AgentId
- Clustered 2-level B$^+$ tree index on Address

Answer the following questions (and explain how you arrived at your solutions).

a. Draw a fully pushed query tree corresponding to the above query.
b. Find the best query plan to evaluate the above query and estimate its cost.
c. Find the next-best plan and estimate its cost.

14.9 None of the query execution plans in Figure 14.3 for queries 14.3 – 14.6 does duplicate elimination. To account for this, let us add one more relational operator, δ, which denotes the operation of duplicate elimination. Modify the plans in Figure 14.3 by adding δ in appropriate places so as to minimize the cost of the computation. Estimate the cost of each new plan.

14.10 Build a database for the scenario in exercise 14.5 using the DBMS of your choice. Use the EXPLAIN PLAN statement (or an equivalent provided by your DBMS) to compare the best plan that you found manually with the plan actually generated by the DBMS.

14.11 Follow exercise 14.10, but use the scenario in exercise 14.6.

14.12 Follow exercise 14.10, but use the scenario in exercise 14.7.

Chapter 15

An Overview of Transaction Processing

The transactions of a transaction processing application should satisfy the ACID properties that we discussed in Chapter 2—Atomic, Consistent, Isolated, and Durable. As transaction designers, we are responsible for the consistency of the transactions in our system. We must ensure that, if each transaction is executed by itself (with no other transactions running concurrently), it performs correctly—that is, it maintains the database integrity constraints and performs the operations listed in its specification (for example, a registration transaction in the Student Registration System correctly updates student and course information.) The remaining properties—atomicity, isolation, and durability—are the responsibility of the underlying transaction system. In this chapter we give an overview of how these features are implemented.

Part 4 of the book gives a much more detailed explanation of these issues. If you intend to study that part, you can omit this chapter. Specifically, this chapter is meant to be the final chapter in an introductory database course, not the first chapter in a transaction processing course.

15.1 ISOLATION

The transaction designer is responsible for designing each transaction so that, if it is executed by itself and the initial database correctly models the current state of the real-world enterprise, the transaction performs correctly and the final database correctly models the (new) state of the enterprise. However, if the transaction processing system executes a set of such transactions concurrently—in some interleaved fashion—the effect might be to transform the database to a state that does not correspond to the real world enterprise it was modeling or to return incorrect results to the user.

The schedule of Figure 2.4 on page 24 is an example of an incorrect concurrent schedule. In that schedule, two registration transactions completed successfully, but the course became oversubscribed and the count of the total number of registrants was only incremented by one. The cause of the failure was the interleaving. Both transactions read the same value of *cur_reg*, so neither took into account the effect of the other. We referred to this situation as a lack of isolation—the I in ACID.

One way for the system to achieve isolation is to run transactions one after the other in some serial order—each transaction is started only after the previous transaction completes. The resulting serial schedule will be correct since we assume that transactions that run by themselves perform correctly. Assuming that the database correctly models the real world when the schedule starts, it will correctly model the real world when each transaction completes.

Unfortunately, for many applications serial execution results in unacceptably small transaction throughput (measured in transactions per second) and unacceptably long response time for users. Although restricting transaction processing systems to run only serial schedules is impractical, serial schedules are important because they serve as the primary measure of correctness. A nonserial schedule is guaranteed to be correct if it has the same effect as a serial schedule.

Note that the implication goes in only one direction. Nonserial schedules that do not have the same effect as serial schedules are *not necessarily* incorrect. We will see that most DBMSs give the application designer the flexibility to run nonserial schedules. First, however, we discuss serializable schedules: schedules that are equivalent to serial schedules.

15.1.1 Serializability

One way to improve performance over serial execution and yet achieve isolation is to guarantee that schedules are serializable. A *serializable schedule* is a schedule that is equivalent to a serial schedule. We discuss the meaning of equivalence below.

As a simple example, assume that transaction T_1 reads and writes only database items x and y, and transaction T_2 reads and writes only database item z. Even if execution of the transactions is interleaved, as in the schedule

$$r_1(x)\ w_2(z)\ w_1(y)$$

T_2's access has no effect on T_1, and T_1's accesses have no effect on T_2. Hence the overall effect of the schedule is the same as if the transactions had executed serially in either the order $T_1\ T_2$ or the order $T_2\ T_1$—that is, in one of the following serial schedules:

$$r_1(x)\ w_1(y)\ w_2(z)$$

or

$$w_2(z)\ r_1(x)\ w_1(y)$$

Note that both of the equivalent serial schedules are obtained from the original schedule by interchanging operations that commute. In the first case, the two write operations have been interchanged. They commute because they operate on distinct items and hence leave the database in the same final state no matter in which order they execute. In the second case, we have interchanged $r_1(x)$ and $w_2(z)$. These operations also commute because they operate on distinct items, and hence, in both orders, T_1 gets back the same value of x and the database is left in the same final state.

Suppose that, in addition, both T_1 and T_2 read a common item, q. Again, the overall effect is the same as if the transactions had executed serially in either order. Thus, the schedule

$$r_1(x) \; r_2(q) \; w_2(z) \; r_1(q) \; w_1(y)$$

has the same effect as does the serial schedule

$$r_1(x) \; r_1(q) \; w_1(y) \; r_2(q) \; w_2(z)$$

in which all of T_1's operations precede those of T_2. The equivalence between the two schedules is again based on commutativity. The new feature illustrated by this example is that operations do not have to access distinct items in order to commute. In this case, $r_1(q)$ and $r_2(q)$ commute because they both return the same value to the transactions in either execution order.

The schedule of the two registration transactions shown in Figure 2.4 on page 24 is not serializable. We cannot obtain an equivalent serial schedule by a series of interchanges of adjacent commuting operations, since a read and a write operation on the same data item do not commute; nor do two write operations on the same item.

In general, we are interested in specifying when a schedule, S, of some set of concurrently executing transactions is equivalent to (i.e., has the same effect as) some serial schedule, S_{ser}, of that set. Informally, what is required is that in both schedules

■ The values returned by the corresponding read operations are the same

■ Updates to each data item occur in the same order.

If each read operation returns the same value in S and S_{ser} the computations performed by the transactions will be identical in both schedules and hence the transactions will write the same values back to the database. Since the write operations occur in the same order in both schedules, they leave the database in the same final state. Thus, S has the same effect as (and hence is equivalent to) S_{ser}.

We say that the schedule of a set of transactions is **serializable** if it is equivalent to a serial schedule in the sense described above. Since in a serial schedule only one transaction is executing at a time, there is no possibility of the transactions affecting one another. Thus, we say they are isolated. Moreover, because of the equivalence between serial and serializable schedules, we say that the transactions in a serializable schedule are also isolated.

Database systems can guarantee that schedules are serializable. By allowing serializable, in addition to serial, schedules, they allow more concurrency and hence performance is improved. These systems also offer less stringent notions of isolation (which we discuss shortly) that do not require that schedules be serializable, and hence they support even more concurrency and better performance. Since such schedules are not necessarily equivalent to serial schedules, correctness is not guaranteed for all applications. Therefore, less stringent notions of isolation must be used with caution.

The part of the transaction processing system responsible for enforcing isolation is called the **concurrency control**. The concurrency control enforces isolation by controlling the schedule of database operations. When a transaction wishes to read or write a database item, it submits its request to the concurrency control. On the basis of the sequence of requests it has granted up to that point and given the fact that it does not know what requests might arrive in the future, the concurrency control decides whether isolation can be guaranteed if it grants that request at that time. If isolation cannot be guaranteed, the request is not granted: the transaction is either made to wait or is aborted.

15.1.2 Two-Phase Locking

Most concurrency controls in commercial systems implement serializability using a **strict two-phase locking protocol** [Eswaran et al. 1976]. This protocol uses locks associated with items in the database and requires that a transaction hold the appropriate lock before it can access the item. When a transaction wishes to read (or write) a database item, it submits a request to the concurrency control, which must grant to the transaction a **read lock** (or **write lock**) on the item before passing the request on to the database system module that performs the access. The locks are requested, granted, and released according to the following rules:

1. If a transaction, T, requests to read an item and no other transaction holds a write lock on that item, the control grants a read lock on that item to T and allows the operation to proceed. Note that since other transactions might be holding read locks at that time, read locks are often referred to as **shared** locks.

2. If a transaction, T, requests to read an item and another transaction, T', holds a write lock on that item, T is made to wait until T' completes (and releases its lock). We say that the read request **conflicts** with the previously granted write request.

3. If a transaction, T, requests to write an item and no other transaction holds a read or write lock on that item, the control grants T a write lock on that item and allows the operation to proceed. Because a write lock excludes **all** other locks, it is often referred to as an **exclusive** lock.

4. If a transaction, T, requests to write an item and another transaction, T', holds a read or write lock on that item, T is made to wait until T' completes (and releases its lock). We say that the write request **conflicts** with the previously granted read or write request.

5. Once a lock has been granted to a transaction, the transaction holds the lock. A read lock on an item allows the transaction to do subsequent reads of that item. A write lock on an item allows the transaction to do subsequent reads or writes of that item. When the transaction completes, it releases all locks it has been granted.

The rules dictate that, if a request does not conflict with a previously granted request from another active transaction, it can be granted. Requests (from different transactions) do not conflict if either of the following holds:

Figure 15.1 Conflict table for a two-phase locking concurrency control. Conflicts between lock modes are denoted by X.

Granted Mode

Requested Mode	read	write
read		X
write	X	X

■ They refer to different data items

■ They are both read requests

Figure 15.1 displays the conflict relation for an item in tabular form. An X indicates a conflict.

The concurrency control uses locks to remember the database operations previously performed by currently active transactions. It grants a lock to a transaction to perform an operation on an item only if the operation commutes with (does not conflict with) all other operations on the item that have previously been performed by currently active transactions. For example, since two reads on an item commute, a read lock can be granted to a transaction even though a different transaction currently holds a read lock on that item. In this way, the control guarantees that the operations of active transactions commute, so at any point these operations can be serialized in any order. This result forms the basis of a proof that any schedule produced by the concurrency control is equivalent to a serial schedule.

A locking control is called **two-phase** if each transaction goes through a locking phase, in which it obtains locks, and then an unlocking phase, in which it releases locks. It is called a **strict** two-phase locking control because each transaction retains its locks until it completes: The second phase is compressed to a single point in time. In a **nonstrict** two-phase locking control, the second phase starts after the transaction has obtained all of the locks it will ever need. During the second phase the transaction can release a lock at any time.

While the nonstrict two-phase protocol guarantees serializability, problems arise when transactions abort. If transaction T_1 modifies a data item, x, and then unlocks it in its second phase, a second transaction, T_2, can read the new value and subsequently commit. Since T_1 unlocked x before completing, it might subsequently abort. Atomicity requires that an aborted transaction have no effect on the database state, so if T_1 aborts, x will be restored to its original value. These events are recorded in the following schedule:

$$w_1(x)\ r_2(x)\ w_2(y)\ commit_2\ abort_1 \tag{15.1}$$

T_2 has written a new value to y, which might be based on the value of x that it read. Since that value was produced by a transaction that subsequently aborts, a violation of atomicity has occurred. For this reason, a transaction holds write locks until it commits even in a nonstrict control. A more complete description of this issue can be found in Section 23.2, and a more complete introduction to concurrency controls can be found in Sections 23.3 and 23.4.

Concurrency controls that use strict two-phase locking produce schedules that are serializable in commit order. By this we mean that a schedule, S, is equivalent to a serial schedule, S_{ser}, in which the order of transactions is the same as the order in which they commit in S. To understand why this is so, observe that write locks are not released until commit time, so a transaction is not allowed to read (or write) an item that has been written by a transaction that has not yet committed. Thus, each transaction "sees" the database produced by the sequence of transactions that committed prior to its completion. Nonstrict two-phase locking protocols produce schedules that are serializable, but not necessarily in commit order.

For many applications, users intuitively expect transactions to be serializable in commit order. For example, you expect that, after your bank deposit transaction has committed, any transaction that commits later will see the effect of that deposit.

A more complete discussion of serializability can be found in Section 23.1.

The idea behind a two-phase protocol is to hold locks until it is safe to release them. Early release of locks can result in an inconsistent database state or cause transactions to return incorrect results to the user. The database community has developed special jargon to describe some of the anomalies that can occur.

■ *Dirty read.* Suppose that transaction T_2 reads an item, x, written by transaction T_1 before T_1 completes. This might happen if T_1 releases the write lock it has acquired on x before it commits. Since the value of x returned by the read was not written by a committed transaction—we refer to such a value as committed— it might never appear in the database. This is what we refer to as a **dirty read**. For example, T_1 might abort after T_2 has read x, yielding the schedule

$$w_1(x)\ r_2(x)\ abort_1$$

When T_1 aborts, the change it made to x is rolled back. Hence, T_2 reads a value that should have never existed in the database. The problem in (15.1) is caused by a dirty read.

■ *Nonrepeatable read.* Suppose that transaction T_1 reads an item, x, and then releases the read lock it has acquired before it completes. Another transaction, T_2, might then write x and commit. If T_1 reacquires a read lock on x and reads it again, the value returned by the second read will not be the same as the value returned by the first. We refer to this as a **nonrepeatable read**. This situation is illustrated by the schedule

$$r_1(x)\ w_2(x)\ commit_2\ r_1(x)$$

Note that, in this example, T_2 has committed prior to the second read and so the second read is not dirty. While a nonrepeatable read might seem to be an unimportant issue (why would a transaction read the same item twice?), it is a symptom of a more serious problem. For example, suppose x is a list of passengers on a flight and y is the count of passengers on the list. In the following schedule, T_2 reserves a seat on the flight and hence adds an entry to x and increments y. T_1 reads both x and y and sees the passenger list before the new passenger was added and the passenger count after it was incremented—an inconsistency.

$$r_1(x)\ r_2(x)\ w_2(x)\ r_2(y)\ w_2(y)\ commit_2\ r_1(y)$$

This schedule is directly related to the previous one. In both cases, locking is not two-phase and T_2 overwrites an item that an active transaction has read.

■ *Lost update.* Suppose that a transaction reads the value of an item, x, and, on the basis of the value read, writes a new value back to x. A deposit transaction in a banking system exhibits this behavior, where x is the balance of the account being credited. If such a transaction releases the read lock it has acquired before acquiring a write lock, two deposit transactions on the same account can be interleaved, as illustrated in the following schedule:

$$r_1(x)\ r_2(x)\ w_2(x)\ commit_2\ w_1(x)\ commit_1$$

Once again, we have considered a case in which T_2 commits before T_1's final operation. The problem is referred to as a **lost update**: the effect of T_2 is lost because the value written by T_1 is based on the original value of x rather than the value written by T_2. Thus, if T_1 is attempting to deposit \$5 and T_2 is attempting to deposit \$10, the final database is only incremented by \$5.

These anomalies, as well as other as yet unnamed anomalies, can cause transactions to return incorrect results and the database to become inconsistent.

15.1.3 Deadlock

Suppose that transactions T_1 and T_2 both want to write items x and y but in opposite order. In one possible schedule T_1 locks and writes x; T_2 locks and writes y; T_1 requests to write y but is made to wait because T_2 has y locked; T_2 requests to write x but is made to wait because T_1 has x locked.

$$w_1(x)\ w_2(y)\ \text{Request\_}w_1(y)\ \text{Request\_}w_2(x)$$

At this point, T_1 is waiting for T_2 to complete, and T_2 is waiting for T_1 to complete. Both will wait forever, because neither will ever complete.

This situation is called a **deadlock**. More generally, a deadlock occurs whenever there is a wait loop—that is, a sequence of transactions, T_1, T_2, ..., T_n, in which each transaction, T_i, is waiting to access an item locked by T_{i+1}, and T_n is waiting to access an item locked by T_1. Although two-phase locking is particularly prone to deadlock, deadlock can occur with any concurrency control that allows a transaction to hold a lock on one item when it requests a lock on another item. Such controls must have a mechanism for detecting a deadlock and then for aborting one of the transactions in the wait loop so that at least one of the remaining transactions in the loop can continue.

With one such mechanism, whenever a transaction is forced to wait the control checks to see whether a loop of waiting transactions will be formed. Thus, if T_1 must wait for T_2, the control checks to see if T_2 is waiting and, if so, for what. As this process continues, a chain of waiting transactions is uncovered and a deadlock is detected if the chain loops back on itself. Another mechanism uses **timeout**. Whenever a transaction has been waiting for a "long" time, the control assumes that a deadlock exists and aborts the transaction. A more complete discussion of deadlock can be found in Section 23.4.2.

Even with detection and abortion, deadlocks are undesirable because they waste resources (the computation performed by the aborted transaction must be redone) and slow down the system. Application designers should design tables and transactions so as to reduce the possible number of deadlocks.

15.1.4 Locking in Relational Databases

Up to this point, our discussion of locking has assumed that a transaction requests access to some named item (for example, x). Locking takes a different form in a relational database, where transactions access tuples. Although tuples can be locked, a transaction describes the tuples it wants to access not using names but using a condition that the tuples satisfy. For example, the set of tuples read by a transaction using a SELECT statement is specified by a selection condition in the WHERE clause.[1]

For example, an ACCOUNTS table, in a banking system might contain a tuple for each separate account, and a transaction T_1 might read all tuples that describe the accounts controlled by depositor Mary as follows:

```
SELECT *
FROM ACCOUNTS A
WHERE A.Name = 'Mary';
```

In this case, T_1 reads all tuples in ACCOUNTS that satisfy the condition that the value of their Name attribute is Mary. The condition A.Name='Mary' is called a **predicate**.

As with nonrelational databases, we can ensure serializability with a locking protocol. In designing such a protocol, we must decide what data items are to be locked. One approach is to always lock an entire table, even if only a few tuples in it are accessed. In contrast to tuples, tables are named in the statements that access them. Thus, the SELECT statement can be treated as a read on the data item(s)—tables—named in the FROM clause. Similarly, DELETE, INSERT, and UPDATE can be treated as writes on the named tables. Hence, the concurrency control protocols described in the previous sections can be used and will yield serializable schedules. The problem is that table locks are coarse: A table might contain thousands of tuples, and locking an entire table because a small number of its tuples are being accessed might result in a serious loss of concurrency.

A second approach is to lock only the tuples returned by the SELECT statement. For example, in processing the above SELECT statement, only tuples describing

---

[1] In the special case that a transaction accesses a tuple using its primary key, we might say that the value of the key is the name of the tuple, and we might consider locking the tuple based on that name. Even in this special case, however, additional considerations apply in relational databases (to prevent the anomaly of phantoms, as discussed later).

Mary's accounts are locked. The problem with this approach is that it can lead to an anomaly called **phantoms**. After the statement has been processed, but before T_1 commits, another transaction can create a new account for Mary, insert a new tuple, t, describing that account in ACCOUNTS, and then commit. That tuple is called a phantom. The important thing to note is that the locks T_1 holds do not prevent the insertion. If T_1 re-executes the SELECT, it returns t in addition to the tuples it returned earlier, and hence the read is not repeatable (although in this case T_1 has not released locks). As with non-repeatable reads, the problem extends beyond situations in which a transaction performs the same read twice. Because of the possibility of phantoms, tuple locking does not guarantee serializable schedules. In general, a phantom occurs when, after a transaction, T, has read the tuples in a table, **R**, that satisfy a predicate, P, another transaction inserts a tuple that satisfies P into **R** before T finishes.

Be aware that, although the simple tuple locking algorithm we have just described can indeed lead to phantoms, when many commercial DBMSs use the term "tuple locking" (or as we shall see later "page locking") to describe a concurrency control algorithm, they mean that they use tuple locks (or page locks) as a part of a more complex locking algorithm, such as that described in Section 24.3.1, which does guarantee serializability. As in all things, caution is in order—"when all else fails, read the manual."

15.1.5 Isolation Levels

Locks impede concurrency and hence performance. It is therefore desirable to minimize their use. Table locking used in a two-phase protocol produces serializable schedules but, because of the size of the item locked, has the greatest impact on concurrency. Tuple locking is more efficient, but can result in nonserializable schedules even when used in a two-phase protocol (because of phantoms). Because locks are held until commit time, strict protocols inhibit concurrency more than nonstrict protocols. For these reasons, most commercial DBMSs allow the application designer to choose the locking protocol: for example, the items to be locked and how long the locks are to be held. These options are often described in terms of ANSI standard isolation levels.

Database systems often support several isolation levels [Gray et al. 1976] and allow application designers to choose a level appropriate to a particular application. The designer should choose a level that guarantees that the application will execute correctly and maximizes concurrency. That choice might permit nonserializable schedules. The ANSI standard isolation levels are specified in terms of certain phenomena (or anomalies) that are to be prevented at each level. A phenomenon that is prevented at one level is also prevented at each stronger (higher) level. These levels are (in the order of increasing strength):

READ UNCOMMITTED. Dirty reads are possible.

READ COMMITTED. Dirty reads are not permitted (but nonrepeatable reads are possible).

REPEATABLE READ. Successive reads of the same tuple executed by a particular transaction will not yield different values (but phantoms are possible).

SERIALIZABLE. Phantoms are not permitted. Transaction execution must be serializable.

The SQL standard specifies that different transactions in the same application can execute at different isolation levels, and each such transaction sees or does not see the phenomena corresponding to its level. For example, a transaction that executes at REPEATABLE READ will see the same value if it reads a particular tuple several times even though other transactions execute at other levels. Similarly, a transaction that executes at SERIALIZABLE sees a view of the database that is serialized with respect to the changes made by all other transactions, regardless of their levels.

While a particular level can be implemented in a variety of ways, locking is a common technique. Independent of the isolation level, database systems generally guarantee that each SQL statement is executed atomically and that its execution is isolated from the execution of other statements. Locking goes beyond that in controlling the way statements of different transactions can be interleaved.

Each level uses locks in different ways. For most levels, locks are acquired by transactions on items they access when executing an SQL statement. Depending on how the item is accessed, the lock can be either a read lock or a write lock. Once acquired, it can be held until commit time—in which case it is said to be **long duration**—or it can be held only as long as the statement is being executed—in which case it is referred to as a **short duration** lock. Write locks at all isolation levels are of long duration. Read locks are handled differently at each level.

READ UNCOMMITTED. A read is performed without obtaining a read lock. Hence, a transaction executing at this level can read a tuple on which another transaction holds a write lock. As a result the transaction might read uncommitted (dirty) data.

READ COMMITTED. Short-duration read locks are obtained for each tuple before a read is permitted. Hence conflicts with write locks will be detected and the transaction will be made to wait until the write lock is released. Since write locks are of long duration, only committed data can be read. However, read locks are released when the read is completed, so two successive reads of the same tuple by a particular transaction might be separated by the execution of another transaction that updates the tuple and then commits. This means that reads might not be repeatable.

REPEATABLE READ. Long-duration read locks are obtained on each tuple returned by a SELECT. Hence a nonrepeatable read is not possible, although phantoms are.

SERIALIZABLE. Serializable schedules can be guaranteed if long-duration read locks are acquired on all tables read. This eliminates phantoms, although it reduces concurrency. A better implementation, involving the use of indices, is described in Section 15.1.7.

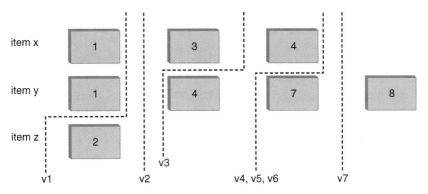

Figure 15.2 Multiversion database.

One particularly troublesome type of nonrepeatable read occurs when a transaction is using a cursor to point to a tuple. At READ COMMITTED that tuple can be changed by a concurrent transaction while the cursor is pointing to it. Some commercial database systems support an isolation level called CURSOR STABILITY, which is essentially READ COMMITTED with the additional feature that a read lock is maintained on a tuple as long as a cursor is pointing at it. Thus, the read of that particular tuple is repeatable if the cursor is not moved.

A more complete discussion of isolation in a relational database system is given in Sections 24.1 and 24.2, which also contain examples of correct and incorrect schedules at each isolation level.

SNAPSHOT **isolation.** An isolation level that is not part of the ANSI standard, but is provided by at least one commonly used DBMS (Oracle), is called SNAPSHOT isolation. SNAPSHOT isolation uses a **multiversion** database: When a (committed) transaction updates a data item, the item's old value is not discarded. Instead, the old value (or version) is preserved and a new version is created. At any given time, therefore, multiple versions of the same item exist in the database. The system can construct, for any i, the value of each item that includes the effects of the ith transaction to commit and of all transactions that committed at a prior time. Figure 15.2 illustrates this situation assuming that transactions are consecutively indexed in the order in which they commit. There, each version of an item is labeled with the index of the transaction that produced it and the versions of the database as a whole are indicated with dotted lines. The version of the database as of the completion of transaction T_4 thus includes three updates to x, two updates to y, and a single update to z. Each database version is referred to as a **snapshot**.

With SNAPSHOT isolation, no read locks are used. *All* reads requested by transaction T are satisfied using the snapshot produced by the sequence of transactions that were committed when T's first read request was made. Since a snapshot once produced is never changed, no read locks are necessary and read requests are never delayed.

The updates of each transaction are controlled by a protocol called **first-committer-wins**. A transaction, T, is allowed to commit if there is no other transaction that (1) committed between the time T made its first read request and the time it requested to commit and (2) updated a data item that T has also updated. Otherwise, T aborts. One implementation of SNAPSHOT isolation (described in Section 24.5) has the nice property that no write locks are needed and hence neither reads nor writes ever wait. However, transactions might be aborted when they complete.

The first-committer-wins feature eliminates lost updates, which occur when two concurrently active transactions that read the same snapshot write to the same data item. Even with first-committer-wins, however, SNAPSHOT isolation allows nonserializable (and hence possibly incorrect) schedules. For example, the schedule

$$r_1(x)\ r_1(y)\ r_2(x)\ r_2(y)\ w_1(y)\ w_2(x)$$

is allowed but is not serializable, because it is not possible to produce an equivalent serial schedule by a series of interchanges of adjacent commuting operations. T_1 and T_2 read the same snapshot, but they write different data items, and so are both allowed to commit.

The implementation of SNAPSHOT isolation is complicated by the fact that a multiversion database must be maintained. In practice, however, it is not possible to maintain all versions. Old versions eventually must be discarded. This can be a problem for long-running transactions since they must be aborted if they request access to a version that no longer exists. A more complete discussion of multiversion concurrency controls and SNAPSHOT isolation can be found in Section 24.5.

15.1.6 Lock Granularity and Intention Locks

To reduce the overhead of maintaining a large number of locks, many commercial concurrency controls lock a unit larger than an individual data item. For example, instead of an item that might occupy only several bytes, the concurrency control might lock the entire disk page on which that item is stored. Since such a control locks *more* items than are actually necessary, it produces the same or higher level of isolation as a concurrency control that locks only the item whose lock has been requested. Similarly, instead of locking a page containing some of the tuples in a table, the concurrency control might lock the entire table.

The size of the unit locked determines the lock **granularity**—it is **fine** if the unit locked is small and **coarse** otherwise. Granularity forms a hierarchy based on containment. Typically, a fine-granularity lock is a tuple lock. A medium-granularity lock is a lock on the page containing a desired tuple. A coarse-granularity lock is a table lock that covers all the pages of a table.

Fine-granularity locks have the advantage of allowing more concurrency than coarse granularity locks, since transactions lock only the data items they actually use. However, the overhead associated with fine granularity locking is greater. Transactions generally hold more locks, since a single coarse-granularity lock might grant access to several items used by the transaction.[2] Therefore, more space is required in the concurrency control to retain information about fine-granularity locks. Also, more time is expended in requesting locks for each individual unit. Because of these tradeoffs, database systems frequently offer granularity at several different levels and different levels can be used within the same application.

Locking at multiple granularities introduces some new implementation problems. Suppose that transaction T_1 has obtained a write lock on a particular tuple in a table and that transaction T_2 requests a read lock on the entire table (it wants to read all of the tuples in the table). The concurrency control should not grant the table lock, since T_2 should not be allowed to read the tuple that was locked by T_1. The problem is how the concurrency control detects the conflict, since the conflicting locks are on different items.

The solution is to organize locks hierarchically. Before obtaining a lock on a fine-granularity item (such as a tuple), a transaction must first obtain a lock on the containing coarse-granularity item (such as a table). But what kind of a lock? Clearly, not a read or write lock, since in that case, there would be no point in acquiring an additional fine granularity lock, and the effective lock granularity would be coarse. For this reason, database systems provide a new type of lock, the **intention lock**. In a system supporting tuple and table locks, for example, before a transaction can obtain a read (shared) or write (exclusive) lock on a tuple, it must obtain an appropriate intention lock on the table containing that tuple. Intention locks are weaker than read and write locks and come in three flavors.

■ If a transaction wants to obtain a shared lock on some tuple, it must first get an **intention shared**, or IS, lock on the table. The IS lock indicates that the transaction *intends* to obtain a shared lock on some tuple within that table.

■ If a transaction wants to obtain an exclusive lock on some tuple, it must first obtain an **intention exclusive**, or IX, lock on the table. The IX lock indicates that the transaction *intends* to obtain an exclusive lock on some tuple within the table.

■ If a transaction wants to update some tuples in the table but needs to read all of them to determine which ones to change (for example, it wants to change all tuples in which the value of a particular attribute is less than 100), it must first obtain a **shared intention exclusive**, or SIX, lock on the table. The SIX lock is a combination of a shared lock and an intention exclusive lock on the table. This allows it to read all the tuples in the table and subsequently to get exclusive locks on those it wants to update.

The conflict table for intention locks is given in Figure 15.3. It shows, for example, that after a transaction, T_1, has been granted an IX lock on a table, another transaction, T_2, will not be granted a shared lock on that table. To understand this, note that the shared lock allows T_2 to read all tuples in the table and that this conflicts

---

[2] For example, the tuples on a disk page are generally elements of a single table, and there is a reasonable probability that a transaction accessing one such tuple will also access another. A single page lock grants permission to access both.

Figure 15.3 Conflict table for intention locks. Conflicts between lock modes are denoted X.

	Granted Mode				
Requested Mode	*IS*	*IX*	*SIX*	*S*	*X*
IS					X
IX			X	X	X
SIX		X	X	X	X
S		X	X		X
X	X	X	X	X	X

with the fact that T_1 is updating one (or more) of them. On the other hand, T_2 can be granted an exclusive lock on a different tuple, but it must first acquire an IX lock on the table. This does not present a problem because, as shown in the figure, IX locks do not conflict. Multiple granularity locks and intention locks are dealt with more fully in Section 24.3.1.

15.1.7 A Serializable Locking Strategy Using Intention Locks

If transactions use only table locks in a two-phase fashion, serializable schedules result. However, such a locking discipline results in low concurrency. On the other hand, page or tuple locking is more efficient, but can produce phantoms. A number of commercial systems use an enhanced fine granularity locking strategy that prevents phantoms and leads to serializable schedules. The essential condition for preventing phantoms is that, after a transaction, T_1, has read the tuples in a table, **R**, that satisfy a WHERE predicate, P, no other concurrently executing transaction, T_2, can insert into **R** a (phantom) tuple, t, that satisfies P until after T_1 terminates.

The strategy depends on how **R** is accessed by T_1. In constructing a query execution plan for an SQL statement that accesses tuples satisfying P, the system determines whether any existing indices can be used. If not, the system must search every page in **R** to locate the tuples that satisfy P. In this case, T_1 acquires an S lock on **R** and holds the lock until it commits. T_2 cannot insert t, since it first needs to acquire a (conflicting) IX lock on **R**. Hence, phantoms cannot occur when no indices are used.

The situation is more involved if T_1 accesses **R** through an index, in which case an entire scan of **R** is not required. For example, if T_1 executes a SELECT statement using predicate P, it acquires only an IS lock on **R**. Assuming that the system implements page locks at the fine granularity level, T_1 must also acquire S locks on the pages of **R** containing the tuples satisfying P that it accesses through the index. Unfortunately, these locks do not prevent phantoms. If T_2 attempts to insert a phantom, t, into **R**, it can obtain an IX lock on **R** since that lock does not conflict with the IS lock obtained by T_1. There is thus no conflict at the table level. If t is stored on a page that is different from the pages locked by T_1, there is no conflict at the page level, either. Hence, it is possible for T_2 to insert t. Some mechanism is needed to prevent such phantoms.

The mechanism used involves locking portions of the index structure itself. When a tuple is inserted into **R**, indices used to access R are updated to include a reference to the new tuple. Hence, if T_1 holds a shared lock on the pages of the index structure that T_2 must update in order to insert a phantom, the insertion cannot be done. In particular, since t satisfies P, the pages of the index that must be updated by T_2 are among those that must be accessed by T_1, and T_1 holds a shared lock on those pages. The details of the locking protocol depend on the type of index used and are discussed in Section 24.3.1.

15.1.8 Summary

The question of how to choose an isolation level for a particular application is far from straightforward. Commercial DBMS vendors usually support a number of options (including, but not limited to, those discussed above) and expect application designers to select the one appropriate for their particular application.

Serializable schedules guarantee correctness for all applications, but might not meet an application's performance requirements. However, some applications execute correctly at an isolation level lower than SERIALIZABLE. For example, a transaction that prints a mailing list of depositors might not need an up-to-date database view. Hence, it can use short-duration rather than long-duration read locks, and can execute at READ COMMITTED. Section 24.2.2 gives examples of applications that run correctly at different isolation levels.

15.2   ATOMICITY AND DURABILITY

Atomicity requires that a transaction either successfully completes and commits or aborts, undoing any changes it made to the database. A transaction might be aborted by the user (perhaps using a cancel button), by the system (perhaps because of a deadlock or because some database update failed a constraint check), or by itself (when, for example, it finds unexpected data). Another way the transaction might not successfully complete is if the system crashes during its execution. Crashes are a bit more complicated than user- or system-initiated aborts, because all of the information stored in main memory is assumed to be lost when the system crashes. Hence, the transaction must be aborted and its changes rolled back using only the information stored on mass storage.

Durability requires that, after a transaction commits, the changes it made to the database are not lost even if the mass storage device on which the database is stored fails.

15.2.1 The Write–Ahead Log

We discuss atomicity and durability in the same section because they are frequently implemented using the same mechanism—the write-ahead log.

A log is a sequence of records that describe database updates made by transactions. Records are appended to the log as the transactions execute and are never changed. The log is consulted by the system to achieve both atomicity and durability. For durability, the log is used to restore the database after a failure of the mass storage device on which the database is stored. Therefore, it is generally stored on a different mass storage device. Typically, a log is a sequential file on disk, and it is often duplexed (with the copies stored on different devices) so that it survives any single media failure.

A common technique for achieving atomicity and durability involves the use of **update** records. As transactions execute database operations that change the database state, update records are appended to the log. No record needs to be appended if the operation merely reads the database. Each update record describes the change made and, in particular, contains enough information to permit the system to undo that change if the transaction is later aborted.

There are several ways to undo changes. In the most common, an update record contains the **before image** of the modified database item—a physical copy of the item before the change. If the transaction aborts, the update record is used to restore the item to its original value—which is why the update record is sometimes referred to as an **undo record**. In addition to the before image, the update record identifies the transaction that made the change—using a **transaction Id**—and the changed database item.

If a transaction, T, is aborted, rollback with the log is straightforward. The log is scanned backwards, and, as T's update records are encountered, the before images are written to the database, undoing the change. Since the log might be exceedingly long, it is impractical to search back to the beginning to make sure that all of T's update records are processed. To avoid a complete backward scan, when T is initiated a **begin record** containing its transaction Id is appended to the log. The backward scan can be stopped when this record is encountered.

Rollback due to a crash is a little more complex than the abort of a single transaction, since now the system must first identify the transactions to be aborted. In particular, the system must distinguish between the transactions that completed and those that were active at the time the crash occurred. All of the active transactions must be aborted.

When a transaction commits, it writes a **commit record** to the log. If it aborts, its updates are rolled back and then an **abort record** is written to the log. Using these records, a backward scan can record the identity of transactions that completed prior to the crash and thus ignore their update records as they are subsequently encountered. If, during the backward scan, the first record relating to T is an update record, T was active when the crash occurred and must be aborted.

Note the importance of writing a commit record to the log when T commits. If we assume that the database is updated immediately when T makes a write request (this is not always the case), all database modifications requested by T will be recorded in mass storage when T requests to commit. However, the commit request itself does not guarantee durability. If a crash occurs after the transaction has made the request, but before the commit record is written to the log, the transaction will be aborted by the recovery procedure and will not be durable. Hence, a transaction has not actually committed until its commit record has been appended to the log on mass store.

One last issue with respect to crashes is that a mechanism must be included to avoid a complete backward scan of the log during recovery. Without such a mechanism, the recovery process has no way of knowing when to stop the scan, since a transaction that was active at the time of the crash might have logged an update record at an early point in the log and then have made no further updates. The recovery process will thus find no evidence of the transaction's existence unless it scans back to that record.

To deal with this situation, the system periodically appends a **checkpoint record** to the log that lists the currently active transactions. The recovery process must scan backward at least as far as the most recent checkpoint record. If T is named in that record and the backward scan did not encounter a commit or abort record for T, then T was still active when the system crashed. The backward scan must continue past the checkpoint record until the begin record for T is reached. The scan terminates when all such transactions are accounted for.

We have assumed that an update record for a database item, x, is written to the mass storage device containing the log at the time the new value of x is written to the mass storage device containing the database. In fact, the update of x and the append of the update record occur in some order. Consider the possibility of a crash occurring at the time the operations are performed. If neither operation has completed, there is no problem. The update record does not appear in the log, but there is nothing for the recovery process to undo since x has not been updated. If the crash occurs after both operations have completed, recovery proceeds correctly, as described above. Suppose, however, that x is updated first and the crash occurs between the update and the log append. Then the recovery process has no way of rolling the transaction back and returning the database to a consistent state since the original value of x appears nowhere on mass store—an unacceptable situation. If, on the other hand, the update record is appended first, this problem is avoided. On restart, the recovery process simply uses the update record to restore x; it makes no difference whether the crash occurred before or after the new value of x was written to the database. If the crash occurred after the update record was appended but before x was updated, the value of x in the database and the before image in the update record are identical when the system is restarted. The recovery process uses the before image to overwrite x—which does not change its value—but the final state after recovery is correct.

Hence, the update record must always be appended to the log before the database is updated. This is referred to as the write-ahead feature, and the log is referred to as a **write-ahead log**.

Recovery from a crash is actually more complex than we have described. For reasons of performance, most database systems maintain copies of database pages in active use in page buffers in main memory. Changes made to the database are recorded in these pages, which need not be transferred to the actual database on mass store immediately. Instead, they might be kept in main memory for some time so that additional accesses to them can be handled quickly. Furthermore, and for similar reasons, log records are not immediately written to the log but are temporarily stored in a log buffer in main memory. To avoid a write to the log for each update record, the entire buffer is written to the log when it is full.

The manipulation of these buffers and their use in updating the log and database on mass storage devices must be carefully coordinated to achieve atomicity and durability. A more complete discussion of this matter can be found in Sections 25.1 and 25.2.

15.2.2 Recovery from Mass Storage Failure

Durability requires that no changes to the database made by a committed transaction be lost. Therefore, since mass storage devices can fail, the database must be stored on different devices redundantly.

One simple approach to durability is to maintain separate copies of the database on different disks (perhaps supported by different power supplies) such that simultaneous failure of both disks is unlikely. Mirrored disks implement this approach. A mirrored disk is a mass storage system in which, transparently to the user, whenever an application requests a disk write operation, the system writes the same information on two different disks. Thus one disk is an exact copy, or a mirror image, of the other.

In transaction processing applications, a mirrored disk system can achieve increased system **availability** since, if one of the mirrored disks fails, the system can continue, using the other one. When the failed disk is replaced, the system then must resynchronize the two. By contrast, when durability is achieved using only the log (as described next), the recovery after a disk failure might take a significant period of time, during which the system is unavailable to its users.

Even when a transaction processing system uses mirrored disks, it must still use a write-ahead log to achieve atomicity—for example, to roll back transactions after a crash.

A second approach to achieving durability involves restoring the information on the disk from the log. Since we do not want recovery to take too long or the log to become too large, the plan is to periodically copy, or **dump**, the entire database contents to mass storage—thus taking a snapshot of the database. Furthermore, in addition to a before image, an **after image** containing the new value of an updated data item is stored in each update record.

To recover from a disk failure, the system first copies the dump file onto the (new) disk. Then it makes two passes through the log—a backward pass, in which it makes a list of all transactions that committed after the dump, and a forward pass, in which it uses the after images of the update records of transactions on the list to roll the database forward from the state recorded in the dump to its committed value at the time of the failure.

An important issue in this approach is how to produce the dump. For some applications, it can be produced off line after shutting down the system: no new transactions are admitted and all existing transactions are allowed to complete. Then no transactions will be executing while the dump is taken, and the state of the database becomes a snapshot resulting from the execution of all transactions that committed prior to the start of the dump. For many applications, however, the system cannot be shut down, and the dump must be taken while the system is operating.

A **fuzzy dump** is a dump taken while the system is operating, and transactions might be executing. These transactions might later commit or abort. The algorithm for restoring the disk using a fuzzy dump must deal properly with the effects of these transactions. A more complete discussion of media failure and dumping can be found in Section 25.4.

15.3   IMPLEMENTING DISTRIBUTED TRANSACTIONS

We have been assuming that the information accessed by a transaction is stored in a single database system. This is not always the case. The information supporting a large enterprise might be stored in multiple databases. For example, a manufacturing facility can have databases describing inventory, production, personnel, billing, and so forth. As these enterprises move to higher and higher levels of integration, transactions must access information at more than one database. Thus, a single transaction initiating the assembly of a new component might allocate the parts by updating the inventory database, specify a particular employee for the job by accessing the personnel database, and create a record to describe the new activity in the production database. Systems of this type are referred to as **multi-database** systems. We will discuss the database and query design issues related to such multidatabase systems in Chapter 18. In this section we discuss transaction-related issues.

Transactions accessing multidatabase systems are often referred to as **global** transactions because they can access all the data of an enterprise. Since the databases often reside at different sites in a network, such transactions are also referred to as **distributed** transactions. Many of the considerations involved in designing global transactions do not depend on whether or not the data is distributed, and so the terms are frequently used interchangeably. Distribution across a network introduces new failure modes (e.g., lost messages, site crashes) and performance issues that do not exist when all databases are stored at the same site.

We assume that each individual database in a multidatabase exports a set of (local) transactions that can be used to access its data. For example, a bank branch might have deposit and withdraw transactions for accessing the accounts it maintains. Each such transaction can be invoked locally to reflect a purely local event (e.g., a deposit is made at the branch to a branch account) or remotely as part of a distributed transaction (e.g., money is transferred from an account at one branch to an account at another). When a transaction at a site is executed as a part of a distributed transaction, we refer to it as a **subtransaction**.

The database at each site has its own local integrity constraints relating data stored there. The multidatabase might also have global integrity constraints relating data at different sites. For example, the database at the bank's main office might contain a data item whose value is the sum of the deposits in the databases at all local branches. We assume that each distributed transaction is consistent. Each subtransaction maintains the local integrity constraints at the site at which it executes, and all of the subtransactions of a distributed transaction taken together maintain the global integrity constraints.

A desirable goal in implementing distributed transactions over a multidatabase system is ensuring that they are globally atomic, isolated, and durable, as well as consistent. We have seen, however, that designers often choose to execute transactions at a single site at a reduced isolation level in the interest of enhancing system performance. With distributed transactions, it is sometimes necessary not only to reduce the isolation level, but also to sacrifice atomicity and isolation altogether. To better understand the underlying issues, we first present the techniques required to provide globally atomic and serializable distributed transactions.

15.3.1 Atomicity and Durability—The Two-Phase Commit Protocol

To make a distributed transaction, T, atomic, either all of T's subtransactions must commit or all must abort. Thus, even if some subtransaction completes successfully, it cannot immediately commit because another subtransaction of T might abort. If that happens, all of T's subtransactions must abort. For example, if T is a distributed transaction that transfers money between two accounts at different sites, we do not want the subtransaction that does the withdrawal at one site to commit if the subtransaction that does the deposit at the other site aborts.

The part of the transaction processing system responsible for making distributed transactions atomic is the **transaction manager**. One of its tasks is to keep track of which sites have participated in each distributed transaction. When all subtransactions of T have completed and T requests to commit, it informs the transaction manager. To ensure atomicity, the transaction manager and the database systems at which the subtransactions execute engage in a protocol, called a **two-phase commit protocol** [Gray 1978, Lampson and Sturgis 1979]. In describing the two-phase commit protocol, it is customary to call the transaction manager the **coordinator** and the database systems the **cohorts**.

In the first phase of the protocol, the coordinator sends a **prepare** message to all of T's cohorts telling them to prepare to commit. Each cohort replies with a **vote** message. A positive vote indicates that the cohort is ready to commit. A negative vote indicates that the cohort has aborted the subtransaction. For example, the *prepare* message from the coordinator might cause the cohort to evaluate a deferred integrity constraint. If the cohort determines that the constraint is violated, the subtransaction is rolled back and a negative vote is sent. Or the cohort might have crashed and the absence of a reply message is interpreted by the coordinator as a negative vote.

Once a cohort at site S replies that it is ready to commit, that decision cannot be reversed (i.e., it must remain ready to commit), since the coordinator bases its commit or abort decision for the distributed transaction on the accuracy of the votes it receives. In particular, the concurrency control at site S is not allowed to subsequently abort the subtransaction. Furthermore, all updates performed by the subtransaction must be stored in nonvolatile memory before the ready vote is sent so that, if the transaction manager decides to commit the distributed transaction but the cohort subsequently crashes, it can commit the subtransaction when it recovers.

If the coordinator receives ready votes from all cohorts, it commits T and sends each cohort a **commit** message, telling it to commit its subtransaction. Since the subtransaction cannot have been aborted after the vote was cast, it can be committed when the message is received. The cohort then sends a **done** message to the coordinator indicating that it has completed its part of the protocol. When the coordinator receives a *done* message from each cohort, the protocol terminates.

If the coordinator receives an abort vote from a cohort, it aborts the distributed transaction and sends **abort** messages to all others. On receiving the *abort* message, a cohort aborts the subtransaction.

For each cohort, the interval between sending a positive *vote* message to the coordinator and receiving the *commit* or *abort* message from the coordinator is called its **uncertain period**, because the cohort is uncertain about the outcome of the protocol. The cohort is dependent on the coordinator during that period because it cannot commit or abort the subtransaction. Locks held by the subtransaction cannot be released until the coordinator replies (since the coordinator might decide to abort and new values written by the subtransaction should not be visible in that case). This negatively impacts performance and the cohort is said to be **blocked**. The uncertain period might be long because of communication delays during the protocol.

There is also the possibility that the coordinator will crash or become unavailable because of communication failures during the uncertain period. Since the coordinator might have decided to commit or abort the transaction and then crashed before it could send commit or abort messages to all cohorts, a cohort has to remain blocked until it finds out what decision, if any, has been made. Again, this might take a long time. Because such long delays generally imply an unacceptable performance penalty, many systems abandon the protocol (and perhaps atomicity) when the uncertain period exceeds some predetermined time, simply arbitrarily committing or aborting the local cohort subtransaction (even though other subtransactions might have terminated in a different way).

In some situations, a site manager might refuse to allow the DBMS to participate in a two-phase commit protocol because of its possible negative effect on performance. In other situations, sites *cannot* participate because the DBMS is an older, **legacy**, system that does not support the protocol. Alternatively, client-side software (such as ODBC or JDBC) might not support the protocol. In this circumstance, global atomicity is not realized.

A complete discussion of the two-phase commit protocol can be found in Section 26.2.

15.3.2 Global Serializability and Deadlock

Each site in a multidatabase system might maintain its own, local strict two-phase locking concurrency control, which schedules operations so that the subtransactions *at that site* are serializable. Furthermore, the control might ensure that deadlocks among subtransactions at that site are resolved.

Global serializability.   To guarantee the serializability of distributed transactions, we must ensure not only that the subtransactions are serializable at each site but that there is some global serialization over *all* sites. For example, we do not want a situation in which the concurrency control at site A serializes the subtransactions of T_1 and T_2 at A in one order while the control at site B serializes the subtransactions of T_1 and T_2 at B in the opposite order. In such a case, no global serialization is possible.

Surprisingly, global serializability can be achieved with no additional mechanisms beyond those we have already discussed:

> If the concurrency control at each site independently uses a strict two-phase locking protocol to serialize the subtransactions locally, and global transactions are committed using a two-phase commit protocol, then global transactions are (globally) serializable in the order in which they have committed. [Weihl 1984]

In Section 26.5 we will demonstrate the truth of this statement.

We have discussed circumstances under which the two-phase commit protocol is not implemented. In such situations, global transactions are not guaranteed to be globally atomic or globally serializable.

Global deadlocks. Distributed systems are subject to a type of deadlock that involves subtransactions at different sites. For example, a subtransaction of T_1 at site A might be waiting for a lock held by a subtransaction of T_2 at A, while a subtransaction of T_2 at site B might be waiting for a lock held by a subtransaction of T_1 at B. Since all subtransactions of a global transaction must commit at the same time, T_1 and T_2 are in a distributed deadlock—they will both wait forever. The system must have some mechanism for detecting global deadlocks and aborting one of the transactions in the wait loop. One simple mechanism is timeout. If a subtransaction at one site is waiting for a sufficiently long time the control at that site aborts the transaction. Section 26.4 will address this issue more fully.

15.3.3 Replication

In a distributed system, replicas of a data item can be stored at different sites in the network. Mobile systems, in which sites might be disconnected from the network for long periods of time, often do this. Before disconnecting, a site makes a copy of data it will use while in the disconnected state. Replication has two potential advantages. It can reduce the time it takes to access the item, since a transaction can access the nearest (perhaps even local) replica. It can also improve the availability of the item in case of failures since, if a site containing a replica crashes, the item can still be accessed using a different replica at another site.

In most implementations of replication, the individual transactions are unaware that replicas exist. The system knows which items are replicated and where the replicas are stored. With a **read-one/write-all** replication algorithm, when a transaction requests to read an item, the system fetches its value from the nearest replica; when a transaction requests to update an item, the system updates all replicas. The portion of the system responsible for implementing the replication algorithm is called the **replica control**.

Read-one/write-all replication has the potential for improving the speed with which a read request can be satisfied over non-replicated systems, since with no replication, a read request might require communication with a distant database. The performance of write requests, however, might be worse, since all replicas must be updated. Hence, read-one/write-all replication has a potential performance benefit in applications in which reading occurs substantially more frequently than writing.

Read-one/write-all systems can be characterized as synchronous update or asynchronous update.

■ **Synchronous-update systems**. When a transaction updates an item, all replicas are updated before the transaction commits. Updates to replicas are thus treated in the same way as updates to any other data item. Synchronous-update systems based on two-phase locking and two-phase commit protocols produce globally serializable schedules.

■ **Asynchronous-update systems**. Only one replica is updated before the transaction commits. The other replicas are updated after the transaction commits by another program that is triggered by the commit operation or that executes periodically at fixed intervals. Hence, even in systems based on two-phase locking and two-phase commit protocols, schedules might not be globally serializable. For example, transaction T_1 might update data items x and y and then commit. Transaction T_2 might then read the value of x from a replica that has been updated and the value of y from a replica that has not.

Asynchronous update systems come in two varieties.

❏ A transaction can lock and update any replica (presumably the nearest one). After the transaction commits, the update is propagated asynchronously to the other replicas. As a result transactions executing concurrently can update different replicas of the same item. The new values produced by these transactions ultimately arrive at all replicas, but perhaps in different orders. Each replica site is then faced with the decision of which update to carry out first or whether to discard an update entirely. A conflict resolution strategy is required to deal with this situation. Since no strategy is guaranteed to be correct for all applications, commercial systems provide several ad hoc strategies, including: "oldest update wins," "youngest update wins," "highest priority site wins," and "user provides a procedure for conflict resolution." Note that this form of replication can give rise to the lost update problem.

❏ A unique replica of each data item is designated the **primary copy**. All other replicas are designated **secondary copies**. Transactions requesting to update an item must lock and update its primary copy. In this way, write conflicts are detected and updates are performed in a specific order. When a transaction commits, the update it has made to the primary copy is propagated to the other replicas. The secondary copies might be updated by a single transaction triggered when the transaction that updated the primary commits. By sequencing updates through the primary copy, the algorithm can ensure that all replicas see the same sequence of updates, and thus no conflict resolution strategy is required. Read requests are satisfied in the conventional way by accessing the nearest replica.

Since asynchronous update produces greater transaction throughput than does synchronous update, it is the most widely used form of replication. However, the designer should be aware that asynchronous-update systems (even primary copy systems) can produce nonserializable schedules and hence can produce incorrect results. A more complete treatment of replication can be found in Section 26.7.

15.3.4 Summary

Many aspects of distributed transaction processing systems are surprisingly simple. The concurrency control at each site can be a strict two-phase locking control. A two-phase commit protocol can be used to synchronize the cohorts at commit time. Global deadlocks can be resolved using timeout.

One result of this simplicity is that distributed transaction processing systems that globally support serializable schedules can be implemented by interconnecting sites containing database managers from different vendors if

■ All the database managers implement strict two-phase locking concurrency controls

■ Each site participates in the two-phase commit protocol

These ideas greatly simplify the design of distributed systems.

Frequently these conditions do not hold. The application at some sites might use one of the lower isolation levels, sites might not participate in a two-phase commit protocol, and/or asynchronous replication might be used. In such situations, distributed transaction execution is not guaranteed to be serializable. Nevertheless, systems might have to be designed under these constraints, and the application designer must carefully assess the implications of nonserializable schedules on the correctness of the database and the ultimate utility of the application.

15.4   BIBLIOGRAPHIC NOTES

A comprehensive discussion of issues related to the implementation of distributed transactions can be found in [Gray and Reuter 1993]. [Ceri and Pelagatti 1984] is more theoretical in its orientation and describes the algorithms underlying the implementation. Two-phase locking was introduced in [Eswaran et al. 1976]. Isolation levels are discussed in [Gray et al. 1976]. The two-phase commit protocol was introduced in [Gray 1978, Lampson and Sturgis 1979]. See [Weihl 1984] for a proof that the two-phase commit protocol together with two-phase locking local concurrency controls guarantees global serializability. One of the first discussions on logging and recovery technology can be found in [Gray 1978]. Excellent summaries of the technology are in [Haerder and Reuter 1983], [Bernstein and Newcomer 1997], and [Gray and Reuter 1993]. Primary copy replication was introduced in [Stonebraker 1979].

15.5   EXERCISES

15.1 State which of the following schedules are serializable.

a. $r_1(x)\ r_2(y)\ r_1(z)\ r_3(z)\ r_2(x)\ r_1(y)$

b. $r_1(x)\ w_2(y)\ r_1(z)\ r_3(z)\ w_2(x)\ r_1(y)$

c. $r_1(x)\ w_2(y)\ r_1(z)\ r_3(z)\ w_1(x)\ r_2(y)$

d. $r_1(x)\ r_2(y)\ r_1(z)\ r_3(z)\ w_1(x)\ w_2(y)$

e. $w_1(x)\ r_2(y)\ r_1(z)\ r_3(z)\ r_1(x)\ w_2(y)$

15.2 In the student registration system, give an example of a schedule in which a deadlock occurs.

15.3 Give an example of a schedule that might be produced by a nonstrict two-phase locking concurrency control that is serializable but not in commit order.

15.4 Give an example of a transaction processing system (other than a banking system) that you have interacted with, for which you had an intuitive expectation that the serial order was the commit order.

15.5 Suppose that the transaction processing system of your university contains a table in which there is one tuple for each current student.

a. Estimate how much disk storage is required to store this table.

b. Give examples of transactions in the student registration system that have to lock this entire table if a table locking concurrency control is used.

15.6 Give an example of a schedule at the READ COMMITTED isolation level in which a lost update occurs.

15.7 Give examples of schedules at the REPEATABLE READ isolation level in which a phantom is inserted after a SELECT statement is executed and

a. The resulting schedule is nonserializable and incorrect.

b. The resulting schedule is serializable and hence correct.

15.8 Give examples of schedules at the SNAPSHOT isolation that are

a. Serializable and hence correct.

b. Nonserializable and incorrect.

15.9 Give examples of schedules that would be accepted at

a. SNAPSHOT isolation but not REPEATABLE READ

b. SERIALIZABLE but not SNAPSHOT isolation. (*Hint:* T_2 performs a write after T_1 has committed.)

15.10 a. Give an example of a schedule of two transactions in which a two-phase locking concurrency control makes one of the transactions wait but a control implementing SNAPSHOT isolation aborts one of the transactions.

b. Give an example of a schedule of two transactions in which a two-phase locking concurrency control aborts one of the transactions (because of a deadlock) but a control implementing SNAPSHOT isolation allows both transactions to commit.

15.11 A particular read-only transaction reads data entered into the database during the previous month and uses it to prepare a report. What is the weakest isolation level at which this transaction can execute? Explain.

15.12 What intention locks must be obtained by a read operation in a transaction executing at REPEATABLE READ when the locking implementation given in Section 15.1.4 is used?

15.13 Explain how the commit of a transaction is implemented within the logging system.

15.14 Explain why the write-ahead feature of a write-ahead log is needed.

15.15 Explain why a cohort in the two-phase commit protocol cannot release locks acquired by the subtransaction until its uncertain period terminates.

15.16 Two distributed transactions execute at the same two sites. Each site uses a strict two-phase locking concurrency control, and the entire system uses a two-phase commit protocol. Give a schedule for the execution of these transactions in which the commit order is different at each site but the global schedule is serializable.

15.17 Give an example of an incorrect schedule that might be produced by an asynchronous-update replication system.

15.18 Explain how to implement synchronous-update replication using triggers.

Part Three

ADVANCED TOPICS IN DATABASES

In this part of the book we discuss a number of more advanced topics. In particular, we study object-oriented databases, semistructured data and XML databases, distributed databases, online analytical processing, and data mining.

Object databases are beginning to find their way into the mainstream both independently and as extensions to existing relational products. In Chapter 16, we will study the principles underlying the object data model and the corresponding query languages, as well as the embodiment of these principles in existing standards.

XML databases represent an emerging field that is expected to become important once the underlying standards and tools are developed. In Chapter 17, we will discuss some of these emerging standards and their applications.

Like object databases, distributed databases are becoming increasingly important for many applications. In Chapter 18, we will discuss distributed database design, query design, and query optimization.

Additional applications of database technology are data warehousing, online analytical processing (OLAP), and data mining. A data warehouse is a database optimized for complex read-only queries typical in decision support applications (e.g., aggregate company sales by region and period. In Chapter 19, we will discuss the data structures, language constructs, and algorithms that simplify such queries and improve system performance.

Chapter 16

Object Databases

In this chapter, we introduce object databases. First we discuss the shortcomings of the relational data model that motivate the need for a richer data model. Unlike relational databases, object databases have a number of standards, which makes the relationships among the different technologies difficult to understand. To navigate the field, we start by introducing a conceptual data model for object databases without reference to any particular standard or language. Then we present the two main standards in the field: ODMG and the object-relational extensions of SQL:1999, explaining their features in terms of the conceptual object model. In the last part of the chapter, we introduce CORBA—a standard promoted by the Object Management Group to facilitate the development of distributed client/server applications. Although CORBA is not a database standard per se, it can be used as a framework for developing distributed object data services, which makes it relevant to this chapter.

16.1 SHORTCOMINGS OF THE RELATIONAL DATA MODEL

Relational DBMSs swept the database market in the 1980s because of the simplicity of their underlying relational model (which proved attractive to application developers) and because tables turned out to be just the right representation for much of the data used in business applications. Encouraged by this success, attempts were made to use relational databases in other applications for which the relational model was not specifically designed—for example, computer-aided design (CAD) and geographical data. It soon became obvious that relational databases are not appropriate for such "nontraditional" applications. Even in their core application area, relational databases have certain shortcomings. In this section, we use a series of simple examples to illustrate some of the problems with the relational data model.

Set-valued attributes. Consider the following relational schema that describes people by their Social Security number, name, phone numbers, and children:

PERSON (SSN: String, Name: String, PhoneN: String, Child: String)

We assume that a person can have several phone numbers and several children, and that Child is a foreign key to the relation PERSON. Thus, the key of this schema consists of the attributes SSN, PhoneN, and Child. Here is one possible relation instance of this schema:[1]

SSN	Name	PhoneN	Child
111-22-3333	Joe Public	516-123-4567	222-33-4444
111-22-3333	Joe Public	516-345-6789	222-33-4444
111-22-3333	Joe Public	516-123-4567	333-44-5555
111-22-3333	Joe Public	516-345-6789	333-44-5555
222-33-4444	Bob Public	212-987-6543	444-55-6666
222-33-4444	Bob Public	212-987-1111	555-66-7777
222-33-4444	Bob Public	212-987-6543	555-66-7777
222-33-4444	Bob Public	212-987-1111	444-55-6666

This schema is *not* in the third normal form because of the functional dependency

$$SSN \rightarrow Name$$

since SSN is not a key and Name is not one of the attributes in a key. Furthermore, it is easy to verify that, if we first decompose this relation into its projections onto SSN,Name,PhoneN and SSN,Name,Child and then join the projections, we get the original relation back. Thus, according to Section 8.9, this relation satisfies the following join dependency:

$$(SSN, Name, PhoneN) \bowtie (SSN, Name, Child)$$

In Section 8.9, we argued that relations that satisfy nontrivial join dependencies might contain a great deal of redundant information (in fact, much more than the amount of redundancy caused by the FDs). Since information redundancy is a cause of update anomalies, relational design theory suggests that we should decompose the original relation into the following three:

PERSON	
SSN	Name
111-22-3333	Joe Public
222-33-4444	Bob Public

---

[1] For brevity, we omit some tuples needed to satisfy the foreign key constraint.

PHONE			CHILDOF	
SSN	PhoneN		SSN	Child
111-22-3333	516-345-6789		111-22-3333	222-33-4444
111-22-3333	516-123-4567		111-22-3333	333-44-5555
222-33-4444	212-987-6543		222-33-4444	444-55-6666
222-33-4444	212-135-7924		222-33-4444	555-66-7777

While this decomposition certainly removes update anomalies, there are still difficulties. Consider the query *Get the phone numbers of all of Joe's grandchildren.* The SQL statement

```
SELECT   G.PhoneN
FROM      PERSON P, PERSON C, PERSON G
WHERE    P.Name = 'Joe Public' AND          (16.1)
          P.Child = C.SSN AND
          C.Child = G.SSN
```

performs the query for the original schema, while the statement

```
SELECT   N.PhoneN
FROM      CHILDOF C, CHILDOF G,
          PERSON P, PHONE N
WHERE    P.Name = 'Joe Public' AND          (16.2)
          P.SSN = C.SSN AND
          C.Child = G.SSN AND
          G.SSN = N.SSN
```

does the same for the decomposed schema. Both of these SQL expressions seem rather cumbersome implementations of the simple query we just stated in English.

One problem is that the redundancy in the original schema for PERSON is solely due to the inability of the relational data model to handle set-valued attributes in a natural way. A much more appropriate schema for the original table would be

```
PERSON(SSN: String, Name: String,
        PhoneN: {String}, Child: {String})
```

where the brackets {} represent set-valued attributes. For instance, Child : {String} says that the value of the attribute Child in a tuple is a *set* of elements of type String. The rows in such a table might look as follows (note the set-valued components):

```
(111-22-3333, Joe Public,
    {516-123-4567, 516-345-6789}, {222-33-4444, 333-44-5555})
(222-33-4444, Bob Public,
    {212-987-1111, 212-987-6543}, {444-55-6666, 555-66-7777})
```

The second problem with the above example is the awkwardness with which SQL handles queries (16.1) and (16.2). Suppose that the type of the attribute Child were { PERSON} rather than {String} and that SQL could treat the value of the Child attribute as a set of PERSON tuples (rather than just a set of strings that represent SSNs). It would then be possible to formulate the query much more concisely and naturally because the expression P.Child.Child can be given precise meaning: the set of all tuples corresponding to the children of the children of P. This would allow us to write the above query in the following elegant way:

```
SELECT    P.Child.Child.PhoneN
FROM      PERSON P                                          (16.3)
WHERE     P.Name = 'Joe Public'
```

Expressions of the form P.Child.Child.PhoneN are called **path expressions**.

IsA Hierarchies.   Suppose that some, but not all, people in our database are students. Since students are persons, we want to factor out the general information pertinent to all persons and have the schema for STUDENT contain only the information specific to students:

```
STUDENT(SSN: String, Major: String)
```

Then we reason that, since a STUDENT is also a PERSON, every student has, for example, a Name attribute. For instance, the query: *Get the names of all computer science majors* can then be written as follows:

```
SELECT    S.Name
FROM      STUDENT S
WHERE     S.Major = 'CS'
```

In SQL-92, the above query would be rejected because the attribute Name is not explicitly included in the schema of STUDENT. However, if the system knew about the IsA relationship between students and persons, it could infer that STUDENT "inherits" Name from PERSON.

The concept of IsA hierarchies is already familiar to us from the entity-relationship model. However, the E-R model does not come with a query language. We are thus compelled to use the relational model and standard SQL, which forces us to write the following, more complex query:

```
SELECT    P.Name
FROM      PERSON P, STUDENT S
WHERE     P.SSN = S.SSN AND S.Major = 'CS'
```

In essence, SQL-92 programmers must include an implementation of the IsA relationship with each query.

Blobs.   The term *blob* stands for **binary large object**. Virtually all relational DBMSs allow relations to have attributes of type blob. For example, a database of movies can have this schema:

```
MOVIE (Name: String, Director: PERSON, Video: blob)      (16.4)
```

The attribute Video might hold a video stream, which can contain gigabytes of data. From the relational point of view, a video stream is a large, unstructured sequence of bits.

There are several problems with blobs. Consider the query

```
SELECT   M.Director
FROM     Movie M
WHERE    M.Name = 'The Simpsons'
```

Some systems might drag the entire tuple containing the blob from disk into main memory to evaluate the WHERE clause. This is a huge overhead. Even when a DBMS is optimized to handle blobs, its options are limited. Suppose that we need only the frames in the range 20,000 to 50,000. We cannot obtain this information if we stay within the traditional relational model. To handle such a query, we need a special routine, frameRange(from, to), perhaps implemented as a stored procedure, which, for a given video blob, returns frames in the specified range.

Would it make sense to add frameRange() as an operator to the relational data model? While this addition would enable anyone to play with video blobs, it would not help with blobs that store DNA sequences or VLSI chip designs. Thus, rather than burdening the data model with all kinds of specialized operations, a general mechanism is needed to let users define such operations separately for each type of blob.

Objects. The shortcomings of SQL just discussed led to the idea of databases that can store and retrieve objects. As explained in the Appendix, an object consists of a set of attributes and a set of methods that can access those attributes, together with an associated inheritance hierarchy.

Attribute values can be instances of complex data types or other objects. For example, the attributes of a person object might include one representing the person's address and one representing her spouse.

Since the value of an attribute might be an instance of an object, the operations defined for the object can be used in queries. Thus, a video object might have a method, frameRange(), which can be used in a query.

```
SELECT   M.frameRange(20000,50000)
FROM     Movie M
WHERE    M.Name = 'The Simpsons'
```

Impedance mismatch in database languages. It is impossible to write complete applications entirely in SQL, so database applications are typically written in a host language, such as C or Java, and access databases by executing SQL queries embedded in a host program. Chapter 10 discussed a number of mechanisms for accessing databases from host languages.[2]

---

[2] While the language of stored procedures, SQL/PSM (see Chapter 10), is computationally complete, it is hardly a suitable replacement for a language like C, C++, or Java.

One problem with this approach is that SQL is set oriented, meaning that its queries return sets of tuples. In contrast, C, Java, and other host languages do not understand relations and do not support high-level operations on them. Apart from this mismatch of types, there is a sharp difference between the declarative nature of SQL (which specifies *what* has to be done) and the procedural nature of host languages (in which the programmer must tell *how* things are to be done). This phenomenon has been dubbed the **impedance mismatch** between the data access language and the host language, and the cursor mechanism (Section 10.2.4) was invented to serve as an adaptor between procedural host languages and SQL.

The possibility of eliminating the impedance mismatch was one reason for the development of object databases in the early days. The basic idea is simple: Take a typical object-oriented language (C++ and Smalltalk were the primary candidates in those days; Java was added in the 1990s) and use *it* as a data manipulation language. Since objects underly both object languages and object databases, no impedance mismatch occurs.

This vision seemed attractive at the time, but there are a number of difficulties. First, there was still a need for a powerful, declarative query language, such as SQL, to support complex data querying. Since C++ or Java could not be easily extended to a declarative query language, the impedance mismatch remained.[3]

Another difficulty was that, instead of just one data manipulation language, SQL (even if mismatched to the host language), we now had as many data manipulation languages as there were host languages. This was not bad in itself, since none of these host languages was new and most programmers were presumably familiar with them. The problem was that the different object languages had somewhat different object models. Thus, it was hard to define a single, unified data model. For instance, if certain objects were created using an application in one host language, accessing them using applications written in other host languages could be problematic.

The two main object database standards discussed in this chapter, SQL:1999 and ODMG, have very different views of the significance of impedance mismatch. Partly because of the above difficulties and partly because of a different design philosophy, SQL:1999 does not aim to eliminate impedance mismatch. In contrast, ODMG sees elimination of this mismatch as a major (even if still elusive) goal.

16.1.1   Object Databases versus Relational Databases

From the previous examples, we can begin to see the broad outlines of the object model and how it relates to the relational model.

■ A relational database consists of relations, which are sets of tuples, while an object database consists of classes, which are sets of objects. Thus, a relational database might contain a relation, called PERSON, with tuples containing infor-

---

[3] In this context, we should mention the ongoing work on the **Java Data Objects Specification**, which is aiming at (among other things) the development of a query language that better blends into the Java syntax.

mation about each person, whereas an object database might contain a class, called PERSON, with objects containing information about each person. A particular relational database can be implemented within the object model by defining a class for each relation. The attributes of a particular class are the attributes of the corresponding relation, and each object instantiated from the class corresponds to a tuple.

■ In a relational database, the components of a tuple must be primitive types (strings, integers, etc.); in an object database, the components of an object can be complex types (sets, tuples, objects, etc.).

■ Object databases have certain properties for which there is no analogy in relational databases:

❑ Objects can be organized into an inheritance hierarchy, which allows objects of a lower type to inherit the attributes and methods from objects of a higher type. This helps reduce clutter in type specifications and leads to more concise queries.

❑ Objects can have methods, which can be invoked from within queries. For instance, the specification of the class MOVIE mentioned earlier might contain a method, frameRange, with a declaration of the form

```
list(VIDEOFRAME) frameRange(Integer,Integer);
```

which states that frameRange takes two integer arguments and returns a list of video frames. Such declarations are made using a special object definition language, which is similar to the data definition sublanguage of SQL.

❑ Method implementations are written in advance using a standard host language (e.g., C++ or Java) and stored on the server. In this respect, methods are similar to stored procedures in SQL databases (Section 10.2.5). However, stored procedures are not associated with any particular relation, while a stored method is an integral part of the respective class and is inherited along the object type hierarchy in a manner similar to that for methods in object-oriented programming languages.

❑ In some object database systems, the data manipulation language and the host language are the same.

16.2   HISTORICAL DEVELOPMENTS

The following brief historical survey can be useful for a better understanding of the evolution of object databases.

Early 1980s: nested relations (also known as non-1NF).   The idea of nested relations was an early approach to dealing with some of the limitations of the relational data model [Makinouchi 1977, Arisawa et al. 1983, Roth and Korth 1987, Jaeschke and Schek 1982, Ozsoyoglu and Yuan 1985]. In a nested relation, attributes can be of type relation. Thus, in the table

111-22-3333	Joe Public	516-345-6789		222-33-4444	Bob Public
		516-123-4567		333-44-5555	Sally Public
222-33-4444	Bob Public	212-987-6543		444-55-6666	Maggy Public
		212-987-1111		555-66-7777	Mary Public

each tuple has four components. The first two are atomic values, as in the traditional relational model. However, the values of the third and fourth attributes are not atomic: they are unary and binary relations, respectively. The unary relation in the third component of the first tuple represents the list of phone numbers of Joe Public, while the fourth component in this tuple is a relation that describes Joe's children (via the Social Security number and name).

Experience has shown that the nested relational model is too limiting and its query languages and schema design theory are too complex.

Mid 1980s: persistent objects.   The idea underlying persistent objects comes from programming languages and traces back to the late 1960s. The early object database systems were, conceptually, just persistent C++ or Smalltalk.

The basic idea is simple and elegant.

1. The user can declare certain C++ or Smalltalk objects as **persistent**.

2. When an application program refers to a persistent object in the program, the system checks if the object is in a main memory buffer. If not, an **object fault** occurs and the system brings the object into memory transparently to the user program.

3. When the program completes, if it has updated any persistent object, the new version of that object is returned to mass storage, again transparently to the user.

Programming languages with persistent objects eliminate impedance mismatch between database data types and the data types of the host language.[4] However, they do not provide a mechanism for high-level declarative querying similar to the SELECT statement in SQL. As a result, all queries must be programmed procedurally using the constructs available in the host language. We will see in Section 16.4.5 that the ODMG standard trades some degree of impedance mismatch for the luxury of declarative query language support.

Early 1990s: object-relational databases.   The basic idea behind **object-relational databases** is that relations are still sets of tuples but tuple components can be

---

[4] Note that persistent data types can reduce impedance mismatch only in a language with a sufficiently rich assortment of data types. For instance, making the native data types persistent in C, which lacks the set data type, is unlikely to help with the problem.

objects. The object-relational model was put to practical use in two early products: UniSQL and Illustra. Object-relational databases are not as general as some of the more recent object databases in which arbitrary objects, not just relations, can exist at the highest level of the data model. However, they come close. The latest releases of most relational database products now support object-relational features, and the SQL:1999 standard has object-relational extensions as well. We cover these extensions in Section 16.5.

Mid 1990s: proliferation of object DBMSs. A number of early object DBMSs, including O_2, GemStone, ObjectStore, Poet, Versant, and others, helped the field mature. Each implementation contributed to the underlying conceptual framework.

Mid to Late 1990s: object data management standards. The field reached a stage when it became apparent that standards were needed to promote user acceptance of the new paradigm. We discuss three of these standards.

ODMG. The ODMG standard (developed by the Object Database Management Group) deals with object database systems and (as a special case) object-relational database systems. Its data model supports objects, and relations are simply special object types. The standard has the following major parts:

❑ ODL—the Object Definition Language: how to specify the database schema.

❑ OQL—the (SQL-like) Object Query Language.

❑ Host language bindings—how to use ODL and OQL from within procedural languages. The standard defines bindings for C++, Smalltalk, and Java. In ODMG, the host language also serves as the object manipulation language.

SQL:1999. The latest incarnation of SQL, SQL:1999 is designed to support a subset of the object-relational data model. The top-level structures are relations containing sets of tuples, but tuple components can be objects. The SQL:1999 standard overlaps with ODMG in object-relational database systems, but the syntax is very different. In addition to generalizing the relational model to be object-relational, SQL:1999 adds a number of other features to the language, such as

❑ Enhancements to SQL data definition, manipulation, and query language (Sections 7.6 and 16.5)

❑ Triggers (Chapter 9)

❑ The SQL Persistent Stored Modules (SQL/PSM) language, discussed in Section 10.2.5, which allows the programmer to write stored procedures[5]

❑ Definition of a call-level interface, SQL/CLI, similar to ODBC (Section 10.6).

❑ Multimedia extensions

---

[5] The ability to define stored procedures was considered of such importance that SQL/PSM was retroactively included in the SQL-92 standard.

CORBA. In parallel to the evolution of object databases, a significant effort was devoted to the development of a standard for client/server systems in which clients can access objects on servers. The Object Management Group (OMG)[6] produced such a standard, called **CORBA**, which stands for *Common Object Request Broker Architecture*. Recent versions of that standard allow clients to transactionally access persistent objects residing on remote servers and to perform those accesses using a declarative query language. Thus, CORBA can provide the functionality of an object database management system. We discuss CORBA further in Section 16.6.

16.3   THE CONCEPTUAL OBJECT DATA MODEL

To avoid becoming lost in the details of the ODMG and SQL:1999 standards, we first present a conceptual view of a data model suitable for object databases. This model, the **Conceptual Object Data Model** (*CODM*), is derived from the work of the research team behind O_2 [Bancilhon et al. 1990], an object DBMS that has had significant influence on the ODMG standard. In fact, CODM is close to ODMG. However, it is not burdened with some of the nitty-gritty details and low-level implementation concerns motivated by the need for compatibility with existing products and standards. In addition, the object-relational extensions of SQL:1999 can be conveniently explained in terms of CODM, which makes the relationship between the two standards easier to understand.

In CODM, every object has a unique and immutable identity, called the **object Id** (**oid**), which is independent of the actual value of the object. The oid is assigned by the system when the object is created and does not change during the object's lifetime. Note the distinction between oids and the primary keys of relations. Like an oid, a primary key uniquely identifies the object. However, unlike an oid, the value of a primary key might change (a person might change her Social Security number). In addition, an oid is an internal object name that normally is not visible to the programmer (and in some languages is not even accessible through an attribute). If repeated references to an object are needed, the oid must be saved in a variable after the object is created or retrieved. A primary key, on the other hand, is visible and can be explicitly mentioned in a query in order to retrieve a specific object.

16.3.1 Objects and Values

Here is an example of an object that describes a person, Joe Public:

```
(#32, [  SSN: 111-22-3333,
         Name: Joe Public,
         PhoneN: {"516-123-4567", "516-345-6789"},          (16.5)
         Child: {#445, #73}] )
```

---

[6] Object Management Group, OMG, and Object Database Management Group, ODMG, are different organizations.

The symbol #32 is the oid of the data object that describes the real-world Joe Public. The rest specifies the *value* part of the object. The oid identifies this object among other objects, and the value provides the actual information about Joe. Observe that the value of the Child attribute is a set of oids of the PERSON objects that describe Joe's two children.

Formally, an **object** is a pair of the form (*oid, val*), where *oid* is an object Id and *val* is a value. The **value** part *val* can take one of the following forms:

- ■ *Primitive value*—such as a member of an Integer, String, Float, or Boolean data type. Example: "516-123-4567".

- ■ *Reference value*—an oid of an object. Example: #445.

- ■ *Tuple value*—of the form $[A_1 : v_1, \ldots, A_n : v_n]$, where the $A_1, \ldots, A_n$ are distinct attribute names and the $v_1, \ldots, v_n$ are values. Example: the entire value part (inside the brackets) of object #32 in (16.5).

- ■ *Set value*—of the form $\{v_1, \ldots, v_n\}$, where the $v_1, \ldots, v_n$ are values. Example: {"516-123-4567", "516-345-6789"}.

Reference, tuple, and set values are called **complex values** to distinguish them from primitive values. The actual ODMG data model includes additional complex value types, such as bags (sets that can have multiple copies of the same element), lists, structures, enumerated types, and arrays. However, we do not consider these here, because they add nothing new to the overall conceptual picture.

Note that the oid part of the object cannot change (if it did, it would indicate a different object). In contrast, the value part of an object can be replaced by another value as a result of an update. For example, if one of Joe Public's phone numbers should change, the value of the PhoneN attribute is replaced by a new value, but the object retains the same oid and is considered to be the same object.

16.3.2 Classes

In object-oriented systems, semantically similar objects are organized into **classes**. For instance, all objects representing persons are grouped into class PERSON.

Classes play the same role in CODM that relations play in relational databases. Whereas in SQL-92 a database is a set of relations and each relation is a set of tuples, in CODM a database is a set of classes and each class is a set of objects. Thus, in SQL-92 we might have a relation called PERSON, with tuples containing information about each person, and in CODM we might have a class called PERSON, with objects containing information about each person.

In this way, a class is a means of organizing objects into categories. A class has a **type**, which describes the common structure of all objects in the class, and **method signatures**, which are declarations of the operations that can be applied to the class objects. We discuss these notions in more detail later on. Here note that only method signatures are part of CODM—method implementations are *not*. A method implementation is a procedure, written in a host language, that is stored on the database server. An ODBMS must provide a mechanism to invoke the appropriate implementation whenever the method is used in the program.[7]

In the relational data model, two tables can be related to each other by means of an interrelational constraint (e.g., a foreign key constraint). In the object data model, one relationship plays a special role. Suppose that, in addition to the PERSON class, which groups together all objects representing persons, we have a STUDENT class, which groups together all objects that represent students. Naturally, every student is a person, so the set of objects that constitute class STUDENT must be a subset of the set of objects that constitute class PERSON. This is an example of the **subclass relationship**, in which STUDENT is a subclass of PERSON. The subclass relationship is also called the IsA relationship or the **inheritance relationship**.

The set of all objects assigned to a class is called the **extent** of the class. To adequately reflect our intuition about the subclass relationship, extents must satisfy the following property:

If C_1 is a subclass of C_2, the extent of C_2 contains the extent of C_1.

For example, since STUDENT is a subclass of PERSON, the set of all students is a subset of the set of all persons.

The query language and the data manipulation languages are aware of the subclass relationship. For example, if a query is supposed to return all PERSON objects that have a certain property and if some STUDENT object has that property, the query will return the STUDENT object in the query result since every student is also a person.

To summarize, a class has a type, which describes the class structure, method signatures (which are often considered part of the type), and an extent, which lists all objects that belong to the class. In this way, class, type, and extent are related, but distinct, notions.

16.3.3 Types

An important requirement of any data model is that the data must be properly structured. Because of the simplicity of the underlying data structure, typing is not a big issue in the relational model. It is more complex in object databases. Consider, for example, the object in (16.5). We can say that its type—let us call it PERSON—is represented by the following expression:

[SSN: String, Name: String, PhoneN: {String}, Child: {PERSON}]   (16.6)

This type definition states that the attributes SSN and Name draw their values from the primitive domain String; the attribute PhoneN must have values that are sets of strings; and the values of the attribute Child are sets of PERSON objects.

---

[7] Typically, this code is executed at the server. However, methods implemented in Java might be executed on the client side because Java provides a mechanism for shipping code between machines.

Intuitively, the type of an object is just the collection of the types of its components. More precisely, complex types suitable for structuring objects can be defined as follows:

■ *Basic types.* String, Float, Integer, and so forth

■ *Reference types.* User-defined class names, such as PERSON and STUDENT

■ *Tuple types.* Expressions of the form $[A_1 : T_1, \ldots, A_n : T_n]$, where A_i is a distinct attribute name and T_i is a type—for example, the type given in (16.6)

■ *Set types.* Expressions of the form $\{T\}$, where T is a type—for example, $\{$String$\}$

Note that (16.6) describes a type in which one relation is nested within another. Each value of Child is a relation: a set of tuples of type PERSON. On the other hand, a string is a basic type, so a value of PhoneN is simply a set of primitive values.

What does it mean for an object to conform to a type? Given the recursive structure of objects and the presence of the IsA hierarchy, the answer to this question is not straightforward. We develop the concept of type in the following paragraphs.

Subtyping. In addition to organizing objects structurally, the type system can tell which types have "more structure" than others. For instance, suppose the type of the PERSON objects is

```
[SSN: String, Name: String, Address: [StNumber: Integer,
                                      StName: String]]
```

This is a tuple type, in which the first two components have basic type and the third has a tuple type.

Consider now the objects of type STUDENT. Clearly, students have names, addresses, and everything else that PERSON objects have. However, students have additional attributes, so an appropriate type might be

```
[SSN: String, Name: String,
 Address: [StNumber: Integer, StName: String],
 Majors: {String}, Enrolled: {COURSE}]
```

Our intuition suggests that type STUDENT has more structure than type PERSON because (1) it has all the attributes of PERSON, (2) the values of these attributes have at least as much structure as the corresponding attributes in PERSON, and (3) STUDENT has attributes not present in PERSON. This intuition leads to the notions of **subtype** and **supertype**: Type T is a *subtype* of (supertype) T' if $T \neq T'$ and one of the following conditions holds:

■ T and T' are reference types, and T is a subclass of T'.

■ $T = [A_1 : T_1, \ldots, A_n : T_n, A_{n+1} : T_{n+1}, \ldots, A_m : T_m]$ and $T' = [A_1 : T_1', \ldots, A_n : T_n']$ are tuple types (note that T includes all attributes of T', that is, $m \geq n$), and either $T_i = T_i'$ or T_i is a subtype of T_i', for each $i = 1, \ldots, n$.

■ $T = \{T_0\}$ and $T' = \{T_0'\}$ are set types, and T_0 is a subtype of T_0'.

According to this definition, STUDENT is a subtype of PERSON because it contains all of the structure defined for PERSON and has additional attributes of its own. Note, however, that having additional attributes is not necessary for a type to be a subtype. For instance

```
[SSN: String, Name: String,
    Address: [StNumber: Integer,  StName: String,          (16.7)
             POBox: String] ]
```

is still a subtype of PERSON even though it does not have attributes beyond those defined for PERSON. Instead, the attribute Address in (16.7) has more structure than the same attribute in PERSON.

Domain of a type.   The **domain** of a type determines all objects that conform to that type. Intuitively the domain of a type, T, denoted $domain(T)$, is the appropriate combination of the domains of the components of T. More precisely,

■ The domain of a basic type, such as Integer or String, is just what we would expect—the set of all integers or strings, respectively.

■ The domain of a reference type, T, is the extent of T, that is, the set of all Ids of objects in class T. For instance, if T is PERSON, the domain is the set of all oids of PERSON objects.

■ The domain of a tuple type, $[A_1 : T_1, \ldots, A_n : T_n]$, is

$$\{[A_1 : w_1, \ldots, A_n : w_n] \mid n \geq 0 \text{ and } w_i \in domain(T_i)\}$$

that is, the set of all tuple values whose components conform to the corresponding types of attributes. Thus, the domain of type (16.6) is the set of all values of the form in (16.5).

■ The domain of a set type, $\{T\}$, is

$$\{\{w_1, \ldots, w_k\} \mid k \geq 0 \text{ and } w_i \in domain(T)\}$$

That is, it consists of sets of values that conform to the given type T. For instance, the domain of type {COURSE} is the set whose members are finite sets of oids for COURSE objects.

It is easy to see that domains are defined in such a way that the domain of a subtype, S, is (in a sense) a subset of the domain of a supertype, S'. More precisely, for any given object, o, in S, either o is already in S' or we can obtain an object, o', in S' by throwing out some components of the tuple subobjects included in o. For instance, a PERSON object can be obtained from a STUDENT object by throwing out the components corresponding to the Majors and Enrolled attributes. Similarly, a PERSON object can be obtained from an object of type (16.7) by throwing out the POBox component from the nested address.

Database schema and instance. In object databases, the **schema** contains the specification for each class of objects that can be stored in the database. For each class, C, it includes

■ The *type* associated with C. This type determines the structure of each instance of C.

■ The *method signatures* of C. A **method signature** specifies the method name, the type and order for the allowed method arguments, and the type of the result produced by the method. For instance, the method `enroll()` has the following signature:

> Boolean enroll (STUDENT, COURSE);

and the method `enrolled()` has the signature

> {COURSE} enrolled (STUDENT);

The signature of `enroll()` says that one must supply an object of class STUDENT and an object of class COURSE to enroll a student. The method returns a Boolean value that indicates the outcome of the operation. The signature of `enrolled()` says that, to check the enrollment of a student, one must supply a STUDENT object and the result will be a set of COURSE objects in which the student is enrolled.

■ The *subclass-of* relationship, which identifies the superclasses of C.

■ The *integrity constraints*, such as key constraints, referential constraints, or more general assertions, which are similar to constraints in relational databases.[8]

An **instance** of the database contains specific objects for the classes specified in the schema. The objects must satisfy all of the constraints implied by the schema, and each object must have a unique oid.

This completes the definition of the conceptual object model. As you can see, most of the notions used in CODM are extensions of familiar concepts from the relational model, but they require considerably more care because of the richness of the data model that underlies them.

16.3.4 Object–Relational Databases

This breed of DBMS arrived in the early 1990s, when a number of vendors began advocating object-relational systems as a safer migration path from relational databases. The main selling point was that such databases could be implemented as conservative extensions to the existing relational DBMSs. After long deliberation, the SQL:1999 working group finally adopted a limited subset of the object-relational data model, which corresponds to a subset of CODM. In general, an object-relational database consists of:

---

[8] The ODMG standard provides means for specifying keys and referential integrity, but it does not define the language for general SQL-style assertions. The SQL:1999 standard inherits its constraint specification language from SQL-92.

■ A set of relations (which can be viewed as classes).

■ Each relation consists of a set of tuples (which can be viewed as instances of the class that represents the relation).

■ Each tuple is of the form (*oid*, *val*), where *oid* is an object Id and *val* is a tuple value whose components can be *arbitrary* values (e.g., primitive values, sets of tuples, and references to other objects).

The main difference between the object-relational and CODM models is that in the former the top-level structure of each object instance is always a tuple while in the latter the top-level structure can be an arbitrary value. However, this restriction on object-relational DBMSs does not significantly decrease the ability to model real-world enterprises.

What differentiates object-relational and traditional relational models is that the tuple components must be primitive values in the relational model whereas they can be arbitrary values in the object-relational model. Thus, the relational model can be viewed as a subset of the object-relational model (and hence of CODM).

We discuss the subset of the object-relational model supported by SQL:1999 in Section 16.5.

16.4   THE ODMG STANDARD

This section provides an overview of the various aspects of the ODMG standard. See [Cattell and Barry 2000] for a definitive guide to ODMG 3.0. We discuss the following:

■ *The data model.* What kinds of objects can be stored in an ODMG database?

■ *The Object Definition Language (ODL).* How are these objects described to the database management system?

■ *The Object Query Language (OQL).* How is the database queried?

■ *The transaction mechanisms.* How are transaction boundaries specified?

■ *Language bindings.* How are ODMG databases used in the "real world"?

The data model underlying ODMG is very close to CODM, although we briefly discuss a few differences in the next section. After that, we present ODL, the Object Definition Language of ODMG—a concrete syntax for describing classes and their types and then discuss the ODMG query language, OQL, and highlight some of its differences from the query language discussed in Section 16.1.

The architecture of an ODMG database.   The overall architecture of an ODMG database is depicted in Figures 16.1 and 16.2. As with relational databases, an application that uses an ODMG database is written in a host language, such as C++. In order to access the database, the application must be linked with the ODBMS libraries and with the code that implements its class methods. In object databases, much of the code that manipulates objects is part of the database itself:

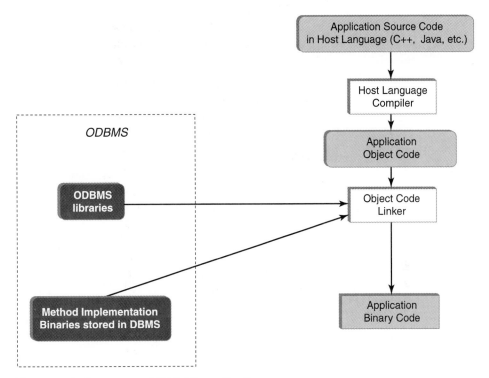

Figure 16.1 Structure of ODMG applications.

Each class comes with the set of methods allowed for the objects in the class. The code for these methods is stored on the database server, and the method signatures are specified as part of the schema using ODL. The ODBMS is responsible for the invocation of the appropriate code whenever a method is called. In principle, methods can execute either at the server or at the client site. However, to execute a method at the client site requires that the ODBMS provide infrastructure for shipping method code to client machines. Because of the difficulty in implementing such infrastructure, commercial ODBMS typically execute methods at the server. Fortunately, the introduction of Java makes code shipping much easier, and we might see more client-side method invocation in future products.

Storing code on the server is reminiscent of stored procedures in relational databases (see Section 10.2.5). However, the important difference is that a method implementation is integral to an object, whereas a stored procedure is an external application routine stored in the database for performance and security reasons.

Elimination of impedance mismatch between the data access language and the host language is one of the most important design goals of ODMG. The immediate practical implication of this goal is that the host language also serves as the data manipulation language. This is achieved using **language bindings**—a set of standards (one per host language) that define how object definitions in C++, Java, and

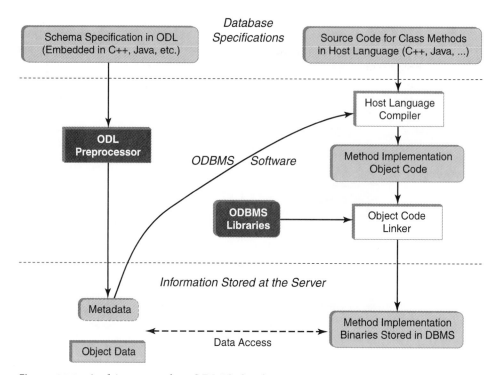

Figure 16.2 Architecture of an ODMG database.

Smalltalk are mapped to database objects. This mapping allows the host program to manipulate database objects *directly* through regular host language statements (assignment, increment, etc.) or by executing methods defined for the corresponding classes. Once such an interaction occurs, the ODBMS is responsible for making sure that resulting changes are made durable when the transaction commits.

Typically, an application finds an object or set of objects in the database using an OQL query. Then the application manipulates and updates those objects with programming language statements and the objects' methods. No special SQL-style update statements are needed, since any updates of an object within the program cause corresponding updates to the copy of the object in the database. For instance, if the host language variable Stud contains the oid of a persistent STUDENT object, the following statement in C++ or Java

```
Stud.Name = "John";
```

changes the name of the student to John both in the program and in the database.[9]

---

[9] Note that ODMG, like C++ and Java, uses double quotes to represent strings. In contrast, strings are set in single quotes in SQL.

Observe that this mode of data access is quite different from the one used in SQL databases. In an SQL database, every query or modification to the data happens through SQL—a language that is very different from a typical host language. This holds true even if the host language is object oriented as is the case with Java, for example, using JDBC and SQLJ, as discussed in Chapter 10. By contrast, in an ODMG database data is modified directly in the host language, the same way as any other object in the program is modified.

ODMG provides special methods that allow the application to send an OQL query (i.e., a SELECT statement) to the database. This facility is viewed as an "ugly duckling" in the overall ODMG scheme of things, since it brings back the infamous impedance mismatch. To address this issue, there is an ongoing **Java Data Objects Specification** effort aimed at the development of an alternative query language—one that better fits with Java syntax. When completed, this specification might replace the current ODMG Java binding.

It follows from the above discussion that a typical application works with two kinds of objects: **persistent** objects, which are stored in the database, and **transient** objects, which are used to hold auxiliary information required by the application logic but are not saved in the database. For instance, a mail-merge application that sends reminders to students who have not paid their tuition queries the database and constructs, for each student, a transient object that contains the information that must be included in the reminder (e.g., name, address, amount of tuition, deadline). Such an object is useful only while the application is active and does not need to be saved. On the other hand, the STUDENT objects might need to be updated and saved to reflect the fact that a tuition notice had been sent. The exact syntax for specifying object persistence is part of the language binding specification, which is discussed in Section 16.4.5.

16.4.1 ODL—The ODMG Object Definition Language

The ODMG Object Definition Language (ODL) is analogous to the data definition sublanguage of SQL. It is used to describe the schema of an object database. As in SQL, schema information defined using ODL is stored in the system catalog and is used at run time to evaluate queries and perform database updates.

ODL and impedance mismatch.   In SQL, the role of the Data Definition Language is very clear—it is the only way to describe data to the database. The role of ODL in ODMG is less obvious. Language bindings allow the programmer to declare database objects and classes directly in the host program using the syntax of the host language (for example, Java), so ODL need not be used for this purpose. This is very different from the mechanism used by embedded SQL, SQLJ, ODBC, or JDBC, where the database schema is defined in a separate language (the DDL subset of SQL) joined to the host language using a call- or statement-level interface. To further complicate matters, very few ODMG vendors have actually implemented ODL in their systems. Why, then, do we bother discussing it?

The role of ODL becomes more clear if we recall that complete elimination of the impedance mismatch is problematic. The idea of using the same language for programming applications and database access sounded very appealing back in the days when people believed that C++ was the only respectable way to program. Objects would be declared uniformly in the host language—independently of whether they were persistent and intended to reside in the database, or transient and intended to be deallocated when the application terminated. However, the arrival of Java made things more complicated. The problem is that Java's object definition facilities are not as extensive as those of C++. Even before Java, Smalltalk (with its own limitations) had a sizable following in the ODBMS application development community, so the question is: How can all of these languages, with their dissimilar object definition facilities, access the same object store? Can a Java application manipulate objects created by a C++ application? Which is the ODMG data model—the one defined by the C++ language binding or the one defined by the Java binding?

These questions are not an issue in SQL databases precisely because there is a single data definition language separate from all host languages. In ODMG, because of the crusade against impedance mismatch, forcing (the same) ODL on each host language is difficult. Nevertheless, ODL is still useful as a way of specifying a reference data model and as a target language for the three language bindings defined by ODMG. So, while ODL might not exist as a software package, it plays an important role in holding the ODMG standard together by providing it with a unifying conceptual foundation. In particular, ODMG specifies that an object created in one language can be accessed by an application written in another language if the object definition belongs to the subset of ODL common to both.

ODL and the ODMG data model.   The terminology used in ODL differs in some respects from that used in CODM, and we highlight the differences as we go.

ODL describes the attributes and methods of each object type, including its inheritance properties. A method is specified by its **signature**, which consists of the method's name, the names, order, and types of its arguments, the type of its return value, and the names of any exceptions it can raise (errors and special conditions).

ODL is an extension of the **Interface Definition Language** (**IDL**) that is used to specify objects in the CORBA standard. Following Java, ODL distinguishes between two kinds of classes. The first is called an *interface*, the second a *class*. To avoid confusion with CODM classes, we call these **ODMG interfaces** and **ODMG classes**, respectively.

In terms of CODM, ODMG interface and class definitions specify

■ A class name (in the CODM sense) along with the relevant part of the inheritance hierarchy

■ A type associated with the class

A collection of such definitions specifies the entire ODMG database schema. The main differences between ODMG interfaces and ODMG classes follow:

■ An ODMG interface cannot include code for methods; only method signatures are allowed (which is why it is called an interface). ODMG classes do include the code for the methods of the class. The signature and the code can be either explicitly specified, using a host language, such as C++ or Java, or inherited from a class higher up in the hierarchy. Also, an ODMG interface does not specify attributes, whereas ODMG classes do.

■ An ODMG interface cannot have its own member objects; that is, object instances of the interface cannot be created. In contrast, an ODMG class can (and usually does) have member objects. Thus, the extent of an ODMG interface consists of the objects that belong to its ODMG subclasses.

■ An ODMG interface cannot inherit from an ODMG class but only from another ODMG interface.

■ An ODMG class can inherit from multiple ODMG interfaces, but it can have at most one immediate ODMG superclass.

The distinction between classes and interfaces exists for two reasons. First, it makes ODL a superset of CORBA's IDL, thereby providing a degree of compatibility with this important standard for distributed systems. Second, it enables ODL to sidestep some of the problems associated with multiple inheritance that arise when a class inherits two different definitions for the same method from different superclasses.

Similarly to CODM, ODMG distinguishes between objects and values. Values are called **literals** in the ODMG terminology. Objects are pairs (*oid*, *val*), as discussed previously. Literals, on the other hand, might have complex internal state, but they do not have oids and they do not have any associated methods. In ODL, objects are created as instances of an ODMG class while literals are instances of types specified using the struct keyword.

The definition for the class PERSON might be

```
// An interface.
// Note: Object is the top interface in ODMG, but a class in Java.
interface PERSONINTERFACE: Object
{    String Name();
     String SSN();
     enum SexType {m,f} Sex();
}
// An ODMG class
// PERSON inherits from PERSONINTERFACE, but has no ODMG
// superclass
class PERSON: PERSONINTERFACE
(    extent PERSONEXT
     keys ( SSN, (Name, PhoneN) ): PERSISTENT; )
// properties of the instances of the type
{    attribute ADDRESS Address;
     attribute Set<String> PhoneN;
// relationships among instances of the type
```

```
        relationship PERSON Spouse;
        relationship Set <PERSON> Child;
// methods of instances of the type
        void add_phone_number(in String phone);
}


// A literal type
struct ADDRESS
{   String StNumber;
    String StName;
}
```

This example defines an interface, a class, and a literal type. The clause PERSON-INTERFACE: Object states that PERSONINTERFACE is a child of Object in the inheritance hierarchy. Object is a built-in interface definition that provides signatures for methods that are common to all objects, such as delete(), copy(), and same_as(). (One object is same_as another if and only if the two have the same oid.) Similarly, PERSON : PERSONINTERFACE states that the class PERSON inherits from the interface PERSONINTERFACE. In our example PERSON is not a child of any ODMG class.

The clauses that begin with extent and keys specify the properties of type PERSON as a whole. extent gives a name to the set of all PERSON objects. This distinction between the class name and the extent name in a Data Definition language is quite unusual from the point of view of relational DBMSs. It is similar to giving one name to the relation schema (i.e., the symbol used in the CREATE TABLE statement) and a different name to the actual relation instance over that schema. From both conceptual and practical viewpoints, the value of extent is questionable.

The keys clause specifies that the extent has two distinct candidate keys: SSN and ⟨Name, PhoneN⟩. In other words, this type cannot have distinct objects with the same SSN or with the same combination of name and phone number.

The remainder of the specification defines the type (in the CODM sense) associated with the interface PERSONINTERFACE, the class PERSON, and the literal type ADDRESS. Every instance of these types is allowed to have several methods and attributes. The method Name() of PERSONINTERFACE returns the primitive type String. The method Sex() returns the enumeration type with possible values m and f. The Address attribute of the class PERSON has the user-defined type ADDRESS, which is the literal type found right under the definition for PERSON. Finally, the PhoneN attribute has the set type, where each member of the set is a string. This type is represented using the ODMG interface set. Note that because only methods can be declared in an interface, Name(), SSN(), and Sex() in the example are methods.

ODMG distinguishes between *attributes* and *relationships*. The value of an **attribute** is a literal (not an object) that is stored within the given object. A **relationship** refers to some other object stored in the database; it specifies how that object is related to the given object. The PERSON definition includes two relationships. Spouse refers to another PERSON object (stored separately) that corresponds to the object's spouse. Child refers to the set of PERSON objects (also stored separately), that lists all children of the given person.

Unfortunately, the use of the ODMG term "relationship" clashes with the use of this term in the E-R model. ODMG relationships and attributes are quite similar except that relationships involve objects rather than values. In contrast, E-R relationships are similar to objects and have their own structure, which is represented using attributes and roles. In fact, it is the E-R notion of role that corresponds to the ODMG notion of relationship, because a role is essentially an attribute whose domain is a set of entities (instead of primitive types, such as integers and strings).

In addition to specifying attributes and relationships, the class definition can also have method signatures (recall that method implementations are provided separately, in the host language). In our example, the signature for the method add_phone_number() has been specified. The keyword in in the parameter list of the method specifies the **parameter passing mode**; here it says that the parameter phone is an input parameter. This feature is borrowed from the CORBA Interface Definition Language (we also saw it in SQL/PSM in Chapter 10). Other parameter passing keywords are out and inout (for output parameters and parameters that can be used for both input and output).

The ADDRESS specification above defines an ODMG literal type (whose instances are "values" in CODM terminology). For this definition, ODMG uses the keyword struct instead of class. Literals have only attributes and no relationships, so the keywords attribute or relationship are not needed in a literal definition.

We continue to develop the above example by (partially) defining another ODMG class, STUDENT:

```
class STUDENT extends PERSON {
    (extent STUDENTEXT)
    . . .
    attribute Set<String> Major;
    relationship Set<COURSE> Enrolled;
    . . .
}
```

The clause STUDENT extends PERSON makes STUDENT a subclass of the class PERSON. Note that ODMG uses the : construct to denote inheritance from an interface and the extends keyword to denote inheritance from a class. Inheritance from a class definition implies inheritance of the method implementations in addition to that of the attributes and method signatures. Furthermore, the extent of STUDENT becomes a subset of the extent of PERSON.

ODMG's inheritance model resembles Java's. An ODMG class can extend only one other ODMG class, but can inherit method signatures from several ODMG interfaces. However, ODMG prohibits *name overloading*: A method with a given name cannot be inherited from more than one class or interface. For example, if LIBRARIAN is defined as a subclass of both FACULTY and STAFF, then FACULTY and STAFF cannot have identically named methods, such as weeklyPay. (Note that, in the case of LIBRARIAN, since multiple inheritance from classes is not permitted, either FACULTY or STAFF or both must be interfaces.)

The relationship Enrolled in the STUDENT definition states that the student is enrolled in a set of courses, where COURSE is an object defined (and stored) separately. The definition of COURSE might be

```
class COURSE : Object {
    (extent COURSEEXT)
    attribute Integer CrsCode;
    attribute String Department;
    relationship Set<STUDENT> Enrollment;
    . . .
}
```

which defines the relationship Enrollment that relates a course to the students enrolled in it.

These relationship declarations automate the enforcement of referential integrity as we know it from SQL. For instance, if a course object is deleted from the database, it is automatically removed from the set of courses that can be returned by the attribute Enrolled of STUDENT objects. Similarly, when a STUDENT object is deleted, it is removed from the set of students enrolled in the appropriate courses.

The ODMG standard does not provide a mechanism, similar to the ON DELETE CASCADE clause in SQL, to react to such deletions. However, almost the same functionality can be obtained with the ODMG *exception* mechanism (which we do not discuss here).

ODL also provides for automatic maintenance of consistency between the values returned by the relationships Enrolled and Enrollment. If john is an object in class STUDENT and john.Enrolled contains the course CS532, but the value of CS532.Enrollment does not include john, the database is inconsistent. To prevent this, the database designer can indicate that the Enrollment relationship is the inverse of the Enrolled relationship, and vice versa.

```
class STUDENT extends PERSON {
    (extent STUDENTEXT)
    . . .
    attribute Set<String> Major;                    (16.8)
    relationship Set<COURSE> Enrolled;
            inverse COURSE::Enrollment;
    . . .
}
class COURSE : Object {
    . . .
    relationship Set<STUDENT> Enrollment;
            inverse STUDENT::Enrolled;
    . . .
}
```

Here, the statement relationship Set<COURSE> Enrolled; inverse COURSE:: Enrollment says that, if a COURSE object, *c*, is in the set *s*.Enrolled, where *s* is

a STUDENT object, then *s* must be in the set *c*.Enrollment. The clause relationship
Set< STUDENT> Enrollment; inverse STUDENT::Enrolled states the opposite inclusion. Note that this constraint is stronger than referential integrity, which can
only guarantee that no student is registered for a bogus course and that course
rosters do not contain phantom students.

16.4.2 OQL—The ODMG Object Query Language

Although objects can be queried directly through their methods and attributes,
ODMG provides a powerful declarative query language to access an object database. As in relational databases, ODMG queries can be issued interactively or
embedded in applications. However, as many vendors do not support the interactive mode, embedded queries are usually used in the real world. The syntax for
embedding queries depends on the host language. Section 16.4.5 illustrates how
this is done in Java. In this section, we discuss the query language itself, independent of the mode.

The ODMG Object Query Language (OQL) is similar in many respects to the
query language subset of SQL. For example, the query

```
SELECT DISTINCT S.Address
FROM PERSONEXT S
WHERE S.Name = "Smith"
```

returns the set of addresses of all persons named Smith.[10] More precisely, it returns a
value of type Set<ADDRESS>. The set type comes with built-in methods that give the
programmer access to the elements of the set to obtain the functionality provided
by cursors in SQL.

Recall that ODMG makes a clear distinction between the name of a class and the
name of the class extent. It is the name of the extent, not of the class, that is used
in the FROM clause. Thus, the above example uses the symbol PERSONEXT, which
represents the extent (i.e., the collection of all objects) of class PERSON.

If, in the above query, the keyword DISTINCT is omitted from the SELECT statement, the query will return a value of type Bag<ADDRESS>, a bag of addresses (a
bag is similar to a set but can have duplicate elements).

Methods can also be invoked in a SELECT statement. Using the example of a
MOVIE object, defined in (16.4), we can write the query

```
SELECT M.frameRange(100,1000)
FROM MOVIE M
WHERE M.Name = "The Simpsons"
```

to invoke the frameRange() method, which returns a set of frame range objects, one
for each movie with the title "The Simpsons." If frameRange() has been redefined
in the inheritance hierarchy, the system will select the correct version based on

---

[10] Note that, unlike SQL, OQL uses double quotes to denote string constants—"Smith" rather than
'Smith'.

inheritance rules. Methods, with or without parameters, can be used anywhere in the query.[11]

SELECT statements that invoke methods can have side effects. For instance, if class PERSON has a method for updating the set of personal telephone numbers, we can write the following OQL query, where an update method is invoked in the SELECT clause:

```
SELECT S.add_phone_number("555-1212")
FROM PERSONEXT S                                           (16.9)
WHERE S.SSN = "123-45-6789"
```

This query changes the database, but does not return anything to the caller.

The ability to call update methods in the OQL SELECT statement blurs the boundary between the data manipulation and query languages.

The syntax of the SELECT statement also includes complex WHERE predicates, joins, aggregates, group-by, order-by, and so forth, as in SQL.

Path expressions.   Path expressions are a key part of OQL; they allow the query to go inside a complex attribute and execute object methods. As noted in Section 16.1, this technique can significantly simplify query formulation. For example,

```
SELECT DISTINCT S.Address.StName
FROM PERSONEXT S
WHERE S.Name = "Smith"
```

returns the set of strings (a value of type Set<String>) corresponding to the street names in the addresses of all persons named Smith.

Relationships can be used in SELECT statements wherever an attribute is allowed. For example, in the following query we are using a relationship, Spouse, instead of an attribute, Address.

```
SELECT S.Spouse.Name()
FROM PERSONEXT S
WHERE S.Name = "Smith"
```

returns the set of names (a value of type Set<String>) corresponding to the spouses of persons named Smith (there can be several Smiths in the database).

Formally, a **path expression** is of the form

$$P.name_1.name_2. \dots . name_n$$

where P can be an object or a variable that ranges over objects and each $name_i$ can be an attribute name, method invocation (with arguments), or relationship name. For instance, the expression M.frameRange(100,1000).play() involves methods.

A path expression must be **type consistent**. In the above example, we used

```
S.Address.StName
```

---

[11] There might be typing restrictions if, for example, the result of a method is used in some other expression, for example, X.age() = Y.frameRange(100,1000) is a type error.

to return the StNames in the addresses of all people named Smith. This expression is type consistent for the following reasons:

■ The variable S refers to an object of type PERSON.

■ The type PERSON has an Address attribute.

■ The subexpression S.Address returns a value of type ADDRESS.

■ The type ADDRESS has an StName attribute.

Earlier, in (16.3), we used the path expression

    P.Child.Child.PhoneN   (16.10)

which was intended to represent the set of phone numbers of all grandchildren of the object P. However, this path expression has a new twist. A person can have more than one child, so the issue here is the nature of the result returned by the subexpression P.Child. Is it a *set of objects*, each of which is of type PERSON, or is it a single *set object* of type Set<PERSON>?

In some object-oriented query languages (e.g., XSQL [Kifer et al. 1992]) P.Child is a set of objects. Thus, in XSQL we can continue to apply Child and later PhoneN to each individual child. In the end, we get the set of all phone numbers of P's grandchildren. However, in OQL P.Child returns a single set object of type Set<PERSON>. Since this set object is *not* of type PERSON, the attribute Child is not defined for it. As far as OQL is concerned, then, expression (16.10) has a type error!

OQL introduces a special operator, flatten, whose purpose is to break up set objects and other aggregate objects, such as lists. For instance, flatten(Set<1,2,3>) is a set of objects {1,2,3}, not a single set object. So, while in XSQL the expression (16.10) is correct, the corresponding expression in OQL is more cumbersome:

    flatten(flatten(P.Child).Child).PhoneN

Nested queries in OQL.   As in SQL, some OQL queries require the nested subquery mechanism. Recall that, in SQL, nested subqueries occur in two places:

■ In the FROM clause, to specify a virtual range for a tuple variable (e.g., query (6.26), page 153)

■ In the WHERE clause, to specify complex query conditions (e.g., query (6.22), page 149)

Nested subqueries can occur in OQL in the FROM and WHERE clauses for the same reasons as in SQL. However, OQL queries can also have nested subqueries in the SELECT clause if there is a need to construct a set object and return it as a result. Clearly, this situation is unique to object-oriented query languages, because set objects cannot occur as components of a tuple in the relational model.

To illustrate, suppose that we need to obtain the list of all students along with the computer science courses they are taking. We want the outcome to be a set of tuples where the first attribute is of primitive type String but the second is of type Set<COURSE>.

```
SELECT struct{ name:    S.Name,
              courses: (SELECT E
                        FROM S.Enrolled E            (16.11)
                        WHERE E.Department="CS")
       }
FROM STUDENTEXT S
```

Here a nested query occurs in the SELECT clause to construct a set to be assigned to the attribute `courses`. The purpose of this nested query is to create a complex nested structure—something that cannot happen in the relational model (and thus is not allowed in SQL, except for subqueries that return a single scalar value). Note that we have used the C-style struct construct to tell OQL that the output of the query is to be treated as a set of complex values.

Aggregation and grouping.   OQL provides the usual aggregate functions such as sum, count, avg, and so forth. From Chapter 6, we know that aggregation is interesting mainly when it is used together with grouping. In SQL, grouping requires a special clause, GROUP BY. Interestingly, OQL grouping can be achieved through nested subqueries in the SELECT clause, and no special grouping clause is required.

To make this concrete, consider query (16.11). Its output is a set of tuples, where the first component is a student name and the second is a set of courses in which the student is enrolled. Thus, the output is *already grouped*. With a small change, we can convert the above example into one that produces a list of students along with the total number of computer science courses in which each is enrolled. The result is similar to an SQL statement that uses a GROUP BY clause.

```
SELECT   name:    S.Name,
         count:   count(SELECT E.CrsCode
                        FROM    S.Enrolled E
                        WHERE   E.Department="CS")
FROM STUDENTEXT S
```

Even though GROUP BY is not necessary in OQL, it is provided along with the HAVING clause. However, it exists not to increase the expressive power of the language or to serve as syntactic sugar—the expressive power does not change, and in most cases GROUP BY does not simplify query formulation. Instead, it is useful as a *hint* to the query optimizer, which uses it to build a better query execution plan.

To explain, consider how a query processor might execute the above query. To answer this query efficiently, the query processor should organize course objects into groups, where each group represents the enrollment course list for a particular student. However, it is unlikely that the query optimizer would figure out on its own that there is a need to group courses around each student, so the probable plan will be to scan STUDENTEXT and execute the subquery for each value of S. On the other hand, the optimizer might process the following query differently:[12]

```
SELECT S.Name, count: count(E.CrsCode)
FROM STUDENTEXT S, S.Enrolled E
WHERE E.Department = "CS"
GROUP BY S.SSN
```

In this query, the FROM clause produces a sequence of oid pairs, $< s, e >$, where e is the oid of a course in which the student with oid s is enrolled.

Because of the GroupBy clause, the optimizer now knows that courses must be grouped around the students who take them, so it might join the classes STUDENT and COURSE using the method that leaves the resulting tuples correctly grouped. One way to do this is to scan the instances of class COURSE and, for each course, c, hash it on the oid of every student who takes c. As a result, the course oids will be placed in buckets in such a way that all courses taken by the same student end up in the same bucket. Therefore, we can compute the join and count the courses taken by each student during the same bucket scan.

16.4.3 Transactions in ODMG

Before a transaction can be initiated, a **database object**, which references the database the transaction is to access, must be open. Creating, opening, and closing of database objects is performed through a built-in interface called DatabaseFactory. Thus, the call

```
db1 = DatabaseFactory.new();
```

creates a new database object and returns a reference, db1, to it. That reference can then be used in the calls

```
db1.open(in String database_name);
```

which opens the database with name *database_name*, and

```
db1.close();
```

which closes it. Only one database can be open at a time.

ODMG has a built-in interface called TransactionFactory, which can be used to create new transaction objects to access the currently open database. Thus, the call

```
trans1 = TransactionFactory.new();
```

creates a new transaction object and returns a reference, trans1, to it. That reference can then be used in calls such as

---

[12] Here we use the so-called "alternative syntax" for GROUP BY, which exists for compatibility with SQL. The "normal" syntax of GROUP BY in OQL is more complex but also more powerful. We do not present it here.

```
trans1.begin();
trans1.commit();
trans1.abort();
```

to perform the indicated operations. ODMG assumes that vendors will provide classes that implement the above interfaces.

16.4.4 Object Manipulation in ODMG

An Object Manipulation Language deals with object creation, deletion, and updating. However, ODMG databases typically do not support a separate data manipulation language because the host language serves that function. ODMG language bindings (discussed next) specify how object manipulation is done using the native syntax of the host language. For instance, to create a new database object, the new constructor is used in C++ and Java. Deletion and modification of an object is done in the host language simply by invoking the methods defined for the corresponding classes.

Another way to update objects is to invoke a method in the SELECT clause, as in (16.9). This technique can be used to update sets of objects that satisfy certain conditions.

16.4.5 Language Bindings

One of the goals of ODMG is to encourage vendors to implement commercial object DBMSs based on the ODMG data model. As with relational databases, most applications of object databases are written in a host language. An important goal of ODMG is to provide uniform ways for such programs to access databases, particularly in C++, Smalltalk, and Java. All of these languages are object oriented and include facilities to specify and create objects similar to those in ODL. To allow these languages to access ODMG databases, **language bindings** have been defined for each. A language binding addresses a number of issues.

■ *Mapping ODL object definitions to the native syntax of the host language.* To better understand this problem, recall that Java, C++, and other host languages do not understand ODL syntax. So how can we use such languages to define ODMG schema? One way is to use a statement-level interface so that ODL statements can be inserted directly into host language programs. The preprocessor then converts these statements into calls to the appropriate database library routines. This is the approach taken by embedded SQL, as discussed in Section 10.2. However, ODMG took a different approach. Instead of modifying the host language, it defines a series of classes and interfaces in the host language, which represent the corresponding concepts in ODL. DBMS libraries then must ensure that operations on instances of such classes in the host language are correctly reflected in the corresponding database objects.

■ *Accessing and querying objects from within the host language.* One way to access the database is by binding a run-time object (defined through the regular mechanisms of the host language) to a database object. Then the database object can be queried and modified by applying the methods supplied with the database object's class to that run-time object. A more powerful way is to access objects by sending OQL queries (i.e., SELECT statements) to the server in a way that is conceptually similar to how this is done in ODBC and JDBC. ODMG bindings use both approaches.

For instance, consider the following class in Java:

```
public class STUDENT extends PERSON {
      public DSet Major;
      // Plus, possibly, other attributes
}
```

Here DSet is an ODMG-defined Java interface that corresponds to the ODL interface Set. DSet is defined because the existing Java interfaces do not provide all of the functionality of Set in ODL. To add a major to a student, we can call a native Java method on a STUDENT object as follows:

```
STUDENT X;
....
X.Major.add("CS");
.....
```

where add is a method that applies to DSet objects. The main design principle behind all language bindings is that the regular host language facilities should be used, with minimal changes, on ODMG objects and thereby eliminate the impedance mismatch. However, a number of facilities needed to implement the standard do not exist in some or all of the host languages. As a result, ODMG language bindings lack syntactic (and sometimes conceptual) unity and their details vary widely from one host language to another. To get a glimpse of the difficulties, we consider a number of issues:

■ *How does the language binding distinguish persistent from transient objects of a particular class?* For instance, an application that enables data entry into the database has both persistent and transient objects. Persistent objects are bound directly to the database objects to be updated. Transient objects do not directly correspond to the information stored in the database, but they are used by the application logic (e.g., to display forms or to hold intermediate results of the computation).

Each language has its own solution to this problem. First, a class must be declared **persistence capable** (which is done differently in each of the three languages). Second, any object of a persistence-capable class that needs to be automatically saved in the database must be made persistent explicitly. In the C++ binding, a special form of the new() method is used for this purpose. In the Java binding, an object becomes persistent via a special method, called makePersistent(), defined in the interface Database, or if it is referenced by an already persistent object. From then on, it is the database's responsibility to make sure that the object is saved in the database.

■ *How do the bindings represent and implement relationships?* None of the three languages, in its original form, implements relationships. The current version of the Java binding does not support them, and the bindings for C++ and Smalltalk implement relationships with specially defined classes and methods.

■ *How are ODMG literals represented?* In C++, literals can be represented using the struct keyword, but in Smalltalk and Java they cannot be represented directly and must be mapped into objects.

■ *How are OQL queries executed?* Again, each language has its own implementation, but they all basically rely on a mechanism similar to that used in JDBC (Section 10.5): A query object is instantiated, and the OQL query is supplied to that object as a parameterized string. The parameters in the query can be instantiated to specific objects using special methods. Then the query is executed with the execute() method of the query object.

■ *How are databases opened and closed, and how are transactions executed?* Each language has predefined classes corresponding to the database and transaction objects of ODL, with appropriate methods for executing the required operations.

A Java binding example.   To make the above discussion more concrete, we discuss how OQL queries can be executed using the Java binding.[13]

The ODMG host language bindings provide two complementary mechanisms for querying objects: OQL queries, using the OQLQuery class, and the methods defined by the DCollection interface. The first extracts sets of objects from the database and assigns them to Java variables; the second queries collections of objects previously retrieved from the database, using the first mechanism, and stored in some Java variables. We illustrate both mechanisms below.[14]

To use the OQLQuery approach, a query object must first be created using the constructor method of class OQLQuery. Some of the methods in this class are

```
class OQLQuery {
    public OQLQuery(String query); // query constructor
    public bind(Object parameter); // supplies arguments
    public Object execute();  // executes queries
    ... ... ...
}
```

The OQLQuery() constructor takes as input a string containing an OQL query (a SELECT statement) and creates a query object. The OQL query itself can be parameterized using **placeholders**—$1, $2, and so forth—which correspond to the ?

---

[13] It is expected that the current Java binding will be replaced with the forthcoming Java Data Objects Specification, mentioned earlier. However, the main principles of database objects access from an application are the same for the current and forthcoming specifications.

[14] Note that this design has a certain amount of impedance mismatch, since it uses a separate language, OQL, to retrieve objects from the database. We discussed this problem on page 497 and mentioned that the forthcoming Java Data Object Specification is intended to overcome this problem.

placeholders in dynamic SQL, JDBC, and ODBC (Chapter 10). These arguments can be replaced with actual Java objects via the method bind(). After all placeholders in the query object are bound, we can execute the query via the method execute().

As an example, the following program fragment computes the set of all courses taken exclusively by computer science students in the spring 1999 semester:

```
DSet students, courses;
String semester;
OQLQuery query1, query2;
query1 = new OQLQuery("SELECT S FROM STUDENT S "
                        + "WHERE \"CS\" IN S.Major");
students = (DSet) query1.execute();
query2 = new OQLQuery("SELECT T FROM COURSE T "
                        + "WHERE T.Enrollment.subsetOf($1) "
                        + "AND T.Semester = $2" );
semester = new String("S1999");
query2.bind(students); // bind $1 to the value of students
query2.bind(semester); // bind $2 to the value of semester
courses = (DSet) query2.execute();
```

The variables students and courses are declared to be of type DSet, which is a Java interface that corresponds to the Set interface of ODL. Conceptually, one can imagine that the Java binding *maps* the interface DSet to the ODL's interface Set.

Next, the variable students is assigned a set object that consists of all objects that represent students in the Computer Science Department. This set object is obtained by first creating an OQL query object and then invoking the method execute() on it.

Note that the target list of the first OQL query consists of just one variable of type DSet. The query returns a set of oids, and assigning the result to a DSet variable makes it possible to access the corresponding objects and apply methods to them. Actually, the signature of execute() says that this method returns a member of class Object, so we have to cast the result to class DSet.

The next step creates another query object and saves it in the variable query2. The method subsetOf() returns the value true or false depending on whether the set T.Enrollment is a subset of the set provided as the parameter $1. The second query is not completely specified—it is a *query template*, since it contains two placeholders. The first, $1, is then bound by the call query2.bind(students) to the object saved in the variable students (which now represents the set of all computer science students). The second placeholder, $2, is bound by the second invocation of bind() to the String object supplied by the variable semester.[15] At this point, the query is fully specified and can be executed using the method execute(). The Object returned as a result of this execution is cast to type DSet before being assigned to courses.

---

[15] Note that the order of the statements query2.bind() matters.

Having obtained the desired collection of courses, we might want to further select a subset of these objects, check the existence of an object with given properties, or process the objects one by one using a cursor-like mechanism. All of this is provided through the interface DCollection, which is a supertype of the interface DSet. Like DSet, DCollection is part of ODMG Java binding. We show part of the interface DCollection:

```
public interface DCollection extends java.util.Collection {
    public DCollection query(String condition);
    public Object selectElement(String condition);
    public Boolean existsElement(String condition);
    public java.util.Iterator select(String condition);
}
```

The most interesting methods here are query(), which provides a powerful way to make subcollections of objects, and select(). The query() method is similar to, but more general than, the selection operator in relational algebra. For instance, the condition argument in the above methods might contain the quantifiers forall and exists. The select() method of DCollection creates a collection specified by the condition supplied as an argument plus an **iterator** object for that collection. An iterator is the embodiment of the familiar notion of a cursor. The Java Iterator interface defines methods that allow the host program to process individual objects in a collection one by one.

Returning to our program, we can take the collection courses computed by the second query and further select those courses that have fewer than three credits:

```
DSet seminars;
seminars = (DSet) courses.query("this.Credits < 3")
```

where this is a variable that ranges over the elements of the collection to which query() is applied. We also assume that the class COURSE has the attribute Credits. Of course, the new collection, seminars, could have been computed by an OQL query directly. However, if we need to compute different subcollections of the collection saved in the variable courses, it might be more efficient to first compute the larger collection and then use the DCollection interface to further query the result.

The other methods specified by the interface DCollection work in similar ways. For instance, selectElement() selects some member of the collection that satisfies the condition passed as a parameter. The method existsElement() tests if the subcollection determined by condition is nonempty.

16.5   OBJECTS IN SQL:1999

Object-oriented extensions in SQL:1999 have gone through many revisions. The final result is a reasonably clean, but rather limited, version of the object-relational model. It was a difficult standardization process, given the requirement to preserve backward compatibility with SQL-92—a language *not* designed with objects in mind.

In this section, we survey the new object-relational extensions of SQL:1999. Unfortunately, at the time of writing, information about the new standard is not easily accessible, and many texts written a few years ago are now out of date. A good description of some aspects of the SQL:1999 object model appears in [Fuh et al. 1999]. Many of the details can be filled in by [Gulutzan and Pelzer 1999].

An SQL:1999 database consists of a set of relations. Each relation is either a set of tuples or a set of objects. An **SQL:1999 object** is a pair of the form (o, v), where o is an oid and v is an SQL:1999 tuple value. An SQL:1999 **tuple value** has the form $[A_1 : v_1, \ldots, A_n : v_n]$, where $A_1, \ldots, A_n$ are distinct attribute names and each v_j takes one of the following values (using the terms introduced in Section 16.3.1):

■ *Primitive values*—constants of the usual SQL primitive types, such as CHAR(18), INTEGER, FLOAT, and BOOLEAN.

■ *Reference values*—object Ids.

■ *Tuple values*—of the form $[A_1 : v_1, \ldots, A_n : v_n]$, where each A_i is a distinct attribute name and each v_i is a value.

■ *Collection values*—includes only the ARRAY construct, which is not very interesting and is not discussed here. The proposed constructs SETOF and LISTOF did not make it into the standard, but they might be included in later editions. In particular, the absence of set-valued attributes greatly limits the usefulness of the SQL:1999 object model and negates some of the benefits of objects discussed in Section 16.1.

As expected of a data model in the object-relational mold, the top-level value of every object in SQL:1999 is a tuple. In contrast, ODMG allows arbitrary values at the top level. Also, because SQL:1999 does not support set values in tuple components, for most practical purposes the tuple constructor is the only way to construct a complex value. However, tuples can be nested inside other tuples to an arbitrary depth.

16.5.1 Row Types

The simplest way to construct a tuple type that can be used in an attribute specification is with the ROW **type construct**. For instance, we can define the relation PERSON as follows:

```
CREATE TABLE PERSON (
    Name CHAR(20),
    Address ROW(Number INTEGER, Street CHAR(20), ZIP CHAR(5)) )
```

We refer to the components of a row type using the usual mechanism of path expressions.

```
SELECT P.Name
FROM PERSON P
WHERE P.Address.ZIP = '11794'
```

A table with row types can be populated with the help of the ROW **value constructor** as follows:

```
INSERT INTO PERSON(Name, Address)
VALUES ('John Doe', ROW(666, 'Hollow Rd.', '66666'))
```

Updating tables with row types is also straightforward.

```
UPDATE PERSON
SET Address.ZIP = '12345'
WHERE Address.ZIP = '66666'
```

When John Doe moves, we can change the entire address as follows:

```
UPDATE PERSON
SET Address = ROW(21, 'Main St.', '12345')
WHERE Address = ROW(666, 'Hollow Rd.', '66666')
        AND Name = 'John Doe'
```

16.5.2 User-Defined Types

Recall from Section 16.3.3 that a type (in CODM) is a set of rules for structuring data. The set of objects that conform to these rules is the type's domain. A class consists of a schema (which includes the type and method signatures) and an extent—a subset of the domain of the type. When we add method bodies to the signatures associated with a type, we get an **abstract data type**. In SQL:1999, abstract data types are called **user-defined types** (or UDT). Here are a few examples of UDT definitions:

```
CREATE TYPE PERSONTYPE AS (
    Name CHAR(20),
    Address ROW(Number INTEGER, Street CHAR(20), ZIP CHAR(5)) );

CREATE TYPE STUDENTTYPE UNDER PERSONTYPE AS (
    Id INTEGER,
    Status CHAR(2) )
METHOD award_degree() RETURNS BOOLEAN;

CREATE METHOD award_degree() FOR STUDENTTYPE
LANGUAGE C
EXTERNAL NAME 'file:/home/admin/award_degree';
```

The first CREATE TYPE statement is similar to the earlier definition of table PERSON, except that now we define a type rather than a table. This type does not have any explicitly defined methods, but we will soon see that the DBMS automatically creates a number of methods for us.

The second statement is more interesting. It defines STUDENTTYPE as a subtype of PERSONTYPE, which is indicated with the clause UNDER. As such, it inherits the attributes of PERSONTYPE. In addition, STUDENTTYPE is defined to have attributes of its own plus a method, award_degree(). The type definition includes only the signature of the method. The actual definition is done using the CREATE METHOD statement (which is associated with STUDENTTYPE through the FOR clause). The statement says that the method body is written in the C language (so that the DBMS knows how to link with this procedure) and tells where its executable can be found. If we specified LANGUAGE SQL instead, we could have defined the method code inside an attached BEGIN/END block using SQL/PSM, the language of stored procedures (see Chapter 10).

User-defined types appear in two main contexts. First, they can be used to specify the domain of an attribute in a table, just like a primitive type, such as integer or character string:

```
CREATE TABLE Transcript (
        Student StudentType,  -- a previously defined UDT
        CrsCode CHAR(6),                              (16.12)
        Semester CHAR(6),
        Grade CHAR(1) )
```

Here we are using the CREATE TABLE statement with the only difference that the attributes can have complex type (such as StudentType above).

Second, a UDT can be used to specify the type of an entire table. This is done through a new kind of CREATE TABLE statement, which, instead of enumerating the columns of a table, simply provides a UDT. This means that all rows of the table must have the structure specified by the UDT. For instance, we can define the following table based on the previously defined UDT StudentType:

```
CREATE TABLE Student OF  StudentType;                   (16.13)
```

Tables constructed via the CREATE TABLE . . . OF statement, as above, are called **typed tables**. The rows of a typed table are **objects**, as described next.

16.5.3 Objects

The only way to create an object in SQL:1999 is to insert a row into a typed table. In other words, every row in such a table is treated as an object with its own oid. The table itself is then viewed as a class (as defined in CODM), and its set of rows corresponds to the extent of the class.

It is instructive to compare (16.13) with the following declaration:

```
CREATE TABLE Student1 (
        Name CHAR(20),
        Address ROW(Number INTEGER, Street CHAR(20), ZIP CHAR(5)),
        Id INTEGER,
        Status CHAR(2) )
```

Note that Student1 contains exactly the same attributes as Student (both names and types). However, Student is a typed table whereas Student1 is not, which means that SQL:1999 considers the tuples of Student—but not the tuples of Student1—to be objects. This disparity (one can even say inconsistency) between the two ways of constructing tables is motivated by the need to stay backward compatible with SQL-92. Note also the difference in the use of StudentType in (16.12) and (16.13). Instances of StudentType in the former are *not* objects, while they *are* in the latter.

The next question is how we get hold of an object. To understand the issue, let us come back to the TRANSCRIPT table in (16.12) and consider the attribute Student. Since the same student is likely to have taken several courses, he has several tuples in TRANSCRIPT. The trouble is that the declaration

    Student STUDENTTYPE

means that this attribute returns STUDENTTYPE values, *not* references to STUDENT-TYPE objects. Thus, information about the same student (name, address, etc.) must be duplicated in each transcript record for him. Clearly, this is the same redundancy we tried to eliminate in Chapter 8. SQL:1999 solves the problem by introducing the explicit **reference type**, which we will discuss further in Section 16.5.6. For now, we have to remember that the domain of a reference type is a set of oids. To reference an object in SQL:1999, we need to obtain its oid, and so we have to look at the mechanism provided for this purpose.

The SQL:1999 standard says that every typed table, such as (16.13), has a **self-referencing column** that holds the tuple oid. The oid is generated automatically when the tuple is created. However, to gain access to the oids stored in the self-referencing column, we have to give the column a name explicitly. The declaration of STUDENTTYPE above does not name the self-referencing column, thus there is no way to refer to the oids of the objects in that table.

Here is a way to take care of the self-referencing column:

    CREATE TABLE STUDENT2 OF STUDENTTYPE   (16.14)
    REF IS stud_oid;

The REF clause gives an explicit name, stud_oid, to the self-referencing column. (Note that this column also exists in (16.13), but is hidden and cannot be referenced.) For most purposes, stud_oid is an attribute like any other. In particular, we can use it in queries (in both SELECT and WHERE clauses), but we cannot change its value because oids are assigned by the system and are immutable.

SQL:1999 takes the approach of C and C++ by distinguishing an object from its reference. This distinction does not exist in ODMG and in true object-oriented languages, such as Java, and is considered by many workers in the field as a drawback.

16.5.4 Querying User-Defined Types

Querying UDTs does not present any new problems. We can simply use path expressions to descend inside the objects and extract the needed information. For instance,

    SELECT T.Student.Name, T.Grade
    FROM TRANSCRIPT T   (16.15)
    WHERE T.Student.Address.Street = 'Hollow Rd.'

queries the TRANSCRIPT relation and returns the names and grades of the students who live on Hollow Road. Note that T.Student returns complex values of type STUDENTTYPE, and inheritance from PERSONTYPE allows us to access the Name and Address attributes defined for it.

Note also that although STUDENT and STUDENT1 have quite different structure, a particular query concerning students would be identical in both cases. Thus

```
SELECT S.Address.Street
FROM X S
WHERE S.Id = '111111111'
```

returns the street name of a student with Id 111111111 regardless of whether X is STUDENT or STUDENT1.

16.5.5 Updating User–Defined Types

Having discussed the data definition aspects of UDTs, we turn to the issue of populating relations based on these UDTs. We have already seen (in Section 16.5.1) how to insert tuples into the PERSON table. By analogy, we can use the same method to insert tuples into the tables STUDENT and STUDENT2. The fact that these relations contain objects (and the extra self-referencing attribute) does not matter because the oids are generated by the system. We have to worry only about the actual attributes. We might try a similar INSERT statement to populate the relation TRANSCRIPT:

```
INSERT INTO TRANSCRIPT(Student, Course, Semester, Grade)
VALUES (????, 'CS308', '2000', 'A')
```

but what should appear as the first component of the VALUES clause? To answer this question, we must wait until Section 16.5.6.

The issue is further complicated by the fact that a UDT is considered to be **encapsulated**, that is, its components can be accessed only through the methods provided by the type. Although we did not define any methods for STUDENTTYPE, the DBMS did it for us. Namely, for each attribute the system provides an **observer method**, which can be used to query the attribute value, and a **mutator method**, which can be used to change that value. Both the observer and the mutator have the same name as the attribute. In the case of STUDENTTYPE, the system provides the following observer methods:

- ■ Id: () $\longrightarrow$ INTEGER. This method returns an integer and, like all observers, it does not take any arguments.[16]

- ■ Name and Status. Both methods have the type () $\longrightarrow$ CHAR(*length*), where *length* is an integer.

- ■ Address: () $\longrightarrow$ ROW(INTEGER, CHAR(20), CHAR(5)).

It should now be clear that query (16.15) uses the observer methods Name and Address. On the other hand, the Grade attribute of the table TRANSCRIPT used in that same query is not part of a UDT, so it does not have an observer method. However, the difference is conceptual and not syntactic, since syntactically we reference Grade in the same way we do Name.

---

[16] The notation () indicates that the method takes no arguments.

The mutator methods are all called in the context of a STUDENTTYPE object and return this same object. However, they take different arguments, and the object they return has its state changed as follows:

■ Id: INTEGER ⟶ STUDENTTYPE. This method takes an integer and replaces the value of Id of the object with that integer. In other words, this mutator method changes the student Id and returns the modified object.

■ Name: CHAR(20) ⟶ STUDENTTYPE. This method takes a string and replaces the value of the Name attribute in the student object. It returns the updated student object. The mutator for Status is similar.

■ Address: ROW(INTEGER, CHAR(20), CHAR(5)) ⟶ STUDENTTYPE. This method takes a row that represents an address and replaces the student address with it.

Note that SQL does not have the public and private specifiers of C++ and Java to control access to methods. Instead, access is controlled through the EXECUTE privilege and the usual GRANT/REVOKE mechanism introduced in Section 4.3.

We are now ready for our first insertion into a UDT:

```
INSERT INTO TRANSCRIPT(Student, Course, Semester, Grade)
VALUES (NEW StudentType()
            .Id(666666666)
            .Status('G5')
            .Name('Vlad Dracula')
            .Address(ROW(666,'Transylvania Ave.','66666')),
        'HIS666',
        'F1462',
        'D')
```
(16.16)

Two things should be noted here. A blank student object in the first component of the inserted tuple is created by a call to StudentType()—a default constructor that the DBMS creates for every UDT. Then the mutator methods are invoked one by one on the newly created object to fill it in with data.[17]

If the student changes the address, name, and grade for the course, we can use the following update statement:

```
UPDATE TRANSCRIPT
SET Student = Student
                .Address(ROW(21,'Main St.','12345'))
                .Name('John Smith'),
    Grade = 'A'
WHERE Student.Id = 666666666
        AND CrsCode = 'HIS666' AND Semester = 'F1462'
```

---

[17] Note that the above syntax is just an indented and more readable form of
NEW StudentType().Id(..).Status(...).Name(...).Address(...).

To change the value of the student object, we use the mutator functions for STU-DENTTYPE, which are generated for us by the DBMS. First, we apply the Address() mutator to change the address and then apply the Name() mutator.

You have certainly noticed that inserting new tuples into relations that involve UDTs is rather cumbersome. However, the ability to associate methods with complex data types can simplify this to some extent. Namely, we can define a special constructor method that takes only scalar values; in this way, a complex object can be created in one call to the constructor.

We illustrate the idea using the language of SQL stored procedures. First, we need to add the following declaration to our earlier definition of STUDENTTYPE:[18]

```
METHOD StudentConstr(name CHAR(20), id INTEGER,
                     streetNumber INTEGER,
                     streetName CHAR(20),
                     zip CHAR(5), status CHAR(2))
RETURNS STUDENTTYPE;
```

Then we define the body of the method as follows:

```
CREATE METHOD StudentConstr(name CHAR(20), id INTEGER,
                     streetNumber INTEGER,
                     streetName CHAR(20),
                     zip CHAR(5), status CHAR(2))
RETURNS STUDENTTYPE
LANGUAGE SQL
    BEGIN
        RETURN NEW STUDENTTYPE()
                .Name(name)
                .Id(id)
                .Status(status)
                .Address(ROW(streetNumber,streetName,zip));
    END;
```

With this new constructor, the insertion of a new tuple into the TRANSCRIPT relation corresponding to (16.16) becomes less of a chore.

```
INSERT INTO TRANSCRIPT(Student, Course, Semester, Grade)
VALUES (StudentConstr('Vlad Dracula', 666666666, 666,
                     'Transylvania Ave.', '66666', 'G5'),
        'HIS666',
        'F1462',
        'D')
```

16.5.6 Reference Types

In schema (16.12) for the TRANSCRIPT relation, the attribute Student has the type STUDENTTYPE. As explained in Section 16.5.3, this prevents sharing of student

---

[18] Like attributes, methods can be added using the ALTER statement in SQL.

objects because every student record is physically stored inside the corresponding transcript record. To enable object sharing, SQL:1999 uses **reference data types**. A reference is an oid, and the domain of a type of the form REF*(udt-xyz)* consists of all of the oids of objects of type *udt-xyz*. We can therefore rewrite our definition of TRANSCRIPT in (16.12) as follows:

```
CREATE TABLE TRANSCRIPT1 (
        Student REF(STUDENTTYPE) SCOPE STUDENT2,
        CrsCode CHAR(6),                                    (16.17)
        Semester CHAR(6),
        Grade CHAR(1) )
```

The type of the Student attribute needs more explanation. First, the type REF(STUDENTTYPE) means that the value of Student must be an oid of an object of type STUDENTTYPE. However, we can create many different tables and associate them with STUDENTTYPE, and each can contain all kinds of students. We might not want Student to refer to just any student. Instead, we might want some kind of referential integrity that ensures that this attribute refers to students described by a *particular* table. The clause SCOPE achieves just that by requiring that the value of Student be not just any oid of type STUDENTTYPE but one that belongs to an existing object in the table STUDENT2.[19] Stay tuned: the choice of STUDENT2, defined in (16.14), over STUDENT is not accidental.

Misfeatures often come on the heels of new features. Here is how query (16.15) looks when applied to the table TRANSCRIPT1, defined in (16.17), which contains an attribute, STUDENT, that has a reference type:

```
SELECT T.Student->Name, T.Grade
FROM TRANSCRIPT1 T
WHERE T.Student->Address.Street = 'Hollow Rd.'
```

Note that we use -> to refer to the attributes of the STUDENTTYPE objects. This is because T.Student returns the *oid* of a student object rather than the object itself. The unfortunate distinction between the references by . and -> comes to SQL:1999 from C and C++, where it exists for historical reasons. Such a distinction is not necessary in an object-oriented language, and it does not exist in OQL or Java.[20]

The general rule for choosing between . and -> is the same as in C and C++. If an attribute has a reference type, then -> is used in path expressions; if it has object type, then . is used. In our case, T.Student has reference type, REF(STUDENTTYPE), so we use T.Student -> Address to descend into the student object. In contrast, query (16.15) uses T.Student.Address, because there T.Student has the type STUDENTTYPE, which is not a reference type.

---

[19] To make all of these requirements consistent, the relation mentioned in SCOPE must be associated with the type mentioned in REF, in a manner similar to the way STUDENT2 is associated with STUDENTTYPE using a CREATE TABLE . . . OF statement.

[20] OQL allows the use of -> but there it is merely an alternative syntax for the dot-notation.

The next important question is how to populate the table TRANSCRIPT1. We have seen examples (in Section 16.5.5) of tuple insertion into complex types. However, in those cases we did not deal with object references. In order to insert a tuple into TRANSCRIPT1, we must find a way to access oids of student objects and assign them to the attribute Student. This is where the self-referencing column, introduced in Section 16.5.3, comes in handy. Recall that table STUDENT2 defined in that section has a self-referencing column, stud_oid, defined by the clause REF IS.[21] Recall also that the table STUDENT in (16.13) has the same type as STUDENT2, except that its self-referencing column is hidden (since we did not give it a name). Thus, we cannot obtain oids of the tuples in STUDENT and assign them as values of the Student attribute in the table TRANSCRIPT1. Precisely because of this handicap, we used STUDENT2 instead of STUDENT in the definition of TRANSCRIPT1.

Assuming that the Id attribute in STUDENT2 is a key, we can now insert a student into TRANSCRIPT1 as follows:

```
INSERT INTO TRANSCRIPT1(Student, Course, Semester, Grade)
SELECT S.stud_oid, 'HIS666', 'F1462', 'D'
FROM STUDENT2 S
WHERE S.Id = '666666666'
```

Observe that we use a SELECT statement to retrieve the oid of the desired student object. This oid becomes the value for the Student attribute. The values for the attributes Course, Semester, and Grade are simply tacked on to the target list.

16.5.7 Collection Types

The most useful collection types, sets and lists, have been left out of the standard for now. When these types become available, data modeling will become more natural and closer to what is possible in ODMG. For instance, instead of creating a separate table for transcripts, we could have extended STUDENTTYPE with the following Enrolled attribute:[22]

```
CREATE TYPE STUDENTTYPE UNDER PERSONTYPE AS (
      Id INTEGER,
      Status CHAR(2)
      Enrolled SETOF(REF(COURSETYPE)) SCOPE COURSE)
METHOD StudentConstr(name CHAR(20), id INTEGER,
                     streetNumber INTEGER,
                     streetName CHAR(20),
                     zip CHAR(5), status CHAR(2))
RETURNS STUDENTTYPE
METHOD award_degree() RETURNS BOOLEAN;
```

---

[21] Note that stud_oid has nothing to do with the attribute Id, which is a regular attribute of STUDENTTYPE whose value has to be set explicitly by the programmer.

[22] To keep the example simple, let us ignore the question of where the grades will be stored in the new design.

In this example, the values of the attribute `Enrolled` must be a set of oids of tuples from the relation Course.

With set collection types, such as the above, a new kind of query becomes possible. For instance, the following query lists, for each student Id, the Id, street, and the courses the student is taking:

```
SELECT S.Id, S.Address.Name, C.Name
FROM Student S, Course C
WHERE C.CrsCode IN
          (SELECT E -> CrsCode
           FROM S.Enrolled E)
```

The `WHERE` clause tests each element of the Cartesian product of Student and Course. The condition uses a nested `SELECT` statement to produce the set of course codes of the courses taken by the student described in a particular row of the product.

The `FROM` clause in that nested `SELECT` statement exhibits a new feature. The range of the variable `E` is a set specified by a path expression, `S.Enrolled`, and each element of that set is a reference to a Course object corresponding to a course in which student `S` is enrolled. This is analogous to the use of a query result in the `FROM` clause in SQL-92, but here, instead of a query, we use a path expression that returns a set of object references.

Since `E` ranges over object references, we must access the attributes of the individual objects using the -> operator, which "dereferences" `E` and produces a particular object in Course.

16.6   COMMON OBJECT REQUEST BROKER ARCHITECTURE

CORBA is designed for an environment in which clients need to access objects residing on servers. One way in which a client can obtain such services is through **remote procedure call (RPC)** [Birrell and Nelson 1984], which will be discussed in Section 22.4.1. The client process executes a procedure call that causes the procedure body to be executed within the server process, which might be on a different computer.

The Object Management Group (OMG) has proposed a new middleware standard, the **Common Object Request Broker Architecture (CORBA)**. Like RPC, CORBA enables clients to access objects that reside on servers, but it is more general and flexible. Even so, it is not a replacement for RPC or similar mechanisms. In fact, CORBA often is implemented on top of RPC.

CORBA is also like RPC in that it provides **location transparency** for distributed computational resources. This means that clients access resources in a location-independent way, and a change in the location of a resource does not affect the clients. Unlike RPC, which is designed to specify remote resources as collections of unrelated procedures, CORBA specifies resources as objects in which related operations are grouped together. It also provides mechanisms for client applications to discover and use remote services that were not available (or even planned) at the time the application was written.

Included in CORBA is a layer called *CORBAservices*, which provides infrastructure for persistence, query, and transactional services—the issues of particular interest to us in this section. CORBA has also become a platform for various application frameworks in areas such as manufacturing, electronic commerce, banking, and healthcare. These frameworks are part of the architectural layer known as *CORBAfacilities*. We do not discuss this layer here, but an introduction to this topic can be found in [Pope 1998].

16.6.1 CORBA Basics

Each server specifies the interfaces to the objects it hosts using a generic **Interface Description Language (IDL)**. IDL is a subset of ODMG's Object Definition Language, ODL, discussed in Section 16.4.1. Like ODL, IDL is used to specify classes and the signatures of their methods. However, IDL classes have no extents and they are called "interfaces" (in agreement with ODL terminology). IDL is also missing constraints and collection types (such as sets), which are present in ODL.

To illustrate the idea, consider a public library server, which provides an interface that allows searching of the library's holdings. Client applications can use these search facilities to enhance the user experience.

```
/* File: Library.idl */
module Library {
  interface myTownLibrary {
    string searchByKeywords(in string keywords);
    string searchByAuthorTitle(in string author, in string title);
  }
}
```

Interfaces are often grouped into modules, which serve several purposes. One important advantage of modules is that they avoid name clashes among interfaces built by different organizations or different units within the same organization. This is possible because the module name is always prefixed to the method names. Thus, the client application refers to a method such as searchByKeywords() as follows:

```
Library_myTownLibrary_searchByKeywords(...)
```

How does a request from an application on a client machine cause the execution of code on the server? This is a matter for the object request broker, discussed next.

Object request brokers.   The new component in the CORBA architecture is the **object request broker (ORB)** that sits between the client and the various servers, as shown in Figure 16.3. When the client executes a method call based on the IDL description, the call goes to the ORB. The ORB is responsible for locating a server that hosts the object and then for making any necessary translations between the client's method call and the method call required by that server's class definition. In other words, the ORB *maps* the IDL language into the language in which the object is implemented. The CORBA standard defines IDL mappings for C, C++, Java, Cobol, Smalltalk, and Ada.

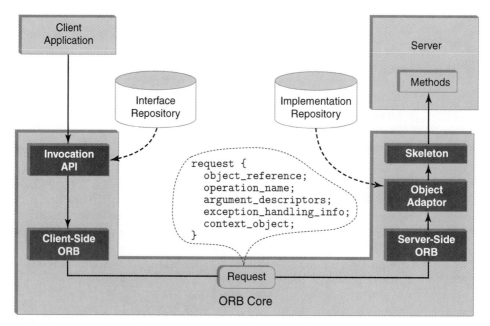

Figure 16.3 CORBA architecture.

The details of a remote call to a server object are as follows.[23] At the time the server is deployed, the IDL definition, `Library.idl`, is compiled by the IDL compiler supplied by a CORBA vendor. The result of the compilation is a pair of files, `Library-stubs.c` and `Library-skeleton.c`. In addition, the method signatures defined by the interface and related IDL information are stored in the **interface repository**.

The file `Library-skeleton.c` contains a **server skeleton**. This is code that maps client requests specified in an operating-system and language-independent form into concrete (operating system and language-specific) calls to the methods `searchByKeywords()` and `searchByAuthorTitle()` on our library server. The skeleton is compiled and linked with the server before the server is deployed. When a server starts, it registers itself with the **object adaptor**, which is part of the ORB that resides on the server. By registering, the server informs the ORB that it can handle calls to certain methods in certain interfaces that are described in the interface repository.[24] Interestingly, several different implementations can be registered to handle the same method call (in the same interface), and it is a job of the object adaptor to choose one. For instance, if the library's catalog is distributed, the object adaptor might satisfy the requests of the library patrons with an implementation

---

[23] We describe the overall process. Some aspects might be specific to a particular CORBA implementation.

[24] Different methods in the same interface can, in principle, be handled by different servers. Likewise, methods in different interfaces can be handled by the same server.

that searches local cached copies of the catalog. On the other hand, staff requests might be satisfied with an implementation that performs distributed search. The object adaptor can decide which implementation to use based on the **context object** that the client includes with the request.[25] The ORB maintains the **implementation repository** to keep track of the available implementations for the different methods on the server.

On the client side, method invocation can proceed in one of the following ways. If the client application knows how to call the server methods (i.e., the name of the method and the types of its arguments), it can use **static invocation**, in which the client is compiled and linked with the **client stub**. In our example, the client stub is stored in Library-stubs.c—one of the files produced by the IDL compiler. With static invocation, the client calls the remote method as if it were a call to a local subroutine. The stub contains code that converts such a call (whose internal format can be OS and language specific) into an OS- and language-independent remote method invocation request that the ORB transmits over the network. Recall that the skeleton on the server then converts this request back into an OS- and language-specific call to a server procedure. The important point here is that the server and the client might execute under different operating systems and can be written in different languages.

Conversion of method calls into a machine-independent format primarily involves the process of **marshaling the arguments**. This is needed because different machines and languages often use different encodings for the data. For instance, some machines use so-called big-endian representation, some little-endian; some machines use 32-bit words, some 64-bit; some computer languages terminate character strings with a null byte, and some do not.

As you can see, sending data "as is" will likely make it unusable for the receiving computer. In CORBA, both client and server follow an agreed-upon protocol for data encoding and decoding. In particular, a method invocation request contains a **descriptor** for each method argument (or method result), which includes the value of the argument and its type and length. Moreover, all of these data items are encoded in a machine-independent network format. It should be clear, however, that the programmer does not deal with this conversion directly. Instead, it is carried out through CORBA library routines that are called (indirectly) by the stub. The overall structure of a method invocation request in CORBA is shown in Figure 16.3.

In some cases, the client does not know how to call methods on the server. This at first might sound like an impossible situation; however, there are very real examples when it might occur and even be useful. Let us come back to the library search application, but now assume that it provides the user with search capabilities

---

[25] CORBA defines an interface, Context, which provides methods for setting arbitrary property name/value pairs. The context object carries with it the collection of all such pairs set by the client. The server can use the Context interface to examine the properties available in the context object and act accordingly. In this way, context objects can be used by the client to supply the server with meta information about the request.

in a number of different catalogs that belong to different libraries. One possibility is that we force all library servers to use the same interface, myTownLibrary, but this might be unrealistic since the libraries are likely to have their own legacy systems, that are expensive to change. Different libraries can also provide different search capabilities—for instance, some might provide search using patterns and wildcards.

If the libraries participating in the search had remained the same, we could have coded all of the different interfaces into our client application and the problem would have gone away. However, we want our application to continue to work when new libraries join or leave the system, and when a new library joins we want it to be searchable by our program. For instance, if yourTownLibrary joins the system, we modify our Library IDL module as follows:

```
/* File: Library.idl */
module Library {
  interface myTownLibrary {
    string searchByKeywords(in string keywords);
    string searchByAuthorTitle(in string author, in string title);
  }
  interface yourTownLibrary {
    void searchByTitle(in string title, out string result);
    void searchByWildcard(in string wildcard, out string result);
  }
}
```

Not only are the method names and the invocation sequences different in the interface to yourTownLibrary, but the result is returned in a different way—as an out parameter instead of the function result. After compiling Library.idl and linking the skeleton with yourTownLibrary's server, we expect the client search application to be able to search both libraries.

To achieve these goals, we design the client application in such a way that it displays a general form to be filled out by the user that contains a number of optional fields, such as book ISBN, author, keywords, and wildcards. The client application then analyzes all interfaces defined in Library.idl and, based on the names of the arguments, constructs appropriate calls to the server. For example, if the user fills out the fields for the author, keywords, and wildcards, the client application might then choose searchByKeywords() in the interface myTownLibrary and searchByWildcard() in yourTownLibrary. If the user enters a title and a wildcard, it might not choose myTownLibrary (because it does not have the right arguments) but searchByTitle() in yourTownLibrary. To make this invocation strategy possible, we can require that the member libraries choose argument names from a fixed vocabulary when they write IDL descriptions of their interfaces. This requirement does not necessitate any changes to the legacy server, but merely instills some discipline in the design of the interfaces.

How can we implement such a flexible method invocation strategy? This is where the interface repository comes in. Instead of using the stub, the client application can use a special **dynamic invocation API**, provided by CORBA, to query the interface repository. This API allows the application to determine all interfaces available in module Library, the methods defined in each interface, the argument names and types for each method, and the method's return value type. Based on the names of the arguments, our search application decides which methods to call and which arguments to provide. It then constructs appropriate request objects using the API call CORBA_Object_create_request(). A request object includes the name of the method to be called, the names and types of its arguments, and the type of the result it returns. A fully constructed request can be used as a parameter to a CORBA API subroutine, CORBA_Request_invoke(), to perform the actual invocation of the method on the server. This request has a machine-independent format, and the above API subroutine transmits it over the network to the server side of the ORB. The latter uses the server skeleton to convert the request into a concrete call to the server method.

It should be noted that static invocation performs the same actions in constructing a request for the ORB. However, since the exact calling sequence of the server method is known in advance, the required sequence of operations is generated automatically by the IDL compiler and constitutes the core of the client stub.

In our discussion of client-side method invocation, we have omitted one ingredient: the actual object on which the client asks the server to perform its operations. An **object reference** that identifies the object in question is part of the client's request for the ORB. How does the client obtain such a reference?

One possible way is to have client and server designers agree on some protocol. For instance, the server might publish object references as strings in some well-known location on the network. In our example, all references to the participating objects can be published in some agreed-upon document on the Web. The string format of a reference can then be converted into an internal binary format used within CORBA via the API call to CORBA_ORB_string_to_object().

A more portable way to obtain object references is to use the *naming service* discussed in the next section.

Interoperability within CORBA.   If there were only one ORB in the world, every object would be able to talk to every other object. In reality, different organizations and companies are likely to deploy their own ORBs, which bind together the objects that implement their business processes. If a group of companies collaborates on a project, they might deploy another ORB specifically for that project. The question is how to communicate with objects that are controlled by different ORBs. An ORB can deliver requests to the objects it controls. However, if an object belongs to a different ORB, a protocol is needed to pass the request to it.

Fortunately, CORBA has a general answer to this question—a **general inter-ORB protocol (GIOP)**. GIOP is essentially a special message format that makes it possible for one ORB to send requests to objects under the scope of another

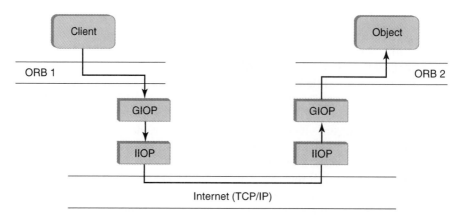

Figure 16.4 Inter-ORB architecture.

ORB, and to receive replies. Since these messages must somehow be delivered using real-world networks, it is necessary to map them into a message format of an existing network, one obvious candidate being the Internet. The **Internet inter-ORB protocol (IIOP)** specifies how GIOP messages are translated into TCP/IP messages so that they can be delivered via the Internet, as illustrated in Figure 16.4.

Similar translation protocols exist for other popular network protocols, such as *Point-to-Point Protocol (PPP)*, which is often used to connect to the Internet using a modem, and other middleware standards, such as the *Distributed Computing Environment (DCE)*.

16.6.2 CORBA and Databases

CORBA has outgrown its initial modest goals and is rapidly becoming a ubiquitous standard for distributed computing. Originally CORBA's purpose was to allow client programs to access objects residing on server computers. However, since objects are persistent, the possibility exists that collections of such objects can be used as a database. To achieve the full functionality of a database system, additional CORBA services beyond those originally provided are necessary. These services are now available through an architectural layer, called *CORBAservices*, which lives above the basic ORB mechanism. Using CORBAservices, it is possible to use ORBs to build a functional database out of disparate objects scattered around the Internet or other networks.

Conceptually, CORBAservices is a set of APIs designed to accomplish specific services, which include event notification services, licensing services (to control the use of certain objects or to charge users for accessing these objects), and life cycle services (to allow copying, moving and deletion of objects). The services that are of particular interest in the database context are

■ *Persistence services.*

■ *Naming services.*

■ *Object query services.*

■ *Transaction services.*

■ *Concurrency control services.*

through which CORBA allows a set of objects, perhaps located at different, geo-graphically separated servers, to act as a database and to be accessed transactionally with the full set of ACID properties enforced.[26]

As an example of a CORBA application using persistent objects, a group of companies might get together to design a new product (a so-called *virtual company*). Each company keeps its part of the design (diagrams, parts lists, documentation, etc.) as persistent objects on its local computer and might implement its objects in a different language and under a different operating system. Using an ORB, an engineer at any one company can access the design objects of any of the other companies and perhaps incorporate them into local documents. The engineer can access any particular design object by name, without knowing on what company's computer it is stored. Query services allow the users to query the entire collection of objects in our virtual company, ORBs allow users to invoke methods on the objects, and transaction and concurrency control services make it possible to write applications that require transactional properties.

Persistence services.   CORBA provides a mechanism that an application can use to interact with remote objects that have made IDL interfaces availble to clients. What is lacking, however, is a standard way for a data store, such as an ODMG database, to export interfaces to its data objects and to allow CORBA clients to manipulate them. Furthermore, there was no standard way for CORBA clients to create or delete objects in a data store. Of course, clients could go outside of CORBA and use, for example, ODBC to talk to databases, but this detracts from the stated goal of CORBA, namely, to provide a unifying object-based interface for building distributed applications. CORBA **persistent state services** (**PSS**) fills these gaps.

The overall architecture of a CORBA persistent state service is shown in Fig-ure 16.5. The basic idea is that persistent objects on the server side are organized into **storage homes**, collections of which are organized into **data stores**. A data store can be anything that provides nonvolatile storage, such as a database or a file system.

On the application side, a program can work with several different data stores simultaneously, as shown in Figure 16.5. To start using a data store, an application must connect to the store using a special method call. Different mechanisms are used to gain access to a storage home, depending on the programming language. In an object-oriented language, such as Java or C++, a storage home corresponds to a public class. To *access* a storage home, the application must have a public class with

---

[26] Observe that there is no need for a separate "object update service," because objects change state when clients invoke methods on them. Such invocations are provided by the ORBs, which are below the CORBA services layer.

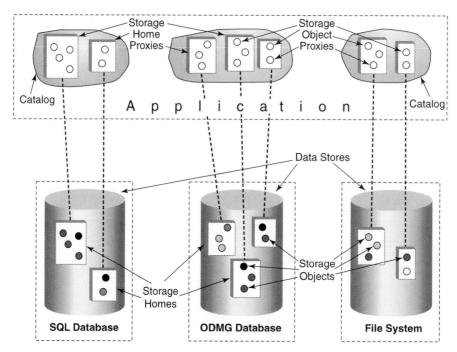

Figure 16.5 Architecture of CORBA persistent state services.

the same name as the storage home, which we call the **storage home proxy**.[27] To *create* a storage home, the programmer must supply a class definition that includes the access methods (both signature and code). The class must then be compiled on the server and registered with the PSS.

The objects that populate a storage home proxy act as proxies of the storage objects on the server. The client application manipulates the proxies directly in the host language by invoking their methods. These methods might directly access a cached copy of a storage object or they might communicate with the server. It is the responsibility of PSS to ensure that any changes to the proxies are reflected on the actual storage objects.

It is easy to see that the design of PSS is influenced by the ODMG architecture and its drive to reduce or eliminate impedance mismatch. Indeed, by manipulating the proxies, the client program has the illusion that it operates on the persistent CORBA objects *directly*, as if they are local objects in the program—it does not use any special API to send query and update requests to the remote objects.

---

[27] In the current version of PSS, this class is called an "instance" of the storage home. We avoid this confusing terminology, because, in the object-oriented setting, an instance is an object that belongs to a class, not a class that is designed somehow to represent another class.

Naming services. Naming services provide a convenient way for programs to refer to (persistent) objects using a well-defined naming mechanism. This mechanism is similar to the way files are named in an operating system. The CORBA namespace is a directed acyclic graph in which each arc is labeled by a simple name. The full object name is the concatenation of all names found on a path from the root of the graph to the object. An object can have more than one full name (depending on the paths followed).

In our library example, instead of using the previously described home-grown protocol for exporting object references (page 527), the server might decide to use the naming service of the ORB, which is defined via the CORBA interface `NamingContext`. The two important methods here are

- `void bind(in Name n, in Object o);`

- `Object resolve(in Name n);`

The first method is used by the server to bind a particular external name[28] (such as `/Library/myTownLibrary/search`) to the concrete object created by the server. The second method is used by the client who passes the published name of an object as an argument to the method and obtains the internal CORBA object reference.

Object query services. Object query services (*OQS*) enable applications to query persistent CORBA objects. OQS draws heavily on the ODMG and SQL standards and provides OQL- and SQL-style querying capabilities to object stores that don't support these query languages.

The overall OQS architecture is depicted in Figure 16.6. A client application passes a query to the query evaluator, whose role is somewhat similar to that of ODBC. It can pass the query to a DBMS with minimal changes, or it might have to break the query into a sequence of requests and manage the query evaluation process. Such query management is required when the DBMS in question does not support all features in the query, if the query evaluator acts as a front end to a non-DBMS data store (e.g., a store of spreadsheets), or if multiple data stores are involved.

In addition, the query evaluator creates an object of type *collection*, whose members are references to the server objects that belong to the query result. The collection object is then passed to the client application for further processing.

Earlier we discussed the collection interface used in the ODMG Java binding (Section 16.4.5) and SQLJ (Section 10.5.9). The CORBA collection interface is similar. It includes the methods for inserting objects into and deleting them from the collection, plus an **iterator method**, which provides cursor-like functionality and allows the application to process the collection one object at a time.

Note that, even though the collection object that represents the query result is usually created by the query evaluator at the client site, the objects that are members of that collection remain in their data stores. When the client invokes the methods

---

[28] The data structure `Name` is defined by CORBA and includes the published object's string name.

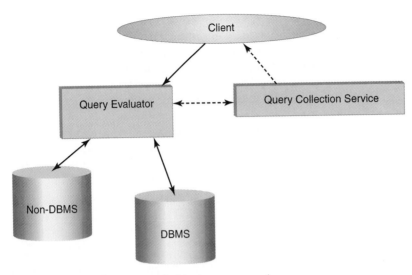

Figure 16.6 Architecture of object query services.

of the query result object, the ORB transmits these requests to the member objects at their servers. Such server-side processing of all requests is common in CORBA. In this case, an ORB serves only as a smart communication channel among objects, but the objects themselves stay on the server.

Transaction and concurrency control services. In Section 15.3.1, we introduced a *transaction manager* module, which orchestrates the execution of a transaction that accesses a number of different databases, perhaps widely distributed geographically, and guarantees that the transaction is atomic (we will return to this in Section 22.3.1). CORBA provides a similar capability, through its **transaction services** (also known as **object transaction services** or *OTS*) for transactions that access a number of different persistent objects or databases, as in Figure 16.5.

Transaction services allow applications to turn a thread of execution into a transaction. A thread can call the begin() method on a special transaction object, after which a transaction context is created for this thread. This context is maintained by the transaction service for the duration of the transaction. The thread can then invoke commit() and rollback() to perform the corresponding transactional operations.

CORBA objects modified by such a transaction must be declared as *transactional* and *recoverable*, which means that they can respond correctly to the commit and rollback commands. Transactional and recoverable objects must reside on **transactional** and **recoverable servers**, which provide the logging and other services (see Section 15.2) needed to implement the commit and rollback commands.

CORBA also provides **concurrency control services**, which allow applications to request and release locks on CORBA objects and to implement the *two-phase locking* protocol (see Section 15.1.2), which ensures transaction isolation. Note that

CORBA-level locking is independent of, and layered on top of, the locking that might be happening in a DBMS that is accessed through CORBA.

Transaction services use the two-phase commit protocol (Section 15.3.1) to guarantee global atomicity of the entire transaction, which might access multiple objects, including persistent objects stored in databases (see Figure 16.5). Any object that is accessed in this way must support the X/Open standard API (Section 22.3.1), which includes commands to commit and rollback databases.

Transaction services implement both the usual flat transaction model (Section 21.1) and the nested transaction model (Section 21.2.3).

Keep in mind that CORBA only *supports* concurrency and transactional semantics—it does not enforce it. In other words, it does not prevent nontransactional CORBA applications from accessing objects nor does it prevent applications that do not use CORBA from accessing those objects. Thus, all applications must agree to use transaction and concurrency control services in order for a CORBA object's semantics to have ACID properties.

16.7   SUMMARY

We began the chapter with a discussion of the limitations of the traditional relational data model and showed how the object-oriented data model deals with them. We then presented a general conceptual data model for object-oriented databases, which fostered an understanding of the common principles behind the different ODBMS implementations and standards. In particular, we discussed two standards, ODMG and SQL:1999, which are very different in their design and philosophy. In the last part of the chapter, we discussed CORBA, which is an emerging infrastructure for building distributed object-oriented data stores. The design of the database-related facilities in CORBA is influenced by the ODMG architecture, but it is still a work in progress and the details might change in the future.

16.8   BIBLIOGRAPHIC NOTES

The emergence of object-oriented databases was preceded by many developments—in particular, the growing popularity of object-oriented languages and the realization of the limitations of the relational data model. The idea of using an existing object-oriented language as a data manipulation language first appeared in [Copeland and Maier 1984]. Nested relations, which represent early attempts to enrich the relational data model, are discussed in [Makinouchi 1977, Arisawa et al. 1983, Roth and Korth 1987, Jaeschke and Schek 1982, Ozsoyoglu and Yuan 1985, Mok et al. 1996].

POSTGRES [Stonebreaker and Kemnitz 1991] was an early proposal for enriching relational databases with abstract data types. Now known as PostgreSQL, this system is a powerful open-source object-relational DBMS that is freely available at [PostgreSQL 2000]. The object database O_2, which strongly influenced the ODMG data model and its query language, is described in [Bancilhon et al. 1990]. The latest version of the ODMG standard can be found in [Cattell and Barry 2000]. A number of problems with the design of the ODMG standard (and some possible solutions) are discussed in [Alagic 1999].

The conceptual data model, presented in Section 16.3, and related issues are discussed more fully in [Abiteboul et al. 1995]. Logical foundations of object-oriented database query languages have been developed in [Kifer et al. 1995, Abiteboul and Kanellakis 1998].

The use of path expressions for querying object-like structures first appeared in the GEM system [Zaniolo 1983]. Path expressions were later incorporated in all major proposals for querying objects, including ODL and the various object-oriented extensions of SQL, such as XSQL, discussed in [Kifer et al. 1992].

The early databases that supported the object-relational data model were UniSQL, POSTGRES, and O_2. Currently, most major relational database vendors (such as Oracle, Informix, and IBM) provide object-relational extensions to their products. Many ideas underlying the design of these systems found their way into the SQL:1999 standard. Further details on the object-relational extensions in SQL:1999 can be found in [Gulutzan and Pelzer 1999].

Since SQL:1999 object extensions are rather new, there are no products that fully conform to this standard. However, IBM's DB/2 comes closest in terms of its syntax and supported features.

A comprehensive guide to CORBA with examples in the C language can be found in [Pope 1998]. Good guides to CORBA for Java and C++ programmers are [Orfali and Harkey 1998, Henning and Vinoski 1999].

This chapter omitted discussion of the database design issues associated with object-oriented databases, which would correspond to the material developed in Chapters 5 and 8 for relational databases. This omission can be filled in with additional reading. The approach to object-oriented database design that is growing in popularity is the **Unified Modeling Language** (**UML**) [Booch et al. 1999, Fowler and Scott 1999].

UML is akin to E-R modeling, but it extends E-R in several directions, most notably by providing the means to specify the external behavior of database objects (i.e., what should be expected of the public methods of such objects). However, E-R modeling has the advantage that it is simpler, and a number of techniques have been developed to adapt it for object-oriented database design [Biskup et al. 1996, Biskup et al. 1996b, Gogola et al. 1993, Missaoui et al. 1995].

While object-oriented E-R style modeling is currently well developed, the corresponding normalization theory has turned out to be much harder than in the relational case. Beginnings of such a theory can be found in [Weddell 1992, Ito and Weddell 1994, Biskup and Polle 2000b, Biskup and Polle 2000a].

16.9 EXERCISES

16.1 Give examples from the Student Registration System where

   a. It would be convenient to use a set-valued attribute

b. It would be convenient to express a relationship (in the ODMG style) between two objects

c. It would be convenient to use inheritance

16.2 Specify an appropriate set of classes for the Student Registration System.

16.3 Give a real-world example of an object that can be stored *directly* in an object database, such as ODMG, but not in an object-relational database.

16.4 Section 16.4.1 has an ODL description of a Person object with the relationship Spouse.

a. How would you express in ODL that a person (possibly) has a spouse?

b. Give an OQL query that returns the name of a particular person's spouse.

16.5 Explain the difference between the oid of an object in an object database and the primary key of a tuple in a relational database.

16.6 Explain the different senses in which the objects in an object database can be considered equal.

16.7 Consider an Account class and a TransactionActivity class in a banking system.

a. Posit ODMG ODL class definitions for them. The Account class must include a relationship to the set of objects in the TransactionActivity class corresponding to the deposit and withdraw transactions executed against that account.

b. Give an example of an object instance satisfying that description.

c. Give an example of an OQL query against that database that will return the account numbers of all accounts for which there was at least one withdrawal of more than $10,000.

16.8 A relational database might have a table called Accounts with tuples for each account and might support stored procedures deposit() and withdraw(). An object database might have a class called Accounts with an object for each account and methods deposit() and withdraw(). Explain the advantages and disadvantages of each approach.

16.9 Suppose that the Accounts class in the object database of the previous example has child classes SavingsAccounts and CheckingAccounts and that CheckingAccounts has a child class EconomyCheckingAccounts. Explain how the semantics of inheritance affects the retrieval of objects in each class. (For example, what classes need to be accessed to retrieve all checking account objects that satisfy a particular predicate?)

16.10 Explain the difference between a set object and a set of objects.

16.11 a. Explain the difference between ODMG attributes and relationships.

b. Explain the difference between ODMG relationships and E-R relationships.

16.12 Explain the concept of type consistency of a path expression.

16.13 Add the appropriate inverse to the Spouse relationship in the PERSON definition given in Section 16.4.1.

16.14 Give an OQL query that returns the names of all spouses of all grandchildren of the person with SSN 123–45–6789 in the PERSON definition given in Section 16.4.1.

16.15 Consider the class PERSON with an additional attribute, age. Write an OQL query that, for each age, produces a count of people of this age. Use two methods: with the GROUP BY clause and without it (using a nested query in SELECT). Describe a plausible query evaluation strategy in each case and explain which query will run faster.

16.16 Write an OQL query that, for each major, computes the number of students who have that major. Use the STUDENT class defined in (16.8) on page 502.

16.17 Use SQL:1999 (with the SETOF construct, if necessary) to complete the schema partially defined in Section 16.5. Include the following UDTs: STUDENT, COURSE, PROFESSOR, TEACHING, TRANSCRIPT.

16.18 Use the schema defined for the previous problem to answer the following queries:

a. Find all students who have taken more than five classes in the mathematics department.

b. Represent grades as a UDT, GRADE, with a method, value(), that returns the grade's numeric value.

c. Write a method that, for each student, computes the average grade. This method requires the value() method that you constructed for the previous problem.

16.19 Use SQL:1999 with the additional SETOF construct to represent a bank database with UDTs for accounts, customers, and transactions.

16.20 Use SQL:1999 and the schema constructed for the previous exercise to answer the following queries:

a. Find all accounts of customers living at the postal ZIP code 12345.

b. Find all customers such that the total value of their accounts is at least $1,000,000.

16.21 E-R diagrams can be used in designing the class definitions of object databases. Design ODMG class definitions for the E-R diagrams in Figure 5.1, Figure 5.5, and Figure 5.12.

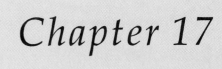

Chapter 17

XML and Web Data

The Web opens a new frontier in information technology and presents new challenges to the existing database framework. Unlike traditional databases, data sources on the Web do not typically conform to any well-known structure, such as a relation or object schema. Thus, traditional database storage and manipulation techniques are inadequate to deal with such data sources. For this reason, there is a need to extend existing database technologies to support the many new Web-based applications in electronic information delivery and exchange in areas such as education, commerce, and government.

17.1 SEMISTRUCTURED DATA

At first sight, the information on the Web bears no resemblance to the information stored in traditional databases. However, certain of its characteristics make it possible to apply many of the techniques developed in databases and information retrieval. First note that much of the Web data is presented in a somewhat structured form. For example, Figure 17.1 shows a student list as a tree encoded in Hypertext Markup Language (HTML), in which different data elements are set out using HTML tags.

To the human eye—albeit not quite so to the machine—the information on this HTML page appears to be a completely structured list of students, which, as shown in Figure 17.2, can be represented using the conceptual object data model (CODM) of Section 16.3. (We used our informal understanding of the document in Figure 17.1 to construct the schema in Figure 17.2.) The actual object appears at the top of the figure. (We represent this object as an oid-value pair, as in Chapter 16.) The schema corresponding to the student list is not explicit in the HTML page, but appears to conform to the schema at the bottom of the figure.

One interesting observation here is that, although the schema (containing attribute names) was not sent with the data, we are able to make a reasonable guess about the structure of the data based on the data itself. This is possible because the designer of the Web page was conscious of the need to make the structure easily understandable to a human and so made the data **self-describing** by including the names of the attributes within the data fields.

Figure 17.1   A student list in HTML.

```
<html>
  <head><Title>Student List</Title></head>
  <body>
    <h1>ListName: Students</h1>
    <dl>
      <dt>Name: John Doe
        <dd>Id: 111111111
        <dd>Address:
          <ul>
          <li>Number: 123
          <li>Street: Main St
          </ul>
      <dt>Name: Joe Public
        <dd>Id: 666666666
        <dd>Address:
          <ul>
          <li>Number: 666
          <li>Street: Hollow Rd
          </ul>
    </dl>
  </body>
</html>
```

Suppose now that the same information is delivered over the Web to a machine (rather than a human) for processing. Unlike the human reader, the machine is less likely to make an intelligent guess about the intended structure of the data received. Furthermore, the schema might not even be well defined, as some students on the list might have additional attributes, such as a phone number, or some addresses might have a variable structure (e.g., post office box instead of street address). Therefore, to facilitate machine-to-machine exchange of information, it is advantageous to agree on a format that makes the data self-describing by distinguishing the attribute names from values within the data.

In sum, Web data *created for machine consumption* is likely to have the following characteristics:

■ It is *object-like*; that is, it can be represented as a collection of objects of the form described by the conceptual data model introduced in Section 16.3.

■ It is *schemaless*; that is, it is not guaranteed to conform to any type structure, unlike the objects discussed in Section 16.3.

■ It is *self-describing*.

Figure 17.2 Student list in object form.

Object:

```
(#12345, ["Students",
          { ["John Doe", "111111111", [123,"Main St"]],
            ["Joe Public", "666666666", [666,"Hollow Rd"]] }
        ])
```

Schema:

```
PERSONLIST [ ListName: STRING,
               Contents:[Name: STRING,
                         Id: STRING,
                         Address:[Number: INTEGER, Street: STRING] ]
             ]
```

Data with the above characteristics have been dubbed **semistructured**. The "self-describing" property may be somewhat misleading, since it can imply that the meaning of the data is carried along with the data itself. In reality, semistructured data carries only the names of the attributes and has a lower degree of organization than the data in databases. In particular, since the schema is absent, there is no guarantee that all objects have the same attributes and that the same attribute in different objects has the same meaning.

In view of our observations, Figure 17.2 is not a completely adequate representation of the original data depicted in Figure 17.1, because neither the object notation nor the schema notation of CODM was designed for self-describing data representation. However, an appropriate notation can be developed by borrowing elements from both the object and the schema notation of CODM. With the new notation, our student list can be represented as schemaless but self-describing as follows:

```
(#12345,
  [ListName:"Students",
    Contents:{ [Name:"John Doe",
                Id: "111111111",                                    (17.1)
                Address:[Number:123, Street:"Main St"]],
               [Name:"Joe Public",
                Id: "666666666",
                Address:[Number:666, Street:"Hollow Rd"]] }
  ])
```

The above syntax is perfectly adequate for representing semistructured data, and it conforms to the best of database tradition. However, this is not the format chosen for data exchange on the Web. The winner is called the **extensible markup**

language (XML)—a standard adopted in 1998 by the World Wide Web Consortium (W3C).

Since its introduction, XML has been steadily gaining momentum and is on the way to becoming the main format for the information intended for both human and machine consumption. The next section introduces the various components of the language and provides examples of its use.

Although at its core, XML data is schemaless, schema-compliant data is always more useful. In particular, the needs of electronic data exchange require stricter enforcement of the formats for transmission than that provided by semistructured data. To help, XML has *optional* mechanisms for specifying document structure. We discuss two such mechanisms: the **document type definition** language (**DTD**), which is part of the XML standard itself, and the **XML Schema**, which is a more recent specification built on top of XML. In the last part of the chapter, we introduce three query languages for XML: a lightweight language called **XPath**, a document transformation language called **XSLT**, and a full-blown language called **XQuery**. For a more in-depth study of semistructured data, we refer the reader to [Abiteboul et al. 2000] and to the other papers in the Bibliographic Notes section.

17.2   OVERVIEW OF XML

XML is not a solution to all of the world's problems, and it is not a revolutionary idea. In fact, it is not even a new idea. Why, then, is it causing a revolution? In a nutshell, XML is a human- and machine-readable data format that can be easily parsed by an application and thus considerably simplifies data exchange. Formats for data exchange were proposed in the past, but they either were nonopen, proprietary standards or did not have the mindshare to gain momentum. XML happened to be in the right place at the right time. People saw what the Web and open standards did for communication, education, publishing, and commerce, and the need to simplify data exchange among software agents became apparent. It also helped that a trusted standards body, the WWW Consortium (W3C) was in place and not affiliated with any particular industry group or government. For the first time a simple, open, and widely accepted data standard emerged, which is giving a boost to a wide range of Web applications.

XML is an HTML-like language with an arbitrary number of user-defined tags and no a priori tag semantics. To better understand what this means, consider HTML, a document format in which various pieces of text are marked with tags that affect the rendering of that text by a Web browser. An important point is that the number of tags in HTML is *fixed* by the HTML definition and each tag has its own well-defined meaning. For instance, any text between the tags <table> and </table> is supposed to be rendered by the browser as a table, and the tag <p> tells the browser to start a new paragraph. In contrast, the repertoire of tags in XML is not set in advance and the user is free to introduce new tag names. Furthermore, there is no set semantics for any XML tag.

The lack of semantics in XML might seem like a step backward. How does the browser know what to do with the documents it receives? The answer is that

Figure 17.3 XML representation of the student list.

```
<?xml version="1.0" ?>
<PersonList Type="Student" Date="2000-12-12">
    <Title Value="Student List"/>
    <Contents>
        <Person>
            <Name>John Doe</Name>
            <Id>111111111</Id>
            <Address>
                <Number>123</Number>
                <Street>Main St</Street>
            </Address>
        </Person>
        <Person>
            <Name>Joe Public</Name>
            <Id>666666666</Id>
            <Address>
                <Number>666</Number>
                <Street>Hollow Rd</Street>
            </Address>
        </Person>
    </Contents>
</PersonList>
```

different semantic layers are supposed to be built on top of XML, and they can be tailored for different categories of applications. Browser rendering is just one such category. The semantics of a document that is intended to be rendered in a browser is represented by a **stylesheet** (Section 17.4.2). However, most XML documents are exchanged by applications that do not display them on the screen for human consumption. In this case, the semantics can depend on the application domain. At this time, whole industries are developing semantic layers for representing information in catalogs, commerce, engineering, and other fields. However, these efforts have the same common need: the ability to define schema. We discuss the structuring mechanisms available in XML in Sections 17.2.4 and 17.3, although it should be noted that, despite the schema, XML data remains semistructured. Compliance with the schema remains optional, and applications are free to ignore part or all of it.

For concreteness, consider the document in Figure 17.3, which is one possible XML representation of the student list from Figure 17.1. The first line is a mandatory statement that tells the program receiving the document (any such program is called **XML processor**) that it is dealing with XML version 1.0. The rest is structured like an HTML document except for the following two important points:

■ The document contains a large assortment of tags chosen by the document author. In contrast, the only valid tags in HTML are those sanctioned by the official specification of the language; other tags are ignored by the browser.

■ Every opening tag *must* have a matching closing tag, and the tags must be properly nested (i.e., sequences such as `<a><b></a></b>` are not allowed). In contrast, some HTML tags are not required to be closed (e.g., `<p>`), and browsers are forgiving even when closing tags are missing.

■ The document has a **root element**—the element that contains all other elements. In Figure 17.3, the root element is `PersonList`.

Any properly nested piece of text of the form `<sometag>...</sometag>` is called an **XML element**, and `sometag` is the **name** of that element. The text between the opening and closing tag is called the **content** of the element. Elements directly nested within other elements are called **children**. For instance, in our example `Name`, `Id`, and `Address` are children of `Person`, which is a child of `Contents`, which is a child of the top-level element, `PersonList`. Conversely, `PersonList` is said to be the **parent** of the elements `Contents` and `Title`, and `Contents` is a parent of `Person`.

XML also defines the **ancestor/descendant** relationships among elements, which are important for querying XML documents and will be revisited in Section 17.4. These relationships have their natural meaning: An ancestor is a parent, a grandparent, and so on, and a descendant is a child, a grandchild, and so on. For instance, `PersonList` is an ancestor of `Person` and `Address`, and `Address` is a descendent of `PersonList`.

An opening tag can have **attributes**. In the tag `<PersonList Type="Student">` of Figure 17.3, `Type` is the name of an attribute that belongs to the element `PersonList` and `Student` is the attribute value. Unlike HTML, all attribute values must be quoted, as shown in the figure, but text strings between tags are not. Also note the element `<Title Value="Student List"/>`, which also contains an attribute. This element does not have a closing tag, but instead is enclosed in `<.../>` and is called an **empty element** because it has no content. In XML, this notation is a shorthand for the combination `<Title Value="Student List"> </Title>`.

Apart from elements and attributes, XML allows **processing instructions** and **comments**. A processing instruction is a statement of the form

```
<?my-command go bring coffee?>
```

and can contain pretty much anything the document author might want to communicate to the XML processor (in the hope that the processor knows what to do with this information). Processing instructions are used fairly rarely. We will encounter one use in Section 17.4.2 in conjunction with XML stylesheets.

A comment takes the following form:

```
<!-- A comment -->
```

It is allowed to occur everywhere except inside the **markups**, that is, between the symbols `<` and `>`, which open or close tags, and in other similar situations. Perhaps surprisingly, a comment is an integral part of the document—the sender is *not* supposed to delete comments prior to transmission, and the receiver is permitted to look inside the comments and use what it finds. Although such treatment of comments goes against prevailing practice in programming and database languages, it is not unheard of in document processing. For instance, JavaScript programs are often placed as comments in HTML documents, and HTML browser is not supposed to ignore them. Instead, it executes JavaScript programs found inside the comments, unless the JavaScript feature is turned off.

Another feature of XML that is worth a brief mention is the CDATA construct. CDATA allows the inclusion of strings of characters containing markup elements that might make the document ill formed. For instance, if we use XML to write a structured guide to Web publishing, we might want to include the following text:

> Web browsers attempt to correct publisher's errors, such as improperly nested tags. For instance, `<b><i>Attention!</b></i>` would be displayed properly by most browsers.

However, such a string would result in an ill-formed document rejected by every compliant XML processor. Here is a convenient and correct way to include such a string:

```
<![CDATA[... <b><i>Attention!</b></i> ... ]]>
```

Finally, a document can have an optional **document type definition** (or *DTD*) which determines document structure. We discuss DTDs in Section 17.2.4.

17.2.1 XML Elements and Database Objects

Let us now evaluate the XML document of Figure 17.3 as a format for sending semistructured data over the Web. It is easy to see that the element names effectively serve as attribute names for the object (XML attribute names can serve the same purpose), so this document is essentially yet another, equivalent textual representation for the self-describing object depicted in (17.1).

Conversion of XML elements into objects. A moment's reflection should convince us that the nested tag structure of XML is well suited to represent tree-structured self-describing objects. Each element in an XML document can be viewed as an object. The tag names of the children elements then correspond to the object attributes' and the elements themselves are the attribute values. For instance, the first Person element in Figure 17.3 can be partially mapped back to an object as follows:

```
{#6543, Name: "John Doe",
     Id: "111111111",
     Address: <Address>
                  <Number>123</Number>
                  <Street>Main St</Street>
              </Address>
}
```

The conversion process is recursive. Simple elements such as Name and Id are converted immediately, by directly extracting their contents. The element Address is left unchanged because it has a complex internal structure, which can be broken further by applying the same conversion procedure recursively. This results in a creation of a new address object:

```
{#098686, Number: "123",
          Street: "Main St"
}
```

Differences between XML elements and objects. Despite the apparent close correspondence between XML elements and structured database objects, there are several fundamental differences. First, XML evolved from and was greatly influenced by SGML [SGM 1986], which is a *document* markup language rather than a *database* language. For instance, XML allows documents of the form

```
<Address>
     Sally lives on
     <Street>Main St</Street>
     house number
     <Number>123</Number>
     in the beautiful Anytown, USA.
</Address>
```

This mixed data/text structure, allowed in XML, is a hindrance when it comes to automated data processing, and is abhorrent to a true database designer.

Second, XML elements are *ordered*, while the attributes of an object in a database are not. Thus, the following two objects are considered the same:

```
{#098686, Number: "123",        {#098686, Street: "Main St",
          Street: "Main St"                Number: "123"
}                               }
```

whereas the following two XML documents are different:

```
<Address>                       <Address>
     <Number>123</Number>            <Street>Main St</Street>
     <Street>Main St</Street>        <Number>123</Number>
</Address>                       </Address>
```

Third, XML has only one primitive type, a string, and very weak facilities for specifying constraints. Fortunately, many of these weaknesses are addressed by the XML Schema specification in Section 17.3.

17.2.2 XML Attributes

We saw the use of XML attributes such as Type and Value in Figure 17.3. An element can have any number of user-defined attributes. However, considering the expressive power of XML elements illustrated earlier, we are left to wonder about the role of XML attributes as a tool for data representation. That is, are they useful in data representation and do they offer anything beyond what elements can offer?

The answer is that XML attributes are sometimes convenient for representing data, but almost everything they can do can also be done with elements. Moreover, with new XML-based standards, such as XML Schema (Section 17.3), we expect that the use of attributes for data representation will decline. Still, they are widely used in a number of XML-based specifications, such as XML Schema and XSLT, which we introduce later in this chapter. We also use attributes extensively in the examples, to illustrate the various features of XML and because this often leads to more concise representation.

In document processing, attributes are used to annotate pieces of text enclosed between a pair of tags with values that are *not* part of that text but are related to it. In the following dialog,

```
<Act Number="5">
    <Scene Number="1" Place="Mantua. A street.">
        .
        .
        .

        <Apothecary Voice="scared">
            Such mortal drugs I have; but Mantua's law
            Is death to any he that utters them.
        </Apothecary>
        <Romeo Voice="persistent">
            Art thou so bare and full of wretchedness,
            And fear'st to die?
            .
            .
            .

        </Romeo>
        .
        .
        .

    </Scene>
</Act>
```

we use attributes to annotate the text with "meta"-information that is not part of the dialog *per se* but is still relevant. They are convenient here because they do not disrupt the dialog flow. In data processing, on the other hand, text flow is a minor concern since computers are unlikely to start appreciating this type of prose in the near future. The concern here is that XML attributes represent yet another, unnecessary dimension in data representation that database programmers have to worry about.

In addition, attribute values can only be strings, which severely limits their usefulness, while XML elements can have children elements, which makes them much more versatile.

Having made these unflattering remarks, we should mention some advantages of attributes. First, the order of attributes in an element does not matter. Thus, the documents

```
<thing price="2" color="yellow">foobar</thing>
```

and

```
<thing color="yellow" price="2">foobar</thing>
```

are considered the same—much as they are in databases. Second, an attribute can occur at most once (i.e., `<thing price="2" price="2">` is not allowed), while elements with the same tag can be repeated, as in Figure 17.3. This constraint can be handy in the right circumstances. Third, attributes can lead to more succinct representation. For instance, `<thing price="2" color="yellow"/>` is much shorter than `<thing><price>2</price><color>yellow</color></thing>`.

A useful feature of XML attributes is that they can be declared to have unique value and they also can be used to enforce limited kind of referential integrity. This cannot be done with elements alone in plain XML. (However, this and much more can be done with the help of XML Schema, discussed in Section 17.3.) After we discuss document type definitions (DTDs) in Section 17.2.4, we will see that an attribute can be declared to be of type ID, IDREF, or IDREFS.

An attribute of type ID must have a unique value throughout the document. This means that if `attr1` and `attr2` are of type ID, it is illegal for both `<elt1 attr1="abc">` and `<elt2 attr2="abc">` to occur in the same document (regardless of whether `elt1` and `elt2` are the same tag, or whether `attr1` and `attr2` are the same attribute). In a sense, ID is a poor cousin of a *key* in relational databases.

An attribute of type IDREF must refer to a valid Id declared in the same document. That is, its value must occur somewhere in the document as a value of another attribute of type ID. Thus, IDREF is a poor cousin of a *foreign key*.

To illustrate, we consider the report document in Figure 17.4. An attribute of type IDREFS represents a space-separated list of strings of references to valid Ids.

In our document, we can declare the attribute StudId of the element Student and the attribute CrsCode of the element Course to be of type ID; the attribute CrsCode of the element CrsTaken to be of type IDREF; and the attribute Members of the element ClassRoster of type IDREFS. As a result, any compliant XML processor will verify that no student or course is declared twice and that referential integrity holds—a course referenced in a CrsTaken element does exist, and all students mentioned in the Members lists are also present in the document.

We can now define an important correctness requirement. An XML document is **well formed** if the following conditions hold:

■ It has a root element.

■ Every opening tag is followed by a matching closing tag, and the elements are properly nested inside each other.

■ Any attribute can occur at most once in a given opening tag, its value must be provided, as discussed above, and this value must be quoted.

Note that the restrictions on ID, IDREF, and IDREFS are not part of the definition of "well-formed," because these attribute types are specified using DTDs, which well-formedness completely ignores.

Figure 17.4 A report document with cross-references.

```
<?xml version="1.0" ?>
<Report Date="2000-12-12">
  <Students>
    <Student StudId="111111111">
      <Name><First>John</First><Last>Doe</Last></Name>
      <Status>U2</Status>
      <CrsTaken CrsCode="CS308" Semester="F1997"/>
      <CrsTaken CrsCode="MAT123" Semester="F1997"/>
    </Student>
    <Student StudId="666666666">
      <Name><First>Joe</First><Last>Public</Last></Name>
      <Status>U3</Status>
      <CrsTaken CrsCode="CS308" Semester="F1994"/>
      <CrsTaken CrsCode="MAT123" Semester="F1997"/>
    </Student>
    <Student StudId="987654321">
      <Name><First>Bart</First><Last>Simpson</Last></Name>
      <Status>U4</Status>
      <CrsTaken CrsCode="CS308" Semester="F1994"/>
    </Student>
  </Students>
  <Classes>
    <Class>
      <CrsCode>CS308</CrsCode><Semester>F1994</Semester>
      <ClassRoster Members="666666666 987654321"/>
    </Class>
    <Class>
      <CrsCode>CS308</CrsCode><Semester>F1997</Semester>
      <ClassRoster Members="111111111"/>
    </Class>
    <Class>
      <CrsCode>MAT123</CrsCode><Semester>F1997</Semester>
      <ClassRoster Members="111111111 666666666"/>
    </Class>
  </Classes>
  <Courses>
    <Course CrsCode="CS308">
      <CrsName>Market Analysis</CrsName>
    </Course>
    <Course CrsCode="MAT123">
      <CrsName>Algebra</CrsName>
    </Course>
  </Courses>
</Report>
```

17.2.3 Namespaces

Namespaces were not part of the original XML specification and were added as an afterthought. However, they have become central to many important standards built on top of XML, so we consider them to be an integral XML feature for all practical purposes.

The driving force behind the introduction of namespaces was the belief that, in the near future, enterprises will start building vocabularies of terms appropriate for the various domains (e.g., education, finance, electronics) and use them as XML tags. In this scenario, naming conflicts between different vocabularies are inevitable, and the integration of information obtained from different sources becomes very hard. For instance, the term Name might have different meanings and structure depending on whether we are talking about people or companies, as we see in these two document fragments:

```
<Name><First>John</First>  <Last>Doe</Last></Name>
<Name>IBM</Name>
```

So it will become harder for an application to process documents that are built out of the vocabularies that contain conflicting tag names.

To overcome this problem, it has been decided that the name of every XML tag must have two parts: the **namespace** and the **local name**, with the general structure *namespace:local-name*. Local names have the same form as regular XML tags except that they cannot have a : in them. A namespace is represented by a string in the form of a **uniform resource identifier** (**URI**) which can be an abstract identifier (a general string of characters serving as a unique identifier) or a **uniform resource locator** (**URL**) (a Web page address).

The overall idea seems simple enough: Different authors use different namespace identifiers for different domains, and thus terminological clashes are avoided. The strategy generally followed since the introduction of namespaces is that authors choose as namespace identifiers the URLs that are under their control. For instance, if Joe Public authors a vocabulary for the school supplies marketed by Acme, Inc., he uses a namespace such as:

```
http://www.acmeinc.com/jp#supplies
```

and for toys the namespace could be

```
http://www.acmeinc.com/jp#toys
```

The WWW Consortium (W3C) recommendation[1] for incorporating namespaces into XML [Nam 1999] goes beyond a simple two-part naming schema—it also fixes a particular syntax for declaring namespaces, their use, and scoping rules. Here is an example:

```
<item xmlns="http://www.acmeinc.com/jp#supplies"
      xmlns:toy="http://www.acmeinc.com/jp#toys">
```

---

[1] The final documents produced by W3C are inconspicuously called "recommendations," but in reality they are as good as standards.

```
<name>backpack</name>
<feature>
     <toy:item>
          <toy:name>cyberpet</toy:name>
     </toy:item>
</feature>
</item>
```

Namespaces are defined using the attribute `xmlns`, which is a reserved word. In fact, W3C has advised that all names starting with `xml` be considered as reserved for the Consortium's use. In our example, we declare two namespaces in the scope of the element `item`. The first one is declared using the syntax `xmlns=` and is called the **default namespace**. Naturally, there can be only one default namespace declaration per start tag (this follows not only because of the semantics but also because XML does not permit multiple occurrences of the same attribute within the same start tag). The second namespace is defined with the xmlns:toy= declaration, identified by the **prefix** `toy`. One can declare several prefixed namespaces as long as the prefixes are distinct.[2]

Namespace declarations. Tags belonging to the namespace `http://www.acmeinc.com/jp#toys`, should be prefixed with `toy:`. In our example, they are the inner tags `toy:item` and `toy:name`. Tags without any prefix (the outer `item`, `name`, and `feature`) are assumed to belong to the default domain.

Namespace declarations have scope, which can be nested like a program block. To illustrate, we consider the following example:

```
<item xmlns="http://www.acmeinc.com/jp#supplies"
     xmlns:toy="http://www.acmeinc.com/jp#toys">
<name>backpack</name>
<feature>
     <toy:item>
          <toy:name>cyberpet</toy:name>
     </toy:item>
</feature>
<item xmlns="http://www.acmeinc.com/jp#supplies2"
     xmlns:toy="http://www.acmeinc.com/jp#toys2">
<name>notebook</name>
<toy:name>sticker</toy:name>
</item>
</item>
```

Here we added one more child element to the outermost `item` element. The child is also called `item`, but it has its own default namespace and a redeclared namespace prefix, `toy`. Thus, the outermost `item` tag belongs to the default namespace

---

[2] Nevertheless, two tags are assumed to belong to the same namespace, even if they have different prefixes, if and only if their prefixes refer to the same URI ("same" meaning that the URIs are equal as character strings).

```
http://www.acmeinc.com/jp#supplies
```

The inner unprefixed `item` tag and its unprefixed child tag, `name`, are both in the scope of the default namespace

```
http://www.acmeinc.com/jp#supplies2
```

Similarly, the tags `toy:item` and `toy:name` inside the `feature` element belongs to the namespace

```
http://www.acmeinc.com/jp#toys
```

The occurrence of `toy:name` at the end of the document belongs to the namespace

```
http://www.acmeinc.com/jp#toys2
```

Observe that, just as the innermost declaration of the default namespace overshadows the outermost declaration, the innermost declaration of the prefix `toy` overshadows the outermost declaration for the same prefix. A namespace-aware XML processor is supposed to understand these subtleties and, in particular, that the two unprefixed occurrences of `item` and `name` are *different tags* since they belong to different namespaces (likewise for the prefixed versions of the tag name). An XML processor that is *unaware* of namespaces will still be able to parse the above document. However, it will think that all unprefixed versions of `item` and `name` are the same and that all occurrences of the prefixed tag `toy:name` are the same. It will just wonder why the name has that weird : inside.

Even though the idea of a namespace seems like motherhood and apple pie—who could possibly be against it—it has been one of the least understood recommendations coming out of W3C [Bourret 2000]. Everyone agrees that tag names should come in two parts, but people have been trying to read between the lines of the recommendation and find things that are not there. One of the most confusing issues is the use of URLs as namespace identifiers. In our everyday experience, a URL points to some Web resource, and, if a URL is used for a namespace, one tends to assume that it is a real address that contains some kind of schema describing the corresponding set of names. In reality, the name of a namespace is just a string that happens to be a URL, and it can be a big disappointment when pointing the browser toward such a URL brings up an unattractive error message.

The idea behind namespaces is nothing more than a mechanism for disambiguating tag names. An XML processor that reads a document encoded with namespaces should "know" how to parse it—that is, how to find its schema (represented as a DTD or an XML schema—the specification languages described later). The information on the schema location can be provided in a special attribute, or it can be part of the convention used in a particular enterprise or community. For example, the toy industry might agree that all toy-related documents should be parsed using the DTD at a particular URL. One convention taking hold right now is that certain vocabularies (such as those used in the XML Schema specification—see Section 17.3) be identified using certain "well-known" namespaces, which prescribe the document schema uniquely.

17.2.4 Document Type Definitions

There are fixed rules that an author must follow in order to create an HTML document that can be properly rendered by the browser. For instance, the table element cannot occur inside the form element. In XML, the author has the ability to specify such rules for any document. This allows XML to be used for a wide variety of document types, such as bills, catalogs, and order forms, which are designed for machine rather than human consumption.

A set of rules for structuring an XML document is called a **document type definition** (**DTD**). A DTD can be specified as part of the document itself, or the document can give a URL where its DTD can be found. A document that conforms to its DTD is said to be **valid**. The XML specification does not require processors to check each document for conformance to its DTD, because some applications might not care if the document is valid. In some cases, the processor does not check validity, instead relying on the guarantee of the sender for this (e.g., in electronic billing, where both sides use software guaranteed to produce valid documents). XML does not even require that the document have a DTD, but it does require that all documents be well formed. (The conditions for well-formedness—proper element nesting and the restrictions on the attributes—have been discussed in Section 17.2.2.)

These two notions of correctness can lead to significant simplification and speedup for XML processors. HTML browser usually tries to correct bugs in the HTML documents and display as much of a buggy document as possible. In contrast, an XML processor is expected to simply reject documents that are not well-formed. A processor that expects valid documents would reject invalid ones (those that do not comply with the DTD) even if they are well formed.

For those who are familiar with formal languages, a DTD is a *grammar* that specifies a legal XML document, based on the tags used in the document and their attributes. For instance, the following DTD is consistent with the document in Figure 17.3:

```
<!DOCTYPE PersonList [
    <!ELEMENT PersonList (Title,Contents)>
    <!ELEMENT Title EMPTY>
    <!ELEMENT Contents (Person*)>
    <!ELEMENT Person (Name,Id,Address)>
    <!ELEMENT Name (#PCDATA)>
    <!ELEMENT Id (#PCDATA)>
    <!ELEMENT Address (Number,Street)>
    <!ELEMENT Number (#PCDATA)>
    <!ELEMENT Street (#PCDATA)>
    <!ATTLIST PersonList Type CDATA #IMPLIED
                         Date CDATA #IMPLIED>
    <!ATTLIST Title Value CDATA #REQUIRED>
]>
```

This example illustrates the most common DTD components: a **name** (Person-List in the example) and a set of ELEMENT and ATTLIST statements. The name of a DTD must coincide with the tag name of the root element of the document that conforms to that DTD. One ELEMENT statement exists for each allowed tag, including the root tag. Furthermore, for each tag that can have attributes, the ATTLIST statement specifies the allowed attributes and their type.

In our example, the first ELEMENT statement says that the element PersonList consists of a Title element followed by a Contents element. A Title element (the second ELEMENT statement) does not contain any elements (it is an empty element). The * in the definition of the Contents element indicates zero or more elements of type Person. If we used + instead of "*", it would mean that at least one Person element must be present. The elements Name, Number, and Street are declared to be of type #PCDATA, that is, a character string.[3]

Following the element list, a DTD contains the description of allowed element attributes. In our case, PersonList is permitted to have the attributes Type and Date, while Title can only have the attribute Value. Other elements are not allowed to have attributes. Moreover, both attributes of PersonList are *optional*, as specified by the keyword #IMPLIED, while the Value attribute of Title is mandatory. All three attributes have the type CDATA, which is, again, a character string. (Note that different syntax is used to declare character string types for elements and attributes.)

Observe that our document in Figure 17.3 is valid with respect to the above DTD, but if we delete, for example, some Address elements from it, it will become invalid, because the DTD says that each person must have an address. On the other hand, if the DTD has

```
<!ELEMENT Person (Name,Id,Address?)>
```

the address field becomes optional since ? indicates zero or one occurrence of the Address element.

It is also possible to state that the order of elements in a person's description does not matter, using the connective |, which represents alternatives:

```
<!ELEMENT Person
      ((Name,Id,Address)|(Name,Address,Id)|(Id,Address,Name)
       |(Id,Name,Address)|(Address,Id,Name)|(Address,Name,Id))>
```

You can see that it becomes rather awkward, however.

DTDs allow the author to specify several types for an attribute. We have seen CDATA. The other frequently used types are ID, IDREF, and IDREFS, mentioned on page 546 in connection with the report document in Figure 17.4. We pointed out that a document of this type needs a mechanism for enforcing referential integrity—much as in the database examples of Chapter 4.

---

[3] PCDATA stands for *parsed character data*.

Figure 17.5 A DTD for the report document in Figure 17.4.

```
<!DOCTYPE Report [
    <!ELEMENT Report (Students,Classes,Courses)>
    <!ELEMENT Students (Student*)>
    <!ELEMENT Classes (Class*)>
    <!ELEMENT Courses (Course*)>
    <!ELEMENT Student (Name,Status,CrsTaken*)>
    <!ELEMENT Name (First,Last)>
    <!ELEMENT First (#PCDATA)>
    .
    .
    .
    <!ELEMENT CrsTaken EMPTY>
    <!ELEMENT Class (CrsCode,Semester,ClassRoster)>
    <!ELEMENT Course (CrsName)>
    .
    .
    .
    <!ELEMENT ClassRoster EMPTY>
    <!ATTLIST Report Date #IMPLIED>
    <!ATTLIST Student StudId ID #REQUIRED>
    <!ATTLIST Course CrsCode ID #REQUIRED>
    <!ATTLIST CrsTaken CrsCode IDREF #REQUIRED>
    <!ATTLIST CrsTaken Semester IDREF #REQUIRED>
    <!ATTLIST ClassRoster Members IDREFS #IMPLIED>
]>
```

Specifically, we want to make sure that the values of the attributes StudId in Student and CrsCode in Course are distinct throughout the document, that the attribute CrsCode in CrsTaken represents a reference to a course mentioned in this document (that there is a Course element with a matching value in its CrsCode attribute), and that the members in a list indicated by Members in ClassRoster refer to student records mentioned in the document (for each such member there is a Student element with the matching value of its StudId attribute). This can be enforced with the DTD shown in Figure 17.5, in which we omit some easily reconstructible parts.

A compliant XML processor that insists on document validity is obliged by this DTD to make sure that no two Student elements have the same value in their StudId attribute (similarly for Course elements).[4] This is because these attributes are declared to have the type ID. Likewise, because the attribute CrsCode of the element CrsTaken is declared as IDREF, referential integrity for course codes is preserved. The attribute Members in ClassRoster is declared as IDREFS, which

---

[4] Actually, a stronger condition is enforced: No StudId attribute of a Student element can have the same value as a CrsCode attribute of a Course element.

represents *lists* of values of type IDREF. This declaration is intended to secure the integrity of references to student Ids.

There are also constraints in the document that beg to be noticed, but they cannot be enforced using DTDs. We discuss these issues in the next section.

17.2.5 Inadequacy of DTDs as a Data Definition Language

XML was conceived as a simplified, streamlined version of SGML [SGM 1986], which was standardized years before the work on XML began. SGML was created for specifying documents that can be exchanged and automatically processed by software agents, and this was the original goal of XML as well. DTDs and the ratio-nale behind their use were borrowed from SGML. Their technical underpinnings come from the theory of formal languages, and general-purpose parsers that can validate any document against any DTD are well known. Such validation has im-portant implications for document processing software. For instance, if an XML processor can expect that the documents it receives have been validated and con-form to the DTD Report described above, it does not need to take care of special cases and exceptions, such as the possibility that a student might have taken a nonexisting course or that a street address is missing.

While the development of XML was going on, new ideas started to emerge. In particular, XML opened up the possibility of treating Web documents as data sources that can be queried (similarly to database relations) and that can be related to each other through semantically meaningful links (similar to foreign key con-straints). At this point, XML began to outgrow its SGML heritage. One of the first enhancements, which came too late to be included in XML 1.0, was namespaces, discussed earlier. A much more significant enhancement is the development of the XML Schema specification (next section), which is designed to rectify many of the limitations of DTD as a data definition language. These limitations include:

■ DTDs are not designed with namespaces in mind. A DTD views xmlns as just another attribute with no special meaning. It is not hard to extend them to include namespaces, but there is a problem of backward compatibility and, in view of other limitations of DTDs, such enhancement is probably a futile exercise.

■ DTDs use syntax that is quite different from that of XML documents. While this is not a fatal drawback, it is not the most elegant feature of XML 1.0, either.

■ DTDs have a very limited repertoire of basic types (essentially just glorified strings).

■ DTDs provide only limited means for expressing data consistency constraints. They do not have keys (except for the very limited ID type), and the mechanism for specifying referential integrity is very weak. The only way to reference something is through the IDREF and IDREFS attributes, and even these are based on only one primitive type, a string. In particular, it is not possible to type the references. One cannot require that the attribute CrsCode of the element

CrsTaken in the report document of Figure 17.4 reference only Course elements. Thus, it is possible for John Doe to have a child element

```
<CrsTaken CrsCode="666666666" Semester="F1999"/>
```

which refers to the student Id of Joe Public instead of a course, and no XML 1.0 compliant processor can detect this problem.

■ DTDs have ways of enforcing referential integrity for attributes but no corresponding feature for elements. For example, the contents of the element Class include the elements CrsCode and Semester (not to be confused with similarly named attributes of the tag CrsTaken). Clearly, we want the content of the element CrsCode to refer to a valid course and match a value of the attribute CrsCode in some Course element. Furthermore, for each pair of values of the attributes in the element CrsTaken, there must be a corresponding pair of CrsCode/Semester tags in some Class element. These constraints cannot be enforced using DTDs.

■ XML data is ordered; database data is unordered (e.g., the order of tuples does not matter). Also, the order of the attributes in a database relation or an object does not matter; the order of elements in XML matters. We already saw that DTDs allow us to specify alternatives, and through them we can state that the order of elements is immaterial (as in the earlier example of the Name, Address, and Id children of the element Person). However, this becomes extremely awkward as the number of attributes grows. For instance, to state that the order among N children elements is immaterial, a DTD must specify $N!$ alternatives.

■ Element definitions are global to the entire document. If a DTD specifies that, for example, Name consists of children elements First and Last, then it is not possible to have a *differently structured* Name element anywhere else in the document. This happens because a DTD can have only one ELEMENT clause per element name. There is no way to localize it with respect to a parent element so that different definitions would apply to different occurrences of Name, depending on where it is nested.

17.3 XML SCHEMA

XML Schema, a data definition language for XML documents, has become a recommendation of W3C as this book was going to press. It was developed in response to the aforesaid limitations of the DTD mechanism and has the following main features:

■ It uses the same syntax as that used for ordinary XML documents.

■ It is integrated with the namespace mechanism. In particular, different schemas can be imported from different namespaces and integrated into one schema.

■ It provides a number of built-in types, such as string, integer, and time—similar to SQL.

■ It provides the means to define complex types from simpler ones.

■ It allows the same element name to be defined as having different types depending on where the element is nested.

■ It supports key and referential integrity constraints.

■ It provides a better mechanism for specifying documents where the order of element types does not matter.

An XML document that conforms to a given schema is said to be **schema valid** and is called an **instance** of the schema.[5] Similarly to DTDs, the XML Schema specification does not require an XML processor to actually use the document schema. It is free to ignore the schema or to use a different one. For instance, the XML processor might want to consider only the documents that satisfy stricter integrity constraints than those given in the schema, or it might decide to enforce only part of the schema. This liberal attitude should be contrasted with databases, where *all* data must comply with the schema. In this sense, XML data as a whole should be considered semistructured (Section 17.1), despite the fact that a schema might partially describe it.

17.3.1 XML Schema and Namespaces

An XML schema document (like a DTD) describes the structure of other (instance) XML documents. It begins with a declaration of the namespaces to be used in the schema, three of which are particularly important.

■ `http://www.w3.org/2001/XMLSchema`—the namespace that identifies the names of tags and attributes used in a schema. These names are not related to, nor do they appear in, any particular document that is an instance of the schema. Instead, they describe the structural properties of documents in general. Remember that there may be no document at the URL `http://www.w3.org/2001/XMLSchema`. The names in this namespace are simply understood by all schema aware XML processors and are referred to as names defined by the XML Schema Specification. For example, the names associated with this namespace include `schema`, `attribute`, and `element`. They do not typically occur in the instance documents, such as the one in Figure 17.4 on page 547. (If they did, they would not describe the structure of the document, would have a different meaning, and would have to be assigned to a different namespace.) Hence, this namespace is typically part of schema documents, but is not used in instance documents.

■ `http://www.w3.org/2001/XMLSchema-instance`—another namespace used in conjunction with `http://www.w3.org/2001/XMLSchema`. It identifies a small number of special names, which are defined in the XML Schema Specification but are used in the instance documents rather than in their schemas (whence the

---

[5] Note that the dichotomy of schema versus instance here is analogous to the terminology that we used in relational and object-oriented databases.

name XMLSchema-instance). One such name, schemaLocation, specifies the location of the schema for the document. Another defines the special null value when it appears in a document. We will discuss these features in due time. This namespace is part of the specification of instance documents.

■ The **target namespace**—identifies the set of names *defined* by a particular schema document, in other words, the user-defined names that are to be used in the instance documents of that particular schema. For instance, in the schema document for Figure 17.4 the names CrsTaken, Student, Status, and so forth, would be associated with the target namespace. (We will soon start developing the various parts of that schema.) The target namespace is declared using the attribute targetNamespace of the opening tag of the schema element—the root tag of every schema document.

The integration with namespaces is one of the important items missing in DTDs: A DTD can define any number of tags, but there is no way to associate those tags with a namespace.

We now begin to develop a schema for the report document of Figure 17.4. Our first example simply declares the namespaces to be used in the schema we are creating.

```
<schema xmlns="http://www.w3.org/2001/XMLSchema"
        targetNamespace="http://xyz.edu/Admin">

    <!-- Nothing here yet -->
</schema>
```

The first namespace declared in this example makes the standard XMLSchema namespace the default. This is handy because in creating the schema, we are likely to use many special tags defined by the XML Schema specification, and making XMLSchema the default namespace will obviate the need for namespace prefixes for them. If, however, we want a different namespace to be the default, we can use

```
xmlns:xsd="http://www.w3.org/2001/XMLSchema"
```

By convention, xsd is the prefix for names in the standard XMLSchema namespace, but this convention is not enforced. In this case, we have to use xsd whenever a name associated with the XML Schema's namespace is used:

```
<xsd:schema xmlns:xsd="http://www.w3.org/2001/XMLSchema"
            xsd:targetNamespace="http://xyz.edu/Admin">

    <!-- Nothing here yet -->
</xsd:schema>
```

The first attribute here says that xsd is the prefix for names associated with the XMLSchema namespace. The second attribute says that the new tags and attributes defined by the above schema document are to be considered as part of the

Figure 17.6 Schema and an instance document.

```
<!-- An XML schema document; located at  http://xyz.edu/Admin.xsd -->
<schema xmlns="http://www.w3.org/2001/XMLSchema"
        targetNamespace="http://xyz.edu/Admin">


    <!-- Nothing here yet -->
</schema>


<!-- An instance-document conforming to the above schema;
     it uses the target namespace defined in that schema -->
<?xml version="1.0" ?>
<Report xmlns="http://xyz.edu/Admin">
        xmlns:xsi="http://www.w3.org/2001/XMLSchema-instance"
        xsi:schemaLocation="http://xyz.edu/Admin
        http://xyz.edu/Admin.xsd">

<!-- Same contents as in the report document of Figure 17.4 -->
</Report>
```

`http://xyz.edu/Admin` namespace. Note that, since `targetNamespace` is a name defined by the XML Schema specification, its use is prefixed with `xsd`.

Suppose now that we have filled in all the blanks in the above schema. How does the fact that we now have a schema for the instance document in Figure 17.4 change this document? We need to add three things to the instance: the declaration of the namespace it uses (in our case, `http://xyz.edu/Admin`), the location of the report's schema, and the `XMLSchema-instance` namespace. The latter is needed because the attribute `schemaLocation`, which specifies the schema location, occurs in instance documents and is part of the `XMLSchema-instance` namespace. To better understand the relationship among the schema, the actual instance document, and the various namespaces, we show the report document and its schema together in Figure 17.6.

Note in the figure that the default namespace in the instance document is `http://xyz.edu/Admin`—the namespace defined in the `targetNamespace` attribute of the schema document.[6] There needn't be anything at this URL because a namespace is just an identifier that is used to disambiguate the names of document tags and attributes. This namespace is chosen as a default in order to minimize the number of namespace prefixes that need to be used in the document. Because the document in Figure 17.6 is supposed to have the same contents as in the report in Figure 17.4, most of the tag and attribute names belong to this default namespace.

---

[6] Most namespaces and document locations used in the examples have been changed to protect the innocent. However, the XMLSchema and XMLSchema-instance namespaces are real.

The attribute `xsi:schemaLocation` is part of the XML Schema specification and belongs to the namespace

```
http://www.w3.org/2001/XMLSchema-instance
```

The value of the attribute is a namespace–URL pair, and it says that the schema for the namespace `http://xyz.edu/Admin` can be found in an XML schema document at the URL `http://xyz.edu/Admin.xsd`. However, as mentioned earlier, XML processors are not bound by these hints. They can choose to ignore the schema or to use a different one.

Before plunging into the specifics of defining the actual schema, we mention one other important detail, the `include` statement. It is easy to see from Figure 17.4 that our report has three distinct components: a student list, a class list, and a course list. Since these components have very different structure, it is reasonable to assume that they might well occur separately in other contexts and that they might have their own schemas. Given this, it is unreasonable for us to copy those schemas over in order to create the schema for the report document. Instead, we can use the `include` statement defined by XML Schema specification:

```
<schema xmlns="http://www.w3.org/2001/XMLSchema"
        targetNamespace="http://xyz.edu/Admin">

    <include schemaLocation="http://xyz.edu/StudentTypes.xsd"/>
    <include schemaLocation="http://xyz.edu/ClassTypes.xsd"/>
    <include schemaLocation="http://xyz.edu/CourseTypes.xsd"/>

    <!-- Nothing here yet -->
</schema>
```

The effect of the `include` statement is to include the schemas at the specified address in the given document. This technique allows for greater flexibility and modularity of XML schemas. Included schemas must have the same target namespace as the including schema. Observe one possibly confusing detail in the above example. We have used the attribute `schemaLocation` without prefixing it with `xsi` and, unlike the previous example, we did not include the `XMLSchema-instance` namespace. This discrepancy has a rational explanation. The `schemaLocation` attribute of the tag `include` belongs to the standard `XMLSchema` namespace (like the `include` tag itself); that is, this attribute is different from the similarly named attribute in the report document above. Since, unlike the report document, our schema does not use any names from the `XMLSchema-instance` namespace, this namespace was not declared.

17.3.2 Simple Types

Primitive types. The dearth of primitive types was one of the criticisms leveled against DTDs. The XML Schema specification rectifies the problem by adding many useful primitive types, such as `decimal`, `integer`, `float`, `boolean`, and `date`, in addition to `string`, `ID`, and `IDREF`. More important, it provides type constructors, such as *list* and *union*, and a mechanism to derive new primitive types from the basic ones. This mechanism is similar to the CREATE DOMAIN statement of SQL (see Section 4.3.6).

Deriving simple types using the list and union constructors.   Note that IDREFS is not one of the primitive types, as it is in DTDs. Here is how this type can be derived using the list constructor:[7]

```
<simpleType name="myIdrefs">
    <list itemType="IDREF"/>
</simpleType>
```

The union type can be useful when there is a need for two or more ways to enter data. For instance, in the United States a telephone number can be 7 or 10 digits long, which can be expressed as follows:

```
<simpleType name="phoneNumber">
    <union memberTypes="phone7digits phone10digits"/>
</simpleType>
```

We will see the definitions of the types phone7digits and phone10digits shortly.

Deriving simple types by restriction.   A more interesting way of deriving new types is via the **restriction** mechanism, which allows us to constrain a basic type using one or more constraints from a fixed repertoire defined by the XML Schema specification. This is how we are going to define the types phone7digits:

```
<simpleType name="phone7digits">
    <restriction base="integer">
        <minInclusive value="1000000"/>
        <maxInclusive value="9999999"/>
    </restriction>
</simpleType>
```

The 10-digit number type is defined similarly. In the definition of phone7digits, we used the tags maxInclusive and minInclusive to define the range of acceptable numbers. XML Schema provides a large number of built-in constraints, such as minInclusive/maxInclusive, to play with [XMLSchema 2000a, XMLSchema 2000b]. Here we mention just a few of the more interesting ones. Suppose that, in addition, we let the user specify phone numbers in the XXX-YYYY format. This can be done in several ways, one being:

```
<simpleType name="phone7digitsAndDash">
    <restriction base="string">
        <pattern value="[0-9]{3}-[0-9]{4}"/>
    </restriction>
</simpleType>
```

---

[7] Unless stated otherwise, all examples of XML schemas assume the standard http://www.w3.org/2000/10/XMLSchema namespace as a default.

Here we used the `pattern` tag to restrict the set of all strings to those that match the given pattern. The language for constructing patterns is similar to that used in the Perl programming language, but the basics should be familiar to anyone with a working knowledge of text editors such as Vi or Emacs. In the above example, [0-9] means "any digit between 0 and 9" and {3} is a pattern modifier that says that only a sequence of exactly three digits is allowed.

Other ways to derive simple types from the basic `string` type include the following:

■ `<length value="7"/>`—restricts the domain to strings of length 7.

■ `<minLength value="7"/>`—restricts the domain to strings of length *at least* 7.

■ `<maxLength value="14"/>`—restricts the domain to strings of length *at most* 14.

■ `<enumeration value="ABC"/>`—allows to restrict the domain to a finite set (see below).

The above constraints are not limited to strings, and `enumeration` is applicable to virtually any base type. Here is an example:

```
<simpleType name="emergencyNumbers">
    <restriction base="integer">
        <enumeration value="911"/>
        <enumeration value="333"/>
        <enumeration value="5431234"/>
    </restriction>
</simpleType>
```

Simple types for the report document.   We now define some simple types for our report document of Figure 17.4. We will later attach these types to the appropriate attributes in the document schema. For easy reference, we summarize all student-related types in Figure 17.8 on page 573 and all course-related types in Figure 17.9 on page 574.

```
<simpleType name="studentId">
    <restriction base="ID">
        <pattern value="[0-9]{9}"/>
    </restriction>
</simpleType>
<simpleType name="studentRef">
    <restriction base="IDREF"
        <pattern value="[0-9]{9}"/>
    </restriction>
</simpleType>
<simpleType name="studentIds">
    <list itemType="studentRef"/>
</simpleType>
<simpleType name="courseCode">
    <restriction base="ID">
```

```
            <pattern value="[A-Z]{3}[0-9]{3}"/>
        </restriction>
    </simpleType>
    <simpleType name="courseRef">
        <restriction base="IDREF">
            <pattern value="[A-Z]{3}[0-9]{3}"/>
        </restriction>
    </simpleType>
```

The first type, studId, defines student Ids as digit strings of length 9; it will be used to specify the domain of values for studId in the report. The second defines the type of *references* to student Ids, the third defines *lists* of references to student Ids, the fourth defines course codes as strings of three uppercase letters followed by three digits, and the fifth is the type for course references. Note also that we have used ID and IDREFS as base types. They have the same semantics as in DTDs, so uniqueness and referential integrity are guaranteed.

Observe that we are already doing better than in the case of the Report DTD shown in Figure 17.5 on page 553. It is impossible for a DTD to say that the attribute Members returns a list of references to students rather than to courses, or to impose a similar restriction on the attribute CrsCode of the tag CrsTaken. In contrast, the above simple types prevent such meaningless references, because the type courseRef is disjoint from the domain of studentId and the domain of studentRef is disjoint from that of courseCode.

Type declarations for simple elements and attributes.   So far, we have been talking about types without attaching them to elements and attributes. Here are some simple cases of type declaration for tags in our report document, which will later become part of the schema document for this report.

```
    <element name="CrsName" type="string"/>
    <element name="Status" type="adm:studentStatus"/>
```

The first declaration states that the element CrsName has a simple content of type string. The last declaration is fancier: It associates the Status tag with a derived type, studentStatus, defined as an enumeration of strings U1, U2, U3, U4, G1, G2, G3, G4, and G5, which represent the various status codes for undergraduate and graduate students.

```
    <simpleType name="studentStatus">
        <restriction base="string">
            <enumeration value="U1"/>
            <enumeration value="U2"/>
                .
                .
                .
            <enumeration value="G5"/>
        </restriction>
    </simpleType>
```

A subtle but very important point in this example is the prefix adm attached to studentStatus—a consequence of the namespace consideration. To understand this better, let us consider the context in which the above statements appear:

```
<schema xmlns="http://www.w3.org/2001/XMLSchema"
        xmlns:adm="http://xyz.edu/Admin"
        targetNamespace="http://xyz.edu/Admin">
    .
    .
    .

    <element name="CrsName" type="string"/>
    <!-- reference to StudentStatus -->
    <element name="Status" type="adm:studentStatus"/>
    .
    .
    .

    <!-- definition of StudentStatus -->
    <simpleType name="studentStatus">
        .
        .
        .

    </simpleType>
    .
    .
    .

</schema>
```

In a schema document the default is typically the standard XMLSchema name-space. This enables us to use frequently occurring symbols, such as element, sim-pleType, name, and type, without a prefix. In addition, a schema document defines a number of types (e.g., studentStatus), elements (e.g., Status), and attributes (see later) that belong to a target namespace (http://xyz.edu/Admin in our case). When we define a new element or type, we use it without a prefix (for example, name="Status" and name="studentStatus") because these names are newly de-fined and hence cannot be part of the default namespace. They are automatically placed in the target namespace. However, how do we *refer* to the names defined within the same schema (for example, our reference to studentStatus in the type attribute)? If we do not use any prefix, the XML processor is supposed to assume that the name belongs to the default namespace. This is precisely what happens with the string type of the element CrsName. Since string is not prefixed, it is assumed to be taken out of the standard XMLSchema namespace, which is correct. In contrast, using studentStatus without a prefix causes the XML processor to assume that this symbol also comes from the default namespace, which is an error since XML Schema does not define studentStatus. Therefore, we need to define a namespace prefix for the target namespace and use it with every reference to a component of the target schema. The purpose of the second occurrence of the xmlns attribute of the schema element in the above example is thus to associate the prefix adm to the target namespace. From now on, we assume that the tar-get namespace has the prefix adm, and we will use it with defined types without mention.

Figure 17.7 Definition of the complex type studentType.

```
<complexType name="studentType">
    <sequence>
        <element name="Name" type="adm:personNameType"/>
        <element name="Status" type="adm:studentStatus"/>
        <element name="CrsTaken" type="adm:courseTakenType"
            minOccurs="0" maxOccurs="unbounded"/>
    </sequence>
    <attribute name="StudId" type="adm:studentId"/>
</complexType>
<complexType name="personNameType">
    <sequence>
        <element name="First" type="string"/>
        <element name="Last" type="string"/>
    </sequence>
</complexType>
```

Next, consider how one specifies the types of some attributes in our document:

```
<attribute name="Date" type="date"/>
<attribute name="StudId" type="adm:studentId"/>
<attribute name="Members" type="adm:studentIds"/>
<attribute name="CrsCode" type="adm:courseCode"/>
```

Notice that these declarations do not associate attributes with elements, so they are not very meaningful at this point. We cannot make the association here because elements that have attributes are considered to have *complex types* (even if they have empty content, such as CrsTaken), so we need to familiarize ourselves with such types first.

17.3.3 Complex Types

Basic example.   So far we have seen how to define simple types—the types of elements that do not contain attributes or children. The fragment of a schema in Figure 17.7 defines a complex type suitable for the Student element in the report document.

This simple example contains two type declarations and many new features. First, the tag complexType is used instead of simpleType to warn the XML processor of things to come. Second, the sequence tag is used to specify that the elements Name, Status, and CrsTaken must occur in the given order. Third, the CrsTaken element (whose type will be defined shortly) is said to occur zero, one, or more times. In general, we can specify any number as a value of minOccurs and maxOccurs. Doing the same with DTDs is possible but extremely awkward, since one must use alternatives (specified using |), which leads to unwieldy schemas. For other elements, we did not specify minOccurs and maxOccurs because they both default to 1 (which we want anyway). Finally, the attribute declaration at the end of the complex type definition associates StudId with the type studentId (Figure 17.8 on page 573), and, because it occurs in the scope of the definition of studentType, it means that every element of type studentType must have this attribute (and no other).

The second type declaration in Figure 17.7 supplies the type for the Name element used in the definition of studentType. This declaration does not introduce new features.

Associating a complex type with an element is no different from associating a simple type with an element. The following statement associates the Student element with the complex type studentType:

```
<element name="Student" type="adm:studentType"/>
```

Special cases. The simple picture just described is complicated by two special cases: How do we define the type of an element that has simple content (just text with no children elements) *and* has attributes, and how can we define the type of an element that has attributes but no content (defined as EMPTY in the DTD). We have seen the first kind of element in the dialog between Romeo and Apothecary on page 545; the second kind is represented by the element CrsTaken of Figure 17.6.

Defining the first type of element is a little awkward, and we skip this topic since it rarely occurs in data representation using XML. On the other hand, defining the type for elements such as CrsTaken is easy:

```
<complexType name="courseTakenType">
    <attribute name="CrsCode" type="adm:courseRef"/>
    <attribute name="Semester" type="string"/>
</complexType>
```

Combining elements into groups. The example of studentType in Figure 17.7 shows how to combine elements into an ordered group using sequence. Tags such as sequence, which describe how elements can be combined into groups, are called **compositors**; they are required when a tag has **complex content**, i.e., when the tag has at least one child element. XML Schema defines several compositors; one provides a way to combine elements into *unordered* sets. Note that the lack of a practical way to specify unordered collections of elements was one of the criticisms of DTDs in Section 17.2.5.

Suppose that we want to allow the street name, number, and the city name to appear in any order in an address. We can specify this using the compositor all:

```
<complexType name="addressType">
    <all>
        <element name="StreetName" type="string"/>
        <element name="StreetNumber" type="string"/>
        <element name="City" type="string"/>
    </all>
</complexType>
```

Unfortunately, there are a number of restrictions on all that make it hard to use in many cases. First, all must appear directly below complexType, so the following is illegal:

```
<complexType name="studentType2">
    <sequence>
        <all>
            <element name="Name" type="adm:personNameType"/>
            <element name="Status" type="adm:studentStatus"/>
        </all>
        <element name="CrsTaken" type="adm:courseTakenType"
                minOccurs="0" maxOccurs="unbounded"/>
    </sequence>
    <attribute name="StudId" type="adm:studentId"/>
</complexType>
```

Second, no element within it can be repeated. In other words, maxOccurs must be 1 for every child of all, so the following is also not allowed:

```
<complexType name="studentType3">
    <all>
        <element name="Name" type="adm:personNameType"/>
        <element name="Status" type="adm:studentStatus"/>
        <element name="CrsTaken" type="adm:courseTakenType"
                minOccurs="0" maxOccurs="unbounded"/>
    </all>
    <attribute name="StudId" type="adm:studentId"/>
</complexType>
```

The third grouping construct of XML Schema is the choice compositor, which plays the same role for complex types as union does for simple types. For instance, in the following example

```
<complexType name="addressType">
    <sequence>
        <choice>
            <element name="POBox" type="string"/>
            <sequence>
                <element name="Name" type="string"/>
                <element name="Number" type="string"/>
            </sequence>
        </choice>
        <element name="City" type="string"/>
    </sequence>
</complexType>
```

choice lets us substitute the post office box for the street address. That is, a valid address must have precisely one of the two possibilities: a post office box or a street address.

Note that a content descriptor, such as a compositor, is required even if the type contains only one child element. For instance,

```
<complexType name="foo">
    <element name="bar" type="integer"/>
</complexType>
```

is illegal, but

```
<complexType name="foo">
    <sequence>
        <element name="bar" type="integer"/>
    </sequence>
</complexType>
```

is correct.

Local element names.   In DTDs, all element declarations are global because only one ELEMENT statement per element name is allowed. Thus, it is not possible to define a valid report document (with respect to *any* DTD) where both Student and Course can have Name as a child element. Indeed, in Figure 17.4 a course name is a string while a student name has complex type personNameType. This was the primary reason for using the tag CrsName instead of Name in the report document. For the same reason, DTDs will not allow us to use the element name Course instead of the name CrsCode for the child element of Class, because the Course child inside the element Courses has a different structure than the CrsCode element inside Class. Thus, if we replace the tag name CrsCode with Course, the DTD must have two different ELEMENT statements for Course, which is impossible.

The XML Schema specification corrects this problem by providing local scope to element declarations. This is done as in any programming language. A declaration of an element type is considered local to the nearest containing <complexType ...> ... </complexType> block. In the report document, this local scoping allows us to rename the CsrName tag to Name and define the following schema:

```
<complexType name="studentType">
    <sequence>
        <element name="Name" type="adm:personNameType"/>
        <element name="Status" type="adm:studentStatus"/>
        <element name="CrsTaken" type="adm:courseTakenType"
            minOccurs="0" maxOccurs="unbounded"/>
    </sequence>
    <attribute name="StudId" type="adm:studentId"/>
</complexType>
<complexType name="courseType">
    <sequence>
```

```
            <element name="Name" type="string"/>
        </sequence>
        <attribute name="CrsCode" type="adm:courseCode"/>
    </complexType>
```

Here both studentType and courseType include a child element, Name. In the first case, this element has a complex type personNameType, which includes two elements: First and Last. In the second case, it has a simple type, string. However, unlike in a DTD the two declarations have different scope and thus their definitions do not clash.

Importing schemas.   In Section 17.3.1, we illustrated the use of the include instruction for constructing a schema out of separate components that reside in different files. This facility supports modular construction of complex XML schemas by small teams of collaborating programmers. Therefore, it requires that the namespace of an included schema be the same as the namespace of the containing schema.

At the same time, the designers of the XML Schema specification understood that the true potential of the Web can be realized only if people can pull together schemas constructed by different groups or organizations. This is the goal of the import statement. As with the include statement, the schemaLocation attribute is provided, but it is optional for import. The only required attribute is namespace, because it is possible to import schemas with different namespaces. In the absence of schemaLocation, the XML processor is supposed to find the schema on its own, possibly deriving it from the namespace using some convention. Even when schemaLocation is provided, the processor is allowed to ignore it or use a different schema. The only thing that the processor must not ignore is the namespace.

In the following example, we use import instead of include:

```
<schema xmlns="http://www.w3.org/2001/XMLSchema"
        targetNamespace="http://xyz.edu/Admin">
        xmlns:reg = "http://xyz.edu/Registrar"
        xmlns:crs = "http://xyz.edu/Courses">
   <import namespace="http://xyz.edu/Registrar"
          schemaLocation="http://xyz.edu/Registrar/StudentTypes.xsd"/>
   <import namespace="http://xyz.edu/Courses"/>
     .
     .
     .
</schema>
```

Here we assume that the instance documents containing student records and courses use different namespaces and that the report processing software knows where to find the schema for course descriptions. Therefore, the schemaLocation attribute is not provided in the second import statement (but it is in the first). The first import statement imports a schema, *Sch*, with target namespace http://xyz.edu/Registrar. The above schema attaches the prefix reg to that namespace so that it can refer to a schema element, x, defined in *Sch* as reg:x.

Deriving new complex types by extension and restriction.* In some cases, the user might need to modify parts of the included or imported schema. This is easy with inclusion because all documents are assumed to be under the author's control. With importing, however, the control is usually with an external entity and the importer might not be allowed to copy the schema, or this might not be desirable. For example, in many cases, the importer just wants to have a "view" of the original schema, so that the importer's schema would change along with that original.

XML Schema provides two mechanisms for modifying imported schema: **extension** and **restriction**. Both are special cases of the notion of *subtype* defined in Chapter 16. **Extending** a schema means adding new elements or attributes to it. **Restricting** a schema means "tightening" its definition in order to exclude some instance documents.

Suppose that foo.edu decides to follow the example of xyz.edu and "XML-ize" their registration system. Overall they like the schema of xyz.edu, but want to add a short course syllabus to every course record. Because xyz.edu is constantly improving its XML student registration tools, foo.edu decides that it can take advantage of these improvements by importing and *extending* the schema rather than copying it over. Specifically, foo.edu wants to extend the type courseType (Figure 17.9, page 574) with an additional element, syllabus. To this end, they create the following schema document:

```
<schema xmlns="http://www.w3.org/2001/XMLSchema"
        xmlns:xyzCrs="http://xyz.edu/Courses"
        xmlns:fooAdm="http://foo.edu/Admin">
        targetNamespace="http://foo.edu/Admin">
   <!-- fooAdm is the prefix to be used with the target namespace -->
   <import namespace="http://xyz.edu/Courses"/>

   <complexType name="courseType">
       <complexContent>
           <extension base="xyzCrs:courseType">
               <element name="syllabus" type="string"/>
           </extension>
       </complexContent>
   </complexType>
   <!-- Now define a Course element for the target namespace
        and associate it with the derived type -->
   <element name="Course" type="fooAdm:courseType"/>
      .
      .
      .
</schema>
```

Notice that the target namespace is now http://foo.edu/Admin—that of the client university and we associate the prefix fooAdm with it. The document uses the import statement to obtain the schema of xyz.edu to use as a basis for constructing a new schema. Since the new schema refers to the names defined in xyz.edu's namespace (such as courseType), we need to associate a prefix with the imported namespace of xyz.edu. We choose xyzCrs.

After defining the namespaces, we define a new type, courseType, using a similar type in the imported schema. The newly defined type is not prefixed, because we want it to belong to the target namespace. However, the base type imported from xyz.edu is prefixed and is referred to as xyzCrs:courseType. To signal the XML processor that a complex type is to be defined by modifying another type, the XML Schema specification requires the <complexContent> ... </complexContent> tag pair. Inside this pair, either an extension or a restriction clause is specified. We use extension in the above example, which means that the specified element, syllabus, is to be added to the contents of the type xyzCrs:courseType to form the new type courseType (in the target namespace http://foo.edu/Admin).

foo.edu might need to make other changes to the schema. For instance, they might generally like the type studentType defined in the namespace http://xyz.edu/Admin (Figure 17.8, page 573), but not that it allows students to take any number of courses (because of maxOccurs="unbounded"). Thus, foo.edu decides to limit this number to 63 by *restricting* the original schema:

```
<schema xmlns="http://www.w3.org/2001/XMLSchema"
    xmlns:xyzCrs="http://xyz.edu/Courses"
    xmlns:fooAdm="http://foo.edu/Admin">
    targetNamespace="http://foo.edu/Admin">

<import namespace="http://xyz.edu/Courses"/>
    .
    .
    .
<complexType name="studentType">
  <complexContent>
    <restriction base="xyzCrs:studentType">
      <sequence>
        <element name="Name" type="xyzCrs:personNameType"/>
        <element name="Status" type="xyzCrs:studentStatus"/>
        <element name="CrsTaken" type="xyzCrs:courseTakenType"
              minOccurs="0" maxOccurs="63"/>
      </sequence>
      <attribute name="StudId" type="xyzCrs:studentId"/>
    </restriction>
  </complexContent>
</complexType>
<!-- Now define a Student element for the target namespace
     and associate it with the derived type -->
<element name="Student" type="fooAdm:studentType"/>
    .
    .
    .
</schema>
```

Analogously to the type extension mechanism, we use the tag `restriction` inside the `complexContent` block. The important difference, however, is that, when restricting a complex type, we must repeat all the element and attribute declarations from the base type. At the same time, we can impose restrictions on the components of the base type, for instance, by replacing `maxOccurs="unbounded"` with the more restrictive `maxOccurs="63"`.

17.3.4 Putting It Together

We have seen a great number of tricks involved in schema definition. We can now combine some of the components and create a complete schema, which consists of a number of type definitions and at least one global declaration of an element—the root element of the document—which associates the name of the root element with a complex type. This type might contain declarations of other elements and attributes, which in turn associate these constructs to their types. Starting with the root element, then, we can descend into its type and find all of its elements and attributes. Repeating this recursively, we can find the elements and attributes at any depth in the document structure.

```xml
<schema xmlns="http://www.w3.org/2001/XMLSchema"
    xmlns:adm="http://xyz.edu/Admin"
    targetNamespace="http://xyz.edu/Admin">

<include schemaLocation="http://xyz.edu/StudentTypes.xsd"/>
<include schemaLocation="http://xyz.edu/CourseTypes.xsd"/>

<element name="Report" type="adm:reportType"/>

<complexType name="reportType">
  <sequence>
    <element name="Students" type="adm:studentList"/>
    <element name="Classes" type="adm:classOfferings"/>
    <element name="Courses" type="adm:courseCatalog"/>
  </sequence>
</complexType>
<complexType name="studentList">
  <sequence>
    <element name="Student" type="adm:studentType"
             minOccurs="0" maxOccurs="unbounded"/>
  </sequence>
</complexType>

<!-- Plus the definition of classOfferings, courseCatalog -->
<!-- the definition of studentType is in the included schema
     http://xyz.edu/studentTypes.xsd -->
</schema>
```

We omit the definition of the lower-level types `classOfferings` and `courseCatalog`, which are defined similarly to `studentList`. Like `studentList`, these types are defined in terms of the types shown in Figures 17.8 and 17.9.

As before, we must be careful about the namespaces, so we define `adm` as a prefix for the target namespace and use it in all references to the names defined in this schema (except in the statements that define these names using the attribute `name`). Recall that the including and included schemas are required to have the same namespace, so one prefix, `adm`, suffices to refer both to the names defined by the including schema (e.g., `adm:courseCatalog`) and the names defined in the included schemas (e.g., `adm:studentType`).

Anonymous types. All types defined so far are **named types**, because each type definition had an associated name, and every new element has an associated named type. Naming is useful when we expect to share the same type among several definitions of elements or attributes. In many cases, however, a type might be one of a kind and not expected to be reused. For instance, in the above combined schema for the report document, the type `reportType` (as well as several other types such as `studentList` and `classOfferings`) is not shared. In this case, **anonymous types** can be convenient.

Anonymous types are defined similarly to named types, except that the `name` attribute is not used and the type definition must be attached to the appropriate `element` or `attribute` definition that uses it. These definitions with attached anonymous types are also slightly different. First, they do not use the `type` attribute to introduce the anonymous type. Second, instead of the empty tags `<element ...` `/>` and `<attribute ... />`, they use tag pairs, and the definition of the anonymous type is physically enclosed by the opening and closing tag. Thus, we can change the definition of the element `Report` in our schema to use an anonymous type as follows:

```
<element name="Report">
  <complexType>
    <sequence>
      <element name="Students" type="adm:studentList"/>
      <element name="Classes" type="adm:classOfferings"/>
      <element name="Courses" type="adm:courseCatalog"/>
    </sequence>
  </complexType>
</element>
```

Similarly, we can change the definitions of the elements `Students`, `Classes`, and `Courses` to use anonymous types. In this case, the contents of the corresponding type definitions are physically included in the above schema.

17.3.5 Integrity Constraints

Earlier we touched upon the issue of referential integrity in XML documents and showed how the XML Schema specification improves upon DTDs in this regard. Even in XML Schema, however, we still use the same special types ID, IDREF, and

Figure 17.8 Student types at `http://xyz.edu/StudentTypes.xsd`.

```
<schema xmlns="http://www.w3.org/2001/XMLSchema"
            xmlns:adm="http://xyz.edu/Admin"
            targetNamespace="http://xyz.edu/Admin">

    <complexType name="studentType">
        <sequence>
            <element name="Name" type="adm:personNameType"/>
            <element name="Status" type="adm:studentStatus"/>
            <element name="CrsTaken" type="adm:courseTakenType"
                        minOccurs="0" maxOccurs="unbounded"/>
        </sequence>
        <attribute name="StudId" type="rpt:studentId"/>
    </complexType>
    <complexType name="personNameType">
        <sequence>
            <element name="First" type="string"/>
            <element name="Last" type="string"/>
        </sequence>
    </complexType>
    <simpleType name="studentStatus">
        <restriction base="string">
            <enumeration value="U1"/>
            <enumeration value="U2"/>
            .
            .
            .
            <enumeration value="G5"/>
        </restriction>
    </simpleType>

    <simpleType name="studentId">
        <restriction base="ID">
            <pattern value="[0-9]{9}"/>
        </restriction>
    </simpleType>
    <simpleType name="studentIds">
        <list itemType="studentRef"/>
    </simpleType>
    <simpleType name="studentRef">
        <restriction base="IDREF">
            <pattern value="[0-9]{9}"/>
        </restriction>
    </simpleType>
</schema>
```

Figure 17.9 Course types at `http://xyz.edu/CourseTypes.xsd`.

```
<schema xmlns="http://www.w3.org/2001/XMLSchema"
            xmlns:adm="http://xyz.edu/Admin"
            targetNamespace="http://xyz.edu/Admin">

    <complexType name="courseTakenType">
        <attribute name="CrsCode" type="adm:courseRef"/>
        <attribute name="Semester" type="string"/>
    </complexType>
    <complexType name="courseType">
        <sequence>
            <element name="Name" type="string"/>
        </sequence>
        <attribute name="CrsCode" type="adm:courseCode"/>
    </complexType>

    <simpleType name="courseCode">
        <restriction base="ID">
            <pattern value="[A-Z]{3}[0-9]{3}"/>
        </restriction>
    </simpleType>
    <simpleType name="courseRef">
        <restriction base="IDREF">
            <pattern value="[A-Z]{3}[0-9]{3}"/>
        </restriction>
    </simpleType>
</schema>
```

IDREFS that are inherited from DTDs. To illustrate the limitation of this facility, let us define the type for the element `Class` in Figure 17.4:

```
<element name="Class" type="adm:classType"/>
<complexType name="classType">
  <sequence>
    <element name="CrsCode" type="adm:courseCode"/>
    <element name="Semester" type="string"/>
    <element name="ClassRoster" type="adm:classListType"/>
  </sequence>
</complexType>
<complexType name="classListType">
  <attribute name="Members" type="adm:studentIds"/>
</complexType>
```

Clearly, if a student claims to have taken a course using a `CrsTaken` child element of `Student`, the corresponding course must have been offered in the specified semester. Such offerings are described by `Class` elements in our document. Given an element such as

```
<CrsTaken CrsCode="CS308" Semester="F1997"/>
```

then, there must exist an element of the form

```
<Class>
   <CrsCode>CS308</CrsCode><Semester>F1997</Semester>
   .
   .
   .
</Class>
```

The problem is that neither `CrsCode` nor `Semester` uniquely determines the `Class` element, so the `ID/IDREF` mechanism is inapplicable.[8] Furthermore, this mechanism does not extend to associating *groups* of values in one part of a document (such as the `CrsCode` and `Semester` attributes of the tag `CrsTaken`) with groups of values in another part (the child elements `CrsCode` and `Semester` of the element `Class`). This is a familiar problem, which in databases is solved using multi-attribute keys.

XML keys.   To address the above problems, the XML Schema specification allows general multi-attribute keys and foreign key constraints in a way that resembles SQL. There is a slight complication, however. SQL deals with flat relations, so to specify a key we simply list the attributes that belong to that key. Similarly, to specify a foreign key constraint in SQL we simply specify a sequence of attributes in both the referencing and the referenced relation. In XML, we are dealing with complex structures, and the notion of a key is more involved. Indeed, a key might be composed of a sequence of values located at different depths inside an element.

Assuming that the frame of reference is the parent element of the `Class` elements, we can say that the key of the collection of `Class` elements is composed of values reachable using the pair of path expressions `Class/CrsCode` and `Class/Semester`. The idea of path expressions is familiar to us from Chapter 16, but in XML they take a more elaborate form. In fact, XML path expressions are part of another specification, called **XPath**, which we study in Section 17.4.1.

To see how complicated a key specification can be, let us expand the definition of `Class` by adding sections and splitting the season from the year in semester names:

```
<Class>
   <CrsCode Section="2">CS308</CrsCode>
   <Semester><Season>Fall</Season><Year>1997</Year></Semester>
   .
   .
   .
</Class>
```

---

[8] In XML Schema, the types ID and IDREF are not restricted to attributes.

Here the set of values that uniquely determines the class is scattered in different places (attributes, element content) and at different levels (in the `Section` attribute of the tag `CrsCode`, in the content of the tag `CrsCode`, in the `Season` child of the `Semester` element, and in the `Year` child of `Semester`). The path expressions needed to reach each of these components are specified in XPath as follows:

```
CrsCode/@Section
CrsCode
Semester/Season
Semester/Year
```

All of these path expressions are relative to `Class` elements in the report document. The first selects the value of the attribute `Section` of the tag `CrsCode`, which must be a child of the current element (assumed to be `Class`). The second selects the content of the `CrsCode` element (i.e., the text between the `<CrsCode>` and `</CrsCode>` tags). The third selects the content of the element `Season`, which must be a child of the element `Semester`, which must be a child of the current element, and similarly for the fourth expression.

XML Schema provides two ways to specify a key. One uses the tag `unique` and is similar to the UNIQUE constraint in SQL; it specifies *candidate keys*, in the terminology of Chapter 4. The other uses the tag `key` and corresponds to the PRIMARY KEY constraint in SQL. In XML, the only difference between `unique` and `key` is that keys cannot have *null values*. (In XML, the value of an element of the form `<footag></footag>` is an empty string and not necessarily a null.) For `footag` to have a null value (called a **nil** in XMLSchema) the following is used:

```
<footag xsi:nil="true"></footag>
```

Here `nil` is a symbol defined in the namespace

```
http://www.w3.org/2001/XMLSchema-instance
```

(and we assume that `xsi` is a prefix that has been defined to refer to that namespace).

Next is an example of a primary key declaration for the `report` document. Declaring candidate keys is similar, except that the tag `unique` is used instead of the tag `key`. Referring to the type `classType` defined at the beginning of this section, we want to specify that the pair of values of tags `CrsCode` and `Semester` uniquely identifies the `Class` element within the document. This is achieved as follows:

```
<schema xmlns="http://www.w3.org/2001/XMLSchema"
        xmlns:adm="http://xyz.edu/Admin">
        targetNamespace="http://xyz.edu/Admin">

  <element name="Report" type="adm:reportType"/>

  <complexType name="reportType">
    <sequence>
      <element name="Students" type="adm:studentList"/>
      <element name="Classes">
```

```
        <!-- Replacing adm:classOfferings with anonymous type -->
        <complexType>
          <sequence>
          <element name="Class" type="adm:classType"
                    minOccurs="0" maxOccurs="unbounded"/>
          </sequence>
        </complexType>
      </element>
      <element name="Courses" type="adm:courseCatalog"/>
    </sequence>

    <key name="PrimaryKeyForClass">
      <selector xpath="Classes/Class"/>
      <field xpath="CrsCode"/>
      <field xpath="Semester"/>
    </key>
  </complexType>

  <complexType name="classType">
    <sequence>
      <element name="CrsCode" type="adm:courseCode"/>
      <element name="Semester" type="string"/>
      <element name="ClassRoster" type="adm:classListType"/>
    </sequence>
  </complexType>
    .
    .
    .
</schema>
```

The above schema lists the relevant type definitions for our report document. The namespace declarations and the type classType have already been discussed. The type reportType is used for the topmost document element, Report. It is a sequence of three elements: Students, Classes, and Courses. The type for Students was defined at the beginning of Section 17.3.4. For easier reference, we expanded the type of the element Classes into an anonymous type and attached it directly to that element. The definition of courseCatalog, the type for the element Courses, is an easy exercise.

The most interesting feature here is the key declaration specified with a key tag and the attribute name indicating PrimaryKeyForClass. Observe that the key declaration appears in the definition of reportType rather than in that of classType, even though the key involves only the classType components. This is intentional, to illustrate the point that XML key declarations are associated with collections of objects (which typically are sets of elements) rather than with types. The xpath attribute of the selector tag specifies a path expression, which identifies the collection of objects to which the key declaration applies. This collection does not need to correspond to a single type. For instance, an XPath expression can return a hetero-geneous set of elements that belong to two or more distinct types (e.g., the union of CrsTaken and Class—see Section 17.4.1). Thus, in XML a key does not need to be associated with a particular single type—quite unlike what we have seen so far.[9] In our case, the selecting path expression is Classes/Class, which is relative to the type reportType. The collection identified by the selector is simply the set of all Class elements in the document (which happens to coincide with the set of all elements of type classType).

Having identified the appropriate collection of objects, we use the subsequent field elements to specify the fields that constitute the key. As explained earlier, these fields can come from different places in an object and can be nested in complex ways. In our case, however, things are simple: The first field in the key is the contents of the child element CrsCode of the element Class, and the second field is the contents of the child element Semester. (Path expressions specified in the xpath attribute of the field clause are relative to the collection of the objects determined by the selector. This is why, for example, the first path expression is simply CrsCode rather than Classes/Class/CrsCode.) Note that, for a path expression to make sense as a specification of a field in a key, it must return precisely one value for each object to which it applies. For instance, the path expression CrsCode returns precisely one value for any given Class element, so the field specification

```
<selector xpath="Classes/Class"/>
<field xpath="CrsCode"/>
    .
    .
    .
```

is allowed. In contrast, the path expression CrsTaken/@CrsCode within the scope of a Student element can return a set of courses taken by the student (refer to studentType defined in Figure 17.8 on page 573), so the field specification

```
<selector xpath="Students/Student"/>
<field xpath="CrsTaken/@CrsCode"/>
    .
    .
    .
```

is not allowed.

Foreign key constraints in XML.   Next, we want to be able to state that every element CrsTaken in a student record refers to an actual class element in the same report. This is akin to a foreign key constraint and is defined using the keyref element, as depicted in Figure 17.10.

A foreign key constraint has a name, a reference identifier, a selector, and a list of fields. Its name is of little importance here. The reference is defined using the attribute refer, and its value must match the name of a key or unique constraint. In our case, it matches the key constraint, PrimaryKeyForClass, for Class elements.

---

[9] Recall that, in the relational model, a key is defined for collections of tuples of a particular schema. In the E-R model, a key is defined for a particular entity or relationship type.

Figure 17.10 Part of a schema with a key and a foreign-key constraint.

```
<schema xmlns="http://www.w3.org/2001/XMLSchema"
    xmlns:adm="http://xyz.edu/Admin">
    targetNamespace="http://xyz.edu/Admin">

  <complexType name="courseTakenType">
    <attribute name="CrsCode" type="adm:courseRef"/>
    <attribute name="Semester" type="string"/>
  </complexType>
  <complexType name="classType">
    <sequence>
      <element name="CrsCode" type="adm:courseCode"/>
      <element name="Semester" type="string"/>
      <element name="ClassRoster" type="adm:classListType"/>
    </sequence>
  </complexType>

  <complexType name="reportType">
    <sequence>
      <element name="Students" type="adm:studentList"/>
      <element name="Classes" type="adm:classOfferings"/>
      <element name="Courses" type="adm:courseCatalog"/>
    </sequence>

    <key name="PrimaryKeyForClass">
      <selector xpath="Classes/Class"/>
      <field xpath="CrsCode"/>
      <field xpath="Semester"/>
    </key>
    <keyref name="NoBogusTranscripts" refer="adm:PrimaryKeyForClass">
      <selector xpath="Students/Student/CrsTaken"/>
      <field name="@CrsCode"/>
      <field name="@Semester"/>
    </keyref>
  </complexType>
</schema>
```

In SQL, this corresponds to the REFERENCES *relation-name* part of a foreign key constraint. Next comes the selector. As in the case of the key constraint, it identifies a **source collection** of elements through its xpath attribute. In our case, the collection in question consists of all CrsTaken elements. Each of these is supposed to reference the key of an object from the **target collection** specified in the key constraint PrimaryKeyForClass.

Finally, we have to specify the foreign key itself, that is, the fields inside the CrsTaken elements (the source collection) that actually reference the fields in the target collection (specified in the key constraint). We do this using the already familiar field tag. As before, this tag provides a path expression (relative to the selected collection of objects) that leads to a value. We want the attributes CrsCode and Semester of the source collection of CrsTaken elements to refer to the fields that constitute the key of the target collection of Class elements. In XPath, we use the path expressions @CrsCode and @Semester to identify these attributes (Figure 17.9). As with fields that form a key, the value of the path expression on any object in the source collection must be unique.

In a similar way, we can specify other key and foreign key constraints in the report document, and replace the constraints previously specified, using the ID and IDREF data types (see exercises 17.5 and 17.7). On the other hand, it is not clear how to specify IDREFS-style referential integrity with the help of the key and keyref tags. For instance, the attribute Members in ClassRoster (at the beginning of Section 17.3.5) has the type studentIds, which is a list of values of type studentRef. Since studentRef is derived by restriction from the base type IDREF (see Figure 17.8 on page 573), studentIds can be seen as a specialized version of IDREFS. We can *try* to specify the desired referential integrity using something like this:

```
<keyref name="RosterToStudIdRef" refer="adm:studentKey">
  <selector xpath="Classes/Class"/>
  <field xpath="ClassRoster/@Members"/>
</keyref>
```

where studentKey is an appropriate key constraint for Student elements. The problem here is that the value of the attribute Members is a *list* while the value of the key attribute StudId in the Student tag is a *single* item. However, it is not possible in XPath to create a reference from the individual components of a list data type (represented by the Members attribute) to other entities in the document (i.e., student Ids defined in the Student elements). The only solution is to use a representation where student Ids are not in a list but occur as individual elements (exercise 17.9).

17.4 XML QUERY LANGUAGES

Why would you want to query an XML document? Will databases soon begin to store XML and speak it fluently?

Storing XML documents in a database specifically designed for this kind of data is not out of the question—methods exist for efficient storage and retrieval of tree-structured objects, including XML documents [Deutsch et al. 1999, Zhao and Joseph 2000]. However, in all likelihood XML documents are going to be stored by mapping them to an existing relational or object-oriented format. On the other hand, recent offerings from all major DBMS vendors already *speak* XML. They can receive XML documents and convert them into relations or objects and provide tools for generating XML from the data already stored in relations or objects. Once generated, an XML document is transmitted to another machine, which either presents it to the user or processes it automatically. To help with this task, the WWW Consortium has developed **document object model** (**DOM**) for XML [DOM 2000], which standardizes the interface by which a client application can access various parts of an XML document and thereby simplifies the task of writing such applications.

What does a query language have to do with all this? Imagine that you are preparing your next semester's schedule and need to find all courses offered in that semester between 3 P.M. and 7 P.M. If the university database server lets you pose such a query, you are in good shape, but more likely it provides a fixed interface that supports only a limited set of queries. In this case, finding what you want might require a tedious process of filling out a series of forms and eyeballing the results, and you might also have to use low-tech instruments, such as pen and paper, to record the needed information.

An alternative is to ask the server for an XML document containing the list of all courses offered this semester and have a client application find the desired information. As mentioned earlier, DOM simplifies this task considerably. Still, it provides only a low-level interface to XML. If your query requires joining information stored in different parts of the document or in separate documents, you might end up writing a fairly large program (and the semester will be over by the time you debug it). An analogy here is using nested loops and if statements to replace a complex SQL query. We will see how a powerful, high-level query language can simplify this task, enabling a new class of client applications capable of processing information in an intelligent and custom-tailored way.

In the remainder of this section, we discuss three query languages for XML: **XPath** [XPath 1999], **XSLT** [XSL 1999], and **XQuery** [XQuery 2001], which is currently work in progress by the W3C Working Group on XML Query Language and will eventually become an official W3C recommendation. XQuery is a successor to the language known as Quilt, described in [Chamberlin et al. 2000, Robie et al. 2000].

XPath is intended to be simple and efficient. It is based on the idea of path expressions, with which we became familiar in Chapter 16, and is designed so that queries are compact and can be incorporated into URLs. Combined URL/XPath expressions became part of the **XPointer** specification [XPointer 2000], which we also introduce briefly. XSLT, on the other hand, is a full-blown programming language with powerful (albeit still limited) query capabilities. In contrast, XQuery is an SQL-style query language designed in the database tradition. It has the most powerful and elegant query capabilities among the languages presented in this section.

17.4.1 XPath: A Lightweight XML Query Language

In an object-oriented language, such as OQL (Section 16.4.2), a path expression is a sequence of object attributes that provides the exact route to a data element nested deep within the object structure. The requirement to provide an exact route is not a problem when the schema of the database is known to the programmer and is not likely to change. However, when the schema is not known and the structure of data needs to be explored (which is often the case in Web applications), merely adopting path expressions from object-oriented languages is not enough.

XPath extends path expressions with query facilities, by allowing the programmer to replace parts of the route to data elements with search conditions. By then examining the data, the XPath interpreter is supposed to find the missing parts of the route at run time. The idea of augmenting path expressions with queries is not new. It appeared in [Kifer and Lausen 1989, Kifer et al. 1992, Frohn et al. 1994] in the context of object-oriented databases and was further developed in works on semistructured data, such as [Buneman et al. 1996, Abiteboul et al. 1997, Deutsch et al. 1998, Abiteboul et al. 2000]. XPath was built on these ideas and became an important basis for many XML extensions.

The XPath data model.   XPath views XML documents as trees and elements, attributes, comments, and text as nodes of those trees. There is a special **root node** in the tree, which should not be confused with the root element of an XML document. This is illustrated in Figure 17.11, which depicts the following XML document:

```
<?xml version="1.0" ?>
<!-- Some comment -->
<Students>
    <Student StudId="111111111">
        <Name><First>John</First><Last>Doe</Last></Name>
        <Status>U2</Status>
        <CrsTaken CrsCode="CS308" Semester="F1997"/>
        <CrsTaken CrsCode="MAT123" Semester="F1997"/>
    </Student>
    <Student StudId="987654321">
        <Name><First>Bart</First><Last>Simpson</Last></Name>
        <Status>U4</Status>
        <CrsTaken CrsCode="CS308" Semester="F1994"/>
    </Student>
</Students>
<!-- Some other comment -->
```

(This document is a fragment of the report document in Figure 17.4, page 547.)

Note that the root node of the XPath tree is different from the node that corresponds to Students, which is the root element of the document. The need for the special root node is apparent from the figure: It serves as a gathering point for all of the document components, including the comments that are allowed to occur outside the scope of the root element.

As usual in a tree, every node except the root node has a parent. A node, *P*, immediately above another node, *C*, is the **parent** of that node, and *C* is a **child** of *P*. However, the XPath specification has an important and sometimes confusing exception: An attribute is *not considered a child of its parent node*. That is, if *C* corresponds to an attribute of *P*, then *P* is a parent of *C*, but *C* is not a child

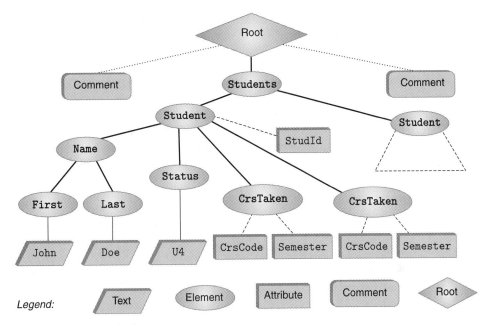

Legend:

| Text | Element | Attribute | Comment | Root |

Figure 17.11 XPath document tree.

of P. Because of the potential confusion due to the peculiar XPath terminology, we use the standard terminology for tree data structures and do regard attributes as children of their parents. To avoid ambiguity, we sometimes talk about e-**children**, a-**children**, and t-**children** when we want to restrict attention to the particular type of children: elements, attributes, or text. For example, Name is an e-child of Student, StudId is an a-child of Student, and John is a t-child of First. When we want to include both element children and text children, we refer to et-**children**. Similarly, ta-**children** refers to text and attribute children, and so on.

The XPath data model provides operators for navigating the document tree and accessing its various components. These operations include accessing the root, the parent of a node, its children, the contents of an element, the value of an attribute, and the like.

We saw some of these operators when we discussed constraints in XML schemas. The basic syntax is that of the UNIX file naming schema: The symbol / represents the root node, . represents the current node, and .. represents the parent node. An XPath expression takes a document tree and returns a set of nodes in the tree. Thus, /Students/Student/CrsTaken is an **absolute path expression** that returns the set of references to nodes that correspond to the elements CrsTaken, which are reachable from the root through a Students child and a Student grandchild. Our tree has three such CrsTaken nodes (one is not shown in the figure). If the current node corresponds to the element Name, then First and ./First both refer to the same child element. If the current node corresponds to the element First, then

../Last is the sibling node corresponding to the element Last. These are **relative path expressions**, since their departure point for navigation is not the root.

To access an attribute, the symbol @ is used. For instance, the set of values of the attribute CrsCode in the above document is obtained using the path expression /Students/Student/CrsTaken/@CrsCode. In our case, this set consists of CS308 and MAT123. Text nodes are accessed using the text() function. For instance, /Students/Student/Name/First/text() represents the collection of nodes, each representing the text content of an element of type First. We have two such nodes in our document; one corresponds to John and the other Bart. If you were wondering, the two comment nodes in the above document can be selected using the expression /comment().

Advanced navigation in XPath. The more advanced features of XPath navigation include facilities to select specific nodes of an XML document as well as facilities to jump through an indeterminate number of children. For instance, to select the second course taken by John Doe, we use the expression /Students/Student[1]/CrsTaken[2]. Here, [1] selects the first of the two Student nodes in the document tree. The expression /Students/Student[1]/CrsTaken then selects all nodes corresponding to CrsTaken in that first Student node. Finally, [2] selects the second of these nodes. Another example of selection of a particular node is /Students/Student/CrsTaken[last()], which is similar to the above except that the main part selects all nodes that correspond to CrsTaken and [last()] selects the last of these nodes in the standard XML ordering of the document components (which is basically an ordering obtained by the depth-first traversal of the document tree). In our case, it selects

```
<CrsTaken CrsCode="CS308" Semester="F1994"/>
```

At times, we might not know the exact structure of the document or specifying the exact navigation path might be cumbersome, so XPath provides several wildcard facilities. One is the *descendant-or-self* operation, //, illustrated by the expression //CrsTaken, which selects all CrsTaken elements in the entire tree. In our particular case, the effect is the same as that produced by /Students/Student/CrsTaken. However, if the document contains elements CrsTaken nested under different types of elements and at different depths, then selecting all such elements without a wildcard is hard and unwieldy.

The descendant operation can be used in relative expressions as well. For instance, .//CrsTaken searches through all descendants of the current node to find the CrsTaken elements.[10] XPath also allows a search through all ancestors (parent, grandparent, etc.) of any given node, but we skip this feature.

---

[10] Note that ./CrsTaken and CrsTaken are the same. However, .//CrsTaken, CrsTaken, and //CrsTaken are all different: the first expression returns all CrsTaken descendants at the current node, the second only the CrsTaken children at the current node, and the third all CrsTaken elements found anywhere in the document.

The third wildcard, *, lets us collect all *e*-children of a node irrespective of type. For instance, `Student/*` selects all *e*-children of the `Student` children of the current node. (In our case, where the current node is the (only) `Students` node, the wildcard selects the two `Name` nodes, the two `Status` nodes, and the three `CrsTaken` nodes.) The expression `/*//*` selects all *e*-grandchildren of the root and their *e*-descendants.

The * wildcard can also be applied to attributes. For instance, `CrsTaken/@*` selects all attributes of the `CrsTaken` nodes that sit below the current node. Note that * does not include the text nodes that could possibly exist among the children of the `Student` element. To select those, the expression `Student/text()` is used.

XPath queries.   We are particularly interested in the features of XPath that give it the ability to select nodes using a query facility. XPath queries are selection conditions that can be applied at any step in the navigation process. To give meaningful examples of XPath expressions with queries, we go back to our report document in Figure 17.4, page 547.

Here is a simple example of a path expression that selects all student nodes where the student has taken a course in Fall 1994:

```
//Student[CrsTaken/@Semester = "F1994"]
```

Here we have a wildcard expression, `//Student`, that selects all `Student` nodes under the root node. The expression inside the square brackets is a **selection condition** that eliminates the nodes that do not satisfy the condition by selecting only those `Student` nodes where the path expression `CrsTaken/@Semester` can be applied and where it returns a set that *includes* F1994.[11] To select elements based on the contents of an element rather than of an attribute, we use the following expression:

```
//Student[Status = "U3" and starts-with(.//Last, "P")
          and not(.//Last = .//First)]
```

This example introduces several features. First, selection conditions can be combined using and, or, and not. Second, to select an element based on the contents of one of its children or descendants, we simply equate the appropriate path expression with another such expression or a constant. Third, XPath has a rich repertoire of various functions that greatly increase its expressive power. For the full list of these functions, we refer you to the XPath specification [XPath 1999].

In the above example, we use the function `starts-with()` to select only those students whose last name starts with P. To summarize the above query, it selects all students who have the status U3, whose last name starts with P, and whose last and first names are different. The other string manipulation functions allow us to check for containment, perform concatenation, determine length, and so forth. For instance, the following query can be used to search for students who have van as part of their name:

---

[11] Note that if a `Student` node has several `CrsToken` children, then the path expression `CrsTaken/@Semester` returns a *set* of nodes.

```
//Student[contains(concat(Name//text()), "van")]
```

Here Name//text() returns the set of all text nodes below the Name element and the concatenation function makes one string out of those nodes—in this case the student's first and last names. Then we check if the result contains van as a substring.

Aggregate functions available in XPath include sum() and count(). For example, the following selects the students who have taken at least five courses:

```
//Student[count(CrsTaken) &gt;= 5]
```

In this expression, CrsTaken returns the set of all *e*-children of type CrsTaken for the current node (which must be a Student node). Thus, Count(CrsTaken) returns the number of these children, which is compared with 5. The obscure >= contraption, stands for >=. This complication is due to the fact that the symbols < and > must be encoded as < and > because they are reserved for tag delimiters.

It should be noted that selection conditions can be applied at different levels and multiple times in a path expression. Thus, the following is legal:

```
//Student[Status="U4"]/CrsTaken[@CrsCode="CS305"]
```

This expression selects all the CrsTaken elements in the document, that occur in Student elements with status U4 and whose CrsCode attribute has the value CS305.

Multiple selection conditions can also be applied at the same level in a path expression, as shown in the following expression which selects all Student elements such that the student took (among other courses) MAT123 in fall 1994:

```
//Student[CrsTaken/@CrsCode="MAT123"]
          [CrsTaken/@Semester="F1994"]
```

The same expression can be written as

```
//Student[CrsTaken/@CrsCode="MAT123"
          and CrsTaken/Semester="F1994"]
```

The or connective—for example, CrsTaken/@CrsCode="MAT123" or CrsTaken/@Semester="F1994"—is also allowed.

There is one other interesting form of selection condition. Suppose that Grade is an optional attribute of CrsTaken. Then

```
//Student[CrsTaken/@Grade]
```

selects all students who have a CrsTaken element with an explicitly specified Grade attribute (regardless of its value). Likewise,

```
//Student[Name/First or CrsTaken]
```

selects those Student elements that have either the element First as a grandchild or the element CrsTaken as a child.

Finally, recall that SQL allows the use of algebraic query operators, such as UNION and EXCEPT. XPath, being a frugal language, allows only the union operator, which is denoted by the symbol |, as in the expression

```
//CrsTaken[@Semester="F1994"] | //Class[Semester="F1994"]
```

The set of nodes selected by this query is a union of elements of different types: The CrsTaken elements pertain to the fall 1994 semester, and the Class elements that describe fall 1994 course offerings. This illustrates how a path expression can return a set containing elements of different types.

XPointer—a Smarter URL. With all of its interesting features, XPath is not an expressive query language. It cannot express joins and is basically suitable only for navigation within tree-structured documents. However, it is precisely this narrow scope that makes XPath suitable as a plug-in component for many XML applications. In Section 17.3.5, we used XPath to express constraints in XML schemas. Its other popular application is to enrich URLs with a simple query facility. A number of extensions to XPath have been developed to facilitate such applications and are going to be standardized in a forthcoming XPointer recommendation from W3C.

XPointer mutated out of the union of URLs and XPath. To understand how XPointer is used, suppose that we need to create a hyperlink from one document to a particular place in another document. Such links are routine in today's HTML documents—a typical example is a table of contents, where clicking on a particular link inside the table takes the user to the corresponding section. In HTML, linking into the middle of a document is done by marking a particular place with an anchor,[12] for example, interesting-place, and then referencing it with the URL syntax *document-url*#interesting-place. The problem is that it is possible to create such a link only if the document author has created the appropriate anchors in advance—an outside viewer of a document cannot arbitrarily bookmark places of interest in a document.

This is where XPath comes in. The idea is to allow the user to concatenate a URL and a path expression. The browser then retrieves the document using the URL and finds the desired place using the path expression. This is precisely what an xpointer is; more specifically, it is an expression of the form:

$$\textit{someURL}\#\texttt{xpointer}(XPathExpr_1)\texttt{xpointer}(XPathExpr_2)\ldots$$

which is processed as follows: First the document at URL *someURL* is found. Then $XPathExpr_1$ is evaluated against it. If a nonempty set of document tree nodes is returned, we are done. Otherwise, $XPathExpr_2$ is tried. If it fails to return a nonempty set, the next path expression is tried, and so on. For instance, assuming that the document in Figure 17.4, page 547, is at URL http://www.foo.edu/Report.xml, we can link directly to the second student transcript as follows:

```
http://www.foo.edu/Report.xml#xpointer(//Student[2])
```

XPointer would be only half-useful if it were not for the ability of XPath to select document nodes based on queries. For instance, we can easily extract the fall 1994 class of MAT123:

---

[12] In HTML, this is specified using the tag <A name="...">.

```
http://www.foo.edu/Report.xml#
            xpointer(//Student[CrsTaken/@CrsCode="MAT123"
                            and CrsTaken/@Semester="F1994"])
```

(This expression should be written in one line; it occupies several lines in the text because of formatting limitations.)

To conclude, we mention that XPointer defines a number of extensions to XPath, such as ranges of document nodes, which we do not discuss here. The interested reader is referred to [XPointer 2000].

17.4.2 XSLT: A Transformation Language for XML*

XSL Transformation (**XSLT**) is a transformation language that is part of **XSL**, the **extensible stylesheet language** of XML. Its original intent was to be a language for converting XML documents into HTML in order to display them with ordinary browsers. However, it is a general transformation language that can produce any type of document (HTML, XML, plaintext) from an XML source. In this capacity, XSLT can be used to query XML documents.

As a query language, XSLT is different from what we have seen so far in this book. Relational algebra, described in Chapter 6, is an **imperative** language, where queries are constructed by specifying the exact sequence of operations that must be performed to obtain the answer. SQL and QBE, discussed in Chapters 6 and 7, are based on relational calculus, which is a subset of predicate logic, and thus belong to the **declarative** group of languages (sometimes called the **logic programming** group). OQL, the object-oriented query language of ODMG discussed in Chapter 16, belongs to the same category.

In these languages, the user specifies the required information and its relationship to the database sources, from which the system must then obtain that information. XSLT, on the other hand, is a **functional** programming language that uses the syntax of XML. Similarly to SQL (and unlike relational algebra), the user specifies the required result indirectly but, instead of a logic-based language such as relational calculus, the result is specified using a collection of recursive functions. Query languages based on functional programming are almost as old as those based on algebra and logic [Shipman 1981]. However, prior to XSLT they had difficulty gaining a foothold in the database world.

XSLT is only one of the two components of XSL. The other is a *formatting* language, which specifies the look of a document when it is rendered in a browser or on paper. The overall process of rendering an XML document consists of transforming it into another document that augments the original document with rendering instructions. The result might lose some of the original contents (e.g., to make it usable in a PDA, such as a Palm Pilot) or it might gain extra content (e.g., a table of contents). When XSL formatting is used, the output document will be in XML format, which can be displayed by some browsers or word processors. Alternatively, XSLT can be used alone to transform input XML documents into a completely different format, such as HTML (to be rendered by an ordinary browser) or LaTeX (for high-quality paper documents).

Formatting is not the subject of this section. Instead, we concentrate on XSLT and, especially, on its use as a query language. Furthermore, we focus on the most interesting of XSLT query capabilities—pattern-based document transformations—and refer the reader to [Kay 2000, XSL 1999] for full details on XSLT.

XSLT basics.   An XSLT program (usually called a **stylesheet**) specifies a transformation of one type of document into another type. As before, we illustrate its various features using the tried and true report document in Figure 17.4, page 547. To process a document, an XML processor needs to know the location of the corresponding stylesheet. This is specified using the xml-stylesheet processing instruction, which must occur in the document **preamble**, between the initial <?xml ... ?> instruction and the first XML tag. For instance, to supply a stylesheet for our report, the document should start as follows:

```
<?xml version="1.0" ?>
<?xml-stylesheet type="text/xsl"
                 href="http://xyz.edu/Report/report.xsl" ?>
<Report Date="2000-12-12">
   .
   .
   .
</Report>
```

The type attribute in the xml-stylesheet instruction says that the stylesheet is a text XSL document, so the XML processor can choose the appropriate parser. The href attribute specifies the stylesheet location. The processor then fetches the stylesheet from the specified site and transforms the document accordingly.

Here is an example of a stylesheet that takes a report (such as the one in Figure 17.4) and extracts the list of all students:

```
<?xml version="1.0" ?>
<StudentList xmlns:xsl="http://www.w3.org/1999/XSL/Transform"
             xsl:version="1.0">
     <xsl:copy-of select="//Student/Name"/>
</StudentList>
```

The effect of the transformation defined by this stylesheet on our report is the following document:

```
<StudentList>
    <Name><First>John</First><Last>Doe</Last></Name>
    <Name><First>Joe</First><Last>Public</Last></Name>
    <Name><First>Bart</First><Last>Simpson</Last></Name>
</StudentList>
```

A stylesheet consists of "examples," which are tags defined in the stylesheet (such as StudentList in our case) and **XSLT instructions** (such as copy-of). The examples are simply copied to the result document, while the instructions extract data items from the source document and place them in the result document. Observe that when viewed as an XML document, our stylesheet has StudentList as its root tag. Thus, like most XML documents, the root tag of a stylesheet contains the declaration of a namespace. StudentList also contains the version attribute required by XSLT. (The XSLT-mandated attributes and the namespace declaration are not copied to the result document.)

The xmlns declaration associates the prefix xsl—a conventional prefix used with XSLT—with the standard namespace that defines the XSLT vocabulary. This vocabulary includes copy-of and other XSLT instructions that we will see shortly. For a rather subtle reason, we cannot use the namespace of XSLT as a default. If we did, StudentList would belong to it (according to the scoping rules for namespace declarations). However, this identifier does not exist in the namespace http://www.w3.org/1999/XSL/Transform and, in fact, was invented just for this example to serve as a top-level tag of the result document.

The copy-of statement is an XSLT instruction that simply copies the elements selected by the XPath expression specified in the select attribute. In our example, the path expression selects all the Name elements that are children of Student, which produces the list of Name elements shown above.

XSLT includes a number of conditional and looping instructions, such as if (an "if-then" without the "else"), choose (an enhanced version of the switch statement in C/C++ and Java), and for-each. Here is an example that uses some of these features:

```
<?xml version="1.0" ?>
<StudentList xmlns:xsl="http://www.w3.org/1999/XSL/Transform"
             xsl:version="1.0">

   <xsl:for-each select="//Student">
     <xsl:if test="count(CrsTaken) &gt; 1">
       <FullName>
         <!-- Last is two levels below Student; use * to skip one level -->
         <xsl:value-of select="*/Last"/>,
         <xsl:value-of select="*/First"/>
       </FullName>
     </xsl:if>
   </xsl:for-each>
</StudentList>
```

The result of applying this transformation to our report is as follows:

```
<StudentList>
   <FullName>
     Doe, John
     Public, Joe
   </FullName>
</StudentList>
```

The for-each statement selects the nodes specified by the corresponding path expression (the set of all Student elements in our case) and then applies the statements that appear inside the `for-each` element. For each student, this program first checks if the student has taken more than one course. (As discussed before, we must encode > using its XML notation, `&gt;`.) Our document has only two students who satisfy this condition: John Doe and Joe Public, for each of whom a block of example tags, `<FullName>` ... `</FullName>`, is copied from the stylesheet to the result document.

Next, we break the structure of the `Name` element in our report and extract the last and first names, discarding the tags. The student names are then displayed in an unstructured textual form. Extraction of the textual contents of an element is achieved using the XSLT instruction `value-of`, which works similarly to `copy-of` except that it extracts the contents of an element rather than the element itself. Had we used `copy-of` instead, the result would have been different:

```
<StudentList>
    <FullName>
        <Last>Doe</Last>, <First>John</First>
        <Last>Public</Last>, <First>Joe</First>
    </FullName>
</StudentList>
```

XSLT templates. The procedural features of XSLT seem powerful, but they are not adequate for dealing with all XML documents. The problem is that the `for-each` instruction can iterate over elements selected by a path expression, but it cannot recursively descend into these elements and transform the document on the way. Since XML documents can be arbitrarily deep, recursive traversal of their structure is essential to extract the desired information. The traversal of XML trees is provided by **pattern-based templates**. The `StudentList` stylesheet described earlier uses a simplified syntax that is a shorthand for the following template:

```
<?xml version="1.0" ?>
<xsl:stylesheet xmlns:xsl="http://www.w3.org/1999/XSL/Transform"
                xsl:version="1.0">
    <xsl:template match="/">
        <StudentList>
            <xsl:for-each select="//Student">
                .......
            </xsl:for-each>
        </StudentList>
    </xsl:template>
</xsl:stylesheet>
```

Essentially, the old stylesheet is wrapped here with the `<xsl:template match="/">`...`</xsl:template>` tag pair, which say that the example part and the instructions in the body of the stylesheet should be applied in the context of the root node of the document.

An XSLT template is a transformation function, which is usually recursively defined in terms of other templates. Inside, a template can use the procedural features

Figure 17.12   Recursive stylesheet.

```xml
<?xml version="1.0" ?>
<xsl:stylesheet xmlns:xsl="http://www.w3.org/1999/XSL/Transform"
                xsl:version="1.0">
  <xsl:template match="/">
    <StudentList>
      <xsl:apply-templates/>
    </StudentList>
  </xsl:template>
  <xsl:template match="//Student">
    <xsl:if test="count(CrsTaken) &gt; 1">
      <FullName>
        <xsl:value-of select="*/Last"/>,
        <xsl:value-of select="*/First"/>
      </FullName>
    </xsl:if>
  </xsl:template>
  <xsl:template match="text()">
    <!-- Empty template -->
  </xsl:template>
</xsl:stylesheet>
```

we have seen already (copy-of, for-each, etc.) or it can call other templates. The interesting aspect of these calls is that typically templates are not called directly but are invoked when their associated XPath expressions match the current node in the document tree.[13] Figure 17.12 shows a template program that achieves the same result as that of the previous stylesheet, which we formulated with the help of the for-each statement. Although the new stylesheet is more complex than the earlier one, it is simple enough and illustrates the main ideas.

The evaluation starts by matching the root node of the document tree in Figure 17.11, page 583, to a path expression specified in the match attribute of one of the templates. In our case, the only expression that matches the root is / in the first template. This template emits the StudentList tag pair, sets the **current** node to the root of the tree, and recursively calls other templates using the apply-templates instruction. The result of this call will be inserted between the StudentList tag pair.

The apply-templates instruction drives the recursive traversal of the document tree. It constructs the set of all *et*-children (i.e., *it ignores the attributes*) of the current context node and applies a matching template to each child.[14]

---

[13] XSLT also has *named templates*, which are called explicitly. However, we do not discuss this mechanism.

[14] These templates are applied independently of each other, but the results are output in the order in which the children appear in the XML tree.

The only *et*-child of the root node is the Students element, and, since our stylesheet does not appear to have a template that matches this node, we seem to be at a dead end. To get out of this complication, we can specify the following template:

```
<xsl:template match="*|/">
    <xsl:apply-templates/>
</xsl:template>
```
(17.2)

which matches any e-node (because of *) or the root node (because of /) and so is applicable. Fortunately, this template is the *default* that XSLT applies when no other template matches the current element node, so we do not have to specify it explicitly (the default for text and attribute nodes is different, as explained below). The above default template does not emit anything and simply continues to apply templates to the *et*-children of Report: Students, Classes, and Courses. This recursive process will reach a dead end while traversing the branches of the document tree that correspond to Classes and Courses, but will yield a useful result on Students.

Let us first consider the transformation of the Students branch. Since our stylesheet has no template that matches Students, the default rule is applied again. It directs the XML processor to apply a matching template to the three Student elements that are children of the element Students. Fortunately, we have an explicit template that matches this time—the second template in the stylesheet. (The actual transformation performed by this template was discussed in connection with the earlier stylesheet, which used the for-each instruction.)

The transformation on the other two branches, Classes and Courses, works similarly, so we consider only Classes. Since nothing matches Classes explicitly, XSLT applies the default template, which in turn applies templates to the *et*-children. Note that the default template ignores attributes and text nodes; however, when it is applied to an element of type CrsCode or Semester (which are descendants of Classes), their *t*-children are affected by the apply-templates statement. The trouble is that XSLT has another default template that applies to attribute and text nodes:

```
<xsl:template match="text()|@*">
    <xsl:value-of select="."/>
</xsl:template>
```

This means that, when this template matches an attribute or a text node, the value of the attribute or the text is copied by the processor to the result document. Unfortunately, in our case this produces spurious text that represents semesters and course codes that are of no interest (recall that we want to see student names only).

The third, empty template in the stylesheet in Figure 17.12 was added precisely to address this problem. The template matches only the text nodes and emits nothing. (We do not need to worry about the attributes here, since <xsl:apply-templates> ignores *a*-children of the current node.) Since we have an explicit rule that matches text nodes, the default rule for these nodes is suppressed.

The algorithm for applying stylesheets to documents is very complicated because of the large number of features available in XSLT. Even the official W3C recommendation [XSL 1999] does not describe it adequately. Here we provide an outline of the evaluation process for simplified pattern-based templates—those that can add at most one element node to the result document and, possibly, invoke `apply-templates`. In particular, we exclude the `for-each` loop.

1. Transformation begins by creating a root for the result document. The process then copies the root of the source document to the result tree and makes it a child of the result document's root node. The source document's root is set to be the *current node* (CN), and the *current node list* (CNL) is initially set to contain only the source root node.

2. *CNL* maintains the collection of nodes in the source document to which templates are to be applied. During the algorithm, *CN* is always the first node in *CNL*. Also, whenever a node, *N*, is placed in *CNL*, its copy (which we denote N^R) is placed in the result document tree. The node N^R can later be deleted or replaced by the application of a template, but such nodes play the role of markers that indicate where changes to the result tree might subsequently occur.

3. The process finds the **best-matching template** for *CN* and applies it to *CN*. The best-matching template is one whose path expression returns the smallest set of source document nodes (by set inclusion) that contains the current node.[15] If there is no template whose path expression returns a set that includes the current node, the appropriate default template is used.

4. Application of a template can lead to the following changes:

   a. CN^R in the result document tree can be replaced by a subtree. For instance, suppose *CN* is the Students node in Figure 17.11. Then the best-matching template in the stylesheet of Figure 17.12 is

      ```
      <xsl:template match="//Students">
          <StudentList>
              <xsl:apply-templates/>
          </StudentList>
      </xsl:template>
      ```

      In this case, CN^R is replaced with the `StudentList` *e*-node and each *et*-child of *CN* in the source tree is copied over to the result tree and becomes a child of `StudentList`. This transformation is shown in Figure 17.13, case (a).

   b. CN^R in the result document tree can be deleted, and its parent might acquire additional children. For instance, the default rule in the stylesheet of Figure 17.12.

---

[15] If there are several such templates, other rules are used to find the best match among them; see [XSL 1999].

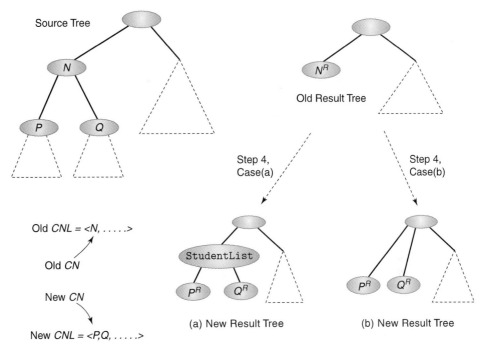

Figure 17.13 Effect of `apply-templates` on the document tree.

```
<xsl:template match="*|/">
    <xsl:apply-templates/>
</xsl:template>
```

deletes CN^R. The *et*-children of CN in the source tree are copied over to the result tree and become children of the parent of CN^R. This transformation is shown in Figure 17.13, case (b).

In both cases, if CN has no *et*-children, CNL will become shorter as a result of the template application. Otherwise (if it does have such children), CNL might grow because CN is replaced in CNL with the list of its *et*-children. The order in which these children are placed in the result tree and in CNL is the same as their order in the source tree. In particular, the first node in CNL becomes the new CN.

In general, the `apply-templates` instruction can have a `select`-attribute:

$$\texttt{<xsl:apply-templates select="}\textit{some path expression}\texttt{"/>} \qquad (17.3)$$

In fact, `<xsl:apply-templates/>` is simply a shorthand for `<xsl:apply-templates select="node()"/>`, where `node()` is an XPath function that returns the set of *et*-children of the given element node. For instance, `<xsl:apply-templates select="@*|text()"/>` applies to attributes (because of the wildcard `@*`) and text nodes (because of the function `text()`), but not to elements.

In general, the transformation (17.3) replaces *CN* with the nodes specified by the `select` attribute—not necessarily the *et*-children of *CN* as in the default case. These nodes are also copied to the result tree, as explained in cases (a) and (b) earlier. The algorithm then proceeds with Step 3.

5. The algorithm terminates when *CNL* becomes empty. In general, however, it might not terminate, and it is the responsibility of the stylesheet author to make sure that it does. For instance, if the path expression in the `select` attribute of `apply-templates` is . (i.e., it refers to the current node), then `apply-templates` will obviously loop forever. A general path expression can refer to parents, ancestors, or siblings of the current node, which makes termination analysis difficult. A simple condition that ensures termination is to require that all path expressions in the `select` attribute search only the subtree of the current node. Therefore, at some point *CNL* will start shrinking and eventually become empty.

Our next example illustrates several advanced features of XSLT. Suppose we want to rewrite the report in Figure 17.4 to get rid of the attributes and replace them with elements, so the record dealing with John Doe is rewritten as follows:

```
<Student>
    <StudId>111111111</StudId>
    <Name><First>John</First><Last>Doe</Last></Name>
    <Status>U2</Status>
    <CrsTaken>
        <CrsCode>CS308</CrsCode><Semester>F1997</Semester>
    </CrsTaken>
    <CrsTaken>
        <CrsCode>MAT123</CrsCode><Semester>F1997</Semester>
    </CrsTaken>
</Student>
```

Furthermore, we want to write this stylesheet in such a way that it does not depend on knowledge of the actual attribute names used in the source document. Thus, if the `Grade` attribute is added to the `CrsTaken` element in the future, our program should still work and transform `<CrsTaken ... Grade="A"/>` into

```
<CrsTaken> ... <Grade>A</Grade></CrsTaken>
```

To accomplish this feat, the stylesheet must be able to emit an element whose name is not known in advance but is computed on the fly based on the attributes found at run time in the source document. Two new features of XSLT make this possible.

■ The `element` instruction tells the stylesheet to copy an element with a given name to the result document. For instance,

```
<xsl:element name="name(current())">
    I do not know where I am
</xsl:element>
```

will copy different elements during evaluation, depending on the current nodes in which it is evaluated. For instance, if during the evaluation, the current node is an attribute named `foo`, the instruction will copy the following element to the result:

```
<foo>
    I do not know where I am
</foo>
```

In this stylesheet, `current()` is an XSLT function that at any particular point during execution returns the current node. The function `name()` is an XPath function that returns the name[16] of the first node in the node set that is passed to the function as an argument. In our case, the argument is always the current node in the evaluation process, so the function returns the name of the current node.

■ The `copy` instruction always outputs the node that is *current* at that particular point in the evaluation process. This feature should not be confused with the `copy-of` instruction, introduced earlier, which outputs the node set returned by its `select` attribute.

Moreover, while the `copy-of` instruction copies nodes together with all of their belongings (attributes, child elements, etc.), the `copy` instruction strips the current node of its attributes and other children.[17] This feature is important to us, since it provides a degree of control over what is to be output and, in particular, enables the stylesheet to intercept attribute nodes and emit them as elements.

The `copy` instruction is also different from the `current()` function. Since it is not an XSLT instruction, it does not copy anything to the result document. Instead, as a function, it returns the current node (with everything in it), and the returned result can be used by XSLT instructions.

One possible solution to our problem (of finding a stylesheet that converts attributes to elements) is shown in Figure 17.14. This stylesheet has two templates. Processing of the source document starts, as usual, with the root. Since none of the explicit templates matches the root, the appropriate default template is used. As seen earlier, the default template (17.2) on page 593 replaces *CN* on *CNL* with the list of its *e*-children and tells the processor to apply matching templates to the list.

---

[16] For an element node, the node name is the name of the tag. For an attribute node, it is the name of the attribute.

[17] Of course, if the current node is a text node or an attribute, there is nothing to strip and the node is copied in its entirety.

Figure 17.14 XSLT stylesheet that converts attributes into elements.

```
<?xml version="1.0" ?>
<xsl:stylesheet xmlns:xsl="http://www.w3.org/1999/XSL/Transform"
                xsl:version="1.0">
    <xsl:template match="node()">
        <xsl:copy>
            <xsl:apply-templates select="@*"/>
            <xsl:apply-templates/>
        </xsl:copy>
    </xsl:template>
    <xsl:template match="@*">
        <xsl:element name="name(current())">
            <xsl:value-of select="."/>
        </xsl:element>
    </xsl:template>
</xsl:stylesheet>
```

In the document in Figure 17.11 on page 583, the only child of the root node is the element Students, so the processor tries to find a matching template for it.

Only the first template in our style sheet matches: The XPath function node() matches every node in the document tree *except* the root and attribute nodes. (The second template selects the document nodes that match the path expression @*, which matches every attribute of the current node.)

The first template copies the current node, N, to the result. Recall that the copy instruction strips the children and the attributes, so only the bare-bones N is copied. Processing the attributes and the *et*-children of N is performed by the two apply-templates instructions within the copy instruction.

The first apply-templates instruction adds the attributes of N (which is the current node) to the beginning of *CNL*. The first node in *CNL* becomes the new current node, *CN*. Assuming that N had attributes, only the second template matches *CN*, so it is used. It outputs the element that has the same name as the current attribute (since the template applies only to attributes and thus current() must return an attribute node) and then makes the value of the current attribute the contents of that element. (For instance, Attr="something" is transformed into <Attr>something</Attr>.)

The second apply-templates inside the copy instruction is already familiar to us. It applies templates to every *et*-child of the current node but not to attribute nodes. As before, only the first template matches such nodes, so they are copied, their attributes are converted into elements, and the process recurs.

Limitations of XSLT. XSLT has a number of features that give it the qualities of a database query language: It can extract sets of nodes from a document, rearrange them, and apply transformations by recursively traversing the document tree. However, XSLT is lacking in certain important ways, which limits its use as a query language.

The most important problem has to do with joining documents or parts of the same document, analogously to the join operation in relational databases. As a simple example, consider taking the report in Figure 17.4 and producing a list of student records where every course taken by the student has the course name attached. To do this, we have to relate the CrsTaken elements and the Course element that have the same course code.

It turns out that formulating such a join-query in XSLT is rather cumbersome. One way is to descend into the Student elements and, for each CrsTaken, use apply-templates with the select attribute pointing to the corresponding Course element. Such an approach is possible, although not very natural, with the help of XSLT variables—a mechanism not discussed in this section. Another way is to use nested for-each loops and XSLT variables that hold sets of document nodes. This method is similar to querying databases by explicitly coding joins as nested loops in embedded SQL.

Fortunately, XSLT is not the last word in XML querying, and a number of other XML query languages have been proposed.

17.4.3 XQuery: A Full-Featured Query Language for XML

XPath and XSLT provide certain query facilities for XML documents. However, we have seen that XPath was designed to be lightweight and so can express only simple queries. XSLT has much greater expressive power, but was not designed as a query language; as a result, it has difficulty formulating complex queries.

Among the many languages specifically designed for querying XML, XQL and XML-QL deserve special mention. XQL [Robie et al. 1998] is an extension of XPath; XML-QL [Deutsch et al. 1998, Florescu et al. 1999] is an SQL-style query language, which also builds on ideas borrowed from languages such as OQL (Chapter 16) and Lorel [Abiteboul et al. 1997]. More recently, the best features of XQL and XML-QL were combined in a language called **XQuery**, which is currently the basis for the design of an official W3C query language for XML [XQuery 2001]. Like XSLT, XQuery uses XPath as a syntax for its path expressions. However, XQuery is generally more succinct and transparent than XSLT when it comes to querying. This section introduces the main features of XQuery.

Selections and joins.   Unlike XSLT, XQuery does not use the verbose syntax of XML, as there is no good reason for any query language to do so.[18] Instead, XQuery statements have some similarity with SQL:

FOR	*variable declarations*
WHERE	*condition*
RETURN	*result*

The FOR clause plays the same role as the FROM clause in SQL, and the WHERE clause is borrowed from SQL with the same functionality. The RETURN clause is

---

[18] At least, not for human consumption. XML-based syntax for XQuery is under development, however. For one thing, it can simplify the job of building parsers for XQuery.

analogous to SELECT: In SQL, it defines the template for the result relation; in XQuery, it specifies the template for the result document.

At a deeper level, XQuery is strongly influenced by OQL, the object-oriented query language for ODMG databases (Chapter 16). This connection will be apparent from the examples. We start with simple queries against the document shown in Figure 17.15, on page 601, which resides at the URL http://xyz.edu/transcripts.xml.

The first query retrieves all students who have ever taken MAT123.

```
FOR $t IN document("http://xyz.edu/transcripts.xml")//Transcript
WHERE $t/CrsTaken/@CrsCode = "MAT123"
RETURN $t/Student
```

The FOR clause declares a variable, $t, and its range—a set of document nodes. This set is specified using the XPath expression //Transcript, which is applied to the document obtained using the function document(). This function, borrowed from XSLT, returns the root of the document specified by the URL. Hence $t ranges over all Transcript nodes in the document. To navigate within document trees, XQuery relies on XPath expressions, which are extended with variables. Thus, $t/CrsTaken/@CrsCode and $t/Student are extended XPath expressions. When $t is bound to a Transcript node in the document tree, the first expression returns the nodes corresponding to the CrsCode attribute of the CrsTaken *e*-children of that node. The second expression returns Student *e*-children of the node.

The WHERE condition selects a subset of the Transcript nodes, where each node has a CrsTaken element with MAT123 as the value of the CrsCode attribute. The variable $t is bound to each such Transcript node in turn, and the RETURN clause is executed for each binding of $t. Each such execution outputs a fragment of the result document, which in our case is the Student element contained within the Transcript node that constitutes the current value of $t. In the example, the following is output:

```
<Student StudId="111111111" Name="John Doe"/>
<Student StudId="123454321" Name="Joe Blow"/>
```

One problem here is that the query does not yield a well-formed XML document. It produces a list of Student elements, which is not contained within a single parent element. This problem is easy to fix by embedding the above query between a pair of tags.

```
<StudentList>
(
    FOR $t IN document("http://xyz.edu/transcripts.xml")
                            //Transcript
    WHERE $t/CrsTaken/@CrsCode = "MAT123"
    RETURN $t/Student
)
</StudentList>
```

Figure 17.15 Transcripts at `http://xyz.edu/transcripts.xml`.

```
<?xml version="1.0" ?>
<Transcripts>
    <Transcript>
        <Student StudId="111111111" Name="John Doe"/>
        <CrsTaken CrsCode="CS308" Semester="F1997" Grade="B"/>
        <CrsTaken CrsCode="MAT123" Semester="F1997" Grade="B"/>
        <CrsTaken CrsCode="EE101" Semester"F1997" Grade="A"/>
        <CrsTaken CrsCode="CS305" Semester="F1995" Grade="A"/>
    </Transcript>
    <Transcript>
        <Student StudId="987654321" Name="Bart Simpson"/>
        <CrsTaken CrsCode="CS305" Semester="F1995" Grade="C"/>
        <CrsTaken CrsCode="CS308" Semester="F1994" Grade="B"/>
    </Transcript>
    <Transcript>
        <Student StudId="123454321" Name="Joe Blow"/>
        <CrsTaken CrsCode="CS315" Semester="S1997" Grade="A"/>
        <CrsTaken CrsCode="CS305" Semester="S1996" Grade="A"/>
        <CrsTaken CrsCode="MAT123" Semester="S1996" Grade="C"/>
    </Transcript>
    <Transcript>
        <Student StudId="023456789" Name="Homer Simpson"/>
        <CrsTaken CrsCode="EE101" Semester="F1995" Grade="B"/>
        <CrsTaken CrsCode="CS305" Semester="S1996" Grade="A"/>
    </Transcript>
</Transcripts>
```

The result is that the FOR clause outputs Student elements one by one and places them as children of StudentList.

In the following examples, we omit the topmost pair of tags when their only purpose is to provide a root element for the query result, as in the above case of StudentList.

The next example illustrates the restructuring capabilities of XQuery. The Transcripts document in Figure 17.15 groups course records around the students who took them. However, the user reading this document might want to reconstruct class lists for each course. In other words, for each course offering in a particular semester, she might want to obtain the list of students who took that course. In XQuery, this can be done directly from the transcripts.xml document, as shown in Figure 17.16. In that query, the variable $c ranges over the set of all distinct CrsTaken nodes in the document transcripts.xml. For each such node, a fragment of the result document is constructed as described in the RETURN clause.

Figure 17.16 Construction of class rosters from transcripts: first try.

```
FOR $c IN distinct(document("http://xyz.edu/transcripts.xml")
                                   //CrsTaken)
RETURN <ClassRoster CrsCode=$c/@CrsCode Semester=$c/@Semester>
    (
        FOR $t IN document("http://xyz.edu/transcripts.xml")
                                   //Transcript
        WHERE $t/CrsTaken/@CrsCode = $c/@CrsCode
               AND $t/CrsTaken/@Semester = $c/@Semester
        RETURN
               $t/Student
               SORTBY($t/Student/@StudId)
    )
</ClassRoster>
SORTBY($c/@CrsCode)
```

The query in Figure 17.16 is almost correct, but it has a flaw that we will explain after discussing the new features it exhibits.

First, observe that the query is nested. The interesting point, however, is that the nesting occurs in the RETURN clause, which corresponds to the SELECT clause in SQL. Recall that SQL bans nested queries (if they return more than one tuple) in the SELECT clause, because they do not make sense in the relational model. Indeed, a nested query typically returns a set of tuples whereas the target list of a SELECT clause in SQL is a template for a single tuple. In contrast, nested queries in the RETURN clause make perfect sense for an XML query language, because the purpose here is to construct a document that can have an arbitrarily complex nested structure. In our case, nesting serves the purpose of embedding student lists into class rosters. We have already encountered the use of nested queries in the target list of a query: This is allowed in the object-oriented query language OQL (see query (16.11) on page 506). Nesting is used there for the same reason it is used in XQuery.

Let us look more closely at the RETURN clause in the query in Figure 17.16, which is executed for each value of the variable $c. First, it constructs the ClassRoster element with the appropriate values for the attributes CrsCode and Semester. Then the nested subquery is invoked to construct the *sorted* list of students who have taken this class (i.e., the given course in the given semester). In it, $t ranges over Transcript elements and the WHERE clause selects those that have a CrsTaken element that matches the semester and course specified in $c. The output consists of elements such as

```
<ClassRoster CrsCode="CS305" Semester="F1995">
    <Student StudId="111111111" Name="John Doe"/>
    <Student StudId="987654321" Name="Bart Simpson"/>
</ClassRoster>
```

which are themselves sorted by the CrsCode attribute that occurs in each roster.

Figure 17.17 Classes at `http://xyz.edu/classes.xml`.

```
<?xml version="1.0" ?>
<Classes>
    <Class CrsCode="CS308" Semester="F1997">
        <CrsName>Market Analysis</CrsName>
        <Instructor>Adrian Jones</Instructor>
    </Class>
    <Class CrsCode="EE101" Semester="F1995">
        <CrsName>Electronic Circuits</CrsName>
        <Instructor>David Jones</Instructor>
    </Class>
    <Class CrsCode="CS305" Semester="F1995">
        <CrsName>Database Systems</CrsName>
        <Instructor>Mary Doe</Instructor>
    </Class>
    <Class CrsCode="CS315" Semester="S1997">
        <CrsName>Transaction Processing</CrsName>
        <Instructor>John Smyth</Instructor>
    </Class>
    <Class CrsCode="MAT123" Semester="F1997">
        <CrsName>Algebra</CrsName>
        <Instructor>Ann White</Instructor>
    </Class>
</Classes>
```

So far so good, except for one thing: John Doe and Bart Simpson received different grades for CS305 in fall 1995, so the FOR clause binds $c to two different CrsTaken elements for that class:

```
<CrsTaken CrsCode="CS305" Semester="F1995" Grade="A"/>
<CrsTaken CrsCode="CS305" Semester="F1995" Grade="C"/>
```

This means that the above ClassRoster element will be output twice. In general, each roster will be output once for every distinct grade received in the corresponding class. One way to overcome this problem is to create a new document that contains a list of all classes and then bind $c to the elements of that list. This can be easily done by selecting all CrsTaken elements from the Transcripts document and then stripping off the Grade attribute from each new one.

We will revisit this idea later, but for now we avoid this problem by assuming that the document in Figure 17.17, which resides at the URL http://xyz.edu/classes .xml, already exists. The following query is a reformulation of the faulty query of Figure 17.16 with slight enhancements intended to illustrate the join operation in XQuery:

```
FOR $c IN document("http://xyz.edu/classes.xml")//Class
RETURN
    <ClassRoster CrsCode=$c/@CrsCode Semester=$c/@Semester>
        $c/CrsName
        $c/Instructor
        (
            FOR $t IN document("http://xyz.edu/transcripts.xml")
                                    //Transcript
            WHERE $t/CrsTaken/@CrsCode = $c/@CrsCode
                    AND $t/CrsTaken/@Semester = $c/@Semester
            RETURN
            $t/Student
            SORTBY($t/Student/@StudId)
        )
    </ClassRoster>
SORTBY($c/@CrsCode)
```

The change in this new query is that the variable $c ranges over the set of all Class nodes of the document in Figure 17.17. Since classes do not occur multiple times there, we no longer have the problem of outputting multiple instances of the same roster (and we do not even need to apply the function distinct()). The result of the new query is enriched by including the course name ($c/CrsName) and the instructor ($c/Instructor) as child elements in each roster. Thus, this query computes a kind of *equijoin* on the attributes CrsCode and Semester between the Transcript elements of the document in Figure 17.15 and the Class elements of the document in Figure 17.17. As remarked at the end of Section 17.4.2, it is difficult to formulate this kind of transformation in XSLT.

Note that in the above query, even if some class has no students, the corresponding element ClassRoster will still appear in the result, albeit with empty contents. This is different from the join operation in relational databases, where a tuple in a CLASS relation with no matching tuples in the TRANSCRIPT relation will not be considered in an equijoin on the attributes CrsCode and Semester. The kind of join produced by the above XQuery example is known in relational databases as an **outer join** (defined in exercise 6.9, Chapter 6). Nevertheless, it is easy to reformulate the query and make it perform a "real" join by adding an appropriate WHERE clause to the outermost FOR statement:

```
FOR $c IN document("http://xyz.edu/classes.xml")//Class
WHERE document("http://xyz.edu/transcripts.xml")
                    //CrsTaken[@CrsCode = $c/@CrsCode
                                and @Semester = $c/@Semester]
RETURN
    <ClassRoster CrsCode=$c/@CrsCode Semester=$c/@Semester>
        $c/CrsName
        $c/Instructor
        (
```

```
              FOR $t IN document("http://xyz.edu/transcripts.xml")
                                          //Transcript
              WHERE $t/CrsTaken/@CrsCode = $c/@CrsCode
                    AND $t/CrsTaken/@Semester = $c/@Semester
              RETURN
                    $t/Student
                    SORTBY($t/Student/@StudId)
      )
   </ClassRoster>
   SORTBY($c/@CrsCode)
```

The purpose of the new WHERE clause is to test whether the document at http://xyz.edu/transcripts.xml has CrsTaken elements that match the attributes CrsCode and Semester for the current value of the variable $c. This test is performed by the path expression //CrsTaken[....] in the first WHERE clause. Only if such elements exist is the corresponding ClassRoster element output. Thus, rosters for the classes with no students will not appear in the result.

The semantics of XQuery.   So far, we have discussed the various examples informally, without explaining how the actual query evaluation mechanism works. We are now going to clarify these issues.

The FOR clause has the following functions:

■ To specify the documents to be used in the query.

■ To declare variables.

■ To bind each variable to its range, which is an *ordered* set of document nodes specified by an XQuery expression. Typically, this is an XPath expression, but, as we shall see later, it can also be a query or a function that returns a list of nodes.

The bindings produced by the FOR clause translate into an ordered list of tuples, each containing a concrete binding for every variable mentioned in the FOR clause. For instance, if the FOR clause declares the variables $a and $b and binds them to the document nodes {v,w} and {x,y,z}, respectively, then the following ordered list of tuples will be produced: {v,x}, {v,y}, {v,z}, {w,x}, {w,y}, {w,z}. Each tuple, such as, {w,x}, provides a concrete binding—$a/w, $b/x—to our variables.

Next, the tuples of bindings are filtered through the WHERE condition. Thus, if the condition is $a/CrsTaken/@CrsCode = $b/Class/@CrsCode and the document nodes w and x are such that w/CrsTaken/@CrsCode = x/Class/@CrsCode, then the tuple {w,x} of bindings for $a and $b is retained; otherwise, it is discarded. The effect of the WHERE clause is thus a selection of an ordered sublist from the original list of tuples.

Finally, for each surviving tuple of bindings the RETURN expression is instantiated. The result is the creation of a fragment for the output document. The process repeats until all eligible tuple bindings are exhausted.

Filtering.   The simplest way to correct the query in Figure 17.16 and to construct class rosters is via the `filter()` function of XQuery. This function takes two arguments, each a set of document nodes. Each node in the first argument represents a document fragment—the subtree rooted at that node—and each node in the second argument stands for itself (i.e., its *children are excluded*).

`filter()` prunes the document fragments supplied as the first argument by deleting all nodes that do not occur in the second argument. The surviving nodes of these document trees are then connected to each other so as to retain the old ancestor/descendant relationships, and the resulting set of document fragments is then returned. For instance, the following `filter()` operation applied to the document in Figure 17.17[19]

```
filter(//Class, //Class|//Class/CrsName)
```

yields the following document fragment:

```
<Class><CrsName>Market Analysis</CrsName></Class>
<Class><CrsName>Electronic Circuits</CrsName></Class>
<Class><CrsName>Database Systems</CrsName></Class>
<Class><CrsName>Transaction Processing</CrsName></Class>
<Class><CrsName>Algebra</CrsName></Class>
```

Note that, even though the node set `//Class` is included in the second argument of the `filter()` expression, its attribute nodes are not explicitly mentioned and thus the attributes do not appear in the output. Likewise, the *e*-child `Instructor` is not included because it is not mentioned explicitly.

Recall the cause of the problem with the query in Figure 17.16. Because of the `Grade` attribute, the variable `$c` may be bound to two different `CrsTaken` elements that have the same values for `CrsCode` and `Semester`. The `filter()` function can help project out the `Grade` attribute and thus eliminate the extraneous bindings for `$c`:

```
LET $trs := document("http://xyz.edu/transcripts.xml")//Transcript
LET $ct := $trs/CrsTaken
FOR $c IN distinct(filter($ct, $ct | $ct/@CrsCode | $ct/@Semester))
RETURN
     <ClassRoster CrsCode=$c/@CrsCode Semester=$c/@Semester>
        (
           FOR      $t IN $trs
           WHERE    $t/CrsTaken/@CrsCode = $c/@CrsCode
                    AND $t/CrsTaken/@Semester = $c/@Semester
           RETURN
                    $t/Student
                    SORTBY($t/Student/@StudId)
```

---

[19] Recall that | in an XPath expression denotes the union of expressions.

```
      )
</ClassRoster>
SORTBY($c/@CrsCode)
```

The only essential difference between the above query and the one in Figure 17.16 is the use of the `filter()` function and the LET clause. The LET clause simply assigns the set of all `Transcript` nodes to the variable $trs and the set of `CrsTaken` children of the `Transcript` nodes to $ct. Here it is used to break up the otherwise very long binding for the variable $c and to simplify the second FOR clause. In other words, if we substitute the values of $trs and $ct wherever these variables occur, we can eliminate the LET statements.

In contrast, the filter expression

```
filter($ct,  $ct | $ct/@CrsCode | $ct/@Semester)
```

is not a syntactic sugar. The first argument here is the set of all `CrsTaken` elements (along with their children), which the three alternatives in the second argument prune by retaining the element node itself and two of its attributes, while leaving out the `Grade` attribute (`CrsTaken` has no *e*-children, so there is nothing else to prune). The result is a list of elements such as

```
<CrsTaken CrsCode="MAT123" Semester="F1997">
<CrsTaken CrsCode="CS305" Semester="F1995">
  .
  .
  .
```

Thus, after pruning, elements such as

```
<CrsTaken CrsCode="CS305" Semester="F1995" Grade="A"/>
<CrsTaken CrsCode="CS305" Semester="F1995" Grade="C"/>
```

become equal, so only one of these will survive the call to the function `distinct()`. This is precisely what the doctor ordered for the query in Figure 17.16.

User-defined functions.   XQuery provides a large number of built-in functions, which include all of the core functions available in XPath. It also provides some other useful functions, such as `distinct()` and `document()`, and others that we will see later.

More interestingly, a query in XQuery can define a number of functions, which can then be called from within the main FOR-WHERE-RETURN query. Functions can call themselves recursively; they can take singleton nodes as well as collections of nodes as arguments; and they can return primitive types, document nodes, or collections of any of these types. The body of a function is an XQuery expression, which can be general (even queries are treated as expressions). An expression can evaluate to an integer, an element, a list of elements, and so on, and the function returns its result.

Here is an example of a function that counts the number of descendant elements and text nodes in a document fragment rooted at node $e:

```
FUNCTION countNodes(AnyElement $e) RETURNS integer {
    RETURN
        IF empty($e/*) THEN 0
        ELSE sum(countNodes($e/*)) + count($e/*)
}
```

This function definition illustrates a great number of features.

■ The declaration `AnyElement $e` says that the argument to the function must be an element. In particular, it cannot be an attribute or a text node, and it cannot be an integer. The function is said to return an integer. We explain a bit later where such types come from.

  The body of an XQuery function is an **XQuery expression**, which evaluates to a value (an integer, a string, a document node, a list of nodes, etc.). The value of that expression is returned. XQuery expressions are explained next.

■ The statement `IF-THEN-ELSE` is a conditional XQuery expression. The part between `IF` and `THEN` must be a Boolean expression—in our case `empty($e/*)`, which uses the built-in function `empty()` to check whether the path expression `$e/*` returns the empty set of document nodes.[20]

  The `THEN` and `ELSE` parts must be XQuery expressions. We do not define the full syntax of XQuery expressions here.[21] Typically they are path expressions (which return a set of document nodes), function calls (which can return a primitive type such as `integer` or `string`, a document node, or a set of nodes in the case of user-defined functions), arithmetic expressions, `IF-THEN-ELSE` conditionals, or full-blown queries (which can return a single document or a list of document fragments).

  In our case, the `THEN` expression is just a constant and the `ELSE` part is an arithmetic expression that makes calls to the aggregate functions `sum()` and `count()`. The function `sum()` applies to a collection of numeric values computed by a recursive call to `countNodes()`, as explained below, and sums them. The function `count()` counts the number of nodes returned by the path expression `$e/*`.

■ The recursive call to `countNodes()` is quite interesting in its own right. Observe that from the signature it appears that this function accepts a single element as an argument. However, seeming to contradict this declaration, the call is applied to a path expression that returns a *set* of document nodes. This is not an error.

> The general convention in XQuery is that, in this case,
> the function is applied to each element in the set and the set   (17.4)
> of results of all such applications is returned.

---

[20] Recall that the wildcard * selects all *e*-children of the current node, so `$e/*` returns the set of all elements that are children of the node assigned to `$e`.

[21] The interested reader is referred to [XQuery 2001].

Figure 17.18 Class rosters constructed with user-defined functions.

```
FUNCTION extractClasses(AnyElement $e)
                  RETURNS LIST(AnyElement){
  FOR $c IN $e//CrsTaken
RETURN <Class CrsCode=$c/@CrsCode Semester=$c/@Semester/>
}


<Rosters>
(
  LET $trs := document("http://xyz.edu/transcripts.xml")
  FOR $c IN distinct(extractClasses($trs))
  RETURN
    <ClassRoster CrsCode=$c/@CrsCode Semester=$c/@Semester>
      (
        FOR $t1 IN  $trs//Transcript[CrsTaken/@CrsCode=$c/@CrsCode and
                                  CrsTaken/@Semester=$c/@Semester]
        RETURN
          $t1/Student
          SORTBY($t1/Student/@StudId)
      )
    </ClassRoster>
)
</Rosters>
```

Thus, countNodes() is applied to *every* document node in its argument set and returns a set of integers, which is then summed by the built-in aggregate function sum() and passed to the arithmetic expression.

In the next example, we come back to the "nearly correct" query in Figure 17.16. Recall that the problem was that a class roster might appear multiple times in the result if at least two students in that class receive different grades. One solution that we came up with was to join transcripts with the document in Figure 17.17. XQuery functions make it possible to create an intermediate document similar to that of Figure 17.17 and join it with Transcripts in the same query, without relying on the existence of another, external document. The solution is shown in Figure 17.18.

The first part of the query defines the function extractClasses(). This function accepts a single element and returns a list of elements. The return type is specified as LIST(AnyElement), where LIST is a list-type constructor and AnyElement is a type of all elements. The result of the function is obtained by evaluating a simple query, which iterates through all CrsTaken descendants of the function argument, strips off the Grade attribute, and outputs the result as a list of Class elements.

The main query appears below the function definition. It returns a document with the top-level tag Rosters, which contains a list of individual elements tagged with ClassRoster. This query is almost identical to the one in Figure 17.16 except

that the variable $c ranges over the result produced by the function extract-
Classes(). Also, the WHERE clause has been eliminated and replaced with a selection condition on the XPath expression that binds the variable $t1. (Selection
conditions in XPath expressions were introduced in Section 17.4.1.)

The last example of user-defined functions illustrates how XQuery can perform
document transformations of the kind discussed in connection with XSLT. Specifically, we rewrite the XSLT stylesheet in Figure 17.14 on page 598, which traverses
an XML document and replaces attributes with elements that have the same name
and content. The XQuery equivalent of that program is as follows:

```
FUNCTION convertAttribute(AnyAttribute $a) RETURNS AnyElement{
  LET $name := name($a)
  RETURN
    <$name>value($a)</$name>
}
FUNCTION convertElement(AnyElement $e) RETURNS AnyElement{
  LET $name := name($e)
  RETURN
    <$name>
      convertAttribute($e/@*)
      IF empty($e/*) THEN $e/text()
      ELSE convertElement($e/*)
    </$name>
}

RETURN convertElement(document("....")/*)
```

The actual query consists of a single call to a previously defined function, con-
vertElement(), which takes as an argument a single element node. In this case, the
argument is the child node of the document root.[22] Note that, since a well-formed
XML document has exactly one topmost element, there is no need for an iteration
construct, such as the FOR clause.[23]

The first function, convertAttribute(), takes an attribute node as an argument
and converts it into the element that has the same name (obtained via a call to
the XPath function name()). The value of the attribute (obtained via the XQuery
function value()) becomes the content of the element.

The second function, convertElement(), does the bulk of the work. It is called
to convert an element node into an attribute-less element with the same name.
For a given element, convertElement() outputs a pair of tags with the same name
(again, using a call to name()) and then converts the element's attributes and finally

---

[22] We ignore the possibility that there might be other children of the root, such as comments and
processing instructions.
[23] Even if the root of the document had multiple e-children, convention (17.4) would allow us to dispense
with the FOR clause.

its *et*-children. To convert attributes, it invokes `convertAttribute()` on the list of attributes of the element.[24] Since `convertAttribute()` takes only a single attribute as a parameter, the function is applied for each attribute separately and yields a list of elements. This behavior follows from the general XQuery convention (17.4) on page 608.

Having finished with attributes, `convertElement()` turns to text nodes and elements. If the element has no *e*-children (as determined by `empty()`),[25] the only child must be a text node (or nothing at all if the element is empty). In the first case, the function emits the text node if it exists; in the second case, it transforms the *e*-children of the current node by calling itself recursively. Again, a list of elements is passed to a function that takes only a single element as a parameter, so this call to `convertElement()` outputs a list of transformed elements.

The above query does not perform quite the same transformation as the XSLT stylesheet in Figure 17.14, on page 598. For instance, if an element has mixed content—its children include elements as well as text nodes[26]—the query ignores the text (because the XPath expression `$e/*` selects only *e*-children) and proceeds to convert the elements. We tackle this problem in the next example, after explaining the relationship between XQuery, XML schemas, and namespaces.

XQuery and data types.   The previous queries showed the use of primitive types, such as `integer`, `AnyElement`, and `AnyAttribute`. However, XQuery goes much further by integrating smoothly with the XML Schema specification and by allowing the importation and use of the types defined in various XML schemas. In fact, the primitive type `integer` used earlier is not a native XQuery type but rather the one defined by the XML Schema specification, so it should be used in conjunction with the corresponding namespace. Likewise, the types `AnyElement` and `AnyAttribute` must be defined in some schema. For simplicity, we pretend that they are part of XML schema specification. We also pretend that the type `AnyText` (that contains all text nodes in a document tree) is defined in the standard XML Schema namespace.

Below is an example that illustrates the integration of XQuery with XML schemas and namespaces and completes the previous example by providing a true XQuery equivalent to the XSLT stylesheet in Figure 17.14 on page 598. First, we need to define a new simple data type that accepts attributes, elements, and text nodes. We assume that this data type is described by the namespace `http://types.r.us/auxiliary`.

```
<schema xmlns="http://www.w3.org/2001/XMLSchema"
        targetNamespace="http://types.r.us/auxiliary">
    <simpleType name="AnyNode">
```

---

[24] Recall that `@*` is an XPath wildcard that returns all the attributes of an element. The XPath function `text()` returns all *t*-children of the current node.

[25] In this case, the element would have the form `<foo>some text</foo>`.

[26] For instance, `<foo>some text<bar>more text</bar>even more</foo>` has mixed content, which consists of two *t*-children and one *e*-child.

```
            <union memberTypes="AnyElement AnyAttribute AnyText"/>
        </simpleType>
    </schema>
```

Assume that this schema is stored in the document found at the URL `http://types .r.us/auxiliary/types.xsd`. Figure 17.19 shows the XQuery expression we are looking for.

The first clause, SCHEMA, tells the XQuery processor where to find the schema used in the query. In our case, this schema contains the definition of the union type `AnyNode`, which we use in the function `convertNode()`. The two NAMESPACE clauses introduce the namespaces used in the query. The namespace XMLSchema is needed for the processor to know that the types `AnyElement`, `AnyAttribute`, and `AnyText` in the query are the primitive types defined by the XML Schema specification and not some other data types. The other namespace, `auxiliary`, associates the name `AnyNode` with the simple type defined in the above schema. Note that this namespace matches the target namespace of the schema document that defines `AnyNode`.

The only other new feature in the query is the operator INSTANCEOF, which tests whether a given node (the value of $n in our case) conforms to a given type. We use this test in the function `convertNode()` to determine whether the argument to the function is an attribute node or an element.

Figure 17.19 XQuery transformation that does the same work as the stylesheet in Figure 17.14.

```
SCHEMA "http://types.r.us/auxiliary/types.xsd"
NAMESPACE aux = "http://types.r.us/auxiliary"
NAMESPACE xsd = "http://www.w3.org/2001/XMLSchema"
FUNCTION convertNode(aux:AnyNode $n) RETURNS aux:AnyNode {
    LET $name := name($n)
    RETURN
        IF $n INSTANCEOF xsd:AnyElement THEN {
            <$name>
                convertNode($n/@*)
                convertNode($n/node())
            </$name>
        } ELSE IF $n INSTANCEOF xsd:AnyAttribute THEN {
            <$name>
                value($n)
            </$name>
        } ELSE $n
}

RETURN convertNode(document("....")/*)
```

The function `convertNode()` works analogously to `convertElement()`, which we discussed earlier. It first checks the argument type. If it is an element, the appropriate pair of tags is created. In between the tags, `convertNode()` is called recursively to convert the attributes of the current element into elements; then it is called to convert all *et*-children of the current node.[27] If the argument is an attribute, the attribute value is output with a pair of tags that have the same name as the attribute. If the argument is neither an attribute nor an element, it must be a text node, in which case the node is simply copied to the result document.

Grouping and aggregation.   Unlike SQL, XQuery does not use a separate grouping operator; instead it relies on a more consistent mechanism that applies aggregate functions to explicitly constructed collections of document nodes. This is achieved with the help of the already familiar LET clause, which declares a variable and initializes it with a collection of nodes specified by an XQuery expression. Interestingly, the use of LET outside of a FOR clause is just syntactic sugar, as we saw in the example on page 606, but its use in the scope of a FOR clause can be essential because grouping cannot be achieved in any other way.

To illustrate, the following query takes the `Transcripts` document in Figure 17.15 on page 601 and produces a document that lists students along with the number of courses each has taken so far.

```
FOR $t IN document("http://xyz.edu/transcripts.xml")//Transcript,
        $s IN $t/Student
LET $c := $t/CrsTaken
RETURN
        <StudentSummary StudId=$s/@StudId Name=$s/@Name
                         TotalCourses=count(distinct($c))/>
SORTBY(StudentSummary/@TotalCourses)
```

Recall that the FOR clause iterates by binding $t to every `Transcript` element of the document. The trick here is that the variable $c is assigned a new list of `CrsTaken` elements each time $t is bound to a new element, because LET occurs in the scope of the FOR clause that binds $t. In other words, for any `Transcript` binding for $t, $c is bound to the list of classes mentioned in that transcript element and the subsequent call to `count()` simply counts the number of distinct elements on the list.

The similarity between the FOR and LET clauses might be deceiving. Both specify variable bindings as collections of document nodes, but FOR binds the variables to the *individual nodes* of a collection *in succession* while LET binds the variables to the *entire collection* of nodes *at once*.

The next query is slightly more complicated, as it involves a join of the `Transcripts` document in Figure 17.15 and the `Classes` document in Figure 17.17. It creates a list of classes along with the average grade in each. To obtain the numeric value for a grade, we use the function `numericGrade()`, which can be easily defined

---

[27] Recall that `node()` is an XPath function that returns all *et*-children of the current node.

as an XQuery function (and is omitted). This example also illustrates another important feature: The binding for the variables in the LET clause (and, for that matter, in the FOR clause) does not need to be specified as an XPath expression, but can be any XQuery expression that returns a list of nodes. In particular, it can be a query as shown below:

```
FOR $c IN document("http://xyz.edu/classes.xml")//Class
-- $g gets the collection of all numeric grades in the class bound to $c
LET $g := (
            FOR $ct IN document("http://xyz.edu/transcripts.xml")
                                        //CrsTaken
            WHERE $ct/@CrsCode = $c/@CrsCode
                    AND $ct/@Semester = $c/@Semester
            RETURN numericGrade($ct/@Grade)
          )
RETURN
    <ClassSummary CrsCode = $c/@CrsCode Semester=$c/@Semester
                    CsrName = $c/CrsName Instructor=$c/Instructor
                    AvgGrade = avg($g)/>
SORTBY(ClassSummary/@CrsCode)
```

This is essentially the same query as the one on page 603, which constructs class rosters by joining the documents transcripts.xml and classes.xml. However, instead of listing all students in the class in the result document, we compute the list of all grades in the class and assign it to a variable, $g, using the LET clause. These grades are then averaged, and the result is assigned as a value of the attribute AvgGrade.

Note that, when the LET clause occurs in the scope of a FOR clause, it introduces a new issue as far as the query semantics is concerned. This happens because now variables are bound both by the FOR and LET clauses. The LET clause is incorporated into the evaluation mechanism as follows. For each tuple of bindings for the variables in the FOR clause, the bindings for the LET variables are determined. Unlike the bindings for the FOR variables, the LET clause bindings are to lists of nodes, which are typically used as arguments to aggregate functions. Thus, the binding for the LET variables is completely determined by the binding for the FOR variables.

The rest of the query evaluation procedure remains unchanged: the WHERE clause filters out tuples of bindings produced by the FOR clause. The only difference is that now the condition in WHERE might also use the variables bound by LET. Finally, for each tuple of bindings for the FOR-variables, the RETURN clause generates a fragment for the result document.

Quantification.   Suppose we want to extract the list of all students who have taken MAT123. In SQL, this requires the EXISTS operator (which is analogous to the XQuery function empty()). XQuery provides similar facilities through the quantifiers: SOME and EVERY, which precisely correspond to the existential quantifier ∃ and the universal quantifier ∀ in relational calculus (Chapter 7). As shown in Chapter 7, explicit use of quantifiers greatly simplifies the formulation of certain queries as compared to their formulation in SQL.

The next query uses the SOME quantifier to return the list of all students who took MAT123.

```
FOR $t IN document("http://xyz.edu/transcripts.xml")//Transcript
WHERE SOME $ct IN $t/CrsTaken
        SATISFIES $ct/@CrsCode = "MAT123"
RETURN $t/Student
```

In many cases, the SOME quantifier can be eliminated from the query. For instance assuming that a student cannot take the same course twice, the above query is equivalent to

```
FOR $t IN document("http://xyz.edu/transcripts.xml")//Transcript,
    $c IN $t/CrsTaken
WHERE $c/@CrsCode = "MAT123"
RETURN $t/Student
```

The analogy between SQL and XQuery should not be taken too far, however. Consider the following queries, which return the course names for classes that have at least one enrolled student: The SQL query

```
SELECT   C.CrsName
FROM     CLASS C, TRANSCRIPT T
WHERE    C.CrsCode = T.CrsCode AND C.Semester = T.Semester
```

and the XQuery query

```
FOR      $c IN document("http://xyz.edu/classes.xml")//Class,
         $t IN document("http://xyz.edu/transcripts.xml")//CrsTaken
WHERE    $c/@CrsCode = $t/@CrsCode AND $c/@Semester = $t/@Semester
RETURN   $c/CrsName
```

Since T does not occur in the SELECT clause and $t does not occur in the RETURN clause, the two are assumed to be existentially quantified. In both cases, a course name is output even if just one matching transcript record is found. If more than one is found, an SQL query processor might or might not output duplicate course names, depending on the inner workings of the query optimizer. (Since SQL is a relational query language, its semantics implies that only one name per course should be output. The possibility of duplicates is an implementation detail.) In contrast, the semantics of the FOR clause in XQuery implies that a course name will be output for *every* matching transcript record. This is because FOR specifies a loop in which the RETURN clause is executed for each binding of $c and $t, and every binding for $c is likely to have multiple matching bindings for $t.

Note that, while SELECT DISTINCT in SQL guarantees that there are no duplicates, the distinct() function in XQuery does not easily achieve the same goal (see exercise 17.30). One way to eliminate duplicates in our example is to use distinct() in conjunction with filter() (see exercise 17.31). Another is to use SOME. Unlike the previous example of students who took MAT123, however, this quantifier is essential and cannot be eliminated simply by moving variables from the WHERE to the FOR clause.

```
FOR     $c IN document("http://xyz.edu/classes.xml")//Class
WHERE
   SOME $t IN document("http://xyz.edu/transcripts.xml")//CrsTaken
   SATISFIES $c/@CrsCode = $t/@CrsCode AND $c/@Semester = $t/@Semester
RETURN $c/CrsName
```

In contrast to the existential quantifier, the universal quantifier, EVERY, cannot be easily eliminated from most queries. As discussed in Chapter 7, the universal quantifier provides a natural way of expressing queries that involve the division operator in relational algebra. Such queries look rather awkward in SQL, because SQL does not support universal quantification directly.[28] To illustrate, the following query retrieves all classes in which every enrolled student took MAT123:

```
FOR $c IN document("http://xyz.edu/classes.xml")//Class
-- $g gets bound to the set of all Transcript elements
-- corresponding to the particular class that binds $c
LET $g := (
    FOR $t IN document("http://xyz.edu/transcripts.xml")
                             //Transcript
    WHERE $t/CrsTaken/@CrsCode = $c/@CrsCode
        AND $t/CrsTaken/@Semester = $c/@Semester
    RETURN $t
          )
-- Take only those $g in which every transcript
-- has a CrsTaken element for MAT123
WHERE EVERY $tr IN $g
    SATISFIES NOT empty($tr[CrsTaken/@CrsCode = "MAT123"])
RETURN $c SORTBY($c/@CrsCode)
```

Here, for every binding of $c to a Class element, $g is bound to the list of transcripts of students who took this class. The outer WHERE clause checks that every student transcript in $g indicates that the student has taken MAT123. (Recall that the XPath expression $tr[CrsTaken/@CrsCode = "MAT123"] returns a nonempty set of nodes

---

[28] We saw in Section 6.2.3 that expressing universal quantification in SQL requires EXISTS, nested subqueries, and double negation. However, SQL:1999 introduces a limited form of universal quantification, the FOR ALL operator, which provides relief for writing many queries that require the division operator of relational algebra.

if and only if $tr is bound to a transcript element that includes a CrsTaken element for the course MAT123.)

17.4.4 Summary

This section presented three query languages for XML. XPath is a lightweight language that is becoming an integral component of a number of XML-related technologies. We have seen several in this chapter: XML Schema, XPointer, XSLT, and XQuery.

XSLT is an XML transformation language. It was not designed as a query language, but, because of its use of XPath and its overall design, it is suitable for many kinds of XML queries, especially those that do not involve document joins.

XQuery is an eclectic language that builds on the ideas developed in the database world. It is still a moving target, and some aspects of its syntax and semantics may change. Even in its present form, however, XQuery illustrates how the ideas developed in relational and object-oriented databases can be applied to querying and restructuring documents.

At present, both XPath and XSLT have the status of W3C recommendations (i.e., standards), and they are already supported by the major Web browsers. At the time of this writing, the XQuery specification is still in a preliminary draft form [XQuery 2001].

17.5 BIBLIOGRAPHIC NOTES

XML attempts to bring some order to the chaotic state of affairs in Web information processing. Conceptually, it is a rewrite and simplification of the well-established SGML standard [SGM 1986]. Version 1 was approved in 1998 and became a widely accepted standard [XML 1998]. As with every new hot topic, a great number of publications appeared in a short period of time. There are too many to list here, so we mention just two recent ones, [Ray 2001, Bradley 2000a].

XML Schema is covered in a number of books, but because, it was a moving target until recently, we recommend the original sources [XMLSchema 2000a, XMLSchema 2000b].

XPath, the XML path expression language, is described in most recent publications on XML. The official W3C recommendation can be found in [XPath 1999]. The original idea of path expressions comes from [Zaniolo 1983]. The idea of enhancing path expressions with query capability was developed by [Kifer and Lausen 1989, Kifer et al. 1992, Frohn et al. 1994, Abiteboul et al. 1997, Deutsch et al. 1998] and others.

XSLT became an official recommendation of W3C in 1999 [XSL 1999], and the latest versions of major browsers, such as Internet Explorer, Mozilla, and Netscape, support it. This subject is covered in several publications, such as [Kay 2000, Bradley 2000b].

The XML query language XQuery is described in [XQuery 2001]. It is an eclectic language that builds on the ideas previously developed for SQL, OQL [Cattell and Barry 2000], XQL [Robie et al. 1998], XML-QL [Deutsch et al. 1998, Florescu et al.

1999], and Quilt [Robie et al. 2000, Chamberlin et al. 2000]. XQuery is still very much a work in progress; the best place to follow its progress is the Web site of the W3C XML Query Working Group, http://www.w3.org/XML/Query.

Finally, [Abiteboul et al. 2000] is an excellent reference that takes the database view of information processing on the Web and covers recent work on semistructured data, including Lorel and XML-QL—two of XQuery's precursors.

17.6   EXERCISES

17.1 Use XML to represent the contents of the STUDENT relation in Figure 4.2, page 59. Specify a DTD appropriate for this document.

17.2 Specify a DTD appropriate for a document that contains data from both the COURSE table in Figure 5.15, page 116, and the REQUIRES table in Figure 5.16, page 117. Try to reflect as many constraints as the DTDs allow. Give an example of a document that conforms to your DTD.

17.3 Restructure the document in Figure 17.4, page 547, so as to completely replace the elements Name, Status, CrsCode, Semester, and CrsName with attributes in the appropriate tags. Provide a DTD suitable for this document. Specify all applicable ID and IDREF constraints.

17.4 Define the following simple types:

   a. A type whose domain consists of lists of strings, where each list consists of 7 elements.

   b. A type whose domain consists of lists of strings, where each string is of length 7.

   c. A type whose domain is a set of lists of strings, where each string has between 7 and 10 characters and each list has between 7 and 10 elements.

   d. A type appropriate for the letter grades that students receive on completion of a course—A, A−, B+, B, B−, C+, C, C−, D, and F. Express this type in two different ways: as an enumeration and using the pattern tag of XML Schema.

17.5 Use the key statement of XML Schema to define the following key constraints for the document in Figure 17.4:

   a. The key for the collection of all Student elements

   b. The key for the collection of all Course elements

   c. The key for the collection of all Class elements

17.6 Assume that any student in the document of Figure 17.4 is uniquely identified by the last name and the status. Define this key constraint.

17.7 Use the keyref statement of XML Schema to define the following referential integrity for the document in Figure 17.4:

    a. Every course code in a `CourseTaken` element must refer to a valid course.

    b. Every course code in a `Class` element must refer to a valid course.

17.8 Express the following constraint on the document of Figure 17.4: No pair of `CourseTaken` elements within the same `Student` element can have identical values of the `CrsCode` attribute.

17.9 Rearrange the structure of the `Class` element in Figure 17.4 so that it becomes possible to define the following referential integrity: Every student Id mentioned in a `Class` element references a student from the same document.

17.10 Write a unified XML schema that covers both documents in Figures 17.15 and 17.17. Provide the appropriate key and foreign key constraints.

17.11 Use XML Schema to represent the fragment of the relational schema in Figure 4.6, page 66. Include all key and foreign key constraints.

17.12 Use XPath to express the following queries to the document in Figure 17.15:

    a. Find all `Student` elements whose Id ends with 987 and who have taken MAT123.

    b. Find all `Student` elements whose first name is Joe and who have taken fewer than three courses.

    c. Find all `CrsTaken` elements that corresponds to semester S1996 and that belong to students whose name begins with P.

17.13 Formulate the following XPath queries for the document in Figure 17.17:

    a. Find the names of all courses taught by Mary Doe in fall 1995.

    b. Find the set of all document nodes that correspond to all course names taught in fall 1996 or all instructors who taught MAT123.

    c. Find the set of all course codes taught by John Smyth in spring 1997.

17.14 Use XSLT to transform the document in Figure 17.15 into a well-formed XML document that contains the list of `Student` elements such that each student in the list took a course in spring 1996.

17.15 Use XSLT to transform the document in Figure 17.17 into a well-formed XML document that contains the list of courses that were taught by Ann White in fall 1997. *Do not* include the `Instructor` child element in the output and discard the `Semester` attribute.

17.16 Write an XSLT stylesheet that traverses the document tree and, ignoring attributes, copies the elements and the text nodes. For instance, `<foo a="1"> the<best quality="S"/>bar</foo>` would be converted into `<foo>the <best/>bar</foo>`.

17.17 Write an XSLT stylesheet that traverses the document tree and, ignoring attributes, copies the elements and *doubles* the text nodes. For instance, `<foo`

```
a="1">the<best/>bar</foo> would be converted into <foo>thethe<best/>
barbar</foo>.
```

17.18 Write an XSLT stylesheet that traverses the document and preserves all elements, attributes, and text nodes, but discards the CrsTaken elements. The stylesheet must not depend on the knowledge of where the CrsTaken element resides in the source document.

17.19 Write a stylesheet that traverses the document tree and, while ignoring the attributes, preserves the other aspects of the tree (the parent–child relationships among the elements and the text nodes). However, when the stylesheet hits the foobar element, its attributes and the entire structure beneath are preserved and the element itself is repeated twice.

17.20 Write a stylesheet that traverses the document tree and preserves everything. However, when it hits the element foo it converts every *t*-child of foo into an element with the name text. For instance,

```
<foo a="1">the<best>bar<foo>in the</foo></best>world</foo>
```

would become

```
<foo a="1">the<best>bar<foo> <text>in the</text>
</foo></best>world</foo>
```

17.21 Consider the relational schema in Figure 4.6, page 66. Assume that the Web server delivers the contents of these relations using the following XML format: The name of the relation is the top-level element, each tuple is represented as a tuple element, and each relation attribute is represented as an empty element that has a value attribute. For instance, the STUDENT relation would be represented as follows:

```
<Student>
    <tuple>
        <Id value="111111111"/> <Name value="John Doe"/>
        <Address value="123 Main St."/> <Status="U1"/>
    </tuple>
        .
        .
        .
</Student>
```

Formulate the following queries using XQuery:

a. Produce the list of all students who live on Main Street.

b. Find every course whose CrsCode value does not match the Id of the department that offers the course. (For instance, the course IS315 in information systems might be offered by the computer science (CS) department.)

c. Create a list of all records from the TEACHING relation that correspond to courses taught in the fall semester.

17.22 Using the document structure described in exercise 17.21, formulate the following queries in XQuery:

    a. Create the list of all professors who ever taught MAT123. The information must include all attributes available from the PROFESSOR relation.

    b. Create the list of all students (include student Id and name) who have taken a course from John Smyth and received an A.

    c. Create the list of all courses in which Joe Public received an A.

17.23 Use the document structure described in exercise 17.21 to formulate the following queries in XQuery:

    a. Create an XML document that lists all students by name and, for each student, lists the student's transcript. The transcript records must include course code, semester, and grade.

    b. Create a document that for each professor lists the name and classes taught.

    c. Create a document that lists every course and the professors who taught it. The course information must include the course name, and the professor information should include the professor's name.

17.24 Use the document structure described in exercise 17.21 to formulate the following queries in XQuery:

    a. List all students who have taken more than three courses.

    b. List all students who received an A for more than three courses.

    c. List all professors who gave an A to more than three students.

    d. List all courses where average grade is higher than B.

    e. List all professors whose given grade (the average among all grades the professor ever assigned to any student) is B or higher. For this problem, you must write an XQuery function that compares letter grades.

    f. List all courses where the average grade is less than the professor's given grade.

17.25 Use the document structure described in exercise 17.21 to formulate the following queries in XQuery:

    a. List all courses where every student received a B or higher.

    b. List all students who never received less than a B.

17.26 Write an XQuery function that traverses a document and computes the maximum branching factor of the document tree, i.e., the maximal number of children (text or element nodes) of any element in the document.

17.27 Write an XQuery function that traverses a document and strips element tags. For instance,

```
<the>best<foo>bar</foo>in the world</the>
```

would become

```
<result>bestbarin the world</result>
```

17.28 Consider a document that contains a list of professors (name, Id, department Id) and a separate list of classes taught (course code, semester). Use aggregate functions to produce the following documents:

a. A list of professors (name, Id) with the number of courses taught. (The same course taught in different semesters counts as one.)

b. A list of departments (department Id) along with the number of different courses ever taught by the professors in them. (Again, the same course taught in different semesters or a course taught in the same semester by different professors is counted as one.)

17.29 Redo exercise 17.28, but now consider the use of the `filter()` function as mandatory.

17.30 Consider the following query:

```
FOR       $c IN document("http://xyz.edu/classes.xml")//Class,
          $t IN document("http://xyz.edu/transcripts.xml")
              //CrsTaken
WHERE     $c/@CrsCode = $t/@CrsCode
AND       $c/@Semester = $t/@Semester
RETURN    $c/CrsName
```

Explain why every course name is likely to be output more than once. Can the use of the `distinct()` function (without any additional features) solve this problem with duplicates? Explain your answer.

17.31 Consider the query in exercise 17.30. Use `filter()` and `distinct()` to get rid of the duplicates in the output.

Chapter 18

Distributed Databases

An increasing number of applications require access to multiple databases located at different sites, perhaps widely separated geographically. These applications fall into two broad categories, each illustrated with an example.

■ *Category 1.* An Internet grocer has established a nationwide network of warehouses to speed delivery of its products. Each warehouse has its own local database, and the merchant has a database at its headquarters. An application that determines the total inventory in all warehouses might execute at headquarters and access all warehouse databases.

■ *Category 2.* When a customer makes a purchase from the Internet grocer, the transaction might involve both the merchant and a credit card company. Information about the purchase might have to be recorded in both the merchant's and the credit card company's databases.

Distributed data is involved in both of these applications. The difference lies in the way each accesses the databases at the individual sites. In category 1, the application is written in terms of a schema that allows it to access the sites at the level of SQL statements. Thus, it might send SELECT statements to each warehouse to obtain the desired information and then take the union of the returned tuples.

Applications in category 2 do not access data in this way. The merchant and the credit card company are separate enterprises and their databases contain sensitive information that neither is willing to share. Furthermore, neither is willing to allow the other to (perhaps inadvertently) introduce inconsistencies into its database. Therefore, the credit card company provides a subroutine (perhaps a stored procedure executed as a transaction) that can be invoked to update its database to record the charges made to a customer's account. Remote sites can invoke the routine, but cannot access the database directly. Since the credit card company creates the routine, its database security and integrity are protected. Thus, in contrast to applications in category 1, direct remote access to the credit card company's database is not possible.

Both of these categories involve distributed data and, if the application requires transactional properties, distributed transactions as well. In Part Four and in the overview of transaction processing in Chapter 15, we deal with these transactional issues. Security in distributed systems is also addressed in Chapter 27.

Only applications in category 1 can access data directly and hence employ database-oriented strategies to improve performance and availability. In this chapter, we discuss such strategies. For example:

- How should a distributed database be designed?

- At what site should individual data items or tables be stored?

- Which data items should be replicated, and at what sites should replicas be stored?

- How are queries that access multiple databases processed?

- What issues are involved in distributed query optimization?

- How do the techniques used for query optimization affect database design?

Why data might be distributed.   Since distribution introduces new problems, why distribute data at all? Why not gather all of the data of a distributed enterprise into a single, central site? There are a number of (possibly conflicting) reasons as to why data might be distributed and where it should be located.

- Data might be placed in such a way as to minimize communication costs and/or response time. This generally means that data is kept at the site that accesses it most often.

- Data might be distributed to equalize the workload, so that individual sites are not overloaded to such a degree that throughput is impaired.

- Data might be kept at the site at which it was created so that its creators can maintain control and guarantee security.

- Certain data items might be replicated at multiple sites to increase their availability in the event of system crashes (if one replica becomes unavailable, an alternate can be accessed) or to increase throughput and reduce response time (since the data can be more quickly accessed using a local or nearby copy).

18.1   THE APPLICATION DESIGNER'S VIEW OF THE DATABASE

An application that directly accesses a database submits SQL statements that have been constructed with some schema in mind. The schema describes the structure of the database seen by the application. We consider three kinds of schemas.

Multiple local schemas.   The distributed database looks to the application program like a collection of individual databases, each with its own schema, as shown in Figure 18.1(a). Such a system is an example of a **multidatabase**. (A more complete discussion of multidatabase systems is given in Section 21.2.2.) If the individual DBMSs have been supplied by different vendors, the system is referred to as **heterogeneous**; if by the same vendor, it is referred to as **homogeneous**.

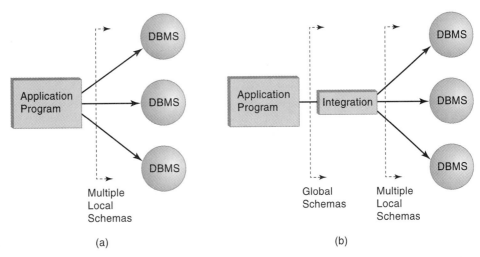

Figure 18.1   Views of a distributed data: (a) Multidatabase with local schemas; (b) Integrated distributed database supporting a global schema.

The application program must explicitly set up a connection to each site that contains data items to be accessed. After a connection has been established, the program can access the database using SQL statements constructed using the site's schema. If data items are moved from one site to another, the program must be changed.

A single SQL statement that refers to tables at different sites—for example, a global join—is not supported. If the application wants to join tables at different sites, it must read the tuples from each table into buffers at the application site (with separate SELECT statements) and explicitly test the join condition for each pair of tuples.

Data at different sites might be stored in different formats. For example, at one site an individual's last name might be stored first; at another it might be stored last. In addition, the types in the individual schema might be different. For example, at one site an Id might be stored as a sequence of characters; at another, as an integer. In these cases, the application must provide conversion routines that can be used at run time to integrate the data.

The application must manage replication. If a replicated item is being queried, the application must decide which replica should be accessed, and, if the item is being updated, it must ensure that the update occurs at all replicas.

The methods we discussed in Chapter 10 for accessing a distributed database using embedded SQL, JDBC, SQLJ, and ODBC all see a distributed database in this way.

Global schema.   The local schema approach provides little support for the application programmer: All of the issues arising from the distributed nature of the database must be handled explicitly in the program. The opposite extreme, in which all issues are hidden from the application and handled automatically, is interesting since it provides an ideal against which distributed database systems can be measured.

In this approach, the application designer sees a single schema that integrates all local schemas. Therefore, we refer to it as a **global schema** and refer to the system as an **integrated** distributed database system.

The integration is done by middleware (as shown in Figure 18.1(b)), which unifies the individual schemas into a single global schema that includes data from all sites. The global schema might include tables that do not appear in any local schema, but which can be computed from tables in local schemas using appropriate SQL statements. In other words, the global schema is a view of the local schemas.

Connections to individual sites are made automatically by the middleware when elements of the global schema are accessed. Hence, the locations of tables are hidden from the application program (this is called **location transparency**). If data items are moved from one site to another, the global schema remains the same and the application program need not be changed. The mapping from global to local schema does need to be changed in the middleware, but doing so is easier than changing a large number of application programs.

As with local schemas, related data at different sites can be stored in different formats and types, which might not match those of the global schema. The middleware provides the conversion routines to integrate the systems under these circumstances.

A related problem is **semantic integration**, which involves at least the issues of value conversion and name conversion. Consider a distributed database that has sites in Europe, Japan, and the United States. Monetary values at all sites can be represented as double-precision numbers, so no format conversion is required. However, 1,000 yen is different from 1,000 euro, as 1,000 euro is different from 1,000 dollars. Thus, a request for a total amount of sales in Tokyo might require currency conversion into yen, while the same request in Amsterdam might require conversion into euro. Attribute name conversion has to deal with cultural differences and individual habits. Even ignoring the possibility that an Amsterdam site might use a different language from a site in New York, we still must deal with the possibility that two different U.S. sites refer to the same attribute as `item#` and `part#`.

Application programs execute SQL statements against the global schema. For example, the application might request the join of two tables, T_1 and T_2, in the global schema. If the tables are stored at the same site, the statement is passed on to that site for processing. If they are stored at different sites (a global join), the middleware must translate the join into a sequence of appropriate SQL statements against the individual databases and perform any other operations needed to compute the join. In a more complex case, both T_1 and T_2 can be views that are populated by the middleware using queries that join relations stored at different sites. We discuss techniques for performing such global joins in Section 18.3.1.

The application designer might choose to replicate certain data items and designate the sites at which the replicas are to reside. However, replication is hidden from the application program. The program accesses a logical data item, and the middleware automatically manages the replication, supplying an appropriate replica to satisfy a query and updating all replicas when appropriate. This is referred to as **replication transparency**.

Restricted global schema. The application designer sees a single global schema, but the schema is the union (as contrasted with a view) of the schemas of individual databases. Thus, the restricted global schema consists of all the tables of the individual databases.

Restricted global schemas are supported by the vendors of some homogeneous systems. The database servers supplied by such a vendor cooperate directly, eliminating the need for middleware, but still function as shown in Figure 18.1(b).[1]

Applications use a naming convention to refer to the tables in each database. Thus, the location of the tables can be hidden from the application (location transparency). A connection to a site is made automatically when a table at that site is accessed.

The application can execute an SQL statement that refers to tables at different sites—for example, a global join. The system includes a global query optimizer to design efficient query plans and provides replication transparency.

18.2 DISTRIBUTING DATA AMONG DIFFERENT DATABASES

In many cases, the distribution of data among different sites is not under the control of the application designer. For example, certain data items might have to be stored at a particular site for security reasons. In other situations, the designer can participate in the decision as to where data is stored or replicated. In this section, we describe several issues related to data distribution.

18.2.1 Fragmentation

The simplest way to distribute data is to store individual tables at different sites. However, a table is not necessarily the best choice as the unit of distribution. Frequently a transaction accesses only a subset of the rows of a table, or a view of a table, rather than the table as a whole. If different transactions access different portions of the table and run at different sites, performance can be improved by storing a portion of the table at the site where the corresponding transaction is executed. When a table is decomposed in this way, we refer to the portions as **fragments**. For such applications, fragments are a better unit of data distribution.

Distributing the fragments of a table has other potential advantages. For example, the time to process a single query over a large table can be reduced by distributing the execution over a number of sites at which fragments are stored. Consider, for example, the query that produces the names and grade point averages of all students at a university. If the STUDENT and TRANSCRIPT tables are stored at the central administrative site, all processing takes place there. If, instead, the tables are fragmented and stored at individual campuses, the DBMSs at each campus

---

[1] The view described here is similar to that supplied by Oracle except that the Oracle implementation supports a certain amount of heterogeneity by allowing limited access to databases from other vendors.

can execute in parallel and together produce the result in less time. Furthermore, distributing fragments might make it possible to improve throughput, provided that a query executed at a site accesses the fragment local to that site. Fragmentation can be either horizontal or vertical.

Horizontal fragmentation.   A table, **T**, is partitioned into fragments

$$\mathbf{T}_1, \mathbf{T}_2, \ldots, \mathbf{T}_r$$

where each fragment contains a subset of the rows of **T** and each row of **T** is in exactly one fragment. For example, the Internet grocer might have a relation

> INVENTORY(StockNum, Amount, Price, Location)

to describe its inventory, together with the location of the warehouse where it is stored. The grocer might horizontally fragment the relation by city, so that, for example, it stores all the tuples satisfying

> Location = 'Chicago'   (18.1)

in a fragment named INVENTORY_CH at the Chicago warehouse, with the schema

> INVENTORY_CH(StockNum, Amount, Price, Location)

(The attribute Location is now redundant and can be omitted.) Because each tuple is stored in some fragment, horizontal fragmentation is lossless. The table can be reconstructed by taking the union of its fragments.

More generally, each fragment satisfies

$$\mathbf{T}_i = \sigma_{C_i}(\mathbf{T})$$

where C_i is a selection condition and each tuple in **T** satisfies C_i for some value of i. Expression (18.1) is an example of a selection condition.

Vertical fragmentation.   A table, **T**, is divided into fragments

$$\mathbf{T}_1, \mathbf{T}_2, \ldots, \mathbf{T}_r$$

where each fragment contains a subset of the columns of **T**. Each column must be included in at least one fragment, and each fragment must include the columns of a candidate key (the same for all fragments).

Thus, the Internet grocer might have a relation

> EMPLOYEE(SSnum, Name, Salary, Title, Location)

to describe its employees at all warehouses. It might vertically fragment EMPLOYEE as

> EMP1 (SSnum, Name, Salary)
> EMP2 (SSnum, Name, Title, Location)

where EMP1 is stored at the headquarters site (where the payroll is computed) and EMP2 is stored elsewhere. Because each column must be in at least one fragment and all fragments include the same candidate key, vertical fragmentation is lossless:

By taking the natural join of its fragments the original table can be reconstructed. Because the candidate key is included in each fragment, vertical fragmentation involves replication. Other columns might be replicated as well. In our case, Name is included in both fragments because it is used by local applications at each site.

Note that the rationale behind vertical fragmentation in the above case is very different from that behind relational normalization, which we discussed in Chapter 8. Indeed, all three relations, EMPLOYEE, EMP1, and EMP2, are in Boyce-Codd normal form, so the algorithms proposed in Chapter 8 leave EMPLOYEE alone.

Mixed fragmentation.   Combinations of horizontal and vertical fragmentation are also possible, but care must be taken to ensure that the original table can be reconstructed from its fragments. One approach is to do one type of fragmentation and then the other. Thus, after our Internet grocer vertically fragments EMPLOYEE into EMP1 and EMP2, it might horizontally fragment EMP2 by location. The fragments corresponding to the Chicago and Buffalo warehouses become

> EMP2_CH (SSnum, Name, Title, Location)
> EMP2_BU (SSnum, Name, Title, Location)

(Once again, the attribute Location might be omitted.) EMP1 is stored at the headquarters site, and EMP2_CH and EMP2_BU are stored at the corresponding warehouse sites.

Derived Horizontal Fragmentation.   In some situations, it might be desirable to horizontally fragment a relation, but the information needed to decide which rows belong in which fragment is not contained in the relation itself. Suppose, for example, that the Internet grocer has more than one warehouse in each city and each warehouse is identified by a warehouse number. Conceptually the database contains two tables:

> INVENTORY(StockNum, Amount, Price, WarehouseNum)
> WAREHOUSE(WarehouseNum, Capacity, Street-address, Location)

The grocer has one database site in each city and wants to horizontally fragment INVENTORY so that a fragment in a particular city contains information about all the items in all the warehouses in that city. The problem is that Location, which identifies the city in which a warehouse is located, is not an attribute of INVENTORY, and so it is not clear how the tuples are to be partitioned.

To solve this problem, we need to know the location of the warehouse that has been identified by a warehouse number. That information is contained in WAREHOUSE. Thus, we need to join the information in the two tables before we can do the fragmentation. We use the *natural join*, since the warehouse number is stored in the two tables using the same attribute name. The rows contained in the fragment of INVENTORY describing Chicago, which we call INVENTORY_CH, are those that join with the rows of WAREHOUSE that satisfy the predicate Location = 'Chicago'. Hence,

$$\text{INVENTORY\_CH} = \pi_A (\text{INVENTORY} \bowtie (\sigma_{\text{Location='Chicago'}}(\text{WAREHOUSE})))$$

where A is the set of all attributes of INVENTORY. The join is used only to *locate* the rows of INVENTORY that we want to include in INVENTORY_CH. Because we do not want to retain any columns of WAREHOUSE, we project the result of the join on the attributes in A. Since

$$\sigma_{\text{Location = 'Chicago'}} \text{WAREHOUSE}$$

is a fragment of WAREHOUSE, the fragmentation of INVENTORY is derived from a fragmentation of WAREHOUSE, and we refer to this type of fragmentation as **derived fragmentation**. INVENTORY_CH is a *semijoin* of INVENTORY with a fragment of WAREHOUSE. We discuss semijoins in Section 18.3.1.

Horizontal fragmentation is used when (most) applications at each site need to access only a *subset of the tuples* in a relation; vertical fragmentation is used when (most) applications at each site need to access only a *subset of the attributes* in a relation. We discuss methods for numerically comparing various possible database designs involving fragmentation in Section 18.3.

Architectures based on the global schema can provide **fragmentation transparency**. This means that the relation appears in its original unfragmented form in the global schema and the middleware transforms any accesses to it into appropriate accesses to its fragments stored in different databases. In contrast, multidatabase systems do not provide fragmentation transparency—each application program must be aware of the fragmentation and use it appropriately in its queries.

18.2.2 Updates and Fragmentation

Although our main interest has been in queries, we note that, when relations are fragmented, update operations sometimes require tuples to be moved from one fragment to another and hence from one database site to another. Suppose that an employee of the Internet grocer is transferred from the Chicago warehouse to the Buffalo warehouse. In the unfragmented EMPLOYEE relation,

        EMPLOYEE (SSnum, Name, Salary, Title, Location)

the value of the Location attribute for that employee's tuple must be changed. If EMPLOYEE is fragmented into EMP2_CH and EMP2_BU, as described earlier, updating the Location attribute for that employee requires moving the corresponding tuple from the Chicago database to the Buffalo database.

The possibility that updates as well as queries might require moving data from one site to another must be taken into account when deciding where to place the data in a distributed database.

18.2.3 Replication

Replication is one of the most used, and most useful, mechanisms in distributed databases. Replicating data at several sites provides increased availability, because the data can still be accessed if some of the sites fail. It also has the potential for improving performance: Queries can be executed more efficiently because the data can be read from a local or nearby copy. However, updates are usually slower because all replicas of the data must be updated. Hence, performance is improved in applications in which updates occur substantially less often than queries. In this section, we discuss performance issues related to the execution of individual SQL statements. In Section 26.7, we will extend the discussion to the performance of transactions that access a database containing replicated data.

Example.   To keep track of its customers, the Internet grocer might have a relation

CUSTOMER(CustNum, Address, Location)

where Location specifies an area serviced by a particular warehouse. The relation is queried at the headquarters site by an application that sends monthly mailings to all customers and each warehouse site queries the relation to obtain information about deliveries in its area. The relation is updated at the headquarters site when (1) a new customer registers with the company or (2) information about a particular customer changes (which happens infrequently).

Intuitively, it seems appropriate to horizontally fragment the relation by Location so that a particular fragment is stored both at the corresponding warehouse and at headquarters. Thus the relation would be replicated, with a complete copy at the headquarters site. We perform an analysis to evaluate that design choice, compared to two others in which data is not replicated. The three choices are as follows:

1. Store the entire relation at the headquarters site and nothing at the warehouses.

2. Store all fragments at the warehouse sites with nothing at headquarters.

3. Replicate the fragments at both sites.

One way to compare the alternatives is to estimate the amount of information that must be transmitted between sites in each case when the specified applications are executed. To do this, we make the following assumptions about table sizes and the frequency with which each application is executed:

■ The CUSTOMER relation has about 100,000 tuples.

■ The mailing application at headquarters sends each customer one mailing each month.

■ About 500 deliveries per day (over all warehouses) are performed, and a single tuple must be read for each delivery.

■ The company gets about 100 new customers a day (and the number of changes to individual customers' information is negligible by comparison).

Now we can evaluate the three alternatives.

1. If we store the relation at the headquarters site, information must be transmitted from there to the appropriate warehouse site whenever a delivery is made—about 500 tuples per day.

2. If we store the fragments at the warehouse sites, information must be transmitted as follows:

❑ From the warehouses to headquarters when the mailing application is executed (about 100,000 tuples per month or 3,300 per day

❑ From headquarters to the warehouses when a new customer registers (about 100 tuples per day)

In total, then, about 3,400 tuples per day must be transmitted.

3. If we replicate the fragments at both headquarters and the warehouses, information must be sent from the headquarters site to the appropriate warehouse site when a new customer registers—about 100 tuples per day.

By this measure, replication appears to be the best alternative. However, other issues might be important, such as the response time of transactions.

1. If we store the relation at headquarters, the time to handle deliveries suffers because of the required remote access. This might not be viewed as important.

2. If we store the fragments at the warehouses and the monthly mailing is done by a single application, the 100,000 tuples that must be sent from the warehouses to headquarters might clog the communication system and slow down other applications. This can be avoided by running the mailing application late at night over the weekend when few other applications are executing.

3. If we replicate the fragments, the time to register a new customer suffers because of the time required to update the tables at both the headquarters and the appropriate warehouse. This might be viewed as important because the customer is online when the update occurs and the time required to update the remote table might make the registration time unacceptably long. However, for this application the customer interaction can be considered complete when the headquarters database is updated. The update at the warehouse site can be performed later because the information is not needed there until some delivery transaction is executed. We discuss such **asynchronous-update replication** in Sections 15.3.3 and 26.7.

We see from this that replicating the fragments still seems to be the best alternative.

18.3   QUERY PLANNING STRATEGIES

A multidatabase system is composed of a set of independent DBMSs. In one type of multidatabase, each DBMS presents an SQL interface to applications. In order to query information stored at multiple sites, the query must be decomposed into a sequence of SQL statements, each of which is processed by a particular DBMS. On receiving an SQL statement, the query optimizer at a site develops a query execution plan, the statement is executed, and results are returned to the application.

Systems that support a global schema contain a global query optimizer, which analyzes a query using the global schema and translates it into an appropriate sequence of steps to be executed at individual sites. Each step can be further optimized by the local query optimizer at a site and then executed. Global query processing thus involves a distributed algorithm that in turn involves direct exchange of data between DBMSs. As a result, in addition to the SQL interface that a DBMS presents to an application, the DBMS presents an interface that supports the direct exchange of data with other DBMSs.

In both cases, we are interested in executing the query efficiently. Since the cost of I/O is so much greater than that of computation, our measure of the efficiency of a query execution plan in Chapter 13 was an estimate of the number of I/O operations it requires. By similar reasoning, the cost of evaluating a query over a distributed database is based on the communication costs involved since communication is both expensive and time consuming.

Our interest in query optimization is threefold. A familiarity with algorithms for global query optimization helps in designing

■ Global queries that will execute efficiently in systems that contain global query optimizers

■ Global queries that will execute efficiently in multidatabase systems that do not contain global query optimizers (Section 18.3.2)

■ Distributed databases on which global queries will execute efficiently (Section 18.3.3)

18.3.1 Global Query Optimization

Planning with joins.   Queries that involve a join of tables at different sites (a global join) are particularly expensive, since information must be exchanged between sites in order to determine the tuples in the result. For example, suppose that an application at site A wants to join tables at sites B and C, with the result to be returned to site A. Two straightforward ways to execute the join that might be evaluated by a global query optimizer are:

1. Transmit both tables to site A and execute the join there. The application program at site A then explicitly tests the join condition. This is the approach used in multidatabase systems that do not support global joins.

2. Transmit the smaller of the tables—for example, the table at site B, to site C, execute the join at site C, and then transmit the result to site A.

To be more specific, we consider two tables, STUDENT(Id, Major) and TRANSCRIPT(StudId, CrsCode), where STUDENT records the major of each student and TRANSCRIPT records the courses in which a student is registered this semester. These tables are stored at sites B and C, respectively. Suppose that an application at site A wants to compute an equijoin with the join condition

$$Id = StudId \tag{18.2}$$

To compare alternative query plans, we must make certain assumptions about table sizes and, in some cases, about the relative frequency of operations on those tables. For this example, we assume that

■ The lengths of the attributes are:

❑ Id and StudId: 9 bytes;

❑ Major: 3 bytes;

❑ CrsCode: 6 bytes.

■ STUDENT has about 15,000 tuples, each of length 12 bytes ($9 + 3$).

■ Approximately 5,000 students are registered for at least one course, and, on average, each student is registered for 4 courses. Thus, TRANSCRIPT has about 20,000 tuples, each of length 15 bytes ($= 9 + 6$). Note that 10,000 students are not registered for any course (this is the summer session).

The join then has about 20,000 tuples (each tuple in TRANSCRIPT corresponds to a tuple in the join), each of length 18 bytes ($= 9 + 3 + 6$).

Based on these assumptions, we can compare the above alternatives.

1. If we send both tables to site A to perform the join, we have to send 480,000 bytes ($= 15,000 * 12 + 20,000 * 15$).

2. If we send STUDENT to site C, compute the join there, and then send the result to site A, we have to send 540,000 bytes ($= 15,000 * 12 + 20,000 * 18$).

3. If we send TRANSCRIPT to site B, compute the join there, and then send the result to site A, we have to send 660,000 bytes ($= 20,000 * 15 + 20,000 * 18$).

Thus, we see that the best of the three is alternative 1.

Planning with semijoins.   Another, often more efficient approach that a global query optimizer might consider is to transmit from site B to site C only those tuples from STUDENT that will actually participate in the join, and then perform the join at site C between those tuples and TRANSCRIPT. This approach involves performing what is called a *semijoin*. The procedure involves three steps.

1. At site C, compute a table, **P**, that is the projection of TRANSCRIPT on StudId— the column involved in the join condition—and then send **P** to site B. Hence, **P** contains the Ids of students who are currently registered for at least one course.

2. At site B, form the join of STUDENT with **P** using join condition (18.2) and then send the resulting table, **Q**, to site C. **Q** contains all of the tuples in STUDENT that participate in the join. In the example, **Q** consists of all tuples in STUDENT corresponding to students registered for at least one course.

3. At site C, join TRANSCRIPT with **Q** using the join condition. The result is the join of STUDENT and TRANSCRIPT, which is then sent to site A.

The result of step 2, the relation **Q**, is called the *semijoin* of STUDENT with TRANSCRIPT. More generally, the **semijoin** of two relations, T_1 and T_2, based on a join condition, is defined to be the projection over the columns of T_1 of the join of T_1 and T_2:

$$\pi_{attributes(T_1)} (T_1 \bowtie_{join\text{-}condition} T_2)$$

In other words, the semijoin consists of the tuples of T_1 that participate in the join with T_2. The idea is then to compute the join of the form

$$T_1 \bowtie_{join\text{-}condition} T_2$$

by first computing a semijoin and then joining it with T_2:

$$(\pi_{attributes(T_1)} (T_1 \bowtie_{join\text{-}condition} T_2)) \bowtie_{join\text{-}condition} T_2$$

It is left to exercise 18.10 to show that the above two expressions are equivalent.

It might seem that we have made a step backward by replacing one join with two. However, step 1 provides a clue—namely, the potential savings in performing a semijoin that lie in the following equivalence:

$$\pi_{attributes(T_1)} (T_1 \bowtie_{join\text{-}condition} T_2)$$
$$= \pi_{attributes(T_1)} (\pi_{attributes(join\text{-}condition)}(T_2) \bowtie_{join\text{-}condition} T_1)$$

In other words, in computing a semijoin of T_1 and T_2 we can first take the projection of T_2 on the attributes mentioned in the join condition and then join the result with T_1 (using the same join condition). We leave the proof of this equivalence to exercise 18.9. This first step potentially cuts communication costs, because the projection of T_2 can be substantially smaller than T_2, so we avoid sending large chunks of data over the communication link. However, we do have to pay for performing the additional join between the result of the semijoin and T_2. If the savings in communication dominate the overhead of the extra join, we come out on top.

In our example, the three steps of the computation correspond to the following algebraic expression:

$$\pi_{attributes(\textsc{Student})} (\pi_{attributes(join\text{-}condition)}(\textsc{Transcript})$$
$$\bowtie_{join\text{-}condition} \textsc{Student})$$
$$\bowtie_{join\text{-}condition} \textsc{Transcript}$$

which, according to the above discussion, must be the same as computing the join of STUDENT and TRANSCRIPT.

It is instructive to compare this approach with the previous ones.

1. In step 1, we send 45,000 bytes ($= 5,000 * 9$).
2. In step 2, we send 60,000 bytes ($= 5,000 * 12$).
3. In step 3, we send 360,000 bytes ($= 20,000 * 18$).

Thus, we send a total of 465,000 bytes ($= 45,000 + 60,000 + 360,000$). Hence, in terms of communication cost, the semijoin alternative is better than the other alternatives we have investigated.

Implementing global joins with replication.   Still another way to implement a global join is to store a replica of one of the tables at the site of the other, thus turning the global join into a local join. In the example, we might store a replica of the STUDENT table at site C perform the join with TRANSCRIPT at site C, and then send the result, 360,000 bytes, to site A.

This approach speeds up the join operation, but slows down updates of the replicated table. In the example, such updates might be rare, because students seldom change their major.

Queries that involve joins and projections.   Most queries involve not only joins but also other relational operators. In the above example, suppose that an application at site A executes a query that returns the majors and course codes of all students who are registered for at least one course. Thus, the row (CS, CS305) will be in the result table if there is at least one computer science (CS) student taking CS305. The query first takes the join of the two tables, STUDENT and TRANSCRIPT, and then projects on Major and CrsCode to obtain the result table, **R**. Our plan is to do the projection at the site at which the join is performed and then send **R** to site A.

In order to re-evaluate the communication costs of the four alternatives we considered in the last section, we need to make one additional assumption—that **R** has 1,000 tuples. Each tuple has a length of 9 bytes, so the size of **R** is 9,000 bytes, making it much smaller than the joined table. That is common in real queries.

1. If we send both tables to site A and do all operations there, we have to send, as before, 480,000 bytes.
2. If we send the STUDENT table to site C, do the operations there, and then send **R** to site A, we have to send 189,000 bytes ($= 15{,}000 * 12 + 1{,}000 * 9$).
3. If we send the TRANSCRIPT table to site B, do the operations there, and then send **R** to site A, we have to send 309,000 bytes ($= 20{,}000 * 15 + 1{,}000 * 9$).
4. If we perform the semijoin as previously described, perform the projection at site C, and then send **R** to site A, we have to send 114,000 bytes ($= 5{,}000 * 9 + 5{,}000 * 12 + 1{,}000 * 9$).

Hence, the semijoin approach is still the best alternative.

We can optimize this procedure by changing step 2 so that, after performing the semijoin to obtain **Q**, we do a projection on **Q** to retain only the columns of STUDENT needed for the query. Only those columns are sent from site B to site C. For example, suppose that STUDENT has additional attributes (such as Address, Date_of_Birth, Entrance_date,) and that, as before, the query requests the Id, CrsCode, and Major of students for each course in which a student is registered. Then, in step 2, we can project on those attributes named in the WHERE and SELECT clauses and send only those to site C.

This idea can be used in all of the approaches discussed so far. Before a table is sent from one site to another to perform a join, all unnecessary attributes can be eliminated.

Queries that involve joins and selections.   A similar idea can be used when the query involves joins and selections. For example, suppose that there is only one warehouse in the Internet grocer application and that the EMPLOYEE relation is vertically fragmented as

```
EMP1 (SSnum, Name, Salary)
EMP2 (SSnum, Title, Location)                                    (18.3)
```

These relations are stored at sites B (headquarters) and C (warehouse), respectively. Suppose that a query at a third site, A, requests the names of all managers whose salary is more than $20,000. (If we had assumed more than one warehouse, the reasoning would have been similar but the arithmetic would have been a bit more complex—see exercise 18.14.)

A straightforward approach is to first perform the join of the tables (to regenerate the EMPLOYEE table) and then use the selection and projection operators on the result to obtain:

$$\pi_{\text{NAME}}(\sigma_{\text{Title='manager' AND Salary>'20000'}} (\text{EMP1} \bowtie \text{EMP2}))$$

Unfortunately, using the semijoin procedure to optimize the join will not reduce communication costs. This is because the two tables are the vertical fragments of the joined table, so EMP1 and EMP2 both contain a candidate key of EMPLOYEE. Hence all tuples of each table must be brought together to reconstruct EMPLOYEE.

Note, however, that the selection condition can be partitioned into selection conditions on the individual tables.

■ Selection condition `Salary > '20000'` on EMP1

■ Selection condition `Title = 'Manager'` on EMP2

Now we can use the mathematical properties of the relational operators to change the order of the join and selection operators (recall the cascading and pushing rules for selection in Section 14.2):

$$\pi_{\text{NAME}}((\sigma_{\text{Salary>'20000'}} \text{EMP1}) \bowtie (\sigma_{\text{Title='Manager'}} \text{EMP2}))$$

Specifically,

1. At site B, select all tuples from EMP1 for which the salary is more than $20,000. Call the result R_1.

2. At site C, select all tuples from EMP2 for which the title is manager. Call the result R_2.

3. At some site (to be determined below), perform the join of R_1 and R_2 and project on the result using the `Name` attribute. Call the result R_3. If this site is not site A, send R_3 to site A.

The only remaining issue is where to perform the join in step 3. There are three possibilities.

1. Plan 1: Send R_2 to site B, and do the join there. Then send the names to site A.

2. Plan 2: Send R_1 to site C, and do the join there. Then send the names to site A.

3. Plan 3: Send R_1 and R_2 to site A, and do the join there

As before, to determine the best plan we must take into account the sizes of the various tables and the size of the result. We make the following assumptions:

■ The lengths of the attributes are

❑ SSnum: 9 bytes;

❑ Salary: 6 bytes;

❑ Title: 7 bytes;

❑ Location: 10 bytes;

❑ Name: 15 bytes.

Thus, the length of each tuple in EMP1 is 30 bytes and in EMP2 is 26 bytes.

■ EMP1 (and hence EMP2) has about 100,000 tuples.

■ About 5,000 employees have a salary of more than $20,000. Therefore, R_1 has about 5,000 tuples (each of length 30 bytes), for a total of 150,000 bytes.

■ There are about 50 managers. Therefore, R_2 has about 50 tuples (each of length 26 bytes), for a total of 1,300 bytes.

■ About 90% of the managers have a salary of more than $20,000. Therefore, R_3 has about 45 tuples, each of length 15 bytes, for a total of 675 bytes.

We can now evaluate the cost of each plan.

1. If we do the join at site B, we have to send 1,300 bytes from site C to site B, and then 675 bytes from site B to site A, for a total of 1,975 bytes.

2. If we do the join at site C, we have to send 150,000 bytes from site B to site C, and then 675 bytes from site C to site A, for a total of 150,675 bytes.

3. If we do the join at site A, we have to send 150,000 bytes from site B to site A, and 1,300 bytes from site C to site A, for a total of 151,300 bytes.

As you can see, the first plan is substantially better than the other two.

To fully appreciate a well-designed query plan, compare the cost of this plan with the cost of the unoptimized plan in which EMP1 and EMP2 are sent, in their entirety, to site A and the query is evaluated there. In that case, 5,600,000 bytes ($= 2,600,000 + 3,000,000$) have to be transmitted!

18.3.2 Strategies for a Multidatabase System

An application accessing a multidatabase system cannot submit an SQL statement over a global schema. Instead, a query involving data at several sites must be constructed using a sequence of SQL statements, each of which is formulated over the schema of a particular DBMS and processed at that site. Although global query optimizers do not exist in such an environment, the application designer can use some of the ideas discussed in Section 18.3.1 to choose a suitable sequence of statements for query evaluation. Unfortunately, the designer is limited in two important ways, which we illustrate using the Internet grocer example.

1. In a multidatabase system, data can be communicated only between a database site and the site at which a query is submitted—site A in the example. With a global query optimizer, on the other hand, database sites cooperate with one another and communicate directly.

2. Even though data cannot be transmitted directly between database sites, we might consider transferring data from one site to another indirectly through site A. This approach is not possible, however. Although site A can receive data from a DBMS (as a result of submitting a SELECT statement), it cannot send data to a DBMS because the application interface is concerned only with processing SQL statements (not receiving data).

This makes it essentially impossible to mimic step 1 of the semijoin procedure (page 634), in which a projection of a table (**P** in that step) is transmitted.[2]

Example. Let us reconsider the fragmented EMPLOYEE table of the previous section and the query at site A that requests the names of all managers whose salary is more than $20,000. If the query were executed in a system with a global optimizer, we would expect the optimizer to choose plan 1, which has a communication cost of 1,975 bytes.

If the same query were executed in a multidatabase system, the application designer could first execute SELECT statements at each site that returned R_1 and R_2 to site A. The program would then perform the necessary processing on these tuples to implement the join operation. The communication cost would be the same as plan 3: 151,300 bytes. Although this strategy would not be as efficient as the best strategy that can be chosen by a global query optimizer, it would certainly be an improvement over the naive strategy that brings EMP1 and EMP2 in their entirety to site A, at the cost of 5,500,000 bytes.

18.3.3 Tuning Issues: Database Design and Query Planning in a Distributed Environment

As in the centralized case, query planning for distributed databases involves evaluating alternatives, among which are

■ Performing operations at different sites

■ Sending partial results or entire tables from one site to another during query execution

■ Performing semijoins

■ Using the heuristic optimization rules for relational algebra (Section 14.2) to reorder operations

Application designers do not have any significant control over the strategies used by a global query optimizer. However, the designer often does have control over the design of the distributed database, and that design can have a significant

---

[2] Site A might try to get around this limitation by dynamically constructing a SELECT statement based on the rows in **P**. For example, if **P** has a single attribute, attr, and the column values are a, b, . . . , then the WHERE clause might contain the terms (attr = 'a' OR attr = 'b' OR . . .). Note that the projection $\pi_{attr}(\mathbf{P})$ is encoded in the WHERE clause of the query. Therefore, transmitting this query to a remote site is tantamount to A sending $\pi_{attr}(\mathbf{P})$ to that site. Therefore, when site A receives the query result, it is conceptually equivalent to receiving the result of the semijoin from the remote site. Unfortunately, this approach works only if the domain of attr is very small.

effect on query planning by changing the alternatives available to the global query optimizer. This is also true if query planning is done manually by the application designer for a multidatabase system.

In the centralized case, the application designer might change the database schema by, for example, adding indices or denormalizing tables (see Sections 8.13, 13.7, and 14.6). In the distributed case, she might have additional choices, such as

■ Placing tables at different sites

■ Fragmenting tables in different ways and placing the fragments at different sites

■ Replicating tables, or data within tables (e.g., denormalizing), and placing the replicas at different sites

As in the centralized case, these choices might speed up certain operations and slow down others. Thus, the designer must evaluate a proposed database design based on the relative frequency of each operation in the application and the importance of throughput and response time for that operation.

In the Internet grocer application, fragmenting the INVENTORY relation speeds up local applications involving delivery of merchandise but slows down global applications that require joining the fragments—for example, computing the total inventory for the company. In evaluating these alternatives, the enterprise might decide that the delivery application must execute quickly but that the total inventory application might execute infrequently with no significant demand on its response time.

The application designer might then consider speeding up the global inventory application by replicating the warehouse inventory information in the headquarters database. But this alternative will probably be rejected because the warehouse inventory information is updated frequently—every time a delivery is made—and the communication cost of updating the replicas is much greater than that of performing the global inventory application. Evaluating such tradeoffs is essential in designing an application that executes efficiently and meets the needs of the enterprise.

18.4   BIBLIOGRAPHIC NOTES

Our description of distributed query processing is based on the implementations of two systems, SDD-1 [Wong 1977, Bernstein et al. 1981] and System R* [Griffiths-Selinger and Adiba 1980]. The theory of semijoins is discussed in [Bernstein and Chiu 1981]. Fragmentation is discussed in [Chang and Cheng 1980, Ceri et al. 1982]. More in-depth study of a number of issues in distributed databases (especially database design and query processing) can be found in specialized texts, such as [Ceri and Pelagatti 1984, Bell and Grimson 1992], and [Ozsu and Valduriez 1991].

18.5 EXERCISES

18.1 Discuss the advantages to the application designer of designing an application as a homogeneous system in which all databases are supplied by the same vendor.

18.2 Explain why a table might be fragmented in the schema of a centralized system.

18.3 Explain whether or not the following statement is true: The join of two tables obtained by a (vertical or horizontal) fragmentation of a table, **T**, can never contain more tuples than are contained in **T**.

18.4 Consider the two examples of query design in a multidatabase system given in Section 18.3.2. Write programs in Java and JDBC that implement both.

18.5 Give an example of a program at site A that requires the join of two tables, one at site B and one at site C. State the assumptions needed to justify the result that, as far as communication costs are concerned, the best implementation is to ship the table at site B to site C, do the join there, and then send the result to site A.

18.6 You are considering the possibility of horizontally fragmenting the relation

> EMPLOYEE (SSN, Name, Salary, Title, Location)

by location and storing each fragment in the database at that location, with the possibility of replicating some fragments at different sites. Discuss the types of queries and updates (and their frequencies) that might influence your decision.

18.7 Suppose that we have a relation

> EMPLOYEE2 (SSnum, Name, Salary, Age, Title, Location)

which is fragmented as

> EMP21 (SSnum, Name, Salary)
> EMP22 (SSnum, Title, Age, Location)

where EMP21 is stored at site B and EMP22 is stored at site C. A query at site A wants the names of all managers in the accounting department whose salary is greater than their age. Design a plan for this query, using the assumptions on page 638 for table and attribute sizes. Assume that the items in the Age column are 2 bytes long.

18.8 Design a multidatabase query plan and a set of SQL statements that implement the query of the previous exercise.

18.9 Use relational algebra to show that step 2 of the method used in Section 18.3.1 to perform a join using a semijoin does in fact generate the semijoin. For simplicity, assume that the join we are attempting is a natural join. That is, prove that

$$\pi_{attributes(T_1)} (T_1 \bowtie T_2) = \pi_{attributes(T_1)} (\pi_{attributes(join\text{-}condition)}(T_1) \bowtie T_2)$$

18.10 Use relational algebra to show that step 3 of the method used in Section 18.3.1 to perform a join using a semijoin does in fact generate the join. For simplicity, assume that the join we are attempting is a natural join. In other words, show that

$$\pi_{attributes(T_1)} (T_1 \bowtie T_2) \bowtie T_2 = (T_1 \bowtie T_2).$$

18.11 Design a query plan for the join example in Section 18.3.1, assuming the same table sizes as in that section, but with the following differences:

a. an application at site B requested the join.

b. an application at site C requested the join.

18.12 Use relational algebra to show that the method of designing horizontal fragmentations described in Section 18.2.1 works as advertised.

18.13 Show that the semijoin operation is not commutative, that is, T_1 semijoined with T_2 is not the same as T_2 semijoined with T_1.

18.14 Use the example schema (18.3), page 637, to design a query for finding the names of all managers (employees with Title = 'manager') whose salary is more than $20,000, but assume that there are three warehouses. Also assume that the total number of employees is 100,000, that 5,000 of them make over $20,000, that the total number of managers is 50, and that 90% of the managers make more than $20,000.

Chapter 19

OLAP and Data Mining

This chapter surveys some concepts and techniques from the emerging fields of *online analytical processing* (OLAP), *data warehousing*, and *data mining*. A good survey of OLAP appears in [Chaudhuri and Dayal 1997]. Data mining, a much larger field than OLAP, spans databases, statistical analysis, and machine learning. Here we only scratch the surface, but we refer you to a collection of articles on applications and current research in [Fayyad et al. 1996] and to a recently published textbook [Han and Kamber 2001].

19.1 OLAP AND DATA WAREHOUSES—OLD AND NEW

Why is so much free material available on the Internet—all for just filling out a form? In fact, the goodies you receive are not free—you are paying for them by providing information about yourself, and, when you buy on the Internet, you are providing even more information about yourself—your buying habits.

You also provide information about yourself when you purchase items in a department store or supermarket with your credit card. In these cases, you are inputting information into a transaction processing system, and the system is saving that information for future use.

What do they do with this information? In many situations, it is combined with what is known about you from other sources, stored in a database, and then used in several ways.

■ It might be combined with information about the purchases of other people to help an enterprise plan its inventory, advertising, or other aspects of its future strategy.

■ It might be used to produce an individualized profile of your buying (or browsing) habits so that an enterprise can target its marketing to you through the mail or in other ways. Perhaps in the future, the people in your zip code area will see different TV commercials based on information about their purchasing habits. Or perhaps you will see TV commercials personalized for you.

These trends in information gathering and assimilation have serious implications for personal privacy. However, that is not our concern in this text.

These types of applications are referred to as **online analytic processing**, or **OLAP**, in contrast with **online transaction processing**, or **OLTP**. The two types of applications have different goals and different technical requirements.

■ The goal of OLTP is to maintain a database that is an accurate model of some real-world enterprise. The system must provide sufficiently large transaction throughput and low response time to keep up with the load and avoid user frustration. OLTP applications are characterized by

   ❏ Short, simple transactions

   ❏ Relatively frequent updates

   ❏ Transactions that access only a tiny fraction of the database

■ The goal of OLAP is to use the information in a database to guide strategic decisions. The databases involved are usually very large and often need not be completely accurate or up to date. Nor is fast response always required. OLAP applications are characterized by

   ❏ Complex queries

   ❏ Infrequent updates

   ❏ Transactions that access a significant fraction of the database

Our example of an OLAP application in Section 1.4 involved managers of a supermarket chain who want to make one-time (not preprogrammed) queries to the database to gather information they need in order to make a specific decision. This illustrates the traditional use of OLAP—ad hoc queries, often made by people who are not highly technical.

The OLAP examples at the beginning of this section describe some of the newer uses. Businesses are using preprogrammed queries against OLAP databases on an ongoing operational basis to customize their marketing and other aspects of their business. These queries are often complex and, since they are key to the business and used operationally (perhaps daily or weekly), are designed and implemented by professionals.

In traditional OLAP applications, the information in the OLAP database is often just the data the business happens to gather during day-to-day operations—perhaps in its OLTP systems. In newer applications, the business often makes an active effort to gather—perhaps even to purchase—the additional information needed for its planned application.

As the *A* in OLAP implies, the goal of an OLAP application is to *analyze* data for use in some application. Thus, there are often two separate but related technical issues involved.

■ *The analysis procedures to be performed and the data required to support those procedures.* For example, a company wants to decide the mix of products to manufacture during the next accounting period. It develops an analysis procedure that requires as input the sales for the last period and the history of sales for the equivalent periods over the past five years.

■ *The methods to efficiently obtain the large amounts of data required for the analysis.* For example, how can the company extract the required sales data from databases in its subsidiary departments? In what form should it store this data in the OLAP database? How can it retrieve the data efficiently when needed for the analysis?

The first issue, analysis, is not a database problem since it requires algorithms specific to the particular business the company engages in. Our interest here is primarily in the second issue—database support for these analytical procedures. For our purposes, we assume that the retrieved data is simply displayed on the screen. However, in many situations—particularly in newer applications—this data is input to sophisticated analysis procedures.

Data warehouses.   OLAP databases are usually stored in special OLAP servers, often called **data warehouses**, which are structured to support the OLAP queries that will be made against them. OLAP queries are often so complex that if they were run in an OLTP environment, they would slow down OLTP transactions to an unacceptable degree.

We will discuss some of the issues involved in populating a data warehouse in Section 19.7. First, we will look at the kinds of data we might want to store in the warehouse.

19.2   A MULTI-DIMENSIONAL MODEL FOR OLAP APPLICATIONS

Fact tables and dimension tables.   Many OLAP applications are similar to the supermarket example of Section 1.4: analysis of sales of different products in different supermarkets over different time periods. We might describe this sales data with a relational table such as that shown in Figure 19.1. Market_Id identifies a particular supermarket, Product_Id identifies a particular product, Time_Id identifies a particular time interval, and Sales_Amt identifies the dollar value of the sales of that product at that supermarket in that time period. Such a table is called a **fact table** because it contains all of the facts about the data to be analyzed.

We can view this sales data as **multi-dimensional**, because the value of the Sales_Amt attribute is a function of the Market_Id, Product_Id, and Time_Id attributes, which form the dimensions. Note that the first three columns in the table are the dimensions and the fourth column is the actual sales data.

We can also think of the data in a fact table as being arranged in a multidimensional cube. Thus, in the supermarket example the data is arranged in the three-dimensional cube shown in Figure 19.2, where the dimensions of the cube are Market_Id, Product_Id, and Time_Id and the individual **cells** within the cube contain the corresponding Sales_Amt. Such a multi-dimensional view can be an intuitive way to think about OLAP queries and their results.

Additional information about the dimensions can be stored in **dimension tables** which describe dimension attributes, such as Market_Id, Product_Id, and Time_Id. For the supermarket example, these tables might be called MARKET, PRODUCT, and TIME, as shown in Figure 19.3. Thus the MARKET table tells what city, state, and

Figure 19.1 The Fact Table for the Supermarket Application.

SALES	Market_Id	Product_Id	Time_Id	Sales_Amt
	M1	P1	T1	1000
	M1	P2	T1	2000
	M1	P3	T1	1500
	M1	P4	T1	2500
	M2	P1	T1	500
	M2	P2	T1	800
	M2	P3	T1	0
	M2	P4	T1	3333
	M3	P1	T1	5000
	M3	P2	T1	8000
	M3	P3	T1	10
	M3	P4	T1	3300
	M1	P1	T2	1001
	M1	P2	T2	2001
	M1	P3	T2	1501
	M1	P4	T2	2501
	M2	P1	T2	501
	M2	P2	T2	801
	M2	P3	T2	1
	M2	P4	T2	3334
	M3	P1	T2	5001
	M3	P2	T2	8001
	M3	P3	T2	11
	M3	P4	T2	3301
	M1	P1	T3	1002
	M1	P2	T3	2002
	M1	P3	T3	1502
	M1	P4	T3	2502
	M2	P1	T3	502
	M2	P2	T3	802
	M2	P3	T3	2
	M2	P4	T3	333
	M3	P1	T3	5002
	M3	P2	T3	8002
	M3	P3	T3	12
	M3	P4	T3	3302

Figure 19.2 Three-dimensional cube for the supermarket application.

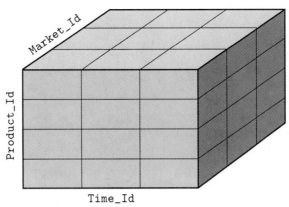

Figure 19.3 Dimension tables for the supermarket application.

MARKET	Market_Id	City	State	Region
	M1	Stony Brook	New York	East
	M2	Newark	New Jersey	East
	M3	Oakland	California	West

PRODUCT	Product_id	Name	Category	Price
	P1	Beer	Drink	1.98
	P2	Diapers	Soft Goods	2.98
	P3	Cold Cuts	Meat	3.98
	P4	Soda	Drink	1.25

TIME	Time_id	Week	Month	Quarter
	T1	Wk-1	January	First
	T2	Wk-24	June	Second
	T3	Wk-52	December	Fourth

region each market is in. In a more realistic example, the MARKET table would contain a row for each supermarket in the chain, which might include many markets in each city, many cities in each state, and many states in each region.

Star schema. The relations corresponding to the supermarket example can be displayed in a diagram, as in Figure 19.4. The figure suggests a star, with the fact table at the center and the dimension tables radiating from it. This type of schema,

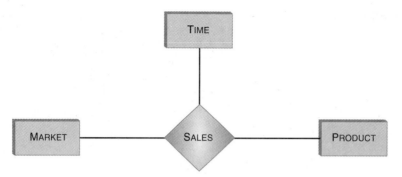

Figure 19.4 Star schema for the supermarket example.

called a **star schema**, is very common in OLAP applications. It is interesting to note that a star schema corresponds to a very common fragment of an entity-relation diagram, where the fact table is a relationship and the dimension tables are entities.

If the dimension tables are normalized (so that each might become several tables), the figure gets a bit more complex and is called a **snowflake schema**. However, for two reasons dimension tables are rarely normalized.

■ They are so small compared with the fact table that the space saved by normalization is negligible.

■ They are updated so infrequently that update anomalies are not an issue. Moreover, in this situation decomposing the relations into 3NF or BCNF might lead to significant query overhead, as explained in Section 8.13.

Instead of a star schema, many OLAP applications use a **constellation schema**, which consists of several fact tables that might share one or more dimension tables. For example, the supermarket application might maintain a fact table called INVENTORY, with dimension tables WAREHOUSE, PRODUCT, and TIME, as shown in Figure 19.5. Note that the PRODUCT and TIME dimension tables are shared with the SALES fact table, whereas the WAREHOUSE table, which describes where the inventory is stored, is not shared.

19.3 AGGREGATION

Many OLAP queries involve **aggregation** of the data in the fact table. For example, the query to find the total sales (over time) of each product in each market can be expressed with the SQL statement

```
SELECT      S.Market_Id, S.Product_Id, SUM(S.Sales_Amt)
FROM        SALES S
GROUP BY    S.Market_Id, S.Product_Id
```

which returns the table shown in Figure 19.6. Here we depict the result table as a two-dimensional cube with the values of the aggregation over Sales_Amt placed

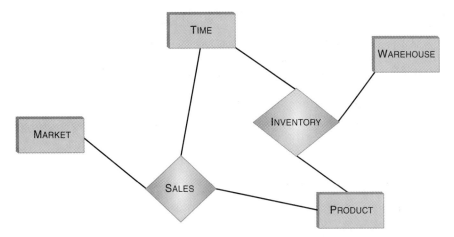

Figure 19.5 Constellation schema for the expanded supermarket example.

Figure 19.6 Query result that aggregates `Sales_Amt` on the time dimension.

		Market_Id		
SUM(Sales_Amt)		M1	M2	M3
	P1	3003	1503	15003
Product_Id	P2	6003	2402	24003
	P3	4503	3	33
	P4	7503	7000	9903

in the cells. Since this aggregation is over the entire time dimension (i.e., the result does not depend on the time coordinate), it produces a reduced dimensional view of the data—two dimensions instead of three.

19.3.1 Drilling, Slicing, Rolling, Dicing

Some dimension tables represent an **aggregation hierarchy**. For example, the MARKET table represents the hierarchy

$$\texttt{Market\_Id} \rightarrow \texttt{City} \rightarrow \texttt{State} \rightarrow \texttt{Region}$$

meaning that supermarkets are in cities, cities are in states, and states are in regions. We can perform queries at different levels of a hierarchy, as shown here:

```
SELECT      S.Product_Id, M.Region, SUM(S.Sales_Amt)
FROM        SALES S,   MARKET M
WHERE       M.Market_Id = S.Market_Id
GROUP BY    M.Region, S.Product_Id
```

Figure 19.7 Query result that drills down on regions.

SUM(Sales_Amt)		Region			
		North	South	East	West
	P1	0	0	4506	15003
Product_Id	P2	0	0	8405	24003
	P3	0	0	4506	33
	P4	0	0	14503	9903

This produces the table of Figure 19.7, which aggregates total sales per product for each region.

When we execute queries that move down a hierarchy—from general to specific, for example, from aggregation over years to aggregation over months—we are said to be **drilling down**. Drilling down, of course, requires access to more specific information. Thus, in order to aggregate over months, we must either use the fact table or a previously computed table that aggregates over days. When we move up the hierarchy (from aggregation over days to aggregation over weeks), we are said to be **rolling up**. It is very common to roll up or drill down using the time dimension—for example, to summarize sales on a daily, monthly, or quarterly basis.

Here is a bit more OLAP terminology. When we view the data in the form of a multi-dimensional cube and then select a subset of the axes, we are said to be performing a **pivot**. The selected axes correspond to the list of attributes in the GROUP BY clause. Pivoting is usually followed by aggregation on the remaining axes.

As an example, the following query performs a pivot of the multi-dimensional cube to view it from the product and time dimensions. It finds the total sales (over all markets) of each product for each quarter (of the current year) and produces the table of Figure 19.8:

```
SELECT      S.Product_Id, T.Quarter,  SUM(S.Sales_Amt)
FROM        SALES S,   TIME T
WHERE       T.Time_Id = S.Time_Id                          (19.1)
GROUP BY    T.Quarter, S.Product_Id
```

If we next ask the same query, but use the GROUP BY clause to group by years instead of by quarters, we are rolling up the time hierarchy.

```
SELECT      S.Product_Id, T.Year, SUM(S.Sales_Amt)
FROM        SALES S,   TIME T
WHERE       T.Time_Id = S.Time_Id
GROUP BY    T.Year, S.Product_Id
```

Figure 19.8 Query result that presents total product sales for each quarter.

SUM(Sales_Amt)		Quarter			
		First	Second	Third	Fourth
	P1	6500	6503	0	6506
Product_Id	P2	10800	10803	0	10806
	P3	1510	1513	0	1516
	P4	9133	9136	0	6137

Figure 19.9 Time hierarchy as a lattice.

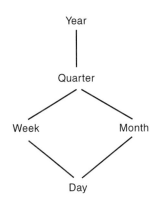

SQL:1999 and some OLAP vendors support a new SQL clause, ROLLUP, to simplify this process (see Section 19.3.2). However, notice that a corresponding drill-down clause is usually *not* provided. The reason is that rollup is not only a convenience but also an optimization device. If the user first asks to aggregate over quarters and then rolls up the result to years, the OLAP system does not need to compute from scratch but can aggregate to the year using the previously computed aggregation results for each quarter. No such optimization is possible for drilling down.

Not all aggregation hierarchies are linear, as is the location hierarchy. The time hierarchy shown in Figure 19.9 for example, is a lattice. Weeks are not contained in months—a week can be in more than one month. Thus, we can roll up days into either weeks or months, but we can only roll up weeks into quarters.

Note that all of the above queries access a significant fraction of the data in the fact table. By contrast, the OLTP query over the database at your local supermarket *How many cans of tomato juice are in stock?* accesses only a single tuple.

Slicing and dicing. We can imagine that the hierarchy for each dimension partitions the multi-dimensional cube into subcubes. Thus, for example, the Quarter level of the time dimension partitions the cube into subcubes, one for each quarter. Queries that return information about those subcubes are said to **slice and dice**.

■ When we use a GROUP BY clause in a query to specify part (or all) of a hierarchy, we are partitioning the multi-dimensional cube into subcubes and so are performing a **dice**. Thus, the query (19.1) performs a dice of the SALES table in the time dimension by partitioning the time dimension into quarters and the cube into one subcube for each quarter.

■ When we use a WHERE clause with an equality condition that compares a dimension attribute to a constant, we are specifying a particular value for that dimension and so are performing a **slice**. If, in the above query, we had asked for the total product sales in each market at time T1, that would have been a slice in the time dimension.

Thus, the difference between dicing and slicing is that dicing partitions the cube into subcubes along the specified dimension whereas slicing selects just one of the subcubes.

19.3.2 The CUBE Operator

Many OLAP queries use the aggregate functions and the GROUP BY clause of the SELECT statement to perform aggregation. However, the standard options for the SELECT statement limit the types of OLAP queries that can be easily formulated in SQL. A number of OLAP vendors (as well as SQL:1999) extend SQL with additional aggregate functions, and at least one vendor allows programmers to provide their own aggregate functions.

One extension is the ROLLUP clause; another is the CUBE operator introduced in [Gray et al. 1997]. Suppose that we want to obtain a table such as that in Figure 19.10—it is similar to the table in Figure 19.6 except that, in addition, it has totals for each row and each column. To construct such a table, we need to use three standard SQL SELECT statements to retrieve the necessary information. The following statement returns the data needed for the table entries (without the totals).

```
SELECT      S.Market_Id, S.Product_Id, SUM(S.Sales_Amt)
FROM        SALES S
GROUP BY    S.Market_Id, S.Product_Id
```

The next statement computes the row totals

```
SELECT      S.Product_Id, SUM(S.Sales_Amt)
FROM        SALES S
GROUP BY    S.Product_Id
```

and the last statement computes the totals for the columns:

```
SELECT      S.Market_Id, SUM(S.Sales_Amt)
FROM        SALES S
GROUP BY    S.Market_Id
```

Figure 19.10 Query result for the sales application in the form of a spreadsheet

SUM(Sales_Amt)		Market_Id			
		M1	M2	M3	Total
	P1	3003	1503	15003	19509
Product_Id	P2	6003	2402	24003	32408
	P3	4503	3	33	4539
	P4	7503	7000	9903	24406
	Total	21012	10908	48942	80862

Three statements are required because the table needs three aggregations—by time, by product Id and time, and by market Id and time—and each is produced by a different GROUP BY clause.

Computing all of these queries *independently* is wasteful of both time and computing resources. The first query does much of the work needed for the second and third queries, so, if we save the result and then use it to aggregate over Market_Id and Product_Id, we can compute the second and third queries more efficiently. Efficient computation of such "data cubes" is important in OLAP, and much research has been dedicated to this issue. See, for example, [Agrawal et al. 1996, Harinarayan et al. 1996, Ross and Srivastava 1997, Zhao et al. 1998].

Economy of scale is the main motivation for the CUBE clause [Gray et al. 1997], which is included in the SQL:1999 standard. When CUBE is used in a GROUP BY clause, as here:

GROUP BY CUBE$(v1, v2, \ldots, vn)$

it is equivalent to a collection of GROUP BYs, one for each of the $2^n - 1$ subsets of $v1, v2, \ldots, vn$. For example, the statement

```
SELECT    S.Market_Id, S.Product_Id, SUM(S.Sales_Amt)
FROM      SALES S
GROUP BY CUBE(S.Market_Id, S.Product_Id)
```

returns the result set of Figure 19.11, which is equivalent to all three of the above SELECT statements and includes all of the values required for the table of Figure 19.10. Note the NULL entries in the columns that are being aggregated. For example, the first NULL in the Product_Id column means that the sales for market M1 are being aggregated over all products.[1]

---

[1] The use of SQL NULL in this context might be confusing, because in this context NULL actually means "all" (it is the aggregation of one of the dimensions).

Figure 19.11 Result set returned with the CUBE operator.

RESULT SET	Market_Id	Product_Id	Sales_Amt
	M1	P1	3003
	M1	P2	6003
	M1	P3	4503
	M1	P4	7503
	M2	P1	1503
	M2	P2	2402
	M2	P3	3
	M2	P4	7000
	M3	P1	15003
	M3	P2	24003
	M3	P3	33
	M3	P4	9902
	M1	NULL	21012
	M2	NULL	10908
	M3	NULL	48092
	NULL	P1	19509
	NULL	P2	32409
	NULL	P3	4539
	NULL	P4	23406
	NULL	NULL	80862

ROLLUP is similar to CUBE except that, instead of aggregating all subsets of its arguments, it creates subsets by moving from right to left. Like CUBE, the ROLLUP option to the GROUP BY clause is included in SQL:1999.

Consider the above SELECT statement in which CUBE has been replaced with ROLLUP.

```
SELECT    S.Market_Id, S.Product_Id, SUM(S.Sales_Amt)
FROM      SALES S                                              (19.2)
GROUP BY ROLLUP(S.Market_Id, S.Product_Id)
```

The syntax here says that aggregation should be computed first with the finest granularity, using GROUP BY S.Market_Id, S.Product_Id, and then with the next level of granularity, using GROUP BY S.Market_Id. Finally, the grand total is computed, which corresponds to the empty GROUP BY clause. The result set is depicted in Figure 19.12. In a larger example (with more attributes in the ROLLUP clause), the result set table would contain some rows with NULL in the last column, some with NULL in the last two columns, some with NULL in the last three columns, and so on.

Figure 19.12 Result set returned with the ROLLUP operator.

RESULT SET	Market_ Id	Product_Id	Sales_Amt
	M1	P1	3003
	M1	P2	6003
	M1	P3	4503
	M1	P4	7503
	M2	P1	1503
	M2	P2	2402
	M2	P3	3
	M2	P4	7000
	M3	P1	15003
	M3	P2	24003
	M3	P3	33
	M3	P4	9902
	M1	NULL	21012
	M2	NULL	10908
	M3	NULL	48092
	NULL	NULL	80862

Note that the ROLLUP operator of OLAP-extended SQL is a generalization of the idea of rolling up the aggregation hierarchy described on page 650. Moreover, the cost savings from reusing the results of fine-grained aggregations to compute coarser-levels of aggregation apply to the general ROLLUP operator. For instance, in query (19.2), aggregations computed for the clause GROUP BY S.Market_ Id, S.Product_Id can be reused in the computation of aggregates for the clause GROUP BY S.Market_Id. These aggregates can then be reused in the computation of the grand total.

Materialized views using the CUBE operator. The CUBE operator can be used to precompute aggregations on all dimensions of a fact table and then save them for use in future queries. Thus, the statement

```
SELECT    S.Market_Id, S.Product_Id, SUM(S.Sales_Amt)
FROM      SALES S
GROUP BY CUBE(S.Market_Id, S.Product_Id, S.Time_Id)
```

produces a result set that is the table of Figure 19.1 with the addition of rows corresponding to aggregations on all subsets of the dimensions. The *additional* rows are shown in Figure 19.13. If this result set is saved as a materialized view, it can speed up subsequent queries.

Figure 19.13 Tuples added to the fact table by the CUBE operator.

RESULT SET	Market_Id	Product_Id	Time_Id	Sales_Amt
	. . .	. . .	. . .	. . .
	NULL	P1	T1	6500
	NULL	P2	T1	10800
	NULL	P3	T1	1510
	NULL	P4	T1	9133
	NULL	P1	T2	6503
	NULL	P2	T2	10803
	NULL	P3	T2	1513
	NULL	P4	T2	9136
	NULL	P1	T3	6506
	NULL	P2	T3	10806
	NULL	P3	T3	1516
	NULL	P4	T3	6137
	M1	NULL	T1	7000
	M2	NULL	T1	4633
	M3	NULL	T1	4610
	M1	NULL	T2	7004
	M2	NULL	T2	4634
	M3	NULL	T2	16314
	M1	NULL	T3	7008
	M2	NULL	T3	1639
	M3	NULL	T3	16318
	M1	P1	NULL	3003
	M1	P2	NULL	6003
	M1	P3	NULL	4503
	M1	P4	NULL	7503
	M2	P1	NULL	1503
	M2	P2	NULL	2402
	M2	P3	NULL	3
	M2	P4	NULL	7000
	M3	P1	NULL	15003
	M3	P2	NULL	24003
	M3	P3	NULL	33
	M3	P4	NULL	9903
	NULL	NULL	T1	16243
	NULL	NULL	T2	27952

(continues)

Figure 19.13 (continued)

RESULT SET	Market_Id	Product_Id	Time_Id	Sales_Amt
	NULL	NULL	T3	24967
	NULL	P1	NULL	19509
	NULL	P2	NULL	32408
	NULL	P3	NULL	4539
	NULL	P4	NULL	24406
	M1	NULL	NULL	31012
	M2	NULL	NULL	10908
	M3	NULL	NULL	48942
	NULL	NULL	NULL	80862

Several materialized views can be prepared (with or without the CUBE operator) and used to speed up queries throughout the entire OLAP application. Of course, each such materialized view requires additional storage space, so there is some limit on the number of materialized views that can be constructed. Since updates are infrequent, the view update problem is not an issue.

19.4 ROLAP AND MOLAP

We have been assuming that the OLAP data is stored in a relational database as one (or more) star schemas. Such an implementation is referred to as **Relational OLAP** (*ROLAP*).

Some vendors provide OLAP servers that implement the fact table as a **data cube** using some sort of multi-dimensional (non-relational) implementation, often with a substantial amount of precomputed aggregation. Such implementations are referred to as **Multi-dimensional OLAP** (*MOLAP*). Note that, in ROLAP implementations, a data cube is a way to think about the data; in MOLAP implementations, the data is actually stored in some representation of a data cube.

One use of the CUBE operator is to compute the aggregations needed to load a MOLAP database from an SQL database. Many MOLAP systems also allow the user to specify certain other aggregations that are to be stored as materialized views. Their databases provide efficient implementations of certain (perhaps non-relational) operations often used in OLAP, such as aggregations at different levels of a hierarchy.

There is no standard query language for MOLAP implementations, but a number of MOLAP vendors (and a number of ROLAP vendors) provide proprietary, sometimes visual, languages that allow technically unsophisticated users to compute tables such as that in Figure 19.10 with a single query, and then to pivot, drill down, or roll up on any table dimension, sometimes with a single click of a mouse.

Not all commercial decision support applications use ROLAP (with star schemas) or MOLAP database servers. Many use conventional relational databases with schemas designed for their particular application. For example, several complex SQL queries used throughout this book can be viewed as OLAP queries (e.g., *List all professors who have taught all courses . . .*). Indeed, any query that uses complicated joins or nested SELECT statements is probably useful only for analysis, since its execution time is too long for an OLTP system.

19.5   IMPLEMENTATION ISSUES

Most of the specialized implementation techniques for OLAP systems are derived from the key technical characteristic of OLAP applications:

> *There is a very large amount of data, but that data is relatively static, with infrequent updates.*

Moreover, many of these techniques involve precomputing partial results or indices, which makes them particularly appropriate when queries are known in advance—for example, when they are embedded into an operational OLAP application. They can also be used for ad hoc (nonprogrammed) queries if the database designer or administrator has some idea as to what those queries will be.

One technique is to precompute some often used aggregations and store them in the database. These include aggregations over some of the dimension hierarchies. Since the data does not change often, the overhead of maintaining the aggregation values is small.

Another technique is to use indices particularly oriented toward the queries that will be made. Since data updates are infrequent, the usual overhead of index maintenance is minimal. Two examples of such indices are *join* and *bitmap* indices.

Star joins and join indices.   A join of the relations in a star schema, called a **star join**, can be optimized using a special index structure, called a **join index**, as discussed in Section 11.7.2. All recent releases of major commercial DBMSs are capable of recognizing and optimizing star joins.

Bitmap indices.   Bitmap indices, introduced in Section 11.7, are particularly useful for indexing attributes that can take only a small number of values. Such attributes occur frequently in OLAP applications. For example, Region in the MARKET table can take only four values: North, South, East, and West. If the MARKET table has a total of 10,000 rows, a bitmap index on Region contains four bit vectors, with a total storage requirement of 40,000 bits or 5K bytes. An index of this size can easily fit in main memory and can provide quick access to records with corresponding values.

19.6   DATA MINING

Data mining is an attempt at knowledge discovery—searching for patterns and structure in large data sets, as contrasted with requesting specific information. If

Figure 19.14 Purchases table used for data mining.

Purchases	Transaction_Id	Product
	001	diapers
	001	beer
	001	popcorn
	001	bread
	002	diapers
	002	cheese
	002	soda
	002	beer
	002	juice
	003	diapers
	003	cold cuts
	003	cookies
	003	napkins
	004	cereal
	004	beer
	004	cold cuts

OLAP is about confirming the known, we might say that data mining is about exploring the unknown.

Data mining uses techniques from many disciplines, such as statistical analysis and artificial intelligence. Our main interest is in understanding these techniques and how they are used to process large data sets.

Associations. One of the more important applications of data mining is finding associations. An **association** is a correlation between certain values in the database. We gave an example of such a correlation in Section 1.4:

> In a convenience store in the early evening, a high percentage of customers who bought diapers also bought beer.

This association can be described using the notation

$$Purchase\_diapers \Rightarrow Purchase\_beer \tag{19.3}$$

To see how this association might have been determined, assume that the convenience store maintains a Purchases table, which it computes from its OLTP system (see Figure 19.14). Based on this table, the data mining system can compute two measures:

■ The **confidence** *for an association*: The percentage of transactions that contain both items among the transactions that contain the items on the left side of the association. The first three transactions of Figure 19.14 contain diapers, and of these the first two also contain beer. Hence the confidence for association (19.3) is 66.66%.

■ *The* **support** *for an association*: The percentage of transactions that contain both items. Two of the four transactions in Figure 19.14 contain both items. Hence the support for association (19.3) is 50%.

The purpose of the confidence factor is to certify that there is certain probability that, if a transaction includes all items on the left side of the association—*Purchase_diapers* in (19.3)—then the item on the right side will appear as well—*Purchase_beer*. If the confidence factor is high enough, the convenience store manager might want to put a beer display at the end of the diaper aisle.

However, confidence alone might not provide reliable information. We need to make sure that the correlation it represents is statistically significant. For instance, the confidence for the association *Purchase_cookies* $\Rightarrow$ *Purchase_napkins* is 100%, but there is only one transaction where napkins and cookies are involved, so this association is most likely not statistically significant. The support of an association deals with this issue by measuring the fraction of transactions in which the association is actually demonstrated.

To assert that the association exists, both of the above measures must be above a certain threshold. Selecting appropriate thresholds is part of the discipline of statistical analysis and is beyond the scope of this book.

An association can involve more than two items. For example, it might assert that, if a customer buys cream cheese and lox, she is likely to also buy bagels (if she buys only cream cheese, she might be planning to use it for a different purpose and therefore not buy bagels).

Purchase_creamcheese AND *Purchase_lox* $\Rightarrow$ *Purchase_bagels*

For such an association, the confidence factor is the percentage of transactions that contain all items in the association among those that contain the first two items.

It is relatively easy for the system to compute the support and confidence for a particular association. That is an OLAP query. However, it is much more difficult for the system to return all possible associations for which the confidence and support are above a certain threshold. That is a data mining query. The idea of mining for association rules and some early algorithms were first introduced in [Agrawal et al. 1993].

We present an efficient algorithm for retrieving the data needed to determine all associations for which the support is larger than a given threshold, T. As we will see, once we have found those associations it is easy to determine which of them has a confidence factor greater than some given threshold.

Assume that we are trying to find all associations $A \Rightarrow B$ for which the support is greater than T. The naive approach is to compute the support for $A_i \Rightarrow B_j$ for all pairs of distinct items, A_i and B_j. However, if there are n items, $n(n-1)$ pairs have to be tried. This is usually too costly.

A more efficient approach, called the **a priori algorithm**, is based on the following observation:

> If the support for an association A $\Rightarrow$ B is larger than T, then the support for both A and B separately[2] must be larger than T.

(Certainly if A and B appear together in R rows, then A and B each appear in at least R rows—and perhaps even more.)

Thus, we first find all individual items whose support is greater than T, which requires n computations. The number of such items, m, is likely to be much less than n. Then we compute the support for every distinct pair of such items, which requires $m(m-1)$ computations. Assume that we find p pairs for which the support is larger than T. Since each pair might lead to two different associations (corresponding to the order of the items), the confidence of $2p$ associations must be computed.

Sequential patterns. Suppose that the table in Figure 19.14 also has columns for `Customer_Id` and `Date`. Now we can make associations concerning the purchases of individual customers over time.

> Is a customer who purchased a particular brand of cheese likely to purchase that brand again at a later date?

> Is a customer who purchased a garbage can likely to purchase fillers for that can at a later date?

Many of the same techniques and measures used for associations can be utilized to discover such **sequential patterns**.

Classification rules. Classification is the use of data about objects in the database to develop rules that can be used to predict future outcomes. For example, a mortgage lender might use the annual income and net worth of a customer to predict whether or not a customer is likely to default on a mortgage. To do this the lender analyzes past records to determine if the association

$$((10,000 \leq \text{P.Income} \leq 50,000) \text{ AND } (\text{P.Networth} \leq 100,000))$$
$$\Rightarrow (\text{P.Default} = \text{'yes'})$$

exists, where P denotes a person. If so, it classifies future customers who satisfy the left-hand side of the association into the category, "likely to default." Classification rules differ from association rules in that they refer to ranges of attribute values rather than a single value. However, the same measures of support and confidence can be used to evaluate a proposed classification.

Machine learning. The field of machine learning (a subfield of artificial intelligence) provides a number of techniques that are useful in data mining. Suppose that the mortgage lender wants to determine which applicants are likely to default

---

[2] The support for a single item such as A is the percentage of transactions that contain A.

on their mortgage, but believes that the classification depends on a larger number of factors than in the previous example and that these factors should not be weighted equally.

To see how a lender might use weights in making a decision, assume he wants to consider only the above two factors: income and net worth. Then he might associate a weight a_1 with the predicate (10,000 $\leq$ P.Income $\leq$ 50,000) and a weight a_2 with the predicate (P.Networth $\leq$ 100,000). The lender might then evaluate the expression

$$a_1 x_1 + a_2 x_2$$

where x_1 has value 1 if the first predicate is true and -1 otherwise, and similarly with x_2 and the second predicate. A customer is considered a bad risk if the value of that expression exceeds some threshold, t, i.e., if

$$a_1 x_1 + a_2 x_2 \geq t$$

and a good risk otherwise. In practice, the lender might want to include a number of other possible factors in this computation. The question is, How should the weights and the threshold be determined?

A technique called **neural nets** allows the lender to use the information in an OLAP database about past customers to "learn" a set of weights that would have predicted their behavior and thus will (hopefully) predict the behavior of new customers. By "learning" we mean that the system uses examples of the characteristics of past customers who did or did not default on their loans to incrementally adjust the weights to give a better prediction of whether or not customers will default.

The above inequality can be viewed as modeling the behavior of a primitive **neuron** (or nerve cell). The neuron "fires" if the weighted sum of its inputs (x_1 and x_2) exceeds the threshold. Using the database containing information about past customers, a simple learning algorithm for a single neuron might be:

1. Initially set the values of all the weights and the threshold to 0.

2. Apply the information about each customer one at a time to the neuron model and see if it gives the correct answer (if the customer defaulted, the sum of the weighted inputs is greater than or equal to the threshold; if the customer did not default, the sum of the weighted inputs is less than the threshold).

   a. If the neuron gives the right answer, leave the values of the weights and the threshold unchanged.

   b. If the neuron gives the wrong answer because the weighted sum of the inputs does not exceed the threshold when it should have (because the customer defaulted), change the values of all the weights and the threshold by the same amount in the direction to make the output exceed the threshold. In particular, increase a_i by d if $x_i = 1$, decrease a_i by d if $x_i = -1$, and decrease t by d.

   c. If the neuron gives the wrong answer because the weighted sum of the inputs exceeds the threshold when it should not have (because the customer did not default), change the values of all the weights and the threshold by the same amount in the direction to make the output be less than the threshold. In particular, decrease a_i by d if $x_i = 1$, and increase a_i by d if $x_i = -1$, and increase t by d.

3. Repeat step 2 (i.e., consider each customer again in each repetition) until the neuron makes relatively few errors and the values of the weights become relatively stable. The neuron is then said to have "learned" the information about those customers. These learned weights can now be used to predict the behavior of new customers.

This algorithm has the property [Novikoff 1962] that if the decision can (always) be correctly made by a single neuron, the values of the weights and threshold will converge to correct values after only a bounded number of weight adjustments. In practice this result is not very useful, because for most applications the required decisions cannot be made (even approximately) by a single neuron model, so a network of such models is used together with a more complex learning algorithm. We do not discuss such networks and their learning algorithms.

We note, however, that the use of neural nets for credit checking is one of the most important commercial successes of both machine learning and data mining.

19.7 POPULATING A DATA WAREHOUSE

Data for both OLAP and data mining is usually stored in a special database often called a **data warehouse**. Data warehouses are usually very large, perhaps containing terabytes of data that have been gathered at different times from a number of sources, including databases from different vendors and with different schemas. Merging such data into a single OLAP database is not trivial. Additional problems arise when that data has to be periodically updated.

Two important operations must be performed on the data before it can be loaded into the warehouse.

1. *Transformation.* The data from the different source DBMSs must be transformed, both syntactically and semantically, into the common format required by the warehouse.

    a. *Syntactic transformation.* The syntax used by the different DBMSs to represent the same data might be different. For example, the schema in one DBMS might represent Social Security numbers with the attribute SSN while another might use SSnum. One might represent it as a character string, another as an integer.

    b. *Semantic transformation.* The semantics used by the different DBMSs to represent the same data might be different. For example, the warehouse might summarize sales on a daily basis, but one DBMS summarizes them on an hourly basis and another does not summarize sales at all but merely provides information about individual transactions.

2. *Data cleaning.* The data must be examined to eliminate any errors or missing information. We might think that data obtained from an OLTP database should be correct, but experience indicates otherwise. Moreover, some erroneous data might have been obtained from sources other than an OLTP database—for example, an incorrect zip code on a form filled in on the Internet.

Often the term "data cleaning" is used to describe both types of operations. Although there is no design theory for performing these operations, a number of vendors supply tools that simplify the task somewhat.

If no data cleaning is necessary and the sources are relational databases that have schemas sufficiently similar to that of the warehouse, the data can sometimes be extracted from the sources and inserted into the warehouse with a single SQL statement. For example, assume that each store, M, in the supermarket chain has an M_SALES table with schema M_SALES(Product_Id, Time_Id, Sales_Amt), which records M's sales of each product for each time period. Then, after time period T4, we can update the fact table (Figure 19.1) stored in the data warehouse with the sales information for market M in time period T4 with the statement

```
INSERT INTO SALES(Market_Id, Product_Id, Time_Id, Sales_Amt)
    SELECT Market_Id = 'M', S.Product_Id, S.Time_Id, S.Sales_Amt
    FROM M_SALES   S
    WHERE S.Time_Id = 'T4'
```

If data cleaning or reformatting is needed, the data to be extracted can be represented as nonmaterialized views over the source databases. A cleansing program can then retrieve the data through the views (without requiring knowledge of the individual database schemas) for further processing before inserting it into the warehouse database.

As with other types of databases, an OLAP database must include a **metadata repository** containing information about the physical and logical organization of the data, including its schema, indices, and the like. For data warehouses, the repository must also include information about the source of all data and the dates on which it was loaded and refreshed.

The large volume of data in an OLAP database makes loading and updating a significant task. For the sake of efficiency, updating is usually incremental: Different parts of the database are updated at different times. Unfortunately, however, incremental updating might leave the database in an inconsistent state. Usually, this is not an important issue for OLAP queries, because much of the data analysis involves only summaries and statistical analyses, which are not significantly affected by such inconsistencies.

Figure 19.15 summarizes the processes involved in loading an OLAP database.

19.8 BIBLIOGRAPHIC NOTES

The term *OLAP* was coined by Codd in [Codd 1995]. A good survey of OLAP appears in [Chaudhuri and Dayal 1997]. A collection of articles on applications

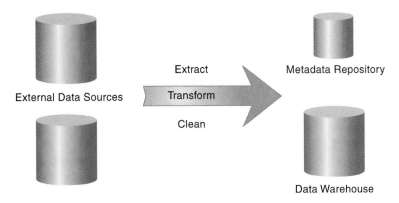

Figure 19.15 Loading data into an OLAP database.

and current research in data mining can be found in [Fayyad et al. 1996]. The CUBE operator was introduced in [Gray et al. 1997]. Efficient computation of data cubes is discussed in [Agrawal et al. 1996, Harinarayan et al. 1996, Ross and Srivastava 1997, Zhao et al. 1998]. The idea of mining for association rules and some early algorithms were first introduced in [Agrawal et al. 1993]. A textbook-style coverage of data mining can be found in [Han and Kamber 2001].

19.9 EXERCISES

19.1 Is a typical fact table in BCNF? Explain.

19.2 Explain why, in an E-R model of a star schema, the fact table is a relationship and the dimension tables are entities.

19.3 Design another fact table and related dimension tables that a supermarket might want to use for an OLAP application.

19.4 Explain why it is not appropriate to model the database for the Student Registration System as a star schema.

19.5 Design SQL queries for the supermarket example that will return the information needed to make a table similar to that of Figure 19.10, except that markets are aggregated by state and time is aggregated by months.
   a. Use CUBE or ROLLUP operators.
   b. Do not use CUBE or ROLLUP operators.
   c. Compute the result table.

19.6 a. Design a query for the supermarket example that will return the total sales (over time) for each supermarket.
   b. Compute the result table.

19.7 Suppose that an application has 4 dimension tables, each of which contains 100 rows.

    a. Determine the number of rows in the fact table.

    b. Suppose that one table has an attribute that can take on 10 values. Determine the size in bytes of a bit index on that attribute.

    c. Determine the maximum size of a join index for a join between one of the dimension tables and the fact table.

    d. Suppose that we use the CUBE operator on this fact table to perform aggregations on all 4 dimensions. Determine the number of rows in the resulting table.

    e. Suppose that we use the ROLLUP operator on this fact table. Determine the number of rows in the resulting table.

19.8 Design a query evaluation algorithm for the ROLLUP operator. The objective of such an algorithm should be that the results of the previously computed aggregations are *reused* in subsequent aggregations and *not* recomputed from scratch.

19.9 Design a query evaluation algorithm for the CUBE operator that uses the results of the previously computed aggregations to compute new aggregations. (*Hint*: Organize the GROUP BY clauses used in the computation of a data cube into a lattice, for example, GROUP BY A < GROUP BY A,B < GROUP BY A,B,C and GROUP BY B < GROUP BY B,C < GROUP BY A,B,C. Describe how aggregates computed for the lower parts of a lattice can be used in the computation of the upper parts.)

19.10 Suppose that the fact table of Figure 19.1 has been cubed and the result has been stored as a view, SALES_v1. Design queries against that table that will return the tables of Figure 19.10 and Figure 19.7.

19.11 We are interested in building an OLAP application with which we can analyze the grading at our university, where grades are represented as integers from 0 to 4 (4 being A). We want to ask questions about average grades for different courses, professors, and departments during different semesters and years. Design a star schema for this application.

19.12 Discuss the difference in storage requirements for a data cube implemented as a multi-dimensional array and a fact table.

19.13 Perform the a priori algorithm on the table of Figure 19.14 to determine all reasonable two-item associations.

19.14 Show that, when evaluating possible associations, the confidence is always larger than the support.

19.15 Give examples, different from those in the text, of syntactic and semantic transformations that might have to be made while loading data into a data warehouse.

Part Four

TRANSACTION PROCESSING

Now we are ready to begin our study of transaction processing.

In Chapter 20, we will give a detailed description of the ACID properties of transactions and how they are related to correct schedules.

In Chapters 21 and 22, we will describe a variety of transaction models and architectures of transaction processing systems.

In Chapters 23 through 26, we will see how each of the ACID properties is implemented in both centralized and distributed systems.

■ Chapters 23 and 24 will discuss the implementation of isolation, first in general terms and then for relational databases. We will look at the various isolation levels supported by SQL and how schedules produced at isolation levels other than SERIALIZABLE can be correct.

■ Chapter 25 will discuss the implementation of atomicity and durability in situations in which a transaction aborts, the system crashes, or the media on which the database is stored fails.

■ Chapter 26 will discuss how the ACID properties are implemented in a distributed environment.

In Chapter 27, we will examine security and Internet commerce, including well-known Internet protocols such as SSL and SET.

Chapter 20

ACID Properties of Transactions

We assume that transactions execute within some application in which there are one or more databases modeling the state of some real-world enterprise.[1] A transaction is a program that can perform the following functions:

1. It can update a database to reflect the occurrence of a real-world event that affects the state of the enterprise the database is modeling. An example is a deposit transaction at a bank: The event is that the customer gives the teller cash; the transaction updates the customer's account information in the database to reflect the deposit.

2. It can ensure that one or more real-world events occur. An example is a withdrawal transaction at an automated teller machine (ATM): The event is the dispensing of cash—if and only if the withdrawal transaction successfully completes.

3. It can return information derived from the database. An example is a transaction that prints out a customer's bank statement.

The difference between the first two functions is that, in the first, the real-world event has already occurred and the transaction simply updates the database to reflect that fact; in the second, the real-world event is triggered from within the transaction.

A single transaction can perform all three functions. For example, a deposit transaction might

1. Update the database in response to a real-world event in which the customer gives cash to the teller

2. Cause the real-world event in which a deposit slip is printed if and only if the transaction successfully completes

3. Return information from the database about the customer's account

---

[1] Some people might say that the database does not *model* the real world but is *part of* it—that the contents of the database in fact *determine* the state of the real world.

In Section 2.3, we saw that the execution of a set of transactions is constrained by certain properties that do not apply to ordinary programs—specifically, the ACID properties. In this chapter, we expand our discussion of that subject.

20.1   CONSISTENCY

Think of a database as playing both an active and a passive role in relation to the real-world enterprise that it models. In its passive role, it maintains the correspondence between the database state and the enterprise state. For example, the Student Registration System must accurately maintain the identity and number of students who have registered for each course, since there is no paper record of the registration. In its active role, it enforces certain rules of the enterprise—for example, the number of students registered for a course must not exceed another number stored in the database, the maximum enrollment for that course (constraint IC2 in Section 2.3). A transaction that attempts to register a student for a course that is already full must not complete successfully.

Consistency is the term that is used to describe these issues, and it has two aspects.

The database must satisfy all integrity constraints.   Not all database states are allowable. There are two reasons for this.

■ *Internal consistency.* It is often convenient to store the same information in different forms. For example, we might store the number of students registered for a course as well as a list whose entries name each student registered for the course. A database state in which the length of the list is not equal to the number of registrants is not allowed (constraint IC3 in Section 2.3).

■ *Enterprise rules.* Enterprise rules restrict the possible states of the enterprise. When such a rule exists, the possible states of the database are similarly restricted. The above rule relating the number of registrants and the maximum enrollment in a course is one example. A state in which the number of registrants is greater than the maximum enrollment is not allowed.

The restrictions are referred to as **integrity constraints** (or sometimes **consistency constraints**). The execution of each transaction must maintain all integrity constraints.

The database must model the state of the real-world enterprise.   The transaction must be **correct** in the sense that it updates the database in such a way as to have the effect stated in its specification. The new database state must reflect the new real-world state—a registration transaction, for example, must increment the database variable that stores the number of students registered for a course and must add that student to the list of registrants. A registration transaction that completes successfully but does not update the database leaves the database in a consistent state, but that state does not show the student as registered. Similarly, a deposit transaction that records your deposit as being in someone else's account leaves the database in a consistent state, but that state clearly does not correspond to the intended state of the real world.

We can determine whether or not all integrity constraints are satisfied by examining the values of the data items in a snapshot of the database (perhaps at a time when no transactions are executing). Unfortunately, this does not tell us whether or not the database state is an accurate reflection of the real-world state of the enterprise. The problem is that it is not enough that the *database state is consistent*—each *transaction must be consistent* as well.

> **Transaction consistency**: The transaction designer can assume that, when execution of the transaction is initiated, the database is in a state in which all integrity constraints are satisfied. The designer has the responsibility of ensuring that, when execution has completed, the database is once again in a state in which all integrity constraints are satisfied and that the new state reflects the transformation described in the transaction's specification.

Note that we are using the word "consistent" in two ways. The database is consistent when all integrity constraints are satisfied; a transaction is consistent when, if run in isolation starting from a consistent database state, it produces a new database state that is also consistent and the new state satisfies the requirements of the transaction's specifications.

Keep in mind that producing consistent transactions is the sole responsibility of the application programmer. The remainder of the transaction processing system takes consistency as a given and provides atomicity, isolation, and durability—the properties needed to ensure that concurrent execution of consistent transactions preserves the relationship between the state of the database and the state of the enterprise in spite of failures.

20.1.1 Checking Integrity Constraints

SQL provides some support for maintaining integrity constraints. When the database is designed, certain integrity constraint can be incorporated as SQL assertions, key constraints, and the like. For example, a PRIMARY KEY constraint can eliminate the possibility that two students are recorded in the database with the same student Id (constraint IC0 in Section 2.3). A CHECK constraint can enforce the relationship between the number of registrants and the maximum enrollment. An ASSERTION can ensure that the room assigned to a particular course is larger than the maximum enrollment. As a transaction is executed, if it accesses data that is included in a constraint specified in the schema, the DBMS automatically checks that the constraint is not violated and prevents any transaction that would cause a violation from completing.

Unfortunately, not all integrity constraints can be encoded in the schema. Even when a constraint can be encoded, the design decision is sometimes made not to do so. Instead, it is checked within the transaction program itself. One reason for such a decision is that constraint checking takes time. When encoded in the schema, constraints are checked automatically whenever a table they reference is modified.

As a result, the check might be performed unnecessarily often. By placing constraint checking in the transactions, it can be carried out only in transactions that might cause a violation. For example, a limitation on the number of students who can register for a course cannot be violated by a transaction that deregisters a student; thus, despite the fact that the number of students in the course is modified, no check should be made (either automatically or otherwise) when this transaction is executed. The advantage of such an approach is that the transaction designer includes constraint checking code only in transactions where constraint violations can occur.

Checking constraints inside transactions has several important drawbacks of its own: It increases the possibility of programming errors and is expensive to maintain. Suppose that at some point constraint IC2 is changed to say that the number of students enrolled in a course should not exceed the room capacity. With internal constraint checking, several transactions might have to be modified, recompiled, and retested. However, if IC2 is specified entirely in the schema, independently of any transaction, changing it is easy and no transaction needs to be modified.

A transaction as a unit of work. The requirement that every transaction preserve integrity constraints limits the designer in specifying the tasks to be done by each of the transactions within an application. To explain this limitation, some authors have defined a transaction as a program that does a "unit of work," meaning that each transaction within an application must do *all* the work required to update the database (and perform other appropriate activities) to maintain the integrity constraints when a real-world event occurs. Thus, for example, it is incorrect to specify that, when a student wants to register for a course, two transactions should be executed—one that updates the count of registrants and one that updates the course roster—because neither of these "transactions" is consistent. The "unit of work" in this case requires updating both, and it must be done by a single transaction, which then preserves the constraints.

20.2 ATOMICITY

The portion of the system responsible for managing transactions and controlling their access to the DBMS is called the **TP monitor**. In addition to consistency, the TP monitor must provide certain guarantees concerning how transactions are executed. One such guarantee is *atomicity*.

> **Atomicity:** The system must ensure that either the transaction runs to completion or, if it does not complete, it has no effect at all (as if it had never been started).

Conventional operating systems usually do not guarantee atomicity. If, during the execution of a (conventional) program, the system crashes, whatever partial changes the program made to files before the crash might still be there when the system restarts. If those changes leave the files in some incorrect state, the operating system takes no responsibility for correcting them.

Such behavior is unacceptable in a transaction processing system. Either a student has or has not registered for a course. Partial registration makes no sense and might leave the database in an inconsistent state. As indicated by constraint IC3, for example, two items of information in the database must be updated when a student registers. If a registration transaction were to have a partial execution in which one update completed but the system crashed before execution of the second update, the resulting database would be inconsistent.

If a transaction successfully completes and the system agrees to preserve its effects, we say that it has **committed**. If the transaction does not successfully complete, we say that it has **aborted** and the system must ensure that whatever changes the transaction has made to the database are undone, or **rolled back**. As we will see in Section 25.2, a transaction processing system includes sophisticated mechanisms for aborting transactions and rolling back their effects.

The above discussion leads to the following important conclusion:

> Atomic execution implies that every transaction either commits or aborts.

Let us look at another example. The withdrawal transaction at an ATM involves (at least) two actions: The account is debited by the amount of the withdrawal and the appropriate amount of cash is dispensed. Its atomic execution implies that, if the transaction commits, both actions occur; if it aborts, neither occurs. (One of these actions is a database update and the other is the real-world event of dispensing cash.)

A distributed transaction is one that accesses databases at different sites. For example, a distributed banking transaction might transfer money between accounts at two different banks. Atomic execution requires that, if the transaction commits, both updates occur; if it aborts, neither occurs.

Why transactions abort.   A transaction might be aborted for several reasons. One possibility is that the system crashes during execution of the transaction (before it commits), or, in the case of a distributed transaction, the system on which one of the database resides crashes. Other possibilities include the following:

1. The transaction is involved in a deadlock and cannot obtain resources to continue execution.

2. Allowing the transaction to complete will cause a violation of an integrity constraint.

3. Allowing it to complete would violate the *isolation requirement*, meaning that there is a possibility of "bad interaction" with another transaction, as described in Section 20.4.

Finally, the transaction itself might decide to abort. For example, the user might push the *cancel* button, or the transaction program might encounter some (application-related) condition that causes it to abandon its computation. Most transaction processing systems have an abort procedure that a transaction can invoke in such cases. Strictly speaking, such a procedure is unnecessary: The transaction can cause the equivalent of an abort by itself, undoing any changes it made to the database and then committing. However, this is a delicate and error-prone task that requires the transaction to remember what database items it has changed and to have sufficient information to enable it to return those items to their previous values. Since the system must contain an abort procedure for dealing with crashes and other conditions anyway, this procedure can be made available to all transactions. The transaction designer can thus avoid having to program the abort.

Programming conventions for bracketing a transaction.   Each transaction processing system must provide a set of programming conventions so that the programmer can specify a transaction's boundaries. These conventions differ from one system to another. For example, the start of a transaction might be denoted by a `begin_transaction` command, and its successful completion might be denoted by a `commit` command.

The invocation of the `commit` command is a *request* to commit. The system might decide to commit the transaction or, for the reasons previously discussed, to abort it. A `rollback` command is provided so that a transaction can abort itself. In contrast to the request to commit, a request to roll back is always honored by the system.

When a distributed transaction requests to commit, the participating sites execute a **commit protocol** to decide whether the request should be granted. In either the distributed or the nondistributed case, if the system decides to commit the transaction, it executes a commit operation. Before the commit is executed, the transaction must be in an uncommitted state (and can still be aborted); after it is executed, the transaction is in a committed state (and can no longer be aborted). The commit operation must be atomic in the sense that no intermediate state separates the uncommitted and committed states. As a result, if the system crashes while the commit is in progress, on recovery the transaction will be either committed or uncommitted. We will discuss the commit operation further in Section 25.2.

20.3   DURABILITY

A second requirement of the transaction processing system is that it not lose information. For example, if you register for a course, you expect the system to remember that fact despite hardware or software failures. Even if an ice storm causes a power blackout the next day and the computer crashes (or even if the crash occurs one microsecond after your transaction commits), you still want to be able to attend class. Conventional operating systems usually do not guarantee durability. Backups might be kept, but no assurances are given that the most recent changes are durable. Hardware failures are not restricted to the CPU and its local memory. The data stored on a mass storage device can also be lost if the device malfunctions. For these reasons, we require

> **Durability.** The system must ensure that, once the transaction commits, its effects remain in the database even if the computer or the medium on which the database is stored subsequently fails.

Durability can be achieved by storing data redundantly on different backup devices. The characteristics of these devices lead to different degrees of system **availability**. If the devices are fast, the system might provide **nonstop** availability. For example, with **mirrored disks** two identical copies of the database are maintained on different mass storage devices; updates are made immediately to both devices. Even though one device might fail, the information in the database is still readily available on the other and service can be provided. As a result, the malfunction might be imperceptible to users. The telephone system has this requirement (although in practice the requirement cannot always be met).

If the backup device is slow, service might be unavailable to users for some period of time after a failure while a **recovery** procedure, which restores the database, is executed. Most airline reservation systems are of this type, much to the chagrin of air travelers who want to make reservations when the system is temporarily unavailable. The Student Registration System is also of this type.

In the real world, durability is relative. What kinds of events do we want the committed data in our system to survive?

■ CPU crash

■ Disk failure

■ Multiple disk failures

■ Fire

■ Malicious attacks

Different costs are involved in achieving durability for each of these events. Each enterprise must decide the degree of durability that is essential to its business, the probability of specific failures that might affect durability, and the level of durability it is willing to pay for.

20.4 ISOLATION

In discussing consistency, we concentrated on the effect of a single transaction. We next examine the effect of executing a set of transactions. We say that a set of transactions is executed sequentially, or **serially**, if one transaction in it is executed to completion before another is started. The nice thing about serial execution is that, if all transactions are consistent and the database is initially in a consistent state, consistency is maintained. When the first transaction in the set starts, the database is in a consistent state and, since the transaction is consistent, the database will be consistent when the transaction completes. Since the database is consistent when the second transaction starts, it too will perform correctly and the argument repeats.

Serial execution is adequate for applications that have modest performance requirements, but it is insufficient for applications that have strict requirements on response time and throughput. Fortunately, modern computer systems consist of a collection of processors—central processing units (CPUs) and I/O processors—that are capable of the **concurrent execution** of a number of computations and

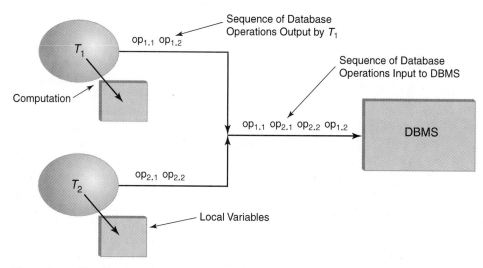

Figure 20.1 Database operations output by two transactions in a concurrent schedule might be interleaved in time. Note that the figure should be interpreted as meaning that $op_{1,1}$ arrives first at DBMS followed by $op_{2,1}$, etc.

I/O transfers. A transaction, on the other hand, is generally a **sequential program** that alternates between computation on local variables, which requires a CPU, and reading or writing information to or from the database, which requires I/O. In either case, the service of only a single processor at a time is necessary. Modern computing systems are therefore capable of servicing more than one transaction simultaneously, and we refer to this mode of execution as **concurrent execution**. Concurrent execution is appropriate in a transaction processing system serving many users. In this case, there are many active, partially completed, transactions at any given time.

In concurrent execution, the database operations of different transactions are effectively interleaved in time, as shown in Figure 20.1. Transaction T_1 alternately computes using local variables and sends requests to the database system to perform operations on the database. For example, an operation might transfer data between the database and local variables, or it might perform some specific update on a database variable. The requests are made in the sequence $op_{1,1}$, $op_{1,2}$, which we refer to as a **transaction schedule**. T_2 performs its computation in a similar way. Since the executions of the two transactions are not synchronized, the order of transfer operations arriving at the database, called a **schedule**, is an arbitrary merge of the two sequences. In Figure 20.1, this sequence is $op_{1,1}$, $op_{2,1}$, $op_{2,2}$, $op_{1,2}$.

When transactions are executed concurrently, the consistency of each transaction is insufficient to guarantee that the database remains consistent. Indeed, although a consistent transaction that starts in a consistent state leaves the database in a con-

Figure 20.2 A schedule in which two deposit transactions are not isolated from one another.

$T_1:$ *step* 1:   *r(bal* : 10)   *step* 2:   *w(bal* : 15)

$T_2:$ *step* 1:   *r(bal* : 10)   *step* 2:   *w(bal* : 30)

sistent state when it commits, its intermediate states during execution need not be consistent. Another consistent transaction that reads the values of variables in such an intermediate state can thus behave unpredictably because it assumes that it starts in a consistent state. Suppose, for example, that the registrar periodically executes an audit transaction that prints student and course records. If that transaction executes after a registration transaction updates the course count and before it updates the class roster, the information printed will be inconsistent: The total number of student records indicating enrollment in the course will be one less than the number of students shown as enrolled in the course in the course record. In this example, the database ultimately reaches a consistent state even though the information printed by the audit transaction is inconsistent.

Concurrent executions can also destroy consistency. In Figure 2.4 on page 24, we showed a concurrent schedule of two registration transactions that exhibits a lost update and hence destroys consistency. The final database does not reflect the state of the real world since it says that 30 students are registered for the course when in fact 31 students are registered. In addition, the database state does not satisfy integrity constraint IC3 because there are 31 entries on the class roster.

Figure 20.2 also illustrates a **lost update**. In this case, the execution of two bank deposit transactions is interleaved. Assume the only integrity constraint to be that the balance of each account is greater than zero. T_1 is attempting to deposit \$5, and T_2 is attempting to deposit \$20. In its first step, each transaction reads the balance as 10. In their second steps, T_2 writes 30 and T_2 writes 15. The final value is 15. T_2's update was lost. Note that the final database state is consistent, because the value of the balance is greater than zero. It is just incorrect: the value of the balance should be 35. If the transactions had executed sequentially, T_1 would have completed before T_2 was allowed to start, T_2 would have read a balance of 15, and both updates would have been reflected in the final database.

The failures we have been describing result from the fact that concurrent transactions are accessing shared data—the database (this is exactly the *critical section problem* discussed in the context of operating systems). For this reason, in studying the correctness of concurrent transaction, we are justified in concentrating on the operations that access the shared data—the database operations.

Atomicity is also complicated by concurrent execution. For example, in Figure 20.3, T_1 is a transaction that eliminates a prerequisite, $course_1$, from another course, $course_2$. T_1 writes the new list of prerequisites to the database with the operation $w(prereq : new\_list)$. The new list is read by the registration transaction T_2, and, based on it, the student is successfully registered. However, after T_2 commits,

Figure 20.3 Schedule illustrating the failure of atomicity when transactions are not isolated.

$$T_1: w(prereq: \ new\_list) \hspace{6cm} abort$$

$$T_2: \hspace{4.5cm} r(prereq: \ new\_list) \hspace{0.8cm} commit$$

T_1 aborts and the original list is reinstated. The fact that the student might successfully register for $course_2$ without having taken $course_1$ (violating constraint IC1) implies that T_1 has had an effect despite having aborted. Thus, T_1's execution is not atomic.

As these examples demonstrate, we must specify some restriction on concurrent execution that guarantees consistency and atomicity. One such *sufficient* restriction is

> **Isolation:** Even though transactions are executed concurrently, the overall effect of the schedule is the same as if the transactions had executed serially in some order.

The exact meaning of this requirement will be made more clear in Chapters 23 and 24. However, it should be evident that, if the transactions are consistent and if the overall effect of a concurrent schedule is the same as that of some serial schedule, the concurrent schedule will maintain consistency. Concurrent schedules that satisfy this condition are called **serializable**.

Note that conventional operating systems usually do not guarantee isolation. Different programs might read and write shared files maintained by the file system. Since the operating system enforces no restriction on the order in which these reads and writes are performed, isolation is not guaranteed when the programs are run concurrently.

20.5 THE ACID PROPERTIES

The features that distinguish transactions from ordinary programs are frequently abbreviated by the acronym ACID [Haerder and Reuter 1983], which denotes the four previously discussed properties of transactions.

A*tomic*. Each transaction is executed completely or not at all.

C*onsistent*. The execution of each transaction in isolation maintains database consistency and moves it to a new state that correctly models the new state of the enterprise.

I*solated*. The concurrent execution of a set of transactions has the same effect as that of some serial execution of that set.

D*urable*. The results of committed transactions are permanent.

It is the transaction designer's job to design consistent transactions. It is assumed that the TP monitor provides the abstraction of atomicity, isolation, and durability. This assumption greatly simplifies the designer's task, since he need not be concerned with failures or concurrent execution. It is the TP monitor's job to guarantee that transactions are atomic, isolated, and durable. The system then guarantees that each schedule maintains database consistency in the following sense:

> When transactions satisfy the ACID properties, the transaction processing system maintains a correct, consistent, and up-to-date model of the real world and supplies responses to users that are always correct and up to date.

Many applications require such a guarantee of correctness. One example is an online, worldwide currency trading system, which must perform in this way at all times since hundreds of billions of dollars may be at stake.

ACID properties in the real world.   In later chapters, we will show that implementing atomicity, isolation, and durability can cause system performance to suffer. For example,

■ Isolation is usually implemented by requiring transactions to obtain locks on the database items they access. These locks prevent other transactions from accessing the items until the locks are released. If locks are held for long periods of time, long waits result and the performance of the system suffers.

■ Atomicity and durability are generally implemented by maintaining a log of update operations. Log maintenance involves overhead.

■ The atomicity of a distributed transaction requires that the transaction either commit at all sites or abort at all sites. Thus, when the transaction completes at one site it cannot unilaterally commit there; instead, it must wait until accesses at all sites have completed. Since locks cannot be released until commit time, this might cause a significant delay.

Even though implementation of the ACID properties involves performance penalties, many transaction processing applications are designed to execute in this way. For some applications, however, the penalties are unacceptable—the system cannot achieve the desired throughput or response time. In such situations, isolation is often sacrificed. It is weakened in order to improve performance. For example:

■ Some applications do not require exact information about the real world. For example, a decision support system for a nationwide chain of department stores might allow store managers to obtain information about the inventory held in each store. Such information is useful in deciding when to purchase additional merchandise. When transactions are completely isolated, the system produces a snapshot of the inventory of all the stores as it exists at an instant of time. However, managers might be able to make adequate purchasing decisions with an approximate snapshot, in which the inventory reported for some stores is an hour or so old while that reported for others is up to date, or in which a few stores do not supply their inventory at all.

■ Some transaction processing applications must model the real world exactly, but execute correctly even though transactions are not completely isolated. Complete isolation guarantees that *any* application executes correctly. It is *sufficient*, but not *necessary*, to guarantee correctness. *Some* applications model the real world exactly even though some transactions are not isolated. (We will give examples of such applications in Section 24.2.2.)

To improve the performance of such applications, most commercial systems offer weaker levels of isolation that do not guarantee serial schedules. One goal of the following chapters is to explore these issues. On the basis of this material, designers can decide whether or not their application requires the ACID properties and whether or not it can afford the required costs.

20.6 BIBLIOGRAPHIC NOTES

Excellent treatments of transactions and their implementation are given in [Gray and Reuter 1993], [Lynch et al. 1994, and Bernstein and Newcomer 1997]. The term *ACID* was coined in [Haerder and Reuter 1983], but the individual components of ACID were introduced in earlier papers, for example [Gray et al. 1976], [Eswaran et al. 1976].

20.7 EXERCISES

20.1 Some distributed transaction processing systems replicate data at two or more sites separated geographically. A common technique for organizing replicated systems is one in which transactions that update a data item must change all replicas. Hence, one possible integrity constraint in a replicated system is that the values of all of the replicas of an item be the same. Explain how transactions running on such a system might violate

  a. Atomicity

  b. Consistency

  c. Isolation

  d. Durability

20.2 Consider the replicated system described in the previous problem.

  a. What is the impact of replication on the performance of a read-only transaction?

  b. What is the impact of replication on the performance of a transaction that both reads and writes the data?

  c. What is the impact of replication on the communication system?

20.3 Give three examples of transactions, other than an ATM bank withdrawal, in which a real-world event occurs if and only if the transaction commits.

20.4 The schema of the Student Registration System includes the number of current registrants and a list of registered students in each course.

    a. What integrity constraint relates this data?

    b. How might a registration transaction that is not atomic violate this constraint?

    c. Suppose the system also implements a transaction that displays the current information about a course. Give a non-isolated schedule in which the transaction displays inconsistent information.

20.5 Give three examples of applications in which certain transactions need not be totally isolated and, as a result, might return data which, although not the result of a serializable schedule, is adequate for the needs of the applications.

20.6 Describe a situation in which the execution of a program under your local operating system is not

    a. Atomic

    b. Isolated

    c. Durable

20.7 At exactly twelve noon on a particular day 100 people at 100 different ATM terminals attempt to withdraw cash from their bank accounts at the same bank. Suppose their transactions are run sequentially and each transaction takes .25 seconds of compute and I/O time. Estimate how long it takes to execute all 100 transactions and what the average response time is for all 100 customers.

20.8 You have the choice of running a single transaction to transfer $300 from one of your savings accounts to another savings account at the same bank or of running two transactions, one to withdraw $300 from one account and a second to deposit $300 in the other. In the first choice the transfer is made atomically; in the second it is not. Describe a scenario in which after the transfer, the sum of the balances in the two accounts is different (from what it was when both transactions started) at the instant the transfer is complete. *Hint:* Other transactions might be executing at the same time that you are doing the funds transfer.

Chapter 21

Models of Transactions

All of the transactions in the Student Registration System are short and make only a small number of accesses to data stored in a single database server. However, many applications involve long transactions that make many database accesses. For example, in a student billing system a single transaction might prepare the tuition and housing bills for all 10,000 students in a university, and in truly large systems a transaction might access millions of records stored in multiple database servers running at different sites in a network. To deal with such long and complex transactions, many transaction processing systems provide mechanisms for imposing some structure on transactions or for breaking up a single task into several related transactions. In this chapter, we describe some of these structuring mechanisms from the point of view of the application designer. In later chapters, we will describe how the mechanisms can be implemented.

21.1 FLAT TRANSACTIONS

The transaction model we have discussed involves a database on a single server. It has no internal structure and so is called a **flat transaction**, which has the form

```
begin_transaction();
      S;
commit();
```

We introduce the `begin_transaction()` statement here, although, if you recall our discussion of transactions in Section 10.2.3, no such statement exists in the SQL:92 standard (a transaction is implicitly started when the previous transaction ends). In this and later sections we talk about transactions in a more general context, and it is useful to describe the abstraction of a transaction explicitly and to use a new syntax for that purpose. `begin_transaction()` informs the DBMS that a new transaction has begun and that the subsequent SQL statements contained in S are part of it.

The transaction alternates between computation using local variables and the execution of SQL statements. These statements cause data and status information to be passed between the database and local variables—which include the in and out parameters of the SQL statements and descriptors. In this simple model, we assume that the transaction accesses a single DBMS. The computation completes when the transaction requests that the server commit or abort the changes to the database that have been made. The DBMS guarantees the transaction's atomicity, isolation, and durability.

To understand the limitations of this model, consider the following situations.

1. Suppose that a travel planning transaction must make flight reservations for a trip from London to Des Moines. The strategy might be to make a reservation from London to New York, then a reservation from New York to Chicago, and finally a reservation from Chicago to Des Moines. Now suppose that, after making the first two reservations, it is found that there are no seats available on the flight from Chicago to Des Moines. The transaction might decide to give up the New York to Chicago reservation and instead choose a route from New York to St. Louis and then to Des Moines.

   There are several options for designing such a transaction. The transaction might abort when it fails to get the Chicago to Des Moines reservation, and a subsequent transaction might be used to route the trip through St. Louis. The difficulty with this approach is that the computation to get a reservation from London to New York and the resulting reservation will be lost, and the subsequent transaction might find that there are no longer seats available on that flight. Another approach is for the transaction to cancel the New York to Chicago reservation and route the trip through St. Louis. While this is a viable approach, in a more involved situation in which a number of computations must be undone, the code for doing this can be quite complex. Furthermore, it seems that with relatively little effort the transaction processing system itself might be able to provide a mechanism for undoing some part of the computation. The system already provides the abstraction of total rollback (abort). What is needed here is a generalization of that abstraction for partial rollback.

2. Since Des Moines does not handle international flights, our traveler must change planes at some point and will probably have to make hotel and auto reservations. Hence, the transaction has to access multiple databases involving different database servers running on machines that might be spread around the world. Despite this multiplicity of database servers, we still want to maintain the ACID abstraction. For example, if we succeed in reserving a seat on the international flight, but the server maintaining the domestic airline's database crashes (making it impossible to arrange a complete trip), we need to abort that reservation. In general, new techniques are needed to guarantee the atomicity, isolation, and durability of transactions that access multiple servers.

3. Arranging a trip includes not only making the necessary reservations but printing and mailing the tickets as well. It is necessary that these jobs get done, but they need not all be done at the same time, particularly since some jobs require mechanical operations and the intervention of humans. Thus, the activities performed by a transaction might be spread out in time as well as in space. Useful here are models that allow a transaction to create other transactions to be executed at a later time. More generally, a model is needed to describe an entire enterprise-wide activity, involving multiple related jobs

performed at different locations and at different times by both computers and humans.

4. Banks post interest at the end of each quarter. One way to do this is to execute a separate transaction for each account, which updates the balance and other relevant account information. If there are 10,000 accounts, 10,000 transactions must be executed. The problem with this approach is that between two successive transactions the database is in an inconsistent state: Interest has been posted in some accounts but not in others. If at that point an auditor were to run a transaction that summed the balances in all accounts, the total would be a meaningless number. A better approach is to post interest to all accounts in a single transaction. Suppose that this is done with a flat transaction and that, after it has posted interest to the first 9,000 accounts, the system crashes. Since the transaction is aborted, all the time and compute cycles it has expended are lost. A model is needed in which a transaction is allowed to preserve partial results in spite of system failures.

The next sections present transaction models that address these and other related issues.

21.2 PROVIDING STRUCTURE WITHIN A TRANSACTION

With the introduction of flat transactions, the application designer is essentially given an all-or-nothing choice: Use flat transactions to get atomicity, isolation, and durability, or design the application without relying on these abstractions. In the remainder of this chapter (and in the following chapters), we will describe models and mechanisms that provide a more refined access to these abstractions. Atomicity, isolation, and durability are made available in different degrees. This flexibility is achieved by introducing structure within a transaction. Structuring implies decomposition: A transaction is broken into parts that relate to each other in various ways. In some cases, the internal structure of a transaction is not visible to other transactions. In other cases it is, and the abstraction of isolation, which is enshrined in ACID, is breached.

In this section we describe models in which the transaction is conceived as a single, tightly integrated unit of work. In Section 21.3 we describe models in which the subtasks of an application are more loosely connected.

21.2.1 Savepoints

Database systems generally provide **savepoints** [Astrahan et al. 1976], which are points in a transaction that serve as the targets of partial database rollbacks. A savepoint marks a particular point in the execution of a transaction. The transaction can specify several different savepoints, which are numbered consecutively, so that they can be distinguished and so that the transaction can refer to a specific one at a later time. They are created using a call to the database server, such as

sp := `create_savepoint()`

where the value returned is the created savepoint's index. A transaction with several savepoints has the form

```
begin_transaction();
    S₁;
    sp1 := create_savepoint();
    S₂;
    sp2 := create_savepoint();
    . . .
    Sₙ;
    spn := create_savepoint();
    . . .
    if (condition) {
        rollback(spi);
        . . .
    }
    . . .
commit();
```

A transaction can request a rollback to a particular previously created savepoint using

```
rollback(sp)
```

where the variable sp contains the target savepoint's index.

The semantics of rollback is that the values of the database items accessed by the transaction, called its **database context**, are returned to the state they had when the savepoint was created—any database changes the transaction made since that savepoint was created are undone. The execution of the transaction then continues at the statement after the rollback statement (not the statement after `create_savepoint()`).

For example, the travel planning transaction might create a savepoint after each individual flight reservation is made. When it is discovered that there are no seats available on the flight from Chicago to Des Moines, the transaction rolls back to the savepoint created after the London to New York reservation was made, causing reversal of the database changes made by the New York to Chicago reservation. The desired effect is as if the transaction had never attempted to route the passenger through Chicago. We will discuss the implementation of savepoints (and, particularly, how isolation is maintained) in Section 23.7.1.

Note that, although the database is returned to the state it had at the time the savepoint was created, the state of the transaction's local variables is not affected by the rollback call (i.e., they are not rolled back). Hence, they might contain values that have been influenced by the values of database items read since the savepoint was created. For example, after creating a savepoint a transaction might read a database item, x, storing its value in local variable $X1$, then calculate a new value in local variable $X2$ and write it back to x. If the transaction subsequently rolls back to the savepoint, x is restored to its original value, $X1$ has the current value of x, and $X2$ has a value that is no longer in the database. The values of $X1$ and $X2$ might influence the subsequent execution of the transaction. This means that rolling back to a savepoint does not create the illusion that execution between savepoint creation and rollback had no effect. Indeed, such an illusion is generally inappropriate—there is no sense in redoing the same computation. The transaction needs to know that rollback has occurred so that a different execution path is taken afterward.

Note that the database state at a savepoint is not durable. If the transaction is aborted or the system crashes, the database is returned to the state it had when the transaction started. Although in one sense an abort can be viewed as a rollback to an (implicitly declared) initial savepoint, there is an important difference between abort and rollback to a savepoint: An aborted transaction does not continue after the abort is executed, whereas a transaction that has been rolled back to a savepoint does continue.

Also, note that after executing the rollback statement `rollback($sp_i$)`, all savepoints created after sp_i but before the rollback are inaccessible, since it makes no sense to roll back to them later in the computation.

21.2.2 Distributed Transactions

Many transaction processing applications have evolved according to very similar scenarios. Over the years, an enterprise develops a number of dedicated transaction processing systems to automate individual activities, such as inventory, billing, and payroll. Such systems might have been developed independently, by different groups, at different times, in different locations, using different hardware and software platforms and different database management systems. Each transaction processing system exports a set of transactions, T_i (which might be stored procedures). In many cases, these systems have been operational for years and are known to be reliable. Therefore, management will not allow them to be modified in any way.[1]

As the requirements for automation increase, the enterprise finds it necessary to integrate these systems in order to perform more complex activities. At this point the systems are referred to as **legacy systems** because they are presented to the application designer as complete, unmodifiable units that must be used in building a larger system. Similarly, their transactions are referred to as **legacy transactions**. Often the properties of legacy systems make integrating them into a larger system difficult.

For example, the inventory and billing systems might form components of a system for automating the sale of an item. If the servers reside on different computers, the first step in the integration is to connect the various sites through a network.

---

[1] In some extreme cases, the person who originally implemented a particular transaction has long since left the company, proper documentation does not exist, and no one else understands how the transaction works.

Figure 21.1 Distributed transaction invoking legacy transactions at several server sites.

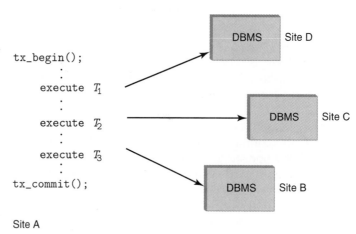

```
tx_begin();
        .
        .
    execute  T₁
        .
        .
    execute  T₂
        .
        .
    execute  T₃
        .
tx_commit();
```

Site A

A transaction in such a system starts at some network site and might access several of the transaction processing systems by initiating the legacy transactions that they export. Although it is possible that all of the individual systems reside on the same machine, this is generally not the case. We refer to such a transaction as a **distributed** or **global transaction**.

The situation is illustrated in Figure 21.1, which shows a new syntax for managing the abstraction of a distributed transaction. This syntax is based on the X/Open standard, which we will discuss in Section 22.3.1. In contrast to begin_transaction(), tx_begin() is not a call to any particular database server. Instead, it is part of the API of the TP monitor, which controls the entire transaction processing system.

You should understand the advantage of constructing a distributed transaction in this way. The transaction sees billing and inventory as abstractions. Its logic can concentrate on integrating the results produced by the legacy transactions without concerning itself with the schema of the local databases, the details of the billing or inventory process, or issues such as atomicity, concurrency, and durability at each site.

For example, a company might have several warehouses at different sites. At each warehouse a transaction processing system maintains a local database for controlling inventory. The president of the company might want to execute a transaction at the main office (site A in Figure 21.1) that produces information based on the total inventory at all warehouses. That transaction causes legacy transactions (T_1, T_2, T_3 in the figure) to be executed at each warehouse (sites B, C, and D in the figure) to gather the inventory information. Each legacy transaction communicates its result back to the transaction at the main office, which integrates the information and produces a report.

A distributed transaction processing application might also be built from scratch, not by integrating legacy systems. One possibility is that the entire distributed transaction resides at a single site. It establishes connections to several DBMSs and has embedded within it SQL statements that are sent to and executed at those servers. In this case, the subtransaction at a particular server is the set of SQL statements that it executes.

In general, a distributed transaction involves a set of subtransactions executed at server modules, which might reside at different sites in a network. Servers might provide access to resources other than databases (such as files). Each subtransaction is a transaction at the server that it accesses and is therefore ACID. When these servers are database systems, we say that the distributed transaction executes in a multidatabase system. A **multidatabase** (sometimes called a **federated database**) is a loose confederation of databases that contain related information.

We assume that the database at each site, referred to as a local database, has **local integrity constraints**. Since each site maintains atomicity and isolation, these constraints are maintained despite the concurrent execution of the subtransactions of multiple distributed transactions at that site. In addition, the multidatabase, consisting of the combination of all local databases, might have **global integrity constraints** relating data at different sites. We assume that a distributed transaction is globally consistent and hence, when it executes in isolation, maintains those constraints as well.

As an example of a global integrity constraint, assume that a bank maintains local databases at all branch offices and that each database contains an item whose value is the assets of that branch. The bank also maintains a database at its central office that contains an item whose value is the total assets of the bank. A global integrity constraint might assert that the value of the total assets item at the central office is the sum of the values of the assets items at all of the local branches. Note that this constraint is not maintained by individual subtransactions. A deposit at a branch initiates a subtransaction at the branch's database that increments the branch's assets but not the total assets item at the central office. To maintain the global integrity constraint, the deposit subtransaction at the branch must be accompanied by a subtransaction at the central office to increment the total assets item by the same amount.

In addition to global consistency, a possible goal of a TP monitor is to ensure that each distributed transaction (including all of its subtransactions) is atomic, isolated, and durable.

■ The atomicity of a distributed transaction implies that each subtransaction is atomic at the server it accesses, and that either all subtransactions commit or all abort. Thus, when a subtransaction of a distributed transaction, T, completes, it cannot immediately commit because some other subtransaction of T might abort (in which case all of T's subtransactions must also abort). We refer to this all-or-nothing commitment as **global atomicity**.

■ Isolation implies not only that each subtransaction is isolated at the server at which it executes (i.e., that each server serializes all the subtransactions that execute at that server) but also that each distributed transaction as a whole is isolated with respect to all others (i.e., that there is some global serialization order among all distributed transactions). Thus, **global serializability** implies that the subtransactions of two distributed transactions, T_1 and T_2, execute in such a way that at all servers it appears that T_1 preceded T_2 or that at all servers it appears that T_2 preceded T_1.

■ The durability of a distributed transaction implies the durability of all of its subtransactions.

Global atomicity and isolation are sufficient to ensure that the concurrent execution of a set of distributed transactions has the same effect as if the distributed transactions had executed serially in some order. Since we assume that each distributed transaction taken as a whole is consistent, serializable execution implies that the concurrent schedule is correct. Later, we will discuss different models in which transactions are not necessarily globally atomic or isolated and in which correctness is not guaranteed.

Models of a distributed transaction.   A distributed transaction can be viewed as a tree. The root of the tree initiates a set of subtransactions, which in turn initiate additional subtransactions, creating a tree of arbitrary depth. Within that general structure are a number of options.

■ The children of a particular subtransaction might or might not be able to execute concurrently.

■ The parent of a set of subtransactions might or might not be able to execute concurrently with its children. In the case in which concurrent execution is possible, the parent might or might not be able to communicate with its children.

■ In some models, only the root can request that the transaction be committed. In other models, an arbitrary subtransaction can request that the transaction be committed, and it is the transaction designer's responsibility to ensure that only one subtransaction makes the request. In still other models, the right to request commit can be explicitly passed from one subtransaction to another.

A number of possible models exist within these options. Two particular variations predominate and can be viewed as extreme cases.

Hierarchical Model. No concurrency is allowed within the transaction. Having initiated a subtransaction, the parent must wait until the subtransaction completes before proceeding. As a result, the parent can neither create additional subtransactions concurrent with the child nor communicate with it. The transaction is committed by the root. Procedure calling is a natural paradigm for communication within this model. TP monitors generally provide a special form of procedure calling known as **transactional remote procedure call (TRPC)**, which, in addition to invoking a procedure, supports the abstraction of a distributed transaction. TRPC will be discussed in Section 22.4.1.

Peer Model. Concurrency is permitted between a parent and its children and among the children. The hierarchical relationship between a parent and its children is minimized: Once created, the child is coequal with, or a peer of, the parent. In particular, a parent and child can communicate symmetrically and any participant can request that the transaction be committed. **Peer-to-peer communication** is the natural paradigm for communication within the peer model. A pair of subtransactions explicitly establishes a connection and then sends and receives messages over the connection. TP monitors generally support peer-to-peer communication, which we will discuss in Section 22.4.2.

Finally, two techniques are generally used to specify the boundaries of distributed transactions. This is referred to as **transaction demarcation**. With **programmatic demarcation**, an application module explicitly informs the TP monitor of the beginning and end of a transaction through the API provided by the monitor. For example, using the X/Open standard, the application invokes `tx_begin()` to start a transaction.

With **declarative demarcation**, the goal is to remove the specification of transaction boundaries from the modules making up the application. Each such module—frequently referred to as a **component** in systems that use declarative demarcation—thus deals only with application-related issues, such as accessing a database and enforcing enterprise rules, but does not specify the transactional context within which it executes. The **container module** that uses the component can specify whether or not the component is to be executed as a transaction. Thus, different modules can use the same component as a transaction all by itself, as a subtransaction, or as a nontransactional part of a bigger transaction. Microsoft Transaction Server (MTS) is a TP monitor that uses declarative demarcation. Enterprise Java Beans (EJB) also provides an interface for declarative demarcation, so TP monitors built with EJB can use this feature.

21.2.3 Nested Transactions

Distributed transactions evolved out of a need to integrate, into a single transactional unit, transactions exported from several servers. Since each server supports the transaction abstraction, (sub)transactions separately control their commit/abort decision. Unfortunately, the transaction designer has little control over the structure of the distributed transaction. The function of each exported transaction is essentially fixed by the way data is distributed across the servers, and distribution might be controlled by such factors as where the data is generated or where it is accessed most often. As a result of this bottom-up approach, the transactions might not reflect a clean functional decomposition of the application.

Because it was not conceived as a way of dealing with multiple servers or distributed data, the nested transaction model evolved differently. Its goal is to allow the transaction designer to design a complex transaction from the top down. The transaction is decomposed into subtransactions in a functionally appropriate way (not dictated by the distribution of data). Furthermore, as with the distributed model, subtransactions control their commit/abort decision, but the handling of the decision is different. Instead of the all-or-nothing approach of the distributed model, individual subtransactions in the nested model can abort without aborting the entire transaction. Even so, the nested transaction as a whole remains globally isolated and atomic.

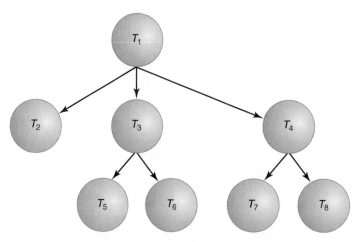

Figure 21.2 Structure of a travel planning transaction.

A number of concrete, detailed models for nested transactions have been proposed. We describe one such model, due to [Moss 1985]. A transaction and all of its subtransactions can be viewed as a tree. The root of the tree is called the **top-level** transaction, and the terms parent, child, ancestor, descendent, and sibling have their usual meanings. Subtransactions that have no children are called leaves. Not all leaves need be at the same level. We assume that the transaction and all of its subtransactions execute at a single site.

The semantics of the nested transaction model can be summarized as follows:

1. A parent can create children sequentially so that one child finishes before the next starts, or it can specify that a set of children execute concurrently. The parent does not execute concurrently with the children; it waits until all children in the set complete and then resumes execution and can create additional children. Note that the tree structure depicting a nested transaction (Figure 21.2) does not distinguish children that execute concurrently from those that execute sequentially.

2. A subtransaction (and all of its descendents) appears to execute as a single isolated unit with respect to its concurrent siblings. For example, in Figure 21.2, if $T2$ and $T3$ execute concurrently, $T2$ views the subtree ($T3$, $T5$, $T6$) as a single isolated transaction; it does not see any internal structure. It follows that the effect of the concurrent execution of a set of siblings is the same as if they had executed sequentially in *some* serial order. Thus, the siblings are serializable with respect to each other.

   In some cases, the serialization order of the siblings affects the final state of the database. For example, in a banking application two concurrent siblings whose task is to write checks from the same account produce the same final balance independent of the actual order (assuming that the initial balance of the account was sufficient to cover both checks). However, the check numbers are dependent on the order. Thus, the nested transaction is not deterministic: The same transaction run at different times can produce different results. If designed correctly, however, all possible results are acceptable to the application.

We can view all nested transactions in a single tree structure with a (fictitious) "mother of all top-level transactions" as a root and all top-level transactions as its children. It then follows that a top-level transaction (and all of its descendents) taken as a single unit executes as a single isolated unit with respect to all other top-level transactions (and all of their descendents). The hierarchical structure within a nested transaction is thus invisible outside of that transaction.

3. Subtransactions are atomic. Each subtransaction can abort or commit independently. The commitment of a subtransaction and its durability are conditional on the commitment of its parent. Hence, a subtransaction is finally committed and made durable when all of its ancestors (including the top-level transaction) commit, at which point the entire nested transaction is said to have committed. If a parent aborts, all of its subtransactions (even those that have committed) are aborted.

4. If a subtransaction aborts, it has the same effect as if it had not executed any database operations. Status is returned to the parent, and the parent can take appropriate action. An aborted subtransaction can thus alter the execution path of the parent transaction and, in this way, can have an impact on the database state. Contrast this to the situation with conventional (flat) transactions, in which an aborted transaction has no effect whatsoever.

5. A subtransaction is not necessarily consistent. However, the nested transaction as a whole is consistent.

The implementation of isolation for nested transactions is more complex than that for flat transactions, since concurrency is possible not only between nested transactions but within them as well. We will discuss this issue in Section 23.7.4.

We illustrate the nested transaction model using our travel planning example. The nested structure of this transaction is shown in Figure 21.2.

Transaction T_1 makes airline reservations from London to Des Moines. It might first create a subtransaction, T_2, to make reservations from London to New York and, when that completes, create a second subtransaction, T_3, to make reservations from New York to Des Moines. T_3, in turn, might create an additional subtransaction, T_5, to make reservations from New York to Chicago, and T_6, to make reservations from Chicago to Des Moines. T_5 and T_6 might be specified to execute concurrently. They might access common data (e.g., the customer's bank account), but their execution is serializable.

If T_6 cannot make reservations from Chicago to Des Moines, it can abort. When T_3 learns of the abort, it can abandon the plan to make reservations through Chicago and hence also abort (thus causing its other child, T_5, to abort and release the reservation from New York to Chicago). When T_1 learns of the abort, it can create a new transaction, T_4, to make reservations from New York to Des Moines through

St. Louis (while still maintaining the reservation between London and New York). If T_4 commits, T_1 can commit and its effect on the database will be the sum of the effects of T_2, T_4, T_7, and T_8. The transaction as a whole is viewed as an isolated and atomic unit by other nested transactions.

21.2.4 Multilevel Transactions*

Multilevel transactions are similar in some ways to distributed and nested transactions: A transaction is decomposed into a nested set of subtransactions. Unlike a nested transaction, however, the motivation for a multilevel transaction is increased performance. The goal is to allow more concurrency in the execution of independent transactions. To understand how this is achieved, it is necessary to look ahead a bit.

Isolation is generally implemented using locks. When a transaction accesses an item, it locks it, forcing other transactions to wait until the lock is released before accessing the item. This prevents one transaction from seeing the intermediate results of another. If a transaction holds the locks it acquires until it commits, isolation is implemented but only a limited amount of concurrency is allowed. The resulting performance enhancement (compared with serial execution) is thus limited.

The multilevel model improves on this situation by allowing the individual subtransactions of a multilevel transaction to commit before the transaction as a whole commits, thus releasing locks, and thereby allowing waiting transactions to progress at an earlier time. This improves performance, but as a result one multilevel transaction can see the partial results produced by another. In contrast, in the nested transaction model the individual subtransactions can only conditionally commit, locks are not released, and one nested transaction cannot see the partial results of another. Nevertheless, the execution of multilevel transactions is atomic and isolated as we will see.

In this section, we discuss the multilevel transaction model based on the work of [Weikum 1991]. We will describe its implementation in Section 23.7.5, where the advantage of the model with respect to performance will become apparent. As with the nested transaction model, we assume that the subtransactions of a multilevel transaction execute at a single site.

The multilevel transaction model.   A multilevel transaction accesses a database over which a sequence of abstractions has been defined. For example, at the lowest level the database might be viewed as a set of pages, which are accessed with read, r, and write, w, operations. At the next higher level, we might see the abstraction of tuples, which are accessed using SQL statements. (This is the level of abstraction generally presented by a DBMS.) A yet higher level might see a more application-oriented interface. For example, in the Student Registration System we might define a set of objects representing course sections and manipulate them with abstract operations for moving students between sections: a test and increment operation, *TestInc*, that conditionally adds another student to a section if there is enough room, and a decrement operation, *Dec*, that removes a student from a section.

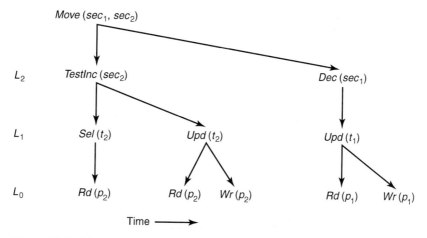

Figure 21.3 *Move* transaction viewed in the multilevel model.

Given these data abstraction levels, a transaction, $Move(sec_1, sec_2)$, that moves a student from section 1 of a large lecture class to section 2 can be structured as shown in Figure 21.3. The application level is the highest level in the figure. It sets the transaction boundaries and invokes *TestInc* to test and increment the count of students in section 2 and, if successful, invokes *Dec* to decrement the count of students in section 1. At level L_2, *TestInc* is implemented by a program that uses a SELECT statement, to retrieve information that determines if the student can be allowed in the section, and an UPDATE statement that increments the count of students in the section. *Dec* is implemented in L_2 using an UPDATE statement that unconditionally decrements the count of students in a section. We assume that section 1 and section 2 information is stored in tuples t_1 and t_2, respectively. At level L_1, these SQL statements are implemented in programs that read and write database pages. Tuple t_1 is stored in page p_1, and tuple t_2 is stored in page p_2. We ignore accesses to index pages in this example.

An operation invoked at some level (except L_0) can be viewed as a subtransaction at the level below. Thus, an invocation of *Upd* at L_2 causes the execution of a subtransaction at L_1 that invokes *Rd* and *Wr*, each of which is implemented as a subtransaction at L_0. Similarly, *TestInc* at L_2 invokes a subtransaction that executes *Sel* and *Upd* at L_1.

When a parent subtransaction creates a child subtransaction, it waits until the child completes. However, in contrast to the nested transaction model, children are not concurrent, which means that a multilevel transaction unfolds sequentially. Two other factors differentiate the multilevel model from the nested model.

1. All leaf subtransactions of the transaction tree are at the same level.
2. Only leaf subtransactions access the database.

Committing a multilevel transaction.   The handling of commitment is a key difference between the nested and multilevel models and is one of the bases for the performance improvement that can be achieved with multilevel transactions. In contrast with the nested model, the commitment of a subtransaction is unconditional. When a subtransaction at any level of a multilevel transaction, T, commits, the changes it has made to the data abstraction on which it operates become visible to other subtransactions at that level, which execute concurrently with T.

Unconditional commitment creates two new problems that must be solved to ensure that the multilevel transaction is atomic and isolated.

■ *Isolation.* Intermediate database states produced by a subtransaction are visible to concurrent transactions before the entire multilevel transaction commits. For example, in Figure 21.3 the section count data item for section 2 is available to concurrent multilevel transactions as soon as *TestInc* commits (before *Dec* starts).

While the transaction as a whole preserves integrity constraints, individual subtransactions might not. Hence, only when the last subtransaction of a multilevel transaction commits can we be sure that the database is in a consistent state. In Figure 21.3, between the execution of the two subtransactions at L_2, the student being moved is not recorded in either section. The resulting section enrollments are not consistent with the total course enrollment, which is presumably stored in some other table. This means that we have to be concerned that concurrent transactions might see inconsistent states.

Even though it appears from this example that multilevel transactions might not be isolated with respect to each other (in the sense that a transaction can access the intermediate results of a concurrent transaction), the implementation of the model, to be described in Section 23.7.5, does guarantee serializability. The transaction *is* isolated in the sense that a schedule has the same effect as if the multilevel transactions had executed in some serial order.

■ *Atomicity.* If a multilevel transaction must be aborted, all of the changes it has made to the database must be undone. With a flat or nested transaction, T, there is no problem. Even though T has updated a data item, x, the new value cannot have been accessed by any concurrent transaction, so one way T can be aborted is by simply writing the old value to x. Think of this as physical restoration. (In Section 25.2.3 we will discuss this approach more completely under the name of *physical logging*.)

Undoing changes made by a multilevel transaction is more complex, since some of its subtransactions might have committed and concurrent transactions might have seen data items they updated. Suppose that a failure condition is detected in a *Move* transaction, T_1, after the decrement subtransaction, D_1, has committed. Since D_1 has committed, so have its children, and thus the new value of t_1 has been made available to concurrent transactions. A simple physical restoration of t_1 to its old value does not always work. For example, suppose that another *Move* transaction, T_2, which moves a student out of the same section,

Figure 21.4 When T_1 aborts, the count for section 1 has been decremented twice. In this case physical restoration yields the wrong result.

T_1: *TestInc(sec$_2$)*   *Dec(sec$_1$)*   *abort*
T_2:   *TestInc(sec$_3$)*   *Dec(sec$_1$)*   *commit*

is executing concurrently with T_1, its decrement subtransaction D_2 is invoked immediately after D_1 commits, and then T_2 commits as shown in Figure 21.4. In this case, the section count has been decremented twice. Since the value of t_1 prior to the execution of D_1 shows neither increment, if we simply restore that value when T_1 aborts, the effect of D_2 will be lost and the database will be in an inconsistent state.

The technique used to solve this problem is called **compensation**. Instead of restoring an old value physically, we undo it *logically* using a **compensating subtransaction**. *Dec* logically undoes a successful *TestInc*, and hence is a compensating subtransaction; *Inc* (increment) logically undoes *Dec*. Similarly, in an airline reservation system, *cancellation* logically undoes *reservation*, which makes a cancellation subtransaction a compensating subtransaction for the reservation subtransaction.

The application designer must supply as part of the application design, a compensating subtransaction for each subtransaction. This is not easily done. If CT is the compensating subtransaction for ST, its action might depend on the state in which ST was executed. For example, *Dec* compensates for *TestInc* only if an increment was actually performed (if not, no compensation is needed). Sufficient information to make compensation possible must be stored in the log when ST commits. For some applications, a compensating subtransaction need not logically undo all database updates made by the subtransaction for which it compensates. In the airline application, for example, *cancellation* might not have to remove the passenger's name from the airline's mailing list. So if atomicity is not required, compensation is not precisely defined but might depend on the application.

In general, to abort a subtransaction $ST_{i,j}$ at level L_i, at a point at which its L_{i-1} subtransactions, $ST_{i-1,1}, \ldots, ST_{i-1,k}$, have committed, we execute compensating subtransactions in reverse order: $CT_{i-1,k}, \ldots, CT_{i-1,1}$, where $CT_{i-1,j}$ compensates for $ST_{i-1,j}$. In Figure 21.3, if *TestInc(sec$_2$)* is aborted before *Upd(t_2)* is invoked, nothing need be done (because *Sel(t_2)* needs no compensation), but if it is aborted afterwards, a compensating update statement must be executed that decrements the count in t_2. If *Move* is aborted after *Dec(sec$_1$)* commits, compensating subtransactions for it and *TestInc(sec$_2$)* must be executed, in that order. We will discuss compensation in more detail in Section 23.6.

21.3   STRUCTURING AN APPLICATION INTO MULTIPLE TRANSACTIONS

In a number of situations, it becomes necessary to decompose into smaller transactions what might ordinarily be a single transaction. For example, a long-running transaction might be decomposed so that locks it has acquired can be released at intermediate points, with the goal of improving performance. Or we might want to commit at intermediate points to avoid losing too much work in the event of a crash. In some situations, what might ordinarily be a single transaction involves subtasks that take place at different times. In this section, we discuss methods for providing such structure. We also discuss workflow management systems, which provide a way to view a complex business activity as a set of subtasks that must be executed in some application-dependent way.

21.3.1   Chained Transactions

Often, an application program consists of a sequence of transactions. For example, in a catalog ordering application there might be a program that consists of a sequence of three transactions: order-entry, shipping, and billing. Between their execution, the program retains information in local variables about the items ordered and the person who ordered them, and may perform some computations with this information.

A trivial optimization, called **chaining**, automatically starts a new transaction when the previous transaction in the sequence commits, thus avoiding the use of `begin_transaction()` (and its associated overhead of invoking the DBMS) for all but the first transaction in the sequence.[2] When chaining is enabled, an application program consisting of a sequence of transactions has the form

```
begin_transaction();
    S_1;
commit();
    S_2;
commit();
      . . .
    S_{n-1};
commit();
    S_n;
commit();
```

where S_i is the body of the ith transaction, ST_i.

The execution of each commit statement makes the database changes caused by the prior transaction durable. Hence, if a crash occurs during the execution of ST_i, all changes made by $ST_1, \ldots, ST_{i-1}$ are preserved in the database when the system

---

[2] Actually, `begin_transaction()` can be dispensed with as well—the first interaction with the server can automatically start a transaction.

is restarted. Of course, information stored by the application in local variables is lost.

Chaining can be viewed from a different perspective when designing long-running transactions, such as the student billing transaction described earlier. Instead of the automatic start of a new transaction, our concern now is to avoid total rollback if a crash occurs. With chaining, a long-running transaction can be decomposed into a sequence of code fragments, $S_1, S_2, \ldots, S_n$, which are chained together as shown above and in which each fragment is a subtransaction. For example, the student billing transaction might be decomposed into 10 subtransactions, each of which does the billing for 1,000 students.

The following considerations arise when a long-running transaction is decomposed into a chain:

1. The good news is that if a crash occurs during a subtransaction, only the results of that subtransaction are lost since the results of prior subtransactions have already been made durable. (This behavior should be contrasted with that of a transaction using savepoints, where the work of the entire transaction is lost in a crash.) The bad news is that the transaction as a whole is no longer atomic. After recovery, the system assumes no responsibility for restarting the chain from the point at which the crash occurred.

2. Since the subtransactions were originally part of a single transaction and so perform a single task, they generally need to communicate with each other. They share access to a common set of local variables, so communication can be easily accomplished. For example, if the student billing transaction is decomposed as described above, a local variable might contain the index of the last student billed. When a new subtransaction starts, it uses that variable to determine which student to bill next. The problem with communication using local variables is that they do not survive a crash, and so, when resuming execution after a crash, it might be difficult to determine which student to bill next.

   As an alternative, the subtransactions might communicate through database variables. For example, the index of the last student billed by a subtransaction might be stored in a database item before the subtransaction commits. If a crash occurs during execution of the next subtransaction, that database item indicates where billing must resume. Note that in this case the database items used for communication are available to transactions executing in other (concurrent) applications. Care must be taken to ensure that the other applications do not tamper with them.

3. The state of that portion of the database accessed by the chained transaction—referred to as its **database context**—is not maintained between one subtransaction and the next in the chain. For example, if locks are used to implement isolation, all of the locks held by subtransaction ST_i are released when it commits. Thus, if ST_{i+1} is the next subtransaction in the chain and it accesses an item that ST_i has accessed, the value that ST_{i+1} sees might be different from the value the item had when ST_i committed (because some other transaction—not

in the chain—modified the item and committed between the time ST_i committed and the time ST_{i+1} requested access to the item). The point here is that, in contrast to a single long-running transaction, each subtransaction in the chain is isolated but the chained transaction as a whole is not.

Another aspect of database context is the state of any cursor that the transaction has opened. Since `commit` closes cursors, any cursor that ST_i opens is not available to ST_{i+1}.

Although isolation is forfeited, chaining can yield a performance benefit. With locking, a long-running transaction can make the portions of the database that it accesses unavailable for long periods. This can create a performance bottleneck, since concurrent transactions are made to wait until the transaction commits and releases its locks. By breaking up the transaction into chained subtransactions, locks are released quickly and the bottleneck is eliminated.

4. Our initial view of chaining was one in which a sequence of individual transactions are processed and chaining automatically starts the next transaction in the sequence when the prior transaction completes. In that case, each individual transaction is consistent and so the database is in a consistent state between transactions. When we view chaining as a mechanism for decomposing a single long-running transaction, the situation is different. Although the entire long-running transaction is consistent, the individual subtransactions might not be. This creates a problem, since a subtransaction releases its database context when it commits, making it visible to other, concurrently executing transactions. These transactions expect to see a consistent database, so we must require that the subtransactions be consistent. The issue of consistency does not arise with savepoints because the entire transaction is isolated and atomic in that case. Since the database context is not released at a savepoint, no concurrent transaction can see an inconsistent state.

The consistency of subtransactions is also required in order to deal with crashes. If a crash occurs, the chained transaction does not run to completion and its partial effects are left visible to transactions in other applications when the system is restarted. Thus, just as the chained transaction is not isolated, it is also not atomic.

Sagas. [Garcia-Molina and Salem 1987] proposed a transaction model, called a **saga**, in which chaining is made atomic through compensation. A compensating transaction is designed for each subtransaction in a chained transaction. If a chained transaction, T_i, consists of subtransactions $ST_{i,j}$, $1 \le j \le n$, and if $CT_{i,j}$ is a compensating transaction for $ST_{i,j}$, an execution of T_i can take two forms. If it completes successfully, this sequence of subtransactions is executed:

$$ST_{i,1}, ST_{i,2}, \ldots, ST_{i,n}$$

If a crash occurs during the execution of $ST_{i,j+1}$, that subtransaction is aborted and the following sequence is executed:

$$ST_{i,1}, ST_{i,2}, \ldots, ST_{i,j}, CT_{i,j}, \ldots, CT_{i,1}$$

In this way, one aspect of atomicity is achieved: If any subtransaction of T_i aborts, all of the changes made by its committed subtransactions are undone. However, it might not be atomic, because before compensation has completed a concurrent transaction might have read some of the changes made by its committed subtransactions. Contrast this with the multilevel model, in which subtransactions are controlled in a way (to be described in Section 23.7.5) that uses compensation to guarantee atomicity and serializability.

An alternate semantics for chained transactions.   From a pedagogical point of view, it is interesting to consider an alternate semantics for chained transactions that deals with some of the issues raised by the conventional interpretation. To distinguish this new semantics from its more conventional counterpart, we use the function call chain(). A chained transaction now has the form

```
begin_transaction();
     S₁;
     chain();
     S₂;
     chain();
     ...
     Sₙ₋₁;
     chain();
     Sₙ;
commit();
```

chain() commits a subtransaction, ST_i (thus making it durable), and starts a new subtransaction, ST_{i+1}, but it does not release the database context and it maintains cursors. For example, when locks are used to implement isolation, those locks held by ST_i are not released but are instead passed on to ST_{i+1}. Thus, if ST_{i+1} accesses an item that ST_i accessed, the value it sees is the same as the value it had when ST_i committed. Since the modifications to the database caused by ST_i are not visible to concurrent transactions, the individual subtransactions need no longer be consistent and ST_i can leave the database in an inconsistent state if ST_{i+1} has been designed to expect that state. Thus, the chained transaction as a whole is isolated, although performance suffers.

Crash recovery is complicated with this semantics. If recovery simply rolls back the subtransaction that was active at the time of the crash, isolation is not supported since transactions that start after recovery can see an inconsistent state. The chained transaction as a whole cannot be rolled back, since earlier subtransactions in the chain have committed. This means that, with the new semantics, a chained transaction must be rolled forward if any one of its subtransactions has committed. If a crash occurs during the execution of ST_{i+1}, the recovery procedure restarts ST_{i+1} and delivers to it the database context held by ST_i when it committed (i.e., the database context as it existed at that point together with the locks held by ST_i). Restarting in this way provides both isolation and atomicity for the chain as a whole. Recall that, in contrast to chained transactions, the system assumes no responsibility for automatically restarting a flat transaction after a crash.

21.3.2 Transaction Scheduling with Recoverable Queues

With chaining, transactions are assembled in a sequence and are processed so that one starts as soon as the previous one completes. Sometimes, however, an application requires that transactions be executed in sequence but not that they be executed as a single unit. Instead, the requirement is that after one transaction completes the next one will *eventually* be initiated and run to completion. So unlike chaining, a substantial interval might elapse between the completion of one transaction and the start of the next.

As we saw earlier, a catalog ordering activity might involve three tasks—placing an order, shipping the order, and billing the customer. These tasks might be performed by three separate transactions. The work performed by the shipping and billing transaction can be executed at any convenient time after the order entry transaction commits. However, it is important that these transactions be executed at some later time, even if the system crashes after the order is taken.

As another example, consider a distributed application in which a transaction, T, at a local site needs to cause some action at a remote site. If the remote action is incorporated into T, the network latency involved in invoking the action and receiving an acknowledgement becomes part of T's response time. If, however, it is not required that the remote action be performed as a single isolated unit together with T, but only that it ultimately be performed, then it can be designed as a separate transaction that T schedules for subsequent execution, and T's response time will not be degraded by network latency.

Applications such as these need some highly reliable mechanism to ensure that the transactions scheduled for future execution are in fact executed. One such mechanism is the **recoverable queue**. A recoverable queue has the semantics of an ordinary queue. Its API allows a transaction to enqueue and dequeue entries. A transaction enqueues an entry describing some work that must be performed (at a later time) if the transaction commits. The information in the entry corresponds to the local state information that must be passed between successive transactions in a chain. At some later time, the entry is dequeued by another transaction that performs the work. This second transaction might be initiated by a server process that repeatedly dequeues entries from the queue and processes them.

As an example, consider an application in which a user wants to make a bid for some item in an Internet auction that will take place the next day. The user executes a transaction that places her bid on a recoverable queue. Later, but before the auction takes place, another transaction removes that bid from the queue and enters it into the auction database. (Note that entries in the auction database can be made in the same order as that in which the bids were made, in accordance with the rules of the auction.) This organization allows the system to respond to the user quickly, as soon as the user's bid has been entered on the queue. The alternate organization, in which the user's initial transaction enters the bid into the auction database, has a longer response time because of the overhead of database operations.

To ensure that an entry enqueued by a committed transaction is eventually processed, the queue must be durable. Durability implies that the queue survives failures, so, as with the database itself, the queue must be stored redundantly on mass storage. Transaction atomicity demands that the *enqueue* and *dequeue* operations be coordinated with transaction commitment in the following ways:

■ If a transaction enqueues an item and later aborts, that item is removed from the queue.

■ If a transaction dequeues an item and later aborts, that item is replaced on the queue.

■ An item enqueued by a transaction, T, that has not yet committed cannot be dequeued by another transaction (since we cannot be sure that T will commit).

Note that it would be possible to implement a queue with such properties directly in the database—a transaction wishing to enqueue an entry simply updates the tables used to implement the queue. The problem is that these tables are used heavily by many transactions. We will see in Chapters 23 and 24 that most implementations of isolation use locking protocols in which transactions updating common data are frequently delayed. From a performance point of view, then, it is desirable to implement the queue as a separate module that is treated as special from the point of view of isolation.

Recoverable queues can implement a variety of scheduling policies, including FIFO (first-in, first-out) and priority ordering. Or a process might be allowed to examine entries in the queue and select a particular entry for dequeueing. Note that, even when a queue has FIFO semantics, the entries might not be processed in FIFO order. For example, transaction T_1 might dequeue the head entry, E_1, from a FIFO queue, and at a later time transaction T_2 might dequeue the new head entry, E_2, from the queue. If T_1 subsequently aborts, E_1 is returned to the head of the queue. The net effect will be that the second entry, E_2, has been serviced, before the first entry, E_1, contradicting the requirements of a FIFO queue.

One way to organize the catalog ordering application is as a pipeline, as shown in Figure 21.5. The order entry clerk initiates a transaction at the order entry server which enters the order, enqueues a shipping entry in a recoverable queue for a shipping transaction, and then commits. At a later time, the shipping server initiates a transaction that dequeues that entry, performs the required operations, enqueues a billing entry in a second recoverable queue for the billing server, and then commits. At a still later time, a billing server initiates a transaction that dequeues the entry, performs the required operations, and then commits. Such an organization is like a pipeline because an entry corresponding to a particular purchase progresses, in sequence, from one queue to the next.

Another way to organize this application is shown in Figure 21.6. An order entry transaction enqueues entries in both a billing recoverable queue and a shipping recoverable queue and then commits. At a later time, a billing transaction can

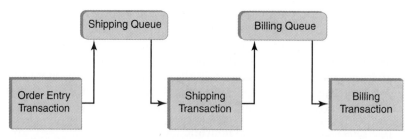

Figure 21.5 A system that uses recoverable queues in a pipeline organization.

Figure 21.6 A system that uses recoverable queues to achieve concurrency.

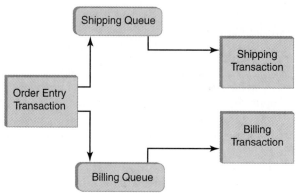

dequeue the entry from the billing queue and perform the appropriate operations, or a shipping transaction can dequeue the entry from the shipping queue and do its work. In this organization, the billing and shipping transactions for the same order can be executing concurrently. (Of course, the customer might be unhappy if he receives the bill before he receives the shipment.)

In the distributed system example, a transaction at central site A might enqueue an entry in a local recoverable queue describing an action that must be performed at remote site B. At a later time, a distributed transaction initiated at B might create a subtransaction at A to dequeue that entry and send it to B for execution.

Recoverable queues used to schedule real-world events.   Another application of the recoverable queue is in achieving atomicity when a transaction is required to perform some real-world action, such as printing a receipt or dispensing cash. In contrast to updating a database, real-world actions cannot be rolled back. Once performed by a transaction, they cannot be reversed by an abort (as a result of a system crash or deadlock, for example). This means that transaction abort is not handled atomically. (What if a transaction in an ATM system dispenses cash and then the system crashes before the transaction commits? The database changes corresponding to the withdrawal are rolled back even though the cash has been dispensed.)

It might appear that the desired semantics—in which the real-world action occurs if and only if the transaction commits—can be achieved using a recoverable queue as follows. The transaction enqueues a request to perform the real-world action on a recoverable queue before committing. If the transaction aborts, the entry is deleted; if it commits, the entry is durably stored for servicing at a later time by a *real-world* transaction that performs the desired action.

Unfortunately, this "solution" only defers the problem to the real-world transaction. What happens if the system crashes while the real-world transaction is executing? We know that the entry will be preserved on the recoverable queue, but how can we tell whether or not the transaction performed the action before the crash? We need to know this to decide if the real-world transaction should be re-executed when the system recovers.

One way to solve this problem requires assistance from the physical device that performs the real-world action. Suppose that the device maintains a counter that it increments each time it performs the action, and suppose that the counter is readable by the real-world transaction. After performing the action, the real-world transaction, T_{RW}, reads the counter and stores its updated value in the database before committing. When recovering after a crash, the system reads the counter and compares its value to the value stored in the database. If the two are the same, no additional real-world actions have been executed since the last real world transaction committed; if not, the device counter must have a value that is one greater than the value stored in the database, indicating that a real-world action was performed but that the corresponding real world transaction, T_{RW}, was aborted as a result of the crash. Hence, the entry that T_{RW} had dequeued was restored to the head of the queue and T_{RW} might or might not have stored the updated value of the counter in the database. Even if it had, that value was rolled back. The system can therefore deduce that the real-world *action* required by the entry at the head of the queue has been performed, but the corresponding real-world *transaction* did not commit.

Recoverable queues used to support a forwarding agent.   Another mechanism used in conjunction with recoverable queues is the **forwarding agent**. Consider a client that wants to invoke a service but determines that the target server is not operational. If the required service can be deferred, the client can enqueue the request for later servicing when the target server becomes available. A forwarding agent is a mechanism that can be used to invoke the target server at a later time. It periodically initiates a transaction that dequeues a request-for-service entry from the queue, invokes the target server, and awaits a response. If the transaction does not complete successfully (e.g., the target server is still not available), it simply aborts and the entry is restored to the queue for later servicing. If the transaction commits, a response entry can be enqueued in a reply queue to be picked up at a later time by the client (see Figure 21.7). Note that the target server cannot (and need not) distinguish between the two circumstances under which it might have been invoked. The service that it performs is independent of whether it was invoked directly by the client or indirectly through the agent.

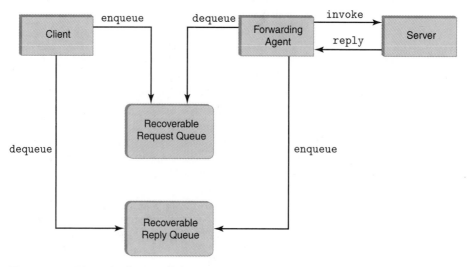

Figure 21.7   Use of a forwarding agent to invoke a server.

Recoverable queues as a communication mechanism.   A recoverable queue can be viewed as a reliable communication mechanism by which modules communicate with each other. Unlike the communication methods discussed previously, in which the communication is *online* or immediate, communication using queues is *deferred*. This situation is analogous to leaving messages in a telephone answering machine. Since the queue is recoverable, the deferred communication can even take place across a crash of the system.

21.3.3   Extended Transactions

The traditional concept of a transaction and its associated ACID properties has proved very useful in many applications, particularly those in which execution time is relatively short (seconds or possibly minutes), the transaction accesses relatively few data items, and the database is local. The Student Registration System is a typical example.

A wide variety of applications, however, do not meet these criteria. For example, in CAD/CAM, office automation, or software development environments, a transaction might last for hours or days and access many data items at different servers. Maintaining isolation and atomicity for such long-running transactions might be too costly in terms of system performance. Isolation implies that database changes made by a transaction, T, are not visible to concurrent transactions until T commits. This means that the concurrent transactions wait and that, when T is a long-running transaction that accesses many data items, performance can suffer. Atomicity requires that either all subtransactions of a transaction commit or all abort. Ensuring atomicity requires that servers engage in an atomic commit protocol (which we will discuss in Chapter 26). Unfortunately, not all servers are willing or capable of participating.

Because of these issues, the transaction model has been generalized into what is called an **extended** (or sometimes **advanced**) **transaction model**. There are several versions of the model which have generally not been developed beyond prototype implementations. The ideas are nevertheless interesting, and they form the basis for the more practical workflow model supported in commercial systems.

The common thread among extended transaction models is that transactions are not ACID. The models are intended to allow the application designer to create transactions that use varying degrees of atomicity and isolation. For that reason, extended transactions must be used carefully to avoid designs that behave incorrectly.

In a manner similar to a distributed transaction, an extended transaction is designed to execute in a multidatabase system composed of a number of database servers. It is composed of subtransactions, and for simplicity we assume that each server exports a set of transactions, which collectively form the library of subtransactions from which an extended transaction is built.

The extended transaction model associates an **execution state** with each subtransaction. Possible execution states include *aborted, committed, executing, not-executed, compensated,* and *prepared-to-commit.* (The prepared-to-commit state will be discussed in Section 26.2.) The fact that a subtransaction can be in the committed state means that the model does not necessarily guarantee isolation. Thus, the database state produced by a committed subtransaction of one extended transaction (which has not yet committed) might be visible to a subtransaction of another extended transaction.

In addition, some extended transaction models allow a committed subtransaction to report logical status, such as *completed successfully* or *completed unsuccessfully.* An unsuccessful completion might be the denial of a bank withdrawal due to insufficient funds. Note, though, that the subtransaction commits in either case.

As with distributed transactions, the application designer must specify the sequence in which the subtransactions of each extended transaction execute. Instead of embedding the sequencing within the transaction program (for example, through the placement of client-to-server remote procedure calls), the extended transaction model uses an external specification. This might take a graphical form, in which subtransactions are nodes and edges indicate the sequencing between subtransactions. Or it might be a set of rules or a control flow language. In any case, the initiation of a subtransaction might be a function of the output or execution state of other subtransactions.

The designer might specify

$$\text{initiate } ST_{i,j} \text{ when } ST_{i,k} \text{ committed} \tag{21.1}$$

where $ST_{i,j}$ and $ST_{i,k}$ are subtransactions of extended transaction ET_i. Here $ST_{i,j}$ starts only if $ST_{i,k}$ commits. If $ST_{i,k}$ aborts, $ST_{i,j}$ is not initiated at all. A specification of the form

$$\text{initiate } ST_{i,r}, ST_{i,k} \text{ when } ST_{i,h} \text{ committed}$$

calls for the concurrent execution of subtransactions $ST_{i,r}$ and $ST_{i,k}$ within a single extended transaction (upon commitment of $ST_{i,h}$). Another choice for the designer is

$$\text{initiate } ST_{i,q} \text{ when } ST_{i,k} \text{ aborted}$$

where $ST_{i,q}$ is a subtransaction that performs the task undertaken by $ST_{i,k}$ in an alternate way. Using this technique, a number of paths leading to the successful completion of an extended transaction can be specified.

For example, $ST_{i,k}$ might be a subtransaction of a trip planning extended transaction that books a New York to Washington air ticket and $ST_{i,q}$ might be a subtransaction that books a New York to Washington rail ticket. The extended transaction might concurrently initiate $ST_{i,k}$ and $ST_{i,q}$, with the requirement that $ST_{i,q}$ commit only if $ST_{i,k}$ aborts.

A subtransaction can be **retriable**, meaning that, even if it initially aborts, it will eventually commit if retried a sufficient number of times. It is not necessary to specify an alternative path in case a retriable transaction aborts. It is only necessary to specify that the subtransaction be retried until it commits. For example, a deposit transaction is retriable but a withdraw transaction is not (sufficient funds might never exist). If all subtransactions of an extended transaction are retriable, the extended transaction can always be completed.

Because the extended transaction model does not necessarily guarantee atomic commitment, a problem arises if an extended transaction fails. For example, a user might decide to cancel an extended transaction at an arbitrary point during its execution, or a (non-retriable) subtransaction for which there are no alternate paths might abort. Subtransactions of the extended transaction that are executing at that point can be aborted, but what about those that have already committed? Their effects must be undone. For example, if the extended transaction ET_i has reserved hotels and transportation for a trip, a subtransaction, $ST_{i,j}$, that reserves a seat on a plane might have committed before the trip is canceled. We faced this problem with multilevel transactions and sagas. We saw in those models that compensation, rather than physical restoration, is appropriate. A similar argument applies in the extended transaction model. The difference is that in the multilevel model compensation guarantees atomicity and serializability. No such assurances are given in the extended transaction model (or in the saga model).

Compensating subtransactions are part of the extended transaction model. An extended transaction that consists only of **compensatable** subtransactions can always be undone. However, some subtransactions are neither compensatable nor retriable. For example, a subtransaction that reserves and pays for a non-refundable ticket is not compensatable (the ticket is non-refundable) and not retriable (there is no guarantee that the ticket will ever become available). Such a subtransaction is often referred to as a **pivot**.

Undoing an extended transaction after a noncompensatable subtransaction has committed is not possible. Instead, it must always be possible to complete the execution at that point. All subsequently executed subtransactions must be retriable (or appropriate alternate paths must be provided). Hence, the execution of an extended transaction consists of the execution of compensatable subtransactions followed by the execution of retriable subtransactions. A single pivot subtransaction can be executed between the two sets.

The extended transaction model assumes the existence of a **run-time controller**, which interprets the sequencing rules and properties of the subtransactions (e.g., retriable, compensatable) and causes each extended transaction to be executed in accordance with them.

21.3.4 Workflows and Workflow Management Systems

A **workflow** is a model of a complex process in an enterprise. It is structured as a set of tasks that must be performed in a specified partial order. A task in the workflow model need not be a subtransaction. For example, the catalog ordering system might include a task executed by a person (not a computer), whose purpose is to pack the merchandise before shipping. Other tasks might be database transactions that delete the merchandise from the inventory database.

A workflow can be viewed as a generalization of an extended transaction, and we will see the role workflows play in application servers in Chapter 22. Workflows as described in this section share many of the properties of these other models, but differ significantly in their emphasis and generality.

A workflow is much less concerned with databases and ACID properties than are the models we have discussed so far. Its concern is automating the execution of complex, long-running enterprise processes involving computational and non-computational tasks in distributed and heterogeneous environments. Isolating the execution of concurrent workflows or guaranteeing their atomicity are not major concerns. Individual tasks within a workflow can be database transactions, which are locally ACID, but the workflow does not distinguish such tasks from other, nontransactional tasks.

Each task in a workflow is performed by an **agent**, which can be a program, a hardware device, or a human. For keeping track of inventory, the agent might be a software system; for packing merchandise, the agent most likely is a human. A workflow might be performed by a number of agents over a significant period of time. Moreover, it is frequently performed in a highly heterogeneous and distributed computing environment, possibly involving legacy systems. In the catalog ordering example, the shipping and billing departments might be totally separate and use different database systems.

Each task has a physical status, such as executing, committed, or aborted. In addition, the completion of a task might generate some logical status information indicating success or failure. In the catalog ordering system, for example, T_4 might discover that the customer has a bad credit rating. It completes in this case, but generates a logical failure status that is due to an application-related condition.

As in the extended transaction model, the tasks in a workflow have to be coordinated. For example, a particular task might be schedulable only after two or

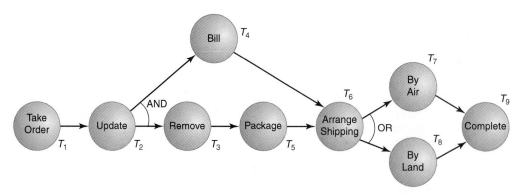

Figure 21.8 Workflow showing the execution precedence relationship between tasks of a catalog ordering system.

more other tasks have completed (an *AND condition*), or perhaps several tasks can be executed concurrently.

Similarly, at a certain point in the execution of a workflow there might be several tasks that essentially accomplish the same goal and only one of them should be executed (an *OR condition*). The choice of which to execute can depend on the logical status or output generated by some prior task in the workflow or on the value of some external variable (e.g., the time of day).

A workflow describing the catalog ordering system is shown in Figure 21.8. Task T_1 takes the order. Task T_2 deletes the item from the inventory database and initiates tasks T_3 and T_4 concurrently. T_3 causes the item to be removed from the warehouse, while T_4 performs the billing function. Task T_5 packages the item when it has been removed. After billing and packaging, task T_6 arranges shipping, which can be by airmail (task T_7) or by land (task T_8)—only one of these alternatives is executed. Finally, when the customer signs the delivery papers the database is updated to indicate that the order has been fulfilled (task T_9).

In addition to logical failure, a task failure can be due to some system-related condition, for example, a server being down. In some applications, such a task is retriable, in which case it is rerun at a later time. Or the customer might decide to cancel the purchase at an arbitrary point, in which case the workflow is said to have failed. Abort is not an appropriate term here, since some tasks might have completed and their results might have become visible.

One way to handle such failures is with compensation, in which a compensating task is specified for each task in the workflow. In case of a run-time failure, compensating tasks are executed for each completed task in the reverse order. For example, a compensating task for T_2 restores the item to the appropriate inventory record. If the failure happened during the execution of T_3 and T_4, these tasks are rolled back and compensating tasks are run first for T_2 and then for T_1.

There are alternative strategies for dealing with failure. If in a workflow some sequence of tasks, T_A followed by T_B, is performed and if, at run time, T_B returns

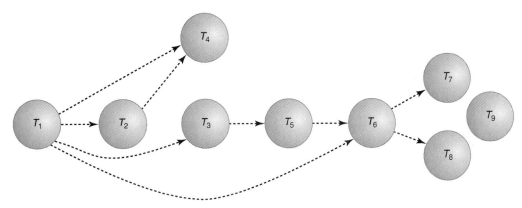

Figure 21.9 Flow of data in the catalog ordering system of Figure 21.8.

a logical failure status, the workflow designer can specify that the compensating task for T_A be performed next, followed by some other sequence of tasks that accomplishes the same goal as those of T_A and T_B, but perhaps in a less desirable way.

The results produced by one task frequently must be supplied as input to another, but this flow is not necessarily the same as the control flow. For example, in Figure 21.8 the customer's name and address, gathered during the execution of T_1, are sent to T_4 and T_6, while the identity of the item is sent to T_2 and T_3. T_2 then sends the item's cost to T_4. This flow of data and goods for the catalog ordering system is shown in Figure 21.9. There is also a formatting issue—the data output by one task might have to be reformatted before it can be input to another task. Such issues come up frequently when information must be passed between legacy systems.

The generality of workflows follows partly from the fact that not all tasks are computational and not all agents are software systems. But even if all tasks are computational, the workflow model follows the extended transaction model in not requiring the ACID properties. Consider the isolation property. As a workflow is executed, individual tasks might release resources they have accessed, making them available to tasks in other workflows. This means that intermediate states of one workflow might be visible to another that is concurrently executing. For example, tasks T_2 and T_4 update different databases. Consider two instances, W_1 and W_2, of the catalog ordering workflow which handle two distinct sales concurrently. If the complete execution of W_2 is carried out between the execution of T_2 and T_4 in W_1, then W_2 will see an intermediate state of the two databases that it could not have seen in any serial execution of the workflows. This might be an acceptable violation of isolation for this application.

As another example, consider that tasks in a business environment often collaborate: Human agents performing different tasks communicate data to each other during the course of execution. Such tasks are not isolated, since data produced by one influences the execution of the other. Nevertheless, this form of communication might be appropriate for some applications.

Still another example of nonisolated behavior is a task updating a file. If files are not locked, an intermediate file state produced by a task in one workflow might be available to tasks in others. Furthermore, file systems generally do not provide atomicity: If the task is aborted for some reason, the file might be left in the intermediate state.

Finally, it might be appropriate to weaken atomicity, since some tasks might not be essential. Our catalog ordering workflow might include a task that adds the customer's name to a mailing list. The failure of that task (e.g., the mailing list database crashes) should not abort the entire workflow: The sale must be completed even if it is not possible to send an advertising brochure at a later time.

Workflow management systems. A **workflow management system (WfMS)** provides support for both specifying a workflow (at design time) and scheduling and monitoring its execution. A workflow specification is generally not concerned with the details of a particular task but rather with the way the tasks are sequenced and the way data flows between them. It might involve the use of a graphical user interface (GUI) through which the workflow designer can draw figures similar to Figures 21.8 and 21.9, or it might support a language in which the rules for task coordination can be expressed as shown in (21.1). For a workflow controller of a transaction processing system (Section 22.2.1), the specification might allow the designer to indicate the sequential or parallel execution of transactions, the use of queues, and the like.

Workflow control involves automating the execution of a workflow by interpreting its specification. This interpretation can involve a number of issues.

Roles, agents, and worklists. Each agent has an attribute indicating a set of roles it can assume. A **role** describes a task the agent can perform, and each task has an associated role. Roles are used by the workflow controller to identify the agents that can perform a task that is ready to be executed. For example, a number of different sales representatives might be capable of performing task T_1 in Figure 21.8. The WfMS might select a particular agent to do the job using an algorithm that balances the load among agents. To facilitate such an assignment, each agent might be associated with a **worklist** enumerating the tasks (from different active workflows) currently assigned to it.

Task activation. The WfMS monitors the physical and logical state of each task and, at a change in state, determines whether the initiation condition for a new task has been satisfied (Have all predecessor tasks completed? Is all input information for the task available?). It then selects and notifies the chosen agent and adds the task to its worklist. The WfMS evaluates logical and physical failure situations and initiates compensating tasks as needed.

State maintenance. Assuming that the durability of the result produced by each task is provided by the server that implements the task, the only other issue related to durability concerns the state of the WfMS itself. If this state and the inputs and outputs of the tasks are durably maintained, the WfMS can resume execution after a system crash. Such resumption is referred to as **forward recovery**.

Filters. Reformatting might be necessary when information from the output of one task is supplied as input to another. The WfMS might provide **filters** for this purpose. Note that the input to a task might be supplied by several prior tasks. The WfMS ensures that all input is present and properly formatted before a task is initiated. Furthermore, a filter might extract information used by the WfMS for task coordination.

Recoverable queues. Recoverable queues might be used by a WfMS as a mechanism for storing information about the tasks of an active workflow and for task sequencing.

The specification of an activity as a workflow is particularly important when the activity is complex and must satisfy a specific set of business rules. For example, management in the enterprise running the catalog ordering system might have a rule that no merchandise can be shipped to any person who does not pass a credit check. Such rules can be incorporated into the workflow so that management can be sure that, even though many instances of the activity are initiated in the course of a day (perhaps using human agents with minimum training), each instance is carried out according to the established policy. To further ensure compliance with business rules, many workflows include tasks that involve management approval of paperwork or other activities in previous tasks.

21.4 BIBLIOGRAPHIC NOTES

The basic idea of a flat transaction has been around for a while. Early descriptions are contained in [Eswaran et al. 1976, Gray 1981, Gray et al. 1976] and an early implementation was presented in [Gray 1978]. A more recent and comprehensive description is found in [Gray and Reuter 1993, Lynch et al. 1994, Bernstein and Newcomer 1997]. Savepoints were introduced in [Astrahan et al. 1976]. A good overview of issues related to distributed transactions over a multidatabase can be found in [Breitbart et al. 1992]. Nested transactions were proposed in [Moss 1985]. Specific models of nested transactions were introduced in [Moss 1985, Beeri et al. 1989, Fekete et al. 1989, Weikum and Schek 1991, Garcia-Molina et al. 1991]. Nested transactions are implemented within the Encina TP monitor [Transarc 1996]. Multilevel transactions have been examined in a number of papers, including [Weikum 1991, Beeri et al. 1989, Beeri et al. 1983, Moss 1985]. A discussion of compensating transactions appears in [Korth et al. 1990]. In [Garcia-Molina and Salem 1987] sagas were introduced. Some examples of extended transaction models are ConTracts [Reuter and Wachter 1991], ACTA [Chrysanthis and Ramaritham 1990], and FLEX [Elmagarmid et al. 1990]. An excellent overview of a variety of transaction models is found in [Elmagarmid 1992]. More recent developments in extended transaction models can be found in [Jajodia and Kerschberg 1997].

General overviews of workflow management can be found in [Georgakopoulos et al. 1995, Khoshafian and Buckiewicz 1995, Bukhres and Kueshn, Eds. 1995, Hsu 1995]. Two main issues have received considerable attention: development of the transaction models suitable for workflows and development of languages for work-flow specification. Discussions of these issues can be found in [Rusinkiewicz and Sheth 1994, Alonso et al. 1996, Georgakopoulos et al. 1994, Alonso et al. 1997, Worah and Sheth 1997, Kamath and Ramamritham 1996]. If business rules are included as part of the workflow, many complex issues arise. First, the specification lan-guage must be rich enough to specify these rules. Second, the workflow must obey the rules, which is a nontrivial achievement. A number of research groups have been investigating formal approaches to workflow specification and algorithms for correct workflow execution. A partial list of this work includes [Orlowska et al. 1996, Attie et al. 1993, Wodtke and Weikum 1997, Singh 1996, Attie et al. 1996, Davulcu et al. 1998, Adam et al. 1998, Hull et al. 1999, Bonner 1999]. Another impor-tant issue—*interoperability* among workflows—has been taken up by the Workflow Management Coalition, which has has published a number of standards in [Work-flow Management Coalition 2000].

21.5   EXERCISES

21.1 The student billing system described in the first section of this chapter can be structured either as a single transaction with a savepoint after each 100 stu-dents or as a chained transaction with a commit point after each 100 students. Explain the differences in semantics between the two implementations. State when the printing of bills takes place in each.

21.2 Explain the difference between each of the transaction models with respect to abort, commit, rollback, and isolation in the following cases:

   a. A sequence of savepoints in a transaction and a chained transaction

   b. A sequence of savepoints in a transaction and a nested transaction con-sisting of subtransactions that are executed serially

   c. A sequence of savepoints in a transaction and a sequence of transactions linked by a recoverable queue

   d. A sequence of chained transactions and a nested transaction consisting of subtransactions that are scheduled serially

   e. A sequence of chained transactions and a sequence of transactions linked by a recoverable queue

   f. A sequence of transactions linked by a recoverable queue and a nested transaction consisting of subtransactions that are executed serially

   g. A nested transaction consisting of a set of concurrently executing siblings and a set of concurrently executing peer-related subtransactions of a distributed transaction

h. A nested transaction consisting of subtransactions that execute serially and a multilevel transaction

21.3 In the Student Registration System design given in Section 12.6, decompose the registration transaction into a concurrent nested transaction.

21.4 In the Student Registration System design given in Section 12.6, redesign the registration transaction as a multilevel transaction.

21.5 Show how the withdraw transaction in an ATM system can be structured as a nested transaction with concurrent subtransactions.

21.6 a. Explain the difference in semantics between the two versions of chaining discussed in the text.

   b. Which of these versions is implemented within SQL?

   c. Give an example of an application where the second version would be preferable.

21.7 Explain how the Student Registration System could interface with a student billing system using a recoverable queue.

21.8 Give three examples of applications in which isolation is not required and a recoverable queue could be used.

21.9 Explain the difficulties in implementing a print operation in a transaction without the use of a recoverable queue. Assume that the transaction does not mind waiting until printing is complete before committing.

21.10 Consider the real-world transaction for dispensing cash discussed in Section 21.3.2. For each of the critical times before, during, and after the execution of the real-world transaction in which the system might crash, describe how the system (after it recovers from the crash) determines whether or not the cash has been dispensed. Discuss some ways in which the cash dispensing mechanism itself might fail in such a way that the system cannot tell whether or not the cash has been dispensed.

21.11 Explain in what ways the execution of each individual SQL statement in a transaction is like a nested subtransaction.

21.12 Show how the credit card validation transaction described in the first paragraph of Chapter 1 can be structured as a distributed transaction.

21.13 The Student Registration System is to be integrated with an existing student billing system (which also bills for meal plans, dorm rooms, etc.). The databases for the two systems reside on different servers, and so the integrated system is distributed. Using your imagination,

   a. Give examples of two global integrity constraints that might exist for the global database of this system.

   b. Give examples of two transactions that access both databases.

21.14 Describe the process that the admissions office of your university uses to admit new students as a workflow. Decompose the process into tasks and describe the task interaction using a diagram similar to Figure 21.8.

21.15 Consider a transaction that transfers funds between two bank accounts. It can be structured into two subtransactions: one to debit the first account and the second to credit the second account. Describe how this can be done in (a) the hierarchical model and (b) the peer model.

21.16 Explain how nested transactions can be implemented using savepoints and procedure calls. Assume that the children of each subtransaction do not run concurrently.

21.17 Describe the similarities and differences between a workflow and an extended transaction.

21.18 Can a session in the Student Registration System be viewed as an extended transaction? Explain your answer.

Chapter 22

Architecture of Transaction Processing Systems

Transaction processing systems are among the largest software systems in existence. They must be built to respond to a wide spectrum of applications, so the demands on them vary greatly. At one extreme are single-user systems accessing a local database. At the other extreme are multiuser systems in which a single transaction can access a heterogeneous set of resource managers that are distributed across a network, and in which thousands of transactions can be executing each second. Many such systems have critical performance requirements and are the foundation of vital enterprises.

To create and maintain such a complex system, a functional decomposition into modules that perform distinct tasks is essential. In this chapter, we discuss the modular structure of these systems, starting with the simplest and introducing new elements of complexity one step at a time. We describe the various tasks that must be performed, show how they are mapped into modules, and explain how these modules communicate in each organization.

22.1 TRANSACTION PROCESSING IN A CENTRALIZED SYSTEM

In a centralized transaction processing system, all of the modules reside on a single computer—for example, a single PC or workstation servicing a single user or a mainframe computer, with many connected terminals that are servicing multiple users concurrently. We consider these two cases separately.

22.1.1 Organization of a Single-User System

Figure 22.1 shows how a single-user transaction processing system might be organized on a PC or workstation. The user module performs **presentation and application services**. Presentation services is generally created by the application generator, described in Section 3.4. It displays forms on the screen and handles the flow of information from and to the user through the forms. A typical cycle of activity might start with presentation services displaying a form, on which the user enters information in textboxes and then clicks the mouse or a pushbutton. Presentation services recognizes the click as an event and call the associated program, referred to as the **event program** in Section 3.6. The presentation services passes the information that has been input in the textboxes in the GUI to event programs,

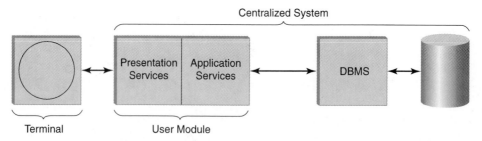

Figure 22.1 Single-user transaction processing system.

which then perform the application services. The programs check the integrity constraints not specified in the schema and execute a sequence of steps in accordance with the rules of the enterprise, updating the database appropriately.

To perform application services, event programs must communicate with the database server. For example, the event program that manages course registration in the Student Registration System has to make sure that a student has taken the prerequisite courses and must add the student's name to the class roster. Its requests to access the database might be specified in embedded SQL statements that are sent to the database server, which translates them into a series of read and write commands that access the database on the mass storage device. The commands are implemented by the underlying operating system.

Note that the user does not interact directly with the database server but instead invokes event programs, which send requests to it. To allow a user direct access to the database server—for example, by specifying the SQL statements to be executed—is dangerous as a careless or malicious user could easily destroy database integrity by writing erroneous data. Even allowing the user read-only access to the data has drawbacks. For one thing, it is generally not a simple matter to formulate an SQL query to return the information a user might want to see. For another, there might be information in the database that some users are not allowed to see—grade information for a particular student that must not be given to any other student but can be made available to any faculty member is one example.

These problems can be solved by requiring that the user access the database indirectly through the event programs supplied by the application (assuming that the user cannot tamper with them). The programs are implemented by the application programmer, who designs each one to verify that accesses to the server are correct and appropriate.

Although the event programs (or portions thereof) can be viewed as transactions, the full power of a transaction processing system is not required in this case. For example, with a single-user system only one transaction is invoked at a time, so isolation is automatic. Mechanisms might still be needed to implement atomicity and durability, but they can be relatively simple since only one transaction at a time is executing.

Although one can argue that single-user systems are too simple to be included in the category of transaction processing systems, they illustrate two of the essential services that must be provided in all of the systems we will be discussing: presentation services and application services.

22.1.2 Organization of a Centralized Multiuser System

Transaction processing systems supporting an enterprise of any size must permit multiple users access to them from multiple locations. Early versions of such systems involved the use of terminals connected to a central computer. In situations in which the terminals and the computer were confined to a small area (for example a single building), communication could be supported over hard-wired connections. More likely, however, the terminals were located at remote sites and communicated with the computer over telephone lines. In either case, a major difference between these early systems and current multiuser systems is that the terminals were "dumb": they had no computing capability. They served as I/O devices that presented a simple, generally textual interface to the user. In terms of Figure 22.1, then, presentation services (beyond those built into the terminal hardware) were minimal and had to be executed at the central site. While such systems could be spread over a substantial geographical area, they were not generally considered distributed since all of the computing and intelligence resided at a single site.

The introduction of multiuser transaction processing systems motivated the development of transactions and the need for the ACID properties. Since multiple users interact with the system concurrently, there must be a way to isolate one user's interaction from another. Because the system is now supporting a major enterprise, as contrasted with an individual's database, issues of atomicity and durability become important.

Figure 22.2, shows the organization of early multiuser transaction processing systems. The user module, containing both presentation services and application programs, runs at the central site. Since a number of users execute concurrently, each user module might be executed in a separate process, as shown. These processes run asynchronously, and they can submit requests for service to the database server at any time. For example, while the server is servicing a request from one application to execute an SQL statement, a different application might submit a request to execute another SQL statement. Sophisticated database servers are capable of servicing many such requests simultaneously, with the guarantee that each SQL statement will be executed as an isolated and atomic unit.

Such a guarantee is not sufficient to ensure that the interactions of different users are appropriately isolated, however. To provide isolation, the application program needs the abstraction of a transaction. A transaction support module is therefore provided within the database server to implement commands such as `begin_transaction`, `commit`, and `rollback` and to provide atomicity, isolation, and durability. This module includes the concurrency control and the log, which we will discuss at length in later chapters.

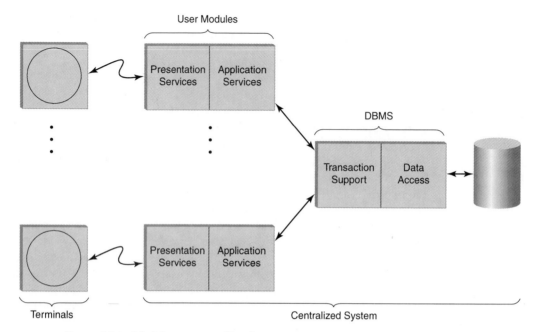

Figure 22.2 Multiuser centralized transaction processing system.

22.2 TRANSACTION PROCESSING IN A DISTRIBUTED SYSTEM

Modern transaction processing systems are generally implemented on distributed hardware involving multiple independent computers at geographically separate sites. The ATM machine is separate from the bank's computer, and a computer at a ticket agent's site is separate from the airline's main reservation system. In some cases, an application might communicate with several databases, each stored on a different computer. The computers are connected in a network, and modules located at any site can exchange messages in a uniform way.

The architecture of these systems is based on the client/server model. With distributed hardware, the client and server modules need not reside at the same site. The location of the database servers might depend on a number of factors, including

■ *Minimization of communication costs or response time.* For example, in an industrial system consisting of a central office, warehouses, and manufacturing facilities, if most of the transactions accessing employee records are initiated at the central office, these records might well be kept at that location and the inventory records kept at the warehouses.

■ *Ownership and security of data.* For example, in a distributed banking system with a computer at each branch office, a branch might insist that the information about its accounts be kept locally in its own computer.

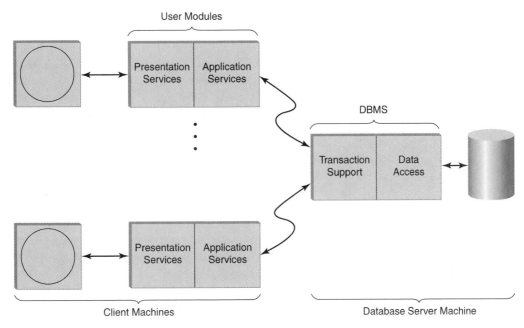

Figure 22.3 Two-tiered multiuser distributed transaction processing system.

■ *Availability of computational and storage facilities.* For example, a sophisticated database server can reside only at a site that includes extensive mass storage facilities.

Keep in mind that, in a distributed system, different software modules reside on different computers. When a transaction processing system is distributed, its *database portion* might still be *centralized;* that is, it might utilize a single database server residing on a single computer. Alternatively, the database might be *distributed;* that is, it might utilize multiple database servers residing on the same or different computers. Thus, a transaction processing system can be distributed but have a centralized database.

22.2.1 Organization of a Distributed System

The organization of a distributed transaction processing system evolved from the multiuser system shown in Figure 22.2. As a first step, terminals are replaced by client computers, so the user module, responsible for presentation and application services, now resides on a client computer and communicates with the database server. This is referred to as a **two-tiered model**. Figure 22.3 shows the organization of a distributed transaction processing system with a centralized database. The application program initiates transactions, which, as shown in Figure 22.2, are handled by the transaction support module to ensure atomicity and isolation.

The database server might export an SQL interface so that an application program on the client computer can send a request to the database server to execute a particular SQL statement. However, several important problems arise when client machines directly use such an interface. One problem has to do with the integrity of the database. As with a single-user system, our concern is that the client machines, which reside at client sites, might not be secure and cannot be trusted. An erroneous application program, for example, can destroy database integrity by submitting an improper update statement.

Another significant problem relates to network traffic and the ability of the system to handle a large number of clients. A user wishing to scan a table might execute SQL statements that cause all of the rows of the table to be transferred from the database server machine to the client machine. Since these machines can be widely separated, considerable network traffic might be required, even though the result of the transaction involves little information. Unfortunately, the network can support only a small number of clients if such requests have to be processed.

One way to address this problem is through stored procedures. Instead of submitting individual SQL statements, the application program on the client computer requests that a particular stored procedure be executed by the database server. In effect, the application program is now provided with a high-level, or more abstract, database interface. Consider a database server for a bank that might make `deposit()` and `withdraw()` stored procedures available to application programs.

Stored procedures have several important advantages.

■ They are assumed to be correct and their integrity can be maintained at the database server. Application programs executed on client computers are prohibited from submitting individual SQL statements. Since the only way the client computer can access the database is through the stored procedures, the consistency of the database is protected.

■ A procedure's SQL statements can be prepared in advance and therefore can be executed more efficiently than interpreted code.

■ The service provider can more easily authorize users to perform particular application-specific functions. For example, only a bank teller, not a customer, can produce a certified check. Managing authorization at the level of individual SQL statements is difficult. A withdraw transaction might use the same SQL statements as those used by the transaction that produces the certified check. The authorization problem can be solved by denying the customer direct access to the database and instead allowing him permission to execute the withdraw stored procedure, but not the certified check stored procedure.

■ By offering a more abstract service, the amount of information that must be communicated through the network is reduced. Instead of transmitting the intermediate arguments or the results of individual SQL statements between the application program on the client machine and the database server, all processing of intermediate results is now done by the stored procedure at the database server, and only the initial arguments and final results pass through

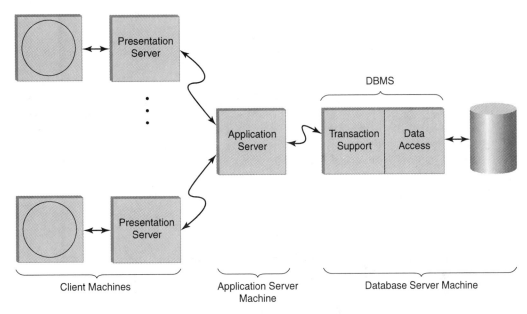

Figure 22.4 Three-tiered distributed transaction processing system.

the network. This is how the table scan described above can be performed. Data communication is thus reduced and a larger number of clients can be served. However, the database server must be powerful enough to handle the additional work that stored procedures require.

The three-tiered model.   The idea of providing higher-level services to the client computer can be carried one step further. Figure 22.4 shows a **three-tiered model** of a distributed transaction processing system, which contrasts with the two-tiered system of Figure 22.3. The user module has been divided into a presentation server and an application server that execute on different computers. Presentation services, at the client site, assembles the information input by the user, makes certain validity checks on the information (e.g., type checking), and then sends a request message to the application server, executing elsewhere in the network.

The application server executes the application program corresponding to the requested service. As before, this program implements the rules of the enterprise, checking conditions that have to be satisfied in order for the request to be executed and invoking the appropriate stored procedures at the database server to carry it out. The application program views the servicing of a request as a sequence of tasks. Thus, in the design of the Student Registration System given in Section 12.6.2, the registration transaction performs (among others) the tasks of checking that the course is offered, that the student has taken all of the course prerequisites, and that the student has not registered for too many courses, before finally performing the task of registering the student.

Each task might require the execution of a complex program, and each program might be a distinct stored procedure on the database server. The application program controls transaction boundaries and hence can cause the procedures to be executed within a single transaction. Moreover, it encourages task reuse: If tasks are chosen to perform generally useful functions, they can be invoked as components of different application programs. In the general case, the transaction is distributed, having the application program as a root, and the stored procedures are the component subtransactions executing on different servers. In this case, more elaborate transaction support is required, which we discuss in Section 22.3.1.

The application can be thought of as a workflow (Section 21.3.4), consisting of a set of tasks that must be performed in some specified order (although all tasks in this case are computational). The application server can be thought of as a workflow controller, controlling the flow of tasks required to implement the user's request.

Figure 22.4 shows a single application server with multiple clients. Since the servicing of a single client request might take a substantial amount of time, a number of client requests might be pending at the same time. Hence, the application server must handle requests concurrently in order to maintain an adequate level of performance. For example, it might be **multithreaded**,[1] with each thread handling a different client. By using threads it is possible to avoid the overhead associated with creating a process for each client. In this way, the system scales better as the number of clients increases.

Furthermore, multiple instances of the application server might exist—particularly if there are many clients. Each instance might reside on a separate computer, and each computer might be connected to a distinct subset of the clients. For example, an application server and the clients it services might be geographically close to one another.

In some organizations, the stored procedures, which implement the tasks invoked by the application program, are moved out of the database server and executed in a separate module called a **transaction server**, as shown in Figure 22.5. The transaction server is generally located on a computer physically close to the database server in order to minimize network traffic, whereas the application server is located near or at the user site. The transaction server now does the bulk of the work, since it submits the SQL statements to the database server and processes the data returned. The application server is primarily responsible for sending requests to the transaction servers.

Although not shown in Figure 22.5, there might be multiple instantiations of the transaction server process. This is an example of a **server class**, which is used when it is expected that the server will be heavily loaded. Members of the class might run on different transaction servers connected to the database server in order to share the transaction load arising from concurrently executing workflows. Each transaction server process might be an instance of a server class. More generally, there might be multiple database server machines storing different portions of the enter-

---

[1] A discussion of threading can be found in the appendix, Section A.3.

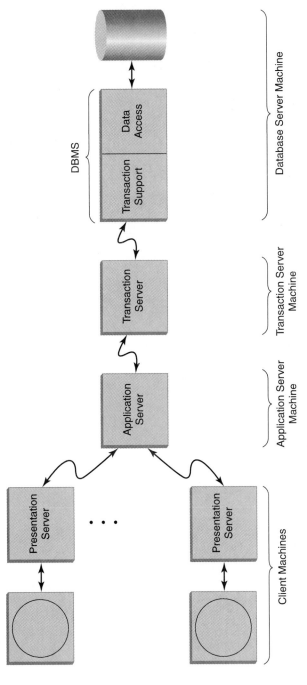

Figure 22.5 Three-tiered distributed transaction processing system with tasks executed in a transaction server.

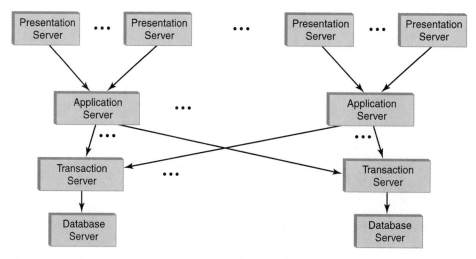

Figure 22.6 Interconnection of presentation, application, and transaction servers in a three-tiered architecture.

prise's database—for example, a billing database on one server and a registration database on another. A particular transaction server might then be capable of executing only a subset of the routines and be connected to a subset of the database servers. In that case, the application server must invoke the appropriate transaction server to get a particular task done. This selective invocation is frequently referred to as **routing**. An application program acting as a distributed transaction routes requests to multiple transaction servers, as shown in Figure 22.6.

Separating the transaction server from the database server is useful in the following situations:

1. Different components of an enterprise use different sets of procedures to access a common database. Separating these sets on different transaction servers allows each component to more easily control its own procedures. For example, the accounting system and the personnel system of a large corporation might use completely different procedures, that access the same data.

2. A single procedure must access several different databases on different server machines.

3. The database server does not support stored procedures.

4. The database server must handle requests arising from a large user population, and hence can become a bottleneck. Moving stored procedures off the database machine eases this load.

Among the advantages of separating the client machines from the application server machine are these:

1. The client computers can be smaller (and hence cheaper). This is particularly important in applications involving hundreds, and perhaps thousands, of client machines.

2. System maintenance is easier, since changes in enterprise rules (causing, changes to the workflow program) can be localized to the application server computer instead of to all client computers.

3. The security of the system is enhanced, since individual users do not have physical access to the application server computer and so cannot easily change the application programs.

Case Study: The three-tiered architecture and levels of software abstraction. CASE
From a software engineering viewpoint, one approach to designing a complex ap- STUDY
plication is to structure it hierarchically as a sequence of levels of abstraction, each
built using the abstractions implemented in the level preceding it. In this view,
the lowest level of an application implements meaningful tasks from which the
application's functionality can be directly constructed. In the Student Registration System, such activities include checking course prerequisites and billing. In
terms of our implementation in Section 12.6.3, this layer consists of the code for the
methods checkCourseOffering(), checkCourseTaken(), checkTimeConflict(),
checkPrerequisites(), and addRegisterInfo(), which interact with the database through individual SQL statements and thus operate on top of the conceptual
level provided by the database. The next level of abstraction might consist of a complete transaction, such as course registration. Our implementation is represented by
the method Register(). Note that this method uses the lower-level tasks, such as
checkCourseOffering() and checkPrerequisites(), and hence is shielded from
database-related concerns (i.e., the actual SQL queries). The top level of abstraction
includes the modules for interacting with the user, for instance, a GUI that allows
the student to fill out the forms required for course registration.

We now see that a correspondence can be established between the levels of abstraction in the application design and the three-tiered architecture. In the Student
Registration System, presentation services sees the abstraction of the total registration interaction provided by the application server. The application server, in
turn, sees the abstraction of the individual billing and registration tasks provided
by transaction servers, which in their turn use the conceptual level abstraction provided by the DBMSs.

Note that there can also be performance benefits when software abstraction layers reside at the corresponding servers in the three-layer architecture. For instance,
the actual code for checking the prerequisites (i.e., for the method checkPrereq-
uisites()) can be kept on the database server as a stored procedure. When this
procedure is called, all the processing is done on the database server and only a
yes or no answer is returned. In contrast, if prerequisite checking were done at the
application server, it would require sending SQL requests to the database, which
might send back potentially large query results and add to network congestion. ■

22.2.2 Sessions and Context

Each of the architectures we have discussed involves **sessions** between clients and servers. A session exists between two entities if they are communicating with one another to perform some job and each maintains some state information, or **context**, concerning its role in that job. Sessions can exist at a number of different levels, which we discuss next.

Communication sessions. In the two-tiered model, presentation servers communicate with database servers; in the three-tiered model, they communicate with application servers, which in turn communicate with database or transaction servers. The handling of a client request often involves the efficient and reliable exchange of multiple messages between communicating modules. In this case, communication sessions are generally established. A session requires that each communicating entity maintains context information, such as the sequence numbers of the messages transmitted in each direction (for reliably transmitting messages), addressing information, encryption keys, and the current direction of communication. Context information is stored in a data structure called a **context block**.

Messages must be exchanged just to set up and take down a session, which makes the cost of these activities nontrivial. As a result, it is wasteful for the presentation server to create a session each time a client makes a request, or for the application server to create a session each time it has to get service from a transaction or database server. Instead, long-term sessions are created between servers each of which carries messages for one client or transaction at a time.

With respect to sessions, one advantage of using a three-tiered model is made apparent by Figure 22.6. A large transaction processing system might involve thousands of client machines and hundreds of transaction servers. In the worst case, each client in a two-tiered model would have a (long-term) connection to each transaction server and the total number of connections would be the product of these two numbers—a potentially large number. The overhead of establishing these connections and the storage costs for context blocks would become excessive.

By introducing the application level, each client now needs to establish a single connection to an application server and the application server needs to establish connections to the transaction servers. However, each connection between an application server and a transaction server can be used by all transactions that are running on that application server. More precisely, if there are n_1 client machines, n_2 application servers, and n_3 transaction servers, the worst case number of connections in a two-tiered architecture is $n_1 * n_3$, whereas the number of connections in a three-tiered architecture is $n_1 + n_2 * n_3$. Since n_2 is much less than n_1, a substantial reduction in the number of connections results. Hence, a three-tiered architecture scales better as the system grows to handle a large client population.

Client/server sessions. A server needs to maintain context information about each client for which it provides a service. Consider a transaction accessing a table through a cursor. In doing so, it executes a sequence of SQL statements (OPEN, FETCH) to create a result set and retrieve its rows. Context has to be maintained by the server so that it can process these statements. Thus, for a FETCH statement the server must know which row was returned last. More generally, if a typical client interaction involves a sequence of requests, the server does not want to have to authenticate the client and determine what it is authorized to do each time a request is made.

The context used by the server for a client/server session can be maintained in a number of different ways.

Stored locally at the server. The server can maintain its client context locally. Each time the client makes a request, the server looks up the client's context and interprets the request using that context. Notice that this approach works well if the client always calls the same server, but care must be taken if the requested service is provided by an arbitrary instance of a class of servers. In that case, successive requests might be serviced by different instances, and context stored locally by one will not be available to another. Furthermore, if the number of clients is large and sessions are long, session maintenance may be a serious burden. This form of context maintenance is often used together with a peer-to-peer communication paradigm (Section 22.4.2).

Context stored in a database. If the server is a DBMS, the context can be maintained in the database itself. This approach avoids the problem of server classes, since all instances of the class can access the same database.

Context stored at the client. The context can be passed back and forth between client and server. The server returns its context to the client after servicing a request. The client does not attempt to interpret the context, but simply saves it and passes it back to the server when it makes its next request. This approach relieves the server of the need to store the context and also avoids the problem of server classes. The context data structure passed back and forth is referred to as a **context handle**. This form of context maintenance is often used together with a procedure calling communication paradigm (Section 22.4.1).

We have so far overlooked an important issue in our discussion of client/server context, focusing only on the context associated with a sequence of requests made by a client to a particular server. More generally, context must be associated with a transaction as a whole (which can include multiple requests to *different* servers and might encompass multiple sessions). The need for this is illustrated in Figure 22.7, in which a client has set up one session with server $S1$ and another session with server $S2$; both servers have used server $S3$ to fulfill the client's requests. The problem is that issues such as isolation and atomicity are associated with the transaction as a whole and not with any particular session. For example, locks (discussed in Chapter 23) are used to implement isolation. $S3$ must use transaction context to determine that a lock acquired in handling a request from $S1$ for a particular transaction can be used in servicing a request from $S2$ for the same transaction.

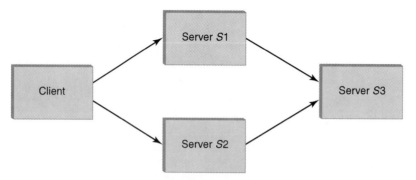

Figure 22.7 Transaction context must be maintained when two servers access the same server on behalf of a single transaction.

22.2.3 Queued Transaction Processing

The two-tiered model shown in Figure 22.3 is referred to as **data centered**, whereas the three-tiered model shown in Figure 22.5 is referred to as **service centered**. In both, the client and server engage in **direct transaction processing**: The client invokes a server and then waits for the result; the service is provided as quickly as possible and a result is returned. The client and server are thus synchronized.

With **queued transaction processing**, the client enqueues its request on a queue of pending requests to the server and then performs other tasks. The request is dequeued when the server is ready to provide the service. Requests from presentation servers for example, are often enqueued in front of an application server until application server threads can be assigned to handle the requests. Later, when the service is completed, the server can enqueue its results on a separate result queue. The result is dequeued still later by the client. The client and server are thus unsynchronized.

With recoverable queues, queue operations are transactional. The handling of a request involves three transactions as shown in Figure 22.8. The client executes transaction T_1 to enqueue the request prior to service; the server then executes transaction T_2, which dequeues the request, services it, and enqueues the result on the reply queue; and the client finally executes transaction T_3 to dequeue the result from the reply queue. Figure 22.8 should be compared with Figure 21.7 on page 706. The main difference is that in Figure 21.7 a forwarding agent is used to dequeue the request from the request queue and invoke a (passive) server whereas in Figure 22.8 the server (actively) dequeues the request.

Queued transaction processing offers a number of advantages. The client can input a request at times when the server is busy or down. Similarly, the server can return results even if the client is unprepared to accept them because it is down or busy. Furthermore, if the server crashes while the request is being serviced, the service transaction is aborted and the request is restored to the request queue. It is serviced when the server is restarted, without any intervention by the client.

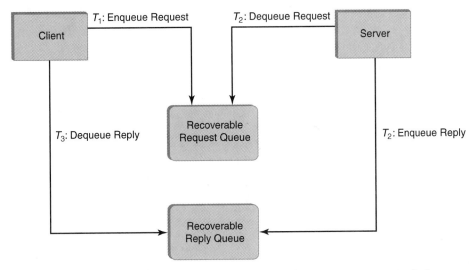

Figure 22.8 Queued transaction processing involves two queues and three transactions.

Finally, when multiple servers become available, the queue can be integrated into an algorithm that balances the load on all servers.

22.3 HETEROGENEOUS SYSTEMS AND THE TP MONITOR

Many current transaction processing systems are **heterogeneous** involving the products of multiple vendors: hardware platforms, operating systems, database managers, and communication protocols. This heterogeneity contrasts with earlier, **homogeneous** systems that involved hardware and software from only a single vendor, which frequently used **proprietary interfaces** designed to interconnect only its own hardware and software products. Even when these proprietary interfaces were published, it was difficult to incorporate products from other vendors into the system, because those other products used different interfaces.

Homogeneous systems have evolved into the more modern heterogeneous systems for the following reasons:

■ Newer applications often require the interconnection of older, legacy systems that had previously operated independently. For example, over the years each department in a company might have developed its own purchasing system. Now the company requires a company-wide purchasing system that interconnects all local systems.

■ There are more vendors supplying hardware and software components, and users demand the ability to incorporate the best ones available regardless of the supplier.

Heterogeneous systems require **open** (nonproprietary) **interfaces**, which vendors agree to implement, and communications software that their products can use to communicate with one another. If a legacy system (such as an old purchasing system) that uses a nonstandard, proprietary interface is to be included, a **wrapper** program can be written as a bridge between interfaces.

To promote the development of open distributed systems in general—and transaction processing systems in particular—various software products have been developed that are frequently referred to as middleware. **Middleware** is software that supports the interaction of clients and servers. Examples of middleware are software modules that support:

■ Communication protocols of various kinds

■ Security of distributed applications, including authentication and encryption

■ Translation of programs and data from the conventions of one module to those of another

■ Atomicity, isolation, and durability of distributed transactions

These software modules can be used in many different distributed applications because of their standardized interfaces.

JDBC and ODBC (Sections 10.5 and 10.6) are two examples of middleware that allow an application to interact with database servers from a variety of vendors. CORBA (Section 16.6), another example, allows applications to access objects distributed through a network.

22.3.1 The Transaction Manager

A major issue in the implementation of distributed transactions is global atomicity. While atomicity at any particular server can be implemented by that server, global atomicity requires the cooperation of all servers involved in the transaction. Cooperation is achieved through the use of a protocol.

When the transaction processing system is homogeneous, the algorithm for implementing global atomicity is usually integrated into the individual servers provided by their vendors. Such systems are sometimes referred to as **TP-Lite**. In heterogeneous systems, this algorithm is often contained in a separate middleware module, shown in Figure 22.9, called a **transaction manager**, which is part of the TP monitor (Section 22.3.2). The figure shows a two-tiered system, but three tiers are also possible. Heterogeneous systems are more complex than homogeneous systems and are frequently referred to as **TP-Heavy**.

In both cases, the module for supporting global atomicity responds to commands from the application program that set the boundaries of a distributed transaction, and coordinates the commitment of its subtransactions. To do this, it must know when the transaction as a whole and of each of its subtransactions are initiated. Here we describe the process as it works in TP-Heavy systems, which, because of their heterogeneity, rely on interface standards. One such standard is the X/Open standard API.

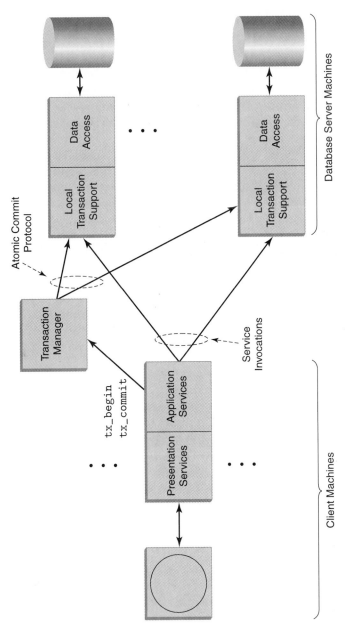

Figure 22.9 Two-tiered multidatabase transaction processing system in which a transaction can access several database servers.

X/Open was defined by X/Open Company Limited, an independent worldwide organization supported by many of the largest information systems suppliers and software companies. Part of this API is the `tx` interface, which supports the transaction abstraction and includes `tx_begin()`, `tx_commit()`, and `tx_rollback()`. These procedures are called from an application program and implemented in the transaction manager. To be specific in describing concepts related to distributed transactions, we base our discussion on this standard.

The application program calls `tx_begin` when it wants the transaction manager to know that it is starting a distributed transaction. The transaction manager records the existence of a new distributed transaction and returns an identifier that uniquely names it. Later, when the application requests service from a resource manager, the communication layer (provided by the TP monitor) informs the transaction manager of the existence of a new subtransaction.

The application calls `tx_commit` to inform the transaction manager of the distributed transaction's successful completion. The transaction manager then communicates with the servers that participated in the transaction in such a way that they all commit or all abort the subtransactions, thus making the distributed transaction globally atomic. An **atomic commit protocol** controls the exchange of messages for this purpose. In this role, the transaction manager is frequently referred to as the **coordinator**. (We will discuss the most commonly used atomic commit protocol in Section 26.2.)

Each of these procedures is a function, which returns a value that indicates success or failure of the requested action. In particular, the return value of `tx_commit()` indicates whether the distributed transaction actually committed or aborted and the reason for an abort. For example, the distributed transaction might abort if the transaction manager discovers that one of the database servers has crashed or that communication to that server has been interrupted.

22.3.2 The TP Monitor

A transaction manager is just one example of an off-the-shelf middleware component that can be used to build a TP-Heavy system. A **TP monitor** is a collection of such components. A number of TP monitors exist. Tuxedo and Encina are early examples. Microsoft Transaction Server (MTS) is a more recent entry into the field, and Java Transaction Service (JTS) is a specification of a Java based TP monitor. All of them include or specify a transaction manager and a set of application-independent services that, though needed in a transaction processing system, are not usually provided by an operating system. As shown in Figure 22.10, a TP monitor can be viewed as a layer of software between the operating system and the application routines.

The TP monitor provides some services similar to those provided by an operating system. The operating system creates the abstraction of concurrently executing *processes* that can communicate with one another, and provides these processes with shared access to the physical resources of the computer system. The TP monitor builds on this abstraction to create the abstraction of *transactions* that execute concurrently in a heterogeneous distributed environment.

The following services are generally provided by a TP monitor.

Figure 22.10 Layered structure of a transaction processing system.

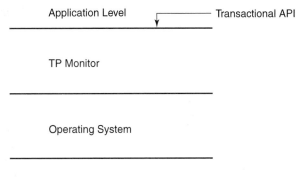

Application Level ⌐──────── Transactional API

TP Monitor

Operating System

Physical Computer System

Communication.   The TP monitor supports the abstractions used by application program modules to communicate with one another. These abstractions are built using the message passing facility provided by the distributed message passing kernel (see the Appendix, Section A.4). Two abstractions often provided are remote procedure call and peer-to-peer communication. Remote procedure call is commonly used by application programs due to its simplicity and its natural relationship to the client/server model. Peer-to-peer communication is more complex, but more flexible. System level modules tend to communicate in this way in order to use the flexibility to optimize performance. Communication with most DBMSs is done through peer-to-peer connections. We discuss communication in Section 22.4.

Global atomicity and isolation.   One goal of a TP monitor is to guarantee global atomicity and isolation. The subtransactions of a distributed transaction might execute at a variety of different resource managers. Frequently these are database managers that implement atomicity and isolation locally. Other resource managers might provide no support for these features. For example, a transaction might access several files maintained by a file server. Access to them should be isolated and atomic. If the file server does not support isolation, a transaction might use a lock manager provided by the TP monitor. A lock in the lock manager is associated with a file in the file server. A transaction that accesses the file is required to set the lock (by calling the lock manager) before calling the file server to do the access, and then to call the lock manager to release the lock when the transaction completes. If all transactions follow this protocol, accesses to the file can be synchronized in the same way as accesses to data items in a database server that provides a concurrency control. (The use of locks in implementing isolation will be discussed more fully in Section 23.5.) Similarly, if the file server does not support atomicity, a log manager might be required.

The transaction manager is important in extending the local isolation and atomicity of each individual server to global atomicity and isolation. To provide this service, it must be informed of the initiation of each subtransaction created by a distributed transaction. Hence, its role is tied in with the communication abstraction used by the application. Each time the application initiates a new subtransaction (by communicating with a server for the first time), the transaction manager is informed. Support for global atomicity thus involves both the transaction manager and the communication facility. This is a complex issue, which we will discuss separately in Section 22.4.1.

Load balancing and routing.   Large transaction processing systems use server classes. If the servers in a class are distributed across a network, availability increases and, since they can execute concurrently, performance is improved. When a client invokes such a service, the TP monitor can route the call to any of the servers in the class. Some TP monitors use load balancing as a criterion in this choice. They might use a round robin or randomizing algorithm to distribute the load across the servers, or they might keep information on the number of sessions (perhaps as measured by the number of peer-to-peer connections) that each server in the class is handling, and choose the one whose load is the smallest. Load balancing can be integrated with queueing when queued transaction processing is provided.

Recoverable queues.   In addition to supporting queued transaction processing, recoverable queues are generally useful for asynchronous communication between application modules and are provided by many TP monitors.

Security services.   The information used in a transaction processing system often needs to be protected. Encryption, authentication, and authorization are the foundation of protection and for that reason are often supported by TP monitors. We will discuss these services in Chapter 27.

Threading.   We have seen (for example, in connection with an application server) that threads reduce the overhead of handling a large number of clients in a transaction processing system. Unfortunately, not all operating systems support them. Some TP monitors provide their own threading in such situations. If so, the operating system schedules a process for execution, unaware that multiple threads exist within it. TP monitor code in the process selects the particular thread to be executed.

Supporting servers.   TP monitors provide a variety of servers that are useful in a transaction processing system. For example, a timing server might keep clocks on different computers synchronized; a file server might be provided as a general utility.

Nested transactions.   Some TP monitors provide support for nested transactions.

As we have introduced a number of terms in this chapter that are often confused, we will review their definitions at this point in our discussion.

▪ A **transaction server** executes the application subroutines that implement the basic units of work from which an application program is built.

▪ A **transaction manager** is a resource manager that supports the atomic execution of distributed transactions.

■ A **TP monitor** provides the transaction manager and the underlying middleware necessary to tie together the modules of the transaction processing system.

■ A **transaction processing system** includes the TP monitor as well as the application code and the various resource managers, such as DBMSs, that make up the total system.

22.4 THE TP MONITOR: COMMUNICATION AND GLOBAL ATOMICITY

The general distributed transaction model presented in Section 21.2.2 involves a set of related computations performed by a number of modules, which might be located at different sites in a network and which communicate with one another. For example, an application module might request service from a database server, or the application itself might be distributed and one application module might call for the services of another.

Consider a course registration application program, $A1$ (perhaps executing in the context of a transaction on an application server), that invokes a stored procedure on a database server, $D1$, to register a student in a course, and then invokes a procedure in a remote application program, $A2$, to bill that student. $A2$ might in turn invoke a stored procedure on a different database server, $D2$, to record the charge. Both $D1$ and $A2$ are viewed as servers by $A1$ (and $D2$ is viewed as a server by $A2$), but only $D1$ and $D2$ are resource managers in the sense that they control resources whose state must be maintained. Although the same communication paradigms can be used for communication among all of these modules (and hence we do not need to distinguish these two cases in this chapter), only the resource managers participate in the atomic commit protocol. If $A1$ is executing in the context of a transaction, T, we say that T **propagates**[2] from $A1$ to $A2$ and $D1$[3] as a result of the invocations made in $A1$.

Although message passing underlies communication, a TP monitor generally offers the application several higher-level communication abstractions. The one chosen generally depends on the application type. In some applications, there is a strict hierarchical relationship between the modules. For example, a client module might request service from a server module and then wait for a reply; in this case, a procedure calling mechanism is particularly convenient. In other applications, a module might treat the other modules it interacts with as peers; in that case, the peer-to-peer communication paradigm is appropriate. In this section, we discuss both of these communication abstractions and their implementation. In addition, we discuss event communication, which is particularly appropriate for handling exceptional situations.

---

[2] The term **spreads** or **infects** are sometimes used.

[3] Some TP monitors permit violations of this general rule. For example, $A1$ can specify that $A2$ not be included in T. Similarly, $A2$ can itself specify that it not be included in T. In addition, commands have been defined that permit a routine to temporarily exclude itself from the current transaction and then resume its participation at a later time.

22.4.1   Remote Procedure Call

A network-wide message passing facility provided by a distributed message passing kernel (see the Appendix, Section A.4) can support communication between modules; however, it suffers from the deficiency that the interface it presents to the modules is not convenient to use. Invoking operating system primitives for sending and receiving a message is neither elegant nor simple. Users prefer the procedural interface of a high-level language and benefit from the type checking automatically provided by a compiler. For these reasons, the goal is to create a procedure calling facility that makes invoking a procedure in a (possibly remote) module similar to calling a local procedure (one linked into the caller's code). Such a facility supports **remote procedure call**, or RPC [Birrell and Nelson 1984, 1990].

Using RPC, a distributed computation takes on a tree structure, since a called procedure in one module can in turn invoke a procedure in another. The procedure that initiates the computation as a whole is referred to as the **root**.

When a procedure is invoked in a module, local variables are allocated as a temporary workspace for it. All of the information necessary to perform the computation is contained in the arguments passed to the procedure. After the computation has been performed and the procedure returns, the local variables are deallocated and hence cannot be used to store context. For this reason, RPC communication is referred to as **stateless**. If context must be maintained over several calls, the called module must store it globally or it must be passed back and forth using a context handle (see Section 22.2.2).

Implementation of remote procedure call.   RPC is implemented using **stubs**. A client stub is a routine linked to a client; a server stub is a routine linked to a server. The routines serve as intermediaries between the client and server as shown in Figure 22.11. A client calls a server procedure using that procedure's globally unique name. This name is a character string known to the users of the system. The call does not invoke the procedure directly however. Instead, it invokes the client stub, which locates the server (using directory services, which we will describe shortly) and sets up a connection to it. It then converts the arguments into a standard format,[4] packs them together with the name of the called procedure into an invocation message, a process called **marshaling of arguments**, and sends the message using a lower-level communication protocol to the server.

In the figure, the server happens to be on a different machine. The server stub receives invocation messages from all clients, unmarshals the arguments in a particular message, converts them to the format expected by the server, and invokes the appropriate procedure using a standard (local) procedure call. The result of this call is returned to the server stub, which sends it back to the client stub using the message passing facility, and the client stub returns it to the client (recall that the client stub was invoked by the client application using a conventional proce-

---

[4] In an alternate organization, the client stub does no conversion, but instead allows the server stub to convert the received arguments to the format the server expects, if such a conversion is necessary.

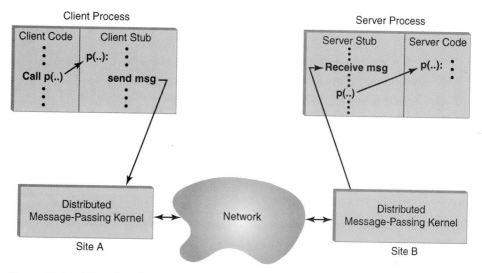

Figure 22.11 Use of stubs to support remote procedure call.

dure call). Thus, RPC is a high-level communication facility implemented by the procedure call mechanism coupled with the message passing facility.

The stub mechanism has several advantages. Only the stubs interfaces to the operating system. It appears to the client and the server that they are communicating with each other through a conventional procedure call. Furthermore, stubs make calls to a server process on a local machine and to one on a remote machine appear identical—as invocations of local procedures linked into the client code. Hence, the client code need not be aware of the physical location of the server: It uses the same mechanism to communicate with a local server as with a remote server. Finally, if modules are moved, the client and server code need not be changed. This feature is generally referred to as **location transparency**.

In connecting clients to servers, stubs must consider the possibility of failure. Failure in a single-site system is relatively infrequent and generally comes in the form of a crash. When the system crashes, the contents of main memory (but not mass storage) are lost, and the system must be restarted. On recovery, there is generally no attempt to resume any procedure that was in progress at the time of the crash.

Failures in a distributed system can include not only the crash of a particular computer but also a communication failure. Such a failure might be relatively permanent (a communication line can be down for an extended period) or transient (a message can be lost but subsequent messages might be transmitted correctly). With hundreds and possibly thousands of connected computers, communication lines, routers, and so forth, the probability of all functioning correctly at any particular time is significantly smaller than that of a crash at a single site. This is why failures are frequent in distributed systems.

Failure is not necessarily total. Large parts of the system might still be functioning, and the application might be required to remain operational despite the failure of some of its components. In contrast to the single-site situation, in a distributed system if a failure interferes with a client/server interaction, it might be possible to continue to provide service. For example, after sending the arguments of a server invocation to the server stub, the client stub must wait for a reply message; if no reply message is received after some timeout period has elapsed, any one of the following situations might have occurred:

■ The invocation message from the client is still in transit.

■ The invocation message from the client has been lost.

■ The server has crashed.

■ The server has started the service, but has not yet completed it.

■ The server has completed its service, but the reply message from the server is still in transit.

■ The server has completed its service, but the reply message from the server has been lost.

Depending on the situation, the client stub might take one of the following actions:

■ Continue to wait.

■ Send another invocation message to the server.

■ Send an invocation message to another server on a different machine capable of performing the same function.

■ Abort the client.

■ Return some error indication to the client.

Unfortunately, the client stub might not know the cause of the delay, and an action appropriate for one situation might compound the problem if the delay was caused by a different situation. For example, the client might wait indefinitely or be aborted prematurely, or a second invocation message might be sent when a reply message has been lost, causing the server to perform the same service twice. While this might be acceptable under certain circumstances—for example, if the client is simply reading some information contained in the server—it might not be acceptable in others—for example, the client is asking to purchase an airline ticket. For these reasons, stub algorithms for dealing with failures can be quite complex.

Directory services.   A server is known to its clients by its interface. The interface is published and contains the information a client needs to invoke the server's procedures: procedure names and descriptions of parameters. As we saw in Sections 16.4.1 and 16.6, an **interface definition language**, or **IDL**, is a high-level language that describes the interface. An IDL compiler compiles the interface description into a header file and server-specific client and server stubs. The header file is included with the application program when it is compiled, and the client stub is linked to the client code in the resulting module. The use of an IDL file to describe the server interface encourages the development of open systems. The client and server can be built by different vendors as long as they agree on the interface through which they communicate.

The server interface, however, does not specify the identity and location of a server process that will actually execute the server code. The location might not be known at compile time, or it might change dynamically. Furthermore, the server might be implemented as a class with instances executing on different nodes in a network. The system must therefore provide a run-time mechanism to bind a client to a server dynamically.

Binding can be achieved by requiring that a server, S, when it is ready to provide service to clients, register itself with some central naming service available to all clients. Such a service is often provided by a separate **name**, or **directory**, **server**.

To register, S supplies to the directory server its (globally unique) name and network address, the interfaces it supports, and the communication protocol(s) it uses to exchange messages with clients (these are the messages used to implement RPC communication). For example, S might accept messages requesting service only over a TCP connection. This is an example of a server (S) acting as a client with respect to another server (the directory server).

The client stub submits a server name or the identification of a particular interface to the directory server and requests the network address and communication protocol to be used to communicate with a server having that name or supporting that interface. Once this information has been provided, the client stub can communicate directly with the server.

Although the directory server is itself a server, it must have some special status since clients and servers have to be able to connect to it without having to use another directory server (to avoid the chicken and egg problem). Hence, it should reside at a well-known network address that can be determined without using a directory server.

A directory server can be a complex entity. One source of that complexity is a result of the central role it plays in distributed computing. If the directory server fails (perhaps because the host on which it resides crashes), clients can no longer locate servers and new distributed computations cannot be established. To avoid such a catastrophe, directory service itself might be distributed and/or replicated across the network. However, this raises new problems: making sure that replicas are up to date and that a client anywhere in the network can locate a directory server that has the information it requires.

The **Distributed Computing Environment** (**DCE**) [Rosenberry et al. 1992] is an example of middleware that supports distributed systems such as TP monitors.[5] Among the services it provides are RPC between modules running on different operating system platforms. Directory services are provided in connection with

---

[5] The TP monitor Encina is based on DCE.

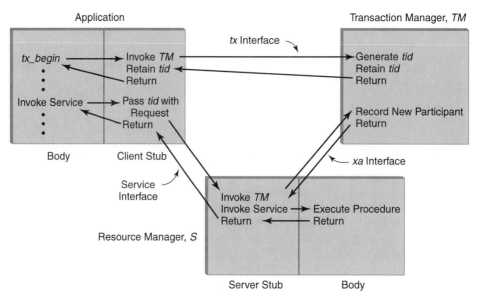

Figure 22.12 Communication with the transaction manager to implement transactional remote procedure call.

this as well as other basic features, such as the security services that we will discuss in Chapter 27.

The Transaction Manager and Transactional RPC. The transaction manager's role in implementing global atomicity is illustrated in Figures 22.12 and 22.13. The X/Open system calls `tx_begin()`, `tx_commit()`, and `tx_rollback()` invoke procedures within the transaction manager (*TM*) which initiate and terminate transactions. When an application initiates a transaction, *T*, it invokes `tx_begin()`. As shown in Figure 22.12, *TM* returns a transaction identifier, *tid*, that uniquely identifies *T*. The transaction identifier is retained in the client stub's data space.

Subsequently, whenever the client invokes a resource manager, *S*, the client stub appends *tid* to the call message to identify the calling transaction to *S*. If this is the first request by *T* to *S*, the server stub notifies *TM* that it is now performing work for *T* by calling *TM*'s procedure `xa_reg()` and passing *tid*. Thus, *TM* can record the identities of all resource managers that participate in *T*. *S* is referred to as a **cohort** of *T*. `xa_reg()` is part of X/Open's `xa` interface between a transaction manager and a resource manager. When a transaction manager and a resource manager both support the `xa` interface, they can be connected in support of distributed transactions even though they are the products of different vendors.

Note that the standard defines both the `tx` interface, between an application and a transaction manager, and the `xa` interface, between a transaction manager and a resource manager, but it does not define an interface between an application and a resource manager. That interface is defined by the resource manager itself.

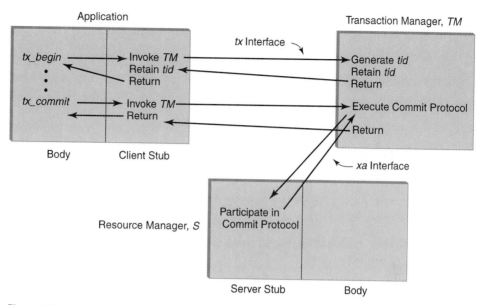

Figure 22.13 Communication with the transaction manager to perform an atomic commit protocol.

Since procedure calling is a synchronous communication mechanism (the caller waits until the callee has completed), when a subtransaction completes its computation all subtransactions it has invoked have also completed. Hence, when the root of the transaction tree finishes its computation, the entire distributed transaction is complete and the root can request that the transaction be committed by calling the transaction manager procedure tx_commit(), as shown in Figure 22.13. (If the client wishes to abort T, it calls tx_rollback().) The transaction manager must then make sure that termination is globally atomic—either all servers invoked by T commit or all abort. It does this by engaging in an atomic commit protocol in which it serves as coordinator and the resource managers serve as cohorts. The most widely used atomic commit protocol, *two phase commit*, will be described in Section 26.2.

To execute a commit protocol, the transaction manager must communicate with all cohorts (e.g., S), as shown in Figure 22.13. It does this by using callbacks that the resource managers have registered with it. In addition to the normal service interface that a resource manager presents to an application, it offers a set of **callbacks** to the transaction manager. These are resource manager procedures that the transaction manager can use for a variety of purposes. Each resource manager might offer different callbacks depending upon the services it is capable of performing. Those that can engage in an atomic commit protocol register callbacks for that purpose.[6] If a cohort does not register such callbacks, it cannot participate in the protocol and global atomicity cannot be guaranteed.

The procedure calling mechanism we have just discussed (involving the use of *tid* and the xa interface) is thus an enhanced version of the RPC mechanism and is one ingredient used to implement global atomicity. It is provided by the TP monitor and referred to as a **transactional remote procedure call**, or **TRPC**.[7]

Global atomicity is implemented by the stubs and the transaction manager. It involves the following:

■ Establishing an identity for T with the transaction manager when T is initiated

■ Inclusion of T's identity as an argument in procedure call messages

■ Notification of the transaction manager whenever a new resource manager is invoked

■ Execution of the atomic commit protocol when the transaction completes (Section 26.2)

An additional obstacle that must be overcome to achieve global atomicity (and that must be handled by TRPC) is caused by failures in the network. We saw in Section 22.4.1 that a number of failure situations might prevent the client stub from receiving a reply to an invocation message sent by it to a server, S, and that these situations are indistinguishable to the client stub. The actions a stub might take can lead to several different outcomes. In particular, if the invocation message is sent a second time, the service might be performed twice, and even if the invocation message is not resent, the stub cannot assume that the service was not performed.

The actions of the stub under these circumstances must ensure that the requested service is performed exactly once at S, allowing the transaction to continue, or that the requested service is not performed at all and (assuming that the service cannot be provided at a different server) the transaction is aborted. Thus, the stub ensures what is called **exactly once semantics**.

The situation is further complicated by the fact that S might have invoked another server, S', in performing the requested service. If the site at which S executes has crashed, and S' executes elsewhere in the network, an **orphan** results: The task at S' has no parent process (i.e., S) to which it reports. The stub has the nontrivial job of guaranteeing exactly once semantics under these circumstances.

A distributed transaction in multiple domains.   Up to this point, we have assumed that the commit protocol for the entire distributed transaction is directed by a single transaction manager. In actuality, a transaction manager's responsibility is limited to a **domain**, which typically includes all of the resource managers at the site at which the transaction manager executes (although other organizations are possible).

---

[6] Callbacks to support distributed savepoints are another example.

[7] TRPC can be implemented as an enhancement of the authenticated RPC to be discussed in Section 27.6.

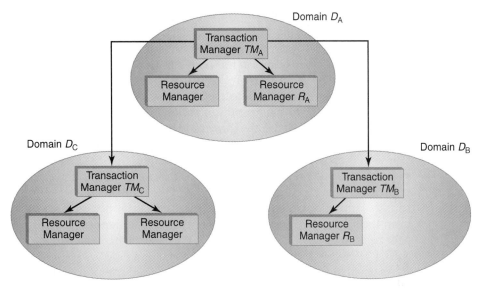

Figure 22.14 Distributed transaction structured as a tree.

Suppose that a participant in a distributed transaction (perhaps an application module or a resource manager) in domain D_A, controlled by transaction manager TM_A, invokes a resource manager, R_B, in a different domain, D_B, controlled by transaction manager TM_B. TM_B will later participate in the atomic commit protocol by becoming the coordinator of R_B and of all other cohorts of the transaction in D_B. Since TM_B acts as the representative of these cohorts with respect to TM_A, it also is a cohort with respect to TM_A. Thus, TM_A must be informed that TM_B is one of its cohorts, and TM_B must be informed of its dual role with respect to R_B and TM_A. In the X/Open model of distributed transactions, the responsibility for spreading this information is placed on a server called the **communication resource manager** and the interface between a transaction manager and the communication resource manager in its domain is called the xa+ interface.

Thus, a distributed transaction is structured as a tree, as shown in Figure 22.14, with resource managers as leaf nodes and transaction managers as interior nodes. (Note that application modules are not part of the tree, since only resource managers need to participate in the atomic commit protocol to determine whether or not to commit the changes made to the resources they manage.) The root of the tree is the transaction manager that controls the domain in which the distributed transaction was initiated. The application program that sets the transaction boundaries sends its request to commit to this transaction manager, which then initiates the protocol. While the figure shows a tree with only two coordinator levels, the number of levels in a general distributed transaction might be arbitrary. The actual exchange of messages along the edges of the tree is described in Section 26.2.1.

22.4.2   Peer-to-Peer Communication

With remote procedure call, a client sends a request message to a server to invoke a procedure and waits for a reply. Hence, communication is synchronous. The subtransaction is performed at the server and a reply message is sent when service is completed. The request/reply pattern of communication is asymmetric, and the client and server do not execute concurrently.

In contrast, **peer-to-peer communication** is symmetric: Once a connection is established, both parties use the same send and receive commands to converse. It is also more flexible, since any pattern of messages between peers can be supported. The send is an asynchronous operation, meaning that the system buffers the message that has been sent and then returns control to the sender. Unlike in RPC, the sender can thus execute concurrently with the receiver. The sender might perform some computation or send additional messages, so a stream of messages might flow from the sender to the receiver before the receiver replies. As with RPC, peer-to-peer communication is supported by a lower-level message passing protocol (such as TCP/IP or SNA).

As usual, flexibility comes at the price of added complexity. Each party must be prepared to deal with the pattern of messages used by the other, which means that there is now more room for error. For example, if each process is in a state in which it is expecting a message from the other before it can continue, deadlock results. Peer-to-peer communication is often supported by TP monitors not only because of its added flexibility, but also because many database servers (often running on mainframes) use this mode of communication.

Establishing a connection.   A variety of peer-to-peer protocols exist. Our discussion in this section is based on IBM's commonly used SNA protocol LU6.2 [IBM 1991] and an API that interfaces to it.

To begin a conversation, a module must first set up a connection to the program it wishes to communicate with. This is done with an `allocate()` command that has as an argument the target program's name. A new instance of the program is created to handle the other end of the conversation. In contrast to RPC, location transparency is not a goal: The requestor explicitly provides the address of the receiving program.

Returning to the example of a distributed computation in Section 22.4, $A1$ might set up a peer-to-peer connection to $A2$. A new instance of the billing program is initiated to receive the messages sent by $A1$ over the connection.

While connections in LU6.2 are half duplex, connections generally might be half or full duplex. With **half duplex**, messages can flow in either direction over the connection, but at any given time one module, A, is the sender (the connection is currently in **send mode** for A) and the other module, B, is the receiver (the connection is currently in **receive mode** for B). A sends an arbitrary number of messages to B and then passes send permission to B. This makes B the sender and A the receiver. When B finishes sending messages, it passes send permission back to A and the process repeats. This contrasts with a **full duplex** connection, in which

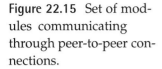

Figure 22.15 Set of modules communicating through peer-to-peer connections.

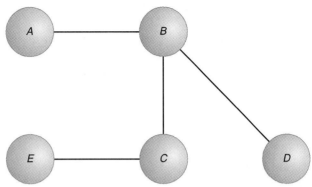

either party can send at any time. With half duplex, the current direction of the connection is a part of its context.

When a routine in module *A*, executing as part of a transaction, sets up a connection to a program instance in module *B*, the transaction propagates from *A* to *B*. Once the connection has been established, *A* and *B* are equal partners and all messages over the connection pertain to that transaction. Client/server context can be conveniently stored for communication over the connection in local variables, so each arriving message can be interpreted with respect to the context. For this reason, protocols built using peer-to-peer interactions are often **stateful**.

A module can engage in an arbitrary number of different peer-to-peer connections concurrently. Because any module participating in the transaction can set up a new connection to any other module, the general structure of a distributed transaction is typically that of an acyclic graph, as shown in Figure 22.15, in which nodes represent the transaction's participants and links represent connections. The graph is acyclic because a new instance of a program is created when a connection is set up. Hence, nodes in the graph represent instances, and it is not possible for a program to set up a connection to an existing instance. In the figure, for example, *C* and *D* might represent different instances of the same program. No node occupies a unique position analogous to the root node of a procedure calling hierarchy.

Distributed commitment.   The rules governing commitment are consistent with the equal status of the participants in a transaction that uses peer-to-peer connections: Any node can request to commit the transaction. In contrast to the hierarchical model of distributed transactions, where only the root module can request to commit, and therefore (since communication is synchronous) all subtransactions must have completed at that time, transactional peers are not synchronized. When a participant decides to commit, its transactional peers might still be executing and not yet ready to commit. Hence, an integral part of committing a transaction is ensuring that all participants have completed. In doing so, the system executes an atomic commit protocol, which guarantees that either all participants commit or all abort. The following description is based on [Maslak et al. 1991].

In a properly organized transaction, a single module, *A*, initiates the commit. All of *A*'s connections must be in send mode at this time. *A* initiates the commit by declaring a **syncpoint**, which causes a **syncpoint message** to be sent over each of *A*'s connections. *A* then waits until the commit protocol completes.

Participant *B*, connected to *A*, might not have completed its portion of the transaction when it receives the syncpoint message. When *B* has completed and all of its connections (other than the connection to *A*) are in send mode, it also declares a syncpoint, which causes a syncpoint message to be sent over all of its connections (other than the connection to *A*). In this way, syncpoint messages spread through the transaction graph. A node that receives a syncpoint message over its only connection (e.g., *E* in the figure) also declares a syncpoint, although no additional syncpoint messages result. Eventually, each peer has declared a syncpoint and all are synchronized at their syncpoint declarations. Now the atomic commit protocol can be completed.

The syncpoint protocol requires that only one module initiate it and that a module declare a syncpoint only if (1) all of its connections are in send mode and it has not yet received a syncpoint message; or (2) all but one of its connections are in send mode, it has received one syncpoint message, and that message arrived over the connection in receive mode. If the protocol is not used correctly, the transaction is aborted. For example, if two participants initiate the protocol by declaring a syncpoint, syncpoint messages converge on some intermediate node over two connections. This violates the protocol and causes the transaction to abort.

The implementation of global atomicity uses a module similar to the transaction manager, called a **syncpoint manager**. A syncpoint manager is associated with a new instance of a program, *A*, when that program accepts a peer-to-peer connection. The syncpoint manager has an associated domain. In a manner similar to the technique used with RPC, each time *A* invokes a resource manager in the domain for the first time, *A*'s syncpoint manager is informed of a new participant in the transaction. Similarly, if *A* sets up a connection to *B*, the syncpoint manager at *A* is informed of the fact that the syncpoint manager at *B* is participating in the transaction. The syncpoint manager must direct the atomic commit protocol among the participants of the transaction in its domain (in this case, *A* is included as a participant) as well as between domains as shown in Figure 22.14. The root of the tree is the syncpoint manager at the participant that declares the initial syncpoint.

When the syncpoint message reaches a leaf node and the subtransaction at that node has completed, a response is sent back up the tree to the root. When all leaves have responded, the root can conclude that the entire transaction has completed. A detailed description of this protocol is provided in Section 26.2.4.)

22.4.3 Handling Exceptional Situations within a Transaction

When modules communicate using RPC the callee, or server, is structured to accept service requests. It exports procedures whose purpose is to service the requests. When no request has been made, the server is idle, waiting for the next one. The situation is similar when peer-to-peer communication is used. In this case, the server accepts a connection and executes a receive command. Once again, however, when no service has been requested, the server is idle.

Both procedural and peer-to-peer communication are useful in designing modules whose primary purpose is to service requests from other modules. However, these modes of communication are often inappropriate for a module that must deal with an exceptional situation but cannot simply wait for that situation to occur because it has other activities to perform.

For example, suppose that a module, M_1, repeatedly reads and records the temperature in a furnace. A second module, M_2, which controls the process that uses the furnace (and perhaps executes on a different computer), might want to be informed of the exceptional case in which the temperature reaches a certain limit. (Perhaps M_2 shuts down the furnace in that case.) Since M_2 must function as a controller, it needs a way to find out when the exceptional case occurs. One way to implement this requirement is for M_2 to periodically call on M_1, using procedural communication, and request that it return the current recorded temperature. Another is for M_2, using a peer-to-peer connection to periodically send a message to M_1 requesting the temperature. These approaches are referred to as **polling**. If it is unlikely that the value ever reaches the limit, polling is wasteful of resources, since M_2 is constantly making requests but the replies indicate that no action need be taken. If M_2 must respond quickly when the value reaches the limit, polling is even more wasteful, since in this case more frequent communication is required.

As a second example, consider a point-of-sales system in which an application module M on a sales terminal responds to service requests from customers input at the keyboard. If the system is about to be taken off line temporarily, an out-of-service message must be printed on the terminal. Unfortunately, however, if M is designed to respond only to inputs from the keyboard, it does not recognize communication coming from the central site, and cannot be notified to print the message. Once again, a convenient mechanism for responding to exceptional situations is needed.

In the above example, it might be possible, using a standard client/server paradigm, to redesign M to respond to a request from the central site (in addition to requests coming from the keyboard). However, this might not be sufficient if the response to the central site is time critical. If the required response time is less than the time allotted to service a keyboard request, an interrupt mechanism is necessary.

Exceptional situations are referred to as **events**. Some TP monitors provide an **event communication** mechanism with which one module that recognizes an event can conveniently notify another module, M, to handle that event. Notification might take the form of an interrupt causing M to execute an event handling routine.[8] If event recognition happens in the context of a transaction, the event handler execution becomes part of that transaction as well. In this way, event handling, like

---

[8] M might also choose to defer executing the event handling routine until a later time, when it explicitly indicates to the TP monitor that it is ready to process any events that have been sent to it.

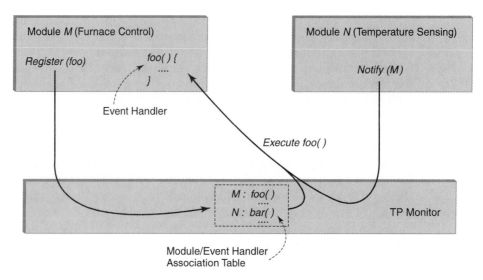

Figure 22.16 Event processing that links an event generating module with an event
handling module.

RPC and peer-to-peer communication, causes a distributed transaction to spread
from one module to another.[9]

The module that agrees to be interrupted uses the event handling API of the TP
monitor to **register** an **event handler** (or callback) that it wishes to execute when
notified of an event. In Figure 22.16, M has registered the handler foo with the TP
monitor. Since M does not wait for the event to occur but continues to engage in its
usual activities, event notification is said to be **unsolicited**.

The system interrupts M when an event it is to handle occurs. It saves M's
current state and passes control to foo. When foo exits, the system, using the saved
state, returns control to the point at which M was interrupted. M can thus respond
immediately when the event occurs. This response is asynchronous, because it
cannot be determined in advance when the event will occur and thus at what point
during M's execution (i.e., between which pair of instructions) foo will be executed.
While fast response is often important, careful design is required to ensure that the
execution of the handler does not interfere with the interrupted computation.

As depicted in Figure 22.16, the event generating module, N, uses the event API
to indicate to the system that an event has occurred and that the module M is to
be interrupted. This process is often called **notification**. Assuming that a handler
has been registered by M, the TP monitor causes it to be executed. The API might
allow a message to be passed to it by the event generating module as an argument.

---

[9] Our discussion is based on event communication in the Tuxedo transaction processing system [An-
drade et al. 1996].

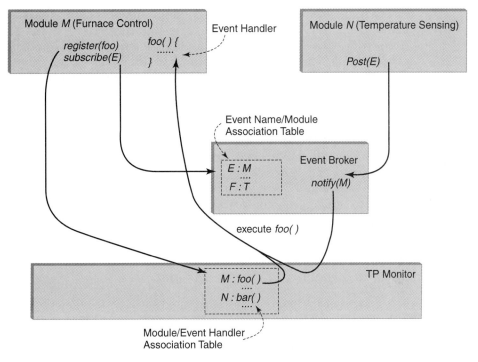

Figure 22.17 Use of an event broker to process event postings.

While this simple form of event communication is useful, it has one important drawback: The event generating module must know the identity of the modules to be notified (there can be more than one). In an application in which the modules that respond to events might change, it is desirable to make the target event-handling modules transparent to the event generating module. This can be done with an event broker.

An **event broker** is a server provided by a TP monitor, which functions as a link between event generating and event handling modules. When an event broker is used, each event is given a name. An event handling module, M, after registering an event handling routine with the TP monitor, **subscribes** to an event, E, by calling the broker using the event API. The name of the event is supplied as an argument. The broker then records the association between the named event and M. An event can have more than one subscriber, in which case a list of event handling modules is associated with it. When the event occurs, the event generating module, N, **posts** the event with the broker (again using broker's API and passing the name of the event an argument). The broker then notifies all modules that previously subscribed to the event. The situation just described is shown in Figure 22.17. Although the figure looks similar to Figure 22.16, notice that the broker keeps an association between named events and event handling modules, and uses `notify` to communicate with an event handling module. The association between the event handling module and the event handling routine is kept in the TP monitor, as before.

As with other forms of communication, communication through events can cause a transaction to spread from one module to another. For example, if the action post(Event) was performed as part of a transaction in the event-generating module, the resulting handler execution can become part of that transaction as well. In some situations, however, the handler's execution should not be part of the transaction that posted the event. For example, a transaction performing some database activities might find an uncorrectable database error, which requires it to abort. Before aborting, the transaction might want to post an event to notify the database administrator of the error. The event handler should not be a part of the transaction; if it were, it would be aborted when the transaction aborts and the database administrator would not be notified. The rules governing when transactions spread as a result of event postings are a part of the protocol implemented by the transaction processing system.

22.5 TRANSACTION PROCESSING ON THE INTERNET

The growth of the Internet has stimulated the development of many heterogeneous distributed transaction processing applications. These applications make use of existing client software (Web browsers) and standard Internet communication protocols to communicate with Web servers that provide transaction processing capability. A Web server has an Internet address (i.e., it is accessible over the Internet), and provides access to the Web using a standard Internet protocol, (e.g., HTTP, SMTP, or FTP).

With such systems, a user can initiate transactions that access databases through Web servers around the world, using her browser as a presentation server. Extensive multimedia catalogs are only a click away; a few more clicks find the cheapest vendor for a particular item, which can be purchased with just a few additional clicks—all while the user is still at home in her pajamas.

In addition, many enterprises have used Internet technology to implement intranets and extranets.

■ **Intranets** interconnect sites within the enterprise via a private network—separate from the Internet but using Internet technology—over which intra-enterprise business can be conducted. A product can be conceived in California, designed in New York, manufactured in Hong Kong, marketed in Chicago, with a centralized accounting function in New Jersey.

■ **Extranets** interconnect the enterprise's vendors and business customers with its intranet. Office supply vendors throughout the world can bid to meet the requirements of a branch of the enterprise in Des Moines.

Transactions play a key role in commerce conducted over a network. One issue that immediately arises is security, since information sent across the Internet can be easily intercepted and perhaps altered and many Internet sites can be broken into by unauthorized users. To deal with security issues, most Web browsers support sophisticated encryption-based security protocols; applications can further increase their security with firewalls and similar mechanisms. We will discuss security issues for Internet transactions in Chapter 27.

22.5.1 Common Architectures

Before we describe Internet transaction processing, we briefly introduce one commonly used architecture by which information is passed between a Web browser and a Web server. A user who wishes to interact with a Web server gives the browser the server's address. This address is in the form of a **uniform resource locator (URL)**—for example, `http://www.somecompany.com`. The browser sets up a connection to that server using the **HyperText Transfer Protocol (HTTP)**. Again using HTTP, the server then returns an appropriate page for the browser to display. The page is written in the **HyperText Markup Language** (HTML), which specifies its display format.

The server can also include with the HTML page one or more programs, called **applets**, written in a language such as Java. Applets execute in a programming environment supplied with the browser. They can animate the HTML page, respond to certain events (such as mouse clicks), and interact with the user and the network in other ways, some of which we discuss below. After sending the page, the server disconnects from the browser.

The browser displays the page when it is received, using the format described in its HTML description, and possibly executes specified applets. The page might include buttons, text boxes, and the like, to be filled in by the user. The user's interaction with the page might trigger the execution of other applets. Associated with the page, but usually hidden from the user, is the URL of a Web server (perhaps different from the one that sent the page) to which the user-supplied information is to be transmitted, and the name of a program on that server to be launched to process that information. The two most popular APIs to invoke programs on the Web server are **Common Gateway Interface (CGI)** and **servlets**.

A *CGI program* can be written in any language—"CGI" refers not to the language in which the program is written but to how the program is called and how the information from the page is passed to it. A *servlet* is written in Java and uses a special Java API to communicate with the client and other programs on the server. Apart from language, the main difference between the two APIs is that the servlet API is much richer. In particular, it provides built-in support for session management, which CGI lacks: A CGI program is invoked on every request from the browser, while a servlet can stay around to process multiple requests from the same client. In spite of these differences, however, the two APIs are similar, and we use CGI as an example.

When the user clicks the *submit* button, the browser sets up a connection to the designated Internet server using HTTP and sends the information. The CGI program is launched on that server and the information is passed to it as an argument. The program processes the information and might perform other actions as well (for example, accessing a database or submitting a request to a transaction processing system). At that point, the program can prepare a new HTML page and send it back to the browser. Once again, the server typically disconnects from the browser and retains no client context. After the user interacts with the new HTML page and clicks its *submit* button, the page can recontact the same or a different server and initiate a new CGI program.

In some applications, the browser might reconnect to the same Web server several times on behalf of the same user (for example, first to read information from a catalog and then to order something). For that reason, the server might want to access context (for example, information that describes the user) that spans the interactions, so it maintains a session with the user that continues over several connections. In other applications, the server might want to maintain context between connections that are days, or even weeks, apart (for example, the user's preferences as expressed in previous orders from the catalog). Context is generally not saved at the server because it must handle thousands of clients concurrently. Maintaining context for all of them wastes resources at the server, particularly since a browser might not reply (perhaps the user becomes bored and points his browser to the Walt Disney site). In Section 22.2.2 we discussed the possibility of storing context at the client. In the case of a browser, this can be done in several ways.

1. *Within a session—hidden fields.* When sending an HTML page to the browser, the CGI program C1 can store context in **hidden fields** in the page. Such fields are not displayed on the screen and so are not visible to the user. After the user fills in the visible fields and clicks the *submit* button, the information on the page (including the contents of the visible and invisible fields) is passed to the CGI program C2 designated on the page. In this way, context known to C1 is passed to C2.

2. *Within a session or between sessions—cookies.* A user's browser maintains a file of **cookies** corresponding to servers that it accessed in the past. Each cookie is a context handle consisting of up to 255 characters of data constructed by the server, describing the user but not normally accessible to him. When the browser connects to a server, it passes the corresponding cookie along with the information input by the user. When the server responds, it returns the (possibly modified) cookie to the browser.

3. *Using servlets.* Servlets have a lifetime that spans an entire client session and hence can maintain client context. In addition, the Java servlet API has built-in support for session management, which may significantly simplify server-side processing.

22.5.2 Organization of Transaction Systems on the Internet

We discuss three possible ways in which a transaction processing system can be organized for an Internet application.

1. The browser acts as presentation server, application server, and transaction server and the database server resides at the Internet site. The Web server at the database site responds to a request from a browser with an HTML page with which the user interacts, together with the application program written as a Java applet. After the user fills in the appropriate fields on the page, the applet executes from within the browser. The applet might access the database at the Internet site. It might initiate a transaction and submit SQL statements for processing by the database server. The applet communicates with the database server using JDBC (see Section 10.5). This model is similar to that of Figure 10.9. The JDBC driver might be downloaded from the Web server with the Java applet, in which case it sets up a network connection to the database server. Or the driver might reside on the Web server and receive commands from the browser as data through the CGI program.

2. The browser acts as the presentation server, and a CGI program at the Web server acts as the application server. When the Web server is contacted, it sends the browser an HTML page with which the user interacts. When the user fills in the page and submits it to the server, a CGI program, which implements the enterprise rules, is launched at the Web server. The program might initiate transactions that contain SQL statements or call stored procedures that reside on the database server, as in Figure 22.4, or it might contain calls to a transaction server, as in Figure 22.5. In the first case, the CGI program might access the DBMS using embedded SQL, or it might use a call-level interface such as JDBC or ODBC. When it completes, it can return an HTML page to the browser.[10]

3. In some applications, a three-tiered transaction processing system might accept requests from both Internet-based and non-Internet-based clients. The non-Internet-based clients connect to the application server as in Figure 22.4. The Internet-based clients connect to the application server through the CGI program on the Web server as shown in Figure 22.18. In this case, the browser is providing presentation services, but the application server views the browser and the CGI program together in the same way as it views non-Internet-based clients: as just another presentation server. For such systems, the CGI program on the Web server processes the information returned from the HTML page and initiates the appropriate application program on the application server using the communication protocol expected by the application server. When the application program completes and returns information to the CGI program, the CGI program prepares the appropriate HTML page and returns that page to the browser.

---

[10] Some commercial application generators optionally support this model by generating applications that execute as CGI programs on a Web server. The application designer uses the application generator to design the forms to be displayed at the client site, together with the appropriate application programs to process the information on them. The application generator then translates that design into equivalent HTML pages and CGI programs. At run time, the system executes as described.

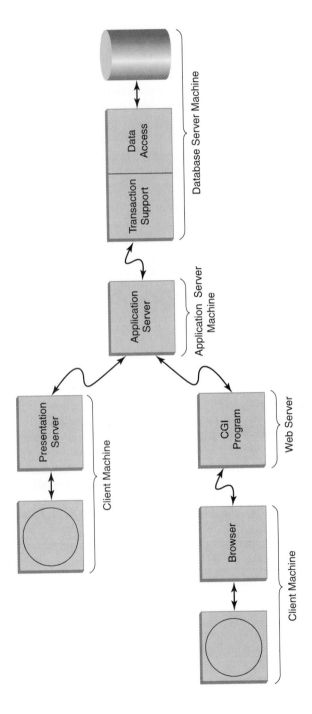

Figure 22.18 An Internet-based client connected to a three-tiered transaction processing system.

22.6 BIBLIOGRAPHIC NOTES

Much of the material in this chapter was drawn from two books. [Gray 1978] is encyclopedic in its coverage of transaction processing systems, and the student is urged to go to this excellent source for additional information. Another excellent source is [Bernstein and Newcomer 1997]. [Gray 1978] gets down to implementation details, but Bernstein and Newcomer focus on a higher level of coverage of much of the same material. Their work includes a very useful discussion of the two-tiered and three-tiered models and a description of several TP monitors. Additional information on Tuxedo can be found in [Andrade et al. 1996]. That on Encina can be found in [Transarc 1996]. RPCs were introduced by [Birrell and Nelson 1984]. A description of IBM's LU6.2, the most commonly used peer-to-peer protocol, can be found in [IBM 1991]. A general discussion of communication techniques, including RPC, can be found in [Peterson and Davies 2000]. The discussion of the handling of exceptional situations is based on the model used in the Tuxedo system [Andrade et al. 1996]. Description of the X/Open model for distributed transaction processing can be found in [*X/Open CAE Specification Structured Transaction Definition Language (STDL)* 1996] and [*X/Open Guide Distributed Transaction Processing: Reference Model*, Version 3 1996b].

Vast literature exists on programming Web applications (including database applications) using CGI and Java servlets. A few recent titles include [Hall 2000, Hunter and Crawford 1998, Sebesta 2001, Berg and Virginia 2000].

22.7 EXERCISES

22.1 Explain the advantages to a bank in providing access to its accounts database only through stored procedures such as `deposit()` and `withdraw()`.

22.2 Explain why the three-level organization of a transaction processing system (including transaction servers) is said to be scalable to large enterprise-wide systems. Discuss issues of cost, security, maintainability, authentication, and authorization.

22.3 Explain what happens in a three-level architecture for a transaction processing system if the presentation server crashes while the transaction is executing.

22.4 Explain why the *cancel* button on an ATM does not work after the *submit* button has been pressed.

22.5 Explain the advantages of including a transaction server in the architecture of a transaction processing system.

22.6 Give an example of a transaction processing system you use that is implemented as a distributed system with a centralized database.

22.7 Give an example in which a transaction in a distributed database system does not commit atomically (one database manager it accessed commits and another aborts) and leaves the database in an inconsistent state.

22.8 Explain whether the system you are using for your project can be characterized as TP-Lite or TP-Heavy.

22.9 List five issues that arise in the design of heterogeneous distributed transaction procession systems that do not arise in homogeneous distributed systems.

22.10 Explain the difference between a TP monitor and a transaction manager.

22.11 Give three examples of servers, other than transaction servers, database servers, and file servers, that might be called by an application server in a distributed transaction processing system.

22.12 Describe the architecture of the student registration system used by your school.

22.13 State two ways in which transactional remote procedure calls differ from ordinary remote procedure calls.

22.14 Suppose that a transaction uses TRPC to update some data from a database at a remote site and that the call successfully returns. Before the transaction completes, the remote site crashes. Describe informally what should happen when the transaction requests to commit.

22.15 Explain the difference between the `tx_commit()` command used in the X/Open API and the COMMIT statement in embedded SQL.

22.16 Propose an implementation of distributed savepoints using the `tx` and `xa` interfaces to the transaction manager. Assume that each subtransaction (including the transaction as a whole) can declare a savepoint, and that when it does so it forces its children to create corresponding savepoints. When a (sub)transaction rolls back to a savepoint, its children are rolled back to their corresponding savepoints.

22.17 Give three advantages of using an application server architecture in a client server system.

22.18 Give an example of an event, different from that given in the text, in which the callback function should not be part of the transaction.

22.19 Explain how peer-to-peer communication can be used to implement remote procedure calling.

22.20 Explain some of the authentication issues involved in using your credit card to order merchandise over the Internet.

22.21 Implement a Web tic-tac-toe game in which the display is prepared by a presentation server on your browser and the logic of the game is implemented within a CGI program on the server.

22.22 Print out the file of cookies for your local Web browser.

22.23 Consider a three-tiered system interfacing to a centralized DBMS, in which $n1$ presentation servers are connected to $n2$ application servers, which in turn are connected to $n3$ transaction servers. Assume that for each transaction the application server, on average, invokes k procedures, each of which is executed on an arbitrary transaction server, and that each procedure, on average, executes s SQL statements that must be processed by the DBMS. If, on average, a presentation server handles r requests per second (each request produces exactly one transaction at the application server), how many SQL statements per second are processed by the DBMS and how many messages flow over each communication line?

Chapter 23

Implementing Isolation

Our university has over ten thousand undergraduate students, and when the deadline for registration approaches, we might expect hundreds of students to be using the Student Registration System at the same time. The system must ensure that such a large number of concurrent users does not destroy the integrity of the database. Suppose, for example, that, because of room size limitations, only 50 students are allowed to register for a particular course (that is one of the integrity constraints of the database), and suppose that 49 have already registered. If two additional students attempt to register concurrently, the system must ensure that no more than one of them succeeds.

One way to ensure the correctness of concurrent schedules is to run all transactions sequentially, one at a time. Thus, when two students try to register for the last opening in a course, the transaction initiated by one of them will execute first and that student will be registered. Then the transaction initiated by the second will execute and that student will be told that the course is full. This type of execution is called **serial**, and the execution of each transaction is said to be **isolated**—the *I* in ACID.

Let us review why isolation is an issue. Recall that our assumption that transactions are consistent—the *C* in ACID—implies that, if the database is in a consistent state and a transaction executes in isolation, it will execute correctly. Since the database has been returned to a consistent state, we can initiate the execution of a second transaction and, because it too is consistent, it will also execute correctly. Hence, if the initial database state is consistent, serial execution of a set of transactions—one transaction at a time—will be correct.

Unfortunately, serial execution is impractical. Databases are central to the operation of many applications and so must be accessed frequently. A system that requires that transactions be executed serially simply cannot keep up with the load. Furthermore, it is easy to see that, in many cases, serial execution is unnecessary. For example, if transaction T_1 accesses tables x and y and if transaction T_2 accesses tables u and v, the operations of T_1 and T_2 can be arbitrarily interleaved and the end result—including the information returned by the DBMS to the transactions and the final database state—will be identical to the serial execution of T_1 followed by T_2 and also identical to the serial execution of T_2 followed by T_1. Since serial execution is known to be correct, the interleaved schedule must be correct as well.

The interleaved execution of a set of transactions is potentially far more efficient than serial execution of that set. Transaction execution requires the services of multiple system resources—primarily CPU and I/O channels—but a transaction frequently utilizes only one of these resources at a time. With concurrent execution of several transactions, we can potentially utilize a number of these resources simultaneously and hence improve system throughput. For example, while the CPU is doing some computation for one transaction, the I/O channel might be providing I/O service for another.

Unfortunately, certain interleaved schedules can cause consistent transactions to behave incorrectly, returning the wrong result to the application and producing inconsistent database states. For that reason, we cannot allow arbitrary interleavings. The first question is how we decide which interleavings are good and which are bad. The next question is how can we implement an algorithm that permits the good interleavings and prohibits the bad. We call such an algorithm a **concurrency control**. These are the questions we address in this chapter.

In most commercial transaction processing systems, concurrency control is done automatically and is invisible to the application programmer, who designs each transaction as if it will execute in a nonconcurrent environment. The concurrency control, while allowing concurrency, ensures that each transaction is isolated from every other transaction. Nevertheless, it is important to understand the concepts underlying the operation of concurrency controls because:

1. Using concurrency control to achieve isolation, in contrast to simply allowing arbitrary interleavings, can result in a significant increase in response time and a significant decrease in transaction throughput (measured in transactions per second). Hence, many commercial systems allow the option (sometimes as the default) of running transactions with a reduced level of isolation. Since the designer might be tempted to use one of these options to increase system efficiency, it is important to understand how these reduced levels of isolation can lead to inconsistent databases and incorrect results.

2. Whether the designer chooses to achieve complete isolation or some reduced level of isolation, the overall efficiency of an application can be strongly influenced by the interaction between the concurrency control and the design of both the tables and the transactions within that application.

Isolation is a complex issue, so we break our discussion into two parts. In this chapter, we are primarily interested in isolation in an "abstract" database system. By abstract we mean a database in which each data item has a name, and read and write operations name the item that they access. Chapter 24 will be devoted to isolation in a relational database system, in which data is accessed using SQL statements that use conditions to identify rows to be addressed. Studying isolation in abstract databases helps us focus on key issues in concurrency control. The specifics of relational databases will lead to a refinement of the techniques developed for the abstract case.

23.1 SCHEDULES AND THEIR EQUIVALENCE

The concurrency controls we are interested in will work in any application. We do not discuss concurrency controls that are designed with a specific application in mind. In particular, we are not interested in controls that utilize information about the computation a particular transaction is carrying out. We are interested in controls that must separate good interleavings from bad ones without knowing what the transaction is doing. For example, a transaction might read the value of a variable in the database. If the concurrency control knows that the variable represents a bank account balance and that the transaction will request the read as a first step of a deposit operation, it might be able to use that information in choosing an acceptable interleaving. However, we assume that this information is not available to the concurrency control.

If we cannot use application-specific information, how do we decide which interleavings are correct? The answer lies in our basic assumption that each transaction is consistent and that therefore serial schedules must be correct. From this it follows that any interleaved schedule that has the same effect as that of a serial schedule must also be correct, and this is the correctness criterion we use. We will refine the notion of "has the same effect as that of a serial schedule" later, but you should understand that this is a conservative notion of correctness. For most applications, there will be many perfectly acceptable executions that are not serial and thus "incorrect" *according to our criteria*, because we assume that the information about what transactions are doing is not available.

We assume that a transaction is a program whose data space includes the database and its local variables. While the local variables are accessible only to that transaction, the database is global and accessible to all transactions. The transaction uses different mechanisms to access the two parts of its data space. The local variables are directly accessible to the transaction (i.e., in its virtual memory), but the database is accessible only through calls to procedures provided by the database manager. For example, at a very low level of implementation detail, the transaction asks the database manager to copy a block of data from the database into its local variables—this is a **read request**; or it asks to overwrite a portion of the database with data stored in local variables—this is a **write request**. At this level, we view the database as a collection of data items and do not presume to know anything about the type of information stored in a data item. Also, we make no assumptions as to where the database is stored. Most likely, it is stored on a mass storage device, but in situations in which rapid response is required it can be stored in main memory.

A transaction, then, is a program in which computations made with the local variables are interspersed with requests for access to the database made to the database manager. Since the computation performed in main memory is invisible to the database manager, its view of the execution of a transaction is a sequence of read and write requests, which we call a **transaction schedule**. If $p_{i,j}$ is the jth request made by T_i, then

$$p_{i,1}, p_{i,2}, \ldots, p_{i,n}$$

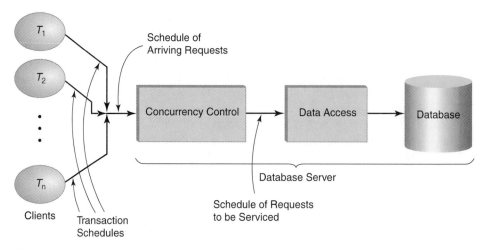

Figure 23.1 Role of a concurrency control in a database system.

is the transaction schedule of T_i, which consists of n requests to the database.

Since transactions execute concurrently, the database manager must deal with a merge of transaction schedules, which we refer to simply as a **schedule**. The database manager has the responsibility of servicing each arriving request, but doing so in the order of arrival might be incorrect. Hence, when a request arrives, a decision must be made as to whether to service it immediately. This decision is made by the concurrency control. If the concurrency control decides that immediately servicing a request might lead to an incorrect schedule, it can delay servicing to a later time or it can abort the requesting transaction altogether.

Hence, the schedule serviced by the database manager might not be the same as the sequence of requests that arrives at the concurrency control. The concurrency control will, in general, reorder the requests. It cannot, of course, reorder the requests of a single transaction. Since we assume that a transaction is a sequential program, it will not submit a request until the previously submitted request has been serviced. The goal of the concurrency control is to reorder requests of *different* transactions in the arriving schedule so as to produce a correct schedule for servicing by the database manager. The system organization is shown in Figure 23.1.

Note that transforming the arriving schedule is not without its costs: A transaction can be either delayed or aborted. Delaying transactions reduces the overall concurrency level within the system and therefore can increase average response time and decrease throughput. Aborting a transaction is worse since it requires that the computation be repeated. Thus, it is important that the concurrency control do no unnecessary transformations, but should recognize as many correct arriving schedules as possible. Concurrency controls are generally incapable of recognizing all correct schedules and therefore sometimes perform unnecessary schedule transformations. The goal in designing a concurrency control is to minimize this waste.

We assume that *the execution of each database operation is atomic and isolated with respect to other database operations.* Although we have assumed that the concurrency control does not know the semantics of transactions (i.e., the nature of the computations), we assume that it does know the effect of each database operation, which we refer to as **operation semantics**. In this chapter, we are mainly concerned with read and write operations. In the next chapter, we will consider the operations performed on a relational database, such as SELECT and UPDATE.

Equivalence of schedules.   Operation semantics is used to determine allowable schedules. To explain how, we must first explain what it means for two schedules to be equivalent. We say that two database operations, p_1 and p_2, **commute** if, for all possible initial database states,

■ p_1 returns the same value when executed in either the sequence p_1, p_2 or p_2, p_1

■ p_2 returns the same value when executed in either the sequence p_1, p_2 or p_2, p_1

■ The database state produced by both sequences is the same

Suppose that p_1 and p_2 are requests made by different transactions and are successive operations in a schedule, S_1. Then S_1 has the form

$$S_{1,1}, p_1, p_2, S_{1,2}$$

where $S_{1,1}$ is a prefix of S_1 and $S_{1,2}$ is a suffix of S_1. Suppose the two operations p_1 and p_2 commute. Then in schedule $S2$

$$S_{1,1}, p_2, p_1, S_{1,2}$$

all transactions perform the same computations as in schedule S_1 since the values returned to each transaction are the same in both schedules. Furthermore, both schedules leave the database in the same final state. Hence, we say that schedules S_1 and S_2 are **equivalent**. Operations that do not commute are said to **conflict**.

Most important, two operations on different data items always commute. Commutativity is also possible between operations on the same item. For example, two read operations on the same item commute. However, a read and a write on the same item conflict because, although the final state of the item is the same independently of the order of execution, the value returned to the reader depends on the order of the operations. Similarly, two write operations on the same item conflict since the final state of the item depends on the order in which the writes occur.

In any schedule, successive operations that commute with each other and belong to different transactions can always be interchanged to form a new schedule that is equivalent to the original. Since equivalence is transitive we can demonstrate the equivalence of two schedules, both of which are merges of the same set of transaction schedules, but which differ substantially in the way the merges are done, using a sequence of such simple interchanges. Unfortunately, this interchange procedure is awkward for use by a concurrency control.

The design of most concurrency controls is based on the following theorem, which is an alternate way to demonstrate the equivalence of two schedules:

> **Theorem (Schedule Equivalence):** Two schedules of the same set of operations are equivalent if and only if conflicting operations are ordered in the same way in both.

Note that we can prove this theorem if we can demonstrate that:

> A schedule, S_2, can be derived from a schedule, S_1, by interchanging commuting operations if and only if conflicting operations are ordered in the same way in both schedules.

since we know that two schedules are equivalent if and only if one can be derived from the other by interchanging commuting operations.

The "only if" part of the theorem follows from the observation that the order of conflicting operations is preserved by the interchange procedure. Thus if conflicting operations were ordered differently in both schedules, S_2 could not have been obtained from S_1 using the interchange procedure.

The "if" part is a little more difficult. It can be demonstrated by showing that *any* schedule, S_2 (of the same set of operations as in S_1), in which conflicting operations are ordered the same way as in S_1, can be generated from S_1 using the interchange procedure. To show this, consider the schedule S_1:

$$\ldots, p_i, p_{i+1}, p_{i+2}, \ldots, p_{i+r}, \ldots$$

Suppose that S_2 is a schedule of the same set of operations, where conflicting operations are ordered the same way as in S_1. Furthermore, suppose that, for all j satisfying $1 \le j \le r - 1$, p_i and p_{i+j} are ordered in the same way in both S_1 and S_2, but that p_i and p_{i+r} are ordered differently. Thus, p_{i+r} is the first operation following p_i in S_1 that is ordered differently in S_2, and so p_{i+r} precedes p_i in S_2. Operations p_i and p_{i+r} must commute, since conflicting operations are ordered in the same way in S_1 and S_2.

Assume now that there is some k satisfying $1 \le k \le r - 1$ such that p_{i+r} does not commute with p_{i+k}. Then, in S_2, the operations must be ordered

$$\ldots, p_{i+k}, \ldots, p_{i+r}, \ldots, p_i, \ldots$$

since conflicting operations are ordered in the same way in both schedules. But this contradicts the assumption that p_{i+r} is the first operation following p_i in S_1 that is ordered differently in S_2.

For this reason, the assumption that there exists a k satisfying $1 \le k \le r - 1$, such that p_{i+r} does not commute with p_{i+k}, is false. Therefore, p_{i+r} commutes with all of the operations in $p_i, \ldots, p_{i+r-1}$, and a series of interchanges of adjacent operations can be used to create a schedule equivalent to S_1 that differs from S_1 only in that p_{i+r} precedes, rather than follows, p_i (as it does in S_2). The interchange procedure can be used repeatedly to reorder the operations that are ordered differently in S_1 and S_2 and thus to transform S_1 into S_2.

23.1.1 Serializability

We have shown that, if conflicting operations are ordered in the same way in two schedules, they are equivalent. Using this rule, we can specify interleaved schedules that are equivalent to serial schedules, and it is these schedules that the concurrency control is designed to permit. We refer to such schedules as serializable [Eswaran et al. 1976].

> A schedule is **serializable** if it is equivalent to a serial schedule in the sense that conflicting operations are ordered in the same way in both.

The notion of a serializable schedule provides the answer to our first question: how are we to decide which interleavings are correct.

> Since a serializable schedule is equivalent to a serial schedule and since we assume that all transactions are consistent, a serializable schedule of any application's transactions is correct.[1]

Serializable schedules are correct for *any* application. However, for a particular application serializability might be too strong a condition (some nonserializable schedules of that application's transactions might be correct) and can lead to an unnecessary performance penalty. Hence, concurrency controls generally implement a variety of isolation levels, the strongest of which produces serializable schedules; the application designer can choose a level appropriate for the particular application. In this chapter, we deal only with serializable schedules. We will discuss less stringent isolation levels in Chapter 24.

To illustrate serializability, suppose that $p_{1,1}$ and $p_{1,2}$ are two successive database operations requested by transaction T_1, and that $p_{2,1}$ and $p_{2,2}$ are two successive operations requested by transaction T_2. One sequence of interleaved operations is

$$p_{1,1}, p_{2,1}, p_{1,2}, p_{2,2}$$

If $p_{2,1}$ and $p_{1,2}$ commute, this interleaved sequence is equivalent to the serial schedule

$$p_{1,1}, p_{1,2}, p_{2,1}, p_{2,2}$$

and is thus correct.

Two transaction schedules are shown in Figure 23.2(a); each displayed on a different line. Time increases from left to right. The total schedule is a merge of the two transaction schedules, with the interleaving indicated spatially. The notation $r(x)$ indicates a read of the data item x; $w(x)$, a write. The value of a data item at any point in the schedule is the value written by the last preceding write or, if there is no preceding write, the initial value.

The schedule in part (a) of Figure 23.2 is interleaved (nonserial) because some of the operations of T_1 occur before those of T_2 and others occur after. The schedule in

---

[1] The converse result, that if a schedule is not serializable, there exists an integrity constraint for which that schedule makes that integrity constraint false, is proved in [Rosenkrantz et al. 1984].

Figure 23.2 (a) *Serializable* schedule; (b) Equivalent *serial* schedule.

T_1:	$r(x)$			$r(y)$	$w(y)$
T_2:		$r(x)$	$w(x)$		

(**a**)

T_1:	$r(x)$	$r(y)$	$w(y)$		
T_2:				$r(x)$	$w(x)$

(**b**)

part (b) is serial, with T_1 completing before T_2 starts. The read and write operations on x executed by T_2 in Figure 23.2(a) commute with the read and write operations on y executed by T_1, and so that schedule can be transformed into the schedule in Figure 23.2(b) using a sequence of interchanges of adjacent commutative operations. Hence, the schedule of Figure 23.2(a) is serializable.

Now consider the two schedules from the point of view of the schedule equivalence theorem. The only conflicting operations in the two transactions are $r(x)$ in T_1 and $w(x)$ in T_2. Since they are ordered in the same way in both part (a) and part (b), the two schedules are equivalent.

Finally, note that although the schedule of Figure 23.2(a) is equivalent to the serial schedule $T_1\ T_2$ in Figure 23.2(b), it is not equivalent to the serial schedule $T_2\ T_1$.

As another example, the schedule shown in Figure 23.3 is not serializable. Since T_2 wrote x after T_1 read x, T_2 must follow T_1 in any equivalent serial order (because its write does not commute with T_1's read and so cannot be interchanged with it). Similarly, since T_1 wrote y after T_2 read y, T_1 would have to follow T_2 in any equivalent serial order. Since T_1 cannot be both before and after T_2, there is no equivalent serial order.

Although the argument for equivalence between a serializable and a serial schedule is based on commutativity and the reordering of operations, the concurrency control does not actually reorder the operations of a serializable schedule before executing it. Since the effect of the serializable schedule is the same as that of the serial schedule, there is no need to reorder the operations. If the concurrency control can determine that the sequence of operations that have arrived is the prefix of a serializable schedule, no matter what operations might be submitted later, it executes the operations as they arrive. If, however, it cannot be certain of this,

Figure 23.3 Nonserializable schedule.

T_1:	$r(x)$			$w(y)$
T_2:		$r(y)$	$w(x)$	

the operations have to be delayed and might need to be reordered so that the total schedule is guaranteed to be serializable. We describe later how this reordering is done.

23.1.2 Conflict Equivalence and View Equivalence

We have said that two schedules are equivalent if conflicting operations are ordered in the same way in both. However, there are actually two different notions of equivalence: the one we have described, called **conflict equivalence** because of its defining property, and a second, called *view equivalence*. Two schedules are **view equivalent** if they satisfy the following two conditions:

1. Corresponding read operations in each schedule return the same values (therefore, all transactions perform the same calculations and write the same values to the database in both schedules).
2. Both schedules yield the same final database state.

The first condition implies that the transactions in both schedules have the same view of the database—hence the name. The second condition is required since although transactions in both schedules write the same values to the database, if the writes occur in different orders the two schedules might leave the database in different final states. The second condition restricts the ordering of write statements to the extent of requiring that the final states be the same: The last operation to write each data item must be the same in each schedule.

The condition for conflict equivalence *is sufficient* to ensure view equivalence, but it is *not necessary*; that is, it is stronger than it need be in some cases. Correspondingly, view equivalence is more general (i.e., weaker) than conflict equivalence. Although two conflict-equivalent schedules are also view equivalent (you are asked to prove this in Exercise 23.6), two view-equivalent schedules are not necessarily conflict equivalent: It might not be possible to derive one from the other by interchanging adjacent operations that commute.

For example, the schedule shown in Figure 23.4 is not conflict equivalent to any serial schedule. The read and write operations on y by T_2 and T_1, respectively, do not commute; hence, if there were a conflict-equivalent serial schedule, T_2 must precede T_1. On the other hand, the two write operations on x by these transactions do not commute either and imply that, in a conflict-equivalent serial schedule, T_1 must precede T_2, which is contradiction. Note, however, that the serial schedule in which the transactions are executed in the order T_2 T_1 T_3 has the same effect as that of the schedule shown in Figure 23.4: x and y have the same final state,

Figure 23.4 Schedule demonstrating that view equivalence does not imply conflict equivalence.

T_1: $w(y)$ $w(x)$

T_2: $r(y)$ $w(x)$

T_3: $w(x)$

and the value returned to T_2 as a result of its read of y is the same in both. The schedule in Figure 23.4 is thus view equivalent to the serial schedule T_2 T_1 T_3 and so is serializable.

Although it might be possible to design concurrency controls based on view equivalence (and perhaps to gain additional concurrency because more serializable schedules are permitted), such controls are difficult to implement. For that reason, concurrency controls are generally based on conflict equivalence. In the remainder of the text, our use of the term "equivalence" will mean conflict equivalence unless we state otherwise.

23.1.3 Serialization Graphs

Another way to think about conflict serializability is based on serialization graphs. A **serialization graph** for a particular schedule, S, of committed transactions is a directed graph in which the nodes are the transactions participating in the schedule and there is a directed edge pointing from the node representing transaction T_i to the node representing transaction T_j,

$$T_i \rightarrow T_j$$

if, in the schedule S,

1. Some database operation, p_i, in T_i conflicts with some operation, p_j, in T_j
2. p_i appears before p_j in S

For example, the serialization graph corresponding to the schedule in Figure 23.2(a) consists of the one edge,

$$T_1 \rightarrow T_2$$

because T_2 wrote x after T_1 read x.

If a directed edge from T_i to T_j appears in a serialization graph for S, we can conclude that T_i must precede T_j in any schedule that is conflict equivalent to S. To see this, observe that, if we attempt to obtain a conflict-equivalent serial schedule by interchanging operations that commute, we cannot interchange the conflicting operations that generated the edge. For example, in any schedule that is conflict equivalent to the schedule of Figure 23.2(a), T_1 must precede T_2 because T_2's write of x cannot be interchanged with T_1's read of x.

The serialization graph for a particular schedule can be used to reason about the serializability of that schedule. For example, the serialization graph for the schedule in Figure 23.3 has two edges:

$$T_1 \rightarrow T_2$$

because T_2 wrote x after T_1 read x, and

$$T_2 \rightarrow T_1$$

because T_1 wrote y after T_2 read y. These two edges form a cycle:

$$T_1 \rightarrow T_2 \rightarrow T_1$$

Figure 23.5 Two serialization graphs.

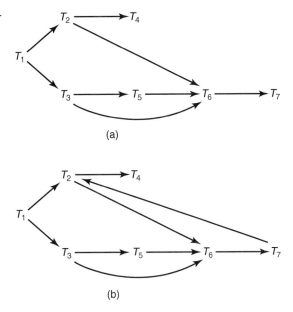

(a)

(b)

Thus, we can conclude that, in any equivalent serial schedule, T_1 must precede T_2 and also that T_2 must precede T_1. Clearly, this is impossible, so we can conclude that there is no equivalent serial schedule and thus that the schedule of Figure 23.3 is not serializable. More generally, we can state the following result:

> **Theorem (Serialization Graph):** A schedule is conflict serializable if and only if its serialization graph is acyclic.

To prove this theorem, note that, if the serialization graph for a schedule, S, has a cycle, we can use the above reasoning to show that it is not serializable. Assume, on the other hand, that the graph is acyclic. Let $T_{i_1}, \ldots, T_{i_n}$, be a topological sort[2] of the transactions in the graph, and construct a serial schedule, S^{ser}, which corresponds to this ordering. The schedule S^{ser} is conflict equivalent to S because, if there is an edge from T_r to T_s in the serialization graph, there exists a conflict between an operation, p_r, of T_r and an operation, p_s, of T_s, and p_r precedes p_s in both S and S^{ser}. Since conflicting operations are ordered in the same way in both schedules, they are equivalent (according to the schedule equivalence theorem on page 766) and thus S is conflict serializable.

The serialization graph in Figure 23.5(a) is a somewhat larger example of a graph that has no cycles and hence corresponds to a serializable schedule. The graph has many topological sorts, and hence there are many conflict-equivalent serial schedules of its transactions. Two of these schedules are

---

[2] A *topological sort* of an acyclic directed graph is any (total) ordering of the nodes in the graph that is consistent with the ordering implied by the edges in the graph. A given acyclic directed graph might have many topological sorts.

$$T_1\, T_2\, T_3\, T_4\, T_5\, T_6\, T_7$$

and

$$T_1\, T_3\, T_5\, T_2\, T_6\, T_7\, T_4$$

The serialization graph in Figure 23.5(b) corresponds to a nonserializable schedule because of the cycle

$$T_2 \rightarrow T_6 \rightarrow T_7 \rightarrow T_2$$

23.2   RECOVERABILITY, CASCADED ABORTS, AND STRICTNESS

Up to this point, our discussion has been motivated by serializability, and we have assumed that all transactions commit. Life gets more complicated when we consider the possibility that a transaction might abort. Additional restrictions must be placed on schedules in that case. When a transaction commits, durability requires that any changes it made to the database be made permanent and must not be lost. When a transaction aborts, it must have the same effect as if it had never been initiated. A transaction that has been initiated but has not yet committed or aborted is said to be **active**.

When a transaction aborts, any changes it made to the database must be nullified. We say that the transaction must be **rolled back**. However, rolling back values the transaction has written to the database might not be sufficient to ensure that the aborted transaction has had no effect. Suppose that T_2 writes a new value to the variable x and that we allow x to be read by transaction T_1 before T_2 terminates, as shown in Figure 23.6(a). The read by T_1 is referred to as a **dirty read**, since T_2 has not committed. If we then allow the sequence of events "T_1 commits, T_2 aborts" to occur, T_2 will have had an effect on T_1 even though we roll x back to the value it had before it was written by T_2. Furthermore, since T_1 has committed, the information it has written to the database—in this case, a new value of y—must be preserved. This creates a serious problem: That value might be a function of the value that T_1 read from T_2, and hence T_2 has (indirectly) affected the database state even though it has aborted.

Figure 23.6 (a) Nonrecoverable schedule; (b) Its recoverable counterpart.

$$
\begin{array}{lllll}
T_1: & & r(x)\ \ w(y)\ \ commit & & \\
T_2: & w(x) & & abort &
\end{array}
$$

(a)

$$
\begin{array}{lllll}
T_1: & & r(x)\ \ w(y) & & abort \\
T_2: & w(x) & & abort &
\end{array}
$$

(b)

Figure 23.7 Nonrecoverable schedule.

$$
\begin{array}{lll}
T_1: & & r(x) \;\; commit \\
T_2: & w(x) & \qquad\qquad\qquad w(x)
\end{array}
$$

Note that, if T_2 does not abort, the schedule in Figure 23.6(a) is serializable, so dirty reads can occur in serializable schedules. Since we generally cannot prevent a transaction from aborting, however, we must design the concurrency control with additional restrictions so that the above situation cannot happen. Specifically, we cannot allow T_1 to commit in the above scenario. If T_1 had not committed, we could have aborted it when T_2 aborted, as in Figure 23.6(b).

A concurrency control is said to be **recoverable** [Hadzilacos 1983] if it does not allow a transaction, T_1, to commit until every other transaction, T_2, that wrote values read by T_1 has committed. (Thus, if T_2 aborts, T_1 can be aborted as well.) We require all our concurrency controls to be recoverable. Schedules produced by a recoverable concurrency control are said to be recoverable schedules.

Note that dirty reads are undesirable even if transactions do not abort. A transaction, T_2, might update a data item several times, and a dirty read by a concurrent transaction, T_1, might see the intermediate value, as shown in Figure 23.7. Intuitively, we conclude that this cannot be a serializable schedule because intermediate values can never be read in a serial schedule. The fact that the schedule in Fig 23.7 is not serializable follows from the fact that the read operation of T_1 conflicts with both writes of T_2.

Even though a concurrency control is recoverable, it might have another undesirable property: cascaded aborts. A concurrency control exhibits **cascaded aborts** if the abort of one transaction causes the abort of one or more other transactions.

Suppose that we allow values written to the database by transaction T_3 to be read by transaction T_2 before T_3 terminates, as shown in Figure 23.8. If T_3 now aborts, T_2 must also abort since it read a value that T_3 wrote. The abort of T_2 forces the abort of T_1 for similar reasons. In a more general case, an arbitrary number of transactions might have to be aborted—an undesirable situation. Thus, we require that our concurrency controls not cause cascaded aborts.

A concurrency control will not cause cascaded aborts if it prohibits dirty reads. This condition is more stringent than that for recoverability, which allows T_1 to read a value written by an active transaction, T_2, but does not allow T_1 to commit until after T_2 commits. However, we choose to require an even stronger condition, called strictness. A concurrency control is said to be **strict** [Hadzilacos 1983] if it does not

Figure 23.8 Recoverable schedule that illustrates a cascaded abort. T_3 aborts, forcing T_2 to abort, which then forces T_1 to abort.

$$
\begin{array}{llll}
T_1: & & r(y) \;\; w(z) & \qquad\qquad\qquad\qquad abort \\
T_2: & r(x) \;\; w(y) & & \qquad\qquad abort \\
T_3: w(x) & & \qquad abort &
\end{array}
$$

Figure 23.9 Schedule illustrating the difficulty of handling rollback.

$$T_1 : \quad w(x) \qquad\qquad\qquad abort$$
$$T_2 : \qquad\qquad\quad w(x) \qquad\qquad\qquad\qquad abort$$

allow a transaction to read *or write* a data item written by an active transaction. A write of a data item written by an active transaction is called a **dirty write**.

Clearly, a strict concurrency control is recoverable and does not exhibit cascaded aborts, but why have we imposed the additional condition on writing? The reason has to do with efficiency in implementing rollback in certain situations. Ordinarily, when we roll back the effect of a write of some data item, x, we expect to restore x to the value it had just before the write occurred. Suppose that we allow the value of x to be changed first by T_1, and then by T_2, as shown in Figure 23.9. If T_1 aborts, we do not have to restore the value of x at all since its value is the one written by T_2 and T_2 has not aborted. If T_2 now aborts as well, we have to restore x to the value it had just before T_1's write (not T_2's). Although we could design the system to perform correctly in all such situations, a strict system is much simpler to design since we can always roll back a write simply by restoring x to its value just before the write occurred. In nonstrict systems, the recovery algorithm is more complex, requiring an analysis of the writes made by a number of transactions.

23.3 MODELS FOR CONCURRENCY CONTROL

In this section we give an overview of several ways in which a transaction can interact with a concurrency control and a database. The interaction with the database can be characterized as either immediate-update or deferred-update.

■ In **immediate-update** systems, a transaction's write operation causes an immediate update of the appropriate data item in the database; its read operation returns the value of the item in the database. It might appear that a read can return a value written by an as yet uncommitted transaction, which means that the concurrency control will not be strict, but we will see that the concurrency control algorithm prevents this.

■ In **deferred-update** systems, a transaction's write operation does not update the appropriate data item in the database immediately; instead, that information is saved in a special area of the transaction called the **intentions list**. A transaction's read operation returns the value of the appropriate data item in the database unless the transaction has written that item, in which case the value from its intentions list is returned. If and when the transaction commits, its intentions list is used to update the database. Note that a value returned by a read is either a value the transaction itself has written or a value written by a committed transaction.

As shown in Figure 23.1, the goal of a concurrency control is to transform the arriving sequence of database requests into a strict, serializable schedule. When a transaction makes a request, the control must decide whether to allow that request to be processed. The control knows the (partial) schedule that has been serviced by the database system up to that point, but has no knowledge of requests that will be arriving in the future. Hence, it must be sure that, no matter what sequence of requests subsequently arrives, the schedule processed by the database system will be serializable. The control's response to a specific request can be one of the following:

1. Allow the request to be processed
2. Make the requestor wait until some other event occurs
3. Deny the request (and abort the transaction)

Concurrency controls differ in the kinds of requests that are always granted (response 1 in the above list), and in the kinds of requests that might be delayed or denied. On this basis, concurrency controls can be characterized as either pessimistic or optimistic.

■ In a **pessimistic** system, whenever a transaction attempts to perform some database operation, it must request permission from the concurrency control. However, the transaction can commit at any time without requesting permission.

■ In an **optimistic** system, a transaction can perform any database operation without requesting permission from the concurrency control. However, the transaction must request permission to commit.

In both systems, a transaction can abort without requesting permission at any time before it commits.

The design of a pessimistic concurrency control is based on the philosophy that a bad thing is likely to happen: the accesses that transactions make to the database are likely to conflict. Hence, a pessimistic control examines each request and allows it to be processed only if it is certain that no subsequent request can cause the schedule to become nonserializable. The control makes "worst case" decisions and is hence called pessimistic. Since the resulting schedules are guaranteed to be serializable, a request to commit can always be granted.

The design of an optimistic control, on the other hand, is based on the philosophy that bad things are not likely to happen: the accesses that transactions make to the database are not likely to conflict. Hence, an optimistic control immediately grants each request for access. When a transaction requests to commit, however, the control must check to make sure that in fact no bad thing happened and if so, the transaction cannot be allowed to commit.

An optimistic algorithm might be appropriate for a large database in which transactions typically access only a few items and those accesses are spread randomly over the database. The more such assumptions are violated, the more likely conflicts will occur; therefore, requests to commit will be denied. In particular, an optimistic algorithm is not appropriate for a database in which **hotspots** exist. These are data items that are heavily accessed in conflicting ways by many transactions.

Concurrency controls are generally characterized by the choices made in these two categories of interaction. The most commonly implemented concurrency control is the immediate-update, pessimistic system, which we describe here in detail. We also discuss, briefly, the deferred-update, optimistic system, since it is useful in some situations. A deferred-update pessimistic system, which we do not discuss is also possible.

23.4 A STRATEGY FOR IMMEDIATE–UPDATE PESSIMISTIC CONCURRENCY CONTROLS

We have already required that our concurrency controls be strict. A transaction must not be allowed to read or write an item in the database that has been written by another transaction that is still active. We justified this restriction as being necessary to ensure recoverability, to prevent cascaded aborts, and to enable efficient rollback. In this section, we discuss additional difficulties associated with immediate update pessimistic systems and propose solutions.

23.4.1 Conflict Avoidance

Suppose that transaction T_2 has written a new value to data item x and that transaction T_1 makes a conflicting request—for example, a request to read x—while T_2 is still active. We have seen that to ensure strictness such a request cannot be granted, but let us ignore strictness for the moment and consider only the requirement of serializability. Since we are assuming an immediate-update system, if T_1's read request is granted, the value written by T_2 will be returned. Hence, if the concurrency control grants the request, it fixes an order between T_1 and T_2 in any serialization: T_1 must follow T_2. If T_1 and T_2 subsequently request access to another data item y, the concurrency control will have to remember the order it had already fixed between them and ensure that the accesses to y do not contradict that order. Thus, if the accesses to y by T_1 and T_2 fix the order "T_2 must follow T_1 in any serialization," the two contradictory orders preclude any serial order equivalent to the resulting schedule.

The problem in the above scenario is actually more serious than it seems. Suppose that, after the accesses to x, T_1 writes a new value to y, then T_1 commits, and finally T_2 requests to read y, as shown in Figure 23.10. The concurrency control cannot grant the read, since the resulting schedule would not be serializable. Since T_2 cannot complete, it must be aborted, but unfortunately that too is impossible since T_1 has read a result (in x) that T_2 wrote and T_1 cannot be aborted (it has already committed).

Figure 23.10 Schedule demonstrating that conflicting requests cannot be granted to active transactions if serializability is to be preserved.

T_1: $r(x)\ w(y)\ commit$
T_2: $w(x)$ `request_r(y)`

Figure 23.11 Schedule demonstrating that conflicting requests cannot be granted to active transactions if serializability is to be preserved.

T_1: $w(x)$ $r(y)$ *commit*
T_2: $r(x)$ request_$w(y)$

The problem can be avoided by delaying T_1's commit, but this only leads to a cascaded abort. To avoid this problem and to ensure serializability, we require that the concurrency control adhere to the following rule:

> The concurrency control grants requests in such a way that it does not determine an ordering among the active transactions.

To enforce this rule, the control will not grant a request to a transaction if it previously granted a conflicting request to another, still active, transaction. In the example, T_1's request to read x is delayed until T_2 is no longer active. Keep in mind that, since transactions are sequential programs, delaying a request actually delays the entire transaction. The schedule produced in this case is

$$w_2(x)\ r_2(y)\ commit_2\ r_1(x)\ w_1(y)\ commit_1$$

where the subscript on an operation identifies the transaction that executes the operation.

Note that the rule precludes more than just dirty reads, as in Figure 23.10. Any request that conflicts with a previously granted request of a still active transaction must be delayed, so the schedule shown in Figure 23.11 is as much a problem from the point of view of the rule as that shown in Figure 23.10.

If the requests made by T_1 and T_2 do not conflict, they can be granted. Requests do not conflict if one of the following conditions is true:

1. The requests refer to different data items.
2. The requests are both read requests.

Figure 23.12 displays the conflict relation in tabular form.

We need to show that a concurrency control based on conflicts produces schedules that are both strict and serializable. The following theorem states that result:

Figure 23.12 Conflict table for an immediate-update pessimistic concurrency control. X denotes conflicts between lock modes.

	Granted Mode	
Requested Mode	read	write
read		X
write	X	X

> **Theorem (Commit Order Serialization):** Concurrency controls that do not grant a transaction's request if a conflicting request has already been granted to another still active transaction produce schedules that are strict and serializable in the order in which the transactions commit (called the **commit order**).

Clearly, all schedules produced by such a concurrency control are strict, since no transaction can read or write an item written by another, still active, transaction. The more difficult part is to demonstrate serializability in commit order. To do this, we must first deal with the fact that schedules can contain operations of transactions that have not completed (previously we have restricted our discussion to schedules produced by completed transactions). When we say that such a schedule is serializable, we mean that it is equivalent to a schedule in which the operations of committed transactions are not interleaved and occur before those of uncommitted transactions. Henceforth, our notion of a serial schedule includes such schedules.

An inductive argument demonstrates the result. The induction is on the number, i, of committed transactions in a schedule. Consider the base case, $i = 1$—that is, only one transaction, T_1, has committed and all others are active. Then the schedule looks as follows: *pre-commit commit$_1$ post-commit*, where *commit$_1$* is T_1's commit operation, *pre-commit* is the sequence of operations (of all transactions) that occur prior to that, and *post-commit* contains all operations that occur after. Neither *pre-commit* nor *post-commit* contain any commit operations. Since, prior to *commit$_1$*, all transactions are active, it follows from our assumptions about the concurrency control that no request in *pre-commit* conflicts with any other request in that part of the schedule. Hence, all operations in *pre-commit* commute. In particular, the operations of T_1 (which are all in *pre-commit*) can be transposed with the operations of other transactions to produce an equivalent serial schedule.

Assume now that all schedules that contain exactly i committed transactions are serializable in commit order. Consider a schedule, S, containing $i + 1$ committed transactions, and let T be the last transaction to commit. Let $S = S_1 \circ S_2$, where S_1 is the prefix of S up to (but not including) T's commit operation. Then S_1 contains i committed transactions and, from the induction hypothesis, is serializable in commit order. Let S_1^{ser} be the serial schedule equivalent to S_1. Thus, S is equivalent to the schedule $S_1^{ser} \circ S_2$. This schedule has the property that all operations of T follow the ith commit. Furthermore, all operations of T must commute with all operations of any uncommitted transactions in S, so the operations of T can be transposed in such a way that they follow those of all committed transactions and precede those of all uncommitted transactions. Once again, every pair so transposed commutes and thus the resulting schedule is serial and equivalent to S.

Because transactions that access only disjoint data items can be ordered arbitrarily, a serializable schedule can be equivalent to more than one serial schedule, but, as we have just shown, one of these serial orders is the commit order.

Although all that we have required is that a schedule be serializable in some order, the user might expect transactions to be executed in commit order. For example, transactions frequently have external actions visible to the user (a deposit

Figure 23.13 Schedule that exhibits deadlock.

$$T_1: \quad w(x) \qquad\qquad\qquad \text{request\_}r(y)$$
$$T_2: \qquad\qquad\quad w(y) \qquad\qquad\qquad\qquad\qquad\qquad \text{request\_}r(x)$$

transaction outputs a receipt), who expects the equivalent serial order to be consistent with these actions. Hence, if a user initiates T_2 after having observed the external actions of T_1, he expects an equivalent serial order in which T_2 executes after T_1 (a withdraw transaction initiated after a receipt has been issued by a deposit transaction should see the result of that deposit in the database). One way to ensure that the order implied by these external actions is the same as the equivalent serial order is to serialize in commit order. Concurrency controls generally serialize transactions in commit order.

23.4.2 Deadlocks

When a transaction makes a request that conflicts with an operation that has been executed by another active transaction, serializability requires that the request not be granted at that time. The requesting transaction might be made to wait until the conflict no longer exists (because the other transaction commits or aborts). However, this can lead to a deadlock, as shown in Figure 23.13. When T_1 requests to read y, it is made to wait (until T_2 commits or aborts). When T_2 later requests to read x, it is made to wait (until T_1 commits or aborts). If no action is taken, both transactions will wait forever—a highly undesirable situation.

More generally, a **deadlock** is said to exist when there is a cycle of transactions waiting for each other.

Concurrency controls that make transactions wait must have some mechanism for dealing with deadlocks. A common one is for the control to construct a data structure representing the *waits_for* relation: If (T_1, T_2) is an element of *waits_for*, then T_1 is waiting for T_2. *waits_for* can be constructed when a conflict is detected. If T_1's request conflicts with an operation previously granted to an active transaction, T_2, (T_1, T_2) is inserted in *waits_for*. Similarly, if T_2 is waiting for T_3, (T_2, T_3) is inserted in *waits_for* and the process continues with T_3 until it either cycles back on itself, and hence detects a deadlock, or terminates on a transaction that is not waiting. If allowing T_1 to wait causes a deadlock, the concurrency control aborts and then restarts one of the transactions in the cycle (often T_1). The abort is not visible to the user who initiated the aborted transaction.

A second mechanism for dealing with deadlock is **time out**. If the time a transaction waits to perform an operation exceeds some threshold, the control assumes that a deadlock has occurred. As a result, it aborts and restarts the transaction.

Finally, a timestamp technique [Rosenkrantz et al. 1978] can be employed to *prevent* (as contrasted with *detect*) deadlock. The concurrency control uses the current value of the clock as the timestamp of a transaction when it is initiated. Assuming that the clock advances more quickly than the rate at which transactions are initiated, each transaction's timestamp is guaranteed to be unique. If a conflict occurs, the concurrency control uses the timestamps of the two transactions involved to make a decision about waits or restarts. For example, it can adopt the policy that an older transaction never waits for a younger one (by aborting the younger one). If a transaction is restarted after an abort resulting from deadlock, it maintains its original timestamp. In this way, the control ensures that a transaction will ultimately complete since it eventually becomes the oldest active transaction.

23.5   DESIGN OF AN IMMEDIATE-UPDATE PESSIMISTIC CONCURRENCY CONTROL

The standard technique for implementing an immediate-update pessimistic concurrency control uses a technique called **locking**. When a transaction makes a request to perform a database operation on a particular item, the system attempts to obtain an appropriate lock on the item for the transaction. For a read operation, it attempts to obtain a **read lock**, and for a write operation, it attempts to obtain a **write lock**. The transaction cannot perform the operation until the lock has been granted. A write lock is stronger than a read lock, since, once a transaction holds a write lock on an item, it can both read and write the item.

On the basis of our previous discussion, we conclude that

■ The concurrency control grants a read lock on a particular item only if no other active transaction has a write lock on that item. Since it will grant a read lock on an item even though another transaction already has a read lock on that item, a read lock is often referred to as a **shared lock**.

■ The concurrency control will grant a write lock on a particular item only if no other active transaction has a read or a write lock on that item. Hence a write lock is often referred to as an **exclusive lock**.

23.5.1   An Implementation Using Lock Sets and Wait Sets

To implement locking, we assume that the concurrency control associates with each locked item, x, a data structure called a **lock set**, $L(x)$, describing the locks held on x by currently active transactions. Given the above rules, it follows that if $L(x)$ is not empty, it can contain either multiple entries describing read locks on x or a single entry describing a write lock on x.

Similarly, we associate with each locked item, x, a data structure called a **wait set**, $W(x)$, which has an entry for each database operation on x that has been requested but for which a lock has not yet been granted. Because of the large number of items generally stored in a database, it is inefficient to maintain lock and wait sets for those not being referenced. Hence, these sets are generally allocated dynamically for an item when it is first referenced, and the overhead of processing a lock request must include the time for managing storage and the space to store entries in the sets.

Finally we associate with each active transaction, T_i, a data structure called a **lock list**, $\mathcal{L}_i$, which is a list of all the entries the transaction has in lock and wait sets of different data items. Note that the lock list of T_i can have at most one item from a wait set, because once a transaction's request is placed in a wait set the transaction is suspended and it is not resumed until the entry in the wait set has been deleted.

A request by T_i to access x can be regarded as a call to a routine in the concurrency control that checks and grants locks. The routine manipulates $L(x)$, $W(x)$, and $\mathcal{L}_i$ by executing the following steps:

1. If T_i already holds a read lock on x, and the request is a read, grant the request. If T_i already holds a write lock on x, and the request is a read or write grant the request.

2. If T_i has not previously been granted an appropriate lock on x, search $L(x)$ and $W(x)$ for an entry that conflicts with the requested access. For example, if T_i requests to read x, a conflicting entry is a write lock held by T_j, $j \neq i$, or a request to write x that has been made by T_j and is pending in $W(x)$. If there are no conflicting entries, grant T_i's request by inserting an entry identifying T_i and the requested lock type in $L(x)$ and in $\mathcal{L}_i$, and resuming T_i. We say that T_i *locks x*.

   If there is a conflicting entry in $L(x)$, delay the request by inserting an entry identifying T_i and the requested lock type in $W(x)$ and in $\mathcal{L}_i$, and blocking T_i. Similarly, if there is a conflicting entry in $W(x)$, delay the request in the same way. T_i is generally made to wait in this latter case to avoid **starving** another transaction, T_j, that is waiting to access x. Starvation occurs if an entry in $W(x)$ is made to wait indefinitely by a sequence of subsequently arriving requests that are serviced first. For example, T_j might be waiting for a write lock while another transaction is holding a read lock. If T_i has made a read request, it can be serviced immediately since it does not conflict with the existing lock. However, if the scheduling algorithm allows T_j's request to be passed over in this way, a sequence of read requests can cause T_j to wait indefinitely. In that case T_j starves and we say that the algorithm is **not fair**. Hence, T_i is made to wait.

3. A deadlock might result if T_i is made to wait. This would be the case if T_j is (transitively) waiting for T_i. The latter can be detected using a *waits_for* relation described in Section 23.4.2. If a deadlock is detected, abort and restart T_i (or some other transaction in the cycle).

4. When T_i commits or aborts, use $\mathcal{L}_i$ to locate and remove all of T_i's entries in lock sets (since T_i is no longer active). If a lock is removed from $L(x)$ and $W(x)$ is not empty, T_i's lock on x conflicts with at least one waiting request and it may now be possible to grant that request (if T_i held a read lock, and read locks are also held by other transactions, it will not be possible to grant requests in $W(x)$). Several strategies can be used to **promote** elements of $W(x)$ to $L(x)$ at this point. For example, a fair strategy is one in which requests in $W(x)$ are examined in *FIFO* (first-in-first-out) order. If a request can be granted, move it to $L(x)$ and examine the next request in $W(x)$. If not, examine no further requests. Alternatively, if the first request in the list is a read, grant all reads in the list. If the first request is a write, grant only that request. This algorithm departs from servicing requests in a FIFO order, but it does not result in starvation. When the promotion process is complete, $\mathcal{L}_i$ is destroyed.

Figure 23.14   An example of a non-serializable schedule involving a transaction that is not two-phase.

$$T_1: \quad l(x) \quad r(x) \quad u(x) \qquad\qquad\qquad\qquad\qquad\qquad l(y) \quad r(y) \quad u(y)$$
$$T_2: \qquad\qquad\qquad\quad l(x) \quad l(y) \quad r(x) \quad w(x) \quad r(y) \quad w(y) \quad u(y) \quad u(x)$$

This concurrency control guarantees that all schedules it permits are serializable, since it grants only those requests that commute with requests previously granted to other active transactions.

The locking algorithm has the property that locks are obtained automatically. A transaction simply makes a request to access a data item, and, when the request is granted, the concurrency control automatically records that the transaction holds the appropriate lock. All locks are held until the transaction completes, at which point the control automatically unlocks all data items locked by the transaction. Since write locks are exclusive and held until termination, automatic locking guarantees strict schedules.

23.5.2 Two–Phase Locking

While the automatic approach to locking is common, some systems allow manual locking and unlocking. In this case, a transaction *explicitly* makes a request to the concurrency control to grant a lock before making a separate request to access the item. As before, an access request is granted only if the concurrency control determines that the requesting transaction currently holds an appropriate lock on the item.

Unlocking can also be manual—except that all locks held by a transaction are released automatically when the transaction terminates. Manual unlocking seems to permit additional flexibility, since, if a transaction releases locks prior to termination, concurrent transactions can access data items at an earlier time than that allowed by automatic unlocking. Unfortunately, however, to enforce strictness a transaction cannot release a write lock early (if it did, another transaction could acquire a lock on the item and access it while the first transaction was still active). Hence, early release applies only to read locks.

Furthermore, unless early release is done properly, it can lead to non-serializable schedules. For example, consider the schedule shown in Figure 23.14, where $l(x)$ is a request to lock x and $u(x)$ is a request to unlock it. T_1 reads x, unlocks it, and then reads y. Between the two accesses, T_2 makes conflicting accesses to both data items. The schedule is not serializable, since each transaction must follow the other in any serial order. This situation could not have happened if locks were handled automatically by the concurrency control, since locks are not released until commit time. We next show that this situation can be avoided in a manual system by requiring that a transaction never lock an item after unlocking any item.

A transaction is said to maintain a **two-phase locking** protocol [Eswaran et al. 1976] if it obtains all of its locks before performing any unlocks (it first goes through a locking phase, then an unlocking phase). The schedule of Figure 23.14 is not two-phase. Automatic locking is two-phase.

> **Theorem (Two-Phase Locking):** A concurrency control that uses a two-phase locking protocol produces only serializable schedules.

A proof of this theorem [Ullman 1982] uses the serialization graph theorem (Section 23.1.3) on page 771: A schedule is conflict serializable if and only if its serialization graph is acyclic. The proof is by contradiction. Assume that the serialization graph for a schedule produced by a two-phase locking concurrency control contains a cycle

$$T_1 \to T_2 \to \cdots \to T_n \to T_1$$

The edge $T_1 \to T_2$ implies that T_1 has an operation in the schedule that conflicts with and precedes an operation of T_2. Because the operations conflict, T_1 must have released a lock and T_2 acquired a lock between execution of the two operations. A similar situation must exist between T_2 and T_3, and the argument can be carried to the conclusion that T_1 released a lock before T_n acquired a lock. The edge $T_n \to T_1$ implies that T_n must have released a lock before T_1 acquired a lock. It therefore follows that T_1 acquired a lock after releasing a lock, in violation of the two-phase locking protocol. Hence, we have produced a contradiction, and we can conclude that the serialization graph for all schedules produced by a two-phase locking concurrency control must be acyclic and thus serializable.

When a two-phase locking protocol is used, one possible equivalent serial order is the order in which the transactions performed their first unlock operations. (You are asked to prove this result in Exercise 23.8.) Thus, if the schedule contains transactions T_1 and T_2 and if T_1's first unlock request occurs before T_2's first unlock request, T_1 precedes T_2 in one equivalent serial order. If the transactions hold all locks until commit time, the serialization is in commit order.

Two-phase concurrency controls that hold *all* locks until commit time (for example, automatic locking) are said to satisfy a **strict two-phase locking protocol**. *The definition of a strict two-phase locking protocol is more restrictive than the definition of a strict concurrency control, since the latter requires the control to hold write locks until commit time but allows read locks to be released early (but still in a two-phase manner).*

Because the equivalent serial order is determined at run time, two-phase locking is referred to as a **dynamic protocol**, in contrast to **static protocols**, in which the order is determined by the order in which transactions are initiated. The timestamp-ordered concurrency control discussed in Section 23.8.1 is an example of a static protocol.

23.5.3 Lock Granularity

We have deliberately referred to the entity being locked as a data item, without explaining what a data item is. We now define a data item to be any entity in the database that can be locked by a concurrency control algorithm—variable, record, row, table, file, and the like. All locking algorithms in this chapter assume that an item has a name that uniquely identifies it. (In Chapter 24, we will see that this is not always the case.) This name is used to reference the item whenever it is accessed. The lock and wait sets of an item are often located by hashing on its name.

The size of the entity locked determines the **granularity** of the lock. Locking granularity is **fine** if the entity is small and **coarse** otherwise. The coarser the granularity, the more conservative the locking algorithm. Thus, in a DBMS that only supports table locks, an entire table is locked when only one row is accessed. Clearly, serializability is unaffected by lock granularity: As long as the items accessed are locked, a two-phase locking concurrency control produces serializable schedules even if some items are locked unnecessarily. Fine granularity locks have the advantage of allowing more concurrency, since transactions need lock only the items they actually access. However, the overhead associated with fine granularity locking is greater. Transactions generally hold more locks, and therefore more space is required to retain information about these locks. Furthermore, more time is expended in requesting locks for each individual item. Coarse granularity locking solves these problems when transactions access multiple items in the same locked entity. For example, a transaction might access multiple rows in the same table. A single table lock makes this possible.

Many systems implement page locking as a compromise, locking the page in which the item is stored, not the item itself. The page address becomes the name of the entity that is locked. Page locking is conservative: not only is the item locked, but all other items stored on the same page are locked as well.

23.6   OBJECTS AND SEMANTIC COMMUTATIVITY*

The design of immediate-update pessimistic concurrency controls is based on the commutativity of database operations. In the simple systems we have been discussing, the only operations are read and write and the only operations on a particular data item that commute are two reads.

If we allow more complex database operations and guarantee that the execution of each complex operation is isolated from the execution of every other complex operation, we can use the semantics of those operations to determine which operations commute and then use that information in the design of the concurrency control. In this section, we discuss object databases (Chapter 16), in which the database operations are methods defined on the objects stored in the database.

As an example of an object database, consider a banking application in which an account object has operations deposit(x) and withdraw(x). We assume that the account balance cannot be negative, so withdraw(x) returns the value OK if there is at least x dollars in the account and the withdraw is successful; it returns NO if there is fewer than x dollars in the account and the withdraw is unsuccessful.

The implementation of both of these operations involves a read of the database (to get the account balance) and a write to the database (to store the new value of the balance). Since a concurrency control for a conventional (non-object database) processes each read and write request separately, it detects a conflict between the read and write operations of any pair of banking operations executed by different transactions on the same account. Suppose, however, that a concurrency control

Figure 23.15 Conflict table for the account object. X denotes conflicts between lock modes.

Granted Mode

Requested Mode	deposit()	withdraw()
deposit()		X
withdraw()	X	X

is prepared to accept requests for method invocations. It can then detect the fact that two deposit() operations on the same account commute—no matter in which order they are executed, they return the same information (nothing) and leave the database in the same final state (the account has been incremented by the values of both deposits). What is wrong with our analysis? Why is the commutativity apparent at the higher level and not at the lower level?

The answer is that, in deciding that two deposit operations commute, we used information drawn from the world of arithmetic: the *semantics* of deposit. Read and write, however, carry very little semantic information: We do not know how the information being read is used in the transaction's computation, and we do not know the relationship between the information read and the information written. Furthermore, since at the lower level the read and write of a deposit are separate operations, we cannot guarantee that operations of other transactions are not interleaved between the two.

The lesson to be drawn here is that more information about operation semantics is available at higher levels, and hence the concurrency control can recognize more commutativity. This allows it to conclude that a larger set of interleaved schedules is equivalent to serial schedules and that less reordering needs to be done. Because reordering involves delays, the use of operation semantics can result in more concurrency and improved performance.

While two deposit operations commute, deposit(y) and withdraw(x) on the same account conflict because withdraw() might return OK if executed after deposit() and NO if executed before (for example, if the balance was $x - y$ dollars before the operations started). Thus, we can construct the conflict table shown in Figure 23.15 and use that table as the basis of a concurrency control design. The rows and columns in the table correspond to the database operations, and for each such operation there is a corresponding lock that the control can grant. For example, when a transaction wants to invoke deposit() on some account, it requests a deposit lock on the account object. If no other transaction has a withdraw lock on that object, the request is granted; otherwise, the transaction is made to wait. Note that this control achieves more concurrency than one based on read and write operations, because the latter does not allow concurrent transactions to execute deposit operations on the same object whereas the control based on Figure 23.15 does.

We can gain even more concurrency if we incorporate two additional concepts into the concurrency control design.

Partial Operations and Backward Commutativity.   We can replace an operation that can have several possible outcomes depending on the initial database state by several operations. For example, we can replace withdraw(x) with

■ withdrawOK(x), which is executed when the balance in the account object is greater than or equal to x dollars

■ withdrawNO(x), which is executed when the balance is less than x dollars

We assume that, when a transaction submits a request to perform a withdraw operation, the concurrency control checks the balance in the account and determines whether to perform a withdrawOK() or a withdrawNO(). These new operations are said to be **partial operations** because each is defined only for a subset of initial states. (Operations that are defined for all states are said to be **total operations**.)

We can define a new type of commutativity, **backward commutativity**, for partial operations and base the concurrency control design on this new definition. Consider the sequence of operations

withdrawOK$_1$(x), deposit$_2$(y)

which is defined only in states for which the balance, z, is at least x dollars. In all such states, the sequence of operations

deposit$_2$(y), withdrawOK$_1$(x)

is also defined because, after the deposit operation, the balance is $z + y$, which is certainly larger than x (and hence withdrawOK(x) is defined). Furthermore, the final database state is the same for both sequences: The balance is $z - x + y$. We say that deposit() backward-commutes through withdrawOK().

More precisely, an operation, p, **backward-commutes** through an operation, q [Weihl 1988], if, in all database states in which the sequence q, p is defined, the sequence p, q is also defined and in both sequences q and p return the same values and the final state of the database is the same.[3] If p does not backward-commute through q, it is said to **conflict** with q. This definition differs from the definition of commutativity for total operations given in Section 23.1. In that definition, two operations commute if they perform equivalent actions when executed in either order starting from *any initial database state*. By contrast, an operation, p, backward-commutes through an operation, q, if they perform equivalent actions when executed in either order starting from *any initial database state in which the sequence q, p is defined*. Thus, the new definition uses the definition of the partial operations.

Note that backward commutativity is not a symmetric relation. For certain operations p and q, p might backward-commute through q but q might not backward-commute through p. For example, we have seen that deposit() backward-commutes through withdrawOK(), but note that withdrawOK() does not

---

[3] A related concept, *forward commutativity*, has also been defined; see exercise 23.19.

backward commute through deposit() because there might be states in which the sequence

$$\text{deposit}_2(y), \quad \text{withdrawOK}_1(x)$$

is defined, but the sequence

$$\text{withdrawOK}_1(x), \quad \text{deposit}_2(y)$$

is not. Some pairs of operations, however, do backward-commute through each other (e.g., two occurrences of withdrawOK()).

A concurrency control design can use the notion of backward commutativity on partial operations in the same way it uses standard commutativity on total operations. For example, if a transaction has a withdrawOK() lock on an account object and another transaction requests a deposit() lock on that object, that request can be granted because deposit() backward-commutes through withdrawOK().

More generally, if a transaction, T_1, has a q lock on an object and another transaction, T_2, requests a p lock on that same object, and if p backward-commutes through q, that request can be granted. Note that, since T_2's operation backward-commutes through T_1's operation, the two operations might have been performed in the opposite order and thus the control has not determined an ordering between T_1 and T_2.

On the basis of these ideas, we can expand the conflict table of Figure 23.15 into the conflict table of Figure 23.16. A space at the intersection of a row and column means that the operation corresponding to the row backward-commutes through the operation corresponding to the column. An X means that the operation corresponding to the row *does not* backward-commute through the operation corresponding to the column.

The small number of conflicts in the table indicates the additional concurrency that will be allowed by a concurrency control that uses that table. However, obtaining this concurrency involves additional run-time overhead. When a withdraw is invoked, the concurrency control must access the database to determine the value of the account balance so that it knows whether to request a withdrawOK() or a withdrawNO() lock. This additional overhead does not occur when the control is based

Figure 23.16 Conflict table for an account object using partial operations and backward commutativity. X indicates that the operation corresponding to the row *does not* backward commute through the operation corresponding to the column.

	Granted Mode		
Requested Mode	deposit()	withdrawOK()	withdrawNO()
deposit()			X
withdrawOK()	X		
withdrawNO()		X	

on the table of Figure 23.15, which involves total, rather than partial, operations, since total operations commute in all states.

23.6.1 Atomicity, Recoverability, and Compensating Operations

In a system in which the database is accessed using only read and write operations, only the write operation modifies the database state. Since a write to a data item, x, conflicts with all other operations on x, once a transaction, T, writes x, no other transaction can access x until T completes (assuming a strict two-phase concurrency control). Hence, if T aborts, it is only necessary to restore x to the value it had before T's write. We have referred to this as physical restoration.

Abort is more complicated in systems that support abstract operations, since two such operations that modify the same data item (such as two deposit operations) might not conflict. Suppose that T_1 modifies x using operation p, then T_2 modifies x using a nonconflicting operation, q, and then T_1 aborts. We cannot simply restore x to the value it had prior to the execution of p, since then the effects of both p and q will be lost. We discussed this issue in connection with multilevel transactions in Section 21.2.4 and concluded that compensation was the appropriate way to undo the effects of an aborted transaction. For every operation, p, there must be a compensating operation, p^{-1}, such that, in all database states in which p is defined, the sequence p, p^{-1} is also defined and the execution of that sequence leaves the database state unchanged. Thus, for example, deposit(x) compensates for withdrawOK(x).

One seeming complication arises if transactions T_1 and T_2 both access the same abstract item, x, using operations p and q, respectively, and then T_1 aborts. Suppose that the operations occurred in the order p, q. The compensating operation for p is p^{-1}, and hence compensation results in the schedule p, q, p^{-1}. How can we be sure that executing p^{-1} after q has modified x will correctly undo the effect of p? How can we even be sure that p^{-1} is defined in the database state that exists after q executes? Fortunately, our concurrency control schedules q only if it backward-commutes through p, and therefore this schedule is equivalent to the schedule q, p, p^{-1}. Since p^{-1} is defined in this schedule, it must be defined in the original one as well. This schedule is equivalent to just q, and so compensation works correctly.

What we have demonstrated in this simple example is recoverability (Section 23.2)—compensation worked correctly and produced atomicity. More generally, consider a transaction, T, with transaction schedule

$$p_1, p_2, \ldots, p_n \tag{23.1}$$

If T aborts after executing some operation, p_i, it is necessary to execute compensating operations for $p_1, p_2, \ldots, p_i$ in reverse order to undo the effects of T up to that point. The transaction schedule in that case is

$$p_1, p_2, \ldots, p_i, p_i^{-1}, p_{i-1}^{-1}, \ldots, p_1^{-1} \tag{23.2}$$

Thus, there are n possible "abort" schedules for T, one for each value of i (depending on when T aborts).

All of these schedules have no net effect on the database. When we execute T, we cannot predict which of its $n + 1$ transaction schedules, (23.1) or (23.2), will occur. Whereas previously an abort operation in a schedule denoted a complex action involving physically undoing all prior changes a transaction had made to the database, (23.2) explicitly describes what the abort operation does, and we no longer need to specify an abort operation in the schedule. The transaction is aborted when this schedule commits. We refer to this as **logical rollback**.

A schedule is recoverable if each aborted transaction has no net effect on the database or on concurrently executing transactions. More precisely, a schedule S is recoverable if, for each aborted transaction T in S, S is equivalent to a schedule in which all operations of T have been deleted.

Consider a concurrency control that deals with compensating operations in the following way:

1. It grants compensating operations without checking for conflicts.[4]
2. It grants forward operations only if they backward-commute through all forward operations that have been granted to active transactions (without considering possible conflicts with previously granted compensating operations of active transactions).

We must now demonstrate that this design works correctly, in the sense that any schedule produced by the control is recoverable and that, after the recovery has taken place, the resulting schedule of transactions that have not aborted is serializable.

Let us take an arbitrary schedule, S, that might have been produced by such a concurrency control and that involves both committed and aborted transactions (and thus contains both forward and compensating operations). Consider the first transaction to abort in S, and let p_i^{-1} be the first compensating operation that that transaction executes. Thus, p_i^{-1} is the first compensating operation in S, and S has the form

$$S_{prefix}, p_i, S', p_i^{-1}, S_{suffix}$$

where S' is the sequence of operations that separates p_i from p_i^{-1}. (Note that S' contains only forward operations, because p_i^{-1} is the first compensating operation in S.) Since the concurrency control would not have scheduled an operation in S' unless that operation backward commutes through p_i, this schedule is equivalent to the schedule

$$S_{prefix}, S', p_i, p_i^{-1}, S_{suffix}$$

which in turn is equivalent to the schedule

$$S_{prefix}, S', S_{suffix}$$

---

[4] If the control were to delay a compensating operation because of some conflict, a deadlock might result such that the abort could not be completed. This is unacceptable.

The transformation has in effect caused p_i and p_i^{-1} to annihilate each other and has thus reduced S to an equivalent schedule that is shorter.

The transformation can now be repeated to eliminate the second compensating operation in S and its matching forward operation. In this manner, all operations of aborted transactions (both forward and compensating) can be eliminated from S, finally producing an equivalent schedule of the transactions that have not aborted. Therefore, S is recoverable. Furthermore, the resulting schedule is conflict equivalent to a serial schedule. The fact that this type of transformation is always possible demonstrates the correctness of the concurrency control.

A schedule that can be reduced by such a transformation to a serializable schedule of transactions that have not aborted is said to be **reducible**. The concurrent execution of transactions $T_1, T_2, \ldots, T_n$ is recoverable if every schedule, in which each transaction, T_j, is represented by one of its transaction schedules, is reducible. All of the schedules produced by the concurrency control described in this section are reducible and hence recoverable.[5]

23.7   ISOLATION IN STRUCTURED TRANSACTION MODELS

In Chapter 21, we introduced a number of transaction models. Having discussed serializability and locking, we can now show how to implement isolation within these models. We will devote all of Chapter 26 to showing how distributed transactions are implemented, so we do not discuss them here.

23.7.1 Savepoints

A savepoint (Section 21.2.1) is a mechanism used within a transaction, T, to achieve partial rollback such that it appears as if the database updates made by the portion of the transaction rolled back never happened. After the rollback completes, the items that have been restored can be unlocked and immediately made available to concurrent transactions. Thus we have the following rules for handling savepoints in concurrency controls based on locks.

1. When a savepoint, s, is created, no change is made to any lock set. However, the concurrency control system must remember the identity of all locks that T_i acquired prior to creating s, so that, if T_i rolls back to s, it can release locks obtained subsequent to the creation. To accomplish this, the control places a marker in the lock list, $\mathcal{L}_i$, containing a number that represents the Id of the savepoint. Lock entries that follow this marker correspond to locks obtained after the creation of s.

2. When the transaction rolls back to s, the locks corresponding to all lock entries following the marker for s in $\mathcal{L}_i$ are released.

It would be a happy result if the above rules preserved isolation in a two-phase locking concurrency control, but this is sadly not the case. A transaction might read

---

[5] A more complete discussion of this subject can be found in [Schek et al. 1993].

a data item, x, after creating a savepoint and then roll back, releasing the read lock. The effect is an early release of a read lock, which allows a non-two-phase schedule to be easily created. To preserve isolation, the second rule should be modified so that write locks are downgraded to read locks and read locks are not released.

23.7.2 Chained Transactions

Chaining can be used to decompose a transaction, T, into smaller subtransactions to avoid total rollback if a crash occurs. In Chapter 21, we discussed two different semantics for how chained transactions deal with the state of database items accessed by the transaction when control moves from one subtransaction in the chain to the next. Using `commit`, the state is not maintained between subtransactions, and, although the individual subtransactions are isolated and serializable, T as a whole is not. Using `chain`, the state is maintained between one subtransaction and the next, and T is isolated and serializable with respect to other transactions.

The `commit` operation is handled in the normal way: All locks are released. For the `chain` operation, locks are not released but are instead passed to the subsequent subtransaction in the chain. Durability is provided in both cases (as described in Chapter 25).

23.7.3 Recoverable Queues

A recoverable queue can be implemented within the database itself (since the database is durable), but performance will suffer thereby. The queue is a hotspot, accessed by many transactions and, since the concurrency control is strict, locks on the queue would be held until commit time, creating bottlenecks.

For this reason, a recoverable queue is implemented as a distinct module. In one possible implementation, a separate lock is associated with each element on the queue and with the queue's head and tail pointers. A transaction wishing to enqueue or dequeue an element must first obtain a write lock on the tail or head pointer, respectively. A pointer is locked only for the duration of the enqueue or dequeue operation, whereas a lock on an element that is enqueued or dequeued is held until commit time. Thus, for example, a transaction, T, might dequeue an element from the queue and release the lock on the head pointer. Another transaction might then dequeue the next element before T commits or aborts.

Note that, since the queue is implemented as a module separate from the database, the requirements of strictness and two-phase locking can be eliminated: the concurrency control is clearly not strict in the way it manipulates the lock on the pointer, and it need not be two-phase. The queue is essentially being treated as an object with known semantics. Using the fact that the queue is used for scheduling work, operations on it are declared to commute—although this is actually not the case (e.g., if the order of dequeue operations is reversed, different information is returned to the callers). As a result, concurrency is enhanced at the expense of isolation. Concurrent transactions might enqueue and dequeue elements on a set of queues in a variety of orders that would not be possible if serializable execution were enforced.

In contrast to its lock on the head or tail pointer, T always retains a write lock on the element it is accessing until it commits. This guarantees, for example, that after T enqueues an element, no other transaction, T', can dequeue that element until after T commits.

23.7.4 Nested Transactions

Nested transactions support concurrent execution of subtransactions. That is, several subtransactions of a top-level transaction can be executing concurrently and can request conflicting database operations. Hence, in addition to the rules governing the granting of locks to concurrent transactions, we must introduce some new rules governing how locks are granted to the subtransactions of a single (nested) transaction.

The nested transaction model discussed in Chapter 21 adheres to the following rules:

1. Each nested transaction in its entirety must be isolated and hence serializable with respect to other nested transactions.

2. A parent subtransaction does not execute concurrently with its children.

3. Each child subtransaction (together with all of its descendents) must be isolated and hence serializable with respect to each sibling (together with all of its descendents).

To implement this semantics, we impose the following rules [Beeri et al. 1989]:

1. When a subtransaction of nested transaction, T, requests to read a data item, a read lock is granted if no other nested transaction holds a write lock on that item and all subtransactions of T holding a write lock on that item are its ancestors (and hence are not executing).

2. When a subtransaction of a nested transaction, T, requests to write a data item, a write lock is granted if no other nested transaction holds a read or write lock on that item and all subtransactions of T holding a read lock or a write lock on that item are its ancestors (and hence are not executing).

3. All locks obtained by a subtransaction are held until it aborts or commits. When a subtransaction commits, any locks it obtained that its parent does not hold are inherited by the parent. When a subtransaction aborts, any locks it obtained that its parent does not hold are released.

Since these rules are a superset of the rules that guarantee isolation among concurrent transactions, the schedules of concurrent nested transactions are serializable. To see that these rules enforce the desired semantics among siblings, observe that no lock held within the subtree rooted at one active sibling can conflict with a lock held within the subtree rooted at another active sibling. Thus, concurrently active siblings are not ordered by the database operations that have been performed within their subtrees. Therefore the siblings are isolated with respect to each other and hence serializable with each other in the order in which they commit.

23.7.5 Multilevel Transactions*

A concurrency control for multilevel transactions can be implemented by two rather elegant generalizations of the conventional, strict two-phase locking concurrency control described in Section 23.4 and 23.5 [Weikum 1991]. The first generalization makes use of the semantics of the operations at each level; the second relies on the fact that multiple levels are involved.

Operation Semantics and Commutativity.　In Section 23.6, we discussed how the commutativity of operations on objects can be used in the design of conflict tables for immediate-update pessimistic concurrency controls. These ideas form a central part of the multilevel model.

Each level in a system that supports multilevel transactions produces its own (interleaved) schedule. Thus, for example, in Figure 21.3, page 695, the schedule at level L_2 of the transaction $Move(sec_1,\ sec_2)$ is the sequence $TestInc(sec_2),\ Dec(sec_1)$. (A reminder: $Move$ moves a student from one course section to another; $TestInc$ conditionally adds one student to a section; and Dec decrements the enrollment in a section.) A more interesting schedule is one that involves the concurrent execution of several multilevel transactions. For example, the L_2 schedule

$$TestInc_1(sec_2),\ TestInc_2(sec_2),\ Dec_2(sec_1),\ Dec_1(sec_1) \tag{23.3}$$

involves the interleaved execution of two transactions, $Move_1(sec_1,\ sec_2)$ and $Move_2(sec_1,\ sec_2)$, each of which moves a student from section 1 to section 2. The interesting aspect of this schedule is that, since the two decrement operations commute, the schedule in (23.3) is equivalent to the schedule

$$TestInc_1(sec_2),\ Dec_1(sec_1),\ TestInc_2(sec_2),\ Dec_2(sec_1) \tag{23.4}$$

and is thus serializable in the order $Move_1,\ Move_2$. Note that, since two $TestInc$ operations on the same tuple do not commute, the schedule is not serializable in the order $Move_2,\ Move_1$ (the initial state might be such that the first to execute succeeds in the increment while the second fails; thus, different results are returned to the caller if the order is reversed).

Suppose now that we examine the schedule (23.3) in terms of the operations that execute at L_1. We see the following:

$$Sel_1(t_2),\ Upd_1(t_2),\ Sel_2(t_2),\ Upd_2(t_2),\ Upd_2(t_1),\ Upd_1(t_1) \tag{23.5}$$

As with the banking application discussed in Section 23.6, since update operations on the same tuple do not, *in general*, commute, this schedule is not serializable in either order. Once again, the more semantics available to the concurrency control, the more concurrency it can detect.

A concurrency control for L_2.　To take advantage of semantics, we can construct a concurrency control for L_2 that uses a conflict table, C_2, in which the row and column operations are those supported at that level. For example, a $Move$ transaction is a program at the *application* level, L_3, containing invocations of $TestInc$ and Dec, which are supported at L_2. The concurrency control at L_2 receives these invocations and

Figure 23.17 Conflict table for an L_2 concurrency control that schedules *TestInc* and *Dec* operations.

	Granted Mode	
Requested Mode	TestInc	Dec
TestInc	X	X
Dec	X	

decides whether they can be serviced using the conflict table C_2, which is shown in Figure 23.17. It issues *TestInc* and *Dec* locks for this purpose. Thus, if *Move* invokes $Dec(sec_2)$, the concurrency control grants a *Dec* lock on sec_2 if no other transaction has a *TestInc* lock on it; otherwise, the *Dec* request must wait. Once the lock has been granted, a program at L_2 can be executed that implements the *Dec* operation by invoking operations at L_1.

Now let us go back to the original example. Although the schedule of (23.3) is serializable in the order $Move_1$, $Move_2$, the two *TestInc* operations do not commute and so impose an ordering on the two transactions. Since the conventional, pessimistic concurrency control described in Section 23.4 does not grant a request if it imposes an ordering among active transactions, the L_2 scheduler does not produce schedule (23.4): As with the conventional concurrency control, not all conflict-serializable schedules can be recognized. However, consider the following interleaved schedule of transactions $Move_1(sec_1, \ sec_2)$ and $Move_2(sec_1, \ sec_3)$

$$TestInc_1(sec_2), \ TestInc_2(sec_3), \ Dec_2(sec_1), \ Dec_1(sec_1) \qquad (23.6)$$

This interleaving is allowed by the L_2 concurrency control, since two decrement operations commute. To see that additional concurrency is gained, realize that we have not indicated when the transactions request to commit. Instead of committing immediately after completing the decrement operation, $Move_2$ might continue to be active for an extended period of time. By recognizing the commutativity of decrement operations, the L_2 concurrency control can avoid delaying Dec_1 until $Move_2$ releases its locks.

Multilevel Concurrency Controls.   It now appears that the strategy for obtaining the best performance is to implement a concurrency control at the highest level, L_n, in the hierarchy (L_2 in Figure 21.3) in order to take advantage of the most semantics. But we have overlooked one important point. In the discussion in Section 23.4 of a conventional, pessimistic concurrency control, we implicitly assumed that the read and write operations scheduled by the concurrency control were totally ordered. Thus, if the control scheduled a write operation after a read operation, it assumed that the read had completed before the write started. With a multilevel concurrency control, this is true when operations conflict but not necessarily true when they do not. Thus, if a transaction, T, executes $TestInc(sec_1)$ and a second transaction requests the same operation, it will be made to wait until T completes because two

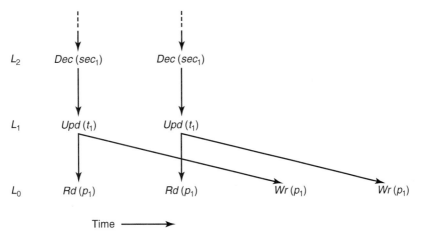

Figure 23.18 Decrement operations do not conflict at L_2, but arbitrary interleaving
at lower levels can lead to problems.

TestInc operations on the same section conflict. Hence, the two operations will be
totally ordered.

However, consider two operations that do not conflict and hence their concurrent execution is permitted by the concurrency control. In Figure 23.18, the L_2
concurrency control has scheduled the concurrent execution of two decrement operations invoked from the application level—the actual transaction program that
runs on top of L_2. (The transaction might invoke other operations as well, but we
do not consider them here.) The decrement operation is implemented by a program (subtransaction) in L_2, and that program invokes operations supported by
L_1. In this case, each instance of the decrement program makes only a single such
invocation—of *Upd*. Each invocation of the *Upd* program in L_1 invokes read and
write operations implemented in L_0.

As shown in the figure, each of the update statements reads the same value of the
enrollment number stored in tuple t_1, decrements that value, and therefore stores
the same value back in t_1. Thus, although two decrement operations have been
performed, the enrollment has only been decremented by one. This is an example
of the lost update problem introduced in Section 2.3. The reason for the lost update
here is that the two *Upd* operations are not isolated with respect to each other.

To avoid this problem, multilevel transactions use a multilevel concurrency
control, which guarantees that the operations *at each level* are serializable and hence
totally ordered. A **multilevel concurrency control** consists of a control at each
level. Thus, the control at L_i schedules the operation invocations it receives from
subtransactions at L_{i+1} in accordance with a conflict table, C_i, which determines
whether or not those operations can be executed concurrently. The control grants
operation locks as described previously and releases them when the subtransaction
at L_{i+1} commits. Figure 23.19 shows this organization.

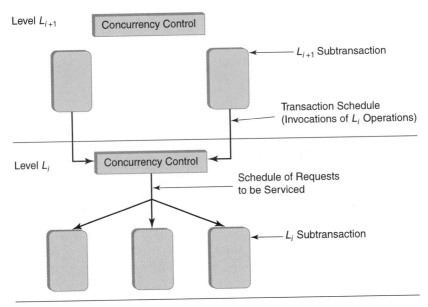

Level L_{i+1}

Concurrency Control

L_{i+1} Subtransaction

Transaction Schedule
(Invocations of L_i Operations)

Level L_i Concurrency Control

Schedule of Requests
to be Serviced

L_i Subtransaction

Figure 23.19 Relationship between levels in a multilevel concurrency control.

A goal of a multilevel concurrency control is to guarantee that operations in-voked by a program at any level are effectively isolated from each other. In other words, an operation invoked by a transaction at the application level is imple-mented by a program—think of it as a subtransaction—in L_n. That subtransaction then invokes a sequence of operations, each of which is implemented by a pro-gram in L_{n-1}. If the L_n concurrency control determines that op_1 and op_2, invoked by two application transactions, can be executed concurrently, then the transaction schedules produced by the subprograms at L_n that implement the operations will be interleaved at L_{n-1}. To guarantee that op_1 and op_2 are effectively isolated, the in-terleaved schedule at L_{n-1} produced by those subtransactions must be serializable, that is, equivalent to a serial schedule of the individual sequences. Note that the equivalent serial order is not important, since op_1 and op_2 commute and therefore both orders produce the same result. The L_n concurrency control requires only that the schedule at L_{n-1} be equivalent to *some* serial schedule.

To make such a guarantee, we need a concurrency control at level L_{n-1} that guarantees that schedules at that level are serializable. The argument now repeats. The L_{n-1} control assumes that the operations it schedules are isolated units when in fact they are not: They are subtransactions at L_{n-2}. Hence, a concurrency control at L_{n-2} is needed to guarantee that these subtransactions are serializable.

Let us follow this reasoning, using Figure 23.18 as an example, and see why the L_0 schedule in that figure cannot be produced by a multilevel concurrency control. Two transactions at the application level (not shown in the figure) concurrently in-voke $Dec(sec_1)$. The L_2 control sees that the two operations commute, so it grants Dec

locks on sec_1 to both transactions, allowing two invocations of the L_2 subtransaction that implements *Dec* to run concurrently. Each subtransaction at L_2 is a program that invokes $Upd(t_1)$. Those invocations are passed to the L_1 control. The first L_2 subtransaction is granted an *Upd* lock on t_1, but the second must wait since *Upd* locks conflict. Thus, only a single invocation of the update subtransaction at L_1 is initiated. It invokes read and write operations on p_1. These are passed to the L_0 control, which grants the locks on p_1 to the update subtransaction and schedules the operations. When the update subtransaction commits, it releases the page locks and returns to the *Dec* subtransaction that invoked it. When *Dec* commits, it releases the *Upd* lock, hence allowing the second invocation of the update subtransaction to commence, and returns to the application transaction that invoked it. In this way, contrary to Figure 23.18, the schedule at L_0 is serializable.

Using the same reasoning as in Section 23.6, we can show that all schedules produced by this concurrency control are recoverable (i.e., compensating operations work correctly and guarantee atomicity when transactions abort).

23.8 OTHER CONCURRENCY CONTROLS

Locking forms the basis of most, but not all, of the concurrency control algorithms in commercial systems. We discuss two nonlocking algorithms in this section: timestamp-ordered concurrency controls and optimistic concurrency controls. The timestamp-ordered algorithm, one of the earlier to be proposed, illustrates the use of timestamps to achieve synchronization. Optimistic concurrency controls are a more recent development and show promise in certain applications. In Chapter 24, we will discuss still another algorithm, multiversion concurrency control, which has been implemented in commercial relational database systems.

23.8.1 Timestamp–Ordered Concurrency Controls

In a **timestamp-ordered concurrency control**, a unique timestamp, $TS(T)$, is assigned to a transaction, T, when it is initiated and the concurrency control guarantees the existence of an equivalent serial schedule in which transactions are ordered by their timestamps. For this reason, timestamp-ordered controls are **static**; that is, the equivalent serial order is determined at the time they are initiated. Transactions are serialized in their initiation order, not necessarily their commit order. Unique timestamps can be generated using a clock. The value of the clock at the time the transaction is initiated is taken as the timestamp. As long as the clock ticks faster than the rate at which transactions are initiated each transaction will get a unique timestamp.[6] We describe an immediate-update version of a timestamp-ordered control; a deferred-update version is also possible.

---

[6] In a network, in which each site generates its own timestamps using its own local clock, uniqueness is not guaranteed by this algorithm. To guarantee uniqueness, the algorithm is modified by assigning to each site a unique identifier. Each site appends its identifier to the value of its clock to form a timestamp. Thus, a timestamp at site i is (c_i, id_i), where c_i is the current value of the clock and id_i is i's unique identifier.

A timestamp-ordered control stores with each data item, x, the following pieces of information:

■ $rt(x)$, the largest timestamp of any transaction that has read x

■ $wt(x)$, the largest timestamp of any transaction that has written to x

■ $f(x)$, a flag that indicates whether the transaction that last wrote x has committed

The maintenance of this information implies additional overhead and hence is a disadvantage of this scheme. Additional space is required for each separately addressable item in the database. Furthermore, since this information is stored in the database, updates to it must be treated like updates to the data items themselves—they must be recorded on disk and they must be rolled back if the transaction aborts. This means that, in contrast to other controls, a read of a data item x causes a write of $rt(x)$. As a result, timestamp-ordered algorithms have not been widely used.

When a transaction, T_1, makes a request to read x, the concurrency control performs the following actions:

R1. If $TS(T_1) < wt(x)$, some transaction, T_2, which must follow T_1 in the equivalent serial (timestamp) order, $(TS(T_2) > TS(T_1))$, has written a new value to x. T_1's read should return a value that x had prior to the write executed by T_2, but that value no longer exists in the database. Thus, T_1 is too old (has too small a timestamp) to read x. It is aborted and restarted (with a new timestamp).

R2. If $TS(T_1) > wt(x)$, there are two cases

❑ If $f(x)$ indicates that the value of x is committed, the request is granted. If $TS(T_1) > rt(x)$, the value of $TS(T_1)$ is assigned to $rt(x)$.

❑ If $f(x)$ indicates that the value of x is not committed, T_1 must wait (to avoid a dirty read).

When T_1 makes a request to write x, the concurrency control performs the following actions:

W1. If $TS(T_1) < rt(x)$, some transaction, T_2, which must follow T_1 in the equivalent serial (timestamp) order, has read an earlier value of x. If T_1 is allowed to commit, T_2 should have read the value that T_1 is requesting to write. Thus, T_1 is too old to write x. It is aborted and restarted (with a new timestamp).

W2. If $rt(x) < TS(T_1) < wt(x)$, a transaction has stored a new value in x that, in a serial schedule ordered on timestamps, overwrites the value that T_1 is requesting to write (since $TS(T_1) < wt(x)$). Furthermore, no transaction with a timestamp between $TS(T_1)$ and $wt(x)$ previously requested to read x (since $rt(x) < TS(T_1)$).

❑ If $f(x)$ indicates that x is committed, any subsequent transaction with a timestamp between $TS(T_1)$ and $wt(x)$ that attempts to read x will be aborted (see R1). Hence, the value that T_1 is requesting to write will not be read by any transaction and will have no effect on the final database state. The request is thus granted, but the write is not actually performed. This action (not per-

Figure 23.20 Sequence of requests accepted by a timestamp-ordered concurrency control. Assuming that $TS(T_1) < TS(T_2)$ and that the initial values of the read and write timestamps of x and y are smaller than both transactions' timestamps, T_1's final write is not performed.

$$
\begin{array}{llllll}
T_1: & r(y) & & & & w(x)\ commit \\
T_2: & & w(y) & w(x)\ commit & \\
& t_0 \quad t_1 & t_2 & t_3 & t_4
\end{array}
$$

forming the write in this situation) is called the Thomas Write Rule [Thomas 1979].

❏ If $f(x)$ indicates that x is not a committed value, T_1 must wait (since the transaction that last wrote x might abort and the value that T_1 is requesting to write becomes the current value).

W3. If $wt(x), rt(x) < TS(T_1)$, there are two cases.

❏ If $f(x)$ indicates that the value of x is not a committed value, T_1 is made to wait since granting the request will complicate rollback (see the discussion in Section 23.2).

❏ If $f(x)$ indicates that the value of x has been committed, the request is granted. The value of $TS(T_1)$ is assigned to $wt(x)$, and the value of $f(x)$ is set to uncommitted. (Later, when T_1 commits, the value of $f(x)$ is set to committed.)

The sequence of requests shown in Figure 23.20 illustrates these rules. Assume that $TS(T_1) < TS(T_2)$, that at time t_0 the read and write timestamps of both x and y are less than $TS(T_1)$, and that both x and y have committed values. Then, at time t_1, rule R2 applies, the read request is granted, and $rt(y)$ is set to $TS(T_1)$. At t_2, using W3, the write request is granted, $wt(y)$ is set to $TS(T_2)$, and $f(y)$ is set to indicate that y is uncommitted. At t_3, W3 again applies, the write request is granted, $wt(x)$ is set to $TS(T_2)$, and, since T_2 immediately commits, both $f(x)$ and $f(y)$ indicate committed values. At t_4, W2 applies since $rt(x)$ has not changed and $wt(x)$ is now $TS(T_2)$. The request is granted, although the write is not actually performed and $wt(x)$ is not updated.

The sequence is thus accepted by a timestamp-ordered control, but we do not refer to it as a schedule since the control does not submit the final write to the database. Note that the sequence is not conflict equivalent to a serial schedule and would not be accepted by a concurrency control based on conflict equivalence. This means that a timestamp-ordered control can accept sequences of requests that are not accepted by a control based on two-phase locking. Exercise 23.38 asks you to provide a schedule accepted by a two-phase locking concurrency control but not a timestamp-ordered control. It follows then that the two controls are incomparable: Each can accept schedules that will not be accepted by the other.

23.8.2 Optimistic Concurrency Controls

In general, an optimistic algorithm consists of several steps. In the first, a task is executed under some (optimistic) assumption that simplifies the performance of the task. For example, in a concurrency control the task is a transaction and the assumption is made that conflicts with concurrent transactions will not occur. Hence we need not be concerned with locking or waiting. Transactions read and write without requesting permission from the concurrency control and, thus, in contrast to lock-based (pessimistic) algorithms, are never delayed. The second step validates the first step by checking to see if the assumption was actually true. If not, the task must be redone, which implies rollback in the concurrency control case. If the assumption is true, validation results in commitment.

This approach stands in contrast to the pessimistic approach, in which execution of the task is done cautiously. No simplifying assumptions are made in the first step, each request for database access is checked in advance, and appropriate actions are taken immediately if conflicts are detected. Hence, no second (validation) step is required in the pessimistic approach.

Since database accesses during the first step are unchecked and conflicts might actually occur, optimistic concurrency controls [Kung and Robinson 1981] generally use a deferred-update approach to avoid propagating the effects of an incorrectly executed transaction to the database. (If an immediate update approach were used, the updates performed by transactions that later roll back would be visible to concurrent transactions and would result in a cascaded abort). The new values of the items written are stored in an intentions list and are not used to update the database immediately. Thus, a third step is needed for a transaction that modifies the database and is successfully validated: Its intentions list is written to the database.

Since rollback is costly, an optimistic algorithm is appropriate only if the optimistic assumption is valid. Note that rollback is more costly with an optimistic algorithm than with a timestamp-ordered algorithm, since the rollback decision is made after the transaction completes. With a timestamp-ordered control a rollback decision is made while the transaction is still executing, which wastes less of the system resources. Rollback can also occur in a pessimistic algorithm, because of deadlock. An important advantage of optimistic algorithms is that deadlocks cannot occur since one transaction never waits for another. In comparing the efficiency of optimistic and pessimistic algorithms, the cost of validation and of managing the intentions list must be weighed against the cost of locking.

Because the database is not modified during the first step (writes may be requested, but are not actually executed), this step is referred to as the **read phase**. The second step is referred to as the **validation phase**, and the third step as the **write phase**. Thus, a transaction's writes are performed (and appear in a schedule) during its write phase. For simplicity, we initially assume that the validation and write phases form a single critical section and hence only one transaction is in its validation or write phase at a time. However, we will modify that assumption shortly. The three phases of a transaction are shown in Figure 23.21(a).

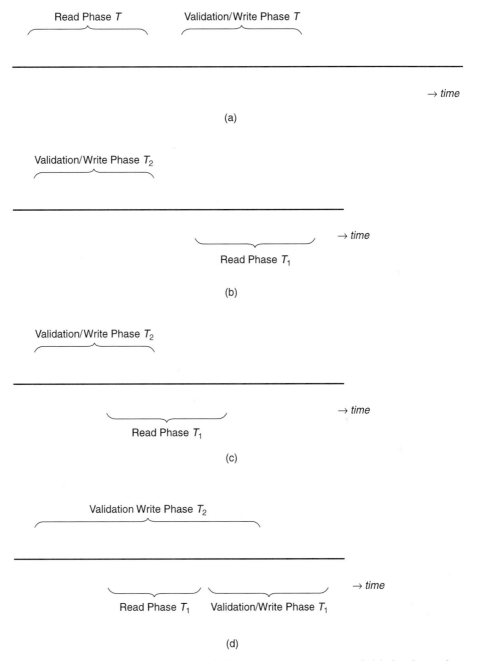

Figure 23.21 Transactions in an optimistic concurrency control: (a) the three phases of a transaction, (b) non-concurrent transactions, (c) T_1 conflicts with T_2 if the set of items read by T_1 overlaps the set of items written by T_2, (d) T_1 conflicts with T_2 if the set of items read or written by T_1 overlaps the set of items written by T_2.

The validation phase ensures that any schedule, S, produced by an optimistic concurrency control is equivalent to a schedule, S^{ser}, in which committed transactions are executed in commit order and hence their operations precede those of uncommitted transactions.

Transaction T_1 will successfully validate, and hence commit, if the operations it executes during its read phase (recall that no write operations are performed on the database during the read phase) do not conflict with operations of transactions that were active during its read phase but committed before T_1 entered its validation phase. If transaction T_2 completes its write phase before T_1 starts its read phase, as shown in Figure 23.21(b), the two transactions are not concurrently active. In this case, all of T_1's operations follow all of T_2's in both S and S^{ser}, and no conflict has taken place. Suppose, however, that T_2 completes before T_1 enters validation, but T_2 had not completed its write phase before T_1 starts its read phase, as shown in Figure 23.21(c). Furthermore, suppose that T_1 reads an item that T_2 writes. T_1's read *might* precede T_2's write, in which case the order of conflicting operations is contrary to the commit order $T_2 T_1$. Therefore, T_1 cannot be allowed to successfully validate. For this reason, the validating transaction tests for conflicts between its read operations and the write operations of concurrent transactions that committed while it is in its read phase: The set of items read by T_1 must be disjoint from the set of items written by any transaction whose write phase overlaps T_1's read phase.

Note that, when T_1 validates, the only check made concerns T_1's read operations. Validation need not check for conflicts involving T_1's write operations. Although a conflict occurs if T_1 writes a record that T_2 reads or writes, the fact that only one transaction at a time can be in its validation/write phase guarantees that T_1's writes (during its write phase) follows T_2's reads (during its read phase) or writes (during its write phase) and hence, assuming that T_1 commits, the operations occur in commit order (i.e., their order is the same in both S and S^{ser}). Thus, even though T_2's read or write conflicts with T_1's write, T_1 can be successfully validated, because these operations need not be interchanged in constructing S^{ser}. (The same point can be made in a different way: T_1's write is performed when T_2 is no longer active, and hence the conflict is of no concern.)

We have made the assumption that only one transaction at a time is in its validation and write phase (this is called **serial validation**). Hence, the equivalent serial order of committed transactions is the order of entry into the validation phase (i.e., the commit order), and no two transactions can simultaneously execute their write phases. Although this assumption simplifies validation, it creates a bottleneck that restricts concurrency.

An alternative, **parallel validation**, avoids the bottleneck by allowing transactions to execute their validation/write phases concurrently. As with serial validation, the order in which transactions start validating is the equivalent serial order. Thus, in addition to the condition that must be met for serial validation, a transaction, T_1, entering its validation phase must be validated against all transactions, T_2, executing their validation or write phases at that time (since these transactions precede T_1 in the equivalent serial order). For this set of transactions, conflicts between write operations (occurring during concurrent write phases) must now be considered. Thus, two conditions must be satisfied before T_1 can commit. The first condition is identical to that of serial validation: If the read phase of T_1 overlaps the validation/write phase of T_2, the set of items read by T_1 must be disjoint from the set written by T_2. In addition, if T_2 enters its validation/write phase before T_1 and the execution of those phases overlap, as shown in Figure 23.21(d), the set of items written by T_1 must be disjoint from the set written by T_2 in order for T_1 to be successfully validated.

23.9   BIBLIOGRAPHIC NOTES

Two excellent books on concurrency controls are [Bernstein et al. 1987, Papadimitriou 1986]. A more theoretical discussion is given in [Lynch et al. 1994].

The concepts of serializability and two-phase locking were introduced in [Eswaran et al. 1976]. The result that if a schedule is not serializable, there exists an integrity constraint that the schedule makes false is proved in [Rosenkrantz et al. 1984]. The concepts of recoverability and strictness were introduced in [Hadzilacos 1983]. Backward and forward commutativity were introduced in [Weihl 1988] and are discussed in more detail in [Lynch et al. 1994]. Our implementation of nested transactions is taken from [Beeri et al. 1989] and the implementation of multilevel transactions is taken from [Weikum 1991]. One of the first timestamp-ordered concurrency controls is described in [Thomas 1979], which also introduced the Thomas Write Rule. Optimistic concurrency controls were introduced in [Kung and Robinson 1981]. Intentions lists were first suggested in [Lampson et al. 1981]. A different approach to designing concurrency controls based on the semantics of the application (as opposed to the semantics of the operations) is discussed in [Bernstein et al. 1999b, Bernstein et al. 1999a, Bernstein et al. 1998, Bernstein and Lewis 1996].

23.10   EXERCISES

23.1 State which of the following schedules are serializable.

    a. $r_1(x)\ r_2(y)\ r_1(z)\ r_3(z)\ r_2(x)\ r_1(y)$

    b. $r_1(x)\ w_2(y)\ r_1(z)\ r_3(z)\ w_2(x)\ r_1(y)$

    c. $r_1(x)\ w_2(y)\ r_1(z)\ r_3(z)\ w_1(x)\ r_2(y)$

    d. $r_1(x)\ r_2(y)\ r_1(z)\ r_3(z)\ w_1(x)\ w_2(y)$

    e. $r_1(x)\ r_2(y)\ w_2(x)\ w_3(x)\ w_3(y)\ r_1(y)$

    f. $w_1(x)\ r_2(y)\ r_1(z)\ r_3(z)\ r_1(x)\ w_2(y)$

    g. $r_1(z)\ w_2(x)\ r_2(z)\ r_2(y)\ w_1(x)\ w_3(z)\ w_1(y)\ r_3(x)$

23.2 Give all possible conflict-equivalent serial orderings corresponding to the serialization graph in Figure 23.5.

23.3 Use a serialization graph to demonstrate that the schedule shown in Figure 23.4 is not conflict serializable.

23.4 Suppose that we declare all of the database integrity constraints in the database schema so that the DBMS will not allow any transaction to commit if its updates violate any of the integrity constraints. Then, even if we do not use any concurrency control, the database always remains consistent. Explain why we must nevertheless use a concurrency control.

23.5 Give an example of a schedule of two transactions that preserves database consistency (the database satisfies its integrity constraints), but nevertheless the final database does not reflect the effect of both transactions.

23.6 Prove that conflict equivalence implies view equivalence.

23.7 Give an example of a schedule in which transactions of the Student Registration System deadlock.

23.8 Prove that with a two-phase locking protocol, one possible equivalent serial order is the order in which the transactions perform their first unlock operation.

23.9 Give an example of a transaction processing system (other than a banking system) that you have interacted with, for which you had an intuitive expectation that the serial order was the commit order.

23.10 Give an example of a schedule that is serializable but not strict.

23.11 Give an example of a schedule that is strict but not serializable.

23.12 Give an example of a schedule produced by a nonstrict two-phase locking concurrency control that is not recoverable.

23.13 Give an example of a schedule produced by a recoverable but nonstrict concurrency control involving three transactions in which a deadlock occurs, causing a cascaded abort of all three.

23.14 Give an example of a schedule, produced by a nonstrict two-phase locking concurrency control, that is serializable but not in commit order.

23.15 Suppose that the `account` object, for which the conflict table is described in Figure 23.16, has an additional operation, `balance`, which returns the balance in the account. Design a new conflict table for this object, including the new operation.

23.16 Consider the following schedule of three transactions:

$$r_2(y)\ r_1(x)\ r_3(y)\ r_2(x)\ w_2(y)\ w_1(x)\ r_3(x)$$

a. Define a serialization between T_1 and T_2.

b. In what apparent order does T_3 see the database?

c. Is the schedule serializable?

d. Assuming that each transaction is consistent, does the final database state satisfy all integrity constraints?

e. Does the database state seen by T_3 satisfy all integrity constraints? Explain.

23.17 Assume that, in addition to the operations read(x) and write(x), a database has the operation copy(x,y), which (atomically) copies the value stored in record x into record y. Design a conflict table for these operations for use in an immediate-update pessimistic concurrency control.

23.18 Suppose that we have a queue object, with operations enqueue and dequeue, in which enqueue always succeeds and dequeue returns NO if there are no items in the queue. Design a conflict table for this object using partial operations and backward commutativity.

23.19 A pair of (partial) database operations, p and q, are said to **forward-commute** if, in every database state in which both p and q are defined, the sequences p, q and q, p are both defined and in both sequences p and q return the same values and the final database state is the same.

a. Describe how forward commutativity can be used in the design of a deferred-update optimistic concurrency control.

b. Give a conflict table for such a control for the account object described in Figure 23.16.

23.20 Design a deferred-update pessimistic concurrency control.

23.21 In an implementation of chained transactions, when a subtransaction chains to the next subtransaction it gives up some of its locks if those locks are not needed in subsequent subtransactions. Explain how this can affect the ACID properties of the overall chained transaction.

23.22 We want to ensure that a set of transactions that use a recoverable queue are isolated. Explain how implementation of the queue should use the locks on the queue pointers and the items in the queue.

23.23 Give an example of a nonserializable schedule in a system that uses a recoverable queue in which locks on the head and tail pointers are given up after the enqueue and dequeue operations complete but before the transaction commits.

23.24 Suppose that the withdraw transaction in an ATM system is structured as a nested transaction with two subtransactions—one that verifies that the PIN number supplied by the user is associated with the given account and a second that debits the balance of the account. Suppose that two such transactions attempt to concurrently withdraw funds from the same account. Explain how a schedule in which the two PIN number verification subtransactions are executed first and the two debit subtransactions are executed next is possible.

23.25 Give an example of a schedule in which a pessimistic concurrency control makes a transaction wait, but later allows it to commit, while an optimistic concurrency control restarts the transaction.

23.26 Give an example of a schedule in which a pessimistic concurrency control makes a transaction wait, but then allows it to commit, while an optimistic concurrency control allows the transaction to commit without waiting.

23.27 Give an example of a schedule that is acceptable (without any delays caused by locks) by an immediate-update, pessimistic, strict two-phase locking concurrency control, while an optimistic concurrency control restarts one of the transactions.

23.28 Can a deadlock occur in the timestamp-ordered control described in the text?

23.29 Give an example of a schedule produced by a timestamp-ordered concurrency control in which the serialization order is not the commit order.

23.30 Give an example of a schedule that is strict and serializable, but not in commit order, and that could have been produced by either a timestamp-ordered concurrency control or a two-phase locking concurrency control.

23.31 Show that the following proposed protocol for a timestamp-ordered concurrency control is not recoverable.

> Store with each data item the maximum timestamp of any (not necessarily committed) transaction that has read that item and the maximum timestamp of any (not necessarily committed) transaction that has written that item.
>   When a transaction makes a request to read (write) a data item, if the timestamp of the requesting transaction is smaller than the write (read) timestamp in the item, restart the transaction; otherwise, grant the request.

23.32 The *Kill-Wait* concurrency control combines the concepts of the immediate update concurrency control and the timestamp-ordered control. As in the timestamp-ordered system, when a transaction, T_1 is initiated, it is assigned a time stamp, $TS(T_1)$. However, the system uses the same conflict table as the immediate-update pessimistic control does and resolves conflicts using the rule

> If transaction T_1 makes a request that conflicts with an operation of active transaction, T_2
>
>   if $TS(T_1) < TS(T_2)$, then *abort T_2*, else *make T_1 wait until T_2 terminates.*

where *abort T_2* is referred to as a *kill* because T_1 kills T_2.

a. Show that the kill-wait control serializes in commit order.

    b. Give a schedule produced by a kill-wait control that is not serializable in timestamp order.

    c. Explain why deadlock does not occur in a kill-wait control.

23.33 The *Wait-Die* concurrency control is another control that combines the concepts of the immediate-update concurrency control and the timestamp-ordered control.

> If transaction T_1 makes a request that conflicts with an operation of active transaction T_2
>
> **if** $TS(T_1) < TS(T_2)$, **then** *make T_1 wait until T_2 terminates,* **else** *abort T_1.*

where *abort T_1* is referred to as a *die* because T_1 kills itself.

    a. Show that the wait-die control serializes in commit order and prevents deadlocks.

    b. Compare the fairness of the execution of the kill-wait and wait-die controls.

23.34 Give a complete description of an algorithm for a parallel validation optimistic concurrency control.

23.35 We are interested in comparing two models for a transaction processing system:

    a. A nested model, similar to that described in the text, except that concurrent execution of children is not allowed. A parent can have only one child executing at a time.

    b. A conventional model, in which whenever a parent in the nested model calls a child, the conventional model calls a subroutine, and whenever a child in the nested model aborts, the corresponding subroutine in the conventional model manually undoes any database updates it has performed and returns with a failed status.

Explain why the nested model is more efficient and allows a higher transaction throughput.

23.36 Suppose that transactions T_1 and T_2 can be decomposed into the subtransactions

$$T_1 : T_{1,1}, T_{1,2}$$

and

$$T_2 : T_{2,1}, T_{2,2}$$

such that the database items accessed by $T_{1,1}$ and $T_{2,1}$ are disjoint from the items accessed by $T_{1,2}$ and $T_{2,2}$. Instead of guaranteeing that all schedules involving T_1 and T_2 are serializable, suppose that a concurrency control guarantees that $T_{1,1}$ is always executed serializably with $T_{2,1}$ and that $T_{1,2}$ is always executed serializably with $T_{2,2}$.

    a. Will T_1 always be serializable with T_2?   Explain.

    b. What minimal additional condition *on the subtransactions* guarantees that the effect of executing T_1 concurrently with T_2 is the same as a serial schedule?

    c. Assuming that the condition of (b) holds, what advantage does the new concurrency control have over a concurrency control that guarantees serializability?

23.37 Suppose that transactions T_1 and T_2 can be decomposed into the subtransactions

$$T_1 : T_{1,1}, T_{1,2}$$

and

$$T_2 : T_{2,1}, T_{2,2}$$

such that each subtransaction individually maintains the consistency constraints of the database. Instead of guaranteeing that all schedules involving T_1 and T_2 are serializable, suppose that a concurrency control guarantees that all subtransactions are always executed serializably.

    a. Will T_1 always be serializable with T_2?   Explain.

    b. Will integrity constraints be maintained by all possible schedules?

    c. What possible problems might arise if the concurrency control schedules transactions in this way?

23.38 Give an example of a schedule that would be accepted by a two-phase locking concurrency control but not by a timestamp-ordered concurrency control.

Chapter 24

Isolation in Relational Databases

LOCKING

In our discussion of isolation up to this point, we have assumed that transactions access items *explicitly*, by name. In a relational environment, a transaction accesses tuples, and describes the tuples it wants to access *implicitly*, using a condition that the tuples satisfy—not by giving their name. Thus, the set of tuples read by a SELECT statement satisfies the selection condition in the WHERE clause.[1]

Consider a table, ACCOUNTS, in a banking system that contains a tuple for each separate account. We might read all tuples in ACCOUNTS describing accounts controlled by depositor Mary using the SELECT statement

```
SELECT *
FROM  ACCOUNTS A
WHERE A.Name = 'Mary'
```

The expression in the WHERE clause is referred to as the **read predicate** (the attributes of the table named in the FROM clause are treated as variables in the predicate), and the statement returns—reads—all tuples that satisfy the read predicate.

Conflicts take a different form with such operations. For example, assume that ACCOUNTS has attributes AcctNumber (the key), Name, and Balance. Also assume that there is a table, DEPOSITORS, containing a tuple for each depositor, with attributes Name (the key) and TotalBalance, in which the value of the TotalBalance attribute is the sum of the balances of all the depositor's accounts. An audit transaction, T_1, for Mary might execute the SELECT statement

```
SELECT SUM(Balance)
FROM  ACCOUNTS A
WHERE A.Name = 'Mary'
```

---

[1] In the special case in which a transaction accesses a tuple using its primary key (for example, Id of the relation STUDENT), we might say that the value of that primary key is the name of the tuple, and we might consider locking the tuple based on that name. As we will see, however, even in this special case additional considerations apply.

and then compare the value returned with the result of executing

```
SELECT D.TotalBalance
FROM DEPOSITORS D
WHERE D.Name = 'Mary'
```

and finally check that the value of TotalBalance is equal to the sum.

Concurrently, T_2, a new account transaction for Mary, might add a new tuple to ACCOUNTS using the statement

```
INSERT INTO ACCOUNTS
VALUES ('10021', 'Mary', 100)
```

and then update TotalBalance by 100 in the appropriate tuple in DEPOSITORS using

```
UPDATE DEPOSITORS
SET TotalBalance = TotalBalance + 100
WHERE Name = 'Mary'
```

The operations on ACCOUNTS performed by T_1 and T_2 conflict, since the INSERT of T_2 does not commute with the SELECT of T_1. If INSERT is executed before SELECT the inserted tuple will be returned by SELECT; otherwise, it will not be returned. Hence, invalid results might be obtained if T_2 is allowed to interleave its execution between the time T_1 reads ACCOUNTS and the time it reads DEPOSITORS. The value of TotalBalance read by T_1 in its second statement will not be equal to the sum of the Balances it read in its first statement. (The operations on DEPOSITORS similarly conflict.)

24.1.1 Phantoms

As with nonrelational databases, we can ensure serializability by the use of a locking algorithm. In designing such an algorithm, we must first decide what to lock. One approach is to lock tables. They have names, and those names are used in the read and write statements that access them. The SELECT statement can be treated as a read on the data item(s)—tables—named in the FROM clause, and DELETE, INSERT, and UPDATE can be treated as writes on the named tables. Therefore the concurrency control algorithms described in Chapter 23 can be used to achieve serializable schedules. As with page locking, table locking is conservative. The problem with this approach is the coarse granularity of the locks. A table might contain thousands (perhaps millions) of tuples. Locking an entire table because one of its tuples has been accessed might result in a serious loss of concurrency.

If, instead of locking tables, we associate a distinct lock with each tuple, lock granularity is fine, but the resulting schedules might not be serializable. For example, suppose that T_1 locks all tuples it has read in ACCOUNTS—those that satisfy the predicate Name = 'Mary'. The ability of a transaction to insert a new tuple into a table is not affected by locks held by other transactions on existing tuples in the table. As a result, T_2 can subsequently construct a tuple, t, that satisfies the predicate and describes a new account for Mary and insert it into ACCOUNTS. Hence, the following schedule is possible

T_1 locks and reads all tuples describing Mary's accounts in Accounts.

T_2 adds t to Accounts and locks it.

T_2 locks and updates Mary's tuple in Depositors.

T_2 commits, releasing all locks that it holds.

T_1 locks and reads Mary's tuple in Depositors.

Here, T_2 has altered the contents of the set of tuples referred to by the predicate Name = 'Mary' by adding t. In this situation, t is referred to as a **phantom** because T_1 thinks it has locked all the tuples that satisfy the predicate but, unknown to T_1, a new tuple, t, that also satisfies the predicate has been inserted by a concurrent transaction. A phantom can lead to nonserializable schedules and hence invalid results. In the example, the value of TotalBalance read by T_1 in its second statement is not equal to the sum of the values of the Balance attributes of the tuples it read in its first statement.

The problem arises because the SELECT statement does not name a specific item. Instead, it specifies a condition, or predicate, that might be satisfied by a number of tuples, some of which might be in a particular table and others might not. While we can set a lock on the tuples that already exist in a table, it is difficult to set a lock on those that do not. To eliminate the possibility of phantoms, we need a locking mechanism that prevents tuples that satisfy a predicate, but are not present in the table (that is, phantoms), from being added to the table.

Although we have illustrated the phantom problem using a SELECT statement, the problem also exists with statements that update the database. For example, an UPDATE statement that updates all tuples in a table satisfying predicate P does not commute with an INSERT statement that inserts a tuple satisfying P into the table. Unfortunately, even if the transaction that does the update acquires locks on all updated tuples, a concurrent transaction can still perform the insert.

One approach to preventing phantoms is to lock the entire table—which will certainly prevent any new tuples, including phantoms, from being inserted. As we shall see in Section 24.3.1, however, table locking is not always necessary since protocols exist that prevent phantoms but do not require that the entire table be locked. Hence, when many commercial DBMSs use the term "tuple locking" (or "page locking") to describe a concurrency control algorithm, they mean that it utilizes tuple locks (or page locks) as a part of such a protocol, which does guarantee serializability. As in all things, caution is in order—"When all else fails, read the manual." Still, there are many situations in which commercial DBMSs lock an entire table in order to prevent phantoms and achieve serializability.

24.1.2 Predicate Locking

One technique for dealing with phantoms is **predicate locking** [Eswaran et al. 1976]. A predicate, P, specifies a set of tuples. A tuple is in the set if and only if the tuples' attribute values make P true. For example, Name = 'Mary' is a predicate that specifies the set of all possible tuples that might exist in Accounts whose Name attribute has value Mary. This set is a subset of the set, D, of all possible tuples that could ever be stored in ACCOUNTS. Hence, P specifies a subset of D, some of whose elements might be in ACCOUNTS and some not.

Predicate associated with an SQL statement.   Each SQL statement has an associated predicate. The predicate associated with a SELECT or DELETE statement is specified in the WHERE clause. In the simplest case, the clause describes constraints on the attributes of the table named in the FROM clause, and the predicate can be associated with that table. However, things can become much more complicated if, for example, the WHERE clause contains a nested SELECT or the FROM clause names several tables. In these cases, several tables are involved, each with an associated predicate. Although we could describe this more general case, we choose not to complicate the discussion since the goal here is only to present predicate locking as a concept.

The predicate associated with an INSERT statement describes the set of tuples to be inserted. In the simple case, in which a single tuple is inserted, the predicate is

$$(A_1 = v_1) \wedge (A_2 = v_2) \wedge \ldots \wedge (A_n = v_n)$$

where A_i is the ith attribute name and v_i is the value of the attribute in the inserted tuple. The predicate specifies the set consisting of a single tuple to be inserted. More generally, the INSERT might contain a nested SELECT statement,

```
INSERT INTO TABLE1 (... attribute list ...)
SELECT ... attribute list ...
FROM TABLE2
WHERE P
```

in which case the predicate P is associated with TABLE2 (since tuples satisfying P are read from that table) and TABLE1 (since tuples satisfying P are written into that table).

An UPDATE statement can be viewed as a DELETE statement followed by an INSERT statement, and hence it has two associated predicates. The first is the predicate P in the UPDATE statement's WHERE clause, which specifies the tuples to be deleted. The SET clause describes how those tuples are to be modified. The resulting set of tuples, described by a predicate, P', are then inserted. For example, the following UPDATE statement posts interest to all of Mary's accounts

```
UPDATE ACCOUNTS
SET Balance = Balance * 1.05
WHERE Name = 'Mary'
```

In this case, the tuples deleted and the tuples inserted satisfy the same predicate, Name = 'Mary'. However, if Mary wants to add her middle initial to her name, we might execute the statement

```
UPDATE ACCOUNTS
SET Name = 'Mary S'
WHERE Name = 'Mary'
```

Now P is Name = 'Mary', but P' is Name = 'Mary S'.

Figure 24.1 Read predicate, P, specifies a subset of D. Some of the tuples in the subset might be in R, others might not.

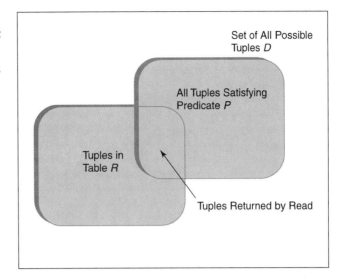

Predicate locks.   A **predicate lock** associated with table R on predicate P locks *all* tuples specified by P, whether or not they are in R. The situation is illustrated in Figure 24.1 for a SELECT statement specifying table R in the FROM clause and predicate P in the WHERE clause. All of the tuples in R that satisfy P are returned by the SELECT statement, but all of the tuples in D satisfying P are locked.

Similarly, for a DELETE statement all tuples in D satisfying P are locked, and the tuples in R satisfying P are deleted. In the case of INSERT, the tuples inserted are locked. For example, the predicate lock associated with the inserted tuple, t, describing Mary's new account in ACCOUNTS locks exactly that tuple.

$$P_t : (\text{AcctNumber} = \texttt{'10021'}) \wedge (\text{Name} = \texttt{'Mary'}) \wedge (\text{Balance} = 100) \quad (24.1)$$

With the UPDATE statement, both P and P' must be locked.

We now interpret the notion of a conflict somewhat more generally. Instead of requiring that conflicting operations name the same data item, we now specify that

> Two operations conflict if at least one is a write and the sets of tuples described by the predicates associated with the operations have non-null intersections.

For example, the SELECT (read) statement that returns all tuples satisfying the predicate Name=`'Mary'` conflicts with the DELETE (write) statement

```
DELETE
FROM ACCOUNTS
WHERE Balance < 1
```

which deletes all accounts satisfying the predicate Balance < 1, since there exist tuples in D satisfying both predicates—for example, the tuple satisfying

AcctNumber = '10000' ∧ Name = 'Mary' ∧ Balance = .5

Such tuples *might* be in ACCOUNTS and hence we cannot be sure that the SELECT commutes with the DELETE. On the other hand, the SELECT does not conflict with

```
DELETE
FROM  ACCOUNTS
WHERE Name = 'John'
```

since the predicates associated with the two statements have a null intersection. Finally, the statement

```
SELECT *
FROM  ACCOUNTS
WHERE Name = 'Mary S'
```

conflicts with the UPDATE statement that adds Mary's middle initial to her Name attribute in ACCOUNTS.

Predicate locking solves the phantom problem, which we explained earlier. When T_1 reads ACCOUNTS, it obtains a read lock on the predicate Name = 'Mary'. Later, when T_2 attempts to insert into ACCOUNTS the tuple t describing Mary's new account, it requests a write lock on predicate P_t (24.1). Since the intersection of the two predicates is not null, a conflict exists and the write lock cannot be granted. The tuple t is a phantom (it does not exist in ACCOUNTS), and the predicate lock on P_t prevents it from being concurrently added.

In an implementation of predicate locking, we associate with each table, R, a lock set, $L(R)$, which contains the locks associated with all requests that have been granted to currently active transactions. Each element of $L(R)$ has a corresponding predicate. When the lock associated with a request for a database operation conflicts with an element of $L(R)$, the concurrency control makes the requesting transaction wait.

With predicate locking, serializable schedules can be guaranteed at a finer granularity of locking than with table locks, since we lock subsets of the set of tuples that might be in R rather than the entire table. Unfortunately, the conflict test—predicate intersection—is expensive to implement, which limits the usefulness of predicate locking. For that reason, commercial DBMSs do not implement predicate locks.

24.2   LOCKING AND THE SQL ISOLATION LEVELS

Most commercial DBMSs guarantee serializability by locking entire tables or by using finer-granularity locking in connection with index locking (which we will describe shortly). Unfortunately, in both cases performance may be inadequate for some applications, creating a considerable incentive to release locks earlier than would be required to achieve serializability.

Early release is possible when weaker levels of isolation [Gray et al. 1976] are used. The SQL standard defines four isolation levels and, as we saw in Section 10.2.3, each transaction can individually choose one of the four. In order of decreasing strength, they are

SERIALIZABLE

REPEATABLE READ

READ COMMITTED

READ UNCOMMITTED

SERIALIZABLE corresponds to the notion of serializable execution discussed in this text and is the only level that guarantees correctness for *all* applications. The enhanced performance that can be achieved with weaker levels is obtained at the risk of incorrect execution.

A given DBMS will not necessarily support all isolation levels. It usually provides a particular level as the default and has mechanisms for requesting one of the other supported levels.

With the exception of SERIALIZABLE, the SQL standard, [SQL 1992], specifies the isolation levels in terms of certain phenomena (sometimes called anomalies) that are to be prevented at each level. A phenomenon that is prevented at one level is also prevented at each higher level.

■ At READ UNCOMMITTED, dirty reads (see Section 23.2) are possible.

■ At READ COMMITTED, dirty reads are not permitted, but successive reads of the same tuple by a particular transaction might yield different values.

■ At REPEATABLE READ, successive reads of the same tuple executed by a particular transaction do not yield different values, but phantoms are possible.

■ At SERIALIZABLE, phantoms are not permitted. Transaction execution must be serializable.

The phenomena allowed and disallowed are summarized in Figure 24.2.

Figure 24.2 Phenomena allowed and disallowed at each isolation level.

Level	Dirty Reads	Nonrepeatable Reads	Phantoms
READ UNCOMMITTED	Yes	Yes	Yes
READ COMMITTED	No	Yes	Yes
REPEATABLE READ	No	No	Yes
SERIALIZABLE	No	No	No

SQL isolation levels do not deal with dirty writes, which, as we saw in Section 23.2, are undesirable for several reasons. While they cannot occur if all transactions run at SERIALIZABLE, they are not explicitly prohibited by the SQL standard at the lower isolation levels (they might, of course, not be allowed in a particular implementation). Note that the schedule in Figure 23.9, page 774, which illustrates a dirty write, does not involve dirty or nonrepeatable reads and hence does not violate the requirements of any of the three lower isolation levels. Since the levels are defined in terms of certain undesirable phenomena, one might think that if dirty reads, nonrepeatable reads, and phantoms are eliminated, the resulting schedules are serializable. The existence of the dirty write phenomenon demonstrates that this is not true.

The SQL standard specifies that different transactions in the same application can execute at different isolation levels, and each such transaction sees or does not see the phenomena corresponding to its level. For example, when a transaction executing at REPEATABLE READ reads a tuple several times, the same value is always returned even though other transactions are executing at other levels. Similarly, a transaction executing at SERIALIZABLE sees a view of the database that is serialized with respect to the changes made by all other transactions, regardless of their levels.

Locking implementation of the isolation levels. By defining isolation levels in terms of behavior, the SQL standard does not constrain the implementation of a concurrency control. In particular, the definition does not imply that the concurrency control must be implemented using locks. Locks, however, form the basis of most concurrency controls, and hence it is useful to consider how the SQL isolation levels can be supported in a lock-based system. We describe an implementation proposed in [Berenson et al. 1995].[2]

Independent of the isolation level, DBMSs generally guarantee that each SQL statement is executed atomically and that its execution is isolated from the execution of other statements. Locking goes beyond that in controlling the way statements of different transactions can be interleaved.

Each level is implemented using locks in different ways. Thus, a lock can be either a conventional lock on an item—a tuple, a page, or a table—or it can be a predicate lock. We describe the implementations using predicate locks, even though we have pointed out that predicate locks are generally not implemented because of their complexity. We have indicated their use for pedagogical reasons. It allows us to be more precise about what needs to be locked. A practical implementation would replace predicate locks with table locks or it would use other techniques (see Section 24.3.1).

A lock can be held until commit time—we refer to such a lock as being of **long duration**—or it can be released after the statement that has accessed the item or predicate has been completed, in which case it is of **short duration**. Short-

---

[2] Be aware that, while many DBMSs implement isolation levels using the locking protocols described below, others use different implementations. In certain situations these different implementations exhibit different behaviors.

duration locks are not sufficient to guarantee serializability. However, by requiring a transaction to request such a lock, the concurrency control can check whether conflicting locks are held by other transactions and force the requestor to wait in that case. If a lock is not requested (as in READ UNCOMMITTED), the existence of a conflicting lock in a lock set is ignored.

All isolation levels use write locks in the same way. Long-duration write locks are obtained on the predicates associated with UPDATE, INSERT, and DELETE statements.

The implementation of a particular level rules out not only the appropriate undesirable phenomenon, but possibly other phenomena as well. Thus, since write locks are of long duration at all levels, dirty writes are ruled out at all levels also. Read locks obtained by a SELECT statement are handled differently at each level.

> READ UNCOMMITTED. A read is performed without obtaining a read lock. Since reading does not involve the locking mechanism, one transaction might hold a write lock on some item or predicate while another reads it. Thus, a transaction might read uncommitted (dirty) data.

> READ COMMITTED. Short-duration read locks are obtained on each tuple, t, returned by a SELECT. As a result, conflicts with write locks are detected and, since write locks are of long duration, dirty reads are impossible. However, since the read lock on t is released when the read is completed, two successive SELECT statements in a particular transaction that both return t might be separated by the execution of another transaction that updates t and then commits. Hence, the value of t returned might be different.

> REPEATABLE READ. Long-duration read locks are obtained on each tuple, t, returned by a SELECT. As a result, a nonrepeatable read of t is not possible. Since the predicate associated with the SELECT is not locked, however, phantoms can occur.

> SERIALIZABLE. All read (and write) locks are long-duration predicate locks, and thus phantoms are not possible. All transactions are serializable.

The use of read locks at each level is summarized in Figure 24.3. Note that, since all write locks are of long duration and all levels other than READ UNCOMMITTED acquire read locks before reading an item, a schedule in which all transactions run at levels higher than READ COMMITTED will be strict.

Figure 24.3 Read locks used in the locking implementation of each isolation level. All levels use long-duration write locks on predicates.

Level	Read Locks
READ UNCOMMITTED	None
READ COMMITTED	Short-duration on tuples returned
REPEATABLE READ	Long-duration on tuples returned
SERIALIZABLE	Long-duration on predicate specified in statement

Since all transactions use long-duration predicate write locks, their write operations are serializable. Hence, a transaction running at SERIALIZABLE (and therefore using long-duration read predicate locks) sees either all or none of the updates performed by a concurrent transaction. That is, it is serialized with respect to all other transactions independent of the isolation level at which they execute. Transactions executing at lower levels, however, do not necessarily see a consistent state, and therefore their updates might cause inconsistencies. SERIALIZABLE transactions might see those inconsistencies, and their computations might be affected as a result.

The read locks acquired at the lower isolation levels are weaker than the long-duration predicate read locks used at SERIALIZABLE and are the source of the performance improvement that these levels can achieve. Since the management of read locks at each level eliminates the anomalies prohibited at that level, transactions executing at different isolation levels can run concurrently and satisfy each level's specification.

The dangers of executing at lower isolation levels. By allowing transactions to run at isolation levels weaker than SERIALIZABLE, nonserializable schedules can be produced. Thus, a transaction might see inconsistent data and, as a result, might write inconsistent data into the database. To see how this can happen at each of the lower levels, consider the following examples.

READ UNCOMMITTED. A transaction, T_2, executing at READ UNCOMMITTED might read dirty values produced by another active transaction, T_1. Such values might never become part of the permanent database and so be meaningless. For example, T_1 might write a value, v, to a data item and later abort. T_2 might read the data item before T_1 aborts and return v to the user. Or T_2 might compute a new value based on v and store it in a different data item, thus corrupting the database since the transaction that produced v aborted.[3] Or T_1 might write v to the data item and then overwrite v with a second value. In this case, v is an intermediate value not meant for external consumption. Even if T_1 writes only final values into the database, if T_2 can see them before T_1 commits, nonserializable schedules can result—for example, the schedule in Figure 24.4 is nonserializable. In the figure, T_1 is a bank transaction that is transferring $100 from an account whose balance is stored in tuple t_1 (initially $1,000) to an account whose balance is stored in tuple t_2 (initially $500). T_2 is a read-only transaction executing at READ UNCOMMITTED that prints out the balance of all accounts. In the schedule shown, T_2 reads an uncommitted value of t_1 and hence does not report the $100 being transferred in either account.

READ COMMITTED. A transaction, T_1, executing at READ COMMITTED uses short-duration read locks on individual tuples. Hence, as shown in Figure 24.5, it is possible for T_2 to update tuple t and then commit between successive reads in

---

[3] To protect against database corruption, transactions running at READ UNCOMMITTED are often required to be read-only.

Figure 24.4 Schedule involving a read of uncommitted data. T_2 executes at READ UNCOMMITTED.

T_1: $r(t_1 : 1000)$ $w(t_1 : 900)$ $r(t_2 : 500)$ $w(t_2 : 600)$ *commit*
T_2: $r(t_1 : 900)$ $r(t_2 : 500)$ *commit*

Figure 24.5 Schedule involving a nonrepeatable read. T_1 executes at READ COMMITTED.

T_1: $r(t : 1000)$ $r(t : 2000)$ *commit*
T_2: $w(t : 2000)$ *commit*

Figure 24.6 Schedule illustrating the lost update problem at READ COMMITTED.

T_1: $r(t : 1000)$ $w(t : 1100)$ *commit*
T_2: $r(t : 1000)$ $w(t : 2000)$ *commit*

T_1. One might not think that this is too serious an issue, since it is unlikely that a transaction will read the same tuple twice. However, incorrect results can occur even when the transaction does not attempt a second read.[4] Figure 24.6 shows a schedule in which T_1 and T_2 are both bank deposit transactions executing at READ COMMITTED that operate on an account whose balance is stored in tuple t. Since T_1's read lock is of short duration, it is possible for T_2 to update t and then commit. As a result, the effect of T_2's update is lost. Note that both transactions read committed data. This is an example of the lost update problem that we introduced in Chapter 2.

Figure 24.7 shows another example of an incorrect schedule at READ COMMIT-TED. Here transaction T_1 sees an inconsistent view of the database. Let us assume that an integrity constraint states that the values of x and y must satisfy $x \geq y$, and initially $x = 10$ and $y = 1$. T_1 reads both x and y, but between the reads (after T_1 has given up its read lock on x), another transaction, T_2, changes both values (such that the new values satisfy the integrity constraint) and then commits. T_1 sees the value of x before T_2 changes it and the value of y after T_2 changes it—a view of the database that does not satisfy the integrity constraint. Since transactions are guaranteed to execute correctly only when they see a consistent view of the database, T_1 might execute in an unpredictable manner and perhaps later write erroneous data into the database. Even if T_2's writes were such that the two values read by T_1 happened to satisfy the integrity constraint, the fact that they came from two different versions of the database (one before the execution

---

[4] This is an example of an ambiguity that results from the informal nature of the way isolation levels are described (in terms of phenomena to be prevented). Does a nonrepeatable read occur only when a transaction attempts a second read and gets a different value, or does it occur whenever, if a second read were attempted, a different value would be read?

Figure 24.7 Schedule illustrating that a transaction executing at READ COMMIT-
TED might see an inconsistent view of the database.

T_1: $r(x:10)$ $r(y:15)$ ...   *commit*
T_2: $w(x:20)$ $w(y:15)$ *commit*

of T_2 and one after) could cause T_1 to execute incorrectly and write erroneous
data to the database.

REPEATABLE READ. Since tuples, but not predicates, have long-duration locks,
phantoms can occur. We saw in Section 24.1.1 that this can cause incorrect
behavior. Note that the example there also involved a transaction seeing an
inconsistent view of the database.

24.2.1 Lost Updates, Cursor Stability, and Update Locks

Figure 24.6 is an example of lost update behavior that occurs because only short-
duration read locks are used at the READ COMMITTED isolation level. A special
case of the lost update problem—when reading is done through a cursor—can be
prevented by an isolation level called CURSOR STABILITY, which is provided instead
of READ COMMITTED in many implementations of SQL.

We have not yet discussed how access through a cursor is affected by transactions
executing at different isolation levels. When a transaction, T_1, opens an INSENSITIVE
cursor over a table, R, a copy of the result set is made and all subsequent FETCH
statements through the cursor are done to the copy. Therefore, no matter at which
isolation level T_1 is executing, the FETCH statements do not see any subsequent
updates to R made by a concurrently executing transaction, T_2 (or even by T_1 itself).

However, if T_1 opens a cursor that is not declared INSENSITIVE (for example, if it is
KEYSET_DRIVEN), pointers to the tuples in R from which the result set is constructed
are returned and all subsequent FETCH operations are done through the pointers.
If T_1 is executed at READ COMMITTED, it acquires only short-duration read locks on
the tuples. If T_1 and T_2 run concurrently, T_1 might fetch some tuples through the
cursor before they are updated by T_2 and others after T_2 has updated them and
committed.[5]

In particular, T_2 might update a tuple while the cursor is pointing at it. That
situation is particularly troublesome if T_1 first reads the tuple and later updates it
before moving the cursor, because, between the read and the update, T_2 might read
the tuple, update it, and then commit. After T_1's update, T_2's update will be lost.
The CURSOR STABILITY isolation level prevents such lost updates.

---

[5] There might be some confusion here because of the requirement in the SQL standard that each SQL
statement be executed in an atomic and isolated fashion. In the case of a cursor, OPEN and FETCH
statement execution is atomic and isolated. Despite that, a transaction, T, that is fetching rows from
the result set of a not INSENSITIVE cursor might read some rows that were updated by a concurrent
transaction and others that were not. In that case, the transactions are not isolated and T might see an
inconsistent view of the result set even though that set was created by an isolated OPEN statement.

Figure 24.8 Schedule illustrating that CURSOR STABILITY is not a panacea.

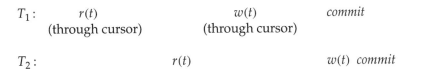

T_1: $r(t)$ $w(t)$ *commit*
         (through cursor)   (through cursor)

T_2: $r(t)$ $w(t)$ *commit*

CURSOR STABILITY is an extension of READ COMMITTED. Hence, it provides a level of isolation whose strength lies between READ COMMITTED and REPEATABLE READ. With CURSOR STABILITY, as long as a cursor opened by transaction T_1 points to a particular tuple, that tuple cannot be modified or deleted by another transaction, T_2. Once T_1 moves or closes the cursor, however, T_2 can modify the tuple.

As with the locking in other isolation levels, CURSOR STABILITY can be implemented with (the equivalent of) long-duration write predicate locks. Read locks are handled as follows:

CURSOR STABILITY. Short-duration read locks are obtained for each tuple read, except if the tuple is accessed through a cursor. A read lock on a tuple referred to by a cursor is a **medium-duration** lock that is retained while the cursor points to the tuple and released when the cursor is moved or closed.

The schedule shown in Figure 24.6 can occur if CURSOR STABILITY is used, because we have implicitly assumed that neither T_1 nor T_2 refers to t through a cursor. Suppose, however, that T_1 is posting interest to all accounts in a bank. It accesses each tuple successively through a cursor, first reading the balance in t and then updating t with a new balance. With CURSOR STABILITY, the read lock that T_1 acquires on t is maintained until it requests to update t, at which point the lock is upgraded to a write lock, which is held until T_1 commits (since write locks are of long duration). Hence, it is not possible for another transaction, T_2, to update t between T_1's read and update.

Consider the situation shown in Figure 24.8. Suppose that T_2 is a deposit transaction that accesses t directly through an index and suppose that it executes at READ COMMITTED or CURSOR STABILITY (it makes no difference in this case since it does not use a cursor). T_2 reads t after T_1 reads it. When T_1 requests to update t, its read lock can be upgraded to a write lock since T_2's read lock is of short duration and so is released when its read completes. Unfortunately, the lost update problem is not solved. The value T_2 writes (after T_1 commits) is based on the value returned by its previous read, not on the new value written by T_1, so T_1's update is lost.

Before we describe how this problem can be solved, consider the other case: T_2 is also executing at CURSOR STABILITY and accesses t through a cursor. Once again, the situation is not a happy one, as both T_1 and T_2 hold their (medium-duration) read locks after reading and a deadlock results when both try to upgrade to write locks. Clearly, CURSOR STABILITY offers only a partial solution to the lost update problem.

Some commercial DBMSs provide additional mechanisms to deal with these problems.

■ In some systems, a transaction, T, can request a write lock on an item at the time it reads the item so that it can update the item later. This avoids the need to upgrade the read lock (and hence avoids the deadlock), but it suffers from the need to lock out all other transactions starting from T's first access, even if those other transactions only want to read the item.

■ Some systems provide a new type of lock, an **update lock**, which can be used by transactions that initially want to read an item but later might want to update it.[6] It allows a transaction to read but not write the item and indicates that the lock is likely to be upgraded to a write lock at a later time. Update locks conflict with one another and with write locks, but not with read locks. For that reason, if T_1 and T_2 both request update locks, the first request will be granted and the other will wait. In this way, both lost updates and deadlocks are avoided. Since update and read locks do not conflict, if T_2 wants only to read t, it can acquire a read lock between T_1's read and write, since T_1 holds only an update lock in that interval. T_1 must upgrade its update lock to a write lock before it writes the item. It might have to wait when it requests the upgrade if other transactions hold read locks.

■ Some systems provide a version of READ COMMITTED called OPTIMISTIC READ COMMITTED. If T_1 executes at this level, it obtains the same short-duration read locks that would be obtained at READ COMMITTED. However, if it later tries to write a tuple, t, that it has previously read, it is aborted if some other transaction has modified t and committed between the time T_1 read t and the time it tried to write it. This approach is called "optimistic" because each transaction optimistically assumes that it need not retain read locks on tuples to prevent lost updates.[7] As with other optimistic algorithms, the transaction is aborted if that assumption turns out to be false. Although OPTIMISTIC READ COMMITTED prevents lost updates, it can still lead to incorrect schedules (see exercise 24.17).

24.2.2 Case Study: Correctness and NonSERIALIZABLE Schedules— The Student Registration System

Although we have given examples of incorrect behavior that can result from executing at any level lower than SERIALIZABLE, the semantics of an application can often be used to show that incorrect behavior cannot occur or has no serious effects. In such applications, transactions can safely execute at levels lower than SERIALIZABLE, thus achieving increased concurrency and better performance. We assume

---

[6] An update lock is sometimes called a *read-with-intention-to-write* lock.

[7] This approach is sometimes called *first-committer-wins* because the first transaction to write a tuple is allowed to commit—*wins*—and the second transaction that attempts to write that tuple is aborted—*loses*. We discuss first-committer-wins further in Section 24.5.3.

that the DBMS uses the locking implementation of each isolation level described earlier in this section.

For example, we might be concerned that the nonserializable schedules allowed by lower isolation levels will result in the violation of some integrity constraints. Recall, however, that many types of integrity constraints can be declared in the database schema and so are automatically checked by the DBMS. Thus, a constraint violation that results from incomplete isolation will be detected by the DBMS and (assuming deferred constraint checking) the transaction will be aborted when it requests to commit.

Therefore, assuming that most integrity constraints will be declared in the schema, the only incorrect schedules we need be concerned with are those that

■ Produce database states that violate integrity constraints not declared in the schema

■ Produce database states that are consistent but incorrect because they do not reflect the desired result of the transaction—for example, a database state resulting from a lost update

■ Return data to the user based on a view of the database that is not obtained from a consistent snapshot—for example, by a read-only transaction executing at READ UNCOMMITTED

When we consider whether or not a specific transaction in some application can safely execute at a lower isolation level, we must investigate its interaction with other transactions in the same application. The following transactions in the Student Registration System, whose schema was given in Section 5.7, illustrate some of the possibilities.

READ UNCOMMITTED. Consider a transaction, T_1, that prints information about the courses in which a student is currently registered. It reads the rows of the TRANSCRIPT table corresponding to the student's Id through a cursor using a sequence of FETCH statements. Such a cursor is likely to be declared INSENSITIVE, and hence a snapshot of the rows pertaining to the student will be obtained when the cursor is opened. However, the problems that might arise are independent of how the cursor is declared.

Suppose that T_1 runs at READ UNCOMMITTED. We need to consider situations in which a concurrent transaction, T_2, might interact with it. Some of these situations are listed below.

■ Suppose that T_2 changes several fields in the same row of TRANSCRIPT with a single UPDATE statement and that row is in the set of rows read by T_1. Since every SQL statement execution is isolated by the DBMS, we are guaranteed that any row seen by T_1 will not be in a state that is the result of the partial execution of T_2's UPDATE statement. The values seen by T_1 will come from a snapshot of the row either before T_2's update occurred or after it completed. Hence, this interaction does not cause a problem.

■ Suppose that T_2 changes several fields in the same row of TRANSCRIPT using *different* UPDATE statements. Since, at READ UNCOMMITTED, T_1 neither checks nor acquires locks, it might retrieve attribute values from a row that T_2 has only partially updated. This situation might be unacceptable, so we must determine, by examining the Design Document for the system, that no transaction operates in this fashion.

■ Suppose that T_2 changes several different rows of TRANSCRIPT using different UPDATE statements. Then T_1 might read one of the student's rows before T_2 has updated it and another after, and hence might report a state that never existed. Similarly, if T_2 inserts or deletes several rows using different SQL statements, T_1 might report a state that never existed. Again, we must determine from the Design Document that no transaction operates in this fashion.

■ Suppose that T_2 updates a row, T_1 subsequently reads that row before T_2 completes (a dirty read), and T_2 later aborts. Thus, the information that T_1 read is later rolled back. We must be certain that, in the rare case that aborted information is returned to the user by T_1, no significant harm is done.

If none of these situations causes a problem, T_1 can execute correctly at READ UNCOMMITTED. As a result, it will neither cause nor experience delays due to locking.

READ COMMITTED.   Consider the transaction T_1, which registers a student for a course, c. To do this, it performs the following sequence of steps (some steps have been omitted):

1. Determine c's prerequisites by reading the table REQUIRES, which has a row for each prerequisite for each course.

2. Check that the student has satisfied each of c's prerequisites by reading TRANSCRIPT to determine if the student has taken each prerequisite and received a grade of at least C.

3. Check that there is enough room in class c and, if so, increment the current enrollment. To do this, T_1 executes

```
UPDATE CLASS
SET Enrollment = Enrollment + 1
WHERE CrsCode = :courseId AND Enrollment < MaxEnrollment
```

where the course code of class c is stored in the host variable courseId, and we assume that CLASS has attributes MaxEnrollment, which contains the maximum allowable enrollment in c, and Enrollment, which contains the number of students currently registered for next semester. (Note that our approach here is different from the design given in Section 12.6.2 where this condition is checked in the schema.)

4. Insert a row in TRANSCRIPT indicating that the student is registered for class c.

Suppose that T_1 is executed at READ COMMITTED. We need to consider the following situations.

▬ While T_1 is reading REQUIRES in step 1 (using short-duration read locks on rows), a concurrent transaction, T_2, might update REQUIRES by inserting new rows corresponding to new prerequisites for c (together with the enforcement dates for these prerequisites) and then commit.

    To make the example more interesting, assume that T_1 reads REQUIRES using a DYNAMIC cursor. If T_1 and T_2 execute concurrently, T_1 might see some, but not all, of the rows that T_2 has inserted. Hence, T_1 is not serializable with respect to T_2.

    However, in this situation nonserializability does not cause a problem because it was specified in Section 3.3 that new prerequisites do not apply to current registrants. Therefore in determining c's prerequisites in step 1, T_1 (using the date attribute of each prerequisite row) ignores any prerequisites that have been added during the current semester. Thus it does not make any difference if T_1 reads some, but not all, of the new prerequisites added by T_2, because it ignores any it does read. For this reason, T_1 executes correctly at READ COMMITTED.

    Note that, if T_1 uses a KEYSET_DRIVEN cursor, the execution is still correct at READ COMMITTED because T_1 does not see *any* of the inserted rows (but the reason is not as interesting—it follows from the semantics of KEYSET_DRIVEN cursors rather than the semantics of the transaction).

▬ After T_1 reads TRANSCRIPT in step 2 and gives up the short-duration read locks on the rows it reads, a concurrent transaction, T_2, might update TRANSCRIPT— for example, by changing a grade in a course the student has taken or by adding a new course, for which that student is being given credit. The change might affect a course that is a prerequisite to c. T_1 does not see the effect of this change, but, if it had been run at the SERIALIZABLE level, it would have obtained (the equivalent of) a long-duration predicate read lock on TRANSCRIPT during step 2. That lock would have prevented T_2 from updating TRANSCRIPT until T_1 had completed. Hence, T_1 would not have seen the effect of T_2 in this case, either, so we conclude that this situation is acceptable at READ COMMITTED.

▬ It might appear that the concurrent execution of two registration transactions attempting to enroll students in c can result in a lost update (as in Figure 24.6). However, a lost update cannot occur in this case, because the check and increment are performed in step 3 as part of the isolated execution of a single SQL statement (note that it is not necessary to rely on the protection afforded by long-duration write locks to ensure this). A similar argument applies to the concurrent execution of a deregistration transaction.

Since none of these situations results in an incorrect schedule, the registration transaction can run correctly at READ COMMITTED. Hence, the read locks acquired in steps 1 and 2 will be released early, improving performance.

REPEATABLE READ.   The only bad situations that can occur in a transaction executing at REPEATABLE READ are those caused by phantoms. Consider a transaction that performs room reassignments. As the new semester approaches, the university might run out of large classrooms and decide to reassign courses originally assigned to large classrooms—but with a small number of registrants—to smaller rooms. The new room must accommodate the students currently registered for the course, and the maximum allowable enrollment for the course must be lowered to the size of that room.

The room reassignment transaction, T_1, performs this function for all courses in a particular time slot. To do this, it performs the following sequence of steps:

1. Identify the courses taught in the designated time slot that satisfy the condition that their maximum enrollment exceed their current registration by some threshold value. To do this, T_1 uses a cursor based on the following query:

   ```
   SELECT    C.CrsCode, C.Enrollment, C.MaxEnrollment,
             C.ClassroomID
   FROM      CLASS C
   WHERE     C.ClassTime = :timeSlot
             AND C.MaxEnrollment - C.Enrollment > :thresh
   ```

   where the time slot and threshold are stored in the host variables `timeSlot` and `thresh`. We assume, as in Section 5.7, that CLASS has attributes `ClassroomId`, which identifies the room in which the course will be taught next semester, and `ClassTime`, which specifies the time slot the course will occupy next semester.

2. For each course identified in step 1, read the tables CLASSROOM and CLASS to determine if there is a smaller room large enough to accommodate the current registrants and that is unoccupied at the specified hour.

3. For each course for which there is a smaller room, update the attribute `ClassroomID` of CLASS to reflect the new room assignment, and update the attribute `MaxEnrollment` of CLASS to reflect the size of the new room.

We first observe that T_1 cannot execute correctly at READ COMMITTED. The short-duration read lock that T_1 obtains in step 1 on CLASS does not prevent a registration transaction from incrementing `Enrollment` between steps 1 and 3. Hence, a course might be assigned to a room too small to accommodate the registered students.

Suppose that T_1 runs at REPEATABLE READ. We need to consider three situations.

■ After T_1 has completed step 1, a concurrent transaction, T_2, might insert a new row into the CLASS table corresponding to a (phantom) new class in the time slot under consideration. Adding such a new class is not only unlikely, but if it happened it would not seriously impact the goal of T_1. The new class will not be considered for room reassignment, but all existing classes will be processed correctly. Furthermore, the effect is the same as if T_2 had executed after T_1 in a serial order.

■ Similarly, after T_1 has completed step 2, a concurrent transaction, T_2, might insert a new row into CLASSROOM corresponding to a (phantom) new room that is available in the time slot under consideration. However, adding a new room is unlikely and will not seriously impact the goal of T_1. Again, the effect is the same as if T_2 had executed after T_1 in a serial order.

CASE STUDY

■ Since T_1 reduces MaxEnrollment, it can conceivably interfere with the correct operation of a registration transaction (executing at READ COMMITTED), which also accesses MaxEnrollment and increments Enrollment for a particular course c. If the two transactions execute concurrently, is it possible to end in a state in which MaxEnrollment < Enrollment for c? No, because the only way that can happen is if the registration transaction increments Enrollment between the execution of steps 1 and 3 in T_1. However, this cannot happen because, in step 1, T_1 obtains a (long-duration) read lock on c's row in relation CLASS.

Since none of these situations causes an incorrect schedule, T_1 can run at REPEAT-ABLE READ instead of SERIALIZABLE. Only those pages or rows that are actually accessed by T_1 need to be read-locked, and so performance is improved.

SERIALIZABLE. Transaction T_1 checks that the number of rows of TRANSCRIPT corresponding to students registered for a particular course this semester is equal to the count of current registrants recorded in that course's row in CLASS. Hence, for each course it performs the following steps:

1. Determine the number of course registrants by counting rows in TRANSCRIPT using

```
SELECT COUNT(*)
INTO :registered
FROM TRANSCRIPT T
WHERE T.CrsCode = :courseId
     AND T.Semester = :this_sem
```

2. Determine the number of course registrants by retrieving the value of Enroll-ment from the appropriate row of CLASS using

```
SELECT C.Enrollment
INTO :enrolled
FROM CLASS C
WHERE C.CrsCode = :courseId
     AND C.Semester = :this_sem
```

3. Compare enrolled with registered.

T_1 must execute at SERIALIZABLE. If it executed at REPEATABLE READ, a registration transaction could be interleaved between steps 1 and 2. Although T_1 would have long-duration read locks on all rows corresponding to students registered for a particular course, the registration transaction could insert a phantom row for a student registering for that course, update the course's row in CLASS, and then commit, releasing all of its locks. The value read by T_1 for the course in step 2 would not be equal to the value it obtained in step 1. To prevent such phantoms, T_1 must run at the SERIALIZABLE isolation level. Note that, if the order of steps 1 and 2 were reversed, this particular interaction could not occur.

We have given some examples where executing at isolation levels lower than SERIALIZABLE produces incorrect results and others where it does not. For any given application, the cautious designer will assume that using lower levels of isolation can produce incorrect results unless it can be demonstrated, using the semantics of the application, that such results are not possible.

Furthermore, note that the errors resulting from choosing an isolation level that is too weak are particularly difficult to track down. They occur in a schedule in which transactions happen to be interleaved improperly. The offending situation might happen rarely if the particular transactions are infrequently invoked, and the effects of the incorrect schedule might not become apparent until long after the execution takes place. For that reason, the system might appear to work correctly for long periods of time until an inconsistent state is suddenly detected. It might be extremely difficult to determine the sequence of events that caused the error.

There is an additional caution from a software engineering viewpoint. Even though the semantics of the initial version of an application might guarantee only correct schedules at lower isolation levels, the semantics of later versions, in which new transactions are added or older transactions are changed, might not. Thus, the reasoning that leads to the decision to execute at a lower isolation level should be carefully documented, perhaps in the Design Document, so that the system maintainers can later determine that the reasoning is still valid for updated versions of the system.

The registration transaction revisited.   The design of the registration transaction given in Section 12.6.2 differs from the design described here in that it assumes that the limit on the number of students that can register for a class is enforced by an integrity constraint in the database schema. Thus, in that design as well (but for a different reason) there is no possibility that the execution of two concurrent registration transactions will cause the limit to be exceeded. Therefore, we might think that the registration transaction in that design can also correctly execute at READ COMMITTED.

However, in Section 12.6.2 we considered some additional conditions that we did not consider here. For example, the transaction checks (within the transaction code) that the registration does not cause the student to exceed the limit of 20 credits per semester. It determines the number of credits for which the student is currently registered by reading TRANSCRIPT. If the constraint is satisfied, it then inserts a new tuple into TRANSCRIPT corresponding to the new course.

If the transaction executes at READ COMMITTED (or at REPEATABLE READ), there is a (rather remote) possibility that the credit limit can be exceeded. If the student initiates two concurrent registration transactions to register for two different courses and neither transaction sees the (phantom) tuple inserted into TRANSCRIPT by the other, they will both commit and, as a result, the credit limit may be exceeded.

Perhaps the designer will decide that this possibility is so unlikely that the registration transaction can safely run at READ COMMITTED. If not, the registration transaction will have to execute at SERIALIZABLE to eliminate phantoms.

Deadlocks in the Student Registration System. Consider the concurrent execution of a registration transaction, T_1, and a deregistration transaction, T_2, for the same course, and assume that the DBMS uses page locking.

■ T_2 first deletes the row in TRANSCRIPT describing the student registered in that course and then decrements Enrollment in CLASS (since there is no point in decrementing Enrollment if the student is not actually registered). Thus, T_2 first obtains a long-duration predicate write lock on TRANSCRIPT and then obtains a long-duration predicate write lock on CLASS. Although we have not discussed the implementation of predicate locks, assume that both locks lock the page being updated.

■ Recall that the registration transaction, T_1, first updates CLASS (since there is no point in inserting a tuple in TRANSCRIPT if there is no room in the course) and then inserts a tuple in TRANSCRIPT. Thus, T_2 first obtains a long-duration predicate write lock on CLASS and then obtains a long-duration predicate write lock on TRANSCRIPT. Again, we assume that both locks lock the page being updated.

Both transactions update the same tuple in CLASS. If T_1 attempts to insert the new tuple in TRANSCRIPT into the page containing the tuple being deleted by T_2, a deadlock might result since T_1 and T_2 obtain their locks in the opposite order. Because long-duration write locks are used at all isolation levels, the deadlock is independent of which level is chosen.

Note that two registration transactions will not deadlock, since they both acquire locks on the two tables in the same order: first on CLASS and then on TRANSCRIPT. Requiring transactions to acquire locks on items in the same order is a standard way to avoid deadlocks.

24.2.3 Serializable, SERIALIZABLE, and Correct

We have used three terms in describing schedules produced by a concurrency control:

■ *Serializable.* Equivalent to a serial schedule.

■ SERIALIZABLE. An SQL isolation level. Dirty reads, unrepeatable reads, and phantoms are not allowed, and schedules must be serializable (as stated in the ANSI specifications [SQL 1992]).

■ *Correct.* Leaves the database in a state that correctly models the real world and satisfies the business rules of the enterprise (as stated in the Specification Document).

These definitions are related as follows (assuming that each transaction is consistent):

■ If a schedule is serializable, it is correct.

▥ If a schedule has been produced by a set of transactions executing at the SERI-
ALIZABLE isolation level, it is serializable (and hence correct).

These implications do not go both ways.

▥ A schedule might be correct, even though it is not serializable.

▥ A schedule might be serializable, even though it has been produced by transactions executing at isolation levels lower than SERIALIZABLE.

The previous section provided examples of these last two points.

Correct, although not serializable.   The registration transaction executes correctly
at READ COMMITTED, even though it is not serializable with respect to a transaction that adds new prerequisites.

Serializable, although some transactions are not SERIALIZABLE.   Schedules in which
all transactions except room reassignment transactions execute at SERIALIZABLE,
and in which room reassignment transactions execute at REPEATABLE READ,
are serializable. This follows because a transaction that creates a phantom (by
adding a new room or a new course) while a room reassignment transaction, T,
is executing can actually be serialized after T since T does not see the phantom.

These examples demonstrate again that correctness can often be obtained without
using the stringent locking protocols required to *guarantee* serializable schedules.

24.3 GRANULAR LOCKING: INTENTION LOCKS AND INDEX LOCKS

In the previous section, we discussed how the performance of a transaction processing system can be improved through the use of isolation levels that do not ensure
serializable execution. Performance can also be affected by lock granularity. In this
section, we consider locking algorithms that allow granularity to be adjusted to the
needs of the transactions. Performance improvements can result, and serializable
behavior is retained.

The designer of a locking system faces a tradeoff between concurrency and overhead in choosing locking granularity. Hence, when implementing a concurrency
control for an application that involves some transactions that access large blocks
of data (e.g., an entire table) and others that access very small blocks (e.g., a few
tuples), it is desirable to use a locking mechanism that allows different granularities.

Granular locking [Gray et al. 1976] is designed to meet this need. A transaction
requiring access to a large block of data can lock the block with a single request; a
transaction requiring access to small amounts of data within a block can lock each
piece individually. In the latter case, several transactions can simultaneously hold
locks on small items within the same block.

As a simple example, a system might provide locks on records and also locks
on specific fields within a record—two locks with different granularity. Suppose
that transaction T_1 has obtained a write lock on field F_1 within record R_1, and
that transaction T_2 requests a write lock on the entire record, R_1. That lock cannot
be granted, since it permits access to F_1. The problem is to design an efficient

mechanism that the concurrency control can use to recognize the lock on F_1 when a lock on R_1 is requested.

The solution is to organize locks hierarchically. Before obtaining a lock on F_1, T_1 must first obtain a lock on R_1. Then, when T_2 requests a lock on R_1, the concurrency control will see the conflict. But what kind of a lock does T_1 get? Clearly, not a read or write lock, since in that case there would be no point in acquiring an additional fine-granularity lock on F_1, and the effective lock granularity would be coarse. DBMSs thus provide a new type of lock, the **intention lock**. Before a transaction can obtain a shared or exclusive lock on an item, it must obtain appropriate intention locks on all containing items in the hierarchy of granularity. Thus, before T_1 can obtain a lock on F_1, it must first obtain an intention lock on R_1. Intention locks come in three flavors.

1. If T_1 wants to read some fields in R_1, it must first get an **intention shared** (or *IS*) lock on R_1. It can then request a shared (S) lock on those fields.

2. If T_1 wants to update some fields in R_1, it must first get an **intention exclusive** (or *IX*) lock on R_1. It can then request an exclusive (X) lock on those fields.

3. If T_1 wants to update some fields in R_1 but needs to read all of the fields to determine which ones to update (for example, it wants to change all fields with values less than 100), it must first obtain a **shared intention exclusive** (or *SIX*) lock on R_1. It can then read all fields in R_1 and request an X lock on the fields it updates. (A SIX lock is a combination of an S lock and an IX lock on R_1.)

Although transactions now must acquire additional locks, performance gains are possible since intentions locks commute with many other lock types. The conflict table for granular locks is given in Figure 24.9. It indicates, for example, that a request for an IX lock on an item is denied if the item is already S-locked. The justification for this is that the S lock allows all contained items to be read whereas the IX lock allows a transaction to request write locks on some of those items. In contrast, a request for an IX lock is granted if the item is already IS locked. The justification for this is that the IS lock allows some subset of the contained items to

Figure 24.9 Conflict table for intention locks. X indicates conflicts between lock modes.

Requested Mode	Granted Mode				
	IS	IX	SIX	S	X
IS					X
IX			X	X	X
SIX		X	X	X	X
S		X	X		X
X	X	X	X	X	X

be S-locked while the IX lock allows some subset of the contained items to be X-locked. These subsets might be disjoint, and if so there is no conflict. If they are not disjoint, the conflict will be detected at the lower level since the transactions will have to obtain S and X locks on the individual contained items.

In the previous example, after T_1 has acquired an IX lock on R_1, no other transaction will be granted an exclusive lock on R_1.

In the general case, the items to be locked are organized in a hierarchy that can be represented as a tree, where the item represented by a node in the tree is contained within the item represented by its parent in the tree. Thus, locking an item in the tree implicitly locks all of its descendents. (Locking a record implicitly locks all of its fields.) The general rule is that, before a lock can be obtained on a particular item (which need not be a leaf), an appropriate intention lock must be obtained on all of the containing items (ancestors) in the hierarchy. Thus, in order to lock a particular item in S mode, a transaction must first acquire IS mode locks on all items on the path to the item from the root in the order they are encountered. The S lock is acquired last to ensure that the transaction cannot actually access the target object until all locks are in place. Locks are released in the opposite order. Similarly, to obtain an X lock on an item, IX locks must be first obtained on all items on the path from the root to the item.

We intentionally based our example on a system using records and fields, rather than tables and tuples, so that phantoms would not be an issue. When we apply the concepts of granular locking to relational databases, that issue arises and we must ensure that phantoms do not occur. The next section discusses an approach to granular locking that does not lead to phantoms and is used in a number of commercial DBMSs.

24.3.1 Index Locks: Granular Locking without Phantoms

We discussed two methods for guaranteeing serializable schedules in a relational database—predicate locking and table locking. We pointed out the deficiencies of each: the computational complexity of predicate locking and the coarse granularity of table locking. The coarse granularity of table locking can be overcome by locking individual tuples, but this can lead to phantoms and nonserializable behavior. Locking the pages on which the tuples are stored (instead of the tuples themselves) is in some ways more efficient, but can also lead to phantoms.

A number of commercial DBMSs eliminate phantoms and guarantee serializable schedules by using an enhanced method of granular locking involving tuples, pages, and tables. The essential requirement for preventing phantoms is that, after a transaction, T_1, has accessed a table, R, using a predicate, P, no other concurrently executing transaction, T_2, can insert into R a (phantom) tuple, t, which also satisfies P, until after T_1 terminates. If the DBMS uses page locking, when T_1 accesses R it locks only those pages actually scanned during the access (unless all pages of R were scanned, in which case it locks R). The phrase "those pages actually scanned during the access" is not as simple as it might seem when the access involves indices.

The method we describe here depends on how R is accessed by T_1. In constructing a query execution plan for an SQL statement that accesses tuples satisfying P, the system determines whether any existing indices can be used. If T_1 has executed a SELECT statement on R and no indices are used, the system must search every page in R to locate the tuples that satisfy P. To perform the search, T_1 acquires an S lock on R. If that lock is held until T_1 commits, T_2 cannot insert t since it would first need to acquire a (conflicting) IX lock on R. Similarly, if T_1 has executed a DELETE statement (we consider an UPDATE statement later) on R with predicate P and no indices are used, it must also search every page in R to locate the tuples that satisfy P. In this case, T_1 acquires a SIX lock on R (recall that a SIX lock is equivalent to both an S lock and an IX lock). Then it obtains X locks on the pages containing tuples satisfying P.[8] Again, T_2 cannot insert t, without acquiring an IX lock on R (which conflicts with the S lock held by T_1). Hence, when no indices are used, granular locking prevents phantoms.

The situation is more involved if T_1 accesses R through an index. In that case, an entire scan of R is not required. If T_1 executes a SELECT on R using predicate P, it acquires only an IS lock on R and S locks on the pages of R containing tuples satisfying P that it accesses through the index. Similarly, if T_1 executes a DELETE on R using predicate P, it acquires only an IX lock on R and X locks on the pages of R containing tuples satisfying P that it accesses through the index.

Unfortunately, this locking protocol does not prevent phantoms. If T_2 attempts to insert a phantom into R, it can obtain an IX lock on R since that lock does not conflict with either the IS or the IX locks obtained by T_1. Hence, there is no conflict at the table level. And, if the phantom that T_2 is attempting to insert will be stored on a page that is different than the pages locked by T_1, there will be no conflict at the page level, either, so it will be possible for T_2 to insert the phantom. Some mechanism is needed to prevent this.

For example, the table STUDENT in the schema for the Student Registration System has an attribute Address (for simplicity we assume that the address simply designates the town), and T_1 might execute the SELECT statement

```
SELECT *
FROM STUDENT S
WHERE S.Address = 'Stony Brook'
```

If there is an index, ADDRIDX, on Address in the relation STUDENT, it will be used to find the students living in Stony Brook. An IS lock will be acquired on STUDENT, and an S lock will be acquired on all pages containing tuples describing students living in Stony Brook. However, these locks will not prevent T_2 from inserting a tuple, t, describing a new student living in Stony Brook, since T_2 needs to obtain only an IX lock on STUDENT and an X lock on the page in which t is to be inserted (this page

---

[8] If the DBMS supports tuple locking, it obtains SIX locks on R and the pages containing tuples satisfying P, and X locks on the tuples.

might be different from all of the pages in which tuples for students living in Stony Brook are stored).

To prevent phantoms, in addition to an appropriate intention lock on the table and page locks on the data pages accessed, a transaction might, in addition, obtain locks on pages of the index structure itself. Two types of indices are used in commercial DBMSs. One type effectively contains a pointer to the only page(s) in which tuples describing students who live in Stony Brook can possibly be stored.[9] Clustered indices, in which the location of a row in the data file is controlled by the value of its search key, fall into this category. An integrated static hash index (in which all rows in a particular bucket are placed in the same page) is another example. In the second type, there is no unique page of STUDENT into which all tuples that describe students living in Stony Brook must be placed. When T_2 requests to insert t, the page in which t is to be stored is determined and a pointer to that page is stored in ADDRIDX. Any secondary index falls into this category.

Our strategy for preventing phantoms depends on the index type. If the index is of the first type, T_1 can delay T_2 by obtaining a long-duration lock (S or X, depending on whether T_1 is executing SELECT or DELETE) on the page(s) of STUDENT containing the tuples that describe students who live in Stony Brook. Since this is the page into which t must be inserted, T_2 is delayed until T_1 completes. For example, in static hashing T_1 acquires an S lock on the bucket to which Stony Brook is hashed.

If the index is of the second type, T_1 acquires long-duration read locks on all leaf pages of ADDRIDX that it accesses while using the index, and T_2 acquires long-duration X locks on all leaf index pages that it updates (e.g., in which it inserts a pointer). Figure 24.10 illustrates the case in which a B^+ tree is used as a secondary index on the STUDENT table for the attribute Address. We have assumed address values a_i, $i > 0$, such that $a_i < a_{i+1}$. In executing the SELECT statement, T_1 obtains a long-duration S lock on the leaf page, A, of the index,[10] which contains pointers to pages B, C, and D in the STUDENT data file that contain the tuples describing the students who live in Stony Brook. An attempt by T_2 at a later time to insert a new tuple describing a student who lives in Stony Brook requires that it insert a pointer to the data page that contains that tuple in every index on STUDENT.

In the case of ADDRIDX, the pointer must be inserted in index page A, since leaf pages are sorted on Address. This requires an X lock on A, which generates a conflict with T_1 and so T_2 is forced to wait. The new tuple is thus prevented from becoming a phantom despite the fact that it might ultimately be stored in a data page other than B, C, or D and the fact that T_1 and T_2 acquire compatible locks (IS and IX) on STUDENT. The lock on A must be retained by T_1 until it commits. Intuitively, by locking the index in this fashion the transaction effectively obtains a predicate lock on the predicate Address = 'Stony Brook'.

---

[9] Note that when a page is locked, any overflow chain associated with the page is locked as well.
[10] More generally, there might be several such leaf pages, but the algorithm is unchanged.

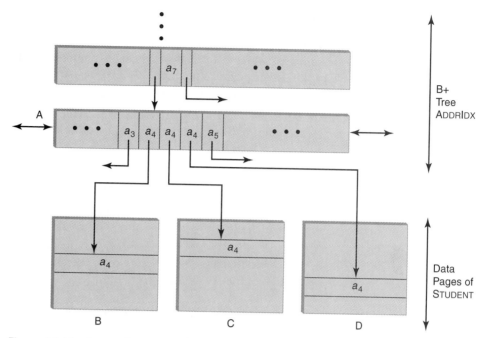

Figure 24.10 An unclustered B$^+$ tree secondary index on the STUDENT table.

Although this method eliminates phantoms caused by INSERT statements, several other issues arise with UPDATE statements. An UPDATE can be treated as if it were a DELETE which deletes the tuples to be updated, followed by an IN-SERT, which inserts the updated tuples. Thus, UPDATE has the interesting property that it is both subject to phantoms, because of its DELETE part, and the cause of phantoms, because of its INSERT part. If an index of the first type is used, a tuple updated by T_1 might have to be moved to a new page in the data file. For example, with hashing, if an attribute of the updated tuple, t', contained in the hash key is changed, t' must be moved to a new bucket. In this case, in order to prevent T_2 from inserting a phantom tuple satisfying the WHERE clause of the UPDATE statement, T_1 must retain a lock on the bucket that originally contained t'. (In addition, T_1 obtains an X lock on the bucket to which t' is moved.) Similarly, if an index of the second type is used and an attribute of t' contained in the search key is changed, the pointer to t' must be moved to a new position. T_1 must retain a lock on the page that originally contained the pointer, to prevent a pointer to a phantom tuple from being inserted later. (In addition, T_1 obtains an X lock on the index page to which the pointer to t' is moved.)

We summarize the protocol when no index is used and when a B$^+$ tree index is used.

Granular Locking Protocol for Relational Databases

■ If no index can be used in the execution of a SELECT, UPDATE, or DELETE statement, the system must search every page in the table named in the FROM clause to locate the tuples satisfying the statement's WHERE clause.

  ❏ A SELECT statement obtains an S lock on the table.

  ❏ An UPDATE or DELETE statement obtains a SIX lock on the table and an X lock on the page(s) containing the tuples to be updated or deleted.

■ If a B$^+$ tree index is used in the access,

  ❏ A SELECT statement obtains an IS lock on the table and an S lock on the page(s) containing tuples satisfying the statement's WHERE clause.

  ❏ An UPDATE or DELETE statement obtains an IX lock on the table and an X lock on the page(s) in which the tuples will be updated or deleted.

  ❏ SELECT, UPDATE, and DELETE statements obtain long-duration S locks on the leaf pages of the B$^+$ tree that were read during their search and long-duration X locks on any pages of the B$^+$ tree that were updated.

This protocol has the property that, when an attempt is made to insert a phantom, lock conflicts will occur

■ At the table level when indices are not involved

■ Along the indexing path when indices are involved

As a result, it does not allow phantoms and produces serializable schedules.

Even when indices are not used, granular locking allows considerably more concurrency than do the methods previously described. In the locking implementation of all isolation levels, including SERIALIZABLE, a write statement requires a long-duration write lock on a predicate. In the absence of indices and granular locks, this is implemented as a long-duration write lock on the corresponding table. With granular locking, a write statement that does not use indices requires only a SIX lock on the table and X locks on the pages containing rows that are updated, inserted, or deleted. These locks prevent concurrent transactions from reading those rows and from changing any rows in the table, but allow concurrent transactions to read any rows in the table other than those in pages that have been updated. Thus, granular locking prevents phantoms at the SERIALIZABLE level (hence ensuring serializability), but locks fewer items than a write lock on the entire table (hence increasing concurrency). If indices are used by the write statement, even more concurrency can be realized.

Note that granular locking can be used at lower isolation levels where phantoms are not an issue. For example, a SELECT statement executing at REPEATABLE READ obtains an IS lock on the table and an S lock on the pages containing tuples satisfying the statement's WHERE clause. In contrast to SERIALIZABLE, however, it does not require long-duration read locks on the leaf pages of indices used by the statement.

Lock escalation. The overhead of granular locking becomes excessive when a transaction accumulates too many fine-grain locks. This overhead takes two forms: the space overhead within the DBMS for recording information about each lock acquired and the time overhead necessary to process each lock request. When a transaction begins acquiring a large number of page (or tuple) locks on a table, it will likely continue to do so. Therefore, it is beneficial to trade in those locks for a single lock on the entire table.

This technique is known as **lock escalation**. A threshold is set in the concurrency control that limits the number of page locks a transaction can obtain on a particular table. When the transaction reaches that limit, the concurrency control attempts to lock the entire table (in the same mode as the page locks). When the table lock is granted, the page locks and the intention lock on the table can be released. Note the danger of deadlock in this scheme. If two transactions are acquiring page locks, at least one of them is a writer, and both reach their threshold, a deadlock results, since neither can escalate their locks to a table lock.

Multilevel control*   Multilevel concurrency control, in which data abstractions are built one on another to an arbitrary depth, has not been widely adopted, but it can be used in abbreviated form within a DBMS. A key issue is that, when a tuple has to be updated, inserted, or deleted, the entire page containing it will generally be exclusively locked so that, for example, information about storage allocation within the page can be adjusted. Thus, the pages accessed by an SQL statement are locked in order to guarantee the isolation of that statement. Maintaining all of these page locks once the statement completes unnecessarily reduces concurrency, however, since they prevent other transactions from accessing the page in what might be totally nonconflicting ways.

To increase concurrency, an SQL statement can be viewed as a subtransaction of a transaction. While the transaction sees the abstraction of SQL statements, the subtransaction sees the abstraction of page reads and writes. The subtransaction can acquire locks on the data pages it accesses and then release them when it completes. The transaction can maintain higher-level locks on tuples and access paths to ensure appropriate isolation.

Table fragmentation.   Table fragmentation is a useful technique related to granular locking. Consider again the table STUDENT. An application wishing to extract information about students living in Stony Brook might execute the statement

```
SELECT *
FROM STUDENT S
WHERE S.Address = 'Stony Brook'
```

An alternative organization of the data is to partition STUDENT into separate tables, called **fragments**, one for each town. For example, we might put all of the tuples satisfying the predicate Address = 'Stony Brook' in one table, STUD_SB, and all tuples satisfying the predicate Address = 'Smithtown' in another, STUD_SM, and so forth. A transaction wishing to retrieve information about students living in Stony Brook now executes

```
SELECT *
FROM STUD_SB
```

We see that a table lock on the fragment is equivalent to a predicate lock on the predicate used to perform the fragmentation. This eliminates the need for index locking as a substitute for predicate locking. Since the original table no longer exists, we are not implementing two different granularities of locking; therefore, a transaction requesting a table lock on a fragment need not get an intention lock at a higher level. Fragmentation was discussed in more detail in Chapter 18. Its advantage is that the table fragments are of finer granularity than the original table, and so a higher degree on concurrency can be obtained. The disadvantage is that queries that span multiple fragments become more difficult to process. For example, a query that retrieves the tuples of all students living in Stony Brook or Smithtown, or a query that uses a predicate that does not involve the attribute Address, must access multiple tables.

24.3.2 Granular Locking in an Object Database*

Many of the ideas in granular locking for relational databases also apply to object databases. Consider a bank account application. A relational database might have a table ACCOUNTS with tuples representing individual accounts. Similarly an object database might have a class ACCOUNTSCLASS in which individual accounts are represented by objects. Just as a tuple is contained in a table, we can view an object as being contained in a class. Furthermore, we can use the same lock modes (shared and exclusive and the corresponding intentions modes) and interpret them in an object database in the same way as they are interpreted in a relational database:

■ In a relational database, locking a table implicitly locks all the tuples in it.

■ In an object database, locking a class implicitly locks all the objects in it.

Thus, in the bank's object database, a granular locking protocol requires that we get the appropriate intention lock on ACCOUNTSCLASS before we can get a lock on a particular account object.

Object databases also support inheritance. Thus, in the bank application, the class hierarchy might include the fact that SAVINGSACCOUNTSCLASS and CHECKING-ACCOUNTSCLASS are subclasses of ACCOUNTSCLASS and that ECONOMYCHECKING-ACCOUNTSCLASS is a subclass of CHECKINGACCOUNTSCLASS. Since an object in the class ECONOMYCHECKINGACCOUNTSCLASS is also an object of the parent classes CHECKINGACCOUNTSCLASS and ACCOUNTSCLASS, a lock on ACCOUNTSCLASS implicitly locks all the objects in CHECKINGACCOUNTSCLASS and ECONOMYCHECK-INGACCOUNTSCLASS. Similarly, before we can get a lock on the ECONOMYCHECKING-ACCOUNTSCLASS class, we must get the appropriate intention locks on both the CHECKINGACCOUNTSCLASS class and the ACCOUNTSCLASS class. Thus, locking a class implicitiy also locks

■ All of its objects

■ All of its descendent classes (and hence all the objects in those classes)

We now summarize our discussion with a (somewhat simplified)[11] protocol for granular locking of object databases.

Granular Locking Protocol for Object Databases

■ Before obtaining a lock on an object, the system must get the appropriate intention locks on the class of that object and on all parent classes of that class.

■ Before obtaining a lock on a class, the system must get the appropriate intention locks on all parent classes of that class.

With these ideas in mind, we see that much of this discussion on isolation and granular locking for relational databases also applies to object databases.

24.4 IMPROVING SYSTEM PERFORMANCE

Performance is a key issue in the design of systems. In this section, we give examples of techniques that can be used to improve the performance of an application running under a locking concurrency control.

■ Transactions should execute at the lowest level of isolation consistent with the requirements of the application.

■ The tradeoff between including integrity constraints in the schema so that the DBMS enforces them and encoding enforcement in the transactions should be examined carefully. For example, some transactions that modify a data item named in a constraint might change it in a way that cannot possibly cause a violation but if the constraint is part of the schema it will be (unnecessarily) checked when the transaction commits. If such transactions are frequently executed, it might be better to restrict constraint checking to the code of transactions that might cause a violation. On the other hand, such a decision should be weighed against the potential maintenance overhead: if later we need to modify the constraint, the code of all transactions that check this constraint must also be changed and recompiled. This would not be necessary if the constraint were part of the schema.

■ Certain integrity constraints should be declared within the database schema so that they are automatically checked by the DBMS, and thus permit a transaction to execute correctly at a lower isolation level than that consistent with the requirements of the application. (The transaction would not execute correctly at that isolation level if those integrity constraints were not checked by the DBMS.) This is essentially an optimistic approach in that it assumes that certain interleavings that cause a database to become inconsistent are unlikely. In the (rare) case in which such interleavings occur, the DBMS aborts the transaction when

---

[11] Some DBMSs might allow different granularities—for example, attribute-level (individual attributes of an object), or database-level. In some DBMSs, a write lock on a class allows the program to change the class declaration, including its methods. Other DBMSs might distinguish between a lock on the class instances, which refers to all of the objects currently in the class (similar to a table lock), and a lock on the class itself, which allows changes to the class definition (similar to a schema lock).

it detects the violation. However, errors that do not result in integrity constraint violations are not detected.

■ Transactions should be as short as possible in order to limit the time that locks must be held. It is particularly important to gather all the needed information interactively from the user before initiating the transaction. Since user interactions take a long time, locks should not be held while they are in progress. It is also desirable to decompose a long transaction into a sequence of shorter ones (assuming that this can be done while maintaining consistency). In the extreme case, each SQL statement becomes a single transaction.

■ The database should be designed so that the transactions invoked most frequently can be efficiently executed. This might involve *denormalization* (see Section 8.13) to avoid expensive joins.

■ Indices should be considered for searches that are performed frequently. In some cases this may mean creating several secondary indices for a particular table, although if the table is updated frequently the overhead of index maintenance should be considered. To avoid multiple indices, an index should be designed to support as many of the searches as possible. With a B^+ tree index this means carefully choosing and ordering the attributes in the search key. For applications sensitive to phantoms, the use of index locking instead of table locks can increase concurrency.

■ Lock escalation is inefficient if the escalation threshold will likely be reached and a table lock will ultimately be acquired. Some databases permit a transaction to explicitly request a table lock before accessing a table (manual locking). Alternatively, if the number of required page (or tuple) locks can be estimated, and it is not too large, the threshold can be set above that value.

■ Lock granularity can often be decreased and hence concurrency increased by fragmenting one or more of the tables.

■ In systems that use page locking, lock conflicts can occur if two transactions access different tuples that happen to be stored on the same page. Putting these tuples on separate pages reduces such conflicts. Similarly if a single transaction accesses a number of tuples, lock conflicts with other transactions can be reduced if all of those tuples are clustered on a small number of pages.

■ A deadlock can occur if one transaction accesses two tables in one order and another transaction accesses them in the opposite order. If possible, transactions that access common resources should all acquire locks on those resources in the same order.

24.5   MULTIVERSION CONCURRENCY CONTROLS

By a **version** of a database we mean a snapshot of the database taken at the time a transaction commits, which contains the results of that transaction and of all transactions that committed at a prior time. Hence, a version contains only committed data. Many versions of a database are produced during the execution of a particular schedule of transactions. In a multiversion DBMS, different versions are retained, and the concurrency control need not use the current one to satisfy a request to read an item.

In this section, we discuss three multiversion concurrency controls. The advantage of these algorithms, all of which have been implemented in commercial systems, is that (in most cases) readers are not required to set read locks. Therefore, a request to read a data item does not have to wait, and a request to write a data item does not have to wait for a reader. This is an important advantage, particularly in the many applications where reading occurs far more frequently than writing. These advantages come at the expense of the additional system complexity required to maintain multiple versions of the database.

Of the three algorithms we discuss, the last two can produce nonserializable schedules and hence incorrect database states. The first algorithm always produces serializable schedules, but can behave unintuitively.

Transaction-level read consistency. The first question that must be addressed in specifying a multiversion concurrency control is "What value is returned to a transaction that requests to read an item in the database?" As with the READ COMMITTED isolation level, multiversion algorithms guarantee that only committed data is returned (because, by definition, a version contains only committed data). Recall, however, that at READ COMMITTED successive reads might return data from different versions and that (from our discussion in Section 24.2.1) when a cursor is used the tuples returned from the result set of a single SELECT statement might come from different versions, even though the result set is computed in an isolated fashion when the cursor is opened. Thus, the transaction might see an inconsistent view of data—a view that does not come from a single database version.

Some multiversion algorithms guarantee a stronger condition on the data returned by such queries. **Transaction-level read consistency** guarantees that the data returned by *all* of the SQL statements executed in a transaction comes from the same version of the database. Transaction-level read consistency, however, does not necessarily guarantee serializability.

The next question that must be addressed is "What version of the database is accessed by an SQL statement?" A multiversion concurrency control might access a version other than the one produced by the last committed transaction. For example, assume that transactions T_1 and T_2 are active in a conventional (single-version) immediate-update pessimistic system. If T_1 has written an item and T_2 makes a request to read the item, a conflict exists and T_2 waits. In a multiversion system, T_2's request might be satisfied using a version that was created before T_1's write (note that this need not be the most recently committed version). T_2 then precedes T_1 in any equivalent serial order.

24.5.1   Read-Only Multiversion Concurrency Controls

In the general case, the design of a multiversion concurrency control that ensures serializable schedules is quite complex. However, there is a special case of a multiversion control, called a **Read-Only multiversion concurrency control**, that is easier to implement and produces serializable schedules.

A Read-Only multiversion concurrency control distinguishes in advance between two kinds of transactions: **read-only**, which contain no write operations, and **read/write**, which contain at least one write operation (and can also contain read operations).

■ Read/write transactions use an immediate-update pessimistic concurrency control. Read and write locks can be managed in a variety of ways depending on the isolation level selected. Transactions access the most current version of the item read or written.

■ All of the reads of a read-only transaction, T_{RO}, are satisfied using the (committed) version of the database that existed when T_{RO} made its first read request. Thus, T_{RO} is serialized immediately after the transaction that created that version—not necessarily in commit order. The effect is as if a **snapshot** of the (committed) database had been taken at the time of T_{RO}'s first read and all subsequent reads are satisfied from that snapshot. Hence, read-only transactions are provided with transaction-level read consistency.

If read/write transactions are executed serializably, all transactions are provided with transaction-level read consistency. In that case, the combined schedule of read-only and read/write transactions is serializable. The equivalent serial order is the commit order of the read/write transactions, with each read-only transaction inserted immediately after the read/write transaction that created its snapshot.

To implement this control, the DBMS maintains multiple versions of the database. We will see in Chapter 25 that DBMSs generally keep version information in their log for recovery purposes, so the maintenance of this information is not unique to multiversion systems. Multiversion systems, however, have the additional requirement of being able to make earlier versions accessible in an efficient manner.

The issue is how to provide the appropriate version to satisfy a particular read request. To do this, the system uses a deferred update technique and maintains a **version counter**, **(VC)**, which is incremented whenever a read/write transaction, $T_{R/W}$, commits. At that time, a new version of each item it has modified is stored in the database and tagged with a version number, N, whose value is obtained from the (incremented) VC. Older versions of the item are retained (perhaps in the log). $T_{R/W}$ has created a new version—or snapshot—of the database, with snapshot number N, consisting of the new versions of the items it has updated and the most recent versions (at the time $T_{R/W}$ commits) of all other items. A snapshot contains only committed values. Each read-only transaction is assigned the snapshot that was current when it made its first read request and all subsequent read requests are satisfied using values drawn from that snapshot.

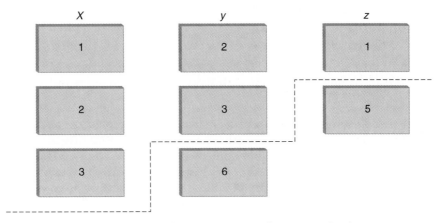

Figure 24.11 Satisfying a read request in a multiversion database.

The situation is illustrated in Figure 24.11. Three items, x, y, and z, of the database are shown. Each item is tagged with a version number. T_{RO} makes its first read request when VC has the value 4. Hence its snapshot number is 4 and it gets the versions of x, y, and z that lie immediately above the dotted line. Versions 5 and 6 might be created while T_{RO} is executing, but it does not see them.

Overhead is involved in storing the version number in each database item. Furthermore, as a practical matter the number of accessible earlier versions might be limited, and hence a (long-running) read-only transaction that draws its information from a very old version might have to be aborted if that version is no longer available.

This control has the highly desirable property that read-only transactions do not have to obtain any locks. For that reason, read-only transactions never have to wait, and read/write transactions never have to wait for read-only transactions. The cost of this property is a more complex concurrency control, the additional storage required to maintain multiple versions tagged with version numbers, and some possible nonintuitive behavior due to the serialization of read-only transactions in an order different than commit order. For example, a read-only transaction that reports bank balances might commit at a later time than a bank deposit transaction but not report the result of the deposit because it executed its first read before the deposit transaction started.

24.5.2 Read–Consistency Multiversion Concurrency Controls

For applications that can tolerate nonrepeatable reads (and hence nonserializable schedules), some commercial DBMSs, such as Oracle, use an algorithm called **Read Consistency** that extends the Read-Only control to deal with read/write transactions.

■ Read-only transactions are treated as in the Read-Only control and therefore are provided with transaction-level read consistency.

■ Write statements in read/write transactions use long-duration write locks applied to the most current version of the item being written. A transaction attempting to write an item that is write-locked by another transaction must wait.

■ Read statements in read/write transactions do not use read locks. Instead, each read request is provided with the value of the most recent version of the requested item.

Read Consistency provides an enhanced implementation of the READ COMMITTED isolation level (and is the implementation of READ COMMITTED provided by Oracle). As with the locking implementation of READ COMMITTED given in Section 24.2, write locks are of long duration and reads return committed values. However, Read Consistency provides transaction-level read consistency for read-only transactions, which is not provided by the locking implementation of READ COMMITTED (nor is it required by the ANSI definition of READ COMMITTED).

A nice property of Read Consistency is that no transaction needs to acquire a lock for a read operation. Hence, reads never wait for writes and writes never wait for reads. As with READ COMMITTED, reads performed by read/write transactions are not repeatable, and so schedules can be nonserializable. For example, the schedule shown in Figure 24.6, which exhibits a lost update, can be produced by this control.

24.5.3 SNAPSHOT Isolation

Still another variation on the same idea is called SNAPSHOT isolation [Berenson et al. 1995]. Variants of SNAPSHOT isolation have been implemented by a number of database vendors, including Oracle. The method is based on the following two principles:

■ All the reads of each transaction are satisfied using the snapshot of the database that was current when that transaction made its first read request. Thus, all transactions are provided with transaction-level read consistency.

■ The writes of each transaction must satisfy the **first-committer-wins** property. A transaction, T_1, is allowed to commit only if there is no other transaction that (1) committed between the time T_1 made its first read request and the time it requested to commit, and (2) updated a data item that T_1 also updated. Otherwise, T_1 aborts. A data item could be either a row or a table. Since tables provide a coarse granularity for determining the interaction between transactions, which negatively affects performance, we will henceforth assume that a data item is a row.

The first-committer-wins property has the important effect of eliminating lost updates. In Figure 24.6 on page 819, T_1 is not allowed to commit because it updated data item t, but T_2 updated t and committed after T_1's first read request and before T_1's commit request.

The first-committer-wins property can be implemented without write locks. When a transaction, T_1, has completed it is validated (as in an optimistic concurrency control but with a different validation criterion) to enforce the first-

Figure 24.12 SNAPSHOT-isolated schedule that is not serializable and leads to an inconsistent database.

T_1: $r(a_1 : 10)$ $r(a_2 : 10)$ $w(a_2 : -5)$ *commit*

T_2: $r(a_1 : 10)$ $r(a_2 : 10)$ $w(a_1 : -5)$ *commit*

committer-wins property. Validation can be implemented by comparing T_1's snapshot number with the version number of each item that T_1 has updated.

◼ Suppose that the version number of some item that T_1 has updated at the time T_1 requests to commit is greater than T_1's snapshot number. This means that some other transaction, T_2, wrote that item and committed after T_1's snapshot was created. In this case, T_1 must be aborted, since T_2 is the first committer—and it wins.

◼ Suppose that, for all items that T_1 writes, the version number at the time T_1 requests to commit is less than or equal to the number of T_1's snapshot. In this case, T_1 is allowed to commit.

As illustrated in Figure 24.11, if the number of T_1's snapshot is 4, and T_1 has written to x and y, then T_1's request to commit will be denied. Although there are no newer versions of x, a newer version of y was created by a different (committed) transaction while T_1 was executing.

As with the optimistic concurrency control algorithm, this control has the property that no locks are needed; hence, neither reads nor writes ever wait, but transactions might be aborted when they complete.

Although SNAPSHOT isolation eliminates many anomalies, it does not guarantee that all schedules will be serializable and hence transactions can perform incorrectly. For example, in Figure 24.12, T_1 and T_2 are two bank withdrawal transactions that are withdrawing funds from different accounts, with balances a_1 and a_2, owned by the same depositor, d. The bank has a business rule that an individual account balance can be negative, but the sum of the balances in all accounts owned by each depositor must be nonnegative. Thus, if d has only two accounts, the constraint is $a_1 + a_2 \geq 0$. Both T_1 and T_2 are consistent: They read the balances in both accounts before making withdrawals and so, when executed in isolation, each maintains the constraint. In the example, each account has $10 initially and each transaction concludes that it is safe to withdraw $15. However, in the schedule shown, which is allowable in SNAPSHOT isolation (because T_1 and T_2 write to different data items), the final values of a_1 and a_2 are both $ - 5$, thus violating the constraint. Note that this schedule is not serializable because T_2 must be after T_1 (T_2 wrote a_1 after T_1 read it) and T_1 must be after T_2 (T_1 wrote a_2 after T_2 read it). (For a continuation of this example, see Exercise 24.27.)

SNAPSHOT **isolation and the isolation-level phenomena.** Even though the example of Figure 24.12 demonstrates that SNAPSHOT isolation can produce nonserializable, and hence incorrect, schedules, note that SNAPSHOT-isolated schedules do not exhibit any of the bad phenomena associated with the lower isolation levels—dirty reads, nonrepeatable reads, and phantoms (as well as dirty writes and lost updates, which are not part of the definitions of the isolation levels).

We need to clarify the statement that SNAPSHOT isolation does not allow phantoms. In a SNAPSHOT-isolated schedule, a transaction, T, might execute a SELECT statement based on a particular predicate, and a concurrent transaction might insert a tuple, t, that satisfies that predicate (seemingly a phantom). T cannot see t even if it rereads the same predicate after the insertion, since all of its reads are satisfied with the snapshot taken when T made its first read. On this basis, one might say that t is not a phantom. We give two examples, one where the insertion of such a tuple does not cause an incorrect schedule and one where it does.

■ The example of a phantom in Section 24.1.1, involving Mary and her accounts, executes correctly at SNAPSHOT isolation. In that example, transaction T_1, which compares TotalBalance with the sum of the balances in all of Mary's accounts, sees inconsistent data because a phantom was inserted between its two SELECT statements. However, SNAPSHOT isolation guarantees transaction-level read consistency. Hence T_1 sees a consistent snapshot of the database as it was when T_1 started. It does not see the phantom, and it does not see the updated value of TotalBalance. Therefore, it executes correctly.

■ Suppose that the bank database has an integrity constraint (corresponding to a business rule of the bank) that no depositor can have more than ten accounts. To enforce this constraint, an add_new_account transaction first executes a SELECT statement using the predicate Name = 'Mary' to determine the number of Mary's accounts. If the number is 9 or less, it inserts a tuple corresponding to a new account for Mary. Now suppose that two instances of the add_new_account transaction, T_1 and T_2, execute concurrently at SNAPSHOT isolation, and that the number of Mary's accounts is initially 9. Each transaction determines the number to be 9 and hence inserts a tuple corresponding to a new account. Mary now has eleven accounts, in violation of the constraint, so the schedule is nonserializable and incorrect.

There is no agreed-upon definition in the literature of what constitutes a phantom. Some sources say that an isolation level permits phantoms if, when a transaction executes the same SELECT statement twice, the second execution can return a result set containing a (phantom) tuple not contained in the result set returned by the first. Using this definition, phantoms are permitted at REPEATABLE READ but not at SNAPSHOT isolation, since a transaction executing the same SELECT statement twice will always obtain the same result set (since both SELECT statements access the same snapshot).

However, the second example illustrates that the effect of phantoms still exists with SNAPSHOT isolation even though, according to the above definition, the insertions do not constitute phantoms. If we had executed the transactions in that

Figure 24.13 SNAPSHOT-isolated schedule that is not serializable and does not exhibit any of the named anomalies.

T_1: $r(x)$ $w(x)$ *commit*
T_2: $r(x)$ $r(y)$ $w(y)$ *commit*
T_3: $r(x)$ $r(y)$ $w(z)$ *commit*

example at REPEATABLE READ, the same (nonserializable) schedule is permitted and we say that phantoms do occur.

Using the definition of phantoms based on the successive execution of SELECT statements, it follows that SNAPSHOT isolation does not exhibit any of the bad phenomena that define the lower isolation levels. Nevertheless, it does not meet the ANSI definition of SERIALIZABLE [SQL 1992], which states that (in addition to not allowing any of the three phenomena) SERIALIZABLE must provide what is "commonly known as fully serializable execution." This is certainly not the case for SNAPSHOT isolation. Schedules that do not contain the three phenomena of dirty reads, nonrepeatable reads, and phantoms are sometimes called **anomaly serializable**. Thus, SNAPSHOT-isolated schedules are anomaly serializable, but might not be serializable.

This again shows that correct execution should not be defined only by the absence of certain specific phenomena. Some authors use the term **write skew** to describe the bad phenomenon exemplified by Figure 24.12, but even adding that phenomenon to the list should not give you much confidence that the list is complete. For example, the schedule shown in Figure 24.13, which is allowable in SNAPSHOT isolation, is not serializable because its serialization graph has a cycle:

$$T_3 \rightarrow T_2 \rightarrow T_1 \rightarrow T_3$$

However, this schedule does not exhibit any of the named phenomena, including write skew (as usually defined).

Conflicts at SNAPSHOT isolation. When we discussed conflicting operations in Chapter 23, we noted that there are three types of conflict between read and write operations (although we did not name them there).

■ *Read/write conflict.* T_2 wrote an item that T_1 had previously read and hence must follow T_1 in any ordering.

■ *Write/read conflict.* T_2 read an item that T_1 had previously written and hence must follow T_1 in any ordering.

■ *Write/write conflict.* T_2 wrote an item that T_1 had previously written and hence must follow T_1 in any ordering.

One reason why schedules produced at SNAPSHOT isolation do not exhibit any of the phenomena associated with the other isolation levels is that the only conflicts that can occur between concurrently executing transactions are read/write conflicts (other types of conflicts are allowed between transactions that are not concurrent with each other).

■ Write/read conflicts cannot occur because T_2 reads the value of the item in the database snapshot taken when T_2 started. Since T_2 and T_1 are executing concurrently, that snapshot does not include the updated value of the item T_1 wrote.

■ Write/write conflicts cannot occur because of the first-committer-wins property.

In the schedule of Figure 24.12, which has a write skew,

■ T_1 has a read/write conflict with T_2 because it wrote a_2 after T_2 read it.

■ T_2 has a read/write conflict with T_1 because it wrote a_1 after T_1 read it.

The schedule of Figure 24.13 is more interesting.

■ T_1 has a read/write conflict with T_2 because it wrote x after T_2 read it.

■ T_2 has a read/write conflict with T_3 because it wrote y after T_3 read it.

■ T_3 has a write/read conflict with T_1 because it read x after T_1 wrote it.

This last conflict does not violate the statement that write/read conflicts cannot occur between concurrent transactions, because T_3 did not execute concurrently with T_1—it started after T_1 committed.

These two examples can be generalized [Fekete et al. 2000] to show that, in every nonserializable SNAPSHOT-isolated schedule, the cycle in the serialization graph consists of at least two read/write conflicts between transactions that execute concurrently and possibly some read/write, write/read, or write/write conflicts between transactions that do not execute concurrently.

Correct execution at SNAPSHOT isolation.   It is interesting to note that all of the four examples given in Section 24.2.2 run correctly at SNAPSHOT isolation.

CASE
STUDY

■ A transaction that prints out the transcript works correctly since it is read-only and sees a snapshot of the database.

■ A registration transaction, T, works correctly because
   ❏ If a transaction, T', changes REQUIRES or TRANSCRIPT after T has made its first read request, the resulting schedule is equivalent to the serial schedule T, T'.
   ❏ If a concurrent registration transaction attempts to enroll students in the same course, it updates the same row of CLASS and only one of the registration transactions is allowed to commit.

■ A transaction, T, that reassigns rooms works correctly because
   ❏ If a transaction, T', changes CLASS or CLASSROOM after T has made its first read request, the resulting schedule is equivalent to the serial schedule T, T'.
   ❏ T cannot interfere with a concurrent registration transaction, since they both update the same row of CLASS and only one is allowed to commit.

Figure 24.14 SNAPSHOT-isolated schedule for a ticket reservation application. The schedule exhibits write skew and is not serializable, but is nevertheless correct.

T_1: $r(s_1:U)$ $r(s_2:U)$ $\quad\quad\quad\quad\quad\quad\quad\quad\quad\quad\quad$ $w(s_2:R)$ *commit*
T_2: $\quad\quad\quad\quad\quad\quad$ $r(s_1:U)$ $r(s_2:U)$ $w(s_1:R)$ *commit*

Figure 24.15 SNAPSHOT-isolated schedule that is serializable but in which T_3 precedes T_1 in the equivalent serial order even though it started after T_1 committed.

T_1: $\quad r(x)$ $\quad\quad\quad\quad$ $w(x)$ *commit*
T_2: $\quad\quad\quad$ $r(x)$ $r(y)$ $\quad\quad\quad\quad\quad\quad\quad\quad\quad\quad$ $w(y)$ *commit*
T_3: $\quad\quad\quad\quad\quad\quad\quad\quad\quad\quad\quad$ $r(y)$ $w(z)$ *commit*

■ The audit transaction works correctly, since it is read-only and sees a snapshot of the database.

An application can run correctly at SNAPSHOT isolation even though some of its schedules exhibit write skew and are nonserializable. For example, consider an application containing a transaction that reserves seats for a concert. The transaction examines the status of a number of seats and reserves one. An integrity constraint asserts that the same seat cannot be reserved by more than one person. Suppose that two ticket reservation transactions execute concurrently and produce the schedule shown in Figure 24.14 (which is virtually identical to the schedule shown in Figure 24.12). Each reads the tuples corresponding to seats s_1 and s_2 and determines that they are both unreserved (U). Then T_1 reserves s_1 by updating its status (to R) in the database; similarly, T_2 reserves s_2. The schedule is correct for this application, even though a write skew has occurred (and hence the schedule is not serializable). Furthermore, if both transactions try to reserve seat s_1, only one of them will commit because of the first-committer-wins rule, preserving the integrity constraint. Hence, any schedule of ticket reservation transactions will execute correctly at SNAPSHOT isolation.

Because of the multiversion aspect of SNAPSHOT isolation, serializable SNAPSHOT-isolated schedules can sometimes yield nonintuitive behavior. For example, the schedule of Figure 24.15 is serializable in the order

$$T_3 \rightarrow T_2 \rightarrow T_1$$

where T_3 precedes T_1 even though it started after T_1 committed.

In practice, many applications run correctly under SNAPSHOT isolation, particularly if most of the integrity constraints are encoded into the database schema (see exercise 24.27). However, the cautious designer will perform a careful analysis of the application before making that design decision. ■

24.6   BIBLIOGRAPHIC NOTES

Phantoms and the use of predicate locks to eliminate them were introduced in [Eswaran et al. 1976]. The definition of the SQL isolation levels can be found in [Gray et al. 1976] and in the ANSI SQL standard [SQL 1992]. The locking implementation of the isolation levels is discussed in [Berenson et al. 1995]. [Gray et al. 1976] contains a good discussion of granular locking. Multiversion concurrency controls are discussed in [Bernstein and Goodman 1983, Hadzilacos and Papadimitriou 1985]. The design of a multiversion, optimistic concurrency control is described in [Agrawal et al. 1987]. SNAPSHOT isolation was first discussed in [Berenson et al. 1995]. [Fekete et al. 2000] discusses the conflict aspects of SNAPSHOT isolation and gives a sufficient condition for a SNAPSHOT-isolated schedule to be serializable. [Bernstein et al. 2000] discusses an approach to proving correctness of schedules at lower isolation levels based on the semantics of the transactions. [Bernstein et al. 1987] contains an excellent summary of many concurrency control algorithms, including index locking. Concurrency control in an object database is discussed in [Cattell 1994].

24.7   EXERCISES

24.1 Suppose that the transaction processing system of your university contains a table in which there is one tuple for each currently registered student.

   a. Estimate how much disk storage is required to store this table.

   b. Give examples of transactions that must lock this entire table if a table locking concurrency control is used.

24.2 Give an example in which phantoms might occur in a nonrelational database consisting of a set of records, where each record has a set of fields.

24.3 For each isolation level weaker than SERIALIZABLE, give an example from a transaction processing system (other than a banking or student registration system) with which you have interacted, of a schedule that produces an erroneous situation.

24.4 Assume that transactions are executed at REPEATABLE READ. Give an example in which a phantom occurs when a transaction executes a SELECT statement that specifies the value of the primary key in the WHERE clause.

24.5 Assume that transactions are executed at REPEATABLE READ. Give an example in which a phantom occurs when a transaction executes a DELETE statement to delete a set of tuples satisfying some predicate, P.

24.6 Assume that transactions are executed at REPEATABLE READ. Give an example in which an UPDATE statement executed by transaction T_2 causes a phantom in an UPDATE statement in transaction T_1.

24.7 Consider a schema with two tables, TABLE1 and TABLE2, each having three attributes, attr1, attr2, and attr3, and consider the statement

```
SELECT T1.attr1, T2.attr1
FROM TABLE1 T1, TABLE2 T2
WHERE T1.attr2 = T2.attr2 AND T1.attr3 = 5
          AND T2.attr3 = 7
```

Give a single INSERT statement that might cause a phantom.

24.8 Explain the difference between a nonrepeatable read and a phantom. Specifically, give an example of a schedule of the SQL statements of several transactions that illustrate the two cases. Specify an isolation level in each case.

24.9 Give an example of a SELECT statement used in an application where the semantics of the application imply that phantoms cannot occur.

24.10 In Section 24.2.2 we argued that a registration transaction executing at READ COMMITTED would not interfere with the correct execution of a room reassignment transaction executing at REPEATABLE READ. Explain why a room reassignment transaction does not interfere with the correct execution of a registration transaction.

24.11 In a DBMS that implements intention locks, explain why two different transactions can both obtain an IX lock on the same table at the same time, without causing a conflict.

24.12 Describe the conditions under which a predicate lock on a table requested by one transaction is denied because a second transaction holds a predicate read lock on the same table.

24.13 For each of the locking implementations of the isolation levels, state whether IS locks are required and when they can be released.

24.14 The following procedure has been proposed for obtaining read locks.

> Whenever an SQL statement reads a set of tuples in a table that satisfies some predicate, the system first gets an IS lock on the table containing the tuples and then gets an S lock on each of the tuples.

Explain why this procedure allows phantoms.

24.15 Give an example of a schedule produced by a read-only multiversion concurrency control in which the read/write transactions serialize in commit order while the read-only transactions serialize in a different order.

24.16 Give an example of a schedule of read/write requests that is accepted by a multiversion concurrency control in which transaction T_1 starts after transaction T_2 commits, yet T_1 precedes T_2 in the serial order. Such a schedule can have the following nonintuitive behavior (even though it is serializable): You deposit money in your bank account; your transaction commits; later you start a new transaction that reads the amount in your account and finds that the amount you deposited is not there. (*Hint:* The schedule is allowed to contain additional transactions.)

24.17 Show that the schedule shown in Figure 24.12 for incorrect execution at SNAPSHOT isolation can also occur when executing at OPTIMISTIC READ COMMITTED (Section 24.2.1) and will also be incorrect.

24.18 Give examples of schedules that would be accepted at:
   a. SNAPSHOT isolation but not REPEATABLE READ
   b. SERIALIZABLE but not SNAPSHOT isolation (*Hint:* T_2 performs a write after T_1 has committed.)

24.19 A particular read-only transaction reads data that was entered into the database during the previous month and uses that data to prepare a report. What is the weakest isolation level at which this transaction can execute? Explain.

24.20 Explain why a read-only transaction consisting of a single SELECT statement that uses an INSENSITIVE cursor can always execute correctly at READ COMMITTED.

24.21 Suppose that a locking implementation of REPEATABLE READ requires that a transaction obtain an X lock on a table when a write is requested. When a read is requested, a transaction is required to obtain an IS lock on the table and an S lock on the tuples returned. Show that phantoms cannot occur.

24.22 Consider an isolation level implemented using long-duration granular locks on rows and tables. Under what conditions can phantoms occur?

24.23 a. Give an example of a schedule of two transactions in which a two-phase locking concurrency control causes one of the transactions to wait, but a SNAPSHOT isolation control aborts one of the transactions.
   b. Give an example of a schedule of two transactions in which a two-phase locking concurrency control aborts one of the transactions (because of a deadlock), but a SNAPSHOT isolation control allows both transactions to commit.

24.24 Explain why SNAPSHOT-isolated schedules do not exhibit: dirty reads, dirty writes, lost updates, nonrepeatable reads, and phantoms.

24.25 Consider an application consisting of transactions that are assigned different isolation levels. Prove that those assigned to SERIALIZABLE can be serialized with respect to all others. In other words, show that, for any SERIALIZABLE transaction, T, and any other transaction, T', any schedule of transactions is equivalent to one in which all operations of T either follow or precede all operations of T'.

24.26 All of the transactions in some particular application write all of the data items they read. Show that, if that application executes under SNAPSHOT isolation, all schedules of committed transactions will be serializable.

24.27 Consider the schedule of two bank withdrawal transactions shown in Figure 24.12 for which SNAPSHOT isolation leads to an inconsistent database. Suppose that the bank encodes, as an integrity constraint in the database schema, the business rule "The sum of the balances in all accounts owned by the same depositor must be nonnegative." Then that particular schedule cannot occur.

   Although the integrity constraint is now maintained, the specification of a particular transaction might assert that, when the transaction commits, the database state satisfies a stronger condition. Give an example of a stronger condition that a withdrawal transaction might attempt to impose when it terminates and a schedule of two such transactions at SNAPSHOT isolation that causes them to behave incorrectly.

24.28 The following multiversion concurrency control has been proposed.

> Reads are satisfied using the (committed) version of the database that existed when the transaction made its first read request. Writes are controlled by long-duration write locks on tables.

Does the control always produce serializable schedules? If not, give a nonserializable schedule it might produce.

24.29 We have given two different implementations of the READ COMMITTED isolation level: the locking implementation in Section 24.2 and the read consistency implementation in Section 24.5. Give an example of a schedule in which the two implementations produce different results.

24.30 The granular locking protocol can exhibit a deadlock between two transactions, one of which executes a single SELECT statement and the other a single UPDATE statement. For example, suppose that one transaction contains the single SELECT statement

```
SELECT COUNT (P.Id)
FROM EMPLOYEE P
WHERE P.Age = '27'
```

which returns the number of employees whose age is 27, and the other contains the single UPDATE statement

```
UPDATE EMPLOYEE
SET Salary = Salary * 1.1
WHERE Department = 'Adm'
```

which gives all employees in the administration a 10% raise. Assume that there are indices on both Department and Age and that the tuples corresponding to the department Adm are stored in more than one page as are those corresponding to age 27.

   Show how a deadlock might occur at isolation levels other than READ UNCOMMITTED.

24.31 Give an example of a schedule executing at SNAPSHOT isolation in which two transactions each introduce a phantom that is not seen by the other transaction, resulting in incorrect behavior. Assume that the data items referred to in the description of SNAPSHOT isolation are rows.

24.32 In an Internet election system, each voter is sent a PIN in the mail. When that voter wants to vote at the election web site, she enters her PIN and her vote, and then a voting transaction is executed.

In the voting transaction, first the PIN is checked to verify that it is valid and has not been used already, and then the vote tally for the appropriate candidate is incremented. Two tables are used: One contains the valid PINs together with an indication of whether or not each PIN has been used and the other contains the names of the candidates and the vote tally for each. Discuss the issues involved in selecting an appropriate isolation level for the voting transaction. Discuss the issues involved in selecting appropriate isolation levels if a new (read-only) transaction is introduced that outputs the entire vote tally table.

24.33 An airlines database has two tables: FLIGHTS, with attributes `flt_num`, `plane_id`, `num_reserv`; and PLANES, with attributes `plane_id`, `num_seats`

The attributes have the obvious semantics. A reservation transaction contains the following steps:

```
        SELECT F.plane_id, F.num_reserv
        INTO :p, :n
        FROM FLIGHTS F
        WHERE F.flt_num = :f
   A.   SELECT P.num_seats
        INTO :s
        FROM PLANES P
        WHERE P.plane_id = :p
   B.   ...check that n < s...
   C.   UPDATE FLIGHTS F
        SET F.num_reserv = :n + 1
        WHERE F.flt_num = :f
   D.   COMMIT
```

Assume that each individual SQL statement is executed in isolation, that the DBMS uses intention locking and sets locks on tables and rows, and that host variable f contains the number of the flight to be booked. The transaction should not overbook the flight.

a. Assuming that the transaction is run at READ COMMITTED, what locks are held at points A, B, and D?

b. The database can be left in an incorrect state if concurrently executing reservation transactions running at READ COMMITTED are interleaved in such a way that one transaction is completely executed at point B in the execution of another. Describe the problem.

c. In an attempt to avoid the problem described in (b), the SET clause of the UPDATE statement is changed to F.num_reserv = F.num_reserv + 1. Can reservation transactions now be run correctly at READ COMMITTED? Explain.

d. Assuming that the transaction is run at REPEATABLE READ and that the tables are accessed through indices, what table locks are held at points A, B, and D?

e. What problem does the interleaving of (b) cause at REPEATABLE READ? Explain.

f. Does the interleaving of (b) cause an incorrect state if the transaction (either version) is run using SNAPSHOT isolation? Explain.

g. To keep track of each passenger, a new table, PASSENGER, is introduced that has a row describing each passenger on each flight with attributes name, flt_num, seat_id. SQL statements are appended to the end of the transaction (1) to read the seat_id's assigned to each passenger on the flight specified in f and (2) to insert a row for the new passenger that assigns an empty seat to that passenger. What is the weakest ANSI isolation level at which the transaction can be run without producing an incorrect state (i.e., two passengers in the same seat)? Explain.

24.34 Two transactions run concurrently, and each might either commit or abort. The transactions are chosen from the following:

$$T_1: \ r_1(x) \ w_1(y)$$

$$T_2: \ w_2(x)$$

$$T_3: \ r_3(y) \ w_3(x)$$

$$T_4: \ r_4(x) \ w_4(x) \ w_4(y)$$

In each of the following cases, state (yes or no) whether the resulting schedule is always serializable and atomic.

a. T_1 and T_2 both running at READ UNCOMMITTED

b. T_2 and T_2 both running at READ UNCOMMITTED

c. T_1 and T_2 both running at READ COMMITTED

d. T_1 and T_3 both running at READ COMMITTED

e. T_1 and T_3 both running at SNAPSHOT isolation

f. T_1 and T_4 both running at SNAPSHOT isolation

Chapter 25

Atomicity and Durability

In previous chapters we made the unrealistic assumptions that transactions always commit and that the system never malfunctions. The reality is quite different: Transactions can be aborted for a variety of reasons, and hardware and software can fail. Such events must be carefully handled to ensure transaction atomicity. Furthermore, a failure might occur on a mass storage device, causing the loss of information written to the database by committed transactions, thus threatening durability.

In this chapter, we discuss the basic problems that must be solved to achieve atomicity and durability and some techniques to do so. Our description is not meant to reflect the design of any particular failure recovery system. Instead, we emphasize principles that underlie the design of a number of such systems.

25.1 CRASH, ABORT, AND MEDIA FAILURE

Although the reliability of computer systems has increased dramatically over the years, the probability of a failure is still very real. A failure might be caused by a problem in the processor or in the main memory units (for example, a power loss) or by a bug in the software. Such failures cause the processor to behave unpredictably, perhaps writing spurious information in arbitrary locations in memory, before finally performing some action that causes it to shut down. We refer to such a failure as a **crash**, and we assume that, when a crash occurs, the contents of main memory are lost. For this reason, main memory is referred to as **volatile storage**. It is possible that a failing processor might initiate a spurious write to the mass storage device, but such an event is so unlikely that we assume that the contents of mass storage survive a crash.

In general, a number of transactions will be active when a transaction processing system crashes, which means that the database will be in an inconsistent state. When the system is restarted after a crash, service is not resumed until after a **recovery procedure** is executed to restore the database to a consistent state. The major issue in the design of a recovery procedure is how to deal with a transaction, T, that was active at the time the crash occurred. Atomicity requires either that the recovery procedure cause T to resume execution so that it can complete successfully—called **rollforward**—or that any effects that T had prior to the crash be undone—called **rollback**.

Rollforward is often difficult, if not impossible. If T is an interactive transaction, resumption requires the cooperation of the user at the terminal. The user must know which of the updates she requested prior to the crash had actually been recorded in the database, and resume submitting requests from that point. Rolling forward a programmed transaction is further complicated by the fact that the local state (the state of T's local variables) might have been in volatile memory at the time of the crash and hence might be lost. T cannot be resumed from the point at which the crash occurred unless its local state is restored. Thus, in order to roll T forward after a crash, special measures must be taken to periodically save T's local state on a mass storage device during transaction execution.

For these reasons, transactions active at the time of a crash are usually rolled back during recovery in order to achieve atomicity. Note that our primary concern here is with the changes T made to the database before the crash. A transaction might have had other, external, effects such as printing a message on the screen or actuating a controller in a factory. External actions are difficult to reverse, although we discussed one technique for handling them in Section 21.3.2.

The rollback mechanism is required to deal not only with crashes but with transaction abort as well. A transaction might be aborted for a number of reasons.

■ A transaction might be aborted by the user—for example, because he entered incorrect input data.

■ A transaction might abort itself—for example, because it encountered some unexpected information in the database.

■ A transaction might be aborted by the system—because the transaction has become deadlocked with other transactions, because the system does not have sufficient resources to complete it, or because of some constraint violation.

Durability requires that the effects of a transaction on a database not be lost once the transaction has committed. Databases are stored on mass storage devices—usually disks. Since crashes typically do not affect these devices, mass storage is referred to as **nonvolatile**. However, it is subject to its own forms of failure, which are referred to as **media failures**. A media failure might affect all or some of the data stored on the device. The redundant storage of data is used to ensure a measure of durability in spite of such failure. The more redundant copies that are kept, the more media failures that can be tolerated. Thus, durability is not absolute, but it is related to the value of the data and the amount of money the enterprise is willing to spend on protecting it. A media failure might occur while transactions are executing, so the recovery procedures for media failure must also provide rollback capabilities.

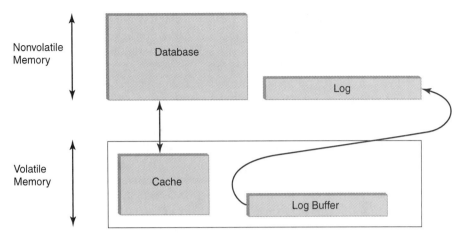

Figure 25.1 Organization of memory.

25.2   IMMEDIATE-UPDATE SYSTEMS AND WRITE-AHEAD LOGS

The mechanism for rollback is different in immediate- and deferred-update systems. Since immediate-update systems are more common, we deal with them first. Our description of such a system proceeds in stages. In this section, we describe a simple, but impractical system to introduce the major ideas. In later sections we discuss some of the complexities that must be dealt with in commercial systems and describe some of the changes that must be made to the simple system to handle them.

Immediate-update systems maintain a **log**, which is a sequence of records. Records are appended to the log as transactions execute and are never changed or deleted. The log is consulted by the system to achieve both atomicity and durability. For durability, the log is used to restore the database after a failure of the mass storage device on which the database is stored. Hence, the log must be stored on a non-volatile device. Typically, a log is a sequential file on disk. In addition, the log is often duplexed (and the copies stored on different devices) so that it survives any single media failure.

The organization of memory is shown in Figure 25.1. For efficiency, the unit of transfer between the database and the database server is the page, and recently accessed pages are kept in a cache in volatile memory. Moreover, information that will eventually be stored in the log is usually first put into a log buffer in volatile memory. The existence of the cache and log buffer complicate the processing required for rollback and commitment. In this section, we assume that neither a cache nor a log buffer is used, but that information is directly read from and written into the database and directly written into the log.

When a transaction executes a database operation that changes the state of the database, the system appends an **update record** to the log (no record need be appended if the operation merely reads the database). An update record describes the change that has been made and, in particular, contains enough information to permit the system to undo that change if the transaction is later aborted. Since the records are appended when the changes are made, the log contains the merge of the update records of all transactions.

In its simplest form, an update record contains the **before-image** of the database item that has been modified—that is, a physical copy of the item before the change was made. If the transaction aborts, the update record is used to restore the item to its original value—hence, the before-image is sometimes referred to as an **undo record**. If the concurrency control enforces serializable execution (i.e., the item was exclusively locked when it was changed and the concurrency control is strict), the new value could not have been viewed by concurrent transactions, and therefore the aborted transaction will have had no effect on other transactions and, after restoration, it will have had no effect on the database either. In addition to the before-image, the update record identifies the transaction that made the change—using a **transaction Id**—and the database item that was changed. We introduce other information contained in the update record as our discussion proceeds.

Because the update record contains a physical copy of the item, this form of logging is referred to as **physical logging**.

If the system aborts a transaction, T, or T aborts itself, rollback using the log is straightforward. The log is scanned backwards, and, as T's update records are encountered, the before-images are written to the database, undoing the change. Since the log might be exceedingly long, it is impractical to search back to the beginning to make sure that all of T's update records are processed. To avoid a complete backward scan, when T is initiated a **begin record** containing its transaction Id is appended to the log. The backward scan can be stopped when T's begin record is encountered. (For easier access, the log records of a transaction can be linked together, with the most recent record at the head of the list.)

Savepoints can be implemented by generalizing this technique. Each time a transaction declares a savepoint, a **savepoint record** is written to the log. The record not only contains the transaction Id and the identity of the savepoint, but might contain information about any cursors open at the time the savepoint was declared. To roll back to a specific savepoint, the log is scanned backward to the specified savepoint's record. The before-image in each of the transaction's update records that are encountered during the scan is applied to the database. Any cursor information in the record is used to re-establish the cursor's position at the time the savepoint was declared.

Rollback because of a crash is a little more complex than the abort of a single transaction, since, on recovery, the system must first identify the transactions to be aborted. In particular, the system must distinguish between transactions that completed (committed or aborted) and those that were active at the time the crash occurred. All of the active transactions must be aborted.

When a transaction commits, it writes a **commit record** to the log. If it aborts, it rolls back its updates and then writes an **abort record** to the log. Both records contain the transaction's Id. After writing a commit or abort record, the transaction can release any locks it holds.

Using these records, the identity of the transactions active at the time of the crash can be determined by the recovery procedure. If, during a backward scan, the first record relating to T is an update record, T was active when the crash occurred and must be aborted. If the first record is a commit or abort record, the transaction completed and its update records can be ignored as they are subsequently encountered.

Note that, for durability, it is important to write a commit record to the log when T commits. Because our simplified view assumes that the database is immediately updated when T makes a write request, all database modifications requested by T will be recorded in nonvolatile memory when it requests to commit. However, the commit request itself does not guarantee durability. If a crash occurs after a transaction makes the request, but before the commit record is written to the log, the transaction will be aborted by the recovery procedure and the system will not provide durability. Hence, a transaction has not actually committed until the commit record has been appended to the log on mass storage.

> Appending a commit record to the log is an atomic action (either the record is in the log or it is not in the log), and the transaction is committed if and only if the action has completed.

Checkpoints.   One last issue must be addressed with respect to crashes. Some mechanism must be included to avoid a complete backward scan of the log during recovery. Without such a mechanism, the recovery process has no way of knowing when to stop the scan, since a transaction that was active at the time of the crash might have logged an update record at an early point in the log and then made no further database updates. The recovery process will find no evidence of the transaction's existence unless it scans back to that record. To deal with this situation, the system periodically writes a **checkpoint record** to the log listing the identities of currently active transactions. The recovery process must (at least) scan backward to the most recent checkpoint record. If T is named in that record and the recovery process did not encounter a completion record for T between the checkpoint record and the end of the log, then T was still active when the system crashed. The backward scan must continue until the begin record for T is reached. It terminates when all such transactions are accounted for. Only the most recent checkpoint record is used (a checkpoint record supersedes the one preceding it). The frequency with which these records are written to the log affects the speed of recovery, since frequent checkpointing implies that less of the log has to be scanned.

An example of a log is shown in Figure 25.2. As the recovery process scans backward, it discovers that T_6 and T_1 were active at the time of the crash because the last records appended for them are update records. It uses the before-images in these update records (in the sequence they are encountered in the backward scan) to roll back the database items to which they refer. Since the first record it encounters for T_4 is a commit record, it learns that T_4 was not active at the time of the crash and therefore ignores T_4's update records. When it reaches the checkpoint record, it learns that, at the time the checkpoint was taken, T_1, T_3, and T_4 were active (T_6 is not mentioned in the checkpoint record since it began after the checkpoint was taken). Thus, it concludes that, in addition to T_1 and T_6, T_3 was active at the time

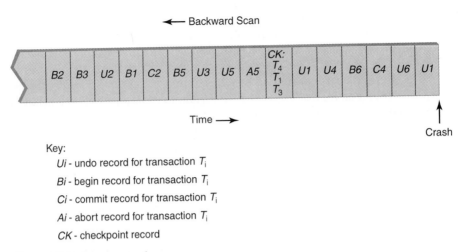

Figure 25.2 Log example.

of the crash (since it has seen no completion record for T_3). No other transaction could have been active and hence these are the transactions that must be aborted. The recovery process must now continue the backward scan, processing all update records for T_1, T_3, and T_6 in the order they are encountered. The scan ends when the begin records for these transactions have been reached.

Write-ahead logging.   We have assumed that an update record for a database item, x, is written to the log at the time x is updated in the database. In fact, the update of x and the append of the update record must occur in some order. Does it make a difference in which order these operations are performed? Consider the possibility that a crash occurs at the time the operations are performed. If it happens before either operation is completed, there is no problem. The update record does not appear in the log, but there is nothing for the recovery process to undo since x has not been updated. If the crash happens after both operations are performed, recovery proceeds correctly, as described above. Suppose, however, that x is updated first and that the crash occurs before the update record is appended to the log. Then the recovery process has no way of rolling the transaction back because there is no before-image in the log that the recovery process can use. Recovery thus cannot return the database to a consistent state—an unacceptable situation.

If, on the other hand, the update record is appended first, this problem is avoided. On restart, the recovery process simply uses the update record to restore x. As shown in Figure 25.3, it makes no difference whether the crash occurred before or after the transaction wrote the new value of x to the database. The original value of x was 3, a transaction updated it to 5, and the crash occurred before the transaction committed. If the crash occurred after the update record was appended but before x was updated (crash 1 in the figure), when the system is restarted the value of x in the database and the before-image in the update record will be identical. The recovery process uses the before-image to overwrite x—which does

Figure 25.3 The recovery procedure can handle database restoration correctly with a write-ahead log.

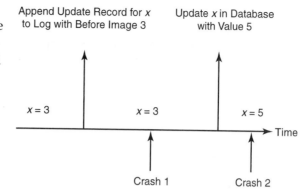

not change its value—but the final state after recovery has completed is correct. If the crash occurred after x was updated (crash 2 in the figure), recovery restores x to 3.

Hence, the update record must always be appended to the log before the database is updated. This is referred to as the write-ahead feature, and the log is referred to as a **write-ahead log**.

25.2.1 Performance and Write–Ahead Logging

While write-ahead logging, as described in the previous section, works correctly, it is unacceptable from a performance point of view since it doubles the number of I/O operations needed to update the database. A log append must now be performed with every database update. To avoid this overhead, database systems generally use a log buffer in volatile memory as temporary storage for log records. The log buffer can be viewed as an extension of the log on mass storage. Log records are appended to the buffer, and when the buffer fills it is appended, or **flushed**, to the log, as shown in Figure 25.1. With a log buffer, the cost of writing to the log is prorated over all log records contained in the buffer.

From the point of view of crash recovery, the difference between the log buffer in volatile memory and the log on mass storage is crucial. The log buffer is lost when the system crashes.

Furthermore, our description has ignored the fact that, to improve performance, most database systems support a cache in volatile store of recently accessed database pages. Thus, when a transaction accesses a database item, x, the database system brings the database page(s) on mass storage containing x into the cache and then copies the value of x into the transaction's buffer. The page is kept in the cache under the assumption that there is a high probability that the transaction will either update x or read another item in the same page at a later time. If so, a page transfer will have been avoided, since the page will be directly accessible (no I/O required) in the cache. For example, a transaction might scan a table through a cursor. After retrieving a row from a page, the next row it fetches most probably will be in the same page.

If x is updated, the cache copy of the page is modified (not the original copy in the database). The cache page is then marked as **dirty**, meaning that the version of the database records that it contains is more recent than the version of those records in mass storage. **Clean** (nondirty) cache pages—pages whose contents have only been read—can simply be overwritten by new pages from the database when space is needed in the cache. Dirty pages, however, must eventually be written back to the database before they can be overwritten in the cache. Decisions concerning which pages should be kept in the cache are made by a page replacement algorithm whose goal is to maximize the number of database accesses that can be satisfied by pages in the cache and at the same time maintain database consistency. A least-recently-used (LRU) algorithm, for example, tends to keep actively used pages in the cache.

Use of the log buffer and the cache complicates write-ahead logging because they affect the time at which the database and the log on mass storage are actually updated. Two properties of the simple scheme described previously must be preserved: the write-ahead feature and the durability of commitment.

The write ahead feature is preserved by ensuring that a dirty page in the cache is not written to the database until the log buffer containing the corresponding update record has been appended to the log. Two mechanisms are generally provided for this purpose. First, database systems generally support two operations for appending a record to the log: one that simply adds the record to the log buffer and one that adds the record to the buffer and then immediately writes the buffer to the log. The latter operation is referred to as a **forced** operation. Whereas a normal (unforced) write simply registers a request with the operating system to write a page to mass storage (the I/O operation is done at a later time), a forced write does not return control to the invoker until the write is complete. Since the log is sequential, when a routine requests a forced write of an update record, of necessity it forces all prior records into the log as well. When the routine resumes execution, it is guaranteed that these records are stored on mass storage. A request can then be safely made to write the corresponding dirty cache page to the database.

The second mechanism involves numbering all log records sequentially with a **log sequence number** (**LSN**), which is stored in the log record. In addition, for each database page, the LSN of the update record corresponding to the most recent update to the page is stored in that page. Thus, if a database page contains database items x, y, and z, and if the item updated most recently is y, the value of the LSN stored in the page is the LSN of the last update record for y.

With the forced write and the LSN, we are in a position to ensure the write-ahead feature. When space is needed in the cache and a dirty page, P, is selected to be written to mass store, the system determines if the log buffer still contains the update record whose LSN is equal to the LSN stored in P. If so, the LSN of P must be greater than the LSN of the last record in the log on *mass storage*. Therefore, the log buffer must be forced to mass storage before the page is written to the database. If not, the update record corresponding to the most recent update to an item in the page has already been appended to the log on mass storage and the page can be written from the cache immediately.

Thus we see that to achieve the write-ahead feature, we must sometimes delay the writing of a cache page containing an updated item until the log buffer containing the corresponding update record has been written to the log. To achieve durability, we must ensure that the *new* values of all items updated by T are in mass store before T's commit record is appended to the log on mass store. Otherwise, if a crash occurs after the commit record has been appended but before the new values are in mass store, the transaction will have been committed but the new values will have been lost, and hence durability in spite of system crashes has not been implemented.

There are two ways to ensure durability: a **force** policy and a **no-force** policy. With a force policy the force operation is extended to writing pages in the cache. Database pages in the cache that have been updated by T are forced out to the database before T's commit record is appended to the log on mass storage. The sequence of events is as follows:

1. If the transaction's last update record is still in the log buffer, force it to the log on mass store. This ensures that all before images are durable.

2. If any dirty pages that have been updated by the transaction remain in the cache, force them to the database. This ensures that all new values are durable.

3. Append the commit record to the log buffer. When it is written to the log on mass store (see below) the transaction will be durable.

Figure 25.4 illustrates the sequence of events for a transaction, T, that has updated an item, x. The update record, with LSN j and before-image x_{old}, is in the log buffer, and the updated page, with the new value, x_{new}, and the LSN of the update record, is in the cache. The page is dirty: It has not yet been written to mass storage. Its original version, with value x_{old} and LSN s, $s < j$, is still on mass storage. The update record must be on mass storage (step 1 in the figure) before the dirty page can be written (step 2) to satisfy the write-ahead property. It may be necessary to force the log buffer to ensure this. Similarly, the dirty page must already be on mass storage before the commit record, with $LSN\ k, k > j$, can be appended to the log buffer, to ensure that it gets to mass storage before the commit record does (step 3). It is necessary to force the dirty page to ensure this.

Note that it is not necessary to force the commit record. However, the transaction is not committed until the commit record has been written to the log on mass store. In some systems, the log buffer is forced when a commit record is appended to the buffer, thus causing the commit to take effect immediately. Other systems do not force the buffer at this time, so a write to the log is avoided but the commit does not take effect until a later time when the log buffer is written to the log. This protocol is referred to as **group commit**, since the group of transactions whose commit records are in the log buffer when the next write occurs all commit at once.

A major drawback of the force policy for ensuring durability is that the writing of dirty cache pages and commit are synchronous. The pages modified by a transaction must be written to the database before the transaction can commit. Since page writes are slow, transaction commit is delayed and response time suffers.

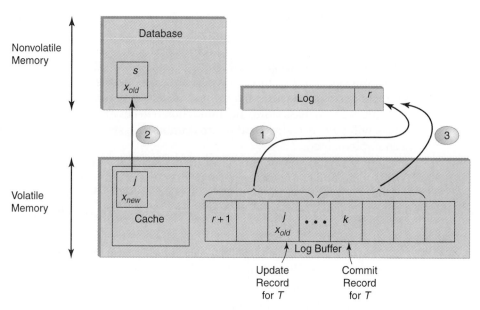

Figure 25.4 Implementing durability using a force policy. It might be necessary to force the pages a transaction has updated out of the cache before the transaction's commit record is written to the log. Before the dirty page updated by T, containing LSN value j, can be written to the database, it might be necessary to force the log buffer (1) so that the update record with LSN equal to j is on mass storage. After the dirty page has been written (2), the commit record for T can be appended to the log buffer (3). The log buffer can be written to the log at some later time.

Another disadvantage of the force policy has to do with pages that are frequently modified by different transactions (for example, those holding system-related information). An LRU page replacement algorithm might choose not to write such a page out of the cache, but with a force policy the page will be written each time a transaction that has modified the page commits. The advantage of a force policy, on the other hand, is that no action need be taken to recover a committed transaction after a crash. At the time the transaction's commit record is written to the log on mass store, all of the new values that it has created have been copied to the database on mass storage as well. With a no-force policy, which we describe in the next section, this is not necessarily the case.

25.2.2 Checkpoints and Recovery

In the previous section, we pointed out that the new value of an item, x, updated by a transaction, T, might still be in a dirty page in the cache when T requests to commit (which means that the copy of this page in the database has not yet been updated). To make T durable, the system must record the new value of x on mass

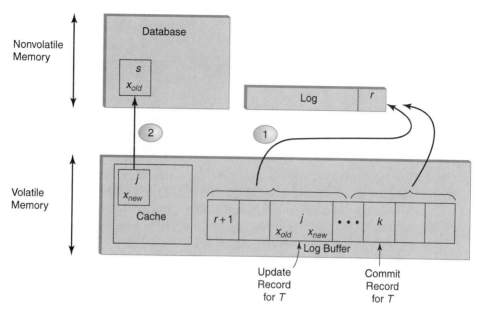

Figure 25.5 Implementing durability using an after-image with a no-force policy. The write-ahead feature requires that, before a dirty page updated by T can be written to the database (2), the corresponding update record must be written to the log on mass storage (1). Although the commit record cannot be written before the update record, the relationship between the time the commit record is written and the time the dirty page is written is not constrained.

store before T's commit record is written to the log on mass store. A common way of guaranteeing that this value is in nonvolatile memory is to store after-images (in addition to before-images) in update records in the log.

In its simplest form, an **after-image**—sometimes called a **redo record**—of an updated item is a physical copy of the item's new value. Because all of T's update records precede its commit record in the log, when T's commit record is written to the log on mass storage, the new values of all database items it has created will be on mass storage as well. Then, even if the database page containing x has not been updated on mass storage at commit time and the system crashes after T commits, the new value of x can be installed in the database page on recovery using the after-image as shown in Figure 25.5. The write-ahead feature still requires that the update record be written to the log on mass storage before the dirty page is flushed to the database, but there is no longer any ordering specified for when the commit record is written. In particular, it can be written out to the log in durable storage before all the cached pages modified by T have been written out.

The obvious advantage of a no-force policy is that a transaction can commit without having to wait until all of the pages it has updated have been forced from the cache. The disadvantage is that, when a crash occurs, recovery is complicated by the following possible situations:

■ Some pages in the database might contain updates written by uncommitted transactions. These pages must be rolled back using the before-images in the log. This problem exists with either a force or a no-force policy.

■ Some pages in the database might not yet contain all the updates made by committed transactions. These pages must be rolled forward using the after-images in the log. This problem exists only with a no-force policy.

We have already dealt with the rollback problem. The question now is how to identify those database pages that must be rolled forward.

One way of doing this is to use a **sharp checkpoint**. Before writing a checkpoint record, *CK*, to the log buffer, processing is halted and all dirty pages in the cache are written to the database. As a result, a recovery process scanning *CK* can conclude that all updates recorded in the log prior to *CK* were written to the database before the crash. If *CK* is the most recent checkpoint record, only updates recorded after it in the log *might* not have been written to the database. Using this information, recovery can proceed in three passes.

Pass 1.   The log is scanned backward to the most recent checkpoint to determine which transactions were active (and must be rolled back) at the time of the crash.

Pass 2.   The log is scanned forward (replayed) from the checkpoint. The after-images in all update records (of commited *and* uncommited transactions) are used to update the corresponding items in the database. At the end of this pass, the database has been brought up to date with respect to all changes made by both committed and uncommitted transactions prior to the crash.

Pass 3.   The log is scanned backward to roll back all transactions active at the time of the crash. The before-image in each update record of these transactions is used to reverse the corresponding update in the database. This pass completes when the begin records of all the transactions have been reached. The effect is the same as if all uncommitted transactions have aborted.

DO-UNDO-REDO is the name given to this general form of recovery. DO refers to the original action of the transaction in updating a data item, UNDO refers to the rollback that occurs in pass 3 if the transaction does not commit, and REDO refers to the rollforward that occurs in Pass 2.

There are three things to consider in using this technique.

■ Transactions that update items and abort after the checkpoint pose a special problem. Their updates were rolled back before the abort record was appended to the log, and, unfortunately, these updates will be restored to the database during pass 2. To ensure that the recovery process handles abort properly a rollback operation should be treated as an ordinary database update performed by the transaction. An aborted transaction that had updated an item, x, will thus have two records in the log for that item, as shown in Figure 25.6:

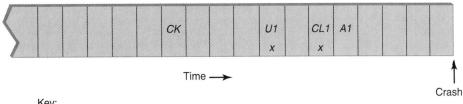

Key:

Ui - update record for transaction T_i

Ai - abort record for transaction T_i

CLi - compensation log record for T_i

CK - checkpoint record

Figure 25.6 Log showing records for an aborted transaction that has updated database variable x. The log contains both an update record and a compensation log record for x.

–An update record associated with the update it performed before aborting, with before-image x_{old} and after-image x_{new}

–A **compensation log record** associated with the reversal of that update during abort processing, with before-image x_{new} and after-image x_{old}

The compensation log record follows the update record in the log, and the abort record for the transaction follows the last compensation log record. The Pass 2 scan first processes the update record and writes its after-image to the database; it then processes the compensation log record and writes its after-image to the database. The final value of x in the database is x_{old}. Since the transaction was not active at the time of the crash, its update and compensation log records are ignored during Pass 3. Because compensation log records can be viewed as update records, they have the nice property of making committed and aborted transactions in the log look the same.

■ Some cache pages updated after the last checkpoint record was written might have been written to the database. Hence, in pass 2 some of the update records encountered describe updates already transferred to the database. Using the after-images in these records to update the database is unnecessary, but not incorrect. In this case, the value of the item in the database and the after-image in the update record are identical, so the use of the after-image has no effect.[1]

■ There is a possibility that the system will crash (again) during recovery, in which case the recovery procedure will be reinitiated. Depending on the pass during

---

[1] Note that several updates of the same database item might have been made after the checkpoint record is written. In that case, the after-image and the item would not be identical. However, after the most recent update record is processed in pass 2, the item will have been brought to the value it had before the crash.

which the second crash occurs, before- or after-images might be applied to the database item a second time. The use of these images, however, is **idempotent**— that is, updating a database item with a particular after image several times has the same effect as that of a single update.[2] A crash during recovery (or, in fact, several crashes) therefore does not affect the outcome. When recovery finally completes, uncommitted transactions have been aborted and updates made by committed transactions have been recorded in the database.

Fuzzy checkpoints.   The use of sharp checkpoints has one major disadvantage. The system must be halted to write dirty pages from the cache before the checkpoint record is written to the log buffer, and such an interruption of service is unacceptable in many applications. The procedure can be modified slightly to deal with this problem, using **fuzzy checkpoints**. The dirty pages are not written from the cache when a checkpoint record is written to the log; instead, their identity is simply noted (in volatile memory), and they are subsequently written to the database (in the background) during normal processing. The only restriction is that the next checkpoint not be taken until all dirty pages noted at the previous checkpoint have been written.

Fuzzy checkpoints are illustrated in Figure 25.7. At the time $CK2$ is appended to the log buffer, all dirty pages that were in the cache when $CK1$ was appended have been written to the database. The modifications to these pages correspond to update records that appeared in the log prior to $CK1$. A database update corresponding to an update record in region $L1$ of the log creates a dirty page, P, that might be in the cache when $CK2$ is appended to the log buffer (P might also have been written by that time, but we cannot be sure). If P is still in the cache when $CK2$ is appended to the log buffer, its identity is noted. We cannot guarantee that it has been written to the database until the next checkpoint record is appended. Since in the figure the system crashes before that happens, we must make the worst-case assumption that update records in regions $L1$ and $L2$ are not reflected in the database.

In order to bring the database to a state that contains all updates done prior to the crash, pass 2 of the recovery procedure must be modified so that the forward scan starts at $CK1$ instead of $CK2$. Pass 1 still completes at $CK2$, since its purpose is to identify transactions active at the time of the crash. Recovery is now slower than with sharp checkpoints. The tradeoff between the speed of recovery and availability during normal operation must now be evaluated to decide whether sharp or fuzzy checkpoints are appropriate for a particular installation.

Archiving the log.   We must deal with one other problem so that our description of logging and recovery is (relatively) complete. We have said that log records are appended to the log and never deleted. What happens when mass storage fills with

---

[2] We used idempotency in the previous paragraph. When an after-image is used to roll forward a page that was actually updated before a crash, the idempotency of the after-image ensures that the update during recovery has no effect.

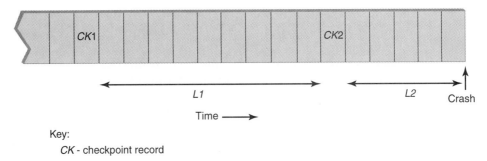

Key:
    CK - checkpoint record

Figure 25.7 Use of fuzzy checkpoints.

log records? You might think that initial portions of the log can simply be discarded, but log records are often held for substantial periods of time for several reasons.

For one, the log contains information that might be useful for reasons other than recovery. For example, it contains the sequence of updates that brought each data item to its current state, which is useful if the enterprise is called upon to explain the state of an item. The log can also be used to analyze performance. For example, if each record contains a timestamp, the response time of each transaction can be calculated. Another reason for not discarding log records is connected with media failure, which we discuss in Section 25.4.

If the log cannot be discarded, an initial portion of it must be moved off line, to tertiary storage (e.g., tape). This is referred to as **archiving**. Only recent log records need to be retained on line, and the question now reduces to deciding at what point a portion of the log can be moved. Certainly, records of active transactions must be maintained on line in order to handle abort and recovery quickly, so portions of the log containing records whose LSN is less than the LSN of the begin record of the oldest active transaction can be archived. However, the need to recover from media failure introduces other constraints, which we discuss in Section 25.4.

25.2.3 Logical and Physiological Logging*

Physical logging has an important disadvantage, particularly in relational databases. A simple update might result in changes to a large number of pages in the database. In that case, the before- and after-images can be large and difficult to manage. For example, the insert of a tuple into a table might require the reorganization of the page to which it is added and the insertion of entries in indices referring to the relation. All regions affected have to be recorded in the before- and after-images, making the update record large and increasing the I/O overhead necessary to manage the log. A technique for overcoming this disadvantage is *logical logging*.

With **logical logging**, instead of storing a snapshot of the updated item in the update record, the operation itself and its inverse are recorded. Hence, the undo record for an operation that inserts row r in table T is *<delete, r, T>* and the redo record is *<insert, r, T>*. Rollback and rollforward now consist of applying the appropriate operation instead of simply overwriting the affected area as in physical logging. In this way, logical logging has the potential of reducing the overhead of log maintenance.

Note, though, that recovery is complicated by the fact that logical operations are not necessarily idempotent. For example, the result of inserting the same row twice is different from inserting it once.[3] It is thus important to know, when processing an update or compensation log record during pass 2, whether or not the updated database page was flushed before the crash. If so, applying the redo operation in pass 2 can produce an incorrect state. In the above example, if the page on which x is stored was written to the database immediately prior to a crash, the logical redo during recovery will cause x to be inserted twice.

Fortunately, the problem is easily overcome using the LSN in the page. If during pass 2 it is found that the LSN in a page is greater than or equal to the LSN of an update record for an item in that page (indicating that the page contains the result of applying the update operation), then the redo operation is not performed.

The second problem is more serious. We have implicitly assumed that logical operations are done atomically—for example, either tuple t has been inserted in a table or it has not. However, several pages might have to be modified in order to do an insertion, and hence the logical operation is not atomic with respect to failure: The system might crash after some, but not all, pages have been written. Hence, the data might be in an inconsistent state on recovery. Inconsistency here takes a different form. For example, the data page containing t might have been written to mass storage, but not the index page that should contain a pointer to t. This is different from the state that might be produced by an inconsistent transaction, since in this case it is not the data values that are inconsistent, but the way they are stored.

The application of a logical operation to an inconsistent state is likely to fail. In the example, the application of a logical redo record in pass 2 might result in two copies of t in the table. This is not a problem when physical logging is used. It is also not a problem for logical logging if the logical operation affects only a single page, since then execution of the operation is atomic and the LSN indicates whether or not it has happened.

To overcome this problem, **physiological logging** can be used. This technique is a compromise between physical and logical logging (the name is an abbreviation of the more descriptive *physical-to-a-page, logical-within-a-page*). A logical operation that involves multiple page updates is decomposed into multiple (logical) mini-operations, in such a way that each mini-operation is confined to a single page (this is the physical dimension to physiological logging) and preserves page consistency. Hence, mini-operations can always be performed on pages, no matter when a failure occurs. The logical operation "Insert t into table T" might be decomposed into the mini-operation "Insert t into a particular page of the file containing T," which is followed by one or more mini-operations, "Insert a pointer to t into a

---

[3] Recall that relational databases do not necessarily check for duplicate rows.

particular page of an index for T." Each mini-operation gets a separate log record, so recovery will work correctly even if a crash occurs while it is taking place. Since logical mini-operations are not necessarily idempotent, LSNs can be used (as described above) to determine which mini-operations have been applied to a page during pass 2.

In the example above, each of the mini-operations is a logical operation that is confined to a single page. The actual insertion of an item into a page involves updating the page's header information (which locates the items and the free space within the page), as well as storing the item in the page. Thus, the page might be completely reorganized. With physical logging, the physical image of all of these changes must be stored in the log record. With physiological logging, only the nature of the mini-operation (e.g., insert), its arguments (e.g., t), and the identity of the page must be stored. If the mini-operation cannot be conveniently represented logically, a physical log record can be used.

25.3 RECOVERY IN DEFERRED-UPDATE SYSTEMS

In a deferred-update system, a transaction's write operation does not update the corresponding data item in the database; instead, the information to be written is saved in a special area of memory called the transaction's intentions list. The intentions list is *not* stored durably. If the transaction commits, its intentions list is used to update the database.

To abort such a transaction, we merely discard its intentions list. Similarly, if the system crashes, no special action need be taken to abort active transactions since they have made no changes to the database.

To achieve durability for committed transactions, the log and log buffer architecture can be used. We assume physical logging for simplicity in the following discussion.

When a transaction updates a data item, in addition to saving the update in the intentions list, the system appends an update record containing an after-image to the log buffer. Neither the write-ahead feature nor a before-image in the update record is required in this case, since the database item is not updated until after the transaction commits. At commit time, the system appends a commit record to the log buffer, which it then forces to the log in nonvolatile memory. Since the update records precede the commit record in the log, the force of the commit record guarantees that all update records are also on nonvolatile storage. After the commit operation has completed, the system updates the database from the transaction's intention list, then releases its locks and writes a **completion record** to the log.

The system might crash between the time the transaction has committed and the time all of its database updates have been made. Since the intentions list is lost, recovery must use the log to complete the installation of the transaction's updates. To speed this process, the system periodically appends to the log a checkpoint record containing the identities of committed transactions whose intentions lists are currently being used to update the database. On restart, the recovery process determines the identities of committed transactions whose intentions lists might not have been completely processed when the crash occurred. It does this by scanning the log backward to the most recent checkpoint record, using completion records and an algorithm analogous to the sharp checkpoint algorithm described previously. It then uses the update records of these transactions to update the database. Thus recovery in a deferred-update system is analogous to pass 2 of recovery in an immediate-update system.

Note that recovery is no longer concerned with rolling back database updates performed by transactions that were active at the time of the crash (pass 3), since active transactions do not update the database. Hence, the checkpoint record lists only incomplete transactions.

25.4   RECOVERY FROM MEDIA FAILURE

Durability requires that no information written by a committed transaction be lost. Therefore, we now consider media failure.

A simple approach to durability is to maintain two separate copies of the database on two different nonvolatile devices (perhaps supported by different power supplies) such that simultaneous failure of both devices is unlikely. Mirrored disks are one way to implement this approach. A mirrored disk is a mass storage system in which, whenever a request to write a record is made, the same record is written on two different disks. Thus one disk is an exact copy, a mirror image, of the other. Furthermore, the double write is transparent to the requestor.

A database stored on a mirrored disk will be durable if a single media failure occurs. In addition the system will remain available if one of the mirrored disks fails, since it can continue to operate using the other. When the failed disk is replaced, the system must resynchronize the two. By contrast, when durability is achieved using a log (as described next), recovery from a disk failure, might take a significant period of time, during which the system is unavailable to its users.

Even when an immediate update system uses a mirrored disk, it must still use a write-ahead log to achieve atomicity. Thus, before-images are still needed to roll back database items when a transaction aborts, and after-images are still needed to roll forward database items when a transaction commits.

A second approach to achieving durability involves restoring the database from the log when a media failure occurs. One way to do this is to play the log forward *from the beginning* using the after-images in the update records. However, this is impractical because of the size of the log. It will take an enormous amount of time, during which the system is unavailable. A solution is to make an archive copy, or **dump**, of the database periodically.

Recovery using the dump depends on how it was taken. For some applications, the dump can be produced off line. The system is shut down at some convenient time by not allowing new transactions to be initiated and waiting until all active transactions have terminated. A dump is then taken, and when it has been completed the system is restarted. To restore the database after a media failure, the system starts with the dump file and then makes two passes through the log records that were appended after the dump record: (1) a backward pass in which it makes a list of all the transactions that committed after the dump was taken and (2) a forward pass in which it copies into the database the redo records of all of the transactions on the list.

Fuzzy dumps.   With many applications, the system cannot be shut down. This calls for a **fuzzy dump**, taken while the system is operating. The fuzzy dump sequentially reads all records in the database, ignoring locks. Thus, transactions can be executing during the dump and can update records and later commit or abort. The dump program can read those records before or after they are written.

Consider an immediate-update system using physical logging. If the two-pass recovery procedure described above were used with a fuzzy dump, the second (forward) pass restores (from the log) the value of each database item written by a transaction that committed after the dump started, whether or not the dump had in fact read that value. As shown in Figure 25.8(a), the value of x recorded in the dump reflects the effect of T, but the value of y does not. Since T commits after the dump starts, however, the after-images of all changes it has made will be used in reconstructing the database starting from the dump. This is unnecessary for x, but rolls y forward to its proper value. The procedure also handles the case shown in Figure 25.8(b), in which a transaction starts after the dump has completed and later aborts, since its update records are ignored in pass 2.

However the two-pass procedure does not handle two situations correctly:

■ The database pages written by a transaction, T, that commits before the dump starts might not be written to the database until after the dump completes. In that case, the dump does not contain the new value written by T, but T is not included in the list of committed transactions, obtained in pass 1, whose update records are used to roll the database forward in pass 2. This happens because the commit record of T precedes the dump record, and the forward scan begins with the dump record.

■ The dump might read a value written by a transaction that is active during the dump but later aborts. In that case, the value recorded in the dump will not be rolled back. This situation is shown in Figure 25.8(c).

To overcome these problems, a fuzzy dump uses the same strategy employed for fuzzy checkpoints.

1. Before starting the dump, the checkpoint record $CK2$, shown in Figure 25.7, is appended to the log, followed by a **begin dump** record. As described in connection with that figure, the presence of $CK2$ in the log ensures that all dirty pages in the cache when $CK1$ was appended have been written to the database and so are recorded in the dump.

2. Compensation log records are used to record the reversal of updates during abort processing.

To restore the database, the system first reloads the dump file. Then it makes three passes through the log.

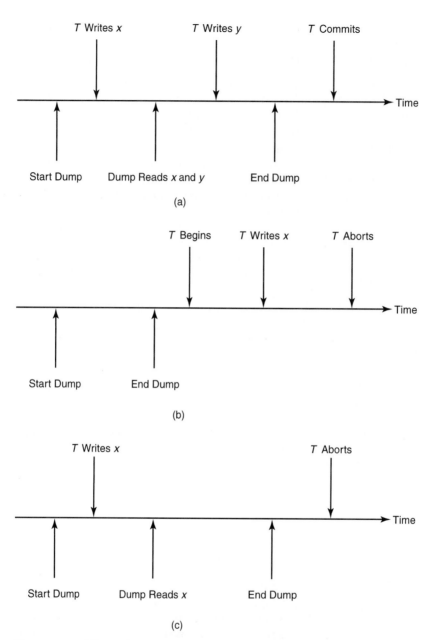

Figure 25.8 Effect of transactions being active while a dump is taken.

Pass 1. This is a backward pass starting at the end of the log and continuing to the most recent checkpoint record. During this pass, the system makes a list, L, of all transactions that were active when the failure occurred.

Pass 2. This is a forward pass starting at the second most recent checkpoint record at the time the dump was initiated ($CK1$ in Figure 25.7) and continuing to the end of the log. During this pass, the system uses the redo records of all transactions to roll the database forward from the state recorded in the dump.

Pass 3. This is a backward pass starting at the end of the log and continuing to the earliest begin record of a transaction in L. During this pass, the system uses the undo records of all transactions in L to roll back their effect.

All redo records (including compensation log records) for updates that might not be included in the dump are replayed in pass 2. Thus, when pass 2 completes the database will be rolled forward from the state recorded in the dump to the state it had when the failure occurred. Only the effects of transactions that were active when the media failed need to be reversed, and they are dealt with in pass 3.

In summary, media recovery requires the most recent dump of the database and that portion of the log containing all update records of all updates that might not be in the dump. Note that the required portion of the log will generally be greater than the portion required for crash recovery. Both portions must include the begin record of the oldest active transaction. However, crash recovery additionally requires that the log contain the two most recent checkpoint records, while media recovery requires the two checkpoint records preceding the start of the dump. Furthermore, if the most recent archived copy of the database is damaged, the same algorithm can be used to restore an earlier copy.

With physiological logging, instead of unconditionally applying before- and after-images during passes 2 and 3, the LSN is used, as described in Section 25.2.3, to determine whether or not an operation should be applied.

25.5 BIBLIOGRAPHIC NOTES

One of the first discussions on logging and recovery technology is in [Gray 1978]. Much of the current technology is based on the implementations of System R [Gray et al. 1981] and Aries (Algorithm for Recovery and Isolation Exploiting Semantics) [Mohan et al. 1992]. Excellent summaries of the technology are in [Haerder and Reuter 1983, Bernstein and Newcomer 1997, Gray and Reuter 1993]. A more abstract view of failures, in which recovery and serializability are integrated into a single model, is described in [Schek et al. 1993].

EXERCISES

25.1   Describe the contents of each of the following log records and how that record is used (if at all) in rollback and in recovery from crashes and media failure.

    a.   Abort record

    b.   Begin record

    c.   Begin dump record

    d.   Checkpoint record

    e.   Commit record

    f.   Compensation log record

    g.   Completion record

    h.   Redo record

    i.   Savepoint record

    j.   Undo record

25.2   Suppose that the concurrency control uses table locks and that a transaction performs an operation that updates the value of one attribute of one tuple in one table. Does the update record have to contain images of the entire table or just the one tuple?

25.3   Suppose that a dirty page in the cache has been written by two active transactions and that one of the transactions wants to commit. Describe how the caching procedure works in this case.

25.4   Suppose that the database system crashes between the time a transaction commits (by appending a commit record to the log) and the time it releases its locks. Describe how the system recovers from this situation.

25.5   Explain why the log buffer need not be flushed when an abort record is appended to it.

25.6   Explain why the LSN need not be included in pages stored in the database when physical logging is used together with a cache and log buffer.

25.7   Suppose that each database page contained the LSN of the commit record of the last transaction that has committed and written a database item in the page and the system uses the policy that it does not flush the page from the cache until the LSN of the oldest record in the log buffer is greater than the LSN of the page. Will the write-ahead policy be enforced?

25.8   The second step of the sharp checkpoint recovery procedure is as follows: The log is scanned forward from the checkpoint. The after-images in all update records are used to update the corresponding items in the database. Show that the updates can be performed in either of the following orders:

a. As each update record is encountered in the forward scan, the corresponding database update is performed (even though the update records for different transactions are interleaved in the log).

b. During the forward scan, the update records for each transaction are saved in volatile memory, and the database updates for each transaction are done all at once when the commit record for that transaction is encountered during the forward scan.

25.9 In the sharp checkpoint recovery procedure, explain whether or not the system needs to obtain locks when it is using the after-images in the log to update the database.

25.10 Consider the following two-pass strategy for crash recovery using a sharp checkpoint and physical logging: The first pass is a backward pass in which active transactions are rolled back. Active transactions are identified as described in Section 25.2. The pass extends at least as far as the begin record of the oldest active transaction or the most recent checkpoint record, whichever is earlier in the log. As update records for these transactions are encountered in the scan, their before-images are applied to the database. The second pass is a forward pass from the most recent checkpoint record to roll forward, using after-images, all changes made by transactions that completed since the checkpoint record was written (compensation log records are processed in the same way as ordinary update records so that aborted transactions are handled properly). Does the procedure work?

25.11 In order for logical logging to work, a logical database operation must have a logical inverse operation. Give an example of a database operation that has no inverse. Suggest a procedure involving logical logging that can handle this case.

25.12 Consider using the crash recovery procedure described in Section 25.2 (intended for physical logging) when logical logging is used. Explain how the procedure has to be modified to handle crashes that occur during recovery. Assume that the effect of each update is confined to a single page.

25.13 Explain why, in a deferred-update system, the write-ahead feature that is a part of immediate-update systems is not used when a database item is updated.

25.14 Explain why in a deferred-update system, the system does not first copy the intentions list into the database and then append the commit record to the log.

25.15 Assume that the system supports SNAPSHOT isolation. Describe how a sharp (nonfuzzy) dump could be taken without shutting down the system.

25.16 a. Explain how the log is implemented in your local DBMS.

b. Estimate the time in milliseconds to commit a transaction in your local DBMS.

25.17 The LSN stored in a page of the database refers to an update record in the log describing the most recent update to the page. Suppose that a transaction has performed the last update to a page and later aborts. Since its update to the page is reversed, the LSN in the page no longer refers to the appropriate update record. Why is this not a problem in the description of logging in the text?

25.18 An airlines reservation system has demanding performance and availability standards. Do the following play a role in enhancing performance? Do they enhance availability? Explain your answers.

a. Page cache

b. Log buffer

c. Checkpoint record

d. Physiological logging

e. Mirrored disk

Chapter 26

Implementing Distributed Transactions

26.1 IMPLEMENTING THE ACID PROPERTIES

A **distributed transaction** is one that accesses resource managers at different sites in a network. When these resource managers are database managers, we refer to the system as a **distributed database system**. Each local database manager might export stored subprograms that a distributed transaction, T, can invoke as subtransactions. Or T might submit individual SQL statements to be executed by the database manager, in which case the sequence of SQL statements submitted to it becomes T's subtransaction at that manager. In general, T's subtransactions might execute in sequence or concurrently, and the results of one subtransaction might influence the execution of another.

Distributed database systems are useful when the organizations they support are themselves distributed and each component maintains its own portion of the data. Communication costs can be minimized by placing data at the site at which it is most frequently accessed, and system availability can be increased, since the failure of a single site need not prevent continued operation at other sites. For example, the Student Registration System might be implemented as a distributed system. Student information might be stored on one computer and the course information on a different computer. The two computers might be located in different buildings on campus.

We discussed the database and query design issues related to distributed database systems in Chapter 18. In this chapter, we discuss transaction-related issues. We refer to the individual database managers that execute subtransactions of a global transaction as **cohorts** of that transaction. A database manager is a cohort of each global transaction for which it is executing a subtransaction and might be a cohort of a number of global transactions simultaneously.

We would like each distributed transaction to satisfy the ACID properties. The module responsible for doing most of this work is called the **coordinator**. In most systems, the transaction manager is the coordinator.

The cohorts of a distributed transaction are scattered across a network. A database manager acts not only as a cohort of distributed transactions initiated at

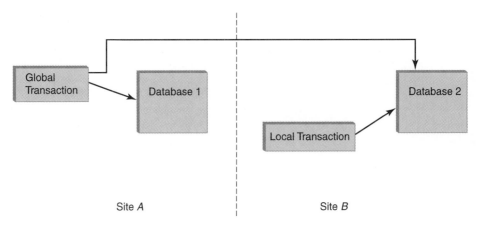

Figure 26.1 Data access paths for a distributed transaction.

arbitrary sites in the network, but also services conventional (single-resource) transactions initiated locally at its site. Since the database manager does not distinguish between local transactions and subtransactions of global transactions, we
frequently refer to both as simply "transactions." The data access paths for a distributed transaction are shown in Figure 26.1.

Consider the nationwide distribution system of a hardware manufacturing company. The company maintains a network of warehouses at different sites throughout the country, and each site has its own local database, which stores information
about that site's inventory. A customer at some site might initiate a transaction requesting 100 dozen widgets. The transaction might read the data item containing
the number of widgets currently in the local warehouse and find that there are
only 10 dozen, which it (tentatively) reserves, and then access data at one or more
of the other warehouses to reserve the additional 90 dozen widgets. After all 100
dozen have been located and reserved, the data items at each of the sites are decremented and appropriate shipping orders generated. If 100 dozen cannot be located,
the transaction releases all reserved widgets and commits, returning failure status
to the customer. In this way, either all sites at which widgets have been reserved
decrement their local databases or none do.

Physical failures are more complex when transactions are distributed. We saw
in Chapter 25 that a crash is a common type of failure. In a centralized system,
all the modules involved in the transaction fail when the computer crashes. With
distributed transactions, the crash of some computer in the network can cause some
subset of modules to fail while the rest continue to execute. Special protocols must
be designed to handle this new failure mode.

A similar situation arises when a communication failure causes the network
to become **partitioned**: Operational sites cannot communicate with one another.
We discuss how to deal with such failures later in the chapter. We assume that a
transaction can abort (and hence must be recoverable) and that once a transaction

commits (at all sites), the system must ensure that database changes at all sites are durable.

If we assume that each site supports the ACID properties locally and ensures that there are no local deadlocks, then the distributed transaction processing system also must ensure the following:

Atomic Termination. Either all cohorts of a distributed transaction must commit or all must abort.

No Global Deadlocks. There must be no global (distributed) deadlocks involving multiple sites.

Global Serialization. There must be a (global) serialization of all transactions (distributed and local).

We discuss each of these issues in this chapter. We also consider data replication and issues related to the distribution of data in a network.

26.2 ATOMIC TERMINATION

To ensure global atomicity, a distributed transaction can commit only if all of its subtransactions commit. Even though a subtransaction has completed all of its operations and is ready to commit, it cannot unilaterally decide to do so, because some other subtransaction might abort (or might already have aborted). In that case, the entire distributed transaction must be aborted. Thus, when a subtransaction has completed successfully, it must wait for all others to complete successfully before it can commit.

The coordinator executes an **atomic commit protocol** to guarantee global atomicity. The communication paths related to the protocol are shown in Figure 26.2. When an application program initiates a distributed transaction, T, it notifies the coordinator, thus setting the initial transaction boundary. Each time T invokes the services of a resource manager for the first time, the manager informs the coordinator that it has joined the transaction. When T completes, the application informs the coordinator, thus setting the final transaction boundary. The coordinator then initiates the atomic commit protocol.

Atomicity requires that, when T completes, either all cohorts must commit their changes or all must abort. In processing T's request to commit, therefore, the coordinator must first determine if all cohorts agree to do so. Some of the reasons a cohort might be unable to commit are:

■ The schema at a cohort site might specify deferred constraint checking (see Section 10.3). When the subtransaction at the site completes, the database manager might determine that a constraint is violated and abort the subtransaction.

■ The database manager at a cohort site might use an optimistic concurrency control. When the subtransaction at the site completes, the manager performs the validation procedure. If validation fails, the manager aborts the subtransaction.

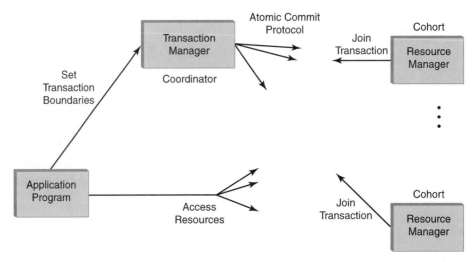

Figure 26.2 Communication paths in an atomic commit protocol.

■ A subtransaction might have been aborted by the (local) concurrency control because of a (local) deadlock or a (local) conflict with some other subtransaction (or local transaction).

■ The cohort site might have crashed and so is unable to respond to the protocol messages sent by the coordinator.

■ Some communication lines might have failed, preventing the cohort site from responding to the protocol messages sent by the coordinator.

26.2.1 The Two-Phase Commit Protocol

The particular atomic commit protocol we describe is called a **two-phase commit protocol** [Gray 1978, Lampson and Sturgis 1979] and is initiated by the coordinator when the transaction requests to commit. To perform the protocol, the coordinator needs to know the identities of all the cohorts of the transaction. Therefore, when the transaction is initiated, the coordinator allocates a **transaction record** in volatile memory, and each time a resource manager joins the transaction, its identification is appended to that transaction's record. Thus, when the transaction requests to commit, the transaction record contains a list of all its cohorts.

We describe the protocol as a series of messages exchanged between the coordinator and the cohorts. These messages are sent by calling procedures provided by the transaction manager and the resource managers.

When the transaction requests to commit, the coordinator starts the first phase of the two-phase commit protocol by sending a **prepare** message to each cohort. The purpose of this message is to determine whether the cohort is willing to commit and, if so, to request that it prepare to commit by storing all of the subtransaction's update records on nonvolatile storage.[1] Having the update records in nonvolatile storage guarantees that, if the coordinator subsequently decides that the transaction should be committed, the cohort will be able to do so, even if it crashes after responding positively to the prepare message.

If the cohort is willing to commit, it ensures that its update records are on nonvolatile storage by forcing a **prepared** record to the log. It is then said to be in the **prepared** state and can reply to the *prepare* message. Each cohort replies to the *prepare* message with a **vote** message.

The vote is **ready** if the cohort is willing to commit and **aborting** if not. Once a cohort votes ready, it cannot change its mind, since the coordinator uses the vote to decide whether the transaction as a whole is to be committed. The cohort is said to have entered an **uncertain period**, because it does not know whether the subtransaction will ultimately be committed or aborted by the coordinator. It must await the coordinator's decision, and during that waiting period it is blocked in the sense that it cannot release locks and the concurrency control at the cohort database cannot abort the subtransaction. This is an unfortunate situation that we will return to in Section 26.6. If the cohort votes aborting, it aborts the subtransaction immediately and exits the protocol. Phase 1 of the protocol is now complete.

The coordinator receives, and records in the transaction record, each cohort's vote. If all votes are ready, it decides that T can be committed globally, records the fact that the transaction has committed in the transaction record, and forces a commit record to the log. The commit record contains a copy of the transaction record.

As with single-resource transactions, T is committed once that commit record is safely stored in nonvolatile memory. All update records for all cohorts are in nonvolatile memory at that time, because each cohort forced a prepare record before voting. Note that we are assuming a general logging system, in which the transaction manager and each of the local database managers have their own independent logs.

The coordinator then sends each cohort a **commit** message telling it to commit. Local commitment is carried out as described in Section 25.2 and involves the forcing of a commit record to the database manager's log (to indicate that the subtransaction is committed), lock release, and local cleanup. After a cohort performs these actions, it sends a **done** message back to the coordinator indicating that it has completed the protocol.

When the coordinator receives a *done* message from each cohort, it appends a **complete** record to the log and deletes the transaction record from volatile memory. The protocol is then complete. For a committed transaction, the coordinator makes two writes to its log, only one of which is forced.

---

[1] A cohort site where only reads have been performed can implement a simplified version of the protocol. See exercise 26.14.

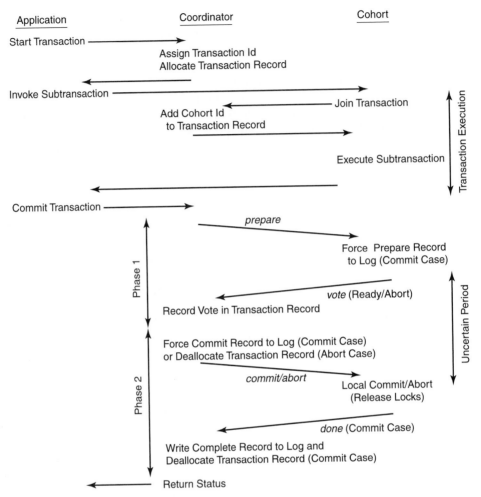

Figure 26.3 Exchange of messages in a two-phase commit protocol.

If the coordinator receives any aborting votes, it deallocates T's record in volatile storage and sends **abort** messages to each cohort that voted to commit (cohorts that voted to abort have already aborted and exited from the protocol). The coordinator does not record the abort in its log because this protocol has the presumed abort property, which we discuss below. The database manager aborts the cohort and writes an **abort** record in its log. The arrival of the *commit* or *abort* message at the cohort ends its uncertain period.

The sequence of messages exchanged between the application, the coordinator (transaction manager), and cohort (resource manager) is shown in Figure 26.3.

Summary of the two-phase commit protocol.   We summarize the two-phase commit protocol here:

Phase 1

1. The coordinator sends a *prepare* message to all cohorts.

2. Each cohort waits until it receives a *prepare* message from the coordinator. If it is prepared to commit, it forces a prepared record to its log, enters a state in which it cannot be aborted by its local control, and sends ready in the *vote* message to the coordinator.

    If it cannot commit, it appends an abort record to its log. Or it might already have aborted. In either case, it sends aborting in the *vote* message to the coordinator, rolls back any changes the subtransaction has made to the database, releases the subtransaction's locks, and terminates its participation in the protocol.

Phase 2

1. The coordinator waits until it receives votes from all cohorts. If it receives at least one aborting vote, it decides to abort, sends an *abort* message to all cohorts that voted ready, deallocates the transaction's record in volatile memory, and terminates its participation in the protocol.

    If all votes are ready, the coordinator decides to commit (and stores that fact in the transaction record), forces a commit record (which includes a copy of the transaction record) to its log, and sends a *commit* message to each cohort.

2. Each cohort that voted ready waits to receive a message from the coordinator. If a cohort receives an *abort* message, it rolls back any changes the subtransaction has made to the database, appends an abort record to its log, releases the subtransaction's locks, and terminates its participation in the protocol.

    If the cohort receives a *commit* message, it forces a commit record to its log, releases all locks, sends a *done* message to the coordinator, and terminates its participation in the protocol.

3. If the coordinator committed the transaction, it waits until it receives *done* messages from all cohorts. Then it appends a complete record to its log, deletes the transaction record from volatile memory, and terminates its participation in the protocol.

The atomic commit protocol across multiple domains. The role of the coordinator of a distributed transaction might be distributed among multiple transaction managers, each in a separate domain (as described on page 744). In this case, the messages of the atomic commit protocol travel over the edges of a tree, as shown in Figure 26.4. Leaf nodes are cohorts, and the root represents the transaction manager that controls the domain containing the application program that initiated the transaction. An interior node in the tree represents a transaction manager that coordinates resource managers in its domain and acts as a cohort with respect to its parent transaction manager.

The application program that initiated the transaction sends its request to commit to the root transaction manager, which then initiates the protocol. It sends *prepare* messages to all of its children (including local resource managers and remote transaction managers). When a transaction manager receives a *prepare* message, it initiates phase 1 of the protocol among its children by sending them *prepare*

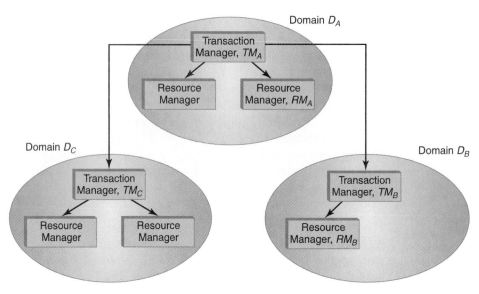

Figure 26.4 Distributed transaction structured as a tree.

messages and awaiting *vote* messages. On the basis of the votes it receives, it responds with an appropriate vote to its parent. While the figure shows a tree with only two coordinator levels, a general distributed transaction might have an arbitrary number of levels.

In the figure, the transaction manager, TM_A, in domain D_A receives the request to commit and sends *prepare* messages to each of its children. When the transaction manager, TM_B, in domain D_B receives the *prepare* message, it executes the first phase of a two-phase commit protocol with its child, RM_B. If it receives a *ready* vote from RM_B, it sends a ready vote to TM_A in response to the *prepare* message. Similarly, TM_C executes the first phase of a two-phase commit protocol among its children. If TM_A also receives a ready vote from TM_C, as well as from the two resource managers at site A, it commits the transaction and sends *commit* messages to all of its children. TM_B and TM_C then execute phase 2 of the protocol among their children. In this way, the *commit* message is propagated down the tree, and then *done* messages are propagated back up. The protocol generalizes in the obvious way to trees with additional levels.

26.2.2 Dealing with Failures in the Two–Phase Commit Protocol

The two-phase commit protocol includes protocols for dealing with various kinds of failures that might occur in a distributed system.

■ A **timeout protocol** is executed if a site times out while waiting for a message. (A timeout might occur either because the sending site has crashed, the message is lost, or the message delivery system is slow.)

■ A **restart protocol** is executed by a site recovering from a crash.

If a site cannot complete the commit protocol until some failure is repaired, we say that the site is **blocked**. When a site blocks, the decision to commit or abort is delayed for an arbitrary period of time. This delay is particularly undesirable at a cohort site that uses a locking concurrency control, since items that the subtransaction has locked remain unavailable to other transactions at that site. For this reason, it is important to understand the circumstances under which the two-phase commit protocol results in blocking. We consider the various failure situations next. We describe these situations as if the protocol tree contains exactly two levels. However, the same decisions are made between a parent and its children at any pair of adjacent levels in a tree with multiple levels.

The cohort times out while waiting for a prepare message.   The cohort can be certain that no decision to commit has yet been taken at any site (since it has not yet voted). It can therefore decide to abort. If a *prepare* message subsequently arrives, the cohort can simply respond with an aborting vote, which will prevent any site from reaching a commit decision (since such a decision requires commit votes from all sites). In this way, global atomicity is preserved.

The coordinator times out while waiting for a vote message.   This situation is similar to the one above. The coordinator can decide to abort and send an *abort* message to all cohorts.[2]

The cohort times out while waiting for a commit or abort message.   This situation is more serious, since the cohort has voted ready and is in its uncertain period. It is blocked until it can determine if the coordinator has made a decision and, if so, what that decision is. The cohort cannot unilaterally choose to commit or abort, since the coordinator might have made a different choice, thus violating unanimity.

The cohort can attempt to communicate with the coordinator, requesting the transaction's status. If this is not possible (the coordinator has crashed or the network is partitioned) the cohort can try to communicate with other cohorts. (To facilitate such communication, the coordinator can provide a list of all cohorts in the prepare message, which the cohort can store in the prepare record that it writes to the log.) If the cohort finds a cohort that has not yet voted, both decide to abort. This is safe, since the coordinator cannot have decided to commit if any cohort has not yet voted. If it finds a cohort that has aborted or committed, it makes the same decision. If all other cohorts it finds are also in their uncertain period, it remains blocked until communication can be established with the coordinator or a cohort that has committed or aborted.

The coordinator times out while waiting for a done message.   The coordinator communicates with the cohort requesting the *done* message. When *done* messages have been received from all cohorts, it deallocates the transaction record.

---

[2] Note that all sites might have sent *commit* messages, but one of the messages was not delivered during the timeout period. In this case, the coordinator aborts the transaction, even though all of the cohorts are operational and voted to commit it—a counterintuitive situation.

The coordinator crashes.   When the coordinator restarts after a crash, it searches its log. If, for some transaction, T, it finds a commit record but no complete record, it must be in phase 2 of the protocol for T. The coordinator restores T's transaction record (found in T's commit record) to volatile memory and resumes the protocol by sending *commit* messages to all cohorts, since the crash might have occurred before the *commit* messages were sent. If the coordinator does not find a commit record for some transaction, two possibilities exist.

■ The protocol was still in phase 1 when the crash occurred.

■ The coordinator has aborted the transaction.

The coordinator cannot distinguish between these two cases, since in both it has not written any records to its log. Fortunately, it does not need to distinguish between them, since in either case the transaction is aborted. If the first case has occurred, then, at some later time, the cohorts will query the coordinator about the transaction's status. Since the coordinator does not find a transaction record for that transaction in its volatile storage, it will reply with an *abort* message. This is allowable, because the transaction was in phase 1 of the protocol when the coordinator crashed, and hence the coordinator had not made any decision before the crash. This reasoning is part of the presumed abort protocol described next.

The cohort crashes or times out while in the prepared state—the presumed abort property.   When a cohort restarts after a crash, it searches its log. If it finds a prepared record but no commit or abort record, it knows that it was in the prepared state at the time of the crash. It requests the transaction's status from the coordinator. The coordinator might also have been restarted (see above), or the cohort might have crashed while the coordinator remained active. If the coordinator finds the transaction record for the transaction in volatile memory, the coordinator can immediately respond to the request. However, if it does not find a transaction record, it presumes (without checking its log) that the transaction has aborted and reports that to the cohort. This feature of the protocol is referred to as **presumed abort** [Mohan et al. 1986].

The presumed abort feature works[3] because the absence of a transaction record indicates that one of the following is true:

■ The coordinator has committed the transaction, received done messages from all cohorts, and deleted the transaction record from volatile memory.

■ The coordinator has crashed, and its restart protocol found commit and complete records for the transaction in its log.

■ The coordinator has aborted the transaction and deleted the transaction record.

---

[3] One dictionary definition of the word *presume* is "to expect or assume, to regard as probably true as in 'innocence is presumed until guilt is proven.'" However, in this case the coordinator definitely knows that the transaction has aborted.

▪ The coordinator has crashed, and its restart protocol did not find any records for the transaction in its log (it aborted the transaction or was in phase 1 of the protocol when it crashed).

Since the cohort is still in the prepared state (and hence has not sent a *done* message), the first and second possibilities are ruled out. Therefore the coordinator can report that the transaction has aborted. This same reasoning applies if the cohort times out in its prepared state and requests the transaction's status from the coordinator. (Note that, when the commit protocol is used across multiple domains, each coordinator in the protocol tree can use the presumed abort property to respond to requests from its cohorts.)

Timeout Protocol for the Two-Phase Commit Protocol

T01. *Cohort times out while waiting for prepare message.* The cohort decides to abort.

T02. *Coordinator times out while waiting for vote message.* The coordinator decides to abort, sends an *abort* message to every cohort from which it received a ready vote, deletes the transaction record from volatile memory, and terminates its participation in the protocol.

T03. *Cohort times out while waiting for commit/abort message.* The cohort attempts to communicate with the coordinator to determine the outcome of the transaction. If it can communicate with the coordinator, the coordinator can use the presumed abort property to formulate its answer. If the cohort cannot communicate with the coordinator, it attempts to communicate with another cohort. If it finds one that has committed or aborted, it makes the same decision. If it finds one that has not yet voted, they both decide to abort. Otherwise the cohort blocks.

T04. *Coordinator times out while waiting for done message.* The coordinator sends a message to the cohort requesting that the *done* message be sent. It maintains the transaction record in its volatile memory until it has received *done* messages from all cohorts.

The protocol for restarting a coordinator or cohort site after a crash can be built on the crash recovery procedure described in Section 25.2.

Restart Protocol for the Two-Phase Commit Protocol

RES1.   If the restarted site is a cohort site and, for some transaction, the site's crash recovery procedure finds a commit or abort record in its log, that transaction has completed, and the procedure takes no additional actions beyond those discussed in Section 25.2.

RES2.   If the restarted site is a cohort and, for some transaction, the site's crash recovery procedure finds a begin transaction record in its log but does not find a prepared record (and hence the cohort has not yet voted), the procedure takes no additional actions beyond those discussed in Section 25.2 (i.e., it aborts the subtransaction).

RES3. If the restarted site is a cohort and, for some transaction, the site's crash recovery procedure finds a prepared record, but no commit or abort record, in its log (and hence the cohort might have sent a ready vote before the crash), the crash occurred during the cohort's uncertain period. The crash recovery procedure restores all the database updates made by the subtransaction. The cohort then follows the protocol TO3.

RES4 If the restarted site is the coordinator and, for some transaction, it finds a commit record, but no complete record in its log, the crash occurred after the coordinator had committed the transaction, but before it had received *done* messages from all the cohorts. When the coordinator is restarted, the transaction record is restored to volatile memory from the commit record. The coordinator then follows the protocol TO4.

26.2.3 Formats and Protocols: The X/Open Standard

The two-phase commit protocol ties together software modules, such as DBMSs and a transaction manager, that might have been provided by different vendors. If these modules are to communicate effectively, and if application programs are to communicate with them, they must agree on communication conventions, sometimes called the **format and protocols** (**FAP**). Standardization of the FAP promotes **interoperability** among products of different vendors.

The X/Open standard permits interoperability by defining a set of function calls for exchanging protocol messages and the formats of those messages. With X/Open, the names of functions called by transactions and implemented in the transaction manager (coordinator) are prefixed with tx—for example, tx_begin() is the function called to start a transaction in Figure 26.3. Similarly, X/Open function calls from the transaction manager to resource managers are prefixed with xa. Thus, when a resource manager (cohort) wishes to join a transaction it calls xa_reg(). When a transaction wishes to commit, it calls tx_commit(). The transaction manager then calls each of the resource managers using xa_prepare() (causing *prepare* messages to be sent) and waits for that function to return. The return value of each call to xa_prepare() is the ready or aborting vote of that resource manager. If all votes are ready, the transaction manager sets the return value of the transaction program's call of tx_commit() to commit and calls each of the resource managers with xa_commit(). If one or more of the return values of xa_prepare() is aborting, the transaction manager sets the return value of the transaction's call of tx_commit() to abort and calls each of the resource managers with xa_abort().

The X/Open standard provides the structure for the implementation of global atomicity when RPC is used to invoke subtransactions. In that case it is the stubs that invoke, for example, tx_begin and xa_reg.

26.2.4 The Peer-to-Peer Atomic Commit Protocol

A variation of the two-phase commit protocol achieves the atomic commitment of transactions that use peer-to-peer communication (Section 22.4.3).[4] Here syncpoint managers perform the function of transaction managers. The syncpoint manager associated with an application program, A, keeps a record of all application programs and resource managers with which A has directly communicated.

Assuming that A initiates the protocol by declaring a syncpoint, all of its connections must be in send mode. The syncpoint manager associated with A starts phase 1 of the protocol by sending *prepare* messages to all resource managers that A has invoked and *syncpoint* messages over all of its connections to other application programs. Then A waits until the protocol completes. When the *syncpoint* message arrives at some other program, B, that program might not have completed its portion of the transaction. When it does and all of its connections (other than the connection to A) are in send mode, it also declares a syncpoint. This causes the syncpoint manager associated with B to send *prepare* messages to all resource managers that B has invoked and *syncpoint* messages to all programs (other than A) with which B has communicated. Then B waits until the protocol completes.

In this way, *syncpoint* messages spread and a tree similar to the one pictured in Figure 26.4 is defined. Assuming that all peers want to commit, each peer eventually declares a syncpoint, all are synchronized at their syncpoint declarations, and the associated resource managers are in a prepared state. Ready *vote* messages propagate up the tree, and phase 1 of the two-phase commit protocol completes. Then phase 2 starts, and the transaction is committed by the tree of syncpoint managers. Commit status is also returned to each program, which can then continue its execution by starting a new transaction.

If a peer decides to abort, local rollback is initiated and abort status is sent to all resource managers, causing them to roll back as well. Abort status is also returned to each program, which can then continue executing by starting a new transaction.

26.3 TRANSFER OF COORDINATION

Generally, the transaction manager associated with the site at which the transaction is initiated becomes the coordinator. It communicates with the cohorts to carry out the atomic commit protocol. The cohorts might be resource managers, but more generally they are transaction managers in a distributed transaction tree.

There are several reasons why basing coordination at the initiator site might not be an optimal arrangement. For one thing, the initiator site might not be the most reliable site involved in the transaction. Consider that the transaction might be initiated as the result of some action at a point-of-sales terminal and involve servers, in the store's main office and at the customer's bank. It might be safer to

---

[4] This description is based on [Maslak et al. 1991].

have coordination located at one of these servers, in which case the protocol can be modified so that coordinator status is transferred from one participant to another.

A second reason for transferring coordination has to do with optimizing the number of messages to be exchanged during the protocol. The two-phase commit protocol (with the presumed abort property) involves the exchange of four messages between the coordinator and each cohort. Optimizations on this are possible. For example, the following modified protocol involves two participants, P_1 and P_2, that can be thought of as transaction managers (each of which controls a set of cohort resource managers) or servers.

1. P_1 initiates the protocol by entering the prepared state (if P_1 is a transaction manager, its cohorts are all in their prepared states). It then sends a message to P_2, which simultaneously says that P_1 is prepared to commit locally and requests P_2 to prepare and commit the transaction as a whole. Thus, the message is a combination of ready vote and *prepare* message and has the effect of transferring the coordinator role to P_2.

2. P_2 receives the message and, assuming it is willing to commit, enters the prepared state. Since it knows that P_1 is prepared at this time, P_2 can decide to commit the transaction as a whole and take the actions necessary to commit the transaction locally. It responds to P_1 with a *commit* message.

3. P_1 receives the message, commits locally, and responds with a *done* message to P_2.

The *done* message is required because of the presumed abort property: P_2, acting as the new coordinator, must remember the transaction's outcome in case the *commit* message is not received by P_1. It can then respond to a query from P_1 asking about the transaction's outcome. The done message indicates to P_2 that it can delete the transaction record from volatile memory. The fact that the protocol has completed with an exchange of only three messages (instead of four) shows that the number of messages exchanged can be optimized.

26.3.1 The Linear Commit Protocol

The **linear commit protocol** is a variation of the two-phase commit protocol that uses transfer of coordination. The cohorts are assumed to be interconnected in a (linear) chain. Assume (arbitrarily) that the leftmost cohort, C_1, initiates the protocol. When it is ready to commit, it goes into the prepared state and sends a message to the cohort on its right, C_2, indicating that it is ready to commit and transferring coordination to C_2. After the message is received, if C_2 is willing to commit, it also goes into the prepared state and relays the message to the cohort on its right, again transferring coordination. The process continues until the message reaches the rightmost cohort, C_n. If C_n agrees to commit, it commits and sends a *commit* message to C_{n-1}, which commits and propagates the message down the chain until it reaches C_1, which then commits. Finally, a *done* message is propagated up the chain from C_1 to C_n to complete the protocol.

If, after receiving the first protocol message, a cohort wants to abort the transaction, it aborts and sends *abort* messages to the cohorts on its left and right. Those cohorts abort and forward the *abort* message further along the chain until it reaches both ends.

The logging, timeout, and recovery protocols used to achieve atomicity for various types of failure are similar to those for the two-phase commit protocol (see exercise 26.11).

The linear commit protocol involves fewer messages than the two-phase commit protocol and hence saves on communication costs. If n is the number of cohorts, the linear commit requires $3(n - 1)$ messages, whereas the two-phase commit requires $4n$ messages (a separate coordinator is involved). On the other hand, the two-phase commit completes after a sequence of four message exchanges (independent of the number of cohorts), since the coordinator communicates with all cohorts in parallel. The linear commit requires a sequence of $3(n - 1)$ exchanges because messages are sent serially.

The concept of linear commit is part of a number of the Internet transaction protocols that we will discuss in Chapter 27.

26.3.2 Two-Phase Commit without a Prepared State

The basic idea in transfer of coordination can be used to adapt the two-phase commit protocol to situations in which (exactly) one of the cohorts, C, does not understand the prepare message and does not have a prepared state (this might be the case if C is an older legacy system). In this case the coordinator executes phase 1 of the protocol with the cohorts that do support a prepared state in the normal way. If all of these cohorts agree to commit, the coordinator sends a commit message to C, which effectively allows C to decide whether the transaction as a whole will be committed. If C responds to the coordinator that it has committed, the coordinator sends commit messages to the other cohorts and completes phase 2 of the protocol. If C responds that it has aborted, the coordinator sends abort messages to the other cohorts.

Note that C does not actually function as a coordinator, since it does not take the steps necessary to handle failures. It does not maintain a transaction record for the distributed transaction; nor does it understand a done message. Thus, it cannot respond to queries from other cohorts if a failure occurs. Hence, coordination is not completely transferred.

26.4   DISTRIBUTED DEADLOCK

Pessimistic concurrency controls that employ waiting are subject to deadlock. Assuming that each local concurrency control does not permit local deadlock, we want to ensure that the overall system is not subject to distributed deadlock. For example, a simple distributed deadlock between two distributed transactions, T_1 and T_2, both of which have cohorts at sites A and B, will result if the concurrency control at site A makes T_1's cohort, T_{1A}, wait for T_2's cohort, T_{2A}, while the concurrency control at site B makes T_2's cohort, T_{2B}, wait for T_1's cohort, T_{1B}. Note that, in the general model of a distributed transaction, the cohorts can run concurrently, whereas a transaction accessing a single database is purely sequential. Hence, in the above example, T_{2A} not only holds some resource for which T_{1A} is waiting, but can actually progress, since it is not delayed by the wait of T_{2B}. Deadlock still occurs, however, since T_2 cannot release its locks until it commits globally, which will not happen if T_{2B} is waiting. Ultimately, in such a situation, all progress in the deadlocked transactions stops.

In general, a distributed deadlock cannot be eliminated by aborting and restarting a single cohort. The statements executed by a cohort are really a subsequence of the statements executed by the transaction as a whole. They cannot be re-executed because other cohorts might have already executed statements that logically follow them. For example, results computed by T_{1A} might have been communicated to T_{1B} before the deadlock occurred. Restarting T_{1A} without restarting T_{1B} makes no sense in that case, so the entire distributed transaction must be restarted.

The techniques to detect a distributed deadlock are simple extensions of those discussed in Section 23.4.2. In one, the system constructs a distributed *waits_for* relation and searches for cycles whenever a cohort is made to wait. For example, a cohort of T_1 informs its coordinator that it is waiting for a cohort of T_2. T_1's coordinator then sends a **probe** message to T_2's coordinator. If T_2's coordinator has also been informed by one of its cohorts that it is waiting for a cohort of T_3, the probe message is relayed by the coordinator of T_2 to the coordinator of T_3. A deadlock is detected if the probe returns to T_1's coordinator.

Another technique uses timeout: whenever the wait time experienced by a cohort at some site exceeds some threshold, the concurrency control at that site assumes that a deadlock exists and aborts the cohort.

Finally, the timestamp technique [Rosenkrantz et al. 1978] described in Section 23.4.2 can be used for distributed transactions with one small generalization. Whenever a distributed transaction is initiated, its coordinator uses the clock at the coordinator site as the basis of a timestamp. To ensure that all timestamps are globally unique, they are formed by appending the coordinator's (unique) site identifier to the low-order bits of the clock value. When the transaction creates a cohort at a site, it sends along the value of its timestamp. With a single, unique timestamp associated with all cohorts of a distributed transaction, the strategy of never allowing an older transaction to wait for a younger transaction eliminates distributed deadlocks.

26.5 GLOBAL SERIALIZATION

In a centralized system, the goal of concurrency control is to respond to requests to access items in the database so as to produce a specified level of isolation. With a distributed transaction, multiple DBMSs are involved, each of which might be supporting a different isolation level. Under such circumstances, the isolation between concurrent distributed transactions is poorly defined. Suppose, however, that we consider the problem of implementing globally serializable schedules. A simple approach is to provide a single control at some central site. All requests (at any site) are sent to this site, which maintains the data structures for implementing the locks for data items at all sites.

Such a system is just a centralized concurrency control in which the data is distributed. Unfortunately, this simple approach has significant drawbacks: It requires excessive communication (with the delays that this implies), the central site is a bottleneck, and the entire system is vulnerable to the failure of that site.

A better approach, and the one generally followed, is for each site to maintain its own local concurrency control. Whenever a (sub)transaction makes a request to perform an operation at some site, the concurrency control at that site makes a decision based only on local information available to it, without communicating with any other site. Each concurrency control separately uses the techniques previously described to ensure that the schedule it produces is equivalent to at least one serial schedule of transactions and subtransactions of global transactions at its site. The overall design of the system must then ensure that global transactions are serialized globally—that is, that there is at least one equivalent serial ordering on which all sites agree.

Our concern, since the sites operate independently and might even employ different concurrency control algorithms, is that there might be no ordering on which all sites agree. Consider global transactions T_1 and T_2 that might have cohorts at sites A and B. At site A, T_{1A} and T_{2A} might have conflicting operations and be serialized in the order T_{1A}, T_{2A}, while at site B conflicting cohorts of the same two transactions might be serialized T_{2B}, T_{1B}. In that case, there is no equivalent serial schedule of T_1 and T_2 as a whole.

We can ensure that local serializability at each site implies global serializability using nothing more than the individual concurrency controls and the two-phase commit protocol. Specifically it can be shown [Weihl 1984] that

> If the concurrency controls at each site independently use either a strict two-phase locking or an optimistic algorithm and the system uses a two-phase commit protocol, every global schedule is serializable (in the order in which their coordinators have committed them).

While we do not prove that result here, it is not hard to see the basic argument that can be generalized into a proof. Suppose that sites A and B use strict two-phase locking concurrency controls, that a two-phase commit algorithm is used to ensure global atomicity, and that transactions T_1 and T_2 are as described above. We argue by contradiction. Suppose that the conflicts described above occur (so that the transactions are not serializable) and that both transactions commit. T_{1A} and T_{2A} conflict on some data item at site A, so T_{2A} cannot complete until T_{1A} releases the lock on that item. Since the concurrency control is strict and a two-phase commit algorithm is used, T_{1A} does not release the lock until after T_1 has committed. Since, T_2 cannot commit until after T_{2A} completes, T_1 must commit before T_2. But if we use the same reasoning at site B, we conclude that T_2 must commit before T_1. Hence, we have derived a contradiction, and it follows that both transactions cannot have committed. In fact, the conflicts we have assumed at sites A and B yield a deadlock, and one of the transactions will have to be aborted.

26.6 WHEN GLOBAL ATOMICITY CANNOT BE GUARANTEED

In practice, there are a number of situations in which an atomic commit protocol cannot be completed and hence global atomicity cannot be guaranteed.

■ **A cohort site does not participate in two-phase commit.** A particular site might not support the protocol. For example, a resource manager might be a legacy system that does not support a prepared state. Alternatively, a site might elect not to participate to avoid the degradation of performance that can occur with blocking. A transaction is blocked during the uncertain period and holds locks that prevent other transactions from accessing the locked items. Since the site cannot control the length of the uncertain period, it is no longer independent: Factors that control access to locked resources are controlled elsewhere. For example, the length of the uncertain period depends on the speed with which other cohorts respond to *prepare* messages and the efficiency of the message passing system. If the coordinator crashes or the network becomes partitioned, a cohort might remain blocked for a substantial period of time.

Cohort sites that elect to participate in the protocol often deal with this problem by unilaterally deciding to commit or abort a blocked subtransaction in order to release locks. Such a decision is referred to as a **heuristic decision**.

Unfortunately, assigning a technical name to the action does not change the fact that global atomicity might be compromised as a result of such an action. A heuristic decision might cause global inconsistency in the database (a subtransaction that updated a data item at one site might commit, but a subtransaction of the same transaction at a different site that updated a related data item might abort). Such inconsistencies can sometimes be resolved in an ad hoc manner by communication among the database administrators at the different sites. Although heuristic decisions do not preserve global atomicity, they are the only way to resolve an important practical problem.

A cohort site might not participate for reasons unrelated to performance. For example, the site might charge a fee to execute a subtransaction and, when the subtransaction completes and returns a result to the application, might demand to collect the fee even if the overall transaction subsequently aborts. Therefore, the site administrator might insist that the subtransaction commit as soon as it completes, without waiting for the transaction to commit or abort globally.

■ **The language does not support two-phase commit.** On the application side, although JDBC, ODBC, and most versions of embedded SQL allow a transaction to connect to multiple DBMSs, they do not support two-phase commit. When a transaction completes, it sends individual commit commands to each DBMS, one at a time. Thus, the all-or-none commit provided by a two-phase commit protocol is not enforced and so the transaction is not guaranteed to be globally atomic. However, a proposed new Java API, **Java Transaction Service (JTS)**, includes a TP monitor (and an appropriate API) that guarantees an atomic commit of distributed transactions using JDBC. Microsoft also has introduced a new TP monitor, **Microsoft Transaction Server** (**MTS**), that includes a transaction manager (and an appropriate API) that guarantees an atomic commit of distributed transactions using ODBC. Furthermore, embedded SQL provided by some database vendors supports two-phase commit among that vendor's DBMS (i.e., in a homogeneous system).

■ **The system does not support two-phase commit.** Support of the two-phase commit protocol requires that the system middleware include a coordinator (transaction manager) and that the application, coordinator, and servers agree on conventions for exchanging protocol messages. For example, the X/Open standard specifies APIs for this purpose (e.g., the tx and xa interfaces). For many applications, such system support is not available and so the two-phase commit cannot be implemented.

26.6.1 Weaker Commit Protocols

If sites do not participate in a two-phase commit protocol (or some other atomic commit protocol), the execution of distributed transactions is not guaranteed to be isolated or atomic. Nevertheless, systems might have to be designed under this constraint. In such cases, the application designer must carefully assess how this affects the correctness of the database and the ultimate utility of the application to its clients.

When the two-phase commit is not supported, one of the following weaker commit protocols might be used.

■ In the **one-phase commit protocol**, the application program does not send commit commands to any site until all subtransactions have completed. Then it sends a separate commit command to each site it accesses. Some sites might commit, and some might abort. A distributed transaction implemented with JDBC might operate in this fashion.

■ In the **zero-phase commit protocol**, each subtransaction commits as soon as it has completed all operations at a site. Again, some sites might commit and some might abort. Note that, after the subtransaction at one site commits, the application program might initiate new subtransactions at other sites. In one variant of this protocol, the application initiates subtransactions one at a time. When one completes and commits, it initiates another.

■ In the **autocommit protocol**, a commit operation is performed immediately (automatically by the system) after each SQL statement. Autocommit is the default in ODBC and JDBC.

None of these protocols guarantees global atomicity, since subtransactions (or operations) might commit at some sites and abort at others.

In the normal case in which all subtransactions commit, if each DBMS uses a strict two-phase locking algorithm or an optimistic concurrency control algorithm, the one-phase commit protocol guarantees global serializability.

> If (1) the concurrency control at each site independently uses either a strict two-phase locking or an optimistic algorithm, (2) the application program uses a one-phase commit protocol, and (3) the subtransactions at all sites commit, then all global schedules are serializable (in the order in which the application programs have committed them).

Thus, the transaction maintains all global and local integrity constraints.

The same reasoning that justifies a similar result for the two-phase commit applies here—with the added restriction that the subtransactions at all sites must commit. If the subtransactions at some sites abort, so that the global transaction is not atomic, the parts of the transactions that do commit are serializable, again using the same reasoning.

With the zero-phase protocol, a subtransaction might commit and release locks at one site before another subtransaction is initiated and acquires locks at another site. Hence, from a global perspective, locking is not two-phase and therefore global serializability is not guaranteed, even if the subtransactions at all sites commit. Transactions might be serializable in different orders at different sites. Each subtransaction maintains the local integrity constraint at the site at which it executes, but the global transaction does not necessarily maintain global integrity constraints.

The zero-phase commit protocol holds locks for a shorter period of time than does the one-phase commit protocol. Thus, it can provide better performance, but global serializability is not guaranteed. Zero-phase commit might therefore be particularly appropriate for applications in which there are no global integrity constraints and so global serializability is not an issue. Local serializability, however, is maintained.

The autocommit protocol holds locks for the shortest possible time and hence yields the best performance, but it does not guarantee even local serializability at each site. For this reason, it is not guaranteed to maintain either global or local integrity constraints.

In the one-phase and zero-phase commit protocols, if the application program requests the subtransaction at some site to commit and that subtransaction instead aborts, the application program is notified of the abort and might be able to achieve the desired result in some other way—perhaps by initiating a new subtransaction at a different site. For some applications, this feature can be a significant advantage compared with the two-phase commit protocol, in which, when a subtransaction at any site aborts, the entire global transaction aborts.

26.7 REPLICATED DATABASES

A common technique for dealing with failures is to replicate portions of a database at different sites in the network. Then, if a site crashes or becomes separated from the network because of a partition, the portion of the database being maintained by that site can still be accessed by contacting a different site that holds a replica. We say that the **availability** of the data has been increased.

Replication can also improve the efficiency of access to data (hence increasing transaction throughput and decreasing response time), since a transaction can access the nearest replica, perhaps one that exists at the site at which the transaction was initiated. For example, in the Internet grocer application discussed in Section 18.2.3, the company has a table describing its customers that is replicated at its headquarters site and at the local warehouse from which a customer's orders are delivered. Transactions involving the delivery of merchandise execute at the warehouse site and use the replica stored there, while transactions involving monthly mailings to all customers execute at headquarters and use the replica stored there.

Of course, replication has its costs. First, more storage is required. Second, the system becomes more complex since we must properly manage access to replicated data. For example, if we allow two transactions to access, and perhaps update, different replicas of the same item, each might be unaware of the effects of the other, resulting in a problem similar to the lost update problem. Thus, a replicated system must ensure that replicas of a data item are properly updated and that appropriate values are supplied to transactions requesting to read that item. In the Internet grocer application, the replicated customer information needs to be updated only when the customer information changes—for example, a change of address, which occurs infrequently.

An item is said to be **totally replicated** if a replica exists at every site. It is said to be **partially replicated** if replicas exist at some but not all sites.

If the DBMS itself does not support replication, the application can replicate the data items. The DBMS is then unaware of the fact that distinct items at different sites are replicas of one another. If $x1$ and $x2$ are replicas of a data item, each transaction must explicitly maintain the integrity constraint $x1 = x2$. A transaction that accesses a replicated data item must specify which replica it wants. A transaction that updates a replicated item must explicitly initiate subtransactions to update each replica.

Instead of requiring transactions to manage replication, most commercial DBMSs provide a special subsystem for this purpose—a **replica control**—which makes replication invisible to the application. The replica control knows where all replicas of a data item are located. When a transaction requests access to an item, it does not specify a particular replica. The replica control automatically translates the request into a request to access the appropriate replica(s) and passes the request to the local concurrency control if the replica is local and/or to the remote site(s) at which the replica resides. We assume that concurrency controls implement a locking protocol, so when replicas are accessed they are locked in the same way as are ordinary data items: A shared lock for read access, an exclusive lock for write access. The concurrency control is unaware that a table might actually be a copy of another table at a different site. The relationship between the replica control and the concurrency control is shown in Figure 26.5.

Replica controls in commercial DBMSs attempt to maintain some form of **mutual consistency**. With **strong mutual consistency**, every committed replica of an item always has the same value as every other committed replica. Unfortunately, performance considerations often make this goal impractical to achieve, and so

Figure 26.5 Relationship between replica control and concurrency control in a replicated database.

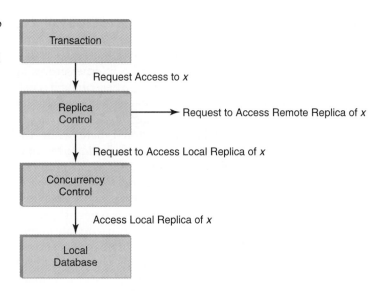

most replica controls maintain the more modest goal, **weak mutual consistency**: All committed replicas of an item *eventually* have the same value, although at any particular time some may have different values. A variety of algorithms are used to maintain these goals.

The simplest replica control system is referred to as a **read-one/write-all** system. When a transaction requests to read a data item, the replica control can return the value of any one—presumably the nearest—of its replicas. With a fully replicated system, transactions that do not update replicated data items need not make any remote accesses and hence can respond rapidly to the user. When, however, a transaction requests to update a data item, the replica control must execute an algorithm that (eventually) causes all replicas of the item to be updated. This is the difficult case, and different algorithms have different characteristics. Generally speaking, read-one/write-all systems yield an improvement in performance over nonreplicated systems (where reads might have to access distant data items) if reads occur substantially more frequently than updates.

Read-one/write-all systems can be characterized as synchronous-update or asynchronous-update depending on the algorithm the replica control uses to maintain mutual consistency. We discuss synchronous-update systems in the next section and asynchronous-update systems in Section 26.7.2.

26.7.1 Synchronous–Update Replication Systems

In a **synchronous-update system**, when a transaction updates a data item, the replica control locks and updates all of the replicas before the transaction commits. As a result the strong form of mutual consistency is maintained. Hence, synchronous replication is also referred to as **eager** replication since replicas are updated immediately. When a transaction reads an item only a single replica is locked.

Assuming that a two-phase locking policy is used, all replicas that are accessed will be appropriately locked before the transaction commits. Hence, transactions execute serializably and database consistency is preserved.

Locking can take one of two forms.

■ *Pessimistically.* All necessary locks are acquired before the transaction proceeds beyond the statement that requested the access.

■ *Optimistic.* Only a single replica is locked, and updated if the access is a write, when the statement is executed. The other replicas are locked and updated later but before the transaction commits.

In either form, a new type of deadlock, **one-item deadlock**, is possible. This occurs if two updaters of the same item run concurrently and each succeeds in locking a subset of the item's replicas. Such deadlocks can be resolved with the usual protocols.

When a transaction commits, we must guarantee that each update of an item is durable. It is not sufficient to simply commit the transaction at the site at which it was initiated and send commit messages to replica sites, since replica site A might crash before receiving the message. If, on recovery, the updated value is not installed at A, a read request for the item by another transaction that is satisfied at A will not return the correct value.

The two-phase commit protocol can be used to ensure that each replica site commits the new value if the transaction commits. The cohorts are the replica sites that the transaction has accessed.[5] Although it is no longer necessary for each cohort to separately evaluate the outcome of distinct subtransactions, the prepared state is necessary to guarantee that all updates are durable before the transaction actually commits.

Unfortunately, eager replication has the effect of requiring the transaction to acquire additional locks, which increases the probability of deadlock. Furthermore, the response time is greatly increased due to the time required to handle lock requests for remote replicas and the fact that the transaction cannot complete until durability at all replica sites is ensured. These factors negatively impact performance, and for this reason synchronous replication has limited applicability.

The Quorum Consensus Protocol.   Although synchronous-update read-one/write-all replication can increase availability for readers, it does not help updaters. Because a (synchronous) update must access all replicas, the update cannot be completed if any site has crashed. We now describe a variant of synchronous replication in which no operation need access all replicas, so a data item might still be available even though some replica is inaccessible. To achieve this goal, we no

---

[5] A replica site at which only reads have been performed can give up its read locks as soon as it receives the prepare message. See exercise 26.14.

longer insist on maintaining (even weak) mutual consistency. Since replicas are no longer identical, the state of a data item must be constructed from its replicas and the replica control is responsible for doing this. Our goal is the same as for read-one/write-all replication: All schedules resulting from the use of the replica control should be equivalent to serializable schedules in which there is only one copy of each data item.

The basic idea of the **quorum consensus** protocol [Gifford 1979] is that, when a transaction makes a request to read (or write) a replicated item, the concurrency control first locks some subset, called the **read quorum** or **write quorum** of the replica before granting the request. If the size of a read quorum is p and the size of a write quorum is q, we require that $p + q > n$ and $q > n/2$, where n is the total number of replicas. Thus, we ensure that there is a nonempty intersection between any read quorum and any write quorum and between any two write quorums for a particular item. As a result, whenever concurrent transactions execute conflicting operations on a replicated item, a lock request will not be granted at the site of at least one replica and one of the operations will be forced to wait. Note that the read-one/write-all system can be viewed as a quorum consensus protocol in which the number of replicas in a read quorum is 1; in a write quorum, n.

Quorum consensus enables us to trade off the availability and the cost of the operations on an item. The smaller the value of p, the more available an item for reading and the lower the cost of a read. Similarly, the smaller the value of q, the more available an item for writing and the lower the cost of a write. The availabilities of read and write are related, however. The more available and efficient read is, the less available and efficient write is.

When a write request is granted (and the transaction commits), only the items in the write quorum have been updated. Hence, mutual consistency is not maintained and replicas at different sites might have different values. We assume that, when each transaction commits, it is assigned a unique timestamp and that each replica of an item has the timestamp of the (committed) transaction that last wrote it. Since each read quorum intersects each write quorum, each read quorum intersects the write quorum of the most recent write. Therefore, at least one item in each read quorum has the timestamp of the last transaction to update the item and, hence, the current value. That timestamp is the largest timestamp in the quorum. The value of the corresponding replica is returned by the replica control to a read request.

We can now summarize the quorum consensus protocol. We assume that an item, R, is stored as a set of replicas in the system and that each replica contains a value and a timestamp. We also assume an immediate-update pessimistic concurrency control and a strict two-phase commit protocol. Finally, we assume that each site maintains a local clock and that the clocks are synchronized to, at least, the extent that the timestamps of transactions are consistent with their commit order.

Quorum Consensus Replica Control Protocol

1. When a transaction executing at site A makes a request to read or write a particular item, the replica control at A sends the request to a (read or write) quorum of sites containing the replica. If the concurrency control at a replica

site can grant the appropriate lock on the replica, the requested operation is performed and a reply is returned to the replica control at site A. If the request is a read, the reply contains the value of the replica and its timestamp.

2. When replies have been received by the replica control at A from a quorum of sites, the transaction proceeds. If the request is a read, the replica control returns to the transaction the value of the replica with the largest timestamp.

3. A transaction commits using the two-phase commit protocol, where the cohorts are all of the sites at which it holds read or write locks.[6] The coordinator obtains a timestamp for the transaction using the local clock and sends it with the prepare message. If the transaction commits, each cohort at which a write occurred updates its replica with the value of the timestamp before unlocking it.

As long as the control can assemble the necessary quorums for all operations, the protocol can proceed even when failures have occurred. When a site fails and is subsequently restarted, some of its replicas might have very old timestamps. The site need take no special recovery action, however, since the values contained in these replicas will not be used by any transaction until after they have been overwritten by some later transaction, at which time they will be current.

26.7.2 Asynchronous–Update Replication Systems

In an **asynchronous-update system**, when a transaction updates a data item the replica control updates some, but not all, of the replicas before the transaction commits. Most often, only a single replica is updated. The other replicas are updated after the transaction commits, and hence only weak mutual consistency is maintained These updates might be triggered by the commit operation or perhaps executed periodically at fixed time intervals. Asynchronous replication is referred to as **lazy**, since replicas are not updated immediately. The updates are not done as a part of the transaction itself, so *the system as a whole might not be serializable and transactions might see an inconsistent state.*

For example, Figure 26.6 shows a schedule in which transaction T_1 updates x_A—the copy of x at site A, and y_B—the copy of y at site B. After T_1 commits, transaction T_2 reads y_B—hence getting the new value of y—and the replica of x at site C, x_C, that has not yet been updated. Thus, T_2 sees a (possibly) inconsistent view of the database. Later, a replica update transaction, T_{ru}, that updates all replicas of x and y, including x_C, is executed.

In the context of replication, **capture** refers to the process by which the replica control recognizes that an update of a replica by an application has occurred and must be propagated to other replicas. Capture can take two forms: The log can be monitored and updates to replicated items noted for later propagation; or triggers can be set in the database to record the changes. **Apply** refers to the process by

---

[6] As before, a replica site at which only reads have been performed can give up its read locks as soon as it receives the prepare message.

which replica sites are informed of the updates they must perform to keep their replicas current.

Different applications are best served by different forms of asynchronous replication. In some cases, the emphasis is on keeping the replicas as tightly synchronized as possible. Although serializability is not ensured, the goal is to minimize the interval between the time one replica is updated and the time the update is applied to the other replicas. A distributed application maintaining account or customer service records might fall in this category, which is variously referred to as **group**, **peer-to-peer**, or **multimaster** replication. In other cases, tight synchronization is not crucial. For example, an organization might have a large sales force in the field that periodically logs in to a central site and downloads a reasonably up-to-date view of the data. The form of replication that is frequently used in this case is **primary copy** replication. A third form of replication is referred to as **procedural** and applies when large blocks of data must be updated.

Primary copy replication.   A particular replica of a data item is designated the **primary copy** [Stonebraker 1979], and other replicas are **secondary copies**. Secondary copies are created by **subscribing** to the changes made at the primary copy. Although a transaction can read any copy, it can update only the primary. In one approach, if transaction T at site A wants to update data item x, it must obtain an exclusive lock on the primary copy of x, x_p, and update it. Even if there is a secondary copy at A, x_A, the secondary is not updated. As a result, if two transactions want to update x, the first must commit before the lock on x_p can be granted to the second. Thus, the write operations of transactions are serialized but read operations are not. In another approach, the application simply transmits updates to the primary copy to be processed later.

T's updates are asynchronously and nonserializably propagated to secondary copies (including x_A) after it commits. Since T and the apply step do not constitute a single isolated unit, replicas are updated in a nonserializable fashion. Reads can be satisfied using arbitrary replicas, so concurrent transactions might see an inconsistent view of the database (as shown in Figure 26.6) and function incorrectly as a result.

Figure 26.6   Schedule illustrating the possibility of inconsistent views with lazy replication. T_1 updates x and y at sites A and B. T_{ru} propagates the updates after T_1 commits. Because propagation is asynchronous, T_2 sees the new value of y but the old value of x.

T_1: $w(x_A)$	$w(y_B)$	*commit*			
T_2:		$r(x_C)$	$r(y_B)$	*commit*	
T_{ru}:				$w(x_C)$ *commit*	

With primary copy replication, all updates are funneled through the primary copy. The site at which this copy exists then executes replica-update transactions to implement the apply step. A single update transaction might update all replicas (as in Figure 26.6), or an individual update transaction for each replica might be used. If the update transactions for each replica are executed serializably in the same equivalent order as that in which the primary copy is updated, the replica control system can guarantee that each secondary copy sees the updates in the same order as does the primary copy. This guarantees weak mutual consistency.

In a variant of primary copy replication, if T at site A requests to update x, and x_A is not the primary copy, it locks both the primary copy of x and x_A and updates them as part of the transaction. Other secondary copies are updated as previously described after T commits. In this way, the user at A can execute subsequent transactions that read x_A without having to wait for the update to propagate back from the primary to A.

In an alternate approach to the apply step with primary copy replication, instead of propagating updates from the primary copy when a transaction completes, the replica control system periodically broadcasts the current value of the primary copy to the secondary copies. The value broadcast should be transactionally consistent, containing all of the updates performed by committed transactions since the last broadcast.

In some implementations, each secondary site can declare a view of the primary item and only that view is transmitted. This is particularly useful if the secondary sites communicate with the primary site through a low-bandwidth (e.g., telephone) connection and it is therefore important that only relevant data be replicated at each site.

In still another approach to the apply step, updates are not automatically propagated from the primary site, and replica sites explicitly request that their view be refreshed. This is referred to as a **pull strategy**, since the secondary sites pull the data from the primary sites. In contrast, in the **push strategy** of the algorithms we have described up to this point, the primary site pushes data out to the secondary. Push strategies reduce the interval in which replica values are inconsistent. In either case, all replicas of an item will eventually contain the same value, so weak mutual consistency is supported.

A pull strategy might be appropriate when secondary sites are mobile (perhaps hand-held) computers used by a large sales force in the field. A salesperson might update his replica when he connects to the network. Since bandwidth is small, he defines a view that includes only information pertaining to his sales region. In this application, the replicas can be slightly (for example, minutes or hours) old. Read accesses predominate. A write occurs only when a new contract is signed and the new information is sent to the primary first and broadcast to (or pulled by) all secondaries later. If the update occurs while the secondary is disconnected, it must be saved until a connection is established.

Group replication. An update can be made to any replica—presumably the nearest one. (Thus, if a database is totally replicated, read/write as well as read-only

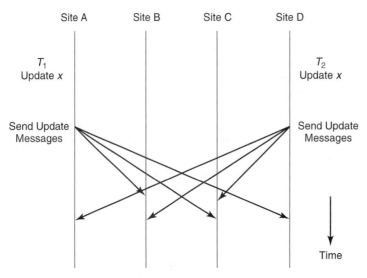

Figure 26.7 With group replication, updates might reach replicas in different orders, leading to violation of mutual consistency.

transactions can be completed using only data at the local site.) The updates made by a transaction, T, are later propagated to the other replicas. Since propagation is asynchronous, global serializability cannot be guaranteed.

   As with primary copy replication, group replication can lead to nonserializable, and hence incorrect, schedules. For example, a schedule similar to the one shown in Figure 26.6 is possible. In addition, without further refinement, it might not even support weak mutual consistency. Figure 26.7 illustrates a situation in which two concurrent transactions, T_1 and T_2, executing at sites A and D, respectively, update different replicas of data item x. As shown, the order of arrival of the messages that propagate those updates might be different at different replica sites. Since the final value of a replica is the value in the last write, mutual consistency is not preserved if replicas are updated in different orders. In the terminology of replication, a **conflict** has occurred and the replica control system must employ a **conflict resolution** strategy to guarantee **convergence** and preserve mutual consistency.

   One algorithm for guaranteeing weak mutual consistency is to associate a unique timestamp with each update and with each replica. An update's timestamp is the time at which it was submitted to the system, and a replica's timestamp is the timestamp of the last update applied to it. Weak mutual consistency can be ensured if a replica site simply discards an arriving update when its timestamp is less than that of the replica's timestamp. This is an example of the Thomas Write Rule [Thomas 1979] we discussed in Section 23.8.1. With this algorithm, the value of each replica eventually converges to the value contained in the update with the largest (most recent) timestamp. Although the rule guarantees weak mutual consistency, lost updates are possible: Two transactions read and update different replicas, but only the result of one survives. For this reason, the algorithm might not be appropriate for some applications.

Unfortunately, no algorithm exists that correctly merges the effects of different transactions in such situations for all applications. In some applications, the appropriate conflict resolution strategy is obvious. For example, if a directory is replicated and concurrent transactions append distinct entries to different replicas, the final value of all of the directory's replicas should contain both entries. Thus, a conflict resolution strategy for a particular application can often be devised. In the general case, a replica control system can notify the user when it detects a conflict and allow the user to resolve it. Since there is no conflict resolution strategy that is guaranteed to be correct, some commercial systems provide several alternative ad hoc strategies, including "Oldest update wins," "Youngest update wins," "Highest priority site wins," and "User provides a procedure for conflict resolution."

Procedural replication.   This form of replication is useful when updates need to be applied to many items in a batch-oriented fashion—for example, if interest has to be posted to each bank account and bank records are replicated at several sites. If each update were separately transmitted over a network, communication costs would be high. An alternative is to replicate a stored procedure at each secondary site and invoke that procedure at all replicas when the data is to be updated.

Summary.   *The tradeoff between synchronous- and asynchronous-update systems is one of correctness versus performance.* Many commercial DBMSs provide both types of replication. The designer should be aware that asynchronous updates can produce nonserializable schedules that might be incorrect and yield an inconsistent database.

26.8   DISTRIBUTED TRANSACTIONS IN THE REAL WORLD

Although the design theory for distributed transaction processing systems might seem complex, its final results are surprisingly simple and practical. If the concurrency control at each site is either a strict two-phase locking pessimistic control or an optimistic control and a two-phase commit protocol is used to synchronize the cohorts at commit time, then distributed transactions will be serializable. Global deadlocks, which might arise as the result of waits imposed by pessimistic controls, can be resolved using timestamps, waits-for graphs, or timeout.

One result of this simplicity is that distributed transaction processing systems can be implemented by interconnecting sites that contain DBMSs from different vendors if the following is true:

1. All the DBMSs implement one of the two specified concurrency controls.
2. Each site participates in the two-phase commit protocol.

These ideas greatly simplify system design.

Atomicity and isolation are properties of a transaction processing system which guarantee that if the transactions of an application are consistent, the application will run correctly. We have now seen that, in order to improve performance, distributed transaction processing systems frequently do not support atomicity and isolation completely. Transactions at a site might not run at the SERIALIZABLE isolation level, the two-phase commit protocol might not be used in committing distributed transactions, or an asynchronous update technique might be used to support replication. Whether these compromises cause incorrect behavior is very much dependent on the semantics of the application. For this reason, in building a particular transaction processing system, these issues must be considered carefully.

26.9 BIBLIOGRAPHIC NOTES

A comprehensive discussion of distributed transactions can be found in [Gray and Reuter 1993]. [Ceri and Pelagatti 1984] is more theoretical in its orientation.

The two-phase commit protocol was introduced in [Gray 1978, Lampson and Sturgis 1979]. The presumed abort property for the two-phase commit protocol was discussed in [Mohan et al. 1986]. A more powerful commit protocol, called three-phase commit, was introduced in [Skeen 1981]. The wound-wait and kill-wait systems, which use a timestamp technique to avoid deadlocks, were introduced in [Rosenkrantz et al. 1978]. A proof that the two-phase commit protocol, together with two-phase locking local concurrency controls, guarantees global serializability was given in [Weihl 1984]. The quorum consensus protocol was introduced in [Gifford 1979]. Primary copy replication was introduced in [Stonebraker 1979], and the Thomas Write Rule is from [Thomas 1979].

26.10 EXERCISES

26.1 Describe the recovery procedure if a cohort or coordinator crashes at the following states within the two-phase commit protocol:

 a. Before the coordinator sends the *prepare* message

 b. After a cohort has voted but before the coordinator has decided commit or abort

 c. After the coordinator has decided to commit but before the cohort has received the *commit* message

 d. After the cohort has committed, but before the coordinator has entered the completion record in the log

26.2 Explain why a cohort does not have to force an abort record to the log during the two-phase commit protocol.

26.3 Explain how the fuzzy dump recovery procedure must be expanded to deal with the two-phase commit protocol in which there might be prepare records in the log.

26.4 Describe the two-phase commit protocol when one or more of the database managers is using an optimistic concurrency control.

26.5 Assuming no failures, describe how the two-phase commit protocol extends to the case in which the distributed transaction is an arbitrary tree of subtransactions.

26.6 Describe how the presumed abort feature is achieved in the protocol of the previous example.

26.7 Describe how the two-phase commit protocol given in the text can be expanded to deal with a cohort site that uses a timestamp-ordered concurrency control.

26.8 Give schedules of distributed transactions executing at two different sites such that the commit order is different at each site but the global schedule is serializable.

26.9 Suppose the concurrency controls at each site of a distributed system independently use a strict two-phase locking concurrency control, an optimistic concurrency control, or a timestamp-ordered control that serializes conflicting transactions in commit order and a two-phase commit protocol is used. Are distributed transactions globally serializable?

26.10 Phase 1 of the extended two phase-commit protocol is identical to Phase 1 of the two-phase commit protocol we have described. Recall that in the two-phase commit protocol described in the text the commit record is written to the log after Phase 1 completes. In the new protocol Phase 2 is as follows:

> *Phase Two.* If the coordinator receives at least one aborting vote during Phase 1, it decides abort and sends an *abort* message to all cohorts that voted ready. If all votes are ready, it sends a *commit* message to each cohort.
>
> If a cohort receives an *abort* message, it rolls the subtransaction back. If a cohort receives a *commit* message, it forces a commit record to its log, releases all locks, sends a *done* message to the coordinator, and terminates.
>
> The coordinator waits until it receives the first *done* message from a cohort. Then it forces a commit record to its log.
>
> The coordinator waits until it receives a *done* message from all cohorts. Then it writes a complete record to its log and terminates.

Describe timeout and restart procedures for this protocol. Show that this protocol blocks only when the coordinator and at least one cohort crash (or a partition occurs) or when all cohorts crash.

26.11 Design a logging, timeout, and restart procedure for the linear commit protocol. Do not assume the existence of a separate coordinator module. Assume that all communication between cohorts is carried on along the chain.

26.12 Consider a distributed transaction processing system that uses a serial validation optimistic concurrency control at each site and a two-phase commit protocol. Show that deadlocks are possible under these conditions.

26.13 Prove that if all sites use optimistic concurrency controls and if a two-phase commit protocol is used, distributed transactions are globally serializable.

26.14 If a cohort in a distributed transaction has performed only read operations, the two-phase commit protocol can be simplified. When the cohort receives the *prepare* message, it gives up its locks and terminates its participation in the protocol. Explain why this simplification of the protocol works correctly.

26.15 Consider the following atomic commit protocol that attempts to eliminate the blocking that occurs in the two-phase commit protocol. The coordinator sends a prepare message to each cohort containing the addresses of all cohorts. Each cohort sends its vote directly to all other cohorts. When a cohort receives the votes of all other cohorts it decides commit or abort in the usual way.

    a. Assuming no failures, compare the number of messages sent in this protocol and in the two-phase commit protocol. Assuming that all messages take the same fixed amount of time to deliver, which protocol would you expect to run faster? Explain.

    b. Does the protocol exhibit blocking when failures occur?

26.16 The *kill-wait* concurrency control of exercise 23.32 is based on locking. When it is used in a distributed system, it is referred to as the *wound-wait* protocol. We assume that a distributed transaction uses RPC to communicate among cohorts so that when the two-phase commit protocol starts all cohorts have completed. The *kill* primitive is replaced by a *wound* primitive.

> If the cohort of transaction T_1 at some site makes a request that conflicts with an operation of the cohort of an active transaction, T_2, at that site, then

$$\textbf{if } TS(T_1) < TS(T_2) \textbf{ then } wound\ T_2 \textbf{ else } make\ T_1\ wait$$

where *wound* T_2 means that T_2 is aborted (as in the *kill-wait* protocol), unless T_2 has entered the two-phase commit protocol, in which case T_1 waits until T_2 completes the protocol.
Explain why this protocol prevents a global deadlock among transactions.

26.17 Suppose the nested transaction model were extended so that subtransactions were distributed over different sites in a network. At what point in the execution of a distributed nested transaction would a cohort enter the prepared state? Explain your reasoning.

26.18 In the text we state that if, in a distributed database system, each site uses a strict two-phase locking concurrency control and the system uses a two-phase commit protocol, transactions will be globally serializable. Does the result also hold if the concurrency controls are not strict (but are two-phase)?

26.19 Explain how to implement synchronous-update replication using triggers.

26.20 Design a quorum consensus protocol in which, instead of a timestamp field, each item has a version number field, which is updated whenever the item is written.

26.21 Consider a quorum consensus protocol in which an item is stored as five replicas and the size of each read and write quorum is three. Give a schedule that satisfies the following conditions:

> Three different transactions write to the item. Then two of the replica sites fail, leaving only three copies—*all of which contain different values.*

Explain why the protocol continues to execute correctly.

26.22 Consider a quorum consensus protocol in which an item is stored as n replicas, and the size of read and write quorums are p and q respectively.
   a. What is the maximum number of replica sites that can fail and still have the protocol work correctly?
   b. What is the minimum value that p and q can have such that $p = q$?
   c. Select p and q so that the maximum number of replica sites can fail and still have the protocol work correctly. For this selection, how many sites can fail?

26.23 Explain why, in a quorum consensus replication algorithm, the clocks at all sites must be synchronized.

26.24 Describe an application of replicated data items in which serializability is not needed.

26.25 In what way is the checkbook you keep at home for your checking account like an asynchronous-update replication system?

26.26 Give an example of a nonserializable schedule produced by a primary copy asynchronous-update replication system.

26.27 The following variant of the primary copy asynchronous update replication protocol has been proposed for totally replicated systems.
   a. A transaction executing at site s_1 updates only the replicas at A before it commits.

       b. After the transaction commits, a second transaction is initiated to update the primary copies of all items updated at A.

       c. After the transaction in step (2) has completed, each primary site propagates the update made at that site to all secondaries (including the one at site A). Updates made to a primary copy by several transactions are propagated to secondaries in the order in which the primary was updated.

    Explain why, in step (2), all primaries must be updated in a single transaction and, in step (3), the update is propagated to site s_1.

26.28 Explain how triggers can be used to implement primary copy replication.

26.29 Describe a design of a logging protocol for distributed savepoints.

Chapter 27

Security and Internet Commerce

AUTHENTICATION, AUTHORIZATION, AND ENCRYPTION

Security is a major issue in the design of applications that deal with privileged information or that support systems on which life and property depend. In most applications, the participants in a transaction must identify each other, with a high degree of certainty, and they might want to ensure that no third party is observing or modifying the information being exchanged. Security issues are particularly important for transactions executed over the Internet because it is relatively easy for imposters to pretend to be particular clients or servers and for eavesdroppers to listen in on the exchanges between participants.

Authentication refers to the process by which the identity of a participant is established. When you perform a transaction at an automated teller machine (ATM), the system establishes your identity using the information on your ATM card and your personal identification number (PIN.) Furthermore, you may want to establish that you are talking to a real ATM and not a "Trojan horse" designed to obtain your PIN. Similarly, when you are considering executing an Internet transaction with Macy's and you have to supply your credit card number to the server, you want to make certain that you are actually talking to that server and not to three students in a dorm room pretending to be Macy's.

Authorization refers to the process that determines the mode in which a particular client is allowed to access a specific resource controlled by a server. The client is assumed to have been previously authenticated. Authorization can be individual (*you* are allowed to withdraw money from your bank account) or group-wide (*all tellers* are allowed to write certified checks), and it is often specified in terms of the functions that the individual or group is allowed to perform. For example, "John is allowed to withdraw money from a specified account."

Encryption is used to protect information stored at a particular site or transmitted between sites from being accessed by unauthorized users. A variety of highly sophisticated algorithms exist to transform this information into a bit stream that is intelligible only to selected users.

Since encryption plays an important role in authentication and authorization, we quickly review its general structure first. Then we discuss authentication and

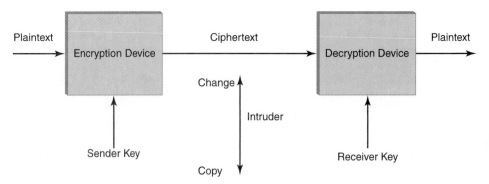

Figure 27.1 Model of an encryption system.

authorization and finally how all three concepts are applied in Internet commerce transactions.

27.2 ENCRYPTION

The general model of an encryption system is shown in Figure 27.1. The information to be sent is generally a string of characters referred to as **plaintext**. It is encrypted by a device (or program) transforming it into **ciphertext**, and it is the ciphertext that is actually transmitted. At the receiving end, the ciphertext is decrypted by another device, transforming it back into the original plaintext.

The goal of an encryption system is to protect information from an **intruder**. Intrusion is generally assumed to take two forms: **passive**, in which an intruder can only copy information in transit; and **active**, in which an intruder can, in addition, modify information in transit, resend previously sent messages that it has copied, or send new messages. While no practical encryption system can completely defend against an intruder with unlimited computational resources (which can be used to analyze the ciphertext), the goal is to make intrusion so difficult that it becomes extremely unlikely that an intruder will succeed.

There are a variety of encryption algorithms, and it is generally assumed that the intruder knows the particular algorithm used in the system under attack. However, each algorithm is parameterized by one or more **keys**, which control the encryption and decryption process. Recovery of the plaintext from the ciphertext without the decryption key is exceedingly difficult. Hence, the strength of the technique depends on keeping the decryption key secret.[1]

We use the notation

$$ciphertext = K_{sender}[plaintext]$$

---

[1] A truly unbreakable encryption system is the **one-time pad** [Stallings 1999, Schneier 1995], which uses a randomly generated key that is as long as the message and is used for one message and then discarded.

to denote that the ciphertext is the plaintext encrypted by the sender with the key K_{sender}. The complete encryption system, including encryption and decryption, can be represented with the notation

$$plaintext = K_{receiver}[K_{sender}[plaintext]]$$

which states that, if the plaintext is first encrypted with K_{sender} and then decrypted with $K_{receiver}$, the result will be the original plaintext.

Symmetric cryptography.   With **symmetric cryptography**, the same key is used for both encryption and decryption ($K_{sender} = K_{receiver}$). The key is known only to the two communicating processes (since it can be used to decrypt the ciphertext).

Several common techniques are used in symmetric cryptography. With a **block cipher**, the plaintext is divided into fixed-size blocks, which are then mapped in a one-to-one fashion into ciphertext blocks. The particular mapping is a function of the encryption algorithm and key. The sequence of ciphertext blocks is the encrypted message. Since the mapping is one to one, the plaintext can be recovered.

A **substitution cipher** is one type of block cipher. A variety of substitution ciphers have been proposed for mapping plaintext blocks. For example, a **monoalphabetic** (sometimes called *simple*) substitution cipher has a block size of one character, and a one-to-one mapping from the set of characters onto itself is used to construct the ciphertext. Thus, if *a* is mapped to *c*, each occurrence of *a* in the plaintext is replaced by *c* in the cipher text.

A **polyalphabetic** substitution cipher is made up of multiple monoalphabetical substitution ciphers. For example, there might be ten different monoalphabetical ciphers. The first character is encrypted with the first cipher, the second, with the second cipher, and so on, until the tenth character, after which the sequence starts over with the eleventh character being encrypted with the first cipher.

A **polygram** substitution cipher is one in which the block size is more than 1. For example, if the block size is 3, the block "cde" might be encrypted as "zyy" and "dce" might be encrypted as "dtr."

A **transposition** cipher is also a block cipher, but in contrast to a substitution cipher, the order of the characters in each plaintext block is altered to produce the ciphertext block—the reordering is the same on each plaintext block and is described by the key. For example, if the block "cde" is encrypted as "dec," "dce" will be encrypted as "ced."

Ciphers that map plaintext blocks into ciphertext blocks are subject to a frequency analysis attack. It is assumed that the intruder knows the block size and can measure the frequency with which each plaintext block is used in normal (unencrypted) communication. The intruder can then compare that with the frequency with which ciphertext blocks appear in an encrypted stream. By matching cipher- and plaintext blocks with similar frequency characteristics, the intruder can greatly reduce the number of alternatives that must be tested to determine which plaintext block maps into a particular ciphertext block. The longer the encrypted stream the intruder can monitor, the more accurate the frequency estimate of the ciphertext blocks and the greater the reduction in computation that will result. The frequency analysis attack renders many substitution and transposition ciphers with small block sizes of little use, since accurate frequency profiles for small plaintext blocks are available.

ANSI's **Data Encryption Standard** (DES) is a symmetric encryption technique that uses a sequence of stages to encrypt a block of plaintext, each stage encrypts the output of the previous stage. All stages use the same block size, and each uses either a substitution or a transposition cipher. The result of combining these two cipher techniques is sometimes referred to as a **product cipher**. DES, which uses a block size of 64 bits and a key of 56 bits,[2] is in wide use, for example, within the banking and financial services industry.

A **bit stream cipher**, is an example of an encryption technique that is not based on blocks. The ciphertext stream is the result of taking the exclusive OR of the plaintext stream and a pseudo-random sequence of bits produced by a random number generator using the key as the initial seed. By using the key with the same generator, the same pseudo-random sequence can be produced at the receiving end to decrypt the ciphertext.

Asymmetric cryptography.   In contrast to symmetric cryptography, **asymmetric cryptography** associates with each user an encryption key and a decryption key. The encryption key is not a secret. A user distributes it openly to anyone who might want to send him a message. The encryption key is therefore a public key, known to potential intruders. The decryption key, however, is private, known only to the user. If M is a (plaintext) message and K_C^{pub} and K_C^{priv} are public and private keys, respectively, of client C, then asymmetric cryptography is described by the relationship

$$M = K_C^{priv}[K_C^{pub}[M]]$$

since using K_C^{priv} to decrypt a message that has been encrypted using K_C^{pub} yields the original plaintext. In other words, the sender uses the recipient's public key to encrypt the message, and the recipient decrypts it with her private key.

If, as is generally the case, information must be transferred in both directions between two processes, each process uses the other's encryption key to encrypt messages. Because the encryption key can be made public, asymmetric cryptography is referred to as **public key cryptography**. (Symmetric cryptography, in which the key is known only to the communicating processes, is referred to as **secret key cryptography**.) The concept of public key cryptography was proposed in [Diffie and Hellman 1976], but almost all public key cryptography systems are based on the RSA algorithm [Rivest et al. 1978]. An excellent description of the mathematics underlying the RSA algorithm and of many other cryptographic algorithms and protocols is given in [Schneier 1995].

We briefly describe the RSA algorithm. To design an encryption/decryption key pair, two large (random) prime numbers, p and q, are selected, and an integer, d,

---

[2] The key has been criticized by cryptographic experts as being too small.

is chosen such that it is relatively prime to $(p - 1) * (q - 1)$. Finally, the integer e is computed such that

$$e * d \equiv 1 \ (mod \ (p - 1) * (q - 1))$$

The encryption key is (e, N), and the decryption key is (d, N), where $N = p * q$ and is referred to as the modulus.

The message to be encrypted is broken into blocks such that each block, M, can be treated as an integer between 0 and $(N - 1)$. To encrypt M into the ciphertext block, C, we perform the calculation

$$C = M^e \ (mod \ N)$$

To decrypt C, we perform

$$M = C^d \ (mod \ N)$$

The protocol works correctly because

$$M = (M^e \ (mod \ N))^d (mod \ N) \tag{27.1}$$

which can be demonstrated using some elementary concepts from number theory.

Although d and e are mathematically related, factoring N (a large integer) to obtain p and q (which can be used to calculate d from e) is extremely difficult. Hence, only the receiver can decrypt messages sent to it.

Public key encryption is a very powerful technique, but it is more computationally intensive than symmetric cryptography (exponentiation of large numbers to large powers is expensive, although not nearly as expensive as factoring a large number, which would be necessary to break the encryption). For that reason, it is generally used to encrypt a few small blocks of information, exchanged as part of a protocol, rather than large blocks of data, which are generally encrypted using symmetric techniques.

27.3 DIGITAL SIGNATURES

One very important use of asymmetric cryptography is to implement **digital signatures**, which can be used as proof of authorship of a document in a way similar to the way handwritten signatures are used in everyday life. As with public key cryptography, the concept was invented in [Diffie and Hellman 1976], but, like public key systems, most digital signature systems are based on the RSA algorithm [Rivest et al. 1978] or on other algorithms developed specifically for signatures.

Digital signatures based on encryption algorithms utilize a property of many asymmetric encryption algorithms: the roles of the public and private keys can be reversed. The private key can be used to encrypt plaintext, and the resulting ciphertext can be decrypted using the corresponding public key. Hence,

$$M = K_C^{pub}[K_C^{priv}[M]] = K_C^{priv}[K_C^{pub}[M]] \tag{27.2}$$

Unlike encryption, here the sender uses her own private key to encrypt the signature, and the recipient uses the public key of the sender to recover the signature.

If the public key algorithm has property (27.2), C (the sender) can prove that she generated the message, M, by encrypting M with K_C^{priv}. If the receiver can recover M using K_C^{pub}, the receiver knows that M could have been generated only by C, since only C knows K_C^{priv}. (Someone else might have actually sent the message, but only C could have generated it.) This technique assumes that the receiver knows C's public key, K_C^{pub}. The process of distributing public keys and related issues are discussed in Sections 27.4 and 27.7.1.

Note that since anyone can decrypt the message with the public key, the message is not hidden. Message hiding is not the purpose of a digital signature protocol.

A problem with this technique is that encrypting and decrypting an entire message using a public key algorithm can be computationally intensive and time consuming. To reduce this time, some function, f, of M is computed—for example, a check sum or a hash—that produces a result that is considerably smaller than M itself. $f(M)$ is sometimes called a **message digest** of M. The message digest function, f, is assumed to be known to the intruder as well as to the communicants. $f(M)$ is encrypted with K_C^{priv} and referred to as a digital signature, which is transmitted along with M. Thus, C sends two items, $K_C^{priv}[f(M)]$ and M, to the receiver. The receiver decrypts the first item using K_C^{pub} and then compares the outcome with the result of applying f to the second item. If the two are the same, the receiver should be able to conclude that M could have been generated only by C. To safely allow such a conclusion, however, we must deal with some other issues.

Consider an intruder that listens to and copies the transmission from C to the server.

1. The intruder might use the signature $K_C^{priv}[f(M)]$ attached to a message M sent by C to sign a different message, M', in an attempt to fool the receiver into believing that C sent M'. The intruder can succeed in this attack if it can construct M' such that $f(M) = f(M')$. To prevent this attack, f is required to be a **one-way function**: f has the property that, given an output, y, constructing an argument, x, such that $f(x) = y$ is computationally infeasible. For example, a one-way message digest function might produce an output string that satisfies the following properties:

   a. All values in the range of f are equally likely.

   b. If any bit of the message is changed, every bit in the message digest has a 50-percent chance of changing.

   Property (b) ensures that $f(M)$ and $f(M')$ are not the same simply because M and M' are related or similar messages. Property (a) guards against the possibility of finding an M' such that $f(M) = f(M')$ simply because f maps a large percentage of messages to $f(M)$.

   Under these conditions, it is extremely difficult for the intruder to construct a message M' such that $f(M')$ is equal to $f(M)$ and hence to find a message, M', to which the signature $K_C^{priv}[f(M)]$ can be attached. Furthermore, the intruder cannot forge the signature that can be used with M', $K_C^{priv}[f(M')]$, since it does not know K_C^{priv}.

2. The intruder might attempt to copy and then resend a signed message a second time,[3] in what is referred to as a **replay attack**. A replay attack can be dealt with by having the client construct a timestamp (using the technique described in Chapter 26) and include it in the message. The digital signature is calculated over the entire message. Assuming that clocks at all sites in the network are roughly synchronized, if the receiver keeps a list of the timestamps of all recently received messages and rejects arriving messages containing timestamps in the list (recall that timestamps are globally unique), it can detect that message's second arrival. The key point here is that the timestamp is not repeating. A replay attack can also be dealt with if each message has a unique sequence number.

In addition to guaranteeing the identity of the signer, the digital signature also guarantees the *integrity* of the message. Although the message is transmitted in the clear, and hence can be read by an intruder, it cannot be changed by the intruder, since the signature of the changed message would be different. (If privacy is desired, the signed message can be encrypted with another key.)

Digital signatures also prevent **repudiation**. The signer cannot deny having constructed the message, since the digital signature accompanying the message could have been constructed only with the signer's private key. Digital signatures are often used in commercial security protocols.

27.4   KEY DISTRIBUTION AND AUTHENTICATION

With both symmetric and asymmetric cryptography, before two parties can communicate they must agree on the encryption/decryption key(s) to be used. Since doing so often involves communicating keys in messages, this phase of a protocol is called **key distribution**. In most situations, key distribution also involves authentication. At the same time that the parties agree on a key, they also make sure of each other's identity.

One might think that key distribution is easy for asymmetric algorithms, since the receiver's encryption key is public knowledge. That is, if C wants to send an encrypted message to S, it simply sends a request in the clear (unencrypted) to S requesting S's public key. S can then send its key (in the clear) to C. Life is not so simple, however. An intruder might intercept S's message and substitute its own public key. If C uses that key, the intruder can decrypt all messages sent from C to S. For this reason, key distribution is complicated by authentication when public key encryption is used: C must be able to authenticate the sender of the key.

---

[3] This attack might be of some value if the message were a request by C to transfer money into the intruder's bank account.

A similar situation exists with symmetric encryption. If a unique (symmetric) key for encrypting and decrypting messages is associated with each process, P, all processes sending to P have to know that key. But then each such sender can decrypt all messages sent to P by the others, since the key is also used for decryption—an unacceptable situation. The common solution to this problem is to associate a unique (symmetric) key, known as a **session key**, with each conversation, or session, between two processes. A session key must be created and distributed to the two processes before the session starts. It becomes a part of the communication context and is discarded when the session completes. Once again, a process using a session key wants to be certain of the identity of the other process that has a copy of that key.

It follows that, in addition to addressing the key distribution problem, we must also be concerned with authentication. Intuitively, when we speak of a client, we think of the individual on whose behalf the client process is running, and we use these concepts interchangeably.

One goal of authentication is to enable a server to positively identify the client that is the source of a message so that it can decide whether to grant the requested service. For example, should the requestor be allowed to withdraw money from Mary's bank account? Another goal is to enable a client to authenticate the server before sending it any important information. For example, am I sending my credit card number to Macy's or to a Macy's impersonator?

To model these situations, we speak of **principals**. A principal might be a person or a process, and the purpose of authentication is to demonstrate that a principal is who it claims to be.

Generally, a person demonstrates that she is who she claims to be by providing something that only she possesses. The simplest, and least secure, of these is a password, in which case the individual possesses some unique knowledge. Unfortunately, passwords often have to be short and relevant (e.g., a pet's name) to be remembered, and therefore can frequently be compromised by an intruder willing to try enough candidates. Also, if a password is sent over the network, it might be intercepted and thereby compromised.

Security can be enhanced by requiring a *physical* item that only the individual possesses, for example a token card. An even more secure technique involves the use of some biological identifier such as a fingerprint or voiceprint. Unfortunately, the cost of biological mechanisms is high, and any computer representation of such characteristics might be copied.

Although passwords play a role in key distribution and authentication protocols, these protocols involve a number of new techniques that employ the exchange of encrypted messages. Since there are only a few messages, the cost of encryption is generally not significant, so the protocols can be based on either symmetric encryption (e.g., Kerberos, as discussed in Section 27.4.1) or public key encryption (e.g., SSL, as discussed in Section 27.7.1). However, because of the heavy computational requirements of public key encryption, the actual exchange of data generally uses symmetric techniques based on session keys.

27.4.1 The Kerberos Protocol: Tickets

As an example of a protocol that uses symmetric cryptography to authenticate a client to a server and distribute a (symmetric) session key for subsequent data exchange, we describe a simplified version of the widely used **Kerberos** system designed at MIT [Steiner et al. 1988, Neuman and Ts'o 1994]. Kerberos is an off-the-shelf middleware module that can be incorporated into a distributed computing system and might be provided by a TP monitor.

The Kerberos protocol involves the use of an intermediary process, called a **key server**. (Actually Kerberos calls its key server the Key Distribution Server, or KDS.) The key server creates session keys on demand and distributes them in such a way that they are known only to the communicating processes. For this reason, it is referred to as a **trusted third party**.

Each user wishing to communicate at some time registers a symmetric **user key** with the key server, KS. User keys are not session keys, but are used only to communicate session keys at the start of a session.

Assume that a client, C, wants to communicate with a server, S. C and S have previously registered user keys $K_{C,KS}$ and $K_{S,KS}$, respectively, with KS. $K_{C,KS}$ is known only to C and KS, and similarly with $K_{S,KS}$. KS is trusted by C in the sense that C assumes that KS will never communicate $K_{C,KS}$ to any other process and that the data structure it uses to store $K_{C,KS}$ is protected from unauthorized access. Similarly, KS is trusted by S.

Kerberos introduces the concept of a **ticket** to distribute a session key. To understand the role of a ticket, consider the following sequence of steps, illustrated in Figure 27.2, which forms the heart of the protocol. (As with the other protocols described here, we omit some minor details.)

1. C sends to KS a message, $M1$ (in the clear), requesting a ticket to be used to authenticate C to S. $M1$ contains the names of the two communicants (C, S).

2. When KS receives $M1$, the following takes place:

   a. KS (randomly) constructs a session key, $K_{sess,C\&S}$.

   b. KS sends to C a message, $M2$, containing two items:

      i. $K_{C,KS}[K_{sess,C\&S}, S, LT]$

      ii. $K_{S,KS}[K_{sess,C\&S}, C, LT]$—the actual ticket

      where LT is the *lifetime* (the time interval) over which the ticket is valid.

3. When C receives $M2$, it performs the following steps:

   a. C recovers $K_{sess,C\&S}$ from the first item using $K_{C,KS}$ (it cannot decrypt the ticket).

   b. C saves the ticket until it is ready to request some service from S.

Observe that KS does not know the actual source of $M1$: it could have been sent by an intruder, I, posing as C. However, KS encrypts $M2$, making the information returned accessible only to C and S.

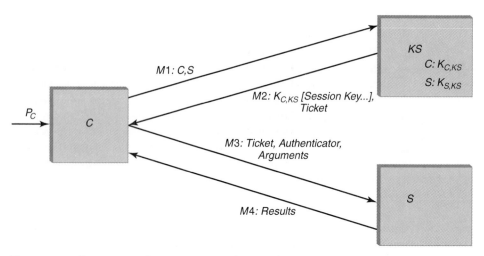

Figure 27.2 Sequence of messages used to authenticate a client in symmetric encryption.

Rather than store its user key, $K_{C,KS}$, in some protected way, C constructs it when needed using the principal's password, P_C, which is supplied to C at login time. This is done with the help of a one-way function, f.

$$K_{C,KS} = f(P_C)$$

Thus, only C (using f) can construct $K_{C,KS}$, and hence only C can retrieve $K_{sess,C\&S}$ from the first item in $M2$: the message sent by KS to the process claiming to be C. Note that the protocol does not send P_C across the network and so avoids the possibility that it might be copied. Furthermore, since C does not store $K_{C,KS}$, the possibility that it might be stolen is reduced.

Later, when C wants to invoke a server operation from S, the following takes place:

4. C sends to S a message, $M3$, containing the arguments of the invocation, (which might or might not be encrypted using $K_{sess,C\&S}$), the ticket, and an authenticator (see below).

Only S can decrypt the ticket and recover the encrypted items. However, the ticket (containing C) alone is not sufficient to authenticate C to S, since I could have copied it in step 2 and replayed it to S with its own invocation. A timestamp might be useful in preventing a replay, but the timestamp cannot be stored in the ticket because the ticket is meant to be used by C multiple times during its lifetime. C therefore sends an authenticator along with its ticket. An **authenticator** consists of C's name together with a (current) timestamp, TS, encrypted with $K_{sess,C\&S}$:

$$authenticator = K_{sess,C\&S}[C,\ TS]$$

and is meant to be used only once. S can decrypt the authenticator by using $K_{sess,C\&S}$ (which it determines by decrypting the ticket).

At this point, S knows that the ticket could have been constructed only by KS, since only KS knows $K_{S,KS}$. Furthermore, since S trusts KS and since each time $K_{sess,C\&S}$ is transmitted it is encrypted by either $K_{C,KS}$ or $K_{S,KS}$, S knows that only C knows $K_{sess,C\&S}$. The authenticator contains some plaintext (e.g., C) encrypted by $K_{sess,C\&S}$, that can be compared with the contents of the ticket (which also contains C). If they match, S concludes that C must have constructed the authenticator. To authenticate C to S (i.e., to be sure that the invocation actually comes from C), however, several possible attacks must be ruled out.

1. I might attempt a replay attack in which it copies both the ticket and the authenticator from $M3$ and uses them at a later time. To combat this, we must make it impossible for an authenticator (in contrast to a ticket) to be used more than once. A new authenticator (with a unique timestamp) is constructed by C for each of its invocations—it is *live* if its timestamp is within the lifetime (LT) of the accompanying ticket. To ensure that a copy of an authenticator is of no value, and that S can defend itself against a replay, S uses the following protocol:

   a. If the received authenticator is not live, S rejects it.

   b. S maintains a list of authenticators it has received that are still live. If the received authenticator is live, S compares it against the list and rejects it if a copy is found. By maintaining lifetime information, S can limit the number of authenticators it has to keep on the list.

2. I intercepts $M3$ (it does not reach S) and tries to use the ticket and authenticator for its own invocation of a service. However, if C has chosen to encrypt the arguments of its invocation with $K_{sess,C\&S}$, then I cannot substitute its own arguments because it does not know $K_{sess,C\&S}$. Sending the entire intercepted message at a later time accomplishes nothing for I since it simply causes C's original request to be serviced.

3. I intercepts $M1$ and substitutes the message (C, I). I's goal in this attack is to fool C into thinking that I is S and to acquire private information about C contained in the arguments that C thinks it is sending to S in $M3$. The protocol defends against this attack by including the server's name in the first item of $M2$. C uses this information to determine the identity of the process that can decrypt its invocation message.

A number of distinct levels of protection can be offered by this protocol. The client can request that authentication occur only when a connection to the server is first established. Or it can request authentication on each call for service. Or it can request that $K_{sess,C\&S}$ be used to encrypt the arguments of the invocation (in $M3$) and the results returned (in $M4$) as well as to encrypt the authenticator.

We have given arguments to demonstrate how Kerberos defends against a variety of attacks an intruder might attempt. Be under no illusions as to whether our discussion constitutes a proof that Kerberos is secure—it does not. Such proofs are the subject of ongoing research.

Single sign-on. Kerberos provides a property, referred to as **single sign-on**, that is becoming important as client interactions become increasingly complex. Complex interactions frequently involve access to multiple resources and hence multiple servers. Each server needs to authenticate the client and, in the worst case, has its own interface for doing so. Furthermore, the password used by the client might be different for each server it accesses. Hence, a client must remember multiple passwords and engage in multiple authentication protocols, and the system administrator must keep the authentication information associated with each server current as client information changes.

With single sign-on, the client needs to authenticate itself only once. Kerberos provides this property by concentrating authentication in an **authentication server** (similar to KS), which authenticates C at login time using the password supplied by the client, as described earlier. Since the identity of the servers the client intends to access might not be known at this time, it is not possible for the authentication server to construct the appropriate tickets (each ticket is encrypted with a particular server's key). Instead, it returns a **ticket-granting ticket** to C, which is used for requesting service from a particular server, called the **ticket-granting server**, TGS—also part of Kerberos. Later C can request the specific tickets it needs (for example, a ticket for S) from TGS using the ticket-granting ticket.

The authentication server generates a session key, $K_{sess,C\&TGS}$, that C can use to communicate with TGS, and returns to C (in a format similar to that of $M2$ in the simplified protocol).

■ $K_{C,KS}[K_{sess,C\&TGS}, TGS, LT]$—$K_{sess,C\&TGS}$ is a session key for communicating with TGS

■ $K_{TGS,KS}[K_{sess,C\&TGS}, C, LT]$—the ticket-granting ticket for TGS

where $K_{TGS,KS}$ is the key that TGS has registered with KS.

Later, when C wants to access a particular server, S, it sends a copy of the ticket-granting ticket together with the server's name (and an authenticator) to TGS. TGS then returns to C (again in a format similar to that of $M2$).

■ $K_{sess,C\&TGS}[K_{sess,C\&S}, S, LT]$—$K_{sess,C\&S}$ is a session key for communicating with S

■ $K_{S,KS}[K_{sess,C\&S}, C, LT]$—the ticket for S

C thus obtains a different ticket for each server it accesses. It engages in a single authentication protocol, and, since the use of tickets is invisible at the user level, the user interface is simplified. Also, since authentication is concentrated in a single server, the administration of authentication information is simplified.

27.4.2 Nonces

A **nonce** is a bit string created by one process in a way that makes it highly unlikely that another process can create the same string. For example, a randomly created bit string of sufficient length created in one process probably will not be created later by another process. Nonces have a variety of uses, one of which is related to authentication.

The problem to be solved with a nonce arises when two processes, P_1 and P_2, share a session key, K_{sess}, and P_1 sends an encrypted message, M1, to P_2 and expects an encrypted reply, M2. How can P_1, when it receives M2, be sure that it was constructed by P_2? It might seem that P_1 can just decrypt M2 using K_{sess} and see if the result makes sense. Often, however, determining whether a string makes sense requires human intervention, and in some cases even that does not help. Consider the case in which M2 simply contains a data string (an arbitrary string of bits) calculated by P_2. I might substitute a random string for M2. When P_1 decrypts that string using K_{sess} it might produce another string that looks like a data string. Unfortunately, P_1 cannot determine whether or not the string is correct without repeating P_2's calculation. Alternatively, I might replay an earlier message sent during the same session and hence encrypted with K_{sess}. In some cases, such a replay might be a possible correct response to M1 and hence P_1 is fooled into accepting it.

In the nonce solution to this problem, P_1 includes a nonce, N, in M1, and P_2 includes $N + 1$ in M2. On receipt of M2, P_1 knows that the sender must have decrypted M1, since $N + 1$, not a simple replay of N, is returned. This implies that the sender knows K_{sess} and is therefore P_2.

In Kerberos, the timestamp TS (which is already part of the authenticator) can be used as a nonce so that no additional items need be added. The server can include $TS + 1$ in M4.

Nonces are often used in cryptographic protocols for a completely different reason. Appending a large random number to the plaintext before encrypting a message makes it considerably harder for an intruder to decrypt the message by guessing parts of its contents—for example, guessing the expiration date or some of the redundant information in a credit card number—and using that information to reduce the cost of a brute force search to discover the key. This use of a nonce is sometimes referred to as adding **salt** to a message. A number of the protocols we discuss later use salted messages, but we omit that part of the protocol in our discussion. In some protocols, a nonce used for this purpose is called a **confounder**.

27.5   AUTHORIZATION

Having authenticated a client, the server must next decide whether the requested service should be granted. Thus, the authorization component of the system must decide, when a request arrives from a client to access a particular object, whether the principal should be allowed the requested access to that object. This is referred to as an **authorization policy**. The modes in which an object can be accessed depend on the type of the object being protected.

If, for example, the resource is a file, the modes of access might be read, write, append, and execute. Operating systems typically control access to files stored in their file system by first requiring that principals authenticate themselves (at login time) and then checking that each access to a file has been previously authorized

Figure 27.3   Access control list for a file.

Id	r	w	a	x
11011	1	1	0	0
00000	1	0	0	0

by the file's owner. The data structure that is generally used to record the system's protection policy (in Windows NT and many versions of UNIX) is the **access control list** (ACL).

Each file has an associated ACL, and each entry on the ACL identifies a principal and contains a bit for each possible access mode. The ith bit corresponds to the ith access mode and indicates whether or not that principal is allowed to access the file in that way. Figure 27.3 shows an ACL for a file. The first five bits contain an Id. Each of the following bits corresponds to an access mode: read, write, append, and execute. The figure indicates that the user with Id 11011 has permission to read and write the file associated with the list.

As a practical matter, it is necessary to introduce the notion of a **group**. For example, it would be awkward to list all principals separately in the ACL of a file that is universally readable. A group is simply a set of principals, and an ACL entry can correspond to it. The access permissions contained in the entry are allowed to all group members. Thus, as illustrated in Figure 27.3, a file that is universally readable, but writable only by its owner, might have an ACL consisting of two entries: one for the owner with Id 11011 and read and write bits set and one for the group containing all principals with only the read bit set. The Id 00000 identifies the group consisting of all users. With the introduction of groups, several entries in an ACL might refer to a particular principal (e.g., a principal might belong to several groups). In this case, the principal is granted the union of the permissions in each such entry.

The structure for storing and enforcing an authorization policy in a transaction processing system is only a minor generalization of the ACL/group structure used by operating systems to protect files. Resources are controlled by servers, so a server (instead of the operating system) is responsible for storing the ACL and enforcing the authorization policy on the resources it controls. Servers export certain methods, making them available for invocation by clients. These methods constitute the modes of access to the resources encapsulated within the server. In short, the authorization policy is formulated in terms of the methods a particular principal can invoke and the particular resources on which to invoke them. In the Student Registration System, for example, the method that changes a grade cannot be invoked by a student, the method that changes the personal information describing a student (e.g., a student's address) can be invoked only by that student, and the method that sets a limit on class enrollment can be invoked by any faculty member.

ACLs can be used in support of this generalization. In one approach, the Student Registration System server might use a single ACL containing an entry for the student group and an entry for the faculty group. The permission bits in each entry correspond to the methods that can be invoked by the clients. An entry needs to have only enough bits so that each exported method can be associated with a distinct bit. In this case, the faculty group is granted permission for the grade change and class enrollment methods, and the student group is granted permission for the personal information method. The additional requirement that the personal information of a particular student be changed only by that student has to be checked separately. The ACL is checked by the server when a method is invoked, and, if the necessary permission has not been granted, an error code is returned to the caller.

Alternatively, we might regard the server as managing a number of distinct resources—class records, personal records—and allocate a separate ACL for each record. In this case, a finer granularity of protection can be enforced. For example, the ACL for a student's personal record contains an entry for only that student.

The SQL GRANT statement is one way that a client can specify an authorization policy for a table. In this case, the access modes correspond to various types of SQL statements. An SQL server might implement the policy using ACLs, in which case the GRANT statement causes a modification to the ACL associated with the table specified in the statement.

Each server is generally responsible for providing its own authorization module, because the objects it controls and the access to them are specific to that server. By contrast, a principal's identity and group membership can be general to all servers. The authorization module within each server, referred to as a **reference monitor**, is responsible for constructing, retrieving, and interpreting access control lists. Middleware modules for doing this might be provided by a TP monitor.

27.6 AUTHENTICATED REMOTE PROCEDURE CALL

A goal of many distributed applications that require authentication and authorization is to hide the complexities of the required protocols from the principal. Once the principal has executed the login procedure, service invocation should be simple and authentication and authorization should be invisible (unless a violation is detected). One way to achieve this goal is by implementing authentication in the RPC stubs, as shown in Figure 27.4, and by presenting the abstraction of an **authenticated RPC** to clients and servers. This is the approach used in the DCE model of distributed computation.

In this approach, middleware provides an API that the client can use to log in and to invoke servers. The API interfaces to the stub, which engages in the exchange of messages (for example, the messages of Figure 27.2). The key server is now referred to as the **security server**, since it implements authentication and plays a role in implementing authorization as well: it keeps track of all groups to which each principal belongs and includes in a ticket sent to a principal a list of that principal's group Ids. Security servers can be obtained as off-the-shelf middleware modules.

Each server is responsible for securely storing a copy of its server key, $K_{S,KS}$, locally and making it available to the server stub when an invocation message

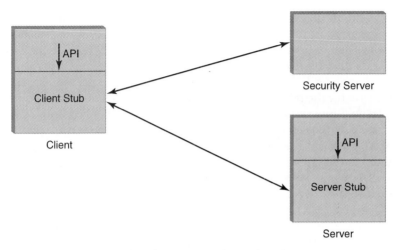

Figure 27.4 Relationship between stubs and authentication.

arrives. The stub can then decrypt the ticket contained in the message to determine the client's identity and the groups to which the client belongs.

The server stub API provides calls that the server can use to retrieve the client's identity and group membership information contained in the ticket from the server stub. Authorization for each client call is provided within the server proper (not the server's stub) by the reference monitor, using the client's (authenticated) identity and group membership information and the access control lists contained within the server.

27.7 INTERNET COMMERCE

Security issues are particularly critical when transactions are executed over the Internet. Authentication is important to prevent one site from successfully impersonating another. Encryption is important to prevent eavesdropping. In addition, there is a general sense of suspicion between the parties participating in Internet transactions, perhaps because there is no face-to-face interaction and because impressive looking websites can be produced by fly-by-night operations. For these reasons, mutual authentication is often required.

We distinguish two kinds of Internet commerce transactions: **customer-to-business (C2B)** and **business-to-business (B2B)**. The security requirements of the two are similar, but we assume that customers have only the security software that comes with their browsers, while businesses can have more sophisticated and specialized protection, such as their own public and private encryption keys, which customers (usually) do not have.

27.7.1 The Secure Sockets Layer Protocol: Certificates

Certificates. Servers (perhaps representing businesses) that want to authenticate themselves to other parties as part of an Internet transaction can use a **certification authority (CA)**, which acts as a trusted third party. A number of companies are in the business of being certification authorities.

The CA uses public key encryption to generate **certificates**, which certify the association between a principal's name (e.g., Macy's) and its public key. The certificate contains (among other items) the principal's name and public key, and it is signed with the private key of the CA. Since the CA's public key is well known (and is most likely prestored in the user's browser), any process in the system can determine the validity of the certificate. Hence, if a client wants to communicate securely with Macy's, it can encrypt a message using the public key found in a valid certificate containing the name "Macy's" and be certain that only a process with knowledge of Macy's private key will be able to decrypt the message. Certificates thus solve the problem of distributing public keys reliably, which is the key distribution problem for asymmetric encryption. They are used in the protocols described below.

Any Internet server, S, that wants to obtain a certificate from a CA, first generates a public and private key and then sends the public key, plus other information, to the CA. The CA uses various means to verify the server's identity (perhaps looking it up in Dun and Bradstreet and communicating with personnel at the server's place of business by phone and ordinary mail) and then issues it a certificate, containing, among other items,

- The CA's name

- S's name

- S's URL

- S's public key

- Timestamp and expiration information

The CA signs the certificate and sends the signed certificate to S in the clear, perhaps by email. S then verifies its correctness (for example, that the public key stored in the certificate is S's public key). Note that a certificate is public information readily available to an intruder. It is, however, of no use to an intruder, because a client who wishes to communicate with S will use S's public key to encrypt a message. Since S's private key is not contained in the certificate, only S can decrypt the message.

The SSL protocol. The **Secure Sockets Layer (SSL)** protocol [Netscape 2000], uses certificates to support secure communication and authentication over the Internet between a client and an Internet server (or between servers). By using certificates, SSL is able to eliminate the need for an online key server (as in Kerberos), which can be a bottleneck in transaction systems that process thousands of transactions per second.[4]

A goal of SSL is to authenticate a server to a client. Since this is done using a certificate, each server that wants to be authenticated must first obtain a certificate. Clients, on the other hand, are not generally registered with certification authorities and hence do not have certificates or the encryption keys associated with them.[5] A logged-in client is typically represented by a browser, which (usually) does not have a private key of its own. Rather, the browser contains the public keys of all certification authorities that have made arrangements with that browser's vendor. The browser does not actually communicate with a CA during the SSL protocol; nor does a CA know any private information about a browser.

The SSL protocol authenticates the server to the client and establishes a session key for their use.[6]

Assume that a browser, C, connects to a server, S, that claims to represent a particular enterprise, E (for example, Macy's). In this case, the protocol consists of the following steps:

1. S sends C a copy of its certificate signed by the CA—in the clear.
2. C validates the certificate using the CA's public key (included in its browser) and hence knows that the public key in the certificate is E's public key.
3. C generates and sends to S a session key encrypted with E's public key.[7]

Note that C, not S, generates the session key because, at this point in the protocol, C can communicate securely with S using E's public key, but S cannot communicate securely with C (nor is there an online key server, as in Kerberos, to generate the session key).

Once the session key has been established, C and S (now known to represent E) can use it to exchange encrypted messages. The protocol is performed invisibly to the application program in a layer of the communication hierarchy between the data transport (TCP/IP) and application levels.

If the browser uses the session key to communicate a credit card number to S, the user can have considerable confidence that that communication is secure. The browser itself generated the session key, which it communicated to S using E's public key, and the user knows that E's public key is genuine because it was

---

[4] Note, however, that certificates have a potentially significant disadvantage in that, once a certificate has been granted to a server by a CA, it is difficult to revoke it later if necessary. By contrast, an online key server can easily stop providing keys for a particular server.

[5] SSL has an optional authentication protocol for clients that do have certificates.

[6] A browser engages in the SSL protocol when it connects to a server whose URL begins with https: (instead of the usual http:), which indicates an SSL-encrypted HTTP protocol.

[7] SSL is actually slightly more complex. C generates and sends to S a **pre-master secret** from which C and S independently, using the same algorithm, generate two session keys—one for communication in each direction. This adds an additional measure of security. The pre-master secret is also used by C and S to verify the integrity of messages in the application part of the protocol.

obtained from a certificate that could have been generated only by the CA. The user trusts the CA to have verified E's identity and included the correct information about E in the certificate, and trusts the browser vendor to have included the correct public key for each CA and a correct implementation of the SSL protocol in the browser.[8] The user must also trust that its browser has not been corrupted, perhaps by some malicious program it downloaded at some earlier time.

At this point, the protocol has authenticated the server to the client, but the client has not been authenticated to the server. For many applications, client authentication is not necessary. For example, most servers will accept a credit card purchase from any browser that can supply the credit card number, without determining that the browser actually represents the card owner. (Most telephone-order catalog companies accept orders under similar conditions.)

For other applications, S does want to ensure that it is talking to a particular client (for example, before sending that client its private portfolio information or accepting a stock trading transaction). One way to provide such authentication is for client and server to agree (perhaps over the telephone) on a password, which the server stores and the client supplies after the session key has been established. Another way is for the client to also have a certificate, so that both client and server can be authenticated.

27.7.2 The Secure Electronic Transaction Protocol: Dual Signatures

Many merchants use the SSL protocol in customer purchase transactions. After the session key is established, the customer sends the details of the items to be purchased and the credit card information to the merchant's server, which completes the transaction by having the credit card approved at some other site representing the credit card company. The only drawback in this is that the merchant learns the client's credit card number.

Of course, in most non-Internet customer–merchant transactions, the merchant obtains a credit card number because the customer hands the merchant her card.[9] However, revealing the credit card number to the merchant is particularly problematic in electronic commerce for two reasons.

■ Only the number, not the card itself, is needed to make a purchase, allowing a dishonest merchant to use it without the cardholders knowledge until the problem is discovered.

■ Furthermore, the anonymous nature of Internet commerce does not promote a trusting relationship between merchant and customer. Hence customers are more comfortable if merchants do not learn their credit card numbers.

---

[8] Although the SSL protocol solves the key distribution problem in which the client obtains the public key of a server, the solution involves another key distribution in which the client has already obtained the public key of the CA.

[9] When you go to a restaurant, for example, you give your credit card to a waitress, who gets the transaction approved and returns a receipt for you to sign. How do you know she has not copied your credit card number?

To encourage electronic commerce over the Internet, protocols having stronger security guarantees have been developed. One is the **Secure Electronic Transaction (SET) protocol** [VISA 2000], jointly developed by Visa and MasterCard. While SSL is a **session-level security protocol**, which guarantees secure communication for the duration of a session, SET is a **transaction-level security protocol**, which guarantees security for a purchasing transaction, including an atomic commit.

The SET protocol is quite complex, with many signatures and much cross checking to increase overall security. Here we present a simplified version that demonstrates the mechanisms by which the credit card number is hidden from the merchant and how the purchasing transaction is committed atomically.

The protocol involves two new ideas:

■ Each customer has her own certificate and hence her own public and private keys. These keys are used to provide one of the unique features of the protocol, the **dual signature**, which considerably increases the security of the transaction.[10] The customer's certificate also contains a message digest of her credit card number and its expiration date. Recall that information in the certificate is unencrypted. Hence, only the digest (not the credit card number itself) can be included. The digest is used to verify that the credit card number supplied by the customer corresponds to a card belonging to the customer.

■ A new server, the **payment gateway**, G, operates on behalf of the credit card company. Thus, SET is a three-way protocol, involving the customer, the merchant, and the payment gateway, which acts as a trusted third party during the protocol and performs the commit operation at the end of the transaction.

The basic idea of the protocol is that customer C sends merchant M a two-part message: The first part contains the purchase amount and C's credit card information encrypted with G's public key (so that M cannot see the credit card information); the second part contains the purchase amount and the details of the purchase (but not the credit card information) encrypted with M's public key. M then forwards the first part of the message to G, which decrypts it, approves the credit card purchase, and commits the transaction.

In one possible attack on a protocol such as this in which there is a two-part message, an intruder attaches the first part of one message to the second part of another. For example, having intercepted the messages for Joe's and Mary's purchases, an intruder can attach the first part of Joe's message to the second part of Mary's, hoping to force Joe to pay for Mary's goods. One way to thwart this type of attack is to have M associate a unique Id with each transaction and to require that C include it in both parts of the message. An attempt to unite the parts of different messages then becomes easily detectable. This does not solve the problem of a dishonest merchant, however, who associates the same Id with two different purchases so that the parts of the two resulting messages can be combined. A new

---

[10] Some versions of SET use a modified dual signature that does not require the customer to have her own certificate (and public and private keys).

mechanism is needed to overcome this type of problem. That mechanism is the dual signature, described next.

Before SET begins, C and M negotiate the terms of a purchase. The protocol begins with a handshake in which C and M exchange certificates and authenticate each other. C sends its certificate to M, and M sends both its certificate and G's certificate to C, at which point C and M know each other's and G's public key. Then the purchase transaction begins.

1. M sends a signed message to C containing a (unique) transaction Id (which is used to guard against replay attacks). C uses the public key in M's certificate to check the signature and hence knows that the message came from M and was not altered in transit.

2. C sends a message to M containing two parts plus the dual signature:

   a. The transaction Id, C's credit card information, and the dollar amount of the order (but not a description of the items purchased)—encrypted with G's public key:

   $$m_1 = K_G^{pub}[trans\_Id,\ credit\_card\_inf,\ \$\_amount]$$

   b. The transaction Id, the dollar amount of the order, a description of the items purchased (but not C's credit card information)—encrypted with M's public key:

   $$m_2 = K_M^{pub}[trans\_Id,\ \$\_amount,\ desc]$$

   The dual signature has three fields:

   a. The message digest, MD_1, of the first part of the message:

   $$MD_1 = f(m_1)$$

   where $f()$ is the message digest function

   b. The message digest, MD_2, of the second part of the message:

   $$MD_2 = f(m_2)$$

   c. C's signature of the concatenation of MD_1 and MD_2:

   $$K_C^{pri}[f(MD_1 \cdot MD_2)]$$

   Thus, the complete dual signature is

   $$dual\_signature = MD_1,\ MD_2,\ K_C^{pri}[f(MD_1 \cdot MD_2)]$$

and the complete message sent from C to M is $(m_1, m_2, dual\_signature)$.

The dual signature binds the two parts of the message. So, for example, an attempt by an intruder or M to associate m_2' with m_1 does not work since its message digest, MD_2', will be different from MD_2. Although MD_2' can be substituted for MD_2 in the dual signature, $K_C^{pri}[f(MD_1 \cdot MD_2)]$ cannot be used as the signature for $MD_1 \cdot MD_2'$, and only C can compute the correct dual signature for the reconstructed message.

3. M decrypts the second part of the message with its private key (but it cannot decrypt the first part, which contains the credit card number). The merchant then

   a. Uses the dual signature to verify that m_2 has not been altered in transit. It first computes the message digest of m_2 and checks that it is the same as the second field of the digital signature (MD_2). It then uses the public key in C's certificate to check that the third field is the correct signature for the concatenation of the first two fields.

   b. Verifies the transaction Id, the dollar amount of the order, and the description of the items purchased.

   Next M sends a message to G containing two parts:

   a. m_1 and the dual signature it received from C:

   $$m_3 = m_1, \; dual\_signature$$

   b. The transaction Id and the dollar amount of the order—signed with M's private key and encrypted with G's public key:

   $$m_4 = K_G^{pub}[trans\_Id, \; \$\_amount, \; K_M^{pri}[f(trans\_Id, \; \$\_amount)]]$$

   The complete message sent from M to G is (m_3, m_4), together with copies of C's and M's certificates.

4. G decrypts the message using its private key.

   a. It uses the dual signature and the public key in C's certificate to verify that m_1 was prepared by C and was not altered (as in step 3a).

   b. It uses the message digest of the credit card information in C's certificate to verify the credit card information supplied in m_1.

   c. It uses M's signature in m_4 and the public key in M's certificate to verify that m_4 was not altered.

   d. It checks that the transaction Id and the dollar amount are the same in m_1 and m_4 (to verify that M and C agreed on the purchase).

   e. Checks that the Transaction Id was never submitted before (to prevent a replay attack).

   f. It does whatever is necessary to approve the credit card request.

   Then G returns a signed *approved* message to M. At this point, the transaction is committed.

5. When M receives the *approved* message, it knows that the transaction has committed. It sends a signed message, to C: *transaction complete. C* then knows that the transaction has committed.

Note how the protocol deals with some other attacks.

1. M cannot attempt to substitute different goods, since the dual signature is over the description agreed to by C. By forwarding the dual signature on to G, M has committed itself to that description.

2. C cannot use m_1', copied from a message submitted by a different customer in an attempt to get that customer to pay for C's purchase by attaching it to m_2. In that case, the dual signature does not help since it is computed by C. However, m_1' and m_2 would have different transaction Ids, so the transaction will be rejected by G.

The atomic commit protocol for SET. When G commits the transaction, it logs appropriate data to make the transaction durable. M might also wish to commit its subtransaction when it receives the approved message from G. Many customers might not want to perform a formal commit, but the exchange of messages between C, M, and G can be viewed as a linear commit protocol and in that context,

■ The messages sent from C to M in step 2 and from M to G in step 3 are *vote* messages. Before sending them, C and M must be in a prepared state.

■ The messages sent from G to M in step 4 and from M to C in step 5 are *commit* messages. G and M must enter appropriate commit records into their logs before sending those messages.

Note that G is a trusted third party, trusted by the other two participants to perform the commit.

27.7.3 Goods Atomicity, Escrow, and Certified Delivery

Some Internet transactions involve the actual delivery of the purchased items. Transactions involving the purchase of downloaded software are in this category. Such transactions[11] should be **goods atomic**, in that the goods are delivered if and only if they have been paid for. In the context of the SET protocol, "paid for" means that the purchase has been approved by the payment gateway; in the context of the electronic cash protocols described in Section 27.7.4, it means that the electronic cash has been delivered to the merchant and accepted by the bank.

Transactions involving the purchase of physical goods are usually not goods atomic. The customer orders the goods and the transaction commits, after which (in most cases) the merchant ships the goods. In Internet commerce, however, the customer might not trust the merchant to send (download) the goods after the transaction commits.

Goods atomicity is not really a new concept. The only original idea is that the event of delivering the goods is part of the transaction in which the goods are paid for. The requirement that the goods be delivered if and only if they are paid for is just the usual definition of atomic transaction execution. The hard part of implementing goods atomicity is that delivery cannot be rolled back, which means

---

[11] The term "transaction" is used loosely in this context. The actual delivery of the goods might occur after the transaction commits but is part of the protocol in which the transaction is embedded.

that, if the goods are delivered before the transaction commits and the transaction subsequently aborts, there is no way to undo the delivery, and the execution is not atomic.

In Section 21.3.2, we considered a situation similar to goods atomicity in which cash is dispensed by an ATM if and only if the withdraw transaction at the bank commits. We discussed how a recoverable queue could be used for that purpose. Both cash dispensing and goods atomicity involve an external event that is supposed to take place if and only if the transaction commits.

The concept of goods atomicity and a protocol for implementing it were developed in connection with the NetBill system [Cox et al. 1995]. The protocol is in some ways similar to SET in that it involves a client, a merchant, and a trusted third party that effectively consummates a credit card transaction through a linear commit protocol. Rather than describe NetBill, we describe how to implement goods atomicity as an enhancement of the SET protocol.

After C and M have agreed on the terms of a transaction, but before C sends a confirmation to M (step 2 of SET), M sends (downloads) the goods to C encrypted with a new symmetric key, $K_{C,M}$, that M has constructed for this purpose. M also sends a message digest of the encrypted goods, so C can verify that the encrypted goods were correctly received. Note that C cannot use the goods at this point since it does not know $K_{C,M}$.

The description, *desc*, that C sends to M (in m_2) includes both a specification of the goods and the message digest of the encrypted goods, signed with C's private key. In effect, C is acknowledging that it has received (in encrypted form) the goods corresponding to the digest. As in step 2 of SET, the complete message is $(m_1, m_2, dual\_signature)$, and this is C's vote to commit. If, on receiving the message from C, M agrees that the description it has received from C is accurate, it constructs the message (m_3, m_4) as in step 3 of SET, but includes two additional items in m_4:

■ $K_{C,M}$

■ The message digest of the encrypted goods signed with C's private key, which it received from C in Step 2, signed again (countersigned) with M's private key

M then sends the message to G (step 3 of SET).

An unscrupulous merchant cannot change the terms of the transaction (perhaps to show a higher price), since the dual signature constructed by C contains the price information. By adding its signature to the message (in m_4) and forwarding it to G, M commits itself to the transaction. Once again, this message is M's vote to commit.

When G receives the doubly signed message from M (step 4 of SET), it knows that both parties are prepared to commit to the terms of the transaction. As with SET, if G is satisfied with the credit card information supplied by C, it commits the transaction, durably stores m_3, m_4, and the dual signature, and sends an *approved* message to M. M, in turn, sends a *transaction complete* message containing $K_{C,M}$ to C, so C can decrypt the goods.

This protocol is goods atomic for the following reasons:

■ If a failure occurs before G commits the transaction, no money is transferred and C does not get the goods since it does not get $K_{C,M}$.

■ If a failure occurs after the commit, the money is transferred, G has a (durable) copy of $K_{C,M}$, and C has an encrypted copy of the goods. C can get $K_{C,M}$ either from M or—if for some reason M does not send $K_{C,M}$—from G, since G knows that the transaction has committed and C's certificate identifies it as the principal who constructed the dual signature.

An important feature of the protocol is that, when the transaction commits, G has a copy of $K_{C,M}$, and hence C can decrypt the goods even if M "forgets" to send the *transaction complete* message containing $K_{C,M}$.

Certified delivery. Another issue in the delivery of goods over the Internet is **certified delivery**. A goods-atomic transaction guarantees delivery to the customer, but we would like to have the additional assurance that the right goods are delivered. How can M defend itself against a charge that the goods it sent do not meet the agreed-upon specifications, and how can C be assured that the specific goods ordered are received? In particular, if there is a dispute between M and C about the delivered goods, and that dispute is to be resolved by an arbiter, how can M and C present their respective cases to the arbiter? For example:

■ Suppose that, after decrypting the delivered goods, C finds that they do not meet their specifications and wants her money back. C can demonstrate to the arbiter that the software does not work, but how can she show that this software is in fact the same software that M sent?

■ Suppose that C is trying to cheat M, and the nonworking software she demonstrates to the arbiter is not the same software that M sent. How can M unmask this attempted fraud?

The enhanced SET protocol meets the requirements of certified delivery. Recall that G durably stored m_3, m_4, and the dual signature when the transaction committed. The dual signature constructed by C was over the specification of the goods contained in m_2. By forwarding the signature on to G, M confirms that the specification is accurate (since it can decrypt m_2 to examine the specification and it can check that the signature is over m_2).

■ C can demonstrate to an arbiter that the encrypted goods she claims to have received from M are actually the goods that were sent by M by simply running the digest function against the goods and comparing the result to the digest in m_4 stored by G. The arbiter can then decrypt the goods using $K_{C,M}$ and test them. C can also provide m_2 containing the specifications and demonstrate that the dual signature was on m_2 and hence agreed to by M. The arbiter is now in a position to judge C's claim.

■ M can defend himself against a claim that the received goods do not meet their specifications since M can also produce m_2. Once again the arbiter can determine that the goods have not been tampered with and then test them against their specifications.

Escrow services.   Another application requiring goods atomicity is the purchase of actual (nonelectronic) goods over the Internet from an unknown person or an auction site. The goods cannot be downloaded, but must be sent by a shipping agent. One participant in the transaction might be suspicious that the other will not abide by the conditions of the purchasing agreement. How can both parties be sure that the transaction is goods atomic and that the goods will be delivered if and only if they are paid for?

One approach that comes close to meeting these requirements uses a trusted third party called an **escrow agent**. A number of companies are in the business of being escrow agents on the Internet. The basic idea is that, after the customer and the merchant have agreed on the terms of the purchase, instead of paying the merchant, the customer pays the escrow agent, which holds the money until the goods have been delivered and accepted by the customer. Only then does the escrow agent forward the payment to the merchant.

We sketch a simplified form of an escrow protocol,[12] leaving out many of the details involving authentication, encryption, and so forth. The protocol involves a customer, C, a merchant, M, and an escrow agent, E. It begins after C and M have reached agreement on the terms of the purchase.

1. C sends E the agreed-upon payment, perhaps using one of the secure payment methods described in this chapter.

2. E durably stores the payment and other information needed for the rest of the protocol and commits the transaction.

3. E notifies M that the payment has been made.

4. M sends C the goods using some traceable shipping agent (such as FedEx or UPS), which agrees to make available to E the status information on the shipment (including confirmation of delivery).

5. When C receives the goods, she inspects them to see if they match her order. This inspection must be completed by the end of a stipulated period, which starts when the goods have been delivered as documented by the shipping agent's tracking mechanism.

    a. If C is satisfied with the goods, the following take place:

        i. C notifies E that the goods have been received and are satisfactory.

        ii. E forwards the payment to M.

    b. If C is not satisfied with the goods, the following take place:

        i. C notifies E that the goods have been received and are not satisfactory.

        ii. C returns the goods to M using some traceable shipping agent.

---

[12] The protocol described is based on the i-Escrow protocol [i-Escrow 2000].

iii. *M* receives the goods, and notifies *E*.[13]

iv. *E* returns the payment to *C*.

c. If, by the end of the inspection period, *C* does not notify *E* as to whether or not she is satisfied with the goods, *E* forwards the payment to *M*.[14]

This protocol reasonably approximates both goods atomicity and certified delivery. For example, *C* has a stipulated inspection period to determine whether or not the goods delivered are the goods ordered. As with the previous goods atomicity protocol, this one relies on a third party, which is trusted by both *C* and *M*, to perform certain specified activities after the transaction commits.

27.7.4 Electronic Cash: Blind Signatures

The Internet purchasing transactions we have discussed so far use a credit card, which, along with a check, is an example of **notational money**. That is, your actual assets are represented by the balance in your bank account; your credit card or check is a *notation* against those assets. At the time you make a purchase, you provide a notation that identifies you and the cost of the goods you are purchasing; the merchant trusts that you will abide by the purchasing agreement and eventually pay for the purchases with real money—that there is enough money in your checking account or that you are in good standing with your credit card company. In either case, your bank balance will eventually be decremented to reflect your purchase.

In contrast to notational money, cash is backed by the government. Although it does not have intrinsic value (it is, after all, just a piece of paper) the public's trust in the stability of the government causes it to be treated as if it had intrinsic value (i.e., as if it were gold). Thus, the merchant knows that he can deposit cash in his account or use it to purchase other goods without having to trust the customer. Cash is often referred to as **token money**. In the world of the Internet, token money is **electronic** or **digital** cash.

Token money offers the participants in a transaction certain advantages over notational money.

■ *Anonymity.* Since the customer is not required to provide a signed record to complete a cash transaction, such a transaction can be performed anonymously. Neither the bank nor the credit card company knows the customer's identity. By contrast, a credit card company keeps records of all customers' purchases, and a bank has access to canceled checks. These records might be made available at a later time to the government, to a court proceeding, or even to someone hoping to pry into an individual's personal life.

---

[13] *M* can inspect the returned goods to see if they are as specified and must complete its inspection by the end of a stipulated inspection period. We omit what happens if *M* finds the returned goods unsatisfactory.

[14] *M* might not send the goods to *C* in step 4, or *C* might not return the goods to *E* in step 5bii. Again, these situations can be resolved using the shipping agent's tracking mechanism.

■ *Small-denomination purchases.* For each credit card transaction, the credit card company charges a fixed fee plus a percentage of the purchase price. Thus, credit cards are not appropriate for purchases involving only a small amount of money, yet many Internet vendors would like to charge a few cents for a page of information they supply to browsers. Small-denomination electronic cash would be useful for such transactions.

Hence there is a need to support transactions based on electronic cash. Such transactions should satisfy the requirement of **money atomicity**: Money should not be created or destroyed. However, since electronic cash is represented by a data structure in the system, there are several ways in which money atomicity might be violated. For example:

■ A dishonest customer or merchant can make a copy of the data structure and use both the original and the copy.

■ Money can be created or destroyed if a failure occurs (e.g., a message is lost or the system crashes). For example, a customer who has sent a copy of the data structure to a merchant cannot determine whether the message was received by the merchant and so decides to reuse the data structure in a different purchase—even though the money was actually received. Alternatively, the message might not have been received, but the customer does not reuse the data structure, failing to realize that the payment had not been made.

What follows is a discussion of an electronic cash protocol designed to support the purchase of arbitrary (not necessarily electronic) goods. Goods atomicity is not a feature of this protocol; instead, the customer trusts that the merchant will send the goods after the transaction commits.

Tokens and redundancy predicates.   This protocol is based on the Ecash protocol [Chaum et al. 1988]. Cash is represented by electronic tokens of various denominations. Each token consists of a unique serial number, n, encrypted with a private key known only to the bank. The terminology here is confusing since it is often said that, in electronic cash protocols, the bank "signs" the serial number to create the token. Here, the meaning of signing differs from that given in Section 27.3, in which a signed item consists of the item followed by an encryption of its digest. In this section, when we say that the bank signs a serial number, we mean that the bank encrypts the serial number with a private key and the result is a token.

How does this scheme prevent intruders from creating counterfeit tokens? After all, a token is just a bit string of a certain length. The fact that the bit string is the encryption of a serial number provides no protection. You might think that we could test the token for validity by decrypting it with the bank's public key and examining the result. However, that key can be applied to any valid or invalid token, yielding a bit string, and we have no way of distinguishing a bit string that is a valid serial number from one that is not.

To prevent intruders from creating counterfeit tokens, we use a technique that requires serial numbers to be bit strings that have some special property that distinguishes them from arbitrary bit strings. For example, it might be required that the first half of the serial number be created at random and the second half be a scrambled form of the first half using a fixed and known scrambling function. Formally, we say that there is some well-known predicate, *valid*, called a **redundancy predicate**, such that, for all valid serial numbers, n, the predicate *valid*(n) is true.

Although it is assumed that the counterfeiter knows the redundancy predicate and the bank's public key for decrypting tokens, she does not know the bank's private key and so cannot produce tokens by encrypting a valid serial number. Hence, in counterfeiting tokens she faces the problem of finding a (fake) token that decrypts to a bit string that satisfies *valid*. The counterfeiter can use a trial-and-error technique to do this, but it is extremely unlikely that the result of decrypting an arbitrarily chosen bit string will satisfy *valid* if the bit string is long enough and if *valid* is such that the number of bit strings of that length that satisfy *valid* is a small percentage of the total number of bit strings of that length.

In its scheme for minting tokens, the bank keeps a set of public/private key pairs and chooses serial numbers that satisfy *valid*. It signs all serial numbers used in creating tokens of a particular denomination, j, with the same private key, K_j^{priv}, from the set and uses a different private key for each denomination. The bank does not keep a list of the serial numbers of the tokens that it has created, but if the numbers are large enough and the number of tokens minted at each denomination is limited, the probability that the bank will choose the same serial number twice can be made vanishingly small. The bank does keep a list of the serial numbers of all tokens deposited and therefore can reject a copy of a token that was deposited already. In this way, it can detect an attempt to use a duplicated token. Any customer or merchant can check the validity and denomination of a token by decrypting it with K_j^{pub} and applying *valid* to the result.

A simple digital cash protocol.   If anonymity is not an issue, the customer, C, the merchant, M, and the bank, B, can use the following simple digital cash protocol.

Creating tokens

1. C authenticates herself to B and sends a message requesting to withdraw some specified amount of cash, in the form of tokens, from her account.

2. B debits C's account and then mints the requested tokens by making up a serial number, n_i, for each token, such that *valid*(n_i) is true. It then encrypts n_i with the private key, K_j^{priv}, corresponding to the token's denomination j, to produce the token $K_j^{priv}[n_i]$.

3. B sends the tokens to C encrypted with a session key generated for B and C's use in the usual manner. A token cannot be sent in the clear because an intruder can copy it and spend the copy before C has a chance to spend the original. (In that case, the original token will be rejected by B when it is later deposited by C). At this point, the token creation transaction is committed.

4. C receives the tokens and stores them in her "electronic wallet."

Spending tokens

1. When C wants to use some of her tokens to purchase goods from M, she establishes a session with M and generates a session key in the usual manner. She then sends a message to M containing a purchase order for the goods and the appropriate number of tokens, all encrypted with the session key.

2. Upon receiving the message from C, M decrypts the tokens and checks that they are valid and are sufficient to purchase the requested goods. M then sends the tokens to B encrypted with a session key.

3. Upon receiving the message from M, B decrypts the tokens and checks that they are valid. It then checks its list of deposited tokens to ensure that the received tokens have not already been deposited. B then adds the received tokens to its list of deposited tokens, credits M's account with the amount of the tokens, commits the transaction, and sends a *complete* message to M.

4. Upon receiving the *complete* message from B, M performs local commit actions and then sends a *complete* message (and the goods purchased) to C.

This protocol does not guarantee goods atomicity or certified delivery. M might not send the goods to C.

As with the SET protocol, the exchange of messages among B, M, and C can be viewed as a linear commit protocol.

An anonymous protocol and blinding functions.   The simple digital cash protocol does not provide anonymity to the customer, because the bank can record the serial numbers of the tokens withdrawn by the customer. When those tokens are deposited by a merchant, the bank could conclude that the merchant sold something to that customer. This exposes some information about the customer's activities that he might prefer to keep private. To provide anonymity, the protocol is modified so that the customer (not the bank) makes up a serial number, n, that satisfies $valid(n)$, scrambles it, and then submits it to the bank. The bank creates the token by signing the scrambled serial number (it does not know what the serial number is), using a private key appropriate to the denomination being withdrawn. Such a signature is called a **blind signature** [Chaum et al. 1988]. The bank does not know the serial number, so it cannot trace it back to the customer when the token is later deposited by the merchant. When the customer receives the blinded token from the bank, it unscrambles it to obtain the token.

To implement a blind signature, the protocol uses a **blinding function**, b (sometimes called a **commuting function**). The function b and its inverse, b^{-1}, have two properties.

■ Given $b(n)$, it is very difficult to determine n.

■ b commutes with the encryption function used by the bank involving the (private) denomination key K_j^{priv}. That is,

$$K_j^{priv}[b(n)] = b(K_j^{priv}[n])$$

and as a result

$$b^{-1}(K_j^{priv}[b(n)]) = b^{-1}(b(K_j^{priv}[n])) = K_j^{priv}[n]$$

Therefore C can recover the token from the blinded token.

Creating tokens

1. C creates a valid serial number, n, satisfying $valid(n)$.
2. C selects a blinding function, b (known only to C), and **blinds** the serial number by computing $b(n)$.
3. C authenticates himself to B and sends a message containing $b(n)$, requesting to withdraw from his account some specified amount of cash in the form of tokens. (As in the simple digital cash protocol, the message is encrypted with a session key.) Since B does not know the blinding function, it cannot determine n.
4. B signs $b(n)$ with a private key, K_j^{priv}, appropriate to the token's denomination, creating the blinded token $K_j^{priv}[b(n)]$. It debits C's account accordingly and returns the blinded token to C, again using a session key. Although B cannot check that C had selected a valid serial number (satisfying $valid(n)$), C has no reason to construct an invalid number because he knows that B will debit his account by the amount of the token and that the token's validity will be checked when he attempts to spend it. At this point, the token creation transaction is committed.
5. C **unblinds** the blinded token by using $b^{-1}(K_j^{priv}[b(n)])$ to obtain $K_j^{priv}[n]$, which is the requested token consisting of a signed valid serial number.

Creating a blinding function. The protocol requires that C create his own blinding function, b, unknown to B. This might seem a difficult task, but it is actually quite easy in the context of the RSA algorithm for public key cryptography. In one scheme for doing this, C first generates a random number, u, that is relatively prime[15] to the modulus N of the bank's keys (see Section 27.2). Because u is relatively prime to N, it has a **multiplicative inverse**, u^{-1}, with respect to N, such that

$$u * u^{-1} \equiv 1 \ (mod \ N)$$

To blind the serial number, n, C computes

$$K_j^{pub}[u] * n \ (mod \ N)$$

and sends the result to B. Hence, the blinding function can be viewed simply as multiplication by a random number.

---

[15] Euclid's algorithm can be used to test whether the random number is relatively prime to N (see [Stalling 1997]).

The signed result, sr, returned by B to C is

$$sr = K_j^{pri}[K_j^{pub}[u] * n]$$

Using equation (27.1) on page 919, it follows that

$$sr = u * K_j^{pri}[n] \ (mod \ N)$$

Informally, we can say that, to unblind the token, C "divides sr by u," but actually C uses the multiplicative inverse, u^{-1}, to recover the token

$$K_j^{pri}[n] = u^{-1} * sr \ (mod \ N)$$

The serial number n can now be obtained using K_j^{pub}.

Spending tokens.   The protocol for spending and validating tokens involves the same steps as those in the simple protocol previously described. Fortunately, we did not assume that B kept a list of the serial numbers of the tokens it generated because, with the anonymous protocol, it does not know what these numbers are. When M submits the token to B for redemption, B simply assumes that, if the serial number satisfies *valid*, it earlier (blindly) signed that serial number. As before, B keeps a list of the serial numbers of tokens that have been deposited, so it will not accept the same token twice.

Money atomicity.   The question is whether the electronic cash protocols achieve money atomicity. Money atomicity has two aspects:

1. Money might be created (outside of any transaction) if a process can make a copy of a token and then spend it. However, the bank will uncover this attempted fraud when it checks the serial number against its list of previously submitted tokens. Counterfeiting is another way of creating money, but, as we saw earlier, success in this is unlikely.

2. Money might be destroyed as the result of a failure, but such problems can generally be dealt with.

   ❑ In the token generation transaction, the bank debits the customer's account, sends the token, and then commits, but the communication system loses the token and it is never delivered to the customer. However, these protocols have the interesting property that, if the customer claims never to have received a token that the bank sent, the bank can simply send the customer a copy of the (blinded) token that it retrieves from its log. Even if the customer is dishonest and now has two copies of the token, only one can be spent.

   ❑ In the token spending transaction, the system crashes after the customer sent the token but before she received a message that the transaction committed. The customer does not know whether the transaction committed before the crash and hence whether the token was actually spent. If she attempts to spend the token again, she might be accused of fraud. However, she can later ask the bank whether a particular token was spent (i.e., is in the list of spent tokens), but this might compromise her anonymity.

27.8 BIBLIOGRAPHIC NOTES

Most of the material in this chapter is well covered by [Stallings 1999]. The concept of public key cryptography was first presented by [Diffie and Hellman 1976], but almost all public key cryptography systems are based on the RSA algorithm [Rivest et al. 1978]. [Schneier 1995] does a good job of describing the mathematics underlying the RSA algorithm and of many other cryptographic algorithms and protocols. Like public-key cryptography, the concept of digital signatures was introduced in [Diffie and Hellman 1976], but, again, most digital signature systems are based on the RSA algorithm [Rivest et al. 1978], or on other algorithms developed specifically for signatures and not appropriate for encryption. The Kerberos system is discussed in [Steiner et al. 1988] and [Neuman and Ts'o 1994] and forms the basis of security as provided in DCE [Hu 1995]. The NetBill system was introduced in [Cox et al. 1995]. [Chaum et al. 1988] introduced the Ecash protocol and blind signatures. Descriptions of the SSL and SET protocols can be found at appropriate sites on the Web, which at publication time were [Netscape 2000] for SSL and [VISA 2000] for SET. The escrow agent protocol is based on the i-Escrow system available through eBay and described at publication time on its Web site [i-Escrow 2000].

27.9 EXERCISES

27.1 Discuss some security issues involved in executing transactions over the Internet.

27.2 Anyone who uses a computer keyboard should be able to easily solve the following simple substitution cipher:

Rsvj ;ryyrt od vjsmhrf yp yjr pmr pm oyd tohjy pm yjr lrunpstf/

27.3 Explain why, in general, short encryption keys are less secure than long keys.

27.4 Why is it necessary, in the Kerberos protocol, to include S in the message sent from KS to C (i.e., message M2)? Describe an attack that I can use if S is not included.

27.5 Explain how timestamps are used to defend against a replay attack in a security protocol.

27.6 Explain how nonces are used to increase security when encrypting messages that are short or that include fields for which the plaintext might be known to an intruder.

27.7 In a system using public key cryptography, site B wants to fool C by impersonating A. B waits until A requests to communicate with B. A does this by sending an "I want to communicate" message to B, stating its name (A) and encrypted with B's public key. Then B springs the trap. It sends an "I want to communicate" message to C claiming it is A and encrypted with C's public key. To ensure that it is actually communicating with A, C replies (to B) with a message obtained by encrypting a large random number, N, with A's public key. If C gets a response containing $N + 1$ encrypted with C's public key it would like to conclude that the responder is A, because only A could have decrypted C's message. C gets such a response. However, it is wrong because the response comes from B. Explain how this could have happened. (*Hint:* The protocol can be corrected if the encrypted text of each message includes the name of the sender.)

27.8 Suppose an intruder obtains a copy of a merchant's certificate.

    a. Explain why the intruder cannot simply use that certificate and pretend he is the merchant.

    b. Explain why the intruder cannot replace the merchant's public key with its own in the certificate.

27.9 Suppose that you use the SSL protocol and connect to a merchant site, M. The site sends you M's certificate. When the SSL protocol completes, how can you be sure that the new session key can be known only to M (perhaps an intruder has sent you a copy of M's certificate)? Can you be sure that you are connected to M?

27.10 Using your local Internet browser:

    a. Describe how you can tell when you are connected to a site that is using the SSL protocol.

    b. Suppose you are connected to a site that is using the SSL protocol. Describe how you can determine the name of the CA that supplied the certificate used by that site.

    c. How many bits are in the keys that your browser uses for SSL encryption?

27.11 Suppose that you obtained a certificate of your own. Explain how you could use that certificate to deal with situations in which an intruder might steal your credit card number.

27.12 Suppose that an intruder puts a virus on your computer that alters your browser. Describe two different ways that the intruder could then impersonate some server site S that you might attempt to communicate with—even though you use the SSL protocol—and obtain your credit card number.

27.13 A merchant using the SSL protocol (without SET) might implement a credit card transaction as follows: The customer purchases an item, and the merchant asks him to send his credit card information encrypted using the session key established with the SSL protocol. When the merchant receives that information, she initiates a separate transaction with the credit card company to have the purchase approved. When that transaction commits, the merchant commits the transaction with the customer. Explain the similarities and differences of this protocol to SET.

27.14 Assume that the merchant in the SET protocol is dishonest. Explain why he cannot cheat the customer.

27.15 Explain why a trusted third party is used in the certified delivery protocol.

27.16 Describe a restart procedure that the merchant's computer can use to deal with crashes during the SET protocol.

27.17 Explain why MD_2 in the SET protocol (Section 27.7.2) must be a part of the dual signature.

27.18 Explain why a forger could not simply submit an arbitrary random number as a token in the electronic cash protocol.

27.19 Assume that, in the anonymous electronic cash protocol, the bank is honest but the customer and the merchant might not be.

  a. After receiving the tokens from the bank, the customer later claims that she never received them. Explain what the bank should then do and why it is correct.

  b. After receiving the message containing the purchase order and the tokens from the customer, the merchant claims to have never received the message. Explain what the customer should do and why.

27.20 Describe the methods used in each of the following protocols to prevent a replay attack:

  a. Kerberos authentication

  b. SET

  c. Electronic cash

A.1 BASIC SYSTEM ISSUES

A transaction processing system might be implemented on a single computer or on a number of computers, perhaps widely separated geographically. A transaction might access a single (local) database residing on the same computer, or it might access a number of (remote) databases on different computers a half the world away. Whatever the case, the ACID properties of transactions must be supported. In this section we review some of the basic concepts and mechanisms used to design such systems.

A.1.1 Modules and Objects

Most large systems are designed with the "divide and conquer" approach. The system is decomposed into simpler modules, which are implemented and debugged separately. Languages that support a module structure allow the programmer to specify a module interface and a module body. The **interface** to a module, $M1$, contains all of the information that another module, $M2$, needs in order to access $M1$. It includes the names of procedures within $M1$ that can be called by $M2$, together with their parameters and types, which make up the syntax of a calling statement (sometimes called the **signature** of the procedure). The interface should also include semantic information: a description (perhaps textual) of what each procedure does.

The interface serves as a contract between the implementor of the module and its users. The implementor guarantees that the module will meet the specifications contained in its interface. $M1$'s interface is often referred to as its **application programming interface** (API) when $M1$ provides services to application-level programs. This situation is shown in Figure A.1.

The interface also includes a description of the mechanism used to return error conditions to the caller. These conditions occur frequently in transaction processing systems—for example, $M1$ might not be initialized when $M2$ makes the call or the arguments supplied to $M1$ might be incorrect.

The **body** of a module contains the procedures that can be called by other modules, procedures that are available for internal use only, and variable declarations. $M1$'s interface can be designed prior to the implementation of its body and stored in a library. The advantage of separating the specification of $M1$'s interface from

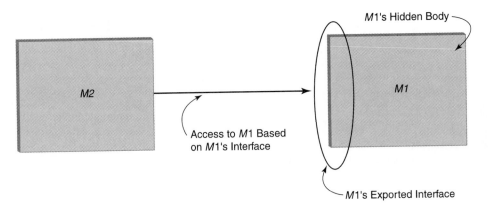

Figure A.1 Module structure.

the implementation of its body is that modules that call $M1$ can be designed and implemented (and even partially debugged) using only its interface. Thus, the implementation of $M1$ and of $M2$ can proceed concurrently.

The body of each module is hidden from other modules. Sometimes we say that the procedures and variable declarations are **encapsulated** within the module. Thus, $M1$'s body can be reimplemented at any time, and, if its interface remains the same, $M2$ need not be changed. This property is often referred to as **implementation transparency**. The variables declared in the module's body are global to $M1$'s procedures. Unlike variables local to a procedure, global variables are permanent and retain their values between calls. The values of the global variables constitute the **state** of the module.

Implementation transparency implies that the users of a module need not be concerned with how the services provided by the module are implemented. Moreover, the users of a module cannot, purposely or inadvertently, destroy the integrity of the variables declared in the module body because these variables are not directly accessible to them. Users can indirectly affect the state of these variables by calling interface procedures, but those procedures preserve data integrity.

The idea of a module can be further refined, leading to the concept of an object. An **object** is a computer representation of some entity that has meaning in a set of applications—for example, a pushdown stack or a pushbutton, which is represented by the picture of a pushbutton that might appear on the forms that are part of the graphical interface to a transaction processing system.

An object is characterized by a set of **attributes** whose values constitute the state of the object, and a set of **methods**, which are the procedures that can be called by other modules and which are described in the object's interface. The attributes of a pushbutton might include its size, location, and color. The methods associated with the pushbutton object might include the procedure that draws its graphical representation on the screen and the procedure that changes that representation when the user clicks it. The procedures and the data structures that encode the attributes are encapsulated within the object.

Some attributes are **public** and can be accessed from outside the object using conventional assignment statements. For example, a clock object might make the variable that stores the current time directly readable by external routines. Other attributes are **private** and can be accessed only by the public object methods. For example, the pushbutton object has a set of private attributes that are related to its graphic display and used by the methods that draw the pushbutton displayed on the screen. Since users cannot access these private attributes, they cannot destroy the display's integrity.

A given application might include many similar objects, such as pushbuttons, that have the same attributes and methods. These objects are instances of an **object class**, or just **class**. Thus there might be a class called pushbutton with the set of methods and attributes described above. A particular pushbutton object is an **instance** of the pushbutton class. Compared with conventional programming languages, an object class is like a data type, and an object in that class is like a variable of that type.

Languages that support objects also support **inheritance**. After an object class has been implemented within the system (perhaps by the system vendor), an application programmer can implement a new object class, which is a **child** of the original object class. The child inherits all of the attributes and methods of its parent and can have additional attributes and methods of its own.

For example, a child of a pushbutton class might be a toggle pushbutton class, in which the color of the pushbutton toggles between red and green when clicked to produce different effects. Since the toggle pushbutton automatically inherits the attributes and methods of its parent, its designer can use the inherited methods for drawing and changing the color of the toggle pushbutton and need not understand the private graphic attributes or other details of maintaining the integrity of the graphic display. Inheritance provides a means for application programmers to easily customize generic object classes for specific applications.

Objects can be viewed as a generalization of a programming language concept called **abstract data types**. Informally, an abstract data type is an object without inheritance. One example is the integer data type built into the hardware of a computer. The integer has a value (its attribute) and some operations: addition, subtraction, multiplication, and division (its methods). It is said to be abstract because its implementation (ones-complement, twos-complement, etc.) is encapsulated and invisible to the programmer who uses it. Most programming languages provide other built-in abstract data types, which are not implemented within the hardware—for example, arrays and records. Again, the implementation of those types is encapsulated and invisible to the programmer who uses them. Some languages allow programmers to define their own abstract data types, for example, a queue. From there it is only a small conceptual step to languages that allow programmers to define their own objects—abstract data types with inheritance, for example, a priority queue that is a child of a queue.

A.1.2 Clients and Servers

One important class of modules in a transaction processing system is **resource managers**. We use the term "resource" in the most general sense to describe hardware or data useful to a number of modules in a system—for example, a database, a login file containing login identifiers and their corresponding passwords, a source of unique numbers, or a printer. A "resource manager" is a module that regulates the use of a resource. It encapsulates the resource and its associated data structures together with a set of procedures that it exports to other modules. These procedures are the methods or abstract operations that are made available to other modules that wish to access the resource. The resource is accessible only through these procedures.

For example, a resource manager managing a database—referred to as a **database manager** or a database management system (DBMS)—is the only module with permission to access the areas on mass storage containing the database. It might, in addition, contain buffers in its address space to hold recently accessed pages—referred to as a **cache memory**. It might provide the service of executing an SQL statement. A login manager might encapsulate a login file and implement services for registering a new user, changing a password, and checking a password. A resource manager's interface is described in an API.

Resource managers provide service to other modules, which might be executing concurrently. Hence, while resource manager RM is providing service to some module M_1, another module, M_2, might also request that RM perform some service. In the simplest case, service is provided in first-in-first-out fashion: M_2's request for service waits until the procedure invoked by M_1 returns. However such discipline, can lead to performance problems in large systems in which the service provided by RM is needed by many other modules. The problem is the same as that caused by the serial execution of transactions: RM can become a bottleneck. The problem can be solved by allowing for concurrent execution of the resource manager's procedures. **Threads** are an example of such a mechanism. We will return to this issue and discuss threads in more detail in Section A.3.

Resource managers are frequently referred to as **servers**. Thus, we refer to a module that manages a database as either a database manager or a database server. The modules that call servers are referred to as **clients**. These names can be somewhat misleading because modules are often organized hierarchically. A module that acts as a server with respect to one module might use the services of other modules, in which case it is a client of those other modules.

Transaction processing systems are often organized as client/server systems. Transactions are invoked by client modules, which call on appropriate server modules when they need to access some resource.

Consider a simple transaction processing system organized as shown in Figure A.2. The user module consists of a presentation server, which controls the information displayed on the screen, and an application server, which executes the application programs. The database server executes SQL statements for the application programs.

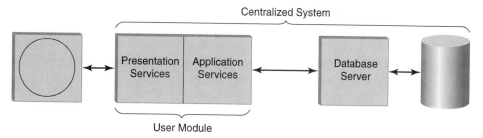

Figure A.2 Simple transaction processing system.

Be aware that the terms **client** and **server** are often used in different contexts. Up to this point, we have used them to refer to *modules*, which might reside on the same or on different computers. In other contexts, these terms might refer to the *computers* on which these modules execute. Thus, we might say that our Student Registration System is a client/server system in which the clients are the PCs used by the students and the server is a mainframe in the registrar's office. In this context, a transaction processing system is a client/server system only if the client and server modules reside on separate computers. A system in which the client and server modules all reside on the same computer would not be called a client/server system in this context. To distinguish between these two usages, we use the terms "client" and "server" to refer to the module organization we have been describing and speak specifically of a client machine and a server machine when referring to hardware. Note that one of the characteristics—indeed, one of the advantages—of the client/server organization is that it can be easily implemented on a single computer or on a network of computers.

A.2 MULTIPROGRAMMED OPERATING SYSTEMS

Modern computer systems incorporate multiple independent processors that can execute simultaneously. Examples include a central processing unit (CPU) and an I/O processor (sometimes called a channel). A **uniprocessor system** has a single CPU, while a **multiprocessor system** has more than one. A conventional multiprocessor system is one in which all processors share access to a common, main memory, and so it is referred to as a **shared memory system**. A variant of this architecture is one in which each CPU has its own private main memory and only the mass storage devices are shared. This type of system is referred to as a **shared disk system**.

There is also the **shared nothing system**, in which separate computer systems are interconnected via communication lines. Each system is self-contained, with its own private main memory and mass storage devices, and nothing is shared. In one variant of this architecture, the individual systems are packaged together in a single box and are homogeneous. Each system is built of the same hardware and controlled by copies of the same operating system, and they communicate over high-speed connections (for example, buses). In another variant, the individual systems are part of a **distributed system**. Distributed systems generally involve heterogeneous hardware and software, they may be geographically distributed, and their communication is slower (perhaps over telephone lines). We return to such systems in the next subsection.

An **operating system** is a program that manages the resources of an individual computer system. These resources include execution time on the system processors, space in memory, and access to physical devices (e.g., a mass storage device or a communication line). The operating system might manage informational resources as well, such as a file system. One goal of an operating system is to use these resources efficiently.

The user and system tasks that are performed under the control of an operating system are executed as processes. A **process** is an executing program that has available to it some data. The data might be directly accessible to the program in its virtual memory, or it might be stored in files that are accessible through the operating system. In addition, data can be global or local. Global data is accessible to all procedures executed by the process, local data is created dynamically when a particular procedure is entered, and released when the procedure returns. Local data is generally stored in a stack and consists of the procedure's parameters and local variables. The program and all of the data it can access are said to reside in the process's **data space**.

In the simplest case, each process has a control point, which is the address of the next instruction to be executed. (We consider processes with multiple control points in Section A.3.) The control point, together with the values of the variables in its data space, are referred to as the process's **state**.

In a **uniprogrammed** operating system, one process is run to completion before another is started. This makes inefficient use of system resources, since many programs are designed in such a way that they can utilize only one physical processor at a time. For example, programs typically alternate between computing (requiring a CPU) and transferring information to and from files (requiring an I/O processor). During the computing phase, I/O devices are idle, while the CPU idles during the I/O phase.

Efficient use of a computer system requires keeping as many physical processors busy as possible. To achieve that, it is desirable for multiple processes to run concurrently. A process might request service from only one (or perhaps a small number) of processors at a particular point in time. However, if many processes are running concurrently, many processors can be utilized simultaneously, resulting in an improvement in system throughput. Operating systems capable of running multiple processes concurrently are referred to as **multiprogrammed** operating systems.

Concurrent execution is important from the user's point of view, since the initiation of a process serving one user does not have to wait for the termination of a process serving another user, as is the case in a uniprogrammed system. The result is improved response time.

Concurrency is particularly important in transaction processing systems that serve thousands of users at the same time. With concurrent transactions execution, the inherent power of a computer system can simultaneously reduce the response times of individual transactions and increase throughput.

Each process executing under the control of a multiprogrammed operating system appears to be running on its own machine. In reality, though, the processes are sharing the existing resources, which are allocated by the operating system (they include time on the CPUs, space in memory, service requests on the I/O processors, etc.). The operating system causes a CPU to be shared by allowing one process, P_1, to run for a period of time, called a **time quantum**, and then interrupting P_1 to give another process, P_2, a chance to run. P_1 is resumed at a later time. This results in a phenomenon called **interleaved execution**. In a multiprocessor system, each CPU is shared in this way.

If the data spaces of P_1 and P_2 are disjoint, their execution is unaffected by interleaving. P_1 cannot tell that it has been interrupted because, when it resumes, the state of its data space is identical to the state that existed immediately prior to the interruption.[1] Data spaces need not be disjoint, however, but may overlap. At one extreme, the overlap between data spaces might be limited to files on mass storage. However, operating systems also allow processes to share parts of their virtual memory. In any case, the operating system is responsible for ensuring that each process is allowed to access only the information in its own data space.

If the data spaces of P_1 and P_2 are not disjoint, these processes are said to *share* access to the data items contained in the intersection. If, when P_2 interrupts P_1, it changes the value of an item in the intersection, the state of P_1's data space when the interrupt occurred will not be identical to the state when P_1 is later resumed, and therefore P_1's execution might be affected by the interleaving. For example, if P_1 reads the item and P_2 writes a new value to the item, a different value will be returned to P_1 depending on whether it was interrupted by P_2 before or after it performed the read. Note that processes have no control over when the interrupt takes place—it is the operating system, in its resource allocation routine, that makes this decision. Thus, in different runs of the same two processes the interleaving might be different. This means that, if data spaces are not disjoint, the processes might behave differently on different runs.

We dealt with the effects of interleaving in the discussion of transaction isolation in Chapter 23 and showed that transactions behave differently depending on how their database operations are interleaved. In that case, the shared data space is the database (the workspaces of different transactions are disjoint).

---

[1] We assume here that the process does not access the system's clock. A process could tell that it had been interrupted if it could detect the passage of time.

Process management in a multiprogrammed operating system is a complex matter. The operating system must maintain a considerable amount of information about each process in its tables, which requires the use of large blocks of memory. This information includes the total amount of resources (e.g., compute time) the process is allowed to use, the amount it has used so far (for accounting and scheduling), the current location of its virtual memory (i.e., its physical address in main memory or on mass storage), its scheduling priority, the files it is allowed to access (so that processes and users can be protected from one another), and so forth. In addition, these tables frequently have to be scanned, causing the operating system to use a large amount of compute time. For example, the system has to frequently scan its process table to determine the order in which processes should be run.

The space and time overhead incurred by a multiprogrammed operating system is thus a function of the number of processes that it supports, and hence that number is limited. This limitation has motivated the need for low-overhead processes and has resulted in the development of threads and multithreaded processes.

A conventional, or **single-threaded**, process has a single control point. As execution proceeds, the control point moves from one instruction or I/O operation to another and defines an execution path. The execution is **sequential**, meaning that at any given time the state of the process determines a unique instruction or I/O operation that the process will execute next. A **multithreaded** process contains several control points that define independent paths of execution called **threads**. When threads are supported in an operating system, it allocates CPUs to them in the same way that it allocates CPUs to processes. In this way, the threads within a process can execute concurrently.

Since at any given time the next instruction to be executed in a multithreaded process can be the next instruction in any of its threads, the execution of the process as a whole is no longer sequential. Also, since the control point of each thread can refer to an arbitrary instruction, several threads might be executing the same procedure. Each thread in a process has access to the global information (data and procedures) in the process's data space, as well as the thread's private stack for local data.

The operating system can manage a multithreaded process with n threads with significantly less overhead than is required to manage n processes.

■ The operating system maintains a single description of the data space for the process as a whole.

■ The operating system accounts for the use of resources for the process as a whole.

■ The access path to files, devices, and the like, is shared by all threads in the process.

■ The operating system can switch execution from one thread in the process to another without an expensive **context switch** between processes.

The advantages of multithreading do not come without a cost. Threads must be carefully programmed to synchronize their access to global data within the process. Furthermore, there is no memory protection between the threads executing within a process, so an error in the execution of one thread in the process can corrupt information in the data spaces of all the other threads.

An application server is an example of a module that might be multithreaded. When a user logs on at a client machine, a session might be established at the application server to handle her. Each session has associated local data (e.g., the user's name and Id) that is used to process the user's requests. A session might continue for a relatively long period of time, since the user might want to perform a sequence of interactions, and each interaction will generally require communication with the user. For example, many students might be using the registration system at the same time to register for several courses. As a result, a large number of sessions are likely to be in progress simultaneously, making it inefficient to dedicate an entire process to just one. Instead, a thread in the application server can be associated with each session, with local information stored in its private stack.

A.4 COMMUNICATION

Multiprogrammed operating systems generally make it possible for processes to communicate with each other. Thus, the system allows for the possibility that processes are not separate and unrelated computations running on behalf of different users but cooperating to perform some complex task. For example, a difficult scientific computation over some two-dimensional space might be divided into several computations over different regions of the space where each is performed by a separate process. Alternatively, a search over a database containing several terabytes of information might be divided among a number of searchers in different processes. Communication between the cooperating processes is needed in these situations.

One way processes can communicate in a shared-memory architecture is through shared regions of their data space. One process can write a message in some shared location, and another process can read the message at a later time. Similarly, the processes can simply access common data structures in the shared portion of their data space so that one process can view modifications made by the other. A set of threads can communicate in this way. Such a mode of communication is particularly effective if the processes interact closely and have a considerable amount of information to exchange.

Shared memory is a very low overhead communication technique. Nevertheless, it has its problems.

■ Some mechanism must be provided for processes to synchronize their access to shared data. For example, the reader of a message should not start reading until after the writer has finished writing. Similarly, when a process updates a data structure the intermediate states produced during the update might not be well formed. Thus, if two processes attempt to access a data structure concurrently, and at least one is performing an update, one or both might behave erroneously.

The code sections that access the data structure are referred to as **critical sections**. Accesses to the data structure need to be isolated for exactly the same reason that transactions accessing common database items need to be isolated. This type of isolation is often referred to as **mutual exclusion**, and we say that execution of critical sections must mutually exclude each other.

■ Shared memory does not generalize to distributed systems, where processes reside on different computers with no shared data space.

To overcome these problems, a multiprogrammed operating system provides an **interprocess communication facility** (**IPC**) that allows processes to exchange messages using *send* and *receive* operations. A process, P_1, can invoke a *send*, designating another process, P_2, to receive a message it has constructed. P_2 can invoke a *receive* indicating its willingness to receive the next message that has been sent to it. Since messages are buffered in the operating system from the time they are sent until the time they are received, the sender and receiver need not have any shared memory.

Computers in a network are interconnected by communication lines. As far as the operating system is concerned, a communication line is simply a new type of I/O device. To support the development of distributed applications, the IPC implemented in the operating system of each computer is extended to allow processes located anywhere in the network to exchange messages in a uniform way. Thus, whether or not the processes are on the same machine, they can use the same commands to communicate. Such systems are referred to as **distributed message-passing kernels**. Since each machine is not necessarily directly connected to all other machines, a **store-and-forward** strategy is used. Messages pass through intermediate machines on a path from source to destination. The route is determined by a distributed algorithm executed in the kernels.

Several grades of message passing service are generally provided to users, the most primitive of which is the **datagram**. In this case, the operating system at the source machine keeps no record of the message after it has been sent into the network. If the message is lost (because of failure or insufficient resources at intermediate machines), the source is not informed. Although loss is unlikely, datagrams are, for this reason, considered (relatively) unreliable. The Internet Protocol (IP) is an example of a protocol providing datagram service.

Message passing systems providing a **virtual circuit** are more reliable. In this case, the source retains a copy of the message until it is acknowledged by the destination and so can resend the message if it is lost. The Transmission Control Protocol (TCP) is built on top of IP and is an example of a protocol providing virtual circuit service. The **socket** structure in UNIX and Windows is a user interface to a distributed message-passing kernel that provides both datagrams and virtual circuits.

Both peer-to-peer and remote procedure call communication (RPC), described in Chapter 22, can be built on top of the message passing service provided by a distributed message-passing kernel. For example, when a remote procedure call is made, the caller (source) sends a message containing the arguments to the callee (destination) and then executes a receive to await a response. When the (remote) procedure completes, the callee sends a response message containing the results back to the caller. In a similar way, peer-to-peer communication is an enhanced version of the message passing facility provided at the operating system level. One such enhancement is its mechanism for transactional synchronization (syncpoint), described in Section 22.4.2.

In contrast to shared-memory communication, message passing generalizes to a distributed system. It also solves the synchronization problems associated with shared memory. For example, instead of client processes directly accessing a shared data structure, the data structure can be managed by a single server. The server accepts messages from the clients (using either peer-to-peer communication or RPC) describing requested accesses and processes them one at a time. If the server is single-threaded, there is no concurrent access to the data structure and there are no synchronization problems. If the server is multithreaded, the threads must be synchronized in their access to the data structure. The communication costs (including those associated with the copying of messages between system buffers and the sender's and receiver's address spaces) and delays associated with transferring messages limits message passing to situations in which the processes interact loosely and the amount of information to be communicated is small.

References

Abiteboul, S., and Kanellakis, P. (1998). Object identity as a query language primitive. *Journal of the ACM* **45**(5): 798–842.

Abiteboul, S., Hull, R., and Vianu, V. (1995). *Foundations of Databases*, Addison-Wesley, Reading, MA.

Abiteboul, S., Quass, D., McHugh, J., Widom, J., and Wiener, J. (1997). The Lorel query language for semistructured data. *International Journal on Digital Libraries* **1**(1): 68–88.

Abiteboul, S., Buneman, P., and Suciu, D. (2000). *Data on the Web*, Morgan Kaufmann, San Francisco.

Adam, N., Atluri, V., and Huang, W. (1998). Modeling and analysis of workflows using Petri nets. *Journal of Intelligent Information Systems* **10**(2): 131–158.

Agrawal, D., Bernstein, A., Gupta, P., and Sengupta, S. (1987). Distributed optimistic concurrency control with reduced rollback. *Distributed Computing* **2**(1): 45–59.

Agrawal, R., Imielinski, T., and Swami, A. (1993). Database mining: A performance perspective. *IEEE Transactions on Knowledge and Date Engineering* **5**(6): 914–925.

Agrawal, S., Agrawal, R., Deshpande, P., Gupta, A., Naughton, J., Ramakrishnan, R., and Sarawagi, S. (1996). On the computation of multidimensional aggregates. *Proceedings of the International Conference on Very Large Data Bases (VLDB)*, Mombai, India, 506–521.

Aho, A., and Ullman, J. (1979). Universality of data retrieval languages. *ACM Symposium on Principles of Programming Languages (POPL)*, 110–120.

Alagic, S. (1999). Type-checking OQL queries in the ODMG type systems. *ACM Transactions on Database Systems* **24**(3): 319–360.

Alonso, G., Agrawal, D., Abbadi, A. E., Kamath, M., Günthör, R., and Mohan, C. (1996). Advanced transaction models in workflow contexts. *Proceedings of the International Conference on Data Engineering (ICDE)*, New Orleans, 574–581.

Alonso, G., Agrawal, D., Abbadi, A. E., and Mohan., C. (1997). Functionality and limitations of current workflow management systems. *IEEE-Expert, Special issue on Cooperative Information Systems* **1**(9).

Andrade, J. M., Carges, M. T., Dwyer, T. J., and Felts, S. D. (1996). *The TUXEDO System, Software for Constructing and Managing Distributed Business Applications*, Addison-Wesley, Reading, MA.

Apt, K., Blair, H., and Walker, A. (1988). Towards a theory of declarative knowledge. In J. Minker (ed.), *Foundations of Deductive Databases and Logic Programming*, Morgan Kaufmann, San Francisco, 89–148.

Arisawa, H., Moriya, K., and Miura, T. (1983). Operations and the properties of non-first-normal-form relational databases. *Proceedings of the International Conference on Very Large Data Bases (VLDB)*, Florence, 197–204.

Armstrong, W. (1974). Dependency structures of database relations. *IFIP Congress*, Stockholm, 580–583.

Astrahan, M., Blasgen, M., Chamberlin, D., Eswaran, K., Gray, J., Griffiths, P., King, W., Lorie, R., McJones, P., Mehl, J., Putzolu, G., Traiger, I., and Watson, V. (1976). System R: A relational approach to database management. *ACM Transactions on Database Systems* **1**(2): 97–137.

Astrahan, M., Blasgen, M., Gray, J., King, W., Lindsay, B., Lorie, R., Mehl, J., Price, T., Selinger, P., Schkolnick, M., Traiger, D. S. I., and Yost, R. (1981). A history and evaluation of System R. *Communications of the ACM* **24**(10): 632–646.

Attie, P., Singh, M., Sheth, A., and Rusinkiewicz, M. (1993). Specifying and enforcing intertask dependencies. *Proceedings of the International Conference on Very Large Data Bases (VLDB)*, Dublin, 134–145.

Attie, P., Singh, M., Emerson, E., Sheth, A., and Rusinkiewicz, M. (1996). Scheduling workflows by enforcing intertask dependencies. *Distributed Systems Engineering Journal* **3**(4): 222–238.

Atzeni, P., and Antonellis, V. D. (1993). *Relational Database Theory*. Benjamin-Cummings, San Francisco.

Avron, A., and Hirshfeld, J. (1994). Query evaluation, relative safety, and domain independence in first-order databases. *Methods of Logic in Computer Science* **1**: 261–278.

Bancilhon, F., and Spyratos, N. (1981). Update semantics of relational views. *ACM Transactions on Database Systems* **6**(4): 557–575.

Bancilhon, F., Delobel, C., and Kanellakis, P. (eds.) (1990). *Building an Object-Oriented Database System: The Story of O2*. Morgan Kaufmann, San Francisco.

Batini, C., Ceri, S., and Navathe, S. (1992). *Database Design: An Entity Relationship Approach*. Benjamin-Cummings, San Francisco.

Bayer, R., and McCreight, E. (1972). Organization and maintenance of large ordered indices. *Acta Informatica* **1**(3): 173–189.

Beeri, C., and Bernstein, P. (1979). Computational problems related to the design of normal form relational schemes. *ACM Transactions on Database Systems* **4**(1): 30–59.

Beeri, C., and Kifer, M. (1986a). Elimination of intersection anomalies from database schemes. *Journal of the ACM* **33**(3): 423–450.

Beeri, C., and Kifer, M. (1986b). An integrated approach to logical design of relational database schemes. *ACM Transactions on Database Systems* **11**(2): 134–158.

Beeri, C., and Kifer, M. (1987). A theory of intersection anomalies in relational database schemes. *Journal of the ACM* **34**(3): 544–577.

Beeri, C., Fagin, R., and Howard, J. (1977). A complete axiomatization for functional and multivalued dependencies in database relations. *Proceedings of the ACM SIGMOD International Conference on Management of Data*, Toronto, Canada, 47–61.

Beeri, C., Bernstein, P., and Goodman, N. (1978). A sophisticate's introduction to database normalization theory. *Proceedings of the International Conference on Very Large Data Bases (VLDB)*, San Mateo, CA, 113–124.

Beeri, C., Mendelson, A., Sagiv, Y., and Ullman, J. (1981). Equivalence of relational database schemes. *SIAM Journal of Computing* **10**(2): 352–370.

Beeri, C., Bernstein, P., Goodman, N., Lai, M.-Y., and Shasha, D. (1983). A concurrency control theory for nested transactions. *Proceedings of the 2nd ACM Symposium on Principles of Distributed Computing*, Montreal, Canada, 45–62.

Beeri, C., Bernstein, P., and Goodman, N. (1989). A model for concurrency in nested transaction systems. *Journal of the ACM* **36**(2): 230–269.

Bell, D., and Grimson, J. (1992). *Distributed Database Systems*. Addison-Wesley, Reading, MA.

Berenson, H., Bernstein, P., Gray, J., Melton, J., O'Neil, E., and O'Neil, P. (1995). A critique of ANSI SQL isolation levels. *Proceedings of the ACM SIGMOD International Conference on Management of Data*, San Jose, CA, 1–10.

Berg, C., and Virginia, C. (2000). *Advanced Java 2 Development for Enterprise Applications*, (2nd ed.). Prentice-Hall, Englewood Cliffs, NJ.

Bernstein, P. (1976). Synthesizing third normal form from functional dependencies. *ACM Transactions on Database Systems* **1**(4): 277–298.

Bernstein, P., and Chiu, D. (1981). Using semi-joins to solve relational queries. *Journal of the ACM* **28**(1): 28–40.

Bernstein, P., Goodman, N., Wong, E., Reeve, C., and Rothnie, J. (1981). Query processing in a system for distributed databases (SDD-1). *ACM Transactions on Database Systems* **6**(4): 602–625.

Bernstein, P., and Goodman, N. (1983). Multiversion concurrency control—Theory and algorithms. *ACM Transactions on Database Systems* **8**(4): 465–483.

Bernstein, P., Hadzilacos, V., and Goodman, N. (1987). *Concurrency Control and Recovery in Database Systems*. Addison-Wesley, Reading, MA.

Bernstein, A. J., and Lewis, P. M. (1996). High-performance transaction systems using transaction semantics. *Distributed and Parallel Databases* **4**(1).

Bernstein, P., and Newcomer, E. (1997). *Principles of Transaction Processing*. Morgan Kaufmann, San Francisco.

Bernstein, A. J., Gerstl, D., Leung, W.-H., and Lewis, P. M. (1998). Design and performance of an assertional concurrency control system. *Proceedings of the International Conference on Data Engineering* (ICDE), Orlando, 436–445.

Bernstein, A. J., Gerstl, D., and Lewis, P. (1999). Concurrency control for step decomposed transactions. *Information Systems* **24**(8): 673–698.

Bernstein, A. J., Gerstl, D., Lewis, P., and Lu, S. (1999). Using transaction semantics to increase performance. *International Workshop on High Performance Transaction Systems*, Pacific Grove, CA, 26–29.

Bernstein, A. J., Lewis, P., and Lu, S. (2000). Semantic conditions for correctness at different isolation levels. *Proceedings of the International Conference on Data Engineering*, San Diego, 507–566.

Birrell, A., and Nelson, B. (1984). Implementing remote procedure calls. *ACM Transactions on Computer Systems* **2**(1): 39–59.

Biskup, J., and Polle, T. (2000a). *Constraints in Object-Oriented Databases* (manuscript).

Biskup, J., and Polle, T. (2000b). Decomposition of database classes under path functional dependencies and onto constraints. *Proceedings of the Foundations of Information and Knowledge-Base Systems.* In Vol. 1762 of *Lecture Notes in Computer Science*, Springer-Verlag, Heidelberg, Germany, 31–49.

Biskup, J., Menzel, R., and Polle, T. (1996). Transforming an entity-relationship schema into object-oriented database schemas. In J. Eder and L. Kalinichenko (eds.), *Advances in Databases and Information Systems*, Workshops in Computing, Springer-Verlag, Moscow, Russia, 109–136.

Biskup, J., Menzel, R., Polle, T., and Sagiv, Y. (1996). Decomposition of relationships through pivoting. *Proceedings of the 15th International Conference on Conceptual Modeling.* In Vol. 1157 of *Lecture Notes in Computer Science*, Springer-Verlag, Heidelberg, Germany, 28–41.

Blaha, M., and Premerlani, W. (1998). *Object-Oriented Modeling and Design for Database Applications.* Prentice-Hall, Englewood Cliffs, NJ.

Blakeley, J., and Martin, N. (1990). Join index, materialized view, and hybrid-hash join: A performance analysis. *Proceedings of the International Conference on Data Engineering (ICDE)*, Los Angeles, 256–263.

Blasgen, M., and Eswaran, K. (1977). Storage access in relational databases. *IBM Systems Journal* **16**(4): 363–378.

Bonner, A. (1999). Workflow, transactions, and datalog. *ACM SIGACT-SIGMOD-SIGART Symposium on Principles of Database Systems (PODS)*, Philadelphia, 294–305.

Booch, G., Rumbaugh, J., and Jacobson, I. (1999). *The Unified Modeling Language User Guide*, Addison-Wesley, Reading, MA.

Bourret, R. (2000). Namespace myths exploded. *http://www.xml.com/pub/a/2000/03/08/namespaces/index.html.*

Bradley, N. (2000a). *The XML Companion.* Addison-Wesley, Reading, MA.

Bradley, N. (2000b). *The XSL Companion.* Addison-Wesley, Reading, MA.

Breitbart, Y., Garcia-Molina, H., and Silberschatz, A. (1992). Overview of multidatabase transaction management. *VLDB Journal* **1**(2): 181–240.

Bukhres, O., and Kueshn, E. (eds.) (1995). *Distributed and Parallel Databases—An International Journal*, Special Issue on Software Support for Workflow Management.

Buneman, P., Davidson, S., Hillebrand, G., and Suciu, D. (1996). A query language and optimization techniques for unstructured data. *Proceedings of the ACM SIGMOD International Conference on Management of Data*, Montreal, Canada, 505–516.

Cattell, R. (1994). *Object Database Management* (rev. ed.), Addison-Wesley, Reading, MA.

Cattell, R., and Barry, D. (eds.) (2000). *The Object Database Standard: ODMG 3.0.* Morgan Kaufmann, San Francisco.

Ceri, S., and Pelagatti, G. (1984). *Distributed Databases: Principles and Systems.* McGraw-Hill, New York.

Ceri, S., Negri, M., and Pelagatti, G. (1982). Horizontal partitioning in database design. *Proceedings of the International ACM SIGMOD Conference on Management of Data*, Orlando, 128–136.

Chamberlin, D., Robie, J., and Florescu, D. (2000). Quilt: An XML query language for heterogeneous data sources. In *Lecture Notes in Computer Science*, Springer-Verlag, Heidelberg, Germany (*http://www.almaden.ibm.com/cs/people/chamberlin/quilt_lncs.pdf*).

Chang, S., and Cheng, W. (1980). A methodology for structured database decomposition. *IEEE-TSE* **6**(2): 205–218.

Chaudhuri, S. (1998). An overview of query optimization in relational databases. *ACM SIGACT-SIGMOD-SIGART Symposium on Principles of Database Systems (PODS)*, Seattle, 34–43.

Chaudhuri, S., and Dayal, U. (1997). An overview of data warehousing and OLAP technology. *SIGMOD Record* **26**(1): 65–74.

Chaudhuri, S., Krishnamurthy, R., Potamianos, S., and Shim, K. (1995). Optimizing queries with materialized views. *Proceedings of the International Conference on Data Engineering (ICDE)*, Taipei, Taiwan, 190–200.

Chaum, D., Fiat, A., and Noar, M. (1988). Untraceable electronic cash. *Advances in Cryptology: Crypto'88 Proceedings.*In *Lecture Notes in Computer Science*, Springer-Verlag, Heidelberg, Germany, 319–327.

Chen, P. (1976). The Entity-Relationship Model—Towards a unified view of data. *ACM Transactions on Database Systems* **1**(1): 9–36.

Chen, I.-M., Hull, R., and McLeod, D. (1995). An execution model for limited ambiguity rules and its application to derived data update. *ACM Transactions on Database Systems* **20**(4): 365–413.

Chrysanthis, P., and Ramaritham, K. (1990). ACTA: A framework for specifying and reasoning about transaction structure and behavior. *Proceedings of the ACM SIGMOD International Conference on Management of Data*, Atlantic City, NJ, 194–205.

Cochrane, R., Pirahesh, H., and Mattos, N. (1996). Integrating triggers and declarative constraints in SQL database systems. *Proceedings of the International Conference on Very Large Data Bases (VLDB)*, Bombay, India, 567–578.

Codd, E. (1970). A relational model of data for large shared data banks. *Communications of the ACM* **13**(6): 377–387.

Codd, E. (1972). Relational completeness of data base sublanguages. *Data Base Systems*. In Vol. 6 of *Courant Computer Science Symposia Series*, Prentice-Hall, Englewood Cliffs, NJ.

Codd, E. (1979). Extending the database relational model to capture more meaning. *ACM Transactions on Database Systems* **4**(4): 397–434.

Codd, E. (1990). *The Relational Model for Database Management, Version 2*. Addison-Wesley, Reading, MA.

Codd, E. (1995). Twelve rules for on-line analytic processing. *Computerworld*, April 13.

Copeland, G., and Maier, D. (1984). Making Smalltalk a database system. *Proceedings of the ACM SIGMOD International Conference on Management of Data*, Boston, 316–325.

Cosmadakis, S., and Papadimitriou, C. (1983). Updates of relational views. *ACM SIGACT-SIGMOD-SIGART Symposium on Principles of Database Systems (PODS)*, Atlanta, 317–331.

Cox, B., Tygar, J., and Sirbu, M. (1995). Netbill security and transaction protocol. *Proceedings of the 1st USENIX workshop on Electronic Commerce*, New York, Vol. 1.

Date, C. (1992). Relational calculus as an aid to effective query formulation. In C. Date and H. Darwen (eds.), *Relational Database Writings*, Addison-Wesley, Reading, MA.

Date, C., and Darwen, H. (1997). *A Guide to the SQL Standard*. (4th ed.), Addison-Wesley, Reading, MA.

Davulcu, H., Kifer, M., Ramakrishnan, C.R., and Ramakrishnan, I.V. (1998). Logic based modeling and analysis of workflows. *ACM SIGACT-SIGMOD-SIGART Symposium on Principles of Database Systems (PODS)*, Seattle, 25–33.

Deutsch, A., Fernandez, M., Florescu, D., Levy, A., and Suciu, D. (1998). XML-QL: A Query Language for XML. *Technical report W3C (http://www.w3.org/TR/1998/NOTE-xml-ql-19980819/)*.

Deutsch, A., Fernandez, M., and Suciu, D. (1999). Storing semistructured data with stored. Proceedings of the *ACM SIGMOD International Conference on Management of Data*, Philadelphia, 431–442.

DeWitt, D., Katz, R., Olken, F., Shapiro, L., Stonebraker, M., and Wood, D. (1984). Implementation techniques for main-memory database systems. *Proceedings of the ACM SIGMOD International Conference on Management of Data*, Boston, 1–8.

Diffie, W., and Hellman, M. (1976). New directions in cryptography. *IEEE Transactions on Information Theory* **IT-22**(6): 644–654.

DOM (2000). Document Object Model (DOM) (*http://www.w3.org/DOM/*).

Eisenberg, A. (1996). New standard for stored procedures in SQL. *SIGMOD Record* **25**(4): 81–88.

Elmagarmid, A. (ed.) (1992). *Database Transaction Models for Advanced Applications*. Morgan Kaufmann, San Francisco.

Elmagarmid, A., Leu, Y., Litwin, W., and Rusinkiewicz, M. (1990). A multidatabase transaction model for interbase. *Proceedings of the International Conference on Very Large Data Bases (VLDB)*, Brisbane, Australia, 507–518.

Eswaran, K., Gray, J., Lorie, R., and Traiger, I. (1976). The notions of consistency and predicate locks in a database system. *Communications of the ACM* **19**(11): 624–633.

Fagin, R. (1977). Multivalued dependencies and a new normal form for relational databases. *ACM Transactions on Database Systems* **2**(3): 262–278.

Fagin, R., Nievergelt, J., Pippenger, N., and Strong, H. (1979). Extendible hashing—A fast access method for dynamic files. *ACM Transactions on Database Systems* **4**(3): 315–344.

Fayyad, U., Piatetsky-Shapiro, G., Smyth, P., and Uthurusamy, R. (eds.) (1996). *Advances in Knowledge Discovery and Data Mining*. The MIT Press, Cambridge, MA.

Fekete, A., Lynch, N., Merritt, M., and Weihl, W. (1989). Commutativity-based locking for nested transactions. *Technical Report MIT/LCS/TM-370.b*, Laboratory for Computer Science, Massachusetts Institute of Technology, Cambridge, MA.

Fekete, A., Liarokapis, D., O'Neil, E., O'Neil, P., and Shasha, D. (2000). Making snapshot isolation serializable. *http://www.cs.umb.edu/ poneil/publist.html*.

Flach, P. A., and Savnik, I. (1999). Database dependency discovery: A machine learning approach. *AI Communications* **12**(3): 139–160.

Florescu, D., Deutsch, A., Levy, A., Suciu, D., and Fernandez, M. (1999). A query language for XML. *Proceedings of the Eighth International World Wide Web Conference*, Toronto, Canada.

Fowler, M., and Scott, K. (1999). *UML Distilled*. Addison-Wesley, Reading, MA.

Frohn, J., Lausen, G., and Uphoff, H. (1994). Access to objects by path expressions and rules. *Proceedings of the International Conference on Very Large Data Bases (VLDB)*, Santiago, Chile, 273–284.

Fuh, Y.-C., Dessloch, S., Chen, W., Mattos, N., Tran, B., Lindsay, B., DeMichiel, L., Rielau, S., and Mannhaupt, D. (1999). Implementation of SQL3 structured types with inheritance and value substitutability. *Proceedings of the International Conference on Very Large Data Bases (VLDB)*, Edinburgh, Scotland, 565–574.

Garcia-Molina, H., and Salem, K. (1987). Sagas. *Proceedings of the ACM SIGMOD International Conference on Management of Data*, San Francisco, 249–259.

Garcia-Molina, H., Gawlick, D., Klien, J., Kleissner, K., and Salem, K. (1991). Modeling long-running activities as nested Sagas. *Quarterly Bulletin of the IEEE Computer Society Technical Committee on Data Engineering* **14**(1): 14–18.

Garcia-Molina, H., Ullman, J., and Widom, J. (2000). *Database System Implementation*, Prentice-Hall, Englewood Cliffs, NJ.

Georgakopoulos, D., Hornick, M., Krychniak, P., and Manola, F. (1994). Specification and management of extended transactions in a programmable transaction environment. *Proceedings of the International Conference on Data Engineering (ICDE)*, Houston, 462–473.

Georgakopoulos, D., Hornick, M., and Sheth, A. (1995). An overview of workflow management: From process modeling to infrastructure for automation. *Journal on Distributed and Parallel Database Systems* **3**(2): 119–153.

Gifford, D. (1979). Weighted voting for replicated data. *Proceedings of the ACM 7th Symposium on Operating Systems Principles*, Pacific Grove, CA, 150–162.

Gogola, M., Herzig, R., Conrad, S., Denker, G., and Vlachantonis, N. (1993). Integrating the E-R approach in an object-oriented environment. *Proceedings of the 12th International Conference on the Entity-Relationship Approach*, Arlington, TX, 376–389.

Gottlob, G., Paolini, P., and Zicari, R. (1988). Properties and update semantics of consistent views. *ACM Transactions on Database Systems* **13**(4): 486–524.

Graefe, G. (1993). Query evaluation techniques for large databases. *ACM Computing Surveys* **25**(2): 73–170.

Gray, J. (1978). Notes on database operating systems. *Operating Systems: An Advanced Course*. In Vol. 60 of *Lecture Notes in Computer Science*, Springer-Verlag, Berlin, 393–481.

Gray, J. (1981). The transaction concept: Virtues and limitations. *Proceedings of the International Conference on Very Large Data Bases (VLDB)*, Cannes, 144–154.

Gray, J., and Reuter, A. (1993). *Transaction Processing: Concepts and Techniques*. Morgan Kaufmann, San Francisco.

Gray, J., Laurie, R., Putzolu, G., and Traiger, I. (1976). Granularity of locks and degrees of consistency in a shared database. *Modeling in Data Base Management Systems*, Elsevier, North Holland.

Gray, J., McJones, P., and Blasgen, M. (1981). The recovery manager of the System R database manager. *Computer Surveys* **13**(2): 223–242.

Gray, J., Chaudhuri, S., Bosworth, A., Layman, A., Reichart, D., and Venkatrao, M. (1997). Data cube: A relational aggregation operator generalizing group-by, cross-tab, and sub-totals. In Fayyad et al. (eds.), *Data Mining and Knowledge Discovery*, The MIT Press, Cambridge, MA.

Griffiths-Selinger, P., and Adiba, M. (1980). Access path selection in distributed data base management systems. *Proceedings of the International Conference on Data Bases*, Aberdeen, Scotland, 204–215.

Griffiths-Selinger, P., Astrahan, M., Chamberlin, D., Lorie, R., and Price, T. (1979). Access path selection in a relational database system. *Proceedings of the ACM SIGMOD International Conference on Management of Data*, Boston, 23–34.

Gulutzan, P., and Pelzer, T. (1999). *SQL-99 Complete, Really*. R&D Books, Gilroy, CA.

Gupta, A., and Mumick, I. (1995). Maintenance of materialized views: Problems, techniques, and applications. *Data Engineering Bulletin* **18**(2): 3–18.

Gupta, A., Mumick, I., and Subrahmanian, V. (1993). Maintaining views incrementally. *Proceedings of the ACM SIGMOD International Conference on Management of Data*, Washington, DC, 157–166.

Gupta, A., Mumick, I., and Ross, K. (1995). Adapting materialized views after redefinitions. *Proceedings of the ACM SIGMOD International Conference on Management of Data*, San Jose, CA, 211–222.

Hadzilacos, V. (1983). An operational model for database system reliability. *SIGACT-SIGMOD-SIGART Symposium on Principles of Database Systems (PODS)*, Atlanta, 244–256.

Hadzilacos, V., and Papadimitriou, C. (1985). Algorithmic aspects of multiversion concurrency control. *SIGACT-SIGMOD-SIGART Symposium on Principles of Database Systems (PODS)*, Portland, OR, 96–104.

Haerder, T., and Reuter, A. (1983). Principles of transaction-oriented database recovery. *ACM Computing Surveys* **15**(4): 287–317.

Hall, M. (2000). *Core Servlets and JavaServer Pages (JSP)*. Prentice-Hall, Englewood Cliffs, NJ.

Han, J., and Kamber, M. (2001). *Data Mining: Concepts and Techniques*. Morgan Kaufmann, San Francisco.

Harinarayan, V., Rajaraman, A., and Ullman, J. (1996). Implementing data cubes efficiently. *Proceedings of the ACM SIGMOD International Conference on Management of Data*, Montreal, Canada, 205–216.

Henning, M., and Vinoski, S. (1999). *Advanced CORBA Programming with C++*. Addison-Wesley, Reading, MA.

Hsu, M. (1995). Letter from the special issues editor. *Quarterly Bulletin of the IEEE Computer Society Technical Committee on Data Engineering*, **18**(1): 2–3, Special Issue on Workflow Systems.

Hu, W. (1995). *DCE Security Programming*. O'Reilly and Associates, Sebastopol, CA.

Huhtala, Y., Karkkainen, J., Porkka, P., and Toivonen, H. (1999). TANE: An efficient algorithm for discovery of functional and approximate dependencies. *The Computer Journal* **42**(2): 100–111.

Hull, R., Llirbat, F., Simon, E., Su, J., Dong, G., Kumar, B., and Zhou, G. (1999). Declarative workflows that support easy modification and dynamic browsing. *Proceedings of the ACM International Joint Conference on Work Activities Coordination and Collaboration (WACC)*, San Francisco, 69–78.

Hunter, J., and Crawford, W. (1998). *Java Servlet Programming*. O'Reilly and Associates, Sebastopol, CA.

IBM (1991). System network architecture (SNA) logical unit 6.2 (LU6.2): Transaction programmer's reference manual for LU6.2. *Technical Report GC30-3084*.

i-Escrow (2000). i-Escrow. (*http://www.iescrow.com*).

Ioannidis, Y. (1996). Query optimization. *ACM Computing Surveys* **28**(1): 121–123.

Ito, M., and Weddell, G. (1994). Implication problems for functional constraints on databases supporting complex objects. *Journal of Computer and System Sciences* **49**(3): 726–768.

Jaeschke, G., and Schek, H.-J. (1982). Remarks on the algebra of non-first-normal-form relations. *ACM SIGACT-SIGMOD-SIGART Symposium on Principles of Database Systems (PODS)*, Los Angeles, 124–138.

Jajodia, S., and Kerschberg, L. (eds.) (1997). *Advanced Transaction Models and Architectures*, Kluwer Academic Publishers, Dordrecht, Netherlands.

Kamath, M., and Ramamritham, K. (1996). Correctness issues in workflow management. *Distributed Systems Engineering Journal* **3**(4): 213–221.

Kanellakis, P. (1990). Elements of relational database theory. In J. V. Leeuwen (ed.), *Handbook of Theoretical Computer Science*, Vol. B *Formal Models and Semantics*, Elsevier, Amsterdam, 1073–1156.

Kantola, M., Mannila, H., Raäihä, K.-J., and Siirtola, H. (1992). Discovering functional and inclusion dependencies in relational databases. *International Journal of Intelligent Systems* **7**(7): 591–607.

Kay, M. (2000). *XSLT Programmer's Reference*. Wrox Press, Paris.

Keller, A. (1985). Algorithms for translating view updates to database updates for views involving selections, projections, and joins. *ACM SIGACT-SIGMOD-SIGART Symposium on Principles of Database Systems (PODS)*, Portland, OR, 154–163.

Khoshafian, S., and Buckiewicz, M. (1995). *Introduction to Groupware, Workflow, and Workgroup Computing*. John Wiley & Sons, New York.

Kifer, M. (1988). On safety, domain independence, and capturability of database queries. *Proceedings of the Third International Conference on Data and Knowledge Bases*, Jerusalem, Israel, 405–415.

Kifer, M., and Lausen, G. (1989). F-Logic: A higher-order language for reasoning about objects, inheritance and schema. *Proceedings of the ACM SIGMOD International Conference on Management of Data*, Portland, OR, 134–146.

Kifer, M., Kim, W., and Sagiv, Y. (1992). Querying object-oriented databases. *Proceedings of the ACM SIGMOD International Conference on Management of Data*, Washington, DC, 393–402.

Kifer, M., Lausen, G., and Wu, J. (1995). Logical foundations of object-oriented and frame-based languages. *Journal of the ACM* **42**(4): 741–843.

Kitsuregawa, M., Tanaka, H., and Moto-oka, T. (1983). Application of hash to database machine and its architecture. *New Generation Computing* **1**(1): 66–74.

Knuth, D. (1973). *The Art of Computer Programming: Vol III: Sorting and Searching,* (1st ed.), Addison-Wesley, Reading, MA.

Knuth, D. (1998). *The Art of Computer Programming: Vol III, Sorting and Searching,* (3rd ed.), Addison-Wesley, Reading, MA.

Korth, H., Levy, E., and Silberschatz, A. (1990). A formal approach to recovery by compensating transactions. *Proceedings of the International Conference on Very Large Data Bases*, Brisbane, Australia, 95–106.

Kung, H., and Robinson, J. (1981). On optimistic methods for concurrency control. *ACM Transactions on Database Systems* **6**(2): 213–226.

Lacroix, M., and Pirotte, A. (1977). Domain-oriented relational languages. *Proceedings of the International Conference on Very Large Data Bases (VLDB)*, Tokyo, Japan, 370–378.

Lampson, B., and Sturgis, H. (1979). Crash recovery in a distributed data storage system. *Technical Report*, Xerox Palo Alto Research Center, Palo Alto, CA.

Lampson, B., Paul, M., and Seigert, H. (1981). *Distributed Systems: Architecture and Implementation (An Advanced Course)*. Springer-Verlag, Heidelberg, Germany.

Langerak, R. (1990). View updates in relational databases with an independent scheme. *ACM Transactions on Database Systems* **15**(1): 40–66.

Larson, P. (1981). Analysis of index sequential files with overflow chaining. *ACM Transactions on Database Systems* **6**(4): 671–680.

Litwin, W. (1980). Linear hashing: A new tool for file and table addressing. *Proceedings of the International Conference on Very Large Databases (VLDB)*, Montreal, Canada, 212–223.

Lynch, N., Merritt, M., Weihl, W., and Fekete, A. (1994). *Atomic Transactions*, Morgan Kaufmann, San Francisco.

Maier, D. (1983). *The Theory of Relational Databases*. Computer Science Press. (Available through Books on Demand: *http://www.umi.com/hp/Support/BOD/index.html*.)

Makinouchi, A. (1977). A consideration on normal form of not-necessarily-normalized relations in the relational data model. *Proceedings of the International Conference on Very Large Data Bases (VLDB)*, Tokyo, Japan, 447–453.

Mannila, H., and Raäihä, K.-J. (1992). *The Design of Relational Databases*. Addison-Wesley, Workingham, U.K.

Mannila, H., and Raäihä, K.-J. (1994). Algorithms for inferring functional dependencies. *Knowledge Engineering* **12**(1): 83–99.

Maslak, B., Showalter, J., and Szczygielski, T. (1991). Coordinated resource recovery in VM/ESA. *IBM Systems Journal* **30**(1): 72–89.

Masunaga, Y. (1984). A relational database view update translation mechanism. *Proceedings of the International Conference on Very Large Data Bases (VLDB)*, Singapore, 309–320.

Melton, J. (1997). *Understanding SQL's Persistent Stored Modules*, Morgan Kaufmann, San Francisco.

Melton, J., and Simon, A. (1992). *Understanding the New SQL: A Complete Guide*. Morgan Kaufmann, San Francisco.

Melton, J., Eisenberg, A., and Cattell, R. (2000). *Understanding SQL and Java Together: A Guide to SQLJ, JDBC, and Related Technologies*. Morgan Kaufmann, San Francisco.

Microsoft (1997). *Microsoft ODBC 3.0 Software Development Kit and Programmer's Reference*. Microsoft Press, Seattle.

Missaoui, R., Gagnon, J.-M., and Godin, R. (1995). Mapping an extended entity-relationship schema into a schema of complex objects. *Proceedings of the 14th International Conference on Object-Oriented and Entity Relationship Modeling*, Brisbane, Australia, 205–215.

Mohan, C., Lindsay, B., and Obermarck, R. (1986). Transaction management in the R* distributed database management system. *ACM Transactions on Database Systems* **11**(4): 378–396.

Mohan, C., Haderle, D., Lindsay, B., Pirahesh, H., and Schwartz, P. (1992). Aries: A transaction recovery method supporting fine-granularity locking and partial rollbacks using write-ahead logging. *ACM Transactions on Database Systems* **17**(1): 94–162.

Mohania, M., Konomi, S., and Kambayashi, Y. (1997). Incremental maintenance of materialized views. *Database and Expert Systems Applications (DEXA)*, Springer-Verlag, Heidelberg, Germany.

Mok, W., Ng, Y.-K., and Embley, D. (1996). A normal form for precisely characterizing redundancy in nested relations. *ACM Transactions on Database Systems* **21**(1): 77–106.

Moss, J. (1985). *Nested Transactions: An Approach to Reliable Computing*. The MIT Press, Cambridge, MA.

Nam (1999). *http://www.w3.org/TR/1999/REC-xml-names-19990114/*.

Netscape (2000). SSL-3 specifications. *http://home.netscape.com/eng/ssl3/index.html*.

Neuman, B. C., and Ts'o, T. (1994). Kerberos: An authentication service for computer networks. *IEEE Communications* **32**(9): 33–38.

Novikoff, A. (1962). On Convergence Proofs for Perceptrons. *Proceedings of the Symposium on Mathematical Theory of Automata*, New York, 615–621.

O'Neil, P. (1987). Model 204: Architecture and performance. *Proceedings of the International Workshop on High Performance Transaction Systems*. In Vol. 359 of *Lecture Notes in Computer Science*, Springer-Verlag, Heidelberg, Germany, 40–59.

O'Neil, P., and Graefe, G. (1995). Multi-table joins through bitmapped join indices. *SIGMOD Record* **24**(3): 8–11.

O'Neil, P., and Quass, D. (1997). Improved query performance with variant indexes. *Proceedings of the ACM SIGMOD International Conference on Management of Data*, Tucson, 38–49.

Orfali, R., and Harkey, D. (1998). *Client/Server Programing with Java and CORBA*. John Wiley, New York.

Orlowska, M., Rajapakse, J., and ter Hofstede, A. (1996). Verification problems in conceptual workflow specifications. *Proceedings of the International Conference on Conceptual Modeling*. Vol. 1157 of *Lecture Notes in Computer Science*, Springer-Verlag, Heidelberg, Germany.

Ozsoyoglu, Z., and Yuan, L.-Y. (1985). A normal form for nested relations. *ACM SIGACT-SIGMOD-SIGART Symposium on Principles of Database Systems (PODS)*, Portland, OR, 251–260.

Ozsu, M., and Valduriez, P. (1991). *Principles of Distributed Database Systems*, Prentice-Hall, Englewood Cliffs, NJ.

Papadimitriou, C. (1986). *The Theory of Concurrency Control*. Computer Science Press, Rockville, MD.

Paton, N., Diaz, O., Williams, M., Campin, J., Dinn, A., and Jaime, A. (1993). Dimensions of active behavior. *Proceedings of the Workshop on Rules in Database Systems*, Heidelberg, Germany, 40–57.

Peterson, W. (1957). Addressing for random access storage. *IBM Journal of Research and Development* **1**(2): 130–146.

Peterson, L., and Davies, B. (2000). *Computer Networks: A Systems Approach* (2nd ed.). Morgan Kaufmann, San Francisco.

Pope, A. (1998). *The CORBA Reference Guide*. Addison-Wesley, Reading, MA.

PostgreSQL (2000). PostgreSQL. *http://www.postgresql.org*.

Pressman, R. (1997). *Software Engineering: A Practitioner's Approach*. McGraw-Hill, New York.

Ram, S. (1995). Deriving functional dependencies from the entity-relationship model. *Communications of the ACM* **38**(9): 95–107.

Ramakrishnan, R., and Ullman, J. (1995). A survey of deductive databases. *Journal of Logic Programming* **23**(2): 125–149.

Ramakrishnan, R., Srivastava, D., Sudarshan, S., and Seshadri, P. (1994). The CORAL deductive database system. *VLDB Journal* **3**(2): 161–210.

Ray, E. (2001). *Learning XML*, O'Reilly and Associates, Sebastopol, CA.

Reese, G. (2000). *Database Programming with JDBC and Java*. O'Reilly and Associates, Sebastopol, CA.

Reuter, A., and Wachter, H. (1991). The contract model. *Quarterly Bulletin of the IEEE Computer Society Technical Commmttee on Data Engineering* **14**(1): 39–43.

Rivest, R., Shamir, A., and Adelman, L. (1978). On digital signatures and public-key cryptosystems. *Communications of the ACM* **21**(2): 120–126.

Robie, J., Lapp, J., and Schach, D. (1998). XML query language (XQL). *Proceedings of the Query Languages Workshop*, Boston (*http://www.w3.org/TandS/QL/QL98/pp/xql.html*).

Robie, J., Chamberlin, D., and Florescu, D. (2000). Quilt: An XML query language. *XML Europe* (*http://www.almaden.ibm.com/cs/people/chamberlin/robie_XML_Europe.pdf*).

Rosenberry, W., Kenney, D., and Fisher, G. (1992). *Understanding DCE*, O'Reilly and Associates, Sebastopol, CA.

Rosenkrantz, D., Stearns, R., and Lewis, P. (1978). System level concurrency control for distributed database systems. *ACM Transactions on Database Systems* **3**(2): 178–198.

Rosenkrantz, D., Stearns, R., and Lewis, P. (1984). Consistency and serializability in concurrent database systems. *SIAM Journal of Computing* **13**(3): 505–530.

Ross, K., and Srivastava, D. (1997). Fast computation of sparse datacubes. *Proceedings of the International Conference on Very Large Data Bases (VLDB)*, Athens, Greece, 116–125.

Roth, M., and Korth, H. (1987). The design of non-1nf relational databases into nested normal form. *Proceedings of the ACM SIGMOD International Conference on Management of Data*, San Francisco, 143–159.

Rusinkiewicz, M., and Sheth, A. (1994). Specification and execution of transactional workflows. In W. Kim (ed.), *Modern Database Systems: The Object Model, Interoperability, and Beyond*, ACM Press, New York, 592–620.

Sagonas, K., Swift, T., and Warren, D. (1994). XSB as an efficient deductive database engine. *Proceedings of the ACM SIGMOD International Conference on Management of Data*, Minneapolis, MN, 442–453.

Savnik, I., and Flach, P. (1993). Bottom-up induction of functional dependencies from relations. *Proceedings of the AAAI Knowledge Discovery in Databases Workshop (KDD)*, Ljubliana, Slovenija, 174–185.

Schach, S. (1990). *Software Engineering*. Aksen Associates, Homewood, IL.

Schek, H.-J., Weikum, G., and Ye, H. (1993). Towards a unified theory of concurrency control and recovery. *ACM SIGACT-SIGMOD-SIGART Conference on Principles of Database Systems (PODS)*, Washington, DC, 300–311.

Schneier, B. (1995). *Applied Cryptography: Protocols, Algorithms, and Source Code in C*. John Wiley, New York.

Sciore, E. (1983). Improving database schemes by adding attributes. *ACM SIGACT-SIGMOD-SIGART Symposium on Principles of Database Systems (PODS)*, New York, 379–383.

Sebesta, R. (2001). *Programming the World Wide Web*. Addison-Wesley, Reading, MA.

SGM (1986). Information processing—text and office systems—Standard Generalized Markup Language (SGML). *ISO Standard 8879*.

Shipman, D. (1981). The functional data model and the data language DAPLEX. *ACM Transactions on Database Systems* **6**(1): 140–173.

Signore, R., Creamer, J., and Stegman, M. (1995). *The ODBC Solution: Open Database Connectivity in Distributed Environments*. McGraw-Hill, New York.

Singh, M. (1996). Synthesizing distributed constrained events from transactional workflow specifications. *Proceedings of the International Conference on Data Engineering*, New Orleans, 616–623.

Skeen, D. (1981). Nonblocking commit protocols. *Proceedings of the ACM SIGMOD International Conference on Management of Data*, Ann Arbor, MI, 133–142.

Spaccapietra, S. (ed.) (1987). *Entity-Relationship Approach: Ten Years of Experience in Information Modeling, Proceedings of the Entity-Relationship Conference*, Elsevier, North Holland.

SQL (1992). ANSI X3.135-1992, *American National Standard for Information Systems—Database Language—SQL*.

SQLJ (2000). SQLJ. *http://www.sqlj.org*.

Stallings, W. (1999). *Cryptography and Network Security: Principles and Practice*, (2nd ed.). Prentice-Hall, Englewood Cliffs, NJ.

Stallman, R. (2000). GNU coding standards. (*http://www.gnu.org/prep/standards.html*.)

Standish (2000). Chaos. *http://standishgroup.com/visitor/chaos.htm*.

Staudt, M., and Jarke, M. (1996). Incremental maintenance of externally materialized views. *Proceedings of the International Conference on Very Large Data Bases (VLDB)*, Bombay, India, 75–86.

Steiner, J. G., Neuman, B. C., and Schiller, J. I. (1988). Kerberos: An authentication service for open network systems. *USENIX Conference Proceedings*, Dallas, 191–202.

Stonebraker, M. (1979). Concurrency control and consistency of multiple copies of data in INGRES. *IEEE Transactions on Software Engineering* **5**(3): 188–194.

Stonebraker, M. (1986). *The INGRES Papers: Anatomy of a Relational Database System*. Addison-Wesley, Reading, MA.

Stonebreaker, M., and Kemnitz, G. (1991). The POSTGRES next generation database management system. *Communications of the ACM* **10**(34): 78–92.

Summerville, I. (1996). *Software Engineering*, Addison-Wesley, Reading, MA.

Sun (2000). JDBC data access API. *http://java.sun.com/products/jdbc/*.

Teorey, T. (1992). *Database modeling and design: The E-R approach*. Morgan Kaufmann, San Francisco.

Thalheim, B. (1992). *Fundamentals of Entity-Relationship Modeling*. Springer-Verlag, Berlin.

Thomas, R. (1979). A majority consensus approach to concurrency control for multiple copy databases. *ACM Transactions on Database Systems* **4**(2): 180–209.

Topor, R., and Sonenberg, E. (1988). On domain independent databases. In J. Minker (ed.), *Foundations of Deductive Databases and Logic Programming*, Morgan Kaufmann, Los Altos, CA, 217–240.

Transarc (1996). Encina monitor programmer's guide and reference. *Technical Report ENC-D5008-06*, Transarc Corporation, Pittsburgh.

Ullman, J. (1982). *Principles of Database Systems*. Computer Science Press, Rockville, MD.

Ullman, J. (1988). *Principles of Database and Knowledge-Base Systems, Volumes 1 and 2.* Computer Science Press, Rockville, MD.

Vaghani, J., Ramamohanarao, K., Kemp, D., Somogyi, Z., Stuckey, P., Leask, T. and Harland, J. (1994). The Aditi deductive database system. *The VLDB Journal* **3**(2): 245–288.

Valduriez, P. (1987). Join indices. *ACM Transactions on Database Systems* **12**(2): 218–246.

Van Gelder, A., and Topor, R. (1991). Safety and translation of relational calculus queries. *ACM Transactions on Database Systems* **16**(2): 235–278.

Venkatrao, M., and Pizzo, M. (1995). SQL/CLI—A new binding style for SQL. *SIGMOD Record* **24**(4): 72–77.

Vincent, M. (1999). Semantic foundations of 4nf in relational database design. *Acta Informatica* **36**(3): 173–213.

Vincent, M., and Srinivasan, B. (1993). Redundancy and the justification for fourth normal form in relational databases. *International Journal of Foundations of Computer Science* **4**(4): 355–365.

VISA (2000). SET specifications. *http://www.visa.com/nt/ecomm/set/intro.html*.

Weddell, G. (1992). Reasoning about functional dependencies generalized for semantic data models. *ACM Transactions on Database Systems* **17**(1): 32–64.

Weihl, W. (1984). *Specification and Implementation of Atomic Data Types*. Ph.D. thesis, Department of Computer Science, Massachusetts Institute of Technology, Cambridge, MA.

Weihl, W. (1988). Commutativity-based concurrency control for abstract data types. *IEEE Transactions on Computers* **37**(12): 1488–1505.

Weikum, G. (1991). Principles and realization strategies of multilevel transaction management. *ACM Transactions on Database Systems* **16**(1): 132–180.

Weikum, G., and Schek, H. (1991). Multi-level transactions and open nested transactions. *Quarterly Bulletin of the IEEE Computer Society Technical Committee on Data Engineering* **14**(1): 55–66.

Widom, J., and Ceri, S. (1996). *Active Database Systems*. Morgan Kaufmann, San Francisco.

Wodtke, D., and Weikum, G. (1997). A formal foundation for distributed workflow execution based on state charts. *Proceedings of the International Conference on Database Theory (ICDT),* Delphi, Greece, 230–246.

Wong, E. (1977). Retrieving dispersed data from SDD-1: A system for distributed databases. *Proceedings of the 2nd International Berkeley Workshop on Distributed Data Management and Data Networks,* Berkeley, CA, 217–235.

Wong, E., and Youssefi, K. (1976). Decomposition—A strategy for query processing. *ACM Transactions on Database Systems* **1**(3): 223–241.

Worah, D., and Sheth, A. (1997). Transactions in transactional workflows. In S. Jajodia and L. Kerschberg (eds.), *Advanced Transaction Models, and Architectures,* Kluwer Academic Publishers, Dordrecht, Netherlands, 3–45.

Workflow Management Coalition (2000). WfMC standards. *http://www.aiim.org/wfmc/standards/docs.htm.*

XML (1998). Extensible Markup Language (XML) 1.0. *http://www.w3.org/TR/REC-xml.*

XMLSchema (2000a). XML Schema, part 0: Primer. *http://www.w3.org/TR/xmlschema-0/.*

XMLSchema (2000b). XML Schema, parts 1 and 2. *http://www.w3.org/XML/Schema.*

X/Open CAE Specification Structured Transaction Definition Language (STDL) (1996a). X/Open Co., Ltd., London.

X/Open Guide Distributed Transaction Processing: Reference Model, Version 3 (1996b). X/Open Co., Ltd., London.

XPath (1999). XML Path Language (XPath), version 1.0. *http://www.w3.org/TR/xpath/.*

XPointer (2000). XML Pointer Language (XPointer), version 1.0. *http://www.w3.org/TR/xptr/.*

XQuery: (2001) A query language for XML. Editors: D. Chamberlin, , D. Florescu, T. Robie, T. Simeon, M. Stefanescu, *http://www.w3.org/TR/xquery.*

XSL (1999). XSL transformations (XSLT), version 1.0. *http://www.w3.org/TR/xslt/.*

Zaniolo, C. (1983). The database language GEM. *Proceedings of the ACM SIGMOD International Conference on Management of Data,* San Jose, CA, 423–434.

Zaniolo, C., and Melkanoff, M. (1981). On the design of relational database schemata. *ACM Transactions on Database Systems* **6**(1): 1–47.

Zhao, B., and Joseph, A. (2000). XSet: A lightweight XML search engine for Internet applications. *http://www.cs.berkeley.edu/~ravenben/xset/.*

Zhao, Y., Deshpande, P., Naughton, J., and Shukla, A. (1998). Simultaneous optimization and evaluation of multiple dimensional queries. *Proceedings of the ACM SIGMOD International Conference on Management of Data,* Seattle, WA, 271–282.

Zloof, M. (1975). Query by example, *NCC,* AFIPS Press, Montvale, NJ.

Index